HANDBOOK OF REGIONAL INNOVATION AND GROWTH

Handbook of Regional Innovation and Growth

Edited by

Philip Cooke

University Research Professor in Regional Development and Director, Centre for Advanced Studies, University of Wales, Cardiff, UK

with

Bjørn Asheim

Professor, CIRCLE (Centre for Innovation, Research and Competence in the Learning Economy) and Department of Human Geography, Lund University, Sweden, and University of Agder, Norway

Ron Boschma

Professor, Department of Economic Geography and Urban and Regional Research Centre Utrecht (URU), Utrecht University, The Netherlands

Ron Martin

Professor, Department of Geography and St Catharine's College, University of Cambridge, UK

Dafna Schwartz

Professor, Department of Business Administration, Ben-Gurion University of the Negev, Beer-Sheva, Israel

Franz Tödtling

Professor and Head, Institute for Regional Development and Environment, University of Economics and Business, Vienna, Austria

Edward Elgar
Cheltenham, UK • Northampton, MA, USA

Published by
Edward Elgar Publishing Limited
The Lypiatts
15 Lansdown Road
Cheltenham
Glos GL50 2JA
UK

Edward Elgar Publishing, Inc.
William Pratt House
9 Dewey Court
Northampton
Massachusetts 01060
USA

Paperback edition 2013
Paperback edition reprinted 2015

A catalogue record for this book
is available from the British Library

Library of Congress Control Number: 2010939195

ISBN   978 1 84844 417 1 (cased)
          978 0 85793 151 1 (paperback)

Typeset by Servis Filmsetting Ltd, Stockport, Cheshire
Printed and bound in Great Britain by the CPI Group (UK) Ltd

Contents

List of figures   ix
List of tables   x
List of boxes   xi
List of contributors   xii
Preface   xv

 1   Introduction to the *Handbook of Regional Innovation and Growth*   1
     Philip Cooke, Bjørn Asheim, Ron Boschma, Ron Martin, Dafna Schwartz
     and Franz Tödtling

PART I   REGIONAL INNOVATION THEORY

     Introduction   27
     Bjørn Asheim and Dafna Schwartz
 2   Schumpeter and regional innovation   32
     Esben Sloth Andersen
 3   Neo-Schumpeterian perspectives on innovation and growth   43
     David Wolfe
 4   Regional agglomeration and growth: the classical approach   54
     Eirik Vatne
 5   Innovation, product life cycle and diffusion: Vernon and beyond   67
     Gunther Tichy
 6   Perspectives on mature Marshallian industrial districts   78
     Marco Bellandi
 7   The new Marshallian districts and their process of internationalization   90
     Fiorenza Belussi

PART II   REGIONAL INNOVATION AND GROWTH DYNAMICS

     Introduction   103
     Philip Cooke, Franz Tödtling and Dafna Schwartz
 8   Innovation and productivity: local competitiveness and the role of space   107
     Roberta Capello
 9   Human capital and labour mobility determinants of regional innovation   119
     Daniel Felsenstein
10   The geography of knowledge flows   132
     Stefano Breschi
11   Regional innovation and diversity   143
     Simona Iammarino

12 Networks of innovation   155
    Elisa Giuliani
13 From regional anchors to anchoring   167
    Lisa De Propris and Olivier Crevoisier

PART III   REGIONAL INNOVATION AND EVOLUTION

    Introduction   181
    Ron Boschma and Ron Martin
14 Technological relatedness, related variety and economic geography   187
    Ron Boschma and Koen Frenken
15 Regional economies as path-dependent systems: some issues and
    implications   198
    Ron Martin
16 Absorptive capacity in a regional context   211
    Maria Abreu
17 Regional knowledge networks   222
    Michael Steiner
18 Regional competitiveness: from endowments to externalities to evolution   234
    Ron Martin
19 Regional cultural economy: evolution and innovation   246
    Al James

PART IV   AGGLOMERATION AND INNOVATION

    Introduction   265
    Philip Cooke and Bjørn Asheim
20 Proximity and innovation   269
    Christophe Carrincazeaux and Marie Coris
21 The changing form and geography of social capital   282
    Stuart Rosenfeld
22 Cluster evolution   293
    Arne Isaksen
23 Transversality and regional innovation platforms   303
    Philip Cooke
24 Technology clusters   315
    Edward Malecki

PART V   REGIONAL WORLDS OF INNOVATION

    Introduction   333
    Philip Cooke and Dafna Schwartz
25 Worlds of production: conventions and the microfoundations of regional
    economies   339
    Peter Sunley

26 Culture as a source for growth and change: some evidence from cultural
   clusters in Andalusia   350
   Luciana Lazzeretti
27 Service innovation   363
   Yuko Aoyama and Rory Horner
28 Regional services innovation   380
   Philip Cooke
29 Open innovation and regional growth   391
   Peter Prud'homme van Reine
30 Foreign direct investment and regional innovation   406
   Philip Cooke and Dafna Schwartz
31 Innovation systems in emerging economies: the case of India   419
   Scott Ptak and Sharmistha Bagchi-Sen
32 Green innovation   434
   Philip Cooke

PART VI   REGIONAL INNOVATION SYSTEM INSTITUTIONS

   Introduction   449
   Dafna Schwartz and Franz Tödtling
33 Regional innovation systems   455
   Franz Tödtling and Michaela Trippl
34 Intermediaries in regional innovation systems: role and challenges for policy 467
   Claire Nauwelaers
35 Regional entrepreneurship   482
   Niels Bosma, Veronique Schutjens and Erik Stam
36 Venture capital in regional innovation and growth   495
   Jesper Lindgaard Christensen
37 Regional entrepreneurship development: promoting spin-offs through
   coaching and mentoring   505
   Magnus Klofsten and Staffan Öberg
38 Regional innovation and incubation: the technological incubators
   programme for entrepreneurship and innovation   514
   Daniel Shefer and Amnon Frenkel

PART VII   REGIONAL INNOVATION POLICY

   Introduction   529
   Philip Cooke and Ron Boschma
39 Regional innovation governance   534
   Martin Heidenreich and Knut Koschatzky
40 Learning regions   547
   James Simmie
41 Regional innovation platforms   556
   Vesa Harmaakorpi, Tomi Tura and Helinä Melkas

42   Regional innovation policy and dramaturgy   573
     Philip Cooke
43   Design-driven regional innovation   587
     Philip Cooke and Arne Eriksson
44   Regional innovation policy between theory and practice   597
     Arnoud Lagendijk

Index   609

Figures

1.1	The waveform evolution of capitalism (1770–2060)	12
2.1	The creation of a new firm in Schumpeter's Mark I model, with no possibility of further expansion	38
2.2	The two feedback loops of an incumbent firm in Schumpeter's Mark II model	39
2.3	Logistic diffusion with added *r*-innovation and *K*-innovation	40
9.1	Relative regional employment in high-tech sectors, 1995–2006	126
9.2	Relative regional capital–labour ratios, 1995–2006	126
9.3	Relative regional real wages, 1995–2006	127
13.1	A typology of regional knowledge anchoring capacities	174
18.1	Clustering, externalities and regional competitive advantage	239
18.2	Regional dynamic comparative advantage	242
19.1	Marshall's triad of external economies of industrial localization	247
19.2	The mechanisms through which locally dominant cultural norms, values and beliefs inform worker and firm behaviour	255
32.1	North Jutland's green regional innovation system	443
33.1	Main structure of regional innovation systems (RISs)	456
34.1	Wallonia innovation system and strategy	477
38.1	Government investment vs private investment in Israeli incubators' projects, 1991–2006	519
39.1	Regional knowledge generation, diffusion and exploitation	539
41.1	The principle of combining industries and areas of expertise in the Regional Development Platform Method	567
41.2	A systemic framework for development of a regional innovation system	569
41.3	The age business core process in the Lahti region	570
42.1	Regional intercluster innovation platform model	577
42.2	The Lahti regional innovation system platform policy toolkit	579
42.3	Regional innovation quadrants	581
42.4	Transversality: key process and practice conceptual framework	583

Tables

7.1	Performance of sampled district firms in the period 2000–02	93
7.2	Export flows	94
7.3	Models of internationalization	94
8.1	Different approaches to innovation and regional growth	108
9.1	Effect of regional human capital stocks, mobility and innovative capacity on regional earnings: spatial panel regressions for Israeli regions, 1995–2006	128
15.1	Some issues in the study of regional path-dependence	200
15.2	Some possible sources of new regional path creation	204
15.3	Path-dependent regional economic evolution: three conceptions	206
20.1	Forms of proximity and dominant spatial configurations according to knowledge base complexity	275
25.1	The four worlds of production	340
28.1	Product or process innovation of firms by sector and region, 2004–06	384
33.1	Types of linkages to external knowledge sources and partners	459
34.1	Rationale and features of regional innovation intermediaries within the old linear and new systemic innovation paradigm	472
37.1	Similarities and differences between coaching and mentoring	509
41.1	Dimensions of proximity and distance in innovation networks	559
41.2	Proximity and distance in innovation according to certain theories and frameworks	561
41.3	The cluster model versus the regional innovation platform model	565
43.1	Lombardy design cluster: leading firms' financial performance	592

Boxes

1.1   Some conceptual issues in regional innovation studies   6
29.1 Contributions of regions to enabling and enhancing open innovation, in
      turn leading to regional growth: sociocultural environment   398
29.2 Contributions of regions to enabling and enhancing open innovation:
      economic environment   399
29.3 Contributions of regions to enabling and enhancing open innovation:
      institutional environment   401
32.1 Moves by California ICT entrepreneurs into clean technologies, 2008   441
34.1 Strategic agenda for regional innovation intermediaries   474

Contributors

Maria Abreu, Research Fellow, Department of Economic Geography, University of Groningen, The Netherlands and Fellow, Programme on Regional Innovation, Judge Business School, University of Cambridge, UK.

Esben Sloth Andersen, Professor, Business School, Aalborg University, Denmark.

Yuko Aoyama, Graduate School of Geography, Clark University, Worcester, MA, USA.

Bjørn Asheim, Professor, CIRCLE (Centre for Innovation, Research and Competence in the Learning Economy) and Department of Human Geography, Lund University, Sweden, and University of Agder, Norway.

Sharmistha Bagchi-Sen, Professor, Department of Geography, University at Buffalo–SUNY, Buffalo, NY, USA.

Marco Bellandi, Professor, Department of Economic Sciences, University of Florence, Firenze, Italy.

Fiorenza Belussi, Associate Professor of Strategic Management and Organization at the University of Padua, Italy.

Ron Boschma, Professor, Department of Economic Geography and Urban and Regional Research Centre Utrecht (URU), Utrecht University, The Netherlands.

Niels Bosma, Research Associate, Urban 7 Regional Research Centre, University of Utrecht, The Netherlands.

Stefano Breschi, Professor, Department of Management and Technology and KITeS, Universitá L. Bocconi, Milan, Italy.

Roberta Capello, Professor, Department of Management, Economics and Industrial Engineering, Polytechnic of Milan, Italy.

Christophe Carrincazeaux, Professor, School of Geography and GRETHA Research Institute, University of Bordeaux, France.

Jesper Lindgaard Christensen, Associate Professor, Business School, Aalborg University, Denmark.

Philip Cooke, University Research Professor in Regional Development and Director of the Centre for Advanced Studies, University of Wales, Cardiff, UK.

Marie Coris, Associate Professor, School of Geography and GRETHA Research Institute, University of Bordeaux, France.

Olivier Crevoisier, Professor, Institute of Economic and Regional Research, University of Neuchâtel, Switzerland.

Lisa De Propris, Senior Lecturer in Industrial Economics, Birmingham Business School, University of Birmingham, UK.

Arne Eriksson, Principal, AKE Konsult, Nyköping, Sweden.

Daniel Felsenstein, Associate Professor, Department of Geography and Institute of Urban and Regional Studies, Hebrew University of Jerusalem, Israel.

Amnon Frenkel, Senior Lecturer, Faculty of Architecture and Town Planning, Technion – Israel Institute of Technology, Haifa, Israel.

Koen Frenken, Professor, Economics of Innovation and Technological Change, Eindhoven Centre for Innovation Studies, Technical University of Eindhoven, The Netherlands.

Elisa Giuliani, Research Associate, Department of Economics, University of Pisa, Italy.

Vesa Harmaakorpi, Professor, Lappeenranta University of Technology, Lahti School of Innovation, Lahti, Finland.

Martin Heidenreich, Professor, Jean Monnet Centre for Europeanisation and Transnational Regulations, Institute for Social Sciences, Carl von Ossietzky University of Oldenburg, Oldenburg, Germany.

Rory Horner, Graduate School of Geography, Clark University, Worcester, MA, USA.

Simona Iammarino, Reader in Economic Geography and Regional Science, Department of Geography and Environment, London School of Economics, UK.

Arne Isaksen, Professor, Working Life and Innovation, Agder University, Grimstad and Research Fellow, NIFU-STEP, Oslo, Norway.

Al James, Lecturer, Department of Geography, Queen Mary University of London, UK.

Magnus Klofsten, Professor, IEI/PIE and Helix Centre of Excellence, Linkoping University, Sweden.

Knut Koschatzky, Professor, Economic Geography, University of Hannover and Head of the Policy and Regions Competence Centre at the Fraunhofer Institute for Systems and Innovation Research, Karlsruhe, Germany.

Arnoud Lagendijk, Lecturer, Regional Development and Policy, Nijmegen School of Management, Radboud University of Nijmegen, The Netherlands.

Luciana Lazzeretti, Professor, Department of Business Economics, University of Florence, Firenze, Italy.

Edward Malecki, Professor, Department of Geography, Ohio State University, Columbus, OH, USA.

Ron Martin, Professor, Department of Geography and St Catherine's College, University of Cambridge, UK.

Helinä Melkas, Professor, Lappeenranta University of Technology, Lahti School of Innovation, Lahti, Finland.

Claire Nauwelaers, Innovation Unit, Regional Development Policy Division, Directorate for Public Governance and Territorial Development, OECD, Paris, France.

Staffan Öberg, Coach Management Leader Centre for Innovation and Entrepreneurship, Linkoping University, Sweden.

Peter Prud'homme van Reine, independent consultant and educator in Innovation Culture and Change. Previously, he was technology manager at Philips Electronics, senior consultant at THT Intercultural Management Consulting (a KPMG company), academic lecturer and researcher (Vrije Universiteit Amsterdam, Universiteit Utrecht, Radboud University Nijmegen and Leiden University School of Management) and director of Nimbas Graduate School of Management.

Scott Ptak, Research Associate, Department of Geography, University at Buffalo–SUNY, Buffalo, NY, USA.

Stuart Rosenfeld, Principal, Regional Technology Strategies Ltd, Carrboro, NC, USA.

Veronique Schutjens, Assistant Professor, Section of Economic Geography, Faculty of Geosciences, University of Utrecht, The Netherlands.

Dafna Schwartz, Professor, Department of Business Administration and Co-director of Bengis Center for Entrepreneurship and Hi-Tech Management, Guilford Glazer Faculty of Business and Management, Ben-Gurion University of the Negev, Beer-Sheva, Israel.

Daniel Shefer, Professor, Urban and Regional Economics, Technion – Israel Institute of Technology, Haifa, Israel.

James Simmie, Professor, Urban Innovation and Competitiveness, Oxford Brookes University, Oxford, UK.

Erik Stam, Associate Professor of Innovation and Organizational Economics, University of Utrecht, The Netherlands.

Michael Steiner, Professor, Department of Economics, Karl-Franzens-University Graz, Austria.

Peter Sunley, Professor, Department of Geography, University of Southampton, UK.

Gunther Tichy, Professor of Economics and Policy, University of Graz, Austria.

Franz Tödtling, Professor and Head, Institute for Regional Development and Environment, University of Economics and Business, Vienna, Austria.

Michaela Trippl, Research Associate, Institute for Regional Development and Environment, University of Economics and Business, Vienna, Austria.

Tomi Tura, Director, Lahti Science and Business Park Ltd, Lahti, Finland.

Eirik Vatne, Professor, Norwegian School of Economics and Business Administration, Bergen, Norway.

David Wolfe, Professor, Co-Director, Program on Globalization and Regional Innovation Systems, Munk School of Global Affairs, University of Toronto, Canada.

Preface

Today, innovation has never been as visibly required nor as much embraced as a competitive strategy by firms and development authorities. There are four huge challenges that call forth expectations of strengthened innovation practice. The first of these in global ranking is the crisis of human-induced climate change which is heating up the average temperature of the planet so inexorably. Innovations to impact upon the amount and nature of energy use, water use and recycling are called for here; in other words a new emphasis on eco-innovation, more integrated and systemic than the environmental technologies of yesteryear. There is good news, in that such innovations are not beyond the leading high-technology edge: many already exist. They need strategic niche management and support for technological integration and human adjustment, including sensible subsidy regimes, to start making major contributions towards crisis mitigation. The second, related crisis concerns energy itself and the evident need to ramp up the use of renewable fuels and to replace fossil fuels in the energy mix. At the time of writing, a polluting crude oil leak from deep wells in the Caribbean has just been capped, albeit temporarily, just as the polluting company announces yet another deep and difficult project in Libya. Such is the difficulty of extraction that it cannot be very long before diminishing returns to investment, or stricter regulation, put an end to such dangerous risk-taking. Then the full attention of the oil giants can be directed towards a post-hydrocarbon innovation future.

The third and fourth crises are even more directly economic and intertwined in nature. The global economy has entered a period of disequilibrium caused ultimately by global trade imbalances. Globalization has resulted in massive trade surpluses in emerging markets like China, with associated trade deficits in mature consumer markets like the US and on a smaller scale the UK. Both are liberal markets that for a quarter of a century experimented with hands-off neoliberal deregulation, most visibly in financial markets. Innovations proliferated, but unlike manufacturing regulatory regimes, without pre-commercial stress testing of products or institutions. A mortgage bubble mutated into a liquidity crisis as banks refused to lend, bringing unprecedented woe to investors and borrowers alike. Sovereign debt default threats rocked the foundations of some countries and the euro economies and the International Monetary Fund (IMF) had to be recapitalized, alongside the introduction of new funds to facilitate emergency lending. It is still unclear whether budgetary cuts to public expenditure will trump public stimulus packages to restore some degree of economic stability. The longer-term disequilibria of globalization, with cheap money flooding Western markets to facilitate historically low bank rates and securitization of hitherto intangible values, and its aftermath, have seriously eroded demand for consumer goods. This has created a major need for innovation, utilizing better, cheaper and cleaner inputs to produce a vast range of consumer products and services.

The best intellectual guide to grappling with such a 'perfect storm' of existential crises is Joseph Schumpeter. The best guide for what to do to restore innovative capability to faltering economies, especially the mosaic of regional and urban economies that increasingly comprise the 'real economy', is Jane Jacobs. The first explained 'creative destruction' of the kind we have recently experienced on a massive scale; the second pointed to 'relatedness' or 'related variety' as the evolutionary way out of the aftermath of creative destruction. This *Handbook of Regional Innovation and Growth* unites these complementary, evolutionary world perspectives in ways that have seldom, if ever, been essayed before. To manage an ambition of this magnitude, great expertise in editing and authoring the necessary contributions was required. The editors and authors had to be familiar with the main lines of reasoning of the founding parents of evolutionary innovation analysis, and with their elaboration on the many dimensions of contemporary economic activity. Accordingly, on my being invited by Edward Elgar to accept the offer of editing the *Handbook*, with the added opportunity of contracting editorial support to achieve the task, clear thinking was called for. As with all academic fields, in evolutionary spatial innovation studies there are circles of interacting, if not like-minded scholars. Within these, there are those whose primary expertise lies in innovation research and those who push back the boundaries on the wider front of evolutionary economic geography.

In the team that 'volunteered' for editorial responsibilities are two leading authors in the influential regional innovation systems field, Bjørn Asheim, Deputy Director of the Centre for Innovation, Research and Competence in the Learning Economy (CIRCLE) at the University of Lund, Sweden, and Franz Tödtling, Head of the Institute for Regional Development and Environment, University of Economics and Business at Vienna, Austria. There are a further two that are leaders in the new and exciting field of evolutionary economic geography, Ron Boschma, Professor, Faculty of Geographical Sciences, University of Utrecht, The Netherlands, and Ron Martin, Professor of Economic Geography, Department of Geography, University of Cambridge, UK co-editors of the definitive *Handbook of Evolutionary Economic Geography*, also published by Edward Elgar. Finally there are Dafna Schwartz who is Professor at the Department of Business Administration and Co-director of the Bengis Center for Entrepreneurship and Hi-Tech Management at Ben Gurion University of the Negev, Beer-Sheva, Israel who is expert in entrepreneurship, innovation, risk capital and innovation as well as a senior researcher in foreign investment in emerging markets, and myself, mainly expert in regional innovation and clusters but also an early proponent and continuing advocate of the virtues of an evolutionary systems approach to regional development and policy.

I felt very comfortable inviting these friends to be my co-editors, and was delighted when they all accepted. This was both because of admiration for their many intellectual achievements and contributions, but also because I knew them all very well, had partnered them in international research projects, co-authored or co-edited books with them, or contributed to their collections. Accordingly, there was a high level of trust in the process, another example of that magic quality that helps make the world go round, as well as infusing many of the accounts that follow. I sketched and circulated a structure for a book of, initially, 42 chapters, suggesting topics and sometimes authors to colleagues, and our comments, restructurings and invitations to authors proceeded. There were successive rounds of inviting authors to contribute as not all those initially approached could fit a *Handbook* commission in to their publishing plans, but most of those approached delivered. Briefly, the book proceeds from the theory and founding parents of regional innovation and growth research, through key concepts from evolutionary dynamics, to varieties or 'worlds' of regional innovation, to regional innovation institutions, to regional governance and policy. Reading every chapter closely in editing the book, it was striking how frequently chapters resonated across the seven main parts of the *Handbook* and how issues raised in one or more early parts of the volume are addressed and often resolved in later chapters. This gives continuity, point of view and backbone to the resulting text, the relative tightness of which will have wide appeal, especially for students and browsers new to the subject. We hope readers will find as much pleasure in reading the *Handbook of Regional Innovation and Growth* as I and my co-editors experienced in its compilation.

Phil Cooke on behalf of Bjørn Asheim, Ron Boschma,
Ron Martin, Dafna Schwartz and Franz Tödtling,
Cardiff, July 2010

1 Introduction to the *Handbook of Regional Innovation and Growth*
Philip Cooke, Bjørn Asheim, Ron Boschma, Ron Martin, Dafna Schwartz and Franz Tödtling

INTRODUCTION

This book marks the maturation of a field of study that is only some twenty years old. Regional innovation systems is taught in university undergraduate and graduate studies courses in numerous social sciences, notably economic geography, regional planning, business economics, innovation systems analysis, development studies, political science, sociology of science, science technology and society, and environmental studies. Moreover, it is increasingly widely applied in regional economic governance practice by development, innovation and enterprise support agencies. It is related to, but has a distinctive lineage from, teaching, research and practice in national, sectoral and technological systems of innovation, as David Wolfe makes clear in Chapter 3. Its origins lie in three related strands of research that pre-date the regional innovation systems discourse (Cooke, 2008).

These are, first, the systems view of planning, dating from the late 1960s as a comprehensive perspective on the integrated analysis and planning of city and regional systems. The importance of this perspective resides in its broad application and integrative perspective, way beyond urban and regional economic processes, in biology and engineering for example. However, with respect to spatial studies its value lay particularly in its insistence on analysis of, for example, land use and transportation interconnections and innovation in these fields, and its interweaving of understanding spatial economic processes with better-informed aspirations to improve them by means of policy and management. These conjoining aspects are central to each of the systems of innovation fields noted above. They are captured by the early terms 'technological paradigm' and 'technological regime' in, for example, Dosi (1982). Here the first refers to the predominating technological profile on the macro-scale, such as 'the Computer Era' or 'the Information Age', which is pervasive in modern working and domestic life and tends accordingly to influence the nature, direction and pace of change (for example, Pavitt, 1984; Carlsson and Stankiewicz, 1991). 'Technological regime' expresses the norms, institutions, organizations and rules that tend to sustain the dominant technological paradigm by means of standards, institutional mindsets, dominant technological discourses, government regulations and organizational preferences. For a swift taste of this relationship, think of the ways in which the fossil fuels 'paradigm' resists the challenging discourse of a potential renewable fuels 'paradigm' by its influence on the predominating fossil fuels regime of subsidies (and their frequent absence for the challenger paradigm), regulations (low renewables requirements), technologies (sunk costs of past and expense of new infrastructures) and economic discourse (for example only 'scale', hence cheapness, matters).

Second, regional innovation systems thinking was influenced by empirical research findings, initially from Italy, that showed economies of scale inside the large or multinational corporation were not the only pathway to economic competitiveness (Bagnasco, 1977; Becattini, 1978; Brusco, 1982). These authors pointed, in different ways, to the success of small and medium-sized enterprises (SMEs) working collaboratively and competitively with success in both mass and specialized markets ('flexible specialization', after Piore and Sabel, 1984). Mass markets included, for example, mass-consumption food production and clothing, the latter marketed through German and American department stores; specialized markets included specialist types of engineering such as agricultural irrigation systems, food packaging machinery, spectacle frames, hiking and skiing boots, luxury footwear, luxury fashion clothing and super-cars (also super-bikes).

This was interesting because the systems of production – diffused, often in the countryside – as Bagnasco and Brusco observed it, concentrated in 'industrial districts' as Becattini saw it, were characterized by often rapid, collectively inspired and managed innovation in products and processes, later also in services, including organizational innovation (for example specialized engineering or production software, telematics and systems). Regions were important to this phenomenon in a multitude of ways. Industrial districts, as one variant of 'Third Italy', were found mainly in a macro-regional belt across north-central Italy, from Marche to Veneto and nearby regions. Some regions like Emilia-Romagna and Tuscany were Communist-governed or 'red'; others, like Veneto, were conservative ('white', Christian Democrat). There were different regional nuances, even between the 'red' modes of economic governance: decentralized in Emilia-Romagna, centralized in Tuscany. Enterprise support services were available, either through the regions or the regionally important business associations. In the 'white' regions chambers of commerce were among the most important support organizations. Thus 'system variety' added interest to the networked concept of SME production. Later, such regionalized SME networks or 'milieux' were discovered in Germany, Switzerland, Sweden, France, Spain and Portugal (notably by the GREMI group; Aydalot, 1986) and then in developing countries (Schmitz, 1995). Accordingly, an influential and related research agenda had opened up.

Finally, the emergent discourse of regional innovation systems, rooted strongly in regional science, applied regional economics and economic geography, as shown in the apparently seminal article (Cooke, 1992) found shared conceptual interests with the national systems of innovation literature. This was principally through connections between the Science Policy Research Unit at Sussex University, notably its director, Chris Freeman, and a graduate course in Regional Economic Development at Cardiff University where, in 1988 he guest-lectured on 'Networks of Innovators', subsequently published as Freeman (1991). The innovation systems perspective, developed from Friedrich List to Joseph Schumpeter, the emphasis on overturning a hegemonic academic and policy discourse favouring the 'linear model' of innovation, and the advocacy of a collective learning approach among interacting users and producers after Lundvall (1985), resonated positively with the lengthily gestating regional innovation systems concept. Systems, networks and interactive learning were the common threads linking the three complementary schools of thought that came to inform the regional innovation systems model of regional economic evolution. Both the systems approach and

Schumpeter's economics were evolutionary, and 'learning', along with 'networking' and 'variety', were cornerstones of the evolutionary view.[1]

KEY THEMES IN THIS HANDBOOK: INNOVATION, PRODUCTIVITY AND GROWTH

No mention has yet been made of the 'growth' aspect in this *Handbook*'s title. In reality it was the title proposed to the lead editor when approached by the publisher with the idea for the project in 2008. Reflecting upon it, all the editors found it valuable to keep 'growth' in the title. The main reason was that it not only adds a valid dimension to the general approach to the chapters assembled in this collection but, importantly, it also gives an answer to the question: what, exactly, is innovation for (for example Moulaert and Sekia, 2003)? The purpose of innovation is growth, measured in terms of productivity, efficiency and effectiveness. The fundamental belief in Porter (1990), for example, is that 'co-location' by firms increase efficiency (for example reducing supply chain costs; accessing talent), start-up activity, innovation and productivity while more generic conditions for growth, such as good infrastructure and education, are insufficient (for empirical support, see Delgado et al., 2010; Spencer et al., 2010). Growth is not only an economic but also a social process. It is itself subject to critique from activists and others who seek certain 'limits to growth'. Reasons for this range from the moral to the environmental, and the two in combination are not unusual. From an evolutionary perspective, growth is a successful indicator of the health of an organism, whether biological or socio-economic. It seems that capitalism, which from a Schumpeterian perspective is fuelled by innovation, must grow in order to survive. Growth is implicit in the notion of markets, the inefficiencies in which stimulate innovative efforts to profit from seeking better alignments between value and price, whether of commodities, companies or currencies. For more citizens to have access to the quality of life of the typical middle-class household of the advanced economies is not a morally indefensible position, given the massive inequalities that exist even in many such countries, let alone between them and the developing world. Such a benign outcome may not be achievable, but that does not make it undesirable. Indeed, it is what democratically elected governments continue to pursue around the world.

Hence, innovation is not simply the pursuit of the new, or an abstraction to satisfy the psychology of novelty. Improving on some technology or process is what most economic activity has been concerned with across geography and its history. Of interest to the project of this book is the extent to which innovation is conceived of in this way, implicitly or explicitly. It would be misleading to say that every contribution addresses this interdependence explicitly. Most focus upon innovation and implicitly assume more or less the above argument (for a widely cited economic geography of endogenous growth theory, see Martin and Sunley, 1998). However some address the innovation growth nexus more overtly, including through the lens of innovation and productivity (Capello's Chapter 8 in this volume), and for the moment it is useful to identify some salient points in her argument. This is important for two reasons: first, it is seldom done in innovation studies in general, let alone regional innovation studies; and second, it reminds us of the two-way implications of the relationship. Thus innovation depends on growth because it carries certain key implications regarding investment, capabilities and organization. Most growth is asserted to come from intra-industry trade among advanced economies, not even from interindustry trade between them and less developed economies (Krugman, 1991). If true, it is because, in effect, advanced economies can afford to trade innovations made affordable by past growth, which is replenished by returns from present investment in future innovation.

Capello's key points about the relationship between productivity and innovation are the following. There are three perspectives on the relationships between regional innovation and productivity, depending what kind of knowledge determinants prevail. Taking a functional approach to understanding knowledge, innovation and productivity relations, the key idea is that science-based innovation in 'scientific regions' short-cuts the invention-to-innovation circuit. Schumpeterian radical innovation may ensue, with associated profits from the increased translational productivity from invention to innovation. Geographical proximity is accordingly crucial to this kind of productivity gain. However, research into innovation shows that it often occurs without science and is thus not confined to 'scientific regions' (Asheim and Gertler, 2005). In this case, it is necessary to take a more structural perspective on the innovation–productivity nexus. Accordingly, the regional system and its entrepreneurship talent, knowledge and industrial assets replace science as the determinant of a virtuous innovation–productivity cycle. Productivity gains are reaped from the rapid recombination of knowledge (innovation) and its commercial exploitation (entrepreneurship), which are regional innovation system processes. Innovation is incremental and productivity gains from the pervasive and rapid knowledge–innovation recombinations that are proximate and systemic. But neither all innovation nor all associated productivity gains are confined to or derived from the region, as an enormous amount of research literature shows (see Cooke, 2009; Ponds et al., 2010; Breschi's Chapter 10 in this *Handbook*). Indeed, not only may innovation involve relational proximity over great distances but its productivity gains involve collective learning processes. Hypothetically, these result in global network hierarchies in which typically factor (for example labour) value is extracted from the 'learning region' and productivity increases are lodged at the top of the hierarchy (innovative region). This is the working out of the law of combined and uneven development, the law of increasing returns to (knowledge) scale, and that of 'cumulative causation'. The question remains, to what extent and at what magnitude may learning gains be repatriated, as seems to happen at least to some extent among returning Taiwanese and Indian migrants from Silicon Valley (Saxenian, 2000)?

Thus treating regional innovation as a means to the end of increasing growth by enhancing productivity opens up an important research agenda. This has been broached somewhat by research that compares productivity gains from innovation *in situ* but little yet seems to have been done in terms of interregional productivity magnitudes deriving from knowledge flows of the kind exemplified by science-intensive innovation activities such as biotechnology. Edquist et al. (2001) conducted research into product and process innovation, focusing on their comparative contribution to productivity and employment. Broadly, they concluded that productivity increased with both types of innovation, although the former contributed more to capital than labour productivity, while this was reversed for process innovation. The reason for these results is clear: by definition a product innovation creates employment while contributing to increased efficiency (greater quality or value at lower cost), whereas process innovation almost always involves labour-shedding. Considered from a regional viewpoint the region where product innovation predominates should always display high job growth (except in recessions) and capital (technological) productivity. The process-innovating region will lose jobs but gain in labour productivity. The nature and quality of regional production then determine regional growth. Schumpeterian regions should, in theory, constantly reap high profits from radical innovations (see the discussion below on the problem of 'what is radical' in innovation studies) and the region should also reap gains from the constant demand for high-value labour. Labour-intensive production will tend to produce the opposite result, except for bursts of labour productivity occasioned by investments in new process technology.

A different question is addressed in comparative productivity research conducted by Van Ark (2005). His spatial productivity question concerned differentials in productivity and productivity growth between the US and the European Union (EU) in the 2000s. His results were interesting and instructive, and add a dimension of understanding to the centrality of innovation to regional increasing returns in productivity and growth. They identified three key influences on the superior productivity profile of the US over the EU in manufacturing and services. First, most innovative technology – especially pervasive, even radical innovations related to information and communication technology (ICT) – originate in the US, where users have an early opportunity to know about and understand their possible contributions to business enhancement. Second, budgets for investment in improved technology are higher in the US; hence early adopters are more numerous. This was particularly so in services, where EU productivity is poor in sectors like banking, which in some large countries remains mainly paper-based. Finally, knowledge spillovers were identified as an asset to early adopters. Thus a new system of, say, e-commerce introduced to a firm or organization might be disruptive, but collective 'learning-by-doing' means that solutions to problems swiftly circulate the office. Logically, therefore, higher growth from productivity gains associated with innovation should accrue to regions with many innovators and early, communicative adopters – a combination of product innovation in one part of the regional system and process innovation amongst the user community. Stasis or comparative productivity decline would be hypothesized for the non-innovating, non-adopting, non-communicating region.

Felsenstein's Chapter 9 in this *Handbook* addresses the issue of human capital and labour mobility in ways directly relevant to this discussion. He, too, draws attention to three perspectives for illuminating understanding of the relationship between innovation and labour as a factor of production. Though the fit is not perfect, there is some resonance with Capello's taxonomy. The first perspective is that of new economic geography (NEG; after Krugman, 1991) which initially accounted for regional innovation in terms of labour pooling behaviour, namely firms and workers seek out regional market-size and pecuniary externality effects, agglomerating where they find a region where industry has a lead over everywhere else (see also Vatne's Chapter 4 on regional agglomeration in this *Handbook*). This is not hugely dissimilar to the sector-function view on regional productivity. In modelling terms, this approach produces naive results, which Felsenstein calls 'catastrophic' agglomeration (and regional desertification) that have to be corrected technically but which still produce misleadingly overconcentrated spatial results. An alternative that does not fall into the trap of overemphasizing a single type of knowledge determinant of regional growth (for example, science region) is new growth theory (NGT) with which Krugman (1991) is also closely associated, along with Romer (1990) on endogenous technological change. Here, by analysing regional externalities interactively with human capital mobility, the approach estimates the way that human and physical capital, labour mobility and innovation impact on regional productivity and growth. In terms of our earlier discussion on this, theory supports the deduction that the higher the average level of human capital, the more rapid the diffusion of knowledge, therefore the higher the level of regional productivity (including earnings). So NGT allows different kinds of regional knowledge and innovation into the innovation–productivity analysis, in common with Capello's structural approach. However, while human and physical capital are found to impact upon regional productivity, the model results are confounded by a 'regional innovation' effect. Thus a third approach receives some degree of support from this inconsistency, namely evolutionary economic geography (EEG). This, like Capello's cognitive approach, sees institutions, organizations and cultural practices as critical in generating regional growth. Thus cultural and institutional proximity are as important as spatial proximity and the region represents an active innovation agent.

LINEAR, INTERACTIVE AND NEOLINEAR INNOVATION MODELS

The preceding section formed a bridge from innovation via productivity to growth as an explanation of the reasoning behind the use of the 'regional innovation and growth' coupling in the title and main thematic of this *Handbook*. This introduction next proposes to draw up a list of a further six key issues in innovation studies that arise from subjects tackled in the chapters that are of wider relevance, although of central importance to regional innovation systems analysis. As in the preceding section, not all chapters will be invoked in constructing analyses and arguments about these as yet unresolved, indeed in quite large part unraised, topics for debate. Each chapter is introduced according to the seven-section structure of the book. Chapters are alluded to where they can help illuminate the specific issues raised, alongside the broader published innovation studies literature. They are intended to stimulate interest, debate and further research (Box 1.1).

BOX 1.1   SOME CONCEPTUAL ISSUES IN REGIONAL
INNOVATION STUDIES

- Beyond the interactive innovation model?
- Radical innovation: how radical is radical?
- The roles of innovator and entrepreneur.
- Path-dependence and new path creation.
- Technological or innovation paradigm and regime?
- System self-organization or system leadership?

The first of these concerns the core concept in evolutionary innovation systems theory and suggests that a re-examination of the received wisdom of the interactive, user–producer critique of the traditional linear model of innovation is now overdue (Lundvall, 1985, 1992). This is for the following reasons. First, in recent research the user–producer interactive innovation model no longer seems to capture the variety of forms that innovation processes may take in time or space. To clarify, when the model was introduced in the 1980s it was because of a perceived necessity to move away from a hierarchical administrative model of the mode of innovation that had appeared with the rise of the modern, especially American, large and increasingly multinational corporation (Hymer, 1976). Conceptually, innovation contained three distinct phases, consisting of invention, innovation and diffusion. In the context of the large corporation this frequently translated into invention being done in the corporate research and development (R&D) laboratory, innovation being done by production engineers, and diffusion being the responsibility of the sales and marketing departments. Each phase was a discrete step. Much responsibility rested on the shoulders of the production engineers, responsible for prototyping, trialling and testing an invention, the scientific origins of which they may only have had a hazy understanding. Some inventions proved unworkable, some R&D projects could seem endless. In this model, the corporate in-house R&D scientist and team were a privileged and expensive elite.

Firms like General Electric, AT&T and RCA were exemplary carriers of this tradition, evolving spatial divisions of labour that separated places where R&D was conducted from places where the other functions occurred. Of course, the needs of everyday practice eroded such rigid conceptual boundaries. Thus university scientists might be given sub-projects where in-house R&D capabilities were lacking; or a scientist or doctor might bring an invention to the corporation for analysis of its potential. Much pharmaceutical invention followed the latter course even though scientific teams were organized like armies of molecule-hunters focused on specific diseases. In those 'linear' times hospital doctors frequently found or made time to conduct patient-based research of an informal kind in the hospital or clinic. In Le Fanu (1999) such 'chance discovery' by scientists and doctors outside corporate pharmaceuticals R&D laboratories accounted for penicillin, cortisone, streptomycin, heart pacemakers and numerous other radical – 'paradigm shifting' as Le Fanu refers to them – treatments for disease. If anything, from the 1940s to the 1990s when productivity requirements brought an end to informal medical research, and biotechnology further 'scientized' it, big pharmaceuticals corporations, despite retaining major R&D laboratories, could be said to be akin to prototype engineering and marketing departments in manufacturing firms. With the aforementioned 'scientization' they are primarily marketing and financing agents for university invention and biotechnological innovation, often by small and medium-sized enterprises (SMEs). Hence, it is arguable that the linear model was never an accurate representation of innovation in 'Big Pharma' and was based on more of an electronics or engineering paradigm.

In engineering, too, the impact of Japanese 'lean production' industrial processes effectively ended the last vestiges of the linear model wherever it might have existed, because here was the apotheosis not of in-house design and production but of the evolution of radically decentralized production by means of outsourcing to increasingly elaborate and globalized supply chains. The manner in which customers and suppliers, now normally independent corporate entities, would negotiate innovation and other product and process qualities had now moved further away from the linear conception presumed of intra-corporate ordering. While subcontracting had been present from the earliest days of the emergence and evolution of capitalism, it had often developed a 'stress' or 'sweating the suppliers' culture. This practice extended, in some industries and economies, even into the 2000s. Not untypically it involved highly capricious requirements being made by customers of suppliers, such as ordering parts, short-term, then changing the order many times before the delivery deadline (Jones, 1984). Accordingly, as in the case of the West Midlands (UK) automotive industry, where it reached its apotheosis, it presaged the oblivion of once important suppliers like Lucas Automotive, on the one hand, and assemblers like Rover, on the other.[2] Elsewhere, notably in the Nordic countries and Germany, with their coordinated rather than 'stressing' or 'cut-throat' forms of supply-chain cost minimization, this was less prevalent. Nevertheless, even in German engineering, notably automotives, despite more benign customer–supplier traditions, organizational innovation occasioned by the rise of Asian luxury car production placed seemingly unsustainable new burdens on suppliers. Hitherto, these had been meticulous executors of blueprints handed down from the customer design engineering department: now, they were themselves required to innovate in fulfilling client requirements. The threat of outsourcing to innovative suppliers outside the region or transplanting supply to newly liberated, low-wage Eastern Europe acted as an incentive.

A common way of innovating organizationally to meet Asian competition was to relax corporate hierarchy slightly, moving towards matrix management, which allowed for greater cross-departmental teamwork, and giving innovation a project-based character. 'Simultaneous engineering' (also known as 'concurrent engineering') brought representatives from marketing departments into project teams with engineers, designers and external suppliers to develop innovations. It is matrix management, and giving innovation a project-based character, that captured the core of user–producer interactive innovation. Thus, the modern marketing manager had become expert in framing issues relating to user needs. Meanwhile, the supplier or producer was increasingly external to the intermediate user corporation. From an innovation perspective, the following question was posed: 'How can the producer know the needs of potential users, when markets separate users from producers?' (Lundvall, 1992, 50). Lundvall's answer is somewhat Nordic: 'The relative importance of product innovations indicates that most markets are organized markets' (Lundvall, 1992, 51). This involves information exchange, cooperation, hierarchy, mutual trust, with durable and selective relationships. This is an important observation of the social embeddedness of markets, against the neoclassical view that they are atomistic and utilitarian, which is what was being critiqued. But while the point is made that we should expect to find user-driven, or customer-driven innovation as it is now commonly referred to, in this, it might at times be more producer-driven (for example see below, also Chapter 43 on design-driven innovation in this *Handbook*). As will by now have become clear, the ensuing complexity was in general beginning to be tackled by 'collaborative manufacturing' (Sabel et al., 1991).

Into this lacuna has stepped a discourse of 'neolinear' innovation models that are in key ways anathema to the notion of durable, loyal and selective principal–agent relations between producers and users presented above. Times have changed and the EU requires competitive tendering, although such rules are not so difficult for firms and organizations to innovate around and there is much regional variation in observing the letter of the law (for example on food procurement; Morgan et al., 2006). But much more far-reaching than the imposition of supranational and national transaction rules since the 1980s has been the wholesale removal of them, particularly during the neoliberal epoch that commenced then. In Engelen and Faulconbridge (2009), reference is frequently made to the geography and variable quality of financial regulation between national regulatory regimes. They note the fact that California and Florida were engines of subprime mortgage demand, but miss the fact that it was geographically variable deregulation that both stimulated 'securitization' of everything, from fish catches to student loan pools, and that it was initially only legal in a handful of US states, mostly in the sunbelt as such. Producer-driven innovation had come to dominate financial services.

Securitization began on Wall Street when Lewis Ranieri, a utility bond manager at Salomon Brothers, innovated the first collateralized mortgage bond (CMB) that fathered the collateralized debt obligations (CDO), which brought the global financial system to its knees. Much lobbying of Washington by Ranieri and others legitimated this risky trade, which along with the Clinton administration's repeal of the Glass–Steagal Act incentivized normal banks to become investment banks, gambling with their investor capital. We might refer to this as 'supply-driven' financial innovation because the normal mortgage market was starved of capital for new loans, while deregulation enabled securitization to provide mortgage firms with instant returns from banks buying the loans and transforming them into tradeable bonds. The user–producer interaction in this kind of innovation gives effectively zero innovation capability to the user. Even over time, the user does not become increasingly familiar with the inner workings of the innovation or, indeed, the codified let alone the tacit knowledge behind it. Ultimately, even the innovators did not understand the basic modelling flaw, which was that the data utilized to estimate CDO probabilities of defaulting were inevitably historically based. Therefore, anything worse than the historical trend could not be predicted or, in a cognitive sense, understood or intuited except by a few heretical 'outsiders' (Patterson, 2010; Lewis, 2010). Without labouring the point, it can be seen that other areas of deregulation such as energy and telecommunications also gave rise to supply-driven innovation opportunities but also casualties in earlier times.

If the user–producer innovation interaction is non-existent in financial innovation, it is only slightly less so in respect of another 'neolinear' variety known as design-driven innovation (Verganti, 2006; see also Chapter 43 on design-driven innovation in this *Handbook*). Verganti holds that design-driven innovation is akin to 'technology-push' innovation as conceived by Dosi (1982) as being capable of provoking regime and/ or paradigm change in dominant technologies and innovation trajectories. Verganti's (2006) field of interest is the Lombardy regional innovation system, particularly its overlapping and interacting design-intensive furniture and kitchenware clusters, where the equivalent to a technological paradigm is a socio-cultural paradigm. Instead of technology, its discourse is meaning, and by changing meanings designers, like technologists, are capable of changing paradigms and regimes through innovations that entrepreneurs commercialize. This innovator–entrepreneur division is quite pronounced here, with 'circles' of external as well as internal designer-innovators iterating rounds of 'meaning analysis' to set an exclusive tone for new ranges of design-intensive products to be 'proposed' to consumer markets (Pisano and Verganti, 2008). In neither supply-driven nor designer-driven innovation models is there significant change in the key source of impulse, the producer, over time.

A third 'neolinear' innovation model is referred to as user-driven innovation. First articulated as such by Von Hippel (1988), his research showed that often technologically radical innovations such as the semiconductor, apparently 'producer-driven' in its design by AT&T's Bell Laboratories (as they were in the 1960s when the innovation occurred) and their leading micro-electronics scientist William Shockley, were largely defined in the extremely detailed specifications of their ultimate user, the US Department of Defense. Other innovations of the time were shown to be considerably more user-driven than believed at the time, notably gas chromatography, thermoplastics and magnetic resonance equipment. However, many of Von Hippel's examples include manufacturer rather than user-driven innovation, suggesting mainly that the kinds of highly techno-logically advanced innovations he is concerned with are less determined by 'producer power' than the two preceding models.

As Verganti (2006) sees it, user-driven innovation, whose main input is market research, the data for which are often highly technical (for example eye-tracking equip-ment) and statistically rigorous consumption analyses, predominates nowadays in mass consumer product markets because competition is so fierce that even marginal nuances concerning packaging, advertisement or product placement design can be advantageous. Contrasting this with what he conceives as 'paradigm-shifting' design-driven innovation which, after Dosi (1982), regarding radical 'technology-push' innovation also inclines to the radical, he sees 'market pull' or user-driven innovation as always incremental. This, however, betrays Verganti's product innovation bias. Contrariwise, if organiza-tional innovation in service markets is considered, the radical nature of the introduction of supermarkets, fast food outlets (including drive-through), budget airlines, mobile telephony and Internet finance, to name a few, would suggest that not all mass market innovation is user-driven, and that such markets can sustain radical innovation. In Von Hippel's (2005) more recent work on the democratization of innovation, he suggests that a notable share of contemporary innovation has become user-driven, citing many leisure industries in support, such as mountain bikes, hiking and mountaineering gear, snowboards, sailboards, microlite aircraft and microbreweries as cases in point. To some extent regional and organic food can be subsumed here. However, the hobbyist tone that many of these entail suggest this to be a noteworthy but limited niche of primarily incremental innovation. Moreover, the commercialization of such products usually reveals that entrepreneurs remain at the heart of the imitation process, expropriating the innovators or recombiners of knowledge, much as Schumpeter predicted.

Finally, attention must be drawn to a variant of user-driven innovation: demand-driven innovation, where increasingly what were perceived as interchangeable terms now denote different scales and kinds of innovation. This is now clarified to mean collectively specified demand for major public investments that may not be forthcoming through markets due to market failure. States, national or regional, must coordinate demand and supply as users defining demand to producers. Hence at times user drivers super-sede producer drivers and vice versa because many technologies and institutions must combine systemically through 'strategic niche management' to achieve success. This is exemplified where regions seek transition towards sustainability. The complexity of this tends to mean that though specific eco-innovations are incremental, in combination their effect is 'paradigm-shifting' under a sustainable technology regime or even produc-tion–consumption 'landscape'. The latter is a long-term expectation in 'co-evolutionary transition' theory, capable of being glimpsed in 'transition regions' which, nevertheless, must coexist with the broader, global, hydrocarbon path-dependence and its prevailing regulatory regime.

It is important to understand the role of discourse articulation in stimulating change from established development paths. Just as neoliberal discourse formed the basis for a thoroughgoing critique of the regulated character of financial markets, so in such sustainability hot spots as Denmark, critical discourses were articulated to undermine prevailing norms (see also 'Green innovation', Chapter 32 in this *Handbook*). The first of these was an anti-nuclear energy discourse; the second was its reverse, a pro-renewable energy discourse. Protest movements acting out the discourse brought reversal of govern-ment policy, suspension of nuclear energy policy and redirection of Denmark's nuclear research towards renewable energy research. In such demand-driven innovation settings, subsidies are a necessary element of 'strategic niche management' and can be found being made to consumption rather than only to production. The Danish case involved what *ex post* is revealed as a successful consumer subsidy policy regime that more than paid for itself in tax returns from wind turbine production. From the early 1970s, government subsidies were made available to users of first-generation wind turbines. This sustained the industry, initially based largely upon domestic demand, and enabled the north and mid-Jutland-based cluster's design to evolve considerably from its path-dependent roots in agricultural and marine engineering where the plough and the ship's propeller were the inspiration.

RADICAL INNOVATION: HOW RADICAL IS RADICAL?

In neo-Schumpeterian innovation theory, innovation can be radical or incremental. Why only these two alternatives? The answer can be found in the intellectual origins provided by Schumpeter's theory of business cycles (see Andersen's Chapter 2 in this *Handbook*). These are waveform fluctuations that can be traced statistically through the evolution of capitalism. Also known as 'long waves', they have been applied in regional science to explain the rise of 'new industrial spaces' such as Silicon Valley (Hall and Markusen, 1985), spatial processes underlying globalization (Dicken, 1986; Knox and Agnew, 1994), regional development (Marshall, 1987) and regional innovation (Martin and Simmie, 2008) among many others. Figure 1.1 presents a stylized representation of these waves since the onset of the Industrial Revolution and into an uncertain future where, nevertheless, the not unreasonable emphasis on nanobiotechnology and neuroscience arises from economic geographer and evolutionary biologist Zack Lynch's BrainWaves weblog.[3] The key point in respect of the neo-Schumpeterian perspective on innovation is that long waves are the linchpin of its scientific theory, analysis and to some extent predictive power. Innovation is the engine of capitalism, long waves set its course for epochal periods, and creative destruction represents the punctuation of its evolution caused by radical innovation.

Accordingly, each of the six epochs in Figure 1.1, with the possible exception of the last one, represent widely accepted as key evolutionary moments of the capitalist era.

Six Long Waves of Techno-Economic Development (1770–2060)

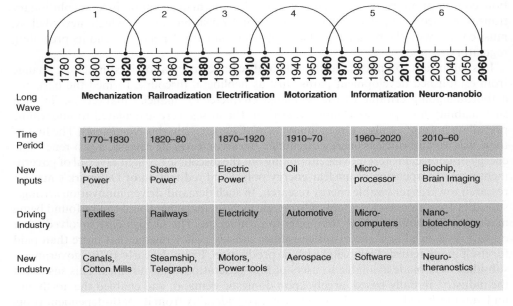

Long Wave	Mechanization	Railroadization	Electrification	Motorization	Informatization	Neuro-nanobio
Time Period	1770–1830	1820–80	1870–1920	1910–70	1960–2020	2010–60
New Inputs	Water Power	Steam Power	Electric Power	Oil	Micro-processor	Biochip, Brain Imaging
Driving Industry	Textiles	Railways	Electricity	Automotive	Micro-computers	Nano-biotechnology
New Industry	Canals, Cotton Mills	Steamship, Telegraph	Motors, Power tools	Aerospace	Software	Neuro-theranostics

Source: Based on Z. Lynch, http://www.neurosociety.com.

Figure 1.1   The waveform evolution of capitalism (1770–2060)

As such, they had sometimes brutal (hand-loom weavers rapidly obsolesced by factory production), sometimes gentler, more long-lasting transitional impacts upon societies in which they occurred (such as the evolution of motorization). To the extent that society's norms had become embedded in the dominant preceding technological regime it could be its regulatory, socio-economic governance instruments that enforced constraints to hold back the negatively perceived impacts of such radical change. In the UK, the Factory Acts moderated the depredations wrought on factory workers; the 'Red Flag Act' set motorized speed limits of 4 mph in the country and 2 mph in towns, with a man walking ahead warning locals by flapping a red flag; while steam still has to give way to sail at sea. Hence the concept of technological 'regime' became an important accompaniment to the concept of 'technological paradigm' associated with the radical innovation and its pervasive influence in itself. As noted, this regime–paradigm distinction weaves through the main elements of the regional innovation systems framework. There, the paradigm is the firm-based 'exploitation' or 'commercialization' subsystem, while the regime is the socio-economic governance subsystem that sustains it.

However, as is well known, for the neo-Schumpeterian school radical innovation is accompanied by incremental innovation, which occurs during the paradigmatic epochs as marginal improvements are made under broadly technologically equilibrium conditions. This is when path-dependence resumes, albeit renewed and redirected, following the punctuated evolution caused by creative destruction. As Martin shows in Chapter 15 of this *Handbook*, elements of this may set in early, such as the QWERTY keyboard still used in iPhones, or late, as in the case of increasingly efficient automotive engines in the face of 'peak oil', global warming and renewable energy vehicles. Late path-dependence is a frequent response to perceived paradigm shift as discussed by Dosi (1982) and Freeman et al. (1982) in respect of advances in clipper ship technology in the face of steam, or piston engine aircraft in the face of jet engines (Geels, 2006). But, in any case, it is a key tenet of neo-Schumpeterian innovation studies that incremental innovation is regular, common and more of a central feature of innovation than radical innovation. In Lundvall (1992) it is clear that this is a necessary consequence of the rise of user–producer innovation relationships. Geographical and cultural proximity are assets in the tacit knowledge exchange this implies: 'distance will play an important role. Being close to advanced users will form a comparative advantage for the producers and vice versa . . . they base their comparative advantage upon geographical and cultural proximity' (Lundvall, 1992, 57–8).

The contrasts between this and 'radical innovation' are stark. Norms, codes and standards become inadequate, producers lack communicability and users become confused. Geographical proximity thus becomes even more important because face-to-face contact, trust and even friendship are the only solvents of cognitive radical innovation blockages. Accordingly, radical innovation is disturbing and unsettling until the new paradigm has demonstrated its value, and hitherto resistant multinationals, for example, start to make acquisitions of new paradigm start-ups.

Hence, there is long-wave-inducing innovation interspersed with epochal passages of incremental innovation or 'normal science', an idea taken from Thomas Kuhn's (1962) pioneering research on the 'structure of scientific revolutions'. Clearly, such a restrictive binary division between these opposites is inadequate, except as a guide to certain interesting cultural and geographical 'infrastructures' of innovation as implied by the user–producer, interactive critique of the prevailing command model of linear innovation then prevalent. Thus not long afterwards Christensen (1997) introduced a more cost-based, middle-range distinction between 'disruptive' and 'sustaining' innovation; the first occurring with the 'democratization' of innovations, creating mass markets by cost reduction that disrupts the market for hitherto dominant technologies. 'Sustaining' innovation is the opposite, where to sustain a presence firms innovate upwards, making more exclusive, expensive products. However, these are fundamentally marketing rather than innovation strategies, since in both cases the 'innovation' to be re-packaged already exists. Nor does this possible solution pretend to have the theoretical depth to trace the socio-technical and economic-geographic implications of creative destruction displayed by the neo-Schumpeterian approach.

Verganti's work on design-driven innovation discussed above also introduces a different, less epochal or long-wave take on radical innovation, which is nevertheless neo-Schumpeterian in its theorization. Design is defined as dealing with the meanings people give to products, and the messages and product languages that can be devised to convey meaning– 'de-sign', 'signing it' and giving it 'sign-ificance': 'design is making sense of things'. It also has paradigmatic representation in distinct design languages. Thus innovation of meanings is incremental if framed within existing aesthetic norms, but radical when significant reinterpretation of meanings is achieved. Radical innovations in meaning are not immediate and imply profound changes in socio-cultural regimes. Product ranges may be transformed from simple tools to 'transition objects' intended to appeal, for example, to child-like affections dormant in adults. The innovation model of a firm such as this means it pushes innovative design onto the market, as 'technology-push' does, with radical effect. The discourse is one of making proposals to the potential consumer or user of the innovation. This is not 'technology-push' but 'design-push' and conceivably 'regime-push'. Design is not inclusive but negotiated by members of knowledgeable 'circles', some with hierarchical structures (Pisano and Verganti, 2008). However, this is clearly not 'epochal' but more 'episodic' radical innovation. It is economic but it is also symbolic, invoking 'creative destruction' in the relatively short-term aesthetic sphere.

Accordingly, from within the same broad theoretical perspective we have, first, an 'epochal', long-wave technological radicalism that has pervasive and transitional effects on communities and markets of many if not all kinds. Contrariwise, in more specialist markets we have 'episodic' radical innovations that are transformative of taste and affection towards objects. These may spawn radical innovation in related fields, even contributing to a broader 'design-intensive' product ethic, while drawing process and content novelty from 'epochal' innovation such as widespread computerization in society. It displays interactive qualities between the design 'paradigm' and the 'regime' of ideas, norms and standards that envelops it cognitively. In these respects, and drawing attention to the possibility of other varieties of radicalism in innovation, this marks an important enrichment of the neo-Schumpeterian perspective on regional innovation.

THE ROLES OF INNOVATOR AND ENTREPRENEUR

This is a lesser order of issue for the perspective informing this *Handbook* than the preceding ones concerning relations between innovation and growth; linear, interactive and neo-linear innovation models; and 'epochal' versus 'episodic' innovation radicalism. It has, nevertheless, long been a grey area in innovation studies where they can be treated as the same thing or even act as substitutes. Thus Garud and Karnøe (2001), in a widely cited review of the literature on path-dependence (see Chapters 14 by Boschma and Frenken, and 15 by Martin, in this *Handbook*) discuss innovation only in terms of entrepreneurship, not innovators. It can, of course seem pedantic to dwell on this, but in the absence of any discussion as to why entrepreneurship is being privileged the reader is justified in querying the usage. For a moment's thought reveals that it is arguable that most entrepreneurs are not innovators or indeed innovative. Those that are can often be seen employing specialist professionals to manage innovation. This is pronounced in fashion design as we have just seen, and can be observed in the haute couture industry studied by Wenting (2008), where signature designers are hired routinely as in-house or freelance consultants. But this separation is not confined to fashion for nowadays innovation in, for instance, the automotive and knowledge-intensive services industries is subject to comparable outsourcing. In automotives, this ranges from the combustion engine consultancy A.V. List in the Steiermark region of Austria, where research, experimentation and examination of engine technology are conducted for leading global brands, to the production and prototype design habitually done by consulting engineers in other parts of the automotive industry (Schamp et al., 2004; Strambach, 2008).

This is unexceptional and yet another marker of the rise of user producer innovation across the economy, as lean production has eroded the hitherto 'M' form of departmentalized corporate hierarchy. This reached its apotheosis in the era of ambitious claims about the virtues of economic and spatial planning. In Chapter 2 by Andersen in this *Handbook*, neglect of innovation in the literature is put down to the interest of 'post-Schumpeterian' regional economists in growth modelling, where innovation was forgotten because its dynamics were also less amenable to formalization. They were more interested in static interdependence between different parts of the industrial system and its translation into policies of regional development planning. According to Andersen, Schumpeter was of the opinion that an innovation could neither be implemented nor financed by its inventor. This is because the inventor of the innovation (or innovator, a term Schumpeter is not recorded as using much, if at all) requires the skills of the entrepreneur to implement the innovation, including borrowing the necessary capital and establishing a new firm to invest it. The entrepreneur may also recombine other innovations in the new firm, but the innovations are by someone else (that is, the Schumpeterian 'inventor'). So, as the word implies, the entrepreneur is the active intermediary (middleman) among the active knowledge source (inventor or innovator), active financial source (bank) and the active market (attracting customers).

This makes sense, even in early capitalism, because engineering skills to invent or innovate were specialized even then, as Uglow (2003) shows for the Boulton and Watt relationship in marketing steam engines, most of which were sold to Cornish tin mines, largely at the behest of the entrepreneur Boulton rather than the engineer Watt. Nowadays, in innovative industry such as digital services or genomics, venture capitalists play a role comparable to that of the Schumpeterian entrepreneur. Typically, they provide finance, are likely to be involved in establishment of a start-up or spin-off firm and will oblige the inventor or innovator to accept that the firm should have both coaching and professional management, something academic entrepreneurs sometimes refuse, thus killing the deal (Hellmann, 2000). In reality, the innovator may be an entrepreneur, but such hybrids are unquestionably a tiny minority. Most entrepreneurship is, again in reality, moderately routine: even venture capitalists, like consultants, have their methodology worked out and it probably does not change much in its essentials. What may distinguish them is their relatively sophisticated knowledge of specific technologies, necessary to help determine investment risk. As today, the Schumpeterian entrepreneur could actually also be a serial entrepreneur, although this was disallowed in his analysis for technical reasons. Finally, this analysis is based on Schumpeter I; in Schumpeter II oligopolistic corporations were increasingly also innovators, meaning that in-house 'entrepreneurship' and use of retained profits, outlawed in Schumpeter I, could be used in innovation investments.

PATH-DEPENDENCE AND NEW PATH CREATION

This is also something of a dependent variable in relation to the bigger picture of 'punctuated evolution' and 'creative destruction'. It arises from the perspective that equilibrium prevails in economic development, but that it is epochally 'punctuated' by radical innovation and relatedness of innovation associated with the 'carrier wave'. The idea of 'path-dependence' (David, 1985) is intended to capture this claimed characteristic of innovation, namely that its resonances may persist right through the long intervals and possibly beyond. This is rather akin to the echoes of the 'Big Bang' that signified the birth of the universe that may still be observed amongst the universe's background noise by astrophysicists. But does it serve the same purpose of confirming one theory and inclining to disprove a competing theory (for example the 'steady-state' origin of the universe)? What is served by showing persistence in a subject-field that is largely devoted to understanding how socio-economic and technical novelty and innovation occur? In one respect, it is a little like listening for the echoes of Big Bang in seeking retrospectively to understand why things are as they are. In David's (1985) study, the focus was the QWERTY keyboard, still utilized in today's digital micro-devices because, although better arrangements have been innovated none has been adopted, largely for institutional, practical reasons at the behest of users. This is helpful, as it underlines the fact that 'institutions matter' in technology analysis and that it is indeed a human artifact rather than a disembodied and societally neutral device or procedure.

Much the same can be said for the subject matter of this *Handbook*, regional innovation and growth. The urban and regional socio-technical paradigm changes, sometimes quite dramatically, as in recessions or lengthier periods of industrial decline. The spatial regime that accompanies it can, according to inherited theory, only change with difficulty and slowly, if at all, because it is institutionally path-dependent. This means that the education system, the standard social norms and expectations, the skills base, even the means to be entrepreneurial or innovative for most firms and people are path-dependent, and the region in question is 'locked in' to an obsolescent socio-technical regime. This is rather a strong explanation that can find good empirical support in some regions, notably older heavy industry regions formed in the early Industrial Age. Yet, as Boschma and Frenken's Chapter 14 in this *Handbook* shows, much evidence is emerging that the more accomplished regional economies are those with relatedness to established industrial structures. In other words, new path creation is possible and actually occurs.

The acid test is, perhaps, coal mining regions. In the UK, France and, to a lesser extent, Germany such regions seem to illustrate the path-dependent, locked-in profile quite well. However, in the Netherlands, where much of the early work on relatedness was conducted, its former coal mining region of Limburg prospers. Why is this? One important reason is that the former state-owned concern Dutch State Mining (DSM) was privatized and chose to diversify, first into chemicals, and more recently into 'biologics' or inputs into biotechnology and pharmaceuticals (for example vitamins). This 'Nokia-type' strategy of internal corporate transformation has also served the region, as well as DSM's shareholders, well. Innovative links with regional, and later global, universities have assisted these efforts. This is an example of what Martin (Chapter 15) refers to as industry-focused evolution from path-dependence, but in a context of radical renewal (not necessarily radical innovation). Indeed it is more akin to Verganti's version of radical innovation in that there is episodic, large firm-led technological paradigm shift, which happens also to be interactive with a relatively modernizing socio-cultural regime in the Limburg region. One hypothesis about the unexpected event has two subelements: first, weak relatedness and, second, an inappropriate socio-cultural (including political) regime. The UK is easily the country that most evolved regional unrelatedness in ushering into old industrial regions branch plants in many kinds of light industry as its regional policy. Germany, by contrast, has not entirely unsuccessfully benefited from path-dependent relatedness among coal, pharmaceuticals, steel and engineering in its policy, and France is somewhere in between.

Thus relatedness offers niche understanding of ways out of negative path-dependence as a policy that encourages entrepreneurship from innovation around established industry branches. The aim is to diversify from an 'industrial monoculture', but not too distantly in terms of industry profiles. This happens more as a norm of regional innovation in the Nordic countries, as three brief sketches show. First, as Chapter 32 on 'Green innovation' in this *Handbook* shows, Jutland, Denmark's expertise in wind turbines, followed by power station design and other eco-innovations, stems from path creation from marine and agricultural engineering. Vastragotland's (Gothenburg region) loss of ship construction was mitigated by the build-up of automotive engineering and the development of technical expertise and innovation in specialized ship component subsystems sold to the Asian shipbuilders who displaced them but still need such expertise. Finland's pulp and paper equipment industry sought less reliance in Finland and in the case of ValMet (Vaasa region) diversified into luxury sports car assembly (Porsche Boxter). When the parent repatriated assembly to south-west Germany in the 2007–09 recession, a contract was won to assemble US firm Fisker's electric sports car. These are sufficiently related business moves to enable rapid adjustment, notably in relation to the engineering skills base of the industry in question. Accordingly, while regional innovation must pay attention to analysis of, especially, negative path-dependence, its prime focus will remain better understanding regional innovation by judicious new path creation.

TECHNOLOGICAL OR INNOVATION PARADIGM AND REGIME?

With its origins in economic geography and applied regional economics, the language of regional innovation systems research is not significantly influenced by that of the national innovation systems approach, part of the origins of which reside in the analysis of science and technology and its relationships to society (but see Asheim and Gertler, 2005; Asheim, 2007 for a more 'national' view of regional innovation). Many early definitions of that field of study betray those origins, giving what Lundvall (1992) refers to as the 'narrow' definition of innovation:

> we may make a distinction between a system of innovation in the narrow sense and a system of innovation in the broad sense. The narrow definition would include organisations and institutions involved in searching and exploring – such as R&D departments, technological institutes and universities. The broad definition . . . includes all parts and aspects of the economic structure and the institutional set-up affecting learning as well as searching and exploring. (Lundvall, 1992, 12)

The narrow definition is influenced by the American perspective of the time, as conveyed by Nelson (1993) and Rosenberg (1994), in which innovation was seen as largely technological. As we have seen, the roles of R&D departments (for example Bell Labs) had been instrumental in evolving the technological lead of US firms and the economy more generally. The phenomenon of computerization and its later 'democratization' in the form of personal computers owed much to military and other government contracts paid to large laboratories from which new technology firms spun out. This, captured in the rise of territorial technology complexes like Silicon Valley, needed to be understood. Economic geographers and regional scientists were in the vanguard in this task (for example Hall and Markusen, 1985; Scott, 1988) but were typically rather technology-struck and descriptive rather than analytical.

Accordingly, the technology emphasis to innovation studies in the narrow sense hung over the field for a long time. Even when more nuanced analyses of systems of innovation emerged in which the enveloping regime of regulations, standards and rules gave social content to the narrow view, thus broadening it out somewhat, the discourse was of technological paradigms and regimes, sometimes techno-economic in the latter case (Dosi, 1982; Freeman et al., 1982). Contrariwise, the broad definition of innovation that Lundvall alludes to in the quotation above was really far too broad, although he nuanced it somewhat by saying that at different epochs different subsystems of the whole economic structure and institutional set-up would be the focus for study of innovation. Thus workshop systems would be the focus in study of the earliest epoch of the Industrial Age; the electrification epoch would put newly emergent R&D labs under the microscope; while the Information Age would highlight universities and academic entrepreneurship. Yet, as is evident, the perspective on technology remains resolutely to the forefront as the broad view of innovation is whittled down to manageability for research purposes. Even then, accounts of national innovation systems such as those in Nelson (1993) could be fairly sprawling and with low analytically based comparability across national cases as a partial consequence. To try to achieve some further kind of manageability, researchers specialized more in technological or sectoral innovation systems analysis (Carlsson and Stankiewicz, 1991; Breschi's Chapter 10 in this *Handbook*) but technology again dominated and the measurements deployed in sectoral comparisons were often not measures of innovation but of invention (patents, R&D expenditures).

Importantly, therefore, regional innovation systems research involved neither only the narrow technology focus nor the complexities of trying to research exemplar subsystems of epochal technology regimes in relation to leading technological paradigms. Crucially, it depended heavily on theory, on the one hand; and tailored empirical research on firm and organizational innovation, on the other. This is not to say that the regional perspective produced results or insights superior to the others, mainly because the focus was different, but rather to say that its methodology was more grounded and its data for testing propositions was focused entirely on processes and institutions responsible for innovation. This is accounted for clearly in chapters in this volume such as Tödtling and Trippl's Chapter 33 (see also Tödtling and Trippl, 2005) and Heidenreich and Koschatzky's (Chapter 39). In the former, the authors emphasize the taxonomic approach to analysis of difference, which enabled research-based testing to eventuate in typologies that were both valuable for comparative analysis and for the design of regional innovation policies. Furthermore, because of the regional science and regional policy origins of the perspective, innovation systems research examined more deindustrializing and rural regional settings than ever occurred in the technology-focused work of national, technological or sectoral systems research. Thus an innovation focus has paid dividends from its comparative and primary empirical emphases, as it has from its encompassing of the study of innovative aspects of regional governance. Heidenreich and Koschatzky note the importance of this in highlighting variability in regional governance powers as key elements in understanding the structure of regional economies, especially in Europe. As they show, there can be swift recovery from economic setbacks where there are political commitments to regional innovation and resources to implement them, and the opposite where these are absent, citing contrasts between Spanish autonomous regions and much weaker governance set-ups in support of their argument. This is extended *a fortiori* to federal governance, where despite the traumas of transition, notable successes have been registered around regional innovation strategies in Thuringia, Saxony and Brandenburg in former East Germany, indicating the advantages of 'regional experimentalism' of the kind that regional innovation analysis is well-attuned to (Sabel, 1995).

It has been noted in the section of this 'Introduction' on neolinear innovation models that there is still much to be gained from adapting foundational concepts such as technological paradigms and socio-technical regimes to less narrow and also less epochal subjects than long waves. Verganti's (2006) adaptation of technological to socio-cultural regime is innovative in the manner that it shows how the broader 'regime' concept, first introduced in international relations studies (Ruggie, 1975) can be usefully deployed more episodically and regionally than hitherto. Similarly 'design paradigm' speeds up the application of what began life, after Kuhn (1962), as a concept denoting less than long-wave longevity. Accordingly, preference should generally be shown for utilizing the terms 'innovation paradigm' and 'innovation regime' where they are found analytically useful. 'Regional innovation paradigm' is not strictly synonymous with 'regional exploitation sub-system' (one of the two subsystems in a regional innovation system, as demonstrated in Tödtling and Trippl's Chapter 33 and Heidenreich and Koschatzky's Chapter 39 in this *Handbook*.) This is because paradigm denotes 'dominance' (prevailing) whereas an 'exploitation subsystem' denotes variety (for example clusters, oligopolies, supply-chain elements coexisting regionally). But as long as usage is clear, reference to, for example, Lombardy's 'design-driven regional innovation paradigm', to paraphrase Verganti (2006), seems unexceptionable. Equally, 'regional socio-cultural regime' adds value and takes innovation away from its hitherto prevailing technological bias. Research on precisely this phenomenon has been conducted in the EU 6th Framework Programme in the Corporate Culture and Regional Embeddedness (CURE) project (http://www.cure-project.eu/; Heidebrink and Soul, 2007). The research reveals significant regional socio-cultural regime distinctiveness interacting in path-dependent and path-creating ways with corporate innovation practices in production, organization and marketing.

SYSTEM SELF-ORGANIZATION OR SYSTEM LEADERSHIP?

Finally, we arrive at a culminating issue that is of wide-ranging importance to regional innovation systems studies, not least because it addresses a conceptual and real issue about systems. This concerns the extent to which 'practice systems', of which regional innovation systems are an exemplar, are intended to achieve optimal efficiency and effectiveness through tending towards autopoiesis or self-organization, or through a hierarchical form of directed organization involving system leadership (Wenger, 2000). Clearly, the latter concept has received much attention in business school literature in the shadow of airport biographies of the likes of 'Neutron Jack' Welch, former chief executive officer (CEO) of General Electric, who is presented as almost single-handedly turning around the fortunes of that company through aggressive cost accounting, including an infamous annual cull of the company's bottom-performing 10 per cent with massive workforce reduction during his period of stewardship. Such beliefs spawned a plethora of consultancy reports and business school articles and books on 'leadership', drawing on heroes as varied as football coach Vince Lombardi, Sun Yat Sen and Antarctic explorer Sir Ernest Shackleton. The business writings of Machiavelli were even pored over for the guidance of modern managers.

In the Welch era, GE's pollution of the Hudson River made the company a target of the US environmental movement, but post-Welch the firm's two key marketing campaigns, 'Ecomagination' and 'Healthymagination', repositioned GE as a champion of green technology and healthcare initiatives. Even so, the company's once huge financial services division, GE Capital, a Welch-inspired innovation supplying 55 per cent of GE revenue, reported $500 billion in debt occasioned by the credit crunch and bad loans. Recourse was required to the US Treasury's Troubled Asset Relief Programme (TARP) for a $3.5 billion loan in 2008. Separately, GE was forced to retreat from the media business, selling its controlling stake in NBC Universal to Comcast. An accounting scandal and dividend cut dented its reputation for financial reliability, and in Britain it was accused of medical censorship after it took a radiologist to court for claiming that there were potentially fatal side-effects to one of its healthcare products. It could be argued that this and other hard-driving corporations, notably Royal Bank of Scotland and Lehman Bros, were not especially advantaged by charismatic leadership in difficult times.

What about softer forms of leadership in more 'loosely coupled systems' typically found in regional innovation systems? Sydow et al. (forthcoming) study this comparatively. They conceive it as involving motivating, involving, empowering, supporting, sense-making, mobilizing, controlling, manipulating, legitimizing and representing. They suggest that it is not so different from internal management in the large corporation; but in one respect more than the others, regional innovation system management, possibly more than clusters, can have parallel and rotating leadership of action lines in pursuit of strategic aims. Stakeholder governance of regional innovation systems means that they are appropriate vehicles for such focal and temporary management of specific actions, and it is a method for keeping commitment from the relatively high-powered individuals who are likely to find themselves invited to serve on innovation system governance networks. This is not self-management; it is leadership by a collective organization responsible for managing, for example industry clusters and it may pass swiftly or rotate among incumbents who are not employed and may not even be reimbursed expenses. Innovation system management is unlike cluster management in being this step nearer to autopoiesis since it is unusual to find a cluster without a cluster-management team in the form of a network (for example the Cambridge Network Ltd) or a common services council (for example Massachusetts Biotechnology Council). Variable governance of multi-client subsystems maintains the loose coupling and related flexibility, variety and reflexivity of regional innovation systems.

The key problem of overpersonalized leadership as revealed in the Sydow et al. (forthcoming) study is that when the charismatic leader steps aside there may not be an equivalent available to replicate any successes of the past; worse, the system may crumble

– precisely the result in the Arizona optronics case that is one of Sydow et al.'s exemplars. Thus while collective leadership might not be autopoiesis of the self-organizing kind that systems thinking tends to favour, it is far less risky than the 'cult of the personality' that is its diametric opposite. This is analysed in relation to Lombardy's design-driven regional innovation paradigm by Pisano and Verganti (2008), where a hierarchical, exclusive circle of experts is deemed the appropriate collaboration model. Given the obvious weaknesses of personality cult 'leadership' – especially for non-corporate, stakeholder, loosely coupled systems – the uncertainties of commitment that can be imagined from a flat-hierarchy, network-managed, loosely coupled arrangement, perhaps Wallin's (2006) model of 'orchestration' is an elegant compromise, embodying the notion of 'conducting' as an expertise distinct from that of being the highly expert leader of the orchestrated woodwind or violin section. The role of 'orchestration' is developed at greater length in Chapters 23 and 42, in this *Handbook*.

NOTES

1. Articulating this took longer. It occurred first in the Introduction to Braczyk et al. (1998), the original manuscript for which was written in 1995, lost by the publisher during an ownership change, then rediscovered 18 months later. It could easily have come second to a rival project with which at least two of the editors of the present volume (Asheim and Cooke) were associated. For also in 1995 a regional innovation systems seminar was held in Oslo, chapters for a book were prepared, and co-editor Keith Smith from the Science, Technology and Economic Policy (STEP) research group in Oslo impressed on authors an evolutionary systems approach to regional innovation. But the project was never completed.
2. Interestingly, this 'stressing' effect was not unknown in 'lean production' as practised by Japanese companies. Thus Cooke and Morgan (1998) reported evidence of, for example, Panasonic requiring annual incremental innovation of parts from its in-house *keiretsu* suppliers (typically a 3 per cent cost reduction and increased quality) to the point where this could not be achieved. The supplier then vacated the market, the customer turning to obliging suppliers elsewhere. Acculturation to this mode of cost control meant suppliers constantly searching for and selecting new customers, often for largely unfamiliar products, something which is now far more widely practised as a survival strategy in European engineering (Knie and Hård, 2010).
3. The term 'neuro-theranostics' refers to treatments that are both therapies and diagnostic treatments in neuro-medicine.

REFERENCES

van Ark, B. (2005), 'In search of the silver bullet for productivity growth: a review article of the power of productivity and transforming the European economy', *International Productivity Monitor*, Centre for the Study of Living Standards, **10**, 79–86.
Asheim, B.T. (2007), 'Differentiated knowledge bases and varieties of regional innovation systems', *Innovation – The European Journal of Social Science Research*, **20**, 223–41.
Asheim, B. and M. Gertler (2005), 'The geography of innovation: regional innovation systems', in J. Fagerberg, D. Mowery and R. Nelson (eds), *The Oxford Handbook of Innovation*, Oxford: Oxford University Press, pp. 291–317.
Aydalot, P. (ed.) (1986), *Milieux Innovateurs en Europe*, Paris: GREMI.
Bagnasco, A. (1977), *Tre Italia: la problematica territoriale dello suilppo Italiano* (Three Italies: the Territorial Problematic of Italian Development), Bologna: Il Mulino.
Becattini, G. (1978), 'The development of light industry in Tuscany', *Economic Notes*, **18**, 107–23.
Braczyk, H., P. Cooke and M. Heidenreich (eds) (1998), *Regional Innovation Systems*, London: UCL Press.
Brusco, S. (1982), 'The Emilian model: productive decentralisation and social integration', *Cambridge Journal of Economics*, **6**, 167–84.

Carlsson, B. and R. Stankiewicz (1991), 'On the nature, function, and composition of technological systems', *Journal of Evolutionary Economics*, **1**, 93–118.

Christensen, C. (1997), *The Innovator's Dilemma*, Boston, MA: Harvard Business School Books.

Cooke, P. (1992), 'Regional innovation systems: competitive regulation in the new Europe', *Geoforum*, **23**, 365–82.

Cooke, P. (2008), 'Regional innovation systems: origin of the species', *International Journal of Technological Learning, Innovation and Development*, **1**, 393–409.

Cooke, P. (2009), 'The economic geography of knowledge hierarchies among internationally networked medical bioclusters: a scientometric analysis', *Tijdschrift voor Economische en Sociale Geografie*, **100**, 332–47.

Cooke, P. and K. Morgan (eds) (1998), *The Associational Economy*, Oxford: Oxford University Press.

David, P. (1985), 'Clio and the economics of QWERTY', *American Economic Review*, **75**, 332–7.

Delgado, M., M. Porter and S. Stern (2010), 'Clusters and entrepreneurship', *Journal of Economic Geography*, **10**, 495–518.

Dicken, P. (1986), *Global Shift*, London: Harper & Row.

Dosi, G. (1982), 'Technological paradigms and technological trajectories: a suggested interpretation of the determinants and directions of technical change', *Research Policy*, **11**, 147–62.

Edquist, C., L. Hommen and M. McKelvey (2001) *Innovation and Employment: Process versus Product Innovation*, Cheltenham, UK and Northampton, MA, USA: Edward Elgar.

Engelen, E. and J. Faulconbridge (2009), 'Introduction: financial geographies – the credit crisis as an opportunity to catch economic geography's next boat?', *Journal of Economic Geography*, **9**, 587–95.

Freeman, C. (1991), 'Networks of innovators: a synthesis of research issues', *Research Policy*, **20**, 363–80.

Freeman, C., J. Clark and L. Soete (1982), *Unemployment and Technical Innovation: A Study of Long Waves and Economic Development*, London: Pinter.

Garud, R. and P. Karnøe (2001), 'Path creation as a process of mindful deviation', in R. Garud and P. Karnøe (eds), *Path Dependence and Creation*, London: Lawrence Erlbaum, pp. 1–38.

Geels, F. (2006), 'Co-evolutionary and multi-level dynamics in transitions: the transformation of aviation systems and the shift from propeller to turbojet (1930–1970)', *Technovation*, **26**, 999–1016.

Hall, P. and A. Markusen (eds) (1985), *Silicon Landscapes*, London: Allen & Unwin.

Heidebrink, L. and P. Soul (2007), 'Business ethics in a regional perspective', *Journal of Economic and Business Ethics*, **8**, 353–6.

Hellmann, T. (2000), 'Venture capitalists: the coaches of Silicon Valley', in C. Lee, W. Miler, M. Hancock and H. Rowen (eds.), *The Silicon Valley Edge*, Stanford, CA: Stanford University Press, pp. 276–94.

Hymer, S. (1976), *The International Operations of National Firms: A Study of Direct Foreign Investment*, Cambridge, MA: MIT Press.

Jones, D. (1984), *Outsourcing in the West Midlands Automotive Industry*, Birmingham: West Midlands Enterprise.

Knie, A. and M. Hård (2010), 'Innovation, the endless frontier: historical networks of engineering science', *Technology Analysis and Strategic Management*, **22**, 433–45.

Knox, P. and J. Agnew (1994), *Geography of the World Economy*, London: Edward Arnold.

Krugman, P. (1991), *Geography and Trade*, Cambridge, MA: MIT Press.

Kuhn, T. (1962) ,*The Structure of Scientific Revolutions*, London: Penguin.

Le Fanu, J. (1999), *The Rise and Fall of Modern Medicine*, London: Abacus.

Lewis, A. (2010), *The Big Short*, London: Penguin.

Lundvall, B. (1985), *Product Innovation and User-Producer Interaction*, Aalborg: Aalborg University Press.

Lundvall, B. (1992), 'User–producer relationships, national systems of innovation and internationalisation', in B. Lundvall (ed.), *National Systems of Innovation*, London: Pinter, pp. 45–94.

Marshall, M. (1987), *Long Waves of Regional Development*, London: Macmillan.

Martin, R. and J. Simmie (2008), 'Path dependence and local innovation systems in city-regions', *Innovation: Management and Policy Practice*, **10**, 183–96.

Martin, R.L. and P.J. Sunley (1998), 'Slow convergence? The new endogenous growth theory and regional development', *Economic Geography*, **74**, 201–27.

Morgan, K., T. Marsden and J. Murdoch (2006), *Worlds of Food*, Oxford: Oxford University Press.

Moulaert, F. and F. Sekia (2003), 'Territorial innovation models: a critical survey', *Regional Studies*, **37**, 289–302.

Nelson, R. (ed.) (1993), *National Innovation Systems*, Oxford: Oxford University Press.

Patterson, S. (2010), *The Quants*, New York: Crown.

Pavitt, K. (1984), 'Sectoral patterns of technical change', *Research Policy*, **13**, 343–73.

Piore, M. and C. Sabel (1984), *The Second Industrial Divide*, New York: Basic Books.

Pisano, G. and R. Verganti (2008), 'Which kind of collaboration is right for you?', *Harvard Business Review*, **86**, 78–86.

Ponds, R., F. van Oort and K. Frenken (2009), 'Innovation, spillovers and university–industry collaboration: an extended knowledge production function approach', *Journal of Economic Geography*, **10**, 231–55.

Porter, M. (1990), *The Competitive Advantage of Nations*, New York: Free Press.

Romer, P. (1990), 'Endogenous technical change', *Journal of Economic Literature*, **98**, 338–54.

Rosenberg, N. (1994), *Exploring the Black Box: Technology, Economics, and History*, Cambridge: Cambridge University Press.

Ruggie, J. (1975), 'International responses to technology: concepts and trends', *International Organization*, **29**, 557–83.

Sabel, C. (1995), 'Experimental regionalism and the dilemmas of regional economic policy in Europe', paper presented to the International Seminar on Local Systems of Small Firms and Job Creation, 1–2 June, Paris, OECD.

Sabel, C., H. Kern and G. Herrigel (1991), 'Collaborative manufacturing: new supplier relations in the automobile industry and the redefinition of the industrial corporation', in H.G. Mendius and U. Wendeling-Schröder (eds), *Zulieferer im Netz – Zwischen Abhängigkeit und Partnerschaft* (Suppliers in Networks – Between Dependency and Partnership), Cologne: Bund Verlag, pp. 374–404.

Saxenian, A. (2000), 'Networks of immigrant entrepreneurs', in C. Lee, W. Miler, M. Hancock and H. Rowen (eds), *The Silicon Valley Edge*, Stanford, CA: Stanford University Press, pp. 248–75.

Schamp, E., B. Rentmeister and V. Lo (2004), 'Dimensions of proximity in knowledge-based networks: the cases of investment banking and automobile design', *European Planning Studies*, **12**, 607–4.

Schmitz, H. (1995), 'Small shoemakers and Fordist giants: tale of a supercluster', *World Development*, **23**, 9–28.

Scott, A. (1988), *New Industrial Spaces*, London: Pion.

Spencer, G., T. Vinodrai, M. Gertler and D. Wolfe (2010), 'Do clusters make a difference? Defining and assessing their economic performance', *Regional Studies*, **44**, 697–16.

Strambach, S. (2008), 'KIBS as drivers of multi-level knowledge dynamics', *International Journal for Services Technology and Management*, **10**, 151–74.

Sydow, J., F. Lerch, C. Huxham and P. Hibbert (forthcoming), 'A silent cry for leadership: organizing for leading (in) clusters', *Leadership Quarterly*, **22.**

Tödtling, F. and M. Trippl (2005), 'One size fits all? Towards a differentiated regional innovation policy approach', *Research Policy*, **34**, 1203–19.

Uglow, J. (2003), *The Lunar Men: The Friends Who Made the Future*, London: Faber & Faber.

Verganti, R. (2006), 'Innovating through design', *Harvard Business Review*, December, Reprint R0612G, 1–9.

Von Hippel, E. (1988), *The Sources of Innovation*, Oxford: Oxford University Press.

Von Hippel, E. (2005), *The Democratization of Innovation*, Cambridge, MA: MIT Press.

Wallin, J. (2006), *Business Orchestration*, London: Wiley.

Wenger, E. (2000), 'Communities of practice and social learning systems', *Organization*, **7**, 225–46.

Wenting, R. (2008), *The Evolution of a Creative Industry*, Utrecht: University of Utrecht.

PART I

REGIONAL INNOVATION THEORY

Introduction
Bjørn Asheim and Dafna Schwartz

LOCATION AND INNOVATION

Regional innovation systems thinking has Schumpeterian origins, but Schumpeter never wrote a theory of regional innovation. Nevertheless, many of the theoretical elements Schumpeter did write about, like creative destruction, evolution and entrepreneurship, are of great interest to regional innovation and growth analysts. Part I of this *Handbook* starts with a chapter by Esben Sloth Andersen (Chapter 2) that pieces together Schumpeter's intentions, perspectives and analyses of regional innovation from the whole range of both his German and English written work. Some surprising conclusions can be drawn from this synthesis. For example, it could have been entirely possible for his *Theory of Economic Development* to have been entitled '*Theory of Economic Evolution*', since the German word *entwicklung* translates as either. Accordingly, the predilections of his translator determined that various fields of development studies that he effectively opened up would be denied their evolutionary origins. Does this matter? For at least three reasons, it does. First, evolutionary economic geography, like evolutionary economics, would have a longer, more integrated pedigree. Second, core concepts in evolutionary economic geography like relatedness, path-dependence and creation, and regional absorptive capacity, would have been researched and elaborated to a far greater extent than their currently embryonic state. Third, policy interventions would have been different if informed by sophisticated, well-grounded theory and empirical results. There would have been less 'parachute policy' for needy regions relying mainly on inward investment, and more intervention in support of evolving 'regional relatedness'.

Andersen shows that Schumpeter had ambitions to develop a theory of location that recognized, allowed for and emphasized two dimensions that evolutionary economic geography claims as key conceptual pillars. The first of these is regional variety, while the second is the cultural and institutional distinctiveness that arises from geographical proximity. As discussed in the Introduction to this *Handbook*, B.-Å. Lundvall, one of the founders of neo-Schumpeterian innovation systems thinking, fully recognized precisely these important elements as crucial for successful incremental innovation, and even more for success in radical innovation. But Schumpeter was thwarted in his ambition to achieve a final locational synthesis by his death shortly after he made a public appeal for a large collection of industrial and locational monographs. These were to be researched using a comparative methodology that would explore the continuing innovation of production and consumption functions and the nature and practices of leading stakeholders in these processes, including entrepreneurs. His outline of evolutionary economics would form the analytical template for these case studies of industrial and *locational* evolution. These results could then be formalized to analyse the broader picture of economic evolution, leading to development of general theories of the evolution of the space economy.

A forerunner sketch of key elements of the locational monographs can be visualized in his analysis of 'railroadization'. Andersen shows how Schumpeter emphasized that: 'rail-roadization is our standard example by which to illustrate the working of our model'. His reason was that many factors 'combine to make the essential features of our evolutionary process more obvious in this than they are in any other case more easily than in any other can the usual objections to our analysis be silenced by a simple reference to obvious facts'. This was particularly intended as a key illustration of the Schumpeterian theory of waveform economic evolution, but he used railroadization more generally, to exemplify nearly all aspects of his evolutionary theory. Hence evolutionary economic geography and regional innovation lay at the heart of Schumpeter's standard model of evolutionary economic growth.

Finally, an aspect of Schumpeter's perspective that remains germane to modern analyses of economic evolution is irreversibility, especially concerning the branching of innovations from platforms of preceding innovations, new path creation or the mutation of clusters by recombination of existing knowledge to form new potential firms, clusters and innovations. Irreversibility as he saw it derives from the imperative for economic agents always to tailor their practice to existing reality. Thus if digitization did not exist there would be no credit cards, mobile telephony or e-mail. Hence it is clear that although the process of economic evolution could have 'searched and selected' myriad trajectories, in reality it only follows one. As Andersen puts it: 'any replay of the film of economic evolution will therefore end up with a different outcome'. This hints at the importance of an evolutionary economics understanding of the mechanisms, capability limitations and institutional blockages that determine the nature and direction of path-dependence in the economic system.

IRREVERSIBILITY, EXTERNALITIES AND INSTITUTIONAL FIT

It is for reasons such as these, concerning fascination of broad and suggestive theoretical problems – like the role of location in economic evolution, for example how to explain cluster evolution in economic space; regional innovation and systemic evolution, for example what spatial specificities underpin repeated innovation; and irreversibility or path-dependence and branching, for example what is the precise role of relatedness in cluster mutation – that the school of neo-Schumpeterian innovation studies developed. It aims to continue his work and solve the many fascinating problems about evolution that he raised. In David Wolfe's Chapter 3, a biography on the neo-Schumpeterian school's sectors of interest in national, technological, sectoral and regional innovation systems is presented. In this, four key elements are of high importance for the project of this *Handbook*. First, Wolfe stresses the ways in which the co-evolving nature of the global macroeconomy towards a knowledge economy places much more emphasis on the exploitation of initially tacit (creative or scientific), subsequently formalized (codified) knowledge for innovation and growth. Clearly, knowledge was exploited in the Industrial Age, but much of it was workshop-based 'learning by doing'. Nowadays, much of the high-value segment of international trade involves the exchange of innovations. The ability to create these is not so much a product of resource-based or cost-based comparative advantage, but a more institutionally founded, knowledge-based constructed advantage. Second, Wolfe draws attention to the relationship in the neo-Schumpeterian school's work between market and institutional (that is, non-market, collective provision like public research, education and procurement) dimensions, and particularly the issue of 'institutional fit' in relation to societal and economic needs. This is also a focus of Heidenreich and Koschatzky's Chapter 39 in Part VII of this *Handbook*. Institutional fit facilitates systemic interactive learning, and in the market the kind of collective entrepreneurship through user–producer interactions that Lundvall emphasizes. In respect of regional innovation systems, Wolfe has a useful focus on the 'increasing returns' dimension of path-dependent positive 'lock-in' that reveals the market success of an innovation, but which may turn negative for the region that fails to renew its market advantage or its institutional fit. Finally, he demonstrates the ways in which network interactions are the means of ensuring refreshment of interfirm and interinstitutional fit, and how geographic proximity of the regional kind facilitates that.

Eirik Vatne's Chapter 4 takes these insights forward in mining the theoretical work of the classic location theorists to extract the relatively limited contribution that they made to regional innovation studies. As Wolfe shows, the classical and neoclassical traditions eschewed the study of 'technology', as it would be referred to, since it was impossible to model and was assumed to be a purchased input accordingly. Nevertheless their perspectives had implications for innovation, not least because their work involved explaining agglomeration, which was an innovative outgrowth of early industrialization, notably in mining and other resource-intensive activity. One aspect to note in Vatne's summary of Von Thunen's land rent theory of growth is how automatic agent response is to market signals. There is none of the sense of drama found in Chapter 2, where Andersen imagines the same situation radically changed because an entrepreneur introduces a railroad between two cities, which can be analysed by means of Schumpeter's evolutionary version of comparative statics. He also points out that Marshall, then an embryonic evolutionary economist, recognized three things salient to this *Handbook*: differentiation and integration (relatedness and its socio-technical organization); collective entrepreneurship and firm interdependence; and the market advantage from innovation that exploits these 'external economies'. These were the source of Marshall's theory of innovation, which stemmed from knowledge interchange within the 'industrial district', and between it and its markets. Agglomeration for him stemmed from the interaction of technological, labour pool, and networking 'externalities' (spillovers). Weber's contribution to innovation theory was rather less, but not negligible. Initially innovation, in the guise of technology, was treated as uniform in his partial equilibrium framework. But key 'agglomeration factors' after transport and labour costs included development of new technology and better work organization (that is, process innovations) facilitating external returns to scale. These were differentiated by Hoover into locational and urbanization economies or, as Vatne terms them, 'Romer externalities' and 'Jacobs externalities' in more modern parlance. But it was Francis Perroux who most clearly utilized Schumpeterian disequilibrium and evolutionary perspectives in his regional development model, as also noted in Andersen (Chapter 2 of this *Handbook*) arguing innovation to be the engine of regional growth.

AGGLOMERATION AND INTERNATIONALIZATION

A further model of regional development that was centred upon regional innovation and growth was Vernon's 'product life cycle'. Gunther Tichy, in Chapter 5, dissects it from its origins in practical regional planning to its demise in the face of organizational innovations in the decades since it was introduced in 1960. The basic thesis of the approach, echoing regional industrial organization of the time, was that innovation and manufacturing (product innovation) occurred in high-income lead markets (for example New York or Los Angeles) but manufacturing quickly moved to cheaper labour zones as standardization of production (process innovation) cheapened the product, thereby also enlarging its market. Tichy then traces the mechanisms causing the demise of the model's explanatory power, showing how new agglomerations may concentrate innovative production, dominant designs might undermine innovator regions, and open innovation means that manufacturing establishes only in low-cost regions (for example Apple products like iPhone and iPad at Foxconn in south China).

We conclude this introduction to the 'Regional Innovation Theory' part of the *Handbook* with two takes on the Marshallian and neo-Marshallian perspectives on regional innovation and growth. Accordingly, this provides an elegant balance of the two main theoretical wellsprings of regional innovation theory: the Schumpeterian or neo-Schumpeterian on the one hand, and the Marshallian or neo-Marshallian on the other. In Chapter 6, Marco Bellandi opens the reflections with an analysis of Marshall's analysis of industrial district processes observed partly through the lens of late-developing Italian experience (Third Italy: Chapter 1, 'Introduction' to this *Handbook*). It is immediately noteworthy that this perspective emphasizes the twofold dimensions of: (1) small and medium-sized enterprise networking making for an externalized, local division of labour; and (2) localized cultural bonds embedding economic activity in local society. The first of these furnishes what elsewhere (Chapter 1, 'Introduction' to this *Handbook*) was specified as the innovation paradigm in relation to the second, the innovation regime, institutionally supporting the paradigm. Of interest here is that these had to be mobilized into a 'world of production' (Sunley's Chapter 25 in this *Handbook*), dominated by large multilocational and mass market firms traversing Vernonesque space. This was not the case with the first industrial districts studied by Marshall in Great Britain. Accordingly, 'flexible specialization' often had to outcompete – with economies of scope (variety, innovation, design) – the predominating economic geography of scale. Globalization now challenges the evolution of this model even further. Design-driven innovation is one response to this (Chapter 1, 'Introduction', and Chapter 43 in this *Handbook*). Internationalization of product cycles is another. Organizational innovation (for example 'orchestration' or 'versatile integration' of small and medium-sized enterprise teams) and the elaboration of variety is yet another, moderating path-dependence and associated 'lock-in' practices and mindsets.

Finally, the newer neo-Marshallian practice is evaluated by Fiorenza Belussi in Chapter 7. This is characterized by major outflows and inflows of knowledge, labour, intermediaries and entrepreneurs. Modern districts are more orchestrated into groups with lead firms acting as knowledge gatekeepers, while the 'gardening' practices of localized intermediaries towards their industrial district are replaced by global trade, currency and investment rules. But in districts that embrace this more global regime, innovation practices are heightened, not least because in some cases (eyeglass frames, kitchenware, ski boots) they seek to maintain global export leadership.

Thus regional innovation theory is found to have firm foundations, notably in the neo-Schumpeterian and neo-Marshallian traditions but also in possibly unsuspected ways through scholars like Hoover, Vernon, Perroux and even Weber. What can be concluded as having a unifying or at least resonating effect upon what are a diverse group of partial equilibrium and disequilibrium evolutionary and classical or neoclassical regional scientists? Three features link them intellectually. First, most obviously for the regional economists, but tellingly also for Schumpeter and Marshall, is a recognition that economic processes interact significantly with geographic and socio-cultural proximity. Second, all are interested in the most pronounced expression of this, which is the nature of agglomeration and the way this evolves in relation to change in innovation paradigms and regimes. Finally, with the exception of the static classicals, there is recognition of the importance and force of innovation as a solvent of path-dependence and a means of accommodating to the turbulence that accompanies economic evolution.

2 Schumpeter and regional innovation
Esben Sloth Andersen

PROPOSING LOCATIONAL STUDIES

The regional patterns of the complex division of labour between firms can be studied from two quite different perspectives. First, one can concentrate on an analysis of the equilibrated functioning of a system with a given division of labour. Second, one can study how this complex system came into being. Here one has to emphasize the sequence of innovative activities and adaptive responses. However, this process often disturbs the static patterns in a radical way – as emphasized by Schumpeter's concept of the process of creative destruction.

The two perspectives suggest a split between economists studying, on the one hand, the maintenance and incremental change of static structures and, on the other hand, the entrepreneurial creation of new structures (and destruction of old ones). But the sole concentration of one or the other research speciality might be harmful to the understanding of the real process of localized evolution. In the 1950s and 1960s, this difficulty was apparently overcome through the work of a group of post-Schumpeterian researchers. These pioneering economists tried to develop a concept of a sequence of evolutionary steps in which radical innovations are followed by manifold incremental innovations and non-innovative adaptations. Such sequences of innovations were underlying Erik Dahmén's (1991) idea of development blocks, Albert O. Hirschman's (1958) idea of an inducement of entrepreneurship and investment decisions through the backward and forward linkages from a particular innovative step, and the growth pole or development pole theories of François Perroux (1988; see Vatne's Chapter 4 in this *Handbook*). However, when later researchers tried to formalize the pioneering post-Schumpeterian theories of localized growth and evolution, the underlying assumptions concerning the presence of innovations were often forgotten. Actually, many researchers were not interested in the causal sequence of decisions about innovations and investments, but rather in the static interdependence between the different parts of the industrial system and their easy translation into regional planning and development planning. Given this background, the time was ripe for Paul Krugman's (1995) intervention in the debate on the future of economic geography and development economics. His explanation of the crises in these fields is that they lack disciplined modelling. However, he forgot the even more important fact that the fields to a large extent had forgotten their Schumpeterian heritage.

The discussion of the Schumpeterian heritage can conveniently start from a provocation that Schumpeter issued shortly before he died. He provoked many of the most talented theorists, statisticians and model builders at an important business-cycle conference. Schumpeter's (1949, 328) paper led up to the 'final thesis' that:

what is really required is a large collection of industrial and locational monographs all drawn up according to the same plan and giving proper attention on the one hand to the incessant change in [or innovation of] production and consumption functions and on the other hand to the quality and behaviour of the leading personnel [including Schumpeterian entrepreneurs].

Thus he suggested that his sketchy evolutionary economics should be used to design case studies of the evolution of industries and localities. The resulting evidence should then supply the stylized facts needed for the modelling of the macroscopic consequences of economic evolution – as well as for the development of theories of the evolution of the economic system in industrial space and geographical space.

The main materials for understanding the proposal of industrial and locational monographs are found in Schumpeter's large book on *Business Cycles: A Theoretical, Historical, and Statistical Analysis of the Capitalist Process* (1939). This book concerns waveform economic evolution, but its topic is presented in a complex and ill-structured way and its theoretical novelties are often hidden in boring historical and statistical accounts. Nevertheless, the suggested 'industrial and locational monographs' and the related modelling efforts can be considered part of the effective completion of *Business Cycles*. Furthermore, a modern implementation of Schumpeter's proposal will also have to take into account his theoretical movement from individual entrepreneurship to innovative oligopolistic competition as the main driver of economic evolution. Since this part of his theory is sketched out in the wide-ranging *Capitalism, Socialism and Democracy* (1942), we face additional difficulties. The present chapter proposes a way of overcoming these difficulties for understanding Schumpeter's approach to regional innovation. At the same time the chapter tries to introduce the interested reader to Schumpeterian concepts and models. The starting point is his basic theory of evolution and his favourite illustrative example.

THE STANDARD EXAMPLE

In order to come to grips with Schumpeter's basic analysis of economic evolution, we can do no better than to consider the age of railroad construction – in both its pioneering and its more mature stages (Andersen, 2002). The pioneering period was the time when the horse-driven mail coaches were outcompeted, schemes for financing railroad projects blossomed and failed, industries supplying and using the railroads were set up, railroad towns mushroomed, and so on. The period of maturation was not least characterized by the routinization of what earlier had been novelties. The maturation period also included the emergence of early forms of the modern corporation, partly as the forced outcome of financial crises and conspicuous examples of creative destruction.

Schumpeter (1939, 304) emphasized that: 'railroadization is our standard example by which to illustrate the working of our model'. His reason was that many factors 'combine to make the essential features of our evolutionary process more obvious in this than they are in any other case'. He added that: 'More easily than in any other can the usual objections to our analysis be silenced by a simple reference to obvious facts.' This standard example was presented in the context of the Schumpeterian theory of waveform economic evolution, but he actually used railroadization to exemplify nearly all aspects of his evolutionary theory.

We can quickly grasp the way the standard example can be used by imagining that we are engaged in a dialogue with Schumpeter, and asking him for answers that can be derived from his basic evolutionary theory as well as for his major examples:

- Can a Schumpeterian innovation be implemented in incremental steps? No. It involves a jump away from old routines. Example? The replacement of the mail coach by the railroad.
- Can the innovation be implemented by its inventor? No. It is carried out by an entrepreneur based on already existing inventions. Example? The use of largely pre-existing technology for the first successful general-purpose railroad: the Liverpool–Manchester line from 1830.
- Can the innovation be induced by consumers? No. It has to be made by an entrepreneur and to be enforced upon consumers. Example? Consumers initially had to be persuaded to use the railroads.
- Can the innovation be implemented within the framework of an already existing firm? No. It presupposes the creation of a new firm. Example? A mail coach firm never moved into the railroad business.
- Can the innovation be implemented with the saved money of an entrepreneur? No. This entrepreneur needs to borrow money for his innovative project. Example? The financing of the railroad projects.
- Can the innovation be implemented by means of unemployed resources? No. The innovative project applies economic resources that were previously used for other purposes. Example? Most of the resources used for railroad projects.

The effects of the railroad innovation quickly spread throughout the economic system. However, the analysis of the overall effects of railroadization becomes highly complex. This suggests that we need limited examples that are provided by relatively remote and isolated economic regions. With respect to such cases, Schumpeter (1939, 102) emphasized that a 'railroad through new country . . . upsets all conditions of location, all cost calculations, all production functions within its radius of influence and hardly any "ways of doing things" which have been optimal before remain so afterward' (p. 102). On one occasion, Schumpeter (1941, 349) chose as his example 'the railroadization of the Middle West as it was initiated by the Illinois Central'. He emphasized that: 'while a new thing is being built and financed, expenditure is on a supernormal level, and through a normal state of incomes we get all those symptoms which we associate with prosperity'. However, the case also demonstrates 'the way in which progress is accomplished in capitalism and the old eliminated'. Thus: 'the Illinois Central not only meant very good business whilst it was built and whilst new cities were built around it and land was cultivated, but it spelled the death sentence for the [old] agriculture of the West'.

The case of the railroadization of the Midwest of the USA serves to demonstrate that it is sometimes, for an epoch of economic evolution, 'easy to locate the ignition of the process and to associate it with certain industries and . . . with certain firms' (Schumpeter, 1939, 102). However, the focus on the great contours of railroadization also implies that we miss details that might also be explained by Schumpeter's theory of economic evolution. For instance, the process of railroadization not only involved an implementation of and adaptation of the railroad innovation; it also involved a large number of minor innovations in practically all sectors of economic life. The study of these innovations can make use of the Schumpeterian theory, but Schumpeter tended to dismiss anything which came close to induced innovation. Thus he ignored such minor innovations that probably were present in the sphere of influence of the Illinois Central Railroad.

Schumpeter's approach demonstrates why he found it advisable to start his analysis of regional innovation and its consequences from highly stylized cases. It is by ignoring the details of railroadization that we can effectively use it to illustrate the Schumpeterian version of the overall process of evolution. The stylized process of railroadization started from a given system of economic routine, including the routines underlying mail-coach-based services for long-distance transportation. Then the economic system became disturbed by the introduction of railroad-based transport services with a large potential and with large resource needs. A major reorganization of the system of economic routine took place through cycles of economic prosperity and recession. The end result was a relatively equilibrated state, partly based on the routines of railroad transportation (combined with horses for short distances). We should note that this state was the starting point for the disturbance created by the addition of cars for transport over short distances. Thereby, a new chapter of the story began.

Let us try to develop a Schumpeterian analysis of a simple economic system in the nineteenth century consisting only of two remote cities, each surrounded by its agricultural district. The privately organized transport system is originally based on horse power. But it becomes radically changed because an entrepreneur introduces a railroad between the two cities. This change can be studied by means of Schumpeter's evolutionary version of comparative statics. Thus we assume that the horse-transport-based economic system is initially in a stationary equilibrium. Then a temporary disequilibrium emerges due to the creation of the railroad and the induced changes throughout the economic system. But gradually emerges a new equilibrium based on a mix of the railroad (for long-distance transport) and horses (for short-distance transport). We should note that the new equilibrium cannot be reached from the old equilibrium by a simple growth process in which the economic system is continuously equilibrated. The reason is that the railroad is obviously not implementable by increasing the number of mail coaches (the original vehicles of long-distance transport).

The general use of horse-based transport influences all production routines and consumption routines of the original economic system. An essential feature is that short-distance transport is much cheaper than long-distance transport. Therefore, both persons and goods are primarily moved over short distances. This implies that economic exchange largely takes place within each city and its agricultural environment. Since the interaction between the two cities is very limited, the producers of each city are not pressed by the competition from the other city. This means that prices of identical products can be different in the two cities.

When planning his innovative project, the railroad entrepreneur can use this information in different ways. First, he will be able to deliver long-distance transport services much more cheaply than the mail-coach firms. This means that he can take over the whole of the demand for their services even if his price is set very much above his costs. Second, he can set his price significantly lower in order to increase the demand for long-distance transport dramatically. The reason is that firms after the creation of the railroad are no longer protected by the given high transport costs between the cities.

The increased competition between the two cities will wipe out low-productivity firms and lead to more intercity exchange than before. Third, the functioning of the railroad will increase the aggregate production of the two cities because of increased division of labour and specialization. This growth will also contribute to the demand for the services of the railroad. While the railroad entrepreneur directly uses such considerations for the planning of his project, they also help him to predict the reactions of the other economic agents. He probably realizes that these reactions are characterized by a basic asymmetry. Those who are influenced negatively and directly by the railroad project can be assumed to react much more strongly and violently that those who receive the widely diffused gains. The entrepreneur must be a man of will and action to overcome the hindrances and to accept that he only gets lukewarm support.

Let us assume that the railroad entrepreneur, sooner or later, succeeds in completing his enterprise by means of borrowed money. His functioning as an entrepreneur is over when the railroad is running and he has paid back the loan. Then he has to find another role in the economic system. He can take the role as the leading manager of the railroad, but it is more likely that he invests his entrepreneurial profit and lives on as a rentier or as the owner of land. Yet another possibility seems to be that the entrepreneur continues as a railroad promoter or by making other innovations. The main reason why Schumpeter rejected this possibility is probably that it would seriously complicate his analysis. For instance, the recurrent innovator would be able to contribute to the finance of subsequent projects. But Schumpeter also could refer to empirical evidence as well as to his psychology of the entrepreneur. In any case, his assumption helps us to concentrate on the reactions to the railroad of all the other agents. For them, the railroad has changed from being a controversial issue to being a fact. It is especially the managers of all the incumbent firms of the economic system who try to adapt to the new situation in the best possible way. Let us examine four of the many possible forms of reactions:

- The mail-coach firms are facing destructive competition from the new railroad. They either close down or engage in other activities.
- The railroad implies demand for more or less directly related activities. Since persons and goods have to be brought to and from the railroad stations of the two cities, an obvious example is the short-distance transport with horses. If we add the increase of economic activity, the net result of the railroad can actually be the increased use of horses in the economic system as a whole.
- The railroad produces extensive, but more diffuse, adaptations among practically all economic agents. Consumers can access the products of the other city more easily and more cheaply, and they might want to visit that city. Some producers can expand their production; others are forced to decrease production or shut down.
- Finally, the railroad opens up the potential for a whole cluster of further innovative activity. Some of these innovations clearly fit the Schumpeterian concept. Others can be described as belonging to the type of adaptive innovations that Schumpeter disliked to think of. In any case, we have to dismiss these possibilities of innovation since they prolong the way back to equilibrium.

Even without further innovation, it is clear that the economic system has to undergo a long process of adaptation to the railroad before it reaches the corresponding equilibrium. Let us ignore the details of this process and simply assume that a stationary equilibrium based on the railroad has been reached. Here all economic agents are engaged in dull routine. However, a new would-be entrepreneur finds this system interesting. He faces two cities that, because of cheap long-distance transport, have differentiated production. If the new entrepreneur is interested in the transport innovation, it must be clear to him that it is very difficult to succeed by further radical improvements of the connection between the two cities. He is, in a sense, a realist and will not even dream about 'innovating' the system back to the time before the railroad. He probably also rejects the possibility of introducing a new means of long-distance transport – even though he might know of one that is potentially better than the railroad. The problem is that the established railroad can respond by a destructive price war. It is instead transport over short and medium distances that provides a promising field of innovation. The background is that an encompassing network of horse transport has emerged within each city and between the city and its agricultural districts. Here it is easier to implement an alternative, and here the opposition against his innovation will be more diffuse. The solution is, therefore, an automobile in the style of the Model 'T' Ford. The reason is that the car has to be affordable by smaller firms and consumers who are not located near the railroad stations. Therefore, it should not be too expensive and it should be usable for the transportation of both goods and persons.

The above analysis of transport innovations sounds like strongly stylized economic history – and so it is. However, is also serves as a simple illustration of Schumpeter's entrepreneurial theory of economic evolution. This illustration demonstrates that his theory depicts an irreversible process of change. This irreversibility emerges from the fact that all economic agents always build their behaviour according to the given situation. While the managers merely adapt to this situation, the entrepreneurs use it as the starting point for their innovative projects. In each situation, there are many ways of making an innovation. If we study a sequence of many innovative steps, it becomes obvious that the process of economic evolution could have followed innumerable trajectories. But it actually only follows one of these trajectories. Any replay of the film of economic evolution will therefore end up with a different outcome. Nevertheless, we know a lot about the evolutionary mechanisms and the engineering problems that constrain the movement of the economic system of routine in the immense space of possibilities.

SUCCESSIVE APPROXIMATIONS TO ECONOMIC EVOLUTION

Business Cycles focuses on the macroscopic consequences of the railroads that emerge from the way innovative projects were financed in the heyday of capitalism. It was the conspicuous success of the Liverpool–Manchester railroad that demonstrated the feasibility of general railroadization. The consequences included several 'manias' of railroad investment in a period in which each railroad project was still so difficult that it must be described as an innovation. Schumpeter (1939, 250) would probably have liked us to consider the financial 'manias . . . induced by a preceding period of innovation which transformed the economic structure and upset the pre-existing state of things'. Changes of the 'industrial and commercial process' are complemented by 'developments in the financial sphere'; and they lead to a 'building boom', to 'speculative excesses' and to 'the stock exchange crisis'.

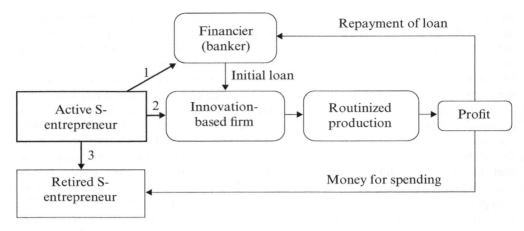

Source: Andersen (forthcoming).

Figure 2.1   The creation of a new firm in Schumpeter's Mark I model, with no possibility of further expansion

However, although Schumpeter wanted to analyse such phenomena, they are much too complex for the introductory study of his evolutionary theory and its consequences for regional evolution. For this purpose, it is more important to consider the basic structure of the evolutionary model that we have studied above. Let us name it Schumpeter's Mark I model or the entrepreneurial model of economic evolution, and compare it with his Mark II model of innovative oligopolistic competition.

In Schumpeter's Mark I model the innovative projects of the entrepreneurs take the form of enterprises that in the end are turned into routinized firms. This definition means that the entrepreneur has nothing to do with the management of the routinized firm that is the outcome of his enterprise. Thus, Schumpeter (1939, 93–6) could assume that enterprise implies that 'New Men' are engaged in the 'construction of New Plant' that is 'embodied in a New Firm created for the purpose'. He considered these assumptions to be devices 'to bring within the reach of theory an important feature of capitalist reality'. A major implication is that would-be entrepreneurs cannot directly reuse the resources of old firms for their new purposes. They instead need credit from financiers, which Schumpeter called banks.

The function of an individual Schumpeterian entrepreneur is summarized by Figure 2.1. The entrepreneur might want to implement an innovative project to create a dynasty, but he might also be motivated by the will to conquer or the joy of creating (Schumpeter, 1934, 93). In any case, he needs a loan from a financier. The granting of this loan presupposes some calculation of expected profit based on the conjecture that everyone else will stick to given routines. The entrepreneur spends the loan to establish a firm that implements a new combination of existing resources. When this task is completed, the entrepreneur retires and enjoys the part of the profit that is not used pay back the initial loan. This explains two characteristics of his basic theory of economic evolution. First, there is nothing automatic about innovation since it implies an individual entrepreneur and an individual banker. Second, the established firms are conservative since they have

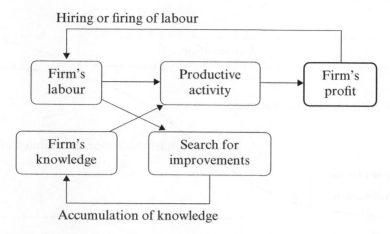

Figure 2.2   *The two feedback loops of an incumbent firm in Schumpeter's Mark II model (the pure labour version)*

no resources for expansion or for significant improvements of their knowledge. These characteristics cover the essence of Schumpeter's account for economic evolution until he changed his assumptions on incumbent firms in *Capitalism, Socialism and Democracy*. This change of assumption has important consequences for the interpretation of regional evolution – which basically becomes more difficult to obtain.

In Schumpeter's Mark II model the innovative projects are part of the oligopolistic competition between incumbent firms. Let us think in terms of a caricature of this model in which production only takes place by means of labour and knowledge (see Figure 2.2). At any point of time, the firm employs labour and has a given stock of knowledge. Labour and knowledge are combined to produce output. Thereby profit is obtained, and this profit is spent with the sole purpose of obtaining a larger profit in the next period. This increase might be obtained through the hiring or firing of employees. But it is even better to direct part of the labour force toward the search for profit-expanding improvements. The resulting increase of knowledge is used for gaining advantages in the market and for a more efficient exploitation of the existing labour force. The restless search for increased profits of incumbent firms is at the centre of the process of economic evolution in the Mark II model. Furthermore, it is the competitive pressures that enforce all industrial firms to engage in the innovative race in some area of business. However, in most areas we see the gradual elimination of the large majority of firms. The result is the oligopolistic competition between a few survivors. Even the position of these survivors is unstable since there is always the possibility that new firms might enter the game. This entry might look like the one in Schumpeter's Mark I model, but the entrant cannot in the long run rest on its initial knowledge. These characteristics of the Mark II model have obvious consequences for regional evolution.

Although Schumpeter presented his Mark II model of economic evolution in *Capitalism, Socialism and Democracy*, it was probably the writing of the historical parts of *Business Cycles* that convinced him of the necessity of developing this model. He had tried to summarize the history of 300 years of capitalist economic evolution in terms of

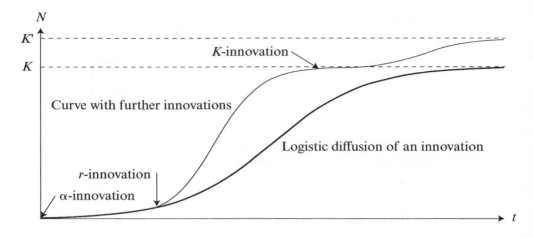

Source: Andersen (2009, 432).

Figure 2.3   Logistic diffusion with added r-*innovation and* K-*innovation*

Mark I, but he had to recognize that incumbent firms are at least the major source of incremental innovations. Since these changes can be described as an adaptive response to given circumstances, they cannot be called Schumpeterian innovations in the narrow sense. However, during the twentieth century, the established firms had increasingly become engaged in a broad range of innovative activities. Thereby they had emerged as the major driver of economic evolution. Schumpeter (1939, 96) considered his Mark I model of entry-based innovation as representing the 'Competitive Capitalism' of the past and he had to recognize the emergence, especially from the 1890s, of 'Trustified Capitalism'. He emphasized that: 'Economic evolution or "progress" would differ substantially from the picture we are about to draw, if that form of organization prevailed throughout the economic organism.' In *Capitalism, Socialism and Democracy* he acknowledged that the change had taken place. However, Alfred Chandler's (1977, Part II) analysis of the history of organizational innovation and adaptation in the railroad business serves to demonstrate that the Mark II model can also be used for the analysis of these relatively early aspects of the age of the railroads.

Although there is some truth in Schumpeter's idea of the historical movement from competitive capitalism to oligopolistic capitalism, a full analysis of the process of railroadization in the nineteenth century presupposes the application of both his models. The most abstract application of the Mark I model describes this model in terms of a single innovative event and an enormously complex process of diffusion and adaptation. The α-innovation was the first modern railroad project (see Figure 2.3). At this level of abstraction, the following railroad projects can be considered simple replications of the first pioneering project. This diffusion roughly followed an S-curve. The formula for such logistic curves is:

$$\frac{dN}{dt} = rN\left(\frac{K - N}{N}\right),$$

where N is the number of completed projects, r is the potency of spread, and K is the carrying capacity of the economic system under investigation. The diffusion of the railroads is determined by r in the beginning of the process, but the speed of diffusion slows down as the number of railroads approaches the carrying capacity. However, it is only at the highest level of abstraction that the story can be told in this way. Even the faintest wish to become realistic suggests that we need to add two less radical types of innovation. The first addition is to recognize that the railroad projects can be innovated in a way that makes it easier to replicate them. These r-innovations increase the speed of diffusion. The second addition becomes more relevant when the number of railroads has approached the carrying capacity of the system. Then it is obvious that the innovative focus turns to the issue of creating room for more railroads. The resulting K-innovations increase the number of railroads that the system can carry.

The idea of r-innovations and K-innovations can be included in Schumpeter's Mark I model. Here these minor innovations are connected to the establishment of new firms that serve as the suppliers of established railroad firms. However, the demand for the output of the new suppliers presupposes that the railroad firms transform themselves. Furthermore, it seems to be a historical fact that the minor innovations often emerged within the railroad companies. Thereby, their behaviour approached that of the Mark II model, which today is commonplace. Actually, it must also have been commonplace for Schumpeter. So we should ask why Schumpeter did not add this degree of realism to the model that he applied for most of his life. He would probably have answered that he actually had added what is presently called r-innovations and K-innovations into his extended concept of routine behaviour. This type of behaviour, however, is placed under the concept of the circular flow that only adapts to given changes of circumstances. When the α-entrepreneur disturbs this system, the consequence is a highly complex process of adaptation that, in the realistic version, includes r-innovations and K-innovations. It is only when this process has reached its end point that another α-innovation is introduced. However, he had to abstain from analysing the details of the complex process of adaptation because he could not perform this analysis precisely and because he did not want to clutter his basic message.

It has probably by now become clear that Schumpeter followed the basic heuristic of modellers: 'Keep It Simple, Stupid' (the KISS principle). This principle explains why he preferred the Mark I model over the Mark II model. It also explains why he tended to abstract from locational issues. For those of us who want to move to the locational studies that he proposed, his basic message was that we should not forget the KISS principle. So why not start with cases for which the Mark I model makes some sense? Such studies have their own complexities. When we have solved some of them, time is ready for entering the strange world of the Mark II model in which the main problem seems to be to explain why dominant firms and dominant regions are not even more dominant than they actually are.

REFERENCES

Andersen, E.S. (2002), 'Railroadization as Schumpeter's standard example of capitalist evolution: an evolutionary-ecological account', *Industry and Innovation*, **9**, 41–78.

Andersen, E.S. (2009), *Schumpeter's Evolutionary Economics: A Theoretical, Historical and Statistical Analysis of the Engine of Capitalism*, London: Anthem.

Andersen, E.S. (forthcoming), *Joseph A. Schumpeter: A Theory of Social and Economic Evolution*, London: Palgrave Macmillan.

Chandler, A.D. (1977), *The Visible Hand: The Managerial Revolution in American Business*, Cambridge, MA: Harvard University Press.

Dahmén, E. (1991), *Development Blocks and Industrial Transformation: The Dahménian Approach to Economic Development*, Stockholm: Almquist & Wiksell.

Hirschman, A.O. (1958), *The Strategy of Economic Development*, New Haven, CT: Yale University Press.

Krugman, P. (1995), *Development, Geography, and Economic Theory*, Cambridge, MA, USA and London, UK: MIT Press.

Perroux, F. (1988), 'The pole of development's new place in a general theory of economic activity', in B. Higgins and D.J. Savoie (eds), *Regional Economic Development: Essays in Honour of François Perroux*, Boston, MA: Unwin Hyman, pp. 48–76.

Schumpeter, J.A. (1934), *The Theory of Economic Development: An Inquiry into Profits, Capital, Credit, Interest and the Business Cycle*, Cambridge, MA: Harvard University Press.

Schumpeter, J.A. (1939), *Business Cycles: A Theoretical, Historical, and Statistical Analysis of the Capitalist Process*, New York, USA and London, UK: McGraw-Hill.

Schumpeter, J.A. (1941), 'An economic interpretation of our time: The Lowell Lectures', *The Economics and Sociology of Capitalism*, Princeton, NJ: Princeton University Press, pp. 339–400.

Schumpeter, J.A. (1942), *Capitalism, Socialism and Democracy*, 1st edn, New York: Harper.

Schumpeter, J.A. (1949), 'The historical approach to the analysis of business cycles', *Essays: On Entrepreneurs, Innovations, Business Cycles, and the Evolution of Capitalism*, New Brunswick, NJ, USA and London, UK: Transaction, pp. 322–9.

3 Neo-Schumpeterian perspectives on innovation and growth
David Wolfe

INTRODUCTION

Traditional neoclassical models and more recent evolutionary, or neo-Schumpeterian, models of economics treat the link between technological innovation and long-term economic growth in significantly different ways. In the neoclassical approach, innovation is viewed largely as an exogenous variable, operating outside of the properties of the general equilibrium models. However, most studies of the innovation process highlight a number of facts that do not fit comfortably into the neoclassical framework. The focus in neoclassical economics is on the static efficiency of an economy in allocating scarce resources at a single point, rather than its dynamic efficiency in generating increasing resources over time. Its assumptions about the presumed rationality of economic agents, the easily codified and undifferentiated nature of technical knowledge, the relatively free access to knowledge by firms, and the largely symmetrical behaviour of identical firms in the innovation process, are challenged by the body of literature associated with the neo-Schumpeterian perspective of evolutionary economics (Nelson, 1994, 297–304; Lundvall, 2006).

The adoption and application of neo-Schumpeterian perspectives over the past two decades 1990–2010 has led to a proliferation of approaches that place the innovation system at the centre of the analysis. The increasing salience of knowledge and innovation in the global economy focuses attention on the innovative capacity of national and regional economies, as well as on the specific dynamics of innovation associated with technological and sectoral systems. Innovation and technical progress are generated by a complex set of structures that produce, distribute and apply various kinds of knowledge. Central issues in this approach concern the degree of complementarity or fit between the various institutions which perform this role and the effectiveness with which they respond to rapid technological change. Over the past two decades 1990–2010, a growing number of policy analysts and government organizations have adopted the innovation systems approach, which focuses on the complex and interdependent role of institutional structures, to examine the relative capacity of national economies. The systems of innovation approach focuses on the nature of the systemic interactions between key actors and institutions that comprise an innovation system. The central tenet of the approach is that what appears at the macroeconomic level as technological innovations emerges out of the interaction of a wide range of economic and social actors, and that many of the market forces which determine the success of these innovations are delimited by a complex set of non-market institutions (Soete et al., 2009; Edquist, 1997, 2005). This chapter explores the evolution of the innovation systems approach, especially in terms of its relation to the neo-Schumpeterian approach to economics, and delineates the application of the approach in terms of national, technological, sectoral and regional systems of innovation.

NEO-SCHUMPETERIAN PERSPECTIVES

A critical difference between the neo-Schumpeterian and neoclassical perspectives is their conception of the origins, nature and accessibility of technical knowledge. In the neoclassical perspective, technology is seen as information that is generally applicable, easy to reproduce and reuse, and is not always distinguished from the general base of scientific knowledge. Firms can produce and use innovations by drawing upon a freely available pool of technological knowledge (Dosi, 1988, 1130). In the evolutionary view, technology consists of an assemblage of practices and components that are created as a means to fulfil a human purpose. Technologies invariably share a common structure; in other words, they are put together or assembled out of pre-existing components or parts. Brian Arthur argues that technologies are organized around a central concept or principle, which realizes its expression in the form of physical components in order for the technology to come into being (Arthur, 2009, 31–5). Technology can be defined as: 'the ability to carry out productive transformations . . . translating materials, energy and information in one set of states into another, more highly valued set of states' (Metcalfe, 1997, 279).

Technology thus consists of three key elements: knowledge, skills and artefacts, and from an evolutionary perspective, technological innovation involves the process of applying knowledge and skills to combine an existing set of artefacts into novel combinations that fill a market demand and thereby create value. The neo-Schumpeterian perspective underlines the fact that innovation involves the commercialization of new knowledge, which is what differentiates it from invention. While the actual process of creating novel combinations of existing artefacts or components is the purview of firms, enhancing the knowledge and skills needed to create these novel combinations is the responsibility of a much wider set of social institutions – hence the importance of the systems of innovation perspective for understanding and analysing the nature of technological change.

From this perspective, the process of technological advance is seen as: 'a phenomenon of organized complexity that results in cumulative and irreversibly long-run change, in which successive events are uncertain, highly contingent and difficult to forecast' (David and Foray, 1995, 17). Despite the dynamic and unpredictable nature of the innovation process, it invariably develops along ordered paths defined by the economic and technical properties of past discoveries. This is one of its central paradoxes. The early stages in the development and diffusion of new technologies are marked by an increase in diversity, in terms of the range of products, processes and services associated with the technology – witness the number of competing types and manufacturers of personal computers competing in the marketplace in the 1970s. In this early stage of the technology, the design is still variable and there is no certainty about which products will dominate the market. However, the cumulative and irreversible character of technological change results from the tendency for markets to lock into particular technologies as their use becomes more widespread. Technologies become more useful and more attractive to end users as this occurs. This phenomenon is referred to as increasing returns. In other words, history matters; additions to technological knowledge are by nature cumulative and the ability to exploit new knowledge depends on the technological capabilities that already exist (Rosenberg, 1994, 15).

THE SYSTEMS OF INNOVATION PERSPECTIVE

As was seen above, the neo-Schumpeterian perspective on innovation emphasizes the evolutionary and uncertain manner in which technologies develop. Innovation and technical progress are increasingly generated by a complex set of structures that produce, distribute and apply various kinds of knowledge and combine that knowledge into new products. This process unfolds through the heuristic search techniques developed by individual firms as part of their routines to develop and exploit the commercial potential of new knowledge. However, these routines are developed in the context of the broader set of social and political institutions that provide many of the key inputs needed to support innovation in the firm – ranging from scientific research and highly qualified labour to the sources of finance and public policy supports that sustain the process. The innovative performance of individual countries, regions or industrial sectors is influenced by the way elements of this institutional system interact with each other in the creation and application of knowledge. A key issue is the degree of complementarity or fit between the various institutions which perform this role and the effectiveness with which they respond to rapid technological change.

The key insight of the systems of innovation approach is the emphasis placed on the systemic nature of the relationship. Systems are defined as a set of interrelated components which share a common boundary and work towards a common purpose. From a biological or engineering perspective, the adoption of a systems approach focuses on the nature of the relationships between the component parts of the system. The dynamic properties of the system are always different than the properties of the individual components, as the properties of the components exert an influence over the character and behaviour of the entire set included in the system. Hence, any change in the character or behaviour of key components in the system is likely to alter the performance of the system as a whole (Carlsson et al., 2002, 234). An innovation system is thus comprised of the relationships among a set of components that interact in the production, diffusion and adoption of new and commercially valuable knowledge (Lundvall, 1992). The systems of innovation approach stresses the social nature of the innovation process wherein innovation results from the interaction among the specific components of invention, research, technical change and learning that comprise the system.

National Systems of Innovation

The national system of innovation was the first application of the concept to gain widespread recognition. Both Christopher Freeman and Bengt-Åke Lundvall trace the roots of the approach back to Friedrich List's concept of national systems of production which took into account the importance of a wide range of national institutions (Freeman, 1997; Lundvall, 2007). The first contemporary use of the term is found in Freeman's study of technological change in the Japanese economy. In that work, Freeman defined national systems of innovation as: 'the network of institutions in the public and private sectors whose interactions initiate, import, modify and diffuse new technologies' (Freeman, 1987, 1). He underlined the role of social and political institutions in supporting the adoption and dissemination of scientific and technical knowledge. His study of the Japanese system of innovation analysed the contribution of four key components to the innovative performance of Japanese firms: the role of government policy; the role of corporate research and development (R&D); the role of the education and training system; and the industrial structure of the Japanese economy.

Lundvall's approach emerged out of the joint effort with colleagues in the Aalborg school to situate their previous research on innovation theories in the context of the national system of innovation. Lundvall first used the concept of the innovation system in the mid-1980s to analyse the interaction between firms and knowledge institutions in the innovation process (Lundvall, 2007). Lundvall and the other researchers at Aalborg stressed the ubiquity of innovation in the modern economy and the need for continuous learning processes and the capacity to employ new techniques, develop new products and adopt new forms of organization in all sectors of the economy. In his refinement of the concept, Lundvall pointed to the interactive nature of the learning process that exists between the producers and users of new technology in defining it as being: 'constituted by elements and relationships which interact in the production, diffusion and use of new, and economically useful, knowledge and that a national system encompasses elements and relationships, either located within or rooted inside the borders of a nation state' (Lundvall, 1992, 2). He starts from the premise that the most valuable resource in the modern economy is knowledge and, consequently, the most important process is learning. The centrality of learning for the innovation process stems from the recognition that the knowledge frontier is moving so rapidly that simple access to, or control over, existing knowledge assets affords a fleeting competitive advantage. The capacity to learn is critical to the innovation process and essential for developing and maintaining a sustainable competitive advantage (Lundvall, 1998, 408).

Both Freeman and Lundvall emphasize the relative importance attached to the patterns of interaction between firms as part of a collective learning process in the acquisition and use of new technical knowledge. This flows from their belief that innovation is increasingly tied to a process of interactive learning and collective entrepreneurship, especially in terms of the relationships between producers and users of new technology. The innovative performance of individual countries is therefore influenced by the way in which elements of this institutional ensemble interact in the creation and application of knowledge. Lundvall and his collaborators suggest that it is helpful to think about two related dimensions of the innovation system. The first involves the structure of the system – what is produced in the system and what innovative competencies are involved in producing these; the second involves the institutional make-up of the system – the ensemble of non-market forces that shape and condition the way in which production and innovation occur (Lundvall et al., 2002, 220).

A third application of the national innovation system concept is provided in the collaborative study of innovation across 15 nations edited by Richard Nelson (1993). In his overview of the key findings of the comparative and cross-national study, Nelson argued that the use of the concept of 'system' to analyse the innovative performance of firms and nations draws attention to the role of a 'set of institutional actors that, together, play the major role in influencing innovative performance' (Nelson, 1992, 349). His analysis of the comparative results singles out a key set of institutional actors that play a consistent role in the various systems. Among those identified are corporate research and development laboratories; the role of universities, or scientific and technical education structures more generally; and the role of governments, and in particular their policies designed to influence the rate and pace of innovation. In comparing the factors that exerted the strongest influence on the innovative performance of national systems in the 15 countries, Nelson identifies the extent of interactive linkages among firms and their upstream suppliers; the role of the education and training system in providing firms with a study flow of workers with the needed skills and knowledge; the contribution of publicly supported universities and public research laboratories; as well as a wide and diverse range of government programmes. Overall, he concludes that the range of institutional structures supporting innovation vary across national systems as a result of the considerable differences in their respective traditions and their developmental trajectories (Nelson, 1992, 373–4). The evidence of this variety serves as a warning against presuming that there is a 'best fit' between socio-political institutional structures and the prevailing technological regime. It cautions against presuming that uniformity exists across respective national models or that they are necessarily converging on a common model.

Sectoral and Technological Systems of Innovation

While Freeman, Lundvall, Nelson and a number of other writers were elaborating the national systems of innovation concept in the late 1980s and early 1990s, parallel work by a number of researchers developed the technological systems approach. In a series of case studies in different sectors of the Swedish economy – factory automation, electronics, materials technology and pharmaceuticals – the researchers led by Bo Carlsson identified a distinct technological dimension that both grounded the firms involved in their national or regional context and influenced the pattern of technological development. Out of these findings, they formulated the concept of technological systems, which is defined as:

> a network or networks of agents interacting in a specific technology area under a particular institutional infrastructure to generate, diffuse and utilize technology. Technological systems are defined in terms of knowledge or competence flows rather than flows of ordinary goods and services. They consist of dynamic knowledge and competence networks. (Carlsson and Stankiewicz, 1991, 111; Carlsson and Jacobsson, 1997, 268)

Technological systems consist of a number of different elements, including knowledge or competence networks, industrial or production networks, and institutional infrastructures that are often spatially correlated. The boundaries of a specific technological system often lie within the boundaries of the national state. However, some are regionally based and are more consistent with regional than national systems. The technological system can also be delineated at three different levels of analysis. The first applies to a specific technology in the sense of a field of knowledge which can be analysed in terms of its application or the range of products in which it is used. The second level of analysis focuses on the product or artefact in terms of the markets for that product and the links to customers. The third level of analysis focuses on an interrelated set of products, which may be complementary or substitutes for each other, and operate under the same institutional arrangements (Carlsson et al., 2002, 238). Carlsson and Stankiewicz distinguish a technological system from a national innovation system in a number of ways: the national system subsumes a wide range of industrial sectors and technological areas of competence; the boundaries of a technological system may be national, regional or, in some instances, supranational; and the technological system places greater emphasis on the problems of the adoption and utilization of technology as opposed to the generation and distribution of knowledge (Carlsson and Stankiewicz, 1991, 112).

A closely related approach to that of the technological system is the idea of a sectoral system of innovation developed by Franco Malerba and others. A sectoral system of innovation is defined as:

> that system (group) of firms active in developing and making a sector's products and in generating and utilizing a sector's technologies; such a system of firms is related in two different ways: through processes of interaction and cooperation in the artefact-technology development and through processes of competition and selection in innovative and market activities. (Breschi and Malerba, 1997, 131)

The primary focus of the sectoral innovation systems (SIS) approach is on the competitive relationships among firms, with specific reference to the selection environment for the firms and their products. In this sense, the SIS approach adopts an explicitly Schumpeterian perspective. Furthermore, the SIS approach is open about the spatial boundaries of the innovation system; the actual boundaries of the system emerge from the specific conditions of the sector under investigation. Some sectors have competitive and organizational boundaries which are not coterminous with the nation-state; sectoral firms may compete in global markets, but from a highly localized or regionalized base. Consistent with other innovation systems approaches, sectoral systems of innovation display specific organizational and institutional features which are the product of the historical and path-dependent trajectory along which the sector has developed.

Regional Systems of Innovation

In tandem with the early work on national systems of innovation and technological systems, a parallel stream developed in the late 1980s, partly in response to the spread of globalization and increased attention to the importance of geographical proximity for innovation. This approach identified the constellation of institutions at the regional level that contribute to the innovation process as the 'regional innovation system'. The focus on the importance of the regional level for analyses of innovation was linked to a growing recognition of the importance of network relations among actors in the innovation process and the tendency for those networks to be spatially grounded. In contrast to the more conventional forms of interfirm relations – markets and hierarchies – this alternative form of resource allocation is characterized by transactions among interrelated groups of firms linked by both cooperative and competitive relations that engage in reciprocal and mutually supportive actions (Powell, 1990). Building on this insight, Cooke and Morgan (1993) identified two different dimensions of the network paradigm: the corporate and the spatial. Within the corporate sphere, network forms of organization represented an important mechanism through which firms can cope with the twin challenges of rapid technological change and increasing economic uncertainty. Within the spatial dimension, the network approach took on increasing importance as regional governments tried to foster the type of industrial culture conducive to innovative behaviour in the emerging knowledge-based economy (Cooke and Morgan, 1993, 544).

Central to this approach is the view that innovation and the dynamics of economic growth are geographically localized. In the context of rapid technological change and concerns over global competition and production, this focus on the regional and local dimension underlines how key elements of innovative sectors are locally influenced and rooted. Complex systems of technology, production processes, industrial organization, and their supporting infrastructures of social and political institutions exhibit distinctive spatial characteristics. Patterns of production relations aggregate over time among interrelated networks of firms, drawing upon the distinctive skills and characteristics of local labour markets in specific regions (Cooke and Morgan, 1998).

Early conceptions of regional innovation systems drew their inspiration in part from this recognition of the growing relevance of regional networks of firms, but also emerged partly in reaction to the 'one size fits all' mentality that characterized much of the thinking about science parks, incubators and clusters. According to one of the early proponents of the regional innovation systems approach, 'RIS [regional innovation system] thinking recognized from the beginning . . . the diversity of regional innovation characteristics of business and regional governance competences and capabilities and advocated diverse policy responses' (Cooke, 2008a, 394). The regional innovation system was defined as: 'the set of economic, political and institutional relationships occurring in a given geographical area which generates a collective learning process leading to the rapid diffusion of knowledge and best practice' (Nauwelaers and Reid, 1995, 13; Cooke, 1998). The strength of the RIS approach lay in its systematic linking of five key concepts derived from theoretical insights in both neo-Schumpeterian economics and economic geography: the concept of the region as a meso-political unit with some capacity to support economic development; the concept of innovation as the process whereby new knowledge is taken up and introduced to the market as new products, processes or forms of business organization; the concept of the network as a set of reciprocal linkages among actors that coalesce to pursue common economic interests; the concept of learning, particularly the institutional aspect, whereby new knowledge, skills and capabilities are incorporated in the routines of firms and innovation support organizations; and finally, the concept of interaction through which firms and relevant supporting organizations associate to pursue collective practices and projects of individual economic or commercial benefit (Cooke, 2005, 88).

Proponents of this approach insisted that regional innovation systems should not be conceived of merely as geographically delimited versions of the national innovation system. The focus on the regional derives from the observation that regions evince distinct differences in terms of their industrial structure, research and technology infrastructure, training and educational institutions, policy supports, broader governance structures and relationships between key actors in the innovation system. In this sense, regional innovation systems are seen as the complex of institutions that support the innovation process within the industrial structure of a given region. The governance of regional innovation systems occurs through a mix of both public and private organizations that can include branches of industry associations and chambers of commerce, as well as public sector development agencies and the broad range of regional levels of government in both traditionally federal systems and more centralized ones that have experienced an increasing degree of decentralization over the past three decades 1980–2010, especially in Europe (Asheim and Gertler, 2005).

The first systematic attempt to analyse and compare regional innovation systems differentiated among a series of case studies along two key dimensions of innovative activity: the governance structure and the business structure. The goal of the typology was to analyse in a consistent fashion the similarities and differences in the degree of institutionalization present in a regional innovation system, or in other words, the degree to which the system has become institutionalized, especially in terms of the level of support found for the innovation process. Drawing upon an earlier framework developed by Cooke, the governance dimension focused on the modes of regional technology transfer, as well as the modes of business interrelationship present in the RIS, and distinguished between three modes of governance: grassroots, network and *dirigiste*. The business innovation dimension was characterized by the prevailing set of relations among firms in the regional economy, in relation both to other regional firms, as well as to firms in the global economy. This dimension was concerned with the role of lead firms in the regional economy, the tendency of firms to obtain R&D from in-house activities as opposed to public research institutions, and the innovative milieu within which firms operate. It distinguished between three such sets of relations: localist, interactive and globalized (Cooke, 1998, 19–24; 2004).

The regional innovation system approach is closely linked in the broader literature on regional economies with a number of complementary approaches that describe industrial districts, innovative milieu, industrial clusters and knowledge-based or creative cities. While each of these approaches has certain benefits, the regional innovation system focuses attention on the particular setting of the regional economy within the broader dynamics of the global economy and the way in which firm interaction within the regional context and the institutional supports for regional firms affects the competitive dynamics of the regional economy. More recent work in the field has stressed the necessity of mobilizing regional knowledge capabilities in support of the innovative activities of firms in the RIS to sustain their position within a rapidly changing global economy. From this perspective the dynamism of the regional innovation system is dependent on the existence of asymmetric knowledge capabilities that are created and sustained through the process of constructing regional advantage. The innovation support capabilities of regional innovation systems depend to an ever greater extent on the degree to which the regional policy framework is effective in expanding the institutional supports within the RIS to sustain these asymmetric knowledge capabilities (Cooke, 2005).

Recent work on regional innovation systems has focused on the way in which regional economies develop new technological and innovative capabilities. Of central interest are the concepts of variety and related variety derived from Jane Jacobs's work on the economy of cities. There is evidence to suggest that the emergence of new technological capabilities and the growth of new industries is strongly shaped or conditioned by the presence of related industries within the regional economy. The creation of new combinations of knowledge is facilitated by the knowledge spillovers that occur between both technologically and physically proximate industries in dynamic and innovative regions.

These new combinations of knowledge in turn become the innovation platforms across older industrial sectors and thus provide a new source of growth for the region. This suggests that thinking about future directions for regional innovation policy should focus on measures to enhance the synergies that can emerge from the presence of related variety across industrial structures within regional economies. This approach can generate significant policy externalities where a new innovation can be applied in a wide range of sectors across the regional development platform (Cooke, 2008b, 28).

CONCLUSION

The value of applying a neo-Schumpeterian approach to understanding modern capitalist economies is in its insights into the competitive dynamics that drive those economies. This approach emphasizes the complex, uncertain and path-dependent nature of technological change and places entrepreneurs and firms at the centre of the process. At the same time, it underlines that firms and entrepreneurs operate in the context of a broader set of institutional supports that comprise the respective innovation systems, which can be analysed at the national, regional, technological and sectoral level. Regardless of which lens one adopts to analyse innovation dynamics, the study of innovation systems offers new criteria for evaluating the effectiveness of government policies in support of firm-based innovation. In the past, government policies were oriented towards overcoming or compensating for market failures; however, the insights afforded by studies of the national innovation system also make it possible to study the nature of systemic failures. The insights generated by this approach prescribe the need for a broader range of policies, which place greater emphasis on the role of social factors and institution building than is found in traditional approaches to science and technology (S&T) policy. It emphasizes that individual agents and firms operate within the framework of existing national and regional policies and institutions which influence and constrain social and economic behaviour. These institutions themselves are the product of path-dependent and evolutionary sequences of development, and the role they play in innovation systems changes slowly as a result. Effective policy-making from an innovation systems perspective recognizes that programme objectives must be matched to the institutional contexts in which they will operate (OECD, 2005, 26).

From this perspective, it recognizes that strategies and policies aimed at promoting the more effective development of innovative capacities do not operate in isolation from each other, but in the context of a broader mix of government initiatives and institutional supports which all exert an influence over firm-based outcomes. Applying the innovation systems approach enables policy-makers to identify sources of success and failure within the broader mix of institutions that facilitate or inhibit the process of innovation, as well as specific structural gaps in the innovation system. It also focuses attention on the need for greater horizontal coordination of policy initiatives and the need to align policies more effectively across multiple levels of governance. A coordinated approach to policy development at the regional and local level requires integrated policy planning at the 'governance' level, across existing programme boundaries as well as levels of government, leading to a more effective degree of 'policy alignment' (OECD, 2007, 122).

REFERENCES

Arthur, B. (2009), *The Nature of Technology: What It Is and How It Evolves*, New York: Free Press.

Asheim, B. and M. Gertler (2005), 'Regional innovation systems', in Jan Fagerberg, David C. Mowery and Richard R. Nelson (eds), *The Oxford Handbook of Innovation*, Oxford: Oxford University Press, pp. 291–317.

Breschi, S. and F. Malerba (1997), 'Sectoral innovation systems: technological regimes, Schumpeterian dynamics and spatial boundaries', in C. Edquist (ed.), *Systems of Innovation: Technologies, Institutions and Organizations*, London: Pinter, pp. 130–56.

Carlsson, B. and S. Jacobsson (1997), 'Diversity creation and technological systems: a technology policy perspective', in C. Edquist (ed.), *Systems of Innovation: Technologies, Institutions and Organizations*, London: Pinter, pp. 266–94.

Carlsson, B., S. Jacobsson, M. Holmén and A. Rickne (2002), 'Innovation systems: analytical and methodological issues', *Research Policy*, **31** (2), 233–45.

Carlsson, B. and R. Stankiewicz (1991), 'On the nature, function, and composition of technological systems', *Journal of Evolutionary Economics*, **1** (2), 93–118.

Cooke, P. (1998), 'Introduction: origins of the concept', in H. Braczyk, P. Cooke and M. Heidenreich (eds), *Regional Innovation Systems: The Role of Governances in a Globalized World*, London: UCL Press, pp. 2–25.

Cooke, P. (2004), 'Introduction: regional innovation systems – an evolutionary approach', in P. Cooke, M. Heidenreich and H. Braczyk (eds), *Regional Innovation Systems, 2nd Edition*, London, UK and New York, USA: Routledge, pp. 1–18.

Cooke, P. (2005), 'Regional knowledge capabilities and open innovation: regional innovation systems and clusters in the asymmetric knowledge economy', in S. Breschi and F. Malerba (eds), *Clusters, Networks and Innovation*, Oxford, UK and New York, USA: Oxford University Press, pp. 80–112.

Cooke, P. (2008a), 'Regional innovation systems: origin of the species', *International Journal of Technological Learning, Innovation and Development*, **1**, 393–409.

Cooke, P. (2008b), 'Regional innovation systems, clean technology and Jacobian cluster platforms policies', *Regional Science Policy and Practice*, **1**, 23–45.

Cooke, P. and K. Morgan (1993), 'The network paradigm: new departures in corporate and regional development', *Environment and Planning D: Society and Space*, **11**, 543–64.

Cooke, P. and K. Morgan (1998), *The Associational Economy Firms, Regions, and Innovation*, Oxford, UK and New York, USA: Oxford University Press.

David, P. and D. Foray (1995), 'Accessing and expanding the science and technology knowledge base', *OECD STI Review*, **16**, 13–68.

Dosi, G. (1988), 'Sources, procedures and microeconomic effects of innovation', *Journal of Economic Literature*, **26**, 1120–71.

Edquist, C. (1997), 'Introduction: systems of innovation approaches – their emergence and characteristics', in C. Edquist (ed.), *Systems of Innovation: Technologies, Institutions and Organizations*, London: Pinter, pp. 1–35.

Edquist, C. (2005), 'Systems of innovation', in J. Fagerberg, D. Mowery and R. Nelson (eds), *The Oxford Handbook of Innovation*, Oxford: Oxford University Press, pp. 514–52.

Freeman, C. (1987), *Technology Policy and Economic Performance: Lessons from Japan*, London, UK and New York, USA: Pinter Publishers.

Freeman, C. (1997), 'The "National System of Innovation" in historical perspective', in D. Archibugi and J. Michie (eds), *Technology, Globalisation and Economic Performance*, Cambridge: Cambridge University Press, pp. 24–49.

Lundvall, B. (1992), 'Introduction', in B. Lundvall (ed.), *National Systems of Innovation: Towards a Theory of Innovation and Interactive Learning*, London: Pinter Publishers, pp. 1–22.

Lundvall, B. (1998), 'Why study national systems and national styles of innovation', *Technology Analysis and Strategic Management*, **10**, 407–21.

Lundvall, B. (2006), 'One knowledge base or many knowledge pools?', DRUID Working Paper No. 06–08, Aalborg and Copenhagen, www.druid.dk.

Lundvall, B. (2007), 'National innovation system: analytical focusing device and policy learning tool', Working Paper R2007:004, Ostersund, Sweden: Swedish Institute for Growth Policy Studies.

Lundvall, B., B. Johnson, E. Andersen and B. Dalum (2002), 'National systems of production, innovation and competence building', *Research Policy*, **31**, 213–31.

Metcalfe, S. (1997), 'Technology systems and technology policy in an evolutionary framework', in D. Archibugi and J. Michie (eds), *Technology, Globalisation and Economic Performance*, Cambridge: Cambridge University Press, pp. 25–46.

Nauwelaers, C. and A. Reid (1995), *Innovative Regions? A Comparative Review of Methods of Evaluating*

Regional Innovation Potential, European Innovation Monitoring System (EIMS) publication no. 21, Luxembourg: European Commission, Directorate General XIII.

Nelson, R. (1992), 'National innovation systems: a retrospective on a study', *Industrial and Corporate Change*, **1**, 347–74.

Nelson, R. (ed.) (1993), *National Innovation Systems: A Comparative Analysis*, New York, USA and Oxford, UK: Oxford University Press.

Nelson, R. (1994), 'What has been the matter with neoclasssical growth theory?', in Gerald Silverberg, and L. Soete (eds), *The Economics of Growth and Technical Change: Technologies, Nations, Agents*, Aldershot, UK and Brookfield, VT, USA: Edward Elgar, pp. 290–324.

OECD (2005), *Governance of Innovation Systems, Volume 1: Synthesis Report*, Paris: Organisation for Economic Co-operation and Development.

OECD (2007), *Competitive Regional Clusters: National Policy Approaches*, OECD Reviews of Regional Innovation, Paris: Organisation for Economic Co-operation and Development.

Powell, W. (1990), 'Neither market nor hierarchy: network forms of organization', in Barry M. Staw and L.L. Cummings (eds), *Research in Organization Behaviour*, vol. 12, Greenwich, CT: JAI Press, pp. 295–336.

Rosenberg, N. (1994), 'Path-dependent aspects of technological change', *Exploring the Black Box: Technology, Economics, and History*, Cambridge: Cambridge University Press, pp. 9–23.

Soete, L., B. Verspagen and B. ter Weel (2009), 'Systems of innovation', Working Paper #2009–062, Maastricht: UNU-Merit.

4 Regional agglomeration and growth: the classical approach
Eirik Vatne

INTRODUCTION

Empirically, a rapid diversification and relocation of economic activities has been observed, as well as the rise of very specialized production sites such as 'Silicon Valleys' of dissimilar types, financial districts or science parks. Dispersion as well as concentration seem to coexist as economic mechanisms. In both cases, a more profound division of labour between firms, regions and nations is under way.

Localized concentration or agglomeration has been an essential part of theories explaining the spatial distribution of production and human settlement. But other lines of economic theory also explain why economic activities are spatially diversifying, caused by comparative advantages, falling distribution costs, the deregulation of national economies and the internationalization of economic activities.

Concepts like agglomeration, industrial districts, production complexes, local innovative milieux, regional innovation systems and business clusters all entail economic activity being spatially unevenly distributed and clustered in territories that are specialized in some way or another. The modern theory of embedded clusters focuses on the competitiveness of firms and competitive advantages resulting directly or indirectly from the firm's localization. The co-location of economic agents can possibly create agglomeration economies. One aspect is the cost advantages and static efficiency brought forward from the increased division of labour, scale economies, lower communication costs and positive externalities. Other economies arrive through dynamic forces such as an increased capability to learn, produce new knowledge and innovate. Regional agglomeration, specialization, innovation and economic growth come together in a modern explanation of regional economic development.

The purpose of this chapter is to bring attention to some of the early models and concepts developed to reveal the social and economic mechanisms behind the clustering of economic activity. In the first part, I will briefly discuss the early contributions to location theory, from von Thünen and Marshall to Weber, Lösch and Isard. Next, I will include a deeper analysis of Perroux's alternative approach to explaining industrial concentration, and draw some lines to modern models of clustering.

The Industrial Revolution, followed by rapid industrialization and urbanization, led to a sharp spatial concentration of economic activities. Nonetheless, early locational analysis focused on a theory of land rent, agricultural production and the influence of transport cost on the spatial distribution of economic activity (for example von Thünen, 1826 [1966]) or, more typically, on a verbal description of specific patterns of location in particular regions.

Johann Heinrich von Thünen's approach was novel for his time. He used deduction, reductionism and normative theory as analytical tools. An outcome of this abstraction was an assumption of a given market price accessible at one point in space (for example a town or larger city), uniform fertility of the soil and the same wage rate over a spatial plain, output per acre depended on unit of labour per acre, and so on. He also introduced a declining marginal product of labour as more labour-intensive methods of production were introduced.

As a consequence of these assumptions, land rent would decrease and labour intensity diminish as a function of distance from the central city and increasing transportation cost. Agricultural production would specialize (or agglomerate) in layers or rings around clustered markets (cities). Labour-intensive production would be produced nearest the market city, and land-intensive production further away.

Von Thünen's main contribution was a first formal theory of location, a theory of factor intensities and an explanation for territorial specialization. On the other hand, location factors like labour productivity, technology and important arguments for external economies were not included (Friedrich, 1929).

AGGLOMERATION AND SCALE ECONOMIES

Alfred Marshall was influenced by von Thünen and his approach with the 'given' technology and variation in transport and labour costs. Marshall used this approach to demonstrate that producers near markets would gain a 'situation' advantage in the same way as a producer located near a specialized labour market, 'especially adapted to his trade' (Marshall, 1890 [1920]).

In his time, Marshall observed a high concentration of specialized industries in specific locations, concentrations that generated specialized labour markets. He also observed that gains in the efficiency of production seemed to be associated with changing the organization of production and the division of labour between individuals and firms. By using an analogy from biology, he proposed that the human economic society would also develop specialized skills, knowledge and machines through a process of separation of work functions and differentiation of production. Parallel to a diversification of the work process, Marshall also observed an integration process through the 'intimacy and firmness of the connections between the separate parts of the industrial organism', and that 'those organisms tend to survive which are best fitted to utilize the environment for their own purpose' (Marshall, 1892 [1922], 120).

Even if we refrain from the biologism of social processes, Marshall pointed out three important aspects of evolutionary development under capitalism: first, that a continuous technological specialization takes place; second, that objects in an economy compete and at the same time are interdependent through a division of labour; and third, that this interdependence produces competitive advantages for the units that are able to take advantage of their environment.

He also argued that an increased division of labour and standardization of production, combined with expanding national and international markets, would support increasing returns to scale and further specialization. Economic growth therefore generates differentiation and integration, and producers would be more specialized and less self-supported. In Marshall's mind, scale economies are first and foremost a result of the size of the market for the products produced, not a product of the size of the factory in itself.

He used this insight to introduce two concepts of scale economies: (1) external economies of scale: 'those dependent on the general development of the industry'; and (2) internal economies of scale: 'those dependent on the resources of the individual houses of business engaged in it, on their organization and the efficiency of the management' (Marshall, 1890 [1920], 266). From this position, Marshall proposed that utilizing the gains of the division of labour could take place either inside large enterprises or through an integrated, cooperating production system inside one industry. In the latter case, external economies would develop most easily if the production system was territorially concentrated.

Marshall's intention was not to develop a location theory but to create a theoretical basis for a microeconomic partial equilibrium theory. His 'spatial' analysis was descriptive, three observations of which have been very important to the development of modern agglomeration theory (Marshall, 1890 [1920], 271).

The first was the development of a specialized labour market. Here, we meet one of the important externalities of human life produced by mechanisms broader than pure economic reasoning. History, culture and social processes influence the development of specialized knowledge, entrepreneurship, skills and cooperativeness. Specialized labour markets are localized.

The second was that localized centres of specialized production would develop a division of labour between firms, splitting up companies and generating a set of more specialized companies that could better exploit scale economies and develop more efficient and novel technology. As a consequence, firms inside an 'industrial district' would access a greater variation of input factors, and at a better price than available in environments without these externalities, given that the advantages of scale economies were transferred to the customer and not kept as monopoly profit.

The third was the advantages of a spatial clustering of persons in the same industry. This concentration would help in developing efficient channels to transmit information and speed up the diffusion of new knowledge of a technological or commercial nature. Together, these circumstances would influence the innovative capabilities of the individuals and firms present in this environment.

In short, these three elements – (1) a local pool of specialized labour; (2) local provision of inputs specific to an industry; and (3) a fast flow of information and ideas – are all basic concepts in the literature on industrial districts, in evolutionary economics and in 'new economic geography'.

AGGLOMERATION AND LOCATION THEORY

Alfred Weber's publication *Über den standort der industrien* (1909 [1929]) was the first attempt to analyse more systematically the existence of spatial concentration of manufacturing. Weber's goal was to 'determine the agglomerations of population' (Weber, 1909 [1929], 6) with the use of 'abstraction from the particular' and the 'precision of mathematics' (geometry). The result was simple models of a partial equilibrium type including location factors such as transport and labour cost and agglomeration economies. In the initial models, no internal scale economies existed and all firms produced with the same technology.

His first model consisted of points of localized raw materials in a geometric space and other points where manufactured goods were consumed (the markets). The problem of minimizing the transport cost of raw material and finished products, given one market point, would determine the site of manufacturing production. Depending on freight cost and transport infrastructure, and the physical appearance of the material (weight, form and weight loss during processing), manufacturing could take place at the raw material point, at the point of consumption or at an intermediate site. Any deviation from the point of minimum transport cost would increase the transport cost in circles around and away from the minimum point. Weber called these circles 'isodapanes'.

If ubiquitous materials[1] like water or air enter significantly into the manufacturing process, giving the finished product greater weight than that of localized (raw) materials, the industry would locate at the market and a concentration of manufacturing would appear at the same point as where the goods are consumed. The first formal argument for the concentration of manufacturing activity was therefore based on economizing with transportation costs.

The second step in Weber's approach was to introduce points in space where a lower labour cost was available. If the savings in labour costs exceed the additional transport cost incurred, the optimal location of manufacturing activity would move to the point of cheap labour.

Next, Weber introduced agglomeration economies and 'the interdependence of production units' as a location factor. Inspired by Marshall's analysis, Weber argued that this factor was unlike the two others: 'by the fact that they result from the social nature of production, and are accordingly not to be discovered by analyzing an isolated process of production' (Weber, 1909 [1929], 125). In Weber's analyses, external economies to scale are defined as a cost advantage that makes production and distribution cheaper if most of an interdependent production system is co-located. Weber's 'agglomeration factor' includes a concentration of production due to an upsizing of a factory with a constant technique, but more important economies of scale in production, purchasing or finance. Social factors of agglomeration, such as the development of new technology, better work organization, and a deeper division of labour, more efficient markets or lower overhead costs for companies sharing public infrastructure, also encourage firms to agglomerate. Interdependencies of this kind could induce savings in production costs for all the firms if they operate in the same location.

Weber's agglomeration factor was introduced in a partial equilibrium model where many firms had found separate minimum cost locations determined by the different markets they served and the surrounding points of localized raw material. Again, Weber used 'isodapanes' around the least-cost location of each firm and identified its critical 'isodapane' where the saving in production cost due to agglomeration would be exactly the same as the increase in transportation cost: 'if its critical isodapane intersects with those of enough other individual units to make up a unit of agglomeration, it will be concentrated with these others' (Weber, 1909 [1929], 137). If those firms moved to this position, they would end up with a lower sum of production, labour and transport costs and still serve the same, separate markets as before.

Formally, the Weberian model is a partial equilibrium model where the initial location is given. Consequently, the revised location is not determined endogenously and simultaneously. Weber says less about the social and economic mechanisms behind these cost savings and his agglomeration economies are also independent of the number of firms producing in the agglomeration. Weber 'seems to have been of two minds, posing broad questions about agglomeration but applying his tools in a manner that could not quite answer them' (Meardon, 2000, 331).

SCALE ECONOMIES AND EXTERNALITIES

Firms may co-locate because they are taking advantage of a specific immobile resource or they are supplying the same local or regional market. In these cases, proximity to other firms does not necessarily gain specific economic advantages for the firms based on interdependencies. If, on the other hand, the productivity in one company is positively influenced by a co-location with other firms, there exist economic advantages of inter-relationships among firms referred to as 'positive external effects'. These effects are collectively produced and spill over to attached participants as a more or less 'free' good.

In Marshall's version, external effects are external scale economies 'dependent on the general development of the industry' in contrast to the internal scale economies of an enterprise. Externalities of this kind are dependent on specialization, mechanization and the division of labour inside complex production systems, often located in the same region but not necessarily so. The implication is that external factors outside the firm, through increasing scale, can directly or indirectly influence the firm's cost structure, productivity and profit margins. Being an active and sometimes also a sleeping partner in such a 'closed' environment allows the firm to access a wider variation of specialized inputs at a lower price or better quality than is available for firms that are not part of this system. Through linkages and business networks, specialization and increasing returns to scale are thereby achieved.

The sources of these benefits are diverse and the social and economic mechanisms behind them are complex and differ substantially. However, as Gordon and McCann argue: 'It is solely the issue of geographical proximity which is the common element determining if . . . [these mechanisms are] grouped together under the general heading of "external economies" of industrial clustering' (Gordon and McCann, 2000, 516).

Edgar Hoover, among others, took Weber's ideas further and divided 'agglomerative forces' into three classes: (1) scale economies inside a firm; (2) 'location economies' related to a specific industry; and (3) 'urbanization economies' available to all kinds of firms in a location as the level of activities increase (Hoover, 1954, 90).

'Internal scale economies' relate to a diminishing marginal cost of production as scale increases, combined with serving a large market. Under these conditions, some firms will produce in large facilities on one or a few site(s) large enough to cause urbanization and a local concentration of production factors. This concentration may allow a development of external economies, but not necessarily.

'Location economies' or 'Romer externalities' are gained through well-known processes of specialization, the division of labour, the development of specialized production equipment, a specialized pool of labour, technological change and so on. 'Urbanization economies' or 'Jacobs externalities' are related to cost sharing in large infrastructure investments like transportation and information networks, scale economies in private and public services used by many industries, dynamic processes of recombination or creativity caused by a heterogeneous environment, and so on.

DIFFERENT CONCEPTS OF EXTERNALITIES

Externalities, in modern welfare theory, are only present if there is a divergence between the private and social costs caused by imperfect markets. The existence of positive or negative externalities of this kind demands direct linkages between firms, as in the symbiotic relation between apple-growers and bee-keepers. These endogenous agglomeration forces are often called 'technological externalities' and could be split into Marshall's three types of externalities: (1) technological spillover, often produced as invisible knowledge leakage when firms learn and innovate; (2) labour market pooling, often produced collectively through the division of labour and specialization also in the workforce; and (3) non-traded inputs, often acquired through social relations and networking (Krugman, 1991). Technological externalities relate to the production function and operate through direct, positive linkages between firms. These externalities will influence the production cost of the firm and thereby change the productivity of related firms.

Tibor Scitovsky's concept of 'pecuniary external economies' does not correspond to the concept of 'technological external economies'. Pecuniary externalities refer to a situation under imperfect competition and underutilized resources, where economic agents are mutually interdependent through market transactions and not directly through linkages. They are said to exist when:

> Investment in an industry leads to an expansion of its capacity and may thus lower the prices of the factors used by it. The lowering of product prices benefits the users of these products; the raising of the factor prices benefits the suppliers of the factors. When these benefits accrue to firms, in the form of profits, they are pecuniary external economies. (Scitovsky, 1954, 147)

If such scale economies exist, the private profitability of an investment carrying pecuniary externalities will underestimate the social utility of this investment. Pecuniary externalities thereby relate to the profit function of the firm and act through the market. Given imperfect competition and increasing returns to scale, pecuniary externalities imply that a firm's choice of location will influence the size of other firms' local market, or lower their costs and by that affect their profitability. This is a sort of cumulative causation effect induced indirectly by forward and backward linkages (see Myrdal, 1957; Hirschman, 1958).

GENERAL EQUILIBRIUM THEORY AND AGGLOMERATION

Weber's partial equilibrium modelling was an inspiration to both economic trade (for example Ohlin, 1933) and location theorists (for example Palander, 1935; Lösch, 1939 [1954]; Isard, 1956), all with ambitions to integrate spatial economics and agglomeration into a general equilibrium model. Unfortunately for their projects, the formalization and tools available in general equilibrium modelling could not cope with the evolutionary dynamics of Marshall's externalities, the lack of perfect mobility of production factors in a spatial economy and the persistent differences in factor prices between regions.

Ohlin's attempt to integrate trade and location theory ended up in eclecticism and a model unsuitable for studying agglomeration. Palander, on his part, gave up the Casselian model and concluded that a static equilibrium model was inappropriate for the spatial economy.

August Lösch's intention was to develop a model that identified the best location to maximize profit in contrast to Weber's minimum-cost location. In his model, demand (production) and supply (consumption), prices and location were simultaneously solved. The model was based on individual producers isolated from each other, carving out an 'ideal' market for themselves in the shape of a hexagon. Included was an assumption of a given 'best-practice' technology used uniformly in space, and a perfectly even distribution of population and raw material. This system determined the spatial structure of an economic landscape and the density of economic agents and includes a theory of endogenous market areas. The spatial structure of producers could be interpreted as the clustering of economic agents in specific agglomerations or crossroads, at regular intervals of central places, but his model did not include scale economies and increasing returns.

Walter Isard's (1956) ambition was to integrate von Thünen's method and Weber's cost minimization with Palander's extension and Lösch's system of market areas into a world with agglomeration economies. He also tried to integrate his space economy into mainstream economics with the use of common neoclassical modelling tools. Static equilibrium, perfect competition and given uniform productivity and technology in space forced him to omit the dynamics of innovation and technical change as part of his model.

Isard had a special interest in the dynamics of the division of labour and interdependences, the location of industrial complexes and the use of input–output relations of the Leontief type. His analysis of technological change therefore used a comparative static framework and gave some insight into evolutionary processes in the development of territorial industrial complexes, but did not explain uneven productivity in different regions due to differentiation in the use of technology.

A more successful attempt to understand agglomeration came with Harold Hotelling's (1929) early use of game theory and the study of spatial competition. His model showed that spatial competition is basically strategic and that the competitive game will lead firms to agglomerate in the centre of the market. His model was later modified, with the result that price competition leads to the spatial dispersal of producers and competition for the market area leads to the agglomeration of producers (d'Aspremont et al., 1979).

Smithies (1941) and Greenhut (1956) also tried to integrate aspects of imperfect competition into location theory, but under the assumption of territorially identical production costs. This consequently led to the exclusion of technological externalities as an important factor of location.

In mainstream economics the study of agglomeration came to a standstill, caused by the recognized problems of integrating increasing returns to scale and imperfect competition into the general equilibrium framework. However, a breakthrough in maths made it possible to model increasing returns and imperfect competition and subsequently led to the development of 'endogenous growth theory', 'new trade theory' and 'new economic geography'. It is outside the scope of this chapter to review these models (but see Felsenstein's Chapter 9 in this *Handbook*). Let us just note that Krugman's approach adopted Marshall's focus on increasing returns to scale and monopolistic market structures.

Krugman's model demonstrates that economic activities will agglomerate in a situation with the combined effect of increasing returns, decreasing or low transportation costs and increasing demand for manufacturing goods (Krugman, 1991; Fujita et al., 1999). In 'new economic geography' or 'spatial economics' models, demand and supply externalities (pecuniary externalities) exist alongside cumulative growth or polarization processes (Myrdal, 1957; Hirschman, 1958), increasing returns on the plant level and a self-reinforcing attraction of 'market potential' in larger regions (Harris, 1954; Pred, 1965).

A parallel theoretical development to explain agglomeration has taken place in regional science and urban economics, but it is again outside the scope of this chapter to review these contributions (see Fujita and Thisse, 2002; McCann, 2008).

DISEQUILIBRIUM THEORY AND AGGLOMERATION

An alternative route to studying agglomeration was to dismiss the neoclassical modelling framework. Francois Perroux was one of the dissenters with an ambition to construct an alternative analytical system, a general theory of interdependence based on asymmetries of economic power between agents. This system includes imperfect competition, a 'domination effect', externalities and the dynamics of innovations, all factors that do not lead to equilibrium but to a state of extended and cumulative changes and the agglomeration of economic power. In Perroux's view, asymmetric power relations are present on all levels – between individuals, firms, regions or nations (see also Andersen's Chapter 2 in this *Handbook*).

On this basis, he constructed a general theory of 'economic space' and 'poles of growth' (*'pôles de croissance'*) (Perroux, 1950), with a later application for regional development (Perroux, 1988). Regional agglomeration was thereby only one special case of the more general growth 'pole' concept.

The first element of his theory builds on a Schumpeterian understanding of the dynamic force of innovations and the evolutionary character of economic development. Perroux argued that innovations are the driving force of economic growth. The productivity of labour and capital will increase through technological and organizational innovations, but growth will be concentrated on specific industries and firms. Better efficiency in production in the growth sector, combined with new products with high demand elasticity, will lead to a situation more like a monopoly than a free market economy. However, the monopoly position is temporary. Temporary super-profit in a firm or an industry will provoke actions in others, but will also 'force' the entrepreneurial firms to reinvest their profit in the development of new products and productivity-improving measures. A cluster of innovative firms or industries of a certain scale will thus be a core in a productivity-gaining process of economic change.

The second element was a domination thesis identifying key sectors of the economy called '*industrie motrice*'. In dominant industries or enterprises, internal scale economies exist, reducing the unit cost of production. The dominant firm can therefore lower its prices and diffuse a cost reduction to other firms through its forward linkages. This would possibly increase the demand and the profit for the whole 'pole' of related industries or firms and implement a cumulative process of growth. Even if the dominant firm keeps the temporary monopoly profit for itself, increased research and development (R&D) activity due to this profit would drive the growth process further. Analysing 'forward and backward linkage effects' would identify whether an industry or a firm is 'dominant' or not. An industry demanding a large set of semi-produced inputs or system supplies would induce expansion or stagnation for many agents and by that dominate a production system.

The third element benefited particularly from Scitovsky's analysis of pecuniary externalities. Under imperfect competition, the profit of a firm is not only a function of its own transactions, but also of the transactions of other firms. Thus, profitability and productivity are not only a function of the innovative actions of a particular firm, but are also induced indirectly via the development of and trading with other firms through linked markets.

Perroux argued that innovations are driving the growth process, and externalities (particularly pecuniary externalities) diffuse growth impulses and promote further economic growth. In an economy characterized by disequilibrium and combined with extensive linkages between firms, the growth injection will therefore be much larger than in an economy without such linkages. Externalities in Perroux's mind are a dynamic force producing much more than static multiplier effects. If market linkages create advantages through interrelations, there must exist increasing returns to scale somewhere in the value chain. The size of the (local) market will also impact on the degree of competition or choice of inputs.

In essence, the growth 'pole' concept puts the focus on technological change, the mutual structural interdependencies in a growth process, the clustering of growth in economic space and why and how specific sectors of the economy or some large firms play a key role in economic progress.

Perroux's analysis of these processes and how they work is, however, diffuse, not very well conceptualized or understood and not formally modelled (Blaug, 1964; Darwent, 1969; Meardon, 2001). His ambition to create a formal, analytical alternative to the neoclassical framework was unfinished. As he developed several ill-defined concepts, many misinterpretations also followed. One critique saw his contribution to economics as more like 'a slogan masquerading as a theory' (Blaug, 1964, 551).

His ideas had first and foremost a strong influence on regional planning and the political interest in creating economic growth in troubled regions of the 1960–1970s (for example Boudeville, 1966). Growth centre policy was the outcome, a policy practice spreading to most Western countries in the 1970s.

In the process of transforming his theory to policy, there was a particular problem related to the confusion of economic and 'banal' or geographical space. Even if economic development is functionally clustered to particular sectors of the economy, there is no one-to-one correspondence that territorial clustering will also follow. With 'economic space' and growth 'pole', Perroux had in mind an abstract, topological space of economic agents. In this space, economic development is clustered – some sectors of the economy or networks of firms grow faster than others. These entities are characterized by innovative strength, dominant actors with propulsive strength and corresponding pecuniary externalities. Externalities generated by a propulsive sector or firm could of course agglomerate in specific regions, but absolutely not by necessity (Perroux, 1950).

His geographical contribution was not a theory of sectoral, regional polarization or location theory, but indications that some sectors of the economy will develop faster in 'a complex industrial "pole" which is geographically concentrated and growing, [then] economic activities are intensified because of proximity and human contacts' (Perroux, 1955 [1971], 287).

In later use of the 'domination thesis', many scholars forgot the 'structural dominance' the leading industry or firm should have and only focused on the size of a 'core firm'. Perroux's dynamic perspective of interrelations and the importance of innovations also disappeared in the later application of his thesis and ended up in static input–output multiplier analysis. The 'pole' concept was also transformed from the French to the English connotation, and deliberately to a place in geographical space instead of economic space.

'OLD' AGGLOMERATION THEORY AND 'NEW' CLUSTER THEORY: THE HERITAGE

Fuzzy concepts and ill-defined models are part of reality in social science. Earlier contributions to the understanding of territorial agglomeration are history, and new approaches lead the contemporary discourse. Still, many of the perspectives and concepts developed in the classical literature have proven to be solid and important to bear in mind today, in spite of their weaknesses.

One obvious lesson is the restriction formalization set for analysing the complex, dynamic processes behind agglomeration. As most of these early contributions were inside the realm of economics, it also illustrates the problem to include social and cultural perspectives or technological change in formal economic modelling. Another insight is that the agglomeration of economic activity is influenced by other aspects than knowledge spillovers, untraded interdependencies and the proximity of related partners. Market potential, transportation costs or internal scale economies are still relevant aspects of agglomerations.

In the end, it is the productivity and profitability of firms that determine whether a cluster of them grows faster in some locations than others. One reason is localized scale economies and cost advantages in production, distribution or financing; another a changing pattern of organization and knowledge production. As the focus of the study of agglomeration has turned more and more towards dynamic, innovative processes, it would also be wise to ask questions about cost efficiencies and economizing with input factors as part of modern cluster theory.

The conceptual differences between internal or external scale economies, location and urbanization economies and technological and pecuniary externalities are also wisdoms from the 'old' school that are important to keep in mind alongside the study of technological externalities, the role of knowledge spillover and the creation of new knowledge. Perroux's focus on the prominence of specific innovative industries or large key firms is still relevant in our study, for example, of the clustering of biotechnological activity and the impact that growth industries have on other sectors of the economy.

In contrast to Perroux's or Isard's focus on large enterprises, industrial complexes, asymmetries in power and location economies, contemporary studies of clustering and innovation seem to be more interested in small-scale, new firm formation, heterogeneity in business services, trust and diverse urbanization economies. This change in focus is relevant and reflects the changing landscape of production and the dismantling of Fordism, but still asymmetries in the power of business relations are an important factor of agglomeration.

The confusing debate on 'economic' or 'banal' (geographical) space is also relevant to the proximity debate, if 'local buzz' or 'global pipelines' are the most important channels for the distribution of information and knowledge, or for the diffusion of growth. Do positive externalities diffuse through territorial or institutional channels, or both? Can Perroux's economic space be compared with Porter's 'industrial clusters', and 'banal' space with Porter's 'regional clusters' (Porter, 1990)? Insights from the debate following Perroux's confused delimitation of agglomerations are therefore still relevant to the debate on the territorial boundary of clusters.

Lastly, we could learn an important lesson from the transformation of Perroux's abstract theorizing of agglomerated, economic growth and the perverted use of his theoretical ideas in public policy. In this transformation, a lot of the dynamic substance of the theory disappeared and ended up as simple beliefs that the implementation of a larger production facility in a locality would generate backward or forward linkages and a cumulative process of localized growth. From this experience, we have learned that it is very difficult to create agglomeration economies by decree.

As thoroughly discussed in other chapters, a regional innovation system (RIS) consists of the institutional infrastructure that supports learning and development of new knowledge or practices within the frame of a region. In an RIS two subsystems of actors are involved: a production system of manufacturing or service firms, and a supportive infrastructure of knowledge-generating agents such as schools universities, research laboratories, technology transfer agencies and so on (Cooke et al., 1998). In addition, an interaction between the two systems must be in place to create a pulsating environment for exchange of ideas, diffusion of knowledge, learning and, in the end, commercial projects of relevance for the economic development of the region.

CONCLUSIONS

In modern debates on regional development and innovation, the coexistence of a knowledge-generating infrastructure and a need for proximity between actors in learning processes have captured a prominent position. The classical location and agglomeration theory did not contemplate too much the importance of these institutions and the nature of knowledge. So, why is this heritage still important for our understanding of regional innovation systems?

First, the roots of modern understanding of the spatial clustering of firms and how they develop interdependencies goes back to Marshall. His understanding of the evolutionary nature of firms and their specialization, the localized nature of labour markets and the importance of skills, or the 'sticky' nature of the diffusion of knowledge and learning, has influenced a broad set of scholars interested in the 'new', 'evolutionary' or 'proper' economic geography, the studies of 'industrial districts' or in the strategic management-based cluster theory. This stream of research is also well integrated in the systemic understanding of the RIS, particularly the operation of the production system of private firms.

Second, Perroux did not succeed in his grand ambition to develop an alternative model of economic development. His understanding of economic growth as an innovation-driven, evolutionary and clustered process integrated in a system of interdependent agents including a key actor has, nevertheless, inspired a further development of this insight. One example is parts of a neo-Schumpeterian approach to understand how technological change relates to economic growth and a clustering of these processes in specific sectors or regions (for example Dosi et al., 1990). In this perspective technological change is related to socio-institutional conditions in specific societies and seen as an evolutionary and uneven development path. This understanding has been used to argue for the existence of 'national systems of innovation' and, later, 'regional innovation systems'.

Lastly, in the modern version of agglomeration or cluster theories, much more emphasis has been put on the role of localized knowledge spillovers and the interactive and knowledge-based nature of production in mature economies. Applications of these insights are also present in the contemporary understanding of regional innovation systems as being foremost, a spatial clustered phenomenon.

NOTE

1. Available everywhere, at roughly the same cost.

REFERENCES

d'Aspremont, C., J.J. Gabszewicz and J.-F. Thisse (1979), 'On Hotelling's "Stability in Competition"', *Econometrica*, **47** (5), 1145–50.
Blaug, M. (1964), 'A case of Emperor's clothes: Perroux's theories of economic domination', *Kyklos*, **17**, 551–64.
Boudeville, J.R. (1966), *Problems of Regional Economic Planning*, Edinburgh: Edinburgh University Press.
Cooke, P., M.G. Uranga and G. Etxebarria (1998), 'Regional systems of innovation: an evolutionary perspective', *Environment and Planning A*, **30** (9), 1563–84.
Darwent, D.F. (1969), 'Growthpoles and growthcentres in regional planning – a review', *Environment and Planning*, **1**, 5–32.
Dosi, G., K. Pavitt and L. Soete (1990), *The Economics of Technical Change and International Trade*, New York: Harvester Wheatsheaf.
Friedrich, C.J. (1929), 'Editor's introduction: the theory of location in relation to the theory of land rent', in A. Weber, *Theory of the Location of Industries*, Chicago, IL: University of Chicago Press.
Fujita, M., P. Krugman and A. Venables (1999), *The Spatial Economy: Cities, Regions, and International Trade*, Cambridge, MA: MIT Press.
Fujita, M.P. and J.F. Thisse (2002), *Economics of Agglomeration*, Cambridge: Cambridge University Press.
Gordon, I.R. and P. McCann (2000), 'Industrial clusters: complexes, agglomeration and/or social networks?', *Urban Studies*, **37** (3), 513–32.
Greenhut, M.L. (1956), *Plant Location in Theory and Practice: The Economics of Space*, Chapel Hill, NC: University of North Carolina Press.
Harris, C.D. (1954), 'The market as a factor in the localization of production', *Annals of Association of American Geographers*, **44**, 315–48.
Hirschman, A.O. (1958), *The Strategy of Economic Development*, New Haven, CT: Yale University Press.
Hoover, E.M. (1954), *Location Theory and the Shoe and Leather Industries*, Cambridge, MA: Harvard University Press.
Hotelling, H. (1929), 'Stability in competition', *Economic Journal*, **39** (153), 41–57.
Isard, W. (1956), *Location and Space-Economy*, Cambridge, MA: MIT Press.

Krugman, P. (1991), 'Increasing returns and economic geography', *Journal of Political Economy*, **99** (3), 483–99.

Lösch, A. (1939), 'Die räumliche Ordnung der Wirtschaft. Eine Untersuchung über Standort, Wirtschaftsgebiete und Internationalen Handel', in W.H. Woglom and W.F. Stolper (transl.) (1954), *The Economics of Location*, New Haven, CT: Yale University Press, pp. 100–130.

Marshall, A. (1890), *Principles of Economics: An Introductory Volume*, 8th edn (1920), London: Macmillan.

Marshall, A. (1892), *Elements of Economics of Industry. Volume I of Elements of Economics*, 3rd edn (1922), London: Macmillan.

McCann, P. (2008), 'Agglomeration economies', in C. Karlsson (ed.), *Handbook of Research on Cluster Theory*, Cheltenham, UK and Northampton, MA, USA: Edward Elgar, pp. 23–38.

Meardon, S.J. (2000), 'Eclecticism, inconsistency, and innovation in the history of geographical economics', *History of Political Economy*, **32** (4), 325–59.

Meardon, S.J. (2001), 'Modeling agglomeration and dispersion in city and country', *American Journal of Economics and Sociology*, **60** (1), 25–57.

Myrdal, G.M. (1957), *Economic Theory and Under-Developed Regions*, London: Gerald Duckworth & Co.

Ohlin, B.G. (1933), *Interregional and International Trade*, Cambridge, MA: Harvard University Press.

Palander, T. (1935), *Beiträge zur Standortstheorie*, Uppsala: Almqvist & Wicksell.

Perroux, F. (1950), 'Economic space: theory and applications', *Quarterly Journal of Economics*, **64** (1), 89–104.

Perroux, F. (1955), 'Note sure la notion de pole de croissance', [Note on the concept of 'growth poles'], English translation in I. Livingstone (ed.) (1971), *Economic Policy and Development*, London: Penguin Books, pp. 307–20.

Perroux, F. (1988), 'The pole of development's new place in a general theory of economic activity', in B. Higgins and D.J. Savoie (eds), *Regional Essays in Honor of Francois Perroux*, Boston, MA: Unwin Hyman, pp. 48–76.

Porter, M. (1990), *The Competitive Advantage of Nations*, New York: Free Press.

Pred, A.R. (1965), 'The concentration of high-value-added manufacturing', *Economic Geography*, **41** (2), 108–32.

Scitovsky, T. (1954), 'Two concepts of external economies', *Journal of Political Economy*, **62** (2), 143–51.

Smithies, D.M. (1941), 'Optimal location in spatial competition', *Journal of Political Economy*, **49** (3), 423–39.

Von Thünen, J.H. (1826), *Isolated State: An English Edition of Der isolierte Staat*, J. Wartenberg and P. Hall (transl.) (1966), Oxford: Pergamon Press.

Weber, A. (1909) *Alfred Weber's Theory of the Location of Industries*, C. Friedrich (transl.) (1929), Chicago, IL: University of Chicago Press.

5 Innovation, product life cycle and diffusion: Vernon and beyond

*Gunther Tichy**

In its condensed form the regional version of the product-cycle hypothesis states that products are invented in lead markets, characterized by high income and information density. They are manufactured there initially, but the more they get standardized the more manufacturing is shifted to low-income regions and countries. This idea was developed by Vernon (1966) in a short article based the author's practical experience. As head of the path-breaking 'Metropolis 1985' project (Vernon, 1960) he became familiar with the difficulties of explaining New York's competitiveness by the traditional comparative cost paradigm. The challenging task of this three-year study was to analyse and forecast the region's economic and demographic features up to 1985. 'Everyone agrees that the metropolitan behemoth surrounding New York Bay is on the move. But there are considerable differences of view over the direction in which it is moving' (Vernon, 1960, 1). The results filled nine volumes, the last one a summary by Vernon (1960) himself.

The metropolitan area study was concerned with population, employment and production growth, with New York's competitiveness and its determinants. The results did not yet turn up as a regional version of the product-cycle hypothesis, but collected some of its most important components: 'The New York area . . . acted as a magnet for many kinds of national-market activities and services that experienced a comparatively fast growth in national employment. The other was a persistent change in the competitive position of the Region's national-market activities; that is, in individual lines there was a slower growth. . . . But the Region's mix has steadily boosted its growth', concluded Lichtenberg (1960, 179) in Volume 7 of the study. '[N]ewly created economic activities seem attracted to the area. . . . There is a considerable group [of firms], however, whose overriding locational need is to be able to tap a pool of facilities – of space, of skills, of suppliers, or freight services – such as the New York area is able to provide, and to share these facilities with other producers' (Vernon, 1960, 68–9). Springing up and being wiped out quickly they develop and manufacture 'products whose characteristics could not be accurately anticipated – products, that is, which were unstandardised' (Helfgott et al., 1959, 11). But even if Vernon emphasizes producing the unpredictable as New York's growth driver, he appears to believe that this strength relies more on availability of facilities and flexibility for product development than on higher innovativeness per se.

This chapter will first sketch the main elements of Vernon's model; the following section will elaborate the critical assumptions responsible for Vernon's regional product cycle. The chapter then pursues the further development in regional and suggestively in macro theory, concentrating on the critical points in traditional and recent applications. A final section concludes.

VERNON'S REGIONAL MODEL OF THE PRODUCT CYCLE

The Metropolis 1985 study was dominated by the question: how can New York grow, given its lack of space and its high costs of production? Vernon's answer was a regional adaptation of the product-cycle hypothesis, developed by Kuznets (1930) and Burns (1934). Characteristics of infrastructure, industries and products such as, for example, information density, supply of services, newness of production, or flexibility came out as important factors explaining New York's competitiveness, with the migration of standardized products to cheaper and less crowded regions as a dampening effect. In the mid-1960s interest shifted from the regional to the international level: in 1965 Hirsch, a doctoral student of Vernon, finished his thesis on 'Location of industry and international competitiveness' (Hirsch, 1967) and Vernon became director of the 1965 Harvard Multinational Enterprise Project, dealing with foreign direct investment and competitiveness in international trade. Both became aware that traditional trade theory, based on comparative advantage, could explain neither American competitiveness in international trade nor the relative labour intensity of American exports (compared to imports; the Leontief paradox). Recognizing that comparative advantage is not static (Hirsch, 1967, v) and that knowledge is not a universal free good, Vernon (1966) introduced product design and development, in addition to capital and labour, as a third factor of production, and developed a demand-driven theory of innovation. Even if entrepreneurs in all countries have equal access to scientific knowledge, those in high-income countries are more likely to be aware of the need for new products.

Consciousness of the need as well as responsiveness to potential demand rely on the ease of communication, which is a function of geographical proximity. High-income consumers will be the first to demand (and are able to buy) advanced new products, and producers in high-income countries, confronted with high wages, will be the first to introduce new labour-saving devices. But new products are not only invented in high-income countries, they are also manufactured there, as their further development and improvement affords specific skills and face-to-face contacts, and initially limited demand impedes mechanization. It is not the supply of factors as such, but the special mix of factors which makes high-income agglomerations competitive. The high cost of production is no problem at this stage as the innovator enjoys monopoly and the price elasticity of new products tends to be low. The more the product gets standardized, scale economies are achieved and demand increases, so face-to-face contacts and tacit knowledge lose importance, but price becomes an argument. The production is shifted to low-wage destinations. Vernon (1966, 200) emphasized that a sufficient level of demand in the recipient region is a necessary precondition for relocation, but that threat – due to inertia – is a more reliable stimulus than opportunity.

In the mid-1960s, as Vernon (1966, 199) became more interested in the impact of the product cycle on international trade, he switched from the two-region to a three-country model, and summarized the results in a famous graph: new products are invented and manufactured initially by the United States, the most innovative country at that time; the rest of the world, unable to invent and produce that specific type of goods, has to import them. As the product matures and 'other advanced' countries' domestic markets grow, they start to manufacture by themselves, substituting imports; the US, however, still remains the main exporter. In the product's standardization phase 'less developed countries' start production, the US becomes a net importer, and other advanced countries' net exports shrink. The empirical evidence for this pattern came out as weak, however, at that time, before the digital revolution facilitated communication and information transfer. Vernon found more evidence for a regional shift of production within the United States to its low-wage south, but for international direct investment there were 'only the barest shreds of corroboratory information' (Vernon 1966, 204).

In the late 1970s Vernon (1979, 255) observed that: 'The last decade has produced a flowering of hypotheses that purport to explain the international-trade and direct-foreign-investment activities in terms of the so-called product cycle'. But he himself had lost his belief in the power of this hypothesis. The rapid spread of multinationals gave Vernon (1971) a striking illustration of the extent to which modern means of communication permit an integrated organization to link resources in different national economies. Multinational firms vastly extended their geographical reach by overseas subsidiaries, standardizing their products on a world basis (Vernon, 1979, 262) by ingathering these subsidiaries under the discipline and framework of a common global strategy and a common global control (Vernon, 1968 [1972], 10). Quick transfer of manufacture of new products to foreign subsidiaries drastically shortened the product cycle. Vernon still adhered to the hypothesis of the home market's importance for innovation, but no longer to manufacturing there after the pilot phase. Furthermore he emphasized that the income gap had decreased, that the home basis of the EU had increased, and that the world had become multi-polar.

VERNON'S FOUR CENTRAL ASSUMPTIONS AND THE CONSEQUENCES

The ensuing discussion on the product cycle suffered from being based on two Vernons. Vernon I's broad socio-economic narrative in Metropolis does not lack qualifications as to supply elements, to innovative activities outside Metropolis, to the variety of goods or to competition, but cannot deduce a strict cycle. Vernon II (1966, 1972) can deduce a deterministic cycle, but at the cost of four strong assumptions: a multinational one-product firm in a three-region world, the identity of product cycle and regional cycle and the ability of the core's firms continuously to provide small demand-driven innovations:

1. The product affords high-income demand and urbanization economies for design and development. The entire product is manufactured by one firm, no intermediate products are bought. As the single product of the single firm is not modified after having reached its dominant design, the life cycle of the product coincides with the life cycle of the firm, the industry and the market.
2. Multinational firms are central, as the transfer of manufacturing is almost exclusively push and rests predominately on direct investment: multinationals shift the manufacture of products to 'other advanced' and later to 'less developed countries' as soon these have reached their dominant design and the demand in the recipient countries is strong enough to afford an own plant.

3. Demand elements dominate (in line with contemporary conceptions; see for example Schmookler, 1966). Innovation occurs where the demand for new products is highest, and manufacturing is transferred to low-income regions with sufficient demand.
4. High-income regions are able to produce 'new' products continuously, thereby staying competitive even if manufacturing of mature products is continuously shifted to the periphery. Combined with the involvement of customers this implies small rather than radical innovations, as radically new products tend to be developed by new firms in new environments (Brezis and Krugman, 1993).

Relaxing these assumptions removes the product cycle as a general and typical phenomenon. Irrespective of the strong assumptions, irrespective of Vernon's own reservations as to the future of the product cycle and in spite of critical objections in the literature, the model was widely applied. It found its way into macroeconomics after having been formally modelled by Krugman (1979) and Grossman and Helpman (1991). In the 1990s most ordinary analyses of advanced countries' competitiveness were based on product-cycle considerations. The formalization of Vernon's hypothesis, however, removed much of its catholic flavour. Since the 1990s a petty version of the product-cycle model stood at the basis of all policy proposals of regional, national and international agencies (Europäischer Rat, 2000; OECD, 2007). Reduced to a technical, more or less deterministic relation, almost a rule of thumb, and demand relegated to the second rank at the expense of supply, 'high technology' replaced 'new products' and 'industries' replaced 'products'; in this concept developed high-tech products swiftly move to emerging countries, so that advanced countries' industries are continuously forced to '[move] up the value chain . . . The survival of growth of industries and firms in high-cost and high-productive economies depends directly on their capacity to innovate and move into new areas of activity' (OECD, 2007, 121).

In geography and regional economics a slightly modified version of Vernon's model came up as the workhorse in the late 1970s. Norton and Rees (1979, 151) underlined that: 'The importance of the product cycle and the spawning effect of growth industries in peripheral locations cannot be overemphasized.' Suarez-Villa (1984), criticizing the dominance of demand elements in the product-cycle literature, has an eye on industries and their strategies, not on product categories: he considers the change of corporate strategies in the course of the product cycle as the relevant aspect. Markusen's (1985) profit-cycle theory explored how, why and when a region's leading industries undergo major changes. She hypothesizes that changing sources of profitability along an industry's evolutionary path will first concentrate and later disperse production geographically, setting in motion a methodically destabilizing process for regional economies. Traditional theories of regional development have not only failed to account for innovation and long-run structural change, but have ignored the role of corporate strategy and the existence of market power as well. Inspired by the manufacturing drain from the American and British (Oakey et al., 1980) industrial belt, the bulk of the regional literature delved into the filtering-down process (Thompson, 1969) from the core regions, mainly by the way of branch plants. Vernon's central question concerning the preconditions of innovation turned up again, but not before the late 1980s (Oakey, 1985; Saxenian, 1994).

WHAT IS LEFT OF VERNON'S REGIONAL VERSION OF THE PRODUCT CYCLE?

Product-cycle ideas are alive today, but it is not Vernon's full model any more. Deliberately selected elements are scattered over a multitude of applications in theory and policy, ranging from growth, development, foreign trade, innovation and technology to regional and urban economics and planning. In particular the policy proposals to sustain industrial countries' competitiveness rely extensively on product-cycle considerations as mentioned above. The following remarks will concentrate on innovation and regional economics, nevertheless.

Where does Innovation Occur?

Vernon (1966, 191–2) was correct in assuming that in principle all enterprises, wherever located, 'can assure equal access to the knowledge that exists in the physical, chemical and biological sciences'. But:

> It is a mistake to assume, however, that equal access to scientific principles in all advanced countries means equal probability of equal application of these principles in the generation of new products. There is ordinarily a large gap between the knowledge of a scientific principle and the embodiment of the principle in a marketable product . . . There is good reason to believe, however, that the entrepreneur's consciousness of and responsiveness to opportunity are a function of ease of communication; and further, that ease of communication is a function of geographical proximity.

This is strongly confirmed by empirical evidence as to the strength of the distance–decay factor (Jaffe and Trajtenberg, 1996; Eaton et al., 1998; Bottazzi and Peri, 2000; Tichy, 2008); Venables (2001) estimated a reduction of technology transfer to 65 per cent when the transfer distance increases from 1000 km to 2000 km. The geographic spread of innovations and the speed of diffusion strongly depend on the receiving country's human capital and complementary assets (Teece, 1986) on the receivers' side, and on innovating firms' (limited) willingness to diffuse their intellectual property (Tichy, 1998). Technologies which are transferred to subsidiaries are about ten years old and licences for innovations are still older (Mansfield et al., 1982).

In the early 1960s Vernon positioned the location of the entrepreneurs that bridge the gap between 'scientific principle and the embodiment of the principle in a marketable product' in the urban economy of Metropolis; in the mid-1960s he favoured high-income USA, even if he accepted that specialized knowledge of European and Japanese firms had led to material- and capital-saving innovations. Hirsch (1967), putting more weight on the supply of skills, preferred small leading countries which lack a broad array of material resources. Oakey (1985) accentuated the compulsion for the core regions to continuously innovate and stressed the importance of innovating high-tech small and medium-sized enterprises (SMEs). More recently, with industries increasingly science-based, science centres evolved as the dominating seedbeds of new products (Zucker and Darby, 2006). Brezis et al. (1993) and Brezis and Krugman (1993) emphasized that revolutionary innovations are most likely implemented in new agglomerations; producers in the established centre may not adopt them: given their experience they remain more productive with the old-established technology.

Duranton and Puga (2001) (see Capello's Chapter 8 in this *Handbook*) formalized a version of the regional product-cycle model in the context of a micro-based general equilibrium model of urban economics, and demonstrated that new firms are established in more diversified areas. Cities no longer differ by sectors but by functions, some 'churning new ideas and new products . . . other cities specialise in more standardised production' (Duranton and Puga, 2001 1471).

Contrary to Vernon, all these later versions of the product cycle call attention to a declining phase and to a potential degeneration of regions to, 'old industrial areas' (Tichy, 1981, 1987). The empirical work of Norton and Rees (1979, 151) and Norton (1981) revealed that the American core regions had lost their innovative capacity in parallel to the manufacturing drain. The machine-tool industry, their core competency, had lost importance, and for the new industries southern and western regions gathered more competencies. Norton (1981) found three explanations: the mobility of mature industries; political maturity as institutional arthritis; and the dispersion of innovative activity. Utterback (1979), however, held that a technical rejuvenation was possible, and stressed the indigenous potential for economic revival.

New Products and the Importance of Dominant Design

Neither in his Metropolis study nor in his 1966 article did Vernon define 'new' products; he only indicated some general characteristics: goods demanded by high-income earners, goods whose restricted demand impedes mechanization, labour-saving devices, products affording specialists and face-to-face contacts, and so on. According to Hirsch most 'new' products follow a product cycle, only 'Certain [first-phase] product groups may be manufactured at less cost in other countries' (1967, 85). Following Kuznets (1953, 254) Hirsch defined 'new' as involving a revolutionary invention or a discovery. The standard geographers' model, as well as the Organisation for Economic Co-operation and Development and European Union (OECD–EU) policy model, rely on the assumption that only high-tech products can follow a product cycle by being invented and temporarily manufactured in high-income agglomerations, before migrating to low-cost destinations after having approached their dominant design.

But what is a 'new' product, what is a 'dominant design', and can dominant designs change? The Kuznets–Hirsch definition of 'new' as involving a revolutionary invention or a discovery applies more to the invention of a new technical principle such as the steam engine, the automobile, the tyre or the integrated circuit (see discussion of 'radical innovation' in Chapter 1, 'Introduction', to this *Handbook*). The invention of a new principle is a rare event, however. Few products, consequently, would follow a product cycle, and besides it is not unlikely that revolutionary technologies are first adopted in new agglomerations. More frequent is the development of products 'new' in a much more restricted sense. Anderson and Tushman (1990) define product innovations as changes that increase the product performance frontier or create new uses that customers value, measuring product performance by speed, cost, usability or any other performance criterion deemed important from a user's standpoint. Not the automobile, but such components as the airbag; not the pneumatic tyre as a principle, but the radial ply tyre;

not the integrated circuit but the compact disk; or, as a non-technical example, specific fads of fashion. Production can easily start in less-skilled locations for products which are 'new' merely in a restricted sense.

Vernon and Hirsch assume a clear break between the phases of the cycle, with the formation of an everlasting dominant design (Abernathy and Utterback, 1978), and the standard product-cycle policy models follow suit. But the majority of products are progressively modified and improved during their life, and firms take pain to differentiate products, and restrict offshoring by keeping the advanced versions at home (Dachs and Zahradnik, 2008; Jungmittag, 2008). Most new products are minor or major enhancements of already existing products; the location of production in these cases depends on whether the enhancement needs a change in production technology. Changes in product characteristics can easily be transferred to a plant at the periphery, while continuous changes in production methods imply that production stays in the agglomeration in which the products were designed. Landes (1969, 100–104) and Gort and Klepper (1982) illustrate how many different approaches proved necessary and how much time was needed to establish a dominant design. But Teece (1987) stresses that innovation can occur lower down in the design hierarchy: the famous DC-3 may have been the dominant design of a passenger plane, but the DC-8 and Boeing 707 jets were later dominant designs of the (same) product, and the wide bodies a yet further one. At the end of the cycle of the 'product DC-3' another 'product' (or dominant design) was invented and produced by the same firm in the same plant.

Recent experience suggests that Vernon's ideas as to the character of the products following a product cycle need adaptations (Tichy, 1991), but are nevertheless more realistic than the perceptions of the familiar OECD–EU policy model. Vernon (1979, 256) is right in ranking an advanced specialized home market higher than technology. High-tech is neither a necessary nor a sufficient condition. Such products may follow a product cycle and are manufactured in agglomerations during their pioneer phase, but this phase may be extremely short, especially if these products address mass markets (see the next subsection). Advanced investment goods, which are in a continuous process of improvement – but not necessarily considered as high-tech by the usual definitions – do not follow a product cycle in most cases.[1]

Filtering Down

The transfer of products from the agglomeration to the periphery has three aspects: Who transfers, what and when? In Vernon's seminal 1966 article the transfer of production to the periphery occurred exclusively by push: whenever the product has entered its mature phase and demand in low-income countries has started to rise, manufacturers shift the production to low-cost destinations. This is possible because Vernon's dominant way of transfer is to subsidiaries of multinational firms. They are specialists in the handling and transfer of information that is less efficiently transmitted through markets than within firms (Magee, 1977, 318). This was true in the 1960s and 1970s when US rust-belt corporations shifted production to branch plants in the periphery (Erickson, 1980). Recent research revealed, nevertheless, that multinationals concentrate foreign direct investment (FDI) on sectors with low research and development (R&D) intensity (Jungmittag, 2008). Other entrepreneurs are even less inclined to transfer manufacturing – they lose scale economies and accumulated learning effects, at least in the short run, and problems and costs of transfer are not easy to anticipate – product-cycle-like transfer is less common than Vernon believed.

But even at Vernon's time the transfer of production by way of multinationals' direct investment (push) was only one of several alternatives, and even then not the most important one. The production of cameras was not transferred to Japan by multinationals' push, nor was the production of consumer electronics to Southeast Asia, nor that of cars to South Korea. Production was pulled away by the attracting countries, not least as a result of deliberate government policy (Ernst, 2000). But this transfer was not simple imitation: the 'new' or modified products were devised by the 'imitators' for a mass market with low prices, designed for simple manufacturing and simple handling. Other forms of pull-transfer are learning effects resulting from training in multinationals' subsidiaries, simple imitation by local producers, licences or franchising. This implies that the transfer of 'standardized' products to non-agglomerations is not the simple mechanical decision that the standard product cycle hypothesis assumes: it affords entrepreneurs and innovations – even if at a lower level – in the country taking over the product. It is a question of terminology whether these 'derivative innovations' are considered as 'new' products or not.

As to the 'what' of transfer, Vernon assumed manufacture of entire products: 'Increasingly corporations manufacture multiple products in multiple branch plants in multiple locations' (Erickson and Leinbach, 1979, 60). But a distinct pattern emerged: branch plants nearest to the headquarters are the smallest, less independent and maintain direct flows of material with the main plant; the most distant plants serve to supply distant markets (Erickson and Leinbach, 1979, 60). Simple processes of manufacturing durables for standardized high-volume consumer markets (for example mobile phones or laser printers), or products facing high demand in the destination countries (for example cars) are typically outsourced entirely (see Chapter 29 on 'Open innovation and regional growth' by Prud'homme in this *Handbook*). But even in these markets innovators tend to apply a strategy of product diversification, manufacturing more sophisticated versions at home. Frequently, they do not transfer entire products, but reduce vertical integration by outsourcing the production of simpler components or even of specific tasks to subsidiaries in low-income countries or to specialists (Baldwin, 2006; Blinder, 2006).

As to the 'when' of transfer, Vernon (1960, 109) held that: "one can only guess at the speed of these processes of birth and maturity and technological shifts'. The general catching up in technology of emerging economies (Comin et al., 2008) and the advances in communication technology suggest an increasing speed, but as a consequence of the wide diversity among products and transfer processes no generalizations are possible. According to Storper and Christopherson (1987), plants may agglomerate in the late phase of the cycle rather than disperse.

SOME CONCLUSIONS

Vernon's basic idea, that new products are invented in high-income markets and manufacture is shifted to less advanced markets after a dominant design has evolved, is a seminal general principle but it is too simple as a description of reality or as a basis for policy prescriptions.

High-income agglomerations and lead markets with specialized skills in a specific technology and sophisticated specific demand are important as a seedbed, but for specific innovations only. Specialization and path-dependence suggest that innovations in a completely new technology are more likely in new places, especially in a science-based knowledge society.

'New' products, as a requirement for high-income countries' competitiveness, do not necessarily involve a revolutionary technology or a discovery, as Vernon and Hirsch assume. Even less are high-tech products essential, as the recent OECD–EU policy model suggests. Skill-intensive specialities addressing specialized demand and based on a considerable part of tacit knowledge are more important than high-tech, traditionally defined.

A dominant design is typical for some products, especially those addressing standardized mass-consumption markets, but they can change from time to time. More products, however, are in a process of continuous development and product diversification, which restricts the transfer to non-technological improvements.

The transfer of entire products may be typical for standardized consumer goods facing a mass market; more often specific product lines, single components or, increasingly, specific tasks are outsourced. The addressee of outsourcing is a specialist in the last case, rather than a low-wage manufacturer, more often residing in an advanced country.

The modifications of the traditional product cycle remove much of its catholic claim. It is no longer possible to explain product cycle, technology cycle, firm cycle, regional cycle and development of countries with one simple theory. The product-cycle hypothesis gave a valuable impetus to urban, regional and international economics to converge within new economic geography, but the range of existing product-cycle models extends from narrative to several types of partial and general equilibrium models, each with different specific types of simplifying assumptions and simplifications, often contradicting each other. This poses no problem: different models, containing different elements of the product-cycle hypothesis, are required to answer the different questions, which the traditional product cycle model tried to answer conjointly.

NOTES

* I am indebted to the editors, to Peter Mayerhofer, Gerhard Palme and Andreas Reinstaller for their substantial critique on a preliminary version; the failures and errors are of course mine.
1. For example paper machines, clothing or industrial textiles, machine tools or high-grade steel.

REFERENCES

Abernathy, William J. and James M. Utterback (1978), 'Patterns of industrial innovation', *Technology Review*, **80** (7), 40–47.
Anderson, Philip and Michael L. Tushman (1990), 'Technological discontinuities and dominant designs: a cyclical model of technological change', *Administrative Science Quarterly*, **35** (4), 604–33.
Baldwin, Richard (2006), 'Globalisation: the great unbundling(s)', Helsinki: Economic Council of Finland.
Blinder, Allan (2006), 'Offshoring. The next industrial revolution?', *Foreign Affairs*, **85** (2), 113–28.
Bottazzi, Laura and Giovanni Peri (2000), 'Innovation and spillovers: evidence from European regions', CESifo Working Paper 340, Munich.

Brezis, Elise S. and Paul Krugman (1993), 'Technology and the life cycle of cities', NBER Working Paper 4561.
Brezis, Elise S., Paul R. Krugman and Daniel Tsiddon (1993), 'Leapfrogging in international competition: a theory of cycles in National Technological Leadership', *American Economic Review*, **83** (5), 1211–19.
Burns, Arthur F. (1934), *Production Trends in the United States*, New York: National Bureau of Economic Research.
Comin, Diego, Bart Hobijn and Emilie Rovito (2008), 'Technology usage lags', *Journal of Growth Economics*, **13**, 237–56.
Dachs, Bernhard and Georg Zahradnik (2008), 'Internationalisation of R&D in ICT', in Huub Meijers, Berhard Dachs and Paul J.J. Welfens (eds), *Internationalisation of European ICT Activities*, Berlin and Heidelberg: Springer, pp. 157–85.
Duranton, Gilles and Diego Puga (2001), 'Nursery cities: urban diversity, process innovation, and the life cycle of products', *American Economic Review*, **91** (5), 1454–77.
Eaton, Jonathan, Eva Gutierrez and Samuel Kortum (1998), 'European technology policy', *Economic Policy*, **13** (27), 403–38.
Erickson, Rodney A. (1980), 'Corporate organization and manufacturing branch plant closures in non-metropolitan areas', *Regional Studies*, **14**, 491–501.
Erickson, Rodney A. and Thomas A. Leinbach (1979), 'Characteristics of branch plants', in R.E. Lonsdale and H.L. Seyler (eds), *Nonmetropolitan Industrialisation*, Washington, DC: Winston/Wiley, pp. 57–78.
Ernst, Dieter (2000), 'Inter-organisational knowledge outsourcing: what permits small Taiwanese firms to compete in the computer industry', *Asia-Pacific Journal of Management*, **17**, 223–55.
Europäischer Rat (2000), 'Schlussfolgerungen des Vorsitzes', http://www.consilium.europa.eu/ueDocs/cms_Data/docs/pressdata/de/ec/00100-r1.d0.htm.
Gort, Michael and Steven Klepper (1982), 'Time paths in the diffusion of product innovations', *Economic Journal*, **92** (3), 630–53.
Grossman, Gene M. and Elhanan Helpman (1991), 'Endogenous product cycles', *Economic Journal*, **101**, 1214–29.
Helfgott, Roy B., W. Eric Gustafson and James M. Hund (1959), *Made in New York: Case Studies in Metropolitan Manufacturing*, Cambridge, MA: Harvard University Press.
Hirsch, Seev (1967), *Location of Industry and International Competitiveness*, Oxford: Clarendon Press.
Jaffe, Adam B. and Manuel Trajtenberg (1996), 'Flows of knowledge spillovers from universities and federal labs: modelling the flow of patent citations across institutional and geographic boundaries', National Bureau of Economic Research Working Paper 5712.
Jungmittag, Andre (2008), 'Trends in foreign direct investment', in Huub Meijers, Berhard Dachs and Paul J.J. Welfens (eds), *Internationalisation of European ICT Activities*, Berlin and Heidelberg: Springer, pp. 132–56.
Krugman, Paul R. (1979), 'A model of innovation: technology transfer and the world distribution of income', *Journal of Political Economy*, **87** (2), 253–68.
Kuznets, Simon S. (1930), *Secular Movements in Production and Prices: Their Nature and their Bearing upon Cyclical Fluctuations*, Boston, MA and New York: Houghton.
Kuznets, Simon S. (1953), *Economic Change*, New York: Norton.
Landes, David. S. (1969), *The Unbound Prometheus: Technological Change and Industrial Development in Western Europe from 1750 to the Present*, Cambridge: Cambridge University Press.
Lichtenberg, Robert M. (1960), *One-tenth of a Nation: National Forces in the Economic Growth of the New York Region*, Cambridge, MA: Harvard University Press.
Magee, Stephen P. (1977), 'Information and the multinational corporation', in Jagdish N. Bhagwati (ed.), *The New International Economic Order: The North–South Debate*, Cambridge: Cambridge University Press, pp. 315–40.
Mansfield, Edwin, Antony Romeo, Marius Schwartz, David Teece, Samuel Wagner and Peter Brach (1982), *Technology Transfer, Productivity and Economic Policy*, New York: Norton.
Markusen, Ann (1985), *Profit Cycles, Oligopoly and Regional Development*, Cambridge, MA: MIT Press.
Norton, R.D. (1981), 'Regional life-cycles and US industrial rejuvenation', in Herbert Giersch (ed.), *Towards an Explanation of Economic Growth*, Tübingen: Mohr-Siebeck, pp. 253–80.
Norton, R.D and J. Rees (1979), 'The product cycle and the spatial decentralization of American manufacturing', *Regional Studies*, **13**, 141–51.
Oakey, Ray (1985), 'High technology industries and agglomeration economies', in Peter Hall and Ann Markusen (eds), *Silicon Landscapes*, Boston, MA: Allen & Unwin, pp. 94–117.
Oakey, Ray, A.T. Thwaites and R.A. Nash (1980), 'The regional distribution of innovative manufacturing establishments in Britain', *Regional Studies*, **14**, 235–54.
OECD (2007), *Staying Competitive in the Global Economy: Moving Up the Value Chain*, Paris: OECD.
Saxenian, AnnaLee (1994), *Regional Advantage: Culture and Competition in Silicon Valley and Route 128*, Cambridge, MA: Harvard University Press.
Schmookler, Jacob (1966), *Invention and Economic Growth*, Cambridge, MA: Harvard University Press.

Storper, Michael and Susan Christopherson (1987), 'Flexible specialization and regional industrial agglomerations: the case of the US motion picture industry', *Annals of the Association of American Geographers*, **77** (1), 104–117.

Suarez-Villa, Luis (1984), 'The manufacturing process cycle and the industrialisation of the United States – Mexico borderlands', *Annals of Regional Science*, **18** (1), 1–23.

Teece, David J. (1986), 'Profiting from technological innovation', *Research Policy*, **15** (6), 285–305.

Teece, David, J. (1987), 'Profiting from technological innovation: implications for integration, collaboration, licensing and public policy', in David J. Teece (ed.), *The Competitive Challenge*, Cambridge, MA: Ballinger, pp. 137–58.

Thompson, Wilbur R. (1969), 'The economic base of urban problems', in Neil W. Chamberlain (ed.), *Contemporary Economic Issues*, Homewood, IL: Irwin.

Tichy, Gunther (1981), 'Alte Industriegebiete in der Steiermark – ein weltweites Problem ohne Lösungsansätze', *Berichte zur Raumforschung und Raumplanung*, **25** (3), 18–26.

Tichy, Gunther (1987), 'A sketch of a probabilistic modification of the product cycle hypothesis to explain the problems of old industrial areas', in Hermann Muegge and Walter B. Stöhr (eds), *International Economic Restructuring and the Regional Community*, Aldershot: Avebury, pp. 285–305.

Tichy, Gunther (1991), 'The product cycle revisited: some extensions and clarifications', *Zeitschrift für Wirtschafts- und Sozialwissenschaften*, **111** (1), 27–54.

Tichy, Gunther (1998), 'Clusters: less dispensable and more risky than ever', in Michael Steiner (ed.), *Clusters and Regional Specialisation: On Geography and Technology Networks*, European Research in Regional Science Vol. 8, London: Pion, pp. 226–37.

Tichy, Gunther (2008), 'Wie mobil sind Ideen? Zur Entwicklung des internationalen Handels in der Wissensgesellschaft', *Wirtschaftspolitische Blätter*, **55** (3), 407–30.

Utterback, James M. (1979), 'The dynamics of product and process innovation in industry', in Christopher T. Hill and James M. Utterback (eds), *Technological Innovation for a Dynamic Economy*, New York: Pergamon Press, pp. 24–37.

Venables, Anthony J. (2001), 'Geography and international inequalities: the impact of new technologies', paper prepared for World Bank annual conference on Development Economics, Washington, DC, May.

Vernon, Raymond (1960), *Metropolis 1985: An interpretation of the findings of the New York Metropolitan Region Study*, Cambridge, MA: Harvard University Press.

Vernon, Raymond (1966), 'International investment and international trade in the product cycle', *Quarterly Journal of Economics*, **80** (2), 190–207.

Vernon, Raymond (1968), 'Economic sovereignty at bay', *Foreign Affairs*, October, reprinted in Vernon (1972), *The Economic and Political Consequences of Multinational Enterprise: An Anthology*, Boston, MA: Division of Research, Graduate School of Business Administration, Harvard University. pp. 3–19.

Vernon, Raymond (1971), *Sovereignty at Bay. The Multinational Spread of U.S. Enterprises*, London: Longman.

Vernon, Raymond (1972), *The Economic and Political Consequences of Multinational Enterprise: An Anthology*, Boston, MA: Division of Research, Graduate School of Business Administration, Harvard University.

Vernon, Raymond (1979), 'The product cycle hypothesis in a new international environment', *Oxford Bulletin of Economics and Statistics*, **41** (May), 255–67.

Zucker, Lynne G. and Michael R. Darby (2006), 'Movement of star scientists and engineers and high-tech firm entry', NBER Working Paper 12172.

6 Perspectives on mature Marshallian industrial districts

*Marco Bellandi**

INTRODUCTION

The contemporary force of social and business relations, overlapping at the local level, is exemplified by industrial districts (IDs) and especially those: (1) whose industry is based mainly on small and medium-sized specialized firms resulting from local agents' entrepreneurial and life projects, where economies of the division of labour can possibly be achieved without the extended hierarchical organization of big firms; and (2) whose social dimension is represented by a local society with a well-defined identity for their localized industries, such as to appear like a 'nation within a nation' within the flux of change and of open relations (Marshall, 1919, 20–21). This chapter is aimed at presenting a conceptual review of some investigations and interpretations specifically concerned with the cases of IDs in 'old' or post-industrialized countries which are 'mature' and 'typical', and in particular with the ways in which such IDs deal with contemporary globalization and innovation challenges.

'Typical' IDs are meant here as localities whose industrial and social features can be more appropriately understood with the help of the so-called 'Marshallian industrial district' (MID) model (Becattini, 2004). They are places (often corresponding to a small to medium-sized city, or a set of such cities and their territories) whose collective capabilities for economic growth and social enrichment are based on the development of locally specific technological and professional capabilities and attitudes. The development goes together with progressive differentiation along the sectoral lines of a related set of specialized industrial and trade activities with a stable connection to an open cluster of market niches at national and international level. The business support of such division of labour is a 'system' of specialized enterprises (normally small and medium-sized enterprises – SMEs) with local roots. This means that the core set of specialized productive activities is organized by means of a decentralized structure made of several firms, intermediate markets, business teams and specific public goods which are provided largely by local social and institutional relations. Examples of such IDs include some rather idealized Italian cases, championing light industrialization processes in the last decades of the twentieth century. They were compact centres of life and work each characterized by strongly focused productive attitudes and capabilities, and a population of very small local firms specialized in a locally integrated industrial field of traditional but upgraded products.[1] Yet, other cases of IDs could be assimilated to MID-like trajectories as well, even when they show more heterogeneous features, possibly emerging from the evolutionary trajectories of the 'idealized' cases.

'Mature' IDs are meant here as the grown-up results of a trajectory of sustained development preserving some general features through years and decades, apart from contingent reactions to temporary crises or incremental adjustments related to organic differentiation. 'Mature typical' IDs are therefore the result of a sustained MID trajectory, and they are not necessarily to be assimilated nowadays to a class of aged and outdated industrial and social systems. However, mature typical IDs meet peculiar problems when confronted with challenges requiring fast and systemic adjustments: inertial factors (complex sets of organizational routines, entrenched cultural habits, institutional fatness) grow with maturity and hamper quick reactivity; systemic adjustment needs coordinated action among key and complementary sources of impulse to change, and in typical IDs there are many such sources, with an ensuing scaling-up of difficulties of coordination. The combination of inertial factors and difficulties of coordination easily explains the risk of lock-in and irreversible decline in the face of tough new challenges.

The chapter opens with a short summary of general stylized facts on the re-emergence of IDs after the golden age of mass production. The following section presents a synthetic assessment of views both on contemporary innovation and internationalization challenges facing mature typical IDs, and on the structural and strategic variations needed for successful reactions to such challenges, possibly giving way to dematuring paths. The chapter then concludes by discussing the interpretative problems involved by the reactions above, in particular if and how the types emerging from such dematuring paths can be read still with the help of the MID model. The last section gives some final remarks.

THE RE-EMERGENCE OF INDUSTRIAL DISTRICTS IN THE PAST DECADES[2]

The idea of the ID as a form of industrial organization and development, suggested by Alfred Marshall in the second half of the nineteenth century, was resurrected and developed at the end of the 1970s, first of all by a handful of Italian scholars such as Giacomo Becattini and Sebastiano Brusco. The resurrected idea helped in understanding the re-emergence of IDs in industrialized countries after the golden age of mass production.[3]

IDs emerging or re-emerging after the golden age of mass production, such as those which grew to international success in some Italian regions (in particular the so-called 'Third Italy') in the 1970s and 1980s, were constantly confronted by the concentrated economic and strategic power of large firms, powerful capitalists and big urban systems.[4] On the market side, the re-emergence was pulled by the increased purchasing power in industrialized countries after the post-Second World War recovery, and its effects in terms of a larger demand for customized goods and services. The demand was raised by expanding segments both of consumers satisfied in their basic needs, and of users of personal services, social services and various artificial aids to remedy weaknesses and handicaps. On the production side, the connection to the changing needs was pushed by the increasing possibilities of capitalist production to exit from the 'factory' and return to 'workshops' within society to acquire artisanship, customized services, and ties with historical-cultural and environmental sources of distinctive experiences. The return to workshops had the support of various technological and organizational developments, but was also the expression of social tendencies. On this last point, in particular, Arnaldo Bagnasco (2003) pointed to the upsurge of international flows of people and communications in the decades of post-Second World War international expansion, placing the traditional forms of regulation of production and social identity under strain, particularly those built around the nation-state. This would have brought about a rediscovery of 'the importance of societal self-organizing capacities, which often have a small organizational size, underlining an image of "small cultural homelands" where to seek further meaning in a world that often appears remote' (Bagnasco, 2003, 96). IDs in the second half of the twentieth century developed faster where, in some regions of industrialized countries, local reserves of socio-cultural and institutional meanings had preserved better. Their success stories could be seen as 'the first precocious examples of local *recentrage* of the social organization' (p. 99), where *recentrage* stands for restoration of an open correspondence between the evolving core of a production system and the reproduction of the social resources necessary for it to work (p. 103).[5]

The study of the development trajectories of strong IDs also suggested a theoretical refinement of Marshall's concepts, that is, the so-called 'Marshallian industrial district', as an ideal-typical model of ID along a steady path of industrial development (the 'MID').[6] The structure is characterized by a certain degree of local dominance by an industrial cluster (local specialization); a decisive but not exclusive role of locally embedded centres of strategy and decision on local private and public investments in technical, human and social capital (endogeneity); and a structured plurality of autonomous centres of business strategy (decision-making decentralization). The effective operation of this structure requires its incorporation into conditions characterized by the right combination of local forces[7] and external conditions.[8] Market and institutional actions by district agents upon and within this incorporated structure combine in district processes of local development such as: a continuous rearticulation of the local division of labour among firms, and related adaptations in the mechanisms for its integration (local intermediate and labour markets, teams, specific public goods and services); the reproduction and renewal of experience-based production knowledge, and spiralling feedbacks with experiment-based knowledge opening to innovations in the local technological and product basis; and the reproduction of appropriate motivational traits, balancing social cohesion and economic mobility. The district processes upon the structure and within the frame conditions propel the realization of potential increasing returns at the local level, and of external economies for local producers. In turn, their realization supports development and change in the same structure.

The accumulation of experiences and growth along an MID-like path resulted in a set of mature typical IDs taking an important role in various industrialized countries or regions in the 1980s and 1990s. Many of them were in Italy, of course, such as Prato, Santa Croce sull'Arno, Carpi, Reggio Emilia, Pesaro, Civitanova Marche, Arzignano, Riviera del Brenta, Como, Lecco, Lumezzane, Seregno, Vigevano, Biella and Valenza Po'. Well-known cases in other industrial countries include, for example: Cholet, Cluses, Oyonnax, Roanne and Morez in France; Elche, Elda, Ibi, Alcoy, Castellon de la Plana and Sabadell in Spain; the Ave Valley in Portugal; the Herning–Ikast-Brande area of Jutland in western Denmark; Gnosjö in Sweden; and Bishu and Tsubame in Japan.[9] These cases of mature typical IDs were characterized by: a strong manufacturing specialization, often in so-called 'traditional' products; import–export relations around the local industrial core of strongly integrated sets of vertically and horizontally related phases of production; local sources of new experience-based knowledge and non-local sources of new experiment-based knowledge; and dense local institutional networks providing governance and specific public goods to the decentralized systems of special-ized SMEs and to the local society.

Contemporary global tendencies have menacing implications for those mature typical IDs in what are now (or are becoming) old or post-industrialized countries (regions): science is more and more interpenetrated with experience-based knowledge along open and non-linear processes of technological and product innovation; the extension of international production fragmentation requires reduction of the degree of local integra-tion of manufacturing *filières*;[10] the unceasing progress in transportation infrastructures increases the integration between local production systems and the mobility of workers within large urbanized (metropolitan) areas at the national and international level;[11] big multinational enterprises (MNEs) have an increasing capacity to tap new sources of cheap labour, capital and land; and some new industrializing localities and regions grow and insert themselves into such global value chains thanks to the combination of strong public hand, a large supply of cheap production factors, and emerging new local forces and markets. Three implications seem plausible:

1.   When the above industrial difficulties combine with social difficulties, such as those brought about by the ever-increasing importance of networks of people and com-munication going beyond the local level (which are another expression of global tendencies), mature typical IDs may go into an irreversible decline.[12]
2.   District forms and district-like processes, together with expanding resources devolved by international public organizations to support local economic develop-ment, are emerging in various new industrializing countries and regions;[13] the decline of mature typical IDs in old or post-industrialized countries may not be the end of IDs as such.
3.   Some IDs in old or post-industrialized countries still survive, and even demature and thrive, when appropriate changes are made to the mix of district structural charac-teristics and processes. Furthermore new industries and forms of local development with some district features combine in various ways and at various territorial scales with typical IDs.

The next section tries to elaborate on the last point, that is, on the bases of progressive reaction of IDs to contemporary challenges. In particular the discussion focuses on IDs with MID-like features[14] and which are mature, according to the definitions provided previously.

CONTEMPORARY GLOBALIZATION AND INNOVATION CHALLENGES[15]

Let us consider a light conceptual framework, based on two reciprocal relations, and aimed at understanding the forms and results of reactions which may be undertaken in mature typical IDs faced within threatening global tendencies:

1.   Without revamped sources of inner local productivity and creativity, interna-tional investment strategies do not lend positive solutions to clusters and localities

hit by globalization challenges, in terms of functional upgrading and local development.

2. Without appropriate international and translocal strategies, the value produced by inner innovation may not only be predated by multinational agents, or spill over too easily to global markets, but may also lack an important bridge to factors needed for local innovation.

The problem confronting many contemporary mature typical IDs, when concerned with international strategies of investment and production, comes from the tradition of strong local production integration. However, the development of relations with foreign suppliers may be favoured by the application of a variety of local team experiences, and of contractual and personal relationships of district entrepreneurs in local and distant trade networks. Secondly, active foreign direct investment (FDI) promoted by larger district firms can take a district form when, for instance, district FDI is concentrated in a (foreign) place with district-like potentialities, and the leading district firms induce other district firms to invest in the same territory.

At the aggregate level such individual actions contribute variously to the ID's prospects. An economic activity which is moved from a locality may either be replaced locally or not. The moved activity may have been embedded in a network of industrial and social relations promoting local productivity, learning, and creativity in the original place, or may instead have maintained a footloose relationship to it. A similar distinction is applied to the moved activity in the receiving locality. The combinations of those processes bring about different results. An embedded activity which moves and becomes footloose is 'delocalized'; while an embedded or footloose activity which moves and is embedded in the new place is 'relocalized'. A cluster where an embedded activity is replaced by a footloose activity is functionally downgraded in its systemic content; while a cluster where a footloose activity is replaced by an embedded activity is functionally upgraded in its systemic content. Finally, local decline is characterized by quantitative shrinking and by functional downgrading in one local cluster (or more), not compensated by upgrading in other local clusters. Instead, local development is characterized by quantitative expansion and by functional upgrading in local clusters and marginal downgrading processes, if any, in other clusters in the same locality.[16]

It is quite clear that the possibilities of combining productive internationalization with new prospects of local development and upgrading in mature typical IDs increase where the resources and capacities for local innovation and renewal are strong. This is the first reciprocal relation of the framework.

Passing to the second relation, let us consider, for example, the case of those many Italian IDs characterized by SME clusters producing highly differentiated goods for the individual and for the house.[17] Here, inner levers of competitive advantage seem to reside nowadays not only in the continuous upgrading of capacities of teams of district firms to produce and sell products of medium to high quality, with highly personalized and craft content. Since the markets for those products are more and more crowded by potential international competitors, the inner levers should be the support to more systematic and effective search of new technologies, products and markets, branching out from the local traditions and constituting new cores of local clusters. This would require increased investments, not only in all the instruments promoting association with taste for beauty and good quality of life, love for well-executed craft jobs and high functionality, certificates of quality of process, environmental safety and ethical responsibility, and reasonable price–quality ratios; but also investments and cultural efforts for increasing the traditionally poor capacity of conversation between SME clusters and the centres of public research and higher education.[18] Here the second reciprocal relation becomes more evident.

An open approach to international production increases the need for SME clusters to contact the world of 'knowledge' centres, even just for help in dense communication with distant and foreign places of production and trade. This provides a robust basis for further and larger collaborative efforts between science and industry at the local level. Furthermore, internationalization capacities and management skills help to combine the peculiar factors of inner productivity, creativity and innovative potential, with foreign resources and opportunities. An effective combination needs appropriate forms of international relations, in particular specific to the features shared by the population of district SMEs. Such features traditionally include individual energy, creativity and simple internal managerial structures, interaction within teams of independent specialized firms, the help of shared trust bases, of cognitive proximity, and of various types of specific public goods providing indivisible assets and rules. Going abroad with a networked structure is consistent with the use of such particular features and of rich pools of district resources; keeping contact with home resources through networked relations reduces the temptation of independent or predatory strategies, whereby for example single entrepreneurs buy cheap in foreign areas and undersell home competitors, including by means of counterfeit brands and misleading advertising. Getting in touch with foreign partners who have or may learn to have similar networked structures and skills helps the building of collaboration and joint infrastructural, production and trade projects on a basis of organizational and institutional similarity.[19]

On the other hand, coming back to the revamping of the inner bases of local productivity and creativity, the constitution and maintenance of some bases demand high levels of urban infrastructure. The local scale and urban quality of an ID are rarely adequate to this purpose. A regional (sometimes a national) milieu hosting dynamic regional cities and districts can offer a solution, if the collaboration among networks of firms, research centres, knowledge services, high-level trade facilities and proactive local and regional policy-makers finds a way to develop and interact together with the preservation of local identities and social cohesion and mobility.[20] This means that networked projects, cross-cluster and trans-local relations at a regional level are also an important part of the recipe for inner levers and drivers.

BEYOND 'OLD' MARSHALLIAN INDUSTRIAL DISTRICTS?

The recent tendencies sketched in the previous section would seem to confirm the need for mature typical IDs in old or post-industrialized countries to change or die; where 'change' means to leave a strictly canonical form, that is, that corresponding to the model of the so-called Marshallian industrial district (MID). This is a legitimate approach, of course,[21] but it also depends on specific conceptual associations, of various type and order.

Ideal Types, Heterogeneity and Empirical Thresholds

The first association concerns what I see as a wrong interpretation of the MID, when it is restricted to a model of local development with a mono-industrial specialization in a well-delimited and not too large urban–rural place, with production processes vertically integrated at the local level, with an industrial structure composed by a population of very small firms with a high degree of turnover, a flat local power structure and a high level of social cohesion and trust. That is a romantic model, 100 per cent specialized, endogenous, decentralized and communitarian.[22]

However, the previous definition indicates that the MID as a model of an evolving socio-economic system needs to incorporate a certain degree of heterogeneity in its key dimensions. Without it, the system crystallizes and is unable to preserve its own identity within the flux of change. This idea is not new, being already suggested by Alfred Marshall, and it is clearly given in a pioneering paper by Giacomo Becattini:

> The Marshallian industrial district is a localized 'thickening' (and its strength and weakness both lie in this spatial limitation) of inter-industrial relationships which is reasonably stable over time. Its composite nature, tending towards the multisectoral, gives it, even in the midst of intense change, a stability which a unit such as a single industry, in the technological sense of the term, lacks; it is therefore possible to study it, in order to ascertain its permanent characteristics, the 'laws' which govern its formation, its maintenance and its decline. Paradoxically, the greater the ability of the district to renew itself, to graft new sectors on to old, to develop its original industry in ever more specialized ways – in accordance with Allyn Young's celebrated model – the more it retains its identity as an industrial district.[23]

The evolutionary perspective has been developed variously, and it includes models of both organic adaptation (steady-state development) and discontinuous adjustment.[24] In this sense, for example, the possibility discussed in the previous section, of district internationalization through translocal and cross-cluster relations, is not something beyond the MID model as such, but a specific manifestation that can be found in some contemporary IDs, and which can be understood also with the help and reference to the overall framework of MID structures and processes. Of course, beyond certain thresholds of sectoral dispersion among the agglomerated activities, dependency on external strategic control and business centralization, clustering and economic development in a place reflect a coalescence of the MID logic with other types of logic; until the disappearance of the MID logic when what prevails is merely the effect of the variable location choices of almost dis-anchored companies and/or of top-down strategies of state departments.

How to define such thresholds? There is no need to say that there are no theoretically definite answers. However, it is also well known that as regards empirical investigation, statistical methods have been developed in Italy, in particular by Fabio Sforzi, and applied (also in other countries) to the large-scale identification and quantitative measurement of industrial districts.[25] They incorporate proxies and thresholds that are more or less directly related to the MID's defining features. However they are necessarily restricted to structural characteristics. Hence, cases on the list of 'statistical' districts may have lost district dynamic capabilities even though they still comply in terms of their aggregate structural characteristics. Alternatively, the list may not include emergent districts which do not (yet) comply with the statistical thresholds defined for one or more of the proxies for structural characteristics.[26] The two problems imply either overinclusive associations or underinclusive ones.

The Changeable Fortunes of Old Champions

Another wrong association concerns cases which are rightly associated to MID structures and processes. Let us come back to the internal managerial structures of the small to medium-sized enterprises (SMEs) which should lead the internationalization processes discussed in the previous subsection. They are necessarily simple; but in many contemporary mature typical IDs they may be too simple or, more precisely, stick to formulae which have worked well in the past, and are clearly outdated in the face of contemporary internationalization challenges. In most successful Italian IDs from the 1960s to the 1990s the core population of SMEs included largely family concerns, centred on and around the business acumen, the technical competence and the entrepreneurial energy of one or two founders. All strategic decisions had the fundamental input of knowledge possessed or directly controlled by the masters. The same can be told of the governance of teams of small firms, relying heavily for 'versatile integration' (Becattini and Rullani, 1996) on the competence of a leading member. This governance model is at odds with the necessities of coping with internationalization challenges. A more open model is requested, where essential cognitive inputs are contributed by a team of members, with differentiated tasks, competences and operative decision fields. If the shift to such a model is blocked within an ID by cultural inertia or business myopia, then the system suffers, not because of the SMEs as such, but in relation to the historically determined models assumed by them, and to the difficulty in enacting a transition to different models. The same could be said of other MID features.

In other words, it is quite easy to associate anecdotal evidence of district failures to inherent problems with the MID model, even when the association is not so stringent. More generally, within the thresholds of approximated MID characteristics, a huge number of different types may be represented. Of course forms and types corresponding to celebrated and highly successful Italian IDs in the 1960s and 1970s are included as well. They demonstrated: a very high degree of manufacturing specialization in the production of personal or household goods, intermediate goods, or light mechanical products and instruments; a core population of small firms running a locally integrated production *filière*; and concerning the processes, a central role of informal rules oriented by strong civic values, competition and cooperation balances, layers of local contextual and external codified knowledge, socio-economic mobility, and so on. They have been important field laboratories for elaborating and testing district theories and the same large-scale statistical methods for specifying IDs. Given their success and the widespread circulation of the studies referring to them, those cases have started to be identified as champions of the MID model, or even with the ID as such.[27] But they were champions, not the ideal-types, and the (relative) decline or even just the transformation of the Italian leading examples do not imply per se the need to throw out the general reference to the MID model.

Dematuring IDs: Between Entering New MID Paths and Coalescing with Different Models

MID general structural and dynamic characters encompass a large set of historically defined cases and types of industrial organization and local development. Those variations can include the characters of mature typical IDs reacting progressively to contemporary challenges and dematuring, that is, finding new combinations of specific industrial structures and strategies, products and markets, and competitive factors. The previous section has illustrated some aspects of such reaction. Furthermore, in the face of contemporary challenges, dematuring together with the convergence to a new MID path may go beyond the set of traditional options. For example, IDs either move from a consumer good specialization, to a machinery specialization, to a combination with more and more articulated and specialized tertiary functions; or increase the importance of medium-sized district firms managing translocal networks of production and distribution:[28]

> with the fast pace of technological change, the borders of traditional sectors become blurred, and the distinctions between manufacturing and tertiary sectors, not to speak of the one between low tech and high tech sectors, become less and less clear and meaningful. New or re-generated IDs may turn to be characterised by an 'industrial' specialisation that has lost its traditional (like in the first and second waves) identity as a locally integrated manufacturing *filière*. (Becattini et al., 2009, xx)

However, in the midst of change, the borders of the MID model may be trespassed as well. Even when falling within the statistical thresholds of 'MID-oriented' district identification, some dematuring IDs need to be seen in terms of coalescence of an MID logic with other types of logic of industrial organization and development. Examples in the present age are easily taken from some cases of Japanese *sanchi* variously related to the networks of large Japanese firms; of Chinese IDs characterized by penetrations of both strong public government and FDIs into local forces; of US 'university-centric industrial districts'; and of some cases of Italian districts too, showing various combinations of these types of IDs.[29]

SOME CONCLUSIONS

A final consideration concerns the fact that 'coalescence' itself is not always stable in character, but something which accompanies the transition of an ID (hit by a strong challenge) towards a new path of development, possibly but not necessarily a new path with MID features. Coming back once again to the internationalization and innovation challenges, let us suppose that actions at a local systemic level and at a cross-cluster translocal level require transitional centralization into the hands of some public or private agencies. They should help and manage the development of many operational aspects needed both for the new local combinations of open science and contextual experience and creativity, and for the building of the new classes of translocal specific public goods (Bellandi and Caloffi, 2008).

One cannot dismiss the risk that the elite of public and private agencies at the local and translocal level will become a centre of power pursuing sectional interests increasingly separated from the communities of people and producers involved. For this reason, participatory methods and democratic legitimacy should be a necessary part of the recipe, as predicated by methods of strategic planning in local economic development.[30] It is however plausible that some among the most successful IDs of the recent past, within MID statistical threshold, are currently suffering from a lack of social and business consensus and experience on the need and opportunity to adopt formal methods of local management, as opposed to the past informal methods of conflict solutions, social ruling and local governance.

NOTES

*   Useful comments by Annalisa Caloffi are gratefully acknowledged.
1.   I will come back more explicitly to such 'champions' in a later section.
2.   This section is based on material taken from Bellandi (2007).
3.   See Becattini (2004).
4.   Nor did the ID as a concept have an easy life in the first years after the re-emergence. A strong push in the international popularity and discussion around IDs was brought about by the contributions of US-based scholars, for example Michael Piore, Charles Sabel and Jonathan Zeitlin, who identified a 'second industrial divide', with the re-emergence of flexible specialization and artisanal modes of production as a viable (but not necessarily dominant) alternative to mass production. Interpretative frames in a similar vein were proposed by Michael Storper, Allen Scott and Michael Best. See Becattini et al. (2009) for illustrations.
5.   For recent publications providing an overview of quantitative empirical research studies and large-scale identification on IDs in Italy see sections 7, 8 and 9 of Becattini et al. (2009).
6.   The term and the model were proposed by Becattini in papers published between the end of the 1970s and the beginning of the 1990s. See Becattini (2004). In fact it has been argued that in Marshall's times, there were many cases of IDs showing oligopolistic forms far from what is now seen as the MID model; see Andrew Popp and John Wilson, and Phil Cooke as well, in Becattini et al. (2009).
7.   In particular: cognitive proximity within a pool of complementary competencies (human capital) and specific means of production (technical capital); shared attitudes towards a role for trust in local exchanges, and diffused entrepreneurship as the expression of life projects featuring a community of local producers (social capital).
8.   In terms of market and technological tendencies (for example variable and differentiated demand, large divisibility of production processes), regional and national cultural and institutional pivots (for example support to social and public formation of production factors, intermediary organizations of small firms), and national and international legal frame works (for example protection against entrenched monopolies, free trade).
9.   See sections 6, 7 and 8 of Becattini et al. (2009). In North America, as in most parts of the industrialized Northern European, Australian and Japanese regions, there are many cases of industrial clusters with ID features within large metropolitan areas (such as those of Orange County, Silicon Valley, and Boston in the USA), but there are only a few cases of strong contemporary MID trajectories as such. See also Storper and Scott (1992), Markusen (1996) and Porter (2003).
10. On international value chains and local systems see Pietrobelli and Rabellotti (2006), Schmitz (2004) and section 10 of Becattini et al. (2009).
11. Globalization 'returns', sometimes with waves of immigrant workers and their families, bringing with them both new energies and particular problems for hosting IDs. See for example the recent reflections on the Prato ID by Gabi Dei Ottati (2009).
12. Differing views on this point have fuelled recent debates: see Amin (2004), Asheim and Herstad (2005) and Storper in Becattini et al. (2009).
13. See section 10 of Becattini et al. (2009).
14. That is (to repeat): a quite high level of local specialization, strategic and value endogenous control, and decentralization in decision-making structures and processes.
15. This section is based on material from Bellandi and Caloffi (2010).
16. See section 10 of Becattini et al. (2009).

17. These constitute a good part of the set of mature typical IDs to which we are referring in this section.
18. See section 5 of Becattini et al. (2009).
19. See references in Bellandi and Caloffi (2008).
20. See for example Cooke et al. (2004 [1998]); refer also to Bellandi and Caloffi (2010).
21. See, among others, Markusen (1996), Giuliani (2005), McCann (2006) and Zeitlin (2007).
22. For reflections on this point refer to Phil Cooke, to Andrew Popp and John Wilson, and to Michael Porter and Christian Ketels, in Becattini et al. (2009).
23. Becattini (2004, 16). It is the English translation of a passage concluding the 1979 Italian paper which opened the international revival of the ID as a concept of contemporary application. The same paper has been translated several times in various languages.
24. See for example Belussi (Chapter 7 in this *Handbook*), Sölvell (2008) and sections 4 and 5 of Becattini et al. (2009).
25. See section 6 of Becattini et al. (2009).
26. White noise in 'statistical' IDs identification is amplified by 'policy-driven' identification (for example in Italy at the level of regional governments). White noise is much greater with so-called industrial or business clusters, since these are subject to worldwide attempts at policy-driven identification. The diffusion of critical assessments is partly related to this burgeoning noise.
27. See Asheim (2000), and Michael Porter and Christian Ketels in Becattini et al. (2009).
28. See De Arcangelis and Ferri (2005).
29. See Cooke and Lazzeretti (2007), and Becattini et al. (2009) sections 5 and 10. Refer also to Chapter 7 by Fiorenza Belussi in this *Handbook*, for a reading of 'new' districts.
30. See Amin (2004) and Bagnasco (2003). See also section 11 of Becattini et al. (2009).

REFERENCES

Amin, Ash (2004), 'Regions unbound: towards a new politics of place', *Geografiska Annaler*, **86** (1), 33–44.
Asheim, Bjorn T. (2000), 'Industrial districts: the contributions of Marshall and beyond', in G.L. Clark, M.P. Feldman and M.S. Gertler (eds), *The Oxford Handbook of Economic Geography*, Oxford: Oxford University Press, pp. 413–31.
Asheim, Bjorn T. and Sverre J. Herstad (2005), 'Regional innovation systems, varieties of capitalism and non-local relations: challenges from the globalising economy', in R.A. Boschma and R. Kloosterman (eds), *Learning from Clusters: A Critical Assessment from an Economic-Geographical Perspective*, Dordrecht: Springer Verlag, pp. 169–202.
Bagnasco, Arnaldo (2003), *Società fuori squadra. Come cambia l'organizzazione sociale*, Bologna: Il Mulino.
Becattini, Giacomo (2004), *Industrial Districts: A New Approach to Industrial Change*, Cheltenham, UK and Northampton, MA, USA: Edward Elgar.
Becattini, Giacomo, Marco Bellandi and Lisa De Propris (eds) (2009), *Handbook of Industrial Districts*, Cheltenham, UK and Northampton, MA, USA: Edward Elgar.
Becattini, Giacomo and Enzo Rullani (1996), 'Local systems and global connections: the role of knowledge', in R. Cossentino, F. Pyke and W. Sengenberger (eds), *Local and Regional Response to Global Pressure: The Case of Italy and its Industrial Districts*, Geneva: International Institute for Labor Studies, pp. 159–74.
Bellandi, Marco (2007), 'Industrial districts and waves of industrialization: a rich and contested terrain', *SR Scienze regionali*, **6**, 7–33.
Bellandi, Marco and Annalisa Caloffi (2008), 'District internationalisation and trans-local development', *Entrepreneurship and Regional Development*, **20** (November), 517–32.
Bellandi, Marco and Annalisa Caloffi (2010), 'Towards a framework for the evaluation of policies of cluster upgrading and innovation', *Revue d'Economie Industrielle*, **129–30**, 259–76.
Cooke, Philip, Martin Heidenreich and Hans-Joachim Braczyk (eds) (2004), *Regional Innovation Systems: The Role of Governance in a Globalized World*, 2nd edn, London: Routledge (1st edn 1998).
Cooke, Philip and Luciana Lazzeretti (eds) (2007), *Creative Cities, Cultural Clusters and Local Economic Development*, Cheltenham, UK and Northampton, MA, USA: Edward Elgar.
De Arcangelis, G. and G. Ferri (2005), 'The specialization of the districts: from typical final goods to machinery for making them?', in Banca d'Italia, *Local Economies and Internationalization in Italy*, Rome: Banca d'Italia, pp. 421–36.
Dei Ottati, G. (2009), 'Italian industrial districts and the dual Chinese challenge', in G. Johanson, R. Smyth and R. French (eds), *Living Outside the Walls: The Chinese in Prato*, Cambridge: Cambridge Scholars Publishing, pp. 26–41.
Giuliani, Elisa (2005), 'Cluster absorptive capacity', *European Urban and Regional Studies*, **12** (3), 269–88.

Markusen, Ann (1996), 'Sticky place in slippery space: a typology of industrial districts', *Economic Geography*, **72** (3), 293–313.

Marshall, Alfred (1919), *Industry and Trade*, London: Macmillan.

McCann, Philip (2006), 'Regional Development: Clusters and Districts', in M. Casson, B. Yeung, A. Basu and N. Wadeson (eds), *The Oxford Handbook of Entrepreneurship*, Oxford: Oxford University Press, pp. 651–70.

Pietrobelli, Carlo and Roberta Rabellotti (eds) (2006), *Upgrading to Compete: Global Value Chains, Clusters, and SMEs in Latin America*, Cambridge, MA: Harvard University Press.

Porter, M.E. (2003), 'The economic performance of regions', *Regional Studies*, **37** (6–7), 549–78.

Schmitz, Hubert (ed.) (2004), *Local Enterprises in the Global Economy: Issues of Governance and Upgrading*, Cheltenham, UK and Northampton, MA, USA: Edward Elgar.

Sölvell, Örjan (2008), *Clusters: Balancing Evolutionary and Constructive Forces*, Stockholm: Ivory Tower Publishing.

Storper, Michael and Allen J. Scott (1992), *Pathways to Industrialization and Regional Development*, London: Routledge.

Zeitlin, Jonathan (2007), 'Industrial districts and regional clusters', in G. Jones and J. Zeitlin (eds), *The Oxford Handbook of Business History*, Oxford: Oxford University Press, pp. 219–43.

7 The new Marshallian districts and their process of internationalization
Fiorenza Belussi

INTRODUCTION

Firms in industrial districts (hereafter 'district firms') are characterized by very complex interactions. Thus, there is an innate level of indeterminacy, diversity, variety and pluralism, which explains why, behind the industrial district (ID) conceptualization, first proposed by Alfred Marshall, we encounter so many morphological varieties. The international literature has stressed three main elements which specifically characterize the ID organizational form: (1) the density of local social and economic networks; (2) the co-presence of rivalry and cooperation; and (3) the active presence of district institutions that support its long-term expansion (Paniccia, 2002; Markusen, 1996; Saxenian, 1994; Sammarra, 2003; Feldman, 2004; Becattini et al., 2003). Industrial districts are geographically bounded spatial systems whose extension can correspond to or cross or overlap the regional boundary (Cooke et al., 1997; Cooke, 1998). The process of globalization of the IDs has broken the self-contained elements of ID working.

Firstly, the local cooperative network which emerged during the development of an enlarged inter-firm division of labour (being at the basis of the social capital embedded in the territory) has been subjected to a process of opening. The new Marshallian districts are now often characterized by inwards and outwards flows of labour forces, entrepreneurs and intermediated activities. Examples of this include the US industrial district of Silicon Valley (Saxenian, 1999) in which a consistent proportion of entrepreneurs and technicians declare a foreign provenance; or the Italian districts of Prato and Arzignano (Belussi and Sedita, 2010), characterized by the phenomenon of 'inverse delocalization', where the strategy of moving immigrants into the ID is even preferred to the more diffused process of offshoring low-cost intermediated activities.

Secondly, if district firms were in the past immersed in a sea of competitive and cooperative relations, as Marshall and then Porter acknowledged, within a flat and a decentralized district structure, today the old Marshallian model has been replaced by the existence of district firm leaders, which increase the stock of local knowledge, acting as knowledge gatekeepers from outside, absorbing and recombining external knowledge flows. This spikier model overlaps with the old Marshallian model of 'distributed' knowledge spillovers and local interactive learning.

Thirdly, if it is true that district firms are located in a territory where public and private institutions have emerged, co-evolving with the local production system and influencing its pattern of evolution (Mistri, 2002), then objectively the role played by local institutions in IDs is diminishing in importance, with the ID model being more and more integrated into a multilevel environment of regional, national and international innovation systems (for a general discussion see Nelson and Sampat, 2001; Cooke, 2001). In the case of Italian IDs, for instance, vocational training centres and agencies providing specialized services to local firms were important in the past, while in United States, public research support, and venture capital initiatives for financing innovative start-up, were behind the success of many high-tech districts. But today, the old function of 'gardening' played by the local institutions (Belussi, 1999; Arrighetti and Serravalle, 1999; Squazzoni and Boero, 2002) does not appear to be so crucial. In fact, advanced services, financial investments and venture capital initiatives are developed in a context of increasing globalization, where new technologies are developed at a global scale and macroeconomic policies dictate the new economic order (in terms of exchange rate, financial interconnectedness, openness of the markets, import and custom regulations, and so on).

DISTRICTS HETEROGENEITY, GLOBALIZATION AND THE TECHNOLOGICAL DYNAMISM OF LOCAL FIRMS

According to Cantwell and Iammarino (1998), globalization appears to be an extraordinary force of change, confronting the identity of IDs and their efficacy as a specific organizational model *tout court*. In fact, as stressed by Simmie and Sennen (1999), Coe and Bunnell (2003) and Lorenzen and Mahnke (2002), transnational networks now connect local clusters, districts and regions, making the spatial distinction blurred.

During 2000–2010, the great pressure towards the globalization of districts has produced two main paths. The first path emerged in order to control district firms' manufacturing costs (and particularly labour costs). This has implied the cutting of the ID local value chain (Sammarra and Belussi, 2006; Mudambi, 2008). The main consequence has been a radical shift in the configuration of the production towards new emerging markets and regions (such as Eastern Europe, India and China). The second path has regarded the possible erosion of the competitive position of firms located in Western IDs in comparison with firms located in newly emerging markets, with a shake-out process involving the weak 'fringe' of the mature Western IDs, or driving the whole ID towards an endless decline – similar to what occurred to the British IDs after the First World War. A large degree of heterogeneity is shown if we compare new Marshallian evolutionary districts, where internal-to-the-firm learning mechanisms are visible, and where new organizational, product and process innovation have been introduced by leading firms, also within old traditional staple districts, technologically inert (Belussi and Sammarra, 2010).

Heterogeneity appears not to be linked to simple explanatory factors. For instance, a variety of growth paths among the Italian IDs were found by Belussi and Gottardi (2000), Belussi and Pilotti (2002) and Belussi and Sedita (2009), regarding the introduction of changes in the firms' governance structure, sector of specialization, innovative capabilities and level of internationalization. The emergence of large innovative groups within the Italian IDs was detected, in particular, by Cainelli and De Liso (2005). Considering the case of IDs located in other countries, Caniëls and Romijn (2005), Guerrieri et al. (2001) and Markusen (1996) discovered the existence of a multiplicity of evolutionary patterns of growth, innovation and learning. Globalization also played a central role in determining the long-term performance of IDs located in developing countries (Guerrieri et al., 2001).

In modern IDs, distance-learning processes, activated by absorbing external knowledge and information (or through the setting of distant research and development and technology collaborations) played a crucial role. They have been illustrated, for instance, by Powell et al. (1996) and by Giuliani et al. (2005). Considering the phenomena of knowledge offshoring and global production subcontracting, we can affirm that spatial proximity (Maskell, 1999) has diminished in importance, while organizational proximity now appears more relevant (Rugman and Verbeke, 2003).

Considering the literature developed around the issue of the internationalization of IDs, it can be observed that many districts have evolved into complex systems with mobile boundaries, which contain dominant networks that dominate the international markets, and that control several global commodity chains (Gereffi et al., 2005; Dicken, 2007). This process is radically transforming the old Marshallian model. Furthermore, instead of a unique stereotype of globalization, a multiplicity of district firm strategies are encountered (Mariotti et al., 2006; Grandinetti and Rullani, 1996; Rullani, 1997; Bell et al, 2001; Maskell, 1999).

RESULTS FROM EMPIRICAL INVESTIGATIONS REGARDING THE ITALIAN IDS

In this section I will briefly discuss the variety of Italian district growth patterns, using mainly the results of two recent large empirical analyses. The first, reported in Belussi and Martone (2003), used the CERVED archive, and regards a stratified representative sample of firms located in 23 low-, medium- and high-tech districts.[1] The second is a qualitative analysis based on secondary sources collected by Belussi et al. (2008). The evolutionary pattern of 12 districts is studied. Information previously gathered has been enriched to provide a matching of the two research pieces.

For the 23 districts analysed[2] (Tables 7.1, 7.2 and 7.3) some short-term trends related to the dynamics of sales, employment and export flows can be indicated, and some 'structural' features linked to the innovative activity of firms and to their pattern of internationalization can also be described.

Districts investigated are located in the north and south of Italy. The modality of low-tech industries[3] covers the majority of the sample. In medium-tech industries there are only four cases. Medium-tech districts are specialized in taps (Cusio Valselsa), knives and cutlery (Lumezzane), marble (Carrara) and tiles (Sassuolo). In Italy high-tech districts are quite uncommon, and this is correlated to the backwardness of the national innovation system. The only case surveyed is the electronic district of Catania, originated around the activities of the French–Italian multinational STMicroelectronics.

Many of these districts have attained a high international reputation and sell their sophisticated products across the world, for example Biella, Prato, Sassuolo, Montebelluna, Belluno, Carrara, Manzano and Matera. Table 7.1 shows that even in years of turbulence, growth and stability still characterizes the Italian districts' model of development.

Decline in sales appears to be a more frequent tendency among firms in Prato and in Belluno, for opposite reasons to the above: in the first case the district has been hit hard by international competition; in the second, a process of centralization around the largest local firm (Lux Ottica), has affected the local subcontractors. Actually Lux Ottica

Table 7.1 Performance of sampled district firms in the period 2000–02

District	Evolution of sales				Firms with positive employment trends (on total sampled)	Firms with innovations introduced in the period 2000–2003 (on total sampled)	Presence of leaders
	Growth	Stability	Contraction	Total			
Low-tech districts							
Small-medium size	33.6	40.3	26.1	100.0	22.7	30.0	No
Large size	35.1	47.8	17.1	100.0	26.2	27.3	Yes
Medium-tech districts							
Small-medium size	28.7	65.4	5.9	100.0	12.8	28.4	Yes
Large size	30.8	54.9	14.3	100.0	20.1	33.3	Yes
High-tech districts							
Small-medium size	35.3	41.2	23.5	100.0	29.4	35.8	Yes
Total	32.7	41.6	25.7	100.0	22.1	29.1	Frequent

Table 7.2   Export flows

District	Changes in export flows 2001 in comparison with 2000				Total
	Growth	Contraction	Stability	The firm does not operate on international markets	
Low-tech districts					
	20.8	8.9	17.4	52.9	100.0
Medium-tech districts					
	14.3	9.0	29.7	48.4	100.0
High-tech districts					
	5.9	5.5	16.7	77.8	100.0
Total	16.9	8.2	20.9	54.0	100.0

Table 7.3   Models of internationalization

District	Presence of MNCs	International outsourcing	Presence of FDI in low-cost countries (low-cost resource-seeking)	Presence of FDI in high-cost countries (market-seeking)	Presence of FDI or joint ventures involving R&D activities (knowledge-seeking)
Low-tech districts					
	Not frequent	Frequent	Not frequent	Not frequent	Not frequent
Medium-tech districts					
	No	Not frequent	Frequent	Yes	Not frequent
High-tech districts					
	Yes	Yes	No	No	Yes

is the largest worldwide multinational that manufactures glasses frames. This firm is also leading many distributive channels in Asia and US.

In the districts considered, sales stability or growth does not impact very positively on local employment, given the ample recourse to international subcontracting and to foreign direct investment (FDI) initiatives. In Table 7.1 only one district seems to perform particularly positively in the years considered: Matera.

A very important aspect to be considered is the innovative capability of district firms. The innovative capability of firms located in industrial districts is the result of a complex process of an original innovative and/or imitative activity. Following the traditional 'quantitative' approach used by several innovation surveys, which combine the two modalities, innovation activity in firms can be roughly measured by the number of technological innovations introduced in the period analysed (2000–2003) by the innovating firms, weighted on the total. Considering this aspect, it can be appreciated how the introduction of innovations among the sampled firms is rather frequent within all the district typologies considered, and also within the low-tech districts. The presence of innovating firms appears to be quite evenly spread across the entire sample, confirming the existence of a high degree of heterogeneity in each considered category. In the period analysed, Italian IDs displayed significant dynamism, underlined by the fact that nearly one firm out of three introduced at least one innovation in product, process or in the organizational field.

The presence of leader firms (large firms with significant innovation capability and high export share) is now characterizing the Italian scene, and particularly the districts characterized by medium technology and by the presence of large size firms, as shown in Table 7.1 in the last column.

Let us consider now the aspect of the internationalization of the Italian IDs. Since the 1970s, high export flows have characterized the Italian model of industrial districts. Recently Lorenzoni (1997), Quadrio Curzio and Fortis (2000) and Caroli and Lipparini (2002) have confirmed the positive international position of Italian districts. It is well known that in newly developing countries, on the contrary, local firms in districts are often quite unspecialized, and incapable of generating significant export flows (Humprey and Schmitz, 2002).

During the 1990s, Italian industrial districts were characterized by a quite open model (Coró and Grandinetti, 1999), not only considering the entity of export flows, but also taking into account the building of international subcontracting chains. A new international division of labour has occurred: thus, all standardized and low-value-added phases related to manufacturing have been gradually relocated abroad in low-labour-cost countries (Belussi and Sammarra, 2010). Initially, outward flows were strategically organized by the district leaders (or by the larger local groups). Subsequently, this process has gradually also involved the great majority of the district firms, including many small local firms. Up to now the delocalization of manufacturing activities abroad has not created too many social conflicts at the local level, undermining the cooperative base of the industrial district model.

More recently, and above all in medium- or high-tech sectors, the internationalization of the district firms has gone further. Several large leading groups have used foreign direct investments and 'pocket multinationals' have emerged in Italian districts, closing the gap with what was occurring at international level (Rugman and Verbeke, 2003; Lorenzen and Mahnke, 2002). In particular, the following cases can be mentioned: Montebelluna (Tecnica, Geox, Stonefly, and so on); Belluno (Lux Ottica); Alto Livenza (Domo group); Manzano (Callegaris); Matera (Natuzzi group); and Cusio Valsesia (Alessi). The entry of multinationals has been reported only in a few cases, among which are: Montebelluna (with the entry of Nike); Mirandola (with the entry of Gambro); and Catania (with the transfer of STMicroelectronics).

Firms in industrial districts are characterised by two distinct typologies: those which have an autonomous capacity of governing global relations; and those which have remained 'local'. This heterogeneity is well depicted in Tables 7.2 and 7.3. In fact, nearly half of the firms interviewed do not operate on international markets. However, many firms interviewed are local subcontractors of leading firms which, in contrast, are fully integrated in international markets. In addition it should be noted that in low-tech districts the strategy of international outsourcing appear as a strategy of diffusion, while in medium-tech districts the recourse to FDI is more frequently selected. The internationalization of the district represents a critical moment in its life cycle: it destroys some existing competences and it generates the development of new functions (logistics, marketing, R&D, and so on). In many cases districts have changed their original specialization, becoming more diversified. Typically, Italian districts are specialized not only in traditional products (those related to the 'Made in Italy' sector), but also in sectors producing basic technology and manufacturing machinery. In 2005–10, mechanical firms in the Italian industrial districts emerged as the most dynamic exporters (Carabelli et al., 2006).

SOME CONCLUSIONS: THE FUTURE OF DISTRICTS

The phenomenum of the globalization of markets is deeply challenging the evolution of modern economic systems. Industrial districts and regions are profoundly affected too.

Despite the fact that many districts entered in the 1990s in a cycle of a negative conjuncture, if we consider the Italian case, there is still a significant heterogeneity exhibited as regards their performances in sales, export, employment and innovation strategies. In contrast to what was advocated by many scholars, industrial district firms show a remarkable resilience, and many firms are still positioned in an expansive trend. In Italy industrial districts in 2000–2010 were also quick in adopting various forms of internationalization. Many firms were typically high exporters; a large number of them were able to activate external linkages focused on the governance of international subcontracting chains; a small number of firms were even able to become 'pocket multinationals'.

The novel emerging forms of internationalization in industrial districts are related to the growth of 'small multinationals' sustained by moderate hierarchies, which use FDI, and mixed intermediate forms of internationalization (joint ventures, subcontracting agreements, productive collaboration agreements and/or technological extension of networks of foreign trade channels, and so on). Among those that go abroad and cooperate with other foreign companies are, especially, large final firms and dynamic subcontractors, pushed by their clients to do this. The internationalization processes analysed consisted of activities that were outsourced by Italian district firms, and transferred abroad through agreements between companies, processing flows, building of commercial channels, and outward FDI. This process only occurred in districts specialized in high-tech products, like biotech or electronics, but spread around within the 'Made in Italy' districts, whose sector of specialization is the production of yarn, clothing, knitting and footwear, and in sectors based on medium-low technologies, like tiles, furniture, marble and mechanical products.

Of course, it is difficult to have a clear vision regarding the possible changing scenario of how territorial proximity will be influenced, modified or even nullified by globalization, and by the adoption of ICT technologies. The use of ICT could dramatically reduce the importance of physical proximity and profoundly affect the strategic importance of size, because in order to benefit from the advantages of internationalization, firms need to reach a certain scale. It is hard to guess whether new technologies could in future replace the role of the 'local community' in responding to the needs of stability, identity, trust, coordination, and sharing risk and knowledge that occur in mercantile and non-mercantile exchanges. Globalization can produce a new geographic space in which 'local' and 'long-distance' networks can flourish and become operative networks.

The important feature of this contribution has been the identification and the discussion of the characteristics of the new Marshallian districts: they are becoming complex learning systems that, on the one hand, produce localized knowledge, and on the other hand, activate processes of learning at the boundaries among distant communities, firms, institutions and networks. In many cases district firms have enlarged their differentiated knowledge base, recombining their existing knowledge with technologies developed elsewhere (Belussi et al., 2008).

The analysis conducted leads to the conclusion that firms in industrial districts, embedded in different regional contexts, are not just becoming local nodes of global networks (Amin and Thrift, 1992). The picture of the transformation of new Marshallian IDs is certainly more complex than that. The density of local relations still appears to be important in order to construct local competitive advantages, based on diversification and differentiation strategies, and on 'related varieties' as assumed by Asheim et al. (2007).

NOTES

1. This research is based on a large number (978) of small and medium-sized firms interviewed by the CERVED researchers.
2. For clarity of the table I have reported here only the aggregated data crossed by district typology.
3. Low-tech districts considered are the following: textiles (Biella and Prato), knitwear (Carpi), clothing (Val Vibrata), wedding-dresses (Putignano), leather (Santa Croce in Florence), footwear (Bari), sports articles and footwear (Montebelluna), spectacles (Belluno), furniture (Alto Livenza and Pesaro), chairs (Manzano in Udine), leather sofas (Matera), tomato processing (Nocerino-Sarnese, in Campania) and ham production (Langhirano-Parma).

REFERENCES

Amin, A. and N. Thrift (1992), 'Neo-Marshallian nodes in global networks', *Internat: Journal of Urban and Regional Research*, **16**, 571–87.
Arrighetti, A. and G. Serravalle (eds) (1999), *Istituzioni intermedia e sviluppo locale*, Rome: Donzelli.
Asheim, B., R. Boschma and P. Cooke (2007), 'Constructing regional advantage: platform policies based on relative variety and differentiated knowledge bases', Evolutionary Economic Geography Paper 07.09, http://econ.geo.uu.nl/peeg/peeg0709.pdf.
Becattini, G., M. Bellandi, G. Dei Ottati and F. Sforzi (eds) (2003), *From Industrial Districts to Local Development: An Itinerary of Research*, Cheltenham, UK and Northampton, MA, USA: Edward Elgar.
Bell J., R. McNaughton and S. Young (2001), 'Born-again global firms: an extension to the born global phenomenon', *Journal of International Management*, **7**, 173–90.
Belussi, F. (1999), 'Policies for the development of knowledge-intensive local production systems', *Cambridge Journal of Economics*, **23**, 729–74.
Belussi, F. and G. Gottardi (2000), *Evolutionary Patterns of Local Industrial Systems: Towards a Cognitive Approach to the Industrial District*, Aldershot: Ashgate.
Belussi, F. and C. Martone (2003), 'Processi di internationalizzazione e delocalizzazione delle Pmi e dei distretti industriali', in AAVV, *Le piccole e medie imprese nell'economie italiana*, Milan: Franco Angeli.
Belussi, F. and L. Pilotti (2002), 'Knowledge creation, learning and innovation in Italian industrial districts', *Geografiska Annaler*, **84**, 19–33.
Belussi, F. and A. Sammarra (eds) (2010), *Business Networks in Clusters and Industrial Districts: The Governance of the Global Value Chain*, London: Routledge.

Belussi, F., A. Sammarra and S.R. Sedita (2008), 'Managing long distance and localised learning in the Emilia Romagna life science cluster', *European Planning Studies*, **16** (5), 665–92.

Belussi F. and S. Sedita (2009), 'Life cycle vs. multiple path dependency in industrial districts', *European Planning Studies*, **17** (4), 505–28.

Belussi, F. and S. Sedita (2010), 'The evolution of the district model: "reverse relocation" and the case of the leather-tanning district of Arzignano', *ERIEP – European Review of Industrial Economics and Policy*, **1**, 15 July, http://testrevel.unice.fr/eriep/index.html/id=3067.

Cainelli, G. and N. De Liso (2005), 'Innovation in industrial districts: evidence from Italy', *Industry and Innovation*, **12** (3), 383–9.

Caniëls, M. and H. Romijn (2005), 'What drives innovativeness in industrial clusters? Transcending the debate', *Cambridge Journal of Economics*, **29**, 497–515.

Cantwell, J. and S. Iammarino (1998), 'MNCs, technological innovation and regional systems in the EU: some evidence in the Italian case', *International Journal of the Economics of Business*, **5**, 383–408.

Carabelli, A., G. Hirsh and R. Rabellotti (2006), 'Italian SMEs and industrial districts on the move: where are they going?', Quaderno SEMeQ, 13, Università degli Studi del Piemonte Orientale.

Caroli, M. and A. Lipparini (eds) (2002), *Piccole imprese oltre il confine. Competenze e processi di internazionalizzazione*, Rome: Carocci.

Coe, N. and T. Bunnell (2003), 'Spatializing knowledge communities: towards a conceptualisation of transnational innovation networks', *Global Networks*, **3** (4), 437–56.

Cooke, P. (1998), 'Global clustering and regional innovation: systemic integration in Wales', in H.-J. Braczyk, P. Cooke and M. Heidenreich (eds), *Regional Innovation Systems*, London: UCL Press, pp. 245–62.

Cooke, P. (2001), 'Regional innovation systems, clusters, and the knowledge economy', *Industrial and Corporate Change*, **10** (4), 945–74.

Cooke, P., M. Uranga and G. Etxebarria (1997), 'Regional innovation systems: institutional and organisational dimensions', *Research Policy*, **26**, 475–91.

Corò, G. and R. Grandinetti (1999), 'Evolutionary patterns of Italian industrial districts', *Human System Management*, **18** (2), 117–29.

Dicken, P. (2007), *Global Shift: Reshaping the Global Economic Map*, London: Sage.

Feldman, M. (2004), 'Knowledge externalities and the anchor hypothesis: the locational dynamics of the US biotech industry', paper presented at the Annual Meeting of the Association of American Geographers, Philadelphia, PA, 14–17 March.

Gereffi, G., J. Humprey and T. Sturgeon (2005), 'The governance of global value chains', *Review of International Political Economy*, **12** (1), 78–104.

Giuliani, E., R. Rabellotti and M.P. van Dijk (eds) (2005), *Cluster Facing Competition: The Importance of External Linkages*, Aldershot: Ashgate.

Grandinetti, R. and E. Rullani (1996), *Impresa transnazionale ed economia globale*, Rome: Nis.

Guerrieri, P., S. Iammarino and C. Pietrobelli (eds) (2001), *The Global Challenge to Industrial Districts: Small and Medium-sized Enterprises in Italy and Taiwan*, Cheltenham, UK and Northampton, MA, USA: Edward Elgar.

Humphrey, J. and H. Schmitz (2002), 'How does insertion in global value chains affect upgrading in industrial clusters?', *Regional Studies*, **36** (9), 1017–27.

Lorenzen, M. and V. Mahnke (2002), 'Global strategies and acquisition of local knowledge: how MNCs enter regional clusters', DUID Working Paper no. 8.

Lorenzoni, G. (1997), *Architetture reticolari e processi di internazionalizzazione*, Bologna: Il Mulino.

Mariotti, S., M. Mutinelli and L. Piscitello (2006), 'Eterogeneità e internazionalizzazione produttiva dei distretti industriali italiani', *L'Industria*, **27** (1), 173–201.

Markusen, A. (1996), 'Sticky places in slippery space: a typology on industrial districts', *Economic Geography*, **72**, 293–313.

Maskell, P. (1999), 'Globalisation and industrial competitiveness: the process and the consequences of "ubifiquation"', in E. Maleki and P. Oinas (eds), *Making Connections: Technological Learning and Regional Economic Exchange*, Aldershot: Ashgate, pp. 35–60.

Mistri, M. (2002), 'Globalizzazione e processi di governance nei distretti industriali', *Argomenti*, **4**, 5–26.

Mudambi, R. (2008), 'Location, control and innovation in knowledge intensive industries', *Journal of Economic Geography*, **8**, 699–725.

Nelson, R.R. and B.N. Sampat (2001), 'Making sense of institutions as a factor shaping economic performance', *Journal of Behavior and Organization*, **44** (1), 31–54.

Paniccia, I. (2002), 'A critical review of the literature on industrial districts, in search of a theory', *Industrial Districts: Evolution and Competitiveness in Italian Firms*, Cheltenham, UK and Northampton, MA, USA: Edward Elgar, pp. 151–86.

Powell, W.W., K.W. Koput and L. Smith-Doerr (1996), 'Interorganisational collaboration and the locus of innovation: networks of learning in biotechnology', *Administartivre Science Quarterly*, **41** (March), 116–45.

Quadrio Curzio, A. and M. Fortis (2000), *Il made in Italy oltre il 2000*, Bologna: Il Mulino.

Rugman, A. and A. Verbeke (2003), 'Multinational enterprises and clusters', *Management International Review*, **43** (Special Issue 3), 151–69.

Rullani, E. (1997), 'L'evoluzione dei distretti industriali: un percorso tra de-costruzione e internazionalizzazione', in R. Varaldo and L. Ferrucci (eds), *Il distretto industriale tra logiche di impresa e logiche di sistema*, Milan: Franco Angeli, pp. 82–113.

Sammarra, A. (2003), *Lo sviluppo dei distretti industriali. Percorsi evolutivi fra globalizzazione e localizzazione*, Rome: Carocci.

Sammarra, A. and F. Belussi (2006), 'Evolution and relocation in fashion-led Italian districts: evidence from two case-studies', *Entrepreneurship and Regional Development*, **18**, 543–62.

Saxenian, A. (1994), *Regional Advantage: Culture and Competition in Silicon Valley and Route 128*, Cambridge, MA: Harvard University Press.

Saxenian A. (1999), *Silicon Valley New Immigrant Entrepreneurs*, San Francisco, CA: Public Policy Institute.

Simmie J. and J. Sennen (1999), 'Innovative clusters: global or local linkages?', *National Institute of Economic Review*, **170**, 87–98.

Squazzoni, F. and R. Boero (2002), 'Economic performance, inter-firm relations and local institutional engineering in a computational prototype of industrial districts', *Journal of Artificial Societies and Social Simulation*, **5** (1), http://jasss.soc.surrey.ac.uk/s/r/l.html.

PART II

REGIONAL INNOVATION AND GROWTH DYNAMICS

PART II

REGIONAL INNOVATION
AND GROWTH DYNAMICS

Introduction

Philip Cooke, Franz Tödtling and Dafna Schwartz

PRODUCTIVITY AND GROWTH

Part II of the *Handbook* is devoted to debates about the relationships between regional innovation and growth, on the one hand, and aspects of industrial organization that they are influenced by, facilitate and form, on the other. Much of this part therefore contains interesting discussions about the meaning of regional innovation and growth for broader evolutionary processes that shape economic geography. It draws on issues foreshadowed in the general introduction to this book (Chapter 1), namely productivity and regional inequality, which will be only briefly summarized here. Then it moves into a group of chapters that investigate debates about the nature of spillovers, especially knowledge spillovers, in the economic geography of agglomeration, and questions whether and in what ways specialization of agglomerations is preferable to their diversification for fostering innovation or not. The conditions under which these debates resolve one way or the other constitute an important inflection point for the evolutionary economic geography project of the book.

To recap, Chapter 8 by Roberta Capello and Chapter 9 by Daniel Felsenstein argue the following. First, there is a high degree of confluence in the views that the relationships between innovation and productivity devolve into three: these are represented, first, by new economic geography (or the functional approach to regional productivity) whereby regional innovation is highly interrelated to issues of market-size and pecuniary externality effects, agglomerating where the lead region is found (rather like Vernon's initial product life-cycle take on innovation). This tends to produce misleadingly over-concentrated (extreme regional disparities) analytical results. A better alternative is new growth theory (NGT), which focuses on impacts of innovation externalities from human capital on endogenous technological change hence regional productivity and growth. This theory supports the deduction that the higher the average level of human capital, the more rapid the diffusion of knowledge, the higher the level of regional productivity (including earnings). This is similar to Capello's structural approach. In other words high human capital, absorbed externalities (for example knowledge spillovers) and communicative or networking power combine to produce regional advantage. But these models are confused by a 'regional innovation' effect which is clarified by evolutionary economic geography (EEG), or Capello's cognitive approach, which sees institutions, organizations and cultural practices as critical to generating regional growth. This is where modelling that includes cultural proxies like 'relatedness' of industry, social networks and spin-off activity is conducted, confirming the advantages for growth from innovation fostered in, or utilized at distance by, agglomeration incumbents.

SPECIALIZATION OR DIVERSIFICATION?

Regions endowed with the above-mentioned assets will forge ahead and maintain a lead over others by replenishing those capabilities, especially in the globalized knowledge economy. Moreover, regions that evolve those capabilities may narrow the lead region's advantage, possibly overtaking it in the long term, especially if the lead region backslides or becomes 'locked in' to negative path-dependence effects. These are guarded against by evolution of firm, knowledge and regional variety, agility and innovation, which assist new, more diversified path creation. Chapters 10 and 11, by Stefano Breschi and Simona Iammarino respectively, address this portrayal of regional economic evolution head-on.

Breschi's interest is in knowledge spillovers in relation to growth, focused on innovation using knowledge from concentrated or dispersed sources. Endogenous growth theory addresses the issue raised in the 'Introduction', Chapter 1, to this *Handbook* regarding the public nature of knowledge. There, the discussion was about the likely impact of university research as spillovers into the regional as opposed to the global economy. Hypothetically, and with some evidentiary support from the 'relatedness' perspective (see Boschma and Frenken, Chapter 14 in this *Handbook*), spillovers can be expected to be a majority, since much research on geographical knowledge spillovers shows there to be a more or less rapid distance–decay effect based on such indicators as patent citations. Geography is thus important to spillover absorption, but the magnitudes of outward leakage or, conversely, inward infusion of valuable knowledge from interregional or international research, publication or patenting partnerships, is simply unknown although likely to be a hot topic, especially in times of straitened research and teaching budgets at research universities.

Endogenous growth theory thus purports to explain how new knowledge is internally generated by investments in R&D, but because ideas are free, its benefits are not confined to regional innovators networked to the knowledge source. Even patenting does not protect; rather, it allows a rent to be charged by the inventor to subsequent users. Incidentally, this also means that in effect the real productivity of this kind of knowledge is also not known. However, to the extent that research has been conducted into this problem, its results are probably an underestimate. Hence, open science increases the productivity of the research process for unknown numbers of firms in the region as well as the broader global economy. In pursuit of some purchase on this question the neoclassicals (for unclear reasons known as MAR, the acronym for economists Marshall, Arrow and Romer) with their knowledge production function econometrics incline to the view that specialization of knowledge spills over most fruitfully for firms (see Vatne's Chapter 4 on 'Romer externalities' in this *Handbook*). Research from a more eclectic viewpoint more in tune with evolutionary economic geography is cited by Breschi as supporting the conclusion that a diversified knowledge base is more friendly to innovation performance (see Vatne's Chapter 4 on 'Jacobs externalities', and Boschma and Frenken's Chapter 14, in this Handbook). However, he also notes research showing that this can vary over time and space, for example Tichy's (see Chapter 5 in this *Handbook*) observations about new agglomerations housing innovations would be illustrative of this 'creative disruption' of an established innovation surface. Accordingly, against an inclination to favour sectoral specialization in understanding innovative performance, Breschi's review conclusions incline towards 'variety' being a better explanation.

VARIETY AND NETWORKS

Simona Iammarino's Chapter 11, on 'Regional innovation and diversity' expressly explores this contention. As she puts it: 'In other words, are the most innovative and fast-growing regions sectorally specialized or diversified?' Her starting premise is that the answer to this question not only may be unknown, but may be unknowable, given the complexity of links between variety and innovation at the regional level. In light of the conclusions of the preceding chapters in Part II, this is a salutary observation. Iammarino points out that even Jane Jacobs did not expect variety or diversity alone to yield up regional growth. Nevertheless she saw the key cross-pollinations being interindustry, unlike MAR for whom they are interfirm, and the former are, she thought, likely to produce the greater regional economic returns. Moreover, Iammarino points out, despite the difficulties posed for analysis by sector, structure and methodology, more and more research results in the burgeoning field of variety and growth incline to the conclusion that variety is more associated with regional economic growth than specialization of industry. But, reiterating Jacobs's injunction that variety is not automatically growth-inducing, she underlines that it must be used and exploited, and therein lies the paradox that some diversified regional economies have poor growth performance. As noted in the 'Introduction', Chapter 1, to this *Handbook* and elsewhere (Chapter 14) there needs to be a distinction between 'diversity' which can run the whole gamut of regional economic structure, and 'variety' which need only be a segment or segments ('revealed related variety') of the regional industrial bandwidth. So the balanced judgement of Iammarino is that variety is a desirable but by no means sufficient condition for regional innovation and growth, and that it may be meaningless unless energized by the regional regime of intermediaries, social capital and forms that comprise it.

This perspective is explored in some detail in Elisa Giuliani's Chapter 12 on 'Networks of innovation'. Innovation is precisely dependent on networks of innovators within firms, and between them and knowledge institutions. It relies on numerous sources that must be connected for the knowledge recombinations opened up by the innovation paradigm to be fully explored and exploited. Such networks display four dimensions around which performance may revolve. These are the following. (1) Network formalization, that is, how legitimate or authoritative is it? (2) Network actors, for example for innovation negotiation, scientists or administrators, and if the latter, budget-controlling or not? (3) Network methodology, that is, should it be understood in terms of process or substance? (4) Network geography, global or 'only' local? Network layers also seem crucial, the thicker the better, that is, market only is thin and probably associational; market plus social is thicker and more 'communitarian'; market, social and policy is thickest and capable of innovation paradigm-regime communication, consensus and committed action. Clearly these thickened networks are a precise model for using and exploiting 'variety' of the kind that Iammarino sees Jacobs recognizing as having major potential for realizing regional innovation and growth.

Finally, in Chapter 13 Lisa De Propris and Olivier Crevoisier inquire about the degree to which agglomeration, whether specialized or diversified, needs regional anchoring elements, apart from the thickened networks that may interweave regional variety for positive innovation purposes. 'Anchoring' has meant three loosely related things over time. Initially it embodied the idea that a regional economy might benefit from having an endogenously evolved industry complex (for example shipbuilding, aeronautics plus suppliers). Subsequently, and in respect of constructing regional advantage based on new industries, the anchor question concerned what would be the supply-side characteristics (for example skills, subsidies, knowledge) that would attract them. Nowadays, anchoring is a territorial or 'space of flows' hub capability in transceiving and transforming global knowledge for innovation. Referencing origination of the anchoring concept in analysis of biotechnology clustering, the authors observe that productivity gains accrue from the lowering of transactions costs, other pecuniary externalities (for example asset sharing), and innovation based on interactive learning. This explanation works *ex post* but the questions of cluster emergence and cluster vulnerability to insufficient 'variety' arise. In other words: how can such clusters be reproduced; and how can they be insured against anchor overspecialization and vulnerability to path-dependence, 'lock-in' and obsolescence, such as occurred in Boston's minicomputer cluster? An answer lies in enhancing the 'process' function of such complexes and looking for innovation gains from related variety (see Chapter 23 on 'Transversality' in this *Handbook*). On the basis of such 'platform-building', strong links can be made to a more diverse range of global industries interested in accessing 'platform technologies'. De Propris and Crevoisier envisage a forerunner of this kind of anchoring in today's Swiss watch-making industry, which is no longer anchored in a sector or even a regionalized supply-chain, but rather in an interlinked arrangement of capabilities stretching across, integrating and adapting various technologies including micro-electronics, optics, micro-mechanics and material sciences, into one nodal innovation system.

Hence, the chapters synthesize a view of the evolution of regional innovation as bifurcating asymmetrically along lines that, on the one hand, underline the importance of industrial specialization for innovation, as espoused not only by MAR but also by Michael Porter in the cluster basket; and on the otherhand, a newer line that advocates, guided by the insights of Jane Jacobs, the virtues of diversification, moderated by theoretical refinement, to the more nuanced concept of 'variety' or, more generally, 'relatedness'. This seems to enhance prospects for regional innovation and growth through territorial knowledge dynamics based on 'transversality' while not condemning the region or, at a smaller scale, the cluster to vulnerability from overspecialization, narrow path-dependence and possible innovation inertia. These findings resonate clearly with those culminating in the chapters on the way neo-Marshallian industrial districts seek to cope with the challenge of globalization: flexibility, agility, design and innovation. To these may be added the promotion and evolution of judicious regionally related variety.

8   Innovation and productivity: local competitiveness and the role of space
Roberta Capello

INTRODUCTION

Innovation, or in more modern terms the smart use of advanced knowledge, is regarded as one of the key drivers of economic growth in the knowledge-driven society. Three different interpretative approaches of innovation and local growth can be distinguished according to the determinants that explain the different degrees of regional innovation, namely:

- A sectoral and functional approach which foresees innovation as the result of the presence of innovative sectors or functions. In this approach, physical proximity among actors facilitates the exchange of tacit knowledge, generating localized knowledge spillovers (see Stefano Breschi's Chapter 10 in this *Handbook*).
- A structural approach that interprets regional innovation as the result of the presence of structural elements in a region that make the area prone to innovation.
- A cognitive approach, that interprets innovation as the result of the presence of collective learning processes and socialization to the risk of innovation (that is, territorialized relations among subjects operating in geographical and social proximity), and of the existence of rules, codes and norms of behaviour which: (1) facilitate cooperation among actors and therefore the socialization of knowledge; and (2) assist economic actors (individual people, firms and local institutions) to develop organizational forms which support interactive learning processes.

These approaches developed in parallel, starting from the 1980s when a scientific wave of reflections on the role of innovation in economic growth pervasively influenced all branches of economics (industrial, regional, traditional macroeconomic economics). Within their own conceptual frames, they found ways to evolve, coexist and influence one another, remaining however quite different in many respects: in terms of local determinants explaining innovation, of elements driving the path to innovation, of interactions from innovation to growth, of the role of space in determining local innovation patterns, of the concept of productivity embedded in each approach.

The aim of the present chapter is to provide an overview of these different approaches, with the aim of highlighting peculiarities and similarities. As the chapter will demonstrate, in only one of these approaches is space considered as a source of dynamic efficiency, as a real resource for generating knowledge, learning and persistent innovation capacity over time. The other two approaches mentioned are rather aspatial, leaving to space the trivial role of a physical container of different structural and sectoral elements that facilitate the development of innovation.

DIFFERENT APPROACHES TO INNOVATION, PRODUCTIVITY AND LOCAL COMPETITIVENESS

The Sector- and Function-based Approach

An approach to the explanation of innovation determinants at the regional level is the sector- and function-based approach (Table 8.1). In the pure sectoral approach elements explaining local innovation capacities were highlighted in the presence of 'science-based' or high-technology sectors; regions hosting these sectors were considered as 'scientific' regions leading the transformation of the economy and economic growth. New jobs were expected mainly from these new sectors, while more traditional sectors were expected to restructure or even to flow offshore, giving rise to serious tensions in local labour markets (Camagni and Capello, 2009).

It soon became evident that the dichotomy was too simplistic, and that many knowledge-based innovations were possible and were actually introduced by 'traditional' sectors – such as textiles and car production – in their path towards rejuvenation. Furthermore, elaboration of technological *filières* (inputs and outputs) inside the value

Table 8.1   Different approaches to innovation and regional growth

	Sector-based, function-based approach	Structural approach	Cognitive approach
Determinants of innovation	Science-based sectors, R&D, higher education functions	Human capital, demographics, research centres, high-value sectors	Collective learning processes
Typology of innovative regions	Scientific regions	Advanced regions	Learning regions
Path towards innovation	Invention–innovation short circuit, spatial spillovers	Knowledge–innovation short circuit	Collective learning, local synergies
From innovation to growth	Radical innovation, Schumpeterian profits	Continuing innovation	Productivity increases
Concept of productivity	Productivity in innovation activities	Productivity of regional innovation systems	Factor productivity generated by innovation
Knowledge transfer	Epidemiological processes	Epidemiological processes	Labour mobility, spin-offs and customer–supplier relationships
Role of space	Proximity economies, specialization advantages and agglomeration advantages	Proximity economies	Uncertainty reduction, relational capital

chain increasingly underlined the relevance of advanced tertiary sectors. These supplied producer services mainly in the form of consultancy for process innovation (proper acquisition and use of advanced technologies, tailor-made software, systems integration in production, administration and logistic processes, organizational support) and for product innovation (marketing, design, testing, advertising, finance, distribution).

A function-based approach was preferred (even though it overlapped conceptually with the previous one). This stressed the importance of pervasive and horizontal functions like research and development (R&D) and higher education. 'Scientific' regions, hosting large and well-known scientific institutions, were studied deeply and relationships between these institutions and the industrial fabric were analysed, with some disappointment where expected but not often visible direct linkages were concerned (MacDonald, 1987; Massey et al., 1992; Monk et al., 1988; Storey and Tether, 1998). Indicators of R&D inputs (like public and private research investment and personnel) and increasingly indicators of R&D output (like patenting activities) were used in order to understand the engagement of firms and territories with advanced knowledge, intended as a necessary long-term precondition for continuing innovation (Dasgupta and Stiglitz, 1980; Antonelli, 1989; Griliches, 1990).

What is striking is the central role played by spatial elements, both evidenced by empirical analyses, and deductively derived from theory. The tendency of high-technology activities to cluster in valleys, corridors, glens and high-tech districts was early empirical evidence. Explanation of the phenomenon was straightforward: externalities coming from the presence of advanced education facilities were invoked to explain these facts, but international accessibility, advanced urban atmosphere, and reconversion of traditional industrial competencies (Malecki, 1980; Saxenian, 1996) were also suggested. Concentrated location facilitates the exploitation of technological and scientific knowledge developed by research centres and universities; it gives easier access to the tacit and uncodified knowledge required for imitation and reverse engineering; and it ensures the ready availability of skilled labour and advanced services.

Moreover, the complex and systemic nature of innovative processes were seen to explain their cumulative character: clusters of incremental innovations follow an initial radical innovation which marks out a 'technological trajectory' along which knowledge grows and develops within well-defined technological boundaries. At the local level, demand for and the supply of innovative factors interact and mutually reinforce each other, increasing innovation performance and productivity. Advanced firms enrich the surrounding environment by diffusing their technological and organizational expertise, while the surrounding environment simultaneously sustains their activity. The outcome is a cumulative region-specific polarization of research and innovation activities which reinforces the natural tendency for innovation to concentrate in space.

The role of agglomeration economies, both urban and sectoral, in explaining the concentration of innovative activity was demonstrated long ago by Marshall. But interest in dynamic agglomeration economies (the agglomerative advantages that foster innovation by firms) has grown considerably in recent years, as recognition has gained ground of the importance of innovation for the competitiveness of local systems. In fact, using both input indicators (for example spending on research and development) and output indicators (for example number of patents) of innovative activity, many studies in the 1980s showed that innovation is concentrated in central and metropolitan areas. Moreover, in all the industrialized countries, analyses of the location of high-tech firms reveal marked polarization effects due to the pronounced preference of these firms for central locations with strong sectoral specialization. Concentration of innovation activities also revealed an innovative capacity which persistently outstrips that of other geographical areas, and they achieve levels of innovation sometimes greatly disproportional to their manufacturing weight. They thus testify to the presence of some form of increasing returns on the concentration of innovative activity.[1]

A modern version of a function-based approach highlights an explicit link between the existence of knowledge-based functions and the creation of entrepreneurial activities as drivers of growth: in the knowledge filter theory, investments in knowledge by incumbent firms and research organizations such as universities generate entrepreneurial opportunities because not all of the new knowledge is pursued and commercialized by the incumbent firms (Acs et al., 2004, 2005; Acs and Plummer, 2005). By so doing, theory moves a step forward by explicitly emphasizing the link between knowledge creation, structural elements and regional growth. Moreover, this particular theory contains some insights into the third – cognitive – approach when it claims that the capabilities of economic agents within the region actually to access and absorb new knowledge and ultimately utilize it to generate entrepreneurial activity is no longer assumed to be invariant with respect to geographic space, as was generally thought. In particular, diversified areas, in which differences among people that foster looking at and appraising a given information set differently, thereby resulting in different appraisal of any new idea, are expected to gain more from new knowledge (see Boschma and Frenken's Chapter 14 in this *Handbook*).

In both sector-based and function-based approaches, space is treated in a widely abstract, indirect and stylized way: concentration and agglomeration of main R&D facilities are by and large assumed to be acceptable starting points for empirical analyses, while knowledge diffusion processes are analysed in terms of pure probability functions, decreasing with physical distance. Spatial spillover effects are considered as a black box, with no reference to real, territorialized channels of direct knowledge interaction (Capello and Faggian, 2005). This approach imposes the same limitations as did Hägerstrand's pioneering model in regard to the spatial diffusion of innovation: the diffusion of knowledge means adoption, and adoption means more innovation and better performance. However, this ignored the most crucial aspect of the innovation process: how people actually learn. This is the aspect of overriding interest not only for scholars but also, and especially, for policy-makers, should they wish to explore the possibilities of normative action to promote local development. What this approach certainly does is to witness that productivity in innovation activities is not invariant over space, and that increasing returns clearly emerge in clustered activities.

The Structural Approach

A different approach to the study of the determinants of innovation capacity at the local level was what can be called the structural approach, characterized by the aim to go in depth into the structural (endogenous) elements that are important for the innovative capacity of a region (Table 8.1). Regions characterized by these elements were considered to be 'advanced regions' responsible for leading innovation activities, productivity increases and local growth.

The main idea of this approach was that certain structural conditions, embedded in the local systems, determined the speed with which each society adopted innovation and exploited it. Each nation and region has its unique 'social filter' that hampers or sustains innovation. This allows identification of 'innovation-prone' versus 'innovation-averse' regions (Rodriguez-Pose, 1999; Crescenzi et al., 2007). These elements have been identified in education, lifelong learning, sectoral composition, use of resources (unemployment) and demographics, particularly migration. In the most innovative places, migration is expected to update the matching of knowledge, skills and competencies in line with the evolution of the technological frontier (Crescenzi et al., 2007).

This approach does not add much to the conceptualization of the way a region learns. The path to innovation is a matter of knowledge, translated easily (and immediately) into (commercialized) innovation thanks to the presence of structural elements. Sometimes it also risks a tautological reasoning by claiming that innovation-prone regions are those more endowed with structural, sectoral and functional activities useful for innovation.

In the structural approach, space is taken into consideration in two ways. First, space is seen as a vehicle for enhancing agglomeration economies, allowing for the operation of 'sharing', 'matching' and 'learning' mechanisms; close proximity becomes a condition for the dissemination of information, through typical epidemiological processes. This approach emphasises that understanding the ways these interactive proximities and densities adjust over time explains regional technological trajectories (Crescenzi et al., 2007). Second, space is seen as a conductor of knowledge spillovers from R&D activities, subject to strong and visible distance–decay effects.

Productivity is also in this approach at the centre of the analysis: in this approach, the interest lies in the understanding of different degrees of productivity in innovation activities developed by regional systems. Innovation productivity is not invariant over space, and shows strong cumulative effects in specific areas with regional-specific elements and factor endowment, such as high human capital, population density, taxes and industry structure. As in the case of the sector- and functional-based approach, once innovation takes place, it acts immediately on growth thanks to (never explicitly mentioned) mechanisms on factor productivity gains.

However, space remains passive in the processes of knowledge creation and innovation. As was the case for the sector- and function-based approach so in this approach space is treated in an indirect and stylized way; it remains a pure container of structural elements, of a socio-economic structure able to develop an endogenously driven accumulation of human capital which ensures long-term positive productivity enhancement and, accordingly, growth. Regional economic growth is made to depend solely on increasing returns to productive resources, to increasing returns that overcome the marginal decreasing returns to scale of single-production resources typical of traditional neoclassical approaches. It is only thanks to a third, rather different approach, a cognitive one, that this limitation is overcome. This is the subject matter of the next subsection.

The Cognitive Approach

Another kind of reflection exists, developed during the mid-1980s but reinforced in the present period, in which a relation-based approach is preferred, concentrated on the identification of a 'cognitive capability' explaining regional innovation (Foray, 2000):

the ability to manage information in order to identify and solve problems or, more precisely in the economic sphere, the ability to transform information and inventions into innovation, hence productivity increases, through cooperative or market interaction (Table 8.1). The 'learning' region (see James Simmie's Chapter 40 in this *Handbook*) is identified as the place where such cognitive processes play a crucial role, combining existing but dispersed know-how, interpretations of market needs, and information flows with intellectual artifacts such as theories and models, and allowing exchange of experiences and cooperation (Lundvall and Johnson, 1994). Especially in contexts characterized by a plurality of agents – like cities or industrial districts – knowledge evolution 'is not the result of individual efforts in R&D within individual firms, but rather the combination of complementary capacities and of widespread interactive learning processes, which involve many "customers" and "suppliers" along a well-defined *filière* or supply chain' (Cappellin, 2003a, 307).

This approach is very different from the previous approaches as far as the path towards innovation is concerned. In the sector-based approach, attention is focused on an invention–innovation short circuit taking place inside individual firms (or their territories) operating on advanced sectors. R&D facilities are strictly linked to production facilities, while firms tend to cluster inside high-tech districts in order to take advantage of all sorts of proximity externalities. In the function-based approach, a sort of division of labour operates between R&D and higher education facilities on the one hand, and innovating firms on the other. Their interaction produces academic spin-off or knowledge spillover flowing from the former to the latter (Acs et al., 1994; Audretsch and Feldman, 1996; Anselin et al., 2000). In the structure-based approach, a knowledge–innovation short circuit is at the basis of the path to innovation. Once structural elements exist (education, human capital, entrepreneurial activities), the existing knowledge is easily turned into commercialized innovation.

In the cognitive approach, attention is focused mainly on the regional or local level at the construction of knowledge through cooperative learning processes, nourished by spatial proximity ('atmosphere' effects), network relations (including long-distance, selective relationships), interaction, creativity and recombination capability. A collective learning process of this kind was first hypothesized by the GREMI group (Camagni, 1991, 2004; Perrin, 1995 [2006]) and subsequently widely adopted as a sound theoretical concept for the interpretation of knowledge-based development and innovation (Keeble and Wilkinson, 1999, 2000; Capello, 1999a; Cappellin, 2003a; Tödtling and Kaufmann, 2001; Cooke et al., 2000; see Tödtling and Trippl's Chapter 33 in this *Handbook*). Relatedness between economic activities in terms of shared competences is an effective knowledge transfer recently highlighted by the evolutionary economic geography (Boschma and Frenken, 2007; Lambooy, 2004; see Boschma and Frenken's Chapter 14 in this *Handbook*).

The cognitive approach gives space a more direct role. Knowledge flows and information channels are investigated and seen as clearly embedded in the territorial structure of an area through:

- the huge mobility of professionals and skilled labour – between firms but internally to the local labour market defined by the district or the city, where this mobility is maximal); and

● the intense cooperative relations among local actors, and in particular customer–supplier relationships in production, design, research and, finally, knowledge creation.

The role of space becomes clear: abstract space becomes real territory, a relational space where functional and hierarchical, economic and social interactions take place and are embedded into geographical space. The local milieu – a 'territory' identified by both geographical proximity (agglomeration economies, district economies) and cognitive proximity (shared behavioural codes, common culture, mutual trust and sense of belonging) – supplies the socio-economic and geographical substrate on which collective learning processes can be incorporated (Camagni and Capello, 2002).

Thus a territory, a milieu, becomes a 'cognitive engine' and possibly an innovation place: its characteristics enhance interaction and cooperation, reduce uncertainty (especially concerning the behaviour of competitors and partners), reduce information asymmetries (therefore reducing mutual suspicion among partners) and reduce probability of opportunistic behaviour under the threat of social sanctioning (Camagni, 1991, 2004) – all elements that are confirmed by many regional economics schools (Bellet et al., 1993; Rallet and Torre, 1995; Cappellin, 2003b).

The foregoing concerning the role of territorial variables and the centrality of local conditions should not be taken as suggesting a return to an anti-historical localism or territorial autarchy. On the contrary, local milieux may be expected to be accessible, open and receptive to external flows of information, knowledge, technologies, organizational and cognitive models, and competent to recombine local knowledge and external knowledge anew. What is really meant by referring to the importance of local territories is the fact that, while some relevant production factors like financial capital, general information, consolidated technologies and codified knowledge are readily available virtually everywhere nowadays, the ability to organize these 'pervasive' factors into continuously innovative production processes and products is by no means ubiquitous or generalized, but exists selectively only in some places where tacit knowledge is continuously created, exchanged and utilized, and business ideas find their way to real markets.

This approach disentangles the cause–effect chain between innovation, factor productivity and regional growth, highlighting the way in which innovation impacts on firms' productivity, and the way in which space helps in this process, being no longer the pure conductor of knowledge, as witnessed in the next section.

SPACE AS A SOURCE OF KNOWLEDGE CREATION: THE *MILIEU INNOVATEUR* THEORY

As said in the previous section, the main feature of the cognitive approach is that space becomes a source of knowledge creation, since it embeds channels of knowledge transfer (see also Chapter 19 in this *Handbook*, 'Regional cultural economy' by A. James). This concept is now acknowledged in many approaches to regional innovation and growth, but finds its roots in the *milieu innovateur* theory of the 1980s (Camagni, 1991).

Learning in a milieu takes place in a spontaneous and socialized manner within the local labour market through forms of stable and enduring collaboration between customers and suppliers based on loyalty and trust. These relations produce a transfer of codified and tacit knowledge between customers and suppliers which triggers processes of incremental innovation and specific technological trajectories. Relations in the local labour market likewise perform an important role in the local production system, because high turnover of skilled labour within the area and scant external mobility cross-fertilize knowledge among firms and upgrade workers' skills. Finally, firm spin-offs – independent firms created by workers previously employed by a local firm (see Cooke's Chapter 32 in this *Handbook*) – also participate in the knowledge socialization process.

The accumulation of knowledge in large firms is ensured by the presence of R&D departments; and it is permanent because large firms are long-lived and develop their own internal capabilities and cultures. By contrast, small firms have very short life cycles, with the consequence that they are unable to develop a solid stock of firm-specific knowledge. This difficulty is remedied by the milieu and by the relations within it, which guarantee continuity of knowledge through labour market stability, high mobility of people within the area, and stable relations between customers and suppliers.

In *milieu innovateur* theory, therefore, collective learning is the territorial counterpart of the learning that takes place within firms. In large firms, knowledge and information are transferred via internal functional interaction among the R&D, production, marketing and strategic planning departments (Camagni, 1991; Capello, 1999a; Keeble and Wilkinson, 1999). In milieux, and in local small firms systems, this function is performed by the already mentioned high level of labour market mobility, by intense innovative interactions between customers and suppliers, and by firm spin-offs.

Milieu theory flanks these channels of learning available to firms with a third and complementary one: learning through 'network cooperation'. Through strategic alliances and/or non-equity cooperation agreements, firms acquire some of the strategic assets that they require externally, thus avoiding the costs of developing them internally. This knowledge acquisition process stands midway between internal learning and collective learning, in that the firm comes into contact with the outside but still maintains a set of selected and targeted relationships. This form of learning assumes an important role in *milieu innovateur* theory because it permits local knowledge – which is produced by socialized and collective processes liable to isolation and lock-in – to enrich and innovate itself. Only through the cooperation with external firms that ensures an influx of new knowledge can a milieu avoid death by entropic (decayed) uniformity. It is with this conceptual tool that the theoreticians of the *milieu innovateur* interpret the growth of small-firm areas, among them the Marshallian industrial district.

However, collective learning is not the only dynamic advantage generated for local firms by the milieu, with its assets of relational capital. A further factor facilitating firms' innovative capacity is reduction of the uncertainty that accompanies innovative processes. In large firms, the functions of information-gathering, the codification of knowledge and the selection of decision-making routines – all of which are geared to reducing static and dynamic uncertainty – are performed by the R&D department, or by the planning unit. In the case of a *milieu innovateur*, they are undertaken in a socialized and collective manner by the milieu itself, in which information rapidly circulates and productivity rises because of geographical and collective proximity (Camagni, 1991).

Finally, the reduction of the costs of *ex ante* coordination among decision-making units, and the facilitation of 'collective action' (undertaken to furnish collective goods or simply to integrate private investment decisions), is a further element enhancing the innovative process in a milieu. Such coordination generally suffers from the availability of limited and costly information, and from the possible existence of opportunistic behaviour. The presence of the milieu reduces these costs because it enables information to circulate more easily. It facilitates the taking of coordinated decisions through proximity and social homogeneity and cohesion, while it discourages opportunistic behaviour by fostering trust and threatening social sanctions. This last social and psychological element is crucial: it derives from the sharing of common values and similar codes of behaviour, and it acts positively by developing trust and loyalty. Conversely, it develops rapid processes of isolation and punishment for opportunistic behaviour.[2] All of these are innovation- and productivity-enhancing characteristics (see the opening paragraph to this chapter).

This milieu externality is an element which occurs in the local environment at the same level as those more traditional elements of static efficiency, such as the industrial atmosphere and the external economies associated with a clustering of small firms: it is independent from a conscious cooperative will by single actors, while its exploitation is set apart from an explicit strategy of each single local actor, when some preconditions are met. In this sense, it is a collective element rather than a cooperative one.

Hence, the existence of these external economies explains higher factor productivity of firms located in milieux rather than elsewhere. Collective learning provides local firms with positive external effects on factor productivity. In particular, the capacity of firms to innovate, in the form of patents, R&D expenditures and expenses for R&D activity in general, are influenced by the know-how present locally, that is, managerial, organizational and scientific knowledge, which cumulates locally thanks to a cross-fertilization process of innovative ideas.

In recent years, econometric empirical analyses have corroborated the theory. In the case of three milieux in Italy, a production function was estimated using data collected at individual firm level in which efficiency parameters of the production factors were connected to the intensity of local spin-offs; to appreciation of the stability and quality of the local labour market; and to the individual forms of specialized knowledge internal to the local area, and the lesser importance of acquiring knowledge from outside (Capello, 1999b). The results showed that labour productivity is subject to increasing returns (given the small average size of firms) which are substantially reinforced by the presence of collective learning processes. Conversely, (intangible) capital productivity is subject to decreasing returns, but is greatly augmented by an increase in the appreciation and use of local specialized knowledge.

CONCLUSIONS

Three approaches highlighted as characterizing the main theories of innovation and productivity in regional growth have been presented in this chapter: the sector- and function-based approach, the structural approach and the cognitive approach. All of them interpret the local determinants of regional innovation capacities, each of them having a different interpretation of the path towards innovation and, especially, each of them based on a different concept of space.

Within the three approaches, only the cognitive one builds upon a concept of space that goes beyond simple geographical proximity, thus requiring a notion of cognitive proximity: abstract space becomes territory, a 'territory' identified by both geographical and cognitive proximity (shared behavioural codes, common culture, mutual trust and sense of belonging).

Only through this approach does space become a source of knowledge creation, since it supplies the socio-economic and geographical substrate on which collective learning processes can be incorporated. Thus a territory becomes a 'cognitive engine' and possibly an innovation place: its characteristics enhance interaction and cooperation, reduce uncertainty, reduce information asymmetries and reduce the probability of opportunistic behaviour under the threat of social sanctioning. All this provides a theoretical justification for explaining why one territory, more than another, is endogenously able to learn and grow through innovation, which in turn, as we have seen, enhances productivity and the prospects for growth.

NOTES

1. For some literature in this field, see Goddard and Thwaites (1986), Oakey et al. (1980), Clark (1971), Malecki and Varaiya (1986), Breschi (2000), Paci and Usai (2000).
2. This recalls the theory of the Marshallian industrial district and the role performed by social and cultural homogeneity in producing forms of transaction regulation which deter opportunistic behaviour. See Camagni and Rabellotti (1997), Arrighetti et al. (2001).

REFERENCES

Acs, Z.J., D.B. Audretsch, P. Braunerhjelm and B. Carlsson (2004), 'The missing link: the knowledge filter and entrepreneurship in endogenous growth', Centre for Economic Policy Research (CEPR) Discussion Paper.

Acs, Z.J., D.B. Audretsch, P. Braunerhjelm and B. Carlsson (2005), 'The knowledge spillover theory of entrepreneurship', Discussion Papers on Entrepreneurship, Growth and Public Policy 2705, Max Planck Institute of Economics.

Acs, Z., D. Audretsch and M. Feldman (1994), 'R&D spillovers and recipient firm size', *Review of Economics and Statistics*, **76** (2), 336–40.

Acs, Z.J. and L.A. Plummer (2005), 'Penetrating the "knowledge filter" in regional economies', *Annals of Regional Science*, **39**, 439–56.

Anselin, L., A. Varga and Z. Acs (2000), 'Geographic and sectoral characteristics of academic knowledge externalities', *Papers in Regional Science*, **79** (4), 435–43.

Antonelli, C. (1989), 'A failure inducement model of research and development expenditure: Italian evidence from the early 1980s', *Journal of Economic Behaviour and Organization*, **12** (2), 159–80.

Arrighetti, A., G. Seravalli and G. Wolleb (2001), 'Social capital, institutions and collective action between firms', paper presented at the EURESCO Conference, Social Capital: Interdisciplinary Perspectives, Exeter, 15–20 September.

Audretsch, D. and M. Feldman (1996), 'R&D spillovers and the geography of innovation and production', *American Economic Review*, **86** (3), 630–40.

Bellet, M., G. Colletis and Y. Lung (1993), 'Introduction' to the special issue on iEconomy and Proximity', *Revue d'Economie Régionale et Urbaine*, **3**, 357–61.

Boschma, R. and K. Frenken (2007), 'Why is economic geography not an evolutionary science? Towards an evolutionary economic geography', *Journal of Economic Geography*, **6**, 273–302.

Breschi, S. (2000), 'The geography of innovation: a cross-sector analysis', *Regional Studies*, **34** (2), 213–29.

Camagni, R. (1991), 'Local milieu, uncertainty and innovation networks: towards a new dynamic theory of economic space', in R. Camagni (ed.), *Innovation Networks: Spatial Perspectives*, London: Belhaven-Pinter, pp. 121–44.

Camagni, R. (2004), 'Uncertainty, social capital and community governance: the city as a milieu', in R. Capello and P. Nijkamp (eds), *Urban Dynamics and Growth: Advances in Urban Economics*, Amsterdam: Elsevier, pp. 121–52.

Camagni, R. and R. Capello (2002), 'Milieux innovateurs and collective learning: from concepts to measurement', in Z. Acs, H. de Groot and P. Nijkamp (eds), *The Emergence of the Knowledge Economy: A Regional Perspective*, Berlin: Springer Verlag, pp. 15–45.

Camagni, R. and R. Capello (2009), 'Knowledge-based economy and knowledge creation: the role of space', in U. Fratesi and L. Senn (eds), *Growth and Innovation of Competitive Regions: The Role of Internal and External Connections*, Berlin: Springer, pp. 146–66.

Camagni, R. and R. Rabellotti (1997), 'Footwear production systems in Italy: a dynamic comparative analysis', in R. Ratti, A. Bramanti and R. Gordon (eds), *The Dynamics of Innovative Regions*, Aldershot: Ashgate, pp. 139–64.

Capello, R. (1999a), 'Spatial transfer of knowledge in high-technology milieux: learning vs. collective learning processes', *Regional Studies*, 33 (4), 353–65.

Capello, R. (1999b), 'SMEs clustering and factor productivity: a milieu production function model', *European Planning Studies*, 7 (6), 719–35.

Capello, R. and A. Faggian (2005), 'Collective learning and relational capital in local innovation processes', *Regional Studies*, 39 (1), 75–87.

Cappellin, R. (2003a), 'Territorial knowledge management: towards a metrics of the cognitive dimension of agglomeration economies', *International Journal of Technology Management*, 26 (2–4), 303–25.

Cappellin, R. (2003b), 'Networks and technological change in regional clusters', in J. Bröcker, D. Dohse and R. Soltwedel (eds), *Innovation Clusters in Interregional Competition*, Berlin: Springer, pp. 53–78.

Clark, N.G. (1971), 'Science, technology and regional economic development', *Research Policy*, 1, 296–319.

Cooke, P., P. Boekholt and F. Tödtling (eds) (2000), *The Governance of Innovation in Europe – Regional Perspectives and Global Competitiveness*, London, UK and New York, USA: Pinter.

Crescenzi, R., A. Rodriguez-Pose and M. Storper (2007), 'The territorial dynamics of innovation: a Europe–United States comparative analysis', *Journal of Economic Geography*, 7, 673–709.

Dasgupta, P. and J. Stiglitz (1980), 'Uncertainty, industrial structure and the speed of R&D', *Bell Journal of Economics*, 11 (1), 1–28.

Foray, D. (2000), *L'Economie de la Connaissance*, Paris: La Découverte.

Goddard, J. and A. Thwaites (1986), 'New technology and regional development policy', in P. Nijkamp (ed.), *Technological Change, Employment and Spatial Dynamics*, Berlin: Springer Verlag, pp. 91–114.

Griliches, Z. (1990), 'Patent statistics as economic indicators: a survey', *Journal of Economic Literature*, December, 1661–707.

Keeble, D. and F. Wilkinson (1999), 'Collective learning and knowledge development in the evolution of regional clusters of high-technology SMS in Europe', *Regional Studies*, 33 (4), 295–303.

Keeble, D. and F. Wilkinson (2000), *High Technology Clusters, Networking and Collective Learning in Europe*, Aldershot: Ashgate.

Lambooy, J. (2004), 'The transmission of knowledge, emerging networks and the role of universities: an evolutionary approach', *European Planning Studies*, 12 (5), 643–57.

Lundvall, B.-Å. and B. Johnson (1994), 'The learning economy', *Journal of Industry Studies*, 1 (1), 23–42.

MacDonald, S. (1987), 'British science parks: reflections on the politics of high technology', *R&D Management*, 17 (1), 25–37.

Malecki, E. (1980), 'Corporate organisation of R&D and the location of technological activities', *Regional Studies*, 14 (3), 219–34.

Malecki, E. and P. Varaiya (1986), 'Innovation and changes in regional structure', in P. Nijkamp (ed.), *Handbook of Regional and Urban Economics*, Amsterdam: North-Holland, pp. 629–45.

Massey, D., P. Quintas and D. Wield (1992), *High Tech Fantasies: Science Parks in Society, Science and Space*, London: Routledge.

Monk, C.S.P., R.B. Porter, P. Quintas, D. Storey and P. Wynarczyk (1988), *Science Parks and the Growth of High Technology Firms*, London: Croom Helm.

Oakey, R., P. Nash and A. Thwaites (1980), 'The regional distribution of innovative manufacturing establishments in Britain', *Regional Studies*, 13, 141–51.

Paci, R. and S. Usai (2000), 'Technological enclaves and industrial districts: an analysis of the regional distribution of innovative activity in Europe', *Regional Studies*, 34 (2), 97–114.

Perrin, J.-C. (1995), 'Apprentissage Collectif, Territoire et Milieu Innovateur: un Nouveau Paradigme pour le Développement', in J. Ferrão (ed.), *Políticas de Inovação e Desenvolvimento Regional et Local*, Edição do Instituto de Ciencias Sociais de Universidade de Lisboa; republished in R. Camagni and D. Maillat (eds) (2006), *Milieux Innovateurs, Economica-Anthropos*, Paris, pp. 99–128.

Rallet, A. and A. Torre (eds) (1995), *Economie Industrielle et Economie Spatiale*, Paris: Economica.

Rodriguez-Pose, A. (1999), 'Innovation prone and innovation averse societies: economic performance in Europe', *Growth and Change*, **30**, 75–105.

Saxenian, A. (1996), *Regional Advantage: Culture and Competition in Silicon Valley and Route 128*, Cambridge, MA: Harvard University Press.

Storey, D.J. and B.S. Tether (1998), 'Public policy measures to support new technology-based firms in the European Union', *Research Policy*, **26** (9), 1037–57.

Tödtling, F. and A. Kaufmann (2001) 'The role of the region for innovation activities of SMEs', *European Urban and Regional Studies*, **8** (3), 203–15.

9 Human capital and labour mobility determinants of regional innovation
Daniel Felsenstein*

INTRODUCTION

This chapter looks at the role of human capital and labour mobility in determining regional innovation and growth. Innovation as a factor in regional growth is not a new notion and has been addressed in many of the classic antecedents of regional growth theory. The Marshallian tradition assumes local knowledge spillovers to be a central factor in the formation of agglomeration in space, supplemented by local labour pooling and non-traded local inputs (Marshall, 1890). The Jacobian tradition similarly sees knowledge transfer as an important input to local growth although its source is somewhat different, emanating from outside the local production environment and grounded in scope and diversified economic activity rather than scale and concentrated production (Jacobs, 1969). However, it has only been since the advent of new growth theory (NGT) that innovation has become an active component in understanding regional growth (Romer, 1986). Prior to NGT, the region was understood as the arena in which knowledge creation took place. Within this environment, tacit and implicit knowledge was produced and exchanged and the demarcation of the region expressed the territorial limits in which growth could be expected.

NGT posits that growth is the result of increasing returns associated with new knowledge or technology. In contrast to previous theory, NGT internalizes (endogenizes) technological progress and knowledge into a model of how markets function. When individuals accumulate new skills and know-how they unwittingly impact on the productivity and human capital levels of others. As such, the production of technological progress becomes endogenized. The increasing returns and spillovers from human capital become the glue that holds cities and regions together. The region has thus progressed from the context in which innovation takes place to a more proactive role as a central component in this change.

However, commentators are not unanimous as to the centrality of the region in creating knowledge spillovers and explaining the existence of clusters of innovative activity. The original new economic geography (NEG) perspective on agglomeration sees these clusters purely as a product of labour market pooling behaviour. In this growth model, firms and workers find it profitable to seek out locations where each are found in abundance (the market size effect), leading them to converge on locations that have an early lead in a particular industry (Krugman, 1991). The theoretical spatial outcome of this NEG approach is the formation of exaggerated 'catastrophic' agglomerations of economic activity in a given region and the 'desertification' of activity in its vicinity. To prevent this from happening, the NEG modelling strategy introduces technical fixes that allow for the existence of workers and firms in peripheral regions. These include distributing immobile low-wage labour across the region and manipulating transport costs to allow firms to cluster and produce under increasing returns. Whatever the cause, the logical conclusion of the NEG approach leads to overconcentration which is only prevented via technical rather than structural reasons. In contrast, the NGT view is that local externalities do not just stem from market size effects or pecuniary externalities but also from knowledge and technological externalities. Thus, while regional agglomeration is the outcome of NEG modelling efforts, under the NGT approach regional agglomeration is an endogenously determined cause of growth (McCann and van Oort, 2009)

Aside from the NGT and NEG approaches, a further perspective on the role of innovation in regional growth is provided the evolutionary economic geography (EEG) approach (Boschma, 2005).This sees local institutions, institutional arrangements and cultural practices as critical in generating regional growth. Under this view, knowledge externalities and spillovers are not just the result of the aggregate concentration of firms and workers but also the product of the cultural and institutional factors that influence knowledge flows. Therefore, cultural and institutional proximity is as important as spatial proximity. The implication of this view is that in contrast to the previous approaches, the region is neither the arena for innovation nor an active input into the production function. Instead it is a unique repository of specific historical and geographic features that cannot be easily reproduced by other places.

In the following sections, I analyse the mechanisms promoting regional innovation. In wake of the interest in the active role of the region as an innovative agent, I first question whether the region is really more than the passive backdrop for the generation of innovation. At essence, I show that this question relates to the way the region is conceived: as an individual unit or as a collective (group). Applying the notions introduced by NGT in a spatial context (Faggian and McCann, 2009), I then proceed to investigate the two specific mechanisms through which knowledge becomes an inherently regional asset. The first is through the generation of local externalities and the second is through human capital mobility and the individual decisions of workers and households. While each of these issues is treated separately, the interdependence between them is highlighted. Finally, I attempt to tie these notions together in a systematic framework by empirically estimating the way that human and physical capital, worker mobility and innovation level impact on regional productivity. Theory points to the fact that the higher the average level of human capital, the more rapid the diffusion of knowledge and the higher the levels of productivity and presumably earnings. Using spatial panel estimation in order to entangle issues of spurious relationships, it is found that both human and physical capital impact on regional productivity, but that a strong regional innovation effect can confound this impact.

REGIONS AS INNOVATORS?

The stylized causality of economic development points to knowledge generating innovation and innovation creating economic growth (Arrow, 1966). However, knowledge does not flow freely along this continuum. It gets caught up at critical junctures that also have a territorial expression, accumulating at some while by-passing others. These critical nodes exist at different spatial scales: cities, metropolitan areas and regions. Along this continuum, the region features as a distinct unit of analysis. However the essence of the nature of a region is not clear. On the one hand, the region can be considered as the mirror image of the national economy, inexorably linked to the vagaries of macroeconomic policy, changing trade patterns and currency rate fluctuations. While regions are always more open than national economies and with freer factor movement, they are nevertheless miniature versions of the national economy. In many countries of all sizes, a booming regional economy can often dictate national macro performance. On the other hand, the region can be conceived as a group unit that comprises districts, municipalities and cities. Groups behave differently to individuals. They have different propensities to self-organize and their level of social cohesion is far more complex. They do not reflect the national economy and need to be given an independent identity.

This is not just idle philosophizing and has some very real consequences. For example, the exact way in which a region is conceived (individual unit or group) can have very real consequences in the measurement of regional inequalities (Portnov and Felsenstein, 2010). A tradition exists in the regional growth literature that treats regions as individual units regardless of their size (Barro and Sala-i-Martin, 1992). As such, when measuring regional convergence for example, large and small regions are assumed to carry equal weight just as tall and short people are treated equally when looking at inequality between them. However, if regions are conceived as groups, then the measurement of interregional inequality calls for taking scale into account. For example, the use of population-weighted indices (such as a weighted Gini index of inequality) would highlight the independence of the constituent parts of the group.

This discussion has a distinct bearing on the role of regional innovation. A particularly fashionable notion in the regional innovation literature relates to the 'learning', 'creative' or 'innovative' region (Cooke and Morgan, 1998; Maskell and Malmberg, 1999; Rutten and Boekema, 2007). These notions all seem to imply that the role of the region as a collective is greater than the sum of its constituent parts. When functioning as an organic unit, the region will be able to achieve higher growth levels than those attainable without collective action. In other words, increasing returns exist to acting 'regionally', and the corollary is that regions are conceived of as groups rather than individual units.

Ironically, however, recent work has begun to call into question the 'regions as innovators' thesis precisely on the grounds of the argument of regions as individual units. At the root of the innovative region concept is the notion of tacit knowledge. This refers to the non-codified informal behaviour, local practices and untraded interdependencies that accompany formal codified production. Tacit knowledge is relatively spatially immobile and context-specific. It is acquired through learning by doing and face-to-face contact and cannot be exchanged over distances. As such, it forms a key determinant of the spatial distribution of innovation. Recently this conception of tacit knowledge being grounded locally has been called into question and has been replaced by the idea that tacit knowledge is produced organizationally and not regionally (Gertler, 2007). According to this view, conventions, norms and business practices (corporate cultures) are developed within a community and not a territory. This organizational space is not territorially bounded and as such, the key ingredient to the 'regions as innovators' thesis – tacit knowledge – has been appropriated to a non-spatial realm. In this organizational space, the key units are atomistic firms which can in theory be scattered across large distances. In this view of the world, if regions are important at all, it is only as locations for these individual units.

Whatever the perspective on the region, a *sine qua non* of innovation research is that knowledge is distributed unequally across space and that it exhibits 'sticky' properties in that it is not always easily transferable (Markusen, 1996; Ratanawaraha and Polenske, 2007). Faggian and McCann (2009) have posited two main processes by which knowledge becomes embodied in a region and becomes part of the regional innovation infrastructure. The first relates to spatially grounded externalities that accompany the production of knowledge, and the second to human capital decisions (with respect to residential location and migration) that lead to a reallocation of production factors as people move in response to economic opportunity. It is to these issues that I now turn.

THE SPATIAL EXTERNALITIES PERSPECTIVE

Marshallian externalities are the natural springboard for any discussion of spatial spillovers. Marshall highlighted local knowledge spillovers, non-traded local inputs and specialized local labour pools in his speculations on the causes of spatial clustering in economic activity. For Marshall: 'if one man starts as idea, it is taken up by others and combined with suggestions of their own; and thus it becomes the source of further ideas' (Marshall, 1920, 271). In identifying the causes of agglomeration, he distinguished between what today are referred to as the roles of 'first' and 'second' nature in economic development (Krugman, 1993). He saw knowledge spillovers and externalities as key second-nature determinants of external returns to scale which accounted for spatial agglomerations. Subsequently, the microeconomic foundations of local spillovers and externalities have been developed. Storper and Venables (2004) have shown how face-to-face contacts among economic agents improve coordination, increase productivity and mitigate the incentives problem, leading to spillovers and greater innovative activity. For them, it is the 'buzz' of the agglomeration (that is, the accidental and non-scheduled spillovers) that gives places an edge. Several commentators point to the importance of 'cafeteria effects' (Charlot and Duranton, 2004; Fu, 2007), where important information is released randomly in both time and space, leading to agglomeration as a strategic response. The more concentrated the agents, the more 'luck' in accessing cafeteria-type information and the more rapid the diffusion and growth of this knowledge. As knowledge percolates, total factor productivity grows. Scale is an important issue here. The larger the agglomeration or the region, the greater the probability of meeting an information-rich contact, so that total factor productivity will vary directly with scale. Conversely, scale may also impose a communication cost. As the proverbial cafe becomes crowded or the agglomeration overheats, total factor productivity will become reduced.

In this externality-based view, knowledge becomes embodied in the region through a cumulative growth process that is internally (endogenously) driven. The stock of regional knowledge accumulates as the level of average human capital rises and as scale increases. The regional knowledge base is not embellished on the basis of transfers or redistribution from other places (via migration) which represents regional accrual via a flow mechanism. Instead, the regional knowledge base grows on the basis of spillovers that are spatially bounded. These are generally intense, frequent and short-term transactions which only add to the importance of proximity and territorial compactness.

The fact that knowledge has spillover effects is non-controversial. It is well accepted that knowledge generates externalities due to its public-good nature, characterized by non-rivalry in consumption and non-exclusivity in production. It is also unchallenged that the marginal cost of transmitting tacit knowledge across space diminishes as frequency of contact increases. Feldman (1994) has added a further twist to this logic by pointing out that proximity reduces the uncertainty and risk inherent in innovative activity. This has been formalized in empirical studies that estimate knowledge production functions with specific reference to spatial units of observation (Jaffe, 1989). From there only a short leap is needed to estimate empirically the spatial extent of innovation spillovers and the break-points beyond which spatial effects are no longer felt (Anselin et al., 1997).

THE HUMAN CAPITAL–LABOUR MOBILITY PERSPECTIVE

At a general economy-wide level, Lucas (1988) has identified human capital as an endogenous source of economic growth. Human capital accumulation affects the productivity of the individual worker and also that of the economy as a whole. However a key element of human capital, in regional growth terms, is its mobility in response to economic opportunity. This mobility can occur over short distances (commuting) or long distances (migration). The former is generally in response to short-term disequilibria between supply and demand, while the latter represents a reallocation of factors of production. In fact, neoclassical theory predicts that labour migration should lower the rate of economic growth. However, if migrants are highly skilled, their propensity to migrate will increase and their effect on the growth of their destinations will be positive (DaVanzo, 1976).

Knowledge therefore can be conveyed across regions through the collective decisions of migrants. The seminal work by Sjaastad (1962) looks at migration as a human capital investment decision with both costs and returns. The utility to individual i from migrating to region j is:

$$U_{ij} = \alpha_{ij}X_i + \beta Z_j + u_{ij} \tag{9.1}$$

where X denotes a vector of personal characteristics, such as age, family size, and so on, and Z a vector of destination characteristics, such wage rates, cost of living etc. The return to personal characteristics varies by person and region. Similarly, the utility in region k is specified as:

$$U_{ik} = \alpha_{ik}X_i + \beta Z_k + u_{ik} \tag{9.2}$$

Individual i will move from region j to region k when:

$$U_{ij} - U_{ir} + C_{jk} > 0 \tag{9.3}$$

where C_{jk} denotes the cost of moving from j to k. Generally, higher-skilled workers will have lower costs and higher returns from migration due to lower information costs, more perfect information and lower psychic costs of attachment to place of origin and its social networks (DaVanzo and Morrison, 1981). High-skilled labour expects more compensation for its investment in education and has higher expected net benefits from migration than non-skilled labour.

While labour mobility is a mechanism for raising the knowledge and innovation level of a region, confusion exists as to the exact causality of this relationship. Is the regional knowledge base the result of labour mobility, or does labour move in response to regional knowledge opportunities? This in itself is tied up with the role of regions in generating human capital (that is, the 'learning region' thesis). As noted earlier, regions have traditionally been considered the territorial unit in which the exchange and production of tacit knowledge takes place and spatially based externalities then ensue. However, another view is that the region functions as a conduit for the flow of highly skilled and mobile labour that replaces similar sized outflows of other (skilled and non-skilled) labour. This is a labour market 'churning' mechanism in which the stock of labour may not grow but its knowledge base will be continually upgraded (Schettkat, 1996). Regions that include a large concentration of knowledge centres and institutions such as corporate and government research and development (R&D) centres, research universities and technological incubators are clear magnets for this kind of 'escalator' effect.

The Greater London metropolitan region has filled this role for some time, with education in the region playing a key role in the career paths of young people seeking to accumulate human capital and job experience. Over time, this skilled labour tends to disperse from the London area as life-cycle patterns change and incumbents can capitalize on the housing market gains and human capital accumulation that they have amassed over their period in the region. The region therefore becomes an active element in interregional or even international flows of mobile labour. Recent work (Faggian and McCann, 2006) has pointed to the 'flow-through' role of the university system for attracting potential high-quality human capital to a region as more important than its traditional function as a node for regional knowledge production and diffusion (Florax, 1992; Felsenstein, 1996). Other evidence shows that for generating new innovations, mobile human capital attracted from other regions is a more potent force than locally bred human capital (Simonen and McCann, 2010).

Increasingly, human capital mobility is international and not just interregional. While international labour mobility may be too small to be detected at the economy-wide level, at the regional level there is a wealth of evidence that immigrants do have a positive effect on wages and innovation levels measured by R&D and patents (Hunt and Gauthier-Loiselle, 2008; Niebuhr, 2010). Evidence from Israel highlights the distinction between economy-wide and regional effects. The country provides an ideal laboratory setting for natural experiments in this area due to mass immigration in the 1990s that boosted the population by 15 per cent. At the national level evidence shows that mass immigration may not have had any adverse effect on manufacturing productivity (Paserman, 2008), employment or wages (Friedberg, 2001). At the regional level the picture is more equivocal. Beenstock and Peleg (2000) have found that regional unemployment and wage rates are not sensitive to immigration. In a small country like Israel, employment is sufficiently mobile between regions to diffuse the effects of immigrants in the local labour market to the national labour market.

SOME EMPIRICAL EVIDENCE

Description of the Data

As shown above, knowledge is the bedrock of innovation. Two mechanisms are behind the process by which knowledge becomes a regional asset. The first is the externality effect whereby a region embellishes its stock of knowledge based on contagion effects between workers and places. Through the generation of externalities within a given region total factor productivity will rise, as will the average level of regional productivity. Similar workers will therefore be more productive and receive higher wages if they operate in regions with large stocks of human capital externalities (Rauch, 1993). The second mechanism relates to the human capital mobility effect and the way knowledge transfers to the region through the agency of individual migration decisions (Sjastaad, 1962). In this section I present empirical evidence relating to these mechanisms and the way regional knowledge stocks are reflected in higher levels of regional wages (and presumably higher levels of regional productivity and growth). Previous work has shown that higher compensation is paid in cities and regions with higher levels of human capital (Glaeser and Mare, 2001). In contrast to previous cross-sectional analyses, I attempt to investigate this connection using spatial panel data for Israeli regions. The object of this empirical study is to show that regions with higher levels of human capital, physical capital and innovation will also have higher productivity levels

The data used in this section relating to regional real earnings, education levels and immigrant population have been described in detail elsewhere (Beenstock and Felsenstein, 2007, 2008). These data represent the physical capital base of the region which reflects the region's knowledge assets, skills and technologies. For innovation levels, I follow a tradition that uses high-tech employment as a proxy measure (Fingleton et al., 2007) and utilize data constructed in earlier work on the regional knowledge base in Israel (Cooke and Schwartz, 2008; Schwartz, 2006). This work regionalizes the CBS Labour Force Survey employment data in order to create EU-equivalent NACE economic sectors.

To describe the data regional shares for innovation, capital–labour ratios and wages are plotted in Figures 9.1–9.3. Each variable portrays a very different regional pattern. Regional innovation levels seem bifurcated with low, stable levels of high tech employment in the peripheral North and South regions and in the metropolitan regions of Haifa and Jerusalem. In contrast there seems to be evidence of regional convergence in high tech between the Central and Tel Aviv regions that function as a single labour market (Figure 9.1). With respect to regional physical capital we observe a picture of 'inverted' regional convergence with regional gaps being visibly smaller in 2006 that in 1995. However, the relatively affluent regions of the centre of the country (Centre, Tel Aviv and Jerusalem) are observed to be leveling-up with the poorer peripheral areas (North and South) and the traditional heavy industry area (Haifa) (Figure 9.2). Historically, regional policy has favoured capital investment in the peripheral regions and subsidized investment there (Schwartz and Keren, 2006). However since the mid-1980s, the map

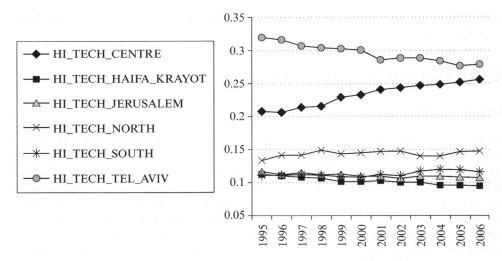

Figure 9.1   Relative regional employment in high-tech sectors, 1995–2006

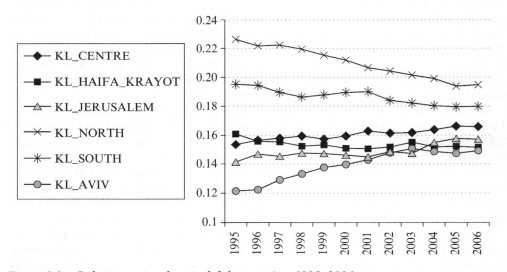

Figure 9.2   Relative regional capital–labour ratios, 1995–2006

of regional assistance has been progressively rolled back and government policy has changed its emphasis. As a result, greater weight has been placed on supporting market forces in trade policy, labour market policy and on more selective regional assistance to R&D and incubator projects (Avnimelech et al., 2007).

Regional real wages are plotted in Figure 9.3. As can be seen, Tel Aviv increases its share of real wages throughout the study period and while there is some shifting in the ranks of the other regions, the overall impression is one of regional stability. The North and South regions' share of real wages are consistently low, with some shifting between

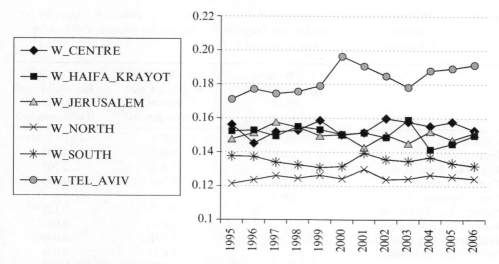

Figure 9.3   Relative regional real wages, 1995–2006

the Centre, Jerusalem and Haifa whose share drops over the study period. In sum, innovation levels and wages seem to be either sclerotic or divergent over the period studied, with most of the divergence coming from the increasing shares captured by the Tel Aviv and Central regions. In contrast, there is a pattern of convergence in regional physical capital but this is in reverse to that anticipated, with the richer, more innovative regions catching up with the poorer that were jump-started in the first place.

Do Innovative Regions Make Workers More Productive?

Given the role of externalities and human capital mobility decisions in generating the regional knowledge base, the question now is what are the relative contributions of regional innovation and stocks of human and physical capital to productivity? Do regions endowed with larger stocks make for more productive workers as a positive process of cumulative causation starts to set in? To test this proposition as predicted by human capital theory, I measure productivity by average wage in the region, human capital by the lagged effect of education, physical capital by the capital–labour ratio, migrant behaviour by the regional share of foreign immigrants and innovation by high-tech employment in the region. Specifically, I posit that:

$$\ln w_{jt} = \alpha_j + \theta_t + \gamma \ln k_{jt} + \delta e'_{jt} + \rho m_{jt} + \tau \ln i_{jt} + u_{jt} \qquad (9.4)$$

where, subscripts *j* and *t* denote region and year respectively, ln *w* denotes wages deflated by national consumer prices, ln *k* denotes the capital–labour ratio, *e'* denotes the lagged regional share of human capital based on the premise that the effects of education are not felt immediately, *m* denotes the regional share of immigrants and ln *i* denotes gross high-tech employment in order to proxy innovation.

Given the structure of the data (observations on six regions for 12 time periods),

Table 9.1   Effect of regional human capital stocks, mobility and innovative capacity on regional earnings: spatial panel regressions for Israeli regions, 1995–2006 (dependent variable = ln earnings)

	1. Without Regional Fixed Effects (Homogenous)	2. Without Regional Fixed Effects (Heterogenous)	3. With Regional Fixed Effects (Heterogenous)
Constant	4.603	6.021	4.670–7.461
Immigrants	0.002	0.001[+]	0.002
High Tech Emp. Share	0.183	1.416	2.705
Capital – Labour	0.291	0.369	0.415
Lag Education	0.030[+]	–	–
Centre – Lag Education	–	0.062	–0.127[+]
Haifa – Lag Education	–	0.073	0.061[+]
Jerusalem – Lag Education	–	0.071	–0.040[+]
North – Lag. Education	–	0.052	0.076
South – Lag Education	–	0.060	0.051
Tel Aviv – Lag. Education	–	0.070	0.036[+]
R^2	0.973	0.941	0.970
DW Statistic	1.977	1.872	2.176
Cointegration Tests			
ADF test	–0.744	–0.574	–3.179
PP test	–1.985	–1.984	–4.326

Notes:
All coefficients significant $p<.01$ except for those marked with [+].
Estimated by EGLS with SUR cross-section dependence.
PP = Philips–Perron cointegration test (null hypotheses of no cointegration).

equation (9.4) calls for panel data estimation. This means testing for non-stationarity in the data. The short panel means lags of greater than one year cannot be used. The coefficients α and θ represent the two-way fixed effects for the six regions and 12 years of data, and μ denotes the residual error. Table 9.1 reports the panel cointegration tests for the effect of regional human and physical capital stocks, mobility and innovative capacity on regional earnings. I present three specifications for equation (9.4), all estimated in first differences and varying in their level of heterogeneity.

Model 1 presents the most homogenous specification. It is estimated without regional fixed effects and assumes human capital is homogenous across regions. Immigrants have a very small but positive effect on productivity. The return to human capital is estimated as rather low, 3 per cent for an extra year of education, and is surprisingly insignificant. It should be noted that human capital and high-tech employment are correlated ($r = 0.65$) and that the high coefficient on the latter may incorporate some of the effect of the former. The elasticity of earnings with respect to physical stock is estimated as 0.290. The test statistics are significant and suggest that the non-stationary variables are cointegrated. However, the DW statistic (slightly above the critical value of 1.8) does not conclusively support this.

In Model 2, human capital is allowed to vary by region but regional fixed effects are not specified. Labour mobility is surprisingly not significant, but the impact of physical capital is more pronounced than in the previous model. The effect of innovation increases dramatically and when returns to human capital are allowed to vary by region, the result is larger estimated coefficients (return to education of 5–7 per cent). The test statistics indicate that the model is cointegrated and the estimated coefficients are not spurious. This goes some way in allaying the concern that the self-selection of high-tech workers in more innovative regions creates the observed productivity effect.

Model 3 is the most homogenous form of estimation. The test statistics for panel cointegration decline seriously and the DW statistic is well over its critical value. The effect of mobility is again significant but the coefficients for human capital are either very small, insignificant (Haifa and Tel Aviv) or with counter-intuitive signs (Jerusalem and Centre). Physical capital stock continues to exert a large and positive influence. In sum, within the constraints of the data we have evidence of both human and physical capital influencing regional productivity. If human capital is treated heterogeneously (left to vary by region) some of its effect becomes confounded with the strong regional innovation effect (see Table 9.1).

CONCLUSIONS

This chapter has highlighted the role played by human capital in generating the regional knowledge base, and the two major mechanisms through which this human capital effect is expressed: spatial externalities and labour mobility. The issue of causality in this relationship is left unresolved; does human capital accumulation spawn innovation or do innovative places attract talent? In reality, both situations occur and from a dynamic perspective the causation is circular.

As the review section has shown, the literature has progressed beyond the primary question of 'Does space matter?' in the generation of regional innovation. Rather, the question would seem to be: what role does the region play in the innovation process? Is it the passive backdrop against which innovation occurs? Or is it an active ingredient in the innovation production function or perhaps a unique repository of non-reproducible traditions and business practices? The policy implications of this dilemma are clear. Only the second option presents intervention possibilities. The first implies that nothing can be done in the face of market forces, while the third points to the futility of trying to replicate non-replicable processes.

This chapter has also discussed whether the innovation and human capital characteristics of a region contribute to productivity. I have tested for the possibility of spurious correlation in this relationship (in that more skilled workers self-select better paying regions) and have found strong effects for both human and physical capital with some of the former confounded with regional innovation. Labour mobility as measured by the import of human capital through migration is only found to have a small effect.

While knowledge spillovers are notoriously difficult to trace, it would seem that knowledge externalities are a prime source of regional productivity gains, and probably more so than labour market processes of human capital migration and mobility. While we may be skeptical of much of the high-tech promotional hype that glorifies the Silicon

Valleys and Research Triangles of the world, the basic story that these accounts tell is not that far from reality. Innovative activity tends to cluster in relatively few choice areas that attract further activity. Similarly, high-skilled labour operates, communicates and enhances its productivity among clusters. This self-entrenching process is at the base of the observed productivity premium and makes it difficult for regions not caught up in this spiral ever to close the gap.

NOTE

*   Thanks to Nadav Ben Zeev for research assistance and to Dafna Schwartz for access to the employment data.

REFERENCES

Anselin, L., Z.J. Acs and A. Varga (1997), 'Local geographic spillovers between university research and high technology innovation', *Journal of Urban Economics*, **42**, 422–48.

Arrow, K. (1966), 'Economic welfare and the allocation of resources for invention', in R. Nelson (ed.), *The Rate and Direction of Inventive Activity*, Princeton, NJ: Princeton University Press, pp. 609–25.

Avnimelech, G., D. Schwartz and R. Bar-El (2007), 'Entrepreneurial high-tech cluster: Israel's experience with venture capital and technological incubators', *European Planning Studies*, **15** (9), 1181–98.

Barro, R.J. and X. Sala-i-Martin (1992), 'Convergence', *Journal of Political Economy*, **100** (2), 223–51.

Beenstock, M. and D. Felsenstein (2007), 'Mobility and mean reversion in the dynamics of regional inequality', *International Regional Science Review*, **30** (4), 335–61.

Beenstock, M. and D. Felsenstein (2008), 'Regional heterogeneity, conditional convergence and regional inequality', *Regional Studies*, **42** (4), 475–88.

Beenstock, M. and M. Peleg (2000), 'Regional economic effects of immigration: Israel 1990–1998', paper presented at SCORUS Conference, Shenzhen.

Boschma, R.A. (2005), 'Proximity and innovation: a critical assessment', *Regional Studies*, **39** (1), 61–74.

Charlot, S. and G. Duranton (2004), 'Communications externalities in cities', *Journal of Urban Economics*, **56**, 581–613.

Cooke, P. and K. Morgan (1998), *The Associational Economy*, Oxford: Oxford University Press.

Cooke, P. and D. Schwartz (2008), 'Regional knowledge economies: an EU–UK and Israeli perspective', *Tijdschrift voor Economische en Sociale Geografie*, **99** (2), 178–92.

DaVanzo, J. (1976), 'Differences between return and non-return migration: an econometric analysis', *International Migration Review*, **10** (1), 13–27.

DaVanzo, J. and F. Morrison (1981), 'Return and other sequences of migration in the US', *Demography*, **18**, 85–101.

Faggian, A. and P. McCann (2006), 'Human capital flows and regional knowledge assets: a simultaneous equation approach', *Oxford Economic Papers*, **52** (3), 475–500.

Faggian, A. and P. McCann (2009), 'Human capital and regional development', in R. Capello and P. Nijkamp (eds), *Handbook of Regional Growth and Development Theories*, Cheltenham UK and Northampton, MA, USA: Edward Elgar, pp. 133–51.

Feldman, M.P. (1994), 'Knowledge complementarity and innovation', *Small Business Economics*, **6** (3), 363–72.

Felsenstein, D. (1996), 'The university in the metropolitan arena: impacts and public policy implications', *Urban Studies*, **33** (9), 1565–80.

Fingleton, B., D.C. Igliori, B. Moore and R. Odera (2007), 'Employment growth and cluster dynamics of creative industries in England', in K.R. Polenske (ed.), *The Economic Geography of Innovation*, Cambridge: Cambridge University Press, pp. 60–86.

Florax, R. (1992), *The University: A Regional Booster*, Aldershot: Avebury.

Friedberg, R. (2001), 'The impact of mass immigration on the Israeli labor market', *Quarterly Journal of Economics*, **116** (4), 1373–1408.

Fu, S. (2007), 'Smart café cities: testing human capital externalities in the Boston Metropolitan Area', *Journal of Urban Economics*, **61**, 86–111.

Gertler, M.S. (2007), 'Tacit knowledge in production systems: how important is geography?', in K.R. Polenske (ed.), *The Economic Geography of Innovation*, Cambridge: Cambridge University Press, pp. 87–111.

Glaeser, E.L. and D.C. Mare (2001), 'Cities and skills', *Journal of Labor Economics*, **19**, 316–42.

Hunt, J. and M. Gauthier-Loiselle (2008), 'How much does immigration boost innovation?', NBER Working Paper No 14312, National Bureau of Economic Research, Cambridge, MA.

Jacobs, J. (1969), *The Economy of Cities*, New York: Vintage.

Jaffe, A.B. (1989), 'Real effects of academic research', *American Economic Review*, **79** (4), 957–70.

Krugman, P. (1991), 'Increasing returns and economic geography', *Journal of Political Economy*, **99**, 483–99.

Krugman, P. (1993), 'First nature, second nature and metropolitan location', *Journal of Regional Science*, **33**, 129–44.

Lucas, R.E. (1988), 'On the mechanics of economic development', *Journal of Monetary Economics*, **22**, 3–42.

Markusen, A. (1996), 'Sticky places in slippery space: a typology of industrial districts', *Economic Geography*, **72** (3), 293–313.

Marshall, A. (1890), *Principles of Economics*, New York: Prometheus Books.

Marshall, A. (1920), *Industry and Trade*, London: Macmillan.

Maskell, P. and A. Malmberg (1999), 'Localized learning and industrial competitiveness', *Cambridge Journal of Economics*, **23** (2), 167–86.

McCann, P. and F. van Oort (2009), 'Theories of agglomeration and regional economic growth: a historical review', in R. Capello and P. Nijkamp (eds), *Handbook of Regional Growth and Development Theories*, Cheltenham UK, and Northampton, MA, USA: Edward Elgar, pp. 19–32.

Niebhur, A. (2010), 'Migration and innovation: does cultural diversity matter for regional R&D activity?', *Papers in Regional Science*, **89** (3), 563–85.

Paserman, D.M. (2008), 'Do high-skill immigrants raise productivity? Evidence from Israeli manufacturing firms, 1990–1999', IZA Discussion Paper 3572, Bonn.

Portnov, B. and D. Felsenstein (2010), 'On the suitability of income inequality measures for regional analysis: some evidence from simulation analysis and bootstrapping tests', *Socio-Economic Planning Sciences*, **44**, 212–19.

Ratanawaraha, A. and K.R. Polenske (2007), 'Measuring the geography of innovation: a literature review', in K.R. Polenske (ed.), *The Economic Geography of Innovation*, Cambridge: Cambridge University Press, pp. 30–59.

Rauch, J.E. (1993), 'Productivity gains from geographic concentration of human capital: evidence from the cities', *Journal of Urban Economics*, **34**, 380–400.

Romer, P.M. (1986), 'Increasing returns and long run growth', *Journal of Political Economy*, **94**, 1002–37.

Ruttan, R. and F. Boekema (2007), *The Learning Region*, Cheltenham, UK and Northampton, MA, USA: Edward Elgar.

Schettkat, R. (1996), 'Flows in labor markets: concepts and international comparative results', in R. Schettkat (ed.), *The Flow Analysis of Labor Markets*, London: Routledge, pp. 18–36.

Schwartz, D. (2006), 'The regional location of knowledge based economy activities in Israel', *Journal of Technology Transfer*, **31**, 31–44.

Schwartz D. and M. Keren (2006), 'Locational incentives and the unintentional generation of employment instability: some evidence from Israel', *Annals of Regional Science*, **40** (2), 449–60.

Simonen, J. and P. McCann (2010), 'Knowledge transfers and innovation: the role of labor markets and R&D co-operation between agents and institutions', *Papers in Regional Science*, **89** (2), 295–309.

Sjastaad, L. (1962), 'The costs and returns of human migration', *Journal of Political Economy*, **70** (5), 80–93.

Storper, M. and A.J. Venables (2004), 'Buzz: face to face contact and the urban economy', *Journal of Economic Geography*, **4**, 351–70.

10 The geography of knowledge flows
Stefano Breschi

INTRODUCTION

Research on the geography of innovation in the past twenty years or so to 2010 has largely revolved around two basic questions. Does knowledge tend to flow more easily across spatially proximate agents than across agents localized far apart in space? To what extent may localized knowledge flows also be characterized as spillovers? The purpose of this chapter is to provide a review of the empirical literature that has attempted to assess the existence and spatial extent of knowledge flows. From a purely methodological perspective, two distinct approaches can be identified in the literature. A first group of studies has adopted a knowledge production function approach, interpreting a positive correlation between regional innovative inputs and outputs as evidence of localized knowledge spillovers. A second group of studies has instead focused on the much more complex task of providing a direct measurement of knowledge flows. Although this group comprises a more heterogeneous set of empirical approaches compared to the studies based on the knowledge production function, a few common features can nonetheless be identified. First, the search for a direct measurement of knowledge flows implies the shifting of the unit of analysis from the level of regions or clusters, to the level of individual innovations or to the level of individual researchers. Second, most of the studies included in this group attempt to disentangle the role that different transmission channels may play in the spatial diffusion of knowledge.

The rest of the chapter is organized as follows. The section below provides a broad review of the studies based on the knowledge production function approach, whereas the following section discusses the most recent studies that have addressed the problem of directly measuring the spatial extent of knowledge flows. A final section concludes.

THE REGIONAL KNOWLEDGE PRODUCTION FUNCTION APPROACH

The Earliest Studies

Originally introduced by Griliches (1979) to estimate the social rate of return to research and development (R&D) and later on refined by Jaffe (1986) to assess the effect on the productivity of firms' R&D of spillovers deriving from the R&D carried out by other firms, the model of the knowledge production function has become the key analytical tool to test empirically the localization of knowledge spillovers, by shifting the unit of analysis from the level of the firm or the industry to the level of the region. According to this spatial reinterpretation, the knowledge production function is just a two-factor Cobb–Douglas production function that relates a measure of regional knowledge output to two input measures: R&D performed by industry, and research performed by universities. Formally:

$$K_{ri} = RD_{ri}^{\alpha_1} \, URD_{ri}^{\alpha_2} \varepsilon_{ri} \tag{10.1}$$

where K_{ri} denotes new knowledge produced by companies located in region r and active in industry (or technology) i, RD_{ri} is industrial R&D of companies located in region r and active in industry (or technology) i, URD_{ri} measures research expenditures undertaken at universities in region r in scientific fields related to industry (or technology) i, and ε_{ri} is a stochastic error term.[1]

Apart from Thompson's (1962) pioneering effort, the seminal contribution to the estimation of a regional knowledge production function is due to Jaffe (1989). His key finding is the existence of a substantial effect of university research on corporate innovation output as measured by the number of patents. Acs et al. (1994) also provide estimates of (10.1) by replacing patent data with a more direct measure of innovation, that is, the number of new commercially introduced products; and more importantly, by estimating separate equations for small and large firms. Their results show not only that large firms rely to a larger extent on internal R&D than small firms, but also that the elasticity of innovation output with respect to university research is significantly greater for small firms than for large ones. This result suggests that small firms, while lacking internal knowledge inputs, are able to innovate by exploiting localized knowledge spillovers from university laboratories.

Feldman and Florida (1994) and Feldman (1993) estimate an innovation production function by including among the explanatory variables a set of measures aimed to capture the effects of other regional knowledge-generating inputs. Their results show that both the presence of specialized business services related to innovative activities, that is, commercial testing laboratories, and a variable measuring the presence of firms in related industries, have a positive and significant impact on the number of new products generated within a region. Audretsch and Feldman (1996b) show that, even after taking account the geographic concentration of production, the degree of spatial concentration of innovations tends to be greater in industries with higher R&D intensity, with a larger fraction of skilled workers in the total workforce, and where the amount of expenditures on university research in related academic disciplines is larger. These results are taken to suggest that the propensity for innovative activity to cluster in space is more attributable to the role of localized knowledge spillovers and not merely to the geographic concentration of production. Along similar lines, Audretsch and Feldman (1996a) divide industries into four groups according to the stage of the industry life cycle and estimate the impact of industry knowledge intensity on the propensity for innovations to cluster spatially, finding rather mixed results. On the one hand, a larger fraction of skilled workers in the total workforce is found to be associated to a larger degree of spatial concentration of innovations in all industries. On the other hand, industry R&D intensity is associated to a larger extent of spatial clustering of innovative activities only in industries in the declining phase, but not in industries in the birth, growth and maturity stages. Similarly, university research leads to a greater spatial concentration of innovations in industries in the birth phase of the life cycle, but not in industries in the growth stage.

Whereas the studies reviewed above adopt US states as the basic spatial unit of analysis, Feldman and Audretsch (1999) collect data on the number of new product innovations at the level of metropolitan statistical areas (MSA). The number of innovations at the city-industry level is then regressed against variables capturing the city specialization in the same industry (that is, locational quotient), the presence within the city of other industries whose science base is related to the industry under consideration and, finally, an index of localized competition among firms in the same industry. The most important result they reach is that diversity matters more than specialization, a finding that is interpreted as evidence that knowledge spills over more across than within industries.

The Spatial Range of Spillovers

Although the earliest wave of studies has provided some evidence that knowledge flows are spatially bounded, there is no indication about how local are localized knowledge spillovers. In other terms, even assuming that the benefits of knowledge spillovers decay with geographical distance, what is their spatial range? After what distance threshold does knowledge produced in a location cease to confer any advantage to companies located elsewhere? In order to answer these important questions, a second wave of studies has embarked upon the task of refining the regional knowledge production function, by collecting information at lower spatial scales of aggregation (for example cities) and by including into the knowledge production function spatially lagged variables designed to capture the spillover effects of university and industry research carried out in other locations within a given distance.[2] This leads to reformulating the regional knowledge production function as follows:

$$K_r = RD_r^{\alpha_1} URD_r^{\alpha_2} KS_r^{\alpha_3} \varepsilon_r \qquad (10.2)$$

$$KS_r = \sum_{s \neq r} w(d_{rs}) RD_s \qquad (10.3)$$

where KS_r represent knowledge spillovers to the region r from private or university research carried out in other regions. Interregional knowledge spillovers are defined as a weighted sum of knowledge-generating inputs, where the spatial weights w are defined as a function of the geographical distance d_{rs} between regions r and s to reflect the idea that the intensity of spillovers should decay with the spatial distance between the sending and the receiving areas.

Anselin et al. (1997) show that university research carried out in counties located within 50 miles from an MSA (and not part of the MSA) has a significant positive effect on innovative output. By contrast, the effect of private R&D seems to be confined within the boundaries of the MSA itself, with no spatial leakage. However, estimates of a model in which the dependent variable is private R&D show that university research has a positive inducement effect only within the MSA itself, while there is indication of spatial spillovers up to 50 miles with respect to private R&D.[3] Using the same data set, Varga (2000) estimates a spatial lag model showing that the number of new products in an MSA is positively related to the average innovation output in MSAs located within a distance of 75 miles. This finding suggests that, in addition to spillover effects originating in the same location, technology transfers from neighbouring areas also have substantial effects on new knowledge creation. Furthermore, by looking at the elasticity of innovation output with respect to university research, he also shows that the effect of additional university R&D spending has a substantial impact only in cities endowed with a critical mass of high-technology employment. For Europe, Bottazzi and Peri (2003) find that interregional knowledge spillovers have a positive effect up to a distance of 300 km, whereas no significant effect is detected beyond that distance. In a similar way, Moreno et al. (2005) show that interregional R&D spillovers rapidly decay with distance, remaining within the range of 250 km. Moreover, they also confirm that, while existing, knowledge spillovers across regions are of very limited magnitude.

Bode (2004) generalizes the previous results by showing that interregional knowledge spillovers contribute to increasing a region's innovative performance only in regions with low R&D intensity, whereas highly innovative regions tend to exploit knowledge spillovers at home. Moreover, the extent of spatial decay of knowledge externalities appears to be rather strong: no more than 2 per cent of all patents are accounted for by research done outside the boundaries even in regions with low R&D intensity, while for regions with high R&D intensity the contribution of spillovers from other areas is virtually zero. More recently, Tappeiner et al. (2008) show that any evidence of spatial correlation of innovation outputs between contiguous regions (that is, spatial spillovers) disappears once variables measuring the social capital available to regional actors are included in the model. From such results, they conclude that interpreting the existence of spatial autocorrelation of innovative activity as evidence of knowledge spillovers is probably misplaced. This phenomenon has more do with cultural and institutional similarity among contiguous regions than with direct knowledge exchanges between them.

The Channels of Knowledge Transmission

In the literature reviewed above, the observed statistical correlation between regional knowledge inputs and outputs has frequently been interpreted as reflecting pure techno-logical externalities. However, a more balanced view should start from acknowledging that the regional knowledge production function is no more than a black box, which is unable to tell anything about the mechanisms through which knowledge is actually transmitted from one agent to the other.[4] In other words, most of the econometric tests produced so far within this approach are observationally equivalent with respect to dif-ferent channels of knowledge transmission. In this respect, the key point to observe is that, while some of these mechanisms are compatible with a spillover interpretation of the observed correlations, many others are not.

To this purpose, it is useful to recall the traditional distinction between pure and pecuniary externalities (that is, agglomeration economies). The former represent dis-embodied knowledge spillovers and occur when firms profit from the R&D activities undertaken by others without compensating them for the benefits received. They occur through non-market interactions that directly affect the production possibilities of firms. On the other hand, pecuniary externalities are by-products of market interac-tions: they affect firms only insofar as those are involved in exchanges mediated by the price mechanism (Ottaviano and Thisse, 2001). The distinction is not just a theoretical or a semantic one, but it may have crucial implications for the design of policy interven-tions. While both types of externalities are likely to be at work, the attention of many geographers of innovation has focused only on pure spillovers, disregarding the importance of pecuniary externalities in explaining why knowledge flows are spatially localized and therefore regions differ in their ability to generate innovations. Once we reject the idea that the evidence produced by the econometric approach based on the knowledge production function can be exclusively interpreted as the result of pure knowledge spillovers, the relevant questions become those of assessing the relative importance of knowledge transfers mediated by market and non-market exchanges, and of identifying the most important channels through which knowledge is transmitted. This requires entering into the black box and telling apart the specific mechanisms through which knowledge travels.

DIRECT MEASUREMENT OF KNOWLEDGE FLOWS

The Use of Patent Citations

In what has become a classical reference, Jaffe et al. (1993) (hereafter, JTH) argue that knowledge flows can be directly measured by patent citations and that the latter provide material for a natural experiment on the role of geography.[5] The JTH experiment consists in comparing the fraction of citing and control patents in terms of the frequency with which they match the cited ones geographically. Control patents are selected in a way that mimics the existing spatial distribution of patenting activity, thereby providing a benchmark against which assessing the extent of spatial co-location between citing and cited patents. The results show that citing patents are up to three times more likely than control patents to come from the same state as the cited ones, and up to six times from the same metropolitan area.[6] JTH results have been widely cited and interpreted as a further proof that knowledge externalities (spillovers) are both important and to a large extent local in nature, thereby providing additional support to the findings of the regional knowledge production function approach.[7] To the extent that patent citations represent uncompensated flows of knowledge, this interpretation seems to be warranted. Yet, in order for this interpretation to be valid, one has to provide an answer to an ancillary question: what are the mechanisms through which knowledge is transmitted from the origin (the cited patent) to the destination (the citing patent)? While JTH are relatively agnostic with respect to this question, subsequent studies have attempted to explore in greater detail the channels through which knowledge flows and the relative role of market versus non-market diffusion mechanisms.

Mobility of Skilled Workers

An important knowledge diffusion mechanism is the localized mobility of individual (skilled) workers. Using a sample of highly cited semiconductor patents, Almeida and Kogut (1999) find evidence of localized knowledge flows only in Silicon Valley, which is also the region with the highest levels of intraregional mobility of engineers across firms. According to these results, the reason why knowledge flows are spatially bounded has to be found in the workings of the labour market for scientists and engineers, rather than in the direct communication taking place over more informal social networks. Knowledge is transferred by individuals who move from one organization to the other, but do not relocate in space. This line of interpretation is supported by the work of Zucker et al. (1998, 2002) on the biotechnology industry. They show that the external knowledge generated by a star scientist located in a region improves the performance only of that company with which the scientist has developed close collaborative relations. The reason, they argue, is that knowledge in this field is characterized by high degrees of natural excludability: anyone wishing to build upon that knowledge must gain access to the research teams and lab setting that generated it. Under these circumstances, star scientists tend to enter into contractual arrangements with firms, in order to extract the supranormal returns from their intellectual capital. In doing so, they also tend to prefer locations within commuting distance from their home or university, thus creating localized effects of university research. In a similar vein, Breschi and Lissoni (2005, 2009) show that the localized mobility of inventors across organizations accounts for a very large fraction of the observed localization of patent citations. This result points out that one of the fundamental reasons for the localization of knowledge flows relates to the low propensity of a special category of knowledge workers (that is, inventors) to relocate in space while moving across firms.

Markets for Technologies

Although market transactions are usually thought to be less sensitive to spatial proximity than non-market relationships, there are reasons to believe that this view is misplaced. In his recent review of the concept, Boschma (2005) points out that besides spatial proximity, other dimensions of proximity such as organizational, social and institutional may be required to solve the problem of coordinating the process of knowledge transfer and sharing among different organizations. In addition to this, the insights of Storper and Venables (2004) as well as of many sociologists (Uzzi, 1997) make clear that market transactions are embedded in a web of social relations that help reducing uncertainty and risks related to opportunistic behaviour. In this respect, the face-to-face contacts that derive from spatial proximity provide an efficient monitoring technology and are instrumental in developing the necessary level of trust among transacting partners. On the empirical side, Mowery and Ziedonis (2004) replicate the JTH methodology by distinguishing between citations that are linked through a licensing contract and those that are not. Their results show that market-based citations are far more spatially localized than non-market (that is, spillover) citations. Precisely because the tacit knowledge necessary to develop the licensed invention is embodied in individuals, access to it requires providing knowledgeable workers with the appropriate incentives to engage in collaborative development. This objective may be achieved by offering those individuals some kind of compensation, such as equity stakes or research contracts (Jensen and Thursby, 2001). This in turn requires that frequent interactions are established, which are most effectively conducted at a short spatial distance.

Social Networks

As argued above, a view has come to prevail in the literature that identifies in the network of informal social relationships the communication channel supporting the localization of knowledge spillovers. Until not so long ago, however, the lack of direct empirical evidence has prevented a clear understanding of two crucial questions. What type of social relations are more likely to transmit relevant knowledge? And even more fundamentally, is there a way to test empirically whether and to what extent social networks actually play an important role in the localized diffusion of knowledge?

A few recent studies attempt to fill this gap. Agrawal et al. (2006) explore the role of social ties between inventors by running a modified JTH experiment, which focuses on citations to patents of mobile inventors, that is inventors who have moved at least once across different metropolitan statistical areas. More specifically, they examine what fraction of citations to patents produced by a mobile inventor while in the new location (after they moved) actually comes from patents in the mover's prior location. Their results show that a disproportionate level of knowledge generated by mobile inventors in their new location flows back to their prior location, thereby providing substantive evidence that co-location facilitates the formation of social relationships that endure over time (that is, after individuals are separated).

This insight has been actually followed by other authors who have started exploring explicitly the professional network represented by co-invention relationships among patent inventors. Building upon an earlier study of Stolpe (2002), Singh (2005) and Breschi and Lissoni (2004) adopt a similar methodology to investigate the role of collaborative networks among inventors in driving the diffusion of knowledge. Their results show that the probability of a knowledge flow sharply decreases with the social distance among inventors, starting from very high levels at low social distances. Moreover, looking at the interaction between social and geographical distances, it emerges that co-invention networks represent channels of interfirm knowledge diffusion that are probably more effective than geographical co-location per se. The probability of a citation link for patent pairs at low social distance, but located in different regions, is several orders of magnitude higher than for patent pairs located in the same region, but linked by a longer social path. At the same time, however, both studies confirm that geography still plays a role in mediating knowledge flows. For patent pairs at high social distances, the odds of a citation link are still much larger for spatially co-located patent pairs than for non co-located pairs.

In a similar vein, Breschi and Lissoni (2005, 2009) replicate the JTH experiment, looking at the population of US inventors in the field of drugs and biotechnology. Differently from the original experiment, however, they distinguish patent pairs (that is, citing–cited and control–cited) according to the social distance that separates them. Without controlling for social distance, their results confirm the original JTH findings about the geographical localization of patent citations. However, once patent pairs at relatively short social distance (that is, lower than six) are removed from the sample, evidence of localization effects considerably weakens to the point of becoming almost insignificant. These results suggest that social proximity, rather than geographical proximity per se, is probably the most important reason explaining why knowledge flows are spatially localized. To put it differently, one can say that spatial proximity is not a sufficient condition to benefit from knowledge flows, although it may be a necessary one.

The role of co-invention networks in spurring innovative performance has been further investigated by Bettencourt et al. (2007) and Fleming et al. (2007), though from a more macro-regional perspective. Bettencourt et al. (2007) investigate the relationship between innovative activity and the population size of metropolitan areas in the US, finding robust evidence of increasing returns to scale: the number of patents increases more than proportionally with metropolitan size.

However, the puzzling result they find is that this increase in patenting rate is not related either to higher productivity or to network effects. On the one hand, the number of patents per inventors stays essentially constant across metropolitan areas, thereby suggesting the absence of positive agglomeration effects. On the other hand, measures of connectivity in the co-invention network are not related in any simple way to the scaling of inventiveness with metropolitan size, thereby suggesting that structural features of metropolitan networks of inventors are unlikely to matter. The origin of the increasing returns with metropolitan size must be found elsewhere. In particular, they show that larger metropolitan areas have disproportionately more inventors and creative workers than smaller ones, which explains why the number of patents increases superlinearly with city size, but that the productivity of single inventors stays constant across the entire urban system.

Exploiting the same data set, Fleming et al. (2007) investigate further the relationship between patent productivity and structural properties of the co-invention network at the level of US MSAs. In particular, they investigate whether a 'small-world' network structure has a positive impact on metropolitan innovation rates. Their results indicate that a short average distance among inventors is associated to higher rates of regional patenting, while network clustering has no statistically significant effect. Consequently, the small-world measure, that is, the interaction between distance and clustering, fails to demonstrate a statistically significant impact.[8]

Evidence from Surveys

A few studies in recent years have adopted an even more direct approach to the problem of studying localized knowledge flows by exploiting information from surveys of inventors. Mariani and Giuri (2007) investigate the geographical breadth of knowledge spillovers by taking the answers of inventors to a question that asks them to rank the importance of close and distant interactions with people working for other organizations as sources of ideas. Their results show that the role of geographical proximity in mediating knowledge spillovers matters for just 4.8 per cent of all patents examined, whereas 15 per cent of all patents rely only on distant sources of knowledge. Science-based patents also tend to build upon more geographically distant sources of ideas. However, after controlling for a number of factors, they show that the most significant explanatory variable of the geographical breadth of knowledge spillovers is the educational background of inventors. The interpretation they give for this result is that highly educated people are more likely to have built over time a geographically dispersed network of collaboration than their less educated peers. Ibrahim et al. (2008) also follow a survey approach to investigate the sources of knowledge that can potentially affect inventors. By comparing cluster- and non-cluster-based inventors, they show that inventors located in clusters benefit to a significantly larger extent from local sources of knowledge, particularly when the source of ideas refers to tacit and non-codified explicit knowledge.

CONCLUSIONS

The review in this chapter has distinguished between two, broadly defined, methodological approaches to the problem of investigating the spatial extent of knowledge flows. One approach has been based upon the estimation of a regional knowledge production function, correlating knowledge-generating inputs and outputs. Despite its undeniable merits, the major limitation of this approach is that it is unable to tell apart the channels through which knowledge is actually transmitted and to distinguish between non-market (that is, pure spillovers) and market-based (that is, pecuniary externalities) transmission mechanisms. The objective of entering into the black box of the knowledge production function and of telling apart the specific mechanisms through which knowledge travels has triggered a second set of studies, whose common denominator is the search for a direct measurement of knowledge flows. Results emerging from these studies show that geography matters because, in addition to mediating the access to publicly available knowledge and ideas, it is also a platform to organize market-based knowledge transactions, such as those that involve the movement of workers across firms and the trade of knowledge between universities and firms, as well as between firms. Confirming the intuitions of many economic geographers, these studies show that social networks represent key drivers of localized knowledge diffusion, but at the same time they also raise a few puzzling questions. On the one hand, the structure of local social networks seems to be far more fragmented and sparse than it has been probably thought so far, thereby implying that knowledge flows are not only spatially, but also socially bounded. In other terms, social ties bound the flows of knowledge within well-defined communities of actors, so that non-member individuals are likely to be excluded from them even if spatially co-located. On the other hand, although social networks appear to mediate the access to knowledge, the empirical evidence about their impact on regional innovative performance is much less encouraging, by failing to show any significant correlation between the structural properties of regional networks and innovation output. In this respect, it must be pointed out, however, that the empirical investigation on the role of networks is still in its infancy and that, no matter how relevant, only one type of social relationship, that is, co-invention, has been investigated so far. Further efforts of data collection, both from archival sources and from specifically designed surveys, are likely to yield large pay-offs in terms of enhancing our understanding of the spatial dimension of knowledge flows.

NOTES

1. In addition to these variables, some studies also include a vector of 'local' economic characteristics Z, aimed to capture additional knowledge externalities deriving, for example, from the presence of firms offering specialized inputs and services or from the availability of a large population of skilled workers.
2. It is worth noting that the need for modelling the geographical scope of knowledge spillovers has emerged also from the empirical observation of strong levels of positive spatial autocorrelation between neighbouring regions (Moreno et al., 2005; OhUallachain and Leslie, 2005).
3. Anselin et al. (2000b) and Anselin et al. (2000a) extend these results by showing that for drugs and chemicals and for electronics there are no knowledge externalities that transcend the geographic scale of the MSA. Moreover, electronics is the only industry in which they can find evidence of positive knowledge externalities for university research.

4. For a more articulated critical overview, see Breschi and Lissoni (2001a, 2001b). See also OhUallachain and Leslie (2007).
5. Whether or not patent citations actually measure knowledge flows is a hotly debated issue, which involves the intricacies of the patent examination procedures. Entering into this debate goes beyond the scope of this chapter. For a discussion, see Jaffe et al. (2000); Alcacer and Gittelman (2006); Breschi and Lissoni (2004).
6. For a recent critique of the JTH methodology, see Thompson and Fox-Kean (2005); Thompson (2006).
7. Similar experiments have been carried out, amongst many others, by Maurseth and Verspagen (2002), Verspagen and Schoenmakers (2004), Branstetter (2006) and MacGarvie (2006).
8. However, it must be pointed out that the largest network component within which they calculate the index of small-world comprises in most cities a very small fraction of all inventors located there. The lack of a significant correlation with regional innovation output is thus hardly surprising.

REFERENCES

Acs, Z.J., D.B. Audretsch and M.P. Feldman (1994), 'R&D spillovers and recipient firm size', *Review of Economics and Statistics*, **76** (2), 336–40.
Agrawal, A., I. Cockburn and J. McHale (2006), 'Gone but not forgotten: knowledge flows, labor mobility, and enduring social relationships', *Journal of Economic Geography*, **6** (5), 571–91.
Alcacer, J. and M. Gittelman (2006), 'Patent citations as a measure of knowledge flows: the influence of examiner citations', *Review of Economics and Statistics*, **88** (4), 774–9.
Almeida, P. and B. Kogut (1999), 'Localization of knowledge and the mobility of engineers in regional networks', *Management Science*, **45** (7), 905–17.
Anselin, L., A. Varga and Z. Acs (1997), 'Local geographic spillovers between university research and high technology innovations', *Journal of Urban Economics*, **42** (3), 422–48.
Anselin, L., A. Varga and Z. Acs (2000a), 'Geographical spillovers and university research: a spatial econometric perspective', *Growth and Change*, **31** (4), 501–15.
Anselin, L., A. Varga and Z.J. Acs (2000b), 'Geographic and sectoral characteristics of academic knowledge externalities', *Papers in Regional Science*, **79** (4), 435–43.
Audretsch, D.B. and M.P. Feldman (1996a), 'Innovative clusters and the industry life cycle', *Review of Industrial Organization*, **11** (2), 253–73.
Audretsch, D.B. and M.P. Feldman (1996b), 'R&D spillovers and the geography of innovation and production', *American Economic Review*, **86** (3), 630–40.
Bettencourt, L.M., J. Lobo and D. Strumsky (2007), 'Invention in the city: increasing returns to patenting as a scaling function of metropolitan size', *Research Policy*, **36** (1), 107–20.
Bode, E. (2004), 'The spatial pattern of localized R&D spillovers: an empirical investigation for Germany', *Journal of Economic Geography*, **4** (1), 43–64.
Boschma, R. (2005), 'Proximity and innovation: a critical assessment', *Regional Studies*, **39** (1), 61–74.
Bottazzi, L. and G. Peri (2003), 'Innovation and spillovers in regions: evidence from European patent data', *European Economic Review*, **47** (4), 687–710.
Branstetter, L. (2006), 'Is foreign direct investment a channel of knowledge spillovers? Evidence from Japan's FDI in the United States', *Journal of International Economics*, **68** (2), 325–44.
Breschi, S. and F. Lissoni (2001a), 'Knowledge spillovers and local innovation systems: a critical survey', *Industrial and Corporate Change*, **10** (4), 975–1005.
Breschi, S. and F. Lissoni (2001b), 'Localised knowledge spillovers vs. innovative milieux: knowledge "tacitness" reconsidered', *Papers in Regional Science*, **80** (3), 255–73.
Breschi, S. and F. Lissoni (2004), 'Knowledge networks from patent data: methodological issues and research targets', in W. Glanzel, H. Moed and U. Schmoch (eds), *Handbook of Quantitative S&T Research: The Use of Publication and Patent Statistics in Studies of S&T Systems*, Berlin: Springer Verlag, pp. 613–43.
Breschi, S. and F. Lissoni (2005), 'Cross-firm inventors and social networks: localised knowledge spillovers revisited', *Annales d'Economie et de Statistique*, **79–80**, 1–29.
Breschi, S. and F. Lissoni (2009), 'Mobility of skilled workers and co-invention networks: an anatomy of localized knowledge flows', *Journal of Economic Geography*, **9** (4), 439–68.
Feldman, M.P. (1993), 'An examination of the geography of innovation', *Industrial and Corporate Change*, **2** (1), 451–70.
Feldman, M.P. and D.B. Audretsch (1999), 'Innovation in cities: science-based diversity, specialization and localized competition', *European Economic Review*, **43** (2), 409–29.
Feldman, M.P. and R. Florida (1994), 'The geographic sources of innovation: technological infrastructure

and product innovation in the United States', *Annals of the Association of American Geographers*, **84** (2), 210–29.

Fleming, L., C. King and A.I. Juda (2007), 'Small worlds and regional innovation', *Organization Science*, **18** (6), 938–54.

Griliches, Z. (1979), 'Issues in assessing the contribution of research and development to productivity growth', *Bell Journal of Economics*, **10** (1), 92–116.

Ibrahim, S.E., M.H. Fallah and R.R. Reilly (2008), 'Localized sources of knowledge and the effect of knowledge spillovers: an empirical study of inventors in the telecommunications industry', *Journal of Economic Geography*, **9** (3), 405–31.

Jaffe, A.B. (1986), 'Technological opportunity and spillovers of R&D: evidence from firms' patents, profits, and market value', *American Economic Review*, **76** (5), 984–1001.

Jaffe, A.B. (1989), 'Real effects of academic research', *American Economic Review*, **79** (5), 957–70.

Jaffe, A.B., M. Trajtenberg and M.S. Fogarty (2000), 'Knowledge spillovers and patent citations: evidence from a survey of inventors', *American Economic Review*, **90** (2), 215–18.

Jaffe, A.B., M. Trajtenberg and R. Henderson (1993), 'Geographic localization of knowledge spillovers as evidenced by patent citations', *Quarterly Journal of Economics*, **108** (3), 577–98.

Jensen, R. and M. Thursby (2001), 'Proofs and prototypes for sale: the licensing of university inventions', *American Economic Review*, **91** (1), 240–59.

MacGarvie, M. (2006), 'Do firms learn from international trade?', *Review of Economics and Statistics*, **88** (1), 46–60.

Mariani, M. and P. Giuri (2007), 'Inventors and the geographical breadth of knowledge spillovers', LEM – Scuola Superiore Sant'Anna – Working Paper, 2007 (26).

Maurseth, P.B. and B. Verspagen (2002), 'Knowledge spillovers in Europe: a patent citations analysis', *Scandinavian Journal of Economics*, **104** (4), 531–45.

Moreno, R., R. Paci and S. Usai (2005), 'Spatial spillovers and innovation activity in European regions', *Environment and Planning A*, **37** (10), 1793–812.

Mowery, D.C. and A.A. Ziedonis (2004), 'The geographic reach of market and nonmarket channels of technology transfer: comparing citations and licenses of university patents', in J. Cantwell (ed.), *Globalization and the Location of Firms*, Cheltenham, UK and Northampton, MA, USA: Edward Elgar, pp. 333–74.

OhUallachain, B. and T.F. Leslie (2005), 'Spatial convergence and spillovers in American invention', *Annals of the Association of American Geographers*, **95** (4), 866–86.

OhUallachain, B. and T.F. Leslie (2007), 'Rethinking the regional knowledge production function', *Journal of Economic Geography*, **7** (6), 737–52.

Ottaviano, G.I. and J. Thisse (2001), 'On economic geography in economic theory: increasing returns and pecuniary externalities', *Journal of Economic Geography*, **1** (2), 153–79.

Singh, J. (2005), 'Collaborative networks as determinants of knowledge diffusion patterns', *Management Science*, **51** (5), 756–70.

Stolpe, M. (2002), 'Determinants of knowledge diffusion as evidenced in patent data: the case of liquid crystal display technology', *Research Policy*, **31** (7), 1181–98.

Storper, M. and A.J. Venables (2004), 'Buzz: face-to-face contact and the urban economy', *Journal of Economic Geography*, **4** (4), 351–70.

Tappeiner, G., C. Hauser and J. Walde (2008), 'Regional knowledge spillovers: fact or artifact?', *Research Policy*, **37** (5), 861–74.

Thompson, P. (2006), 'Patent citations and the geography of knowledge spillovers: evidence from inventor- and examiner-added citations', *Review of Economics and Statistics*, **88** (2), 383–8.

Thompson, P. and M. Fox-Kean (2005), 'Patent citations and the geography of knowledge spillovers: a reassessment', *American Economic Review*, **95** (1), 450–60.

Thompson, W. (1962), 'Locational differences in inventive effort and their determinants', in R. Nelson (ed.), *The Rate and Direction of Inventive Activity*, Princeton, NJ: Princeton University Press, pp. 253–72.

Uzzi, B. (1997), 'Social structure and competition in interfirm networks: the paradox of embeddedness', *Administrative Science Quarterly*, **42** (1), 35–67.

Varga, A. (2000), 'Local academic knowledge transfers and the concentration of economic activity', *Journal of Regional Science*, **40**, 289–309.

Verspagen, B. and W. Schoenmakers (2004), 'The spatial dimension of patenting by multinational firms in Europe', *Journal of Economic Geography*, **4** (1), 23–42.

Zucker, L.G., M.R. Darby and J.S. Armstrong (1998), 'Geographically localized knowledge: spillovers or markets?', *Economic Inquiry*, **36** (1), 65–86.

Zucker, L.G., M.R. Darby and J.S. Armstrong (2002), 'Commercializing knowledge: university science, knowledge capture, and firm performance in biotechnology', *Management Science*, **48** (1), 138–53.

11 Regional innovation and diversity
Simona Iammarino

INTRODUCTION

Much of the literature on agglomeration economies has dealt with the question of whether a specific regional industrial structure enhances knowledge diffusion, innovation and local economic growth. The question at the core of these studies is whether firms learn more from local firms in the same industry – that is, regional specialization; or from local firms in other industries – regional diversity. In other words, are the most innovative and fast-growing regions sectorally specialized or diversified? A conclusive answer to such a question has not been found – and indeed cannot be. In fact, an evolutionary interpretation of these issues indicates that there is no univocal causal relationship between regional industrial structure and economic growth, and that the links between diversity and innovation at the spatial level are far more complex than assumed by a mechanicistic view of the 'structure–conduct–performance' type.

Indeed, regions show degrees of diversity within and across their boundaries because of the evolutionary nature of the technological capabilities of firms and other economic actors, of technological regimes underlying industrial structures, and of integration and alignment of (local and non-local) knowledge flows at the regional system level. The evolutionary path of such key factors is strongly influenced by the social, cultural and institutional features of the region, giving rise to spatial diversity at two different levels: interregional, that is, creating specialized as well as diversified regions; and intraregional, that is, leading over time to either more specialization or more diversification. Even in this latter case, however, as pointed out by Jane Jacobs who first recognized the economic potential of regional diversity for growth, diversity per se does not necessarily evolve into 'diversity for growth'. Complementarity and relatedness between old and new knowledge, and openness of interactive learning modes and networks, are crucial to ensure local economic growth and institutional upgrading.

This chapter first summarizes the debate on specialization versus diversification as promoters of regional growth, whilst the following section explains the roots of regional diversity by looking at the evolutionary nature of innovation processes. The chapter then debates the increasing interdependence of innovation sources internal to the region and external to its boundaries, that is, the co-evolution of local and global networks for knowledge creation, and their relevance for regional diversity conducive to growth. A final section presents some concluding remarks.

REGIONAL DIVERSITY AND GROWTH

Diversity is natural to regions, within and across their boundaries. Jane Jacobs first made this observation with reference to big cities that she described as 'natural generators of diversity and prolific incubators of new enterprises and ideas of all kinds' (Jacobs, 1961, 189). Even regions in the same country or economic areas, such as the European Union, show striking and persistent differences in socio-economic endowments, technological profiles, productivity levels and growth rates.

Contrary to the Marshallian tradition, according to which agglomeration externalities stem mainly from specialization,[1] thus accruing to spatially proximate firms that operate in the same industry, Jacobs (1969) put the emphasis on the role of urbanization economies, and therefore sectoral diversity, to promote local economic growth. She argued that urban diversity, in terms of productions, facilities, skills, tastes, needs and cultures, generates cross-fertilization of ideas, and that ideas developed in one sector can be fruitfully applied to many other economic activities co-located in the same urban area. Whilst interfirm knowledge spillovers are essentially intra-industry in the Marshallian tradition, they are inter-industry in Jacobs's view, according to which it is the exchange of complementary knowledge and experience across different sectors that yields greater economic returns.

What Jacobs described in her books were essentially large metropolitan centres, but her argument on diversity spurring knowledge transfer and diffusion and therefore growth has been applied to geographical scales other than the urban area. There are obviously differences between urbanization and diversification economies, as the first often imply the latter, but the reverse does not generally hold. For example, both London and the region of Baden-Württemberg are considered to be highly industrially diversified, but the forces of spatial agglomeration and the mechanisms for spillovers follow different channels. Moreover, the issue is further complicated by the fact that while there is evidence to suggest that the link between innovation and cities can be strong, particularly with respect to certain sectors (for example Duranton and Puga, 2001; Acs, 2002), there is also much support for the fact that cities do not always seem to be innovation cores, nor does innovation necessarily concentrate in cities (for example Simmie and Sennet, 1999).

Following the integration of the new developments in economic geography and endogenous growth theories in the early 1990s, the debate on specialization versus diversification has heated up, prompting a plethora of empirical studies aimed at answering the critical question: is there a causal relationship between regional industrial structure, innovativeness and, ultimately, local economic growth?

Some empirical studies have advocated dynamic agglomeration externalities across industries (inter-industry spillovers) as a primary source for regional economic growth (for example Glaeser et al., 1992; Feldman and Audretsch, 1999; Paci and Usai, 2008). Some others have found dynamic agglomeration externalities to be particularly strong within the same sector, supporting the view of localization economies and intra-industry spillovers as a major engine for localized growth (for example Henderson et al., 1995; Forni and Paba, 2001). Other scholars have obtained mixed results for different sectors within the same region, with sectoral diversity having positive (for example Combes, 2000, for services) as well as negative (for example Combes, 2000; Blien and Suedekum, 2005, for manufacturing) effects on growth, also in dependence on the industry life cycle (for example Audretsch and Feldman, 1996). Recent contributions have shown that the results on the supposedly causal connection between structure and performance at the regional level are actually highly dependent on methodological choices, varying sensitively to the adoption of different geographical units of analysis, estimation methods, variable specification, sectoral aggregation, and so on (for example Combes, 2000; van Oort, 2004; Mameli, 2007; Mameli et al., 2008).

Yet, in the main, the evidence of a positive impact of regional diversity on growth seems to be prevailing against the hypothesis of localization economies and intra-industry spillovers.[2] Thus, can we conclude that there is a causal nexus between (a diversified) regional economic structure and growth? Jacobs herself pointed out that the fact of being diverse does not automatically generate benefits, and indeed we can notice that different diversified urban regions display technology gaps and divergent growth rates. In other words, to assume that diversification externalities automatically result in knowledge spillovers is misleading. One major issue is to clarify what exactly diversity means, and to what extent it does occur. Jacobs in fact stressed that, in order to reap the benefits from diversity, 'various efficient economic pools of use' are needed, and that in districts or regions lacking the ability to create such effective pools of use and economic interactions, diversity may be associated with stagnation and decline (Jacobs, 1961, 194).

Beyond methodological differences, most of the studies on agglomeration economies and their impact on economic growth, in spite of their emphasis on the relevance of knowledge, tend to be largely unconcerned with the interplay between industries, technology and regional environments. They are mainly engaged in identifying localized knowledge spillovers, irrespective of the characteristics of any functional dimension of knowledge and innovation processes (Iammarino and McCann, 2006).

This is also reflected in the almost invariable choice of employment growth as the dependent variable in the models tested by the agglomeration literature, which does not account for productivity growth or employment dynamics caused by technological change (Cingano and Schivardi, 2004). Most empirical findings do not explain how knowledge spillovers arise, nor do they shed light on the mechanisms by which the main knowledge flows occur (Breschi and Lissoni, 2001; Mameli, 2007). The deterministic assumption of 'structure–conduct–performance' underlying much of the literature so far can be neither confirmed nor rejected irrefutably: sectoral concentration or diversity in regional industrial structures is only part of the story accounting for regional innovativeness and growth.

Therefore, it is possible to argue that there are factors contributing to either regional specialization or diversification but, in either case, not to growth. There is no conclusive evidence on the one-way link between structure and dynamics of regional comparative advantages, innovation and performance. Rather, what emerges in the actual world is the coexistence of different regional specialization patterns, any of which may lead to success or failure in the competitive struggle. To understand the links between diversity and growth it is therefore necessary to go into the meaning of 'regional diversity' in more depth, taking into account the specific characteristics of innovation processes and their dynamics.

INNOVATION AND DIVERSITY

As we have seen, both Marshall's and Jacobs's dynamic agglomeration externalities predict an impact of geography on innovation and growth (Glaeser et al., 1992, 1128).

The major function of geographical space is, explicitly or implicitly in both theories, that of facilitating learning, knowledge flows and the building up of capabilities among the co-located economic actors. Regional diversity, both intra- and interregional, is rooted in the evolutionary nature of capabilities of firms and other economic actors, of industry specificities and technological regimes, and of regional systemic integration.

Firstly, in an evolutionary framework the nature and the sources of continuity in the behavioural patterns of the individual organization – particularly the firm – are at the core of the analysis (Nelson and Winter, 1982).[3] The capabilities idea takes into account the firm's specific assets, generally difficult to imitate or protect by strong intellectual property rights. Likewise, it encompasses the tacit elements of innovation – skills acquisition, knowledge and learning – represented by routines. The concept of capabilities – beyond its strong micro-foundations – has been used variously across different units of analysis from individual to global, to describe a large variety of processes and functions. The main extensions to orthodox static notions of capabilities involve both interactive and dynamic capabilities. The interactive dynamic capabilities of firms represent the extent to which the firm is able to integrate, build and reconfigure internal and external competences to address rapidly changing environments, that is, changes in the capabilities of other actors – for example consumers, clients, suppliers, public research organizations, and so on – in real time (see among others Malerba, 1992; Teece et al., 1997; von Tunzelmann and Wang, 2007; von Tunzelmann, 2009).

Despite their highly situated (within the firm) character, the processes of capabilities accumulation allow for the identification of commonalities within and across industries (technological dimension) and systems (organizational or geographical dimension). That is, firms attempt to imitate and adopt certain processes of capability accumulation observed in other firms, industries or regions. These changes may or may not be conveyed to other firms in the same industry or region – it is likely that some will not be, accounting for diversity in competences and capabilities at the micro-level even within the same geographical location.

Secondly, the evolution of firms in a specific industry is shaped by the underlying conditions affecting the creation and reproduction of knowledge; that is, 'technological regime' (Winter, 1984), a particular combination of appropriability of the returns to innovation, technological opportunities, degree of cumulativeness of technical knowledge, and characteristics of the knowledge base. The interdependence between industry and geography thus has various layers: if, on the one hand, industry-specific knowledge conditions help to explain regularities in industrial patterns across different regions, on the other hand cross-sectoral region-specific advantages (that apply to both specialized and diversified locations) underlie intra-industry heterogeneity across space (for example Breschi and Malerba, 1997, 2005; Bottazzi et al., 2005). The overall process of industrial evolution is characterized by structural change, with the emergence of new industries and the regeneration or decline of old ones. Radical innovation will often lead to the creation of new economic activities, spurring regional diversification; conversely, incremental innovation acts as the growth engine of existing activities in specific institutional contexts, strengthening regional specialization (Verspagen, 2000).

Thirdly, by the same token, highly situated (within the region) capabilities refer to the overall ability of the local system to engage in innovative and organizational processes and to make institutional change (that is, 'social capabilities' for growth; see Abramovitz, 1986), accounting for diversity of capabilities at the meso or regional level (Cooke, 2001).

The region as a whole builds on interactive dynamic capabilities because its agents are able to deploy interorganizational routines effectively: these links, networks and collective learning processes act at the region or system level (for example Eisenhardt and Martin, 2000; Leoncini et al., 2003).

Nevertheless, in line with Jane Jacobs's observation of stagnant diversified cities, the possibility exists that regions, like firms, may neither accumulate knowledge efficiently, nor be able to learn and develop capabilities. There are in fact serious complications to the functions of integration and alignment of the multiplicity of interactions in a specific regional system (von Tunzelmann, 2009). One of the major problems is that, in this complex structure of interrelations, the capabilities of one type of regional actor (for example producers) may evolve in a different direction to those of another type of actor (for example consumers or policy-makers). Problems in governance structures and lack of alignment in means and objectives for knowledge creation may prevent different types of regional organizations from evolving along the same trajectory, generating a waste of resources and precluding – even more so in the presence of high regional diversity – the achievement of those 'efficient economic pools of use' noted by Jacobs as a precondition to reap the benefits of diversity (Storper and Harrison, 1991; von Tunzelmann, 2009).

Firm-level capabilities, technological regimes, system integration, and their dynamics explain the variety of regions, underlying the balance between sources of innovation in each particular spatial context. Such a balance changes over time following changes in each of the three factors and influencing the extent of diversity at both intra- and interregional level. The regional industrial pattern is thus likely to be transformed by: the adaptation of actors to changes in the external environment; diversification brought about by scientific discoveries and technical progress; creation of new interorganizational linkages; upgrading and acquisition of competencies; and alterations of the institutional and cultural support for innovative activities.

A critical observation, which bears important implications for the argument of coordination and alignment of regional capabilities, regards knowledge complementarities. As recognized by Jacobs herself, knowledge spills over effectively only when complementarities exist among industries in terms of shared competences and capabilities. Such complementarities are captured by the notion of 'related variety' (Boschma, 2005; Frenken et al., 2007; Boschma et al., 2009; Boschma and Iammarino, 2009).[4] To understand diversity, both intra- and interregional, it is essential to distinguish between different forms of regional variety, because they involve different economic effects. Knowledge will only spill over from one sector to another when they are complementary in terms of competences and capabilities.[5] Hence, related variety is needed in order to enable effective connections and innovation governance: some degree of cognitive proximity is required to ensure that effective communication (of both information and knowledge) and interactive learning take place, avoiding knowledge and information misalignment and/or cognitive lock-in (Swann, 1997; Nooteboom, 2000). Thus, it is neither regional diversity (which may involve too wide cognitive distance) nor regional specialization (which may result in a too narrow cognitive base) per se that stimulate innovation. Rather, local specialization in related variety is more likely to induce effective interactive learning and to facilitate collective coordination of innovation processes (Boschma, 2005). As such, the concept of related variety goes beyond the traditional dichotomy of localization versus diversification externalities (Boschma and Iammarino, 2009).

The idea of innovation based on related variety is close to the Schumpeterian definition of innovation, in which innovation is driven by interaction and feedback mechanisms that cross industry boundaries, and stems from the recombination of old and new pieces of knowledge in entirely new ways (Kline and Rosenberg, 1986). The impact of related variety on regional growth is arguably particularly strong in key sectors that lead structural change brought about by shifts in technological paradigms and alterations in the conditions affecting the creation and reproduction of knowledge across industries, that is, technological regimes. Such key sectors (today, for example, microelectronics, information and communication technology (ICT, new materials, biotechnology) are characterized by high pervasiveness, horizontal effects and inter-industry cross-fertilization among emerging technologies and capabilities (Dosi, 1982; Bussolati et al., 1995). Thus, it is not diversity per se, but diversity 'in what' that matters in accruing benefits to the region.

Yet, the generation and diffusion of innovation across space is dependent not only on purely economic factors but also on social, cultural and institutional characteristics of the regional system. This implies that regional diversification can actually come about from mechanisms other than shifting the local production structure towards general purposes or cutting-edge technologies. Regional advantage can be 'constructed' on the basis of new Schumpeterian combinations of valuable, scarce, non-imitable and context-specific resources – for example combinations of skills, talent, creativity and quality – which may generate increasing diversity conducive to growth in lagging rural areas as well as in declining industrial regions (Braczyk et al., 1998; Cooke, 2007; Rutten and Gelissen, 2008). The role of general-purpose technologies in such cases would be still critical in terms of providing platforms for regional technological upgrading and diversification of the original local knowledge base (Cooke, 2007).

INNOVATION SOURCES, OPENNESS AND DIVERSITY

The relationship between regional diversity, innovation and growth has often been considered by treating the specificities of the regional economic environment as essentially a closed entity. However, firms can learn from a variety of non-local firms and organizations as well as from co-located actors. The literature on agglomeration economies briefly rehearsed above has mostly neglected linkages across regions, overlooking the fact that new diversity may stem from the establishment of extra-local linkages. The economic geography of innovation is paying increasing attention to the importance of such linkages – and thus to how diversity may occur – as a way to prevent regional stagnation and to spur diversity conducive to growth (for example Asheim and Isaksen, 2002; Cooke, 2002; Bathelt et al., 2004; Belussi et al., 2008).

Regional systemic advantages (or disadvantages) derive from attributes such as 'untraded interdependencies', formal and informal flows of knowledge, interactive learning and network intensity, which generate the bulk of territorial externalities (Saxenian, 1994; Storper, 1995, 1998). However, the existence of spatially localized interdependencies and relations does not necessarily imply that innovation depends principally on them: knowledge circulation within the region is complementary to that occurring across regions, and to the linkages between local and non-local actors (Wolfe and Gertler, 2004). Being able to build new competences and capabilities involves the ability to establish links at all levels, from the 'global' to the 'local'. Such linkages can be established through many different channels: trade exchanges, inward and outward foreign direct investment, involvement in global production networks, technological alliances, and integration in knowledge networks that, beyond firms, may encompass a variety of regional organizations. The extent to which a region attracts innovative resources from elsewhere, and transmits new ideas and innovation outwards – spurring its external integration – depends first and foremost upon its extant absorptive capacity and knowledge base (for example Simmie, 2003; Morgan, 2004).

The notion of regional absorptive capacity, in conjunction with that of openness and attractiveness, has been effectively applied to explain diversity in the context of industrial clustering (for example Bell and Albu, 1999; Arita and McCann, 2000, 2002; Owen-Smith and Powell, 2004; Giuliani et al., 2005; Iammarino and McCann, 2006; Morrison, 2008; Belussi and Sammarra, 2010) and regional innovation systems (for example Cooke et al., 1998; Cooke, 2001; Asheim and Isaksen, 2002; Cantwell and Iammarino, 2003; Cantwell and Piscitello, 2005; Doloreux and Parto, 2005; Iammarino, 2005; von Tunzelmann, 2009).

In the cluster literature, global firms can assume a critical role in bridging capabilities at both the micro and the spatial system level. Multinational enterprises (MNEs) can be seen as 'internal' actors, contributing to the creation and diffusion of new technical knowledge within the cluster; and at the same time as 'external' players, channelling knowledge created elsewhere (within the firm) into the local system. MNEs can act as gatekeepers that import knowledge that may (or may not) diffuse to other co-located firms, depending on the regional absorptive capacity and on the complementarity between the knowledge inflows and the local knowledge base; they can even influence the circulation of knowledge in the cluster without being necessarily located *in situ* (as in the case of global buyers or distributors). Related variety brought into the region through extra-regional channels may enhance diversification into new applications and new sectors while building and extending on the local knowledge base, thus helping to produce diversity conducive to growth.

The literature on the growing role played by global firms as creators of innovation in regional systems of innovations (RSIs) has provided further evidence on the interaction between local and global sources of innovation and regional diversity. Multinational enterprises' locational choices for innovative activities are moulded by the interaction and the intensity of diversification and specialization economies at the spatial level, giving rise to geographical hierarchies within and across national boundaries. Internationally integrated networks within the MNE, and interfirm networks established between foreign and local firms, may lead to an improvement of capabilities both of the MNE and of the host region, amplifying the advantages of geographical agglomeration in some particular lines of technological development, thus reinforcing or broadening the existing sectoral pattern of technological specialization of regional systems (Cantwell and Iammarino, 1998, 2000, 2001; Cantwell and Noonan, 2001).

More particularly, it has been shown that a region at the top of the geographical hierarchy is more likely to attract a broad range of both indigenous and foreign MNE innovative activities, as MNEs located there will generally try to extend their established lines of technological expertise through intrafirm networks. Examples of such core regional systems in Europe are found in the South East of England, Lombardia in Italy and Baden-Württemberg in Germany, which pull in the development efforts of a broad range of large firms, both national and foreign, generally extending their own lines of technological competence by drawing on the capabilities to be found locally in such centres of all-round excellence. Therefore, it is argued that, in such cases, spillover effects are mainly due to a high dynamism in terms of technological and productive activities (particularly services), general infrastructure, financial facilities, openness to external networks, business climate, corporate and enterprise culture. These regions have been labelled as higher-order locations in the geographical hierarchy, both within the national boundaries and even in the wider European context. Intermediate regional locations, such as the West Midlands and the North West in the UK or Piemonte in Italy, attract innovative activities more for a specific set of specialized expertise which can be accessed by asset-seeking MNEs. By locating research facilities in such regions, aligned with sectoral-specific local strengths, MNEs may be able to upgrade their own technological capabilities in some particular technological fields (Cantwell and Iammarino, 1998, 2000).

However, in line with the evolutionary economic geography framework, the sectoral patterns of regional technological activities gradually change as new industries develop and new technological linkages are forged between sectors. Specialization and diversification tend to move along a cumulative path in which the creation of new technological competencies depends on the pattern of advantages previously established. In other words, along with the related variety argument rehearsed above, diversification is one of the possible forms of incremental change in the composition of the regional innovation base, whilst in other cases regional profiles may be reinforced and concentrated in their established areas of technological expertise.

Multinational firms may fit into regional profiles of specialization, thus supporting the process of local technological concentration. In contrast, depending upon the initial regional technological profile, MNEs may spur the diversification of the regional knowledge base. Yet, in spite of a high degree of technological diversity, some higher-order RSIs, especially those characterized by more mature clusters of activity, which have become more narrowly specialized in their technological activities, might experience a slower process of convergence between old and new technologies because of a lock-in trend due to both the initial technological profile and the institutional environment. Other higher-order RSIs which have broadened their profiles, moving into complementary trajectories and achieving institutional integration, might experience a faster process of convergence between old and new technologies, reaching a greater potential for 'diversity for growth' (Cantwell and Iammarino, 2001, 2003).

To sum up, the local technological profiles in the principal EU regions are distinctive, and the fact that only some RSIs are able to adjust to the highest technological opportunities confirms that the location-specific nature of technological change might imply more diversity, and eventually the rise and the decline of technological poles within the area. As a consequence, a 'competitive bidding' between regional systems of innovation is likely to occur: the advantages and disadvantages of competition and gains in competence may clearly be more or less balanced out, depending on the capabilities, structures and institutional alignment and integration of the regional innovation system; in other words, on its overall capacity and speed to react to major technological changes.

CONCLUSIONS

Paraphrasing Jacobs, 'regional diversity itself permits and stimulate more diversity' (Jacobs, 1961, 190). However, as also stressed by Jacobs, diversity per se is not a sufficient condition for regional innovativeness and growth. Indeed, even the fact that diversity is a necessary condition for regional growth implies a qualification of what diversity is exactly, and how it occurs. As we have seen, for the benefits of diversity to be accrued, the complementarity among industries that make up the local industrial structure is essential. The notion of related variety – that is, a certain degree of cognitive proximity and shared competences and capabilities between new knowledge applications and the existing regional knowledge base – helps identify 'which' diversity translates into 'diversity for growth' at the regional level.

Related variety yields greater returns not only because it ensures the 'various efficient economic pools of use' stressed by Jacobs (1961, 194), but also because it facilitates the alignment and integration of means and objectives across regional institutional networks – or prevailing modes of contemporary regional governance covering functional, resource and spatial matters related to the deployment of innovation processes within the region.

Furthermore, industrial diversity occurs increasingly as a result of heterogeneous and interdependent knowledge sources, some of them endogenous to the regions, some extra-regional. The co-evolution of local and global knowledge linkages and networks for knowledge creation – with its variety of mechanisms, among which we have highlighted in particular the role of MNEs as generators of new knowledge within and between regional systems – is another precondition for spurring diversity conducive to growth. The balance between internal and external sources of innovation and the degree of closure versus openness of innovation models at both organizational and spatial system level are a major factor underlying the rising intra- and interregional diversity and the formation of regional hierarchies, leading to 'more similar but less equal' patterns of regional evolution.

Thus, following evolutionary formulations, the regional economic structure does not appear to show a deterministic link but rather a complex interaction with innovativeness and performance, which gives rise to distinct localized evolutionary paths. A range of complementary and integrated local and non-local capabilities and linkages, alignment of institutional objectives and networks, and openness and external integration are all necessary conditions for 'diversity for growth' in regional systems.

NOTES

1. See Chapter 10 in this *Handbook* for regional specialization.
2. See, for a comprehensive review of the empirical literature, Mameli (2007); and Duranton and Puga (2001) for a review of the advantages and disadvantages of specialization and diversity in urban agglomerations.
3. See Chapter 14 in this *Handbook* for a comprehensive view of evolutionary economic geography.
4. See Chapter 14 of this *Handbook* for an in-depth discussion of the related variety concept.
5. Related variety is not defined in terms of input–output linkages among sectors. It is relevant to draw a distinction between the economic dimension and the cognitive one, because business networks do not necessarily coincide with knowledge networks (see, for example, Giuliani, 2007).

REFERENCES

Abramovitz, M. (1986), 'Catching up, forging ahead, and falling behind', *Journal of Economic History*, **46**, 385–406.
Acs, Z. (2002), *Innovation and Growth of Cities*, Cheltenham, UK and Northampton, MA, USA: Edward Elgar.
Arita, T. and P. McCann (2000), 'Industrial alliances and firm location behaviour: some evidence from the US semiconductor industry', *Applied Economics*, **32**, 1391–1403.
Arita, T. and P. McCann, (2002), 'The relationship between the spatial and hierarchical organization of multiplant firms: observations from the global semiconductor industry', *Journal of International Management*, **8**, 121–39.
Asheim, B.T. and A. Isaksen (2002), 'Regional innovation systems: the integration of local "sticky" and global "ubiquitous" knowledge', *Journal of Technology Transfer*, **27**, 77–86.
Audretsch, D.B. and M.P. Feldman (1996), 'R&D spillovers and the geography of innovation and production', *American Economic Review*, **86** (3), 630–40.
Bathelt, H., A. Malmberg and P. Maskell (2004), 'Clusters and knowledge: local buzz, global pipelines and the process of knowledge creation', *Progress in Human Geography*, **28** (1), 31–56.
Bell, M. and M. Albu (1999), 'Knowledge systems and technological dynamism in industrial clusters in developing countries', *World Development*, **27** (9), 1715–34.
Belussi, F. and A. Sammarra (eds) (2010), *Business Clusters and Industrial Districts: The Governance of the Global Value Chain*, London and New York: Routledge.
Belussi, F., A. Sammarra and S.R. Sedita (2008), 'Managing long distance and localised learning in the Emilia Romagna life science cluster', *European Planning Studies*, **16** (5), 665–92.
Blien, U. and J. Suedekum (2005), 'Local economic structure and industry development in Germany: 1993–2001', *Economics Bulletin*, **15** (17), 1–8.
Boschma, R.A. (2005), 'Proximity and innovation: a critical assessment', *Regional Studies*, **39** (1), 61–74.
Boschma, R.A., R. Eriksson and U. Lindgren (2009), 'How does labour mobility affect the performance of plants? The importance of relatedness and geographical proximity', *Journal of Economic Geography*, **9** (2), 169–90.
Boschma, R.A. and S. Iammarino (2009), 'Related variety, trade linkages and regional growth in Italy', *Economic Geography*, **85** (3), 289–311.
Bottazzi, G., G. Dosi and G. Fagiolo (2005), 'On sectoral specifities in the geography of corporate location', in S. Breschi and F. Malerba (eds), Clusters, Networks and Innovation, Oxford: Oxford University Press, pp. 54–79.
Braczyk, H.J., P. Cooke and M. Heidenreich (eds) (1998), *Regional Innovation Systems*, London: UCL Press.
Breschi, S. and F. Lissoni (2001), 'Knowledge spillovers and local innovation systems: a critical survey', *Industrial and Corporate Change*, **10**, 975–1005.
Breschi, S. and F. Malerba (1997), 'Sectoral systems of innovation: technological regimes, Schumpeterian dynamics and spatial boundaries', in C. Edquist (ed.), *Systems of Innovation*, London: Pinter, pp. 130–56.
Bussolati, C., F. Malerba. and S. Torrisi (1995), 'L'evoluzione del sistema industriale italiano e l'alta tecnologia', Liuc Papers, no. 25, serie Economia e Impresa, 5.
Cantwell, J.A. and S. Iammarino (1998), 'MNCs, technological innovation and regional systems in the EU: some evidence in the Italian case', *International Journal of the Economics of Business*, Special Issue, **5** (3), 383–408.
Cantwell, J.A. and S. Iammarino (2000), 'Multinational corporations and the location of technological innovation in the UK regions', *Regional Studies*, **34** (3), 317–22.
Cantwell, J.A. and S. Iammarino (2001), 'EU regions and multinational corporations: change, stability and strengthening of technological comparative advantages', *Industrial and Corporate Change,* **10** (4), 1007–37.
Cantwell, J.A. and S. Iammarino (2003), *Multinational Corporations and European Regional Systems of Innovation*, London, UK and New York, USA: Routledge.
Cantwell, J.A. and C.A. Noonan (2001), 'The regional distribution of technological development: evidence from foreign-owned firms in Germany', in M.P. Feldman and N. Massard (eds), *Knowledge Spillovers and the Geography of Innovation*, Dordrecht: Kluwer Academic Publishing, pp. 155–72.
Cantwell, J.A. and L. Piscitello (2005), 'Recent location of foreign-owned R&D activities by large multinational corporations in the European regions: the role of spillovers and externalities', *Regional Studies*, **39** (1), 1–16.
Cingano, F. and F. Schivardi (2004), 'Identifying the sources of local productivity growth', *Journal of the European Economic Association*, **2**, 720–42.
Combes, P.P. (2000), 'Economic structure and local growth: France, 1984–1993', *Journal of Urban Economics*, **47**, 329–55.

Cooke, P. (2001), 'Regional innovation systems, clusters, and the knowledge economy', *Industrial and Corporate Change*, **10** (4), 945–74.

Cooke, P. (2002), *Knowledge Economies: Clusters, Learning and Competitive Advantage*, London: Routledge.

Cooke, P. (2007), 'To construct regional advantage from innovation systems first build policy platforms', *European Planning Studies*, **15** (2), 124–46.

Cooke, P., M. Gomez Uraga and G. Etxebarria (1998), 'Regional innovation systems: an evolutionary perspective', *Environment and Planning A*, **30**, 1563–84.

Doloreux, D. and S. Parto (2005), 'Regional innovation systems: current discourse and unresolved issues', *Technology in Society*, **27** (2), 133–53.

Dosi, G. (1982), 'Technological paradigms and technological trajectories: a suggested interpretation of the determinants and directions of technical change', *Research Policy*, **11**, 147–62.

Duranton, G. and D. Puga (2001), 'Nursery cities: urban diversity, process innovation, and the life cycle of products', *American Economic Review*, **91**, 1454–77.

Eisenhardt, K.M. and J.A. Martin (2000), 'Dynamic capabilities: what are they?', *Strategic Management Journal*, **21**, 1105–21.

Feldman, M. and D. Audretsch (1999), 'Innovation in cities: science-based diversity, specialisation and localised competition', *European Economic Review*, **43**, 409–29.

Forni, M. and S. Paba (2001), 'Knowledge spillovers and the growth of local industries', CEPR Discussion Paper No. 2934.

Frenken, K., F.G. van Oort and T. Verburg (2007), 'Related variety, unrelated variety and regional economic growth', *Regional Studies*, **41** (5), 685–97.

Giuliani, E. (2007), 'The selective nature of knowledge networks in clusters: evidence from the wine industry', *Journal of Economic Geography*, **7**, 139–68.

Giuliani, E., R. Rabellott and M.P. van Dijk (eds) (2005), *Clusters Facing Competition: The Importance of External Linkages*, Aldershot: Ashgate.

Glaeser, E.L., H.D. Kallal, J.A. Schinkmann and A. Shleifer (1992), 'Growth in cities', *Journal of Political Economy*, **100**, 1126–52.

Henderson, J.V., A. Kuncoro and M. Turner (1995), 'Industrial development in cities', *Journal of Political Economy*, **103**, 1067–85.

Iammarino, S. (2005), 'An evolutionary integrated view of regional systems of innovation: concepts, measures and historical perspectives', *European Planning Studies*, **13** (4), 495–517.

Iammarino, S. and P. McCann (2006), 'The structure and evolution of industrial clusters: transactions, technology and knowledge spillovers', *Research Policy*, **35** (7), 1018–36.

Jacobs, J. (1961), *The Death and Life of Great American Cities*, New York: Random House.

Jacobs, J. (1969), *The Economy of Cities*, New York: Random House.

Kline, S.J. and N. Rosenberg. (1986), 'An overview of innovation', in R. Landau and N. Rosenberg (eds), *The Positive Sum Strategy: Harnessing Technology for Economic Growth*, Washington, DC: National Academy Press, pp. 275–306.

Leoncini, R., S. Montresor and G. Vertova (2003), 'Dynamic capabilities: evolving organisations in evolving (technological) systems', Working Paper 0304, University of Bergamo, Department of Economics.

Malerba, F. (1992), 'Learning by firms and incremental technical change', *Economic Journal*, **102**, 845–59.

Mameli, F. (2007), 'Agglomeration economies and local growth in Italy', unpublished PhD dissertation, University of Reading.

Mameli, F., A. Faggian and P. McCann (2008), 'Employment growth in Italian local labour systems: issues of model specification and sectoral aggregation', *Spatial Economic Analysis*, **3** (3), 343–60.

Morgan, K. (2004), 'The exaggerated death of geography: learning, proximity and territorial innovation systems', *Journal of Economic Geography*, **4**, 3–21.

Morrison, A. (2008), 'Gatekeepers of knowledge within industrial districts: who they are, how they interact', *Regional Studies*, **42** (6), 817–35.

Nelson, R.R. and S.G. Winter (1982), *An Evolutionary Theory of Economic Change*, Cambridge, MA: Harvard University Press.

Nooteboom, B. (2000), *Learning and Innovation in Organizations and Economies*, Oxford: Oxford University Press.

Owen-Smith, J. and W.W. Powell (2004), 'Knowledge networks as channels and conduits: the effects of spillovers in the Boston biotechnology community', *Organization Studies*, **15** (1), 5–21.

Paci, R. and S. Usai (2008), 'Agglomeration economies, spatial dependence and local industry growth', *Revue d'EconomieIndustrielle*, **123** (3), 87–109.

Rutten, R. and J. Gelissen (2008), 'Technology, talent, diversity and the wealth of European regions', *European Planning Studies*, **16** (7), 985–1005.

Saxenian, A. (1994), *Regional Advantage: Culture and Competition in Silicon Valley and Route 128*, Cambridge, MA: Harvard University Press.

Simmie, J. (2003), 'Innovation and urban regions as national and international nodes for the transfer and sharing of knowledge', *Regional Studies*, **37** (6–7), 607–20.

Simmie, J. and J. Sennet (1999), 'Innovative clusters: theoretical explanations and why size matters', *National Institute Economic Review*, **4/99** (170), 87–98.

Storper, M. (1995), 'The resurgence of regional economies, ten years later: the region as a nexus of untraded interdependencies', *European Urban and Regional Studies*, **2**, 191–221.

Storper, M. (1998), *The Regional World: Territorial Development in a Global Economy*, New York: Guilford.

Storper, M. and B. Harrison (1991), 'Flexibility, hierarchy and regional development: the changing structure of industrial production systems and their forms of governance in the 1990s', *Research Policy*, **20**, 407–22.

Swann, G.M.P. (1997), 'Towards a model of clustering in high-technology industries', in G.M.P. Swann, M. Prevezer and D. Stout (eds), *The Dynamics of International Clusters: International Comparisons in Computing and Biotechnology*, Oxford, UK and New York, USA: Oxford University Press, pp. 52–76.

Teece, D.J., G. Pisano and A. Shuen (1997), 'Dynamic capabilities and strategic management', *Strategic Management Journal*, **18**, 509–33.

van Oort, F. (2004), *Urban Growth and Innovation: Spatially Bounden Externalities in the Netherlands*, Aldershot: Ashgate.

Verspagen, B. (2000), 'Economic growth and technological change: an evolutionary interpretation', Ecis and MERIT, April.

von Tunzelmann, N. (2009), 'Regional capabilities and industrial regeneration', in M. Farshchi, O. Janne and P. McCann (eds), *Technological Change and Mature Industrial Regions: Firms, Knowledge and Policy*, Cheltenham, UK and Northampton, MA, USA: Edward Elgar, pp. 11–28.

von Tunzelmann, N. and Q. Wang (2007), 'Capabilities and production theory', *Structural Change and Economic Dynamics*, **18**, 192–211.

Winter, S.G. (1984), 'Schumpeterian competition in alternative technological regimes', *Journal of Economic Behavior and Organization*, **5** (3–4), 287–320.

Wolfe D.A. and M.S. Gertler (2004), 'Clusters from the inside and out: local dynamics and global linkages', *Urban Studies*, **41**, 1071–93.

12 Networks of innovation
Elisa Giuliani

INTRODUCTION

Innovation is nowadays considered an engine of economic growth (Fagerberg et al., 1994; Silverberg and Verspagen, 1994). As suggested by Freeman and Perez (1988), a chief explanation for this is that, when a new techno-economic paradigm emerges and displaces an old one, the new paradigm opens up an unprecedented range of new investment opportunities which, after a period of adjustment, lead to a new wave of growth. New techno-economic paradigms are technological revolutions like the introduction of electricity, or the information technologies that have pervasive effects in the economy by raising productivity, but also by leading to the emergence of new industries as well as to changes in the institutional systems and in the functioning of society. While these revolutions happen only episodically, they are nevertheless based on an underlying process of continuous exploration and innovation carried out by firms, public institutions and other actors in the economy in the search for new solutions to problems. A key characteristic of innovation is that it is widely recognized as being a social process, involving the interaction, alliance and cooperation, and thus the networking, of different actors, being rarely the result of an individual effort by a single firm (Freeman, 1991).

This chapter presents a literature review about innovation networks, with a particular focus on regional networks.[1] The chapter is organized as follows. I first introduce the concept of 'network' as a governance structure and outline the various strands of literature about innovation networks. The following section focuses on the origins of the idea of innovation networks in regional studies, spanning studies of the industrial districts of the British industrial revolution, to more contemporary studies of regions and industrial districts in the 1970s–1990s. I then discuss the most recent advancements in the study of innovation networks in regional contexts, which have increasingly applied quantitative methods to the analysis of innovation networks. A final section concludes briefly.

NETWORKS OF INNOVATION

Economists have traditionally looked at firms as isolated and atomistic rational actors. According to this view, the way in which firms interact is solely through the market, which is driven by prices. Even within the less orthodox transaction cost economics (Coase, 1937; Williamson, 1975) firms (hierarchies) and markets are seen as the only two possible governance structures, the former being particularly appropriate to face problems of opportunism and asset specificity; the latter being appropriate when transactions are non-repetitive, involve no asset specificity and thus keep transaction costs to a minimum. For a long time, economists did not contemplate the fact that parallel to market transactions, firms may be embedded in a web of social and personal relations, bound to influence their economic behaviour. In fact: 'they have implicitly accepted the presumption . . . that "market processes" are not suitable objects of sociological study because social relations play only a frictional and disruptive role, not a central one, in modern societies' (Granovetter, 1985, 504).

Organizational sociologists spotted the limitations of economic theory and brought forward the idea that, in modern economies, firms are neither isolated actors, nor are they connected only through arm's-length transactions (that is, through the market). In contrast, they are embedded in systems of social relations, which shape the organization of production, distribution and consumption. In this respect, Granovetter (1985) questions the validity of the market–hierarchy dichotomy, by arguing that opportunism can be pervasive even within the same corporation, while it can be kept at bay in the market, if firms are embedded in networks of social relations that monitor and sanction opportunistic behaviours and malfeasance. Hence, transaction costs can be kept to a minimum when firms are embedded in social networks (Gulati, 1995). The presence of social networks in the market has now been widely documented by several scholars. Powell (1990) considers networks to be a distinguished form of governance, which is entirely different from either markets or hierarchies, as: 'In network modes of resource allocation, transactions occur neither through discrete exchange [as in markets] nor by administrative fiat [as in hierarchies], but through networks of individuals engaged in reciprocal, preferential, mutually supportive actions' (p. 303). The key issue is that firms use networks as these deliver some advantages vis-à-vis other governance structures (Powell, 1990). First, they permit the informal exchange of unique and idiosyncratic assets such as knowledge or know-how, which market mechanisms are unlikely to transact. Second, they are a relatively loose and rapid way to put individuals or organizations in contact, even when these are not formally connected to each other. Third, they have the power to maintain stable and high-quality relationships over time, fostering trust and reciprocity – issues that are never contemplated in traditional economic theory.

The advantages of networks are particularly striking in the innovation processes. Innovation is in fact widely recognized as being a social process, involving the interaction, alliance and cooperation of different actors, and thus rarely being the result of an individual effort by a single firm (Freeman, 1991). Works by Pavitt (1984), Freeman (1987), von Hippel (1988) and Lundvall (1988), to cite a few prominent ones, have been among the first to show empirically that the innovative process has numerous, often interconnected, sources. These pioneering contributions and ideas became mainstream thinking in the 1990s, when scholars progressively converged to the idea that 'the locus of innovation is found in a network of inter-organisational relationships' (Powell et al., 1996, 119). Since the 1990s, a massive amount of work has been carried out to analyse the motivations, conditions and effects of 'innovation networks'.[2] Studies on this are growing in number and have taken different directions; below is an attempt to classify some of the key streams of literature on the topic.[3]

The Degree of Formalization of the Network

While most of the original research on networks emphasizes personal and informal linkages, a vast majority of interorganizational studies about innovation networks are based on formal linkages such as cooperative agreements, co-patenting activities, strategic alliances, and the like (Hagedoorn, 1993, 2002; Powell et al., 1996; Ahuja, 2000), most likely because large-scale and longitudinal relational data are more easily available in the form of formal agreements. However, formal networks coexist with a more invisible set of informal networks, as illustrated in several studies, including: the work on know-how or information trade (von Hippel, 1987, 1988; Carter, 1989; Schrader, 1991; Sattler et al., 2003); that of economic geographers on the processes of collective learning (Capello, 1999; Lawson and Lorenz, 1999; Capello and Faggian, 2005); and more sociological contributions on the motivations of knowledge transfer across organizations (for example, Bouty, 2000). Recent studies have compared the nature and characteristics of informal and formal knowledge networks between the same set of actors, revealing that these follow very different patterns (for example Bonte and Keilbach, 2005; Allen et al., 2007).

Type of Actors

Innovation networks – especially informal ones – are primarily formed by individuals (for example inventors, academic researchers, managers, technicians, and so on), which are taken as the unit of analysis in several works on intra- or interorganizational networks (Allen, 1977; Zucker and Darby, 1996; Bouty, 2000; Saxenian and Hsu, 2001; Reagans and McEvily, 2003; Singh, 2005; Lissoni, 2008). In other cases, particularly when networks are formal, the unit of analysis is organizations, with a significant amount of studies focusing on interfirm innovation networks (Powell et al., 1996; Mowery et al., 1996, 1998), or on networks formed by different organizations such as firms, universities, public research institutes or other public organizations (Owen-Smith and Powell, 2004; Giuliani and Arza, 2009).

Method or Approach to Analysis

A relevant distinction is about the methodological approach adopted to investigate innovation networks. On the one hand, scholars analyse innovation networks by taking a qualitative, process-oriented case-study approach, which explores the motivations that lead to the formation of ties, the nature of ties, how and why ties are maintained over time; as for example in the ethnographic studies of Hagardon and Sutton (1997) or Uzzi and Lancaster (2003), or those of the French research group (GREMI) on the innovative milieu (Camagni, 1991). On the other hand, scholars have adopted a more structuralist approach based on social network analysis (SNA) (Wasserman and Faust, 1994; Carrington et al., 2005),[4] according to which it is the structure of a network in which one is embedded that matters, as 'players with well structured networks obtain higher rates of return' (Burt, 1992, 61). This second stream has been powerful in analysing the determinants or consequences of networks and of their members' positions within networks (for example Burt, 1992; Zaheer and Bell, 2005).

Geographic Scope

A context in which innovation networks have been intensively studied is that of regional clusters (see the following section). However, recent works have suggested the need to move beyond the local context and to analyse distant networks, connecting regional clusters with other actors at a national or international levels (Amin and Thrift, 1992; Bell and Albu, 1999). In this respect, particularly informing are the works by Saxenian and colleagues on linkages between technical communities of different clusters (Saxenian and Hsu, 2001; Saxenian, 2006); those by Schmitz and colleagues on the insertion of industrial clusters in global value chains (Schmitz, 2004; Pietrobelli and Rabellotti, 2007); by Giuliani on technological gatekeepers (Giuliani and Bell, 2005; Giuliani, 2011); and by Bathelt, Maskell and colleagues on 'local buzz' and global knowledge pipelines (for example Bathelt, 2005; Maskell et al., 2006).

The rest of this chapter focuses on this last point, and will therefore review the literature of innovation networks by taking a regional perspective.

INNOVATION NETWORKS IN A REGIONAL PERSPECTIVE

It is probably fair to mention that the pioneering ideas of innovation networks in industrial districts were already present in the work of Alfred Marshall (1920). Although his language did not explicitly refer to 'innovation networks' as such, he clearly suggested that firms and employees are advantaged by working close by, because geographical proximity gives them opportunities to exchange 'ideas' and learn from each other, as suggested in the following quote:

> so great are the advantages which people following the same skilled trade get from near neighbourhood to one another. The mysteries of the trade become no mysteries; but are as it were in the air, and children learn many of them, unconsciously . . . Good work is rightly appreciated, inventions and improvements in machinery, in processes and the general organisation of the business have their merits promptly discussed: if one man starts a new idea, it is taken up by others and combined with suggestions of their own; thus it becomes the source of further new ideas. (Marshall, 1920, 271)

Through these words Marshall described one of the sources of external economies, the knowledge spillovers, which allow district firms to improve their production techniques and achieve productivity gains that isolated or geographically dispersed firms would rarely attain. While recent historical accounts about the 'collective invention' of the British industrial revolution have provided support to his view (Allen, 1983; Nuvolari, 2004), it was only in the 1970s that scholars started to study innovation networks in contemporary regional or subregional areas.

Since the end of the 1970s, industrial districts became studied in Italy (Bagnasco, 1977; Brusco, 1982; Becattini, 1989), in Europe more widely (Aydalot and Keeble, 1988; Camagni, 1991) and in North America (Piore and Sabel, 1984; Saxenian, 1991, 1994), not only because of their capacity to compete on international markets as well as (or even better than) large firms, but also because they turned out to be significant wellsprings of product and process innovations. As will be discussed in the rest of this section, the chief explanation for these places to be wellsprings of innovation is considered to be the presence of multiple localized networks, which enhance the diffusion of tacit knowledge and the circulation of contextual skills among co-located firms and institutions. This issue has been subject to the study of numerous scholars and schools of thought (see Boschma, 2005; Tödling et al., 2009), among which are: the innovative milieux and 'collective learning' approach (Aydalot and Keeble, 1988; Camagni, 1991; Lawson and Lorenz, 1999; Capello and Faggian, 2005); the regional innovation system approach (Cooke, 2001, 2008; Cassiolato et al., 2003); the Italian school of industrial districts (Bellandi, 1989; Belussi and Gottardi, 2000); the California school of economic geography (Storper, 1997; Scott, 1998); and the regional economists' tradition of localized knowledge spillovers (Jaffe et al., 1993; Audretsch and Feldman, 1996). However, in my view, all these different streams do overlap to a certain extent with respect to the mechanisms that have been associated with the formation of innovation networks, which are discussed below:

1. Market relationships. Regional clusters of firms are typically characterized by networks formed through market mechanisms (Storper, 1997: 'traded interdependencies'), based on user–producer production linkages, on the mobility of skilled workers, or on the generation of spin-off firms. These networks have been considered a significant channel for the diffusion of knowledge and for the generation of interorganizational innovations in regions and subregional areas (Saxenian, 1991; Almeida and Kogut, 1999; Morgan, 1999). The diffusion of knowledge through local market linkages is facilitated by the geographical proximity of firms and other organizations, which eases the transfer of tacit knowledge and promotes innovation accordingly. For this reason, scholars have at times implicitly assumed that market and innovation networks are almost overlapping phenomena (Gelsing, 1992, 117).
2. Social ties. What really seems to make a difference in regions and subregional areas are networks originating from non-market relationships, and stemming from the cultural and social proximity of entrepreneurs and workers of a given regional area. Traditional accounts of Italian industrial districts are based on the idea that social relationships – based on kinship, friendship and, more generally, on common historical roots – coexist with market relationships. Becattini (1990) defines the Italian industrial district as a 'socio-territorial entity which is characterised by the active presence of both a community of people and a population of firms in one naturally and historically bounded area' (p. 38). In line with most of the organizational sociology literature, the presence of social ties is considered to reduce transaction costs and thus increase the efficiency of district firms. In addition, the presence of a social glue between the actors of a district is considered to favour processes of cooperation, leading to the formation of interorganizational innovation networks. As suggested by Dei Ottati in a work about Italian industrial districts, 'it is the cooperative dimension, reflected in the inter-personal and inter-organisational relations occurring in the district, that allows the division of innovative labour among a multiplicity of actors – a process that can be named "collective innovation"' (adapted and translated from Dei Ottati, 1995). Social ties are a predominant explanation in the formation of innovation networks in most of the leading schools of thought or approaches to the study of regional economies. Among many others, Storper (1997) includes this dimension in the famous concept of 'untraded interdependencies'; while Saxenian (1994) uses it to describe the way engineers interact with each other in the high-tech cluster of Silicon Valley.
3. Policy-driven ties. Beside spontaneous processes of collective innovation related to the presence of market and/or social networks, scholars have emphasized the

importance of public institutions and policies in fostering the formation of innovation networks at the regional level (see works on regional innovation systems
by Cooke et al., 1997; Cooke, 2001, 2008; see also Bianchi and Bellini, 1991) and
the subregional level (see works on local innovation systems by Mytelka, 2000;
Cassiolato et al., 2003).

All these studies have contributed to generate an incredibly rich and descriptive
account of 'innovation networks' – although rarely named as such – in regional and
subregional areas. They have thoroughly described the collective mechanisms through
which innovation is generated as well as the factors that facilitate the formation of innovation networks (geographical proximity, socio-economic relations, market linkages,
policies, and so on), generating a conceptual link between these factors and a number of
beneficial effects for firms and regions in general (efficiency gains, reduction of transaction costs, innovation). However, these studies have some important limitations. They
have, by and large, been based on a deductive approach, rarely demonstrating the
causal relations between the structural organization of interfirm linkages (networks),
their drivers and/or expected positive or negative results (Gordon, 1991, 176). Rather,
they have used 'networks' as a generic and broad interpretative factor of the positive
relationship between geography and innovation, often leading to the generalization that
the denser the networks the better for the economic growth and innovation of the region
or cluster (exceptions to this view include Grabher, 1993; Scott, 1998). This is in line
with Grabher (2006), who suggests that: 'although networks were rarely theorized in an
explicit fashion, they denoted an integral ingredient in these Marshallian accounts that
envisioned networks mainly in a rather generic sense as a shorthand for all sorts of ties
that did not adhere to a straightforward market logic' (p. 172). Similarly, Glückler (2007)
points out that much of the use of networks in economic geography has often been meta-
phorical and little formalized. Recent contributions have addressed these limitations
and are opening up a new way for measuring and assessing the importance of networks
for innovation in regions and subregional areas, as discussed in the section that follows.

INNOVATION NETWORKS WITH A REGIONAL PERSPECTIVE: NEW APPROACHES

Dissatisfied by the existing approaches to the study of innovation networks, in recent
years scholars have proposed a methodological shift in the analysis of networks. They
have searched for an inductive approach to research, which could explore more rigor-
ously the (causal) relationship between 'networks' and their drivers and/or consequences.
The methodological shift falls within the structuralist tradition and it is based on the
application of methods of social network analysis to regional studies – which has so far
been undertaken by only relatively few researchers (Reid et al., 2008, 347). Some of the
key findings of this literature (and directions for further research) are discussed below:

1.   Understanding the structure of innovation networks. The structure of a network
     refers to the way the linkages between the actors that form part of a network are
     distributed. This is not a trivial aspect because, as suggested by Newman (2003, 180):

'real networks are non-random in some revealing ways that suggest both possible mechanisms that could be guiding network formation, and possible ways in which we could exploit network structure to achieve certain aims'. On this basis, scholars have investigated the structural properties of innovation networks within and across regional clusters, and have found that different types of network structures may also lead to different types of rewards (and constraints) for its members. One of the key finding of this literature is that innovation-related knowledge is diffused in a rather structured, selective and uneven way within industrial clusters and it is thus not pervasive or collective as presumed by conventional theories – leaving a number of firms isolated from the local knowledge network, even when these are geographically proximate or have established other types of business linkages with the nearby firms (see works by Giuliani, 2003, 2007; and Morrison and Rabellotti, 2009 on the wine industry; Boschma and Ter Wal, 2007 on the footwear industry; Sammarra and Biggiero, 2008 on the aerospace industry; Steiner and Ploder, 2008 for a study of the region of Styria in Austria; and Ter Wal, 2008 for a study of information technology – IT – and life sciences co-inventor networks in Sophia-Antipolis).

2. Analysing the relationship between network position and firms' characteristics. The analysis of the structural properties of networks reveals that actors are not equally positioned within a network.[5] Some may be more central than others – for example by having more ties to other actors of the network – and this means that they can better access the valuable knowledge circulated through the network or exert power on the network members. The position of the actors in a network has been associated with firms' innovative performance (see for example McDermott, 2007; Giuliani, 2008) or with other firm-level characteristics (Steiner and Ploder, 2008).

3. Comparing different networks. Social network analysis permits the comparison of different types of networks formed by the same set of actors. Among other things, this helps to illuminate what type of networks (for example market, friendship, professional) are most likely to carry knowledge that is relevant to achieve innovative results. First attempts in this direction find that networks that have been conventionally considered as almost overlapping with knowledge networks (for example business networks) are instead very different (see for example Giuliani, 2007; see also Boschma and Ter Wal, 2007 and Morrison and Rabellotti, 2009 for the structural comparison of networks that are carriers of different types of knowledge). Further work is needed to unravel this question.

4. Analysing network evolution over time. A key innovative step ahead has to do with the study of network evolution over time. While previous studies have taken a historical or descriptive perspective on this (Guerrieri and Pietrobelli, 2001; Iammarino and McCann, 2006), recent research has explored whether network analysis could offer an alternative view. Because of the general lack of longitudinal network data at the regional level, scholars have so far used primarily co-inventor networks based on patent data (see for example Cantner and Graf, 2006 who study the evolution of the networks of inventors in Jena; Fleming and Frenken, 2007 who compare the evolution of co-inventor networks in Silicon Valley and Boston; Ter Wal, 2008 on IT and life sciences co-inventor networks in Sophia-Antipolis over a period of 30 years), while still very little is found on the evolution of informal networks (for an

exception see Giuliani, 2010 on a Chilean wine cluster). This is certainly one of the most promising open lines of research.

Because SNA is rapidly becoming adopted by economic geographers (and other scholars working on innovation networks with a regional perspective), it is fair to mention that this approach has been persistently criticized by many. One such criticism is that studies using social network analysis tend to give prominence to the structure of relationships, while neglecting processes, content of ties and characteristics of actors (see Smith-Doerr and Powell, 2003). For example, Gossling et al. (2007) argue that: 'although the structural account has produced many valuable insights on networks, it has an important drawback: it frequently treats network interaction and interactions in networks as a black box' (p. xiv). However, I maintain here that, as far as regional studies are concerned, the adoption of SNA and the subsequent concepts' simplification and operationalization have not (yet) taken a blind quantitative drift (in this respect, see the work by Fleming and Frenken, 2007).

CONCLUSIONS

This chapter has shown that networks are pervasive in the economy and that they significantly shape the behaviour of economic actors. In particular, it has reviewed studies that have looked at innovation as a social process, thus being the result of interorganizational networking. Emphasis has been placed on innovation networks within the context of regions and similar geographically bounded areas, where the literature has both implicitly and explicitly demonstrated the importance of networks for innovation. I would like to conclude this chapter with some words for (young) scholars who intend to explore this process using new methods, such as those of social network analysis, to study innovation networks in regional and subregional areas. SNA is currently becoming a real methodological fad, it has boomed in the field, to a certain extent because it is relatively easy to use, highly intuitive and permits nice visualizations of networks. However, it would be a real pity if the opportunities offered by using SNA get wasted by: (1) reducing it to a mere tool of network visualization and mapping, that has nothing to add either to theory or to more standard empirical analysis; or (2) taking the quantitative drift of mere structural analysis, forgetting context, content of ties and qualities of actors in the network.

NOTES

1. In this chapter I will use the expression 'regional' to indicate subnational territories, and 'subregional' to indicate industrial agglomerations like industrial districts, local systems of production, milieux, clusters, and so on. These concepts have been variously defined in the literature, although scholars have not necessarily agreed on definitions. As shown by Giuliani (2005) scholars have used different terms to express similar concepts and, in contrast, similar terms have been adopted to express very different concepts. For this reason, I will not attempt here to define each of these 'subregional' agglomerations, pointing the interested reader to more specific works on this.
2. An innovation network is defined here as a set of actors (individuals, firms and other organizations) linked to each other with the purpose of transferring or exchanging knowledge or technological assets that lead

to some form of innovative output. This broad definition includes for example formal networks based on research and development (R&D) agreements between firms; the transfer of knowledge through labour mobility or spin-offs; as well as informal networks based on the transfer of technical know-how or joint problem-solving. On this basis, through these networks, actors may search for radical as well as incremental innovations. This chapter focuses mostly on interorganizational networks.

3. For a comprehensive review, see Ozman (2009).
4. SNA is focused on uncovering the patterning of interaction of people and other types of actors, including organizations (firms, universities, and so on). It is based on the intuitive notion that the way an agent operates and succeeds depends in large part on how that agent is tied into the larger web of social connections. The study of the pattern of interaction is guided by formal theory organized in mathematical terms (essentially, graph theory), and it is grounded in the systematic analysis of empirical data.
5. The position of an actor in a network refers to the way it connects to other members of the network. Positions can be measured differently. One of the most frequent ways through which network position is evaluated is through degree of centrality, measured on the basis of the number of direct linkages established by an actor with other members of the network. Scholars have identified several other measures of centrality (see Wasserman and Faust, 1994) and also several other ways to identify distinguished positions in a network – as for example Burt (1992)'s structural holes.

REFERENCES

Ahuja, G. (2000), 'Collaboration networks, structural holes, and innovation: a longitudinal study', *Administrative Science Quarterly*, **45**, 425–55.

Allen, J., A. James and P. Gamlen (2007), 'Formal versus informal knowledge networks in R&D: a case study using social network', *R&D Management*, **37** (3), 179–96.

Allen, R.C. (1983), 'Collective invention', *Journal of Economic Behaviour and Organization*, **4**, 1–24.

Allen, T.J. (1977), *Managing the Flow of Technology: Technology Transfer and the Dissemination of Technological Information within the R&D Organization*, Cambridge, MA: MIT Press.

Almeida, P. and B. Kogut (1999), 'Localization of knowledge and the mobility of engineers in regional networks', *Management Science*, **45**, 905–16.

Amin, A. and N. Thrift (1992), 'Neo-Marshallian nodes in global networks', *International Journal of Urban and Regional Research*, **16**, 571–87.

Audretsch, D. and M.P. Feldman (1996), 'R&D spillovers and the geography of innovation and production', *American Economic Review*, **86**, 630–40.

Aydalot, P. and D. Keeble (1988), *High Technology Industry and Innovative Environments: The European Experience*, London, UK and New York, USA: Routledge.

Bagnasco, A. (1977), *Tre Italie: la problematica territoriale dello sviluppo italiano*. Bologna: Il Mulino.

Bathelt, H. (2005), 'Cluster relations in the media industry: exploring the "Distanced Neighbour" paradox in Leipzig', *Regional Studies*, **39** (1), 105–27.

Becattini, G. (1989), 'Sectors and/or districts: some remarks on the conceptual foundations of industrial economics', in E. Goodman, and J. Bamford (eds), *Small Firms and Industrial Districts in Italy*, London: Routledge, pp. 123–35.

Becattini, G. (1990), 'The Marshallian industrial district as a socio-economic notion', in F. Pyke, G. Becattini and W. Sengenberger (eds), *Industrial Districts and Inter-firm Co-operation in Italy*, Geneva: International Institute for Labour Studies, pp. 37–51.

Bell, M. and M. Albu (1999), 'Knowledge systems and technological dynamism in industrial clusters in developing countries', *World Development*, **27**, 1715–34.

Bellandi, M. (1989), 'Capacita' innovativa diffusa e sistemi locali di imprese', in G. Becattini (ed.), *Modelli Locali di Sviluppo*, Bologna: Il Mulino, pp. 149–72.

Belussi, F. and K. Caldari (2009), 'At the origin of the industrial district: Alfred Marshall and the Cambridge school', *Cambridge Journal of Economics*, **33** (2), 335–55.

Belussi, F. and G. Gottardi (2000), *Evolutionary Patterns of Local Industrial Systems: Towards a Cognitive Approach to the Industrial District*, Aldershot: Ashgate Publishing.

Bianchi, P. and N. Bellini (1991), 'Public policies for local networks of innovators', *Research Policy*, **20**, 487–97.

Bonte, W. and M. Keilbach (2005), 'Concubinage or marriage? Informal and formal cooperations for innovation', *International Journal of Industrial Organization*, **23** (3–4), 279–302.

Boschma R.A. (2005), 'Proximity and innovation: a critical assessment', *Regional Studies*, **39** (1), 61–74.

Boschma, R.J. and A.L.J. Ter Wal (2007), 'Knowledge networks and innovative performance in an industrial district: the case of a footwear district in the south of Italy', *Industry and Innovation*, **14** (2), 177–99.

Bouty, I. (2000), 'Interpersonal and interaction influences on informal resource exchanges between R&D researchers across organizational boundaries', *Academy of Management Journal*, **43**, 50–65.

Brusco, S. (1982), 'The Emilian model: productive decentralization and social integration', *Cambridge Journal of Economics*, **6**, 167–84.

Burt, R.S. (1992), *Structural Holes: The Social Structure of Competition*, Cambridge, MA: Harvard University Press.

Camagni, R. (1991), *Innovation Networks. Spatial Perspectives*, London, UK and New York, USA: Belhaven Press.

Cantner, U. and H. Graf (2006), 'The network of innovators in Jena: an application of social network analysis', *Research Policy*, **35** (4), 463–80.

Capello, R. (1999), 'Spatial transfer of knowledge in high technology milieux: learning versus collective learning processes', *Regional Studies*, **33**, 353–65.

Capello, R. and A. Faggian (2005), 'Collective learning and relational capital in local innovation processes', *Regional Studies*, **39** (1), 75–87.

Carrington, P.J., J. Scott and S. Wasserman (2005), *Models and Methods in Social Network Analysis*, New York: Cambridge University Press.

Carter, A.P. (1989), 'Know-how trading as economic exchange', *Research Policy*, **18**, 155–63.

Cassiolato J.E., H.M.M Lastres and M.L. Maciel (2003), *Systems of Innovation and Development: Evidence from Brazil*, Cheltenham, UK and Northampton, MA, USA: Edward Elgar.

Coase, R. (1937), 'The nature of the firm', *Economica*, **4** (16), 386–405.

Cooke P. (2001), 'Regional innovation systems, clusters and the knowledge economy', *Industrial and Corporate Change*, **10**, 945–74.

Cooke, P. (2008), 'Regional innovation systems: origin of the species', *International Journal of Technological Learning, Innovation and Development*, **1**, 393–409.

Cooke, P., M. Gomez Uranga and G. Etxebarria (1997), 'Regional innovation systems: institutional and organizational dimensions', *Research Policy*, **26**, 475–91.

Dei Ottati, G. (1995), *Tra mercato e comunità aspetti concettuali e ricerche empiriche sul distretto industriale*, Milan: Franco Angeli.

Fagerberg, J., B. Verspagen and N. von Tunzelmann (1994), *The Dynamics of Technology, Trade and Growth*, Aldershot, UK and Brookfield, VT, USA: Edward Elgar.

Fleming, L. and K. Frenken (2007), 'The evolution of inventor networks in the Silicon Valley and Boston regions', *Advances in Complex Systems*, **19**, 53–71.

Freeman, C. (1987), *Technology Policy and Economic Performance: Lessons from Japan*, London: Pinter.

Freeman, C. (1991), 'Networks of innovators: a synthesis of research issues', *Research Policy*, **20**, 499–514.

Freeman, C. and C. Perez (1988), 'Structural crises of adjustment, business cycles and investment behaviour' in G. Dosi, C. Freeman, R. Nelson, G. Silverberg and L. Soete (eds), *Technical change and Economic Theory*, London: Pinter, pp. 590–608.

Gelsing, L. (1992), 'Innovation and the development of industrial networks', in B.-Å. Lundvall (ed), *National Systems of Innovation: Towards a Theory of Innovation and Interactive Learning*, London: Pinter, pp. 116–28.

Giuliani, E. (2003), 'Knowledge in the air and its uneven distribution: a story of a Chilean wine cluster', paper presented at the DRUID Academy Winter 2003 PhD Conference, Aalborg, Denmark, 16–18 January.

Giuliani, E. (2005), 'Cluster absorptive capacity: why some clusters forge ahead and others lag behind', *European Urban and Regional Studies*, **12** (3), 269–88.

Giuliani, E. (2007), 'The selective nature of knowledge networks in clusters: evidence from the wine industry', *Journal of Economic Geography*, **7**, 139–68.

Giuliani, E. (2008), 'What drives innovative output in emerging clusters? Evidence from the wine industry', SPRU Electronic Working Papers, 169, Falmer, UK.

Giuliani, E. (2010), 'Network dynamics in regional clusters: the perspective of an emerging economy', Papers in Evolutionary Economic Geography (PEEG) 1014, Section of Economic Geography, Utrecht University.

Giuliani, E. (2011), 'The role of technological gatekeepers in the growth of industrial clusters: evidence from Chile', *Regional Studies*, forthcoming.

Giuliani, E. and V. Arza (2009), 'What drives the formation of "valuable" university–industry linkages? Insights from the wine industry', *Research Policy*, **38**, 906–21.

Giuliani, E. and M. Bell (2005), 'The micro-determinants of meso-level learning and innovation: evidence from a Chilean wine cluster', *Research Policy*, **34** (1), 47–68.

Gluckler, J. (2007), 'Economic geography and the evolution of networks', *Journal of Economic Geography*, **7** (5), 619–34.

Gordon, R. (1991), 'Innovation, industrial networks and high technology regions', in R. Camagni (ed.), *Innovation Networks: Spatial Perspectives*, London, UK and New York, USA: Belhaven Press, pp. 174–95.

Gossling, T., L. Oerlemans and R. Jansen (2007), *Inside Networks: A Process View on Multi-organisational Partnerships, Alliances and Networks*, Cheltenham, UK and Northampton, MA, USA: Edward Elgar.

Grabher, G. (1993), 'The weakness of strong ties: the lock-in regional development in the Ruhr area', in G. Grabher (ed.), *The Embedded Firm*, Oxford: Routledge, pp. 255–77.

Grabher, G. (2006), 'Trading routes, bypasses, and risky intersections: mapping the travels of 'networks' between economic sociology and economic geography', *Progress in Human Geography*, **30** (2), 163–89.

Granovetter, M. (1985), 'Economic action and social structure: the problem of embeddedness', *American Journal of Sociology*, **91**, 481–510.

Guerrieri, P. and C. Pietrobelli (2001), 'Models of industrial clusters' evolution and changes in technological regimes', in P. Guerrieri, S. Iammarino and C. Pietrobelli (eds), *The Global Challenge to Industrial Districts: Small and Medium-Sized Enterprises in Italy and Taiwan*, Cheltenham, UK and Northampton, MA, USA: Edward Elgar, pp. 899–914.

Gulati, R. (1995), 'Does familiarity breed trust? The implications of repeated ties for contractual choices in alliances', *Academy of Management Journal*, **38** (1), 85–112.

Hagardon, A. and R.I. Sutton (1997), 'Technology brokering and innovation in a product development firm', *Administrative Science Quarterly*, **42** (4), 716–49.

Hagedoorn, J. (1993), 'Understanding the rationale of strategic technology partnering: interorganizational modes of cooperation and sectoral differences', *Strategic Management Journal*, **14**, 371–85.

Hagedoorn, J. (2002), 'Inter-firm R&D partnerships: an overview of major trends and patterns since 1960', *Research Policy*, **31** (4), 477–92.

Iammarino, S. and P. McCann (2006), 'The structure and evolution of industrial clusters: transactions, technology and knowledge spillovers', *Research Policy*, **35**, 1018–36.

Jaffe, A.B., M. Trajtenberg and R. Henderson (1993), 'Geographic localization of knowledge spillovers as evidence from patent citations', *Quarterly Journal of Economics*, **188**, 577–98.

Lawson, C. and E. Lorenz (1999), 'Collective learning, tacit knowledge and regional innovative capacity', *Regional Studies*, **33** (4), 305–17.

Lissoni, Francesco (2008), 'Academic inventors as brokers: an exploratory analysis of the KEINS database', CESPRI Working Papers 213, CESPRI, Centre for Research on Innovation and Internationalisation, Universita' Bocconi, Milan, Italy.

Lundvall, B.-Å. (1988), 'Innovation as an interactive process: from user–producer interaction to the national system of innovation', in G. Dosi, C. Freeman, R. Nelson, G. Silverberg and L. Soete (eds), *Technical Change and Economic Theory*, London: Pinter, pp. 349–69.

Marshall, A. (1920), *Principles of Economics*, London: Macmillan.

Maskell, P., H. Bathelt and A. Malmberg (2006), 'Building global knowledge pipelines: the role of temporary clusters', *European Planning Studies*, **14**, 997–1013.

McDermott, Gerald (2007), 'The politics of institutional renovation and economic upgrading: recombining the vines that bind in Argentina', *Politics and Society*, **35** (1), 103–43.

Morgan, K. (1999), 'The learning region: institutions, innovation and regional renewal', *Regional Studies*, **31** (5), 491–503.

Morrison, A. and R. Rabellotti (2009), 'Knowledge dissemination and informal contacts in an Italian wine local system', PRIN Working Papers 1, Dipartimento di Scienze Economiche, Bologna University, Bologna.

Mowery, D.C., J.E. Oxley and B.S. Silverman (1996), 'Strategic alliances and interfirm knowledge transfer', *Strategic Management Journal*, **17**, 77–91.

Mowery, D.C., J.E. Oxley and B.S. Silverman (1998), 'Technological overlap and interfirm cooperation: implications for the resource-based view of the firm', *Research Policy*, **27**, 507–23.

Mytelka, L. (2000), 'Local systems of innovation in a globalized world economy', *Industry and Innovation*, **77** (1), 15–32.

Newman, M.E.J. (2003), 'The structure and function of complex networks', *SIAM Review*, **45** (2), 167–256.

Nuvolari A. (2004), 'Collective invention during the British Industrial Revolution: the case of the Cornish pumping engine', *Cambridge Journal of Economics*, **28**, 347–63.

Owen-Smith, J. and W.W. Powell (2004), 'Knowledge networks as channels and conduits: the effects of spillovers in the Boston biotechnology community', *Organization Science*, **15**, 5–21.

Ozman, M. (2009), 'Inter-firm networks and innovation: a survey of literature', *Economics of Innovation and New Technology*, **18** (1), 39–67.

Pavitt, K. (1984), 'Sectoral patterns of technical change: towards a taxonomy and a theory', *Research Policy*, **13**, 343–73.

Pietrobelli, C. and R. Rabellotti (2007), *Upgrading to Compete. Global Value Chains, SMEs and Clusters in Latin America*, Cambridge MA: Harvard University Press

Piore, M.J. and C.F. Sabel (1984), *The Second Industrial Divide: Possibility for Prosperity*, New York: Basic Books.

Powell, W.W. (1990), 'Neither market nor hierarchy: network forms of organization', *Research in Organizational Behavior*, **12**, 295–336.

Powell, W.W., K.W. Koput and L. Smith-Doerr (1996), 'Interorganizational collaboration and the locus of innovation: networks of learning in biotechnology', *Administrative Science Quarterly*, **41**, 106–45.

Reagans, R. and B. McEvily (2003), 'Network structure and knowledge transfer: the effects of cohesion and range, *Administrative Science Quarterly*, **48**, 240–67.

Reid, N., B.W. Smith and M.C. Carroll (2008), 'Cluster regions: a social network perspective', *Economic Development Quarterly*, **22** (4), 345–52.

Sammarra, A. and L. Biggiero (2008), 'Heterogeneity and specificity of inter-firm knowledge flows in innovation networks', *Journal of Management Studies*, **45** (4), 800–829.

Sattler, H., S. Schrader and C. Lüthje (2003), 'Informal cooperation in the US and Germany: cooperative managerial capitalism vs. competitive managerial capitalism in interfirm information trading', *International Business Review*, **12** (3), 273–95.

Saxenian, A. (1991), 'The origins and dynamics of production networks in Silicon Valley', *Research Policy*, **20**, 423–37.

Saxenian, A. (1994), *Regional Advantage Culture and Competition in Silicon Valley and Route 128*, Cambridge, MA: Harvard University Press.

Saxenian, A. (2006), *The New Argonauts: Regional Advantage in a Global Economy*, Cambridge, MA: Harvard University Press.

Saxenian, A.L. and J.-Y. Hsu (2001), 'The Silicon Valley–Hisinchu connection: technical communities and industrial upgrading', *Industrial and Corporate Change*, **10** (4), 893–920.

Schmitz, H. (ed.) (2004), *Local Enterprises in the Global Economy: Issues of Governance and Upgrading*, Cheltenham, UK and Northampton, MA, USA: Edward Elgar.

Schrader, S. (1991), 'Informal technology transfer between firms: cooperation through informal trading', *Research Policy*, **20**, 153–70.

Scott, A.J. (1998), *Regions and the World Economy: The Coming Shape of Global Production, Competition and Political Order*, Oxford: Oxford University Press.

Silverberg, G. and B. Verspagen (1994), 'Learning, innovation and economic growth: a long-run model of industrial dynamics', *Industrial and Corporate Change*, **3**, 119–223.

Singh, J. (2005), 'Collaborative networks as determinants of knowledge diffusion patterns', *Management Science*, **51** (5), 756–70.

Smith-Doerr, L. and W.W. Powell (2003), 'Networks and economic life', in N.J. Smelser and R. Swedberg (eds), *The Handbook of Economic Sociology*, Princeton, NJ: Russell Sage Foundation/Princeton University Press, pp. 379–402.

Steiner, M. and M. Ploder (2008), 'Structure and strategy within heterogeneity: multiple dimensions of regional networking', *Regional Studies*, **46** (2), 793–815.

Storper, M. (1997), *The Regional World Territorial Development in a Global Economy*, New York: Guilford Press.

Ter Wal, A.L.J. (2008), 'Cluster emergence and network evolution: a longitudinal analysis of the inventor network in Sophia Antipolis', paper presented at the 25th DRUID Summer Conference, Copenhagen.

Ter Wal, A.L.J. and R.J. Boschma (2007), 'Co-evolution of firms, industries and networks in space', Papers in Evolutionary Economic Geography # 07.07, Urban and Regional Research Centre, Utrecht University.

Tödtling, F., P. Lehner and A. Kaufman (2009), 'Do different types of innovation rely on specific kinds of knowledge interactions?', *Technovation*, **29**, 59–71.

Uzzi, B. and R. Lancaster (2003), 'Relational embeddedness and learning: the case of bank loan managers and their clients', *Management Science*, **49**, 383–99.

von Hippel, E. (1987), 'Cooperation between rivals: informal know-how trading', *Research Policy*, **16**, 291–302.

von Hippel, E. (1988), *The Sources of Innovation*, New York: Oxford University Press.

Wasserman, S. and K. Faust (1994), *Social Network Analysis: Methods and Applications*. Cambridge, MA: Cambridge University Press.

Williamson, O. (1975), *Markets and Hierarchies, Analysis and Antitrust Implications: A Study in the Economics of Internal Organization*, New York: Free Press.

Zaheer, A. and G.G. Bell (2005), 'Benefiting from network position: firm capabilities, structural holes, and performance', *Strategic Management Journal*, **26**, 809–25.

Zucker, L.G. and M.R. Darby (1996), 'Star scientists and institutional transformation: patterns of invention and innovation in the formation of the biotechnology industry', *Proceedings of the National Academy of Sciences*, **93**, 12709–16.

13 From regional anchors to anchoring
Lisa De Propris and Olivier Crevoisier

INTRODUCTION

The current debate on regional development and innovation dynamics often refers to the metaphor of the 'anchor' to describe a tension or a balance between the local and the global forces shaping economic activities. In this chapter, a critical review of the current literature will show how this term is used in different ways depending on the correspondence and interplay between the local and global scales.

One can distinguish a first meaning in which anchoring consists of the historical position of a production system within a region due to a process of (mainly local) accumulation of knowledge and capital (for a recent review, see Becattini et al., 2009). A second idea emerged when the necessity to understand the location dynamics of new industries and what factors were determining industries' location choices became a prime concern for regional growth (Feldman, 2003). In this case, the focus shifted from the endogenous process of cumulated firm capacity to the drivers and players able to attract a critical mass of entrepreneurial vibrancy to a particular place and to retain it. Finally, we would argue that with today's (alleged) hypermobility of capital, knowledge and people, anchoring is becoming more related to the permanent interplay of economic activities across space, namely within and between places, than to any local accumulation.

SYSTEMIC INNOVATION, INDUSTRIAL AND REGIONAL TRAJECTORIES

The concept of 'regional anchors' was first coined by Feldman (2003) as she wanted to understand how emerging industries, like biotechnologies, could be anchored in a particular region, trigger a process of firms' clustering and become, thereby, engines of regional growth. Indeed the context of this contribution is the debate that throughout the 1990s and early 2000 developed around the forms and the dynamics of localized processes of innovation and learning. In the literature these were described by four main models: industrial districts, clusters, innovative milieux and regional innovation systems. These in different ways are organizational models that describe localized systems of firms and interfirm networking able to create the socio-economic conditions leading to superior innovation performance.

In a post-Fordist economy where the segmentation of production processes underpins flexible and modular value chains, the disintegration of production functions mirrors a disintegration of knowledge and competences. So much so that high levels of functional specialization necessarily lead to fast-moving and cumulative processes of learning, especially in relation to tacit knowledge. At the same time, the systemic nature of production reflects the systemic nature of the innovation process across firms. Indeed, firms do not innovate in isolation, but contribute to a collective process of learning, advancement and adoption.

The common ground across the four models above is an understanding that a critical mass of specialized firms in a context of systemic production could bring benefits thanks to external and agglomeration economies. These, in fact, reduce the transaction costs associated with firms' networking, increase firms' efficiencies – for instance through pecuniary externalities (for example pooling of specialized labour and the sharing of common inputs) – and drive sustained radical and incremental innovations. Nevertheless, these models differ, both in the way the place, the industry and the community is argued to co-evolve or not, that is, the determinants of their trajectory; and in the way the systemic 'plumbing' of information and knowledge transfers and spillovers is able to absorb, adopt and integrate the knowledge and information coming into the system through its external 'pipelines'.

The so-called 'Marshallian industrial district' (MID) describes a model of a local production system where a localized industry is embedded in a community of people so that both co-evolve over time. An MID: 'has an economic and social identity shaped by an industrial atmosphere; the latter coinciding with a set of shared cognitive, moral and behavioural attitudes drawing on locally dense cultural interactions, and which orientate technical, human and relational investments towards forms consistent with local accumulation' (Becattini et al., 2009, xviii).

On the other hand, innovative milieux (IMs) can be defined as: 'sets of localised players in which interactions between players develop thanks to multilateral learning processes. The latter generate innovation specific externalities and converge towards more and more performing forms of common resources management' (Maillat et al., 1993). In this model, rich learning interactions develop primarily among local players. External links are seen as less frequent and above all monofunctional. Links between local players can be both mercantile and non-mercantile relationships (Kebir and Crevoisier, 2008). The emphasis on the extension and interconnectivity of the networks of information and knowledge is particularly relevant in this model.

In the MID and IM models, the processes of knowledge creation and transfer build on existing competences and embedded knowledge because their life cycle starts with an 'accident of history' in a particular place. Indeed one of the most debated issues within these streams of literature has been how they can be created. Indeed in both cases, the drivers of their innovation processes are assets or resources that are 'embedded' within a place and within the community in that place. These resources coincide with the 'knowledge in the air' suggested by Marshall and the 'shared know-how' in industrial districts; while more recently, Kebir and Crevoisier (2008) argue that:

> culture can be distinguished from the other resources that are mobilised because of its intrinsic link to the societies and communities that produce it . . . Society, culture, etc. thus appear as substrates of economic factors while at the same time they are subject to modification by the economy. In this context, culture produces the knowledge and practices that are necessary in order to establish social links, rules, codes of conduct and the forms of language needed in order for exchanges to take place. (p. 307)

Systemic learning and innovation processes are taking place with respect to activities (sectors or technologies) that are embedded in the socio-economic fabric of places;

they draw, build and expand, combining internal, cumulated and tacit knowledge with external more codified information.

The IM and MID models have, however, been shown to be somewhat inadequate when trying to explain the emergence of new industries and evolutionary patterns that can take a new industry to locate in some place rather than elsewhere. At the zenith of the debate on the knowledge economy, we witnessed not only a change in the production organization paradigm with the demise of the Fordist model and the emergence of flexible specialized models (Piore and Sabel, 1984), but also successive and fast-moving shifts in the technological paradigm itself. Indeed, the focus on high-tech industries and, at the same time, the rise of new industries, like biotechnology, have both suggested that the economic growth of localities could be shaped for the future regardless of their past in some sense. In other words, the position acquired by a region thanks to past learning would no longer matter, or may even become a disadvantage for the initial rooting of a new industry.

Models of local production organization that could endorse this view were Porter's clusters and the Cooke's regional innovation systems (RISs). Clusters are geographical agglomerations of small and large firms, specialized in related industries comprising buyer–supplier networks in a context of cooperation and trust (Porter, 1990). Their key features are the spatial co-location and vertical disintegration of the value chain; which means that they can represent a model of local organization where the industry is not in symbiosis with the place, but can be added to a place. It could be argued that any firm agglomeration can be to some extent a cluster, insofar as it contains a set of input–output relations, and this explains why the term has been widely used to label phenomena that below the surface are very different. There is no doubt that the fact that conceptually clusters can be set up in a proactive way has enabled the term to be used to explain the genesis of some industries in some specific places. In other words, the cluster model provides a framework to understand and explain the emergence and accumulation of one or a few related new industries in a particular place.

The RIS model provides a more sophisticated framework to explain not only the geographical clustering of industries but also the systemic nature of their innovation processes by spelling out the synergies between firms and the innovation infrastructure (Braczyk et al., 1998). The latter is particularly apt to present a possible path for the emergence of high-tech localized industries and to explain their dynamics. In RISs, the nodes of the innovation process are the firms and the innovation-intensive institutions, either public or private, that form the innovation infrastructure. In its conceptualization, an RIS combines local and 'wider, global innovation interactions' (Cooke, 2001) that enable the systemic innovation process to be constantly fed by new ideas and knowledge coming from outside so as to remain on the innovation frontier.

One can notice that these representations of regional trajectories were elaborated at the end of the 1980s, when production factors were mainly considered as immobile. More precisely, in the four models, capital is considered as a pure follower of entrepreneurial dynamism and accumulates somewhat automatically within the region. Collective knowledge is considered as the main externality and as it is collective, it cannot move. This accumulation through history is the base of technological and regional trajectories (Crevoisier and Jeannerat, 2009).

With growing concern over technological change and the emergence of new industries, these models could partially provide explanations by integrating entrepreneurial projects and the local capacity to appropriate knowledge generated elsewhere. Development is still driven by the past, but further steps depend highly on the local capacity to combine traditional knowledge with new technologies.

ATTRACTING THROUGH SPACE AND ANCHORING EMERGING INDUSTRIES

The technological leaps that have characterized the last couple of decades to 2010 have seen the emergence of completely new industries including information and communication technology (ICT) and, more recently, biotechnologies. The latter in particular has attracted the attention of Feldman (see Feldman, 1999, 2003; Feldman and Lowe, 2007; Lowe and Feldman, 2008), who has taken this new sector as an opportunity to understand how regional economic development can be driven by the 'anchoring' of a new and growing industry. As it was becoming increasingly accepted that the presence of competitive local production systems contributed to regional growth and competitiveness (Porter, 1990), scholars like Feldman started to question 'how clusters are formed, how new industries become anchored in a local economy and, as a result, how locations may reap the resulting economic rewards' (Feldman, 2003, 311). Indeed since these new industries were embryonic and still footloose, the question was to understand how they could be encouraged to root in one place rather than another. This was particularly relevant for those regions lacking some form of pre-existing competitive advantage and eager to attract a critical mass of firms and innovation activities that could finally grow into a regionally immobile competitive advantage.

According to Feldman (2003), the agglomeration of firms in a sector in a particular place can be engineered by means of a 'regional anchor'; her argument stems from the 'anchor tenant hypothesis'. She uses the metaphor of the shopping centre to build her argument. She argues that when one looks at what determines the success of a shopping centre, one finds that it often depends on the presence of an 'anchor tenant' which is able to guarantee a certain volume of customers for itself and, more importantly, for the other tenants – smaller, less known or less attractive brands. The anchor tenant creates a positive externality for all the shops in the shopping centre; in fact it acts as a magnet both for the other tenants which see their business guaranteed by the critical mass of customers the anchor tenant is able to attract and, of course, as just mentioned, it is a magnet for customers.

The anchor hypothesis proposed by Feldman is conceptually attractive in the way it models almost a mechanical synergy between the presence of a regional anchor and the emergence and growth of a clustered new industry. The role of anchor tenants in a regional system of innovation can be assumed by universities and government labs (Feldman, 2003) if and when they have the ability to generate start-ups or attract firms. Her application of this hypothesis to the biotech industry in Cambridge, MA and Berkeley, CA (Feldman and Lowe, 2007; Lowe and Feldman, 2008), and of the ICT industry in Washington, DC makes it all the more relevant. Other studies have produced similar findings. Sable (2007) looks at the development of the biotech industries in San Diego and Boston and finds that in both cases local universities played key roles as anchoring players, especially as hubs of scientific knowledge, catalysts of social network-ing (social capital) between entrepreneurs and the academia, and engines of innovation spillovers; indeed: 'the basic science base in the university milieu is also a magnet for biotechnology entrepreneurs' (Sable, 2007, 40). Mayer (2006) on the other hand argues that the growth of the Portland's high-tech industries was driven not by universities but by two lead firms, Intel and TekTronix: one an external firm whose location in Portland generated significant spin-offs, and the other an indigenous large firm whose downsizing spawned start-ups. Indeed, regional anchors trigger a process of knowledge specializa-tion and regional agglomeration as they attract talents, expertise, innovations and new firms related to a particular sector. This process aims, therefore, to create a regional competitive advantage where before there was none, and this can be done because it is driven by a new industry which in itself constitutes a technological leap. Feldman and Lowe (2007) argue that regulations can also act as catalysts stimulating and steering the agglomeration of an industry in a particular place through setting up a favourable business environment for it.

However, how sustainable is regional growth if it depends uniquely on the regional anchor? Indeed, Feldman (2003) herself is aware that 'if the anchor leaves the mall, the viability of the smaller stores is threatened' (p. 322). This means that the ability of a regional anchor to trigger a process of regional specialization that leads to sustainable regional growth is likely to depend on the ability of a place not only to attract such a firm, but more importantly to retain it.

The current literature has provided ample evidence of how attempts to fast-track regional economic development through 'flagship catalysts' can prove to be short-lived. There is some evidence that, for instance, technopoles have in some cases failed to deliver the expected regional growth, because they have been like 'cathedrals in the desert' (Cooke, 2001), that is, they have been unable to set up linkages and synergies with the contiguous economy.

Another route to leapfrog technological change and to trigger the development of an industry in a region has been through the location of a foreign firm; the technological know-how and the international linkages of the latter are often expected to generate localized dynamic spillovers through the creation of a local supply chain (De Propris and Driffield, 2006). Numerous examples demonstrate that the footloose nature of the foreign multinational firm prevents it from totally rooting in the local economy, especially if there is a technological gap between the foreign firm and the host economy (ibid.), since the latter is unable to engage in a mutually dependent relationship. In the case of Ireland, the location of multinational firms has been short-lived and with a less than expected impact on the local economy.

It could be argued, therefore, that the sustainability of the 'anchor tenant' à la Feldman very much depends on the strategic rationale motivating the attraction of the catalyst firms: whether this is short-term employment creation or long-term sustained industrial growth. Besides, it could be suggested that the anchoring of a new industry to a particular place also depends on the knowledge and network infrastructures underpin-ning the local system of innovation. In other words, in order to be effective, a proactive attempt to promote regional growth through regional anchors must be coupled with the enhancement and strengthening of the regional innovation system. This means support-ing the synergies and interdependences between universities, the government and the business community (also referred to as the 'triple helix'; see Etzkowitz and Leydesdorff, 2000), since these cement and underpin the systemic nature of the innovation process.

The argument is, therefore, that if regional growth is pursued through the anchoring of a new industry, this means transforming mobile factors into immobile factors to sustain a local process of firm agglomeration and knowledge accumulation. In fact, in a global context where products, services, labour, capital and knowledge move quickly and freely, regional competitive advantages coincide with locally differentiated and distinctive resources and competences. This means: embedding skilled labour and capital; transforming codified into tacit knowledge; supporting dense and deep local networking that mirrors knowledge and information sharing; and creating hard and soft infrastructures for innovation. Clearly, such regional innovation hot spots are not isolated, but have constantly to interface with other innovation systems in the same or related sectors. Moreover, such a local capacity to innovate, that is, to build collective differentiating knowledge and resources, has to be conceptualized as an endogenous, autonomous entrepreneurial force. Otherwise, there is no explanation as to why development occurs in such a place and not elsewhere.

EMBEDDEDNESS AND MOORING

Feldman's contribution describes 'anchoring' as a process that enables a place to secure the presence of a catalyst player (or of an otherwise mobile resource) able to generate knowledge externalities which almost mechanically germinate through knowledge spillovers leading to new firms' formation. Key to this view is the idea that anchoring means attracting, harbouring or pegging a resource that could otherwise move elsewhere. Nevertheless, we would argue that this anchoring process cannot occur in a vacuum; rather there exist pre-existing and embedded layers of social, institutional and economic linkages that characterize the fabric of the local place and qualify its ability to engage with the catalyst firm.

The term 'embeddedness' can be defined as the presence in a system or community of personal relations and structures so as to activate trust-based transactions. It is well known that the latter underpins the cooperative context where innovation takes place and flourishes. Indeed innovation is more and more proceeding through knowledge spillovers and shared tacit information; here cooperation and trust enable sustained and dense knowledge flows.

The superior performance of such highly innovative places (MID and IM) has attracted outside firms to look into locating there in order to access knowledge and competences which would otherwise be unreachable, and hence a 'locational' advantage in Dunning's well-known ownership–location–internalization framework. Indeed, it is well known that the casual and spontaneous sharing of tacit knowledge and the inevitable knowledge spillovers decay with distance from the centre of the system. This means that co-location is necessary to be part of this systemic and geographically bound microcosmos. This explains why such places have attracted outside firms, interested in sourcing competences and knowledge (De Propris et al., 2008).

If one wishes to carry on with the nautical metaphor, such places are attractive to firms who are interested in 'mooring' in a certain place to access its embedded knowledge.

Whether mooring is sufficient to become part of the socio-economic community of these places and to penetrate its unwritten rules and codes so as to benefit from wider innovation, is debatable. Current studies suggest that location choices driven by knowledge sourcing embody a high degree of commitment on behalf of the multinational firm, because only an 'embedded' behaviour in reality enables true and long-lasting knowledge externalities to bear fruit. Embedded local communities can be cautious of new, outside players and request evidence of commitment to avoid 'hit and run' strategies. The location and 'anchoring' of a lead firm in a context where there is already a system of dynamic innovation can be extremely beneficial to activate technological leaps as 'imported' knowledge is accessed (via the lead firm), adjusted and combined (across the local knowledge basis) with existing and embedded competences.

ANCHORING AS THE CORE OF TERRITORIAL DEVELOPMENT IN A MOBILE WORLD

When related to embeddedness, anchoring appears to relate to the existence of some social fabric compared with economic and innovation processes. Feldman stresses the relevance of external links in a world characterized by mobile firms, knowledge and people. Paradoxically, as resources and production factors have been able to move increasingly more freely, it has become crucial for local systems to have the capacity to engage with these (potentially) mobile factors. In this framework, anchoring coincides precisely with the capability of a local system to access, interact and 'capture' knowledge, information, ideas or any form of tangible and intangible asset from other places or other firms to be fed into its local innovation system.

The concept of anchoring is also present in the current literature in relation to the challenges that local production systems face as globalization forces them to be more open, outward-looking and multi-located than ever. In this stream of literature, anchoring assumes a different meaning from the one introduced by Feldman, in that it relates the image of anchoring to the locally embedded nature of tacit knowledge and learning, which are key elements of firms' and regions' innovation processes. In this alternative perspective, anchoring coincides with the deep and complex roots that businesses have in a local context, whilst at the same time engaging in open, multi-local networks. In this context, the notion of anchoring must be distinguished from that of mobility if we wish to understand the processes of learning within space. Mobility is usually understood as a physical movement across space; on the other hand, anchoring is the other, inseparable face of mobility. Indeed, mobility means the relocation of economic activities to other places, or the interspatial transfer of information and knowledge. To some extent, this suggests a separation between the 'spaces' involved. We argue, on the contrary, that anchoring refers to the fact there are forms of linkages and relations that can occur between a context of localized knowledge and its various elements during their immobile phase. In other words, relations develop and coexist at different geographical scales, whereby mobile – or potentially mobile – elements will maintain relations both with those elements that are immobile and rooted in a location, and with those that are outside it. Anchoring therefore becomes decisive, because the easier mobility becomes, the more crucial the reasons behind such mobility seem to be.

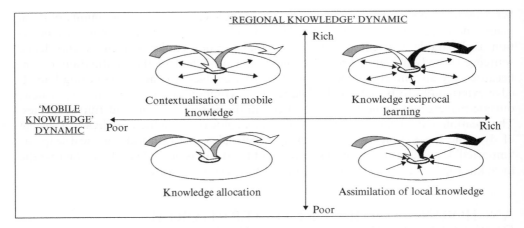

Source: Crevoisier and Jeannerat (2009).

Figure 13.1   A typology of regional knowledge anchoring capacities

The notion of anchoring (Berset and Crevoisier, 2006) is close but different to that of embeddedness. Embeddedness, in fact, refers to a condition where economic actors interact and relate to each other in a context that has a specific historical origin and development, as well as precise spatial coordinates. In other words, firms' embeddedness refers to their belonging to a certain place. Instead, anchoring embodies the idea that there exists an aspect of mobility between places, namely a tendency to open or a movement towards a 'new' context. For example, knowledge can move from the context where it is generated and 'embedded' to feed into another context's knowledge system. Anchoring is the way in which the outgoing knowledge interacts with the external knowledge in ways that necessarily impact on the initial embedded knowledge. This means that if we want to understand the mobility and anchoring of knowledge, we have to take into account the context in which knowledge is initially generated, the context of where it is transferred to and the way this knowledge evolves when interacting with its new context.

It can be argued that various contexts of local knowledge creation will mobilize and integrate mobile knowledge generated elsewhere in differing ways. In some places, for instance, mobile skilled workers may only come, work and leave without having learnt anything new from local people and without having taught anything new to them. This is a simple allocation among various places. On the contrary, some places may learn a great deal from people coming from elsewhere and may also provide a rich learning experience to those people. What becomes decisive is the local capacity to interact with mobile elements in a rich and complex manner (see Figure 13.1). One of the most crucial challenges currently facing knowledge-intensive regions is to gain a position 'on the global map' of knowledge flows, in particular ensuring the movement and anchoring of knowledge in their specific sectors.

In traditional cluster or innovation system policies, the rationale for policy-making has been to intervene in terms of the research and training infrastructure to provide skills and competences complementary to local activities, and to support the local provision of whatever set of knowledge is more needed and relevant for local firms. In other words, cluster policies have been seen as systemic (De Propris, 2007) and space-bound. In reality, this alone might not be sufficient to ensure the competitiveness of local production systems, as the self-contained nature of their innovative dynamism is increasingly less relevant. In a world where it is becoming easier and easier to mobilize very different, and complementary, knowledge from other places, the focus should be on building local capacities to access and mobilize external knowledge.

The anchoring role of lead firms here is to dovetail the local circuits of embedded and cumulative competences and specializations with the global circuit knowledge creation and transfer. In this framework, the anchor firm becomes a firm that is secured in the local system whilst being able at the same time to network globally through two-way channels, especially of knowledge. Giblin (2011) suggests that lead firms that are able to engage with the local and global networks act more as enablers than gatekeepers, and their role is to 'pollinate' the local context with inputs, ideas and innovations.

A good example of this is the Swiss micro-technology industry. It mainly consists of integrating various technologies, including micro-electronics, optics, micro-mechanics and material sciences, into one miniaturized system. The country is far too small to produce all the competences needed, therefore mobilizing external knowledge is key to the competitiveness of such a sector. The development of this industry is the result of a combination of an embedded set of skills derived from the long Swiss tradition in watch-making with a new set of knowledge accessed and captured through distant connections with complementary places and clusters.

As Dankbaar (2007) explains, enterprises that simply delocalize many of their activities due to cost-saving strategies or to access competencies have some difficulties, for example, in maintaining their 'core knowledge'; this is knowledge that their delocalized partners are seeking to anchor. These dynamics are becoming a major challenge for mobility and anchoring strategies. Local institutional capacities of value creation, value enhancement and value 'capture' (Coe et al., 2008) determine the ways in which local innovation systems realize knowledge mobility and anchoring.

In such an approach, regional development is no longer centred on integrated production systems or value chains. Today, nearly all value chains are organized across space, often spreading across several continents. Long-distance interactions develop rapidly and help increase local specialization into global production networks.[1] Multiscalar and multispatial relations become crucial. Of course, these relations are neither compulsorily cooperative nor egalitarian (Weller, 2006). Regional competitiveness relies heavily on the local capacity to take part in such long-distance interactions.

CONCLUDING REMARKS

Despite the vibrant debate of the concept of anchoring and its various interpretations, it still remains an intriguing and controversial issue. The metaphor has captured the imagination of scholars troubled by the challenges and opportunities that globalization is offering, especially for the economic development of regions and places. The sharp increase in the mobility of production factors over the period 1990–2010 has radically changed the scale and the 'space' of innovation and of capital accumulation. Localities and regional systems that have been and are still developing along trajectories of cumulative innovation and knowledge, find themselves part of multiregional and multiscalar systems. Long-distance exchanges force economic actors to identify forms of proximities that are not geographical but are still able to generate comfortable relationships.

In this framework, anchoring provides a conceptual link between local and global. Feldman's conceptualization stresses the stability and stillness that the idea of 'dropping an anchor' depicts; on the other hand, anchoring could also be seen as the mobility to float whilst still having a firm anchor in the home place. Although this brief discussion has probably opened rather than closed the debate, it has hopefully provided a critical overview on the current views.

NOTE

1.　For more details, see the special issue of *Environment and Planning A* (2006); and a special issue of *Journal of Economic Geography* (2008).

REFERENCES

Becattini, G., M. Bellandi and L. De Propris (2009), 'Critical nodes and contemporary reflections on industrial districts: an introduction', in G. Becattini, M. Bellandi and L. De Propris (eds), *A Handbook of Industrial Districts*, Cheltenham, UK and Northampton, MA, USA: Edward Elgar, pp. xv–xxxv.

Berset, A. and O. Crevoisier (2006), 'Circulation of competencies and dynamics of regional production systems', *IJMS: International Journal on Multicultural Societies*, **8** (1), 61–83.

Braczyk, H., P. Cooke and M. Heidenreich (1998), *Regional Innovation Systems*, London: UCL Press.

Coe, N., P. Dicken and M. Hess (2008), 'Global production networks: realizing the potential', *Journal of Economic Geography*, **8** (3), 271–95.

Cooke, P. (2001), 'Regional innovation systems, clusters and the knowledge economy', *Industrial and Corporate Change*, **10** (4), 945–74.

Crevoisier, O. and H. Jeannerat (2009), 'Territorial knowledge dynamics: from the proximity paradigm to the multi-location paradigm', *European Planning Studies*, **17** (8), 1223–41.

Dankbaar, B. (2007), 'Global sourcing and innovation: the consequences of losing both organizational and geographical proximity', *European Planning Studies*, **15** (2), 271–88.

De Propris, L. (2007), 'Reconciling cohesion and competitiveness through EU cluster policies?', *Policy Studies*, **28** (4), 327–45.

De Propris, L. and N. Driffield (2006), 'The importance of clusters for spillovers from foreign direct investment and technology sourcing', *Cambridge Journal of Economics*, **30** (2), 277–91.

De Propris, Menghinello S. and R. Sugden (2008), 'The internationalisation of production systems: embeddedness, openness and governance', *Entrepreneurship and Regional Development*, **20**, 493–515.

Environment and Planning A (2006), Theme Issue: *Global Production Networks*, **38** (7), 1193–1305.

Etzkowitz, H. and L. Leydesdorff (2000), 'The dynamics of innovation: from national systems and "Mode 2" to a Triple Helix of university–industry–government relations', *Research Policy*, **29**, 109–23.

Feldman, M. (1999), 'The new economics of innovation, spillovers and agglomeration: a review of empirical studies', *Economics of Innovation and New Technology*, **8**, 5–25.

Feldman, M. (2003), 'The locational dynamics of the US biotech industry: knowledge externalities and the anchor hypothesis', *Industry and Innovation*, **10** (3), 311–28.

Feldman, M. and N. Lowe (2007), 'Consensus from controversy: Cambridge's Biosafety Ordinance and the anchoring of the biotech industry', *European Planning Studies*, **16** (3), 395–410.

Giblin, M. (2011), 'Managing the global–local dimensions of clusters and the role of "lead" organisations: the contrasting cases of the software and medical technology clusters in the West of Ireland', *European Planning Studies*, **19** (1), 23–42.

Journal of Economic Geography (2008), Special Issue: *Global Production Networks: Debates and Challenges*, **8** (3), 267–440.

Kebir, L. and O. Crevoisier (2008), 'Cultural resources and regional development: the case of the cultural legacy of watchmaking', *European Planning Studies*, **16** (9), 1189–1205.

Lowe, N. and M. Feldman (2008), 'Constructing entrepreneurial advantage: consensus building, technological uncertainty and emerging industries', *Cambridge Journal of Regions, Economy and Society*, **1**, 265–84.

Maillat, D., M. Quévit and L. Senn (1993), 'Réseaux d'innovation et milieux innovateurs: Un pari pour le développement regional', Neuchâtel: GREMI, EDES.

Mayer, H. (2006), 'What is the role of universities in high-tech economic development? The case of Portland, Oregon, and Washington, DC', *Local Economy*, **21** (3), 292–315.

Piore, M. and C. Sabel (1984), *The Second Industrial Divide*, New York: Basic Books.

Porter, M. (1990), *The Competitive Advantage of Nations*, New York: Free Press.

Sable, M. (2007), 'The impact of the biotechnology industry on local economic development in the Boston and San Diego metropolitan areas', *Technological Forecasting and Social Change*, **74**, 36–60.

Weller, S. (2006), 'The embeddedness of global production networks: the impact of crisis in Fiji's garment export sector', *Environment and Planning A*, **38** (7), 1249–67.

PART III

REGIONAL INNOVATION
AND EVOLUTION

Introduction
Ron Boschma and Ron Martin

RELATEDNESS AND PATH-DEPENDENCE

Two recurring themes in this *Handbook* are relatedness of industry, by means of which regional growth is assisted, and path-dependence, by means of which it can be constrained. Exploration of the first is a relatively recent phenomenon, pioneered by Ron Boschma and Koen Frenken, but already it is a core body of theory and empirical research in evolutionary economic geography. The main mechanism by which relatedness influences regional growth is through knowledge transfer between firms, one result of which can be innovation. The key agents of such transfer are employees developing their careers by changing jobs in neighbouring areas and new companies being formed by the spin-off process that may also be a vehicle for innovations. Path-dependence is a more established concept arising in economic history, particularly the branch interested in the history of innovation. It has been analysed fruitfully by Ron Martin and colleagues in the context of evolutionary economic geography and particularly regional development, adaptation and change.

The authors of Chapter 14 indicate the pivotal position occupied by the idea of 'related variety' in evolutionary economic geography. Comparable to 'proximity' as presented in Chapter 20 of this *Handbook*, it has numerous dimensions, notably the cognitive, social, organizational, institutional and geographical. Much research effort is exercised in relation to both concepts, seeking to assess the relative importance of each in understanding, for example, the evolution of agglomerations or clusters, the core problematic of economic geography. In doing this, light is cast on the role of numerous other of the key process elements of interest to evolutionary economic geography, such as innovation, technology, knowledge spillovers, learning and the creation of new regional developmental pathways. In order to illustrate this, the authors take the two most frequently identified types of relatedness – geographical and cognitive – as their main focus. They then apply these perspectives to issues of externalities and regional growth, on the one hand, and technological change in new path creation, on the other.

With respect to externalities and regional growth, Boschma and Frenken note in Chapter 14 that a key research question has been the extent to which firms in agglomerations benefit most, if at all, from 'Romer externalities' of localization (after Vatne, Chapter 4, this *Handbook*) or 'Jacobs externalities' of urbanization. Specialization and diversification are again key dynamics of growth and agglomeration, but again, while it might seem that specialization would logically require less interindustry knowledge transfer effort to the extent that similar specialist technologies were being utilized, the gains from efforts, conceivably by intermediary agencies, to assist knowledge transfers among different industries might yield the greater reward. However, the authors also place strong emphasis on technological relatedness, even among diverse industries, as being a necessary but insufficient condition for cognitive proximity – meaning clarity of understanding the other's business model, processes and potential – to result in innovation-led profitability. Empirical research is reported as suggesting the advantage from the absorption of knowledge spillovers from regional (and extraregional) industry that is cognitively relatively proximate in some way (technological, inputs, skills), is positive and significant, whereas those from Romer externalities are less so.

These analyses are static so the authors turn their attention to the dynamics of technological relatedness and regional branching (new path creation). This is prefaced by discussion of relatedness in the short and long term, one hypothesis being that constructing advantage from related variety only brings short-term advantage. Long term, some wholly new branches are needed to sustain regional growth. This is clearly an open question, warranting deep thought, because at the heart of spatial evolution is a notion of an industrial ecosystem, which means that complementarities foster growth while unrelatedness destroys it. As noted in Chapter 23 in this *Handbook* on 'transversality' in regional innovation and growth, keeping industry conscious of regional relatedness is one of the key tasks of the advanced regional development agency. This applies to the periods of 'normal science' or unpunctuated regional equilibrium, which is the short term, especially in respect of 'episodic' radical innovation. But such multilevel interaction between regime elements and paradigm elements is extremely important during more 'epochal' creative destruction inflections. Because the 'relatedness' perspective can appear 'disembedded' from neo-Schumpeterian concerns about innovation and policy, it can also appear to be vulnerable to randomness in its predictive qualities. However, this aspect improves with the introduction of a dynamic element into the analysis represented in such branching processes as entrepreneurship, merger and acquisition, and exploitation of industrial density. These are also mechanisms that contribute to regional path-dependence, which imposes a heavy effect on regional evolution such that new path creation is generally influenced by its industrial legacy. This makes the Silicon Valley phenomenon really an extreme exception to the rule of regional development, which is one reason why it has never been replicated.

The idea of the regional economy as a path-dependent system is the subject of Chapter 15 by Ron Martin. Among the conceptual issues that the concept raises are questions such as the extent to which the regional economy and its 'regime' are uniform, or composed of elements on different paths; to what extent are paths articulated even if they are on different paths; indeed, can regional evolution be characterized as systemic at all? Clearly these are salient questions because articulation would suggest relatedness, and disarticulation its opposite. Hypothetically, therefore, the disarticulated region would be expected to be weaker in economic terms than the systemically articulated one. Once again, as with the question, 'how radical is radical?' raised in Chapter 1 of this *Handbook*, much depends on refinements of conceptual degree and intensity. Thus it may be unnecessarily misleading to inquire whether regions display path-dependence on certain industries or not. Many are multilocational, such that electrical engineering or automotive components were until the 1990s produced in almost every county of Great Britain and location quotients (measures of concentration) could be quite high in peripheral regions. But their industrial volume and density were far from equally distributed. Moreover, the presence of automotive engineering in Cornwall, or until the 1980s in Renfrewshire and East Lothian, Scotland was a product of late path-dependence, if it could even be termed path-dependence at all. Yet both Scottish plants were systemically integrated to the nearby British Steel strip mill for 20 years, although suppliers refused to leave the West Midlands. Accordingly, the lack of spin-offs or significant network externalities make it seem inappropriate to discuss Linwood and Bathgate in terms of path-dependence. This helps to illuminate what qualifies a region to be so discussed. One element is clearly 'agglomeration', another may be 'origins' or 'embeddedness', meaning inquiry about why key events first occurred, evolved and diversified or 'branched' in a particular region. Martin's chapter suggests this is the predominant way in which regional path-dependence is conceived and researched, in terms of either industry 'selection' of one from a number of candidate regions, or why a region 'specializes' in a specific industry.

However, a second approach involves the quest for regional path-interdependence between industries; in other words its entire 'paradigm' and 'regime' evolution such as would allow profiling systemic regional articulation. This question is also asked from different angles in research cited in Chapter 1, 'Introduction', to this *Handbook* investigating 'regional varieties of capitalism' and 'regional corporate cultures'. Regional path-interdependence introduces the historical dimension quite profoundly. Chapter 23 on 'transversality' introduces some evidence for this in small, Nordic regions. Here early path-dependence (for example ships' propellers; plough design) remains embedded in later path-dependent industry (wind turbine blades) in North Jutland, while forestry (pulp and paper) reveals early path-dependence and examples of flexography (packaging, printing, film scripts) are later emanations of an initial resource endowment in Värmland, Sweden. Connecting to the earlier discussion of 'epochal' and 'episodic' radical innovation, both transitions described above have 'origins' in 'epochal' exploitation of natural resources ('mechanization' in Figure 1.1, Chapter 1 in this *Handbook*) but have been 'episodically' innovated according to opportunities arising from intersections of epochs (for example 'mechanization' and 'electrification' for windmills; 'mechanization' and 'informatization' for graphics). Of course, path-dependence with renewal also applies to epochal long waves and their aftershocks. This seems more satisfying than the 'randomness' that some path-dependence analyses share with some 'relatedness' perspectives as indicated in the taxonomy of path-dependence in Martin's (Chapter 15) Table 15.3.

ABSORPTIVE CAPACITY AND KNOWLEDGE DYNAMICS

Relatedness and path-interdependence are intimately bound up with absorptive capacity, which is the subject of Chapter 16 by Maria Abreu in this *Handbook*. The capability to adopt innovations from elsewhere without misunderstandings is a valuable asset for firms in supply chains (vertical absorptive capacity) as well as related industries in a region (lateral absorptive capacity). The second is probably the harder competence, but arguably the more rewarding. The 'learning' advantage claimed for absorptive capacity – namely, the more pre-learning of a subject, the more that can subsequently be learnt – is one of the core assumptions of the neo-Schumpeterian innovation framework and evolutionary economic geography more generally. Ideas like 'learning by doing' and 'learning by interacting' have been common currency between them and the neoclassical school for decades, as Abreu shows. Moreover, she also shows that its progenitors later demonstrated absorptive capacity to be a fundamental explanatory element in the understanding of path-dependence. This is because it allows for better prediction of future innovation and purposeful expectations. Such is the prospective influence of cumulativeness of the process, Abreu shows, that it can lead to the potential 'lock-out' of firms that do not invest in absorptive capacity. To repeat, this is difficult, but even more so for lateral absorptive capacity, except insofar as it is moderated by the constraints of geographical proximity. Even then, it must be further assumed there is worthwhile cross-sector knowledge to be learned in or nearby to the region and a competent regional 'regime' to help communicate it, for the transaction costs of true lateral absorptive capacity can be formidable indeed, and 'knowledge filtering' is a practical necessity. Abreu demonstrates conceptual mechanisms for facilitating such lateral controls, notably in respect of asymmetrical and symmetrical filtering. This has obvious theoretical value for assessment of methods by which regional knowledge spillovers involve magnitudes of both regional knowledge leakages and infusions.

Returning to the issue of lateral knowledge transfer, the 'regional regime' has a key role to play in, for example, facilitating organizational structures and management practices that assist knowledge transfer. This can include job rotation, communities of practice and cross-functional communication mechanisms from websites to professional or scholarly publications aimed at promoting knowledge transfer. Regions that have such cultures are advantaged, especially under the learning and innovating conditions operating in a globalized knowledge economy. Abreu expresses the conviction that regional innovation systems have these cross-fertilization and cross-pollination capabilities and that, fundamentally, that is their *raison d'être*. She also cites literature that equates high human capital with high regional absorptive capacity, echoing Felsenstein's analysis in Chapter 9 of this *Handbook*. This also adds further support to the importance of knowledge-based regional networks for regional innovation and growth anatomized by Giuliani in Chapter 12 of this *Handbook*. Finally, the manner in which knowledge filters empirically through networks of knowledge-based 'gatekeeper' firms to their associated firms lends support to the idea expressed in De Propris and Crevoisier's Chapter 13 on the importance of 'anchor' firms for regional innovation and growth.

This analysis of regional absorptive capacity, regional innovation systems and knowledge-based networks links seamlessly to Michael Steiner's Chapter 17 on 'Regional knowledge networks'. What is the added value of these beyond the virtues expressed in cited chapters, and the vast literature upon which they draw regarding varieties of network interaction for regional innovation and growth? The key lies in the emphasis in Steiner's analysis upon knowledge networks. Introduced in Abreu's chapter, here they are more deeply explored from the perspective that innovation is intimately influenced by the capabilities of economic agents to combine different pieces of knowledge efficiently. This is entirely consistent with the neo-Schumpeterian perspective on innovation and the innovator's role in facilitating entrepreneurship. As well as being important as sources and means of knowledge filtering to entrepreneurs, networks are also types of governance, set between states and markets due to their associative qualities and fully consistent also with the notion of functional regional innovation systems. As such they actually bridge various practice and policy chasms left by market failure on the one hand, and state failure on the other. This involves important knowledge-interpretative functions such as internalization and recontextualization of knowledge, as implied in regional absorptive capacity. A number of questions arise concerning 'who' and 'why' regarding network membership, and 'what' regarding traffic that is carried by them. They are more or less exclusionary and self-selecting because they enhance access to valuable intangible goods – technical, market and contractual knowledge foremost – for incumbents. How knowledge circulates is highly exclusive and contractualized according to some empirical accounts; more informal and open according to others – even in the same industry, notably biotechnology. This suggests that confidential, high-value-adding, intellectual property knowledge is likely to be more circumscribed than knowledge that ranks as gossip. But it may be influenced by sector, some having less excludability than others, or less expensive origins; or it may vary by region, some being more open, sociable and trusting than others, as the social capital literature implies (see Rosenfeld's Chapter 21 in this *Handbook*). Tacitness gives geographic proximity its *raison d'être* even if the tacit dimension of knowledge is not clearly demarcated from the codified dimension in all contexts.

REGIONAL COMPETITIVENESS AND CULTURE

Key points raised in Part III of the *Handbook* – notably relatedness, path-interdependence, absorptive capacity, knowledge and networks – contribute to regional innovation and growth, expressed in shorthand as 'regional competitiveness', something that as Ron Martin in Chapter 18 of this *Handbook* notes is not clearly defined but nevertheless much aspired to. This is not a new thing, even if the rhetoric is; regions have always been required to have export firms that, on quality or price or, increasingly, interweaving aspects of both, can prosper in extraregional, preferably overseas, markets. Of course, the competitiveness drive is ultimately self-defeating, since by definition it erodes all but the strongest competitor. Nevertheless it has the virtue of stimulating paradigm and regime ingenuity to innovate ever-new and better ways of making or doing things. This, as Schumpeter knew, is the wellspring or engine of capitalism, and just as the ultimate opposite to competition is not cooperation but monopoly, so the monopolist gives way by inertia or regulation to new waves of competitiveness, according to capitalist rules. Competitiveness is thus the way in which capitalism renews itself. A region's firms must constantly improve their productivity (unit labour costs) in their industry or move to higher-productivity industries where, conceivably, competition may be less (for example Christensen's sustaining strategy of moving upwards into luxury from mass markets). Martin goes on to show how Porter's and Krugman's notions of regional competitive advantage work by emphasizing regional externalities like 'regional regime' and 'regional production characteristics' as key to increasing regional productivity that produces regional competitiveness. To this Martin adds path-dependent regional stock assets (such as past innovations, technical know-how, and so on) regional absorptive capacity and relatedness to yield a post-Porter approach that stresses – as do the chapters in Part II of this *Handbook* – adaptability, agility, flexibility and versatility of regional firms in a dynamic theory of regional comparative advantage. Finally, in Chapter 19, Al James presents an important analysis of the 'regional culture of production' dimension of dynamic comparative advantage. These influence relatedness, regional absorptive capacity and knowledge networks in telling and detailed ways. Thus, in line with the earlier judgement of Silicon Valley's exceptionalism James characterizes it thus:

In Silicon Valley, a distinctive regional Californian counterculture – characterized by an openness to experimentation, the glorification of risk-taking, an acceptance of failure as a learning process, rapid change as the norm, a rejection of traditional social hierarchy, and greater loyalties to transcendent technologies than individual employers – is argued to have underpinned a regional, decentralized, network-based industrial system of learning.

This is different even from other high-tech locations in the US and encourages us to pause in reflection about the simple-mindedness of many ministerial injunctions to emulate it in, for example, the more deindustrialized parts of Great Britain. Yet, certain kinds of modern economic activity take root even there, mainly where there is path-dependent relatedness, notably renewable energy innovation in former coalfields, high-quality organic food production in hitherto 'food deserts', and diversified tourism where once the masses relaxed before the innovation of the package holiday. It would be repetitive to list again the key themes for regional innovation and growth covered in the chapters in this section; all, from relatedness to regional culture, are essential to an understanding of the keys to accomplishment in this complex and evolving field.

14 Technological relatedness, related variety and economic geography
Ron Boschma and Koen Frenken

INTRODUCTION

In economic geography, increasing attention is paid to the relevance of relatedness for learning and regional development. Relatedness between actors is thought to affect the nature and scope of knowledge spillovers. Relatedness may comprise of many dimensions, such as the cognitive, social, organizational, institutional and the geographical dimension (compare with Chapter 20 on proximity by Carrincazeaux and Coris in this *Handbook*). Being proximate in these dimensions will enhance the probability of agents to interact and exchange knowledge in an effective manner (Boschma, 2005). That is, distances on at least some of these dimensions need to be overcome in order to connect firms, and to enable interactive learning.

In this chapter, we will concentrate on the cognitive and the geographical dimension for reasons of simplicity, but also because these two dimensions have attracted most attention in the recent empirical literature in economic geography. We briefly outline the main theoretical ideas behind the regional-economic relevance of technological relatedness, and we will present a body of empirical work in economic geography that has made an attempt to measure technological relatedness in various ways, and to test its importance for firm and regional performance. More precisely, we discuss in the next section how the notion of related variety has contributed to the literature on externalities and regional growth. In the following section, we take a more dynamic perspective on this issue, and discuss how new growth paths in regions emerge (that is, how new industries emerge and develop in regions), and how technological relatedness might be a key input in this process of regional diversification. The final section draws some conclusions.

RELATED VARIETY AND REGIONAL GROWTH

In the spatial externalities literature, a key question is whether firms in big agglomerations benefit from the local co-presence of other firms. Studies have demonstrated that knowledge spillovers are often geographically localized (Audretsch and Feldman, 1996). In addition, this literature has incorporated a sectoral dimension, investigating whether firms in big agglomerations learn principally from other local firms in the same sector, or from other local firms in a wide range of other sectors (Glaeser et al., 1992; Feldman and Audretsch, 1999). To put it simply, the former form of spatial externalities has been labelled localization economies (see Vatne's Chapter 4 in this *Handbook* on 'Romer externalities'), while the latter form has been associated with Jacobs's externalities (Van Oort, 2004).

While the work of Jane Jacobs is seminal in economic geography, the spatial externalities literature has not well specified the meaning behind Jacobs's externalities (but see Iammarino's Chapter 11 in this *Handbook*). For one thing, one can seriously question whether knowledge spillovers across sectors will occur in diversified regions just because sectors are each other's neighbours.More precisely, this literature largely ignores an insight derived from evolutionary economics: that is, that the relatedness between technologies used in sectors in a region may strongly affect the scope and nature of knowledge spillovers (for example Carlsson and Stankiewicz, 1991; Breshnahan and Trajtenberg, 1995). When applying this insight to the spatial externalities literature, one may expect that the extent to which the variety of technologies present in a region is related will positively affect the scope for knowledge spillovers, as local firms in different but related activities can profit more from mutual spillovers than local firms that are active in unrelated industries.

Frenken et al. (2007) proposed the notion of related variety to incorporate this relatedness effect in the spatial externalities literature. This notion builds on the ideas of Nooteboom (2000), among others, who argued that knowledge is more likely to spill over across two sectors when their cognitive distance is neither too large nor too small. That is, some degree of cognitive proximity between the two sectors ensures effective communication and common understanding, and some degree of cognitive distance is needed to avoid cognitive lock-in. Related variety in a region may capture this delicate balance between cognitive proximity and distance across sectors in a region, in contrast to Jacobs's externalities (in which regional diversity per se involves too much cognitive distance) and localization economies (in which regional specialization produces too much cognitive proximity). Then, the higher the number of technologically related sectors in a region, the more variety in related sectors, the more learning opportunities there are for sectors in that region, the more intersectoral knowledge spillovers are likely to take place, resulting in higher regional growth.

Empirical studies have investigated the significance of related variety for regional growth in the Netherlands, Sweden, Great Britain, Spain, Italy, Finland and Turkey. A major challenge is to measure the degree of (technological) relatedness between sectors. Some have followed Frenken et al. (2007) by taking the Standard Industrial Classification (SIC) as a starting point. They look at the degree of variety of sectors at a low digit level (for example five-digit) that share the same at a higher digit level (for example, two-digit). Five-digit sectors (for example sub-branches in chemicals) that share the same two-digit class (for example chemicals) are assumed to show some degree of cognitive proximity because they share competences in the same two-digit class, but they also show some degree of cognitive distance at the five-digit level. Then, the more variety there is at the five-digit level within each two-digit sector in a region, the more related variety (and real learning opportunities) in a region, which is calculated as an entropy measure in each region. However, this measure of relatedness between sectors is not unproblematic. One reason is that the predefined relatedness measure based on SIC codes does not fully capture the degree of technological relatedness between sectors (see for example Breschi et al., 2003). Therefore, others have used a measure of revealed relatedness between sectors in a region, based on frequently found combinations of products at the plant level (Neffke et al., 2009), or based on the intensity of labour flows between sectors (Neffke and Henning, 2009). Most of these studies have found some empirical evidence for the importance of related variety for regional growth (Essletzbichler, 2007; Boschma and Iammarino, 2009; Bishop and Gripaios, 2010).

The next step is to account for the fact that new and related variety may also be brought into the region through intersectoral linkages with other regions. This may be done by simply looking at possible knowledge spillover effects from technologically related sectors in neighbouring regions. More preferably, one should include network data that identify actual knowledge flows, which allow assessing of the economic effects on regional growth of interregional network linkages between technologically related sectors. This would enrich the agglomeration externalities literature, which simply assumes rather than measures knowledge flows between sectors, and which arbitrarily predefines regions at whatever spatial scale, as if all connections exist within the boundaries of these spatial entities. Boschma and Iammarino (2009) have made an attempt to estimate the effects of knowledge spillovers between related sectors across regions on regional growth in Italy. Based on actual trade data, they found a positive correlation between employment growth of Italian regions on the one hand, and the degree of technological relatedness between existing sectors in Italian regions and their import sectors on the other hand. This outcome might indicate that a region benefits from extraregional knowledge when it originates from (import) sectors that are related or close, but not quite similar to existing sectors in the region. However, this issue of economic effects of related flows within and across regions on regional growth is still unexplored.

Another issue is the treatment of related variety as static and given. On longer time-scales, related variety in regions itself is likely to be subject to change and, as such, becomes a dependent variable in its own right (Boschma and Frenken, 2011). A key question that follows from this is how related variety itself can be explained as an outcome of a historical process of regional development. One can question to what extent the technological relatedness between sectors in a region can help us to understand the development opportunities of each single region through diversification into new, related industries. Moreover, the long-term evolution of related variety in a region is not only affected by the entry of new industries, but also by the decline and exit of old industries. Here again, the notion of technological relatedness might be highly relevant: can we understand the loss of old industries in a region from the level of technological relatedness between the old industry and other sectors in the region? And finally, how will changes in related variety affect overall regional growth? Saviotti and Frenken (2008) have claimed that related variety might be a source for regional growth in the short run, but not so much in the long run, because long-term sustainable regional growth requires now and then the development of new sectors that are quite unrelated to pre-existing sectors in the region. To these topics, we now turn.

TECHNOLOGICAL RELATEDNESS AND REGIONAL BRANCHING

Since Schumpeter, it is common knowledge that regional economies are subject to structural change in the long run; that is, sectors come and go. Economic geographers embraced these Schumpeterian ideas quite prominently at a very early stage (Lambooy, 1984; Markusen, 1985). A widely accepted view in the 1980s and 1990s was that new industries developed in new growth regions like Silicon Valley, but not in old industrial regions because of high wages, labour unions and congestion. This literature tended to assume that new industries almost started from scratch, and more or less ignored the question of whether pre-existing regional industrial structures might boost the emergence and growth of new industries.

As stated before, the spatial externalities literature has emphasized the blessings of a highly diversified economy in large cities, which would positively affect this process of regional diversification. Henderson et al. (1995) claimed that young (high-tech) industries needed diversified cities where they could exploit Jacobs's externalities (that is, benefits from interindustry spillovers) (see also Duranton and Puga, 2001; Neffke et al., forthcoming). However, more recently, the notion of relatedness has been introduced to explain regional diversification, claiming that the entry of new sectors might depend on the presence of technologically related industries in a region, not on a wide range of industries per se.

From an evolutionary perspective, one would expect that a set of related industries in a region is rather persistent over time because regions are more likely to expand and diversify into sectors that are closely related to their existing activities. From the entrepreneurship literature, we know that setting up a new firm is a very risky and uncertain event, and few firms survive their first years of existence. Due to this uncertainty, entrepreneurs will show a propensity to stay close to their existing competences, and to exploit their social networks in their own region (Dahl and Sorenson, 2010; Stam, 2010). There is quite robust evidence from many empirical studies that the performance of new firms tends to increase when the entrepreneur has a pre-entry background in an industry that is technologically close to the new venture, because that still enables the entrepreneur to use the previously acquired knowledge.

In their diversification strategies, also firms tend to rely and build on their existing competences, which have proven successful in the past. The reason for this is that, as argued by Nelson and Winter (1982), intrafirm diversification is not without problems, because search by firms for new markets and new technologies is accompanied by fundamental uncertainty. Search for new technologies and new markets is therefore more likely undertaken locally; that is, directed to technologies and markets with which firms have become familiar in the past, and in which no major switching costs are involved. Penrose (1959) conceived firm growth as a progressive process of related diversification, in which firms diversify into products that are technologically related to their current products.

This is in line with studies that found that mergers and acquisitions (M&As) show higher levels of performance when they connect firms with technologically related knowledge bases (see for example Piscitello, 2004; Cassiman et al., 2005). Ahuja and Katila (2001), for instance, found that a moderate level of overlap between the knowledge bases of the acquired and the acquiring firm had a positive effect on the subsequent innovation output of the acquiring firm, in contrast to very high and very low levels of overlap between their knowledge bases (that is, high and low cognitive proximity, respectively). Since most new divisions are established inside existing plants, it is a localized phenomenon not only in cognitive-market terms but also in geographical terms (Frenken and Boschma, 2007). Related diversification by means of M&As may also have a geographical bias. Studies have demonstrated that geographical proximity may be a determinant of M&As within countries (see Rodriguez-Pose and Zademach, 2003). In sum, there are good reasons to believe that related diversification at the firm level (both through internal and external growth) is expected to have a geographical bias, although systematic empirical evidence is still lacking.

Besides the fact that related diversification through entrepreneurship and firm diversification may have a regional bias (that is, spin-offs often locate near their parents, and new divisions are often established inside plants, respectively), there are also other reasons, more at the regional level, why this is the case. When a region specializes in a particular knowledge base, this will act as both an incentive and a selection mechanism for local firms (Maskell and Malmberg, 1999, 2007). That is, it offers opportunities to local firms for further improvements in familiar and related fields of knowledge, but less so to non-local firms that are distanced on various dimensions (Gertler, 2003). And creation of new knowledge that is unrelated to this regional knowledge base is more likely to be selected out (Boschma, 2004). In addition to that, the remaining mechanisms through which knowledge is transferred from old to new related sectors (that is, labour mobility and social networks) also tend to have a local bias, although not exclusively so (Capello, 1999; Boschma and Frenken, 2011). That is, most employees change jobs within the same labour market area, and social networks that channel knowledge flows tend to be local (Breschi and Lissoni, 2003).

There is increasing empirical evidence that this process of related diversification (or branching) occurs indeed at the regional level. There is a vast literature in economic geography and economic history that reports in detail how regions have reinvented themselves by moving from old to new activities now and then (see for example Porter, 1990; Glaeser, 2005). More recently, quantitative studies have investigated the diversification process in many countries and regions systematically over a longer period with the assistance of revealed relatedness measures. These studies confirm that countries and regions are indeed more likely to expand and diversify into sectors that are closely related to their existing activities. Hausmann and Klinger (2007) investigated how countries diversified their export portfolios in the period 1962–2000, making use of United Nations (UN) Commodity Trade Statistics. They found a strong tendency of the export mix of countries to move from current products towards related products, rather than goods that are less related. Neffke et al. (2009) did a long-term analysis of 70 Swedish regions in the period 1969–2005. They found systematic evidence that a sector had a higher probability to enter a region when this sector was technologically related to other pre-existing sectors in that region, as compared to unrelated sectors.

These studies also tend to demonstrate that countries and regions have a different capacity to diversify successfully into related activities, depending on the degree of related variety: the higher the number of related industries in a region, the higher the number of possible recombinations, and thus the higher the probability that regions will diversify successfully into related products. Hausmann and Klinger (2007) found evidence that richer countries were indeed positioned in the more dense parts of industry space, which meant more opportunities to diversify and sustain economic growth; in contrast to poorer countries, having less potential to diversify into related products because of a thinner base of related industries to start from. Although their methodology and focus was different, Neffke et al. (2009) found in their Swedish study a similar outcome: the probability of a new sector to enter a region increased quite dramatically with the number of technologically related sectors in that region. Neffke et al. (2009) also investigated the probability of a sector to exit a region. Interestingly, they found systematic evidence, based on more than 3000 exit events, that a sector had a higher probability to disappear from a region, the lower the number of technologically related industries in that region. This comes as no surprise, because the more embedded a sector is with other technologically related sectors in that region, the more it can potentially benefit from related variety externalities.

Another finding of Neffke et al. (2009) was that the overall technological coherence for all Swedish regions was on average relatively high and rather stable over a period of 35 years, meaning that regions were characterized by a rather coherent set of related industries over time. On average, the entry of new sectors (though technologically related to other sectors in a region) tended to lower the technological coherence in Swedish regions, and thus added new (but related) variety in regions. This stood in contrast to the exit of sectors, which were, on average, less technologically related to other sectors in a region and thus performed a variety-destroying effect in regions. The net effect of all entries and exits resulted in a rather stable technological coherence for all Swedish regions, despite the fact that this coherence was constantly redefined as a result of creative destruction.

These outcomes lend support to the fact that the rise and fall of industries is strongly conditioned by the industrial past of regions. In other words, the Schumpeterian process of structural change seems to be subject to a path-dependent process that tends to manifest itself at the regional level. This is an important outcome, because previously, it was thought that path-dependent processes in regions were revealed by the persistence of regions to excel in specific sectors or technologies over time (Storper and Scott, 1992; Rigby and Essletzbichler, 1997; Martin and Sunley, 2006). Now, we have some evidence that the process of structural change itself (in terms of entry and exits of sectors) is subject to path-dependence, as regions tend to diversify into related activities and deindustrialize in unrelated activities. Having said that, the question remains whether these findings (though quite robust in the Swedish case) can be replicated in other countries. Another open question is through which kinds of (knowledge transfer) mechanisms old sectors are connected to new related sectors.

Entrepreneurship is most likely to be a key transfer mechanism through which relevant knowledge is transferred and diffused from old to new sectors at the regional level. This occurs when new firms in a newly emerging industry are set up by entrepreneurs who previously acquired knowledge and experience in a related industry in the same region (Klepper and Simons, 2000). There is indeed increasing evidence that experienced entrepreneurs who originate from related industries play a crucial role in the formation of new industries in regions. However, the relevance of technological relatedness is not only shown in old sectors giving birth to new sectors. More importantly, longitudinal studies have demonstrated that this branching process also increases the probability of survival of the new industry (Klepper, 2007). To be more precise, experienced entrepreneurs (that is, those with a pre-entry background in related industries) show a higher survival rate in the early development stage of a new industry, as compared to other types of entrants, because they can still exploit related competences and skills. This has been observed, for example, in the evolution of the British car industry, in which early entrants had a higher survival rate when the entrepreneur previously worked in related industries like bicycle making, coach making and engineering, and when the firm had been founded in a region that was well endowed with these related industries (Boschma and Wenting, 2007). In other words, these outcomes support the earlier finding that regions tend to diversify into new but related industries.

But there may be other knowledge transfer mechanisms through which regions might branch into new industries, such as labour mobility (Frenken and Boschma, 2007; Boschma and Frenken, 2011). Labour mobility is considered to be a mechanism through which knowledge diffuses. As most employees change jobs within a region, labour flows may bring growth to that region (see for example Almeida and Kogut, 1999; Heuermann, 2009). However, little to no attention has been paid to the effects of labour flows between firms of related industries. Boschma et al. (2009) have stated that the economic effects of labour flows cannot be accurately assessed without paying attention to the extent to which the inflow of new knowledge is related to the existing knowledge base of the firm. In an empirical study of more than 100 000 job moves in Sweden, they indeed found evidence that the inflow of employees with skills that were related to the skill portfolio of a plant had a positive effect on productivity growth of the plant, while the hiring of new employees had a negative effect when it concerned either skills that were already available in the plant, or skills that were unrelated (that is, very different) to those present in the plant. Similar findings have been found in a recent study on labour mobility in Denmark (Timmermans and Boschma, 2010). However, the importance of these related knowledge flows through labour mobility for the emergence and growth of new industries still needs to be explored. For instance, we do not (yet) know whether new entrants in newly emerging industries are more inclined to hire labour from related industries, and if so, whether this will make a difference economically. In other words, regional branching through labour mobility is as yet an unexplored research field.

The concept of relatedness has also found its way in network analysis. Networks are considered to be a major channel of knowledge diffusion (see for example Powell et al., 1996; Sorenson et al., 2006; Ter Wal, 2009). The extent to which networks will matter for new knowledge creation and innovations may again depend on the degree of technological relatedness among the partners, among other factors. There is likely to be an optimal level of cognitive proximity stemming from the need to keep some cognitive distance to stimulate new ideas, and to secure some cognitive proximity between network partners for the purpose of effective communication (Boschma and Frenken, 2010). Empirical studies have confirmed that collaborative research projects like technological alliances tend to generate more radical knowledge when they consist of agents that bring in related competences (see for example Gilsing et al., 2007). Broekel and Boschma (2009) found a similar positive effect on firm performance when investigating the ego-networks of firms in the Dutch aviation industry.

There is, however, no literature yet on the relationship between industry life cycles and network dynamics (Boschma and Frenken, 2010). As explained earlier, new industries generally emerge from a recombination of technologies. Therefore, we expect new entrants with links to technologically related industries to have a higher survival rate, at least during the first years of formation. With the progressive technological development in the industry, the knowledge base of firms is progressively codified. This means that with cognitive proximity between firms rising as firms become technologically more proximate, the geographical distance of network relations is expected to increase over time (Menzel, 2008). This has indeed been observed in the evolution of the German inventor network in the biotech sector (Ter Wal, 2009). In combination with increasing social proximity, cluster firms in that industry will also become more connected with each other. So, next to increasing numbers of global links, the local density of network links is expected to increase over time as well. One can also expect the probability to survive a shake-out in the industry to be dependent on the firm's degree of interconnectedness in the interfirm network. This means that the average degree of interconnectedness of firms will increase over time, while the falling number of firms will increase the density of relations. As the number of firms in an industry declines over time, the remaining firms are typically embedded in strong social networks and interlocking corporate boards, which tend to resist structural change. Such resistance can be further reinforced by increasing organizational proximity, due to mutual financial participation between cluster firms. All these processes will further increase the cognitive proximity between cluster firms, which will result in an excess of cognitive proximity. Such structures typically explain the inability of old industrial regions to renew themselves successfully (Hassink, 2005). The solution to such a regional lock-in phenomenon clearly lies in trying to reorganize network relations, such that interactions can take place between actors that are less proximate in cognitive space, yet not too distant. Put differently, to foster innovation, new technologies need to be explored to examine the potential of recombinations between different technologies. Such cognitive widening is most likely to be realized through the establishment of networks outside the region.

CONCLUDING REMARKS

This chapter has given some examples of how the evolutionary concepts of technological relatedness and related variety have been successfully applied in economic geography more recently. These include: (1) the spatial externalities literature, which is preoccupied with the question whether (related) variety in urban economies matter for growth; (2) the emerging regional diversification literature, which is about the explanation of new growth paths in regions, and which tests the idea that regions are more likely to diversify into sectors that are technologically close to their existing activities; (3) the entrepreneurial literature that focuses on spin-off companies and experienced entrepreneurs that have acquired knowledge in related industries, and which seem to play a quite crucial role in the process of regional branching; (4) the labour mobility literature, which focuses on how related labour flows might matter for regional development; and (5) the emerging network literature in economic geography, which deals with the question of whether local 'buzz' or global pipelines matter for regional growth, and whether networks should consist of (local and non-local) partners that bring in related competences. And linking network dynamics to the industry life-cycle approach, one could test whether cognitive proximity levels between cluster firms will increase over time, with detrimental effects on their performance levels.

In other words, we believe that the study of technological relatedness and related variety opens up new and promising directions of research in evolutionary economic geography. In this respect, there are many research challenges ahead of us. Among others, we have to define and measure technological relatedness and related variety more accurately, in order to capture better the knowledge spillover effects of related variety.

Another challenge is to investigate in detail the key mechanisms that operate as effective channels of knowledge transfer between old and new industries, and to what extent these operate at the regional level. There is some evidence that experienced entrepreneurs and diversifiers play a crucial role in the early stages of the industry life cycle, but only a limited number of industries have been investigated so far. And no empirical studies have yet been conducted that have assessed the importance of labour mobility and social networking in the context of an industry life-cycle approach, and whether connections with related activities are crucial in this respect.

REFERENCES

Ahuja, G. and R. Katila (2001), 'Technological acquisitions and the innovation performance of acquiring firms: a longitudinal study', *Strategic Management Journal*, **22**, 197–220.

Almeida, P. and B. Kogut (1999), 'Localization of knowledge and the mobility of engineers in regional networks', *Management Science*, **45**, 905–17.

Audretsch, D.B. and M. Feldman (1996), 'Spillovers and the geography of innovation and production', *American Economic Review*, **86**, 630–40.

Bishop, P. and P. Gripaios (2010), 'Spatial externalities, relatedness and sector employment growth in Great Britain', *Regional Studies*, **44** (4), 443–54.

Boschma, R.A. (2004), 'Competitiveness of regions from an evolutionary perspective', *Regional Studies*, **38** (9), 1001–14.

Boschma, R.A. (2005), 'Proximity and innovation: a critical assessment', *Regional Studies*, **39** (1), 61–74.

Boschma, R., R. Eriksson and U. Lindgren (2009), 'How does labour mobility affect the performance of plants? The importance of relatedness and geographical proximity', *Journal of Economic Geography*, **9** (2), 169–90.

Boschma, R.A. and K. Frenken (2010), 'The spatial evolution of innovation networks: a proximity perspective', in R.A. Boschma and R. Martin (eds), *The Handbook of Evolutionary Economic Geography*, Cheltenham, UK and Northampton, MA, USA: Edward Elgar, pp. 120–36.

Boschma, R. and K. Frenken (2011), 'Technological relatedness and regional branching', in H. Bathelt, M.P. Feldman and D.F. Kogler (eds), *Beyond Territory: Dynamic Geographies of Innovation and Knowledge Creation*, Routledge, Taylor & Francis, forthcoming.

Boschma, R.A. and S. Iammarino (2009), 'Related variety, trade linkages and regional growth in Italy', *Economic Geography*, **85** (3), 289–311.

Boschma, R.A. and R. Wenting (2007), 'The spatial evolution of the British automobile industry', *Industrial and Corporate Change*, **16** (2), 213–38.

Breschi, S. and F. Lissoni (2003), 'Mobility and social networks: localised knowledge spillovers revisited', CESPRI Working Paper No. 142.

Breschi, S., F. Lissoni and F. Malerba (2003), 'Knowledge-relatedness in firm technological diversification', *Research Policy*, **32**, 69–87.

Breshnahan, T.F. and M. Trajtenberg (1995), 'General purpose technologies: engines of growth?', *Journal of Econometrics*, **65** (1), 83–109.

Broekel, T. and R. Boschma (2009), 'Knowledge networks in the Dutch aviation industry: the proximity paradox', Papers in Evolutionary Economic Geography 09.15, Utrecht.

Capello, R. (1999), 'Spatial transfer of knowledge in high technology milieux: learning versus collective learning processes', *Regional Studies*, **33** (4), 353–65.

Carlsson, B. and R. Stankiewicz (1991), 'On the nature, function and composition of technological systems', *Journal of Evolutionary Economics*, **1**, 93–118.

Cassiman, B., M.G. Colombo, P. Garrone and R. Veugelers (2005), 'The impact of M&A on the R&D process: an empirical analysis of the role of technological and market relatedness', *Research Policy*, **34** (2), 195–220.

Dahl, M.S. and O. Sorenson (2010), 'Home sweet home: entrepreneurs' location choices and the performance of their ventures', Research Paper, Aalborg University.

Duranton, G. and D. Puga (2001), 'Nursery cities: urban diversity, process innovation, and the life cycle of products', *American Economic Review*, **91** (5), 1454–77.

Essletzbichler, J. (2007), 'Diversity, stability and regional growth in the United States, 1975–2002', in K. Frenken (ed.), *Applied Evolutionary Economics and Economic Geography*, Cheltenham, UK and Northampton, MA, USA: Edward Edgar, pp. 203–29.

Feldman, M.P. and D.B. Audretsch (1999), 'Innovation in cities: science-based diversity, specialization and localized competition', *European Economic Review*, **43**, 409–29.

Frenken, K. and R.A. Boschma (2007), 'A theoretical framework for evolutionary economic geography: industrial dynamics and urban growth as a branching process', *Journal of Economic Geography*, **7** (5), 635–49.

Frenken, K., F.G. Van Oort and T. Verburg (2007), 'Related variety, unrelated variety and regional economic growth', *Regional Studies*, **41** (5), 685–97.

Gertler, M.S. (2003), 'Tacit knowledge and the economic geography of context or the undefinable tacitness of being (there)', *Journal of Economic Geography*, **3**, 75–99.

Gilsing, V., B. Nooteboom, W. Vanhaverbeke, G. Duysters and A. van den Oord (2007), 'Network embeddedness and the exploration of novel technologies: technological distance, betweenness centrality and density', *Research Policy*, **37**, 1717–31.

Glaeser, E.L. (2005), 'Reinventing Boston: 1630–2003', *Journal of Economic Geography*, **5**, 119–53.

Glaeser, E.L., H.D. Kallal, J.A. Schinkmann and A. Shleifer (1992), 'Growth in cities', *Journal of Political Economy*, **100**, 1126–52.

Hassink, R. (2005), 'How to unlock regional economies from path dependency? From learning region to learning cluster', *European Planning Studies*, **13** (4), 521–35.

Hausmann, R. and B. Klinger (2007), 'The structure of the product space and the evolution of comparative advantage', CID Working Paper no. 146, Center for International Development, Harvard University, Cambridge, MA.

Henderson, J.V., A. Kuncoro and M. Turner (1995), 'Industrial development in cities', *Journal of Political Economy*, **103**, 1067–85.

Heuermann, D.F. (2009), 'Reinventing the skilled region: human capital externalities and industrial change', working paper, University of Trier, Trier.

Klepper, S. (2007), 'Disagreements, spinoffs, and the evolution of Detroit as the capital of the US automobile industry', *Management Science*, **53**, 616–31.

Klepper, S. and K.L. Simons (2000), 'Dominance by birthright: entry of prior radio producers and competitive ramifications in the US television receiver industry', *Strategic Management Journal*, **21**, 997–1016.

Lambooy, J.G. (1984), 'The regional ecology of technological change', in J.G. Lambooy (ed.), *New Spatial Dynamics and Economic Crisis*, Tampere: Finnpublishers, pp. 63–77.

Markusen, A. (1985), *Profit Cycles, Oligopoly and Regional Development*, Cambridge, MA: MIT Press.

Martin, R. and P. Sunley (2006), 'Path dependence and regional economic evolution', *Journal of Economic Geography*, **6** (4), 395–437.

Maskell, P. and A. Malmberg (1999), 'Localised learning and industrial competitiveness', *Cambridge Journal of Economics*, **23** (2), 167–86.

Maskell, P. and A. Malmberg (2007), 'Myopia, knowledge development and cluster evolution', *Journal of Economic Geography*, **7** (5), 603–18.

Menzel, M.P. (2008), 'Dynamic proximities: changing relations by creating and bridging distances', Papers in Evolutionary Economic Geography, no. 08.16, Department of Economic Geography, Utrecht University.

Neffke, F. and M.S. Henning (2009), 'Skill relatedness and firm diversification', Papers on Economics and Evolution, no. 09.06, Jena, Max Planck Institute of Economics.

Neffke, F., M. Henning and R. Boschma (2009), 'How do regions diversify over time? Industry relatedness and the development of new growth paths in regions', Papers in Evolutionary Economic Geography, no. 9.16, Utrecht University.

Neffke, F., M. Svensson Henning, R. Boschma, K.J. Lundquist and L.O. Olander (forthcoming), 'The dynamics of agglomeration externalities along the life cycle of industries', *Regional Studies*.

Nelson, R.R. and S.G. Winter (1982), *An Evolutionary Theory of Economic Change*, Cambridge, MA, USA and London, UK: Belknap Press.

Nooteboom, B. (2000), *Learning and Innovation in Organizations and Economies*, Oxford: Oxford University Press.

Penrose, E. (1959), *The Theory of the Growth of the Firm*, Oxford: Oxford University Press.

Piscitello, L. (2004), 'Corporate diversification, coherence and economic performance', *Industrial and Corporate Change*, **13** (5), 757–87.

Porter, M. (1990), *The Competitive Advantage of Nations*, New York: Free Press.

Powell, W.W., K. Koput and L. Smith-Doerr (1996),' Interorganizational collaboration and the locus of innovation: networks of learning in biotechnology', *Administrative Science Quarterly*, **41**, 116–45.

Rigby, D.L. and J. Essletzbichler (1997), 'Evolution, process variety, and regional trajectories of technological change in US manufacturing', *Economic Geography*, **73** (3), 269–84.

Rodriguez-Pose, A. and H.M. Zademach (2003), 'Rising metropolis: the geography of mergers and acquisitions in Germany', *Urban Studies*, **40** (10), 895–923.

Saviotti, P.P. and K. Frenken (2008), 'Trade variety and economic development of countries', *Journal of Evolutionary Economics*, **18** (2), 201–18.

Sorenson, O., J.W. Rivkin and L. Fleming (2006), 'Complexity, networks and knowledge flow', *Research Policy*, **35** (7), 994–1017.
Stam, E. (2010), 'Entrepreneurship, evolution and geography', in R. Boschma and R. Martin (eds), *Handbook on Evolutionary Economic Geography*, Cheltenham, UK and Northampton, MA, USA: Edward Elgar, pp. 139–61.
Storper, M. and A.J. Scott (eds) (1992), *Pathways to Industrialization and Regional Development*, London, UK and Boston, MA, USA: Routledge.
Ter Wal, A.L.J. (2009), 'The spatial dynamics of the inventor network in German biotechnology: geographical proximity versus triadic closure', Utrecht: Department of Economic Geography.
Timmermans, B. and R. Boschma (2010), 'Labour mobility and plant performance in Denmark: the significance of related inflows', Utrecht University.
Van Oort, F.G. (2004), *Urban Growth and Innovation: Spatially Bounded Externalities in the Netherlands*, Aldershot: Ashgate.

15 Regional economies as path-dependent systems: some issues and implications

Ron Martin

[I]f there is one single area of economics in which path dependence is unmistakable, it is in economic geography – the location of production in space. The long shadow cast by history over location is apparent at all scales, from the smallest to the largest. (Krugman, 1991, 80)

Although the assertion that 'history matters' has come to be coupled frequently with references to the concept of path dependence, the precise meaning of the latter – and hence the significance of the former expression – more often than not remains rather cloudy . . . A clearer grasp of what the term 'path dependence' is about therefore ought to be part of the historical social scientist's tool-kit. (David, 2007, 92)

INTRODUCTION

A key research question that has attracted increasing attention in economic geography concerns how the economic landscape evolves through time, and why that evolution takes certain spatial forms and historical trajectories rather than others (see Boschma and Martin, 2007, 2010). There is a growing consensus that 'history matters' in regional development, and the notion of path-dependence, originally developed in economics by Paul David and Brian Arthur in the mid- to late 1980s, is now widely viewed as a 'foundational concept' for giving analytical content to this belief.[1] Indeed, it has been argued that to be ontologically convincing the theorization of regional growth and development has to be firmly rooted in the idea of path-dependent economic evolution (Scott, 2006). Certainly economic geographers now freely employ the concept in their theoretical and empirical work and in recent years the literature on regional path-dependence has grown apace (for some examples, see: Cooke and Morgan, 1998; Glasmeier, 2000; Walker, 2001; Bathelt and Boggs, 2003; Fuchs and Shapira, 2005; Gertler, 2005; Hassink, 2005; Hassink and Shin, 2005; Boschma and Frenken, 2006; Martin and Sunley, 2006; Scott, 2006; Belussi and Sedita, 2009; Lagerholm and Malmberg, 2009; Martin, 2010; Martin and Sunley, 2010).

However, the fact that the idea of path-dependence now 'figures prominently in the analytical consciousness' of economic geographers does not mean that the definition, meaning, theorization or explanatory significance of the concept are settled matters. To say that regional development is a path-dependent process, or that a regional economy is a path-dependent system, is not of itself self-explanatory. The basic notion of regional path-dependence may be intuitive enough, namely that the form and performance of a regional economy today is somehow to be understood in terms of that region's development in the past; or, loosely speaking, that where a regional economy gets to is determined by how it got there. Every regional economy inherits the legacies of its own past, and those legacies 'condition' and shape in various ways and to various extents the activities that can be carried out in the current period; which activities and outcomes will then, in their turn, form part of the evolving historical sequence of events and outcomes that will influence future activities and development in the region. But such statements raise a whole series of fundamental issues that go to the heart of how we conceptualize regional path-dependence. These critical issues have only just begun to be interrogated (see Martin, 2006; Martin and Sunley, 2006, 2010; Martin, 2010), but their resolution would help to provide 'a clearer grasp' (to use David's phrase) of what the concept of 'regional path-dependence' is about, and hence enhance its explanatory purchase. It is not possible in this necessarily brief chapter to discuss all of the relevant issues, so what follows is not intended to be an exhaustive discussion.[2]

UNRAVELLING THE NOTION OF REGIONAL PATH-DEPENDENCE

Many of the basic mechanisms that make for path-dependence – natural resource endowments, various forms of increasing returns, external and network economies, sunk costs, learning effects, imitative behaviour, self-reinforcing expectations – have a quintes-sentially local dimension in their form and operation (Sydow et al., 2009). In this way, path-dependence can be seen as a process or effect that is locally contingent and locally emergent, and hence to a large extent 'place dependent' (Martin and Sunley, 2006). But this still leaves open the question of the different components of a regional economy on which these place-dependent mechanisms operate. Regional economies are complex, composite ensembles of firms, industries, institutions, infrastructures and cultures, and this systemic complexity renders the notion of regional path-dependence both compli-cated and contentious (Table 15.1). Do all of the components of a regional economy (firms, industrial sectors, technologies, institutions) display path-dependence? Can different paths coexist within a region? To what extent is there 'path-interdependence' amongst different industries or technologies in a region? In what sense can we talk of the path-dependent evolution of a regional economy as a whole, as an aggregate system?

Most applications of the notion of path-dependence in geographical work have tended to be 'single-industry'-orientated. One variant focuses on the spatial evolution of a given industry across different locations or regions. This approach is akin to Arthur's (1994c) model of industrial location wherein, over time, local spin-offs and local network exter-nalities provide two possible mechanisms that lead, in a path-dependent manner, to the concentration of an industry in particular locations (regions). Examples of this type of enquiry are Klepper's (2007) study of the locational dynamics of the US automobile industry, and Boschma and Wenting's (2007) analysis of the spatial evolution of the automobile sector in the UK. Such studies require an explanation of why path-dependent processes within a given industry emerge in (or 'select') certain locations or regions but fail to materialize in (or 'select') others. A second variant is concerned with the path-dependent evolution of a particular industry in a specific region. This has probably been the main use of path-dependence as an explanatory notion by economic geographers, and is typically deployed in studies of highly specialized economic spaces such as Porter-type business clusters, industrial districts, high-technology localities and regional innovation systems. Kenney and von Burg's (2001) account of the evolution of Silicon Valley, Bathelt and Boggs's (2003) analysis of the evolution of Liepzig's media cluster, and Belussi and

Table 15.1   Some issues in the study of regional path-dependence

Key issues	Main research questions
The regional economy as a multiscalar path-dependent system	Path-dependence may characterize a region's firms, its industries and the regional economy as a whole. How are the paths at these different scales related? Is a certain threshold of interaction and interrelatedness between firms and industries within a region required before it displays aggregate path-dependence?
The pervasiveness of path-dependence in the economic landscape	Is it a fundamental feature of regional development – i.e. inevitable and indeed necessary for regional growth to take place? Or is it more typical of economically specialized regions and localities, and less likely to emerge in areas with diverse economic-technological structures?
Sources of regional path-dependence	Regions differ markedly in economic structure, institutions, connections to other regions and beyond, etc., so the nature and sources of path-dependence might be expected to vary from region to region. In what ways is path-dependence a place-dependent process? Is a single, overarching theory possible?
Regional path-dependence as the co-evolution of paths	Can different paths coexist within a region, and how do these interact – what is the nature of 'inter-path coupling'? How do the various industrial and technological paths co-evolve in a region?
The 'depth' of regional path-dependence	Path-dependence may exhibit different degrees of 'depth' or historicity. What factors determine the 'depth' of regional path-dependence? What are the consequences for regional development of strong versus weak historicity?
Form of regional economic evolution implied	Does path-dependence imply a developmental trajectory characterized by punctuated equilibrium; or one of slow, incremental mutation and cumulative transformation?
The geographies of new path creation	Where and when do new industrial and technological paths emerge? Is new path emergence itself a path-dependent and place dependent process? What is the role of radical versus incremental innovation in path evolution?

Source: Adapted from: Martin and Sunley (2006).

Sedita's (2009) work on Italian industrial districts, typify this approach to regional path-dependence. These studies typically invoke localized network externalities to explain the local path-dependent development of the industry in question. Yet another approach has been to look for evidence of persistent technological regimes in manufacturing sectors across regions and to interpret technological differences as evidence of path-dependence (Rigby and Essletzbichler, 1997; Essletzbichler and Winther, 1999).

By comparison, much less attention has been given to a third possible approach to regional path-dependence, where interest is in how a regional economy, as a whole, evolves through time. This, potentially, is the most interesting test of the path-dependence idea; but it is also the most problematic. The focus here is on the evolution of the region's entire industrial–institutional system. The difficulty is that there need not be any isomorphism between the degree of path-dependence across different industries in a region, nor across different scales of observation (from firms to industries). Indeed, different industries within a region may be subject to quite different sources or mechanisms of path-dependence: some may be resource-based, others subject to particular externalities of localization, some tied to the inertia of large sunk costs of physical or infrastructural capital investments, still others subject to technological 'lock-in', and so on. The more economically diverse a region is, therefore, the more likely it is to contain multiple instances of path-dependence. These multiple simultaneous paths may of course be wholly unrelated. But a more likely scenario is where there is at least some degree of multiple related path-dependence across the regional economy.

Of relevance to this issue, Bassanini and Dosi (2001) argue that systems may be composed of path-dependent entities (such as firm or industries), but whether or not the system as a whole will be path-dependent depends on the structure of the interactions between the constituent entities. They contend that when such interactions are strong – above a certain 'threshold' – path-dependence among the constituent entities induces path-dependence at the level of the 'aggregate' system, although as they acknowledge, there is no *a priori* way of specifying what that 'interaction threshold' has to be before aggregate path-dependence outcomes become observable.[3] In most regions there will be groups of interrelated or complementary industries and activities, linked either by direct input–output relationships, or by various indirect (or untraded) interdependencies and externalities. In other words, various networks and structures of interrelatedness can emerge between different sectors and activities within a region, thus suggesting the possibility of what we might call 'path-interdependence', that is, situations where the path-dependent trajectories of particular local industries are to some degree mutually reinforcing, and co-evolving. Unravelling the path-dependent dynamics of such regional economies remains a conceptual and empirical challenge.

THE STRENGTH OR HISTORICAL 'DEPTH' OF REGIONAL PATH-DEPENDENCE

Another critical issue in regional path-dependence has to do with the 'strength' of the historical causality or 'conditioning' that the notion of path-dependence implies. How much of a region's previous developmental history is relevant in explaining the form and performance of a region's economy at any given point in time? One of the defining ideas of the path-dependence perspective, especially in David's work, is that early decisions and outcomes matter more. Such decisions serve to 'select' one developmental path which, because of the positive feedback and self-reinforcing mechanisms typically regarded as causing path-dependent dynamics, becomes progressively reinforced, rendering a switch to some alternative trajectory less and less likely. This idea of the importance of 'remote historical events' in shaping the course of subsequent economic change is what can be termed 'initial event' or 'early path-dependence', defined as a process in which, typically, once an early path becomes established, thereafter the outcome is simply reproduced or 'locked in' (see Page, 2006). This accords with David's famous QWERTY keyboard example, and is the interpretation of path-dependence often used to depict the 'lock-in' of regional industrial specialisms and industrial location patterns.

However, regional economic trajectories may be shaped not by early industrial or technological decisions, but by more recent outcomes. In the case of such 'recent path-dependence' (Page, 2006), even minor recent 'deviations' and 'perturbations' in economic activity (whether happenstance or deliberate in origin) can prevent 'lock-in' to a stable configuration, and instead promote more or less continual industrial or technological change, mutation and evolution (see also below). The notion of recent path-dependence thus runs counter to common conceptions of path-dependence which emphasize the importance of early decisions, but it may well be the form of historicity that operates in a surprising number of cases, and especially in those industries and activities where knowledge and technology change rapidly, and thus in regional economies based on such activities. At the very least, the notion focuses attention on the depth of path-dependence processes and dynamics: that is, on how far back past outcomes (investments, innovations, locational decisions, and so on) continue to exercise influence over economic activity. Or to put it more graphically, the depth of path-dependence has to do with the length of the 'memory' in the regional development process.

Clearly, between the two types of early and recent path-dependence there are varying degrees of 'historicity'. Although not referring explicitly to path-dependence, but in the context of conveying the importance of history in the economic process, Kaldor (1985 [1994]) captures the basic issue in this way: 'Taking the very near future, anything that can be produced is determined, or rather limited, by the heritage of the past . . . and its influence will determine future events to an extent that varies *inversely* with the distance of the future from the present' (Kaldor, 1985 [1994]; reprinted in Buchanan and Yoon, 1994, 109–10).

What matters is the strength of this 'inverse' relationship – the 'decay rate of historicity', so to speak. For some economic processes – and for some regional economies – the temporal decay in the influence of the past on the present may be slow, and early developments continue to shape and limit current developments (coal-mining communities, and other forms of natural-resource-based local economic specialization, would be archetypical examples). In such cases it might be valid to talk of path-dependent 'lock-in' to a stable, even static, economic configuration. But for other processes – and for other regional economies – the decay rate may be steeper: recent events have much greater influence, so that a region's development trajectory can change over time, though still in a path-dependent manner. And even if a region's industrial specialism remains outwardly the same, the industry in question may undergo considerable change in terms of products, technologies used, constituent firms and so on. The notion of the 'depth' of path-dependence would thus seem to be of fundamental importance for studying regional growth and development, and bears crucially on the issue of what sort of regional economic evolution is implied by path-dependence (see below). Thus far, however, it is a notion that has received surprisingly little attention.

REGIONAL PATH CREATION: WHERE AND WHY DO NEW PATHS EMERGE?

Another intriguing and challenging aspect of path-dependence is that it is not self-evident how one should conceptualize the 'starting point' of an industrial or technological path;

that is, how a new path is created. This problem carries over with an additional dimension to the study of regional path-dependence: why do particular industrial or technological paths emerge in particular locations rather than in some others? The conceptualization of path creation has been a neglected aspect of path-dependence research in general (Garud and Karnøe, 2001), and of regional path-dependence more specifically (Martin and Sunley, 2006, 2010). Reflecting its origins in the work of David and Arthur, the typical assumption has been that new industrial and technological paths arise or emerge at random, as key 'breakpoints' triggered by happenstance, accidental or serendipitous events, discoveries or inventions. This assumption has been carried over into economic geography via the notion of 'windows of locational opportunity', to argue in effect that the geographical emergence of new industrial and technological paths is likewise a basically chance process – that the locational window is essentially 'open' everywhere (Boschma and van de Knaap, 1997). Under this 'virgin landscape' assumption (Martin, 2010), where new paths emerge is essentially unpredictable.

Now it may well be that some new industrial and technological paths are genuinely random or happenstance in their origin and location. Certainly many will appear to be unpredictable. But because an event is *ex ante* unpredictable does not mean that it cannot be given an *ex post* explanation. Many apparently random new paths can in fact be traced to some purposive act or antecedent condition: indeed, as Garud and Karnøe (2001), among others, argue, 'purposive deviation' from established norms, conditions and patterns of behaviour is in fact a common way by which economic agents explore new technological, product or industrial possibilities and eventually succeed in establishing new pathways of economic development. And in a similar way, where these new paths emerge may not simply be a random process.

In his work on path-dependence in industrial locations, Arthur (1994b, 1994c) argued that the role of history is strongest precisely when the geographical emergence of a new industry is a purely random event. But he also recognized two other possibilities: his so-called case of 'pure necessity' (where the location of firms is the result of 'determinate economic forces', such as raw material sources, and where, curiously, he argues that history has no role to play); and 'chance-and-necessity' (in which geographical attractions interact with chance events, and history is partially responsible for the outcome). In fact, as economic geographers are increasingly realizing, the 'windows of locational opportunity' for the creation of new industrial or technological paths are not equally open everywhere, and may even be firmly closed in some locations and regions, so that where new industrial paths emerge need not be a chance event (Martin and Sunley, 2010). A region's previous development path may promote and facilitate the emergence of a new industrial or technological path, or it may deter and inhibit it. It is sometimes claimed by economic geographers that 'new industries are not born in old industrial regions', the argument being that 'new industries' – especially those requiring advanced knowledge and skills; or different work, innovation and business cultures; or different institutional set-ups – will not be attracted to, or will find it difficult to become established in, precisely those locations whose path-dependent development histories have been built around industries based on 'old' knowledge, skills, technologies, and business and work cultures. However, whilst this characterization has some striking examples to support it, it is far from being a universal rule. New regional development paths can be created in several different (and overlapping) ways (see Table 15.2), and 'old' regions are not necessarily excluded from

Table 15.2   Some possible sources of new regional path creation

Source of new industrial/ technological path	Process
Radical Schumpeterian general innovation	Major Schumpeterian innovation may diffuse and trigger new industrial/technological paths in certain regions
Indigenous creation	Emergence of new technologies and industries from within the region, the result of accidental or purposive innovative breakthroughs, that may have no local antecedents there
Branching into related, complementary or more advanced sectors	Emergence of new activities and/or technologies as developments, offshoots, mutations or variants of existing activities/technologies in the region
Spin-offs into new activities	Spin-off and spin-outs of new ventures from existing firms, to form possible bases of new activities and/or technologies in the region
Implants of firms from elsewhere	Importation of a new firm or plant may act as the catalyst of new industrial or technological path in the region
Reorientation of existing sector(s)	Major realignment of existing sector(s) as a result of technological, competitive or other 'shock' to the region

these processes: in such regions the industrial, technological and skill legacies inherited from the past can sometimes be recombined, or selectively upgraded and reorientated to form the potential bases for new industrial paths to develop.

In fact, examples can be found where new industrial paths have developed out of 'old' activities in 'old' regions, for example through industrial mutation, branching processes or spin-outs from existing firms, into new related sectors or activities that draw on but reconfigure, upgrade or reorient old activities. What might matter in such instances is the pre-existing degree of technological variety in the region (see Boschma and Frenken, Chapter 14 in this *Handbook*). Also, the movement into a region of a large or significant 'lead' firm that then attracts related or similar firms, or a network of specialist suppliers, can act as a catalyst for the emergence of a new development path there. What can often be found on close examination is that new path creation is itself a path-dependent process, either in a positive, or indeed negative, way, and hence also a place-dependent process. While it is possible to conceptualize a variety of ways in which regional path creation can occur, along the lines suggested in Table 15.2, why such mechanisms occur in some places and not others can only be explained by detailed research on a case-by-case basis, and different causal processes may operate in different locations. The emergence of clean energy clusters in the US and UK, for example, appears to reflect both 'pure necessity' and 'previous path'-type processes: some clusters are emerging in locations where favourable specific natural resource conditions exist (as in the case of solar energy, wind

energy and wave energy technologies); others are developing in high-technology locations where pre-existing relevant knowledge and expertise are being utilized and adapted;
and still others are developing in locations where old non-renewable energy industries
are reorientating around renewable energy based activities (see 'Green innovation',
Chapter 32 in this *Handbook*).

PATH-DEPENDENCE AND THE EVOLUTIONARY DYNAMIC OF REGIONAL ECONOMIES

A constant theme of work using the concept of path-dependence is that it is key for
understanding the evolution of the economy. Remarkably, however, little discussion has
been directed in economic geography or regional studies to the question of what sort of
evolution the concept implies. In fact, the path-dependence models developed by David
and Arthur are multiple equilibrium models: path-dependence is essentially about the
historically contingent selection of, and convergence to, one of a number of possible multiple long-run stable equilibrium states, or 'basins of attraction'.[4] Indeed, David (2005)
explicitly refers to his approach as 'path-dependent equilibrium economics'. This raises
some fundamental questions about how path-dependence relates to notions of economic
evolution (see Martin, 2010).

As Page (2006) points out, path-dependence can be of two main types. A process
is 'outcome-dependent' if the outcome in a given period depends on past outcomes.
A process is 'equilibrium-dependent' if there is convergence to a long-run stable distribution over outcomes, and this long-run distribution depends on past outcomes.
Equilibrium dependence implies outcome dependence, but outcome dependence does
not necessarily imply equilibrium dependence. The canonical path-dependence model is
of the equilibrium-dependence type, and leads to a view of economic evolution as one of
'punctuated equilibrium' (David, 2007, 187) in which long periods of stability ('lock-in'
to particular technologies, institutions and regional industrial patterns) are spasmodi-
cally disrupted by (radical) external path-breaking technological or industrial 'shocks'
(Table 15.3). David (1993, 39) even claims that this aspect of path-dependence 'may open
a way for the formulation of dynamic models that are compatible with "stage theories"
of development'.

This interpretation of path-dependent economic evolution may fit the historical
succession of certain key, economy-transforming, Schumpeterian 'general-purpose
technologies', which tend to hold sway for quite long periods until replaced by some
radical new alternative. And the economic landscape – the regional patterns and paths
of economic activity and development – can certainly be dramatically transformed by
such historic 'punctuations'. But the problem with this 'punctuated equilibrium' view
of path-dependent economic evolution is that by emphasizing stable reproduction – via
self-reinforcing mechanisms – it gives little recognition to other types of industrial and
technological change.

In some cases, regional industrial or technological development might be better
described as some sort of cyclical process (Audretsch and Feldman, 1996; Brezis and
Krugman, 1997; Heblich et al., 2008; Martin and Sunley, 2010), whereby the path-
dependent development of a particular industrial–technological configuration in a region

Table 15.3   Path-dependent regional economic evolution: three conceptions

Type of evolution	Process
Punctuated equilibrium	Regional economies evolve by means of moving from one path dependent stable (equilibrium) industrial/technological configuration to another as result of spasmodic external shocks
Cyclical replacement/regeneration	Regional economies evolve through the succession of path-dependent industrial-technological cycles, whereby the exhaustion of one cycle ushers in the conditions for the establishment of a new cycle
Cumulative mutation/adaptation	Regional economies evolve through a process of more or less continual industrial and technological mutation and adaptation, in which incremental innovation and firm population dynamics play key roles

eventually becomes exhausted – innovation may slow or cease, negative externalities may set in, or some other endogenous process of industrial maturation or sclerosis takes hold – and the stage is set for the potential reorientation of the regional economy around a new set of industries or technologies (which may, of course, draw upon elements of the old industries and technologies).

A third, and arguably more likely, evolutionary pattern is that of continuous cumulative change, mutation, experimentation and adaptation. This seems to typify many industries, technologies, institutions and regional economies (see Cooke and Eriksson's Chapter 43 in this *Handbook*). Discontented with the overemphasis on continuity in standard path-dependent explanations of institutional evolution, political scientists and historical sociologists have recently argued that through processes of 'layering' (addition of new micro-components), 'conversion' (changes in function of existing components) and 'recombination' (combining new and old properties and features), institutions can and do change incrementally, and that such incremental change can be cumulative and transformational (Stark and Bruszt, 2001; Boas, 2007; Schneiberg, 2007).

Similar processes take place within firms, within industries and in regional economies. Being composite entities consisting of various industries, numerous firms and a range of technologies, regions are subject to the two basic evolutionary mechanisms found in many systems (Endler and McLellan, 1988): changes in the population of entities making up the system (in the case of a regional economy, changes in its population of firms); and changes in the characteristics of the entities of a system (changes in products, technologies, business methods, and so on of those firms). As a result, a region's industrial system, and its developmental path, can evolve incrementally and cumulatively over time. New firms are added, older ones may disappear, and some firms will innovate and adapt in order to remain competitive. Indeed, for most industries in most regions, external competition, shifting markets, and technological and regulatory developments constantly confront firms with the need to innovate and adapt in order to compete and survive. How such basic interacting evolutionary processes drive regional path-dependence, and how the latter in turn conditions the local operation and impact of those forces, are issues in much need of detailed conceptual and empirical enquiry, and this implies a close integration of path-dependence ideas with those relating to the processes of innovation, entrepreneurship and learning within regional economic contexts. Regional cumulative incremental (and adaptive) economic evolution is necessarily path-dependent, being conditioned and shaped by the inherited legacies of past developments; and because it is path-dependent, this form of evolution combines continuity and change.

A CONCLUDING NOTE: SOME IMPLICATIONS OF REGIONAL PATH-DEPENDENCE FOR REGIONAL POLICY

Notwithstanding the fact that the concept of regional path-dependence is complex and open to critical interrogation, it nevertheless suggests that the role of history and historicity in regional economic development should be an integral part of regional policy analysis. Path-dependence of one kind or another would seem integral to the process of regional development, and thus to our understanding of that process. Hence the existence of path-dependence frames the potential and possibilities for policy intervention. How far and in what ways it does so will depend on the nature, depth and extent of the path-dependence mechanisms at work in a regional economy.

The 'depth' (or degree of 'historicity') of regional path-dependence is of importance because it can constrain the scope for policy-makers to influence regional economic outcomes. The greater the 'depth' (historicity) of the path-dependence mechanisms at work in a regional economy – the stronger is the process of 'early or initial' path-dependence or, as some might put it, the stronger the degree of 'lock-in' to some initially selected path or state – the more difficult it is likely to be for policy-makers to change radically the direction of a region's development path. Conversely, where path-dependence is of the 'recent' type, policy action may be expected to have greater leverage in shaping regional outcomes.

The concept of path-dependence further suggests that policy attempts to create new industrial paths or clusters in a region are less likely to succeed if those industries or clusters have no local antecedents or favourable inherited legacies – no previous related or relevant industries, technologies, competencies, skills or institutions – on which they can draw and from which they can develop. Policies to redevelop a region's economy are more likely to succeed if they take proper account of, and build upon, the legacies (specifically, of course, the strengths and competences) inherited from the region's previous developmental history (see Sydow et al., 2010). At the same time, a path-dependence approach may help identify appropriate moments of policy action, such as when a new technological or industrial path appears to be emerging in a region. Policy intervention at this stage can help establish the new path, for example by promoting externalities of various kinds, or perhaps even steer it in a particular direction. More generally, path-dependence suggests an important role for regional policies that are aimed to foster and facilitate constant cumulative innovation and adaptation in a region's economy so that its industrial development paths do not get 'locked in' and the region does not lose its dynamic competitiveness (Boschma, 2004; Martin, Chapter 18 in this *Handbook*).

NOTES

1. David's own work on path-dependence has been prolific, amounting to some 40 or so papers (for examples see: David, 1985, 1988, 1993, 1994, 2005, 2007). Arthur's major contributions are collected in Arthur (1994a). Other notable works on path-dependence in economics include Magnusson and Ottosson (1997, 2009), Durlauf and Young (2001), Garud and Karnøe (2001), Castaldi and Dosi (2006). The concept has become frequently used far beyond economics, in historical sociology, political science, archaeology, organizational science and management studies (see Magnusson and Ottosson, 2009). Some authors have even used the idea to prosecute a 'new social economics' (Blume and Durlauf, 2001; Durlauf and Young, 2001).
2. The interested reader is referred to Martin and Sunley (2006), Martin (2010) and Martin and Sunley (2010) for detailed discussions of the concept of regional path-dependence, its definition, the range of causal processes involved, and the problems the concept raises. What follows here is intended to summarize but also build on these accounts. One critical issue not covered in what follows is the role of purposive human agency in shaping path-dependent processes and outcomes (see, for example, Sydow et al., 2010).
3. This arguments resonates with that by Metcalfe et al. (2006) who contend that insufficient consideration has been given to the evolution of the macro-level economy as a whole, the dynamics of which are not simply reducible to, nor the straightforward summation or average of, micro-level developments, but involve effects that only emerge at the system-wide level.
4. Both the non-ergodic multiple absorbing state Markov process model used by David, and the Polya probability model used by Arthur, have this equilibrium property.

REFERENCES

Arthur, W.B. (1994a), *Increasing Returns and Path Dependence in the Economy*, Ann Arbor, MI: Michigan University Press.
Arthur, W.B. (1994b), 'Industry location patterns and the importance of history', *Increasing Returns and Path Dependence in the Economy*, Ann Arbor, MI: Michigan University Press, pp. 49–67.
Arthur, W.B. (1994c), 'Urban systems and historical path dependence', in *Increasing Returns and Path Dependence in the Economy*, Ann Arbor, MI: Michigan University Press, pp. 99–110.
Audretsch, D.B. and M. Feldman (1996), 'Innovative clusters and the industry life cycle', *Review of Industrial Organisation*, **11**, 253–73.
Bassanini, A.P. and G. Dosi (2001), 'When and how chance and human will can twist the arms of Clio: an essay on path dependence in a world of irreversibilities', in R. Garud and P. Karnøe (eds), *Path Dependence and Creation*, London: Lawrence Erlbaum, pp. 41–68.
Bathelt, H. and J.S. Boggs (2003), 'Towards a reconceptualization of regional development paths: is Leipzig's media cluster a continuation of or a rupture with the past?', *Economic Geography*, **79** (2), 265–93.
Belussi, F. and S.R. Sedita (2009), 'Life cycle vs. multiple path dependency in industrial districts', *European Planning Studies*, **17** (4), 505–28.
Blume, L. and S. Durlauf (2001), 'The interactions-based approach to socioeconomic behavior', in S. Durlauf and H.P. Young (eds), *Social Dynamics*, Cambridge, MA: MIT Press, pp. 15–44.
Boas, T.C. (2007), 'Conceptualising continuity and change: the composite-standard model of path dependence', *Journal of Theoretical Political Science*, **19**, 33–54.
Boschma, R.A. (2004), 'Competitiveness of regions from an evolutionary perspective', *Regional Studies*, **38** (9), 1001–14.
Boschma, R.A. and K. Frenken (2006), 'Why is economic geography not an evolutionary science?', *Journal of Economic Geography*, **6**, 273–302.
Boschma, R. and B. van der Knaap (1997), 'New technology and windows of locational opportunity', in J. Reijnders (ed.), *Economics and Evolution*, Cheltenham, UK and Northampton, MA, USA: Edward Elgar, pp. 171–202.
Boschma, R. and R.L. Martin (2007), 'Constructing an evolutionary economic geography', *Journal of Economic Geography*, **7**, 537–48.
Boschma R. and R.L. Martin (eds) (2010), *Handbook of Evolutionary Economic Geography*, Cheltenham, UK and Northampton, MA, USA: Edward Elgar.
Boschma, R.A. and R. Wenting (2007), 'The spatial evolution of the British automobile industry: does location matter?', *Industrial and Corporate Change*, **16** (2), 213–38.
Brezis, E.S. and P.R. Krugman (1997), 'Technology and the life cycle of Cities', *Journal of Economic Growth*, **2**, 369–83.

Buchanan, James M. and Yong J. Yoon (1994), *The Return to Increasing Returns*, Ann Arbor, MI: University of Michigan Press.

Castaldi, C. and G. Dosi (2006), 'The grip of history and the scope for novelty: some results and open questions on path dependence in economic processes', in A. Wimmer and R. Kössler (eds), *Understanding Change: Models, Methodologies and Metaphors*, Basingstoke: Palgrave-Macmillan, pp. 99–128.

Cooke. P. and K. Morgan (1998), *The Associational Economy*, Oxford: Oxford University Press.

David, P.A. (1985), 'Clio and the economics of QWERTY', *American Economic Review*, **75**, 332–7.

David, P.A. (1988), 'Path dependence: putting the past into the future of economics', The Economic Series Technical Report 533, Institute for Mathematical Studies in the Social Sciences, Stanford University, CA.

David, P.A. (1993), 'Historical economics in the long run: some implications of path dependence', in G.D. Snooks (ed.), *Historical Analysis in Economics*, London: Routledge, pp. 29–40.

David, P.A. (1994), 'Why are institutions the "carriers of history"? Path dependence and the evolution of conventions, organisations and institutions', *Structural Change and Economic Dynamics*, **5** (2), 205–20.

David, P.A. (2005), 'Path dependence in economic processes: implications for policy analysis in dynamical systems contexts', in K. Dopfer (ed.), *The Evolutionary Foundations of Economics*, Cambridge: Cambridge University Press, pp. 151–94.

David, P.A. (2007), 'Path dependence: a foundational concept for historical social science', *Cliometrica*, **1**, 91–114.

Durlauf, S. and H.P. Young (eds) (2001), *Social Dynamics*, Cambridge, MA: MIT Press.

Endler, J.A. and T. McLellan (1988), 'The process of evolution: towards a new synthesis', *Annual Review of Ecological Systematics*, **19**, 395–421.

Essletzbichler, J. and L. Winther (1999), 'Regional technological change and path-dependency in the Danish food processing industry', *Geografiska Annaler*, **81A**, 179–96.

Fuchs, G. and P. Shapira (eds) (2005), *Rethinking Regional Innovation and Change, Path Dependency or Regional Breakthrough?* New York: Springer Verlag.

Garud, R. and P. Karnøe, P. (2001), 'Path creation as a process of mindful deviation', in R. Garud and P. Karnøe (eds), *Path Dependence and Creation*, London: Lawrence Erlbaum, pp. 1–38.

Gertler, M. (2005), 'Tacit knowledge, path dependency and local trajectories of growth', in G. Fuchs and P. Shapira (eds), *Rethinking Regional Innovation and Change, Path Dependency or Regional breakthrough?* New York: Springer Verlag, pp. 23–42.

Glasmeier, A. (2000), *Manufacturing Time: Global Competition in the Watch Industry, 1795–2000*, New York: Guilford Press.

Hassink, R. (2005), 'How to unlock regional economies from path dependency? From learning region to learning cluster', *European Planning Studies*, **13** (4), 521–35.

Hassink, R. and D.-H. Shin (2005), 'The restructuring of old industrial areas in Europe and Asia', *Environment and Planning, A*, **37**, 571–80.

Heblich, S., D. Audretsch, O. Falck and M. Feldman (2008), 'The lifecycle of regions', paper presented at DRUID Conference.

Kaldor, N. (1985), 'Inter-regional trade and cumulative causation', in *Economics Without Equilibrium*, New York: M.E. Sharpe, pp. 57–79. Reprinted in J.M. Buchanan and Y.J. Yoon (eds) (1994), *The Return to Increasing Returns*, Ann Arbor, MI: University of Michigan Press, pp. 107–20.

Kenney, M. and U. von Burg (2001), 'Paths and regions: the creation and growth of Silicon Valley', in R. Garud and P. Karnøe (eds), *Path Dependence and Creation*, London: Lawrence Erlbaum, pp. 127–48.

Klepper, S. (2007), 'Disagreements, spinoffs, and the evolution of detroit as the capital of the US automobile industry', *Management Science*, **53**, 616–31.

Krugman, P. (1991), 'History and industry location: the case of the manufacturing belt', *American Economic Review*, **81**, 80–83.

Lagerholm, M. and A. Malmberg (2009), 'Path dependence in economic geography', in L. Magnuson (ed.), *The Evolution of Path Dependence*, Cheltenham, UK and Northampton, MA, USA: Edward Elgar, pp. 87–107.

Magnusson, L. and J. Ottosson (eds) (1997), *Evolutionary Economics and Path Dependence*, Cheltenham, UK and Lyme, NH, USA: Edward Elgar.

Magnusson, L. and J. Ottosson (eds) (2009), *The Evolution of Path Dependence*, Cheltenham, UK and Northampton, MA, USA: Edward Elgar.

Martin, R. (2006), 'Path dependence and regional economic evolution', *Journal of Economic Geography*, **6**, 395–437.

Martin, R.L. (2010), 'The Roepke Lecture in Economic Geography – Rethinking regional path dependence: beyond lock-in to evolution', *Economic Geography*, **86**, 1–27.

Martin, R.L. and P.J. Sunley (2006), 'Path dependence and regional economic evolution', *Journal of Economic Geography*, **6**, 395–438.

Martin, R.L. and P. Sunley (2010), 'The place of path dependence in an evolutionary perspective on the economic landscape', in R. Boschma and R.L. Martin (eds), *Handbook of Evolutionary Economic Geography*, Cheltenham, UK and Northampton, MA, USA: Edward Elgar, pp. 62–92.

Metcalfe, J.S., J. Foster and R. Ramlogan (2006), 'Adaptive economic growth', *Cambridge Journal of Economics*, **30**, pp. 7–32.

Page, S.E. (2006), 'Path dependence', *Quarterly Journal of Political Science*, **1**, 87–115.

Rigby, D.L. and J. Essletzbichler (1997), 'Evolution, process variety, and regional trajectories of technological change in US manufacturing', *Economic Geography*, **73**, 269–84.

Schneiberg, M. (2007), 'What's on the path? Path dependence, organisational diversity and the problem of institutional change in the US economy, 1900–1950', *Socio-Economic Review*, **5**, 47–80.

Scott, A.J. (2006), *Geography and Economy*, Oxford: Oxford University Press.

Stark, D. and L. Bruszt (2001), 'One way or multiple paths? For a comparative sociology of East European capitalism', *American Journal of Sociology*, **106**, 1129–37.

Sydow, J., F. Lerch and U. Staber (2010), 'Planning for path dependence? The case of a network in the Berlin–Brandenburg optics cluster', *Economic Geography*, **86**, 173–96.

Sydow, J., G. Schreyogg and J. Koch (2009), 'Organizational path dependence: opening the black box', *Academy of Management Review*, **34**, 689–709.

Walker, R. (2001), 'The geography of production', in E. Sheppard and T. Barnes (eds), *A Companion to Economic Geography*, Oxford: Blackwell, pp. 113–32.

16 Absorptive capacity in a regional context
Maria Abreu

INTRODUCTION

Absorptive capacity was famously defined by Cohen and Levinthal (1989) as the ability by a firm to 'identify, assimilate and exploit knowledge from the external environment' (Cohen and Levinthal, 1989, 569). In essence, the firm needs to achieve a sufficient level of previous knowledge in order to be able to adopt innovations developed elsewhere, interpret the results of basic science and follow its own research and development (R&D) programme. While the concept has intuitive appeal at the firm level, extending it to more aggregate dimensions such as regions or countries is not entirely straightforward. The regional development literature has always understood the importance of pre-existing conditions for facilitating the regional growth process. These include education and learning, R&D organizations, government agencies, networks of firms, and local rules, norms and traditions. These factors are variously known as regional capabilities, initial conditions and historical settings; the absorptive capacity literature aims to understand the pre-existing conditions that are relevant to the knowledge creation process.

As we will see, the concept has immense intuitive appeal but is, in part for historical reasons, difficult to define precisely. It has evolved sometimes in tandem but often independently in fields as diverse as development economics, industrial organization and management science. The aim of this chapter is to present a critical review of the absorptive capacity literature, considering strands from different disciplines and providing an overview of the historical evolution of the concept. It discusses the issues involved in the operationalization of the concept at the level of the firm, problems of identification, and aggregation to the regional, sectoral and country levels. The chapter concludes by discussing the multilevel nature of the absorptive capacity concept.

ANTECEDENTS AND HISTORY OF THE CONCEPT

Part of the difficulty in defining 'absorptive capacity' lies in the varied use of the term across different research streams and over time. In the 1960s it appears in the development and macroeconomics literatures, where it is taken to mean the conditions needed to ensure the effective use of external resources such as international aid and expertise by developing countries. In the 1980s and 1990s it is used by Cohen and Levinthal (1989, 1990, 1994) to denote firm-level characteristics that are necessary for technology adoption; while in recent years the concept has been extended to include networks and other relationships with the external environment. These have in turn been used to formulate new aggregate constructs.

Absorptive Capacity in the Development Literature

The concept of absorptive capacity has been used in development economics since the 1960s to denote country-level characteristics which are necessary for the effectiveness of international aid. These characteristics are typically macroeconomic variables such as fiscal and monetary policy, allocative mechanisms such as the quality of the management of government agencies, and local constraints such as education and managerial skills (World Bank, 2004). Although different in its scope, the concept as used in the development literature is not far removed from the sense in which it is used in the innovation literature, since in both cases absorptive capacity denotes the ability by economic actors to overcome constraints to the productive use of external resources.

A parallel stream of research within the macroeconomics growth literature, also originating in the 1960s, has focused on the human capital dimension, and argued that a certain level of human capital is needed before a country can adopt foreign technology and use foreign expertise. While not using the term 'absorptive capacity' explicitly, Nelson and Phelps (1966) apply this idea in a model of technology diffusion, where the growth rate of technology is a function of the interaction between the technological distance to the technology leader and the level of human capital of the adopter. Along similar lines, Abramovitz (1986) argues that economic convergence is a function of the 'social capability' of technologically backward countries, by which he means the level of education of the population and the quality of its commercial, industrial and political institutions. He notes that: 'a country's potential for rapid growth is strong not when it is backward without qualification, but rather when it is technologically backward but socially advanced' (Abramovitz, 1986, 388).

Absorptive Capacity as Firm-Level Concept

By the time Cohen and Levinthal published a series of seminal papers on absorptive capacity, the importance of investment in R&D for subsequent knowledge creation had already been expounded by, among others, Tilton (1971), Allen (1977) and Mowery (1983). The notion that previous experience leads to increased productivity and incremental innovation in the form of 'learning by doing' had also been discussed in the economics literature (Arrow, 1962a), and studies in the cognitive and behavioural sciences had shown that prior knowledge facilitates the learning of new, related knowledge (Bower and Hilgard, 1981; Ellis, 1965).

The contribution of Cohen and Levinthal was to show how the accumulation of absorptive capacity could be a rational strategy for industrial competitiveness. In a seminal paper in the *Economic Journal*, Cohen and Levinthal define absorptive capacity as the ability to: 'identify, assimilate and exploit knowledge from the environment – what we call a firm's "learning" or "absorptive capacity"' (Cohen and Levinthal, 1989, 569). Absorptive capacity allows the firm to adopt innovations developed elsewhere and acquire knowledge that can be used in the innovation process. In their model, absorptive capacity is a function of a firm's previous investment in R&D and the 'ease of learning' of the external knowledge relevant to the firm. The characteristics determining the 'ease of learning' include the complexity of the knowledge to be assimilated, the degree to which the knowledge is targeted to the needs of the firm, the degree to which knowledge is cumulative in the relevant field, and the pace of advance of knowledge in the field. Crucially, Cohen and Levinthal show that increased intra-industry R&D spillovers need not reduce incentives to invest in R&D, because increased spillovers raise the benefits of R&D through the development of absorptive capacity. This finding runs contrary to previous research on R&D spillovers (Arrow, 1962b).

In a further paper, written from a management science perspective, Cohen and Levinthal (1990) further develop their concept of absorptive capacity, now more broadly defined as: 'the ability of a firm to recognise the value of new, external information, assimilate it, and apply it to commercial ends' (Cohen and Levinthal, 1990, 128). The concept is extended to include: the human capital and training of the firm's employees, both of which increase the depth and breadth of knowledge available within the firm; organizational aspects within the firm that allow knowledge to be shared and to reach the appropriate user; management techniques such as job rotation that encourage knowledge sharing; and access to networks to allow the identification of the knowledge relevant to the firm's innovation process.

In a follow-up article (Cohen and Levinthal, 1994), the authors argue that the creation of absorptive capacity is a path-dependent process, both because knowledge creation is cumulative in itself and because absorptive capacity allows the firm to predict better the nature of potential technological advances, affecting its expectations. They extend their 1989 model to allow for past behaviour, uncertainty and competitive interaction, and find that the cumulativeness of the process can lead to the potential 'lock-out' of firms that do not invest in absorptive capacity.

In their papers Cohen and Levinthal emphasize the importance of both the depth of knowledge, in the sense that new discoveries are not possible without sufficient foundations, and the breadth of knowledge, where knowledge is sufficiently diversified to allow new and original connections to be made. Diversity of knowledge is particularly important in settings where there is substantial uncertainty about the knowledge domains from which potentially useful information may be gleaned in the future. By the same principle, a firm's absorptive capacity is more than the sum of the absorptive capacities of its individual workers, since organizational aspects that increase the diversity of the knowledge available in the firm and encourage cross-functional relationships can enhance overall absorptive capacity.

Extensions to the Concept

Over the years a number of authors have sought to extent the conceptual framework developed by Cohen and Levinthal (1989, 1990). Several important extensions stand out. While in Cohen and Levinthal (1989, 1990) the focus is on the internal characteristics of the firm, Lane and Lubatkin (1998) shift the framework to consider the characteristics of both the recipient or 'student' firm and the source or 'teacher' firm, developing the idea of 'relative absorptive capacity'. Following the insights in Cohen and Levinthal (1990) on the balance between depth and diversity of knowledge, Lane and Lubatkin (1998) also show that learning is greatest when the student and teacher firms share a similar form of basic knowledge but differ in their types of specialized knowledge.

Similarly, Dyer and Singh (1998) extend the concept of absorptive capacity to capture the relationship between partner firms. 'Partner-specific absorptive capacity' is defined as: 'the ability to recognise and assimilate valuable knowledge from a particular alliance partner' (Dyer and Singh, 1998, 665). The development of this partner-specific absorptive capacity requires the implementation of processes that allow firms to identify and transfer knowledge across organizational boundaries. Partner-specific absorptive capacity increases in the extent to which partner firms have developed overlapping knowledge-bases and have put in place mechanisms for frequent interactions. The difference between this approach and that of Lane and Lubatkin (1998) is that the concept of 'partner-specific absorptive capacity' assumes that knowledge flows in both directions, while in 'relative absorptive capacity' knowledge exchange is a one-way process.

Although Cohen and Levinthal (1990) had already identified the organizational aspects of absorptive capacity, Van den Bosch et al. (1999) analyse them in more detail. Different organizational forms are better for different aspects of absorptive capacity; for instance, functional forms tend to promote efficiency of absorption, while matrix forms – where individuals are assigned to functional departments but work within temporary units or projects – offer greater scope and flexibility of absorption.

In a wide-ranging review of the absorptive capacity literature, Zahra and George (2002) argue that concept can be decomposed into 'potential' and 'realized' absorptive capacity. Potential absorptive capacity covers the acquisition and assimilation of knowledge, while realized absorptive capacity covers knowledge transformation and exploitation. The authors thus add a fourth component, transformation of knowledge, to the three previously considered in the literature: the acquisition, assimilation and exploitation of external knowledge. They argue that realized absorptive capacity has received the most attention, particularly in empirical studies, but potential absorptive capacity is crucial in allowing firms to build a competitive advantage, particularly in environments of high uncertainty.

FIRM-LEVEL STUDIES

Despite the four major extensions of the concept discussed above, much of the empirical literature has focused on the Cohen and Levinthal (1989, 1990) framework. Two major issues complicate the task of empirical analysis. The first concern is how to operationalize the concept when in many cases the variables of interest, such as human capital and skills, are unobservable. The second relates to the dual role of R&D and other variables in the innovation process; these variables are both a direct input into the innovation process and a key component in the formation of absorptive capacity, leading to identification problems (Schmidt, 2005).

Operationalizing the Concept at Firm Level

A large proportion of the empirical literature has examined the role of R&D in building absorptive capacity. Prior related R&D is often operationalized using R&D intensity, defined as a percentage of sales or the share of R&D employees in total employees (Stock et al., 2001; Fritsch and Lukas, 2001). The results indicate that R&D intensity has a positive impact on cooperation and new product development, suggesting that R&D is an important component of absorptive capacity. The cumulative nature of absorptive capacity has led some researchers to capture it by using a measure of R&D persistence, with somewhat mixed results. For example, Wakelin (2001) shows that the rate of return to R&D is higher for innovative firms, while Cefis and Orsenigo (2001) show that innovators and non-innovators have a high probability to be unaffected. Geroski et al. (1997), however, find that few firms are persistently innovative. The evidence for absorptive capacity as measured by the presence of an R&D department is stronger. Veugelers (1997) finds that external R&D has a positive effect on internal R&D only if a firm has a full-time R&D department; while Bougrain and Haudeville (2002) show that the presence of a formal design office in small and medium-sized enterprises (SMEs) has a positive impact on their ability to exploit external knowledge.

A second important component of absorptive capacity is the human capital embodied in individual workers. The human capital variable is often operationalized by using the level of education of employees and their access to training. For instance, Rothwell and Dodgson (1991) find that SMEs rely on educated technicians, engineers and other specialists in order to access external knowledge, while Gambardella (1992) shows that in-house scientific research programmes facilitate access to external knowledge. The role of gatekeepers in the development of absorptive capacity has also been extensively analysed. Gatekeepers are individuals who are at the interface of the firm and the external environment, or at boundaries between units of the firm, and who are able to identify, assimilate and transmit external knowledge. The presence of key scientists who act as gatekeepers has been found to increase patenting activity and promote R&D alliances (Furukawa and Goto, 2006; Fritsch and Lukas, 2001).

An important component of absorptive capacity is the existence of organizational structures and management practices that aid the transfer of knowledge within the firm. Cohen and Levinthal (1990, 1994) stress the importance of job rotation and cross-functional teams for the development of absorptive capacity. Cross-functional communication mechanisms promote the flow of knowledge within the firm, as do organizational structures that are horizontal, flexible and participative (Daghfous, 2004). A similarity in organizational forms, particularly in terms of knowledge-processing systems and compensation policies based on publications and external reputation, increase the scope for knowledge transfer between two firms (Lane and Lubatkin, 1998). Knowledge management tools such as corporate universities, communities of practice, group benchmarking and learning systems also contribute to absorptive capacity (Mahnke et al., 2005).

A final component is access of the firm to networks that can be used to identify and transfer knowledge. Firms in industries where there is substantial interdependence are better able to identify and absorb new knowledge, since they have access to a number of overlapping networks (DeFillippi and Arthur, 1994). However, the optimal geographical dimension of networks for the development of absorptive capacity is not clearly defined. Abreu et al. (2008) find that different geographies of networks are important for different types of innovation, with local networks having a positive impact on process innovation, national networks having a positive impact on service innovation, and international networks being important for goods innovation. Freel (2003) shows that the impact of networks of different geographical scales varies by industrial sector. The optimal network density may also depend on the degree of heterogeneity of firms: high-density networks may only be beneficial if firms are sufficiently heterogeneous, for instance if they differ in their type of specialized knowledge (Meagher and Rogers, 2004; Lane and Lubatkin, 1998).

Capturing the Dual Role of R&D

A key aspect of the absorptive capacity literature is the dual role played by R&D and other variables in the innovation process. These variables are both a direct input into innovation and a determinant of absorptive capacity, the latter of which is necessary to identify, assimilate and use external knowledge, and hence to innovate. However, this duality is difficult to operationalize in practice. In Cohen and Levinthal (1989, 1990) the issue is addressed by estimating a model of R&D investment, where the decision to invest in R&D in order to build absorptive capacity, and the decision to invest in order to increase the direct input into the innovation process, are considered simultaneously. Another option is to focus on the innovation process and account for the dual role of R&D by including an interaction term between R&D and a proxy for external knowledge (Jaffe, 1986; Veugelers, 1997). This, however, leads to further difficulties. Absorptive capacity is a multidimensional concept and including interaction terms between external knowledge and a number of other absorptive capacity determinants such as human capital, training and organizational aspects quickly leads to intractability. A number of papers have addressed this by using principal components and factor analysis (Lin et al., 2002; Liao et al., 2003; Jansen et al., 2006).

A further solution to the problem is to model the complementarities between internal and external knowledge directly. Arora and Gambardella (1994) do this by estimating a count model of the number of collaborative agreements that a firm enters into, as a function of its ability to screen and use the knowledge resulting from the collaborative links. The results support the hypothesis of complementarities. Kaiser (2002) models complementarities between cooperation choice and innovation expenditures using a simultaneous equations framework, and finds that cooperating firms invest more in R&D than non-cooperating firms. Cassiman and Veugelers (2002) use a multivariate probit model to show that firms that use only internal or external innovation strategies introduced fewer new or improved products than firms that used both strategies, suggesting complementarities between the two types of innovation activities.

ABSORPTIVE CAPACITY AND THE REGION

Although most of the literature on absorptive capacity has been conducted at the firm level, some of the findings of this literature are relevant for regional economics. For instance, suggestions that improvements in human capital, training of employees and the provision of intermediaries who can play the role of gatekeepers to improve access to external knowledge, can help to enhance the productivity of firms in a region, are highly relevant to regional policy. A sparse but growing literature has also directly considered the aggregation of the concept of absorptive capacity to a regional level where, in a development that parallels the contribution of Cohen and Levinthal (1989), 'regional absorptive capacity' is more than just the sum of the absorptive capacities of the individual firms located in the region. Insights from the regional innovation systems literature are particularly relevant in making the transition to an aggregate concept.

Regional Innovation Systems

The regional innovation system (RIS) literature has its roots in the innovation system approach introduced by Freeman (1987) in a study of the economy of Japan, and later developed by Lundvall (1992) and Nelson (1993). Freeman (1987) defined a national system of innovation as: 'the network of institutions in the public and private sectors whose activities and interactions initiate, import and diffuse new technologies' (Freeman, 1987, 1). The systems approach emphasizes the non-linear and path-dependent nature of the innovation system; the interconnectedness between organizations such as firms, research centres, universities, schools and government agencies; and institutions such as common habits, rules, norms and laws that regulate the interactions between individuals, groups and organizations. The focus is on a broad conceptual framework that can be used to understand innovation and learning, rather than on a theoretical model where all linkages are perfectly defined. A regional innovation system is one that lies within a set of spatial boundaries, defined by a geography within which there is some coherence or inward orientation with respect to innovation processes (Asheim and Isaksen, 2002).

The RIS literature is highly relevant to the task of extending the absorptive capacity concept to the regional level because it has identified the organizations, institutions and linkages that are needed to promote the process of knowledge exchange across organizational boundaries in the region. Important aspects of regional innovation systems include linkages between universities and firms, the role of universities in providing public spaces for other economic actors to meet, relationships of firms with their customers and suppliers, and the role of government legislation in providing support for innovation (Asheim and Gertler, 2004). The literature has also considered the boundaries of the regional innovation system; in particular, the issue of linkages to organizations outside the region. For instance, Balthelt et al. (2004) argue that both local and global linkages can coexist in a context where local interactions create a 'buzz' that adds to local innovation processes, while channels of communication or 'pipelines' to actors outside the region are developed in order to access knowledge that is external to the region.

Regional Studies of Absorptive Capacity

Following the principle of extending absorptive capacity from the individual to the firm level, absorptive capacity at the regional level can be thought of as a function of the absorptive capacities of the firms located in the region, institutional features that promote knowledge exchange within firms in the region, and the links to organizations external to the region (Narula, 2004).

The literature on absorptive capacity at the regional level is still very recent and sparse. A number of studies have used insights from the firm-level literature and the RIS literature to estimate regional knowledge production functions which incorporate determinants of absorptive capacity at the regional level. The issues of operationalization and the dual role of R&D discussed above in the context of firm-level studies are also very relevant here. Roper and Love (2006) address the issue of the dual role of the absorptive capacity variables by including interaction terms between human capital and the levels of public and private R&D spending at the regional and national levels. They find some evidence to suggest that regional human capital facilitates knowledge transfer to a region. A similar result is reported by Tondl and Vuksic (2003) for higher education in the Eastern European regions, while Girma and Wakelin (2000) find that firms in the less developed regions in the UK are less likely to benefit from spillovers; in both cases knowledge transfer is assumed to occur via foreign direct investment (FDI).

In a separate strand of the literature, a number of studies have analysed absorptive capacity within industrial clusters. Giuliani (2005) presents a conceptual framework for analysing 'cluster absorptive capacity', which includes the knowledge bases of firms in the cluster, the intracluster knowledge exchange system and the number of links of cluster firms with external sources of knowledge. Through reviewing existing studies of clusters, she finds support for the hypothesis that greater cluster absorptive capacity leads to cluster growth. In a related study, Giuliani and Bell (2004) analyse a wine cluster in Chile and find that external knowledge flows tend to reach firms with very advanced absorptive capacity. These firms take on the role of gatekeepers and further diffuse knowledge within the cluster. Agrawal and Cockburn (2003) also find support for this hypothesis, showing that anchor tenants with high levels of absorptive capacity facilitate the flow of university research to local economies.

Absorptive Capacity at the Sectoral and Country Level

In addition to aggregation to the regional level, absorptive capacity has also been used as a sectoral and country-level concept. Much of the country-level literature is based on a characterization of absorptive capacity in the social capabilities tradition of international macroeconomics. This idea has been further developed in the endogenous growth literature, which emphasizes the importance of human capital and institutions. In a review of the literature, Keller (2004) shows that the pattern of worldwide technical change is mostly due to technology diffusion, driven in part by cross-country differences in absorptive capacity. Grifith et al. (2003) build on the same ideas by interacting R&D with external knowledge in a model of technology growth, and find support for the 'two faces of R&D' hypothesis, as well as an important role for human capital in developing absorptive capacity. This last study is conducted at the sectoral level across a number of Organisation for Economic Co-operation and Development (OECD) countries.

CONCLUSIONS

This chapter has reviewed the literature on absorptive capacity, starting with its historical antecedents in the development economics and international macroeconomics literatures; the seminal work of Cohen and Levinthal (1989, 1990, 1994), who argued that prior related knowledge was needed before a firm could adopt external knowledge and develop its own R&D programme; and recent conceptual extensions. While most of the empirical literature has been conducted at the firm level, a number of recent studies have sought to extend it to higher levels of aggregation. The empirical literature has also identified ways to overcome difficulties in estimating models based on a concept that is difficult to operationalize, and one which is based on the idea that variables have dual roles in the innovation process.

The review suggests that the concept may be relevant at a number of different levels of aggregation, or indeed as a multilevel concept (Van den Bosch et al., 2002). In their seminal contribution Cohen and Levinthal (1990) show how absorptive capacity at the level of the firm is composed of the absorptive capacities of individual employees, plus firm-level variables such as internal communication processes and links to external sources of knowledge. Giuliani (2005), Roper and Love (2006) and others show how absorptive capacity can be extended to a regional level by including the absorptive capacity of individual firms, interfirm variables such as knowledge transfer channels, and links to external knowledge sources. A similar aggregation process can be applied to the sectoral level (Griffith et al., 2003) and the country level (Keller, 1996). The analysis of the components of absorptive capacity at different levels of spatial and sectoral aggregation remains a fruitful area for future research.

REFERENCES

Abramovitz, M. (1986), 'Catching up, forging ahead, and falling behind', *Journal of Economic History*, **46**, 385–406.

Abreu, M., V. Grinevich, M. Kitson and M. Savona (2008), 'Absorptive capacity and regional patterns of innovation', DIUS Research Report No. 08/11, London.

Agrawal, A. and I. Cockburn (2003), 'The anchor tenant hypothesis: exploring the role of large, local, R&D-intensive firms in regional innovation systems', *International Journal of Industrial Organization*, **21**, 1227–53.

Allen, T. (1977), *Managing the Flow of Technology*, Cambridge, MA: MIT Press.

Arora, A. and A. Gambardella (1994), 'Evaluating technological information and utilizing it', *Journal of Economic Behaviour and Organization*, **24**, 91–114.

Arrow, K. (1962a), 'The implications of learning by doing', *Review of Economic Studies*, **29**, 155–73.

Arrow, K. (1962b), 'Economic welfare and the allocation of resources for invention', in R. Nelson (ed.), *The Rate and Direction of Inventive Activity*, Princeton, NJ: Princeton University Press, pp. 609–25.

Asheim, B. and M. Gertler (2004), 'The geography of innovation: regional innovation systems', in J. Fagerberg, D. Mowery and R. Nelson (eds), *The Oxford Handbook of Innovation*, Oxford: Oxford University Press, pp. 291–317.

Asheim, B. and A. Isaksen (2002), 'Regional innovation systems: the integration of local "sticky" and global "ubiquitous" knowledge', *Journal of Technology Transfer*, **27**, 77–86.

Balthelt, H., A. Malmberg and P. Maskell (2004), 'Clusters and knowledge: local buzz, global pipelines and the process of knowledge creation', *Progress in Human Geography*, **28**, 31–56.

Bougrain, F. and B. Haudeville (2002), 'Innovation, collaboration and SMEs internal research capacities', *Research Policy*, **31**, 735–47.

Bower, G. and E. Hilgard (1981), *Theories of Learning*, Englewood Cliffs, NJ: Prentice-Hall.

Cassiman, B. and R. Veugelers (2002), 'Complementarity in the innovation strategy: internal R&D, external technology acquisition and cooperation', CEPR Discussion Paper No. 3284, London.

Cefis, E. and L. Orsenigo (2001), 'The persistence of innovative activities: a cross-countries and cross-sectors comparative analysis', *Research Policy*, **30**, 1139–58.

Cohen, W. and D. Levinthal (1989), 'Innovation and learning: the two faces of R&D', *Economic Journal*, **99**, 569–96.

Cohen, W. and D. Levinthal (1990), 'Absorptive capacity: a new perspective on learning and innovation', *Administrative Science Quarterly*, **35**, 128–52.

Cohen, W. and D. Levinthal (1994), 'Fortune favors the prepared firm', *Management Science*, **40**, 227–51.

Daghfous, A. (2004), 'Absorptive capacity and the implementation of knowledge-intensive best practices', *SAM Advanced Management Journal*, **69**, 21–7.

DeFillippi, R. and M. Arthur (1994), 'The boundaryless career: a competency-based perspective', *Journal of Organizational Behavior*, **15**, 307–24.

Dyer, J. and H. Singh (1998), 'The relational view: cooperative strategy and sources of interorganizational competitive advantage', *Academy of Management Review*, **23**, 660–79.

Ellis, H. (1965), *The Transfer of Learning*, New York: Macmillan.

Freel, M. (2003), 'Sectoral patterns of small firm innovation, networking and proximity', *Research Policy*, **32**, 751–70.

Freeman, C. (1987), *Technology Policy and Economic Performance: Lessons from Japan*, London: Pinter.

Fritsch, M. and R. Lukas (2001), 'Who cooperates on R&D?', *Research Policy*, **30**, 297–312.

Furukawa, R. and A. Goto (2006), 'The role of corporate scientists in innovation', *Research Policy*, **35**, 24–36.

Gambardella, A. (1992), 'Competitive advantages from in-house scientific research: the US pharmaceutical industry in the 1980s', *Research Policy*, **21**, 391–407.

Geroski, P., J. Van Reenen and C. Walters (1997), 'How persistently do firms innovate?', *Research Policy*, **26**, 33–48.

Girma, S. and K. Wakelin (2000), 'Are there regional spillovers from FDI in the UK?', GLM Research Paper, Nottingham.

Giuliani, E. (2005), 'Cluster absorptive capacity: why do some clusters forge ahead and others lag behind?', *European Urban and Regional Studies*, **12**, 269–88.

Giuliani, E. and M. Bell (2004), 'The micro-determinants of meso-level learning and innovation: evidence from a Chilean wine cluster', *Research Policy*, **34**, 47–68.

Griffith, R., S. Redding and J. Van Reenen (2003), 'Mapping the two faces of R&D: productivity growth in a panel of OECD industries', *Review of Economics and Statistics*, **86**, 883–95.

Jaffe, A. (1986), 'Technological opportunity and spillovers of R&D: evidence from firms' patents, profits and market value', *American Economic Review*, **76**, 984–1001.

Jansen, J., F. Van Den Bosch and H. Volberda (2006), 'Exploratory innovation, exploitative innovation, and performance: effects of organizational antecedents and environmental moderators', ERIM Report Series, Rotterdam.

Kaiser, U. (2002), 'An empirical test of models explaining research expenditures and research cooperation: evidence for the German service sector', *International Journal of Industrial Organization*, **20**, 747–74.

Keller, W. (1996), 'Absorptive capacity: on the creation and acquisition of technology in development', *Journal of Development Economics*, **49**, 199–227.

Keller, W. (2004), 'International technology diffusion', *Journal of Economic Literature*, **42**, 752–82.

Lane, P. and M. Lubatkin (1998), 'Relative absorptive capacity and interorganizational learning', *Strategic Management Journal*, **19**, 461–77.

Liao, J., H. Welsch and M. Stoica (2003), 'Organizational absorptive capacity and responsiveness: an empirical investigation of growth-oriented SMEs', *Entrepreneurship Theory and Practice*, **28**, 63–85.

Lin, C., B. Tan and S. Chang (2002), 'The critical factors for technology absorptive capacity', *Industrial Management and Data Systems*, **102**, 300–308.

Lundvall, B. (ed.) (1992), *National Systems of Innovation: Towards a Theory of Innovation and Interactive Learning*, London: Pinter.

Mahnke, V., T. Pedersen and M. Verzin (2005), 'The impact of knowledge management on MNC subsidiary performance: the role of absorptive capacity', *Management International Review*, **45**, 101–20.

Meagher, K. and M. Rogers (2004), 'Network density and R&D spillovers', *Journal of Economic Behaviour and Organization*, **53**, 237–60.

Mowery, D. (1983), 'The relationship between intrafirm and contractual forms of industrial research in American manufacturing, 1900–1940', *Explorations in Economic History*, **20**, 351–74.

Narula, R. (2004), 'Understanding absorptive capacities in an "Innovation Systems" context: consequences for economic and employment growth', DRUID Working Paper, Oslo.

Nelson, R. (ed.) (1993), *National Systems of Innovation: A Comparative Study*, Oxford: Oxford University Press.

Nelson, R. and E. Phelps (1966), 'Investment in humans, technological diffusion, and economic growth', *American Economic Review*, **56**, 69–75.

Roper, S. and J. Love (2006), 'Innovation and regional absorptive capacity: the labour market dimension', *Annals of Regional Science*, **40**, 437–47.

Rothwell, R. and M. Dodgson (1991), 'External linkages and innovation in small and medium-sized enterprises', *R&D Management*, **2**, 125–38.

Schmidt, T. (2005), 'What determines absorptive capacity?', unpublished manuscript, ZEW, Mannheim.

Stock, G., N. Greis and W. Fischer (2001), 'Absorptive capacity and new product development', *Journal of High Technology Management Research*, **12**, 77–91.

Tilton, J. (1971), 'International diffusion of technology: the case of semiconductors', Brookings Institution, Washington, DC.

Tondl, G. and G. Vuksic (2003), 'What makes regions in Eastern Europe catching up? The role of foreign investment, human resources and geography', ZEI Working Paper, Bonn.

Van den Bosch, F., H. Volverda and M. Boer (1999), 'Coevolution of firm absorptive capacity and knowledge environment: organizational forms and combinative capabilities', *Organization Science*, **10**, 551–68.

Van den Bosch, F., R. Van Wijk and H. Volberda (2002), 'Absorptive capacity: antecedents, models and outcomes', ERIM Report Series, Rotterdam.

Veugelers, R. (1997), 'Internal R&D expenditures and external technology sourcing', *Research Policy*, **26**, 303–15.

Wakelin, K. (2001), 'Productivity growth and R&D expenditure in UK manufacturing firms', *Research Policy*, **30**, 1079–90.
World Bank (2004), 'Aid effectiveness and financing modalities', background paper for Development Committee, Washington, DC.
Zahra, S. and G. George (2002), 'Absorptive capacity: a review, reconceptualization, and extension', *Academy of Management Review*, **27**, 185–203.

17 Regional knowledge networks
Michael Steiner

Knowledge has long been acknowledged as the major source of regional economic development and growth; originally conceived as an exogenous factor it has from an evolutionary and institutional perspective been interpreted as an endogenous element of economic activity, thus recognizing that knowledge changes economic activity and economic activity changes knowledge (for recent surveys regarding the links between innovation, knowledge and regional development, and addressing subtle questions of top-down and bottom-up perspectives, see Howells, 2005, and Johansson and Karlsson, 2009).

This interdependency leads to the necessity of new forms of economic institutions where the dichotomy between market and hierarchy is challenged by hybrids in the form of networks. Networks facilitate frequent and proximate relations between economic actors that can contribute to the development of a shared cognitive frame – they thus serve to integrate the positive externalities of innovation, technological knowledge and development activities (Maskell and Malmberg, 1999). The emphasis lies on the interactive character of innovation which involves the sharing and the exchange of different forms of knowledge between actors (Lawson and Lorenz, 1999) – knowledge and competence is developed interactively and within subgroups of a regional economy (Lundvall, 2002). This interaction has often been interpreted also as a result of a 'associative-relational' mode of organization – networks then are a specific form of 'associative governance' (Cooke, 1998; Cooke and Morgan, 1998; Morgan, 2004).

The recent debate has concentrated on the economic character of such networks, stemming from the necessity of coordinating institutions for knowledge generation and diffusion on the one side, and from the incentive structure for firms in order to take part in such networks on the other side.

The first aspect – why there is a need for networks as hybrid institutions beyond firms and markets – points to the complexity of cooperation (Axelrod, 1997) as a phenomenon that cannot be explained solely by individual decision-making: strong rationality is not sufficient for relatively effective economic behaviour. Especially if the focus is on learning and knowledge, markets alone will not suffice for such forms of interaction and additional institutions will be needed (Bünstorf, 2003): individuals and firms alone are not capable of producing sufficient amounts and varieties of knowledge. This is not only – as Arrow (1962) pointed out – due to the externalities connected with knowledge, but also because of uncertainties, asymmetries and costs of transacting knowledge.

The original idea goes well back to Adam Smith who in 1776 interpreted the modern process of innovation as being based on the division of labour, and emphasized the social nature of the innovation process (Smith, 1776 [1904]). The division of labour produces efficiency gains – from specialization as well as from professionalization – but at the same time requires a supporting framework in order to achieve to connect the component contributions of the different agents. This aspect of connectivity becomes even stronger as soon as knowledge and skills are concerned. Because of their public character they cannot be effectively coordinated by conventional markets – for this we need specific institutional arrangements.

Helmstädter (2003) points to additional problems of 'knowledge sharing' transcending the usual problems of the 'division of labour' and asking for new and specific forms of institutions so far neglected by new institutional economics: 'The new institutional economics deals with institutions that govern the interactions taking place under the division of labour but leaves aside the division of knowledge activities that go with it' (Helmstädter, 2003, 14). Whereas the division of labour involves differentiation and separation of mode and product, knowledge sharing involves internalization and recontextualization. Therefore: 'Cooperation is the basic institution of the process of the division of knowledge' (p. 32). Networks may be regarded as such coordinating institutions for knowledge sharing, providing a cognitive framework for transforming information into useful knowledge (Audretsch and Lehmann, 2006; Steiner, 2006). In addition networks lead to coordination that not only improves the capabilities of each firm but implies capabilities that are not isolated to any one firm, and offer the benefit of specialization and variety generation (Kogut, 2000).

The new understanding of networks as guiding institutions for learning and knowledge exchange leads to further reflections concerning the forms, channels and incentives of knowledge exchange also from a micro perspective, and reiterates the question of the extent of market exchange of specialized knowledge versus institutionalized coordination and cooperation.

The incentive question – 'Why do firms participate in networks?' – has been answered by a list of the benefits associated with networks and interfirm linkages (Ahuja, 2000, surveying a vast literature): they help firms to develop and absorb technology, learn new skills, obtain access to needed assets, make it easier to withstand environmental shocks, improve survival prospects and financial performance. This then of course leads to the opposite question: 'Why do not all firms participate in networks?' One possible answer is that not all firms are attractive enough to be accepted in networks. This leads to further questions of excludability and control of network structures and the three dilemmas of knowledge sharing (Dyer and Nobeoka, 2000): how to motivate members to participate and share their knowledge; how to prevent free-riders; and how to reduce the search costs of finding valuable knowledge.

A different answer is given by focusing on social structure perspectives looking primarily at the sociological determinants of linkage formation opportunities. Here the emphasis is on existing network structures within regions, and path-dependency of network formation restricting the opportunities available for future and potential members. Ahuja (2000) develops an integrative framework which enables us to recognize the duality of the network formation process: on the one hand there are inducements and incentives for the firms to take part in networks; on the other hand networks always reflect prior patterns of interfirm relationships which determine the possibilities of linkages.

Similarly, Stuart (1998) argues that the motives for alliance formation are twofold: one is attribute-based and looks at specific firm characteristics that affect firms' propensity to enter networks (size, age, scope, research and development intensity); the other consists of technological network positions and alliance opportunity sets. That implies that a firm's proclivity to enter networks is strongly influenced by its position in the market, and that models of social structure have to be applied to the analysis of economic markets.

If networks are primarily knowledge-exchange-oriented, how does knowledge exchange take place? This exchange occurs through interaction, and the structure of the interaction has a strong influence on the amount of knowledge diffusion. In the background still looms the question as to the public-good character of knowledge and the amount of spillovers – the positive externalities of scientific discoveries which are a free good for all potential users and, as such, a major factor of endogenous growth especially of geographically restricted space. This automatic and pervasive free-good character of knowledge even within close spatial boundaries with identifiable market exchange can be questioned (Zucker et al., 1998): there are degrees of 'natural excludability' depending how well known the techniques of replication are, how strongly the information is embodied in particular individuals, and how strongly the access to a research team is controlled. Giuliani (2005) accentuates these two explanatory approaches. The first attributes knowledge with a highly public nature, so that learning and knowledge sharing within networks is externality-driven. Here collective learning processes are tied to a given territory, and local interactions not just unstructured and unplanned, but also relatively broad and diffuse (Camagni, 2002; Malmberg, 2003). The alternative approach points to the necessity to include specific features of the firm and firm-level learning in order to understand the interaction of firm-level and network-level learning. The knowledge diffusion is rather selective and strongly structured by the relative distance of firms' knowledge bases and dependent on the position of firms within networks and their absorptive capacity (Giuliani and Bell, 2005).

The second position implies a stronger strategic behaviour of firms within networks: firms try to establish a variety of types of interactions and relationships, each having different impacts on the knowledge generation and diffusion process. Mariotti and Delbridge (2001) write of the necessity for firms – in the face of knowledge ambiguity, knowledge-related barriers, tacitness and knowledge complexity – to engage in the management of a portfolio of ties. Organizations, therefore, are likely to engage in interorganizational relations that show a variety of types of ties: these can have quite different dimensions and can be defined according to the character of social relations between actors, the regulation of the relationship and also, of course, the nature of information exchange (Mariotti and Delbridge, 2001, 13). Owen-Smith and Powell (2004) argue that especially in science-driven fields, organizations that develop ties to different kinds of organizations and carry out multiple types of activities are likely to become central players in such networks.

These are strong arguments in favour of very conscious activities in the selection of networks and in their specific formation and resulting structure. The heterogeneity not only in the portfolio of different ties but also in that of collaborators leads to 'creative abrasion' (Powell and Grodal, 2005, 59): broader networks offer more experience, different competencies and additional opportunities, leading to a synthesis from multiple points of view.

Once networks are strongly influenced by the changing behaviour of firms – as pointed out at the beginning, knowledge changes economic activity and economic activity changes knowledge – they themselves are subject to change. The ongoing interaction between network members and the network is itself a force for the adaptation of networks to changing conditions of competition, technology and social structure.

THE REGIONAL DIMENSION OF KNOWLEDGE NETWORKS

Are knowledge networks necessarily 'regional', that is, do they have a limited geographical extension and consist primarily of members coming from a restricted space? Three arguments are usually put forward to support this regional dimension: the need for proximity in knowledge exchange; the decay of knowledge in space; and the embeddedness of economic ties in social relations.

The first argument strongly relies on the original Marshallian reason for co-location of industries where strong technological spillovers are in support of agglomerative tendencies: knowledge is 'in the air' once firms are in close spatial contact (Marshall 1890/1920), in a similar line of argument to the well-known literature on central places, growth poles, industrial districts and so on (for a recent overview and interpretation in the light of new regional growth theories, see McCann and von Oort, 2009). Proximity is also necessary for frequent face-to-face contacts between persons in different organizations, transferring especially the 'tacit' dimension of knowledge (Polanyi, 1962); this tacit knowledge dominates especially the early stages of the innovative process, and is hard to exchange from a distance (Feldman, 1994; Jaffe et al., 1993).

This need for proximity has been questioned on several accounts. First, there is no clear distinction between codified and tacit knowledge (Breschi and Lissoni, 2009). Second, information and communication technologies (ICTs) make it easier to convey knowledge over long distances and also tentatively to codify tacit knowledge (Amin and Cohendet, 2004). And third, the increased international competition between firms and the general tendency of globalization forces them also to look for international strategies and partners in knowledge-intensive activities such as R&D (Hagedoorn, 2002); extra-network relations therefore become more and more important. From this it might be concluded that knowledge exchange is important and also organized in different forms of networks, but it lacks a necessary spatial dimension in the sense of close geographical proximity.

On several accounts Torre (2008) counters these arguments; his reasoning results in a limited albeit still existing need for at least temporary proximity. The distinction between codified and tacit knowledge has certain limits but can be upheld. More important is the ambivalent character of specifically tacit knowledge in its geographical consequence. Either knowledge has a public-good character, in which case it is open for spillover phenomena leading to incentives of collocation. Or it is – because of its tacitness not easily conferrable and hence appropriable – to be considered as a private good underlying the rules of market exchange or cooperative interaction and becoming neutral to distance (Torre, 2008, 874). There are examples of cooperation and of knowledge exchange where proximity is never necessary, but this applies to very specific cases. Epistemic communities – groups of individuals whose communication entirely rests on ICT – do not need physical face-to-face contacts; similarly the ubiquity of single actors via portable phones, Internet and email is certainly a possible way to cooperate. Yet these are rather restricted forms of economic activities, mostly exercised by individual persons (seldom by firms), and not representative of most forms of production-related exchange of knowledge. So the total absence of geographical proximity is rather an exception (Torre, 2008, 877): there is a need for face-to-face contacts demanding geographical proximity. But this need is not permanent, or restricted to certain phases in the life cycle of products (innovation and also the last stage), to times of conflict solution, and to certain phases of interaction of firms (definition of guidelines, of organizational framework, negotiations) and can be organized via mobility of the involved persons. Therefore, geographical proximity is necessary but only for limited time spans (Torre, 2008, 885).

More in favour of proximity over longer time spans is the argument that small and medium-sized enterprises (SMEs) use collocation. Big firms have more opportunities to fulfil the challenges of temporary proximity (delocalizing part of their staff, sending research teams to other locations) than SMEs, which therefore are in stronger need of collocation. Also, spin-offs and newly founded firms stay in close vicinity to their cooperation partners. Since the larger part of networks consists of SMEs, this results finally in close proximity of the majority of firms in networks (without actually being in need of permanent collocation) (Torre, 2008, 885).

This argument is reinforced by the 'knowledge spillover theory of entrepreneurship' (Audretsch, 1995). Contrary to the usual assumption of knowledge production function approaches, it is not firms that exist exogenously and then produce and apply knowledge but: 'it is the knowledge in the possession of economic agents that is exogenous, and in an effort to appropriate the returns from that knowledge, the spillover of knowledge from its producing entity involves endogenously creating a new firm' (Audretsch, 1995, 179–80). Especially for spin-offs and for newly founded firms there is a strong tendency for spatial proximity to networks as the original source of knowledge. Entrepreneurship then can be interpreted as a conduit of knowledge spillover (Audretsch and Aldridge, 2009).

The same question but with different emphasis is treated in the discussion of the spatial scope of knowledge spillovers, with the basic argument that they have a limited range and decay with distance. Research has centred specifically on the impact of university and private R&D institutions on regional (innovation) productivity, resulting in limited spread effects (Anselin et al., 1997; Acs, 2002) and hence spatial concentration (for the empirics, see below).

To summarize so far: the pure character of knowledge alone is not sufficient for the regional dimension of knowledge networks; yet the at least temporary need of face-to-face contact for most economic activities, and the need of SMEs and spin-offs to collocate, does support the formation and subsistence of regional networks. This is also tentatively supported by the spatial decay of knowledge.

If knowledge alone is not sufficient, then what leads to and reinforces the apparent regional dimension of networks? The literature basically points to a combination of agglomerative forces (outside of knowledge spillovers), the embeddedness in social networks and the conditioning of the role of institutions. Extending the basic idea of economies of agglomeration, externalities are widely reinforced by informal and non-economic dimensions. Amin and Thrift (1994) use the term 'institutional thickness' to address the existence of a supporting environment beyond firms (institutionalized cooperations and networks). Knowledge-based innovation is a territorially embedded process and can only be understood by including the social and institutional conditions of every region (Asheim, 1999; Rodriguez-Pose and Crescenzi, 2008). Geographic agglomeration sets a framework for economic interaction and (material and immaterial) linkages between economic actors. This coincides with the view that: 'spatialities and temporalities are not neutral frames, but constitutive elements of socioeconomic transformation' (Colletis-Wahl et al., 2008, 22).

Gordon and McCann (2000, 15) define in this context three theoretical approaches which reflect different (more or less idealized) perspectives of agglomeration: the model of pure agglomeration, the industrial-complex model and the social-network model. It is the third one – relying on trust and social embeddedness as the dominant link between the firms in networks (and therefore not on deliberate economic decisions based on the minimization of different transaction costs) – that most favours the exchange of knowledge. However, such exchange is based on strong interpersonal relationships that transcend firm boundaries and allow for diverse forms of knowledge sharing. Following Iammarino and McCann (2005), traditional and recent approaches of social networks may be differentiated. The traditional approach corresponds to the 'Marshallian-stimulated' industrial districts where knowledge is mainly codified and oriented to process innovation transferred by personal contacts and social and political lobbying. While in the traditional approach the network seems to be based on geographical prox-imity rooted in historical experience, the new approach of social networks seems to be based on relational and organizational proximity. The links between actors are then all the stronger the more they are based on elements of social embeddedness: norms, sets of common assumptions, habits formed by culture, history and, of course (but not neces-sarily), spatial proximity. They form social capital that favours the explicit and implicit sharing of knowledge. New physical technologies are not just there, innovations do not just happen, but they need social technologies as pathways to coordinate human action. Rodriguez-Pose (1999, 82) – pointing to the complex institutional process that shapes the capacities and attitudes towards innovation – speaks of the '"social filters" . . . that either favour or deter the development of successful regional innovation systems'.But this does not imply that these regional networks only rely on their internal knowledge and capacities to generate innovation: they have also to create and maintain capacities to gain knowledge from the outside and to gain access to innovations produced else-where. Rodriguez-Pose and Creszenzi (2008, 54) point to several important questions of spillover analysis beyond the specific regional dimension: what is the balance between internally generated and externally transmitted knowledge? What are the conditions – again regionally and externally – that maximize the diffusion of knowledge? What is the distance that knowledge can travel without decay?

This leads to the important question of extraregional flows and exchanges of people, goods and knowledge. In an extension (and critique) of the 'new regionalism' literature and the relational view of regional development, Wai-Chung Yeung (2009, 327) revisits 'the role of transregional processes – a combination of intra-, inter-, and extra-regional mechanisms – in shaping regional development trajectories'. The 'concept of strategic coupling' as a key transregional process connects actors and forces internal to regions with extraregional flows spearheaded by global production networks. International partnerships, indigenous innovation and production platforms are the essential forms of 'strategic coupling'.

MEASURING KNOWLEDGE IN NETWORKS: EMPIRICAL EVIDENCE

If networks are dominated by knowledge-intensive exchange which has strong regional dimensions, are there any empirical approaches to identify and measure knowledge spillovers and knowledge exchange and to reveal their mechanisms? Despite the theoretical assumption in new economic geography that agglomerative scale effects are dominated by knowledge-driven productivity increases, there stands Krugman's (1991, 53) warning that empirical measurement is impossible because 'knowledge flows are invisible, they leave no paper trail by which they may be measured and tracked'. The warning was – with much effort and some results – ignored.

An early attempt (even before Krugman's warning) was Jaffe's (1989) approach to look at spatially concentrated patent activities in specific technology fields and to derive from such clustering of technological activities spillovers that are spatially close. This basic approach was taken over and refined by Acs et al. (1992), Audretsch and Feldman (1996, 2004) and Feldman (1994); they reveal strong spatial concentrations of different indicators of innovative activity and acknowledge the role of agent interaction and proximity, yet without being able to show the concrete mechanisms of spillovers.

Another approach to finding empirical support for spatially bounded knowledge consisted in measuring the distance knowledge is able to travel: the 'decay function' – where innovative spillovers cease to exist – allows us define the outer limits of potential knowledge networks. The question remains open (Döring and Schnellenbach, 2006 deny a consensus about the spatial range that can be attributed to knowledge spillovers). The distance varies between continents – Varga (2000) finds a range of 75 miles radius for the US; Greunz (2003) and Moreno et al. (2005) a range between 190 and 300 km for Europe – and depends which order of neighbourhood is included, which model is applied and how distance is measured (for example radius or trip-length). Rodriguez-Pose and Crescenzi (2008, 63), in an attempt to quantify the concept of 'proximity' for the EU-25, find a 180 minute trip time limit for interregional knowledge flows and propose the idea of '"human embodied" transmission technology because it allows the maximization of face-to-face contacts between agents'.

Does knowledge exchange prove to be worthwhile and profitable from a micro-perspective, what is the result of these cooperations for the specific firms? This question has been looked at in diverse case studies from quite different angles. They mostly question the public character of the knowledge produced in universities and other 'public' knowledge-generating institutions; they find that it is market exchange between specific partners rather than general spillovers. Zucker et al. (1998, 66) look at the specific form of cooperation between 'star scientists' and firms: 'they are not simply located in the same geographic area . . . but are deeply involved in their operations as principals, employees, or consultants'. Citing ample evidence they show that apparent geographically localized knowledge spillovers in fact represent specific market exchange where the information is rather embodied in particular individuals tied to particular locales. Stuart (2000), again with ample cited evidence, confirms that this kind of cooperation does have positive effects on a number of different measures of firms' performance. In a survey of empirical studies on the role of networks in innovation – mostly using patents as the dependent variable and formal relationships as the independent variable – Powell and Grodal (2005, 67) find a virtuous cycle: 'External linkages facilitate innovation, and at the same time innovative output attracts further innovative ties.'

How does knowledge exchange take place, how do firms in networks learn from each other? Steiner and Hartmann (2006) – based on concepts of organizational learning – identify different forms of learning in networks and between firms. Organizational learning – as the outcome of overlapping activities of individual, firm and interfirm learning – requires the presence of specific systems for the transformation and combination of these related spheres. For organizational learning in networks, two learning systems are particularly relevant: informal learning, comprising meetings in bars or at conferences, communities of practice, networks with fellow graduates and social networks on the one hand; and participative learning systems in the form of R&D teams at interfirm level, interfirm teams working on a joint project, participation in benchmarking clubs, or joint preparation of tenders in consortia on the other hand. Based on in-depth interviews with leading firms they quantify the relative importance of these different forms of learning within specific technological networks, concluding that participative learning systems dominate informal ones.

A rather recently applied tool for the identification of quantifiable forms and contents of interaction within networks is social network analysis (Krätke, 2002; Giuliani, 2005; Gay and Dousset, 2005; Steiner and Ploder, 2008; Reid et al., 2008). Social network analysis has proved to be a helpful tool in discussing the structure of networks and allowing the mapping and measuring of the relationships (communication and transaction) between different actors, and revealing the existence, context and portfolio of relations between actors in a regional network.

The basic insights gained by this approach relate both to the structure of the network as well as to the specific position of firms within specific networks. It also allows differentiating between different forms of interaction – material supplier relations, but especially also different forms of knowledge exchange such as competitive and pre-competitive R&D contacts, and different time dimensions and intensity of these interactions.

Giuliani and Bell (2005) found that in the Chilean wine cluster under scrutiny, suppliers of machinery and materials, as well as consultants, seemed to be important sources of knowledge and technical change. In Reid et al.'s (2008, 5) analysis of the northwestern Ohio greenhouse cluster it could be shown that suppliers communicate with a wide variety of growers and, consequently, that these suppliers are important in the transmission of information from grower to grower. Steiner and Ploder (2008) combine social network analysis with regression analysis and qualitative interviews to reveal different forms and contents of interaction within a given network of machinery, automobile firms and R&D institutions. They show that in its regional dimension the network is strongly based on knowledge-intensive relations: while the firms do have extensive supplier relations, these are relatively weak within the region and within the network. However, their knowledge-oriented relations – differentiated according to competitive and pre-competitive research – are to a large degree regionally concentrated. The interactions of firms are strongly structured, revealing distinct leading actors in the network.

A further approach – again rather recently applied – to identify and measure knowledge in and between firms is a modified version of capital reporting. Intellectual capital reports are usually intended to complement conventional financial reporting, assessing the intangible assets of organizations. But they can also be used to reveal the potential for knowledge generation and knowledge sharing of firms and – adequately modified – can also be applied to knowledge-intensive networks. Based on the basic differentiation of components of intellectual capital as human, structural and relational capital (Edvinsson and Malone, 1997), each component can be used also for network analysis. Hartmann et al. (2007) take an existing competence centre and its corresponding network of scientific and company partners as their unit of analysis. The mission of the competence centre is the application of a science-based methodology to industrial problems and the transfer of research findings to its network partners. Yet the applied methodology reveals that the relational capital – cooperation with other networks and organizations – is quite intensive and can be considered as an indicator of knowledge spillovers extending far beyond the original network.

Are there any empirical approaches to reveal evidence of transregional flows of knowledge between regional networks? This still remains a challenge for research. Some tentative steps have been taken. Crescenzi et al. (2007) discuss – extending the question of the travelling distance of knowledge – the extent of interagglomeration flows, and undertake a comparative analysis of the territorial dynamics of innovation between Europe and the United States. Focusing on the role of agglomeration and the density of economic interactions as the key catalysers of innovation, they use a knowledge production function approach to analyse the territorial dimension of knowledge production in the European Union (EU) and the US. Their main result is that knowledge production is governed by different geographical processes: whereas in the US the generation of innovation occurs in self-contained geographical areas, the process in Europe is much more linked 'to proximity to other innovative areas and to the capacity to assimilate and transform interregional knowledge spillovers into innovation' (Crescenzi et al., 2007, 703).

Gay (2008), using network mapping, tries to compare leading indicators for innovation across national borders. By connecting core regions and technological alliances across Europe, tentative evidence of leading and lagging regions with different degrees of innovativeness can be revealed. The analysis underlines the importance of continuous acquisition of technologies and products through alliances on a transregional and transnational level.

Steiner et al. (2010) – again based on social network analysis in combination with regression analysis and qualitative research – compare medium-technology networks of four European regions in order to explain differences in their specific innovation network structures. Based on differences in their level of agglomeration, the structure of economic sectors, their formal knowledge base and institutional development the importance of technology-specific, firm-specific and region-specific factors is exploratively investigated. It can be shown in this comparative four-region case study that regions increasingly rely on knowledge instead of material linkages, and that firm characteristics determine the position of organizations within the networks.

REGIONAL KNOWLEDGE NETWORKS: A DIFFERENTIATED PICTURE

Altogether this leads to a differentiated picture of regional knowledge networks. Networks are based on knowledge that can be measured – knowledge networks are no longer an empirical black box. They comprise both material and immaterial ties between firms, yet links in the form of various knowledge exchanges are the essential element. The regional dimension is essential for networking; this is partly due to its knowledge content but also to the social embeddedness of economic relations taking place on a regional level. But regional networks are not self-contained and self-sufficient entities – the relational view has to be extended; transregional knowledge flows are an essential element of innovative potential. Networks have different forms and structures. Knowledge sharing in networks is no automatic process. Depending on their capabilities and their strategies not all firms participate to equal intensity and with equal knowledge in networks. They also assume different positions in networks: neither knowledge nor power are equally distributed. The behaviour of firms and agents follows different strategies and is guided by the desire to generate a portfolio of ties and interactions. It is also dependent on changing opportunities and social relations. Networks are dynamic systems, they evolve according to the changing needs of the firms involved.

REFERENCES

Acs, Z.J. (2002), *Innovation and Growth in Cities*, Cheltenham, UK and Northhampton, MA, USA: Edward Elgar.

Acs, Z.J., D.B. Audretsch and M.P. Feldman (1992), 'Real effects of academic research: comment', *American Economic Review*, **82**, 363–7.

Ahuja, G. (2000), 'The duality of collaboration: inducements and opportunities in the formation of interfirm linkages', *Strategic Management Journal*, **21**, 317–43.

Amin, A. and P. Cohendet (2004), *Architectures of Knowledge: Firms, Capabilities and Communities*, Oxford: Oxford University Press.

Amin, A. and N. Thrift (eds) (1994), *Globalisation, Institutions and Regional Development in Europe*, Oxford: Oxford University Press.

Anselin, L., A. Varga and Z. Acs (1997), 'Local geographic spillovers between university research and high technology innovations', *Journal of Urban Economics*, **42**, 422–48.

Arrow, K.J. (1962), 'Economic welfare and the allocation of resources for invention', in R. Nelson (ed.), *The Rate and Direction of Inventive Activity*, Princeton, NJ: Princeton University Press, pp. 619–22.

Asheim, B. (1999), 'Interactive learning and localised knowledge in globalising learning economies', *Geojournal*, **49** (4), 345–52.

Audretsch, D.B. (1995), *Innovation and Industry Evolution*, Cambridge, MA: MIT Press.

Audretsch, D.B. and T.T. Aldridge (2009), 'Knowledge spillovers, entrepreneurship and regional development', in R. Capello and P. Nijkamp (eds), *Handbook of Regional Growth and Development Theories*, Cheltenham, UK and Northampton, MA, USA: Edward Elgar, pp. 201–10.

Audretsch, D.B. and M. Feldman (1996), R&D spillovers and the geography of innovation and production, *American Economic Review*, **86**, 630–40.

Audretsch, D.B. and M. Feldman (2004), 'Knowledge spillovers and the geography of innovation', in J.V. Henderson and J.F. Thisse (eds), *Handbook of Urban and Regional Economics*, Vol. 4, Amsterdam: Elsevier, pp. 2713–39.

Audretsch, D.B. and E.E. Lehmann (2006), 'The role of clusters in knowledge creation and diffusion: an institutional perspective', in B. Asheim, P. Cooke and R. Martin (eds), *Clusters and Regional Development: Critical Reflections and Explorations*, Oxford: Routledge, pp. 188–98.

Axelrod, R. (1997), *The Complexity of Cooperation*, Princeton, NJ: Princeton University Press.

Breschi, S. and F. Lissoni (2009), 'Mobility of skilled workers and co-invention networks: an anatomy of localized knowledge flows', *Journal of Economic Geography*, **9** (4), 439–68.

Bünstorf, G. (2003), 'Processes of knowledge sharing: from cognitive psychology to economics', in E. Helmstädter (ed.), *The Economics of Knowledge Sharing*, Cheltenham, UK and Northampton, MA, USA: Edward Elgar, pp. 74–99.

Camagni, R. (2002), 'On the concept of territorial competitiveness: sound or misleading?', *Urban Studies*, **13**, 2395–2412.

Colletis-Wahl, K., J. Corpataux, O. Crevoisier, L. Kebir, B. Pecqueur and V. Peyrache-Gadeau (2008), 'The territorial economy: a general approach in order to understand and deal with globalization', in M.J. Aranguren Querejeta, C. Iturrioz Landart and J.R. Wilson (eds), *Networks, Governance and Economic Development, Bridging Disciplinary Frontiers*, Cheltenham, UK and Northampton, MA, USA: Edward Elgar, pp. 21–39.

Cooke, P. (1998), 'Introduction: origins of the concept', in H.J. Braczyk, P. Cooke and M. Heidenreich (eds), *Regional innovation systems: The Role of Governances in a Globalized World*, London: UCL Press, pp. 2–28.

Cooke, P. and K. Morgan (1998), *The Associational Economy: Firms, Regions and Innovation*, Oxford: Oxford University Press.

Crescenzi, R., A. Rodríguez-Pose and M. Storper (2007), 'The territorial dynamics of innovation: a Europe–United States comparative analysis', *Journal of Economic Geography*, **7**, 673–709.

Döring, T. and J. Schnellenbach (2006), 'What do we know about geographical knowledge spillovers and regional growth? A survey of the literature', *Regional Studies*, **40**, 375–95.

Dyer, J.H. and K. Nobeoka (2000), 'Creating and managing a high-performance knowledge-sharing network: the Toyota case', *Strategic Management Journal*, **21**, 345–67.

Edvinsson, L. and M.S. Malone (1997), *Intellectual Capital*, New York: Harper.

Feldman, M. (1994), *The Geography of Innovation, Economics of Science, Technology and Innovation*, Dordrecht: Kluwer.

Gay, B. (2008), 'Competitive intelligence and network mapping of interfirm alliances; strategic implications', Groupement de Recherches Economiques et Sociale, Cahier No 2008-05.

Gay, B. and B. Dousset (2005), 'Innovation and network structural dynamics: study of the alliance network of a major sector of the biotechnology industry', *Research Policy*, **34** (10), 1457–75.

Giuliani, E. (2005), 'The structure of cluster. Knowledge and networks: uneven and selective, not pervasive and collective', DRUID Working Paper No. 05-11.

Giuliani, E. and M. Bell (2005), 'The micro-determinants of meso-level learning and innovation: evidence from a Chilean wine cluster', *Research Policy*, **34** (1), 47–68.

Gordon, I.R. and P. McCann (2000), 'Industrial clusters: complexes, agglomeration and/or social networks?', *Urban Studies*, **37**, 513–32.

Greunz, L. (2003), 'Geographically and technologically mediated knowledge spillovers between European regions', *Annals of Regional Science*, **37**, 657–80.

Hagedoorn, J. (2002), 'Inter-firm R&D partnerships: an overview of major trends and patterns since 1960', *Research Policy*, **31**, 477–92.

Hartmann, C., A. Niederl and M. Breitfuss (2007), 'Pilot RICARDA Intellectual Capital Report for the Polymer competence Center Leoben', mimeo, Joanneum Research Graz.

Helmstädter, E. (ed.) (2003), *The Economics of Knowledge Sharing, A New Institutional Approach*, Cheltenham, UK and Northampton, MA, USA: Edward Elgar.

Howells, J. (2005), 'Innovation and regional economic development: a matter of perspective?', *Research Policy*, **34** (8), 1220–34.

Iammarino, S. and P. McCann (2005), 'Firm location and technology: stylised constructs and illusory policies', paper presented at the 4th European Meeting on Applied Evolutionary Economics (EMAEE) in Utrecht, 18–25 May.

Jaffe, A.B. (1989), 'Real effects of academic research', *American Economic Review*, **79** (5), 957–70.

Jaffe, A.B., M. Trajtenberg and R. Henderson (1993), 'Geographic localization of knowledge spillovers as evidenced by patent citations', *Quarterly Journal of Economics*, August, 577–98.

Johansson, B. and C. Karlsson (2009), 'Knowledge and regional development', in R. Capello and P. Nijkamp (eds), *Handbook of Regional Growth and Development Theories*, Cheltenham, UK and Northampton, MA, USA: Edward Elgar, pp. 239–55.

Kogut, B. (2000), 'The network as knowledge: generative rules and the emergence of structure', *Strategic Management Journal*, **21**, 405–25.

Krätke, S. (2002), 'Network analysis of production clusters: the Potsdam/Babelsberg film industry as an example', *European Planning Studies*, **10**, 27–54.

Krugman, P. (1991), *Geography and Trade*, Cambridge, MA: MIT Press.

Lawson, C. and E. Lorenz (1999), 'Collective learning, tacit knowledge and regional innovative capacity', *Regional Studies*, **33**, 305–17.

Lundvall, B.-Å. (2002), 'The learning economy: challenges to economic theory and policy', in G.M. Hodgson (ed.), *A Modern Reader in Institutional and Evolutionary Economics, Key Concepts*, Cheltenham, UK and Northampton, MA, USA: Edward Elgar, pp. 26–47.

Malmberg, A. (2003), 'Beyond the cluster: local milieus and global connection', in J. Peck and H. Yeung (eds), *Remaking the Global Economy*, London: Sage, pp. 61–82.

Mariotti, F. and R. Delbridge (2001), 'Managing portfolios of ties in inter-firm networks', presented at the Nelson and Winter Conference, Aalborg, Denmark.

Marshall, A. (1890/1920), *Principles of Economics*, London: Macmillan.

Maskell, P. and A. Malmberg (1999), 'Localized learning and industrial competitiveness', *Cambridge Journal of Economics*, **23**, 167–85.

McCann, P. and F. van Oort (2009), 'Theories of agglomeration and regional economic growth: a historical review', in R. Capello and P. Nijkamp (eds), *Handbook of Regional Growth and Development Theories*, Cheltenham, UK and Northampton, MA, USA: Edward Elgar, pp. 19–32.

Moreno, R., R. Paci and S. Usai (2005), 'Spatial spillovers and innovation activity in European regions', *Environment and Planning A*, **37**, 1793–1812.

Morgan, K. (2004), 'The exaggerated death of geography: learning, proximity and territorial innovation systems', *Journal of Economic Geography*, **4**, 3–21.

Owen-Smith, J. and W.W. Powell (2004), 'Knowledge networks in the Boston biotechnology community', *Organization Science*, **15** (1), 5–21.

Polanyi, M. (1962), *Personal Knowledge: Towards a Post-critical Philosophy*, London: Routledge.

Powell, W.W. and S. Grodal (2005), 'Networks of innovators', in J. Fagerberg, D.C. Mowery and R.R. Nelson (eds), *The Oxford Handbook of Innovation*, Oxford: Oxford University Press, pp. 56–85.

Reid, N., B.W. Smith and M.C. Carrol (2008), 'Cluster regions: a social network perspective', *Economic Development Quarterly*, **22** (4), 345–52.

Rodríguez-Pose, A. (1999), 'Innovation prone and innovation averse societies: economic performance in Europe', *Growth and Change*, **30**, 75–105.

Rodríguez-Pose, A. and R. Crescenzi (2008), 'Research and development, spillovers, innovation systems, and the genesis of regional growth in Europe', *Regional Studies*, **42**, 51–67.

Smith, Adam (1776), *An Inquiry into the Nature and Causes of the Wealth of Nations*, 5th edn, Edwin Cannan (ed.) (1904), London: Methuen & Co.

Steiner, M. (2006), 'Do clusters think? An institutional perspective on knowledge creation and diffusion in clusters', in B. Asheim, P. Cooke and R. Martin (eds), *Clusters and Regional Development: Critical Reflections and Explorations*, London: Routledge, pp. 199–217.

Steiner, M., J.A. Gil, O. Ehret, M. Ploder and R. Wink (2010), 'European medium-technology innovation networks: a multi-methodological multiregional approach', *International Journal of Technology Management*, **50** (3–4), 229–62.

Steiner, M. and C. Hartmann (2006), 'Organizational learning in clusters: a case study on material and immaterial dimensions of cooperation', *Regional Studies*, **40** (5), 493–506.

Steiner, M. and M. Ploder (2008), 'Structure and strategy within heterogeneity: multiple dimensions of regional networking', *Regional Studies*, **42** (6), 793–815.

Stuart, T.E. (1998), 'Network positions and propensities to collaborate: an investigation of strategic alliance formation in a high-technology industry', *Administrative Science Quarterly*, **43** (3), 668–98.

Stuart, T.E. (2000), 'Interorganizational alliances and the performance of firms: a study of growth and innovation rates in a high-technology industry', *Strategic Management Journal*, **21**, 791–811.

Torre, A. (2008), 'The role played by temporary geographical proximity in knowledge transmission', *Regional Studies*, **42**, 869–89.

Varga, A. (2000), 'Local academic knowledge spillovers and the concentration of economic activity', *Journal of Regional Science*, **40**, 289–309.

Yeung, H.W.-C. (2009), 'Regional development and the competitive dynamics of global production networks: an East Asian perspective', *Regional Studies*, **43** (3), 325–51.

Zucker, L.G., M.R. Darby and J. Armstrong (1998), 'Geographically localized knowledge: spillovers or markets?', *Economic Inquiry*, **36**, 65–86.

18 Regional competitiveness: from endowments to externalities to evolution
Ron Martin

Regional competitiveness lacks a clear, unequivocal and agreed meaning within the academic literature. It is perhaps not surprising therefore that the policy discourse around regional competitiveness is somewhat confused. (Bristow, 2005, 289)

INTRODUCTION: THE 'COMPETITIVENESS IMPERATIVE'

Recent years have seen a surge of academic and policy attention devoted to the notion of 'competitiveness': nations, regions and cities, we are told, have no option but to strive to be economically competitive in order to survive in today's marketplace. This credo of competitiveness has attracted a veritable host of believers and followers. Economists and experts everywhere have elevated 'competitiveness' to the status of a natural law of the modern capitalist economy. Policy-makers at all levels have been swept up in this competitiveness fever: to assess a country's competitiveness and to devise policies to enhance it have become officially institutionalized tasks in most of the Organisation for Economic Co-operation and Development (OECD) nations (*Policy Studies*, 2008). At the same time, city and regional authorities have themselves become increasingly occupied with knowing the relative 'competitive standing' of their local economies compared with that of others, and with devising policy strategies to move their area up the 'competitiveness league table'.

Why has this concern with 'competitiveness' become so prominent in policy-making circles? There is little doubt that the popularity of the notion has been inextricably linked to what is viewed as accelerating globalization and technological change. Globalization is seen not only as an ineluctable process, but also as one that brings with it expanding trade and increasingly intense competition between nations, necessitating the pursuit of efficiency, flexibility and technological innovation in order to remain 'competitive' in the global economy.[1] As Michael Porter expressed the situation, in his highly influential book *On Competition*:

Competition has intensified dramatically over the last decades, in virtually all parts of the world . . . Very few industries remain in which competition has not intruded on stability and market dominance. No company, and no country, can afford to ignore the need to compete. Every company, and every country, must try to understand and master competition. (Porter, 1998a, 84)

In numerous publications since that book, Porter has also argued that the same imperative applies *a fortiori* at the subnational scale: no region, city or indeed locality can afford to ignore the need to compete (Porter, 1998b, 2000, 2001). Every region must try to understand and master competition.

However, whilst the intensity and sources of competition have undoubtedly increased as globalization has surged, the 'regional competitiveness' issue is hardly new, even if the language used is. Few, if any, regional or city economies are self-sufficient, and the need to trade has meant that to a large degree the wealth of regions and cities has long depended on their industries being able to produce goods and services that compete in external markets. Export activity has consistently been a key driver of overall regional economic performance, and historically, regional economies have risen and fallen according to their ability to capture and dominate export markets in the face of competition from other regions seeking to supply the same goods and services more efficiently or effectively. The fact that regions 'compete' in some sense is probably not in question: territorial 'competition', at a whole variety of geographical scales, would seem to be an ineluctable fact of economic life. But precisely how regions (and cities) 'compete' – how we define, conceptualize and measure 'regional competitiveness' – is a more elusive issue. In part this difficulty reflects the debate in economic circles surrounding the basic idea of competitiveness itself. No sooner had Michael Porter's book on *The Competitive Advantage of Nations* (1990) appeared, than Robert Reich (1990), in his review of it, was moved to complain that: 'National competitiveness is one of those rare terms of public discourse to have moved directly from obscurity to meaninglessness without any intervening period of coherence'. And not long after, Paul Krugman (1996a, 1996b, 1997) argued that whilst the notion was relevant to the individual firm, it had little meaning at the national level, where it conjured up a misleading neo-Mercantilist image of international trade as a zero-sum game (see also Rapkin and Strand, 1995).

It is not surprising, then, that the application of the notion to regions and cities should prove contentious and difficult to pin down (see for, example, Steinle, 1992; Cheshire and Gordon, 1995; Duffy, 1995; Storper, 1995, 1997; Begg, 2002; *Urban Studies*, 1999; Camagni, 2003; Boschma, 2004; Gardiner et al., 2004; Kitson et al., 2004; Malecki, 2004; Porter, 1998a, 1998b, 2000, 2001; *Regional Studies*, 2004; Bristow, 2005, 2010; Martin, 2006; Saxenian, 1996; Simmie et al., 2006; Thomas et al., 2008; Martin and Sunley, 2011). It was probably the diversity of definition and interpretation of the idea of regional competitiveness found in this literature that led Bristow (2005, 89) to conclude that the notion 'lacks a clear, unequivocal and agreed meaning'. Her complaint is that:

> Regions are conceived as independent, collective entities competing in directly commensurable terms in a manner directly equivalent to firms. Regions are treated as clearly defined, internally coherent, atomistic and bounded spatial entities with quantifiable attributes that are in their exclusive possession, for each of which a desirable competitive advantage can be identified. Thus, competition is conceived of as occurring among places that begin competing on a level playing field, with fortune favouring the entrepreneurial . . . What is missing is any effort to conceptualise regions as territorially defined social aggregations with very different economic and political structures. (Bristow, 2005, 296)

Bristow's critique raises some fundamental issues. She is right to point to the lack of any clear and agreed definition of the notion of regional competitiveness, and to the simplified treatment of regional economies in such discussions, often as if they are no different from firms. However, it is not true that most notions of regional competitiveness conceive of regional economies competing 'on a level playing field' – to the contrary. Equally, it is not the case that all discussions of regional competitiveness ignore regional differences in economic, social and political structures, arrangements and characteristics.

Indeed, it is precisely around the role of such characteristics in explaining regional competitiveness that much of the disagreement over the concept revolves. My aim in the brief discussion that follows is to provide an evaluative 'road-map' to this disagreement, with the goal of revealing some guideposts for how the conceptualization of 'regional competitiveness' might be taken forward.

IN WHAT SENSE DO REGIONS 'COMPETE'?

Regions, as complex economic entities, do not 'compete' in the same way that firms do. A regional economy is neither a scaled-up version of a firm (to assume so would be to commit the fallacy of composition), nor a scaled-down version of the national economy (regional authorities typically have limited policy agency compared to the nation-state – they cannot set their own interest rates or exchange rate, and usually have only limited taxation powers). Unlike firms, regions do not go out of business. They may become economically depressed, with slow growth, poor employment prospects, high unemployment, low incomes, and so on. And such conditions may be difficult to overcome. But unproductive regional economies do not simply disappear like uncompetitive firms can do. At the very least, public transfers, automatic fiscal stabilizers and subventions usually provide a 'floor' to such economies.

What can and does happen, however, is that a region may lose an entire industry because its firms in that industry lose their (international) competitiveness, and thence their shares of export markets, to more competitive rivals that have emerged elsewhere. Whilst this may not be a zero-sum game problem in the strict sense, it is certainly the case that the growth of a competitor industry in one region can result in the loss of that industry in another region. This problem can be particularly acute for regions because regional economies typically are more specialized, or at least have a narrower range of industries and services, than the national economy, are more open, and more vulnerable to sector-specific shocks and adverse trends in export and import markets. And the loss of an industry can have serious consequences for a region's economy as a whole.

As Cellini and Soci (2002) point out, although the definition of competitiveness has attracted debate and division, one theme nevertheless tends to recur, namely some reference to an economy's 'ability to produce goods and services that meet the test of international markets, while at the same time maintaining high and sustainable levels of income and employment' (see also Aiginger, 2006). In this sense, the levels of prosperity and employment enjoyed by a region's population will depend on the ability of the region's firms to produce goods and services that 'meet the test' of external markets. A region's 'competitiveness' is determined by the productivity, in the widest sense, of its firms, workers and other economic, social, institutional and infrastructural assets. The attractiveness of a region to highly productive firms and workers is clearly one aspect of regional 'competitiveness', and regions may compete directly one with another to attract mobile workers and capital, and firms may actively play off regions against each other in the pursuit of the most favourable tax rates, regulatory concessions, capital grants, and so on (Malecki, 2004). Such interregional, interplace competition can be wasteful of local resources, and may end up as expensive zero-sum games. But what really matters for the notion of regional competitiveness is the productivity, in the widest sense, of a region's entire socio-economy, the efficiency with which its human, physical and environmental resources are utilized and sustained. There are essentially two main explanations of what determines a region's overall productivity: one emphasizes the role of specialization in those activities in which the region's 'endowments' are most productively employed; the other emphasizes the importance of the 'externalities' that derive from the localized clustering (geographical concentration) of similar and related firms in a region (see also Capello's Chapter 8 in this *Handbook* on this).

ENDOWMENTS AND REGIONAL COMPARATIVE ADVANTAGE . . .?

According to conventional Ricardian comparative advantage theory, regions will tend to specialize in and thus export those activities which they are more efficient in, compared to all their other activities. A region need not have an absolute efficient advantage in producing any product over all other regions (countries): it need only be relatively more efficient in producing some products than others in order to benefit from trade. The question is what determines comparative advantage: why is a region efficient – more productive – in certain sectors of activity compared to other regions and nations? In traditional comparative advantage theory a nation's pattern of specialization and exports is shaped by its endowments of the classic production factors of land (including raw materials, climatic advantages), labour (having particular skills) and capital, and the costs of those factors. The assumption is that regions tend to be more differentiated than nations in terms of basic factor endowments. At the same time, the significance of their specific basic factor endowments is rendered the more important by virtue of their being subject to nationally set currency and exchange rates, which cannot be manipulated on a region-by-region basis. According to regional comparative advantage theory, then, regions specialize in those goods and services in which they have the highest productivity, which in turn reflects their specific basic factor endowments and their associated costs. And, according to traditional comparative advantage theory, these endowments are assumed to be pre-given and fixed.

But the traditional idea of regional comparative advantage has been heavily criticized in recent years. Conventional comparative advantage theory, as applied to national economies, assumes zero factor mobility. As Krugman (2005) argues, while this may be reasonable for national economies – capital movements between nations rarely account for more than a fifth of investment, and labour mobility is low – for regions this assumption is much less valid. Interregional movements of capital (firms and investment finance) and labour (workers and entrepreneurs) within a country can be substantial; indeed, as noted above, regional authorities may actively compete over attracting capital and workers. This means that it is unrealistic to think of these two standard factor endowments as being fixed or pre-given in a regional context. Movements of labour and capital will not only be sensitive to regional differences in comparative advantage, economic growth and productivity, but will also tend to accentuate those differences. A significant difference in total factor productivity between two regions could lead to sustained movements of labour and capital out of the less productive region into the more productive region, and such movements will tend to reinforce the productivity of firms in the more prosperous region relative to firms in the less prosperous. For these reasons, Krugman suggests that factor mobility makes interregional growth rates much more sensitive than international growth rates to differences in productivity (efficiency), so that regional competitiveness necessarily also has to do with the relative attractiveness of regions to labour and capital.

Camagni (2003) goes even further. He argues that interregional factor mobility can in fact mean that if a region falls behind in its productivity compared to other regions it can become locked into a vicious spiral of cumulative decline: capital and labour move out to other regions, productivity falls further behind, leading to a further exodus of capital and labour and ideas, and thence to even further falling behind in productivity, and so on. The more that regional wages are set nationally, so there is little scope for wage reductions to compensate for low productivity, combined with the fact that regions are not able to devalue their exchange rate in order to re-establish (price) competitiveness, the more that a region's decline in productivity, once initiated, becomes self-reinforcing, leading to progressive regional decline. For this reason he argues that for regions, what matters is absolute advantage, not comparative advantage.

. . . OR EXTERNALITIES AND REGIONAL COMPETITIVE ADVANTAGE?

The most sustained rejection of the idea of regional comparative advantage, however, has been that of Michael Porter (1990, 1998a, 1998b). According to Porter, comparative advantage theory is both unrealistic and outmoded as a definition and explanation of 'competitiveness' and trade. He criticizes the theory on various grounds: its static nature; its neglect of economies of scale; its assumptions that technologies are identical everywhere, that products are undifferentiated, that there is no intra-industry trade, and that the pool of national (or regional) factor endowments is pre-given and fixed; and for making no reference to firm strategy. In his view:

> All these assumptions bear little relation, in most industries, to actual competition. At best, factor comparative advantage theory is . . . useful primarily for explaining broad tendencies in the patterns of trade (for example, its average labour or capital intensity) rather than whether a nation exports or imports in individual industries. (1990, 12)

He suggests that Ricardian factor comparative advantage has long been an incomplete explanation for competitiveness and trade, especially in those industries and segments of industries involving sophisticated technology and highly skilled employees, precisely, he says, the sectors that are now most important to national productivity. As more and more industries have become knowledge-intensive, he argues, so the role of factor costs has weakened even further.

In his view, while productivity is key to national and regional competitiveness, this is not attributable to specialization on the basis of comparative endowment advantages: 'Access to labour, capital and natural resources', he argues, 'does not determine prosperity, because these have become widely accessible' (Porter, 1998a, 7). Rather, he argues, 'competitiveness arises from the productivity with which firms in a location can use inputs to produce valuable goods and services' (p. 7). The roots of regional productivity ('competitiveness') lie not in local factor endowments, but rather in the localized

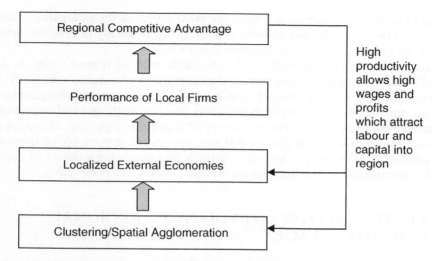

Figure 18.1   Clustering, externalities and regional competitive advantage

externalities that derive from the geographical 'clustering' of similar and interrelated firms, and especially from local knowledge spillovers. Clusters – geographically proximate agglomerations of similar and related firms, in competition and possibly also in collaboration with one another – intensify the interactions and hence the importance of the four key elements in what Porters calls the 'competitiveness diamond': firm strategy and rivalry, demand conditions, factor input conditions, and related and supporting industries.[2] In particular, the interactions and the various externalities associated with the local clustering of the firms promote innovation amongst the firms involved, which in turn raises their productivity and performance, which in their turn improve regional competitive advantage (Figure 18.1).

Interestingly, in what is a marked turnaround in his thinking about the relevance of the idea of competitiveness at the regional scale, Krugman (2005) also defines it as productivity, and follows Porter in stressing the importance of local external economies (of the sort highlighted by Porter) in promoting the productivity of a region's firms. He also stresses the importance of so-called regional 'fundamentals': local characteristics external to firms which have to do with region-specific cultural, social, institutional, environmental and governance assets and arrangements, which serve to differentiate one region from another. As examples of fundamentals he cites high-quality education institutions; a local culture of entrepreneurship; sustained public policy differences, such as differences in tax rates; and the quality of social and physical infrastructures. Such fundamentals, unlike labour and capital, are relatively immobile between regions, and constitute key external resources on which local firms can draw directly or indirectly as sources of competitive advantage.

What these various conceptualizations represent, then, is a distinct move away from endowment-based notions of regional comparative advantage to externalities-based notions of regional competitive advantage, though both approaches essentially define regional competitiveness as regional productivity. Moreover, in both Porter's and Krugman's versions of the externalities-based perspective, considerable emphasis is accorded to spatial agglomeration. This is the main source of the externalities that are considered to be key to the productivity of local firms, especially in export-orientated industries, and hence of the regional economy as a whole.

However, neither approach really deals adequately with what must surely be a key aspect of regional competitiveness, namely the adaptability of a region's economy; how adaptable its firms are, and its ability to create new firms in response to changing market conditions, the rise of new competitors elsewhere and the challenges and opportunities presented by new technologies. Porter's theory of regional competitive advantage goes some way towards this goal in the sense that it stresses the importance of innovation for the upgrading of the cluster industry. But it is far from being a theory of dynamic regional competitiveness. That requires an explicit evolutionary perspective.

FROM EXTERNALITIES TO EVOLUTION: REGIONAL DYNAMIC ADVANTAGE

As noted above, Porter's dismissal of comparative advantage theory was in part based on the charge that it is static. However, this is an outdated criticism (Davies and Ellis, 2000). Recent years have seen the rethinking of comparative theory advantage to incorporate two key advances: a redefinition of 'endowments' to include the whole range of 'soft' resources, especially knowledge, competences and capabilities, as well institutional and cultural features (and thus aspects akin to Krugman's 'fundamentals'); and a recognition that comparative advantage is a dynamic process, not a static state of affairs.

A central role is now accorded to past technological change as manifested in the endogenous cumulated stock of knowledge, skills and technical assets, both within and outside the individual firm (Nelson, 1995, 1996). The potential for productivity growth in an economy depends in part at least on differences in the scope for 'learning' across different firms, sectors and economies (regional and national). Learning effects are a key source of technical advance, and hence of productivity growth. If the potential for such learning effects differs across sectors, then different patterns of specialization will produce different time paths of productivity growth in the economy, and hence of comparative advantage. Thus technological innovation and spillovers of knowledge figure just as importantly in the new comparative advantage theory as they do in Porter's cluster theory (see Maneschi, 1998; Redding, 1999). If learning effects and interfirm knowledge spillovers are localized, as many scholars argue, then productivity rises faster in the region that first develops an industry or specialism. And such a competitive lead is likely to be self-reinforcing. As Krugman graphically puts it:

> Like a river that digs its own bed deeper, a pattern of specialization, once established, will induce relative productivity changes that strengthen the forces preserving that pattern. Clearly, history matters here even for the long run . . . Comparative advantage is created over time by the dynamics of learning, rather than arising from underlying [regional] characteristics. (Krugman, 1987 [1990], 47)

Such a rethinking of comparative advantage gives it a direct link with competence theories of the firm (see Hunt and Morgan, 1995). For these authors, rather than being a theory of national specialization, trade and competitiveness, the new 'comparative advantage of competition' is seen as having micro-foundations, in the sense that what matters is not only the full range of resources and assets available to a firm, but how that firm uses and deploys those resources strategically to gain a competitive advantage over other, rival firms. Ultimately, the source of a firm's competitive advantage lies in its dynamic capabilities or organizational processes that create, integrate, recombine and release resources (Ambrosini and Bowman, 2009; Eisenhardt and Martin, 2000). Without such capabilities, firms are likely to enjoy only a short-term competitive advantage and will fail to respond to their constantly changing environments. Such capabilities are typically shaped both by internal processes, such as path-dependent learning, management practice, cognition and strategy; and by external factors and resources such as the local business environment (Ambrosini and Bowman, 2009). Hunt and Morgan (1995) use the term 'resource advantage theory of competition' to distance this new view of comparative advantage from the traditional model. Since each firm in an industry is a unique entity in time and space as result of history, firms will differ in the resources and assets available to them, how these are deployed, and hence in competitive advantage. Furthermore, this conception of comparative advantage is necessarily dynamic:

> Competition, then, consists of the constant struggle among firms for a comparative advantage in resources that will yield a superior marketplace position of competitive advantage, and thereby superior financial performance. Once a firm's comparative advantage in resources enables it to achieve superior performance through a position of competitive advantage in some market segments or segments, competitors attempt to neutralize and/or leapfrog the advantaged firm through acquisition, imitation, substitution or major innovation. The comparative advantage theory of competition is, therefore, inherently dynamic. (Hunt and Morgan, 1995, 8)

If a wider view, then, is taken of 'endowments' or resources, and learning, technology and a region's externalities and fundamentals are included in those resources, the idea of comparative advantage takes on renewed relevance in discussions of regional competitiveness. Furthermore, it becomes a dynamic concept. In his cluster theory, Porter puts great emphasis on innovation and upgrading as key to maintaining the competitiveness of firms, of clusters, and thus of regions over time. A dynamic, resource-based notion of comparative advantage has an even greater emphasis on innovation. What is essential to dynamic regional comparative advantage is adaptation to constantly changing markets, competition and technology. How well firms adapt to the ever-shifting threats and opportunities that arise in the global economy determines whether they remain competitive in their respective industries and markets (Figure 18.2).

The dynamic competitiveness of a region will depend on the adaptability of its constituent firms. If those firms are slow to adapt, then the regional economy as a whole will lose its competitiveness, and is likely to fall behind in terms of prosperity, wages and employment. The adaptability of firms depends in large part on their innovative capacity, and it is here that a region's assets, externalities and fundamentals assume importance, since these can shape the propensity for and nature of innovative activity by local firms. However, what also matters for the dynamic comparative advantage of a region is not just that its firms adapt, but also that its economic structure – its particular mix of economic activities and specialisms – also adapts and evolves. The most successful dynamically competitive regions appear to be those that manage to reconfigure their economic structures over time, replacing declining or maturing sectors by new ones. Regional

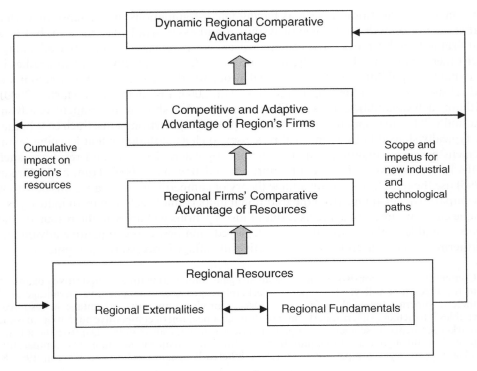

Figure 18.2   Regional dynamic comparative advantage

dynamic competitiveness is thus an evolutionary process in a double sense: in terms of the innovative upgrading of existing firms and activities, and in terms of the creation and development of new firms and activities. With regard to the latter, new regional industrial and technological path creation assumes key importance (see Martin's Chapter 15 in this *Handbook*). New paths of regional industrial and technological development can arise for several reasons: indigenous innovative activity, branching into new or related sectors, attracting major firm implants, purposive deviation from existing activities, public policy initiatives, to name but some. What is clear is that understanding regional competitiveness calls for an evolutionary perspective (see Boschma, 2004; Martin, 2006).

A CONCLUDING NOTE: THE POLICY DIMENSION

It has become somewhat fashionable to talk of 'constructing regional advantage' (Asheim et al., 2009). Following the discussion of this chapter, it might be argued that three main (and interdependent) policy foci are needed to help enhance and improve a region's competitive performance: policies aimed at tackling weaknesses and inadequacies in regional 'fundamentals'; those aimed at enhancing the external economies associated with the region's existing and potential industries and clusters; and those aimed at improving the adaptive capability of a region's economic asset base and fundamentals (firms, industries, workers, institutions; infrastructures, governance arrangements, and so on). Different regional authorities may be expected to assign different relative emphasis to these groups of policy, but in almost all regions, policies will be needed on all three fronts.

As Krugman (2005) remarks, regional external economies are difficult to identify, even after the fact, and harder still to predict. Many policy-making bodies have seized upon the promotion of clusters as the basis for, or least as a major plank in, their efforts to promote and enhance the competitiveness of the regions under their jurisdiction (OECD, 2007). But, as Krugman (2005) also argues, cluster policies should only be a part, and possibly a relatively minor part, of the overall policy armoury. Cluster-based regional competitiveness policy is not without its limitations and problems, and is prone to encourage exaggerated expectations, especially about creating new clusters from scratch and their alleged role as arenas of innovation (Martin and Sunley, 2003, 2011; Simmie, 2006; Asheim et al., 2006).

What also matters, or indeed matters more, are policies that focus on promoting continual improvement, upgrading and innovation across all aspects of a region's resource and asset base so as to increase and maintain the adaptability of a region's firms, industries, workers and institutions. A region's comparative advantage, using that concept in the new, wider sense, is a dynamic process, not a static state. We need better to understand the process of regional economic adaptation, and why some regions seem to be more adaptive than others. Adaptation makes for regional resilience in the face of major changes in the wider competitive, market and technological environment (Simmie and Martin, 2010; Martin, 2011). Furthermore, a dynamic comparative advantage perspective on regional competitiveness throws the issue of sustainability into stark relief. Rapid growth and development can impose strains and pressures on the environmental, social and physical resources of a region, and even give rise to negative externalities and an erosion in the quality of local fundamentals, thereby undermining the comparative advantage in resources on which local firms can draw to enhance their competitive and adaptive advantages. Taking a dynamic or evolutionary view of regional competitiveness, as regional adaptive advantage, thus has far-reaching implications for policy.

NOTES

1. The rise of the so-called BRIC economies (Brazil, Russia, India and China) is repeatedly highlighted as a key development driving this new competitive challenge.
2. More elaborate versions of the basic cluster model include the local institutional set-up, and government policies, as additional components of the 'diamond'.

REFERENCES

Aiginger, K. (2006), 'Competitiveness: from a dangerous obsession to a welfare creating ability with positive externalities', *Journal of Industrial Competition and Trade*, **6**, 161–77.
Ambrosini, V. and C. Bowman (2009), 'What are dynamic capabilities and are they a useful construct in strategic management?', *International Journal of Management Reviews*, **11**, 29–49.
Asheim, B., R. Boschma and P. Cooke (2009), 'Constructing regional advantage: platform policies based on related variety and differentiated knowledge bases', Utrecht University Papers in Evolutionary Economic Geography 07.09.

Asheim, B., P. Cooke and R. Martin (eds) (2006), *Clusters and Regional Development*, London: Routledge.

Begg, I. (ed.) (2002), *Urban Competitiveness: Policies for Dynamic Cities*, Bristol: Policy Press.

Boschma, R. (2004), 'Competitiveness of regions from an evolutionary perspective', *Regional Studies*, **38**, 1001–14.

Bristow, G. (2005), 'Everyone's a "winner": problematising the discourse of regional competitiveness', *Journal of Economic Geography*, **5**, 285–304.

Bristow, G. (2010), 'Resilient regions: re-"place"ing regional competitiveness', *Cambridge Journal of Regions, Economy and Society*, **3**, 153–67.

Camagni, R. (2003), 'On the concept of territorial competitiveness: sound or misleading?', *Urban Studies*, **39**, 2395–411.

Cellini, R. and A. Soci (2002), 'Pop competitiveness', *Banca Nazionale del Lavoro Quarterly Review*, **55** (220), 71–101.

Cheshire, P. and I.R. Gordon (eds) (1995), *Territorial Competition in an Integrating Europe*, Aldershot: Avebury.

Davies, H. and P. Ellis (2000), 'Porter's competitive advantage of nations: time for the final judgement?', *Journal of Management Studies*, **37**, 1189–214.

Duffy, H. (1995), *Competitive Cities: Succeeding in the Global Economy*, London: Spon.

Eisenhardt, K. and J. Martin (2000), 'Dynamic capabilities: what are they?', *Strategic Management Journal*, **21**, 1105–21.

Gardiner, B., R.L. Martin and P. Tyler (2004), 'Competitiveness, productivity and economic growth across the European regions', *Regional Studies*, **38**, 1045–67.

Hunt, S.D. and R.M. Morgan (1995), 'The comparative advantage theory of competition', *Journal of Marketing*, **59**, 1–15.

Kitson, M., R.L. Martin and P. Tyler (2004), 'Regional competitiveness: an elusive yet key concept?', *Regional Studies*, **38**, 991–9.

Krugman, P. (1987), 'The narrow moving band, the Dutch Disease, and the competitive consequences of Mrs Thatcher: notes on trade in the presence of dynamic scale economies', reprinted in P. Krugman (1990), *Rethinking International Trade*, Cambridge, MA: MIT Press, pp. 63–89.

Krugman, P. (1996a), 'Making sense of the competitiveness debate', *Oxford Review of Economic Policy*, **12**, 17–25.

Krugman, P. (1996b), 'Competitiveness: a dangerous obsession: myths and realities of US competitiveness', in *Pop Internationalism*, Cambridge, MA: MIT Press, pp. 3–33.

Krugman, P. (1997), *Pop Internationalism*, Cambridge, MA: MIT Press.

Krugman, P. (2005), 'Second wind for industrial regions?', in D. Coyle, W. Alexander and B. Ashcroft (eds), *New Wealth for Old Regions*, Oxford: Princeton University Press, pp. 35–47.

Malecki, E. (2004), 'Jockeying for position: what it means and why it matters to regional development policy when places compete', *Regional Studies*, **38**, 1101–20.

Maneschi, A. (1998), *Comparative Advantage in International Trade: A Historical Perspective*, Cheltenham, UK and Lyme, NH, USA: Edward Elgar.

Martin, R.L. (2006), 'Economic geography and the new discourse of regional competitiveness', in S. Bagchi-Sen and H. Lawton-Smith (eds), *Economic Geography: Past, Present and Future*, London: Routledge, pp. 159–72.

Martin, R.L. (2011), 'Regional economic resilience, hysteresis and recessionary shocks', *Journal of Economic Geography*, forthcoming.

Martin, R.L. and P. Sunley (2003), 'Deconstructing clusters: chaotic concept or policy panacea?', *Journal of Economic Geography*, **3** (1), 5–35.

Martin, R.L. and P. Sunley (2011), 'Regional competitiveness: clusters or dynamic comparative advantage?', in R. Huggins and H. Izushi (eds), *Competition and Competitive Advantage: The Ideas of Michael Porter*, Oxford: Oxford Unversity Press, pp. 211–37.

Nelson, R. (1995), 'Co-evolution of industry structure, technology and supporting institutions, and the making of comparative advantage', *International Journal of the Economics of Business*, **2**, 171–84.

Nelson, R.R. (1996), 'The evolution of comparative or competitive advantage: a preliminary report on a study', *Industrial and Corporate Change*, **5**, 597–617.

OECD (2007), *Competitive Regional Clusters: National Policy Approaches*, Paris: OECD.

Policy Studies (2008), Special Issue: Understanding Competition States, *Policy Studies*, **31** (1).

Porter, M.E. (1990), *The Competitive Advantage of Nations*, New York: Free Press.

Porter, M.E. (1998a), *On Competition*, Cambridge, MA: Harvard Business School Publishing.

Porter, M.E. (1998b), 'Location, clusters and the new economics of competition', *Business Economics*, **33** (1), 7–17.

Porter, M.E. (2000), 'Location, competition and economic development: local clusters in the global economy', *Economic Development Quarterly*, **14** (1), 15–31.

Porter, M.E. (2001), 'Regions and the new economics of competitiveness', in A.J. Scott (ed.), *Global City Regions*, Oxford: Blackwell, pp. 139–52.

Rapkin, D.P. and J,R. Strand (1995), 'Competitiveness: useful concept, political slogan or dangerous obsession', *International Journal of Political Economy Yearbook*, **8**, 1–20.

Redding, S. (1999), 'Dynamic comparative advantage and the welfare effects of trade', *Oxford Economic Papers*, **51**, 15–39.

Regional Studies (2004), Special Issue on Regional Competitiveness, *Regional Studies*, **38** (9).

Reich, R. (1990), 'But now we're global', *The Times Literary Supplement*, 31 August.

Saxenian, A.-L. (1996), *Regional Advantage: Culture and Competition in Silicon Valley and Route 128*, Cambridge, MA: Harvard University Press.

Simmie, J. (2006), 'Do clusters or innovation systems drive competitiveness?', in B. Asheim, P. Cooke and R. Martin (eds), *Clusters and Regional Development: Critical Reflections and Explorations*, London: Routledge, pp. 164–87.

Simmie, J. and R.L. Martin (2010), 'The economic resilience of regions: towards an evolutionary approach', *Cambridge Journal of Regions, Economy and Society*, **3**, 27–44.

Simmie, J., R.L. Martin, P. Wood, J. Carpenter and A. Chadwick (2006), *The Competitive Performance of English Cities*, London: Department of Communities and Local Government.

Steinle, W.J. (1992), 'Regional competitiveness and the single market', *Regional Studies*, **26**, 307–18.

Storper, M. (1995), 'Competitiveness policy options: the technology-regions connection', *Growth and Change*, Spring, 285–308.

Storper, M. (1997), *The Regional World: Territorial Development in a Global Economy*, New York: Guilford Press.

Thomas, H., A. Beer and D. Bailey (2008), 'A tale of two regions: comparative versus competitive approaches to economic restructuring', *Policy Studies*, **29**, 357–70.

Urban Studies (1999), Special Issue on Competitive Cities, *Urban Studies*, **36** (5–6).

19 Regional cultural economy: evolution and innovation
Al James

INTRODUCTION

> Increasingly the . . . cultural dimension is critical for defining and understanding the dynamics of regions. Regional economies consist of more than just aggregations, or even networks of firms, and their employees; they are also constituted by the cultural traditions and institutional structures that facilitate and regulate economic behaviour. (Wolfe, 1997, 4)

It is widely accepted that fundamental changes within advanced economies since the 1970s herald a new era of capitalist economic development. Variously conceptualized in terms of a shift to a post-Fordist regime of accumulation, the Fifth Kondratiev, the knowledge economy or the new economy, whatever the label used the emergent geography of this new order is marked by a decisive reagglomeration of production. Characteristic in their high rates of technological learning and innovation, the workings of these 'regional industrial complexes', 'new industrial spaces', or 'new industrial districts' have become a fixation for policy-makers and academics keen to explore their potential as tools to stimulate economic growth.

In particular, scholars have drawn on the work of Alfred Marshall (1890 [1952]) on nineteenth-century industrial districts, in which he theorized a 'triad of localisation externalities' that develop as firms collocate spatially (see Figure 19.1). By many producers sharing the fixed costs of and access to common factors of production – land, labour, energy, transportation and other infrastructures – Marshall argued that the supply of such resources is enhanced as capital and labour migrate to these areas to take advantage of the larger combined markets for their services. Localization externalities therefore allow small firms to enjoy the benefits of scale economies usually denied to them because of internal restrictions on growth. Updating Marshall's original ideas to contemporary economic conditions, a major research stream on regional development in the 1980s sought to explain the rise of the region in terms of the 'hard' economics of: vertical disintegration of production and a complex interfirm division of labour; the formation of external economies of scale and scope; dense networks of 'traded' input–output linkages; and the growth of a local institutional infrastructure of specialized services and distribution networks. Indeed, the current widespread policy appetite for the latest version of this mode of thinking – Michael Porter's well-known 'cluster' concept (see for example Porter, 1990, 1994, 1998) – underscores the continued relevance of Marshallian external economies for understanding contemporary regional dynamism.

Developing alongside these economistic variants of neo-Marshallian regional theory, however, and gaining considerable momentum in the early 1990s, there has emerged an alternative research stream within the regional industrial development literature that moves beyond a focus on 'hard' agglomeration economies and 'traded' material linkages

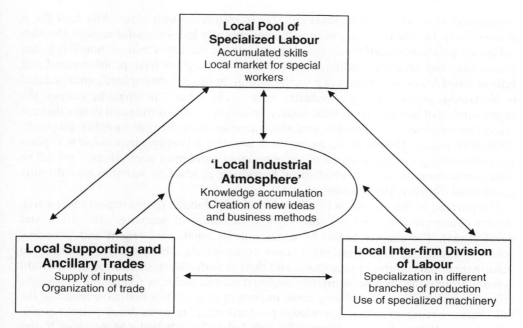

Source: Martin and Sunley (2001, 7), based on Marshall (1890 [1952], Book Four, Ch. 10).

Figure 19.1   Marshall's triad of external economies of industrial localization

to explore how 'untraded' socio-cultural characteristics of regional industrial agglom-erations foster and support (and in some cases constrain) learning and innovation, and hence economic growth and development (see Storper, 1995a; MacKinnon et al., 2002). This focus on the 'cultural economy' of learning and innovation in regional industrial systems is itself part of a broader 'cultural turn' in the social sciences during the 1990s which rejected the ontological binary of 'culture' and 'economy' as self-determining, discrete sets of institutions, each with their own rationalities and conditions of existence (see Amin and Thrift, 2004; Crang, 1997; Sayer, 1997). Instead, scholars have embraced a range of more fluid and hybrid conceptions of 'the economic' that emphasize its mutual constitution by, and hence fundamental inseparability from, 'the cultural'. Rooted in earlier analyses of the socio-cultural foundations of regional development in north-east and central Italy through the 1970s and 1980s (see, for example, Brusco, 1986; Pyke et al., 1990; Trigilia, 1990), there is now an expansive interdisciplinary regional research literature spanning economic geography, economic sociology, regional science and evo-lutionary economics in which scholars have analysed the importance of regionally spe-cific cultures in shaping local knowledge production, employment relations, industrial adaptation and patterns of regional economic development.

Specific research questions within this literature include: how do different regional cultures in otherwise similar regional agglomerations of 'hard' economic institutions give rise to different patterns of economic growth and development? How do cultural norms, values, beliefs and taken-for-granted assumptions facilitate and constrain processes of knowledge production, learning, innovation and entrepreneurship within regional economies? How are these regional cultures (re)produced over time? And how far is it possible to realign regional cultures in economically less successful regions through deliberate policy interventions designed to emulate the success of more dynamic regional economies elsewhere? In tackling these questions, researchers have problematized and reformulated Marshall's notion of a socio-cultural 'industrial atmosphere', encapsulated in his famous phrase 'secrets of industry were . . . in the air', in which he stressed the inseparability of industry from local society, traditions, social norms and values that are critical for economic coordination, and which arise spontaneously and unplanned (Scott, 2000, 107). Indeed, there is now a strong consensus that it is simply impossible to explain the continuing growth advantage of some regional economies over others if we fail to take into account the ways in which firms' knowledge production activities are culturally constituted (Storper, 1997; Saxenian, 1994).

The purpose of this chapter is to offer a broad introduction to this important research stream concerned with the regional cultural economy of learning, innovation and development. The chapter begins by setting out its intellectual origins and 'founding parents'; explaining core conceptual frameworks which scholars have developed to theorize regional cultures of innovation and their growth effects; summarizing important debates around the need to 'demystify' regional culture and how to ground 'innovative milieux' empirically; and outlining some important case studies that have analysed the links between regional culture, knowledge production and regional development (specifically Silicon Valley, Boston's Route 128, Salt Lake City, Oxford's Motorsport Valley and Cuba's bioscience cluster). The chapter concludes by charting two newly emergent research agendas around gendered cultural economies of learning within high-tech regions; and a decentring of the mainstream research literature (with its almost exclusive focus on the Global North) to regional industrial systems in the Global South, in order to expose the limits of Western-centred readings of regional cultural economy, learning and development.

CORE CONCEPTS: FROM TRANSACTION COSTS TO REGIONAL CULTURAL (DIS)ADVANTAGE

The rise of culturally sensitive approaches to understanding the different factors and conditions that affect regional growth and development can be understood as a critical response to one particular economistic variant of neo-Marshallian regional development theory, known as 'the Californian school'. Drawing on empirical work in California's Orange County in the 1980s, Allen Scott and his colleagues argued that the success of regional industrial agglomerations was ultimately a function of the transaction cost reductions that accrue to firms as a function of their close proximity (for example Scott, 1986, 1988; Storper and Walker, 1989). Their argument was threefold. First, instability of markets and an accelerated pace of technological change are met by a disintegration of the production process, and hence a deepening in the social division of labour. This then allows firms to maximize the benefits of specialization and to minimize exposure to risks of overcapacity, labour-force hoarding and dangers of technological lock-in, and hence to become more flexible. Second, as interfirm transactions become more important, so the costs of transport, communication, information exchange, search and scanning become more significant. The increased costs associated with increased external transactions are argued to create a 'spatial pull'; that firms will seek to agglomerate to minimize the costs of those transaction costs through external economies of scale. Third, spatial agglomeration supports in turn the growth of specialized institutions, which further lower transaction costs and increase economic efficiency. These include a myriad of specialized consulting, market research, public relations and venture capital firms, which provide technical, financial and networking services which firms cannot afford individually.

In response, critics argued however that we cannot only theorize the development of regional industrial agglomerations in terms of reductions in the unit costs of production within a given technology (see, for example, Martin and Sunley, 1996; Storper, 1995a). There are three main overlapping critiques. First, the argument that the institutional forms that prevail within these regions are those that deal most efficiently with reducing transactions costs is criticized as functionalist: the existence of all regional economic and social institutions cannot be assumed to be predicated on the minimization of transaction costs per se (Yeung, 2000). Second, critics argued that firms are much more than mechanistic production functions or simple expressions of an abstract capitalist, profit-maximizing imperative. To reduce the inner workings of the firm to a black box in this way says little of how and why entrepreneurs do (or do not) create companies, enter markets, interact with one another or take risks. Critics instead highlight the need to analyse the multiple and competing economic, social, cultural and political motives and logics underpinning firms' strategic behaviour (see Schoenberger, 1994, 1997). And third, critics argued that external economies, cost–price benefits to firms, and 'traded' input–output links as structures in themselves cannot explain the ongoing learning and innovation capacity of particular regional industrial economies, nor why some remain competitive and continue to grow whilst others do not. Arguably, it was Annalee Saxenian's (1994) seminal work on the divergent regional economic growth trajectories of California's Silicon Valley and Boston's Route 128 through the 1980s that demonstrated this last point most explicitly (see also discussions by Gertler, 1995; Oinas, 1995; Storper, 1995b).

By the early 1980s, following periods of sustained economic growth through the 1970s, Silicon Valley and Route 128 both faced economic downturns, primarily due to the decentralization of routine assembly operations to other regions and the loss of commodity chip markets to the Japanese. Through the 1980s, however, while Silicon Valley rebounded with a new generation of computer and semiconductor start-up companies, impressive technological performance and stabilized world market shares in semiconductors, Route 128 floundered.[1] In short, transaction cost analyses could not explain this divergence. What was it about these two similar regional industrial agglomerations of 'hard' economic institutions, both theoretically gaining the transaction cost reductions that stem from firms' spatial agglomeration, that had produced regional economic growth and advance in Silicon Valley yet relative regional decline in Route 128? Whilst not denying the reality of transaction cost reductions, Saxenian argued that the divergent performance of these two otherwise similar regional economies over the late 1980s and early 1990s demonstrated the crucial importance of local cultural determinants of regional industrial adaptation and economic growth. While these had previously been acknowledged as merely superficial disparities between 'laid-back' California and the more 'buttoned-up' East Coast, Saxenian argued instead that variations in industrial cultures across the two regions fundamentally shaped local patterns of learning, entrepreneurship, knowledge production and regional adaptability:

> The experience of Route 128 and Silicon Valley in recent decades suggests that there are important regional sources of competitive advantage. Their differences in performance cannot be explained by approaches that view firms as separate from the social structures and institutions of a local economy. Variations in local institutions and corporate forms shape regional capacities for adaptation . . . These institutions shape and are shaped by the local culture, the shared understandings and practices that unify a community and define everything from labour market behaviour to attitudes towards risk taking. (Saxenian, 1994, 6–7)

In Silicon Valley, a distinctive regional Californian counterculture – characterized by an openness to experimentation, the glorification of risk-taking, an acceptance of failure as a learning process, rapid change as the norm, a rejection of traditional social hierarchy, and greater loyalties to transcendent technologies than individual employers – is argued to have underpinned a regional, decentralized, network-based industrial system of learning. Interfirm flows of embodied information, ideas and know-how through informal social networks, hobbyist clubs, professional societies and high rates of cross-firm labour mobility helped to promote innovation and flexible adjustment among producers of complex related products, imperative under current conditions of shrinking product life cycles, fragmenting markets and an intensification of global competition (Saxenian, 1994; cf. Florida and Kenney, 1990). In addition, the development of shared social identities amongst young, single male engineers around the project of advancing new technologies effectively blurred the work–home boundary and enabled a regularity of long unsocial work hours, and the completion of large workloads in short periods of calendar time.

In contrast, a traditional conservative East Coast business culture in Route 128 – characterized by strong civic ties, self-sufficiency, risk-aversion, a stigmatization of failure, respect for traditional social hierarchies, stability and corporate loyalty – is argued to have sustained relatively integrated corporations; a strict separation of work and social life; 9–5 work hours; lower levels of interfirm networking and labour mobility; an isolation of producers from external sources of know-how and information; and hence lower rates of regional learning, innovation and economic growth. The strength of Saxenian's analysis is that she is able to control for industrial sector, products (in general terms), historical period, position in the business cycle, political events, and nation-state, since these are shared in common between the two regions.[2] Her evidence base is also impressive: repeat interviews over the course of a decade with over 150 local entrepreneurs, chief executive officers (CEOs), vice-presidents (VPs), venture capitalists and other industry-watchers.

In a nutshell, Saxenian showed persuasively and originally how regional processes of entrepreneurship, innovation, adaptability and growth in the knowledge economy are based on a whole series of socio-cultural understandings and practices that go far beyond the basic factors of production outlined by the narrow economism of the Californian school. She also drew attention to the reflexive, mutually constitutive nature of the relationships between: local shared cultural understandings; industrial structure; observed business practices; and regional institutions, including public and private organizations such as universities, business associations, local governments, professional associations and other forums which sustain patterns of social interaction and knowledge exchange within the region (Saxenian, 1994, 8).

CONCEPTUALIZING THE REGIONAL CULTURAL ECONOMY OF INNOVATION AND GROWTH

Building on Saxenian's earlier study of regional cultural (dis)advantage, other scholars have developed a wide range of theoretical frameworks and conceptual tools to help advance our understanding of the significance of 'untraded' socio-cultural and relational characteristics of regional industrial systems, and their role in enabling and constraining processes of learning, innovation and growth. As part of this, researchers have drawn heavily on the work of four key figures.

First, scholars have drawn on the work of Karl Polanyi on 'embeddedness'. In his book *The Great Transformation* (1944) Polanyi rejected the then dominant view of the economy as 'natural', pre-given, self-regulating and inevitable in form, instead arguing that markets are socially constructed and governed. Second, Polanyi's ideas were later reworked and reintroduced to social science in the mid-1980s by the sociologist Mark Granovetter, with 'embeddedness' broadly defined as the set of concrete social relationships between economic and non-economic actors (individuals as well as aggregate groups of individuals), which in turn create distinctive patterns of constraints and incentives for economic action and behaviour (see Granovetter, 1985; Zukin and DiMaggio, 1990; Oinas, 1997; Hess, 2004). Third, in conceptualizing the socio-cultural construction of regional industrial systems, scholars have also drawn on the earlier (1919) work of Thorstein Veblen (dubbed 'old institutionalism'). Here, 'institutions' are interpreted as socio-cultural repertoires, routines and conventions that provide cognitive frameworks or templates of meaning through which economic identities and particular actions and preferred behaviours are legitimated. As such, they are an important factor in determining the path-dependence of regional economic trajectories, because they serve to transmit knowledge, attitudes and values from one generation to the next (Martin, 2000, 81–2). And fourth, scholars have also married neo-Marshallian ideas with a reformulation of Joseph Schumpeter's writings, particularly his famous (1934) work *The Theory of Economic Development*. Schumpeter argued that economic growth requires innovation: that is, the generation of higher-quality products at lower unit costs than had previously been available; and that its pace and direction are affected by the institutional framework in which it occurs (Wolfe and Gertler, 2001). Neo-Schumpetarian accounts therefore emphasize the locally based determinants of entrepreneurship and technological change, and how different institutional environments and institutional arrangements differently promote and constrain innovation and growth (Martin, 2000, 80–81).

Differently incorporating these earlier ideas, a series of overlapping concepts have been developed to deal with different dimensions of the regional cultural economy – innovation and growth nexus. Here I briefly introduce three such core concepts (but see Storper, 1995a and MacKinnon et al., 2002 for fuller reviews). First, the concept of the 'innovative milieu' has been particularly prominent, developed by the GREMI group, an association of principally French–Italian–Swiss regional economists, centred in Paris[3] (for example Camagni, 1995; Capello, 1999; Maillat, 1995). 'Innovative milieux' are defined as: 'the complex network of mainly informal social relationships on a limited geographical area, which enhance the local innovative capability through synergetic and collective learning processes' (Camagni, 1991, 3). Here, then, innovation is grounded in intergenerational transfers of know-how, imitation of successful managerial practices, interpersonal face-to-face contacts, formal and informal cooperation between firms, and the circulation of tacit knowledge (ibid.). A shared social and cultural environment is also argued to enable economic actors to process and use imperfect information more effectively by reducing uncertainties when searching, screening, transcoding and selecting information, and therefore to learn and innovate more effectively (for example Keeble and Wilkinson, 1999).

Notions of a socio-cultural 'innovative milieu' overlap with a second core concept in regional cultural economy: that of the region as a 'nexus of untraded interdependencies' or 'relational assets' as articulated by Michael Storper. These ideas take as their focus a set of shared qualitative rules or socio-cultural 'conventions' which regulate interactions and allow economic actors to understand, interpret and effectively use knowledge; to deploy it in economically useful ways; and hence ultimately to make learning possible within the region (see Storper and Salais, 1997). Specific conventions include accepted norms and values around, for example, class hierarchy, reciprocity and trust, cheating, association, social closure, labour, political exchange, voice and the common good (Storper, 1997, 14), and for Storper these are territorially bounded in 'regional worlds of production'. The central argument here is that: 'agglomeration does not ensure learning or determine its content. [Rather] the use and development of information in such a way that technological learning takes place has to do with the qualitative behaviours of agents in a network' (Storper, 1997, 135). Storper argues that it is therefore difficult to explain the continuing competitive advantage of certain regional economies over others if their cultural conventions, rules of behaviour and explicit accord are not taken into account.

Strongly overlapping with notions of 'innovative milieu' and 'untraded interdependencies', a third core concept within the regional cultural economy literature is that of 'institutional thickness' (Amin and Thrift, 1994, 1995), which stresses the commonly available and institutionalized nature of regional assets which are argued to enhance firm-level capabilities and stimulate 'a diffused entrepreneurship'. Institutional thickness is comprised of four main elements: (1) a strong local presence of 'hard' institutional arrangements (firms, business associations, financial institutions, unions, educational institutions, and so on); (2) high levels of interaction amongst those institutions based on networking, cooperation and exchange; (3) well-defined structures of coalition-building and governance to avoid institutional conflict; and (4) a strong sense of place or belonging, supporting mutual awareness of a common enterprise or 'industrial purpose'. Institutional thickness, then: 'refers, at least potentially, to locally generated cultures serving as a base for economic activity and economic innovation' (Amin and Thrift, 1997, 154).

These three overlapping frameworks therefore have varying emphases: for example, on the role of non-firm institutions and organizations (for example government, training organizations, development agencies, universities) in shaping regional innovative capacity versus the role of networking and intensity of interaction between individual firms. Nevertheless, all three are united in their recognition of regional processes of learning, innovation, development and growth as culturally, relationally and institutionally embedded. Reinforcing this consensus, other scholars have explored how shared commonalities of language, codes of communication, conventions, norms and personal knowledge of each other based on a past working history all help to create a sense of trust upon which effective interfirm cooperation is predicated, given the scope for opportunism offered by the necessary incompleteness of contracts in an uncertain post-Fordist climate of demand (see for example Lorenz, 1992; Gertler, 1995). In combination, these various links and relationships are increasingly regarded as the intangible essence of the competitive firm and the competitive region: a socio-cultural 'glue' which holds dynamic regional economies together beyond mere specialization and interlinkage and which maintains their distinctive mix of competitive and cooperative interfirm relations (Brusco, 1990; Pyke and Sengenberger, 1992; Malecki, 1999).

CRITIQUE AND DEBATE: DEMYSTIFYING THE LINKS BETWEEN REGIONAL 'CULTURE', INNOVATION AND ECONOMIC GROWTH

However, despite the consensus that distinctive regional 'cultures' play a vital role in facilitating processes of social learning and economic growth, the origins of these cultures remain somewhat obscure (Wolfe and Gertler, 2001, 16). Notwithstanding the plethora of conceptual frameworks as introduced above, and a diverse range of empirical case studies, the exact nature of the mechanisms and processes by which regional culture structures promote innovative activity more successfully in some regions than in others are still far from clear (Asheim, 1996). There is often circularity: that innovation occurs because of the presence of a certain cultural 'milieu', and that cultural 'milieux' are what exist in regions where there is innovation (Storper, 1997). Indeed while it is Saxenian who takes us furthest away from this unsatisfactory state of affairs, even she stands accused of not thoroughly establishing the causal links between the competitive culture she describes and the successful growth of Silicon Valley as a regional economy (see Markusen, 1999, 879). It is in this context that Meric Gertler has called for a demystification of regional 'culture' in studies of contemporary economic relations (see Gertler, 1997, 48), and to counter tendencies within the literature to dehumanize and misrepresent regional culture 'as something ethereal and eternal, divorced from historical material practice' (Sayer and Walker, 1992, 178).

One excellent body of research that has sought to demystify the regional cultural economy of learning, innovation and growth is that developed by Nick Henry and Steve Pinch on Oxford's 'Motor Sport Valley'. This world-leading regional agglomeration of small firms clustered within a 50 mile radius around Oxfordshire is where three-quarters of the world's single-seater racing cars are designed and assembled, and the vast majority of the most competitive Formula One racing cars are designed and assembled (Pinch and Henry, 1999, 816). Rejecting narrow economistic explanations that explain the sustained growth of this region as a function of external scale economies, this work instead seeks to ground the rather esoteric socio-cultural notions of 'innovative milieu' and 'untraded interdependencies' by documenting empirically the everyday activities, human interactions and causal agents through which tacit knowledge and cultural conventions (about how to construct the 'best' racing cars in the world) are generated and disseminated within this world-leading 'regional world of production'. In summary, Henry and Pinch trace the embodied 'churning of knowledge' across firms through: the rapid and continual transfer of designers, engineers, managers and drivers (every 3.7 years on average); high rates of firm death and new firm formation in which key personnel are 'recycled'; interlocking company directorships; information 'leakage' through links with component suppliers; and the dissemination of new practices and technologies through gossip, rumour and mutual observation in pit lanes, on test tracks and at race meetings, encouraged by large numbers of specialist magazines and extensive press and TV coverage (see Henry et al., 1996; Henry and Pinch, 2000).

Other work has also sought to elucidate more clearly the embodied mechanisms and everyday practices through which locally dominant socio-cultural norms, values, beliefs and conventions come to shape routine intra- and interfirm learning and innovation behaviours, and the effects of this 'cultural-embeddedness' on firms' observed performance. James's (2005, 2007) empirical analysis of the regional high-tech industrial agglomeration centred on Salt Lake City, Utah offers some useful insights here. This research explores how a locally dominant set of regional cultural norms, values and evaluative criteria associated with the Church of Jesus Christ of Latter-day Saints (informally, the 'Mormon Church' of which over 75 per cent of Utah's general population are members) come to inform the behaviour of local computer software firms. Based on a regional survey of 105 software firms, 20 corporate case studies and 100 in-depth interviews, this research documented how Mormon ethics of mutual obligation, self-sufficiency, anti-debt and prioritization of family over work in some ways support firms' abilities to access external sources of information, knowledge and competencies. One example concerns enhanced levels of cooperation between similarly Mormon-founded and -managed firms premised on cultural trust rooted in a common cultural background. At the same time, however, these same Mormon cultural norms and values also generate self-identified constraints on firms' innovative capacities: for example as a function of reduced weekly work hours in the context of time-based competition; and an unwillingness to seek external debt finance for growth (see James, 2007). Importantly, this work also measured the consequences of this cultural embedding for firms' overall performance across a series of innovation and growth metrics.[4] Controlling for age, the analysis documented that for four of the five performance metrics used, the Mormon-founded and -managed firms tended to perform less well than their non-Mormon counterparts, as a function of their cultural embedding in the region (see James, 2005).[5]

The causal mechanisms through which these cultural influences on firms' learning and innovation behaviours and overall performance are (re)produced on an everyday basis are shown in Figure 19.2. As identified through the Utah case, the major mechanism centres on members of a particular regional culture who also occupy positions of power within local firms, and who have significant influence on the opinions and behaviour of others. These include firms' founders, managers and other opinion leaders. Fundamentally, because what the firm understands itself to be is produced through the actions of its employees, the cultural identities and commitments of these key individuals are closely entwined with (although not identical to) corporate identities and commitments (Schoenberger, 1994, 1997). As such, regional cultural values and conventions

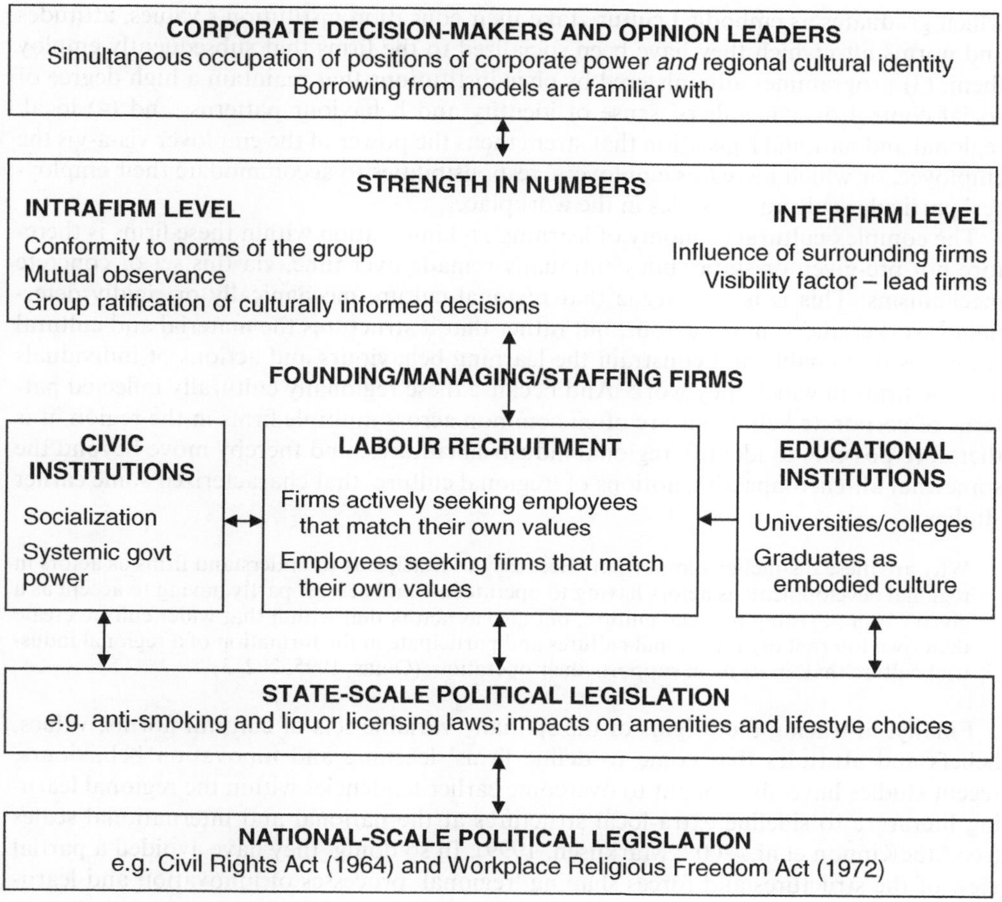

```
┌─────────────────────────────────────────────────────────────────────────┐
│              CORPORATE DECISION-MAKERS AND OPINION LEADERS                │
│   Simultaneous occupation of positions of corporate power and regional    │
│                          cultural identity                                │
│                    Borrowing from models are familiar with                │
└─────────────────────────────────────────────────────────────────────────┘
                                    ↕
┌─────────────────────────────────────────────────────────────────────────┐
│                          STRENGTH IN NUMBERS                              │
│  INTRAFIRM LEVEL                                    INTERFIRM LEVEL        │
│  Conformity to norms of the group          Influence of surrounding firms │
│  Mutual observance                            Visibility factor – lead firms │
│  Group ratification of culturally informed decisions                      │
└─────────────────────────────────────────────────────────────────────────┘
                                    ↑
                    FOUNDING/MANAGING/STAFFING FIRMS
                                    ↓
┌──────────────┐  ┌──────────────────────────┐  ┌──────────────────┐
│   CIVIC      │  │     LABOUR RECRUITMENT    │  │   EDUCATIONAL     │
│ INSTITUTIONS │  │                           │  │  INSTITUTIONS     │
│              │  │ Firms actively seeking    │  │                   │
│ Socialization│◄►│   employees that match    │◄─│ Universities/colleges │
│              │  │   their own values        │  │                   │
│ Systemic govt│  │ Employees seeking firms   │  │ Graduates as      │
│ power        │  │   that match their own    │  │   embodied culture │
│              │  │   values                  │  │                   │
└──────────────┘  └──────────────────────────┘  └──────────────────┘
      ↕                       ↑                          ↕
┌─────────────────────────────────────────────────────────────────────────┐
│                  STATE-SCALE POLITICAL LEGISLATION                       │
│   e.g. anti-smoking and liquor licensing laws; impacts on amenities and   │
│                          lifestyle choices                                │
└─────────────────────────────────────────────────────────────────────────┘
                                    ↕
┌─────────────────────────────────────────────────────────────────────────┐
│                NATIONAL-SCALE POLITICAL LEGISLATION                      │
│   e.g. Civil Rights Act (1964) and Workplace Religious Freedom Act (1972) │
└─────────────────────────────────────────────────────────────────────────┘
```

Source: James (2007, 409).

Figure 19.2   The mechanisms through which locally dominant cultural norms, values and beliefs inform worker and firm behaviour

come to inform decision-making processes, corporate strategy and observed behaviour, through definitions of what has value and what does not. Fundamentally, however, culture is a group property and as such, what counts in terms of cultural values limiting firm behaviour is not only whether the firm's decision-makers embody those values, but whether those values are ratified by the wider work group and accepted by the majority as a valid basis for action. This second 'strength-in-numbers' mechanism also includes everyday processes of conformity to the group, mutual observance and peer pressure.

Reinforcing these effects are a series of secondary reinforcing mechanisms involving: (1) culturally motivated job search and labour recruitment practices, in which firms seek employees that match their existing corporate culture, and employees seek firms that match their own personal values; (2) educational and skilling mechanisms, in which graduates as embodied culture take their education institution's values, attitudes and norms into which they have been socialized to the firms that subsequently employ them; (3) programmes administered by civic institutions that maintain a high degree of social control over members' sense of identity and behaviour patterns; and (4) local, regional and national legislation that strengthens the power of the employer vis-à-vis the employee, or which increases employers' responsibilities to accommodate their employees' particular cultural lifestyles in the workplace.

The complex cultural economy of learning and innovation within these firms is therefore not pre-given or static, but continually remade over time, via this set of concrete mechanisms. This is not to argue that regional culture mechanically or rigidly determines worker and firm behaviour, but rather that it structures the material and cultural resources that enable and constrain the learning behaviours and actions of individuals and the firms in which they work. And because these regionally culturally inflected patterns of corporate behaviour are often common across multiple firms in the region, it is therefore possible to identify regional industrial cultures, and thereby move beyond the somewhat all-encompassing notions of 'regional culture' that characterized some earlier studies:

> Why are these distinctions important? Because . . . it helps us to understand firms as actors in regional development: as actors having to operate in – and at least partly having to accept as a given – a pre-existing regional culture, but also as actors that within that wider culture create their own internal organizational cultures and participate in the formation of a regional industrial culture that, in its turn, supports their operation. (Oinas, 1995, 202–3)

Finally, in tracing the origins of the spatially variable sets of cultural norms, values, beliefs and attitudes that come to define firms' learning and innovation behaviours, recent studies have also sought to overcome earlier tendencies within the regional learning literature to sideline extra-local structures at the national and international scales (see MacKinnon et al., 2002; Markusen, 1999). In so doing, they have avoided a partial view of the structures and forces shaping 'regional' processes of innovation and learning, based on a misplaced conception of regions as 'closed systems' or mere 'containers of intangible assets and structures' (Yeung, 2005, 47; see also Bathelt et al., 2004; Bunnell and Coe, 2001). A useful example here is the recent work of Meric Gertler on cultural conflicts between German producers and Canadian users of advanced industrial manufacturing technologies around purchasing practices, contracting procedures, training and labour practices, operating manuals and service expectations. This work highlights the role of national institutional and regulatory structures in reproducing regional cultural 'differences in expectations, characteristic workplace practices and norms, attitudes, managerial routines, and transactional behaviours – in short, what appear to be substantially different industrial or business "cultures" in North America and Germany' (Gertler, 2004, 81). The economic consequence of these cultural differences was a series of misunderstandings, disappointments, conflicts and, in some cases, termination of the relationship between technology producer and user. In a similar vein, Sadler and Thompson (2001) have explored the ways in which national institutions of organized labour also contribute to the formulation, maintenance and dissolution of regional industrial cultures. Their analysis focuses specifically on the activities of the Iron and Steel Trades Confederation in Teesside, northeast England, and how nationally led centrist labour politics came together with local paternalistic capital–labour relations and localistic forms of self-identification to create a distinctive regional industrial culture. In so doing, they also open up contemporary debates around regional cultural economies of learning and adaptability to old industrial regions.

EMERGING RESEARCH: DIVERSE REGIONAL CULTURAL ECONOMIES OF LEARNING AND INNOVATION

Research over the two decades to 2010 has therefore reinterpreted Marshall's original speculations about 'industrial atmosphere' to emphasize the socio-cultural foundations of industrial organization and corporate behaviour that are critical to understanding learning and innovation processes within regional economies, and hence regional economic development. In addition to the work reviewed above, a series of newly emergent research streams are currently extending ideas of regional cultural economy in exciting new directions. Motivated by the dramatic increase in female labour force participation rates that has accompanied the transition to the new economy, one new research stream explores the gendering of innovation and learning within regional industrial systems. Building on Doreen Massey's earlier analysis of the gendering of organizational cultures in high-tech firms – or what she terms masculinized 'high-tech monasteries' – in Cambridge (Massey, 1995), Gray and James (2007) have examined the implications of such cultures for firms' capacities to access, assimilate, reconfigure, transform and apply external sources of new knowledge and competencies to commercial ends.[6] Key dimensions of this include: the routine difficulties experienced by female professionals in articulating their ideas and making their voices heard relative to male colleagues; and the constraints imposed by gendered norms around parenting in which women assume the majority share of household care and hence find it more difficult than working fathers to engage in after-work networking activities of tacit knowledge transfer (for example, after-work socializing, and attendance at conferences, workshops and seminars). Gray and James argue that these – and other – gendered constraints significantly limit female information technology (IT) workers' abilities to contribute to the kinds of routine activities widely theorized to underpin learning and innovation within and between firms in high-tech regional economies.

Building on this work, subsequent comparative research on gendered work–life conflict amongst IT workers in Cambridge and Dublin has explored how worker uptake of a preferred set of firm-provided 'work–life balance' (WLB) arrangements (particularly, flexitime, teleworking and compressed work weeks) in turn enhances firms' innovative capacities (see James, 2009). Based on a cross-regional survey of 150 IT companies (with combined employment in Cambridge and Dublin of 8068 workers), 54 per cent of managers identified 'an improved corporate environment for learning and creativity' as a consequence of their WLB provision, consistent with measured improvements in firm performance (productivity, revenue growth, workforce diversity) over the same time period (2004–07). In addition, this work has also documented gendered patterns of cross-firm, embodied knowledge transfer in response to uneven WLB provision, and their mediation by different labour market intermediaries, such as GirlGeeks and Women in Technology. Of 162 highly qualified, female IT technical workers surveyed in Cambridge and Dublin, one-third identified 'poor WLB provision' in their previous company as a very important reason for leaving (push); and two-thirds identified 'better WLB provision' as a very important reason for moving to their current company (pull) (see James, 2009). These figures are particularly significant, given average company tenures of 3.5 years within this cohort. This research stream also extends to the USA. Most notably, Chris Benner's (2003) work on the role of female-dedicated labour market intermediaries in facilitating the diffusion of female expertise, skills and knowledge in Silicon Valley highlights further the crucial role of female cross-firm learning communities in promoting knowledge exchange and economic growth within high-tech regional economies.

In addition to this emerging focus on gender, a second new stream of research on regional cultural economies of innovation is concerned with decentring the traditional focus of academic analysis to non-Western regional economies in the Global South (see Murphy, 2008; cf. Park and Markusen, 1995). One important study here is Simon Reid-Henry's (2008) analysis of culturally embedded innovation processes in Cuba's 'Science Pole', which transposes the study of high-tech regional cultures to a developing-world and socialist country context. The study explores the particular relationship between state socialism and local ethics of improvisation (known locally as *'aprovechando'*), conduct of the self (*'consagración'*), and glorification of risk-taking in shaping the research activities of local biotechnology companies. Cuba's 'experimental milieu' was able to replicate many features of regional economies studied in the Global North, albeit from within a very different cultural framework (for example, Cuban scientific research was closely supervised by the state, which was invested in the biotechnology project at all levels, and insisted that research took place in a manner orientated to state-defined needs). By the end of the 1980s, 42 research and production centres were clustered together in the Western Havana Scientific Pole, and their knowledge production activities generated a number of scientific and commercial breakthroughs (such as the world's first Meningitis B vaccine, a recombinant Hepatitis B vaccine and the cholesterol-busting Policosanol), and accounted for over US$100 million in annual export earnings (Reid-Henry, 2008, 1969). Into the 1990s, Cuba's biotechnology cluster continued to attract international acclaim, based on 'proof that developing countries, too, could be innovative' (Reid-Henry, 2008).

As such, this work usefully exposes and challenges a uniformity in the regional innovation literature: 'in which a specifically Western and capitalist economic culture is often uncritically established as an *a priori* norm for regional economic success' (Reid-Henry, 2008, 1968–9). Annalee Saxenian's latest research on cross-regional cultural economies of learning amongst internationally mobile high-tech entrepreneurs ('the new Argonauts') circulating between Silicon Valley and their home countries in China, India, Taiwan and South Korea, also challenges the Global North bias of the regional innovation literature (see Saxenian, 2005). Yet these studies are relatively few in number and much remains to be done in deepening our knowledge and understanding of the cultural economy of learning and innovation in regional economies in the Global South. Crucially, this process of 'theorizing back' (Yeung, 2007) demands that we go further than the creation of an expanded series of add-on case studies to reinterpret or affirm apparently 'universal' Western knowledge. Rather, it requires that we use those case studies to transform existing theoretical accounts and to challenge our taken-for-granted core concepts (Appadurai, 2002; Robinson, 2003).

CONCLUDING COMMENTS

In the context of the shift to a globalized, post-Fordist knowledge economy, the relationship between private sector innovation and regional growth has become a central avenue of inquiry for scholars across a range of disciplines. Building on an earlier interest in agglomeration economies and 'traded' input–output linkages, scholars have broadened their analyses to examine how 'untraded' socio-cultural, institutional and relational characteristics of regional industrial agglomerations foster and support conditions conducive to learning, innovation, entrepreneurship and growth. This chapter has provided an introductory overview to this rich body of literature, focused on the core theoretical frameworks, conceptual tools and some innovative empirical studies that have advanced our understanding of the regional cultural economy of learning, innovation and development. The central argument is that is simply impossible to explain fully the continuing competitive advantage of certain regional economies over others unless we take into account the shared cultural understandings, norms, values, beliefs, customs and conventions which reflexively shape the decision-making processes, social interactions and everyday learning behaviours of knowledge workers and the firms in which they work. That said, much remains to be done in demystifying these cultural–economic relationships, not least in enabling informed, culturally sensitive policy interventions in pursuit of sustainable regional economic growth.

NOTES

1. This divergence in the regional economic performance of Silicon Valley and Boston's Route 128 through the 1980s was manifest empirically in multiple ways (see Saxenian, 1994, 2). For example, while both regions employed high-tech workforces of roughly the same size in 1975, from 1975 to 1990 Silicon Valley generated 150 000 net new tech jobs, three times the number generated in Route 128 over same period. For the period 1986–90, the market value of technology firms in Silicon Valley increased by $25 billion compared with a $1 billion increase for technology firms in Route 128. In 1990 Silicon Valley-based producers exported $11 billion of electronics products compared with $4.6 billion from Route 128. And while Silicon Valley was home to 39 of the US's top 100 fastest-growing electronics corporations in 1990, this compares with only four in Route 128.
2. Nor could Silicon Valley's superior performance could be attributed to differentials in real-estate costs or wage levels. Land and office space were actually more expensive in most of Silicon Valley than in Route 128 during the 1980s, and the wages and salaries of production workers, engineers and managers were also higher. Nor were there any significant differences in tax rates between California and Massachusetts. Nor could their differences in regional performance be traced to patterns of defence spending. While Route 128 has historically relied more heavily on military spending than has Silicon Valley, and hence was made more vulnerable to defence cutbacks, Route 128's downturn began in 1984 at a time when the value of prime defence contracts to the region was still on the increase.
3. GREMI stands for Groupement de Recherche Europeén sur les Milieux Innovateurs.
4. Five metrics were employed: (i) linear revenue growth since start-up; (ii) assumed exponential revenue growth since start-up; (iii) research and development (R&D) intensity I (R&D expenditure to annual revenue); (iv) R&D intensity II (R&D employment to total employment); and (v) productivity in terms of revenue per employee.
5. The most striking differences in performance for medium-sized firms (20–99 employees) as revealed through the survey (N = 105) and in-depth case study (N = 20) datasets include: exponential growth rates, where the non-Mormon-founded and -managed firms outperform their Mormon counterparts three times over; Type I R&D intensities (non-Mormon firms two times greater). And for firms in the smaller employment category (less than 20 employees): non-Mormon firms exhibited productivity figures over two times greater than their Mormon counterparts (see James 2005, 2007 for more detail).
6. The evidence base for this study comprised: in-depth interviews with 88 employees in ten leading firms

(by 2002 workforce size and establishment revenues) in Cambridge's software and telecommunication sectors, with female and male human resources managers, chief executive officers, engineers, scientists and technologists.

REFERENCES

Amin, A. and N.J. Thrift (1994), 'Living in the global', in A. Amin and N.J. Thrift (eds), *Globalization, Institutions and Regional Development in Europe*, Oxford: Oxford University Press, pp. 1–22.

Amin, A. and N.J. Thrift (1995), 'Globalisation, institutional "thickness" and the local economy', in P. Healey, S. Cameron, S. Davoudi, S. Graham and A. Madani-Pour (eds), *Managing Cities: The New Urban Context*, Chichester: John Wiley, pp. 91–108.

Amin, A. and N.J. Thrift (1997), 'Globalisation, socioeconomics and territoriality', in R. Lee and J. Wills (eds), *Geographies of Economies*, London: Arnold, pp. 147–57.

Amin, A. and N.J. Thrift (eds) (2004), *The Cultural Economy Reader*, Oxford: Blackwell.

Appadurai, A. (2002), 'Deep democracy: urban governmentality and the horizon of politics', *Public Culture*, **14** (1), 21–47.

Asheim, B.T. (1996), 'Industrial districts as "learning regions": a condition for prosperity?', *European Planning Studies*, **4**, 379–400.

Bathelt, H., A. Malmberg and P. Maskell (2004), 'Clusters and knowledge: local buzz, global pipelines and knowledge creation', *Progress in Human Geography*, **28** (1), 31–56.

Benner, C. (2003), 'Learning communities in a learning region: the soft infrastructure of cross-firm learning communities in Silicon Valley', *Environment and Planning A*, **35** (10), 1809–30.

Brusco, S. (1986), 'Small firms and industrial districts: the experience of Italy', in D. Keeble and E. Wever (eds), *New Firms and Regional Development in Europe*, London: Kroom Helm, pp. 184–202.

Brusco, S. (1990), 'The idea of the industrial district: its genesis', in F. Pyke, G. Becattini and W. Sengenberger (eds), *Industrial Districts and Inter-Firm Co-operation in Italy*, Geneva: International Institute for Labour Studies, pp. 10–19.

Bunnell, T.G. and N.M. Coe (2001), 'Spaces and scales of innovation', *Progress in Human Geography*, **25** (4), 569–89.

Camagni, R. (1991), 'Local "milieu", uncertainty and innovation networks: towards a new dynamic theory of economic space', in R. Camagni (ed.), *Innovation Networks: Spatial Perspectives*, London: Belhaven Press, pp. 121–44.

Camagni, R. (1995), 'The concept of the innovative milieu and its relevance for public policies in European lagging regions', *Papers in Regional Science*, **74** (4), 317–40.

Capello, R. (1999), 'Spatial transfers of knowledge in high technology milieux: learning versus collective learning processes', *Regional Studies*, **33** (4), 353–65.

Crang, P. (1997), 'Introduction: cultural turns and the (re)constitution of economic geography', in R. Lee and J. Wills (eds), *Geographies of Economies*, London: Arnold, pp. 3–15.

Florida, R. and M. Kenney (1990), 'Why Silicon Valley and Route 128 won't save us', *California Management Review*, **33** (1), 68–88.

Gertler, M.S. (1995), 'Discussion of *Regional Advantage: Culture and Competition in Silicon Valley and Route 128* by AnnaLee Saxenian', *Economic Geography*, **71**, 199–207.

Gertler, M.S. (1997), 'The invention of regional culture', in R. Lee and J. Wills (eds), *Geographies of Economies*, London: Arnold, pp. 47–58.

Gertler, M.S. (2004), *Manufacturing Culture: The Institutional Geography of Industrial Practice*, Oxford: Oxford University Press.

Granovetter, M. (1985), 'Economic action and social structure: the problem of embeddedness', *American Journal of Sociology*, **91**, 481–510.

Gray, M. and A. James (2007), 'Connecting gender and economic competitiveness: lessons from Cambridge's high tech regional economy', *Environment and Planning A*, **39** (2), 417–36.

Henry, N. and S. Pinch (2000), 'Spatialising knowledge: placing the knowledge community of Motor Sport Valley', *Geoforum*, **31** (2), 191–208.

Henry, N., S. Pinch and S. Russell (1996), 'In pole position? Untraded interdependencies, new industrial spaces and the British Motor Sport Industry', *Area*, **28** (1), 25–36.

Hess, M. (2004), '"Spatial" relationships? Towards a reconceptualization of embeddedness', *Progress in Human Geography*, **28** (2), 165–86.

James, A. (2005), 'Demystifying the role of culture in innovative regional economies', *Regional Studies*, **39** (9), 1197–216.

James, A. (2007), 'Everyday effects, practices and causal mechanisms of "cultural embeddedness": learning from Utah's high tech regional economy', *Geoforum*, **38**, 393–413.

James, A. (2009), 'The impacts of work–life balance on learning and innovation in regional economies', Queen Mary University of London / Economic and Social Research Council, report available at http://www.geog. qmul.ac.uk/docs/13292.pdf.

Keeble, D. and F. Wilkinson (1999), 'Collective learning and regional development in the evolution of regional clusters of high technology SMEs in Europe', *Regional Studies*, **33** (4), 295–304.

Lorenz, E.H. (1992), 'Trust, community, and co-operation: toward a theory of industrial districts', in M.J. Storper and A.J. Scott (eds), *Pathways to Industrialisation and Regional Development*, New York, USA and London, UK: Routledge, pp. 195–204.

MacKinnon, D., A. Cumbers and K. Chapman (2002), 'Learning, innovation and regional development: a critical appraisal of recent debates', *Progress in Human Geography*, **26** (3), 293–311.

Maillat, D. (1995), 'Territorial dynamics, innovative milieus and regional policy', *Entrepreneurship and Regional Development*, **7**, 157–65.

Malecki, E.J. (1999), 'Knowledge and regional competitiveness', paper presented at the International Symposium, Knowledge, Education, and Space, Heidelberg, Germany, September.

Markusen, A. (1999), 'Fuzzy concepts, scanty evidence, policy distance: the case for rigour and policy relevance in critical regional studies', *Regional Studies*, **33** (9), 869–84.

Marshall, A. (1890), *Principles of Economics: An Introductory Volume*, 8th edn (1952), London: Macmillan.

Martin R.L. (2000), 'Institutionalist approaches in economic geography', in E. Sheppard and T.J. Barnes (eds), *A Companion To Economic Geography*, Oxford: Blackwell, pp. 77–94.

Martin, R.L. and P. Sunley (1996), 'Paul Krugman's geographical economics and its implications for regional development theory: a critical assessment', *Economic Geography*, **72**, 260–93.

Martin, R.L. and P. Sunley (2001), 'Deconstructing clusters: chaotic concept or policy panacea?', paper presented to the Regional Studies Association annual conference, 21 November, London.

Massey, D. (1995), 'Masculinity, dualisms and high technology', *Transactions of the Institute of British Geographers*, **20**, 487–99.

Murphy, J.T. (2008), 'Economic geographies of the Global South: missed opportunities and promising intersections with development studies', *Geography Compass*, **2–3**, 851–73.

Oinas, P. (1995), 'Discussion of *Regional Advantage: Culture and Competition in Silicon Valley and Route 128* by AnnaLee Saxenian', *Economic Geography*, **71**, 202–4.

Oinas, P. (1997), 'On the socio-spatial embeddedness of business firms', *Erdkunde*, **51**, 23–32.

Park, S.O. and M. Markusen (1995), 'Generalising new industrial districts: a theoretical agenda and an application from a non-Western economy', *Environment and Planning A*, **27**, 81–104.

Pinch, S. and N. Henry (1999), 'Paul Krugman's geographical economics, industrial clustering and the British motor sport industry', *Regional Studies*, **33** (9), 815–27.

Polanyi, K. (1944), *The Great Transformation: The Political and Economic Origins of Our Time*, New York: Farrer & Rinehart.

Porter, M.E. (1990), *The Competitive Advantage of Nations*, London: Macmillan.

Porter, M.E. (1994), 'The role of location in competition', *Journal of the Economics of Business*, **1** (1), 35–9.

Porter, M.E. (1998), *On Competition*, Boston, MA: Harvard University Press.

Pyke, F., G. Becattini and W. Sengenberger (1990), *Industrial Districts and Inter-Firm Co-operation in Italy*, Geneva: International Institute for Labour Studies.

Pyke, F. and W. Sengenberger (eds) (1992), *Industrial Districts and Local Economic Regeneration*, Geneva: International Institute for Labour Studies.

Reid-Henry, S. (2008), 'Scientific innovation and non-Western regional economies: Cuban biotechnology's "experimental milieu"', *Environment and Planning A*, **40**, 1966–86.

Robinson, J. (2003), 'Postcolonialising geography: tactics and pitfalls', *Singapore Journal of Tropical Geography*, **24** (3), 273–89.

Sadler, D. and J. Thompson (2001), 'In search of regional industrial culture: the role of labour organisations in old industrial regions', *Antipode*, **33**, 660–86.

Saxenian, A. (1994), *Regional Advantage: Culture and Competition in Silicon Valley and Route 128*, Cambridge MA: Harvard University Press.

Saxenian, A. (2005), *The New Argonauts: Regional Advantage in the Global Economy*, Cambridge, MA: Harvard University Press.

Sayer, A. (1997), 'The dialectic of culture and economy', in R. Lee and J. Wills (eds), *Geographies of Economies*, London: Arnold, pp. 16–26.

Sayer, A. and R. Walker (1992), *The New Social Economy: Reworking the Division of Labour*, Oxford: Blackwell.

Schoenberger, E. (1994), 'Corporate strategy and corporate strategists: power, identity, and knowledge within the firm', *Environment and Planning A*, **26** (3), 435–51.

Schoenberger, E. (1997), *The Cultural Crisis of the Firm*, Oxford: Blackwell.

Schumpeter, J. (1934), *The Theory of Economic Development*, Cambridge, MA: Harvard University Press.

Scott, A.J. (1986), 'Industrial organization and location: division of labour, the firm, and social process', *Economic Geography*, **62**, 215–31.

Scott, A.J. (1988), *New Industrial Spaces: Flexible Production, Organisation and Regional Development in North America and Western Europe*, London: Pion.

Scott, A.J. (2000), 'Economic geography: the great half century', in R.L. Clark, M. Feldman and M. Gertler (eds), *Handbook of Economic Geography*, Oxford: Oxford University Press, pp. 18–44.

Storper, M.J. (1995a), 'The resurgence of regional economies, ten years later: the region as a nexus of untraded interdependencies', *European Urban and Regional Studies*, **2**, 191–222.

Storper, M.J. (1995b), 'Discussion of *Regional Advantage: Culture and Competition in Silicon Valley and Route 128* by AnnaLee Saxenian', *Economic Geography*, **71**, 199–207.

Storper, M.J. (1997), *The Regional World: Territorial Development in a Global Economy*, New York: Guilford Press.

Storper, M.J. and R. Salais (1997), *Worlds of Production: The Action Frameworks of the Economy*, Cambridge MA: Harvard University Press.

Storper, M.J. and R. Walker (1989), *The Capitalist Imperative: Territory, Technology and Industrial Growth*, New York: Blackwell.

Trigilia, C. (1990), 'Work and politics in the Third Italy's industrial districts', in F. Pyke, G. Becattini and W. Sengenberger (eds), *Industrial Districts and Inter-Firm Co-operation in Italy*, Geneva: International Institute for Labour Studies, pp. 160–84.

Veblen, T. (1919), *The Place of Science in Modern Civilisation*, New York: B.W. Huebsch.

Wolfe, D.A. (1997), 'The emergence of the region state', paper prepared for the Bell Canada Papers 5, The Nation State in a Global Information Era: Policy Challenges, John Deutsch Institute for the Study of Economic Policy, Queen's University, Kingston, Ontario.

Wolfe, D.A. and M.S. Gertler (2001), 'Innovation and social learning: an introduction', in M.S. Gertler and D.A. Wolfe (eds), *Innovation and Social Learning: Institutional Adaptation in an Era of Technological Change*, Basingstoke: Palgrave, pp. 1–24.

Yeung, H.W. (2000), 'Organizing "the firm" in industrial geography I: networks, institutions and regional development', *Progress in Human Geography*, **24** (2), 301–15.

Yeung, H.W. (2005), 'Rethinking relational economic geography', *Transactions of the Institute of British Geographers*, **30**, 37–51.

Yeung, H.W.C. (2007), 'Remaking economic geography: insights from East Asia', *Economic Geography*, **83**, 339–48.

Zukin, S. and P. DiMaggio (eds) (1990), *Structures of Capital: The Social Organisation of the Economy*, Cambridge: Cambridge University Press.

PART IV

AGGLOMERATION AND INNOVATION

Introduction
Philip Cooke and Bjørn Asheim

PROXIMITY AND INNOVATION

Part IV is devoted to understanding the manner in which innovation is facilitated and enhanced by distinctive kinds of proximity in agglomerations. It begins with Chapter 20 on the relationships between proximity and innovation by Christophe Carrincazeaux and Marie Coris, representatives of the French originators of the 'proximity debate' in the early 1990s.

This influential approach is consistent with the core theoretical elements underpinning the theoretical frame of this *Handbook*, namely an interest in the interactions between, for example, relatedness, knowledge spillovers and lateral absorptive capacity in agent recombination of knowledge for innovation, on the one hand, and the institutional structure that sustains such interactions systemically, on the other. This is expressly related with the new economic geography (NEG) perspective in its original formulation, being formed in the interplay between agglomeration and dispersion. However, the simplistic and traditional binary division between centripetal and centrifugal forces or 'core' and 'periphery' thinking is subsequently exposed to critique by the proximity model. For example, what is the extent of proximate technological externalities, that is, how local is local and what are the knowledge transfer mechanisms, and are they always positive in their effect on innovation? Research on this line promises to shed light on the recurrent problem of measurement of regional knowledge spillover leakage (and infusion) with respect to innovation.

One way in which progress is made here is that the Proximity School privileges the coordination of agents over economic geography's perennial neurosis about scale. This means that spatial configurations are constructed from social interactions, rather than the reverse. It means analysing the interaction between knowledge and its communication space. The former is composed of 'combinatorial knowledge' and new or 'technological knowledge', both of the Schumpeterian kind. Innovation arises from a double interaction among combinations of pre-existing knowledge and between these and new knowledge, hence the emphasis on coordination skills. Many of these are tacit; accordingly geographic proximity is important up to a point because modes of communication, identification and application may express 'localized discourses' among cross-functional 'communities of practice'. In these respects, geographical proximity is moulded by relational (that is, cognitive) proximity, meaning that the space of innovation may display a variable geometry. This must be analysed in its changing forms by concrete research to identify the dynamic interplay between complementary and substitutable proximities. This requires careful conceptual refinement of the phases of innovation: hence, a science-based sector might privilege geographic proximity for research and development (R&D) but distant networks for innovation and other near-market activities. Contrariwise, a symbolic knowledge sector might privilege distant networks for determination of a creative artifact's value, but geographic proximity for realization of such value (art auction proximity).

SOCIAL CAPITAL AND CLUSTER INNOVATION

The idea that knowledge plays a crucial role in proximity dynamics is underlined in Stuart Rosenfeld's Chapter 21 in this *Handbook*, an analysis of the role of social capital in regional innovation. He sets the following agenda for regional development theory and practice. First, to design interventions that develop social capital and increase rates of learning, networking, innovation and sustainable growth, and to ensure inclusivity. Second, and imaginatively, assessing how the geometrically increasing use of social networking is affecting the geography and meaning of social capital. Rosenfeld notes that the concept was popularized (though not invented by) Jane Jacobs as her correlate of the medium by means of which regional diversity stimulated innovation (see Chapter 11 of this *Handbook* by Iammarino for further detail). It could also be observed in the innovation practices of industrial districts in the 'Third Italy' where learning, networking and trust were evident in the interfirm and intracommunity interactions, expressing their high social capital. The 'leakage' of knowledge among agents in the region is discounted by Marshallian gains as employees, if not employers, interact and 'educate one another' through Bellandi's 'underground learning'.

As in Carrincazeaux and Coris's (Chapter 20) perspective on proximity, Rosenfeld, after Maskell, sees the boundaries of the cluster being set by the extent of learning knowledge of consequence to its innovation and renewal. Nevertheless, in US high-tech clusters, social capital is insufficient to prevent interregional leakage of value-adding innovation based on localized knowledge. Whether leakage is significantly moderated by pecuniary R&D and non-pecuniary network inputs to research university locales remains a mystery. The advent of 'social networking' among large swathes of the world's affluent youth, especially, has been a remarkable cultural phenomenon, but does it influence core innovation interactions? The jury is out but, admittedly middle-aged, expert opinion is reported by Rosenfeld as unanimous that that face-to-face interaction reveals more: notably the subtleties of tone, meaning and context crucial to interpretation of uncertain knowledge. Measurement of social capital effects awaits Krugman's hope that dreary old economic measures can be found to measure a phenomenon that leaves no paper trail. The best results emerge from tailored surveys, which are nevertheless resource-intensive but show measurable social capital to be a real presence in market transactions. Indeed, as James (Chapter 19, this *Handbook*) recalls Karl Polanyi's observation, market transactions would not exist in the absence of social capital.

The questions centred upon social capital and agglomeration surface clearly in Arne Isaksen's examination of processes associated with cluster emergence in Chapter 22. This has recently been the subject of a book-length treatment by Dirk Fornahl and colleagues, cited in Chapter 1, 'Introduction', to this *Handbook*. One key issue that had tended to be overlooked in earlier research on the subject was: what is the nature of a cluster, as distinct from an agglomeration, or simple co-location? The answer is that interactions, including but also transcending arm's-length exchange, occur between cluster incumbents. That is, social capital stimulates cooperation, tighter collaboration, formal and informal networking, and exchange of favours based on trust and recipriocity. Instead of this, questions used typically to be posed regarding the numbers of firms that constitute a cluster, reminiscent of Zeno's paradox of the bees: that is, how many make a swarm? Accordingly, Krugman's above-mentioned desire to find such social interactions in dreary economists' data before handing over to the social anthropologists is likely to remain unfulfilled. Accordingly, Isaksen rightly notes that research has hardly scratched the surface of the issue of cluster evolution, that is, their origins and development over time, compared to the now well-explored question of why industries cluster.

Although the question of cluster emergence suggests a facile adaptation of product life-cycle theory to a new problem, in fact what is called for is further reflection upon path-dependence and, indeed, diversified path-interdependence (Martin's Chapter 15 in this *Handbook*) to try to unpick the evolutionary mechanisms involved. Nevertheless emergence, growth, maturity and decay or renewal make evolutionary life-cycle reasoning to some degree unavoidable, moderated by recognition of the indeterminacy of outcomes and avoidance of all teleologies. This is achieved by adoption of a regional innovation systems frame of reference regarding interactions between 'innovation paradigm' and 'regional innovation regime'. Logically speaking 'regional regime' variety is a powerful intervening variable in the key inflections of cluster evolution. This would be especially true in 'episodic' radical innovation contexts that renew paradigms, and even in 'epochal' innovation contexts, though more dependently. Here, Isaksen stresses two initiating conditions: first, certain prerequisites or assets exist; second, triggering events stimulate entrepreneurship. In the 'Third Italy', prerequisites included the onset of the 'flight from the soil' by artisan farmers, on the one hand, and economic modernization (housing, automation and urbanization) on the other.

The 'Tuscan', 'Emilian' and 'Marche' models displayed the response of many of the former (artisan farmers) turning to innovative opportunities in the latter (ceramics, white goods, furniture, leather) aided by the European Common Market and US demand. Yet their regional regimes have ranged from left centralism to left decentralism to relative conservatism, and clusters and districts also displayed paradigm variety. The Emilian model is represented by varieties of fine engineering districts and decentralized support services; the Tuscan model had a 'counter-regime' character of entrepreneurship in the face of 'democratic centralism' and official disdain for small businesses; while the 'Marche model' evolved with a responsive regional regime and strong, often religious, conduits to regional credit. The last-named fared badly in 2008–09 when private credit froze, whereas the Emilian model was more resilient because of its cooperative financing traditions. The 'Tuscan model' is different, declining in employment due to varieties of 'hollowing-out' in production, but experiencing innovative bank financing to bolster its interlocking equity model of 'directed networks'. These are all mature cluster regions facing decline or renewal; as such they continue to represent an invaluable laboratory for the study of regional diversity in cluster life cycles. Isaksen illustrates this stage of the cluster life cycle by reference to the end of Oslo's offshore engineering due to cognitive lock-in favouring traditional oil-rigs over an innovative submarine robotics paradigm. Accordingly, cluster renewal seems intimately bound up with regional regime governance of either the 'anchor firm' kind denoted in De Propris and Crevoisier's Chapter 13 in this *Handbook*, or more public orchestration to increase 'relatedness'.

TRANSVERSALITY AND TECHNOLOGY

This is more deeply examined in Philip Cooke's Chapter 23 on transversality in this *Handbook*. Transversality is the regional regime or regional economic governance methodology for securing regional innovation by enhancing relatedness. It embraces the intermediary concept of 'innovative platform' that refers to the combination of interacting regional clusters and/or other forms of related regional industrial organization (for example oligopolies, supply-chains, networks). Transversality not only refers to recombinant regional innovations arising from cross-fertilization of knowledge among distinct industries, but it also embraces the idea of 'joined-up governance' among distinctive policy jurisdictions of relevance to regional innovation and growth. A variety of regional regimes for promoting transversality can be identified on the basis of regionally informed economic governance research. These range from the reactive, seeking solutions to the loss of a core cluster; to varying degrees of proactivity, either seeking to variegate a specific path-dependence or deal with a temporary regional paradigm shock; to committed proactivity to furthering regional innovation by stimulating cross-sectoral knowledge recombinations. Of special interest to the regional innovation and growth interest of this *Handbook* is the repositioning of regional regime governance towards the centre of the regional innovation process. From being a passive 'supporter', 'promoter', 'encourager', 'assistant' or 'partner' in the old rhetoric of supply-side regional economic assistance, the regional regime becomes more of a demand-side 'catalyst' for regional innovation.

Finally, in Chapter 24 we come to Edward Malecki's take on the position of technology clusters in the menagerie of organizational forms taken, notably at the leading edge in this case, of regional innovation and growth. The 'red thread' running through Part IV of the *Handbook* is the role of human organizational capability in fruitfully coordinating knowledge, utilizing social capital in geographic proximity, to evolve, refresh and retain spatial agglomerations with the characteristics of 'innovative clusters'. The technology cluster is the apotheosis of that exercise in spatial complexity, combining as it does both the 'networks' (social capital) and 'scaffolds' (coordination, proximity) that complexity theorists habitually see as separating order from chaos in natural and social scientific affairs. As Malecki states, technology clusters are different from the rest because they remain in relatively immature stages of the 'cluster life cycle'. They are also highly research- and knowledge-absorbent, a further differentiating feature. They vary in assets like entrepreneurship or networking propensity according to national and regional regimes as well as the innovation paradigm to which they belong. They can generally be distinguished by their 'entrepreneurial ecosystem' of research and technology; sources of risk finance; and an entrepreneurial or technical culture. Their success often means that they suffer 'diseconomies of agglomeration' in congestion and other infrastructural inefficiencies. Start-up and spin-off activity tends to be rife at the cluster emergence and early growth stages of technology cluster life cycles. Some display advanced learning in recombinatorial knowledge skills; others are advanced in complex system integration. On the question of transferability of such entrepreneurial ecosystems, Malecki is agnostic, but it could be argued that with advanced knowledge plus venture capital and talent, it can be emulated in a different form, perhaps best exemplified by the Israeli experience of evolving high-tech mini-clusters (see Chapter 38 on incubation policy by Shefer and Frenkel in this *Handbook*).

20 Proximity and innovation
Christophe Carrincazeaux and Marie Coris

INTRODUCTION

The idea that geographical concentration is essential in the dynamic process of innovation is widely shared. It has largely been assumed since the 1980s that agents must be close in order to innovate. The spatial agglomeration of innovative activities underpins the idea that there is a causal relationship between innovation processes and location. But correlation is obviously not causality. Thus, without denying the role of geographical proximity for innovation, it is necessary to understand this link better.

The link between geographical proximity and innovation is one of the major issues addressed by the French School of Proximity since its origin (RERU, 1993). In this chapter, we try to synthesize the major proposals of the French School of Proximity. We firstly present the 'proximist approach' in order to define its specificities, particularly in relation to other approaches, such as new economic geography and the literature on 'localized innovation systems'. Secondly, we outline the main contributions (both theoretical and empirical) of the French School of Proximity to the analysis of the relationship between proximity and innovation. Finally, we conclude with the unresolved debates and limits of the proximist approach.

GEOGRAPHICAL PROXIMITY IN INNOVATION

Two main explanations of the agglomeration of innovative activities can be distinguished in the economic literature: the first one is centred on externalities and the second one on local institutions. The French School of Proximity follows these lines but utilizes normal assumptions on the nature and geographical extent of externalities and widely accepted perspectives on the local dimension of innovative systems. It is proposed to go back to a microeconomic analysis of coordination based on knowledge dynamics.

Geographical Proximity Matters for Innovation

The importance of proximity in the innovation process is usually justified by the use of technological externalities or by the localized nature of innovation systems. According to the new economic geography (NEG), the agglomeration process is the outcome of interplay between agglomeration and dispersion forces (Fujita and Thisse, 2009). For the geography of innovation, the differentiated sensitivity of firms' activities to technological externalities leads to different spatial models when analysed through a centre–periphery framework (Charlot and Duranton, 2006; Ota and Fujita, 1993). The characterization of externalities is central here and has been a source of debate. Krugman (1991) first criticized the use of technological externalities (because of the poor theorization of their

269

effects) before recognizing the role of pure knowledge externalities (Fujita and Krugman, 2004). The debate seems to be closed nowadays, but two problems remain open. The first refers to the spatial extent of such externalities: the transmission channels are not clearly defined, nor is the level of spatial analysis, which is a key issue for these models. The second problem that remains insufficiently explored concerns the assumption of a constantly positive dimension of technological agglomeration.[1]

Numerous contributions have addressed[2] and continue to address[3] the issue of advantages of local specialization as compared to diversity of economic activities. They lead to very different results depending on the methods used to measure diversity (Beaudry and Schiffauerova, 2009) and do not solve the question of the nature of externalities. During the 1990s, an impressive empirical literature on the role of distance in localized knowledge spillovers (LKS) developed, and many syntheses were proposed (see Chapter 10 by Breschi in this *Handbook*; Feldman, 1999; Breschi and Lissoni, 2001 among others). Key issues were already addressed in the seminal article by Jaffe (1989) in which he proposed to evaluate spillovers from university research to industrial innovation through patents. Subsequent studies were based on different estimations of technological distance (hesitations between industrial sectors or technological classes) or geographical distance (estimation on areas or regions with different size or estimation based on distance between zones[4]), always leading to the relevance of LKS. Despite their significant outputs, these approaches were criticized and new methods were used in more recent research in this field. Breschi and Lissoni (2001), for instance, insist on the strong tendency to overestimate the role and nature of (tacit) knowledge in the location process, and claim a better understanding of mechanisms at stake.

Work on LKS remains prominent, being more oriented towards detailed analysis of the transmission channels through the use of relational data.[5] According to those approaches, geographical proximity matters for innovation; but to what extent, remains in debate (see for example Johnson et al., 2006).

The role of geographical proximity is also stated in the more heterogeneous literature on localized innovation systems. The concept of 'innovation system' refers to a dynamic process ensuring consistency of the different actors and institutions that participate in and delimit the range of innovative activities (see Chapter 33 by Tödtling and Trippl in this *Handbook*). For the geography of innovation, the question arising is that of the appropriate level of analysis – always relative – for any innovation system and, therefore, the importance of local dynamics in the innovation process. The reference to the nature of knowledge remains a rationale for the local dimension of these systems, but the institutional context adds a more collective dimension in analyses of innovation.

The theory of innovation renewal in the 1980s (Dosi, 1988) supported the integration of the institutional paradigm in the emergent geography of innovation. From industrial districts to the GREMI V and VI programmes in the 2000s, the innovative milieu approach made a significant contribution to the integration of space and innovation (Crevoisier, 2004).

During the 1990s, the acceleration of the globalization process, of markets and technologies, and the rise of competition from newly industrialized countries led to new questions for developed countries. The knowledge economy became the backbone of the competitive advantage of nations. Competitiveness and the knowledge economy are the basis for the concepts of clusters[6] (Porter, 1990) and regional innovation systems (Cooke et al., 2007). These regional systems would then be the pertinent spatial scale for innovation dynamics (Asheim and Coenen, 2005; Asheim, 2007), even though the issue of the relevant scale remains in question (Doloreux and Parto, 2005).

Coordination through Proximity

The debate on the local dimension of economic interactions became the *raison d'être* of the French School of Proximity in the early 1990s (Carrincazeaux et al., 2008). The starting point was criticism of the postulated local relationships of the majority of spatial approaches. As illustrated quite well by the above brief review, it is always possible to identify local interdependencies in innovation, and some local consistency, since spatial limits are previously identified. The proximity approach seeks to overcome this determinism, taking coordination of agents as a starting point. The French School approach tries to infer the role of local space (here in innovation activities) from proximity relations between agents, organizations and institutions. The space is no longer postulated, but built upon the need for coordination. The proximity approach is thus more a method of understanding or analysing innovation at the local level than a theory in itself. It seeks to go beyond the narrow vision of localized externalities, for which their nature and spatial extent remain a challenge, by analysing first the coordination process of innovative activities.

The nature of interactions relies primarily on the knowledge base. The bridge between geography and innovation is made through the association between the nature of knowledge and communication in space. The qualification of knowledge (or type of externalities when the approaches are focused on knowledge diffusion) is then at the core of the analysis, according to the interactions needed. The literature on the subject is extremely rich in typology from the basic distinction between knowledge (tacit) and information, and numerous syntheses have been proposed (Amin and Cohendet, 2004), modes of coordination and governance being associated with the type of knowledge used (Antonelli, 2005). For the geography of innovation perspective, the link between type of knowledge and type of interaction is also well documented. On the basis of the LKS approach, many contributions have been made on the complexity of the knowledge base (for example the evolutionary perspective of Breschi and Malerba, 1997), on localized systems of innovation (Tödtling et al., 2006) or proximity in the innovation process (Kirat and Lung, 1999). Asheim (2007) and Cooke et al. (2007), for instance, mobilize the distinction between analytical, synthetic or symbolic knowledge for which geography may have some importance.

The proximity approach isolates two key dimensions in terms of the complexity of the knowledge base (Carrincazeaux et al., 2001): on the one hand, the need for associating dissimilar capabilities or skills (labelled combinatorial complexity); on the other hand, the need for implementing new knowledge (technological complexity). This distinction, closed to that of synthetic and analytical knowledge, is more oriented towards a distinction between technological and organizational skills, in order directly to take into account the context of coordination.

Technological complexity is defined as the renewal frequency of the knowledge base.[7] It refers to the technological aspects of learning. This implies taking into account the degree of skills novelty that may affect existing routines for coordination. The frequency of such renewal depends on the level of technological opportunities in innovation and the degree of standardization of production. This complexity refers indirectly to the tacit nature of knowledge if one accepts the hypothesis that the degree of novelty may be associated with the development of new routines, uncertain and not codified by definition. This characteristic of knowledge cannot be directly linked with its scientific character, which in turn is often associated with a higher degree of codification. The hypothesis made here is the opposite, whereby new knowledge departs from standardized routines in coordination.

Symmetrically, combinatorial complexity reflects the difficulty of ensuring consistency of diverse and numerous pieces of knowledge. This complexity has two quantitative and qualitative dimensions. The qualitative side is fundamental because the difficulty of combination is mainly due to the heterogeneity of skills. One can therefore expect an amplification of combinatorial problems with increasing diversity in pieces of knowledge to merge. The quantitative nature of the coordination must not be forgotten: combinatorial constraints are not the same when several dozen engineers or technicians must interact; information and communication technology (ICT) may be limited in that case for communication from a distance.

Then the problem arises of involved actors, agents or institutions in innovative interactions (with whom to coordinate), for example the articulation of different functions both internal and external to the firm. We thus define critical interfaces as critical nodes of coordination and, therefore, key moments of the innovation process, in which proximity relations can be critical in the direction of learning process. This definition is designed to take into account the diversity of the sources of technology and the specific modes of coordination developed.

The approach developed by the French School of Proximity intends to overcome the issue of externalities (in essence external to the firm) to address the spatial dimension of coordination in a process of knowledge creation.

DYNAMICS OF PROXIMITY AND VARIETY IN SPATIAL PATTERNS OF INNOVATION

For the French School of Proximity, geographical proximity matters in the innovation process but it is not always a necessity. Location does not necessarily imply local relationships, and existing local relationships do not prove that innovation relies on the local dimension. Geographical proximity by itself is far from sufficient; and local and global relations are often complementary in the innovation process (Lung et al., 1999). In this respect, territory is viewed as a layering (which may be only temporary) of different forms of proximity, geographical and organizational.

We can try to synthesize the proximity approach on innovation by two major proposals, made at the theoretical level and empirically tested (Bouba-Olga et al., 2008, Carrincazeaux et al., 2008):

● Co-location is not a permanent support for innovation. From this stems the notion of temporary geographical proximity reconciling geographical proximity and relations from a distance.

- Proximity in coordination is not necessarily geographical. This is the (dynamic) interplay between complementarity and substitutability in different forms of proximity that arises from the diversity of spatial patterns of innovation and their trajectories.

Temporary Geographical Proximity

The French School of Proximity first questions and then refutes the *doxa* of 1980–90 that any innovation process is based on co-location of actors involved in this process. Thus the assumption that the location of actors in the innovation process depends on knowledge tacitness has been discussed (Rallet, 1993; Kirat and Lung, 1999; Lung et al., 1999): the location of actors does not only depend on the split between tacit knowledge sharing (co-location) and codified knowledge sharing (distant coordination supported by ICT). This is verified, firstly, because both types of knowledge are strongly interlinked; and secondly, because physical proximity is not the only possible support for tacit knowledge exchange.

The concept of temporary proximity allows a solution to the proximity–distance dilemma (Torre, 2008; Maskell et al., 2006). Thus, without denying its role, geographical proximity is not necessarily permanent, including activities associated with tacit knowledge exchange. Temporary relations can take different forms (Wickham and Vecchi, 2008) and enhance the performance of local clusters. Temporary proximity can bring knowledge externalities, particularly through trade fairs and conferences. For the coordination of innovation, it seems useful to distinguish two main forms of non-permanent proximity:

- Temporary geographical proximity reflects the needs for physical interaction when dealing with certain phases of a project: it is temporary regarding the entire production process since it requires the temporary co-location of staff concerned. It is usually provided by the delegation of staff from one entity to another or between specific places. Rychen and Zimmermann (2008) propose to identify different kinds of places ensuring the interface between different partners.
- Transitory geographical proximity means occasional needs for physical interaction expressed at different times of the production process. These interactions usually take the form of meetings and are mainly provided through business travel.

This distinction is useful when it is related to the complexity of the knowledge base. A situation simultaneously involving high-technological and combinatorial complexity is generally associated with a need for permanent geographical proximity. In intermediate situations, technological or combinatorial complexities being lower, temporary or transitory proximity are sufficient. Thus, in the case of high combinatorial complexity, transitional co-location through meetings may be an efficient coordinating mode. Knowledge is shared by agents (low technological complexity), and only a few meetings may be required. A strong technological complexity will be associated with temporary co-location for the creation and transfer of emerging knowledge.

These situations fundamentally depend on the critical interfaces that can act in different ways depending on the stages of the innovation process. This is well known in assembly industries in particular, with the development of modularity in the automotive and aerospace industries (Frigant and Layan, 2009); or in the software sector for example, in accordance with the stages of development and interactions with customers (Coris, 2008).

Even if it is neither a necessary nor a sufficient condition, geographical proximity still matters. Then the 'imaginary geography' of the Internet, assuming that ICT would lead to the death of proximity, collapses (Rallet and Torre, 2007). But it is not necessarily permanent. It is thus of interest to consider other supports for coordination in the innovation process, that is, to recognize that geographical proximity is only one possible form among others.

Forms of Proximity and Spatial Configurations of Innovation

The main contribution of the French School of Proximity is derived from the reflection on spatial and non-spatial forms of coordination (Rallet and Torre, 2005). While geographical proximity refers to the relative positioning of located agents, non-geographical proximity, through its various declensions, reveals the relative positioning of agents in terms of potential coordination. The basic argument can be stated as follows: the rationality of agents is situated in the sense that it depends on the context of interactions; the location of agents is inferred from coordinating needs, which can result in the mobilization of different forms of proximity. Geographical proximity becomes a form of coordination among others in the innovation process.

If this reflection is an important contribution, it is also a fundamental limit as proximity can be defined in various ways, following the specific needs of each analysis. The proximity school developed many debates about the possible forms of proximity: geographical, organizational and institutional initially, and then only organizational and geographic. Along with these basic definitions, many typologies have been proposed, considering that proximity can be technological, cognitive, relational, virtual and so on (see Chapter 14 by Boschma and Frenken in this *Handbook*). A summary of these theoretical elaborations is proposed by Carrincazeaux et al. (2008).

We here consider it relevant to separate the conceptual aspects of proximity from the empirical use of the concept. It may be useful to distinguish numerous forms of proximity in order to address some specific issues, but from a theoretical point of view the identification of canonical forms (geographic, organizational or institutional) remains essential. This is always a source of discussion as revealed in the typology proposed by Boschma (2005), for example, about the negative effects of proximity.

We go back here to the initial concepts developed by the French School in the 1990s. We should recall that coordination through proximity is not limited to relations with external organizations. The Proximity School considers the innovation process in its entirety, the internal organization of the firm being a key determinant of its external relations. The firm can thus even be seen as a localized innovation system (Quéré, 2008). Resources to coordinate are both internal and external to the organization. The distinction between these two levels being fundamental, it is therefore necessary to isolate a proximity dedicated to the organizational dimension (and/or interorganizational relationships), labelled 'organizational proximity'.

Organizational proximity refers to the coordination mode within an organization, seen as an 'area of definition of practices and strategies of agents within a set of rules driven by institutions' (Kirat and Lung, 1999). It is specific to an organization[8] since

Table 20.1   Forms of proximity and dominant spatial configurations according to knowledge base complexity

		Technological complexity	
		Strong	Weak
Combinatorial complexity	Strong	Geographical proximity *Agglomeration, clusters* (1)	Organizational proximity *Nomad organization/transitory* (4)
	Weak	Institutional proximity *Reticular organization/ temporary* (3)	Weak need for proximity *Distant interactions* (2)

it refers to interactions made among its members, and hence organizational routines. Because inter-organizational relations allow the building of routines and collective learning, proximity also emerges as an organizational form at the interorganizational level. In connection with the innovation process, it refers specifically to the notion of combinatorial complexity of the knowledge base, that is, the ability to coordinate diverse sources of knowledge in its two dimensions, quantitative and qualitative.

Institutional proximity is defined as 'agents' adherence to the same representations, rules of actions and thinking patterns' (Kirat and Lung, 1999). More generally, it expresses the coordination potential between agents (belonging or not to the same organization[9]) or organizations. Institutional proximity takes on two dimensions: the social (in terms of social networks) and the cognitive (close to Rallet and Torre's notion of similarity and symbolizing knowledge base sharing or common representations). For the innovation process, it refers more specifically to the technological complexity of the knowledge base, that is, the production and absorption of new knowledge. It also refers to combinatorial complexity when coordinating knowledge held by heterogeneous agents (organizationally or geographically 'distant') whose 'positions' can only be partially defined by the formal institutions governing the innovation process (regime of intellectual property rights, for example).

By crossing the two dimensions – complexity of the knowledge base, and the three forms of proximity – we can draw a broad typology illustrating the diversity of spatial patterns of innovation. It is summarized in Table 20.1, where each combination of technological and combinatory complexity levels is associated with dominant proximity or spatial configurations. In order to avoid a too deterministic interpretation, each of the four broad configurations is first discussed; later, we consider the dynamics of proximity, that is, the interplay between forms of proximity leading to sectoral variability and spatial trajectories of innovation.

The first configuration, (1), is the emblematic notion of clusters: the need for intensive interactions between partners involved in the innovation process is satisfied through geographical proximity. However, the critical assessment of clusters proposed by Torre (2006) pointed out that geographical proximity is not in itself a factor of coordination: insufficient in itself, it must be enabled by the existence of organizational and institutional proximity. We must therefore reverse causation traditionally established: it is not agglomeration in one place (geographical proximity) which generates cooperation, even if it can help, but its association with other forms of proximity (organizational or institutional).[10]

In the opposite case, (2), linking low levels of combinatory and technological complexity, it appears that geographical proximity, including transitory or temporary, is not a location constraint. Stated otherwise, the co-location has little interest insofar as the need for interactions may occur at a physical distance, through virtual communication tools (ICT), and be supported by known standards. However, the agglomeration of innovation activities can also be observed in that case. We can here supplement the earlier remarks by recalling that proximity deals with coordination, but location is of course a more complex process including traditional economic factors such as the attractiveness of local areas in terms of land tax or local labour markets, for example. Thus it is always difficult to infer the role of knowledge from observed agglomeration when taking coordination as a starting point. This point is clearly shown by Cooke (2008) for whom efficiency of the local milieu for biotech firms' performances relies more on traditional agglomeration effects than on local cooperative links.

The two intermediate situations have different meanings in terms of proximity. In situation (3) of high-technological complexity with low combinatorial complexity, innovation relies more on the nature of knowledge than on its combination. Indeed, interactions are based on common or sufficiently codified practices. In that case, geographical proximity can be activated on a temporary basis to ensure creation and transmission of knowledge (high technological complexity). Coordination needs to be supported by strong institutional proximity; collective learning involves here the sharing of a common cognitive basis. The establishment of a common language is based, on the one hand, on informal ties (especially interpersonal) and formal ones (the regime of intellectual property rights for example); and on the other hand, on the ability to regulate conflicts resulting from asymmetrical positions in the knowledge chain. We can associate this situation to the concept of the network which stresses the existence of specific relationships between partners belonging to different organizations within an area which may be geographically widespread (see Chapter 12 by Giuliani in this *Handbook*).

Finally, the 'nomad organization' also corresponds to a network organization, but based on a transitory geographical proximity (occasional meetings of partners). On the one hand, the low complexity of knowledge facilitates distant coordination, but on the other hand, sharing knowledge among partners implies a strong organizational proximity. This networking would probably fit the various sites of one organization, or for different firms whose recurrent cooperation over time leads to the establishment of organizational proximity.

The approach is also dynamic as proximity relations are built over time and evolve. First insights on this topic have highlighted how learning about just-in-time systems was first made possible through geographical proximity in Japan, and in the USA in a different institutional context. Transfer in Europe could be performed without this geographical constraint since a background of organizational and institutional proximity helped to overcome this constraint (Lung, 1995). Thus learning and trajectories are at the heart of articulation between the canonical forms of proximity.

The sectoral dimension is also of major importance. This fact can be illustrated by pointing out that empirical studies often focus on a particular sector. These sector-specific properties affect both the knowledge base and the nature of interactions that support the innovation process. This implies important sector variability in the knowledge base complexity and critical interfaces. A French empirical study among 600 research and development (R&D) units (Carrincazeaux, 2002) shows that proximity effects vary among sectors and that the proximity constraint does not operate at the same stages of the innovation process.

CONCLUDING REMARKS: QUESTIONS AND OPEN DEBATES

The proximity approach evolves fruitfully through a dialogue between concepts and empirical analysis. If the method is now rather stabilized in the French School, many questions remain open and should be addressed in future research.

The Local and the Global

One major evolution of the literature is to take into account that relationships are simultaneously local and global; that these are not substitutes, but complementary (the ubiquity of agents for Torre and Rallet, 2005). Numerous works using proximity concepts try to deepen this issue (see, for example, Lagendijk and Lorentzen, 2007; Vale and Caldeira, 2007; Cooke, 2008), showing that the competitive advantage of clusters relies also on their ability to develop non-local relations.

From Proximity to Proximities

The major contribution of the proximity approach lies in its ability to consider the diversity of possible situations through the interplay between static and dynamic forms of proximity (the locus of proximity relations varies greatly among activities and time). However, the definition of different proximities is a constantly renewed debate, between theoretical discussions (the holistic institutional approach against the interactionist view of coordination between agents) and empirical studies (numerous variations in qualifying proximity through studies). The major challenge is certainly to stabilize the 'canonical' forms of proximity, the backbone of the approach, with possible variations following distinct fields of application.

Proximity and Internal–External Interactions

When dealing with externalities, the approach is focused, by definition, on the environment of the innovation process. The proximity approach tries to deal simultaneously with internal and external dimensions of organizations by directly studying the innovation process. In other words, proximity relations also reflect how organizations manage internal and external relationships. This allows thinking of different configurations in firms' spatial organization of the innovation process (anchorage, globalization or offshoring).

The Negative Effects of Proximity

The negative dimensions of proximity are traditionally addressed in terms of negative externalities (dispersion forces for NEG, the debate on specialization and diversity, or environmental externalities, for example). Following these lines, the French Proximity

School produced studies on conflicts and proximity (Torre and Zuindeau, 2009). Work is less advanced in the field of innovation. The contribution by Boschma (2005) gives some insight in this domain by underlining lock-in effects associated with proximity and the lack of flexibility induced by an 'excess' of proximity. He considers that dynamics of innovation may be limited by too much cognitive, organizational, social, institutional or geographical proximity. Some contributions, more based on agglomeration effects, try to put the stress on reduced economic performance in relation to regional agglomeration of innovative activities. This is the case for Antonelli et al. (2008), which develops the idea of diminishing returns in the concentration of innovation; or Carrincazeaux and Gaschet (2007), for which regional concentration of resources in innovation does not necessarily lead to superior economic performance.

The Determinism of Knowledge

One major criticism that can be made of the approach presented here is undoubtedly the deterministic nature of knowledge in proximity relations. If the traditional opposition between tacit and codified knowledge is enriched, the fact remains that it is from the nature of knowledge and interactions that the proximity constraint is inferred. Some authors argue that the geography of innovation does not rely on knowledge, but rather on social networks, regardless of the knowledge involved (Grossetti, 2008). These approaches to the geography of innovation are sometimes in conflict. We uphold the idea that knowledge plays a critical role in proximity dynamics. But it is clear that the bridge from the need for proximity (determinism of knowledge) to the spatial organization of agents (the geography of innovation) is not immediate, involving other dimensions, relational and institutional.

Articulating Approaches, Articulating Levels

The proximity approach is of course not a complete theory of the location of innovative activities. It simply provides a framework to analyse coordination through proximity relations, a framework that needs to be integrated into a broader vision of the geography of innovation. Beyond the debate between approaches, it is undoubtedly in this dialogue that our understanding of the geography of innovation will improve. A large research field is open within which to articulate the different levels of analysis between coordination through proximity, embedding in relational networks and innovation systems frameworks. It is from the articulation of these different levels that a better understanding of the obvious diversity of configurations in the geography of innovation will emerge. The proximity approach offers a specific entry to avoid considering space as given, and tries to derive spatial configurations of innovation from the analysis of coordination.

NOTES

1. Fujita (Fujita and Krugman, 2004) considers also negative effects of technological agglomeration (lock-in process).
2. Works from Glaeser et al. (1992) and Henderson et al. (1995) are emblematic as they offer an original theorizing and empirical analysis of externalities in American urban growth. The distinction between

MAR (Marshall–Arrow–Romer, specialization and local monopoly) and Jacobs (diversity) externalities leads to a centre–periphery model.
3. For instance, the nature of variety is taken into account in the evolutionary economic geography (EEG) (Boschma and Frenken, 2006, 2007; Frenken et al., 2007) and tries to isolate in agglomeration effects aspects of, on the one hand, urbanization effects (size and urban density, unrelated variety) or, on the other, intersectoral spillovers (related variety).
4. Acs et al. (1992, 1994); Anselin et al. (1997).
5. Following Jaffe et al. (1993), patents data or scientific publications (Breschi's Chapter 10 in this *Handbook*; Hoekman et al., 2009; Autant-Bernard et al., 2007) offer new ways to deal with the geography of collaborations and knowledge spillovers in innovation.
6. The literature on clusters is certainly most heterogeneous. Martin and Sunley (2003) consider the success of the cluster concept to include its use as that of a brand useful in justifying local policy.
7. For a detailed presentation of the framework, see Carrincazeaux et al. (2001) and Carrincazeaux (2002).
8. This meaning diverges from Rallet and Torre (2005) whose definition of organizational proximity refers to 'adherence' (similarity being a second dimension). The adherence logic fails to differentiate between the inside and the outside of organizations (considered in a broad sense in their mind, including social networks and communities), whereas we believe that organizational frontiers are of importance to understand, for example, external cooperation, and to identify critical interfaces, or knowledge that must be kept inside the organization (know-how, confidentiality, and so on).
9. 'Organization' can be defined in the broad sense of communities or networks that are not explicitly, nor necessarily, closed.
10. Agglomeration of innovative activities in cities (the 'Clusties' for Gaschet and Lacour, 2007) does not necessarily signify local interactions but the search for communication and infrastructure nodes in order to benefit from temporary or transitory geographical proximity (in other words, a 'simple' agglomeration effect).

REFERENCES

Acs, Z.J., D.B. Audretsch and M.P. Feldman (1992), 'Real effects of academic research: comment, *American Economic Review*, **82** (1), 363–7.
Acs, Z.J., D. Audretsch and P. Feldman (1994), 'R&D spillovers and recipient firm size', *Review of Economics and Statistics*, **76**, 336–40.
Amin, A. and P. Cohendet (2004), *Architectures of knowledge: Firms, Capabilities, and Communities*, Oxford: Oxford University Press.
Anselin, L., A. Varga and Z. Acs (1997), 'Local geographical spillovers between university research and high technology innovations', *Journal of Urban Economics*, **42**, 422–48.
Antonelli, C. (2005), 'Models of knowledge and systems of governance', *Journal of Institutional Economics*, **1** (1), 51–73.
Antonelli, C., P. Patrucco and F. Quatraro (2008), 'The governance of localized knowledge externalities', *International Review of Applied Economics*, **22** (4), 479–98.
Asheim, B. (2007), 'Differentiated knowledge bases and varieties of regional innovation systems', *Innovation*, **20** (3), 223–41.
Asheim, B.T. and L. Coenen (2005), 'Knowledge bases and regional innovation systems: comparing Nordic clusters', *Research Policy*, **34** (8), 1173–90.
Autant-Bernard, C., J. Mairesse and N. Massard (2007), 'Spatial knowledge diffusion through collaborative networks', Introduction to Special Issue of *Papers in Regional Science*, **86** (3), pp. 341–50.
Beaudry, C. and A. Schiffauerova (2009), 'Who's right, Marshall or Jacobs? The localization versus urbanization debate', *Research Policy*, **38** (2), 318–37.
Boschma, R. (2005), 'Proximity and innovation: a critical assessment', *Regional Studies*, **39** (1), 61–74.
Boschma, R.A. and K. Frenken (2006), 'Why is economic geography not an evolutionary science? Towards an evolutionary economic geography', *Journal of Economic Geography*, **6** (3), 273–302.
Boschma, R.A. and K. Frenken (2007), 'A theoretical framework for evolutionary economic geography: industrial dynamics and urban growth as a branching process', Papers in Evolutionary Economic Geography, no. 07.01, Faculty of Geographical Sciences, Utrecht University.
Bouba-Olga, O., C. Carrincazeaux and M. Coris (2008), 'La proximité 15 ans déjà: avant propos', *Revue d'Economie Régionale et Urbaine*, **3**, 279–87.
Breschi, S. and F. Lissoni (2001), 'Knowledge spillovers and local innovation systems: a critical survey', *Industrial and Corporate Change*, **10** (4), 975–1006.

Breschi, S. and F. Malerba (1997), 'Sectoral innovation systems: technological regimes, Schumpeterian dynamics, and spatial boundaries', in C. Edquist (ed.), *Systems of Innovation. Technologies, Institutions and Organisations*, London: Pinter Publishers, pp. 130–56.

Carrincazeaux, C. (2002), 'The role of geographical proximity in the organisation of industrial R&D', in M. Feldman and N. Massard (eds), *Knowledge Spillovers and The Geography of Innovation: Institutions and Systems of Innovation*, Dordrecht: Kluwer, pp. 145–78.

Carrincazeaux, C. and F. Gaschet (2007), 'A typology of European regions according to their knowledge base', EURODITE report no. D4b, EURODITE Integrated Project (6th FP).

Carrincazeaux, C., Y. Lung and A. Rallet (2001), 'Proximity and localisation of corporate R&D activities', *Research Policy*, **30** (5), 777–89.

Carrincazeaux, C., Y. Lung and J. Vicente (2008), 'The scientific history of the French School of Proximity: interaction- and institution-based approaches to regional innovation systems', *European Planning Studies*, **16** (5), 617–28.

Charlot, S. and G. Duranton (2006), 'Cities and workplace communication: some quantitative French evidence', *Urban Studies*, **43** (8), 1365–94.

Cooke, P. (2008), 'Distinctive proximities: between implicit and explicit knowledge in ICT and biotechnology innovation', *Revue d'Economie Régionale et Urbaine*, **3**, 381–440.

Cooke, P., C. De Laurentis, F. Tödtling and M. Trippl (eds) (2007), *Regional Knowledge Economies*, Cheltenham, UK and Northampton, MA, USA: Edward Elgar.

Coris, M. (2008), 'Proximité et délocalisations: le cas du logiciel', *Revue d'Economie Régionale et Urbaine*, **3**, 361–80.

Crevoisier, O. (2004), 'The innovative milieus approach: toward a territorialized understanding of the economy?', *Economic Geography*, **80** (4), 367–79.

Doloreux, D. and S. Parto (2005), 'Regional innovation systems: current discourse and unresolved issues', *Technology in Society*, **27** (2), 133–53.

Dosi, G. (1988), 'Sources, procedures and microeconomics effects of innovation', *Journal of Economic Literature*, **26**, 1120–71.

Feldman, M.P. (1999), 'The new economics of innovation, spillovers and agglomeration: a review of empirical studies', *Economics of Innovation and New Technology*, **8**, 5–25.

Frenken, K., F. Van Oort and T. Verburg (2007), 'Related variety, unrelated variety and regional economic growth', *Regional Studies*, **41**, 685–97.

Frigant, V. and J.-B. Layan (2009), 'Modular production and the new division of labour within Europe: the perspective of French automotive parts suppliers?', *European Urban and Regional Studies*, **16** (1), 11–25.

Fujita, M. and P. Krugman (2004), 'The new economic geography: past, present and the future', *Papers in Regional Science*, **83** (1), 139–64.

Fujita, M. and J.F. Thisse (2009), 'New economic geography: an appraisal on the occasion of Paul Krugman's 2008 Nobel Prize in Economic Sciences', *Regional Science and Urban Economics*, **39**, 109–19.

Gaschet, F. and C. Lacour (2007), 'Les systemes productifs urbains: Des clusters aux clusties', *Revue d'Economie Regionale et Urbaine*, **4**, 707–28.

Glaeser, G.L., H.D. Kallal, J.A. Scheinkman and A. Shleifer (1992), 'Growth in cities', *Journal of Political Economy*, **100** (61), 1126–52.

Grossetti, M. (2008), 'Proximities and embedding effects', *European Planning Studies*, **16** (5), 629–42.

Henderson, V., A. Kuncoro and M. Turner (1995), 'Industrial development in cities', *Journal of Political Economy*, **103** (51), 1067–90.

Hoekman, J., K. Frenken and F.G. Van Oort (2009), 'The geography of collaborative knowledge production in Europe', *Annals of Regional Science*, **43** (3), 721–38.

Jaffe, A. (1989), 'Real effects of academic research', *American Economic Review*, **79**, 957–70.

Jaffe, A.B., M. Trajtenberg and R. Henderson (1993), 'Geographic localization of knowledge spillovers as evidenced by patent citations', *Quarterly Journal of Economics*, **108** (3), 577–98.

Johnson, D.K.N., N. Siripong and A.S. Brown (2006), 'The demise of distance? The declining role of physical proximity for knowledge transmission', *Growth and Change*, **37** (1), 19–33.

Kirat, T. and Y. Lung (1999), 'Innovation and proximity: territories as loci of collective learning processes', *European Urban and Regional Studies*, **6** (1), 27–39.

Krugman, P. (1991), *Geography and Trade*, Cambridge, MA: MIT Press.

Lagendijk, A. and A. Lorentzen (2007), 'Proximity, knowledge and innovation in peripheral regions: on the intersection between geographical and organizational proximity', *European Planning Studies*, **15** (4), 385–99.

Lung, Y. (1995), 'Modèles industriels et géographie de la production', in A. Rallet and A. Torre (eds), *Economie régionale & économie industrielle*, Paris: Economica, pp. 85–119.

Lung, Y., A. Rallet and A. Torre (1999), 'Connaissances et proximité géographique dans les processus d'innovation', *Géographie, Economie, Société*, **1** (2), 281–306.

Martin, R. and P. Sunley (2003), 'Deconstructing clusters: chaotic concept or policy panacea?', *Journal of Economic Geography*, **3** (1), 5–36.

Maskell, P., H. Bathelt and A. Malmberg (2006), 'Building global knowledge pipelines: the role of temporary clusters', *European Planning Studies*, **14** (8), 997–1013.

Ota, M. and M. Fujita (1993), 'Communication technologies and spatial organization of multi-unit firms in metropolitan areas', *Regional Science and Urban Economics*, **23**, 695–729.

Porter, M.E. (1990), *The Competitive Advantage of Nations,* London: Macmillan.

Quéré, M. (2008), 'Knowledge and innovation: promoting a system approach of innovation processes', *Economics of Innovation and New Technology*, **17** (1–2), 137–52.

Rallet, A. (1993), 'Choix de proximité et processus d'innovation technologique', *Revue d'Economie Industrielle*, **3**, 365–86.

Rallet, A. and A. Torre (2005), 'Proximity and localization', *Regional Studies*, **39** (1), 47–59.

Rallet, A. and A. Torre (eds) (2007), *Innovations et proximité*, Paris: L'Harmattan.

RERU (1993), Special Issue 'Économie de Proximités', *Revue d'Économie Régionale et Urbaine*, **3**.

Rychen, F. and J.B. Zimmermann (2008), 'Clusters in the global knowledge-based economy: knowledge gate-keepers and temporary proximity', *Regional Studies*, **42** (6), 767–76.

Tödtling, F., P. Lehner and M. Trippl (2006), 'Innovation in knowledge intensive industries: the nature and geography of knowledge links', *European Planning Studies*, **14** (8), 1035–58.

Torre, A. (2006), 'Collective action, governance structure and organizational trusts in localized systems of production: the case of the AOC organization of small producers', *Entrepreneurship and Regional Development*, **18**, 55–72.

Torre, A. (2008), 'On the role played by temporary geographical proximity in knowledge transmission', *Regional Studies*, **42** (6), 869–89.

Torre, A. and A. Rallet (2005), 'Proximity and localization', *Regional Studies*, **39**, 47–60.

Torre, A. and B. Zuindeau (2009), 'Proximity economics and environment: assessment and prospects', *Journal of Environmental Planning and Management*, **52** (1), 1–24.

Vale, M. and J. Caldeira (2007), 'Proximity and knowledge governance in localized production systems: the footwear industry in the north region of Portugal', *European Planning Studies*, **15** (4), 531–48.

Wickham, J. and A. Vecchi (2008), 'Local firms and global reach: business air travel and the Irish software cluster', *European Planning Studies*, **16** (5), 693–710.

21 The changing form and geography of social capital

Stuart Rosenfeld

Social capital has become, over the past two decades to 2010, a standard tool for economic development. Despite lack of consensus on precisely what social capital is and therefore how to measure it, city, state and regional governing agencies have come to understand and appreciate its contributions to competiveness, and they believe they need it to succeed in today's economy. The challenges for regional development are to design interventions that develop social capital and increase rates of learning, networking innovation and sustainable growth and to ensure inclusivity. Further, regional development must consider how the geometrically increasing use of instantaneous communications is affecting the geography and meaning of social capital.

Given an exhaustive literature on social capital and its impacts on learning and innovation in regional economies, this chapter will only summarize the highlights. Then it will speculate on how the widespread diffusion of technologies and talent, the digitalization of information and the instantaneity of communications are affecting the geography of the relationships and norms that characterize social capital. It will consider the effects of social capital on access to and the distribution of power and wealth in a region and, finally, suggest interventions to influence social capital in ways that accelerate innovation and sustainable growth and retain wealth in a region. Finally, it will conclude with some general findings and observations.

REVIEWING SOCIAL CAPITAL, *CIRCA* 1980–2000

Initially 'social capital' was a term used predominantly by sociologists to describe the levels of trust, cooperation and community that exist in a place. Jane Jacobs (1961) may have coined the term 'social capital' in 1962 when she ascribed the transfer of and response to information in close-knit communities as a city's irreplaceable social capital. It took a while, however, for planners and economists to recognize the value of trust and cooperation in a market economy assumed to be driven by competition.

The growing interest in policies to build cooperation and trust to complement and counterbalance the more natural competition originated in Europe, most notably in northern Italy. Regions around the world sought ways to imitate the associational behaviors observed in that region, and the networking that appeared to be embedded in its economic and social fabric (Piore and Sabel, 1984). Among the most important lessons emerging from the rediscovery of Europe's industrial districts and their subsequent reincarnation as industry clusters were the ways that socialization and networking increased learning, innovation and competitiveness.

After Harvard sociologist Robert Putnam and AnnaLee Saxenian made the connection between social capital and economic growth explicit, social capital – initially confined to academic discussions – became the term of choice in economic development. Putnam (1993) found that social capital accounted for differences in the strengths of the economies of northern and southern Italy, which corroborated and provided another theoretical foundation for the documented successes of networking and cooperation within northern Italy's industrial districts.

AnnaLee Saxenian (1994) found that the computer business grew rapidly in northern California because of the close relationships among workers. She found that, by contrast, the computer business declined in Massachusetts largely because of the relative absence of close relationships among firms and workers. In the former case, and for reasons discussed by James in Chapter 19 of this *Handbook*, people socialized and traded information, and as a result news about products moved quickly through the business society.

As these concepts moved from the realm of academia into the literature of practitioners, social capital became part of mainstream policy discussions and began to fuse the interests of sociologists and economists, theorists and practitioners. Since the early 1990s there have been thousands of papers, books and articles on the topic in academic journals and popular magazines, as well as seminars and conferences (Landabaso et al., 2004).

SOCIAL CAPITAL AND LEARNING

One of the leading economic benefits of clusters is opportunities for knowledge spillover and know-how trading. Any disadvantages associated with the leakage of proprietary knowledge are easily outweighed by the advantages of learning about new technologies and techniques through formal and informal means. Among the earliest and most widely cited connections between social capital and learning were those documented by Alfred Marshall (1936): 'When large masses of men in the same locality are employed in similar tasks,' he wrote, 'it is found that, by associating with one another, they educate one another.'

The strength of industrial districts today continues to be closely tied to the exchange of information. The high levels of trust that exist in districts 'allow people to exchange commercial information, pass on design ideas, knowledge of technical processes, etc' (Pyke and Sengeberger 1992, 19). Bellandi (1989, 136–52; see also Bellandi's Chapter 6 in this *Handbook*) called it 'underground learning':

> The processes of transmission of ideas; for example, through interfirm mobility of skilled workers; the exchange of ideas within social institutions, like families, clubs, and so on . . . whether they are organized or spontaneous relationships, personal contact within the agglomeration encourages constant intercommunications from ideas.

Maskell (2000) further developed the 'learning-based theory' of clusters, contending that learning helps explain the existence of clusters plus their internal organization and boundaries. Over time, the learning and knowledge spillover that occurs more readily within industrial concentrations has become a pre-eminent part of regional cluster strategies. The mechanisms include, for example: participation in local associations; networks of firms around, for example, marketing, supply chains or shared resources; interfirm mobility of personnel with tacit knowledge; informal social activities. They often involve 'gatekeepers', which can be local institutions, lead firms, network brokers or community leaders.

SOCIAL CAPITAL AND INNOVATION

Perhaps the most highly sought-after outcome of social capital is innovation, the driving force of regional economies. The idea that innovations result from lonely scientists working day and night in basements or garages is, if not a myth, an exception to the rule. The vast majority of innovations are collaborative and iterative, with many people modifying and improving on each other's ideas before eventually producing a marketable concept.

Porter (1990, 120) writes: 'good ideas are imitated and improved upon by local competitors, raising the overall rate of innovation. The stock of knowledge and skill in the national industry accumulates as firms imitate each other and as personnel move among firms. While an individual company cannot keep all the knowledge and skills to itself, the whole national industry benefits through faster innovation.' The 'clusters of innovation' projects he helped to organize in five large US metropolitan areas, which were based on the geographic concentrations of cluster-based research, led to a range of recommendations that included institutions for collaboration and 'an organization dedicated to mobilizing these groups', both forms of social capital (Porter et al., 2001).

Most of the early literature on regional innovation systems, however, focused on learning and knowledge spillover within the systems and paid scant attention to social capital as a community or regional asset. The systems were institution-driven, with the strongest rates of innovation in systems with access to knowledge, willingness to network, and with the capabilities and proper incentives for learning – and forgetting (Lundvall, 1992).

Agencies that fund research today favor, and sometimes require, collaborative proposals involving teams of researchers from universities, companies and research centers located in many places. In Europe, Eureka began supporting collaborative research and development (R&D) in 1985; and in 1990 the US Congress released a study 'Using R&D consortia for commercial innovation' (Webre, 1990) leading to increased support for such consortia. Even head-to-head competitors have realized the value of cooperation and have become partners, as they did by participating in the creation of Sematech in 1989, a US collaboration of multiple companies and universities to conduct research in microelectronics.

A book by Lewis Branscomb and James Keller (1998) written in the early period of the Internet concluded that geographic proximity was extremely important to innovation. Fountain (1998), a contributing author, concluded: 'Dense social networks can encourage experimentation and entrepreneurship among actors because of the mix of collaboration and competition within the network.' But resource-driven research via networks of institutions does not assure collaboration. Research networks can become bogged down in disputes over contracts, coordination, credit and lack of trust.

In recent years, cluster and regional innovation strategies have converged, perhaps best demonstrated in the Organisation for Economic Co-operation and Development's (OECD, 2001) *Innovative Clusters: Drivers of National Innovation Systems.* Many of the case studies describe how communications technologies opened up access to information, but find that face-to-face contact still is needed because 'we know more than we can tell'. Proponents of regional innovation systems have discovered that successful systems, like clusters, are economic ecosystems that tend to be 'embedded in a social/institutional infrastructure that fosters co-operation, trust and reciprocity, and facilitates the flow of strategic information, alliances, sharing of resources, skills, and exploits efficiently collective external economies' (Landabaso and Rosenfeld, 2009).

The other important issue for regional development to consider is the stickiness of innovation. Regions can use their stock of social capital to generate good ideas, but if the ideas translate into jobs elsewhere they add little to the regional economy. Only a very small proportion of patents are commercialized, and a much smaller number become 'gazelles', or high-growth companies. In the biotech industry, for example, in 2001 only 100 biotech-related drugs out of more than 150 000 patented had reached market in the previous 30 years – and most of those led to production elsewhere (Cortright and Mayer, 2001).

Most analyses of regional innovation use patents filed per capita as a proxy for innovation, a measure that overemphasizes top-down, research-driven innovation. This measure almost always favors places with strong research universities or corporate research divisions. Innovations that occur in less populated areas or within user-driven industries such as cultural sectors and fashion are often overlooked and ignored in innovation strategies, although the exchange of knowledge and networking may be more important to these industries than it is to research-driven innovation.

EFFECTS OF INSTANTANEOUS COMMUNICATIONS ON RELATIONSHIPS AND GEOGRAPHY

Regional economies, clusters and social capital have been dramatically transformed by the instantaneous information access and communications brought about by 'social networking' via the Internet, satellite-based phone service, laptops and a host of handheld devices. Most of the widely cited theories about and research on clusters and on social capital occurred between the 1960s and mid-1990s, before the advent of instantaneous access to almost any source of public information or to any person. There now are thousands of websites and blogs claiming to build, promote and support social capital, turning it into a minor industry.

Since 2000, analysts have been predicting the 'death of distance', writing that it will no longer matter where you live or where you work. The evidence appeared to be overwhelming. Communications technologies are quickly penetrating even the poorest nations and rural regions. In 2008, three-quarters of the population of North America, three-fifths of Oceania, and almost half of Europe, including children, were Internet users, and more than 3 billion mobile phones were in use. Today, 'social capital' is often measured in numbers of 'friends' on Facebook, MySpace, or, for those over 40, Plaxo and Linked-In. A vast majority of under 30-year-olds in developed countries now Tweet and Facebook daily. Bloggers by the thousands comment on nearly every event, product or idea. New generations are using these technologies to create ties to a much larger and more diverse population.

Broadband access also has been a boon for less populated places, making it possible for people to perform certain functions and create new businesses from a distance. Research often involves collaboration across disciplines, universities and laboratories located on multiple continents.

But most businesses still believe that despite its obvious value, communication technologies have certain limitations for the depth of relationships that creates trust, transmits tacit knowledge and drives innovation, three of the most highly valued outcomes of social capital. Maryann Feldman (2002) writes: 'the tacit nature of knowledge and the social nature of the innovation process limit the impact of the Internet'. She finds, confirming similar conclusions by Kevin Morgan, David Wolfe and others, that face-to-face communication reveals subtleties of tone, meaning and context that are crucial when working with uncertain knowledge. Once knowledge can be codified, then distance becomes less important.

Geography is also important to understanding the context for information acquired, knowledge of the firm and its environment from which the knowledge comes; knowing what one firm is good at and not good at, who is reliable and who is not (Brown and Duguid, 2000). This ambient knowledge that comes from informal knowledge makes it possible to assess the value of and applications for information.

Similarly, broadband and wireless have not yet replaced the informal – also 'wireless' – exchanges that take place at breaks, meals and drinks at conferences, coffee shops, pubs or social events. A *Financial Times* headline claimed: 'A teleconference is never as good as a dinner' – that technology works best as a supplement to face-to-face encounters (Case, 2007, 7). Even using video-based technologies that reveal body language and expressions, interactions are less effective than teams that have had face-to-face contact, and are more likely to result in conflict.

Proximity is particularly important to user-driven innovation and creativity. It is no accident that so much of New York's new media cluster is located in south Manhattan; Bangalore's software houses on Church Street; microbreweries in Portland, Oregon; and designers in Milan (see Chapter 43 on design-driven innovation in this *Handbook*). In each case, physical proximity to discriminating customers, competitors and other entrepreneurs provides advantages that cannot be replicated by teleconferences and e-mails. The owner of a web design company who moved from Connecticut to Silicon Valley now has 85 percent of his customers located within a one-hour drive. 'Before, in order to take a meeting, I had to schedule it two weeks in advance and buy a plane ticket. Now I can just meet people for coffee. It really facilitates business.' (Tam, 2006). The 350 new media companies in East and West Sussex, UK, share 'the benefits of a close corporate neighbourhood which is real and not just virtual' (Beavis, 1998).

Innovation based on creativity depends even more on person-to-person interactions than does scientific research, which can be separated into tasks. In Milan, the presence of manufacturers who know the value of design establish very personal relationships with designers, even treating them as a member of the family. Local buzz is crucial; but although buzz can be tweeted instantaneously, it is the personal informal meetings in which secrets are passed on among friends and acquaintances. 'It's a very personal relationship between designer and manufacturer. It is what ties everything together' (Michael Graves, in Verganti, 2006).

MEASURES OF SOCIAL CAPITAL

If social capital is an asset worth developing, then regions would benefit from knowing how much they have, how they compare to other places, and how it influences their economy. Measurement of value, or even presence of social capital, however, has proven elusive. Paul Krugman (1991, 54) wrote that:

> knowledge flows [in contrast to labour pooling] are invisible; they leave no paper trail by which they may be measured and tracked, and there is nothing to prevent the theorist from assuming anything about them that she likes . . . A sociologist might be able to help with survey methods; but I would like to get as far as possible with drab, down-to-earth economic analysis before turning to the other social sciences.

Economists, however, have not made much progress: 'Sharing activity is not captured as a transaction in the firm's financial records and therefore it is not reported as economic activity in the standard economic statistics' (Carter, 1989). The vast majority of analyses of social capital have relied on social science, anecdotes, case studies, interviews and surveys; or, in efforts to quantify the asset, proxies, as in Saxenian (1994) on Silicon Valley and more recently Elizabeth Currid's (2007) on the creative sector in New York City. Some research studies use such proxies as membership or participation rates in various organizations or events, including fraternal organizations, clubs, professional or industry associations, or even organized sports such as bowling or football.

The Australian Bureau of Statistics developed a comprehensive and complex set of indicators for measuring social capital that included hundreds of measures organized into four general categories: network qualities (level of participation and religious affiliation); network structure (source of support in crisis and geographic mobility); network transactions (for example attendance at community events and taking action with others to solve social problems); and network types (for example group homogeneity and links to institutions) (Edwards, 2004). Survey validity depends on the rates and randomness of business responses – which are often less than 25 percent. Cooke and Clifton (2002) conducted a survey of small and medium-sized organizations (SMEs) in the United Kingdom to determine the impact of social capital on performance and, based on a 14 percent response rate, learned that the use of social capital is ubiquitous but that most of it is related to traded transactions.

Other studies have bypassed the aggregate measurement issues to learn whether stronger relationships, such as participating in networks or business associations, or attending trade or professional events, leads to various types of economic outcomes. One assessment of five cluster-based projects in the Northwestern region of the United States that used pre-and post-intervention surveys found that informal learning was the most highly valued outcome, exceeding harder market outcomes (Rosenfeld, 1996).

SOCIAL EXCLUSIVITY, INCLUSIVITY, AND ISOLATION

Which people and businesses gain and which people lose in regional economies depends to a large extent on connections, relationships and trust. These factors affect the exchange of knowledge, employment opportunities and possibilities for collaboration.

Inevitably, discussions of social capital lead to the limitations and potential costs of social capital. 'The downside of social capital is that the same strong ties, which are needed for people to act together, can also exclude non members such as the poor' (Portes and Landolt, 1996). If defined by social norms, social capital can also not only promote positive behaviors but also reinforce bad behavior (Durlauf, 1999). Does social capital, for example, perpetuate racial inequality?

There is nothing inherently fair about social capital. The ties that help members of a group can also enable it to exclude members. One study of social capital in poor communities worries that: 'double sided, dialectical, multidimensional, historical, and intra- and extra-institutional, social capital unfolds in multi-group settings in which one group, intentionally or not, may secure advantages that disable others' (Lopez and Stack, 2002). The authors find that social capital can be marginal if dominant stakeholders or cultural mismatch obstruct cooperation, or empowering if it leads to engagement and integration and builds common norms.

Ensuring that social capital empowers is particularly relevant to developing countries. One study from Chile concluded that:

> the distribution of social capital tends to accentuate social inequalities. People with higher income and education accumulate more of that capital. On the contrary, lower levels of education and incomes are associated with less social trust and a weaker sentiment of reciprocity . . . the accumulation of social capital may deepen existing inequalities. (Lechner, 2000)

Strong social capital and trust limited to a community is also insufficient if it lacks connections to distant markets, sources of knowledge and different ideas. Research in Merseyside, UK warns against taking too limited a view of social capital and working within neighborhoods without making connections to the larger power structure or to new or different ideas (Hibbitt et al., 2001). Bourdieu (1985) noted that even very dense social networks might not generate economic returns if they lack access to other forms of capital resources.

In a study of poor rural communities in the United States, Cynthia Duncan (2000) concluded that a 'lack of trust and cooperation in the community's social climate infects formal and informal relationships at all social levels . . . Nothing is based on merit, everything depends on whom you know and whom you owe.' 'Clearer understanding of social capital', she wrote, 'will facilitate efforts to ameliorate persistent poverty and underdevelopment'.

Geography matters in labor markets and for learning about employment opportunities. Hearing about a new job before it is advertised and having a known name for making the first contact is a decided advantage. Social capital also influences an individual's employment and advancement opportunities. Employment, promotions and deal-making all are very dependent on interpersonal relationships and word-of-mouth communications. Most employers, especially in small companies, rely on referrals and recommendations from people they trust rather than taking the time to sift through the massive information available in job banks or employment services (Reich, 2000). Employees in northeast Mississippi's furniture clusters are constantly changing jobs based on opportunities they hear about from friends and acquaintances. In emerging sectors organized around freelancers and microenterprises, personal connections are crucial.

INTERVENING FOR INNOVATION AND SUSTAINABLE REGIONAL DEVELOPMENT

If social capital, however defined and measured, is considered to be important, if not critical, to innovation and regional growth, then what policies will increase it? For the most part, government agencies worldwide have supported the concept of social capital. Indeed, most of the early strategies to develop networks and clusters targeted ways to build social capital, generally by supporting networks, industry associations, and cluster organizations. Initially, efforts to create or strengthen the associational infrastructure were assumed to lead to higher levels of social capital. Later, governing agencies paid more attention to inclusiveness and looked for ways to democratize social capital. More recently, funders began looking for ways to introduce sustainability and social responsibility.

The first set of interventions took shape in the 1990s, based on the economic successes of northern Italy. In places without industrial districts and their well-developed social structure, imitators found that replicating the networked economy demanded more time and resources than most SMEs were able to invest. Therefore the earliest incentives reimbursed the costs of a neutral network facilitator or manager and provided grants to develop collaborative activities. In many places these networks grew larger, took on more collective activities, possibly required dues, and began to resemble regional business associations. At about the same time, regional innovation strategies led to a parallel set of actions to support collaborative research and development and interinstitutional learning by restricting certain research funds to joint proposals.

As strategies moved from networks to clusters, states and regions shifted their emphasis to cluster associations to build social capital. Public sector support shifted from individual business networks to cluster associations that were expected to build trust among their members and facilitate learning, benchmarking and networking. In some places, the associational infrastructure took on a new, more exclusive form, a 'cluster competitiveness council' composed of key stakeholders who could influence policy and attract resources, rather than an inclusive community of interest intended to build social capital and trust.

Public sector support, however, was generally short term, with the expectation that the associations would become financially self-sufficient based on an annual dues structure, payment for services and/or contracts or grants from other sources. The 'Green Book', an international analysis of cluster activities, finds that 89 percent of all cluster initiatives have a facilitator to manage the activity, most of whom are at least part time and have an office. The majority of the initiatives surveyed were financed by government and less than one-third by industry (Ketels et al., 2004). A major limitation of this strategy was that social capital, and often the very definition of clusters, was embedded in memberships rather than community or region.

A third set of interventions have focused on achieving greater inclusiveness. These interventions come from government agencies and private foundations with social goals. They typically bring non-government organizations and non-profits into the system to integrate marginalized and immigrant populations or to introduce sustainability goals. Although there is a growing sense of social responsibility within the private sector, these interventions are most successful if they add value to the firm, such as by filling labor market shortages, reaching new markets because of branding and goodwill, or reducing costs.

A fourth intervention is investing in local amenities that encourage socialization and networking. As quality of place became more important to talented people and mobile high-technology and creative companies, places began investing in creating the cultural and social 'scenes' to attract them. Despite communication technologies, innovation and creativity have become more clustered, not less, and the social environment has become a critical factor in where they cluster.

A final intervention is targeting resources to build social capital in less-favored and less-populated regions. The European Union has made large investments in regional innovation and cluster strategies for less-favored regions that have included various forms of social capital development. In the US, private foundations have been the most important resources for building social capital. The biggest challenge has been achieving sustainable results that outlast the funding.

CONCLUSIONS

Learning is the most fundamental outcome of social capital. The real strength of clusters lies in the tacit knowledge that resides within the employees of companies in the cluster, and its dispersion across companies and institutions. Tacit knowledge is unwritten, unspoken and a hidden storehouse of knowledge based on a person's emotions, experiences, insights, intuition, observation and internalized information. By its very definition it requires a level of social capital and resists transfer electronically. It requires personal interactions to get at the knowledge that emerges only when the person is asked the right question or to solve a particular problem.

Location still matters. Trust is built on a history of reciprocation or upon shared values and interests. 'Civic capital', as David Wolfe (Wolfe and Nelles, 2008) puts it, 'consists of interpersonal networks and solidarity within a community based on shared identity, expectations, or goals, and *tied to a specific region or locality.*' Virtual communities can add value through access to a broader set of ideas but they cannot communicate experiences.

Creativity thrives with face-to-face interaction. Richard Florida (2002) has argued that social capital can stifle innovation if it leads to conformity and insulation from outside information and connections. His conclusion was based largely on the results of Putnam's civic capital index which seemed to show that high measures of social capital were inversely related to high levels of innovation. Others, however, have shown that places that lack measurable forms of social capital may still have high levels that resist measures. Moreover, the measures used for innovation are biased against smaller communities and more rural regions where innovation occurs 'off the books' rather than being filed for patent.

Inclusiveness spurs innovation. One of the strengths of weak ties over strong ties in generating new ideas and connections is that it adds diversity to the relationships. Similarly, networks and associations that include members from different backgrounds and with dissimilar experiences can inspire members to question the basic framework of the problems being addressed and lead to new solutions and opportunities.

Social capital must encompass both global pipelines and local buzz. 'Local buzz' depends on social capital and firms that understand it and are ready to use it (Bathelt et al., 2002). But the value of local buzz depends on getting continuing new infusions of knowledge from outside the region, through the global pipelines to external suppliers, customers, partners, new employees and professional colleagues, and by participating in international events. This prevents the cluster and region from becoming too insular.

Tweeting is an important complement to, but does not yet replace talking. Having large numbers of 'friends' can move information very quickly but does not provide the deeper kinds of tacit knowledge that drive innovation, learning and growth. Tweeting is more about getting people's attention than about seeking information; looking for attention rather than querying. Open social structures operate differently than spatially bound social networks.

We do not yet know the effects of technology on the social capital of the next generation. Changes are occurring too rapidly in the use of communications technologies to know what they hold in store for the future, when today's youth enter the labor market. Research assesses the last generation of communications technologies, not this year's. Young people depend far more and in different ways on their handheld devices and computers than the adult population, and very differently to the mature adult population. Websites and blogs are already using a different definition of social capital (Twitter, 2009). With hundreds of millions of people Facebooking, tweeting and blogging daily, digital social networks may become an efficient source of some forms of buzz.

Social capital is prevalent in and is as important to less populated areas as it is to large metropolitan areas. The popular view of a spiky economy with the world's largest cities being the spikes is based more on scale and availability of data from large cities than true differences. There is more social capital – as there is more of almost everything – in regions with large, dense populations. But trust and networks can have as great a relative impact on the economies of less populated regions, which desperately need the economies of scale associated with networks and the access to global knowledge that spreads informally.

REFERENCES

Bathelt, H., A. Malmberg and P. Maskell (2002), 'Clusters and knowledge: local buzz, global pipelines and the process of knowledge creation', Aalborg: DRUID Working Paper No 02-12.
Beavis, S. (1998), 'Cluster companies benefit from being neighbours in reality', *Financial Times*, 18 November.
Bellandi, M. (1989), 'The industrial district in Marshall', in E. Goodman and J. Bamford (eds), *Small Firms and Industrial Districts in Italy*, London: Routledge, pp. 31–68.
Bourdieu, P. (1985), 'The forms of capital', in John Richardson (ed.), *Handbook of Theory and Research for the Sociology of Education*, New York: Greenwood Books, pp. 241–58.
Branscomb, Lewis B. and James H. Keller (eds) (1998), *Investing in Innovation: Creating a Research and Innovation Policy that Works*, Cambridge, MA: MIT Press.
Brown, J.S. and P. Duguid (2000), 'Mysteries of the region: knowledge dynamics in Silicon Valley', http://www.sloffi.com/mysteries.htm.
Carter, A. (1989), 'Knowhow trading as economic exchange', *Research Policy*, **18**, 155–63.
Case, A. (2007), 'A teleconference is never as good as a dinner', *Financial Times*, 12 February.
Cooke, P. and N. Clifton (2002), 'Social capital and small and medium enterprise performance in the United Kingdom', in P. Nijkamp, R. Stough and H. de Root (eds), *Entrepreneurship in the Modern Space Economy*, Dordrecht: Kluwer, pp.107–35.
Cortright, J. and H. Mayer (2001), *Signs of Life: The Growth of Biotechnology Centers in the US*, Washington, DC: Brookings Institution.

Currid, E. (2007), *The Warhol Economy: How Fashion, Art and Music Drive New York City*, Princeton, NJ: Princeton University Press.

Duncan, C. (2000), *Worlds Apart: Why Poverty Persists in Rural America*, New Haven, CT: Yale University Press.

Durlauf, S.N. (1999), 'The case "against" social capital', *Focus*, University of Wisconsin-Madison Institute for Research on Poverty, **20** (3), 1–5.

Edwards, R.W. (2004), *Measuring Social Capital: An Australian Framework and Indicators*, Canberra: Australian Bureau of Statistics.

Facebook Statistics, retrieved at http://www.facebook.com/press/info.php?statistics.

Feldman, M.P. (2002), *The Internet Revolution and the Geography of Innovation*, Oxford: Blackwell Publishers.

Florida, R. (2002), 'When social capital stifles innovation', *Harvard Business Review*. Vol. 80 (No. 8 August).

Fountain, J.E. (1998), 'Social capital: a key enabler of innovation', in L. Branscomb and J. Keller (eds), *Investing in Innovation: Creating a Research and Innovation Policy that Works*, Cambridge, MA: MIT Press, pp. 85–111.

Hibbitt, K., P. Jones and R. Meegan (2001), 'Tackling social exclusion: the role of social capital in urban regeneration on Merseyside – from mistrust to trust?', *European Planning Studies*, **9** (2), 141–61.

Jacobs, J. (1961), *The Death and Life of Great American Cities*, New York: Random House.

Ketels, C., O. Solvell and G. Lindqvist (2004), *Cluster Initiative Green Book*, Stockholm: Ivory Tower Press.

Krugman, P. (1991), *Geography and Trade*, Cambridge, MA: MIT Press.

Landabaso, M., A. Kuklinski and C. Romain (2004), *Europe: Reflections on Social Capital, Innovation and Regional Development*, Poland: Wyzsza Szkola Biznesu National-Louis University.

Landabaso, M. and S. Rosenfeld (2009), 'Public policies for industrial districts and clusters', in Giacomo Becattini and Marco Belandi (eds), *The Handbook of Industrial Districts*, Cheltenham, UK and Northampton, MA, USA: Edward Elgar, pp. 739–53.

Lechner, N. (2000), 'La trama social como paisaje cultural', Translated in A. Arcocena and B. Stutz (eds), 'Innovation systems and developing countries', Aalborg: DRUID Working Paper No 02-05.

Lopez, M.L. and C.B. Stack (2002), 'Social capital and the culture of power: lessons from the field', in M. Warren, J.P. Thompson and S. Saegert (eds), *Building Social Capital to Combat Poverty*, New York: Russell Sage Foundation, pp. 31–59.

Lundvall, B. (ed.) (1992), *National Systems of Innovation*, London: Pinter Publishers.

Marshall, A. (1936), *Principles of Economics: An Introductory Volume*, 8th edn, London: Macmillan.

Maskell, P. (2000), 'Towards a learning-based theory of the cluster', paper presented at the World Conference on Economic Geography, Singapore, December.

Organisation for Economic Co-operation and Development (2001), *Innovative Clusters: Drivers of National Innovation Systems*, Paris: OECD.

Piore, M. and C.F. Sabel (1984), *The Second Industrial Divide*, New York: Basic Books.

Porter, M. (1990), *The Competitive Advantage of Nations*, New York: Basic Books.

Porter, M.E., Council on Competitiveness and Monitor Group (2001), *Cluster of Innovation Initiative: Regional Foundations of US Competitiveness*, Washington, DC: Council on Competitiveness.

Portes, R. and P. Landolt (1996), 'The downside of social capital', *American Prospect*, **26**, 18–22.

Putnam, R.D. (1993), *Making Democracy Work: Civic Traditions in Modern Italy*, Princeton, NJ: Princeton University Press.

Pyke, F. and W. Sengenberger (1992), *Industrial Districts and Local Economic Regeneration*, Geneva: International Institute for Labour Studies.

Reich, R. (2000), *The Future of Success: Working and Living in the New Economy*, New York: Vintage Books.

Rosenfeld, S. (1996), 'Does cooperation enhance competitiveness? Assessing the impacts of inter-firm collaboration', *Research Policy*, **24**, 247–63.

Saxenian, A. (1994), *Regional Advantage: Culture and Competition in Silicon Valley and Route 128*, Cambridge, MA: Harvard University Press.

Tam, P. (2006), *Wall Street Journal*, 5 October, p. B1.

Twitter (2009), 'Social capital on twitter: analytics of flow', Social Media Consulting and Strategy by a Social Interaction Design Specialist Social Capital; at http://www.gravity7.com/blog/media/2009/04/social-capital-on-twitter-analytics-of.html, 8 April.

Verganti, R. (2006), 'Innovating through design', *Harvard Business Review*, December, Reprint R0612G, 1–9.

Webre, Philip (1990), 'Using R&D consortia for commercial innovation: SEMATECH, X-ray lithography, and high-resolution systems', Washington, DC: Congress of the United States, Congressional Budget Office.

Wolfe, D.A. and J. Nelles (2008), 'The role of civic capital and civic associations in cluster policy', in C. Karlsson (ed.), *Handbook of Research on Innovation and Clusters*, Cheltenham, UK and Northampton, MA, USA: Edward Elgar, pp. 374–92.

22 Cluster evolution

Arne Isaksen

INTRODUCTION

Much of the literature of clusters focus on the question, 'Why do industries cluster?' A general answer is that industries cluster to gain competitive advantage from external economies and increasing returns for firms (Asheim et al., 2006). Firms can more easily benefit from knowledge spillovers, skilled labour, specialized inputs, adapted local infrastructure and so on if located in close proximity to similar firms, service industries, universities and research and development (R&D) institutes.

This chapter poses a somewhat different question: 'How do clusters emerge, grow, decline and eventually renew themselves?' This question has been relatively neglected in cluster studies until recently, compared with the question of how cluster firms gain competitive strength (Bergman, 2008; Lorenzen, 2005). This second question requires an evolutionary approach which typically distinguishes between different life-cycle stages of clusters. Clusters are seen to follow a general model that resembles industry, technology or product cycles, and the model is abstracted from empirical observations (Bergman, 2008). We should however stress that individual clusters do not follow a predetermined life cycle as all clusters have some unique characteristics that influence their development. In the words of Belussi and Sedita (2009), cluster processes follow differentiated path-dependencies (on 'path-interdependence', see Martin's Chapter 15 in this *Handbook*). To organize the discussion, this chapter nevertheless employs a stylized cluster life cycle consisting of four phases: (1) emergence; (2) growth; (3) maturity; (4) decline and possibly renewal (see for example Feldman and Francis, 2006). The fourth phase points to the fact that some clusters are locked into decline while others manage to restructure and enter into a new growth phase.

The chapter will complement the evolutionary approach with an institutional approach. Italian industrial districts, which include local concentrations of traditional manufacturing industries, have mainly grown spontaneously through local spin-offs and entrepreneurial activity (Amin, 2000). The institutional approach is more appropriate in analysing clusters that are deliberately initiated, or at least supported by policy measures, such as careful planning by local government, universities and firms. The chapter makes use of the regional innovation system (RIS) concept to study the institution-building development of clusters. An RIS consists, in principal, of two subsystems (Cooke et al., 2000). The first consists mainly of firms in the main industrial clusters of a region and includes their support industries, customers and suppliers. The second subsystem is the knowledge infrastructure that supports regional innovation in several industries and clusters (that is, research and higher education institutions, technology transfer agencies, vocational training organizations, business associations, and so on). In a working RIS, continuous innovation and entrepreneurial activity are stimulated by interfirm collaboration, knowledge flow between firms and knowledge organizations, and by socio-cultural structures and institutional environments. The development from a spontaneously emerging cluster to a more planned RIS is one way to strengthen the innovation capability and competitiveness of cluster firms (European Commission, 2002). Thus, the development of a supportive infrastructure of knowledge organizations, policy instruments and socio-cultural structures is one set of explanations for why some emergent clusters grow over a long time.

The chapter will in addition make use of the knowledge base approach, which in the case of cluster evolution to some extent coincides with the distinction between the evolutionary and the institutional approach. The evolutionary approach is highly relevant in analyses of clusters that build on experience-based knowledge, while the institutional approach may be particularly relevant in explaining the growth of R&D-based clusters. Companies and industries usually employ several types of knowledge; however knowledge bases refer to the crucial knowledge that is required by specific firms and industries in order to perform innovation activities.

Two main types of knowledge bases are distinguished here: analytical and synthetic (for example Asheim et al., 2007). These are ideal types rarely found in pure forms in firms and industries, but firms may rely heavily on one specific knowledge base in some phases of an innovation process (Moodysson, 2008). In short, analytical knowledge includes scientific knowledge which is mainly codified. Knowledge creation is to a large degree based on the development and testing of formal, scientific models. Synthetic knowledge includes experience-based knowledge, which has much larger tacit elements and which is quite context-specific. Learning often starts out from practical challenges inside firms or at customers, which are solved through the combination of well-known knowledge and through trial and error. The relevance of knowledge bases in this context refers to the fact that clusters based on analytical (R&D-based) knowledge, such as biotechnology clusters, will often have very different life cycles compared to clusters building on more experience-based knowledge bases.

CLUSTER EMERGENCE

The emergence of clusters is often explained by anecdotal evidence, such as the activity by some pioneer entrepreneurs (Feldman and Francis, 2006). In more analytical terms, we can distinguish between particular prerequisites or assets present in a locality prior to the emergence of the cluster, like some location factors; and the triggering events that turn the location factors into new productive use, and thus initiate the cluster development. Prerequisites include factors like the availability of raw materials, specific knowledge in R&D organizations or experience-based know-how, or the specific or sophisticated needs of a certain group of geographically concentrated customers or firms (European Commission, 2002, 14).

Triggering factors are often the activity of entrepreneurs. Hence, Feldman and Francis (2006) point to the fact that entrepreneurs and new-firm formations often spark the emergence and growth of clusters. Active entrepreneurship may be in response to some exogenous shock, such as a technological or market opportunity. Entrepreneurs are often 'home-grown' and have some location inertia; individuals start companies based on previous knowledge, experience and contacts in a specific locality. Thus, clusters often emerge where entrepreneurs with relevant skills are located. Some areas may then obtain a 'first-mover' advantage in particular industries (Storper, 1997). 'First-mover' advantages cause an early development and accumulation of specific knowledge and skills which further strengthen the advantage of the 'pioneer areas', among other things by spin-off activities and knowledge spillovers.

The growth of industrial districts in the Third Italy (north-east and central parts of Italy) from the 1960s illustrates important factors that may bring about clusters relying mostly on experience-based knowledge. The Third Italy demonstrated job growth in the manufacturing industry in the 1960s and 1970s contrary to other parts of Italy (Becattini, 1990). The growth took place in traditional and design-intensive sectors such as textiles and clothing, footwear, furniture, ceramic goods and mechanical engineering. The growth also occurred in small and medium-sized enterprises (SMEs) that were concentrated in specific areas where the firms formed local networks.

The growth of the industrial districts is explained by a combination of general and specific (triggering) factors. The general factors refer to increased market possibilities outside Italy due to better transportation infrastructure and the enlarged market in the European Union; plus increased demand for more niche products, such as quality products in small batches where SMEs have an advantage compared to larger firms; and technological innovations, that is, computerized production equipment that makes small-batch production more efficient (Amin, 2000). The growth of the industrial districts, however, is also based on a number of social and cultural factors that are territorially specific (Asheim, 2000). These are related to the existence of specific competence, such as tradition and knowledge in entrepreneurship and management of small firms coming from a specific form of farming, that is, share cropping (Brusco, 1986); old knowledge and networks in trade and export (Becattini, 1990); and traditions in craft work and the early existence of technical schools. The industrial districts are also seen as egalitarian societies characterized by local identity and solidarity, which stimulates local collaboration and knowledge spillovers (Amin, 2000). Lastly, the early growth of the industrial districts was promoted by the tradition of family firms, which are flexible towards market changes, and by a reserve of unemployed and underemployed in small-scale farming who could work for low salaries.

The growth of R&D-based clusters can often be explained by the same set of arguments, that is, existing knowledge in a region that becomes a crucial basis for new-firm formations. Thus, Feldman (2007) explains the emergence of the Capitol biotechnology cluster in Maryland, USA by 'three exogenous sets of factors that sparked the nascent entrepreneurial talent in the region' (p. 241). The factors relate to the existence of some large government laboratories and a large amount of R&D funding in the region, new public actions that were designed to stimulate the commercializing of research findings, and new opportunities for the private sector to commercialize new technologies in cooperation with public organizations. These factors initiated local, entrepreneurial activity in biotechnology as the region had a large number of scientists, engineers and students with relevant knowledge. This further led to the building of institutions, such as incubator facilities, networks and infrastructure; state funding and tax initiatives, Venture capital was attracted from outside and created by successful local entrepreneurs as a consequence of the cluster emergence. The result was a virtuous, self-sustaining cycle of biotechnology industrial growth in the Capitol region. Public policy seems more important for the emergence of this R&D-based cluster than in the industrial district cases. Dedicated public policy may, in particular, be a proximal cause for the emergence of clusters in coordinated market economies (as in the Nordic countries) rather than in liberal market economies (as the USA and Britain) (Feldman and Francis, 2006).

CLUSTER GROWTH

The second stylized life-cycle phase is the growth of clusters. The growth is usually explained by the formation of progressively more local externalities or localization economies that form a self-sustaining process. The first local externalities often include: (1) the establishment of several specialized suppliers and service firms, frequently originating from spin-off processes and vertical disintegration of firms; (2) the creation of a specialized local labour market; and (3) the emergence of knowledge spillovers (Storper and Walker, 1989, 80–82). Growing clusters are thus characterized by the fact that firms benefit from information, know-how and knowledge from more and more other cluster participants, and take part in intended and unanticipated learning processes. Increasing local externalities may lower the barriers of local entrepreneurship and attract external firms due to advantageous location factors. Successful entrepreneurs may start new companies and become serial entrepreneurs. Some growing clusters also establish a reputation as the place to be for a particular technology (Feldman and Francis, 2006, 118).

Alongside the growth of a cluster, specific cluster organizations establish, or existing organizations adapt to the need of cluster firms. Cluster organizations may advance local collaboration, learning processes and technological knowledge spillovers, as well as the creation of localized forms of knowledge. The formation of organizations may constitute the first development towards regional innovation systems (RISs). These may be of two main types: related to a narrow and a broad definition of RIS (cf. Lundvall, 2007).

The narrow definition includes mainly R&D activities in universities, research institutes and firms' R&D departments. This definition can in particular be linked to analytical-knowledge clusters, in which firms often need to be in contact with advanced research institutions. Although the contact usually involves partners in different parts of the world, firms also benefit from close geographical distance to R&D institutes, both to gain early access to new research results and to recruit highly educated labour. Such advantages partly explain why firms in new, knowledge-intensive industries, such as biotechnology, often cluster close to some universities and research institutes (Cooke, 2002, 130–31). The interest in the role of research universities for cluster growth was accentuated by the seminal work on Silicon Valley by Saxenian (1996). Saxenian demonstrates that Stanford University and its Industrial Park played a distinctive role in the emergence and growth of the electronics and computer industry in Silicon Valley, among other things as a seedbed for entrepreneurs, new technology and venture capital. The University of California at Berkeley also became an important centre for education and research in the fields of semiconductor and computer science during the 1960s and 1970s. Location in, for example, a prestigious research park also signals quality and credibility to potential clients.

The broad definition of an RIS includes all actors and activities that affect learning, knowledge creation, and innovation in a region, and relates more to synthetic-knowledge clusters than the narrow definition. The RIS includes then a wide set of actors, for example actors occupied with vocational and higher education, training and technological diffusion, and not only those primarily engaged with R&D. An example of organizations in RISs broadly defined is centres of real services that were set up in some industrial districts in the Third Italy during the 1980s. The network of firms in traditional industrial districts, as presented above, first of all carried out incremental changes in products and processes by use of the experience-based competence of entrepreneurs and skilled workers (Brusco, 1990). However, districts had to upgrade during the 1980s in order for firms to carry out more radical innovations, which were necessary to meet increased competition from low-cost countries and to introduce more advanced technology. The upgrading took place through the establishment of centres for real service. The centres have specialized competence for the dominating industrial sectors in the districts, such as information about markets and technological development, and may assist in exporting or in introducing new production equipment. The centres supply the system of firms with professional competence that small firms often cannot possess themselves, and thus raise the innovative capability of the local networks of small firms (Brusco, 1990).

MATURITY

The different cluster life-cycle stages overlap. However, some characteristics of clusters are developed over time. We will here focus on three general characteristics of mature clusters. These are further discussed in the next section on cluster decline and renewal as the characteristics contribute in explaining why some clusters manage to develop into new growth areas and others do not. The first characteristic of mature clusters includes the development over time of supporting informal institutions or social capital. Social capital theory emphasizes the role of institutions (that is, norms, values and informal sanctions) for the maintenance of social relations. Many studies demonstrate that social relationships facilitate access to important resources and information, and produce benefits of trust between actors, which can enhance productivity and innovation. In economic terms social capital can reduce transaction costs because of the prevalent norms and sanctions that guide economic exchange (Halpern, 2005). The argument is that trust, reputation and informal sanctions can supplement formal contacts, the legal systems and formal sanctions. Social institutions foster dense, informal relations between personnel in firms and organizations, which are coordinated by routines or conventions that work best in the context of proximity (Storper, 1997). Social capital can then raise the innovation capability of individual firms and industries in a region by facilitating the flow of knowledge between different actors.

These arguments coincide with the strict definition of true clusters by Malmberg and Power (2006). The definition includes the usual criterion that clusters consist of spatial agglomerations of similar, related and interlinked economic activity. However, the authors also maintain that: 'there should be some form of self-awareness among the cluster participants and some joint policy action' (Malmberg and Power, 2006, 57). This points to the fact that actors in a mature cluster are aware of being involved in a common enterprise, and this awareness help to initiate and coordinate economic activity among cluster participants.

This first characteristic of mature clusters makes these more locally embedded through the development of informal institutions that by their nature are mostly locally confined. The second characteristic, however, points in the other direction, that is towards more extraregional relations or global pipelines (Bathelt et al., 2004). Thus, firms in mature cluster are increasingly incorporated in national and global supply chains and knowledge networks. Cluster firms more and more find their suppliers of components, modules, services and scientific knowledge outside the cluster boundary, as they carry out more worldwide sourcing. Cluster firms are also increasingly seen to be part of global networks governed by large corporations.

The Italian industrial districts, for example, have been much influenced by globalization forces from the early 1990s (Belussi and Sedita, 2009). Less strategic activities have been outsourced to areas with lower labour costs, mostly in Eastern Europe. Some districts engage in forms of 'non-local' learning, in which firms, and some gatekeeper firms in particular, explore, select, transcode and recombine knowledge coming from outside the cluster. The challenge of the districts is to become nodes of global networks, in both absorbing knowledge from outside and keeping their historical and social identity. Another type of economic globalization is detected in particular in R&D-based industries under the term 'born global' (Bell et al., 2001; see also Chapter 30 of this *Handbook* on micro-multinational FDI). Many smaller technology-based firms embark on rapid internationalization of products and services in order to utilize a sophisticated, internal knowledge base and target highly specialized, global market niches, which means that also quite young clusters may have extensive international linkages.

A third characteristic of mature clusters is that they are often organizationally rich: they have a high density and mix of private and public supporting organizations (Tödtling and Trippl, 2004; see also Chapter 33 in this *Handbook*). Such clusters then often constitute well-developed RISs. However, a problem arises if many of the organizations and networks are too much geared towards the demand in the old industries; a situation further analysed in the next section.

CLUSTER DECLINE AND RENEWAL

The decline of regional clusters is often analysed by use of the concept of negative lock-in (for example Hassink, 2005). Negative lock-in is the other side of the coin of cumulative learning and path-dependency that typify previous stages of dynamic clusters, which then are characterized by positive lock-in. Negative lock-in, thus, characterizes situations in which regional industrial development become 'locked in' by the very socio-economic and institutional conditions that once led to the growth of a cluster. The initial strength of the regional cluster in the past, such as unique know-how and skill, a specialized infrastructure of firms, knowledge organizations and education institutions, close interfirm networks and strong political support, may turn into inflexible obstacles to innovation (Grabher, 1993).

Clusters may in general have three main blocking events that cause the decline of jobs and competitive strength, which are structural, endogenous and exogenous events. The first refers to the fact that the core firms in a cluster may be part of a generally stagnant or declining industrial sector (Isaksen, 2003). Firms have a tendency to stay in a sector and a technological trajectory as long as possible, and thus the development of clusters often follows the life cycle of its dominant products. The tendency of firms to stick to 'normal business' reflects the fact that firms, and network of firms, often enter into an evolutionary path in which each step takes the development in a direction from which it is difficult to return, and which then limits future options (Storper and Walker, 1989).

A second blocking event refers to endogenous factors in clusters, such as internal rigidities, a lack of local collaboration and/or local rivalry, too inward-looking firms and organizations, and failures to build capabilities in important new technologies (Porter, 2008, 259–61). Clusters can then lose out in competition to other, more efficient clusters. The last blocking event refers to exogenous factors which can make the specific resources and knowledge of a cluster irrelevant. Exogenous factors can, for example, be technological discontinuities in an industrial sector or a large shift in buyers' needs (Porter, 2008).

The lock-in concept has, in particular, been used to explain the decline of classical, old industrial areas (Hassink, 2005). Political lock-ins are above all seen to hinder restructuring processes in these areas when powerful actors in the RIS (such as large firms, labour unions, education institutions and politicians) are occupied with preserving existing industrial structures. Old industrial clusters most often, but not exclusively, build on experience-based knowledge. Analytical-knowledge clusters are in general younger, and many are still in the growth stage. Such clusters are also generally more open to new, extraregional knowledge due to the codification possibilities of analytical knowledge, and the fact that R&D personnel are often members of epistemic communities, in which other participants may be dispersed throughout a wide geographic area (Moodysson, 2008). Epistemic communities consist of persons with similar knowledge bases, who exchange mainly analytical knowledge, and which then lead to the inflow of new scientific knowledge in R&D-based clusters, in particular. Synthetic-knowledge clusters more often contain local communities of practice, which include groups of people performing similar tasks, and which is more exposed to cognitive lock-in.

The offshore engineering sector in Oslo, the capital region of Norway, illustrates the negative lock-in of a rather knowledge-intensive sector. The offshore engineering sector in this region lost much of its competitive strength vis-à-vis other parts of Norway by the end of the 1990s (Isaksen, 2003). The region dominated the sector in Norway until the mid-1990s with about 60 per cent of all jobs. Then an absolute and relative decline started, and the Oslo region had 30 per cent of all offshore engineering jobs in Norway in 2001. This sharp decline reflects a lock-in of dominating firms in this area of building large, fixed and floating platforms, while a new 'techno-economic path' consisting of smaller and simpler installations and subsea solutions was favoured. The blocking events are related to relatively low R&D activity in the Oslo firms due to losses on contracts at the end of the 1990s, and long geographical distances between the engineering work in Oslo and the platform construction along the west coast of Norway, which may hamper knowledge flow and mutual learning. The decline in the Oslo region may also point to a near-monopoly situation with regard to platform construction by two former dominating companies in Oslo, which hampered competition and the innovation pressure for these two companies.

Why do some clusters manage to renew their activities and endure so much longer than others? Thus, under certain conditions clusters that seemingly are at the 'end' of their life cycle are able of renewing themselves and entering new growth phases (Tödtling and Trippl, 2004). Renewal builds basically on the ability of core cluster firms, or the ability of clusters as such, to change from one dominant type of products, technologies or sectors to others, or move up the quality ladders for specific types of products. These capabilities are stimulated by the existence of a strong RIS which is not too closed and inward-looking (Tödtling and Trippl, 2004). Such a situation may be achieved through related variety in the regional industry and knowledge infrastructure, and by strategic networks to extraregional knowledge sources.

Related variety refers to a situation in which a region has a local mix of several industrial sectors and where these sectors complement each other in terms of knowledge and other common input factors (Frenken et al., 2007; and see Chapter 14 by Boschma and Frenken in this *Handbook*). The relatedness enables knowledge spillovers and learning between complementary sectors and may cause additional economic growth. New industries often emerge out of recombination of existing industries, and related variety may thus form the root of new industries that are closely related to their present portfolio of industries (Boschma and Frenken, forthcoming). Related variety allows higher absorptive capacity of regions and more rapid diffusion of innovations among related firms and industries (Giuliani and Bell, 2005). Such processes may in some cases lead to regional branching in which clusters in one industry stimulate spin-offs and innovation cross-fertilization via knowledge spillovers in other industries (Boschma and Frenken, forthcoming). Old clusters may then give birth to new clusters in neighbouring sectors.

Development of related variety may, thus, represent one solution to negative lock-in situations. Another main way out of such situations includes to strengthening extraregional relations. Participation in global value chains and knowledge networks constitutes a central arena of learning for firms and knowledge organizations. Regions should in particular have some resourceful firms or organizations that participate in global 'learning' networks and act as gatekeepers of knowledge within the region (Giuliani and Bell, 2005). Such firms bring in advanced, external knowledge which is adapted and diffused to other regional firms, provided that local knowledge spillovers exist, and some firms have adequate internal resources or absorptive capacity to be able to identify and use the external knowledge. Boschma and Frenken (forthcoming) maintain that the extraregional knowledge most effectively supports regional industrial growth if it is related and close to existing regional knowledge bases, but not too similar to these.

CONCLUSION

This chapter employs an evolutionary and institutional approach in the analysis of the development of clusters, and distinguishes between clusters dominated by different knowledge bases. We underline that clusters do not follow a predefined life cycle, but rather propose a framework that may be useful in analysing the development of specific clusters. The emergence and growth of clusters relies normally on the ability of entrepreneurs, firms and other cluster participants to exploit specific location factors and to stimulate and utilize localization economies. Localization economies may, however, be linked to close regional networks that include 'ties that blind'. Innovation possibilities are then restrained by too inward-looking RISs containing a permanent core of firms and organizations, which may lead to negative lock-in situations. We lastly propose that delocking is stimulated by a related variety of regional industrial sectors and extraregional networks.

REFERENCES

Amin, A. (2000), 'Industrial districts', in E. Sheppard and T.J. Barnes (eds), *A Companion to Economic Geography*, Oxford: Blackwell, pp. 149–68.

Asheim, B.T. (2000), 'Industrial districts: the contribution of Marshall and beyond', in G.L. Clark, M.P. Feldman and M.S. Gertler (eds), *The Oxford Handbook of Economic Geography*, Oxford: Oxford University Press, pp. 413–31.

Asheim, B.T., L. Coenen, J. Moodysson and J. Vang (2007), 'Constructing knowledge-based regional advantage: implication for regional innovation policy', *International Journal of Entrepreneurship and Innovation Management*, **7** (2–5), 140–55.

Asheim, B., P. Cooke and R. Martin (2006), 'The rise of the cluster concept in regional analysis and policy: a critical assessment', in B. Asheim, P. Cooke and R. Martin (eds), *Clusters and Regional Development: Critical Reflections and Explorations*, London: Routledge, pp. 1–29.

Bathelt, H., A. Malmberg and P. Maskell (2004), 'Clusters and knowledge: local buzz, global pipelines and the process of knowledge creation', *Progress in Human Geography*, **28**, 31–56.

Becattini, G. (1990), 'Italy', in W. Sengenberger, G.W. Loveman and M.J. Piore (eds), *The Re-emergence of Small Enterprises: Industrial Restructuring in Industrialised Countries*, Geneva: International Institute for Labour Studies, pp. 144–72.

Bell, J., R. McNaughton and S. Young (2001), '"Born-again global" firms: an extension of the "born global" phenomenon', *Journal of International Management*, **7**, 173–89.

Belussi, F. and S.R. Sedita (2009), 'Life cycle vs. multiple path dependency in industrial districts', *European Planning Studies*, **17** (4), 505–28.

Bergman, E.M. (2008), 'Cluster life-cycle; an emerging synthesis', in C. Karlsson (ed.), *Handbook of Research on Cluster Theory*, Cheltenham, UK and Northampton, MA, USA: Edward Elgar, pp. 114–32.

Boschma, R. and K. Frenken (forthcoming), 'Technological relatedness and regional branching', in H. Bathelt, M.P. Feldman and D.F. Kogler (eds), *Dynamic Geographies of Knowledge Creation and Innovation*, London: Routledge.

Brusco, S. (1986), 'Small firms and industrial districts: the experience of Italy', in D. Keeble and E. Wever (eds), *New Firms and Regional Development in Europe*, London: Croom Helm, pp. 184–202.

Brusco, S. (1990), 'The idea of the industrial district: its genesis', in F. Pyke, G. Beccatini and W. Sternberger (eds), *Industrial Districts and Inter-firm Co-operation in Italy*, Geneva: International Institute for Labour Studies, pp. 10–19.

Cooke, P. (2002), *Knowledge Economies: Clusters, Learning and Cooperative Advantage*, London: Routledge.

Cooke, P., P. Boekholt and F. Tödtling (2000), *The Governance of Innovation in Europe: Regional Perspectives on Global Competitiveness*, London: Pinter.

European Commission (2002), *Regional Clusters in Europe*, Observatory of European SMEs 2002/No. 3, Luxembourg: Enterprise Publications.

Feldman, M.P. (2007), 'Perspectives on entrepreneurship and cluster formation: biotechnology in the US Capitol region', in K. Polenske (ed.), *The Economic Geography of Innovation*, Cambridge: Cambridge University Press, pp. 241–60.

Feldman, M. and J.L. Francis (2006), 'Entrepreneurs as agents in the formation of industrial clusters', in B. Asheim, P. Cooke and R. Martin (eds), *Clusters and Regional Development: Critical Reflections and Explorations*, London: Routledge, pp. 115–36.

Frenken, K., F. Van Oort and T. Verburg (2007), 'Related variety, unrelated variety and regional economic growth', *Regional Studies*, **41** (5), 685–98.

Giuliani, E. and M. Bell (2005), 'The micro-determinants of meso-level learning and innovation: evidence from a Chilean wine cluster', *Research Policy*, **34**, 47–68.

Grabher, G. (1993), 'The weakness of strong ties: the lock-in of regional development in the Ruhr area', in G. Grabher (ed.), *The Embedded Firm: On the Socioeconomics of Industrial Networks*, London: Routledge, pp. 255–77.

Halpern, D. (2005), *Social Capital*, Cambridge: Polity Press.

Hassink, R. (2005), 'How to unlock regional economies from path dependency? From learning region to learning cluster', *European Planning Studies*, **13** (4), 521–35.

Isaksen, A. (2003), '"Lock-in" of regional clusters: the case of offshore engineering in the Oslo region', in D. Fornahl and T. Brenner (eds), *Cooperation, Networks and Institutions in Regional Innovation Systems*, Cheltenham, UK and Northampton, MA, USA: Edward Elgar, pp. 247–73.

Lorenzen, M. (2005), 'Editorial: why do clusters change?', *European Urban and Regional Studies*, **12** (3), 203–8.

Lundvall, B.-Å. (2007), 'National innovation systems – analytical concept and development tool', *Industry and Innovation*, **14** (1), 95–119.

Malmberg, A. and D. Power (2006), 'True clusters: a severe case of conceptual headache', in B. Asheim, P. Cooke and R. Martin (eds), *Clusters and Regional Development: Critical Reflections and Explorations*, London: Routledge, pp. 50–69.

Moodysson, J. (2008), 'Principles and practices of knowledge creation: on the organization of "buzz" and "pipelines" in life science communities', *Economic Geography*, **84** (2), 449–69.

Porter, M.E. (2008), *On Competition*, updated and expanded edition, Boston, MA: Harvard Business Press.

Saxenian, A.L. (1996), *Regional Advantage: Culture and Competition in Silicon Valley and Route 128*, Cambridge, MA: Harvard University Press.

Storper, M. (1997), *The Regional World: Territorial Development in a Global Economy*, New York: Guilford Press.

Storper, M. and R. Walker (1989), *The Capitalist Imperative. Territory, Technology, and Industrial Growth*, New York: Basil Blackwell.

Tödtling, F. and M. Trippl (2004), 'Like phoenix from the ashes? The renewal of clusters in old industrial areas', *Urban Studies*, **41** (5–6), 1175–95.

23 Transversality and regional innovation platforms
Philip Cooke

INTRODUCTION

Two new terms enter this discourse, the first ('transversality') being recent as of early 2010, the second ('platforms') being extant in the regional innovation context since approximately 2005 (Harmaakorpi and Melkas, 2005; Harmaakorpi, 2006). In that context it was also deployed in the work of an academic commission set up by the European Union (EC, 2006; see also the early conceptualization of 'constructed advantage' in Foray and Freeman, 1993) and subsequently in various policy forums. It ties in also to the notion of general-purpose technologies but has a much broader geographical innovation focus than is implied by that (Helpman, 1998). It is important to the project of this *Handbook* because of three reasons.

First, intellectually, transversality and platforms tie together two elements that have been key to regional innovation thinking from the outset, especially that strong variant associated with regional systems of innovation perspectives (Cooke, 1992, 2001). These are the understanding of process and the understanding of policy. They intertwine, but in conventional analysis they are normally separate. Central to their contemporary intertwining is the evolutionary economic geography concept of 'related variety' as discussed in the chapters by Iammarino, Boschma and Martin, and others in this *Handbook*.

It will be recalled that the concept takes inspiration from Jane Jacobs rather than authors with a more specialization perspective on the wellsprings of regional innovation and growth. Her argument was the evolutionary one that favoured variety or diversity to be prime in understanding the creation of novelty. In Andersen's Chapter 2 in this *Handbook*, it will also be recalled that creativity and its sometime successor 'creative destruction' were conceived by Schumpeter as interactive. The key interaction was perceived to be between the 'innovator' with the creative idea, and the 'entrepreneur' who managed its implementation. Other important actors include bankers, consumers and, we might add, the regulators who often set the scene in favour of, but also against the implementation of innovations.

Of importance to the strength of 'related variety' as a concept are two things: first, does it match reality, in process terms? And second, if it does, as a reasonably persuasive and growing body of evolutionary economic geography evidence increasingly points to, are policy-makers taking steps to take advantage of it for their citizens by formulating and implementing policies that seek to further it? Of massive interest to innovation policy theory is the question of whether, policy-makers being knowledgeable of the academic debate about the importance of related variety or not, evidence can be found that they see virtue in implementing related variety 'platform policies'. In what follows this chapter will show that, somewhat against the grain, leading exponent innovation policy agencies can be found investing in 'transversality' between industries in pursuit of innovative cross-fertilization or cross-pollination opportunities that support business and other kinds of institutional innovation.

But before this is further explored, two further bonuses from transversality and platform thinking were promised. We have seen the prospect that process and policy can be integrated in this, as in other policy models, and the case has yet to be made that this is true regarding transversality. But what does it tell us, if true, about the current condition of the economic geography landscape? It suggests that at the end of the first decade of the twenty-first century it is in transition in very significant ways. A number of crises contributing to general politico-economic turbulence have to be faced and new models found to facilitate this, both conceptually and in practical terms. Returning to the specialization–diversification debate, it suggests that specialization theory has reached the end of its particular economic policy road. Throughout the era increasingly referred to as that associated with a great experiment in neoliberal ideology about the superior 'intelligence' of markets over hierarchies (like states and the public sector) or networks (such as prevail in associative economies like Germany and the Nordic countries; Lowenstein, 2001; Tett, 2009; Akerlof and Shiller, 2009), market specialization was revered. In the innovation field Michael Porter's theory and policy advice favouring 'clusters' was taken up enthusiastically nearly everywhere nationally and regionally in the developed and developing worlds. Ideas associated with Jane Jacobs were out in the cold. But now disaffected agencies everywhere are looking for a more appropriate model of sustaining innovation in more turbulent times.

And this is the third bonus: turbulent times have led to a major reappraisal of past practice in light of the four crises that have constituted a 'long emergency' (Kunstler, 2005) in recent times. These emergencies are, first, the climate change crisis with widespread consensus that human consumption of products and services that produce globally significant and measurable greenhouse gas emissions must be moderated in major ways. Second, the energy crisis, which sees an ever-rising trend in the consumer price of hydrocarbons to fuel mobility and, in its by-products, much of the rest of the economy, has led to demands for a turn towards a post-hydrocarbon economic landscape. Third, the financial crisis brought the global economy to its knees in 2007–09, due to an under-regulated and over-risky experiment with financial innovations that were, critically and unlike manufactured products, untested before being sold to consumers. This demands rebalancing away from its overspecialization effects. And finally, the extended and broader economic crisis that is intimately connected to globalization and 'devil-take-the-hindmost' Ricardian liberal trade calls for response to demands for the rebalancing through reindustrialization of the West. As argued in the chapter on 'Green innovation' (Chapter 32 in this *Handbook*), a key call has been for 'greener economies' based in 'green engineering', 'renewable energy' and recycling that benefit from eco-innovations as composites of relevant related variety industries. Transversality and platforms are intimately linked to the quest for a way out of these four apocalyptic crises.

In what follows, the next section presents the main lineaments of the argument in favour of regional innovation platforms with reference to literature reporting such developmental policy trajectories in Finland. It rests on a critique, briefly outlined, of specialization theory and policy as represented by 'clusters' and 'clustering' measures. The third section of the chapter then leads a search for the conceptual origins in policy theory for transversality, noting that ideas of 'policy mix' have evolved as governance and government have sought, far from successfully, against the linear 'silo-model' of administrative management and in favour of a more lateral 'joined-up' model. Fourthly, some examples of transversality in policy-making are shown, as is their variety away from a central template. Some indication of the relative robustness of the transverse model in innovation indicators is provided. Finally, conclusions and directions for future thought and exploration are suggested.

THE REGIONAL DEVELOPMENT PLATFORM METHOD

Many recent policy assessments in advanced economies have also called into question the way regionalization of innovation through cluster policy has been implemented (Roper et al, 2005; Asheim et al., 2006). Some of these can be summarized as pointing to disaffection with 'sectoral' thinking, 'picking winners' and even the utilization of 'retro-models' like 'clusters' when industry increasingly thinks in lateral 'platform' ways encompassing notions of 'knowledge spillovers' and 'related variety' of the kind discussed in Iammarino's and Boschma and Martin's chapters. Remarkably,'cluster-building', which seems a coherent viewpoint, turns out to rely heavily on only one highly specific case, which Porter (1990) discusses at length (Chapter 5, pp. 210–25). This is the only one of three industry accounts that is substantially place-based. It is the Italian ceramic tile industry, which in 1987 was 85 per cent dependent on production and 75 per cent for employment from one small town, Sassuolo, in Emilia-Romagna. Good, representative case studies are often the only way to test theory where large datasets, often not designed for purpose, fail in this task, but they can run the risk of being 'the sample of one'.

Superficially, Sassuolo fits Porter's 'diamond' notion almost too well, particularly in the way it accounts for so much Italian national production, has final firms in competition, with subcontractors selling contractually to them, and backward integration of the value chain from ceramics to the innovative design and global marketing of firing equipment needed to produce ceramics. But as a reading of Russo's (1985) classic article on Sassuolo shows, locally and nationally contingent events and processes like Italy's 'economic miracle', stupendous housing boom, and housing legislation allowing subsidies favouring use of ceramics, on the one hand, and industrial relations conflicts, on the other, created a space from which hitherto ceramics-free Sassuolo could benefit. Why Sassuolo? Because the appropriate clays existed only there and in the nearby Apennine mountains.

A second weakness in understanding of the issue of geographical scale. In Porter (1990) the cluster definition stretches alarmingly from the local to the national and back again with bewildering facility. Of course, building on the previous point, where a local cluster has the inordinate impact that Sassuolo ceramics exerts upon the national ceramics sector, that may just be acceptable logic. But most industry is nothing like that. So, initially at least, Porter's cluster notion caused enormous confusion until in Porter (1998) he more or less put things right with his spatially more informed definition of the cluster as: 'a geographically proximate group of interconnected companies and associated institutions in a particular field, linked by commonalities and complementarities' (Porter, 1998, 199). This conforms to dictionary definitions of 'cluster' as 'concentration', 'clump' or 'bunch', all denoting gathering or huddling in geographic space. But, even then, on the same page he retreats from the sensible to the risible: 'The geographic scope of a cluster can range from a single city or state to a country or even a network of neighbouring countries' (ibid.).

But this is not the only flaw in Porter's cluster concept, for whether or not there is a reality behind what Porter is trying to get at, we argue clearly that clusters in the sense of industrial districts do, in fact, exist. Evidence, such as that found on the nature and extent of groups of collaborating firms that compete against other collaborating groups in the same district, is exemplified with infinite pains in Becattini (2001) or Dei Ottati (1994) for the woollen textile district of Prato near Florence. Dei Ottati (1994) examined in depth the distinctive kinds of trustful and more sceptical relationships among individual firms, banks and intermediaries for the same place. Astonishingly, in Becattini (2001) a detailed account is given of how, why and through whom the Chinese 'districts within a district' came about in Prato from 1989 to 1993:[1]

> By December 1993 the Chinese community officially numbered over 1400 residents, a negligible figure in itself for somewhere the size of Prato, but one that stands out noticeably if it is borne in mind that . . . in 1989 there were only 40 . . . the Prato Chinese are part of a galaxy of similar communities that have settled in the surrounding area (Camp Bisenzio, Signa, Lastra a Signa etc.) that can be reckoned to number some tens of thousands . . . this community has rapidly and efficiently inserted itself into Prato's manufacture of clothing goods, where it has carved out a number of niches (handbags, gloves, etc.) in which with several hundred small firms, it has a far from negligible importance. (Becattini, 2001, 161–2)

Porter's methodology excludes this kind of knowledge because he takes an operational definition of what counts as clustering, namely secondary data that show high location quotients for specific sectors and subsectors. Occasionally, as in Porter (1998), diagrams of cluster circuitry are drawn but they are not based on intrafirm interviews that would enable his researchers to acquire knowledge of precisely which interfirm transactions are, say, preferential contracts with neighbours; which favour exchange relations with local significant others; whether a firm was a spin-out from another in the locality; and what kinds of relationships exist, if any, with local business support agencies, lawyers, banks, venture capitalists and the like. In other words, Porter cannot prove that anywhere, anything he asserts to be a cluster actually is one. All that can be said from location quotient data is that there is a higher than average specific industrial agglomeration in location x or y, which actually does not get us very far beyond Weber or Lösch (see Vatne's Chapter 4 in this *Handbook*).

Three final qualifiers are, first, because of the static definition of cluster deployed by Porter (1998) none of the dynamism that such spin-out, networking and project-focused activity that the neo-Marshallians routinely find in industrial districts would be available to Porter's methodology even were he bold enough to venture inside a few factory gates. Second, static cluster accounts give a foreshortened sense of the time it takes for clusters to form. Most of the Italian ones date to at least early post-Second World War or the 1960s 'economic miracle' era, and many say that they can be traced back to the Renaissance (see also Isaksen's Chapter 22 in this *Handbook*). Hence presenting clusters as a policy panacea is to engage in an exercise in shaky optimism, which policy organizations are beginning to discover, as we shall see. Finally, Porter's definition is, as we have also seen, a market-driven one with reliance on rivalry and competitive advantage. However, arguably some of the most interesting new cluster forms, such as those that typify biotechnology or clean technology (Feldman and Francis, 2003; Cooke, 2008), are science-driven, not primarily market-driven. Indeed most firms in biotechnology clusters do not even make profits, but have discovered a new business model in which pharmaceuticals firms and research councils invest in ideas.

Regional Development Platform Theory

Not surprisingly, policy-makers and academics have been searching for a more appropriate developmental model. In what follows, a summary is provided of thinking behind the evolution of a post-cluster 'platform policy' concept. This was deployed to identify a new economic base in a region which had seen the disappearance from Finland to Eastern Europe of its once-dominant furniture industry. It is clearly evolutionary rather than neoliberal in its underlying theoretical assumptions. Among its key theoretical elements are the following:

- Regional trajectories are 'path-dependent' over time with specific asset and capability configurations that relate to each other historically and potentially.
- Regional capabilities renew or atrophy, also being collective not individual processes and outcomes.
- Regional competitive (or more accurately, 'constructed') advantage rests on valuable, scarce, non-imitable and non-substitutable resources – for example specific combinations of talent, environment, knowledge and so on.
- Regional dynamic capabilities are processes or routines that integrate and reconfigure assets to meet or create market opportunities.
- Key regional process assets are: knowledge, innovation, networking, leadership and envisioning capabilities.

The organizational basis for integrating these process or routine capabilities is a 'regional innovation system'. This connects organizational and enterprise assets in a collective manner with a view to exploiting and renewing trajectories over time by reconfiguring dynamic capabilities. This process is subject to 'governance' of a facilitative rather than a determinative kind, relying upon vision and leadership that express the dynamic capabilities of the region's actors, routines and processes.

Regional Development Platform Methodology

Within a framework of regional innovation systems (RISs) and evolutionary economics the key aim is to explore market potentials of regional assets and capabilities:

- These explorations define regional development platforms in conceptual terms.
- Regional development platforms are asset configurations evolved from path-dependencies aimed at examining and exploiting market potential.
- Regional platform actors include firms, intermediaries, knowledge centres, research, cultural and talent formation organizations.

● Regional platforms comprise industry, knowledge and contextuation in, for example, techno-economic paradigm change or 'global megatrends' of consequence to the specific region.

Among the guiding principles of this are the following: understanding the 'drivers' of paradigmatic global change; understanding specific regional trajectories, especially regarding agglomeration; avoiding regional lock-ins; defining competitive asset configurations; forming multi-actor innovation networks to exploit such configurations; improving absorptive capacities among network members; utilizing and enhancing regional social capital; promoting leadership and foresight; and engaging multilevel governance in the exploitable platforms. These activities are performed by, *inter alia*: analysts, expert panels, scenario designers, system designers and knowledge intermediaries or entrepreneurs. All this activity is directed at identifying (with 'related variety' to the fore) the existing and future core competencies of the region.

Regional Development Platform Implementation

The region of Lahti was explored and found to be weak in modern talent, knowledge and educational performance. Locked in to a declining mass-market furniture manufacturing profile, the region's leaders sought to envision a new future by:

● Analysis of innovation potential related to regional expertise.
● Grading expert panels regionally: entrepreneurship, growth potential, firm-size balance, global perspective, innovativeness, knowledge-intensity, leadership capability, educational quality, research and technology-transfer expertise.
● Comparing industry grades and identifying leaders, then stimulating 'related variety' by innovation system building around potential 'platforms'.
● Platforms integrating global megatrends to 'related variety' around, for example, the healthcare industry integrating materials, mechatronics and nanotechnology.

In the first documented case of utilizing this approach in Finland (Harmaakorpi, 2006), the key actors diversified away from a declining furniture industry by identifying future advantage in the healthcare industry. The new platform included firms in plastics, construction, furniture and metal, public healthcare organizations, higher education and research organizations, the 'governance' leader – the regional development agency, incubators and talent development centres.

What were the effects and process evaluation results? The effects included changed assumptions by key actors and raised awareness of the key importance of innovation institutions. Old industrial policy mentalities and measures were transcended. A previous perception that absence of clusters and dynamic lead industries or firms (for example Nokia) doomed the region, was transformed by application of policy platform methodology to exploit 'related variety'. Finally, the existential power of multi-actor networks was discovered and entrenched in the region. What problems had to be overcome? Foremost, 'knowledge' access, flow and integration asymmetries were overwhelming. Second, creative, imaginative thinking about the future lacked specificity to enable platform-envisioning to evolve. Among the process innovations developed in this regard was the 'Living Laboratory' in which scripted dramas of institutional resistance to change were acted out (Harmaakorpi and Melkas, 2005). This was because of the realization that in the external world of the policy platform rather than the internal world of the individual or firm far greater knowledge depth and complexity must be handled to enhance 'visualization' and 'potentialization' for the region. Finally this new process proceeded raggedly, and in time-consuming ways that subsequent experience may show can be foreshortened. The novelty of terms and concepts makes it initially difficult for outsiders to understand that clear communication is vital.

Constructing Regional Advantage

The approach taken in the above is a good example of 'constructing regional advantage' (CRA) as evolved in the European Commission's deliberations about improving the elaboration and delivery of regional innovation policies. This embodies key concepts such as 'related variety' among sectors, innovating in the neighbourhood of current assets and not 'leapfrogging' into generically fashionable new industries, regional policy platforms and a vision-led implementation methodology. In the CRA approach (EC, 2006) the envisioning process is conducted as follows:

1. Animation of a 'conversation' process by a legitimate agent (for example a 'seeker', 'researcher,' consultant or regional development agency; for all these points, see also 'Regional innovation policy and dramaturgy', Chapter 42 in this *Handbook*).
2. Facilitator for envisioning 'conversations' with a view to achieving consensus (narrative approach).
3. Conversation process involves identifying 'related variety' assets upon which CRA can be built to achieve the consensus vision.
4. Expert panels focus deeper on specific economic assets and their enhanced exploitation and/or recombination to meet new opportunities.
5. Search, identification and elaboration of vision.
6. Selection of actions for implementation.
7. Appointment of 'leaders' to conduct implementation.
8. Use of vision steering methodology such as 'balanced scorecard'.[2]
9. Feedback of measurements to management.
10. Monitoring and learning for vision steering.

We have thus illustrated a way in which this was actually achieved in Finland. Interestingly it has now also been performed in neighbouring Estonia with comparable results and a comparable set of envisioned directions to help diversify the economy of that small, neighbouring state (Watkins and Agapitova, 2004)

TRANSVERSALITY

We have seen that traditional sector and cluster policies reached a point in their evolution where significant growth or employment gains were less forthcoming than previously thought likely or experienced. Three reasons help to explain this. First, economic context is important and in a general downturn of the severity of that in 2007–09, conditions for sector or cluster growth were generally poor. Second, more directly, it swiftly became clear that risk-finance, even for established let alone new business ventures, largely dried up due to cautious investor practices. Finally, the model of vertically drilling down in relatively narrow fields, even involving partnership with similar overseas initiatives, was producing diminishing returns. Accordingly, some innovative regional policy regimes, as we have seen, began exploring the innovative potential of horizontal interactions among different regional and extraregional sectors or clusters.

Where industries share aspects of technologies, skills or markets, firms in them understand each other even though they are in different subsectors. They gain from knowledge spillovers (Breschi's Chapter 10 in this *Handbook*) if they have the required absorptive capacity (Boschma and Frenken's Chapter 14 in this *Handbook*). New empirical research had also demonstrated the importance for growth and productivity of combinative as compared to cumulative knowledge (Cooke et al., 2010). As noted already, one area where this was found to happen was among firms involved in eco-innovation. This was because their technology and skill-sets typically crossed industry boundaries, making use of advances in each to create innovative solutions. Thus solar energy now uses thin-film polymers but also silicon for substrates and advanced glass for reflectors, while wind turbines use composite materials for blades, gears from crane technology, turbines and concrete for towers. Among regional development agencies shown by research to promote platform interactions among different regional industries, historically first have been those influenced by climate change concerns and actions to promote 'green' production and consumption of, for example, energy. However, subsequent research efforts have shown that 'innovation platforms' and the wider cross-pollination perspective referred to as transversality are by no means limited to agencies with green agendas. A subsidiary idea of relevance to the quest for transversality in policy-making is found in new literature on 'policy mix' whereby policy fields are integrated around key policy 'hot topics' where they are of consequence to the policy issue being focused upon (Nauwelaers's Chapter 34 in this *Handbook*).

VARIETY OF TRANSVERSALITY TYPES

In researching the phenomenon thus far, five styles of transversality programme have been identified, each at different stages of fulfilment. This does not mean that Europe is made up of 100 categories of regional policy style, although it is important to recognize that a uniform national context, while influential, may also give rise to distinctive approaches. These qualitative judgements will be a product of intensive face-to-face interviews with exemplar cases of each, including the possibility of changing category titles and types. The five types I presently hypothesize to remain reasonably instructive after the more targeted research here proposed are as follows.

Reactive Platform Response

This takes at least two subforms observed so far. First, a local crisis such as the loss of a major employer or industry may give rise to a process, animated by the innovation agency, of exploring the application of existing skills to new industries. A 'living lab' of practical applications focused around economic scenarios or profiles leads to some or many firms perceiving ways that they can adapt to rising or possibly demand-led markets such as healthcare or environment. Advanced expertise is called in as needed. Firms innovate into mixed broad 'platforms' where their capabilities fit best. Implementation of this crisis-response mode of transversality is mature in the real-world case of the Lahti furniture industry, as discussed above.

Second, a widespread regional crisis of established clusters in traditional industries leads firms alongside their development and technology agency partners to a quest for a new platform. Panel discussions identify a new cluster composed of capabilities from three or four others. The regional development agency animates interactions among firms, finds support through European Union (EU) and national funding, and ensures actor-commitment. Implementation is immature in the real-world case of the new marine technology platform being constructed at Ancona in the Marche region of Italy (OECD, 2010)

Reactive–Proactive Peripheral Region

In this case a region is peripherally located and perceived, as well as perceiving itself, not to have the quality of institutions to warrant advanced research investment by the state. Accordingly, it is reactive to the peripherality perception by utilization of social capital and exercise of local proactivity, connecting regional industries and investing in regionally funded research and innovation. Medium-tech industry is clustered, branded and transversalized. New knowledge-creating institutions and various user-driven living labs give advantage to the regional platform. Implementation is mature in the real-world case. The exemplar region is Värmland in Sweden. Here interconnectivity of clusters and sectors is organized through established 'innovation platforms' at the industry interfaces. In such innovation platforms, a number of combinative knowledge transfer institutions may be found. An important regional industry is the manufacture of pulp and paper which an earlier cluster initiative branded 'The Paper Province'. It shares an innovation platform with another branded cluster known as 'The Packaging Arena' (TPA). Within the platform are found the following institutions: 'The Packaging Greenhouse', which is a laboratory for formulating and testing ideas about new forms and requirements for packaging; 'The Packaging Media Lab', where design, customer preference and consumer testing (for example eye-tracking) are conducted and 'acted out' in demonstration studios; 'The Do-tank Design Studio' where tested designs and layouts are prototyped; 'The Flexography Institute', where research into accurate graphic representations on varieties of flexible and inflexible paper surfaces is conducted; and 'The Service Research Institute', part of Karlstad University's consumer studies research unit which is co-located in the city centre headquarters of TPA. Strong cross-fertilization links to other regional and extra-regional clusters include those to agro-food, steel and engineering and information and communication technology (ICT) in Värmland, and 'The Printed Electronics' cluster at Norrköping in Ostragotland region. In 2010 Värmland Region and Karlstad University announced ten new 'Cluster Chairs' to further promote regional innovation transversality.

Proactive Narrow Growth Region

Here, the region is economically successful but overdependent upon vulnerable, large-scale supply chains in medium- and high-tech industries. The regional government is able to pool EU, national and regional development funds and embark on a strategy process. It commissions new regional indicators, on the one hand, and envisions interactions among firms in its narrow base, on the other. It then focuses on hub, system and SME innovator firms in the dominant sectors and constitutes them as a group. The group is charged with discovering transversality within itself. This involves technologies, platform potential, barriers and methodologies for identifying lead innovations. Implementation of the actual interfirm knowledge interactions in the real case of Midi-Pyrénées in France was anticipated in early 2010.

Proactive Broad Base 'Green'

The region has a political regime that pursues a green agenda. To that end it promotes a process of matching clusters and sectors against green economy targets such as becoming a producer of renewable energy, organic food, biofuels, green engineering and so on. Various existing industry aids are tailored in support of this agenda and firms committing to a shift in business focus towards finding markets for such output receive financial support. Where interactions outside an established sector are required, these may be facilitated by the regional development agency. Implementation in the real case of Lower Austria's EcoPlus platform is mature.

Proactive Broad Base

Here the prime aim is not specifically to pursue a green agenda, though where this fits it is included. Rather, this approach elaborates on the previous one by aligning all main regional industries against a portfolio of all main advanced technologies utilized in the region and, to some extent, outside. The regional development agency (RDA) then takes on a role greater than animation or facilitation – it becomes a catalyst for innovation. This is done by adopting a 'matrix' approach, bringing together examples of innovations in one industry and evolving a discourse with other industry firms that may see potential in adapting them to their own industry or cluster. Out of these 'panel conversations' emerge many innovations new to the firm or sector, which may have disruptive potential in the new sector even though they might only have been incremental innovations in the existing sector. This approach involves the RDA stimulating firms to explore 'white spaces' between distinctive industries. Implementation in the real case is mature, having begun with the establishment of Bayern Innovativ (BI) in Germany in 1995. Interestingly, as in some of the other transversality types discussed, a strong creative element underpins platform management. Thus BI sees its role as not 'leadership' but 'orchestration' of regional innovation interests (see also Wallin, 2006). Each event BI organizes – some 400 annually – has a narrative 'red thread' running through it that attracts participants. For instance, an 'Innovative Materials' event aimed at vehicle and new materials manufacturers played on the theme of 'Light Living and Leisure' to connect engineering with wider societal issues, attracting 450 participants and key presentations on fibre composites, aluminium and new alloys from the likes of Audi, BMW, Daimler, Opel and Porsche alongside materials specialists like Huber, Voith and ThyssenKrupp. Of some 1000 cooperations arising from events like this, BI estimates some 10 per cent turn into actual commercial innovations (Cooke, 2010).

CONCLUSIONS AND FURTHER RESEARCH

It is clear that a number of European regional innovation policy agencies have conducted post-cluster innovation strategies based on horizontal knowledge interactions among unlike industrial firms. Service innovation businesses are of central importance in many of these instances, as are creative management models ranging from 'living labs' to dramaturgy and orchestration. This is an interesting evolutionary process within the knowledge economy, where becoming a 'services firm' or 'systems integrator' is one form of survival strategy where mass production manufacturing has become uncompetitive, as pioneered by, for example, the computer giant IBM before 2000. Acording to Schamp et al. (2004) many automotive manufacturers are largely such systems integrators, having outsourced vast amounts of the equipment manufacture of their product to elaborate supply chains. Comparable processes are under way in today's aerospace industry. The fields of corporate disintegration of functions and regional integration of new industry platforms will make an interestingly contradictory set of evolutionary learning and innovation processes over the coming decades. Many different aspects of new innovation processes and policies warrant investigation. One of these suggests that as market solutions to innovation demands face increasing pressures from regulators and consumers alike, RDAs may, hypothetically, take on a role that is more proactive than simply reactive. In transversality contexts the RDAs take an obviously catalytic position on stimulating the dynamics of horizontal knowledge flows. Interesting issues of capabilities, talent requirements, governance, supply-side versus demand-side measures, and policy mixes for innovation support arise, and also warrant further research investigation.

NOTES

1. By 2010 Chinese residents in Prato numbered some 35 000.
2. Balanced scorecard is a management system based on a measurement methodology that enables organizations to clarify their vision and strategy and translate them into action (see Kaplan and Norton, 1996).

REFERENCES

Akerlof, G. and R. Shiller (2009), *Animal Spirits; How Human Psychology Drives the Economy and Why it Matters for Global Capitalism*, Princeton, NJ: Princeton University Press.
Asheim, B., P. Cooke and R. Martin (2006), *Clusters and Regional Development: Critical Reflections and Explorations*, London: Routledge.
Becattini, G. (2001), *The Caterpillar and the Butterfly*, Florence: Felice le Monnier.
Cooke, P. (1992), 'Regional innovation systems: competitive regulation in the new Europe', *Geoforum*, **23**, 365–82.

Cooke, P. (2001), 'Regional innovation systems, clusters and the knowledge economy', *Industrial and Corporate Change*, **10**, 945–74.

Cooke, P. (2008), 'Cleantech and an analysis of the platform nature of life sciences: further reflections upon platform policies', *European Planning Studies*, **16** (3), 1–19.

Cooke, P. (2010), 'Matrix policy: rationales and good examples', in A. Eriksson, V. Allee, P. Cooke, V. Harmaakorpi, M. Sotaranta and J. Wallin (eds), *The Matrix: Post-cluster Innovation Policy*, Stockholm: Vinnova.

Cooke, P., C. De Laurentis, S. MacNeill and C. Collinge (2010), *Platforms of Innovation: Dynamics of New Industrial Knowledge Flows*, Cheltenham, UK and Northampton, MA, USA: Edward Elgar.

Dei Ottati, G. (1994), 'Co-operation and competition in the industrial district as an organisational model', *European Planning Studies*, **2**, 371–92.

European Commission (EC) (2006), *Constructing Regional Advantage*, Brussels: DG Research.

Feldman, M. and J. Francis (2003), 'Fortune favours the prepared region: the case of entrepreneurship and the Capitol Region biotechnology cluster', *European Planning Studies*, **11**, 757–64.

Foray, D. and C. Freeman (1993), *Technology and the Wealth of Nations: The Dynamics of Constructed Advantage*, London: Pinter.

Harmaakorpi, V. (2006), 'Regional development platform method as a tool for regional innovation policy', *European Planning Studies*, **14**, 1093–112.

Harmaakorpi, V. and H. Melkas (2005), 'Knowledge management in regional innovation networks: the case of Laths', *European Planning Studies*, **15**, 641–60.

Helpman, E. (ed.) (1998), *General Purpose Technologies and Economic Growth*, Cambridge, MA: MIT Press.

Kaplan, R. and D. Norton (1996), *The Balanced Scorecard*, Boston, MA: Harvard Business School Press.

Kunstler, J. (2005), *The Long Emergency: Surviving the Converging Catastrophes of the Twenty-First Century*, New York: Grove Press.

Lowenstein, R. (2001), *When Genius Failed: The Rise and Fall of Long-term Capital Management*, New York: Random House.

Organisation for Economic Co-operation and Development (OECD) (2010), *SMEs, Entrepreneurship and Local Development in the Marche Region, Italy*, Paris: OECD.

Porter, M. (1990), *The Competitive Advantage of Nations*, New York: Free Press.

Porter, M. (1998), *On Competition*, Boston, MA: Harvard Business School Press.

Roper, S., J. Love, P. Cooke and N. Clifton (2005), *The Scottish Innovation System: Actors, Roles and Policies*, Edinburgh: Scottish Executive.

Russo, M. (1985), 'Technical change and the industrial district: the role of interfirm relations in the growth and transformation of ceramic tile production in Italy', *Research Policy*, **14**, 329–43.

Schamp, E., B. Rentmeister and V. Lo (2004), 'Dimensions of proximity in knowledge-based networks: the cases of investment banking and automobile design', *European Planning Studies*, **12**, 607–24.

Tett, G. (2009), *Fool's Gold: How Unrestrained Greed Corrupted a Dream, Shattered Global Markets and Unleashed a Catastrophe*, London: Little Brown.

Wallin, J. (2006), *Business Orchestration*, London: Wiley.

Watkins, A. and N. Agapitova (2004), 'Creating a 21st century national innovation system for a 21st century Latvian economy', Research Working Paper 2357, Washington, DC: World Bank.

24 Technology clusters
Edward Malecki

The idea of a technology cluster began in the USA with observations of the development and growth of companies in California's Silicon Valley, south of San Francisco, and Route 128 outside Boston, Massachusetts beginning in the 1960s. The patterns seen in these two regions – universities, spin-off firms, entrepreneurs, venture capital – soon became the archetypes for growth elsewhere.[1] Early on, the phenomenon of new technology-based firms (NTBFs) was a novelty. As industrial restructuring took place in many industrialized countries during the 1970s and 1980s, clusters of technology-based industries grew in importance as potential sources of prosperity. Researchers and policy-makers alike looked to these two originators of technology-based regional development.

Early interest focused on the phenomena of technical entrepreneurship and spin-off identified in the two regions (Cooper, 1971; Cooper and Bruno, 1977; Cooper and Komives, 1972; Roberts and Wainer, 1968). Indeed, the field of entrepreneurship studies largely grew from the experience of these regions. By the mid-1980s, the examples of the unplanned Silicon Valley and Route 128, and the planned Research Triangle Park in North Carolina, were well known, producing inspiration for imitators elsewhere (Dorfman, 1983; Hall and Markusen, 1985; Rogers and Larsen, 1984; Miller and Coté, 1987; Smilor et al., 1988). The Silicon Valley model truly became the archetype, seen in the titles of numerous books and articles.[2]

Technology clusters differ significantly from other industrial clusters in that they are more tied to the early stages of industry life cycles, and their resources at the regional level support growth and innovation (St John and Pouder, 2006). The principal activity of technology-based sectors is research, and their main input as well as output is knowledge. For firms, locating near sources of knowledge (such as universities and research centers) and clustering in specialized labor markets maximizes opportunities for collective learning and for exploiting entrepreneurial opportunities (Audretsch et al., 2006; Di Tommaso et al., 2006).

In addition to technology, such clusters also exhibit a culture that favors entrepreneurs. Several cultures can be identified: national, regional and university. The national culture reflects the tolerance of failure necessary for entrepreneurship. Perhaps more importantly, the national innovation system (NIS) provides the framework of research institutions and support needed for science and technology from which NTBFs are generated (Mowery and Sampat, 2005). The regional culture – and, more broadly, the regional innovation system (RIS) – is about institutions but also about the culture of networking, or its absence (Asheim and Gertler, 2005). An RIS must be an innovation-prone, rather than innovation-averse, region (Rodriguez-Pose, 1999). The combination of the specific NIS and local institutions make each cluster unique (Breschi and Malerba, 2001). Finally, the culture of local universities determines whether academic entrepreneurship can take place. Not all universities are the equal of Massachusetts Institute of

Technology (MIT) and Stanford as entrepreneurial universities (Castells and Hall, 1994; Etzkowitz, 2002, 2003; Roberts, 1991), and many do not have the autonomy to be.

Following a review of the characteristics of technology clusters, this chapter examines the archipelago of islands of innovation comprised of technology clusters. It examines the role of universities and of venture capital. This is followed by a review of the challenges of creating technology clusters through policies, such as science parks.

WHAT HAPPENS INSIDE TECHNOLOGY CLUSTERS?

Technology clusters are 'well-functioning' regional innovation systems (Chaminade and Vang, 2008). As clusters, they function through the fundamental processes of agglomeration and localized learning among companies, suppliers and service providers, firms in related industries, and associated institutions such as universities, standards agencies and trade associations (Porter, 2000). Porter and most other cluster researchers rarely distinguish between technology clusters and other types, and rarely explain details about the formation of a cluster and of its evolving networks, spin-offs or long-run evolutionary paths (Asheim et al., 2006). Recent research has differentiated among clusters, based on the generalization that all clusters are not alike. Firms and industries vary greatly in their technological regimes and knowledge characteristics (St John and Pouder, 2006; Iammarino and McCann, 2007).

In general, a technology cluster has: (1) a flow of people and ideas (technology), usually from research at one or more world-class universities; (2) sources of finance for entrepreneurs; and (3) an entrepreneurial or technical culture that provides the linkages usually found in an RIS or 'entrepreneurial ecosystem' (Bahrami and Evans, 1995). Within this system must be a culture of networking or 'organic interdependence', as Paniccia (2006) calls it. In addition, science-based industrial districts have other attributes, including knowledge institutions, venture capital, magnets for talent and an urban 'buzz' (Panniccia, 2006, 107–8).

However, clustered companies also face costs or 'negative externalities': technological isomorphism rather than diversity, labour cost inflation, overspecialization, institutional and industrial lock-in, and local congestion. A common feature of all technology clusters – and global cities as well – is the divide in the social conditions found within them, affecting particularly those who work in low-wage service jobs. These problems are not new; Saxenian (1985) saw them decades ago. In addition, Folta et al. (2006) have found that the largest clusters generally present diseconomies of agglomeration.

The technological context of technology clusters has been largely overlooked. Indeed, technological opportunities vary greatly among industries. In newer industries, technological opportunities are more numerous and open up more possibilities for benefits from research and development (R&D) (Klevorick et al., 1995). The stage of the industry life cycle, in turn, influences strongly the degree to which start-ups and growth can take place in a cluster (Cooper and Folta, 2000).

Among the most important processes in a technology cluster is localized learning and the competitiveness that results from it. The essential characteristic of such clusters is that they are the locations of first-movers in their industries (Maskell et al., 1998). Firms learn in innovative clusters through user–producer relationships, formal and informal collaborations, interfirm mobility of skilled workers, and the spin-off of new firms from existing firms, universities and public research centers (Breschi and Malerba, 2001).

Together, an entrepreneurial infrastructure and leading-edge technological knowledge engender a recombinatorial ability that enables firms and institutions in a cluster to reorient themselves to new opportunities. Silicon Valley has evolved through four generations of information and communication technology (ICT) industries (Hulsink et al., 2008). Likewise, a virtuous circle of regional dynamics in the Boston area has led to a different, but equally competitive, model based on skills in systems integration (Best, 2000; Kenney and von Burg, 1999). The view of innovation as synthesis and integration stresses mid-level innovation, in addition to scientific knowledge (Bhidé, 2008).

The early technology clusters in the USA were a result of firms exploiting opportunities in ICT (including semiconductors, electronics, computers, software and telecommunications). A second generation of clusters soon followed in biotechnology. These two industries are very different, both in their sources of knowledge and in the degree to which customers are important (Cooke et al., 2007). Importantly, biotech and its support networks are not as clustered as those in semiconductors and telecommunications, and they operate more as an archipelago of knowledge nodes (Kenney and Patton, 2005; Moodysson, 2008). The key nodes in the biotech archipelago are a small set of 'bioscience megacenters' identified by Cooke (2004a): Boston, San Francisco and Silicon Valley, San Diego, Toronto, Montreal, Munich, Stockholm and Cambridge.[3]

Newer industries that are spawning general-purpose technologies, such as nanotechnology and 'green' environmental technologies, are different again (Youtie et al., 2008). Nanotechnology relies strongly on cutting-edge research as well as on large facilities found in few locations (Avenel et al., 2007). Robinson et al. (2007) identify three centers in Europe: Grenoble, Delft and Twente. At the same time, scientific strength is critical. Beijing ranks first in the world among locations of authors of scientific papers on nanotechnology; the top four are in Asia (Matthiessen et al., 2006; Miyazaki and Islam, 2007). Illustrating path-dependence, both Boston and the San Francisco Bay area are also among a small number of the leading centers of biotechnology and the newer high-tech field of nanotechnology. Interviews by Feldman (2000, 353) confirm that scientist-entrepreneurs in biotechnology 'typically want to stay where they are'. In nanotechnology, Darby and Zucker (2003, 18) conclude that: 'Where commercial opportunity is built on fast-advancing academic science it is generally more economical to establish commercial laboratories and even manufacturing facilities near the universities than to try to move the scientists and their network to an existing firm location.'

Over time, mainly through (im)mobility of workers, firms in a cluster tend to develop a cluster-specific, interfirm stock of knowledge that is distinct from that anywhere else in the industry. Henry and Pinch (2006) call this a 'cluster-level architectural knowledge system'. Knowledge flows across cluster boundaries are minimal, leading to the creation of 'spatial knowledge monopolies' (Cooke, 2005). These reflect a combination of both local networks of local industrial knowledge and networks (or pipelines) to global knowledge.

The Advantage of Urban Areas

Clusters of innovation and creativity are generally found in large urban agglomerations, in part because several universities and research institutions tend to be found in such areas (Castells and Hall, 1994). Major universities and institutes, no matter how prominent, rank somewhat lower if located in small cities. For example, Oxford ranks 26th and Cambridge, UK 29th among world research centers (Matthiessen et al., 2006). Clusters in large urban areas possess the ideal of agglomeration beneficial for exchange of tacit knowledge and connectivity within global networks which facilitates exchange of codified knowledge (Capello, 1999). Simmie (2006, 178) notes that 'local agglomeration economies are still important', adding that city size provides the kinds of assets required by innovating firms.

Innovation, as measured by patents and competitive exports, is more concentrated in relation to population in large cities (O'hUallachain, 1999; Simmie, 2006). Hilpert (2003) has identified several 'islands of innovation' in Europe, including Greater London, Greater Paris, the Amsterdam–Rotterdam corridor, the Rhine–Ruhr Area, the Rhine–Main Area around Frankfurt, the conurbations of Stuttgart and Munich, and the Milan–Turin Area, as well as Lyon and Grenoble.

In small cities, where local 'buzz' is present to a lesser degree than in large ones, firms must rely more on channels or pipelines to knowledge elsewhere (Bathelt et al., 2004). In small as well as large cities, universities act as pipelines connecting the locality to global knowledge in a variety of scientific fields (Benneworth and Hospers, 2007). However, not all urban agglomerations are equally creative, and not all urban agglomerations are sites of collective learning. Saxenian (1994, 1999) draws a sharp contrast between Silicon Valley, characterized by active networking, collective learning and continual innovation, and Route 128, where a culture of large firms was seen to be dominant, dampening knowledge-sharing and entrepreneurship.

The *entrepreneurial ecosystem* of Silicon Valley favors new, small firms, but it is also a constellation of specialized enterprises with which large firms link (Bahrami and Evans, 1995). A fluid regional labor market for global talent, although somewhat less fluid since 2001, adds to the advantages of the Silicon Valley model (Kogut, 2003). Saxenian (1994) regards Boston's profile as lower, largely because its culture is more conservative and less network-rich than that of Silicon Valley, resulting in a less entrepreneurial milieu. Boston's economy, however, has remained adaptive and innovative, thanks to strong universities which create and maintain both human capital and global links (Bathelt, 2001; Glaeser, 2005).

To what extent can the model of Silicon Valley and its processes of entrepreneurship and innovation be transferred to other places? The economic factors that give rise to the start of a cluster can be very different from those that maintain it. Agglomeration economies, external effects and increasing returns arise 'almost naturally' after a cluster has taken off. The more difficult task – and the most risky – is to get new clusters started. At that stage, 'old economy' factors such as firm-building capabilities, managerial skills, a substantial supply of skilled labor and connection to markets were critical for the take-off of 'new economy' clusters, including Silicon Valley in 1970. These initial factors are different from those that keep an entrepreneurial ecosystem going (Bresnahan et al., 2001).

Silicon Valley's labor market is unlike that in other regions of the USA. Intraregional mobility of engineers is high only in Silicon Valley; in other regions, the internal labor markets of large corporations dominate (Almeida and Kogut, 1999). Power and Lundmark (2004) find similar mobility within the ICT cluster of Stockholm. Contrast this picture of knowledge flows with that of high-tech firms in a mature industry in which firms are multinational and plants are large. McCann and Arita (2006) show that the clusters in the semiconductor industry's 'industrial complex' clusters are intended to keep knowledge from flowing out. In such complexes, labor mobility is low.

Universities: Key Institutions of Technology Clusters

Universities are central to the development of technology clusters because the creation of knowledge is fundamental to research in universities and research institutes. The determination of which universities are 'major' has been aided by the Academic Ranking of World Universities prepared annually since 2003 by the Graduate School of Education, Shanghai Jiao Tong University.[4] This ranking, more comprehensive and with a more transparent methodology than most, has been very influential (Deem et al., 2008). Most significantly, it stresses the fact that not all universities are first-rank, that some are better than others, and that the NIS under which a university operates is powerfully influential on its status.

Castells and Hall (1994, 231) identify three functions of universities in the development of a technology cluster. First, the most important role is to generate new knowledge, both basic and applied. Second, universities train the labor force of scientists, engineers and technicians, who are the key ingredients for the growth of new technologies. Third, universities may play a direct entrepreneurial role, supporting the spin-off of their research into the local network of firms and NTBFs. The highly knowledge-intensive environments of major research universities present opportunities for entrepreneurship (Audretsch et al., 2006). Setting up a university-based industrial park or incubator is an example of this role. Another is for universities to allow and encourage their faculty members to set up new firms, whether by leaving the university to start a company, or by working part-time in both worlds. In either case, spin-off firms act as a knowledge bridge between universities and firms (Benneworth and Charles, 2005).

Together with government and industry, universities form a *triple helix* of interaction to create a support structure for firm formation and regional growth. 'Collective entrepreneurship' takes place through collaboration among university, industry and government actors. The result is a self-sustaining dynamic in which industrial actors become increasingly prominent in the formation of new firms (Etzkowitz and Klofsten, 2005).

Smilor et al. (2007) illustrate the emergence of high-tech clusters in three US regions: San Diego, North Carolina's Research Triangle and Austin, Texas. In all three cases, they identify a planned and coordinated strategy to economic development, centered around one or more major research universities. De Laurentis (2006) found that strong university involvement and an active business sector matched local, regional and national government efforts in both Cambridge, UK and Stockholm. Because of their key role as creators of knowledge and of human capital, universities are central to the technology-based policies of nations and regions.

The Importance of Venture Capital

A technology cluster must include opportunities for new firms to exploit technological opportunities. New firms require sources of finance in order that their entrepreneurial founders are able to devote sufficient time to their new ventures. Venture capital is rooted in local networks and knowledge, providing on the one hand investment opportunities for investors and venture capital firms on behalf of investors, and on the other hand, venture capitalists providing an array of management advice and networking to entrepreneurs (Zider, 1998; Zook, 2005). Informal investors – angels as well as others – are also likely to be found within active technology clusters (Sorheim and Landström, 2001). Early access to venture capital has given Silicon Valley start-ups substantial first-mover advantage (Zhang, 2007).

Cooke et al. (2002) conclude that the research–venture capital model is present and explains innovation in all technology clusters. In some cases, public venture capital has substituted for private capital. What is most important is the level of cooperation among regional actors: higher education and research laboratories, private industry and governments at all levels. The 'American system' of technology-based entrepreneurship achieves high performance because it 'is resolutely decentralized, both geographically and economically' (Katz-Bénichou and Viens, 2005, 259). Cooke (2007b, 175) adds that, in biotechnology:

> All the best performing locations have this combination of generous public research funding by arm's-length bodies, peer-reviewed knowledge claims, venture capital and its early and late stage financial instruments, and vigorous DBFs [dedicated biotechnology firms] seeking markets for innovative and effective treatments. Notice that direct state or big pharma involvement are absent from these elements, something less well performing European economies have failed until recently to recognize.

Where private capital and a free-spirited entrepreneurial culture are absent, public venture capital can substitute for private capital in places where start-up activity is sufficiently high (Cooke et al., 2002). However, it must be integrated both to the culture of start-ups and to their need for active 'coaching' (Clarysse and Bruneel, 2007). Coaching includes a variety of non-financial support, such as screening and signaling, monitoring and support in a variety of business areas, such as strategic planning and obtaining additional financing (Maunula, 2006). Generally, the venture capital model of financing NTBFs has been unique to Silicon Valley and a few other places – mainly China, India, Israel and Taiwan – from which students and professionals have been to Silicon Valley (Saxenian, 2006). In Europe, venture capital has maintained a lower profile (Martin et al., 2002). Ties to national and local systems of innovation continue to be very influential (Petit and Quéré, 2006).

Dispersion of R&D: Centers of Excellence

The example of Silicon Valley and other knowledge-based regions has led to a 'global competition of high-tech centres' (Anttiroiko, 2004). In part, such plans are based realistically on the widespread dispersion of R&D away from large, central facilities near corporate headquarters to new locations (Boutellier et al., 2000). The locations of new R&D sites include, first, manufacturing plants and local customers in new markets; and second, the attraction of technical know-how and expertise available in only a few centers of excellence around the world.

Firms believe they must tap into many sources of expertise because knowledge is increasingly diverse and dispersed (Chesbrough, 2003). No single source – even the best in the world – is sufficient. Increasingly, technologies and lead consumers are found outside the megacenters of an industry. In order to plug into new pockets of knowledge, a firm needs a location in a cluster that is a source of knowledge. Korean and Taiwanese firms, for example, have taken advantage of the Silicon Valley's ecosystem by locating their R&D there and becoming embedded in the ecosystem (Poon et al., 2006).

Clusters in new economy sectors are found mainly in large cities and university towns, and rarely in rural areas or in industrial cities. The new economy innovation system relies more on venture capital and entrepreneurship (including serial start-ups and incubators), and much less on public sector bodies than in the 'normal' regional innovation system (Asheim and Gertler, 2005). The biotechnology sector is an example of this. There are many more 'concentrations', if not full clusters, of biotech expertise, usually located at universities and distant from the core regions and their venture capitalists and other entrepreneurial support networks (Kenney and Patton, 2005). Therefore, some emerging biotechnology and nanotechnology clusters are found outside the traditional cores of high technology (Youtie et al., 2008).

University-based clusters in small or suburban regions include Cambridge and Oxford in the UK as well as Turku, Finland. Large urban regions have many of the characteristics of Silicon Valley, such as Boston, Helsinki and Stockholm. Finally, a number of places have been the products of policy attempts to build high-tech growth, based usually on science parks and related developments.

CREATING CLUSTERS

The attempt to assemble and create the conditions for a successful, self-sustaining cluster is an example of constructed advantage (Cooke and Leydesdorff, 2006). For example, both Grenoble and Silicon Valley are examples of spontaneous clusters, yet both benefitted significantly from government research (Locke and Schöne, 2004; Malecki and Moriset, 2008). However, an absence of spontaneity has led many countries and regions to attempt to create policy-driven clusters (Chiaroni and Chiesa, 2006). Constructed or policy-driven clusters, however, still depend strongly on local conditions. In particular, it is important for a cluster not to remain dependent on government or public support. This has been difficult for cultures in which entrepreneurship is held in lower regard than in the USA, such as France and Germany (Locke and Schone, 2004).

Moreover, policy is both explicit and implicit, with both intended and unintended spatial effects. Sternberg (1996) concludes that, overall, regional disparities – that is, clusters in some places and not in others – are not reduced by policies; core regions dominate everywhere. As Chiaroni and Chiesa (2006) point out, a major problem for policy-driven clusters is how to grow in the long term, when public funding declines. The most important objective for policy should be to promote diversity and excellence in science at academic and research institutions (Autant-Bernard et al., 2006). In other cases, a combination of favorable local conditions is 'primed' by policy initiatives. This would seem to be the case with Leuven (Belgium), where several innovative clusters have developed (Hinoul, 2008).

A convergence of policies is aimed toward the same goal: to foster a larger number of academic spin-offs. However, the contrasting cases of the UK, where technology transfer was pushed as a third stream of income for universities, and of France, where policies are strictly top-down and 'attempt to create entrepreneurial universities in a system without autonomy', suggest that imitation varies greatly (Wright et al., 2007, 63).

European Silicon Valleys

The Silicon Valley phenomenon sparked a pair of reactions in Europe. The first was the early focus on technology, specifically information technology (IT). The second reaction was to the new, flexible, entrepreneurial firm model, which contrasted starkly with the model of the engineering graduate in Europe, who looked forward to a secure job in a large corporation (Locke and Schöne, 2004).

The distinctive nature of the USA also means that non-US cases are important as role models for other regions. Thus, we see Cambridge in the UK as an exemplar, beginning with 'The Cambridge Phenomenon' (Segal Quince Wicksteed, 1985; Keeble et al., 1999; Koepp, 2002; Athreye, 2004). The entrepreneurial ecosystem of Grenoble, like that of Boston and Silicon Valley, is the outcome of an industrial and entrepreneurial development that began decades ago (Malecki and Moriset, 2008). Grenoble is one of seven European regional 'success stories' and one of only two (along with Cambridge) that is characterized by an absence of direct state funding (Brioschi and Cassia, 2006).

A vibrant entrepreneurial culture has grown in Grenoble from the seedbed of national laboratories and research centers, aided by proactive regional policies (De Bernardy, 1999). The success of many other start-ups shows that the region has succeeded in shifting from finance based on government funds to venture capital (Brioschi and Cassia, 2006; Lawton Smith, 2003). These have spanned the technologies from IT to nanotechnology. The high degree of specialization in a narrow, cutting-edge sector – although Grenoble also has built a presence in biotechnology (Cooke, 2004b) – gives the cluster international visibility and strengthens synergies, cooperation and spin-offs.

Based on decades of research on industrial districts in Italy and elsewhere, Paniccia (2006) identifies the science-based or technology agglomeration, which is based on venture capital and the very active role of knowledge institutions, as one of two types most able to absorb and adapt to fluctuations in the economic cycle.[5] When created in remote locations, technology clusters are unable to benefit from – or to create – 'buzz'. Likewise, their pipelines to the outside world are smaller than would be the case if located more centrally in their national territories.

Large as well as small firms are critical to technology clusters and innovation systems. Foray (2007) underscores the importance of large 'anchor tenant' (AT) firms, suggesting that they improve the links between local universities and local firms. The ATs, in turn, invest in R&D and knowledge creation, providing opportunities for entrepreneurs (Audretsch et al., 2006). For example Munich, the leading high-tech region in Germany, is characterized by large firms such as Siemens and its links with SMEs for their knowledge and research (Sternberg and Tamásy, 1999).

The Science Park Model

Science parks (also research parks and technology parks) have proliferated in attempts to imitate the successes in the USA and the success of Stanford Industrial Park (later renamed the Stanford Research Park) (Gibb, 1985). The International Association of

Science Parks (IASP) in early 2009 had 350 members in 72 countries. Macdonald and Deng (2004, 3), however, conclude that 'it would seem that the science park offers little advantage at all'.

Regions in Asia have enthusiastically created their own versions of Silicon Valley (Rowen et al., 2006). Many of the more successful ones are by US-educated Asians who can combine their cultural knowledge of their native country with an understanding of the American business model (Saxenian, 2006). Taiwan's Hsinchu region near Taipei is both a successful imitator and a partner of Silicon Valley (Saxenian, 2006; Sum, 2003). Hsinchu Science-based Industrial Park (HSIP) has become a prototype within Asia. Firms in HSIP have developed a large number of global as well as local links (Wang, 2005).

China has established a large number of science parks, with the aim of sparking learning both from multinational corporations and from local R&D (Walcott, 2003), and touts both Beijing and Shenzhen as 'China's Silicon Valley' (Sum, 2003; Zhou, 2008). China also has created dozens of 'Returning Students Science Parks' to attract foreign-educated Chinese to return home, bringing with them their contacts abroad and cross-cultural knowledge (Saxenian, 2006). India also is building technology parks to lure back native talent. The science parks and high-tech campuses that have mushroomed in the main cities of India, however, remain enclaves or 'islands' with infrastructure provided by foreign investors themselves, surrounded by its absence (Audirac, 2003).

Despite their importance as agglomerations, even the best technology clusters in China and India are not (yet) environments for collaboration and collective learning. Zhongguancun, the ICT complex in Beijing, is home to several successful firms, but is an 'environment hostile to collaboration' (Zhou, 2008, 91). Bangalore likewise falls far short in terms of the interactive learning characteristic of self-sustaining clusters and well-functioning regional innovation systems. Universities focus almost exclusively on providing qualified graduates for local firms. As a result, they play little role in supporting innovation and generating research results for local firms (Chaminade and Vang, 2008). 'Local start-ups remain distant from customers and lack the interaction and learning that characterize a local technical community' (Saxenian, 2006, 320–21).

CONCLUSIONS

The landscape of technology clusters – or what Cooke (2002) calls *knowledge economies* – will continue to be uneven, because private venture capital is so central to innovation and entrepreneurship. Public funding is able to level the playing field somewhat, by supporting the infrastructure for R&D. Therefore, few places have the network architecture, culture of innovation and entrepreneurship – an entrepreneurial regional innovation system (ERIS) – and a knowledge base to attract global companies on a scale to rival Silicon Valley (Cooke, 2008).

'There is no "complete recipe" for the replicability of successful clusters' (Breschi and Malerba, 2001, 832). Moreover, the Silicon Valley model appears to apply to a lesser degree to biotechnology, and perhaps even less to nanotechnology. Regardless of the technology, the success of a technology cluster ultimately depends on its government and institutions to demonstrate the ability to embody intelligence and ability to follow a 'high road', knowledge-based development trajectory (Komninos, 2004; Malecki, 2004).

Technology clusters are complex – complex as outcomes of scientific and technological activity, and complex as social creations of entrepreneurship, institutions and culture. The geographical pattern of technology clusters is an outcome of the location of innovative sectors and of their phases in product and profit cycles. These, in turn, create a variable geography of creativity and entrepreneurship (Iammarino and McCann, 2007). As new industries emerge, new patterns are created. However, the 'old' technology clusters and their universities and research institutions also possess the capability to create new technologies and therefore new firms, thereby remaining technology clusters in newer technologies and industries.

There remains the elusive property of synergy, or the ability for all the ingredients and actors to act as a functioning system (Castells and Hall, 1994; Simmie, 2006). The challenge to create synergy and systemic dynamics is daunting. Castells and Hall (1994) emphasize the importance of time for a technopolis to develop: at least 20 to 30 years. Both Sophia-Antipolis, near Nice, France, dubbed Telecom Valley, and the entrepreneurial clusters in IT and biotechnology in the Washington, DC region took nearly 30 years to mature into well-functioning, innovative and entrepreneurial systems (Feldman et al., 2005; Lazaric and Thomas, 2006). Notably in the Washington case, universities were absent from the process of cluster formation, demonstrating that the recipe is not inflexible.

The global recession that began in 2008 suggests that technology clusters as they evolved during the second half of the twentieth century may not be a model for the twenty-first century. Even in Silicon Valley, venture capital now is more difficult to find. For example, the managed economy may return to take precedence over the entrepreneurial economy, to use the terminology of Audretsch and Thurik (2001). Scientific research will not end and entrepreneurship to exploit opportunities will not end, but both are likely to be subject to a more 'managed' policy environment as well as less 'irrational exuberance' (Schiller, 2000).

NOTES

1. For a review of much of this early work, see Malecki (1981). For a history of the early years of Silicon Valley, see Lécuyer (2006).
2. For example, titles include: *Silicon Valley Fever* (Rogers and Larsen, 1984), *Growing the Next Silicon Valley* (Miller and Coté, 1987), *The Silicon Valley Edge* (Lee et al., 2000), *Understanding Silicon Valley* (Kenney, 2000), *Cloning Silicon Valley* (Rosenberg, 2002), *Clusters of Creativity* (Koepp, 2002), *Building High-Tech Clusters: Silicon Valley and Beyond* (Bresnahan and Gambardella, 2004).
3. A longer list includes 17 bioscience clusters, including three clusters in the USA (Boston, San Francisco and San Diego), two in Canada (Toronto and Montreal), four in Germany (Munich, Berlin, Rhine Neckar – Heidelberg, and Rhineland), two in Sweden (Stockholm–Uppsala and Lund–Medicon), three in the UK (Cambridge, Oxford and Scotland), as well as Zurich, Singapore and Jerusalem (Cooke, 2007a, Table 11). A later list (Cooke, 2007b) adds Paris (Evry) and three others in the USA (Washington, DC, Raleigh-Durham and Seattle).
4. http://ed.sjtu.edu.cn/en/.
5. The other is the canonical industrial district, found mainly among the family-based firms in Italy.

REFERENCES

Almeida, P. and B. Kogut (1999), 'Localization of knowledge and the mobility of engineers in regional networks', *Management Science*, **45**, 905–17.

Anttiroiko, A.-V. (2004), 'Editorial: global competition of high-tech centres', *International Journal of Technology Management*, **28**, 289–323.

Asheim, B., P. Cooke and R. Martin (2006), 'The rise of the cluster concept', in B. Asheim, P. Cooke and R. Martin (eds), *Clusters and Regional Development: Critical Reflections and Explorations*, London: Routledge, pp. 1–29.

Asheim, B. and M.S. Gertler (2005), 'The geography of innovation: regional innovation systems', in J. Fagerberg, D.C. Mowery and R.R. Nelson (eds), *The Oxford Handbook of Innovation*, Oxford: Oxford University Press, pp. 291–317.

Athreye, S. (2004), 'Agglomeration and growth: a study of the Cambridge hi-tech cluster', in T. Bresnahan and A. Gambardella (eds), *Building High-Tech Clusters: Silicon Valley and Beyond*, Cambridge: Cambridge University Press, pp. 121–59.

Audirac, I. (2003), 'Information-age landscapes outside the developed world', *Journal of the American Planning Association*, **69**, 16–32.

Audretsch, D.B., M.C. Keilbach and E.E. Lehmann (2006), *Entrepreneurship and Economic Growth*, Oxford: Oxford University Press.

Audretsch, D.B. and A.R. Thurik (2001), 'What's new about the new economy? Sources of growth in the managed and entrepreneurial economies', *Industrial and Corporate Change*, **10**, 267–315.

Autant-Bernard, C., V. Mangematin and N. Massard (2006), 'Creation of biotech SMEs in France', *Small Business Economics*, **26**, 173–87.

Avenel, E., A.V. Favier, S. Ma, V. Mangematin and C. Rieu (2007), 'Diversification and hybridization in firm knowledge bases in nanotechnologies', *Research Policy*, **36**, 864–70.

Bahrami, H. and S. Evans (1995), 'Flexible re-cycling and high-technology entrepreneurship', *California Management Review*, **37** (3), 62–89.

Bathelt, H. (2001), 'Regional competence and economic recovery: divergent growth paths in Boston's high technology economy', *Entrepreneurship and Regional Development*, **13**, 287–314.

Bathelt, H., A. Malmberg and P. Maskell (2004), 'Clusters and knowledge: local buzz, global pipelines and the process of knowledge creation', *Progress in Human Geography*, **28**, 31–56.

Benneworth, P. and D. Charles (2005), 'University spin-off policies and economic development in less successful regions: learning from two decades of policy practice', *European Planning Studies*, **13**, 537–57.

Benneworth, P. and G.-J. Hospers (2007), 'The new economic geography of old industrial regions: universities as global–local pipelines', *Environment and Planning C: Government and Policy*, **25**, 779–802.

Best, M.H. (2000), 'Silicon Valley and the resurgence of Route 128: systems integration and regional innovation', in J.H. Dunning (ed.), *Regions, Globalization, and the Knowledge-Based Economy*, Oxford: Oxford University Press, pp. 459–84.

Bhidé, A. (2008), *The Venturesome Economy: How Innovation Sustains Prosperity in a More Connected World*, Princeton, NJ: Princeton University Press.

Boutellier, R., O. Gassmann and M. von Zedtwitz (2000), *Managing Global Innovation*, Berlin: Springer.

Breschi, A. and F. Malerba (2001), 'The geography of innovation and economic clusterings: some introductory notes', *Industrial and Corporate Change*, **10**, 817–33.

Bresnahan, T. and A. Gambardella (eds) (2004), *Building High-Tech Clusters: Silicon Valley and Beyond*, Cambridge: Cambridge University Press.

Bresnahan, T., A. Gambardella, A. Saxenian and S. Wallsten (2001), '"Old economy" inputs for "new economy" outcomes: cluster formation in the new Silicon Valleys', Stanford Institute for Economic Policy Research (SIEPR) Discussion Paper No. 00-43, Stanford University, CA, USA.

Brioschi, M.S. and L. Cassia (2006), 'Common trajectories of regional competitiveness in the knowledge economy: a European investigation', *Industry and Innovation*, **20**, 387–401.

Capello, R. (1999), 'Spatial transfer of knowledge in high technology milieux: learning versus collective learning processes', *Regional Studies*, **33**, 353–65.

Castells, M. and P. Hall (1994), *Technopoles of the World: The Making of 21st Century Industrial Complexes*, London: Routledge.

Chaminade, C. and J. Vang (2008), 'Globalisation of knowledge production and regional innovation policy: supporting specialized hubs in the Bangalore software industry', *Research Policy*, **37**, 1684–96.

Chesbrough, H.W. (2003), *Open Innovation: The New Imperative for Creating and Profiting from Technology*, Boston, MA: Harvard Business School Press.

Chiaroni, D. and V. Chiesa (2006), 'Forms of creation of industrial clusters in biotechnology', *Technovation*, **26**, 1064–76.

Clarysse, B. and J. Bruneel (2007), 'Nurturing and growing innovative start-ups: the role of policy as integrator', *R&D Management*, **37**, 139–49.

Cooke, P. (2002), *Knowledge Economies: Clusters, Learning and Cooperative Advantage*, London: Routledge.

Cooke, P. (2004a), 'The molecular biology revolution and the rise of bioscience megacentres in North America and Europe', *Environment and Planning C: Government and Policy*, **22**, 161–77.

Cooke, P. (2004b), 'The accelerating evolution of biotechnology clusters', *European Planning Studies*, **12**, 915–20.

Cooke, P. (2005), 'Regionally asymmetric knowledge capabilities and open innovation: exploring "Globalisation 2" – a new model of industry organization', *Research Policy*, **34**, 1128–49.

Cooke, P. (2007a), 'European asymmetries: a comparative analysis of German and UK biotechnology clusters', *Science and Public Policy*, **34**, 454–74.

Cooke, P. (2007b), *Growth Cultures: The Global Bioeconomy and its Bioregions*, London: Routledge.

Cooke, P. (2008), 'Regional innovation systems, clean technology and Jacobian cluster-platform policies', *Regional Science Policy and Practice*, **1**, 23–45.

Cooke, P., C. Davies and R. Wilson (2002), 'Innovation advantages of cities: from knowledge to equity in five basic steps', *European Planning Studies*, **10**, 233–50.

Cooke, P., C. De Laurentis, F. Tödtling and M. Trippl (2007), *Regional Knowledge Economies: Markets, Clusters and Innovation*, Cheltenham, UK and Northampton, MA, USA: Edward Elgar.

Cooke, P. and L. Leydesdorff (2006), 'Regional development in the knowledge-based economy: the construction of advantage', *Journal of Technology Transfer*, **31**, 5–15.

Cooper, A.C. (1971), 'Spin-offs and technical entrepreneurship', *IEEE Transactions on Engineering Management*, **18** (1), 2–6.

Cooper, A.C. and A.V. Bruno (1977), 'Success among high-technology firms', *Business Horizons*, **20** (2), 16–22.

Cooper, A. and T. Folta (2000), 'Entrepreneurship and high-technology clusters', in D.L. Sexton and H. Landström (eds), *The Blackwell Handbook of Entrepreneurship*, Oxford: Blackwell, pp. 348–67.

Cooper, A.C. and J.L. Komives (eds) (1972), *Technical Entrepreneurship: A Symposium*, Milwaukee: Center for Venture Management.

Darby, M.R. and L.G. Zucker (2003), 'Grilichesian breakthroughs: inventions of methods of inventing and firm entry in nanotechnology', NBER Working Paper No. 9825, Cambridge, MA: National Bureau of Economic Research.

De Bernardy, M. (1999), 'Reactive and proactive local territory: co-operation and community in Grenoble', *Regional Studies*, **33**, 343–52.

Deem, R., K.H. Mok and L. Lucas (2008), 'Transforming higher education in whose image? Exploring the concept of the 'world-class' university in Europe and Asia', *Higher Education Policy*, **21** (1), 83–97.

De Laurentis, C. (2006), 'Regional innovation systems and the labour market: a comparison of five regions', *European Planning Studies*, **14**, 1059–84.

Di Tommaso, M.R., D. Paci, L. Rubini and S.O. Schweitzer (2006), 'Is distance dead? High-tech clusters, analysis and policy perspectives', in C. Pitelis, R. Sugden and J.R. Wilson (eds), *Clusters and Globalisation: The Development of Urban and Regional Economies*, Cheltenham, UK and Northampton, MA, USA: Edward Elgar, pp. 281–308.

Dorfman, N.S. (1983), 'Route 128: the development of a regional high technology economy', *Research Policy*, **12**, 299–316.

Etzkowitz, H. (2002), *MIT and the Rise of Entrepreneurial Science*, London: Routledge.

Etzkowitz, H. (2003), 'Research groups as "quasi-firms": the invention of the entrepreneurial university', *Research Policy*, **32**, 109–21.

Etzkowitz, H. and M. Klofsten (2005), 'The innovating region: toward a theory of knowledge-based regional development', *R&D Management*, **35**, 243–55.

Feldman, M.P. (2000), 'Where science comes to life: university bioscience, commercial spin-offs, and regional economic development', *Journal of Comparative Policy Analysis*, **2**, 345–61.

Feldman, M.P., J. Francis and J. Bercovitz (2005), 'Creating a cluster while building a firm: entrepreneurs and the formation of industrial clusters', *Regional Studies*, **39**, 129–41.

Folta, T.B., A.C. Cooper and Y. Baik (2006), 'Geographic cluster size and firm performance', *Journal of Business Venturing*, **21**, 217–42.

Foray, D. (2007) 'University–industry knowledge transfer in Switzerland', in S. Yusuf and K. Nabeshima (eds), *How Universities Promote Economic Growth*, Washington, DC: World Bank, pp. 47–70.

Gibb, J.M. (ed.) (1985), *Science Parks and Innovation Centres: Their Economic and Social Impact*, Amsterdam: Elsevier.

Glaeser, E.L. (2005), 'Reinventing Boston, 1630–2003', *Journal of Economic Geography*, **5**, 119–53.

Hall, P. and A. Markusen (eds) (1985), *Silicon Landscapes*, London: Allen & Unwin.

Henry, N. and S. Pinch (2006), 'Knowledge and clusters', in C. Pitelis, R. Sugden and J.R. Wilson (eds), *Clusters and Globalisation: The Development of Urban and Regional Economies*, Cheltenham, UK and Northampton, MA, USA: Edward Elgar, pp. 114–32.

Hilpert, U. (2003), 'Globalisation and selective localisation of industry and innovation: the role of government in regionalising socio-economic development', in U. Hilpert (ed.), *Regionalisation of Globalised Innovation: Locations for Advanced Industrial Development and Disparities in Participation*, London: Routledge, pp. 3–28.

Hinoul, M. (2008), 'Creating the dynamic technology region: the knowledge pearl Leuven – Flanders', in W. Hulsink and H. Dons (eds), *Pathways to High-Tech Valleys and Research Triangles*, Berlin: Springer, pp. 99–116.

Hulsink, W., D. Manuel and H. Bouwman (2008), 'Clustering in IT: from Route 128 to Silicon Valley, from DEC to Google, from hardware to content', in W. Hulsink and H. Dons (eds), *Pathways to High-Tech Valleys and Research Triangles*, Berlin: Springer, pp. 53–77.

Iammarino, S. and P. McCann (2007), 'The structure and evolution of industrial clusters: transactions, technology and knowledge spillovers', *Research Policy*, **35**, 1018–36.

Katz-Bénichou, G. and G. Viens (2005), 'High-technology clusters in France: two unusual models – an empiric study', in M.R. Di Tommaso and S.O. Schweitzer (eds), *Health Policy and High-Tech Industrial Development*, Cheltenham, UK and Northampton, MA, USA: Edward Elgar, pp. 258–77.

Keeble, D., C. Lawson, B. Moore and F. Wilkinson (1999), 'Collective learning processes, networking and "institutional thickness" in the Cambridge region', *Regional Studies*, **33**, 319–32.

Kenney, M. (ed.) (2000), *Understanding Silicon Valley: The Anatomy of an Entrepreneurial Region*, Stanford, CA: Stanford University Press.

Kenney, M. and U. von Burg (1999), 'Technology and path dependence: the divergence between Silicon Valley and Route 128', *Industrial and Corporate Change*, **8** (1), 67–103.

Kenney, M. and D. Patton (2005), 'Entrepreneurial geographies: support networks in three high-technology industries', *Economic Geography*, **81**, 201–28.

Kleverick, A.K., R.C. Levin, R.R. Nelson and S.G. Winter (1995), 'On the sources and significance of inter-industry differences in technological opportunities', *Research Policy*, **24**, 185–205.

Koepp, R. (2002), *Clusters of Creativity: Enduring Lessons on Innovation and Entrepreneurship from Silicon Valley and Europe's Silicon Fen*, Chichester: John Wiley.

Kogut, B. (2003), 'The Internet has borders', in B. Kogut (ed.), *The Global Internet Economy*, Cambridge, MA: MIT Press, pp. 1–40.

Komninos, N. (2004), 'Regional intelligence: distributed localised information systems for innovation and development', *International Journal of Technology Management*, **28**, 483–506.

Lawton Smith, H. (2003), 'Knowledge organizations and local economic development: the cases of Oxford and Grenoble', *Regional Studies*, **37**, 899–909.

Lazaric, N. and C. Thomas (2006) 'The coordination and codification of knowledge inside a network, or the building of an epistemic community: the Telecom Valley case study', in W. Dolfsma and L. Soete (eds), *Understanding the Dynamics of a Knowledge Economy*, Cheltenham, UK and Northampton, MA, USA: Edward Elgar, pp. 129–56.

Lécuyer, C. (2006), *Making Silicon Valley: Innovation and the Growth of High Tech, 1930–1970*, Cambridge, MA: MIT Press.

Lee, M.-C., W.F. Miller, M.G. Hancock and H.S. Rowen (eds) (2000), *The Silicon Valley Edge: A Habitat for Innovation and Entreprenership*, Stanford, CA: Stanford University Press.

Locke, R.R. and K. Schöne (2004), *The Entrepreneurial Shift: Americanization in European High-Technology Management Education*, Cambridge: Cambridge University Press.

Macdonald, S. and Y. Deng (2004), 'Science parks in China: a cautionary exploration', *International Journal of Technology Intelligence and Planning*, **1**, 1–14.

Malecki, E.J. (1981), 'Science, technology and regional economic development: review and prospects', *Research Policy*, **10**, 312–34.

Malecki, E.J. (2004), 'Jockeying for position: what it means and why it matters to regional development policy when places compete', *Regional Studies*, **38**, 1101–20.

Malecki, E.J. and B. Moriset (2008), *The Digital Economy: Business Organization, Production Processes and Regional Developments*, London: Routledge.

Martin, R., P. Sunley and D. Turner (2002), 'Taking risks in regions: the geographical anatomy of Europe's emerging venture capital market', *Journal of Economic Geography*, **2**, 121–50.

Maskell, P., H. Eskelinen, I. Hannibalsson, A. Malmberg and E. Vatne (1998), *Competitiveness, Localised Learning and Regional Development: Specialisation in Small Open Economies*, London: Routledge.

Matthiessen, C.W., A.W. Schwarz and S. Find (2006), 'World cities of knowledge: research strength, networks and nodality', *Journal of Knowledge Management*, **10** (5), 14–25.

Maunula, M. (2006), 'The perceived value-added of venture capital investors: evidence from Finnish bio-technology industry', Discussion papers 1030, Helsinki: The Research Institute of the Finnish Economy (ETLA), www.etla.fi/files/1556_Dp1030.pdf.

McCann, P. and T. Arita (2006), 'Clusters and regional development: some cautionary observations from the semiconductor industry', *Information Economics and Policy*, **18**, 157–80.

Miller, R. and M. Coté (1987), *Growing the Next Silicon Valley*, Lexington, MA: Lexington Books.

Miyazaki, K. and N. Islam (2007), 'Nanotechnology systems of innovation: an analysis of industry and academia research activities', *Technovation*, **27**, 661–75.

Moodysson, J. (2008) 'Principles and practices of knowledge creation: on the organization of "buzz" and "pipelines" in life science communities', *Economic Geography*, **84**, 449–69.

Mowery, D.C. and B.N. Sampat (2005), 'Universities in national innovation systems', in J. Fagerberg, D.C. Mowery and R.R. Nelson (eds), *The Oxford Handbook of Innovation*, Oxford: Oxford University Press, pp. 209–39.

O'hUallachain, B. (1999), 'Patent places: size matters', *Journal of Regional Science*, **39**, 613–36.

Paniccia, I. (2006), 'Cutting through the chaos: towards a new typology of industrial districts and clusters', in B. Asheim, P. Cooke and R. Martin (eds), *Clusters and Regional Development: Critical Reflections and Explorations*, London: Routledge, pp. 90–114.

Petit, P. and M. Quéré (2006), 'The "industrialization" of venture capital: new challenges for intermediation issues', *International Journal of Technology Management*, **34**, 126–45.

Poon, J.H., J.-Y. Hsu and S. Jeongwook (2006), 'The geography of learning and knowledge acquisition among Asian latecomers', *Journal of Economic Geography*, **6**, 541–59.

Porter, M. (2000), 'Location, clusters, and company strategy', in G.L. Clark, M.P. Feldman and M.S. Gertler (eds), *The Oxford Handbook of Economic Geography*, Oxford: Oxford University Press, pp. 253–74.

Power, D. and M. Lundmark (2004), 'Working through knowledge pools: labour market dynamics, the transference of knowledge and ideas, and industrial clusters', *Urban Studies*, **41**, 1025–44.

Roberts, E.B. (1991), *Entrepreneurs in High Technology: Lessons from MIT and Beyond*, Oxford: Oxford University Press.

Roberts, E.B. and H.A. Wainer (1968), 'New enterprises on Route 128', *Science Journal*, **4** (December), 78–83.

Robinson, D.K.R., A. Rip and V. Mangematin (2007), 'Technological agglomeration and the emergence of clusters and networks in nanotechnology', *Research Policy*, **36**, 871–9.

Rodriguez-Pose, A. (1999), 'Innovation prone and innovation averse societies: economic performance in Europe', *Growth and Change*, **30**, 75–105.

Rogers, E.M. and J.K. Larsen (1984), *Silicon Valley Fever: Growth of High-Technology Culture*, New York: Basic Books.

Rosenberg, D. (2002), *Cloning Silicon Valley: The Next Generation High-tech Hotspots*, London: Reuters.

Rowen, H.S., M.G. Hancock and W.F. Miller (eds) (2006), *Making IT: The Rise of Asia in High Tech*, Stanford, CA: Stanford University Press.

Saxenian, A. (1985), 'The genesis of Silicon Valley', in P. Hall and A. Markusen (eds) *Silicon Landscapes*, London: Allen & Unwin, pp. 20–4.

Saxenian, A. (1994), *Regional Advantage: Culture and Competition in Silicon Valley and Route 128*, Cambridge, MA: Harvard University Press.

Saxenian, A. (1999), 'Comment on Kenney and Von Burg, "Technology, entrepreneurship and path dependence: industrial clustering in Silicon Valley and Route 128"', *Industrial and Corporate Change*, **8**, 105–10.

Saxenian, A. (2006), *The New Argonauts: Regional Advantage in a Global Economy*, Cambridge, MA: Harvard University Press.

Schiller, R.J. (2000), *Irrational Exuberance*, Princeton, NJ: Princeton University Press.

Segal Quince Wicksteed (1985), *The Cambridge Phenomenon: The Growth of High Technology in a University Town*, Cambridge: Segal Quince Wicksteed.

Simmie, J. (2006), 'Do clusters or innovation systems drive competitiveness?', in B. Asheim, P. Cooke and R. Martin (eds), *Clusters and Regional Development: Critical Reflections and Explorations*, London: Routledge, pp. 164–87.

Smilor, R.W., G. Kozmetsky and D.V. Gibson (eds) (1988), *Creating the Technopolis*, Cambridge, MA: Ballinger.

Smilor, R., N. O'Donnell, G. Stein and R.S. Wellborn (2007), 'The research university and the development of high-technology centers in the United States', *Economic Development Quarterly*, **21**, 203–22.

Sorheim, R. and H. Landström (2001), 'Informal investors – a categorization, with policy implications', *Entrepreneurship and Regional Development*, **13**, 351–70.

St John, C.H. and R.W. Pouder (2006), 'Technology clusters versus industry clusters: resources, networks, and regional advantages', *Growth and Change*, **37**, 141–71.

Sternberg, R. (1996), 'Government R&D expenditure and space: empirical evidence from five industrialized countries', *Research Policy*, **25**, 741–58.

Sternberg, R. and C. Tamásy (1999), 'Munich as Germany's no. 1 high technology region: empirical evidence, theoretical explanations and the role of small firm/large firm relationships', *Regional Studies*, **33**, 367–77.

Sum, N.-L. (2003), '(Re-)Imagining "Greater China": Silicon Valley and the strategy of siliconization', in C.R. Hughes and G. Wacker (eds), *China and the Internet: Politics of the Digital Leap Forward*, London: RutledgeCurzon, pp. 102–26.

Walcott, S.M. (2003), *Chinese Science and Technology Industrial Parks*, Aldershot: Ashgate.

Wang, W.-C. (2005), 'Glob@lizing the network economy: local advantage for high-technology development', in A. Lagendijk and P. Oinas (eds), *Proximity, Distance and Diversity: Issues on Economic Interaction and Local Development*, Aldershot: Ashgate, pp. 169–89.

Wright, M., B. Clarysse, P. Mustar and A. Lockett (2007), *Academic Entrepreneurship in Europe*, Cheltenham, UK and Northampton, MA, USA : Edward Elgar.

Youtie, J., M. Iacopetta and S. Graham (2008), 'Assessing the nature of nanotechnology: can we uncover an emerging general purpose technology?', *Journal of Technology Transfer*, **33**, 315–29.

Zhang, J. (2007), 'Access to venture capital and the performance of venture-backed start-ups in Silicon Valley', *Economic Development Quarterly*, **21**, 124–47.

Zhou, Y. (2008), *The Inside Story of China's High-Tech Industry: Making Silicon Valley in Beijing*, Lanham, MD: Rowman & Littlefield.

Zider, B. (1998), 'How venture capital works', *Harvard Business Review*, **76** (6), 131–9.

Zook, M.A. (2005), *The Geography of the Internet Industry: Venture Capital, Dot-Coms, and Local Knowledge*, Oxford: Blackwell.

PART V

REGIONAL WORLDS OF INNOVATION

Introduction

Philip Cooke and Dafna Schwartz

CONVENTIONS AND CONTEXT

A substantial portion of innovation research and practice is focused upon new technology businesses. This is not surprising since, increasingly, entrepreneurship is the handmaiden of commercialized recombined new and existing knowledge, as Schumpeter (Mark 1) correctly observed. Intellectually, the transformation of, for example, laboratory discoveries of genetic sequences and associated molecules that may interrupt or prevent disease into therapeutic treatments by dedicated biotechnology firms is interesting for three reasons. First, it shows how the most advanced science-based research is now often to be found in the laboratories of research institutes inside leading research universities rather than corporate laboratories. This represents a geographical shift in the centre of gravity of 'translational' knowledge in the life sciences, which attracts agglomerations of entrepreneurial businesses as innovation systems theorems predict. However it does not do so uniformly, which hints at crucial qualitative elements that need to be teased out of the data to explain the marked spatial unevenness of contemporary knowledge dynamics (see also Isaksen's Chapter 22 on 'Cluster evolution' in this *Handbook*).

Second, new agglomerations of the kind under inspection tend to be exemplars of clustering, embracing the collaborative networking based on high-trust learning and associated social capital that exercises many of the accounts in the preceding sections of this *Handbook*. Accordingly, new organizational forms and mechanisms of communication of cumulative and combinative knowledge – external to the corporate management confines of the large or multinational firm – come into play. Whereas large corporations are universally understood to have competitive advantage because their legal and administrative conventions, identity and path-dependence lends them their 'corporate culture', clusters have to work out their conventions by trial and error. This can involve 'translation' issues, negotiation of meanings in 'transition zones' among scientists, investors and entrepreneurs that are managed through corporate divisions of labour within frameworks of shared meanings acquired by practice and in-house training in the large corporation.

Yet, for all such potential pitfalls, innovation is often more efficient and effective in clusters than corporations, otherwise they would not thrive. This hints further at some key advantages of agglomeration for knowledge economy innovation which seem to include: externalized, Marshallian 'in the air' or 'cloud-type' knowledge access advantage; relational commitments substituting for formalized transactions; and increasing returns to learning yielding greater creativity than scaleable corporate efficiency.

Finally, chapters in this *Handbook* on the competitive strategies of neo-Marshallian clusters by Bellandi (Chapter 6) and Belussi (Chapter 7) remind us that learning is also organizational in that regional competitiveness (Martin, Chapter 18) depends upon innovative versatility, agility and flexibility towards meeting customer needs. For many such product and process innovations, the research literature (for example Sydow et al., cited in Martin, Chapter 15) reveals such clusters to be substantially less path-dependent and prone to mission 'lock-in' than corporations.

In Chapter 25, the first chapter in of Part V on 'Regional Worlds of Innovation', Peter Sunley frames propositions such as these according to the well-known Storper and Salais 'worlds of production' grid. Crucially, however, Sunley proceeds to push beyond its categories to explore the conventions and production culture implications of the approach in an illuminating critique. As will become clear, the chapter is an organizational prelude to a number of chapters that explore changing 'worlds of innovation' in sectors such as services, culture and processes such as 'open innovation' that are less commonly analysed in regional innovation studies than are new or advanced manufacturing. In brief, the worlds of production approach went beyond the binary cluster–corporation organizational contrast adumbrated above, to demonstrate a further two dimensions to the debate, arguing for diversity in multiple pathways to modern industrial organization through distinctive models of coordination (Carrincazeaux and Coris, Chapter 20, this *Handbook*) based on conventions that enhance collective communication and cognition.

Production (and associated innovations) can be standardized or specialized, as delineated above, but the extra dimensions proposed are that they can be dedicated or generic. The four resulting cells of production occupy different worlds, the specialized and dedicated product being highly uncertain and reliant on untraded (trust, discretion and so on) interdependencies between customer and supplier. Contrariwise, the standardized and generic product sells to a mass market mainly competitive on price. The grid is really a set of four cost–quality resolution vectors. Is it useful to the project of understanding key tensions and their conceivably impermanent solvents in regional innovation and growth? As with all ideal types, it is informative but rigid; hence it is not clear whether for firms the categories are path-determined or capable of mutation, and how the latter might work. There is reference to firm experimentation to settle on appropriate production conventions but the evolutionary mechanisms and whether or not (re)location is involved are not explored.

Nevertheless, different regions are said to possess the requisite conventions and culture for each 'world of production', and 'lucky' are those with highly 'relational' regional regimes (equivalent to 'cloud-type' settings above). This implies that as the global innovation paradigm becomes more knowledge-intensive, relational regional regimes are absolutely advantaged, which is at least an interestingly testable proposition, which is strongly supported by, for example, research on the 'creative class'. A large measure of this advantage in a globalized knowledge economy is that Schumpeterian entrepreneurial imitation becomes almost impossible, securing regional competitiveness for innovative clusters and regions in the face of 'global shift'. The study of innovation can potentially make important inroads into understanding varieties of regional creativity and its associated culture and conventions.

Accordingly, one of the worlds of production increasingly explored in economic geography is that of culture itself. Luciana Lazzeretti (Chapter 26 in this *Handbook*) undertakes this task, advocating an evolutionary economic methodology with a focus on explaining the production and reproduction of Flamenco in Andalusia. An important point here is that the production of culture can stimulate innovation that in the guise of creative industries can regenerate or otherwise renew geographic spaces. What context and convention makes for a hub in a global–local network of cultural econo-mies? Lazzeretti notes that for 'high cultural' hubs, it is essential to be a culturally dis-tinctive, 'paradigmatic' locale – renaissance city, Art Deco district and so on – with an institutional 'regime' that recognizes the cultural economic potential to translate the production of culture into communications, conferences, events and destinations. The key conventions are sensibilities to specific heritage, framing of experience and project-ing of learning opportunities. This represents a transition in conventions from 'economic enhancement of culture' (culture as factor of production) to 'cultural enhancement of economy' (culture as creative capacity). Within the latter, certain practices occur that represent a convention of openness to improvization: for example, co-location of optical physics and art restoration in Florence cross-fertilized 'episodic' radical innovation in laser cleaning instrumentation. By contrast, the Andalusian Flamenco 'brotherhoods' and 'fraternities', framed by a context of 'sacred and profane' festival culture, are closed and display high social capital but mainly incremental, organizational innovation. For example, foundations and institutions to preserve, learn and reproduce traditions would be a case in point.

INNOVATION IN SERVICE INDUSTRIES

If 'closed societies' represent excellent starting points for understanding the distinctive-ness of particular production cultures in geographic space, the difficulties of penetrat-ing them for research purposes need also to be understood. Yuko Aoyama and Rory Horner's Chapter 27 in this *Handbook* on service innovation is more a case of exploring *terra incognita*, so little has there been investigation of this largest part of most econo-mies in the relevant literature. Their chapter is a valuable review of the existing service innovation literature, which contains relatively little on regional services innovation. This is tackled in the succeeding Chapter 28, where some interesting and important comparisons on levels and types of regional services innovation are presented. Chapter 27 reviews the literature that has discovered service industry innovates in branding advertising and financial intermediation; it also expends research budgets in conducting various kinds of knowledge-intensive activities related to financial analysis, engineering consultancy and design-related activities (KIBS). Indeed Lazzeretti's cultural economy and creative industries were shown to be capable of sustaining innovation. Measurement can be difficult and misleading since indicators were historically devised with manufac-turing in mind. Thus service innovation is measured at a tiny fraction of total research and development (R&D) in typical national statistics. Nevertheless, digital services are largely part of the 'informatization' long wave and therefore contribute to that radical overarching paradigm, though it is notable that innovations like e-commerce depend entirely on innovations from the mechanization and motorization eras for product delivery.

When we examine aspects of regional services innovation (Chapter 28 by Philip Cooke) we find a complex picture involving interesting and instructive contrasts with typical regional innovation profiles. Thus one of these is that some service industries are measured as more innovative than some engineering industries. As noted in Chapter 27, many services innovations are organizational, including budget airlines, online banking and online insurance, which all gained competitiveness by removing vast layers of administrative overhead, increasing capital productivity and identifying unserviced market segments (for example hard-to-insure drivers). Each of these fields benefited from deregulation in air transport and financial services markets; accordingly they can, to a considerable extent, be considered instances of 'supply-side driven innovation' discussed in Chapter 1, the 'Introduction' to this *Handbook*. The geography of such innovations is interesting because, on the one hand, low overhead means headquarters locations are not directly growth locations; but on the other, airports, where the service is consumed, clearly are – tourist destinations too. Moreover, such airports are as likely to be regional as national 'hubs' due to cost considerations. Also because of some degree of call-centre service associated with some such services innovation, notably in finance, low-labour-cost regions domestically and abroad benefit, contingent on language and communication skills.

One of the possibly surprising findings of a comprehensive comparison of innovation indicators across manufacturing and services is that in the UK, London is the least innovative geographical area. This has been known for some time with respect to manufacturing innovation, something that is habitually put down to its deindustrialization and 'tertiarisation' over many years. But London is also the least innovative services region in the UK, including the creative industries. Accordingly, a new picture emerges of the UK's capital city as the location of a huge density of un-innovative administrative, banking and retail jobs interspersed with a few 'village' hotspots that may gain disproportionate attention in the relevant research literature. Around London, in the East and South-East are found higher than average innovation indicators in services, especially creative and KIBS, as well as manufacturing. The broad regional profile of a metropolitan 'doughnut' of command and administration functions surrounded by a semi-rural idyll including islands of high creativity and innovativeness seems inescapable. It is also rather common, since land rents and congestion in central metropoles discourage 'cloud-type' set-ups but favour corporate and, to some extent, government administration willing and able to pay for expensive real estate. Returning momentarily to Peter Sunley's review of 'regional worlds of innovation', certain spatial conventions arise from these diverse contexts, notably the metropolis as the scene of the 'dull compulsion' of 'standardized' administrative commuting, sugared with opportunities for cultural consumption. Meanwhile, innovators and 'creatives' inhabit 'specialized' metropolitan enclaves and ex-urban satellites easily accessible for occasional face-to-face investor contact, or the same cultural consumption experience hosted by the metropolis.

OPEN, EMERGING AND GREEN INNOVATION

Moving on, and capturing one of Aoyama and Horner's Chapter 27 service industry innovations, in Chapter 29 of this *Handbook* Peter Prud'homme van Reine explores 'regional open innovation'. Open innovation involves corporate outsourcing of innovation services to knowledge-intensive clusters where firms expert in the task in hand perform the service at considerably less cost than it could be undertaken in-house by the customer corporation. It is the equivalent for manufacturing firms of outsourcing the management of their supply-chain, procurement process or design engineering requirements to consultants or other intermediaries, something in which they have been engaged since the onset of 'lean production' in the 1990s. Silicon Valley is a classic space of open innovation whose conventions are characterized by: open information flow and learning among firms and between firms and regional universities; rapid response capabilities to changing contractual market opportunities; willingness to experiment and take risks; organizational hierarchies; and ready occupational mobility. As suggested in introducing James's Chapter 19 in this *Handbook*, this is a uniquely framed 'cloud-type' learning space although elements of it have been emulated elsewhere (see Shefer and Frenkel's Chapter 38 in this *Handbook*). Open innovation can thus be intraregional or interregional.

The latter can be influenced by 'quality of place' conventions, referring to aspects including aesthetic design and architecture, high-grade natural environment, recreational facilities, the presence of a diverse set of creative people, housing conditions, smart infrastructure, vibrant city life, symbolic capital and a regional 'brand'. Yet other cases show multinationals establishing networks of entrepreneurs centred in technology hubs in several regions around the world, each hub focusing on its regional technological specialism. Alternatively corporates have mapped the main global locations of their research 'centres of excellence' onto globally excellent research regions. This strongly suggests a potential list of such locations in the convention mapping of multinational capital; talent, technology and tolerance being the main criteria.

Open innovation is merely one way in which foreign investment and regional innovation interact. In Philip Cooke and Dafna Schwartz's Chapter 30 on foreign direct investment, a number of other factors are brought into play. One of the most interesting recent features is that foreign direct investment (FDI) is increasingly conducted by micro-multinationals (as discussed in Isaksen's Chapter 22 on 'born global' small and medium-sized enterprises, or SMEs). This is not only a phenomenon whereby European or North American SMEs locate in Chinese or Indian 'quality-of-place' locations, as Chinese SMEs also increasingly locate in, for example, Italian industrial districts (numbering 3000 in Prato, near Florence, alone in 2007). The authors quote David Teece as averring that this process of cluster upgrading occurred at the behest of large foreign investors or final customers in the past. The Chinese insertion (convention displacement) into the hitherto partly-obscured 'world' of the Italian industrial district would also make an excellent 'production conventions' candidate since the Chinese seem to have been readily able not only to absorb Italian practice but also to transcend it with their own. This inverts the normal line of reasoning in FDI research which asks how FDI knowledge influences the host region by asking how regional knowledge influences FDI.

This is addressed in Scott Ptak and Sharmistha Bagchi-Sen's Chapter 31 on regional innovation in India, introducing the idea of the 'international system of innovation' to supplement it. This is not least because emerging economies find difficulties in framing these rather complex system-entities. It is well known that Indian science and technology innovation is blessed with excellent endogenous research institutions, but it benefits also for innovation in centres like Bangalore, Hyderabad and Mumbai from its 'to and fro brain drain' relationship with Silicon Valley and its technologies and venture capital expertise. This too is an interesting research candidate for studying the economic geography of regional socio-cultural conventions (convention mutation). By this point, these do not appear to pose any significant barrier to global knowledge flows, as the chapters in this section of the *Handbook* consistently show.

Finally, Chapter 32 on 'green innovation' or regional eco-innovation by Philip Cooke indicates that one way in which conventions are absorbed, reutilized and innovated is through branching from path-dependence. Some regions envision their futures according to normative frames such as 'sustainability', 'healthiness' or 'cleanliness', and are able to pursue collective learning and entrepreneurship practices that realize such visions without losing contact with their founding technologies. The evolution of regional eco-innovation systems in regions such as (once again) northern California and north Jutland, Denmark bear witness to the power of the evolutionary perspective in tracing various cluster relatedness mutations that have underpinned their accomplishments in transitioning from fully carbonized to 'green' innovation.

25 Worlds of production: conventions and the microfoundations of regional economies
Peter Sunley

INTRODUCTION

The regional worlds of production framework seeks to explain the wide and resolute diversity of regional economies. It emerged in economic geography during the 1990s and emphasized the need to understand the conventions and shared understandings that reduce uncertainty and allow economic agents to coordinate their activities. While the approach did not attract a large number of advocates, it nevertheless had a profound impact through its emphasis on the cultural dimensions of economic activity and its claim that dynamic regional economies do not benefit just from traditional agglomeration economies but also from various forms of untraded interdependencies. More recent approaches have developed and extended these important, if somewhat elusive, topics by asking how routines and conventions change through time, how they are related to individual behaviour and cognition, how they shape innovation and creativity, and how we can better integrate macro, meso and micro institutional perspectives. While the concept of worlds of production itself has not been adopted widely and explicitly developed in economic geography, it would be a mistake to think that its concerns are declining in importance and anachronistic. The difficult issues that the concept raised remain central to explaining why and how regional economies remain distinctive and why patterns of growth and regional specialization remain both pronounced and fine-grained in a globalizing economy.

THE WORLDS OF PRODUCTION APPROACH

The worlds of production approach was partly a reaction to the notion that industrial organization was shifting from a dominant Fordist method of mass production to a new post-Fordist flexible system based on networks of small firms (see Storper and Salais, 1997). The worlds of production framework cast doubt on this view and explicitly denied that there was one best method of production organization. Instead it emphasized the increasing diversity and variety of production systems and it argued that modern capitalism allows multiple pathways to competitive advantage. Diversity is inherent because different types of product, Storper and Salais (1997) argued, require different types of production system if they are to be produced effectively and efficiently. Productive activity is collective and relies on the coordination of agents, technologies and organizations within what was termed an action framework.

These frameworks rested on the notion of conventions; indeed the worlds of production approach can to a certain degree be seen as an offshoot of the French 'economics of conventions' school. Conventions were defined as shared understandings and norms

Table 25.1   The four worlds of production

	Specialized products *Economies of variety*	Standardized products *Economies of scale*
Dedicated products *Uncertainty*	Interpersonal world	Market world
Generic products *Predictability*	Innovation model or world of intellectual resources	Industrial world

of behaviour that allow actors to reduce uncertainty about each other's decision-making (Biggart and Beamish, 2003). According to Storper (1996, 767): 'Conventions, as rules-of-thumb, constitute veritable guides to "what to do" – action frameworks – which differ from one basic kind of product to another: hence they are cognitive worlds in which actors exist.' Conventions then are the glue that allows actors to behave in a coordinated and collective manner in order to produce products of a certain agreed quality. They act to reduce cognitive distance between people's understandings and resolve the uncertainties in making and marketing a product:

> This resolution comes about, essentially, when actors generate conventions or rules of thumb, which coordinate their activities as producers and as users. Each such set of conventions describes a framework for action, different for each kind of product, which we label a world of production. The theoretical notion of a 'world' is meant to convey the inter-linkage of people, organizations, objects and ideas, with a certain indivisibility and wholeness. (ibid.)

On these foundations, the worlds of production approach also tried to identify different ideal types of production organization. These types are classified according to two dimensions of product characteristic; firstly, whether the product is standardized or specialized; and secondly whether it is generic or dedicated (see Table 25.1). On the first dimension, a standardized product is produced using widely diffused production methods, and competition around the sale of that product focuses on price. In contrast, a specialized product is made with technology and know-how that is restricted, so that competition is centred on quality. On the second dimension, a generic product has well-known characteristics and can be sold in a predictable market. A dedicated product, in contrast, is oriented towards niche markets and it is a customized product that emerges from interpersonal negotiations. Whereas generic products are subject to predictable risk, those in the dedicated category are subject to more radical uncertainty. As a consequence some worlds rely mainly on traded interdependencies while others require more untraded relationships.

Within these four worlds it is argued that combinations of conventions mesh together in a cohesive manner and are manifested in different qualities of products and different levels of organizational performance. Thus the industrial world is said to be dominated by conventions of price and efficiency, while the interpersonal world is typified by the communication of quality to clients. This demands the cultivation of relationships and loyalty, as often occurs in specialized Marshallian districts. The intellectual world, it is argued, is dominated by scientific method and distributed professional scientific virtual communities.

This categorization has seen several applications in studies of food value chains where authors have described the differing conventions and understandings of quality and markets typical of different parts of food supply chains (see Murdoch and Miele, 1999; Ponte, 2009). But in general the theory has not been extensively used in economic geography, which begs the question: why? Certainly, the definitions of specific industrial worlds are questionable. Of course, the worlds described are ideal types and it was recognized that many actual systems are hybrids of these ideal types. But the notion of a convention proved ambiguous and hard to identify empirically and their explanation seemed a little too neat and tidy.

Storper (1996) argued that the connections between conventions and products should not be drawn too tightly but, at its heart, the idea that conventions are derived from product-based action spaces seemed highly functional or dependent on a mysterious *deus ex machina*. The connections between the character of a product and its system of production seemed too close. Conventions are actually likely to be shaped by a whole range of different processes and factors including regulatory contexts, institutional regimes and workplace relationships. It seemed too simple to suggest that these cohere in a neat way around the form of the product. Storper (1996, 115) himself noted the complication that: 'There is no strict identity between product and organization – in a world of highly differentiated products, a similar group of outputs may be produced in somewhat different organizational configurations.' But what was lacking here was a clear explanation of the casual mechanisms that ensured that conventions were matched to, or concordant with, products. Storper briefly argues that there can be interaction between product demand and supply architectures: 'Products do not automatically call forth an appropriate organizational structure; in many cases, organizations have to experiment in order to find the structure that meets the requirements of products they have chosen to produce, and sometimes they fail because they are not able to get into the appropriate world' (Storper, 1997, 114). Underlying this interaction is the notion that if these become too discordant then it is impossible to produce the product, so that a particular system would disappear. So this appears to invoke an underlying evolutionary logic, but this was not explicitly developed.

REGIONAL WORLDS OF PRODUCTION

The worlds of production framework was advanced in economic geography through Storper's (1997) thesis on regional economic development. Here he developed some aspects of the product-based approach by arguing that economies are composed of three sets of fundamental social relations: technologies, organizations and territories. In some regions, as a consequence of various types of agglomeration effects, strong interdependencies emerge between these three sets of social relations and act to shape each other's trajectories and pathways of development. These agglomeration effects are of two types. The first are localized input–output relations that allow close relationships between producers and users of products and have become essential to information exchange and learning. The second are what he termed 'untraded interdependencies'. These consist of conventions and relations that permit some localities to learn more rapidly and so to become more reflexive. Thus, in this view: 'The status of the region is now not merely as a locus of true pecuniary externalities, but for the lucky regions – as sites of important stocks of relational assets' (p. 44).

While technologies and organizations are increasingly stretched across various locations, and products, firms and factor markets are geographically extensive, this approach nevertheless argued that the regional dimension of conventions was significant and becoming ever more so to the contemporary globalizing economy. Territories are made by technologies and organizations but also have important feedbacks on them. Indeed, Storper (1996, 41) suggested that territorial effects could spill across different regional industries. In his words: 'the ensemble of conventions and relations that come into existence in a territorially defined economy may cut across the array of production systems and activities found there, affecting the evolutionary pathways of a variety of sectors in a regionally or nationally common way'. However, the regional world framework idea was most widely applied to specialized clusters of particular industries, and indeed most of the examples cited are quite localized clusters (or 'interpersonal worlds') such as Silicon Valley and Italian industrial districts.

The regional world framework was appealing and was widely used as a justification for a more culturally informed approach in economic geography (see Gertler, 1997; Amin, 1999; James et al., 2008). Parts of this approach took up the rather enigmatic idea of 'relational assets' with enthusiasm, despite the fact that many economic geographers probably lacked the necessary methodological skills to study such cultural features properly. Most geographical accounts interpreted these as relationships based on trust and familiarity that ease the local exchange of tacit knowledge. This was defined as knowledge that is hard to codify and which is best exchanged through face-to-face contact. Thus it appeared to capture the hard-to-imitate, locationally sticky advantages localized in particular territories (for example, see Maskell and Malmberg, 1999). Tacit knowledge has been widely applied in attempts to explain the advantages of specialized industrial clusters. However, this interpretation of relational assets has since been questioned as the idea of localized tacit knowledge exchange has been subject to a vigorous debate in recent years. Critics have argued that tacit and codified knowledge are often inseparable and tacit knowledge is not bounded and synonymous with a local geographical scale or a certain form of geographical proximity (Boschma, 2005; Gertler, 2008; but see Carrincazeaux and Coris's Chapter 20 in this *Handbook* on the resolution of this in the French debate). Instead there has been an emphasis on the ways in which regional economies depend on global exchanges and flows of knowledge, so the picture of how relational assets shape the economic character of regional and urban economies has become more complex.

On the other hand, of course, it is important not to exaggerate the critique: if tacit knowledge exchange does depend on face-to-face contact then it will tend to have a significant local dimension. Regular personal meetings with others outside of a region or city are of course perfectly possible but they do incur a much higher cost in terms of both time and money. In addition, tacit knowledge is not the only advantage of face-to-face contact: Storper and Venables (2004) have described how it can produce 'buzz' through several interlinked motivational and psychological effects.

In hindsight, the regional version of the worlds of production thesis was interpreted in a way which narrowed its meaning. As we have seen, this account argued that the dynamic, high-growth worlds are primarily constituted by untraded interdependencies which are distinguished from traded interdependencies. The untraded variety represent social understandings and relationships that support and smooth the operations of markets and facilitate the exchange of knowledge. In this way the approach drew on economic sociology's picture of embeddedness and emphasized those social networks and non-economic factors, such as regard and friendship, which reduce the frictions of doing business and help to make markets work. Yet this focus on networks and social relationships, which has become central to relational economic geography, ironically tended to begin by distinguishing markets from their supportive social contexts. The distinction between markets and their cushioning social contexts is counterproductive as it implies that markets are in essence pure and abstract economic forces (Peck, 2005). In this way it tends to lose sight of the original insight of the conventions approach that markets are themselves socially constructed and highly diverse in their character (see also, James, Chapter 19 in this *Handbook*). In economic geography, it became more common to emphasize untraded relationships rather than look at the way in which traded and untraded are inseparable and impossible to disentangle.

The fundamental difficulty at the heart of regional world of production is that identifying the key object of study, the economic convention, is far from easy. The definition of conventions is evidently broad and, at times, conventions and relations are used interchangeably. According to Storper and Salais (1997), conventions include the practices, routines, agreements, and their associated informal and institutional forms which bind actors together through mutual expectations. This includes shared, tacit, taken-for-granted, mutually coherent norms and expectations, as well as formal institutional rules and codified standards. It also includes practices and routine actions as well as cognitive frameworks.

Given such a range, it is tempting to conclude that worlds of production are actually defined by, and consist of, institutional rules. However, the world of production approach has had an unnecessarily uneasy relationship with other institutionalist approaches. Storper (2009), for instance, believes that such approaches tend to miss the more micro-scale or bottom-up collective cultures. Martin (2000), however, notes that institutional approaches recognize the importance of both institutional arrangements, or formal organizations, as well as institutional environments which consist of rules and standards. In this view, conventions and cultures are a key part of this environment. Hodgson (2006), for instance, defines conventions simply as specific instances of institutional rules and routines, implying that regional production cultures are just one dimension of a broader institutional geography. Furthermore, Gertler (2010) has recently called for a revival of institutional approaches in economic geography based on interactions between institutional rules at various scales. This means that we need to know more about the ways in which regional institutions mediate between national frameworks and firm-level practices, and thereby shape economic activities in specific times and places. Hence the study of regional economic culture should be better connected to the ways in which national types of capitalism are persistent but also becoming more differentiated and mixed in a globalizing economy (see Christopherson, 2002; Peck and Theodore, 2007). But at the same time, the concept of an institutional rule needs careful differentiation in order to avoid conflating different types of social entity. Rodriguez-Pose and Storper (2006) show that both societies and community can provide important benefits for economies. So while conventions may be one type of institutional rule, there is nevertheless value in distinguishing different types of formal institutional rule and standards from more informal and community-based conventions and relations.

The initial industrial world of production framework emphasized dense and cohesive routines and standards and conveyed a sense of collective order and stable relations, rather than of change. Because perceptions are framed by agreed conventions, change and learning are presented as highly path-dependent (see Martin on path-dependence in Chapter 15, this *Handbook*). As Biggart and Beamish (2003, 453) note, in a conventions approach: 'the potential for coordinated human interaction pivots on both the stability and predictability of the systems within which humans reside, but the price to be paid is resistance to change'. Storper (1997), however, tried to counter this by claiming that some types of regional worlds facilitate reflexivity in which actors are aware of changes and able to respond. A learning economy is the outcome of heightened reflexivity in which actors can distance themselves from practices and shape future outcomes:

> Those firms, sectors, regions, and nations which can learn faster or better (achieving higher quality or cheaper price for a given product or service) become competitive because their knowledge is scarce and therefore cannot be immediately imitated by new entrants or transferred, via codified or formal channels, to competitor firms, regions, or nations. (Storper, 1997, 31)

On this basis, however, it is argued that there are not only different worlds of production but also distinctive worlds of innovation in which there are different types of innovation challenges (Storper, 1993, 1996). While this is intriguing and potentially important it is unlikely that different innovation systems can be derived directly from the characteristics of their products, and most work on regional innovation systems points to a wider range of institutional determinants. It is very difficult in empirical work to distinguish conventions and action frameworks that allow reflexivity from those that do not. Furthermore, the focus on conventions and collective relations inherited from dominant products seems better suited to explaining the path-dependent nature of innovation trajectories, rather than explaining how departures and radical innovations emerge. The relations between conventions and innovations certainly require more attention as it remains unclear how conventions and expectations can be simultaneously sufficiently stable to allow coordination and sufficiently flexible to construct organizational and product innovations.

Explaining how economic rules and conventions change through time is, of course, far from easy. Recent evolutionary approaches in economic geography have used a similar notion to that of conventions, namely firm routines which are understood as dispositions to generate a certain behaviour, rather than the behaviour itself (Hodgson, 2006; Hodgson and Knudsen, 2004). Some evolutionary approaches have adopted a generalized Darwinian worldview and argued that these dispositions are analogous to genes, and subject to variation, selection and replication or retention (for example, see Boschma, 2004; Boschma and Martin, 2007). This certainly offers a more dynamic model of conventions and routines and how they change, although it has its own limitations and, in particular, tends to use the metaphors of 'selection' and 'variation' to summarize a wide variety of different economic and social processes. There is also considerable ambiguity about the relations between routines and behaviour (see Becker, 2004, 2005). As a consequence, it seems that for all of their potential importance, there are a great many questions about the evolution of regional conventions and relational assets that remain unanswered.

SEARCHING FOR REGIONAL CONTEXT

Given these unresolved issues, it is appropriate that Storper (2009) has recently argued that searching for what makes regional economies different is akin to searching for 'dark matter'.[1] By this he means an elusive and not directly observable variable that can be seen to be having a significant, if poorly understood, effect. In this sense regional context or culture is deeply enmeshed with economic activity, but continues to be hard to pin down and substantiate with evidence. The ambiguities surrounding its meaning appear to have limited the amount of rigorous empirical and comparative research that unequivocally demonstrates the extent of variations in production cultures and assesses their outcomes (for an exception see Gertler, 2003, 2004). However, in recent years there has been some progress in economic geography's understanding of economic conventions and cultures, and there are now several research directions that promise to reveal more about these issues and possibly further our understanding of their formation and consequences.

First, it is striking that the worlds of production approach called for a dialogue between cognitive science and economic geography. There are signs that this dialogue is developing with the recent growth of interest in behavioural economics and its insights into the characteristics of individual economic behaviour. It is also, to a certain degree, a contextual approach as one of its core themes is situationalism – the idea that decisions are conditioned by cognitive anchors, cues, frameworks and limited information. In this perspective, economic agents make their choices and decisions on the basis of bounded rationality, imperfect information and local points of reference or anchors (Clark, 1998). Storper (2009) concludes that behavioural economics shares a number of themes with a conventions framework. First, valuable specialized information is not uniformly available but is shaped by participation in divisions of labour and by people's positions in social networks. Second, actors engage in limited search behaviour and rely heavily on reference points even when these are arbitrary and ephemeral. Third, networks affect how actors frame their preferences and choices as economic goals are significantly influenced by comparison and emulation. Most decision-making is not about maximization but it is done using heuristics or rules of thumb, and decisions are also strongly affected by the ways in which stimuli affect emotions. Together these themes suggest that agents' search behaviour, goal formation, choice and evaluation behaviours are all influenced by rules of thumb and framing that are strongly shaped by network and geographic environments.

Behavioural economics is clearly helpful in explaining the sources of non-rational behaviour and suboptimal decision-making. It also provides a series of theoretical justifications for focusing on the ways in which decision-making is related to heuristics and biases and is inherently situated and conditional. To what degree behavioural economic theory can help in the explanation of differences at an urban and regional scale is an open and pressing question, however. Some behavioural approaches seem to argue that human decision-making is everywhere the same and that deep structures in the human mind are essentially common and universal. Thus stylized behavioural tendencies are situated in the long history of human evolutionary experience rather than in positions in regional economies and divisions of labour (Strauss, 2008). Accordingly, the interaction of cultural and cognitive behavioural approaches will be far from straightforward, but it is nevertheless a dynamic and potentially important research agenda. Economic geography will need to examine how far local and regional economic differences can be explained using behavioural theories, and move beyond the fundamental but base point recognition that all economic agents are imperfectly knowledgeable, fallible, malleable and emotional.

Future progress on these agendas will need to resolve some of the ambiguities concerning the relations between cognition and behaviour that have beset cultural approaches and evolutionary economic accounts. The initial worlds of production view tended to see action as an outcome of conventions, that is, it pictured a cognitive framework as an access code that is followed to produce coordinated collective behaviour. Similarly, much of the evolutionary work on routines conceives of behaviour in terms of the enactment of collective dispositions that are only boundedly rational. But this type of explanation can suffer from infinite regress and a failure to explain the origins of routines beyond saying that they are inherited from earlier routines or copies of others' routines. Convention-based approaches are also more comfortable with boundedness in decision-making than with individual agency and entrepreneurial responses to circumstances.

More recently, however research has argued that cognition cannot be seen as primarily a gatekeeper as it is too interlinked with practice. Indeed an increasing amount of work has tried to examine how cognitive structures themselves change as a result of behaviour. For instance, the idea that learning is situated has become influential in economic geography in recent years and emphasizes the notion of learning-by-doing and learning through participation in a knowledge community or collectivity of some kind (Wenger, 1998). This perspective argues that learning occurs through participation as agents are socialized into close and dense communities at work. In some cases of course communities may be access nodes to wider circuits and global flows of knowledge (Bathelt et al., 2004). The idea of communities of practice is clearly not applicable to all types of economic activity as it is best suited to craft and skilled work, and there are rather a variety of forms of economic collectivities in which agents learn and accumulate different types of knowledge (Amin and Roberts, 2008: Gertler, 2008). But the principle that learning is situated and embodied in types of practice suggests that the relationships between conventions, routine and practice are liable to change in an interactive and reflexive manner.

Such practice-based accounts tend to emphasize that cognitive rules change as a consequence of behaviour, so that there is a recursive relationship between action and conventions. Pentland and Feldman (2005), for example, argue that there are two parts to cognitive rules: ostensive and performative. The ostensive dimension may be a standard procedure or a shared norm. The performative aspect refers to specific actions that are inherently improvizational and subject to adjustments. As a result routines may be more facilitating of change than some accounts suggest. In this view, actors may follow scripts but they can also improvise, and these 'scripted improvizations' are the sources of many innovations. It is possible that some regionally and locally based knowledge communities will have greater rates of innovation because they follow heuristics that allow greater rates of improvization and more 'mindful deviations' from established routines and ways of doing things (Garud and Karnøe, 2001). The ways in which regional and local contexts may shape the conditions for these scripted improvizations have only begun to be considered, but the approach does allow for a stronger appreciation of the iterative interactions between routines, conventions and creativity.

Despite these promising signs it is undeniable that understanding regional worlds and their implications for growth remains an immensely difficult challenge. One of the key lessons of the regional world debate is that it is highly unlikely that we will ever understand regional industrial contexts if we try to understand them in isolation from institutions at other scales and as separate from other types of context. Not only do we need to know how firms interact with their local and regional contexts, we also need to recognize that the externalization and fragmentation of many firms raises an even more complex and hard-to-trace set of effects.

As Storper (2009) argues, it is increasingly evident that this regional context is interacting in complex ways with other more distributed contexts and frameworks. However the growth of global production chains and fragmented firm networks is making the search for understanding economic cultures and conventions more, rather than less, important. One of the reasons for this is that there is often an exchange of cultures and routines between transnational firms and local economies so that global firms can absorb as well as modify regional conventions and routines. Secondly, as Gereffi et al. (2005) have argued, global value chains and networks are governed and managed in diverse ways. Some are relational and depend on negotiated contracts and mutually beneficial learning with suppliers, while others are modular and have been decomposed into codified transfer of information. But this distinction should not be overdrawn as most firm networks combine different aspects of management and governance, including the accumulation of conventional understandings, routines and cultures. Economic geographers need to know more about these conventions and knowledge within fragmented and externalized production chains and how they interrelate with conventions and routines developed at regional scales (see Chapter 35 on regional entrepreneurship and Chapter 43 on design-driven innovation in this *Handbook*).

CONCLUSIONS

In retrospect, the worlds of production and related contextual approaches widened the perspective and research agenda of regional economic geography. They raised a wide set of significant, and difficult, issues concerning the micro-features and cultures underlying the style and trajectories of regional economic growth. As I hope to have shown, for various reasons there has been a lack of research into these questions and understanding these 'regional worlds' continues to be an important challenge. However, this review suggests that the way in which these worlds are conceived needs to be refashioned and reworked. First, the notion of conventions and routines need to be understood in ways which provide more room for evolution and change as well as inertia and resistance. The literatures on evolutionary economic geography and situated learning are both potential resources for this task. Second, the insights of behavioural economics should be used to highlight key areas for study in understanding the importance of cognition and situated practice. Third, the study of regional economic cultures needs to be connected to institutional approaches in economic geography, and the artificial separation between formal organizations and collective cultures needs to be dismantled. As part of this, the interactions between regional economic cultures and conventions and the routines, expectations and understandings created by firms and by production networks need to be more carefully and thoroughly investigated.

NOTE

1. Storper uses the metaphor of astronomical 'dark matter' that is non-luminous and not directly observable, but detectable through its gravitational influence.

REFERENCES

Amin, A. (1999), 'An institutionalist perspective on regional economic development', *International Journal of Urban and Regional Research*, **23**, 365–78.

Amin, A. and Roberts, J. (eds) (2008), *Community, Economic Creativity, and Organization*, Oxford: Oxford University Press.

Bathelt, H., A. Malmberg and P. Maskell (2004), 'Clusters and knowledge: local buzz, global pipelines and the process of knowledge creation', *Progress in Human Geography*, **28**, 31–56.

Becker, M. (2004), 'Organizational routines: a review of the literature', *Industrial and Corporate Change*, **13**, 643–77.

Becker, M. (2005), 'A framework for applying organizational routines in empirical research: linking antecedents, characteristics and performance outcomes or recurrent interaction patterns', *Industrial and Corporate Change*, **14**, 817–46.

Biggart, N. and T. Beamish (2003), 'The economic sociology of conventions: habit, custom, practice, and routine in market order', *Annual Review of Sociology*, **29**, 443–64.

Boschma, R. (2004), 'Competitiveness of regions from an evolutionary perspective', *Regional Studies*, **38**, 1001–14.

Boschma, R. (2005), 'Proximity and innovation: a critical assessment', *Regional Studies*, **39**, 61–74.

Boschma, R. and R. Martin (2007), 'Constructing an evolutionary economic geography', *Journal of Economic Geography*, **7**, 537–48.

Christopherson, S. (2002), 'What do national labor market practices continue to diverge in the global economy? The missing link of investment rules', *Economic Geography*, **78**, 1–20.

Clark, G. (1998), 'Why convention dominates pension fund trustee investment decision-making', *Environment and Planning A*, **30**, 997–1015.

Garud, R. and P. Karnøe (2001), 'Path creation as a process of mindful deviation', in R. Garud and P. Karnøe (eds), *Path Dependence and Creation*, Hillsdale, NJ: Lawrence Erlbaum Associates, pp. 1–38.

Gereffi, G., J. Humphrey and T. Sturgeon (2005), 'The governance of global value chains', *Review of International Political Economy*, **12**, 78–104.

Gertler, M. (1997), 'The invention of regional culture', in R. Lee and J. Wills (eds), *Geographies of Economies*, London: Edward Arnold, pp. 47–58.

Gertler, M. (2003), 'The undefinable tacitness of being (there): tacit knowledge and the economic geography of context', *Journal of Economic Geography*, **3**, 75–99.

Gertler, M. (2004), *Manufacturing Culture: The Institutional Geography of Industrial Practice*, Oxford: Oxford University Press.

Gertler, M. (2008), 'Buzz without being there? Communities of practice in context', in A. Amin and J. Roberts (eds), *Community, Economic Creativity, and Organization*, Oxford: Oxford University Press, pp. 203–26.

Gertler, M. (2010), 'Rules of the game: the place of institutions in regional economic change', *Regional Studies*, **44**, 1–15.

James, A., R. Martin and P. Sunley (2008), 'The rise of cultural economic geography', in R. Martin and P. Sunley (eds), *Economic Geography: Critical Concepts in the Social Sciences, Volume Four The Cultural Economy*, London: Sage, pp. 3–18.

Hodgson, G. (2006), 'What are institutions?', *Journal of Economic Issues*, **40**, 1–25.

Hodgson, G. and T. Knudsen (2004), 'The firm as an interactor: firms as vehicles for habit and routines', *Journal of Evolutionary Economics*, **14**, 281–307.

Martin, R.L. (2000), 'Institutional approaches in economic geography', in E. Sheppard and T. Barnes (eds), *A Companion to Economic Geography*, Oxford: Blackwell, pp. 77–94.

Maskell, P. and A. Malmberg (1999), 'Localised learning and industrial competitiveness', *Cambridge Journal of Economics*, **23**, 167–85.

Murdoch, J. and M. Miele (1999), '"Back to nature": changing "worlds of production" in the food sector', *Sociologica Ruralis*, **39**: 465–83.

Peck, J. (2005), 'Economic sociologies in space', *Economic Geography*, **81**, 129–75.

Peck, J. and N. Theodore (2007), 'Variegated capitalism', *Progress in Human Geography*, **31**, 731–72.

Pentland, B. and M. Feldman (2005), 'Organizational routines as a unit of analysis', *Industrial and Corporate Change*, **14** (5), 1–23.

Ponte, S. (2009), 'Governing through quality: conventions and supply relations in the value chain for South African wine', *Sociologica Ruralis*, **49**, 236–57.

Rodriguez-Pose, A. and M. Storper (2006), 'Better rules or stronger communities? On the social foundations of institutional change and its economic effects', *Economic Geography*, **82**, 1–25.

Storper, M. (1993), 'Regional "worlds" of production: learning and innovation in the technology districts of France, Italy and the USA', *Regional Studies*, **27**, 433–55.

Storper, M. (1996), 'Innovation as collective action: conventions, products and technologies', *Industrial and Corporate Change*, **5**, 761–90.

Storper, M. (1997), *The Regional World: Territorial Development in a Global Economy*, New York: Guildford Press.

Storper, M. (2009), 'Regional context and global trade', *Economic Geography*, **85**, 1–21.

Storper, M. and R. Salais (1997), *Worlds of Production: The Action Frameworks of the Economy*, Cambridge MA: Harvard University Press.

Storper, M. and T. Venables (2004), 'Buzz: face-to-face contact and the urban economy', *Journal of Economic Geography*, **4**, 351–70.

Strauss, K. (2008), 'Re-engaging with rationality in economic geography: behavioural approaches and the importance of context in decision-making', *Journal of Economic Geography*, **8**, 137–56.

Wenger, E. (1998), *Communities of Practice: Learning, Meaning and Identity*, Cambridge: Cambridge University Press.

26 Culture as a source for growth and change: some evidence from cultural clusters in Andalusia
Luciana Lazzeretti

INTRODUCTION

Culture[1] in these last few years has been recognized as a flywheel of economic development (Power and Scott, 2004) in both industrialized and underdeveloped countries, and cultural clusters and districts have widely diffused in regions and cities at an international scale (Scott, 2005). In Europe this phenomenon has developed particularly due to the substantial and heterogeneous cultural, artistic, environmental and human heritage, which consistently contributes to the variety of forms of local development (OECD, 2005, 2007). The issue of the economic enhancement of art and culture was originally tackled by studies in cultural economics (Towse, 2003), but was later integrated with contributions from creative economy (Florida, 2002), a subject field that highlighted the role of the human factor and of the creative class and put creative cities side by side with cultural cities and industries as the main protagonists of the knowledge economy's development (Cooke and Piccaluga, 2006).

The production of culture, as well as its role as a flywheel of economic development, have also turned into an increasingly important resource for innovation, because this is able to activate new industrial *filières* and can regenerate not only products but also places and industries (Cooke and Lazzeretti, 2008). In fact, culture becomes the engine of a creative process which combines and recombines new with pre-existing cognitions, offering a completely different wisdom. 'Add new work to another', wrote Jacobs (1969, 59): in the same way, the creative city functions as an open system that attracts talented people from various backgrounds and stimulates their creative capacities.

The investigation in this chapter is structured as follows. First, after presenting the main characteristics of culture as a strategic resource for facing the challenges of the new millennium, I focus on the evolution of the ways culture has been 'enhanced' and on the different roles it played for local economic development and innovation processes; I use an integrated approach combining the cluster-district approach with the perspectives offered by culture and creative economics. In the following section, I analyse two different phases in the evolution of culture enhancement: the first, which may be called the 'economic enhancement of culture' and is widely recognized, is characterized by the spread of several forms of cultural clusters and districts; while the second, the 'cultural enhancement of economy', considers culture as a resource for innovation, in other words, emphasizes the creative capacity of culture (CCC) (Lazzeretti, 2009). This new phase has developed following various paths, characterized by either renewing (of cities and economies) or novelty (cross-fertilization and serendipity). Finally, I analyse two cases of cultural clusters in Andalusia: the Semana Santa and the Feria de Abril in Seville, and the wider Flamenco cluster.

CULTURE AS A STRATEGIC RESOURCE OF THE SECOND MODERNITY

The start of this millennium, which was identified as a 'second modernity' (Ruccio and Amariglio, 2003), sees the challenges of profound changes being marked by the setting up of new technological, productive and consumption paradigms and by a pervasive, increasing sense of uncertainty (Bauman, 2000). Old and new economies coexist in the same competitive scenario (Daniels et al., 2007), and the effects of globalization are progressively leading to an urbanized vision of the world. China's economic achievement and the recent economic and financial crises are questioning the effects of globalization, and a rediscovered strategic value is given to the territorial and social dimensions of economy (Asheim et al., 2006; Scott and Garofoli, 2007), particularly to the role of human factors and local and virtual communities (Okamoto, 2001). There is a great need for exploring fresh ideas, innovative actors, new combinations of different factors of production, and original organizational models (Moulaert and Sekia, 2003). Culture turns into a possible answer to these needs, a useful tool to face the challenge of uncertainty, because of its tangible and intangible assets and its creative capacity to rejuvenate places, sectors or professions, and to generate ideas and innovations.

The lesson learnt by cultural districts and clusters taught us that culture can be a flywheel for economic development (Santagata, 2006), capable of linking local networks with global networks. Culture is both local and global: while its idiosyncratic value contributes to identification of a specific high cultural (HC) place (such as Donatello's David for Florence or the Giralda tower for Seville), at the same time its significance crosses local boundaries and makes it a key part of mankind's heritage. HC places, just like creative cities, can also be the meeting points for artists (O'Hagan and Kelly, 2007) and work as a hub and spoke (Markusen, 1996) linking local and international networks. Stable or temporary artistic networks find a chance to take shape on the occasions of cultural events, so these produce positive externalities and knowledge spillovers (Maskell et al., 2006) which amplify the effects typical of traditional agglomeration economies in cultural clusters.

However, the strategic importance of culture is also due to the huge variety of its exploitable resources (Towse, 2003). These are the 'tangible' resources, like art goods, architectural assets, museums, libraries (which constitute the 'economics of heritage') and the 'intangible' resources, like performing arts (music, theatre and dance), universities, art fairs, and generally all cultural events. The culture of the past, whose traces are left in art masterpieces and all other cultural artefacts, is enhanced and at one with the culture of today's artists, and takes on a different symbolic meaning according to places and to communities.

The variety of culture can then be expressed on different levels, and involve at the same time diverse units of analysis with an economic, territorial or social nature. The phenomenon of cultural enhancement applies to products or professional sectors, but also to clusters, quarters, cities and regions, as well as to cultural institutions and public bodies (Cooke, 2008); likewise, it exerts a pull on many branches of learning – from the humanistic and artistic disciplines to the economic, social and technological fields – which combine differently depending on the case.

This is not all. Culture is a collective and public good (Bellandi, 2003), a meeting point between the public and the private (public and private museums, or public institutions and foundations) where it is possible to try out complex governance models of support to cultural policies (Mommas, 2004).

Finally, culture is a transverse strategic resource; it favours exchange and dialogue, it can promote technological applications, as in design, a creative cross-sector technology ranging over architectural, industrial, fashion and brand design, which is sometimes seen at the heart of strategic renewal (Ravasi and Lojacono, 2005). Culture may induce processes of trespassing among different paradigms – those explained by the lesson of Hirschman (1981) – and promote a cross-fertilization among apparently far-off and dissimilar sectors (Martin, 1999). Culture creates a sort of strategic openness which fuels dialogue and conversation, sets up creative environments inside firms and other contexts, and thus provides the conditions for change (Lester and Piore, 2004). In conclusion, culture plays an important 'bridging' function as it connects concepts, places and paradigms from different backgrounds. Its significance is not exhausted by the emergence of a new important cultural and economic sector; thanks to its multifaceted and all-purpose character it also crystallizes as an extraordinary civilization-rebalancing factor.

THE PATHS TO CULTURE ENHANCEMENT[2]

As seen above, culture is a strategic resource for this millennium, as it can be usefully exploited to produce growth, change, new ideas and innovations. Consequently, it now has a twofold role, which has developed in the course of time following a dialectical relationship of culture and economy. This relationship went through two main stages: the first is represented by the well-established 'economic enhancement of culture', and the second by the emergence of what we called the 'cultural enhancement of economy' (Lazzeretti, 2009). In the first case, culture was basically seen as an asset and trusted to generate economic development and employment just like any other factor of production. In the second case, instead, it is appreciated as a creative capacity, and its strategic role for innovation is particularly stressed.

The theoretical approaches which contributed to this issue are mainly culture and creative economics (Florida, 2002; Towse, 2003), the local economic development approach (Becattini et al., 2009) and, more recently, urban and innovation economics, and economic geography following an evolutionary approach (Boschma and Frenken, 2006; Frenken et al., 2007). This exemplifies the main aspects involved in the two evolutionary stages of the relationship between economy and culture.

The Economic Enhancement of Culture

Within the economy of culture, a first important step was to move from the preservation to the economic enhancement of culture. A variety of scholars contributed to this multidisciplinary debate (for example, Ginsburgh and Throsby, 2006). Culture and economy were combined in a successful paradigm, which was first built in the US, later in Europe and, more recently, also in transition and developing countries (Power and Scott, 2004).

The initial purpose for this field of research was to prove that culture could be considered a factor of production, showing that it played an important role in the traditional cultural industries or in non-profit sectors. In this regard, an exemplary case is that of museums, non-profit institutions where an object of preservation can turn into the target of various forms of economic enhancement.[3]

At that time, however, some idiosyncratic resources took up a strategic value, and simultaneously cultural districts and clusters, with their different connotations, became an emerging phenomenon which emphasized the role of culture as a flywheel of economic development. Some American scholars (for example Frost-Kumpf) defined the cultural district as a 'well-recognized, labelled, mixed-use area of a city in which a high concentration of cultural facilities serves as the anchor of attraction' for other activities (Frost-Kumpf, 1998, 29); some authors worked out taxonomies meant to differentiate cultural districts from institutional, industrial, urban or museum districts (Santagata, 2002); others drew attention to their role in territorial marketing, or pointed out the importance of their resources (Kebir and Crevoisier, 2008).[4]

I intend to contribute to this debate with an analysis of the 'cultural districtualization processes', drawing from the literature covering industrial districts and dynamic processes of district evolution (Becattini et al., 2009). My colleagues and I developed the cultural districtualization (CD) model, specifically designed for cities of art (Lazzeretti, 2003, 2008), following a multidisciplinary methodology which combines the district approach with cluster theory (Porter, 1998), and that we called the cultural, artistic and environmental heritage (CAEH) method. According to this perspective, the cultural district is considered as a complex and articulated model, which is not necessarily the only one of its kind; in fact, it is possible to come across more simplified forms that do not present all typical processes described in the industrial district literature.

The concepts that led our reasoning were therefore essentially two: the CAEH, that is the set of resources necessary to define a HC place;[5] and the HC cluster, that is the set of actors involved in the economic enhancement of the resources. These two concepts merge into the synthetic definition represented by the 'HC local system', which is in fact our unit of analysis:

> An HC local system is characterised by the presence, in its territory, of a large endowment of a set of artistic, natural and cultural resources which identify it as a HC Place, and of a network of economic, non economic and institutional actors who carry out activities concerning the conservation, enhancement, and economic management of these resources and which represent in their totality the HC Cluster. (Lazzeretti, 2003, 638)

So, we have privileged the 'local production system' over the local community also for the analysis of the degree of cultural 'districtualization' of HC places. We have identified degrees and forms of the CD by ascertaining the existence of at least three basic elements: the HC place (identified through its idiosyncratic resources); the economic enhancement of cultural resources (identified through the local clusters of economic, non-economic and institutional actors); and a specific localization of resources and actors (geographical proximity). We have successfully tested this model in many empirical analyses, particularly in the sectors of art restoration, museums, music and cultural events of two laboratory cities (Florence and Seville), and their regions (Tuscany and Andalusia).[6]

The Cultural Enhancement of Economy

A further step in this stream of studies was to start considering culture as a source of innovation capable of generating new ideas and improvements, of rejuvenating mature sectors or creating new ones. Some analyses were so much concerned with the role of creativity that their focus gradually shifted from the cultural district to the creative district (OECD, 2005) of the US, Europe and, finally, Asia – as demonstrated by Scott's (2005) work on the Hollywood film district, which was replicated for the Indian newborn district of Bollywood. So, as scholars had formerly studied the economy of culture by focusing on cultural heritage and performing arts, now academics interested in creative economy are attracted by these particular industries, the knowledge economy and information and communication technology (ICT). Moreover, while there is a distinction between cultural economy and creative industries, the two terms are often used as equivalents; clearly the creative industries represent an emerging reality of modern economy.[7]

In parallel to the rise of concern for creative districts and creative industries, a renewed attention was given to the concept of the creative city, which is sometimes associated with the notions of the cultural city in the new millennium (Hubbard, 2006) and the city of knowledge. This revised concept was soon related to the creative industries (Hall, 2000), and later to the creative class (Florida, 2002). Florida's contributions gave rise to a particularly intense debate on this issue (Glaeser, 2005; Storper and Scott, 2009), and generated a huge quantity of empirical research. On this point, we should not forget that attention has recently shifted to an entrepreneurial approach that links creativity, new firm formation, entrepreneurship (Lee et al., 2004) and urban regeneration (OECD, 2007).

In this context, our contribution follows two paths: on the one hand, the survey of clustering events in creative industries, on an urban and national level (Lazzeretti et al., 2008); and on the other hand, the examination of the 'creative capacity of culture' (CCC) in 'art city' cultural clusters (Lazzeretti, 2009). By CCC, which is the leading concept in this line of reasoning, we intend the ability to rejuvenate places, sectors or professions, and to generate ideas and innovations through processes of cross-fertilization and serendipity. It involves searching out new and different relationships, and preferably the 'unusual' relatedness which is at the basis of the innovation process. The CCC is founded on a multifaceted idea of proximity, diversified not only on a geographical basis, as explored in the CD model, but also cognitively (Boschma, 2005; Boschma and Frenken, Chapter 14, in this *Handbook*).[8] The main objective becomes the search for 'relatedness', which constitutes the *incipit* (opening) of development paths for CCC.

According to this perspective, we identified four development paths, which wind between renewing and novelty, and are differently associated to the main typologies of innovation (rejuvenation, incremental innovation, radical innovation).

Urban renewal

Urban renewal was extensively explored by urban planners and then applied to initiatives of place-marketing and 'experience economy' (Pine and Gilmore, 1999). An OECD report (2007), which was specifically devoted to this issue, recognized three main urban regeneration strategies:

- City branding. Place branding tries to apply the same methodology employed in product marketing to geographical locations, and to create and nurture the narratives that give meanings to a place (Julier, 2005); it underlines its core benefits and style culture.
- Physical renovation and flagship developments. Physical renovation, such as flagship city centre development, was conceived to bring branding images into reality by giving them a material form. According to this strategy a primary role is taken by architects who are asked to furnish places with a new image and a new symbolic value; an exemplary case is that of the Bilbao Guggenheim museum (Plaza, 2006). An example of flagship development can be drawn from the 'waterfront city promotion' (the 'Baltimore model').
- Culture-led and -driven strategies. They regard the organization of exhibits and events. Museums of contemporary art are in this respect of particular importance in attracting mass tourism and entertainment (Griffiths, 1995); also, international events, such as the Olympic Games and the World Expos, represent a chance of great consequence for urban regeneration, and for the reactivation of other economic *filières*. The Quarter Museum in Vienna constitutes a good example of this strategy (Mommas, 2004).

Economic renewal

This path is not as well systematized, but no less important than that of 'urban' renewal. It pertains to the idea that culture can rejuvenate not only places, but also products, professions and sectors that are mature or declining. It can be achieved through:

- Industry regeneration. A first case deserving mention is design, which from many viewpoints may well represent a new cross-sector technology. Design can be successfully combined with the new ICTs, and its planning capability is improved owing to the simulation of a product's virtual progress report, or it can gather new materials for the implementation of new products, as is the case for the shipbuilding industry.
- Profession rejuvenation. Even professions can be rejuvenated and find a resurgence if revitalized by new technology and creativity. An emblematic case is the high-tech artistic craft of the Florentine restorers, who work at a high specialization level and, because of their localization in the historical centre of the city, are considered at the same time a creative class, a creative firm and a source of urban regeneration.[9]

Cross-fertilization

A third path is specifically associated with novelty rather than with regeneration. Jacobs (1961) had already stressed the importance for innovation of cross-fertilization of ideas among industries, as well as among economic actors, and the wider community. The central points to consider are the 'relatedness', and the ability to search and build new relationships. Even this kind of path was not sufficiently codified, so that I can only refer to a few examples drawn from our past research:

- Inside a cultural cluster or district. Cross-fertilization can arise with regard to different professional abilities (specializations) within a single productive *filière* or the same cluster or district; relatedness is based essentially on social and physical proximity (see the cluster of art restoration).

- Among 'related' cultural cluster or sectors. Another relevant example is given by relatedness among cultural clusters in the same city. The case might be that of institutional actors who belong to different clusters, so that they work as 'connection knots'. This certainly occurs with the clusters of fashion, museums and music in art cities. Besides, it is possible to have cluster-to-cluster relationships outside the city, relating the same kind of actors from different places, and even from different countries, as in the case of the relationships entertained by Florentine and Chinese restorers.
- Among 'unrelated' clusters or sectors. In the case of a multifaceted city, sectors which are apparently uncorrelated can have an opportunity of exchange just because of co-location. An example is that of cross-fertilization between the biomedical and health diagnostics sector and the sector of cultural assets, once again in the city of Florence. The presence in the same territory of institutes of applied physics and institutions for preservation, obviously together with a considerable art heritage, was probably at the origin of the implementation of laser technologies of optometry for cleaning stone materials (Lazzeretti, 2009).
- Across time. The last typology we recall is a kind of cross-fertilization which finds its roots in the legacy of tacit knowledge about the old and the new, the first and the second modernity: the rebirth of a creative district. This is the case, for instance, of BHM jewellery, a classical Marshallian manufacturing district which has been revived as an urban cluster founded on design, marketing and the new and distinct ethnic community of Indians, who brought about a whole set of relationships, especially at an international level (De Propris and Lazzeretti, 2009).

Serendipity
The last path is very different from the previous ones and is quite hard to trace. Usually, the term 'serendipity' is described as the capacity of discovering pleasing or valuable things by chance. In this case, the CCC has to do with the discovery of an unusual correlation that is the basis for an innovative idea, which may be connected with new uses for a product, diversification or technological correlations:

- New uses. Coca-Cola, for example, was originally invented as a medicament and only later used as a soft drink; nonetheless, its formula is still a secret.
- Multiplicity of interests. Diversity may also have a positive role, which makes sense with the lesson by Pasteur when he links his original idea of 'protection by inoculation with germs of weakened virulence' to his array of interests and his ability to make associations.
- Technological correlations. The laser-cleaning technologies in art conservation are emblematic. They were discovered by chance while using them to make a holographic archive of statues and monuments (Asmus et al., 1973). Another example is that of the metal-detector technology applied to airports: it was conceived by a jewellery firm and implemented for the selection process of metallic alloys to weigh gold carats.

THE ENHANCEMENT OF CULTURE: SOME EVIDENCE FROM CULTURAL CLUSTER IN ANDALUSIA

After the overview of culture as a resource to growth and change, I now briefly consider a case study, that of some cultural clusters in Andalusia, which can appropriately be interpreted referring also to the evolution of the culture-economy relationship, as described above.

The recent investigations in the field of economy of culture have moved the focus to the performing arts and the analysis of events (Lorenzen and Frederiksen, 2005; Belussi and Sedita, 2008), while creative economy has underlined the importance of studying artists (O'Hagan and Kelly, 2007) or creative industries (Lazzeretti et al., 2008). The field of research is maybe traced following emotions, but it is also questioned with a more aware and critical attitude towards the applications of the so-called 'experience economy' (or 'experience consuming'), and an increasing demand for an 'authenticity' legitimation (Gilmore and Pine, 2007). Compared to these trends, popular festivals and traditions attract a new kind of interest, because of both their multifaceted character (music and songs, dance and theatre, and so on) and their legitimizing authenticity, deriving from the anthropological tradition as well as from the participation of local communities.

An exemplary case in this regard is offered by the 'sacred and profane' rituals of the Andalusian region, whose symbolic value for the collective imaginary is so great as to associate them with the image of Spain itself. The so-called *economia de la fiestas*[10] (Aguilar Criado, 2002) is not only interesting from a socio-anthropological point of view, but it has an economic importance as well; and its financial outcome is visible not only in cultural tourism, but even in other, different sectors. In previous studies of cultural districts, we took Seville as a laboratory city: we measured the spring festivals – the Semana Santa and the Feria de Abril – as constituting the case for an 'economic enhancement of culture' based on an intangible cultural resource, and identified the actors' clusters and relationships (Lazzeretti et al., 2003). Later, our surveys moved from the cities to whole regions – particularly to the regional cluster of flamenco – and went deeper into the analysis of resources: *palos*,[11] flamenco artists and festivals. Among the actors we identified in the cultural cluster, a special strategic role was detained by the 'social actors', a category expressing both the social capital (with the community of Seville's citizens, the gipsy ethnic community, the *hermandades* (brotherhoods) and *cofradías* (fraternities), H&C[12]) and their human capital (artists, musicians, dancers and singers). The social actors are capable of playing a part in the economic enhancement of cultural resources, together with the economic and non-economic actors in the cluster, but they are also capable, as creative actors, of generating new ideas and rejuvenating sectors and places (resulting in the 'cultural enhancement of economic').

The cluster we first examined was that of the Feria de Abril. During the working days, usually on the second week after Easter, Sevilla is the stage for an ephemeral city with more than one thousand *casetas*, which are mostly private (one-, multi-*familiares* or other associations' *casetas particulares*) and create the festival environment, whose heart is located in the Barrio de Los Remedios (Aguilar Criado, 2002). Several economic activities are performed both inside and outside the *recinto ferial*: music and multimedia, restaurants, public services, tourism and flamenco fashion (such as *trajes de flamencos, calzados, complementos*). The demand for all this business is essentially internal, but there is a large external demand which should also be further developed.

Anyway, the Feria is overshadowed by the great festivities of the imposing Semana Santa, which involves, because of a great variety of purposes, more than 500 000 Sevillians and tourists (Pavon, 2006). The Semana has two main events, the *escenificación* (staging), and the organization of processions, particularly on Holy Thursday and on Good Friday (Moreno Navarro, 2001).

At this time, there is a break in ordinary life and the city becomes a unique, special theatre. An estimated number of 100 000 persons animate the processions, among them *nazarenos, costaleros, musicos, acolitos* and various other people involved, for example those who transport the statues of sacred images on special floats called *pasos*.

In this regard, we identified a cluster of art restoration and the actors whose activities could be connected prevalently to the economic enhancement of the Semana Santa (especially artistic artisans and the H&C) (Lazzeretti et al., 2003); we studied their characteristics, localization and collaboration behaviours.[13] Again, we found out that although the main actor is certainly the community of citizens parading or witnessing the parade, the directors of the event, the coordinators of the social as well as the economic networks, are the H&C. The role of the confraternities in Andalusia is still strong and has a considerable influence on the social relations system and is at the basis of political and religious power; to belong to these associations is one of the principal ways of expressing the cultural identity of people in Andalusia.

However, the red thread linking Andalusian 'sacred and profane' rituals and traditions is certainly flamenco, which represents one of the most important idiosyncratic resources in the region and was recently considered also important from an economic point of view (Acuña Arenas, 2006). The word '*flamenco*' comes from Hispano-Arabic *fellahmengu*, which means 'expelled peasant'. The musical genre 'flamenco' probably derives from an Islamic sort of one-string singing, which became known as the music of the gypsies by the beginning of the fifteenth century. Flamenco involves singing, dance and guitar simultaneously. Its evolution goes together with the history of Andalusia; its success grew progressively, and so strongly that it was recently nominated to become one of the resources to be safeguarded as part of mankind's world heritage.[14] Flamenco is a typical strategic cultural resource with both a local and a global significance, and was the object of many interventions for economic enhancement. Cultural and artists foundations were established some years ago, among them the Fundación de Arte Flamenco Cristina Heeren, which started its activity of preservation and teaching of flamenco in 1997, supported also by foreign associations such as the American Friends of Flamenco. In 2006, the first flamenco museum, the Museo del Baile Flamenco, was opened in Seville by the private foundation of the *bailadora* Christina Hoyos. It is an experience museum, an interactive museum supported by new technologies, where many events are organized and training activities are constantly carried out (Grotsch, 2006).

We also found a case of urban regeneration. In Jerez de la Frontera, local institutions promoted the creation of a Ciudad del Flamenco, which has a national auditorium and an advanced art school for flamenco, as well as a documentation centre and a museum of flamenco. Here, a public-architecture official competition, organized in collaboration with the review *Arquitectura Viva*, was announced in 1993, won by the

Swiss Jacques Herzog and Pierre de Meuron, and the laying of the first stone took place in 2005.[15]

Flamenco is a widespread resource of Andalusia: we can find more than 80 different *palos* and over 20 important festivals in this region,[16] and they are mainly concentrated in the Seville–Cadiz–Jerez triangle. Similarly, the places of origin of most of the artists involved are in this area, while the highest concentration of flamenco *tablaos* is in Malaga (Pollutri, 2007).

To sum up, these first investigations allowed us to identify a predominant 'art production' cluster, involving the gipsy community and the interlinked social and family networks. Local music distribution is represented only by small and medium-sized firms, while the large flamenco recording companies are either in Madrid, or in France and in the US, countries which count on a vast audience of flamenco devotees (equally present in the Northern European countries and in Japan). Flamenco travels through the web and has an increasing number of dedicated sites. At present, it appears as the local product of an ethnic community, but it has full potentialities to be enhanced on a global level, and to set off, starting from the music sector, creative *filières* of great consequence. We think that flamenco constitutes an interesting case deserving attention which, if adequately managed, might favour the economic development of Andalusia. This region would then become not only an important HC cluster, but also an international 'HC hub' connecting local networks with global networks.

NOTES

1. I refer to a broad concept of culture, associated with the cultural, artistic and environmental heritage (CAEH), a concept employed in the cultural districtualization (CD) model. This takes into account both tangible and intangible cultural resources having a high idiosyncratic value, that is those able to mark a high cultural (HC) place from one which is not. Culture is not only an asset that can generate economic development, but also a creative capacity able to give birth to new ideas and innovation.
2. This section is an extensive rework of Lazzeretti (2009).
3. As is well known, museum institutions are a symbol of preservation, but they have been through some sort of deep transformation. At first, museums were studied merely as the constituents of a non-profit sector, and only later were they looked upon as applying managerial and entrepreneurship approaches. It is important to consider how museums can take a wide variety of forms, from the large art museums, like the Louvre or the Uffizi, to the systems of museums disseminated over a certain area, like the systems and networks set in many parts of Tuscany. The visible outcome of their transformation is that some museums turned into 'entertainment' parks, others into multifunctional service poles or educational centres, while a few even took on a straight entrepreneurial significance, performing a strategic role in the marketing policies of certain business groups (see for example the Salvatore Ferragamo Shoe Museum that opened recently in Florence). Museums play the part of a main character in culture performance, as they are not only a resource but also a source of regeneration for particular cities and economic activities, like the case of the Bilbao's Guggenheim (Plaza, 2006).
4. A close examination of the literature on cultural districts and clusters can be found in Cinti (2008).
5. Artistic resources are meant as the set of art goods and works of art in the strict sense (for example monuments, architectural complexes, artworks, buildings, archaeological sites); cultural resources refer to that set of activities, behaviours, habits and ways of life that makes one place different from any other (for example universities and research centres, traditional arts and crafts, contextual knowledge, events and manifestations, or the neighbourhood 'atmosphere'); among the human resources fall those expressly ascribable to human capital (for example artists, writers, scientists, artisans); environmental resources refer to typical elements of the urban, natural and environmental landscape (for example urban morphology, ornamental gardens, parks, streets, squares, neighbourhoods, characteristic flora and fauna).
6. A synthesis of the principal empirical researches may be found in Lazzeretti (2008).

7.   According to the British Department for Culture, Media and Sport, the creative industries include: adver-
     tising, architecture, the art and antiques market, crafts, design, designer fashion, film and video, interac-
     tive leisure software, music, the performing arts, publishing, software and computer services, television
     and radio (DCMS, 2001).
8.   Cognitive proximity can be found, for instance, in temporary networks of artists who come in contact
     for the organization of cultural events (projects, exhibits and festivals) or, on a virtual level, in epistemic
     communities like open source software.
9.   In fact, at first the artisan worker was associated with the traditional cultural firm, therefore it was seen
     merely as an actor in the cluster of art restoration whose activity contributed to the enhancement of a
     territorial resource, art. Instead, the same artisan firm can also be regarded as a cultural resource for the
     urban neighbourhood it occupies, because it contributes to revitalize that special place. Another notewor-
     thy fact was that most Florentine restoration workers employ sophisticated technologies and have a high
     professional qualification, acquired either in the workshop or by attending high-level training courses in
     local centres (such as the Workshop for Hard Stones, Opificio delle Pietre Dure). This is a case in which
     art, culture and technology intermingled and gave new impulse to an old profession, as well as to the
     Florentine central neighbourhoods in which the workshops are located, whose atmosphere was certainly
     enlivened (Lazzeretti, 2003).
10. The *economia de la fiestas* deals with the economic and social aspects associated with the cultural events
     between sacred and profane that characterize the Andalusian tradition, most of which are somehow
     related to the *tauromachia* ('the fighting of the bull'), the flamenco or the religious festivals. These events
     are common in small and large, urban and rural centres, and they largely supply the symbolic capital of
     the city, or region. While numerous anthropological and sociological studies have been carried out on this
     issue, there are only few economic investigations, due mainly to the difficulties in collecting information
     about an essentially black economy; the sector is not even covered by official statistics.
11. A *palo* can be defined as a musical form of flamenco. The rhythmic patterns of the *palos* are also often
     called *compás*. A *compás* is characterized by a recurring pattern of beats and accents (for example,
     alegrias, bulerias, tangos, fandangos, Sevillanas, Malagueña).
12. The *hermandades* and *cofradías* (H&C) are associations of lay-persons whose scope is worship and chari-
     table activities, that depend on the ecclesiastic institutions and are placed under the rules of current canon
     and diocesan laws. The term *hermandad* indicates the set of different types of religious confraternities:
     there are in fact *hermandades de gloria, hermandades sacramentales, hermandades de penitencia*; only the
     latter parade at the Semana Santa.
13. In the historical centre we found a substantial subcluster of 51 firms specialized in custom products
     of a traditional type (*pasos*, altars, crowns, banners, metal figurines, flags, cord belts, goblets, crosses,
     thuribles, rulebooks, canes, diadems, and the like) with not only local, but also national and sometimes
     international clients. However, they do not seem to collaborate directly; H&C divide the work between
     the firms and take on the role of focal actors in the *filière* by means of the trust relations they hold with
     them. They have custody and control of the artistic patrimony carried in procession, usually the property
     of the Church, and organize the event by coordinating the different activities that involve not only the
     firms, but also the community of citizens of Seville all year round (Lazzeretti, 2008).
14. The main stages of flamenco's success can be briefly described. The first *cantaores* appeared in eighteenth-
     century Triana, Jerez and Cadiz and marked the passage of flamenco from folklore to an art genre. Then,
     with the late nineteenth-century *cafès cantantes*, it reached all parts of Andalusia and took on a profes-
     sional feature. In the twentieth century Madrid became a centre for *cantaores*, flamenco performances
     and theatres flourished and the first competition, La Copa Pavòn, took place. The Opera Flamenca,
     dating back to the 1920s, constituted a development but there was also a commercialization of flamenco
     (fandango); its public grew, it was performed in large arenas (*plaza de toros*), and also enlarged abroad.
     Flamenco dance established, as well as later, in the 1950s, *troupes* and *tablaos*. By then, it was popular all
     over the world. The first handbook on flamenco art was published in 1956, and in the same year the first
     national competition was held in Cordoba; in 1958 the University of Jerez introduced a chair on *flamen-*
     cologia. The 'age of contamination' started in the 1970s, and a debate developed on the *nuevo flamenco*
     between orthodox and heterodox supporters. Festivals gained a growing importance. In 2009 the Junta of
     Andalusia applied to the United Nations Educational, Scientific and Cultural Organization (UNESCO)
     for the nomination of flamenco for World Heritage designation, but the application was rejected since it
     was not considered under risk of extinction.
15. See http://ciudaddelflamenco.jerez.es/en_proyecto.htm.
16. Over 250 flamenco festivals were surveyed by specialized reviews (ACADAP, 2005). The most important
     ones for the Andalusian region are the following: Bienal de Sevilla, Festival de Jerez, Potaje de Utrera,
     Bienal de Malaga, Festival Internacional de la Guitarra de Cordoba, and Festival de Cante Jondo de
     Mairena de Alcor.

REFERENCES

ACADAP (2005), *Plaza Abierta: guia internacional de Flamenco*, Madrid: ACADAP.

Acuña Arenas, T. (2006), 'El flamenco como recurso economico', Direccion regional de commercio de Sevilla.

Aguilar Criado, E. (2002), 'La economía de la Fiesta', in J. Hurtado Sánchez (ed.), *Nuevos aspectos de la religiosidad sevillana Fiesta, Imagen, Sociedad*, Nodo Área de Cultura y Fiestas Mayores, Ayuntamiento de Sevilla, Sevilla.

Asheim, B., P. Cooke and R. Martin (2006), *Clusters and Regional Development: Critical Reflections and Explorations*, London: Routledge.

Asmus, J.F., G. Guattari, L. Lazzarini, G. Musumeci and R.F. Wuerker (1973), 'Holography in the conservation of statuary', *Studies in Conservation*, **18**, 49–63.

Bauman, Z. (2000), *Liquid Modernity*, Cambridge: Polity Press.

Becattini, G., M. Bellandi and L. De Propris (eds) (2009), *The Handbook of Industrial Districts*, Cheltenham, UK and Northampton, MA, USA: Edward Elgar.

Bellandi, M. (2003), 'Beni pubblici specifici e sviluppo sostenibile', *Sviluppo Locale*, **22**, 3–23.

Belussi, F. and S.R. Sedita (2008), 'The management of events in the Veneto performing music cluster: bridging latent networks and permanent organisation', in P. Cooke and L. Lazzeretti (eds), *Creative Cities, Cultural Clusters and Local Economic Development*, Cheltenham, UK and Northampton, MA, USA: Edward Elgar, pp. 237–57.

Boschma, R.A. (2005), 'Proximity and innovation: a critical assessment', *Regional Studies*, **39** (1), 61–74.

Boschma, R.A. and K. Frenken (2006), 'Why is economic geography not an evolutionary science? Towards an evolutionary economic geography', *Journal of Economic Geography*, **6** (3), 273–302.

Cinti, T. (2008), 'Cultural clusters and cultural district: the state of art', in P. Cooke and L. Lazzeretti (eds), *Creative Cities, Cultural Clusters and Local Economic Development*, Cheltenham, UK and Northampton, MA, USA: Edward Elgar, pp. 70–92.

Cooke, P. (2008), 'Culture, clusters, districts and quarters: some reflections on the scale question', in P. Cooke and L. Lazzeretti (eds), *Creative Cities, Cultural Clusters and Local Development*, Cheltenham, UK and Northampton, MA, USA: Edward Elgar, pp. 25–47.

Cooke, P. and L. Lazzeretti (eds) (2008), *Creative Cities, Cultural Clusters and Local Economic Development*, Cheltenham, UK and Northampton, MA, USA: Edward Elgar.

Cooke, P. and A. Piccaluga (2006), *Regional Development in the Knowledge Economy*, London: Routledge.

Daniels, P., A. Leyshon, M. Bradshaw and J. Beaverstock (2007), *Geographies of the New Economy*, New York: Routledge.

De Propris, L. and L. Lazzeretti (2009), 'Measuring the decline of a Marshallian industrial district: the Birmingham jewellery quarter', *Regional Studies*, **43**, 1135–54.

Department of Culture, Media and Sport (DCMS) (2001), *The Creative Industries Mapping Document*, London: HMSO.

Florida, R. (2002), *The Rise of Creative Class*, New York: Basic Books.

Frenken, K., F.G. van Oort and T. Verburg (2007), 'Related variety, unrelated variety and regional economic growth', *Regional Studies*, **41** (5), 685–97.

Frost-Kumpf, H.A. (1998), *Cultural District: The Arts as a Strategy for Revitalizing our Cities*, Washington, DC: Institute for Community Development and the Arts, Americans for the Arts.

Gilmore, J.H. and B.J. Pine (2007), *Authenticity: What Consumer Really Want*, Boston, MA: Harvard Business Press.

Ginsburgh, V. and D. Throsby (eds) (2006), *Handbook on the Economics of Art and Culture*, Amsterdam: Elsevier.

Glaeser, E. (2005), 'Review of Richard Florida's *The Rise of the Creative Class*', *Regional Sciences and Urban Economics*, **35**, 593–6.

Griffiths, R. (1995), 'Cultural strategies and new model of urban intervention', *Cities*, **12** (4), 253–65.

Grotsch, K. (2006), 'Un protomuseo. El museo del baile flamenco', *Cuadernos de economia de la cultura*, **6**, 139–50.

Hall, P. (2000), 'Creative cities and economic development', *Urban Studies*, **37** (4), 639–49.

Hirschman, A.O. (1981), *Essays in Trespassing: Economics to Politics and Beyond*, Cambridge, MA: Cambridge University Press.

Hubbard, P. (2006), *City*, London: Routledge.

Jacobs, J. (1961), *The Death of the Life of American Cities*, New York: Random House.

Jacobs, J. (1969), *The Economy of Cities*, New York: Random House.

Julier, G. (2005), 'Urban design scapes and the production of aesthetic consent', *Urban Studies*, **42** (5–6), 698–888.

Kebir, L. and O. Crevoisier (2008), 'Cultural resources and regional development: the case of the cultural legacy of watchmaking', in P. Cooke and L. Lazzeretti (eds), *Creative Cities, Cultural Clusters and Local Economic Development*, Cheltenham, UK and Northampton, MA, USA: Edward Elgar, pp. 48–70.

Lazzeretti, L. (2003), 'City of art as a HC Local System and cultural districtualisation processes: the cluster of art-restoration in Florence', *International Journal of Urban and Regional Research*, **27** (3), 635–48.

Lazzeretti, L. (2008), 'The cultural districtualisation model', in P. Cooke and L. Lazzeretti (eds), *Creative Cities, Cultural Clusters and Local Development*, Cheltenham, UK and Northampton, MA, USA: Edward Elgar, pp. 93–120.

Lazzeretti, L. (2009), 'The creative capacity of culture and the new creative *milieu*', in G. Becattini, M. Bellandi and L. De Propris (eds), *The Handbook of Industrial Districts*, Cheltenham, UK and Northampton, MA, USA: Edward Elgar, pp. 281–94.

Lazzeretti, L., R. Boix and F. Capone (2008), 'Do creative industries cluster? Mapping creative local production systems in Italy and Spain', *Industry and Innovation*, **15** (5), 549–67.

Lazzeretti, L., T. Cinti and N. Villanova (2003), 'Il cluster dell'artigianato artistico della *Semana Santa*', Working Paper n. 11, University of Florence, Deparment of Business Economics.

Lee, S.Y., R. Florida and J.A. Zoltan (2004), 'Creativity and entrepreneurship: a regional analysis of new firm formation', *Regional Studies*, **38**, 879–91.

Lester, R.K. and M.J. Piore (2004), *Innovation: The Missing Dimension*, Cambridge, MA: Harvard University Press.

Lorenzen, M. and L. Frederiksen (2005), 'Management of project and product experimentation: examples from music industry', *European Management Review*, **2** (3), 198–211.

Markusen, A. (1996), 'Sticky places in slippery space: a typology of industrial districts', *Economic Geography*, **72** (3), 293–313.

Martin, R. (1999), 'The new geographical turn in economics: some critical reflections', *Cambridge Journal of Economics*, **23**, 65–91.

Maskell, P., H. Bathelt and A. Malberg (2006), 'Building global knowledge pipelines: the role of temporary cluster', *European Planning Studies*, **14** (8), 997–1013.

Mommas, H. (2004), 'Cultural clusters and post-industrial city: towards the remapping of urban cultural policy', *Urban Studies*, **41** (3), 507–32.

Moreno Navarro, I. (2001), *La Semana Santa de Sevilla. Conformacion, Modification y Significationes*, Sevilla: Libano.

Moulaert, F. and F. Sekia (2003), 'Territorial innovation models: a critical survey', *Regional Studies*, **37**, 289–302.

O'Hagan, J. and E. Kelly (2007), 'Geographic clustering of economic activity: the case of prominent western visual artists', *Journal of Cultural Economics*, **31**, 109–128.

OECD (2005), *Culture and Local Development*, Paris: OECD.

OECD (2007), *Competitive Cities. A New Entrepreneurial Paradigm in Spatial Development*, Paris: OECD.

Okamoto, Y. (2001), 'The evolution of ID and the role of community', *Journal of International Economic Studies*, **15**, 167–78.

Pavon, E.H. (2006), 'Desarrollo de sistemas culturales territoriales. Las actividaded economicas vincultadas a la cultura. Estudio de caso. La Semana Santa de Sevilla: economia de una tradition popular', *Cuadernos de Economia de la Cultura*, 4–5 June, pp. 83–102.

Pine, B.J. and J.H. Gilmore (1999), *The Experience Economy: Work is Theatre and every Business a Stage*, Cambridge, MA: Harvard Business Press.

Plaza, B. (2006), 'The return on investment of the Guggenheim Museum, Bilbao', *International Journal of Urban and Regional Research*, **30** (2), 452–67.

Pollutri, D. (2007), 'Il flamenco come risorsa culturale ed economica dell'Andalusia', Doctoral thesis, University of Florence.

Porter, M.E. (1998), *On Competition*, Boston, MA: Harvard Business School Press.

Power, D. and A.J. Scott (2004), *Cultural Industries and Production of Culture*, London, UK and New York, USA: Routledge.

Ravasi, D. and G. Lojacono (2005), 'Design and designers for strategic renewal', *Long Range Planning*, **38**, 51–77.

Ruccio, D.F. and J. Amariglio (2003), *Postmodern Moments in Modern Economics*, Princeton, NJ: Princeton University Press.

Santagata, W. (2002), 'Cultural districts, property rights and sustainable economic growth', *International Journal of Urban and Regional Research*, **1** (26), 9–23.

Santagata, W. (2006), 'Cultural districts and their role in developed and developing countries', in V. Ginsburgh and D. Throsby (eds), *Handbook on the Economics of Art and Culture*, Amsterdam: Elsevier, pp. 101–18.

Scott, A.J. (2005), *On Hollywood. The Place, the Industry*, Princeton, NJ: Princeton University Press.

Scott, A.J. and G. Garofoli (eds) (2007), *Development on the Ground: Clusters, Networks and Regions in Emerging Economies*, London, UK and New York, USA: Routledge.

Storper, M. and A.J. Scott (2009), 'Rethinking human capital, creativity and urban growth', *Journal of Economic Geography*, **9** (2), 147–67.

Towse, R. (ed.) (2003), *A Handbook of Cultural Economics*, Cheltenham, UK and Northampton, MA, USA: Edward Elgar.

27 Service innovation
Yuko Aoyama and Rory Horner

INTRODUCTION

Today, industry executives view service innovation as the next new wave of potential growth (*BusinessWeek*, 2007). Corporate giants such as IBM and GE recognized that their highest growth in revenue was coming from their service activities, and established sections and personnel dedicated to exploring how service innovation can revolutionize the way we view corporate organization. In academic literature, however, innovations in services have long been a neglected aspect of research on innovation. New knowledge that leads to product innovation is assumed to reside largely in the manufacturing sector. The conceptualization of services has long been found to be highly problematic (Castells, 1980; Stanback, 1980; Gershuny, 1978; Daniels, 1993; Sayer and Walker, 1992), and whether it has a distinct contribution to a regional economy has been debated in the literature.

Service innovation is a combination of two highly contested concepts, and the term is used and interpreted in multiple ways by firms and scholars. While no one disputes the importance of services in our economy,[1] research on service innovation is at its early development phase (Drejer, 2004; Bryson and Monnoyer, 2004). In this chapter we explore various aspects of service innovation, firstly as a conceptual problem, and secondly, its multiple usage and application. We also discuss the potential contributions and implications of service innovation to regional development.

UNPACKING SERVICE INNOVATION

Service innovation is mired in 'conceptual confusion' (Chesbrough and Spohrer, 2006, 36). While there is a consensus over service innovation's potential in adding new knowledge and insights on technological and organizational change, the jury is still out on its actual impacts. The debate still remains at the abstract level, and we have yet to see the radical break or an outcome or product of this new orientation.

What is Service?

The service sector as a concept has its origin in the establishment of industrial classification system by the US Census, which opted to use services initially as a residual category to agriculture and manufacturing. This legacy continues to be highly problematic for researchers attempting to reconceptualize services (Daniels and Bryson, 2002; Chesbrough and Sphorer, 2006; Freel, 2006). At best, services are diverse and heterogeneous; at worst, conceptually incoherent. Aside from various descriptive characteristics, such as its intangibility (Johne and Storey, 1998), perishability and heterogeneity

(Nijssen et al., 2006), many services also require simultaneity – co-presence of provider and buyer (Petit, 1986; Johne and Storey, 1998).

Services have been viewed as auxiliary, even parasitical, to manufacturing (Kuznets, 1971; Williams, 1996, 1997 – in Kay et al., 2007). Services have often been associated with lack of innovation and low productivity growth (Miles, 2000). Their largely 'residentiary' (non-exportable) characteristics (North, 1955; Tiebout, 1956) allegedly limit their growth potential. Yet, recent literature suggests that certain service segments are exportable (Wood, 2005), exhibit high productivity as well as employment growth (see, for example, Beyers, 2002) and can serve as engines of economic growth. With the gradual shift in competitiveness from manufacturing to knowledge-based services in the advanced industrialized economies, the knowledge and service functions of selling a product – such as branding, advertising and financial packages – are now recognized as critical sources of profitability, along with various producer services that are involved in the process (such as accounting and management consultancy) (Daniels and Bryson, 2002; Lundquist et al., 2008). Hansen (1998), for example, argued that producer services indeed play a pivotal role in economic growth, through expanding the division of labor, which in turn contributes to increasing returns.

The literature therefore increasingly emphasizes convergence (Hirschorn, 1988) or a complementary relationship between services and manufacturing connected through linkages (Cohen and Zysman, 1989). Howells (2004) for example discusses the cases of IBM and Siemens, both of which derive over half of their revenue from service activities, while a company such as International Computers Limited (ICL) in the United Kingdom (owned by Fujitsu) has completely abandoned manufacturing. The deepening of the division of labor (specialization) combined with increasing service–manufacturing integration means that services are integral aspects of production functions. Howells (2004) used the term 'services "encapsulation"' to describe instances where services act as 'wrappers' to tangible products. Two instances of service encapsulation have been identified: one where existing services encapsulate new goods (or services), and another where new services encapsulate old goods (or services). Howells (2004) also used 'servicisation of manufacturing' to refer to the process in which value is primarily added by service activities within manufacturing. For example, in the automobile industry, products are increasingly packaged with financing or leasing schemes, as well as repair and maintenance services. Aside from product characteristics, the availability and quality of these services often serve as decisive factors for whether consumers make a purchase. High-tech products that cannot be sold without being combined with high-quality services also fit this profile.

What is Service Innovation?

While service innovation has been neglected as a theme, the recent growth of attention both by academics and industries has led some to argue that the question of 'whether services can be innovative is no longer an issue' (Miles, 2000, 16). In general, innovation is a strong disequilibrating factor in the process of economic growth (Verspagen, 1997; Howells, 2005), and is deeply linked to economic performance. Whereas any innovation is difficult to define and measure (see chapters in Parts I and VI in this *Handbook* for discussion on innovation), the issue of definition and measurement is compounded for service innovation. In this chapter we examine several attempts to characterize service innovation, the role of research and development (R&D) facilities, and reverse product life-cycle theory, as well as various attempts at expanding the notion of service innovation.

R&D and service innovation

It has often been assumed that service firms perform (and rely) less on technological and scientific knowledge (and therefore on formal R&D facilities) (Johne and Storey, 1998; Freel, 2006) and more on the 'talent' of human capital. Evidence suggests that the service share in R&D is significantly lower than its share of output and employment in many Organisation for Economic Co-operation and Development (OECD) countries, and this is particularly the case for the European Union (EU) as compared to that in the United States (Miles, 2007). As a result, research on R&D has been conducted almost exclusively on the manufacturing sector (Gadrey et al., 1995). Due to the more informal nature of service innovation, service activities are 'less likely to collaborate with either universities or public sector agencies' (Freel, 2006, 342).

The manufacturing bias in research on R&D, however, is gradually being eroded as the share of service sector R&D has grown over recent decades (Jankowski, 2001). For example, Microsoft was the fifth-largest R&D spender in the United States in 2006 (Miles, 2007). Service firms in finance, media and retail are increasingly investing in R&D, and the share is expected to grow.[2] The emergence of industrial R&D outsourcing, known as contract R&D have resulted in the migration of some R&D from manufacturing to service sector status (Miles, 2000; Parthasarathy and Aoyama, 2006). Finally, it is now recognized that various services support innovation, including management consultancies, information technology (IT) facilities management, training, engineering and design services.

The role of R&D in the service sector may still be significantly underestimated, in part due to the different use of terminologies between sectors (Miles, 2000; Tether, 2005). For example, distribution, marketing and design are generally not understood as conducting R&D; instead, terminologies such as project development, quality management or business re-engineering are used in place of R&D (Miles, 2000, 382). The data also often fail to capture service innovation taking place in the manufacturing and extractive sectors.

The distinction between product and process innovation used in reference to the manufacturing sector activities blurs when it comes to service innovation (Gallouj, 1998). Nijssen et al. (2006) explored similarities and differences between product and service innovation, and argued that whereas R&D is more important for product innovation than service innovation, in both cases success requires strong commitment and involvement of top management, careful alignment of corporate culture and systems, often in a formalized, structured and proactive manner, and being executed by high-quality development staff. Service innovations are seldom stand-alone; they are often complementary and combined with new product development or services.

Some service innovation also takes place without any links to manufacturing. It can result from either bundling or unbundling of existing services, with examples of the former being head-hunters, Club-Med, 'fitness centers', a comprehensive tourist service, and teleshopping; and examples of the latter being charter air service, fast food restaurants and publishing firms (Gallouj and Weinstein, 1997). Since many service innovations are easily imitable and not patentable, it is difficult to use measures that are used in the manufacturing sector to assess incidences of service innovation, and track its evolutionary trajectory and the process of diffusion and adoption.

Reverse product life-cycle theory
While some argue for the specificity of service innovation, others argue that there is nothing distinctive or unique about service innovation (Tether, 2005). Barras (1986, 1990) argued that service innovation is characterized by the reversal of the life cycle that applies to the manufacturing sector. During the first stage of the reverse cycle, applications of new technologies increase the efficiency in delivery of the existing service; the second stage entails quality improvement in services; and in the third stage a new service is generated. His model was designed to parallel the product life cycle of the capital goods sector, through applications of technologies toward service efficiency in the consumer sector, followed by improved quality and, ultimately, new product introduction. The process innovation phase of service innovation is characterized as incremental, which will then be followed by a more radical, product innovation (Gallouj, 1998).

Criticisms exist of this 'reverse life-cycle' model, however (see Miles, 2000; Gallouj and Weinstein, 1997). First and foremost, service innovation allegedly does not depend on an evolutionary model of technological innovation. Secondly, because Barras's model was based exclusively on the development and diffusion of the fifth Kondratieff wave (that is, information technologies) from the 1970s onwards, it remains unclear whether this model can be applied to other technologies. The examples employed emphasize the process of diffusion within the service sector of technology-oriented innovation (such as the introduction of ATMs – automatic teller machines; online insurance quotes) largely derived from the manufacturing sector. Thus, non-technological forms of service innovation seem to be omitted from consideration.

Expanding the notion of innovation
Service innovation represents an attempt to broaden our conceptualization of innovation. Some situate services as intermediaries and orchestrators of innovation (Miles, 2000). Muller and Zenker (2001) situate knowledge-intensive business services (KIBS) as 'bridges for innovation' (p. 1503) by exchanging complementary knowledge with manufacturing firms, and playing an important role as 'co-innovators'. Similarly, Wood (2005) argued that: 'KIBS are seen to be innovative primarily to the extent that they support technological change,' (p. 441). This view would suggest that, whereas services may be critical for innovation, they still are held in an auxiliary, subordinate role to manufacturing.

Hipp and Grupp (2005) argue that the concept of innovation cannot be transposed directly to the service sector. For one thing, service innovation does not necessarily depend on manufacturing activities; and for another, typically it does not depend on a classic organizational form. In identifying service innovation, Hipp and Grupp (2005) use a broad definition, including modifications that lead to a greater flexibility in customization, improvements in user-friendliness, safety, reliability, availability (timeliness and speed), and customer as well as employee productivity. Customization and customer integration is critical to customer satisfaction, which may or may not be induced by exacting duplication of services. As a result, services are often viewed as being oriented toward 'continuous' rather than 'incremental' change (Tether, 2005).

Service innovation includes both incremental and radical innovation to service systems. The interactive nature of service innovation is particularly important in constructing a customized solution to a particular problem (Gallouj and Weinstein, 1997; Vang and Zellner, 2005). This type of innovation is called 'customized innovation'. In this context, service innovation is emphasized as 'ad hoc innovation', which occurs serendipitously. Service innovation typically involves multiple stakeholders, with various suppliers as well as customers. As Gershuny (1978) noted in his book *After Industrial Society? The Emerging Self-Service Economy*, customers are increasingly taking the service functions upon themselves. Since integration is one of the major goals in service innovation, know-how of successful interfirm (as well as supplier–customer network) coordination is viewed as a critical aspect of service innovation (Andersen et al., 2000; Bryson and Monnoyer, 2004).

Ultimately, service is a process itself, 'by which customers evaluate, purchase and consume' (Johne and Storey, 1998). It is comprised of 'dynamic configurations of people, technologies, organizations, and shared information that create and deliver value to customers, providers, and other stakeholders' (IfM and IBM, 2008, 1). To this end, Vargo et al. (2008) advocate for the service-dominant (SD) logic conceptualization of value-creation, while Ordanini and Pasini (2008) introduce services-oriented architecture (SOA). Both of these attempts represent new organizational frameworks that are intended to improve the quality of service provisions.

In sum, service innovation improves access by customers and thereby creates values for suppliers, by improving customer integration at the front end and operational efficiency at the back end. From the supply side, global competition is intensifying; from the demand side, the demand for achieving seamless integration in spite of increasing complexities that result from global sourcing is high. In such a market context, developing service provisions that are 'definable, repeatable and scalable' are critical not only for businesses to capture markets successfully, but also for non-profit organizations and governmental agencies.[3]

These attempts, however, lead to difficulties in distinguishing conceptually between innovation and customization. Does a successful customized solution count as innovation, even if it has not been articulated into a transferable formula? Without an articulated and transferable formula, service innovation becomes too often understood only by its success. For example, research on tourism innovation often claims a successful destination development as evidence of service innovation. Yet it is unclear which aspects of services were deemed innovative. Furthermore, in some instances, new contents are deemed as an aspect of service innovation in some cultural industries such as fashion, media, film and video games. It is also unclear whether all new content can be claimed as innovation, and if not, what makes certain content innovative. Perhaps echoing these concerns, the OECD (2006) uses the definition developed by the Dutch government that emphasizes the 'new and considerably changed' aspects of services as service innovation, and de-emphasizes the incremental aspect of service innovation.[4]

EXAMPLES OF SERVICE INNOVATION

In this section we will examine some key examples of service innovation. The existing literature offers various typologies of analysis conducted on service innovation (Gallouj,

1998; van Ark et al., 2003; Drejer, 2004; Hipp and Grupp, 2005). In aggregate, service innovation is a multidimensional concept that includes technological, organizational, network and value chain configurations, customer interactions and delivery systems dimensions (Kuusisto, 2005). Service innovations can be paradigmatic (such as new technologies or regulatory changes), supplier-dominated (such as those based on technological innovations of the manufacturers), customer-led or organizational. Also, service innovation includes innovation that takes place in the client's organization as a result of influences from services suppliers (van Ark et al., 2003, 16–18). In the following we examine innovation by service categories, namely retail, user-led services, logistics, tourism, contract R&D services and finance.

In principle, service innovation includes non-technological forms of innovation, yet it is difficult to imagine contemporary service innovation without information technology (IT). Although some claims exist that service innovation does not necessitate IT, IT's various applications, such as e-tailing, e-logistics, open source movements, and so on, have undoubtedly provided an impetus to begin exploring the nature and extent of service innovation activities. IT allows close integration of clients, customers and users to the provision of goods and services.

Retail Innovation

Retail innovation generally involves new formats at the front end, and can be combined with distribution innovation at the back end. The rise of chain stores in the United States in the 1930s, and neighborhood convenience store franchise chains in Japan in the 1990s, as well as wholesale membership clubs in the United States in the 1990s, all represent successful retail formats newly introduced to these markets. Retail innovation can also involve branding or pricing strategies. For example, Zara, a clothing producer and retailer originating from Spain, successfully established its brand by implementing a quick-response supply chain that minimized manufacturing-to-sale time in order to adapt and capture fashion trends. Japan's convenience stores are known for their disproportionately large IT investment in relation to floor space compared to any other forms of retail outlets in Japan, as a strategy to shorten the time required for restocking. The point-of-sale (POS) system was developed by Seven Eleven Japan in 1982, intended to improve delivery efficiency through delivery trip rationalization and cost reduction (Hashimoto, 1998). Wal-Mart's trademark 'every-day-low-price' (EDLP) strategy, combined with a factory-direct distribution model, revolutionized the American retailing scene. As in the case of Wal-Mart and Procter & Gamble, however, the factory-direct model typically requires large retailers and large manufacturers, with both having significant market share. Incentives are the highest under 'bilateral oligopoly'. Once implemented, large retailers using online networks can drive their goods suppliers to adopt the IT network and contribute to innovation diffusion (Miles, 2000).

The onset of the Internet in the 1990s gave rise to electronic commerce (e-commerce), which is a form of long-distance purchase. E-commerce can be classified into business-to-business (B2B) (typically procurement), business-to-consumer (e-tailing), and consumer-to-consumer (for example, eBay, craigslist). Those markets with previously restricted geographical boundaries, such as the auction of used books, music tapes or other collectibles, have now acquired nationwide or even global audience. In the category of business-to-consumer e-commerce, initial competition between brick-and-mortar and e-tailers (made famous by the rivalry between Barnes & Noble and Amazon.com[5]) gave way to multichannel retailing ('brick-and-click'), in which sellers use both offline and online storefronts to serve consumers. Japan's convenience stores with e-commerce terminals, and the German department store Karstadt's acquisition of long-standing mail order firm Quelle, are such examples. Service innovation through e-commerce included not only geographical expansion of the customer base (for example particularly consumer-to-consumer exchanges, which used to be largely geographically constrained), but also allowed the delivery of mass-customized services (for example Amazon.com's suggestions for next purchase), and resulted in the expansion of the self-service economy (that is, individual stock-trading on the Internet versus hiring fund managers; or making flight reservations versus using travel agents).

User-led Service Innovation

The role of the industrial or professional user in business innovation research tradition-ally focused on product development in the manufacturing sector (see, for example Gross, 1989; Anderson and Crocca, 1993; von Hippel et al., 1999). Today, we observe various service innovations that have been led by the users as well. As exemplified by Linux, the Internet offers the unparalleled opportunity to connect previously disconnected individu-als around the world to engage in a common project. In many cases, what used to be the 'provision' of digital products and contents is shifting to peer-to-peer 'sharing', in which information, knowledge and digital products are co-developed, shared and distributed freely. In some cases, process has become increasingly, and even at times purely, interac-tive. Open-source development (such as Linux) can be seen as an extreme case of 'lead user involvement' in which user communities undertake innovation on their own.

The open-source project is essentially a creation of a 'regulated commons' (de Laat, 2005), in which communal collaborative effort takes place with anyone from any part of the world who has access to the Internet. In addition, corporations today hope to find business opportunities in open-source projects, taking advantage of the demand conceived and the innovation conducted by user communities. For example, the sale, distribution and support of Linux are increasingly being taken over by various corpora-tions (for example IBM, HP, Novell and Red Hat) for commercial purposes. The user-innovation 'tool-kit' approach goes one step further and advocates that corporations abandon their efforts to understand users, and outsource innovation tasks to users by allowing them to conduct problem-solving themselves (Riggs and von Hippel, 1994; von Hippel and Katz, 2002; Jeppesen, 2005; Piller and Walcher, 2006). It advocates for the potential of user-led innovation in avoiding lock-ins and inside-the-box thinking, with an assumption that firms and users have distinctive product ideas. Through various 'crowd-sourcing' strategies (see, for example, Surowiecki, 2004; Howe, 2008), the proponents of the tool-kit approach advocate for actively employing the wisdom of the masses in inducing innovation.

User-created content is another emerging aspect of user-led innovation. Web 2.0 refers to the new generation of digital integration that takes advantage of new online medium and web-based communities such as online forums, blogs, *wikis*, video-sharing sites and social networking sites. Many were initially developed as peer-to-peer sites, but some are increasingly being adopted by firms and institutions. For example, YouTube not only gave rise to ultra-low-budget, home-made movies,[6] but it is also beginning to be used by corporations, international organizations (such as the World Bank to publicize its World Development Report) and universities (to recruit applicants) for marketing and advertising. Video game industries today, for example, actively take advantage of user-led modifications (known as 'mods') to improve the entertainment value of games (see Aoyama and Izushi, 2008).

Logistics Innovation

Previously considered as a service that provides simple transporting and warehousing of goods, the logistics industry in the contemporary economy has emerged as a strategic and knowledge-intensive industry with a considerable degree of sophistication, and it provides critical services to all sectors of the economy. Along with a shift in the industry's best practices from a supply-push value-chain philosophy to demand-pull logistics, building reliable 'quick response' supply chains with minimal inventory and maximum flexibility became of paramount importance across various sectors (Feldman et al., 1996; Berglund et al., 1999; Arntzen and Shumway, 2002; Hadjiconstantinou, 1999). Globalization of sourcing and markets has further contributed to the growing importance of logistics efficiency. The logistics industry enables long-distance and increasingly cross-border coordination of production.

The Internet revolutionized logistics not only by providing new tools and by improving transparency, but also by allowing the rise of new e-logistics providers, which can be divided into those that provide logistics services exclusively in virtual space (non-asset-based), and those that provide services in both virtual and geographic spaces (asset-based) (Lieb and Schwarz, 2001). The rise of e-logistics providers suggests that organizational dissociation of the physical movement of goods and the related transmission and processing of information is being accelerated by the introduction of B2B e-commerce (Evans and Wurster, 1997; Jallat and Capek, 2001). Purely virtual e-commerce providers include Internet brokers, online auctions and online exchanges. Internet brokers match buyers and sellers and provide market information exclusively online (Lucking-Reiley and Spulber, 2001; Jallat and Capek, 2001), while online auctions (both forward and reverse auctions) typically restrict participants.[7] Online exchanges, which bring together many buyers and sellers in a single marketplace, are usually organized either as a vertical marketplace (by industrial sector such as automobile and steel) or as a horizontal marketplace (process that cuts across industrial sectors, such as office supply procurement). Some online exchanges are set up exclusively to trade less-than-truckload (LTL) spot markets for small shipments, or conducting freight aggregation.[8] The use of e-logistics providers is becoming increasingly widespread; for example, General Electric estimates that roughly one-third of its spending is already conducted through online auctions (GE Global Exchange Services, 2002).

Tourism Innovation

Among the most significant tourism innovations is destination creation through the innovative combination of various tourism objectives (sun and beach, cultural, heritage, and eco-tourisms). Some are creations of a unique environment (such as Las Vegas or Orlando), and others market regional cultures and heritage through public–private partnerships that organize festivals (such as Mardi Gras in New Orleans and flamenco festivals in Andalusia, Spain).[9] Not only is the Internet actively used by local tourism boards and local businesses to market these touristic spaces, but user-created contents are also articulating spaces that are distinct from the former (Zook and Graham, 2007). For example, Google Maps allows users to identify locations on a map and insert personal comments and photos. These user-created spaces are distinctive from, and sometimes complement, but at other times run counter to largely corporate-driven geographic information on the web.

New business models that create novel organization (either through new business start-ups or through significant corporate reorganization) are considered an aspect of service innovation. In tourism, the emergence of low-cost airlines (for example Southwest Airlines in the USA, Ryanair in Europe) offered a new business model that focused on the niche market of budget travelers. All-inclusive resorts developed by Club Med also represent a new business model. Online travel websites that allow airlines and hotels to sell unsold seats and rooms at discount prices (such as Hotwire.com and Lastminute.com) or those that allow consumers to auction for prices (such as Priceline.com) also represent a new business model. Existing firms also adopt new business models, however. The frequent-flyer programs offered by various airlines, for example, were designed to develop loyal customers in what was viewed as a largely undifferentiated service.

Contract R&D Services

With respect to those that induce corporate reorganization, outsourcing of service functions prompted organizational change, particularly with respect to functions that were previously viewed as inappropriate for outsourcing for various reasons (such as business processes or R&D). The emerging service dominant logic (SDL) view today is a response to various global trends, including demographic shift, growth of self-service, web-based technologies, outsourcing and offshoring, service industrialization, servicization of manufacturing, the rise of globally integrated enterprises, Internet collaborations and web-based service. Tidd and Hull (2006) examined intrafirm configurations as an aspect of service innovation, and concluded that cross-functional teaming and physical co-locations characterize many of the successful corporate restructurings.

As firms focus on core competence and outsource other functions, opportunities for providing business process and R&D services have grown phenomenally in the decade to 2010 (Miles, 2001; quoted in Wood, 2005). In addition, technological convergence required the design of new protocols, as previously incompatible voice and data equipment of vertically integrated manufacturers needed to be converted to open standards for products to communicate with one another. These technological and institutional transformations opened up opportunities for Indian firms; one type of R&D services becoming increasingly popular in India involves a sale and transfer of an intellectual property (IP) block in return for a one-time payment plus volume-based royalty to the provider. An IP block typically incorporates some kind of embedded systems design and development, which is a combination of hardware and software dedicated to perform a specific task without human interventions. Multinational Enterprises (MNEs) leverage market uncertainty by purchasing R&D services when they find themselves behind in certain technological areas where they had failed to anticipate growth.

For India, the rapid growth of R&D service exports is largely attributed to embedded systems, which are digital replacements of what were previously mechanical and electrical functions. Embedded systems designers adapt software abstractions for data transmission to meet real-time constraints, power requirements and safety considerations in various domains while interacting with the physical world through sensors and actuators (Lee, 2000). Embedded systems are part of everything from consumer goods, such as cellphones and microwave ovens; to transport equipment, such as automobiles and aircraft; to industrial process control systems. In sum, R&D services in embedded systems involve firms offering design services, and executing specific contracts for customers, as well as firms that generate IP blocks that go into various embedded systems to derive revenue either from a one-time license fee or from recurring volume-based royalty payments, or a combination of both.

Financial Innovation

Tufano (2003) defines financial innovation as: 'the act of creating and popularizing new financial instruments as well as new financial technologies, institutions and markets'. Frame and White (2004) categorize four types of financial innovations: new financial products (for example adjustable-rate mortgages, exchange-traded index funds); new financial services (for example online securities trading, internet banking); new production processes in finance (for example electronic record-keeping for securities, credit scoring); and new organizational forms in the financial industry (for example electronic exchanges for trading securities, Internet-only banks). Although some aspects of financial innovations are clearly unique to the industry, they carry many similar characteristics to other service innovations, including a general absence of dedicated R&D facilities, innovations that are relatively easily imitable (disclosure is often required by regulations) and, in spite of the recent growth, patents remain uncommon for financial innovations (Lerner, 2002).

Financial innovations are often driven by multiple forces (Tufano, 2003). They can be motivated by the desire to circumvent financial regulations and taxes (Miller, 1986). They are also spurred by developments in underlying technologies, which allow lenders to overcome asymmetric information problems and permit organizational innovation (Frame and White, 2004). Furthermore, unstable or volatile macroeconomic conditions, including fluctuating prices, interest rates and exchange rates, tend to induce financial innovation.

Some consider financial innovations to be a mechanism that improves the overall welfare of the economy (Merton, 1992; Frame and White, 2004), while various social costs, including the sense of inequity in the society, have also been noted (Tufano, 2003). The difficulty in accessing data is the biggest challenge in furthering research on financial innovation (Frame and White, 2004; Tufano, 2003).

SERVICE INNOVATION AND REGIONS

How do service innovations link to regions? Since service innovation covers a broad range of phenomenon, its multifaceted nature makes it difficult to conclude that a particular spatial trajectory is emerging as a result of service innovation. Nevertheless, there are at least two key roles of service innovation in regions: first, by contributing to regional economic growth and job creation; and second, through generating localization economies by creating a cluster of knowledge. The geographic perspective on service innovation is still in development. Although there is an extensive literature on regional innovation systems (see Asheim and Coenen, 2005; Asheim and Isaksen, 2002; Cooke, 2001; Cooke et al., 1997), few specifically identify service innovations as drivers of regional innovation and growth. The regional aspects of services are most often discussed within the framework of understanding the advanced producer services (or knowledge-intensive business services – KIBS), yet the emphasis is primarily on service activities and the role of regions, rather than service innovation and the role of regions (see, for example, Wood, 2006a, 2006b). While clustering of services is observed (see for example, Isaksen, 2004; Keeble and Nachum, 2002; Hermelin and Rusten, 2007), it remains entirely unclear as to how specific geographies of services mirror the geography of service innovation.[10] For example, do offshore finance locations such as Cayman Islands also serve as the locations of innovation? How do we explain a myriad of retail and distribution innovations by Wal-Mart, which is headquartered in the remote town of Bentonville, Arkansas?

Wood (2005, 429–30; 2006) renders such 'sector-based views' obsolete, and instead advocates for a 'service-informed perspective', which he claims is critical in regional innovation systems. The latter offers a perspective on innovation that combines market characteristics with expertise profiles; services represent essential expertise that serve as critical resources to regional innovation. Wood (2005) claimed that, today: 'competitive polarization between regions is being driven much more by knowledge-based service functions than the invention or adoption of new technologies' (p. 441). Similarly, Breschi and Malerba (2001) argue that the flow of knowledge, combined with spillovers, is most critical to regional innovation systems. This suggests the renewed significance of cities (Daniels and Bryson, 2002), driven by the concentration of talent (Florida, 2002). Indeed, Breschi and Malerba (2001) argued that innovative processes are geographically concentrated because of necessary specialized inputs, services and resources. Recent work on related variety (see Boschma and Iammarino, 2009) confirmed the strength of Jacobian externalities – what role do services, and service innovation play in such context?

There are counter-examples, however. Bryson and Monnoyer (2004), for example, implicated that when standardization is accomplished, services move away from the core urban areas, whereas service innovation may very well stay in the urban core. Globalization complicates the picture further. Some services such as global consultancies function as important 'conduits of innovative ideas and methodologies between global and national scales' (Wood, 2006a, 55) and are therefore essential in supporting 'regional adaptability' (Wood, 2005, 431). Wood (2005, 431) argued that the supplier–customer relations have 'inherent geographic dimensions', which are articulated by the exchange of expertise across scales. However, manifestation of such geographic dimensions is left open for speculation.

The geographic dimensions of service innovation are made even more difficult to pin down due to significant IT involvement in many service innovations. For example, whereas e-commerce may compete against the 'Main Street' shopping districts to some extent, the increasing integration that resulted in 'click-and-brick' may work to solidify competitiveness of those who engage in multichannel retailing. While some innovations such as those in logistics go hand in hand with globalization and expand the reach of services, other innovations, such as content creation and contract R&D services, depend on the availability of specialized expertise, which are found clustered in certain locations. Some service innovation knowledge is decentralized, coordinated and integrated not by the traditional firm boundaries but along the value or supply chain across firms. The territoriality of service innovation may take a network form, and span across various suppliers and include customers and end-users. Furthermore, because service innovation is more difficult to standardize and therefore codify than manufacturing innovation, it can be assumed that knowledge involved in service innovation is by an order of magnitude more tacit. The involvement of the user exacerbates the complexity further, although clearly this would follow the geography of online populations. Combined, tendencies in service innovation make its geography even more difficult to substantiate.

CONCLUSION AND FUTURE RESEARCH AGENDA

There are three recent and noteworthy developments: in research, policy and institution building. On the policy front, innovation policies have neglected service innovation (Wood, 2005). Myriads of unresolved issues exist in the conceptualization and implementation of effective service innovation promotion. Aside from a few insights, such as the negative role of regulations (see Miles, 2000), we know little about how service innovations are conceived and how they become successful. Recently, efforts by various European governments and the OECD have begun to highlight the importance of service innovation, and in particular, to focus on the promotion of KIBS as regional innovation policy (Kuusitu, 2005; Mas-Verdú, 2007; OECD, 2006). Without proper conceptualization for policies, however, service innovation will continue to lack an appropriate institutional mechanism for its protection and promotion.

On research, Miles (2000) argued that time is ripe for a marriage between service innovation literature and the mainstream innovation studies. However, evidence so far suggests that significant challenges remain in relation to such a marriage. Research on service innovation today still remains more a point of departure for various highly relevant questions. Missing are the analytical frameworks of concrete sets of knowledge, including how service firms innovate and how services facilitate innovation.

To respond to the knowledge gap, new research units are being formed that specifically focus on service innovation. Service science combines 'fundamental science and engineering theories, models and applications with facets of the management field, particularly knowledge, supply chain, and change management, in order to enhance and advance service innovation' (Paton and McLaughlin, 2008, 26). Bitner and Brown (2008) offer a worker-centered definition: 'service science aims to harness the power of science and engineering to support knowledge workers within complex service environments through knowledge-centered technological and architectures and solutions, while ensuring that "workers" are managed toward maintaining and developing knowledge-driven value-added' (Paton and McLaughlin, 2008, 78). Chesbrough and Spohrer (2006, 36) advocate for an academic discipline dedicated to 'service science', claiming: 'there is no academic community of scholars that shares a common mission to understand the roots of this arena of economic activity, or how to advance it'. Academics and practitioners agree that an interdisciplinary approach is required in better understanding service innovation (Hipp and Grupp, 2005; IfM and IBM, 2008). Various units now exist in management, engineering and computer services with little coordination and consolidation of knowledge. For example, the University of California at Berkeley organized Services Science, Management and Engineering (SSME) program, a teaching and research collaboration among several units on campus, including the Haas School of Business, the School of Information, the School of Engineering, and the Center for Information Technology Research in the Interest of Society (CITRIS). The purpose of the program is to train experts who specialize in creating new organizational models and business processes.

The University of Cambridge's Institute of Manufacturing and IBM organized a symposium that combined education, research, business and government sectors in developing a perspective for service innovation (see IfM and IBM, 2008). According to the white paper produced as an outcome of the symposium at Cambridge, service innovation represents a co-evolution of customer demand, technology, business models, governance and organizational innovation. However, among the 35 academic research clusters mentioned by IBM, economic geography is not included as a discipline that can contribute to service innovation research. This is ironic, as one of the oldest scholarly activities on services, the Service Sector Research Unit (now renamed as the Services and Enterprise Research Unit) at the University of Birmingham was established in 1993, and drew skills exclusively from faculty in geography. A significant portion of economic geographers on both sides of the Atlantic today specialize in one or more segments of the service economy. As economic geographers, we must take it upon ourselves to ensure that as a community we continue to engage in this fertile area of service innovation research with a multidisciplinary community of scholars, as service innovation will undoubtedly comprise an important driver of economic growth.

NOTES

1. According to the International Labour Organization (ILO, 2007), service jobs outnumbered those in agriculture or manufacturing sectors for the first time in human history in 2006.
2. Miles (2007) discusses examples from the UK, including the Royal Bank of Scotland, HSBC, Tesco, Royal & Sun Alliance (insurance), Reed Elsevier (publishing), BT and Reuters.
3. Miles (2007) examines only market services, leaving out non-market services such as health and education.
4. The definition adopted by the OECD (2006) comes from van Ark et al. (2003, 16), which states that service innovation is: 'a new or considerably changed service concept, client interaction channel, service delivery system or technological concept that individually, but most likely in combination leads to one or more (re)new(ed) service functions that are new to the firm and do change the service/good offered on the market and do require structurally new technological, human, or organizational capabilities of the service organization'.
5. At the onset of Internet retailing in 1997, competition between Amazon.com and Barnes & Noble bookstores initially positioned brick-and-mortar retail trade in competition against e-commerce development. Amazon was the first business-to-consumer online store, opened 22 months ahead of Barnes & Noble's e-commerce site. The competition between online and real-world booksellers set the tone for subsequent views toward e-commerce development, positioning store and non-store retailing in direct competition.
6. Known as 'mumblecore', the American independent film movement in the 2000s relies on affordable digital video technologies for production and new outlets such as YouTube for distribution.

7. In traditional forward auctions, one seller offers a product on which potential buyers bid. In reverse auctions, the buyer specifies a product requirement, and potential suppliers make their price offers.
8. In the automobile industry, trucks commonly travel at 40 percent capacity, according to Ford Motors Company (Cohen, 2002).
9. See Zukin (1993) for an analysis of Disney World, Fox Gotham (2002) for research on Mardi Gras in New Orleans, and Aoyama (2009) for flamenco festivals in Andalusia, Spain.
10. Muller and Zenker (2001) discuss the role of KIBS in regional and national innovation systems, but rely on findings that are self-reported.

REFERENCES

Andersen, B., J. Howells, R. Hull, I. Miles and J. Roberts (eds) (2000), *Knowledge and Innovation in the New Service Economy*, Cheltenham, UK and Northampton, MA, USA: Edward Elgar.
Anderson, W. and W. Crocca (1993), 'Engineering practice and codevelopment of product prototypes', *Communications of the ACM*, **36** (4), 49–56.
Aoyama, Y. (2009), 'Artists, tourists, and the state: cultural tourism and the flamenco industry in Andalusia, Spain', *International Journal of Urban and Regional Research*, **33** (3), 80–104.
Aoyama, Y. and H. Izushi (2008), 'User-innovation in the video game industry', DIME Working Paper, http:// www.dime-eu.org/files/active/0/AoyamaIzushiPAPER.pdf.
van Ark, B., L. Broersma and P. den Hertog (2003), *Service Innovation, Performance and Policy: A Review*, The Hague: Ministry of Economic Affairs.
Arntzen, B. and H. Shumway (2002), 'Driven by demand: a case study', *Supply Chain Management Review*, January/February, 34–41.
Asheim, B. and L. Coenen (2005), 'Knowledge bases and regional innovation systems: comparing Nordic clusters', *Research Policy*, **34**, 1173–90.
Asheim, B. and A. Isaksen (2002), 'Regional innovation systems: the integration of local "sticky" and global "ubiquitous" knowledge', *Journal of Technology Transfer*, **27** (1), 77–8.
Barras, R. (1986), 'Towards a theory of innovation in services', *Research Policy*, **15** (4), 161–73.
Barras, R. (1990), 'Interactive innovation in financial and business services: the vanguard of the services revolution', *Research Policy*, **19** (3), 215–37.
Berglund, M., P. van Laarhoven, G. Sharman and S. Wandel (1999), 'Third-party logistics: is there a future?', *International Journal of Logistics Management*, **10** (1), 59–70.
Beyers, W. (2002), 'Services and the new economy: elements of a research agenda', *Journal of Economic Geography*, **2** (1), 1–29.
Bitner, M. and S. Brown (2008), 'The service imperative', *Business Horizons*, 50th Anniversary Issue, Jan./ Feb., 39–47.
Boschma, R. and S. Iammarino (2009), 'Related variety, trade linkages and regional growth in Italy', *Economic Geography*, **85**, 289–311.
Breschi, S. and F. Malerba (2001), 'The geography of innovation and clustering: some introductory notes', *Industrial and Corporate Change*, **10** (4), 817–33.
Bryson, J. and M. Monnoyer (2004), 'Understanding the relationship between services and innovation: the RESER review of the European service literature on innovation', *Service Industries Journal*, **24** (1), 205–22.
BusinessWeek (2007), 'Services innovation: the next big thing', *BusinessWeek*, 29 March.
Castells, M. (1980), *The Urban Question*, Cambridge, MA: MIT Press.
Chesbrough, H. and J. Spohrer (2006), 'A research manifesto for services science', *Communications of the ACM*, **49** (7), 35–40.
Cohen, N. (2002), 'E-commerce and the environment', in D. Pamlin (ed.), *Sustainability at the Speed of Light: Opportunities and Challenges for Tomorrow's Society*, Solna, Sweden: WWF, pp. 62–75.
Cohen, S.S. and J. Zysman (1989), *Manufacturing Matters*, New York: Basic Books.
Cooke, P. (2001), 'Regional innovation systems, clusters and the knowledge economy', *Industrial and Corporate Change*, **10**, 945–74.
Cooke, P., M. Uranga and G. Extebarria (1997), 'Regional innovation systems: institutional and organisational dimensions', *Research Policy*, **26** (4–5), 475–91.
Daniels, P. (1993), *Service Industries in the World Economy*, Oxford: Blackwell.
Daniels, P. and J. Bryson (2002), 'Manufacturing services and servicing manufacturing: changing forms of production in advanced capitalist economies', *Urban Studies*, **39** (5–6), 977–91.
de Laat, P. (2005), 'Copyright or copyleft? An analysis of property regimes for software development', *Research Policy*, **34** (10), 1511–32.

Drejer, I. (2004), 'Identifying innovation in surveys of services: a Schumpeterian perspective', *Research Policy*, **33**, 551–62.

Evans, P. and T. Wurster (1997), 'Strategy and the new economics of information', *Harvard Business Review*, **75** (5), 71–82.

Feldman, M., M. Bell and L. Salamon (1996), 'The distribution industry: an engine for Maryland growth', Baltimore, MD: Institute for Policy Studies, Johns Hopkins University.

Florida, R. (2002), *The Rise of the Creative Class*, New York: Basic Books.

Fox Gotham, K. (2002), 'Marketing Mardi Gras: commodification, spectacle, and the political economy of tourism in New Orleans', *Urban Studies*, **39** (10), 1735–56.

Frame, W.S. and L.J. White (2004), 'Empirical studies of financial innovation: lots of talk, little action?', *Journal of Economic Literature*, **42** (1), 116–44.

Freel, M. (2006), 'Patterns of innovation in knowledge-intensive business services', *Industry and Innovation*, **13** (3), 335–58.

Gadrey, J., F. Gallouj and O. Weinstein (1995), 'New models of innovation – how services benefit industry', *International Journal of Service Industry Management*, **6** (3), 4–16.

Gallouj, F. (1998), 'Innovating in reverse: services and the reverse product cycle', *European Journal of Innovation Management*, **1** (3), 123–38.

Gallouj, F. and O. Weinstein (1997), 'Innovation in services', *Research Policy*, **26**, 537–56.

GE Global Exchange Services (2002), 'GE GSN: the world's largest private Web marketplace', http://www.gxs.com/downloads/cs_gsnq202.pdf.

Gershuny, J. (1978), *After Industrial Society? The Emerging Self-Service Economy*, London: Macmillan and New York: Humanities Press.

Gross, P. (1989), 'Marketing pull/technology push: GE's ultem resin', *Research Technology Management*, **32** (2), 30–31.

Hadjiconstantinou, E. (ed.) (1999), *Quick Response in the Supply Chain*, Berlin: Springer Verlag.

Hansen, N. (1998), 'Do producer services induce regional economic development?', *Journal of Regional Science*, **30** (4), 465–76.

Hashimoto, Kenji (1998), 'Shutoken ni okeru kobiniensu sutoa no tenpo ruikeika to sono kuukanteki tenkai: POS deta ni yoru uriage bunseki wo tsujite', *Chirigaku Hyoron* (Geographical Review) **71A** (4), 239–53.

Hermelin, B. and G. Rusten (2007), 'The organizational and territorial changes of services in a globalized world', *Geografiska Annaler*, **89** (s1), 5–11.

Hipp, C. and H. Grupp (2005), 'Innovation in the service sector: the demand for service- specific innovation measurement concepts and typologies', *Research Policy*, **34** (4), 517–35.

Hirschorn, L. (1988), 'The post-industrial economy: labour skills and the new mode of production', *Service Industries Journal*, **8**, 19–38.

Howe, J. (2008), *Crowdsourcing*, New York: Crown Business.

Howells, J. (2004), 'Innovation, consumption, and services: encapsulation and the combinatorial role of services', *Service Industries Journal*, **24** (1), 19–36.

Howells, J. (2005), 'Innovation and regional economic development: a matter of perspective?', *Research Policy*, **34**, 1220–34.

IfM and IBM (2008), 'Succeeding through service innovation: a service perspective for education, research, business and government', Cambridge: University of Cambridge Institute for Manufacturing.

ILO (2007), 'Global Employment Trends Brief 2007', Geneva: ILO.

Isaksen, A. (2004), 'Knowledge-based clusters and urban location: the clustering of software consultancy in Oslo', *Urban Studies*, **41** (5–6), 1157–74.

Jallat, F. and M. Capek (2001), 'Disintermediation in question: new economy, new networks, new middlemen', *Business Horizons*, **44** (2), 55–60.

Jankowski, J. (2001), 'Measurement and growth of R&D within the service economy', *Journal of Technology Transfer*, **26**, 323–36.

Jeppesen, L. (2005), 'User toolkits for innovation: consumers support each other', *Journal of Product Innovation Management*, **22** (4), 347–62.

Johne, A. and C. Storey (1998), 'New service development: a review of the literature and annotated bibliography', *European Journal of Marketing*, **32** (3–4), 184–251.

Kay, D., J. Pratt and M. Warner (2007), 'Role of services in regional economy growth', *Growth and Change*, **38** (3), 419–42.

Keeble, D. and L. Nachum (2002), 'Why do business service firms cluster? Small consultancies, clustering and decentralization in London and southern England', *Transactions of the Institute of British Geographers*, **27** (1), 67–90.

Kuusisto, J. (ed.) (2005), 'Knowledge-intensive service activities in the Finnish forest and related engineering and electronics industries cluster', OECD Sectoral Case Studies in Innovation: Knowledge Intensive Service Activities, http://www.sc-research.fi/fi/uutiset/docs/FORENEL050319a.pdf (accessed 12 May 2009).

Kuznets, S. (1971), *Economic Growth of Nations: Total Output and Production Structure*, Cambridge, MA: Belknap.

Lee, E. (2000), 'What's ahead for embedded software?', *IEEE Computer*, **33**, 18–26.

Lerner, J. (2002), 'Where does State Street lead? A first look at finance patents, 1971–2000', *Journal of Finance*, **57** (2), 901–30.

Lieb, R. and B. Schwarz (2001), 'The Year 2001 Survey: CEO perspectives on the current status and future prospects of the third party logistics industry in the United States', Accenture Consulting and Northeastern University, http://web.cba.neu.edu/~rlieb/2001ceopaper.dot.

Lucking-Reiley, D. and D. Spulber (2001), 'Business-to-business electronic commerce', *Journal of Economic Perspectives*, **15** (1), 55–68.

Lundquist, K., L.-O. Olander and M. Henning (2008), 'Producer services: growth and roles in long-term economic development', *Service Industries Journal*, **28** (4), 463–77.

Mas-Verdú, F. (2007), 'Services and innovation systems: European models of technology centres', *Service Business*, **1**, 7–23.

Merton, R. (1992), 'Financial innovation and economic performance', *Journal of Applied Corporate Finance*, **4** (4), 12–22.

Miles, I. (2000), 'Services innovation: coming of age in the knowledge-based economy', *International Journal of Innovation Management*, **4** (4), 371–89.

Miles, I. (2001), 'Services innovation: a reconfiguration of innovation studies', PREST Discussion Paper Series, no. 01-05, University of Manchester.

Miles, I. (2007), 'Research and development (R&D) beyond manufacturing: the strange case of services R&D', *R&D Management*, **37** (3), 249–68.

Miller, M. (1986), 'Financial innovation: the last twenty years and the next', *Journal of Financial and Quantitative Analysis*, **21** (4), 459–71.

Muller, E. and A. Zenker (2001), 'Business services as actors of knowledge transformation: the role of KIBS in regional and national innovation systems', *Research Policy*, **30** (9), 1501–16.

Nijssen, E., B. Hillebrand, P. Vermeulen and R. Kemp (2006), 'Exploring product and service innovation similarities and differences', *International Journal of Research in Marketing*, **23** (3), 241–51.

North, D. (1955), 'Location theory and regional economic growth', *Journal of Political Economy*, **63** (3), 243–58.

OECD (2006), *Innovation and Knowledge-Intensive Service Activities*, Paris: OECD.

Ordanini, A. and P. Pasini (2008), 'Service co-production and value co-creation: the case for a service-oriented architecture (SOA)', *European Management Journal*, **26** (5), 289–97.

Parthasarathy, B. and Y. Aoyama (2006), 'From software services to R&D services: local entrepreneurship in the software industry in Bangalore, India', *Environment and Planning A*, **38** (7), 1269–85.

Paton, R. and S. McLaughlin (2008), 'Services innovation: knowledge transfer and the supply chain', *European Management Journal*, **26** (2), 77–83.

Petit, P. (1986), *Slow Growth and the Service Economy*, London: Frances Pinter.

Piller, F. and D. Walcher (2006), 'Toolkits for idea competitions: a novel method to integrate users in new product development', *R&D Management*, **36** (3), 307–18.

Riggs, W. and E. von Hippel (1994), 'Incentives to innovate and the sources of innovation: the case of scientific instruments', *Research Policy*, **23** (4), 459–70.

Sayer, A. and R. Walker (1992), *The New Social Economy: Reworking the Division of Labor*, Cambridge, MA: Basil Blackwell.

Stanback, T. (1980), *Understanding the Service Economy*, Baltimore, MD: Johns Hopkins University Press.

Surowiecki, J. (2004), *The Wisdom of Crowds*, New York: Doubleday.

Tether, B. (2005), 'Do services innovate (differently)? Insights from the European Innobarometer Survey', *Industry and Innovation*, **12** (2), 153–84.

Tidd, J. and F. Hull (2006), 'Managing service innovation: the need for selectivity rather than "best practice"', *New Technology, Work and Employment*, **21** (2), 139–61.

Tiebout, C. (1956), 'Exports and regional economic growth', *Journal of Political Economy*, **64** (2), 160–64.

Tufano, P. (2003), 'Financial innovation', in G. Constantinides, M. Harris and R. Stulz (eds), *Handbook of the Economics of Finance*, Amsterdam: North-Holland, pp. 307–36, http://www.econ.sdu.edu.cn/jrtzx/upload-file/pdf/books/handbook/10.pdf.

Vang, J. and C. Zellner (2005), 'Introduction: innovation in services', *Industry and Innovation*, **12** (2), 147–52.

Vargo, S., P. Maglio and M. Archpru Akaka (2008), 'On value and value co-creation: a service systems and service logic perspective', *European Management Journal*, **26** (3), 145–52.

Verspagen, B. (1997), 'European "regional clubs": do they exist, and where are they heading?', MERIT Working Paper 2/97-010, Maastricht: MERIT.

von Hippel, E., S. Thomke and M. Sonnack (1999), 'Creating breakthroughs at 3M', *Harvard Business Review*, **77** (5), 47–57.

Williams, C. (1996), 'Understanding the role of consumer services in local economic development: some evidence from the Fens', *Environment and Planning A*, **28**, 555–71.

Williams, C. (1997), *Consumer Services and Economic Development*, London: Routledge.

Wood, P. (2005), 'A service-informed approach to regional innovation – or adaptation? *Service Industries Journal*, **25** (4), 429–45.

Wood, P. (2006a), 'The regional significance of knowledge-intensive services in Europe', *Innovation*, **19** (1), 51–66.

Wood, P. (2006b), 'Urban development and knowledge-intensive business services: too many unanswered questions?', *Growth and Change*, **37** (3), 335–61.

Zook, M. and M. Graham (2007), 'Mapping DigiPlace: geo-coded Internet data and the perception of place', *Environment and Planning B*, **34** (3), 466–82.

Zukin, S. (1993), *Landscapes of Power: From Detroit to Disney World*, Berkeley and Los Angeles, CA: University of California Press.

28 Regional services innovation
Philip Cooke

INTRODUCTION

This subject has been touched upon but seldom reviewed or investigated from a regional innovation and growth perspective. This is curious, given that in many regions and countries employment and gross domestic product (GDP) from services outweighs income earned from other sectors of the economy. However, it would not be untrue to say that services innovation is a relatively minor part of the literature on innovation and innovation systems overall. That is, it is pronounced neither in the sectoral or technological systems of innovation literature nor in that on national innovation systems. One honourable exception to this situation is Ian Miles, who has worked consistently in the field for many years, making valuable contributions to thinking about services innovation, albeit from an evolutionary but non-spatial perspective. Attention will be devoted to the findings on services innovation by Miles and colleagues in the review section of this chapter that follows this introduction.

In this chapter, the focus will be on innovative services rather than services in general. It is a curious and complicated category because it ranges from the corner newsagents to the largest global finance houses. Some parts of the sector are considered largely uninnovative, notably localized consumer services. Other parts are considered highly innovative but leave few markers in terms that mainstream innovation systems researchers find interesting, notably (until recently) research and development (R&D) expenditure, patents and publications. Nevertheless, in recent years some progress has been made in the latter regard, for example: services now appear in the European Union's Community Innovation Survey; R&D equivalent expenditure for financial services is subject to accounting in some countries; and progress has been made generally in identifying innovative service industries and their comparative innovation rates with respect to, for example, manufacturing industry. As this chapter will show, some possibly surprising results of this recent work indicate that some service sectors are significantly more innovative than even engineering, which among manufacturing industries is normally considered by experts to be something of a Schumpeterian innovation bellwether. It is even possible to display (for the UK only) some data on the regional distributions of services and non-services innovation and I do so below. Finally, in a more textured account of service innovation, the chapter references industries for which innovation scores tend to be high and where some research has been conducted: these are creative industries, healthcare services and aspects of financial services.

SERVICES INNOVATION: A REVIEW

In this section I begin with an overview of some key characteristics of the services economy as a prelude to a general review of key aspects of service industry innovation characteristics. First, as already alluded to, the services economy is heterogeneous. Bryson and Daniels (2007) stress that even within the same service activity significant variations render comparisons difficult. Service firms are segmented by firm size and different sizes of firm reveal distinctive ways of operating, types of clients and geographic markets. Most firms, like the corner newsagent, provide a local service with no export potential, even outside the neighbourhood, let alone the national economy. This scale issue explains why such firms are seldom innovative in the sense of offering new knowledge combinations on commercial markets. This does not mean that innovation is especially difficult in services, for some quite startling increases in growth and productivity within specific markets are registered. Three of these, all associated with large or relatively large firms which nevertheless began small, exemplify this.

Budget airlines are a service industry innovation that developed a significantly different model from their scheduled airline competitors. Two of the most important involved more efficient, hence productive use of capital through tighter flight scheduling and minimization of costs in terms of staffing and services provided. Charging for services that hitherto were covered in ticket prices meant the latter could be reduced radically and revenue accrued by far greater passenger numbers accordingly. Another innovation occurred in the provision of insurance services; thus firms that began to sell insurance online could cut costs by removing 'bricks and mortar' with associated overhead. Alternatively, a third instance is found in a firm like Admiral that innovated by selling insurance to customers, like younger driving offenders, who had been unable to buy car insurance from the incumbents. The freeing-up of various market constraints in Europe and North America made such innovations feasible. Thus, as Bryson and Daniels (2007) make clear, while heterogeneity within services makes across-the-board policy formulation difficult, in specific segments, regulation and deregulation by governments is often the key to innovation and growth.

A second characteristic of services, noted tellingly in research by Van Ark (2005), is that labour productivity lags behind the rest of the economy and varies enormously in the transatlantic comparative analyses of service industry productivity he has conducted. Ostensibly this looks like what is known as 'Baumol's disease' (see for example Baumol et al., 1989), whereby 'progressive' services that are absorptive towards innovation, particularly technological innovation, are differentiated from 'non-progressive' services where such innovation is not possible. This describes a condition in which a faster rate of growth in productivity in manufacturing is associated with a proportionate rise in services occupations and labour. This lowers growth in services productivity and raises inflation accordingly.

However, Van Ark's work tends to undermine this thesis at least in large measure because it shows significantly different rates of productivity performance in the same service industries as between, for example, the European Union (EU) and the US. This is explained in terms of three interrelated technological phenomena. Firstly, American services firms invest more in technology, like for like. Thus US banks buy more computer networks or automatic tellers than European banks. Secondly, US service firms are also early adopters of relevant technological innovations because more of them are produced in the US, thus disadvantaging European users even if they are more eager adopters. Finally, knowledge spillovers explain part of the lag in the sense that workers are more technologically 'savvy' and unafraid to exchange tips with each other for utilizing new technologies in the workplace. Accordingly, even when there was a European catch-up in the early 2000s this was followed by a falling-behind in the later 2000s as later-round innovations were absorbed in the US. In regional terms, Californian banks are shown to be advanced technology users because much of the relevant innovation also occurs in the state.

Productivity is clearly influenced in major ways by innovation. Some services are highly innovative, others are not. What does the research literature tell us about services innovation? According to Andersen et al. (2000), Boden and Miles (2000) and Metcalfe and Miles (2000), services industry includes transport and telecommunications, retail and real estate, finance and hospitality, computer services and consultancy services, public and community services, and assorted recreational and artistic activities. As we have seen, they display considerable distinctiveness with, for example, education and knowledge-intensive business services having large shares of graduates. Contrariwise, hotel and hospitality services tend to have lower, though rising shares of employees with higher education qualifications. Some services, such as finance, are important investors in new technologies, but this varies by country and region. Geographical proximity to innovation was shown from Van Ark's work to be a major element in the explanation for regional services innovation variations. Although it is thought that services are primarily a matter of producing instantly consumed intangible goods, this is far from the truth. Software packages are tangible and portable, as are many creative industry products both based on software, such as computer games, and not, such as works of art, musical scores and, of course, books. Indeed, research to be discussed later suggests that the differentiation of services from manufacturing innovations is substantially less than traditionally considered. Having said that, interesting and contradictory processes can be observed in interactions between them. For now, let two opposite examples suffice to illustrate this point.

In researching Cooke et al. (2010) in Bavaria, Germany the following organizational move between services and manufacturing had been observed. Automotive systems company Robert Bosch, in supplying BMW with electronic control systems, had traditionally sourced its semiconductor system designs from Siemens and later, after it had divested its semiconductors division, the new entity Infineon. The logic of this was that microelectronic systems design services were not a core competence of Bosch, but were of Infineon. However, it had become apparent that, despite their luxury status and reputation for automotive engineering excellence, BMW cars scored less well on electronics, with lower reliability than desired. Accordingly, Bosch had 'retooled' itself with an internal automotive microelectronics system design capability, the better to embed that service into its automotive control system modules. Contrariwise, in the aerospace industry of Midi-Pyrénées at Toulouse, EADS, the producer of Airbus aeroplanes, decided to relinquish its last remaining design and manufacturing mandate, namely aeronautics control systems. Although it had traditionally been responsible for this function it decided to outsource it to Tier 1 supplier Thales. This was the upshot of an embarrassing failure of communication concerning software design between separate EADS software design houses in France and Germany. This caused a two-year delay in the introduction of the A380 'SuperJumbo' Airbus. Its rationale was that it was now to be seen ultimately as a services company supplying systems integration services. Thales, not EADS, was deemed to have greater competence in the design of aircraft control systems since it designed them for numerous military and civilian clients.

It is clear from these two fairly randomly selected illustrations that the borderline between services and manufacturing can be quite fragile in connection with high-tech services like control system software design. In this respect, as Metcalfe and Miles (2000) say, technology-based services are not so dissimilar from high-tech manufacturing. However, other services operate differently, with fewer investments in R&D and intellectual property tools like patents. Nevertheless, as will be seen later, some services both invest in patents and, more frequently, copyrights and trademarks. Metcalfe and Miles argue that there is greater focus upon organizational innovation involving training and skills upgrading of the kind discussed in The Packaging Arena laboratories in Sweden (see 'Transversality and innovation platforms', Chapter 23 in this *Handbook*). Generally, services are perceived to have weak links to university research and associated innovation, with more of what innovation does occur being done in almost accidental ways.

It is probable that service innovation, where it occurs, is more user or consumer-driven than has traditionally been considered the case with manufacturing innovation (see also Chapter 22 in this *Handbook*). The latter has, not least through the Schumpeterian 'innovation as creative destruction' metaphor, itself drawing upon the engineering model effects of the opening of railways in the US Midwest, been heavily influenced by innovation in manufacturing products and systems (see Andersen's Chapter 2 in this *Handbook*). Here, as is revealed in the conceptual progress of the systems of innovation field itself, a linear model of innovation prevailed. Andersen (this volume) draws attention to the producer-driven technological innovations in passenger rail transport, their testing for supremacy in the races between competing locomotives at the Rainhill Trials of 1829 on Merseyside, UK, and the consumer discomforts of the early railway trains. In other words, the customer was the last interest group to be considered in the design of this radical innovation. One hundred and fifty years later, the predominant innovation model had shifted towards a more nuanced user–producer interactive type, especially as outsourcing, of the kind discussed in the Bosch and Airbus cases above, had grown rapidly under the regime of Japanese 'lean production' or 'Toyotism' (Dohse et al., 1985).

Here, supplier and client firms would habitually innovate in project-based teams involving 'concurrent' or 'simultaneous engineering'. Inside such teams would be engineers from both supplier and customer firms, and service personnel such as marketing specialists, all responsible for designing innovations through intense user–producer interactions (Cooke and Morgan, 1998). But services firms, even innovation-users like banks and financial services, typically bought 'turnkey solutions' until they found they needed to upgrade their 'absorptive capacity' to clarify the particularities of their business requirements of the system being designed (Cohen and Levinthal, 1989; Abreu, Chapter 16 in this *Handbook*). Now, more and more, user-driven innovation has risen in prominence in areas like public procurement, especially of 'green' products and services (including 'green' software and systems designs) or retailing, where consumer concerns about food quality, plastic packaging and fair trade imports are highly influential. It is likely that as advanced economies increasingly become service economies, such user-driven innovation in fields like healthcare, where they are powerful lobbyists, or education will grow in importance. This entails not reversion to, but rather reversing the old linear model somewhat; yet not overturning the interactive one but expressing a new hybrid linear-interactive 'designer' model, as pioneered in the biopharmaceuticals industry from discoveries made in post-genomic biotechnologies.

REGIONAL CHARACTERISTICS OF SERVICES INNOVATION

The content of Table 28.1 is drawn from Chapain et al.'s (2010) final report to the UK National Endowment for Science, Technology and the Arts (NESTA) which mapped the interactions between creative industry innovation activity and innovative activity in the rest of British industry at regional level. The data sources utilized included mainly the EU Community Innovation Survey accessed as raw data from the UK Office for National Statistics, and survey data from questionnaire–based research conducted as part of the project. For the first time, a picture is provided of British regional variation and comparative performance in the creative industries versus all industries, on the one hand, and the segments of the rest of the British industrial and service economy, on the other. The data draw attention to a number of crucial findings about innovation, which is defined in both comparator sets as new products or processes in manufacturing or services commercially available on their relevant markets during the period 2004–06. The definition of creative industries is taken from the UK Department of Culture, Media and Sport. This definition includes nine creative sectors: advertising; architecture; arts and antiques; designer fashion; video, film and photography; music and the performing arts; publishing; software, computer games and electronic publishing; and radio and TV.

Table 28.1   Product or process innovation of firms by sector and region, 2004–06

%	Creative Industries	Engi-neering	Other manu-facturing	Retail & distri-bution	KIBS	Other services	All
North East	37	35	45	18	31	18	24
North West	37	38	37	27	30	14	26
Yorkshire & Humberside	36	39	33	19	31	20	24
East Midlands	38	38	48	25	32	16	28
West Midlands	39	40	47	20	35	16	27
East	38	47	44	25	36	23	30
London	19	33	41	19	30	18	22
South East	43	44	38	19	30	18	27
South West	35	41	38	25	36	21	28
Wales	34	41	40	17	31	18	25
Scotland	37	38	40	18	31	18	24
UK	34	39	39	21	31	18	26

Source: EU Community Innovation Survey, Office for National Statistics.

First, it is noticeable that creative industry innovation rates are generally high in all regions except London, which drags the British average down sufficiently that all other regions exceed the British average of 34 per cent of firms reporting creative innovations during the period in question. The data clearly leave a huge open question about the role of agglomeration generally in processes of innovation. However, London performs moderately in all kinds of innovation, scoring below the British average for innovation in all industries. This suggests the following well-known fact, reported in the Department of Trade and Industry (DTI, 1999) report on biotechnology, namely that in general London is not a particularly innovative place in terms of the weight of innovative activity in its overall economic make-up. Simply, it means that London's innovativeness, in the pockets where it exists, is massively outweighed by swathes of uninnovative economic activity, mostly in services like public administration, banking and tourism, that are largely moribund in either creative or innovative terms. The less-considered aspect in this analysis of London's laggardliness is that it is even less innovative in creative industries than it is in nearly all the other sectors, except 'other services'. Even in knowledge-intensive business services (KIBS), where it might be thought that London's global financial hub function gives it major potential innovation significance, it falls slightly below the British average, like the South East and North West. So London has scale, market size and talent but is, in overall terms, rather stagnant creatively speaking. Of course, what this shows is that London's creativity occurs in niches such as the City and Canary Wharf for banking and finance, Mayfair for hedge funds, and Soho for film and video, with various tiny outliers like Clerkenwell, Dalston and Shoreditch in various facets of the creative industries. But these float on a sea of creative mediocrity.

Second, as noted, all other British regions score at or above the British average of 34 per cent of firms reporting creative innovations. There is relatively remarkable homogeneity in the regional scores, except for the South East where 43 per cent report creative innovations. This is in line with the theoretical insights of evolutionary economic geography, whose forerunners Myrdal and Hirschman both predicted that innovative activity would locate in satellites at some commutable distance from 'primate' cities because of diseconomies of scale and agglomeration in metropolitan locations. As discussed in Cooke and Schwartz (2008), with empirical support from Israel, the UK and the EU, this phenomenon occurs in many European and, we might add, US metropolitan systems. Think only of Silicon Valley's satellite status to San Francisco, or Cambridge, MA's to Boston (as well as many other smaller satellites such as Amherst, Waltham and Worcester); Cambridge and Oxford in relation to London; Uppsala to Stockholm; and Rehovot and Herzliah in relation to Tel Aviv, to recognize the phenomenon.

Finally, attention must be drawn to the regional and British average reported creative innovation rate compared to that for UK industry as a whole. Thus, we see that innovation in all British industries is reported by 26 per cent of firms, while creative industry innovation is reported by 34 per cent. Creative innovation is accordingly among the highest to be recorded among industry sectors in Britain. Schumpeterian innovator sectors like engineering and other manufacturing are at the level of Britain and most of its regions are proportionately higher than creative industry innovators. But perhaps more surprising is that most regions, except London and the South West marginally, report higher creative industry innovator firm shares than innovations from their KIBS sectors. In overall UK terms 31 per cent of KIBS firms reported innovations compared to 34 per cent in creative industries.

THE REGIONAL DIMENSION OF SERVICES INNOVATION

Statistically, the question of whether there is a regional dimension to services innovation is settled. Table 28.1 shows it to be regionally somewhat homogeneous in the UK, but far lower than average in London. So once again, because of their heterogeneity, it is impossible to give an unequivocal answer either way. Moreover, statistics such as these may mask varieties of innovative niche performance in regions because of scale effects. This was suggested as one factor in London's apparent mediocrity. Nevertheless evolutionary economic geography suggests that metropoles are not likely to be as innovative as certain of their satellites. For example, it is well known that heavily science-based innovation such as occurs in biotechnology produces highly skewed spatial outcomes. Research shows not only that research services in this field are concentrated in a few globally significant locations like Massachusetts, especially Greater Boston; northern California, here Greater San Francisco; and in Europe, East Anglia, centring upon Cambridge and Bavaria, with Munich at its heart. A few other centres can be identified, but particularly in healthcare biotechnology where new therapeutic treatments represent the absolute leading edge of research-based innovation, these regions predominate and on key innovation indicators are drawing away from the rest. This is most pronounced in the case of Massachusetts, which in the 1990s was behind northern California (San Francisco plus Silicon Valley) but which by the mid-2000s had surpassed it on the key indicators, notably R&D expenditure and new therapeutic treatments (Cooke, 2007). Cambridge (UK) is also well ahead on such indicators compared to its nearest competitor Oxford; as is Stockholm compared to its rival Medicon Valley (Lund plus Copenhagen), despite its lesser biotechnology variety. Evidence shows that these knowledge infrastructures exert significant locational attraction upon pharmaceuticals laboratories (Abramovsky et al., 2007)

These are exemplary cases of a number of evolutionary economic geography concepts operating in the services innovation sphere. First, they display increasing returns to economic scale of the kind identified by evolutionists such as Myrdal and Hirschmann (see Andersen's Chapter 2 in this *Handbook*) and then rediscovered by new neoclassical Nobel laureate Paul Krugman (1995). The point here is that the more assets a region evolves, the more attractive it becomes as a location for related user assets, particularly advanced services like software, imaging, assay and trialling businesses. It also further stimulates Metcalfe and Miles's (2000) 'infrastructural services' such as business angels and venture capital, patent search, audit and legal services, and specialist management accountancy, market research and events management businesses. Second, services geographical proximity of this kind (see Chapter 20 by Carrincazeaux and Coris in this *Handbook*) enhances knowledge spillovers (see Breschi's Chapter 10 in this *Handbook*). These flow around the research, innovation and infrastructural services 'platform' (Chapter 23 on transversality in this *Handbook*) informally by means of social networks and formally by means of buyer–supplier transaction interactions. Even if the latter are confidential, knowledge about their content leaks out through the aforementioned social 'irrigation channels' (Owen-Smith and Powell, 2004). They constitute the 'public-goods' dimension of such platforms, where 'free-rider' opportunities may offer locational advantage. As a measure of willingness to pay by firms for access to such spillovers, Cooke et al. (2007) found UK land rents to be typically two to three times higher than regional norms in such locations.

Finally, these are regions of high related variety. Often dubbed 'biotech clusters', as if biotechnology were a single toolbox that famously ministers and other policy-makers mistakenly believe cannot be supported everywhere, on closer inspection they are shown to be highly diverse. Mention was made earlier of the great variety of infrastructural services enjoyed by such megacentres, but typically they also house varieties of supplier bioservices and application types. Among these are businesses supplying bioreactors (for cell or tissue growth at scale), biologics (medicinal products like vaccines, proteins or cells), screening and sequencing of genes, and nanobiotechnology (for example atomic-scale drug delivery services). Applications of bioscientific knowledge likely to be found in such platforms are agrofood biotechnology (functional foods and healthy food additives), transgenics, bioenergy technologies (for example algae for fuel and even prototype algae-battery technologies) and bioremediation (environmental clean-up by bacteriological methods, for example), even biosecurity (DNA fingerprinting, molecular or biomarkers, and biometrics for identification). Many such firms are intermediary service suppliers to final service or product innovator firms. They are accordingly exemplary instances of the increasingly service-like nature of innovation in the knowledge economy.

Of course the role of education services cannot be overlooked in the explanation for why geographical proximity is of such advantage to services platforms of the kind described. At the heart of these knowledge agglomerations are normally world-class research universities that produce many hundreds if not thousands of highly qualified graduate and postgraduate students every year. To take some illustrative examples: Cambridge, Massachusetts boasts Harvard University whose Medical School (actually located in Boston) alone accounts for some 10 per cent of published articles in the leading bioscientific journals and the Massachusetts Institute of Technology (MIT), home of the Whitehead Institute, co-leader of the Human Genome project. Boston is home to healthcare biotechnology powerhouses like Boston University and Tufts University. Large teaching hospitals like Massachusetts General, and Brigham & Women's, coexist with the many celebrated research institutes of the platform, like the Dana–Farber Cancer Institute, Joslin Diabetes Centre and the Beth Israel Deaconess Medical Centre (cardiovascular, gastrointestinal, and so on). Cambridge, UK has among its key institutions the University Biotechnology Institute, Sanger Institute, co-leader of the Human Genome project, and Medical Research Council Molecular Microbiology Research Institute with its 13 Nobel laureates. Addenbrooke's and Papworth research hospitals are co-located. In both these leading cases it may be said that:

> The mysteries of the trade become no mysteries; but are as it were in the air, and children learn many of them unconsciously. Good work is rightly appreciated, inventions and improvements in machinery, in processes and the general organization of the business have their merits promptly discussed: if one man starts a new idea, it is taken up by others and combined with suggestions of their own; and thus it becomes the source of further new ideas. And presently subsidiary trades grow up in the neighbourhood, supplying it with implements and materials, organizing its traffic, and in many ways conducing to the economy of its material. (Marshall, 1890, 271)

But other service industries commonly display locational economies associated with a concentration of related-variety economic and institutional activities in a specific place (Malmberg and Maskell, 2002). Services drivers from geographical proximity include: the accessibility to firms of dedicated infrastructure and collective goods, informal as well as formal; specialized local labour market assets, as in the case of the popular music cluster described by Maskell and Lorenzen (2004); and high 'relational' goods based on trust due to reciprocity and repeated favour exchanges among firms and institutions. To the extent that these reduce transaction costs, they facilitate interactions and strengthen long-term business linkages. By virtue of the instantaneity of the consumption of many services firms, locational economies from geographical proximity and related variety endow them with even higher efficiency gains and market advantage than even manufacturing firms are perceived to gain from location in specialized clusters.

In summary, there are three key advantages of geographical proximity. First, specialized labour market assets. Although we have seen this asset contributing to the strength of key biotechnology platforms, it is even more relevant for the creative industries. Here products and services tend to have very short shelf-lives. Moreover, interactions will often be organized in projects assembling 'pick-up' teams with complementary talents and experience of such working arrangements. In the creative-industry context, the 'Jacobian' recomposition of such teams is a key driver of service and product innovations under conditions of instant user-consumption of the service (for example a film), and the imperative constantly to be creatively novel and original. However, such are the search and screening costs to access appropriately talented labour that these service innovations would probably be impossible, even with the virtual electronic infrastructures nowadays ubiquitous, outside the relational space of face-to-face contact provided by the geographical proximity of the platform. Transaction cost barriers are largely overcome in the formative process of project envisaging and orchestration by such advantaged innovation settings as these 'Schumpeterian hubs' (Wolfe, 2009).

Second, the advantage of spatially bounded knowledge spillovers for innovation must be heavily emphasized. It is often argued that these are relatively unimportant because in an era of globalization and open innovation (Chesbrough, 2003) relevant knowledge may be 'picked up' practically anywhere in the world. All that is needed is the mechanism of 'relational proximity' to substitute for geographical proximity. This is, however, not a well-founded argument for three reasons. First, since time immemorial 'out of sight, out of mind' has been a prevailing mantra. It is simply difficult to the point of impossibility to keep up at fever pitch the kind of innovation relationships described above at great distance. Second, geographical proximity is not intrinsically causative of knowledge spillovers, relational capital is centrally involved: it is simply easier to arrange and exploit in geographic proximity. Third, relational proximity, like geographical proximity, is a non-uniform medium. For some orchestration stages, distant interaction may suffice (for example when buying a service on a website) but for more serious and demanding projects like designing a service, plotting a business coup or signing a deal, meetings must take place. That the global frequency of business meetings has exploded in the knowledge economy suggests, once again and from a different angle, the importance of geographical proximity to KIBS in the knowledge economy. Such co-location assets apply especially in financial services as well as the fine arts, performing arts, film, music and designer fashion industries (see, on the last-named, Wenting, 2008).

Finally, as noted above, the importance to services innovation of appropriate, even as in the case of biotechnology dedicated, institutional support infrastructures must be re-emphasized. As shown, the initial and successful agglomeration of firms induces a process of institution-building of a private and public nature. Institutional support infrastructures include private, marketized intermediary services and, where markets are weak or failed, judicious public institutional support. The latter include education and training institutions and regional or urban development agencies; the former, for example, private lobbying organizations, and chambers of commerce (Lorenzen and Frederiksen, 2008). Many studies on clusters in service industries have underlined this, including Amin and Thrift (1992), Keeble and Nachum (2002) and Grabher (2002).

CONCLUSIONS

This chapter has shown that services industry innovation exists and is quite extensive, with up to one-third of UK regional creative industry firms reporting creative innovations in the mid-2000s. It also shows that huge centres of services employment – London being the anatomized case, but many other metropoles could be included – are not only not very creatively or otherwise innovative, but are positive laggards compared to their outlying regions; and especially for creative industry, compared to their surrounding region. In the British case the surrounding region is shown to be considerably more creative in terms of proportional firm reportage of innovation than the capital itself.

This last is a particularly interesting finding because it supports long-held theoretical positions within evolutionary economic geography. The main one of these is that metropoles service much routine economic activity both directly and indirectly. They are home to banks and civil services, which are among the least innovative of industries. That judgement has to be slightly adjusted in light of the recklessness of banks that became gamblers with their own and especially other people's money in the neoliberal era from 1980 to 2008 – the Reagan-to-Bush era – when the crossover line between banking and investment banking was deregulated with dire global economic consequences. But generally the core idea was that the metropole had such assets as banks which traditionally gave short-term credit to businesses which, because of high land rents and the need to be close to sources of important business or research knowledge, chose to locate in satellite cities at a distance of approximately 50 miles outside the main city. This hypothesis has been shown to be an excellent locational predictor of the locational behaviour of, especially, high-tech firms. But to this can now be added for Britain, creative industry firms too.

Future research could usefully explore this thesis further, ascertaining the extent to which it is caused by diseconomies of (metropolitan) agglomeration, the absence of high-grade research and related infrastructures to facilitate innovation in large cities, or the pull-effect of knowledge-intensive laboratories and intermediaries at bearable cost in the satellite cities that are recipients of innovative firms. Other questions devolve on the extent to which satellite hierarchies change over possibly short spans of time, and what the reasons might be for that, if found. Finally, does innovation not officially registered occur to any great extent in the parts of the service economy that are widely believed to be uninnovative? Are, for example, the consultants that charge governments very large sums of money to conduct studies or install often failed information technology systems really innovators or not? And similarly, to what extent should their clients be attributed such innovations, where they work, rather than have them disappear into the KIBS category?

REFERENCES

Abramovsky, L., R. Harrison and H. Simpson (2007), 'University research and the location of business R&D', *Economic Journal*, **117**, C114–C141.
Amin, A. and N. Thrift (1992), 'Neo-Marshallian nodes in global networks', *International Journal of Urban and Regional Research*, **16**, 571–87.
Andersen, B., J. Howells, R. Hull, I. Miles and J. Roberts (eds) (2000), *Knowledge and Innovation in the New Service Economy* Cheltenham, UK and Northampton, MA, USA: Edward Elgar.
van Ark, B. (2005), 'In search of the silver bullet for productivity growth: a review article of the power of productivity and transforming the European economy', *International Productivity Monitor*, Centre for the Study of Living Standards, **10**, 79–86.
Baumol, W., S. Blackman and E. Wolf (1989), *Productivity and American Leadership: the Long View*, Cambridge, MA: MIT Press.
Boden, M and I. Miles (eds) (2000), *Services, Innovation and the Knowledge Economy*, London: Continuum.
Bryson, J. and P. Daniels (2007), *The Handbook of Service Industries*, Cheltenham, UK and Northampton, MA USA: Edward Elgar.
Chapain, C., P. Cooke, L. De Propris, S. MacNeill and J. Mateos-Garcia (2010), *Creative Clusters and Innovation: Putting Creativity on the Map*, London: NESTA.
Chesbrough, H. (2003), *Open Innovation*, Boston, MA: Harvard Business School Press.
Cohen, W. and D. Levinthal (1989), 'Innovation and learning: the two faces of R&D', *Economic Journal*, **99**, 569–96.
Cooke, P. (2007), *Growth Cultures*, London: Routledge.
Cooke, P., C. De Laurentis, S. MacNeill and C. Collinge (2010), *Platforms of Innovation: Dynamics of New Industrial Knowledge Flows*, Cheltenham, UK and Northampton, MA, USA: Edward Elgar.
Cooke, P., C. De Laurentis, F. Tödtling and M. Trippl (2007), *Regional Knowledge Economies*, Cheltenham, UK and Northampton, MA, USA: Edward Elgar.
Cooke, P. and K. Morgan (1998), *The Associational Economy*, Oxford: Oxford University Press.
Cooke, P. and D. Schwartz (2008), 'Regional knowledge economies: an EU–UK and Israel perspective', *Tijdschrift Voor Economische en Sociale Geografie*, **99**, 178–92.
Department of Trade and Industry (DTI) (1999), *Biotechnology Clusters*, London: DTI.
Dohse, K., U. Jurgens and T. Malsch (1985), 'From "Fordism" to "Toyotism"? The social organization of the labour process in the Japanese automobile industry', *Politics and Society*, **14**, 115–46.
Grabher, G. (2002), 'Cool projects, boring institutions: temporary collaboration in social context', *Regional Studies*, **36**, 205–14.
Keeble, D. and L. Nachum (2002), 'Why do business service firms cluster? Small consultancies, clustering and decentralization in London', *Transactions of the Institute of British Geographers*, **27**, 67–90.
Krugman, P. (1995), *Development, Geography and Economic Theory*, Cambridge, MA: MIT Press.
Lorenzen, M. and L. Frederiksen (2008), 'Why do cultural industries cluster? Localization, urbanization, products and projects', in P. Cooke and L. Lazzeretti (eds), *Creative Cities, Cultural Clusters and Local Economic Development*, Cheltenham, UK and Northampton, MA, USA: Edward Elgar, pp. 198–211.
Malmberg, A. and P. Maskell (2002), 'The elusive concept of localization economies: towards a knowledge-based theory of spatial clustering', *Environment and Planning A*, **34**, 429–49.
Marshall, A. (1890), *Principles of Economics*, London: Macmillan.
Maskell, P. and M. Lorenzen (2004), 'The cluster as market organization', *Urban Studies*, **41**, 991–1010.
Metcalfe, S. and I. Miles (eds) (2000), *Innovation Systems in the Service Economy*, Dordrecht: Kluwer.
Owen-Smith, J. and W. Powell (2004), 'Knowledge networks as channels and conduits: the effects spillovers in the Boston biotechnology community', *Organization Science*, **15**, 5–21.
Wenting, R. (2008), *The Evolution of a Creative Industry: The Industrial Dynamics of Fashion Design*, Utrecht: University of Utrecht Press.
Wolfe, D. (2009), *21st Century Cities in Canada: the Geography of Innovation*, Ottawa: Conference Board of Canada.

29 Open innovation and regional growth

Peter Prud'homme van Reine

INTRODUCTION

The concept of open innovation, launched by Chesbrough (2003), has quickly gained acceptance among researchers (Christensen et al., 2005; Gann, 2005) and practitioners (Kirschbaum, 2005), and its introduction has resulted in a growing body of literature and ongoing research (Chesbrough et al., 2006; Cooke, 2005a, 2005b, 2007a; Chesbrough and Schwartz, 2007; Fleming and Waguespack, 2007).

Defined as: 'The use of purposive inflows and outflows of knowledge to accelerate internal innovation and expand the markets for external use of innovation', open innovation assumes that companies should use not just internally developed ideas, but also ideas developed externally, and should create external paths for ideas to go to market in addition to the internal path for innovation. This is in contrast with the 'old' model of closed innovation, which assumed that innovation processes need to be controlled by the company for example by investing in internal research and development (R&D) and by controlling intellectual property to protect innovations coming out of these investments (De Jong et al., 2008).

Creation and sharing of knowledge in networks is essential to make open innovation strategies work (OECD, 2008). Although research on open innovation and regional knowledge networks is still in an early stage (Simard and West, 2006), three relevant bodies of literature for understanding how open innovation impacts regional growth can be identified:

- The literature on knowledge transfer in networks (March, 1991; Powell et al., 1996; Dyer and Singh, 1998; Levin and Cross, 2004) and the concept of dynamic capabilities (Teece and Pisano, 1996; Teece et al., 1997). 'Dynamic capabilities' refers to the ability to integrate, build and reconfigure internal and external competencies to address rapidly changing environments (Teece et al., 1997). Dynamic capabilities partly reside in knowledge networks resulting in what has been called 'dynamic knowledge capabilities' (Dawson, 2000) of firms and their networks, which are a prerequisite for open innovation strategies.
- The literature on regional advantage (Saxenian, 1994, Florida, 2000), emphasizing the role of sociocultural factors in interorganizational networks in innovative regions, and the literature on regional competitiveness (Porter, 1998, 2002), emphasizing the role of clusters as centers of innovation.
- The literature on regional innovation systems (Braczyk et al., 1998; Cooke, 1992, 2001; Cooke and Morgan, 1994; Cooke et al., 2004; Asheim and Isaksen, 2002), which emphasizes the influence of the institutional environment on knowledge networks and regional innovativeness.

The literature on regional advantage, regional competitiveness and regional innovation systems and how they relate to open innovation and regional growth will be discussed in the following sections.

REGIONAL ADVANTAGE, REGIONAL COMPETITIVENESS AND OPEN INNOVATION

Saxenian (1994), in her comparative study of Silicon Valley and the Boston area, analyzed the role of regional interorganizational networks in making regions innovative, emphasizing the role of regional culture and human capital. She argues that Silicon Valley pioneers created a decentralized system characterized by open information flow and learning between firms and between firms and regional universities (for example Stanford University) and the ability to respond rapidly to changing markets by putting together people with different backgrounds and starting new companies very quickly. The cultural dimension also shows up in the willingness to experiment and take risks, in the relatively flat organizational hierarchies, in the informality of work styles and in occupational mobility (see also James's Chapter 19 in this *Handbook*). Although Saxenian did not use the term 'open innovation', she describes how Silicon Valley firms were successful by competing intensely, while collaborating in informal and formal ways with one another and with regional universities, to learn about fast-changing markets and technologies. Loosely coupled work teams in companies were reflected in the organization of the regional economy, leading to a 'culture of collaboration' typical of what Chesbrough (2003) later called open innovation.

Intraregional

A good example of 'open innovation' described by Saxenian is the partnership between HP and chipset designer Weitek, which started at the end of the 1980s to speed up innovation in HP's workstations. Weitek got access to HP's manufacturing capabilities and to the needs and plans of HP as a leading customer. HP got access to Weitek's design talent. Both parties were looking for a long-term partnership but made sure to maintain their own competitive position. Weitek sold chipsets made on HP's equipment to third parties, including competitors of HP, and built alliances with them as well. HP continued to work with other chip design companies. Saxenian (1994, 156): 'The openness of this partnership ensured that the design and manufacturing innovations that it produced would diffuse rapidly throughout the region and the industry.' Not just HP, but also companies based in the region such as Sun and Cisco opened up innovation, which in turn contributed to further regional growth. Being part of Silicon Valley's regional network-based system, participating in face-to-face communication and collective learning, was beneficial for speed in the new competitive environment based on continuous cycles of innovation. Interfirm supplier networks reinforced the regional advantage of Silicon Valley as an attractive location for innovative companies.

Although criticized for giving a too romantic picture of Silicon Valley's culture of collaboration and overlooking the high degree of fragmentation that is present in the region as well, Saxenian made an important contribution by emphasizing the influence of sociocultural aspects such as culture and identity and human capital on opening up innovation. At the same time, the strong influence of sociocultural factors makes it difficult to replicate the success of a single region.

Interregional

A further insight is that benefiting from opening up innovation is not just about a culture of cooperation in the region, but also requires maintaining open boundaries to benefit from global connections and cultural diversity. For Silicon Valley companies such as HP, investing in local ties with suppliers and universities in the regions where they are located is part of their globalization model (Saxenian, 1994). Recently (2009), Intel announced that it would strengthen joint research with European universities, open innovation and collaboration with industry and academia, participation in EU framework programs and cooperative standards development work with industry partners.

Silicon Valley's immigrant entrepreneurs and engineers also contribute to maintaining open boundaries. They not only bring cultural diversity, but they also connect Silicon Valley to for example Taiwan and India, by informal social and professional ties and formal corporate alliances and partnerships, thereby facilitating flows of capital, skills and technology (Saxenian, 1999, 2000).

Another contribution of the regional advantage literature is the concept of 'quality of place' (Florida, 2000), as a factor contributing to an open creative environment and vital in attracting and retaining knowledge workers and in supporting innovative companies and industries. 'Quality of place' encompasses a wide range of aspects including architecture, attractive natural environment, recreational facilities, the presence of a diverse set of creative people, housing conditions, smart infrastructure, vibrant city life, symbolic capital and a regional 'brand'. In Silicon Valley, quality of place advantages seem to have played a role in attracting talent during the initial development of the region as an open innovative environment. Quality of place is not included in most of the scholarly work on innovation systems, probably because of its 'fuzziness' and the heavy criticism of researchers on Florida's work for shortcomings in its methodology. However, in empirical accounts of open innovation, quality of place comes forward as an important characteristic of regional advantage (Asheim et al., 2006).

Competitive Advantage

The regional advantage literature is closely linked to competitive advantage literature (Porter, 2002) with its emphasis on clusters as centers of innovation. Porter's concept of clusters as 'geographic concentrations of interconnected companies institutions in a particular field' that 'promote both competition and cooperation' (Porter, 1998), is relevant for open innovation and regional growth, because clusters are often geographically centered: 'Paradoxically, the more complex, knowledge-based, and dynamic the world economy becomes, the more competitive advantage comes from local things e.g. knowledge, relationships, and motivation' (Porter, 1998). Porter argues that 'geographic, cultural, and institutional proximity provides companies with special access, closer relationships, better information, powerful incentives, and other advantages that are difficult to tap from a distance', not just leading to increased productivity of companies based in a region, but also driving the direction and pace of innovation and stimulating the formation of new businesses in the cluster. Porter and Stern (2001), building further on the cluster national competitive advantage model (Porter, 1990), focus on the dynamics of strong innovation clusters in capturing locational advantages in innovation. The link with open innovation is in the advice not just to manage the innovation process in the company, but also to access and augment locational strengths by managing the process of how companies enhance and take advantage of opportunities in the external environment for innovation. Several factors are identified as relevant for shaping competitive innovative capabilities (Porter and Stern, 2001): the presence of sophisticated and demanding local customers; human resources capital (for example cooperation with educational institutes to provide a pool of highly trained engineers and scientists); risk capital available for innovation; innovation infrastructure (for example strong university–industry linkages); and the industrial context (industry associations, networks with supplier companies and related companies in the value chain, competitors).

The regional and competitive advantage literature contributes to understanding the relationship between open innovation and regional growth by showing differences between regions and pointing at relevant factors such as culture, human capital, quality of space, risk capital, infrastructure, industrial context and interaction with customers. However, it does not fully answer where regional advantage regarding open innovation comes from. Success cases cannot simply be copied. Cooke and Leydesdorff (2006) argue that Porter largely ignored funding and policy support by the public sector.

I now turn to the literature on regional innovation systems which gives a more systemic approach to understanding regional competitiveness in terms of (open) innovation.

REGIONAL INNOVATION SYSTEMS AND OPEN INNOVATION

Research on regional innovation systems starts from a regional science and economic geography perspective to look for a generic framework to understand regional competitiveness in terms of innovation (Cooke, 1992; Braczyk et al., 1998). The regional innovation systems approach is an example of a systems approach to innovation which acknowledges that innovations are carried out through a network of various actors supported by an institutional framework (Edquist, 1997). Regional innovation systems are defined as interacting knowledge generation and exploitation subsystems linked to global, national and other regional systems (Cooke et al., 2004). Asheim and Coenen (2006) argue that a regional innovation system is in place when the following two subsystems of actors are systematically engaged in interactive learning:

- The regional supportive infrastructure or knowledge generation subsystem, which consists of public and private research laboratories, universities and colleges, technology transfer agencies, vocational training organizations, and so on.
- The regional production structure or knowledge exploitation subsystem, which consists mainly of firms, especially where these display clustering tendencies.

Authors on regional innovation systems have identified several elements of the institutional context that influence knowledge creation and knowledge sharing, and finally innovation, sometimes directly, sometimes via their impact on networks: knowledge institutes, governance and policies, financial infrastructure and industry context (competition, interaction between companies in the value chain, presence of focal firms). The literature on regional innovation systems, and the literature on networks, capabilities and regional advantage and competitiveness, are clearly linked (Asheim et al., 2006). Early publications on regional innovation policies point already at the importance of networks between firms and regional policies conducive to meeting the needs of small firms (Piore and Sabel, 1984; Cooke and da Rosa Pires, 1985), and criticize innovation policies leading to centralized and hierarchical structures (Cooke, 1985). Systemic institutional networking interaction and learning are key in the regional innovation systems approach, linking it to the national systems of innovation literature focusing on networks (Freeman, 1987, 1988) and interactive learning (Lundvall, 1992). The regional innovation systems literature is also inspired by the work on clusters; however, characteristic for a regional innovation system is that it is able to support several clustered and non-clustered industries.

The interest in open innovation strategies boosts the interest in the regional innovation systems approach, because regional policies can strengthen open innovation potential by facilitating connectivity and knowledge flows in networks, and open innovation practices can in turn strengthen regional competitiveness by attracting global talent and outsourcing contracts to the region.

Large international companies, in their search for new knowledge, create distributed R&D networks by creating their own R&D facilities abroad and/or outsourcing research and innovation contracts to knowledgeable regions with clusters of entrepreneurial, knowledge-intensive outsourcing firms (for example Silicon Valley and Boston in the case of biotechnology), and by building networks to access regional knowledge capabilities (Cooke, 2007b). Procter & Gamble has networks of 'technology entrepreneurs' who work out of 'connect and develop' hubs in several regions around the world, where each hub focuses on products and technologies that are specialties of its region (Huston and Sakkab, 2006). Another example is how the Swiss company Novartis mapped the main global locations of its Centres of Excellence onto globally excellent research bioregions (Cooke, 2007b). Cooke (2001) makes a distinction between hierarchical regional innovation systems characterized by a strong coordination of innovation policies by state agencies, and heterarchical regional innovation systems characterized by distributed governance involving a wide range of market and non-market networks. Regional innovation systems are often initiated by bottom-up processes, but need support from public innovation systems, and institutional and organizational support from the private sector.

Conditions for higher regional innovation potential (Cooke, 2005a) include: interactive innovation between firms; innovation support organizations; a regional university–industry strategy; consultative and networking based innovation policies; the availability of regional private and public finance; regional influence on infrastructure policies; and a cooperative culture, interactive learning and consensus approach at the institutional level. A strength of the regional innovation systems approach is that it also addresses the importance of the integration between local 'sticky' and global 'ubiquitous' knowledge (Asheim and Isaksen, 2002).

Cooke (2005b, 2007a) argues that open innovation is one of the challenges that underline the importance for global competitiveness of regional innovation systems, and clusters within them. He introduces the regional knowledge capabilities model of regional growth, which connects knowledge capabilities residing in networks and open innovation. Open innovation in networks of universities, research institutes, industry, government and financiers leads to the transformation of dynamic knowledge networking capabilities into a regional capability. So, regional knowledge capabilities are rooted in open innovation. In a next stage, companies tap into regional knowledge capabilities and systematic innovation strengths of successful regions in order to overcome intrafirm knowledge asymmetries. Asymmetric knowledge at the regional level then actually gets reinforced by open innovation, leading to accumulation of human capital in 'network nodes'. The result is a spiral of growth operating through these network nodes in global–regional innovation systems. Cooke uses biotechnology as the example for this process, but finds evidence that 'open innovation' from knowledge-capable regional clusters can be seen in other sectors as well: the automotive sector (Schamp et al., 2004), information and communication technology (ICT) (Chesbrough, 2003), electronics (Van den Biesen, 2004) and media (Grabher, 2002).

Important for understanding the connection between regional innovation systems, regional advantage and competitiveness, and open innovation is the concept of 'constructed advantage', introduced by Foray and Freeman (1993) and reintroduced by de la Mothe and Mallory (2003) in relation to regional growth. Constructed advantage is the development of systematic regional innovation capabilities by designing regional innovation systems in such a way that they match regional capabilities. Constructed advantage differs from 'regional advantage' because it describes and explains how to construct regional advantage proactively and gives more attention to the role and impact of public policy. De la Mothe and Mallory propose that the right environmental conditions for creation and exchange of knowledge can give a region 'constructed advantage' in promoting distributed (or open) innovation. Characteristics of regional constructed advantage are: robust and active governance (matching of 'top-down' policy-making and program design with 'bottom up' leadership and action), regional heterogeneity, human talent, creativity, proactive relationships, open and distributed networks between firms, universities and regional governments, a spirit of collaboration, opportunity for business development, risk capital and market access, and coordination between national and regional actors. Moreover, constructed advantage results in the agglomeration of foreign investments, industrial concentration and talent in areas that have well-prepared and culturally conducive institutions (de la Mothe and Mallory, 2006).

Lakoff (2008) has applied the constructed advantage concept to open innovation in a new upcoming region. Cooke and Leydesdorff (2006) compare constructed advantage and another model for regional development, the 'Triple Helix' model of university–industry–government relations (Etzkowitz and Leydesdorff, 1997). The Triple Helix model is based on the added value of close interactions between knowledge institutes, industry and government for example by stimulating university–industry–society knowledge transfer, funding research and subsidizing infrastructure in order to stimulate innovation and growth. The Triple Helix model can be seen as one form of constructing regional advantage but is probably too consensus-focused (Cooke, 2005b). Cooke and Leydesdorff (2006) conclude that constructed advantage based on regional innovation systems that transceive over long distances as well as through regional networks seems to have become the model of choice for achieving accomplished regional economic development.

Cooke (2007c) brings together open innovation and the regional and competitive advantage, regional innovation systems and constructed advantage approaches by describing the process of open innovation as: 'creating constructed advantage through enhancing regional knowledge capabilities by creating spatial knowledge domains institutionalized as Regional Innovation Systems'. Constructed advantage can be used to understand the impact of open innovation strategies on regional growth, and to assess regional innovation policies and innovation strategies of companies, knowledge institutes and other relevant organizations. Cooke (2007c) provides the following list of aspects of the regional environment that need to be addressed to construct regional advantage in terms of innovation:

- Economy – regionalization of economic development; 'open systems' interfirm interactions; integration of knowledge generation and commercialization; smart infrastructures; strong local and global business networks.
- Governance – multilevel governance of associational and stakeholder interests; strong policy-support for innovators; enhanced budgets for research; vision-led policy leadership; global positioning of local assets.
- Knowledge infrastructure – active involvement of universities, public sector research, intermediate agencies, consultancies, and so on.
- Community and culture – cosmopolitanism; sustainability; talented human capital; creative environment; social tolerance.

This list brings together many elements addressed by the networks, capabilities, regional advantage and competitiveness and regional innovation systems literature discussed in this chapter. 'Community and culture' encompasses elements emphasized by Saxenian (culture, identity and global–local connections) and Florida (quality of space and 'creative environment'). 'Economy' encompasses Porter's emphasis on industrial structure, interaction with customers and financial infrastructure.

ENABLING AND ENHANCING OPEN INNOVATION: CONSTRUCTING REGIONAL ADVANTAGE

We have seen that knowledge capabilities, residing in networks of open innovation, contribute to regional growth and that regional innovation systems contribute to how networks are organized and to constructing regional advantage, potentially leading to a spiral of innovation and regional growth.

As Tödtling and Trippl (2005) have argued, there can be no uniform 'ideal' model of innovation policy that applies to all types of regions, so that region-specific solutions are required that account for divergent regional conditions. This is valid for open innovation as well. Based on the previous discussion, however, it is possible to identify which issues need to be taken into account for a region to enable and enhance open innovation. Boxes 29.1, 29.2 and 29.3 list these issues and the contributions regions can make to enable and enhance open innovation in such a way that it results in regional growth.

BOX 29.1   CONTRIBUTIONS OF REGIONS TO ENABLING
AND ENHANCING OPEN INNOVATION, IN
TURN LEADING TO REGIONAL GROWTH:
SOCIOCULTURAL ENVIRONMENT

Open Innovation and Regional Culture and Identity

- Open innovation thrives in a culture characterized by cosmopolitanism, openness for global interaction, social tolerance and making use of diversity. However open innovation also requires a shared identity and shared goals as a region, and relying on home base strengths.
- The solution of this seeming contradiction is in the need to balance deep and wide network ties. While relying too much on deep ties with the same partners in the region may lead to overembeddedness (Boschma, 2005), relying too much on wide ties may lead to a loss of identity and regional strengths.
- The contribution of the region is in stimulating global linkages between regional clusters and innovation partners elsewhere, and in attracting global talent and outsourcing contracts to the region.

Open Innovation and Quality of Place

- Open innovation thrives in an environment with high 'quality of place' that attracts knowledge workers: good living conditions, attractive natural environment, climate, cultural activities, presence of creative people, working conditions, and a good regional image or 'brand'.
- Talented people have high expectations of quality of space, but also have high expectations of opportunities of business performance and achievement.
- The role of the region is in providing conditions for high quality of place and opportunities to perform and achieve in business.

Open Innovation and Developing Human Capital in the Region

- A sufficient pool of talented human capital is a prerequisite for open innovation but open innovation requires more than the presence of 'footloose' professionals with entrepreneurial skills. Inventive regions need technicians, related technical support workers and 'footloose' professionals (Ceh, 2001). Strong interaction between craftsmen, engineers and scientists, and entrepreneurs is necessary to go though the cycle of generating ideas, making prototypes and turning ideas into profitable business. For example, future leaders of open innovation communities must first make strong technical contributions before they can take a boundary-spanning position to integrate their communities (Fleming and Waguespack, 2007).

- The contribution of the region is in investing in human capital to provide the right combination of technological and entrepreneurial human capital, for example by providing high-level education and practical education and training in entrepreneurship, and in facilitating networks between entrepreneurs and technologists.

BOX 29.2   CONTRIBUTIONS OF REGIONS TO ENABLING AND ENHANCING OPEN INNOVATION: ECONOMIC ENVIRONMENT

Open Innovation and Interaction with Competitors

- Open innovation is about combining the development of internal knowledge and exploiting external knowledge, and open innovation communities typically are simultaneously collaborative and competitive (Porter et al., 2005) – whoever makes the best use of internal and external ideas will win. Opening up innovation processes and outsourcing go together with nurturing the internal capabilities that provide the essential underpinnings of competitive advantage (Chesbrough and Teece, 1996), to avoid losing leadership in key technologies (Stefik and Stefik, 2006).
- Open innovation does not make internal R&D a thing of the past: creating an open innovation environment requires a willingness to strive for balance between internal and external R&D. Internal R&D is needed to claim a part of the significant value created by external R&D (Chesbrough, 2003).
- Creating an open innovation environment does not imply completely giving up control of intellectual property: there will always be a level of 'closedness' in innovating firms (Christensen et al., 2005). Open innovation implies profiting from others' use of own innovation processes, and buying others' intellectual property (IP) when it enhances the own business model (Chesbrough, 2003). Unused IP does not have to stay on the shelves, because methods for evaluating IP and a market for IP have been developed (Dankbaar and Vissers, 2008).
- Creating an open innovation environment requires dismissing the NIH ('not invented here') and the NSH ('not sold here') syndromes (Herzog, 2008). The role of the region is in encouraging collaborative attitudes, trust-based networking and practices of sharing IP in projects to enable open innovation, for example by training activities and facilitating pre-competitive cooperative research, and ensuring that there is sufficient competition at the regional level.

Open Innovation and Interaction between Lead Firms, SMEs and Start-ups in the Region

- Lead firms and entrants differ in their abilities to exploit the opportunities that innovation offers (Chesbrough, 1999). Big companies can afford to invest in innovation because of their market power, leading to spin-offs and knowledge spillovers. Small and medium-sized enterprises (SMEs) are better positioned to create radically new markets. Open innovation benefits from the presence of lead firms in a region, such as HP and Intel in Silicon Valley (Saxenian, 1994), Nokia in Finland (Porter and Solvell, 2000), Philips and DSM in the south-east Netherlands (van der Meer, 2007; Kirschbaum, 2005) and Qualcomm in the San Diego region (Lakoff, 2008), provided that the network ties between big and small companies (internal or external) result in inter-dependency so that the strengths of both can be used to exploit open innovation opportunities.
- The role of the region is in stimulating the interaction and knowledge flow between lead firms, SMEs and start-ups. One example is the participation of regional development organizations in open innovation campus initiatives in the south-east Netherlands, where lead companies Philips and DSM share research and business facilities with other large companies, SMEs, start-ups and spin-offs; incubator facilities and collaborative research institutes and programs are financed jointly by public and private parties (Collins, 2006) and former Philips and DSM employees act as coaches of starting entrepreneurs.

Open Innovation and Interaction in the Value Chain between Suppliers and Customers in the Region

- Open innovation between suppliers and customers has the potential to capture value through regional value chain linkages. Open innovation with suppliers in the region makes it possible to include knowledge from these partners early in the development process, to speed up the learning curve. Customers can make suppliers more innovative by challenging them to come up with new ideas or improved specifications.
- The role of the region is in facilitating network organizations in certain clusters, policies to upgrade the capabilities of regional suppliers so that they can participate in open innovation with partners in the value chain, in helping suppliers and customers to come to new forms of sharing value and risk, and in providing a framework through which consumers and users can participate in the innovation process, for example by acting as the launching customer in innovation projects.

BOX 29.3   CONTRIBUTIONS OF REGIONS TO ENABLING AND ENHANCING OPEN INNOVATION: INSTITUTIONAL ENVIRONMENT

Open Innovation and Regional Financial Infrastructure

- Venture capital (venture capitalist companies, venturing arms of corporations, regional banks and private investors) stimulates open innovation by facilitating continuation of successful development paths and investing in a broader knowledge base to open up new fields and opportunities in the region (Chesbrough, 2003; Owen-Smith and Powell, 2004). Even in the Internet industry, venture capital investments tend to be regionally focused because of the importance of local knowledge (Zook, 2005).

- Venture capital can play a broader role than just that of financial investor, by opening up wide networks that are normally difficult to access for start-ups. Start-ups and university spin-offs are often based on scientific ideas and need additional business expertise. Venture capital companies can provide experienced board members and a wide range of business contacts via regional and global networks.

- Open innovation requires a regional finance infrastructure balancing public sector and private sector facilitation. Public finance is necessary to get new initiatives through the phase between incubator and independent start-up company, and to finance a regional infrastructure conducive for open innovation.

- In regions where venture capitalism is less well established, venture capital can be raised in a joint effort between lead companies, regionally embedded banks and public finance. For example in the south-east Netherlands region, lead companies Philips and DSM have created corporate venture capital divisions (van der Meer, 2007; Blau, 2006) and partner with regionally rooted banks and development organizations to stimulate academic entrepreneurship via incubator initiatives (Van den Berg et al., 2005).

Open Innovation and Regional Knowledge Infrastructure

- Proximity of universities enhances open innovation because of the easy access to knowledge and a pool of qualified personnel. However, participation of universities in open innovation networks via contract research, incubators and spin-offs may result in universities and/or university researchers protecting their own intellectual property rights instead of sharing these with regional companies, which may actually be at the expense of open innovation. The role of the region is in establishing connections between universities and the companies around them, and in helping universities and companies to manage IP rights in such a way that revenues are shared and that IP supports open innovation rather than hinders it.

- Open innovation can be seen as a company's effort to profit from external knowledge without making heavy internal investments in long-term research (De Wit et al., 2007), but companies cannot totally rely on external knowledge sources if they want to distinguish themselves from competitors. The role for the region is to establish a regional open innovation environment in which long-term investment in fundamental research and in society are seamlessly connected to realizing short-term results and economic returns, for example via public–private partnerships which bundle top research institutes with large companies, SMEs and start-ups, to boost fundamental research and application in products and services.

Open Innovation and Regional Governance

- Open innovation benefits from regional policies either in a direct way (by subsidies for open innovation initiatives such as consortia and open innovation institutes) or in a more indirect way (by reducing barriers for start-up companies). Regional policies to create conditions for open innovation need to address all issues mentioned in this box and in Boxes 29.2 and 29.3, varying from 'soft' cultural to 'hard' economic issues.
- Open innovation thrives in regions that balance informal and formal network ties that match decisive policy-making and program design with 'bottom-up' consultation and leadership, and connect regional actors with national policy frameworks and institutions. An example of combined informal and institutionalized cooperation is the Brainport Foundation in the south-east Netherlands: a close cooperation between companies, knowledge institutes and regional authorities, with a board that represents these three parties. Brainport has embraced the open innovation approach in the region and its development program addresses stimulating innovation (via knowledge creation, exchange and transfer); developing human capital via education and stimulating entrepreneurship; creating and strengthening networks in business and international cooperation; and improving both 'quality of space' and hard infrastructure.

CONCLUSION

Until recently, the focus of open innovation research has been on global networks, but the potential impact on regional growth is enormous. A regional open innovation strategy can be a double-edged sword. Developing regional knowledge capabilities is a prerequisite for open innovation strategies of companies in a region, which contributes in itself to regional growth by maximizing the value captured from knowledge spillovers, and maximizing the value captured from external transfer in open innovation networks within the region. Successful open innovation in a region further strengthens regional knowledge capabilities which, if properly supported by policies to establish the region globally, in turn will attract knowledge workers and companies with capabilities to capture regional knowledge to the region. Companies already thriving in the regional open innovation network will strengthen their connections to other knowledgeable regions globally, leading to a spiral of growth. The model is attractive for regional authorities because regional advantage for open innovation can be constructed and can occur in regions with different characteristics. However, regional stakeholders need to be aware that open innovation potentially increases creativity and efficiency of the innovation process, but that it also increases its complexity (Fredberg et al., 2008). Regional constructed advantage for open innovation needs a coordinated and sustained effort by companies, knowledge institutes, financiers and regional governments on a wide range of issues: building knowledge capabilities and a strong infrastructure, attracting human capital, and developing a socio-cultural environment which is open for diversity and combines high quality of space with business opportunities. It also requires facilitating interaction in networks and finding the right balance between open and closed innovation to ensure sustainable regional development.

Open innovation is still a relatively new model and there are many areas for future research. The impact of open innovation on emerging cross-border regions such as the Öresund region (Denmark–Sweden) and the Eindhoven–Leuven–Aachen triangle (Netherlands, Belgium, Germany) seems to be a particularly interesting topic for further research.

REFERENCES

Asheim, B.T. and L. Coenen (2006), 'The role of regional innovation systems in a globalising economy', in G. Vertova (ed.), *The Changing Economic Geography of Globalization*, London: Routledge, pp. 148–65.

Asheim, B., L. Coenen, J. Moodysson and J. Vang (2006), 'Constructing knowledge-based regional advantage: implications for regional innovation policy', *International Journal of Entrepreneurship and Innovation Management*, **7** (2–5), 140–55.

Asheim, B. and A. Isaksen (2002), 'Regional innovation systems: the integration of local "sticky" and global "ubiquitous" knowledge', *Journal of Technology Transfer*, **27**, 77–86.

Blau, J. (2006), 'Open innovation goes global', *Research-Technology Management*, **49** (5), 4–5.

Boschma, R.A. (2005), 'Proximity and innovation: a critical assessment', *Regional Studies*, **39** (1), 61–74.

Braczyk, H., P. Cooke and M. Heidenreich (eds) (1998), *Regional Innovation Systems*, London: UCL Press.

Ceh, B. (2001), 'Regional innovation potential in the United States: evidence of spatial transformation', *Regional Science Papers*, **80**, 297–316.

Chesbrough, H. (1999), 'The organizational impact of technological change: a comparative theory of national institutional factors', *Industrial and Corporate Change*, **8** (3), 447–85.

Chesbrough, H. (2003), *Open Innovation: The New Imperative for Creating and Profiting from Technology*, Boston, MA: Harvard Business School Press.

Chesbrough, H. and K. Schwartz (2007), 'Innovating business models with co-development partnerships', *Research Technology Management*, **50** (1), 55–9.

Chesbrough, H. and D. Teece (1996), 'When is virtual virtuous? Organizing for innovation', *Harvard Business Review*, Jan.–Feb., 65–73.

Chesbrough, H., W. Vanhaverbeke and J. West (2006), *Open Innovation: Researching a New Paradigm*, Oxford: Oxford University Press.

Christensen, J., M. Olesen and J. Kjaer (2005), 'The industrial dynamics of open innovation: evidence from the transformation of consumer electronics', *Research Policy*, **34** (10), 1533–49.

Collins, L. (2006), 'Netherlands "technopole" takes open innovation to next stage', *Research-Technology Management*, **49** (2), 2–4.

Cooke, P. (1985), 'Regional innovation policy: problems and strategies in Britain and France', *Environment and Planning C: Government and Policy*, **3**, 253–67.

Cooke, P. (1992), 'Regional innovation systems: competitive regulation in the new Europe', *Geoforum*, **23**, 365–82.

Cooke, P. (2001), 'Regional innovation systems, clusters and the knowledge economy', *Industrial and Corporate Change*, **10**, 945–74.

Cooke, P. (2005a), 'Regional knowledge capabilities and open innovation: regional innovation systems and clusters in the asymmetric knowledge economy', in S. Breschi and F. Malerba (eds), *Clusters, Networks and Innovation*, Oxford: Oxford University Press, pp. 80–112.

Cooke, P. (2005b), 'Regionally asymmetric knowledge capabilities and open innovation: exploring "Globalisation 2" – a new model of industry organisation', *Research Policy*, **34**, 1128–49.

Cooke, P. (2007a), 'Theorizing regional knowledge capabilities: economic geography under open innovation', in J. Surinach, R. Morano and E. Vaya (eds), *Knowledge Externalities, Innovation Clusters and Regional Development*, Cheltenham, UK and Northampton, MA, USA: Edward Elgar, pp. 19–41.

Cooke, P. (2007b), *Growth Cultures: The Global Bioeconomy and its Bioregions*, New York: Routledge.

Cooke, P. (2007c), 'To construct regional advantage from innovation systems first build policy platforms', *European Planning Studies*, **15** (2), 179–94.

Cooke, P., M. Heidenreich and H. Braczyk (2004), *Regional Innovation Systems*, 2nd edn, London: Routledge.

Cooke, P. and L. Leydesdorff (2006), 'Regional development in the knowledge based economy: the construction of advantage', *Journal of Technology Transfer*, **31**, 5–15.

Cooke, P. and K. Morgan (1994), 'The regional innovation system in Baden-Württemberg', *International Journal of Technology Management*, **9**, 394–429.

Cooke, P. and A. da Rosa Pires (1985), 'Productive decentralization in three European regions', *Environment and Planning A*, **17**, 527–54.

Dankbaar, B. and G. Vissers (2008), 'The changing role of the firm', in R. Smits, S. Kuhlmann and P. Shapira (eds), *The International Handbook of Innovation Policy*, Cheltenham, UK and Northampton, MA, USA: Edward Elgar, pp. 53–76.

Dawson, R. (2000), 'Knowledge capabilities as the focus of organizational development and strategy', *Journal of Knowledge Management*, **4** (4), 320–27.

De Jong, J., W. Vanhaverbeke, T. Kalvet and H. Chesbrough (2008), *Policies for Open Innovation: Theory, Framework and Cases*, Helsinki: VISION Era-Net.

De Wit, J., B. Dankbaar and G. Vissers (2007), 'Open innovation: the new way of knowledge transfer?', *Journal of Business Chemistry*, **4** (1), 11–19.

Dyer, J. and H. Singh (1998), 'The relational view: cooperative strategy and sources of interorganizational competitive advantage', *Academy of Management Review*, **23** (4), 660–79.

Edquist, C. (ed.) (1997), *Systems of Innovation: Technologies, Institutions and Organisations*, London: Pinter.

Etzkowitz, H. and L. Leydesdorff (1997), *Universities and the Global Knowledge Economy: A Triple Helix of University–Industry–Government Relations*, London: Pinter.

Fleming, L. and D.M. Waguespack (2007), 'Brokerage, boundary spanning, and leadership in open innovation communities', *Organization Science*, **18** (2), 165–84.

Florida, R. (2000), 'Competing in the age of talent: quality of place and the new economy', report prepared for the R.K. Mellon Foundation, Heinz Endowments, and Sustainable Pittsburgh.

Foray, D. and C. Freeman (1993), *Technology and the Wealth of Nations: The Dynamics of Constructed Advantage*, London: Pinter.

Fredberg, T., M. Elmquist and S. Ollila (2008), 'Managing open innovation, past findings and future directions', VINNOVA Report VR 2008:02.

Freeman, C. (1987), *Technology Policy and Economic Performance: Lessons from Japan*, London: Pinter.

Freeman, C. (1988), 'Japan, a new system of innovation', in G. Dosi, C. Freeman, R. Nelson, G. Silverberg and L. Soete (eds), *Technical Change and Economic Theory*, London: Pinter, pp. 31–54.

Gann, D.M. (2005), 'Open innovation: the new imperative for creating and profiting from technology', *Research Policy*, **34** (1), 122–3.

Grabher, G. (2002), 'Cool projects, boring institutions: temporary collaboration in social context', *Regional Studies*, **36**, 205–14.

Herzog, P. (2008), *Open and Closed Innovation, Different Cultures for Different Strategies*, Wiesbaden: Gabler-Verlag.

Huston, L. and N. Sakkab (2006), 'Connect and develop: inside Procter & Gamble's new model of innovation', *Harvard Business Review*, March, 58–66.

Kirschbaum, R. (2005), 'Open innovation in practice', *Research Technology Management*, **48** (4), 24–8.

Lakoff, S. (2008), 'Upstart startup: "Constructed advantage" and the example of Qualcomm', *Technovation*, **28** (12), 831–7.

Levin, D.Z. and R. Cross (2004), 'The strength of weak ties you can trust: the mediating role of trust in effective knowledge transfer', *Management Science*, **50** (11), 1477–90.

Lundvall, B.-Å. (ed.) (1992), *National Systems of Innovation*, London: Pinter.

March, J.G. (1991), 'Exploration and exploitation in organizational learning', *Organization Science*, **2** (1), 71–87.

van der Meer, H. (2007), 'Open innovation – the Dutch treat: challenges in thinking in business models', *Creativity and Innovation Management*, **16** (2), 192–202.

de la Mothe, J. and G. Mallory (2003), 'Industry–Government relations in a knowledge-based economy: the role of constructed advantage', PRIME Discussion Paper 02-03, University of Ottawa: Program of Research in Innovation Management and Economy.

de la Mothe, J. and G. Mallory (2006), 'Constructing advantage: distributed innovation and the management of local economic growth', *Prometheus*, **24** (1), 23–36.

OECD (2008), *Open Innovation in Global Networks*, Paris: OECD Publications.

Owen-Smith, J. and W. Powell (2004), 'Knowledge networks as channels and conduits: the effects of spillovers in the Boston biotechnology community', *Organization Science*, **15** (1), 5–21.

Piore, M. and C. Sabel (1984), *The Second Industrial Divide*, New York: Basic Books.

Porter, K., K. Whittington and W. Powell (2005), 'The institutional embeddedness of high-tech regions: relational foundations of the Boston biotechnology community', in Stefano Breschi and Franco Malerba (eds), *Clusters, Networks, and Innovation*, Oxford: Oxford University Press, pp. 261–296.

Porter, M. (1990), *The Competitive Advantage of Nations*, New York: Free Press.

Porter, M. (1998), 'Clusters and the new economics of competition', *Harvard Business Review*, Nov.–Dec., 77–90.

Porter, M. (2002), 'Regional foundations of competitiveness and implications for government policy', paper presented at the Department of Trade and Industry Workshop on Regional Competitiveness, London: DTI.

Porter, M. and O. Solvell (2002), 'Finland and Nokia', Harvard Business School Case Study.

Porter, M. and S. Stern (2001), 'Innovation: location matters', *MIT Sloan Management Review*, **42** (4), 28–36.

Powell, W., K. Koput and L. Smith-Doerr (1996), 'Interorganizational collaboration and the locus of innovation: networks of learning in biotechnology', *Administrative Science Quarterly*, **41** (1), 116–45.

Saxenian, A. (1994), *Regional Advantage: Culture and Competition in Silicon Valley and Route 128*, Cambridge, MA: Harvard University Press.

Saxenian, A. (1999), *Silicon Valley's New Immigrant Entrepreneurs*, San Francisco, CA: Public Policy Institute of California.

Saxenian, A. (2000), 'Networks of immigrant entrepreneurs', in C. Lee, W. Miller, M. Hancock and H. Rowen (eds), *The Silicon Valley Edge*, Stanford, CA: Stanford University Press.

Schamp, E., B. Rentmeister and V. Lo (2004), 'Dimensions of proximity in knowledge-based networks: the cases of banking and automobile design', *European Planning Studies*, **12**, 607–24.

Simard, C. and J. West (2006), 'Knowledge networks and the geographic locus of innovation', in H. Chesbrough, W. Vanhaverbeke and J. West (eds), *Open Innovation: Researching a New Paradigm*, Oxford: Oxford University Press, pp. 220–40.

Stefik, M. and B. Stefik (2006), *Breakthrough: Stories and Strategies of Radical Innovation*, Cambridge, MA: MIT Press.

Teece, D. and G. Pisano (1996), 'The dynamic capabilities of firms: an introduction', *Industrial and Corporate Change*, **3** (3), 537–56.

Teece, D., G. Pisano and A. Shuen (1997), 'Dynamic capabilities and strategic management', *Strategic Management Journal*, **18** (7), 509–33.

Tödtling, F. and M. Trippl (2005), 'One size fits all? Towards a differentiated regional innovation policy approach', *Research Policy*, **34** (8), 1203–19.

Van den Berg, L., P. Pol, W. van Winden and P. Woets (2005), *European Cities in the Knowledge Economy*, Aldershot: Ashgate Publishing.

Van den Biesen, J. (2004), 'University–industry relations and innovation strategy in Philips worldwide: an R&D outsourcing approach', presentation to EU Conference, The Europe of Knowledge 2020: A Vision for University-based Research and Innovation, Liège Convention Centre, 25–28 April.

Zook, M.A. (2005), *The Geography of the Internet Industry: Venture Capital, Dot-coms and Local Knowledge*, Oxford: Blackwell Publishers.

30 Foreign direct investment and regional innovation
Philip Cooke and Dafna Schwartz

INTRODUCTION

Until about 1960, even in relatively open economies like the UK or USA, foreign direct investment was rather uncommon. Some large companies with oligopolistic characteristics invested directly in foreign countries because their control of markets was extremely powerful. Oil companies fall squarely into this category and most of what used to be known as the 'Seven Sisters' had refineries as well as distribution networks in many overseas countries.[1] Large companies connected to or reliant upon oil behaved similarly, notably Dupont and ICI in petrochemicals and Ford and General Motors in automotives. Apart from specialist turbine manufacturers like Westinghouse or European electrical engineering firms like Philips, Siemens and Ericsson there was by no means as much foreign direct investment (FDI) in productive capital as nowadays. National economies reigned supreme. This changed in waves from the 1960s, causing a rise in scholarly writing on the subject by the likes of Stephen Hymer (1976) who, effectively, coined the term. Subsequent waves occurred in Europe in the period preceding establishment of the Single European Market in 1992, in Eastern and Central Europe in the 1990s, and in the 2000s massive FDI investments were made in South and East Asia, echoing the more liberal trade regulations of the World Trade Organization and its predecessors, which contributed to the onset of globalization.

As we shall see, by no means all FDI is conducted by multinational corporations (MNCs), which are traditionally defined as follows: enterprises operating in several countries but managed from their home country. Moreover, any firm or group that derives a quarter of its revenue from operations outside of its home country is considered an MNC. According to United Nations (UN) data, some 35 000 firms have direct investment in foreign countries, and the largest 100 of them control about 40 per cent of world trade. In this chapter we will devote attention to the relationships of FDI to regional innovation in two principal ways. The first perspective concentrates on how FDI assists regional innovation. That is, to what extent does FDI contribute to, for example, skills upgrading, supply chain innovation enhancement opportunities and knowledge spillovers in host regions. This phenomenon is noted by leading management theorist David Teece as follows: 'many national systems of production became transformed by increased "outsourcing" and "offshoring" during the 1980s and 1990s (in part due to the global distribution of knowledge effectuated by the MNC itself)' (Teece, 2006).

The other perspective inquires how regional knowledge influences FDI, for example in relation to talent, entrepreneurship and research. These, it is widely held, with much empirical research support, advantage regions that possess them in significant ways regarding FDI (Abramovsky et al., 2007). These authors show, for example, that UK regions with university departments of chemistry scoring 5 or 5* in that country's Research Assessment Exercise attracted twice the average of pharmaceuticals research and development (R&D) laboratories and three times the norm for foreign pharmaceuticals research laboratories. They show that knowledge spillovers from such high-grade research are sufficient to attract overseas and domestic pharmaceuticals firms to the regions that boast it. The knock-on effects on regional innovation systems effects are plain to see. They include job opportunities for graduates, likely customers for university spin-out firms (see Klofsten and Öberg's Chapter 37 in this *Handbook*) and innovation opportunities for incumbent users of such research.

The final main section of this chapter focuses on new forms of FDI observable in the 2010s. These all show FDI moving down the corporate scale to small and medium-sized enterprises (SMEs), and include: financial foreign direct investment (FFDI) which has grown apace as investors in innovation (for example venture capitalists) have focused their attentions on globally innovative regions; entrepreneurial FDI (EFDI), in which, in the main, businesses invest outside their home base to access entrepreneurship that they hope will make their firms grow faster; and finally the practices of micro-multinational companies, where SMEs, notably small high-technology firms, seek out inward investment opportunities in foreign countries. The chapter ends with conclusions and suggestions for further research.

REGIONAL POLICY AND INCENTIVES

The debate in the academic literature over the desirability of using incentives to attract FDI investment to promote growth in specific locations has not yet been settled, whether with regard to particular countries (for example Vietnam – Mai, 2002; Puerto Rico – Guimaraes et al., 1998; Pelzman, 2003; The USA – Axarloglou, 2005, 2007; Bartik, 2005; Peters and Fisher, 2004) or specific regions or localities within, for example, the European Union (Boldrin and Canova, 2001; Hubert and Pain, 2002), particular regions in a country (for example, China – Démurger, 2001; Germany – Schalk and Unitiedt, 2000; the United Kingdom – Wren, 2003; Brazil – Christiansen et al., 2003; Israel – Schwartz and Keren, 2006); zones within the United States (Tumer and Cassell, 2007); metropolitan areas in the United States (Spelman, 2006); localities within a metropolitan area or inner city (Wassmer and Anderson, 2001); or other renewal areas (Adair et al., 2003).

Incentives

Many countries and regions have been implementing various policies and incentives to encourage investment FDI and other investments at the national level, and in many cases to attract the investment to specific depressed regions. It is generally accepted that incentives have had some success in inducing investment in preferred locations (see McGreevy and Thomson, 1983; Rainey and McNamara, 1999; Rees and Miall, 1981). However, their effect is found not to be determinant in the location decisions of firms; rather that primary location factors play a more important role (Guimaraes et al., 1998; Howland, 1985; Mai, 2002; Oman, 2000). Studies show that effects depend on context, and only certain forms of incentives, at certain times, exert the expected positive influence on the local value of commercial and manufacturing property (Wassmer and Anderson, 2001).

Cases have been documented where incentives seem to achieve the economic goal of raising investments, but fail to secure the basic goal of creating competitive capability in priority regions. This is reflected in unchanged technology and no reduction in regional income disparities (Haddad and Hewings, 1999; Schalk and Unitiedt, 2000), often having only limited effects on local long-run employment and wages (Axarloglou, 2007; Cannon, 1980), and often providing jobs that do not improve the job opportunities for local residents (Bartik, 2005). Peters and Fisher (2004) conclude that: 'after decades of policy experimentation and literally hundreds of scholarly studies, none of these claims is clearly substantiated' (p. 35).

The competition for FDI between locations within a country – regions or subnations – can exert a heavy economic toll and raises its cost, as in the case of Brazil (Christiansen et al., 2003). The higher costs occur when subnations compete between themselves for FDI and consequently offer very generous incentive packages to FDI. There are cases where incentives were offered to relocate between subnations within Brazil. Killian (2006) analyses the consequences of international tax competition, presenting the case of US multinationals in Ireland, and finds that not only does this competition 'harm' the home country, but it also has a negative impact on the host country. Nevertheless, the attraction of FDI to needy host economies has been a well-used instrument in the regional policy toolbox, and what is often missing from analyses such as the foregoing is any serious attention to its innovation impact upon regional performance.

HOW FDI ASSISTS REGIONAL INNOVATION

Throughout the second half of the twentieth century, especially in the regions that powered the first Industrial Revolution in coal, steel, shipbuilding and textiles – industries that were in decline as foreign resources and production were opened up – the attraction of FDI was part of the armoury of regional policy wherever it was practised. Hitherto, when the relatively few FDI firms entering host countries had arrived, they either located straightaway in prosperous regions (for example Hoover and Firestone at Perivale, West London) or soon moved there, as with Ford moving from Manchester to Dagenham, East London. Accordingly, regional policy in the 1950s and 1960s tended to focus on indigenous firms that were booming, seeking to entice them to development areas with available labour, cheap rents and grants for equipping factories. In this way, companies like Burberry, Alexon and Daks, all UK clothes manufacturers, came to the declining coalfield districts like the Rhondda in South Wales; Tri-ang, the UK toy manufacturer, and Thorn Electrical, invested in nearby Merthyr Tydfil; while the Sobell TV division of the UK's General Electric Corporation (GEC) invested in Aberdare. Tri-ang also opened in Belfast, then rapidly losing employment in its shipyards, while in the 1960s British Leyland and the Rootes Group invested in automotives in Scotland.

Foreign investments were mainly from the US and included firms in pharmaceuticals such as Bristol-Myers Squibb, Eli Lilly and Baxter Healthcare on Merseyside, and domestic appliances such as Hoover in South Wales and Scotland, or aerospace as with Rockwell Collins in North Wales or Honeywell in Scotland. However, that profile changed dramatically in the 1970s, accelerating through the following decade to peter out in the 1990s. This was the inward investment that arrived in large tranches into these development regions from Asia, mainly Japan, but in the late phase including South Korean, Singaporean and Taiwanese FDI into the UK and, to a lesser extent, France and Germany. Sony was one of the pioneers, opening its Trinitron TV plant in South Wales in 1974 to be followed by Hitachi, Matsushita and, in North Wales, Sharp. Toshiba opened in the South West of England along with many others in Telford in the West Midlands, England, and Oki and Mitsubishi in Scotland. Elsewhere in Europe, Sony invested in TV plants in Bayonne in south-west France and Stuttgart in Baden-Württemberg, Germany. Düsseldorf became the main European mainland centre for Japanese services companies.

But these were outnumbered in jobs totals by the automotive industry investments, many like Nissan, Toyota and Honda in Britain, but also others like Mazda with facilities in Germany, and Toyota in France. Like their predecessors such firms engaged in FDI to expand their markets in the host economies, the main ones at the time being the US and Europe. They located in regions where there was either not a strong trade union presence or where, if it existed, 'no-strike' deals could be negotiated. Smoothness in production scheduling was augmented by the unusual practice of stimulating supply chains composed of Japanese, indigenous or FDI firms from elsewhere to invest in these preferred regions.

Thus the Sony supply-chain in Wales stimulated laminates, glass, components suppliers and metals firms from Germany, Sweden and Japan to join indigenous suppliers of items like remote controls in South Wales. But even the wider supply-base in the UK constituted less than half of Sony's European supply chain, and the question is begged of the extent to which host region innovation was enhanced by such developments.

Therefore, let us look first at issues concerning skills upgrading, supply-chain elaboration and knowledge spillovers in relation to inward investment and regional innovation. A good place to start is Ireland, where FDI rose at 27 per cent per year in the 1990s. It is generally agreed to have contributed significantly to the rapid economic growth of Ireland's 'Celtic Tiger' economy (Krugman, 1997; Sweeney, 1998; Kirby, 2002). According to most accounts of the Irish economic miracle, a sequence of events may be traced from approximately 1987, when unlike much of Europe and elsewhere, Ireland's economy failed to grow even though its government had borrowed heavily on global markets to invest in economic growth. However, like numerous other development economies at the time, monetarist interest rate increases had made such loans acutely difficult to service. Crisis was averted by a social partnership agreement among government, trade unions and industry that held down wages in an orderly process of restoring economic balance. European regional development funds were available for Ireland to access in substantial amounts from roughly this time. Unlike many previous recipients, Ireland's strategic priority focused on building human capital rather than opening new highways. New tertiary educational institutions were established regionally, with a focus on information and communication technology (ICT) training. But still the development that would absorb newly skilled graduates failed to materialize. Accordingly, thousands of medium-to-high-skilled young workers emigrated to ICT employment opportunities in the US, Germany and the UK.

Then, coinciding with new European Union Single Market legislation, FDI began to be directed towards regions or countries with especially favourable grants and conditions regimes. Ireland had one of the lowest corporation tax rates (10 per cent, later rising to 12.5 per cent) as well as aid for industrial sites, training and equipment. ICT companies from the US and Japan invested in assembly plants such as Apple at Cork; Digital (DEC) at Limerick; Hewlett-Packard at Kildare, Galway and Dublin; Dell at Limerick; and IBM at, for example, Dublin and Galway. Some limited supply-chain development occurred but it was more pronounced in Ireland's burgeoning software cluster in which some 9000 indigenous employment opportunities were created for firms supplying the likes of Microsoft, Oracle and IBM (Lotus) (O'Malley and O'Gorman, 2001). Few of the hardware firms survive as manufacturing plants, following a process of exit by routine computer assemblers to even lower-wage regions in Eastern Europe or Asia, experienced also by Scotland (van Egeraat and Jacobson, 2004).

With respect to the quest for knowledge spillovers from a globally excellent knowledge institution, and possibly the last high-profile action to attract FDI to Ireland to enhance regional innovation, was the attraction of Massachusetts Institute of Technology (MIT)'s celebrated Media Lab to Dublin to act as a new media hub. Media Lab Europe was launched in 2000 as a research and innovation laboratory in the fields of digital technologies. Initial funding for the lab came from the Irish government and it was expected to become gradually self-financing through securing corporate funding for its research activities. However, in 2005 the board of directors of Media Lab Europe announced that the company would go into voluntary solvent liquidation. The decision was taken because its principal stakeholders, the Irish government and MIT, had not reached agreement on a new funding model for the organization. Numerous spin-out firms nevertheless survived the bankruptcy, but at an estimated cost of €70 million for 50 digital micro-firms the developmental benefit was clearly somewhat limited (Bayliss, 2007). Nevertheless, a key lesson regarding the tying in of affordable university research and knowledge economy innovation had been learned: namely that FDI in advanced sectors is more a taker than a maker of regional innovation.

In 2010, Bell Labs, a department of Alcatel-Lucent, announced a doubling of the number of researchers to 70 at its Dublin research centre, first established in 2005. Bell Labs Ireland would focus on 'open innovation' into 'Green Touch' energy-efficient telecommunications devices (see Prud'homme's Chapter 29 in this volume). Alcatel-Lucent also has research centres in the US, China, India, Germany, France and Belgium. The original investment included the establishment of a Centre for Telecommunications Value Chain-Driven Research (CTVR) at Trinity College Dublin. Cosmopolitanism, with half the workforce international and half from Ireland, and a university-like ambience, even though Bell Labs had in 2008 eschewed the basic physics research that had made it famous in favour of telecom applications research, suggested that access to postdoctoral ICT talent was now an important locational driver. Until its demise, Nortel's large optronics laboratory near Queen's University, Belfast had displayed a comparable rationale. Accordingly, Bell Labs signifies a shift of FDI sentiment towards regional innovation as more of a handmaiden to FDI rather than the reverse, of which Ireland had once been a leading exponent. Nevertheless, it is hard to draw a hard-and-fast line between the two conditions, given that ICT FDI only began flowing into Ireland when human capital had been upgraded at public expense through the Regional Technology Colleges.

HOW REGIONAL KNOWLEDGE INFLUENCES FDI

We have seen that the hope that FDI can establish a platform for regional innovation and growth is largely unfounded, and theory and policy have had to be significantly revised accordingly. We saw how the experience of developing countries has been if anything worse than that in more advanced economies. However, this judgement needs to be framed in the perspective that applies to economic development more generally. This is that it is heavily influenced by the cyclical economic context in which it is conceived and implemented. Computer hardware assemblers sought a base in the newly liberated European Single Market in 1992. Companies scanned the European space and identified peripheral Ireland as an advantageous location, for reasons discussed. Recall that these included an educated workforce, relatively generous state support of many kinds, plus the unique advantage of a low corporate taxation rate. To that may be added the global economic advantage of being an English-speaking country, a perceived source of further reduced transaction costs. However, it is noteworthy that once cheaper locations in Eastern and Central Europe, where Slavonic languages were the main native languages, proved no barrier to the rapid uprooting of some plants subsequently to be relocated there. Cheap labour costs for assembling routine and mature products proved to be the main locational attraction for that kind of FDI, as demonstrated in the 1970s and 1980s by, for example, Fröbel et al. (1980) and Massey (1984).

However, as was also shown by the example of more recent FDI projects, the new approach to successful attraction of technically complex FDI lay in development of endogenous talent pools whose scarcity made it imperative for FDI to be knowledgeable of their location worldwide. Such talent pools, arising from advanced teaching and research in centres of university excellence, might be ethnically diverse but nevertheless moderately well embedded and available for hire. These might, under the emergence of an 'open innovation' regime, be advantageous as centres of technological entrepreneurship of interests to the inward investor.

Recognition of this is an interesting and important theoretical and policy insight. Three elements are of importance in this respect. First, it suggests that policy can create 'evolution spaces' based on the development of advanced knowledge platforms centred upon university centres of global research excellence. These may concentrate a critical mass of talented labour, some 'ahead of the curve' entrepreneurial spin-outs from academe, and a few 'spin-ins' attracted by talent, knowledge spillover and market opportunities, especially if globally advanced FDI is present and associated 'soft infrastructure' in financial, legal and accountancy services supportive of technology clusters. Second, if the advanced knowledge field is relatively broad, as are many associated with new, general-purpose technologies like biotechnology, nanotechnology, clean technologies and digital media, there are 'related-variety' opportunities for innovative applications among diverse clusters. This is important both theoretically and in policy terms (see Chapter 23 on transversality in this *Handbook*). Third, it requires exquisite foresight capabilities on the part of scientists, entrepreneurs and, because it will have to pay the bills, the economic governance system.

This implies what is now well known as the 'Triple Helix' model (Etzkowitz and Leydesdorff, 1997), but actually it is an evolutionary step beyond that, into a process model involving the 'orchestration' of diverse, conflicting and competing interests rather than the harmonious process of the Triple Helix that are implied here (Wallin, 2006). Orchestration is neither a 'leadership' nor a 'consensus' process model. Rather, it recognizes that diverse interests have their respective competences and capabilities, but so does the orchestrator. The orchestrator will not be as competent as the player of a specific role, thus no competition here; nor should the orchestrator have rivals among the orchestrated, hence no conflict there. Finally, since it is a distinctive diversity-integrating position, it should be unifying in effect. On that basis regional orchestration first defines the value-creation priorities of region, governance, industry science and other interests to be orchestrated. In other words it defines how the region orchestrates stakeholders, including customers, employees, unions, suppliers, competitors and other internal groups. Orchestration involves awareness that the process may affect the innovation environment and even create newly conflicting interests, or impose regional risks. But equally it may facilitate new, unanticipated ways of creating value. Accordingly, it must be subject to continual review in light of such possible changes in perceived business conditions. Few regional innovation agencies yet practice orchestration, as described, but the few that do have a far more transformative effect upon regional innovation than is the case with more conventional approaches. As noted in Chapter 23 on transversality in this *Handbook*, the leading orchestrator agency creates some 1000 innovation cooperations every year, of which 10 per cent are estimated to result in commercial innovations.

Regions that have attracted enormous quantities of FDI because of their pre-existing skills, entrepreneurship and research include, in relation to ICT, Bangalore, Hyderabad, Mumbai and Delhi in India; Shanghai and Beijing in China; and Singapore and Taiwan. In medical biotechnology, it is Greater Boston, and to a lesser extent San Francisco and San Diego in the US; Cambridge in Europe; and Singapore again in this field. For agrofood biotechnology; Saskatoon, Canada; Scania, Sweden; and Wageningen, the Netherlands. All of these identified locations have three common features. First, their offer to the world is consciously defined and presented through a governance structure; they are branded distinctively and have their evolved identity. Second, for the most part they possess an organization that 'orchestrates' collective interests. This may take private forms (San Diego Connect; the Cambridge Network Ltd) public–private forms (the Massachusetts Biotechnology Council; Scania Food Innovation Network) or public forms (Wageningen Food Valley; Singapore Biopolis). They combine the co-evolving innovation mix, discussed above, of high-grade research, entrepreneurship and platform presence of indigenous and FDI MNCs – hence they have regional social capital and global reach in knowledge and markets.

NEW FORMS OF FDI IN THE KNOWLEDGE ECONOMY

The growing role of knowledge in the economy (Cooke and Leydesorff, 2006) has changed the global nature of FDI flows: the type, sectors' locations and the mutual reciprocal relationship with the host location. The flow of FDI in this context is to locations that have knowledge assets which the FDI source can also benefit from. The innovation spillover in these cases is not only from the FDI source to the host location, but also from the host location to the FDI source. This type of relationship is more of the 'win–win' type of situation with mutual reciprocal relationships. In this section we will elaborate two types of FDI (financial FDI and micro-multinationals), using Israel as a case study. Though Israel is a small country with limited resources, it stands out as one of the world's most competitive. It has even been called 'the world's most vital place for entrepreneurship' economies (Haour, 2005).

Financial FDI: Capital Providers, Venture Capital Funds and Private Equity Funds

A new form of FDI in the era of the knowledge economy is the flow of venture investments to emerging markets and to small, innovative high-tech centers around the globe, to benefit from the accumulation of entrepreneurship, technology and innovation in the host location. The providers of this capital are financial and risk intermediaries like venture capital (VC) funds and private equity funds that support venture investments.

In this subsection we demonstrate this new form by using the Israeli experience over the two decades to 2010, demonstrating the role of the government as a trigger in this process (Avnimelech et al., 2008; Avnimelech and Schwartz, 2009; Agmon and Messica, 2008; Schwartz, 2009; Schwartz and Bar-El, 2007). 'The Israeli case is an example of a successful government intervention that helps bring into Israel the all important financial (and risk) intermediation that reduces the trading cost for Israeli innovative firms in the global markets' (Agmon and Messica, 2008).

In 1993 the Israeli government decided to encourage the formation of a VC industry through a special programme called Yozma (which means 'initiative' in Hebrew), and $100 million was allocated for that purpose. Although the country enjoyed a relatively high level of R&D activities at the time with civilian, military and government R&D support programs that were in place, the overall conditions were not ripe for venture investments. Under the Yozma initiative, ten venture capital funds were formed. Each of these funds was a partner of a major Israeli financial institution with leading foreign venture investors, of which the government's share was a maximum of 40 per cent and the private investors' share 60 per cent. A significant attraction of the Yozma programme was the private investors' option to buy out the government's share at a predetermined price over a period of five years.

Thus the Yozma programme did not simply supply risk-sharing to investors, it also provided an upside incentive: that private investors could leverage their profits through the acquisition of the government shares. In addition, Yozma was allowed to invest a certain portion of its capital directly in start-ups. The Yozma programme immediately proved to be extremely successful. Ten VC funds were formed and 15 direct investments were made by Yozma itself and major international venture investors were attracted from the USA, Germany, Japan, the Netherlands and Singapore: Daimler-Benz, DEG (Germany), Advent (USA), Van Leer Group (Netherlands), Oxton (US/Far East), AVX, Kyocera (Japan), CMS (USA), TVM (Germany), Singapore Tech, Vertex International Funds (Singapore), and Walden (US). Nine of the ten funds exercised their option and bought out the government's share. Nine out of the 15 investments (made by Yozma directly) enjoyed successful exits, either through public sales (initial public offerings, IPOs) or through acquisition.

Yet another example is that of India where, unusually, a significant portion of FDI is owned by Indian expatriates in innovation hotspots such as Silicon Valley. This phenomenon evolved as follows. As described by Saxenian (2000), the dynamic economic growth entailed by innovations in microelectronics led to severe skills shortages by the 1980s. According to census statistics approximately one-third of the area's scientists and engineers were non-American in origin. Of these, two-thirds were Asian, mainly Indians and Chinese. Of these 55 per cent of Indian workers and 40 per cent of Chinese had graduate qualifications, compared to only 18 per cent in the indigenous population. Despite this, many found that they could not achieve promotion to managerial positions. From the 1990s some of these educated workers became entrepreneurs, raising venture capital from indigenous investors. By the end of the 1990s some 9 per cent of Silicon Valley start-ups were Indian-owned and 20 per cent were Chinese.

Thereafter, during the 1990s Indian entrepreneurs in particular engaged in what became known as the 'to and fro brain drain', whereby they became frequent, temporary return migrants to their country of origin (Balasubramanyam and Balasubramanyam, 2000). Some set up branches of their US employer or their own start-ups, while others set up new ventures in talent pool regions around Bangalore and Hyderabad where FDI microelectronics firms like Texas Instruments had become established earlier. But yet others brought tranches of the profits they had made from their microelectronics businesses and established Indian-based venture capital firms that targeted indigenous Indian start-up companies. In the high-technology belt of 1990s and 2000s India there was a great global demand for indigenous software skills. Accordingly, many of the new ventures were set up either as suppliers to US FDI software firms like Oracle and Novell or, increasingly, Indian giants like Infosys and Wipro. Many of these were able to access Indian venture capital originating in Silicon Valley but having been transplanted as a new business service to the region by 'to and fro brain drain' migration.

Entrepreneurship by R&D FDI Centres

There is a growing number of multinational corporations that are locating and organizing their R&D either directly or by 'open innovation' (see Chapter 29 by Prud'homme in this *Handbook*) in emerging market economies in order to gain competitive capabilities (Baskaran and Muchie, 2008). Even though countries compete for R&D FDI investments by offering different incentives (Guimon, 2009), the distribution of R&D FDI centres has not been equitably spread across regions; rather, they are concentrated in a small number of locations facilitating the emergence of new centres and clusters of knowledge across the globe

Analyses of flows of R&D FDI across the globe from 2002 to 2005 show that North America has been the source of one-half of all R&D FDI and that the Asia Pacific, especially China and India, has been the overwhelming destination for most R&D FDI, accounting for more than one-half of all investment and almost three-quarters of the jobs created. Another destination is Israel, which is considered to be a hub of innovation. Studies analysing the flow of R&D FDI show that the weakness or strength of national innovation systems (NISs) influences the nature and volume of the R&D inflow (Baskaran and Muchie, 2008). Therefore, one of the conclusions is that an efficient policy of promoting R&D-intensive FDI has to be connected to the local innovation policy – national and regional (Guimon, 2009, for Spain and Ireland). Another conclusion is the need to include in the policy measures 'after-care services', since R&D-intensive FDI tends to be evolutionary rather than purely greenfield (Guimon, 2009). Taking Israel as an example, where many multinational firms have R&D centres, in many cases the international firm acquires domestic companies and transforms them into local research facilities. In Israel in 2007 there were at least 110 foreign R&D centres, employing over 35 000 workers. The number had grown to 210 centres by 2010, many of them specialized in high-technology fields where Israel has competitive advantage.

Micro-multinational Firms

Before this current term to describe SMEs that have multiple global locations evolved, they were more familiarly known as 'mid-size multinationals'. Certain regions pioneered this phenomenon, one of them being Catalonia in Spain. Here the lead FDI industry was textiles and clothing. Encouraged by the Catalan government, SMEs engaged in capital export to produce cheaper fashion goods in foreign countries with low labour costs. These moves were often orchestrated by a regional design or technology centre. Thus Fitex, the private Catalan technology centre, manages with government support a platform of ten supply chain firms in China; as does another one named Cettemsa. These early 'mid-size multinationals' were not strictly speaking all multinationals in the accepted meaning of the term. Rather, they organized, with the assistance of intermediaries, logistics, training, ICT management, fashion innovation and retailing. They were thus able to gain many of the integrated supply-chain features that at a larger scale the true multinational would typically arrange in-house. That is not to say that all large multinationals only engage in FDI to reorganize their internal production structures; many of course also outsource to local producers. This is something that makes the practices of Catalan clothing firms – some of which, such as Mango, have grown to be significant multinational retailers as well as producers – interesting emulators of that large-firm-initiated competitive strategy.

The micro-multinationals tend nowadays to be technology-intensive or knowledge-intensive businesses. Three features characterize their method of operation. First, during the 2000s it became important for certain smaller technology firms to locate in benign investment environments. Such investor-intensive locations as California and Massachusetts were perceived to have better risk-capital, better managerial and better innovation support infrastructures. For a short-lived period in the mid-2000s there was a fashion for smaller biotechnology firms to 'decapitate' themselves by keeping research in bioscientific knowledge centres like Cambridge, UK and translocating other parts of the business through various co-ownership strategies to the 'better business environments' of the US (Cooke, 2007). Meanwhile, and not without irony, a number of similar moves by US biotechnology start-ups, seeking to access what they perceived as a better regime of public innovation support from the likes of Scottish Enterprise, also ensued. This was because their experience was that US venture capital interest in biotechnology had evaporated.

A second reason for the micro-multinational phenomenon is that the enhancement of various forms of low-cost software and interactive communication systems known as Software as a Service (SaaS) enabled 'virtual businesses' to come into existence. Often themselves software design companies, they would typically have no physical office, would employ software engineers from numerous different countries, and would have international clients for whom they produced technical or design solutions.

Finally, the onset of the 'knowledge economy' and a business mindset of innovating through exploiting pure knowledge in its many forms was a third reason for small-firm internationalization. Thus a category of 'knowledge entrepreneurs' dealing in intellectual property, ranging from problem-solving to 'open innovation' knowledge supply-chain activity (Prud'homme's Chapter 29 in this *Handbook*), to making money from litigating patent 'squatters' (that is, firms inadvertently or otherwise infringing valid but dated patents) had emerged, many with global reach (Porter and Cooke, 2007).

CONCLUSIONS

The chapter has presented the trend in FDI over time. It has presented the expectations of policy-makers from the FDI source to contribute to the growth of their location, particularly to growth rather than innovation. Studies and literature to be pursued in further research have been presented that seek to evaluate the effectiveness of government interventions and new trends in FDI in the era of the knowledge economy. As part of the new FDI trends many governmental experiences and the role of government as a trigger to encourage new types of FDI in support of the high-tech sector were elaborated on. It remains an interesting and important research field. More research is clearly needed on innovation gains to regions from pursuing an FDI strategy. As noted in the cases of Ireland and Scotland, even when the original innovation impulse of FDI had passed and its incumbents had moved on, not insubstantial innovation gains in surviving smaller firm and institutional profiles could be identified. FDI remains a potent aspect of the global economy and its geography, and new directions and scales of FDI and its contribution to innovation and growth are sorely needed. This means studies not only of Asian and Latin American recipient regions, but also of the impact of small, specialist micro-multinationals on the innovation profile of both their home and host regions.

NOTE

1. This term was coined by Italian magnate Enrico Mattei and referred to Exxon (Esso), Shell, BP, Gulf, Texaco, Mobil and Socal (Chevron). With Exxon's acquisition of Mobil and Chevron's of Gulf and Texaco they became Four Sisters who now control only 10 per cent of world oil and gas reserves. In a *Financial Times* article the New Seven Sisters, controlling 30 per cent of the world's oil and gas reserves, were said to be: Aramco of Saudi Arabia, CNPC of China, Gazprom of Russia, NIOC of Iran, PDVSA of Venezuela, Petrobras of Brazil, and Petronas of Malaysia (Sulzberger, 1979; Beltrame, 2007).

REFERENCE

Abramovsky, L., R. Harrison and H. Simpson (2007), 'University research and the location of business R&D', *Economic Journal*, **117** (519), C114–41.
Adair, A., J. Berry and S. McGreal (2003), 'Financing property's contribution to regeneration', *Urban Studies*, **40** (5–6), 1065–80.
Agmon, T. and A. Messica (2008), 'Venture capital funds, financial foreign direct investment and the generation of local comparative advantage in the technology sector in Israel', *Contributions to Political Economy*, **27** (1), 57–73.

Avnimelech, G. and D. Schwartz (2009), 'Structural transformation of regional venture capital industry: evidence from Israel', *Innovation: Management, Policy and Practice (IMPP)*, **11** (1), 60–73.

Avnimelech, G., D. Schwartz and M. Teubal (2008), 'Entrepreneurial high-tech cluster development', in C. Karlsson (ed.), *Handbook of Research on Innovation and Clusters: Cases and Policies*, Cheltenham, UK and Northampton, MA, USA: Edward Elgar, pp. 124–48.

Axarloglou, K. (2005), 'What attract foreign direct investment inflows in the United States', *International Trade Journal*, **19** (3), 285–304.

Axarloglou, K. (2007), 'Do all foreign direct investment inflows benefit the local economy?', *World Economy*, **30** (3), 424–45.

Balasubramanyam, A. and V.N. Balasubramanyam (2000), 'The software cluster in Bangalore', in J.H. Dunning (ed.), *Regions, Globalization and the Knowledge-Based Economy*, Oxford: Oxford University Press, pp. 349–63.

Bartik, T.B. (2005), 'Solving the problems of economic development incentives', *Growth and Change*, **36** (2), 139–67.

Baskaran, A. and M. Muchie (2008), 'Foreign direct investment and internationalization of R&D: the case of BRICS economics', Working Paper No. 7, Development, Innovation and International Political Economy Research (DIIPER), Aalborg University, Denmark.

Bayliss, D. (2007), 'Dublin's digital hubris: lessons from an attempt to develop a creative industrial cluster', *European Planning Studies*, **15**, 1261–72.

Beltrame, S. (2007), 'The new Seven Sisters', *Financial Times*, 11 March.

Boldrin, M. and F. Canova (2001), 'Inequality and convergence in Europe's regions: reconsidering European regional policies', *Economic Policy*, **32**, 205–52.

Cannon, J. (1980), 'The impact of investment incentives on manufacturing change: the Georgian Bay region of Ontario', *Canadian Geographer*, **24** (2), 131–48.

Christiansen, H., C. Oman and A. Charlton (2003), 'Incentives-based competition for foreign direct investment: the case of Brazil', Working Papers on International Investment, OECD.

Cooke, P. (2007), *Growth Cultures: The Global Bioeconomy and its Bioregions*, London: Routledge.

Cooke, P. and L. Leydesorff (2006), 'Regional development in the knowledge-based economy: the construction of advantages', *Journal of Technology Transfer (JTT)*, **31** (1), 5–16.

Démurger, S. (2001), 'Infrastructure development and economic growth: an explanation for regional disparities in China?', *Journal of Comparative Economics*, **29**, 95–117.

van Egeraat, C. and D. Jacobson (2004), 'The rise and demise of the Irish and Scottish computer hardware industry', *European Planning Studies*, **12** (6), 810–34.

Etzkowitz, H. and L. Leydesdorff (eds) (1997), *Universities in the Global Knowledge Economy*, London: Pinter.

Fröbel, F., O. Kreye and J. Heinrichs (1980), *The New International Division of Labour*, Cambridge: Cambridge University Press.

Guimaraes, P., R.J. Rolfe and D.P. Woodward (1998), 'Regional incentives and industrial location in Puerto Rico', *International Regional Science Review*, **21** (2), 119–38.

Guimon, J. (2009), 'Government strategies to attract R&D-intensive FDI', *Journal of Technology Transfer*, **34** (4), 364–80.

Haddad, E.A. and G.J.D. Hewings (1999), 'The short run regional effects of new investments and technological upgrade in the Brazilian automobile industry: an interregional computable general equilibrium analysis', *Oxford Development Studies*, **27** (3), 359–83.

Haour, G. (2005), 'Israel, a powerhouse for networked entrepreneurship', *International Journal of Entrepreneurship and Innovation Management*, **5** (1–2), 39–68.

Howland, M. (1985), 'Property taxes and the birth and intraregional location of new firms', *Journal of Planning Education and Research*, **4** (3), 148–56.

Hubert, F. and N. Pain (2002), 'Fiscal incentives, European integration and the location of foreign direct investment', *Manchester School*, **70** (3), 336–63.

Hymer, S. (1976), *The International Operations of National Firms: A Study of Direct Foreign Investment*, Cambridge, MA: MIT Press.

Killian, S. (2006), 'Where's the harm in tax competition? Lessons from US multinationals in Ireland', *Critical Perspectives on Accounting*, **17** (8), 1067–88.

Kirby, P. (2002), *The Celtic Tiger in Distress*, London: Palgrave.

Krugman, P. (1997), 'Good news from Ireland: a geographical perspective', in A. Gray (ed.), *International Perspectives on the Irish Economy*, Dublin: Indecon, pp. 38–53.

Mai, P.H. (2002), 'Regional economic development and the foreign direct investment flows in Vietnam 1988–98', *Journal of the Asia Pacific Economy*, **7** (2), 182–202.

Massey, D. (1984), *Spatial Divisions of Labour*, London: Macmillan.

McGreevy, T.E. and A.W.J. Thomson (1983), 'Regional policy and company investment behaviour', *Regional Studies*, **17**, 347–58.

O'Malley, E. and C. O'Gorman (2001), 'Competitive advantage in the Irish indigenous software industry and the role of inward foreign direct investment', *European Planning Studies*, **9**, 303–21.

Oman, C. (2000), 'Policy competition for foreign direct investment: a study of competition among governments to attract FDI', Development Centre Studies, Development Centre of the Organisation for Economic Co-operation and Development (OECD), Paris.

Pelzman, J. (2003), 'The continuing saga of gimmicky investment plans targeting Puerto Rico', *Tax Notes International*, **11**, 551–4.

Peters, A. and P. Fisher (2004), 'The failures of economic development incentives', *Journal of the American Planning Association (JAPA)*, **70** (1), 27–37.

Porter, J. and P. Cooke (2007), 'From seekers to squatters: the rise of knowledge entrepreneurship', *CES-Ifo Forum*, **8**, 21–8.

Rainey, D.V. and K.T. McNamara (1999), 'Taxes and the location decision of manufacturing establishments', *Review of Agricultural Economics*, **21** (1), 86–98.

Rees, R.D. and R.H.C. Miall (1981), 'The effect of regional policy on manufacturing investment and capital stock within the UK between 1959 and 1978', *Regional Studies*, **15** (6), 413–24.

Saxenian, A. (2000), 'Networks of immigrant entrepreneurs', in C.-M. Lee, W.F. Miller, M.G. Hancock and H.S. Rowen (eds), *The Silicon Valley Edge: A Habitat for Innovation and Entrepreneurship*, Stanford, CA: Stanford University Press, pp. 248–75.

Schalk, H.J. and G. Unitiedt (2000), 'Regional investment incentives in Germany: impacts on factor demand and growth', *Annals of Regional Science*, **34** (2), 173–95.

Schwartz, D. (2009), 'Venture capital and business development in Israel', in J. Osmond (ed.), *Regional Economies in a Globalising World*, Cardiff: Institute of Welsh Affairs, pp. 76–9.

Schwartz, D. and R. Bar-El (2007), 'Venture investments in Israel – a regional perspective', *European Planning Studies*, **15** (5), 623–44.

Schwartz, D. and M. Keren (2006), 'Location incentives and the unintentional generation of employment instability: some evidence from Israel', *Annals of Regional Science*, **40** (2), 449–60.

Spelman, W. (2006), 'Growth, stability, and the urban portfolio', *Economic Development Quarterly*, **20** (4), 299–316.

Sulzberger, C. (1979), *The Last of the Giants*, London: Macmillan.

Sweeney, P. (1998), *The Celtic Tiger*, Dublin: Oak Leaf Press.

Teece, D. (2006), 'Reflections on the Hymer thesis and the multinational enterprise', *International Business Review*, **15**, 124–39.

Tumer, R.C. and M.K. Cassell (2007), 'When do states pursue targeted economic development policies? The adaptation and expansion of state enterprise zone programs', *Social Science Quarterly*, **88** (1), 86–104.

Wallin, J. (2006), *Business Orchestration*, London: Wiley.

Wassmer, R.W. and J.E. Anderson (2001), 'Bidding for business: new evidence on the effect of locally offered economic development incentives in a metropolitan area', *Economic Development Quarterly*, **15** (2), 132–48.

Wren, C. (2003), 'Investment scale as a signal in industrial assistance schemes in employment objectives', *Economica*, **70** (278), 331–52.

31 Innovation systems in emerging economies: the case of India

Scott Ptak and Sharmistha Bagchi-Sen

Today, it is generally accepted that innovation-led economic growth is the most critical component for rising standards of productivity and general welfare among nations (Edquist, 1997). The 'innovation system' (IS) approach created by the works of Freeman (1982), Dosi et al. (1988) and Lundvall and Johnson (1994) helps to explain the process by which innovation generates this economic development. Combining a network and evolutionary economic approach, this model is a useful tool for analyzing the way in which discoveries happen, are disseminated, commercialized and utilized in various places and at various scales. The IS model is especially pertinent in understanding growth in today's knowledge-based economy because a clearer understanding about how innovation works means an increased opportunity to control the outcome of the innovation process. Local, regional, national and even international policies throughout the world aim to harness this power of innovation. In this context, developing countries face unique obstacles and opportunities for achieving growth through innovation.

The experience of India demonstrates one way that such an emerging economy has embraced these challenges and opportunities to become one of today's most relevant hubs for global innovation. India has reined in the processes of the innovation system at various spatial scales to further its goals of economic growth and technological upgrading.

This chapter begins with a short focus on the innovation system literature, followed by a direct application of this literature to the challenges and obstacles of operating a successful innovation system in a developing country. The chapter then focuses on India's successes – and shortcomings – in overcoming these obstacles in transforming innovation into economic development. The chapter concludes with a future research agenda and policy implications for pursuing economic growth through the innovation system in emerging economies.

INNOVATION SYSTEMS: CONCEPT AND SCALES

The innovation system approach attempts to describe the process of knowledge-based economic development through the evolutionary economic perspective. Innovation refers not only to the generation of knowledge, but also to the transportation of an idea into the economic realm in the form of a marketable product, service or process (Nelson and Rosenberg, 1993). It is not a specific definition limited to those revelations at the world threshold of technology; rather innovation can also include those factors 'influencing . . . technological capabilities' (Nelson and Rosenberg, 1993). Innovation is not an isolated single action, but rather a process which requires the involvement of a large network of actors and other institutions governed by a framework of rules and procedure, and influenced by the socio-political and spatial environments in which interactions between actors occur (Lundvall and Johnson, 1994). The relevant actors, institutions, rules, procedures and environmental characteristics will vary depending on the specific time, spatial scale and time period analyzed. As an obvious example, the actors, institutions, rules, procedures and environments relevant in bringing about modern innovation today at a local scale in the Indian automotive hub of Chennai will differ markedly from those relevant at bringing about national innovation in the German States during the Industrial Revolution (Freeman, 1987).

These differences perpetuate because actors relate not only to one another but also to their disparate environments in the innovation process (Storper, 1991). Taking their cue from the biological sciences, scholars in the IS literature have used the terms 'knowledge ecology' or 'ecosystem' (Papaioannou et al., 2009) to draw an analogy between these interactions and those between plants, animals, humans and the broader physical environment. It is here that the term 'system' is used to denote the interaction of the actors with the broader environment. While the majority of actors within an innovation system hardly see it as their individual goal (or power) to spur widespread economic growth through innovation, the competitive market environments and other institutional infrastructure within a socio-spatial environment often works to direct micro-goals of individuals, firms, localities, regions and even nations into this macro-reality. The goal of policy-makers concentrated on knowledge-based economic development then has been to pursue a particular outcome by bolstering or manipulating components of the relevant 'system' to achieve a desired outcome: economic development.

The socio-spatial 'embeddedness' of the learning and innovation processes necessarily implies that innovation cannot be understood generally at one static spatial level (Carlsson and Stankiewicz, 1991). Instead, scholars have sought to understand the processes of the innovation system on three spatial scales: through the national innovation systems (NISs), the regional innovation systems (RISs), and the more emergent international innovation system (IIS).

The National Innovation System

Within the innovation system literature, the NIS scale is perhaps the most widely cited. It seeks to understand in either specific or broad terms how innovations are developed, diffused and utilized within a nation, and subsequently, how these innovations can effect economic development. Lundvall (1992), the first to coin the term 'national innovation system', understands the NIS in a broad sense as including: 'all parts and aspects of the economic structure and the institutional set-up affecting learning as well as searching and exploring – [including especially] the production system, the marketing system and the system of finance [of a country]'. He advocates an inclusive view of what constitutes an NIS, indicating that the topic must be: 'kept open and flexible regarding which subsystems should be included and which processes should be studied' (Lundvall, 1992).

Archibugi and Michie (1997) have divided this broad scope of 'subsystems' affecting learning into two categories with regard to the NIS. Nation-specific factors play a crucial role in shaping technological change. These nation-specific factors are often institutional, like a country's education system, certain public support to industrial innovation or defense-related technology contracting. But there are also historical factors to consider, an appeal to evolutionary economic thinkers who understand that a nation's trajectory can also affect innovation. For an institutional backbone, a successful NIS has a good education system, science and technology capabilities, industrial structure, ability to identify strengths and weaknesses of its own, capability in creating a supported environment to allow interaction within the innovation system, and a good ability to absorb technologies from abroad (Archibugi and Michie, 1997).

At a more nuanced level, for an NIS to be effective, it needs to have active participation from government (including sponsored public research institutes), industry, and academia, the three components loosely referred to as the 'Triple Helix' of innovation (Etzkowitz and Leydesdorff, 1997). Industry serves important functions as a commercializer of knowledge, a developer of knowledge through in-house R&D operations (especially in developed countries), and an absorber or transmitter of foreign technology. Determinants of the success of industry in performing these functions include: the level of education and experience possessed by the employees, especially at the managerial level; whether a given business has contact with foreign companies, either in exporting or importing (for technology transfer); the relative size of firms within the industry (as greater resources allow firms to invest more heavily in in-house R&D, or to procure technology from abroad); and the relative abundance or scarcity of interfirm connections.

By way of policy formulation, central and regional governments also play important roles in the NIS, acting as: coordinators among research producers; subsidizers of industry or learning institutions; promoters of technology transfer (through import–export regimes, FDI policies and direct sponsorship of other programs); providers of broader institutional policies and the 'learning environment' (including education and legal protections for producers); and more recently, the designers of medium- or long-term visions for technological upgrading (Arocena and Sutz, 2005). Public policy reach must also try to cure the bureaucratic and infrastructural bottlenecks that constrain entry of foreign investment and trade; and also in many cases to provide seed capital to new ventures, since this sector is often ill-served by the private marketplace (Wessner and Shivakumar, 2007). Universities, the bastions of academia, and public or private research institutes, are also essential ingredients to a successful NIS. Such centers of learning not only train a qualified workforce, but often participate directly in discovery and invention, creating spin-off companies that allow an idea to move from the academic to the economic realm.

The Regional Innovation System

While the physical and political boundaries of the modern nation-state allow for a somewhat precise definition of the 'national' in 'national innovation system', the conceptual boundaries of the 'region' have never been mapped to any real degree of specificity. Cooke et al. (1997) defines the region as a: 'territor[y] smaller than [its] state possessing supralocal governance capacity and cohesiveness differentiating [it] from [its] state or other regions'. A more precise, inflexible definition of the region lies, if not outside the realm of practicality, then certainly outside the scope of this chapter.

For our purposes, it is only important to note that the RIS, operating within and dependent on the NIS, operates with its own specific nuances. The RIS is interconnected with the broader NIS in its firm connections and dependency on the national institutional set-up including, especially, national policies of education, legal regimes, taxation, FDI policies, import–export schedules, and so on. However, the localization of actors within the region and the specific institutions, cultures and factor-specific conditions of a region mean that the RIS differs markedly from the NIS. While regions are influenced by the NIS, they have a particular ability to 'go their own way' and depart from the national average (Fischer, 2002).

There is a long history of attempts to explain, in theoretical terms, the innovation system at the regional or local level (see Marshall, 1898; Amin and Robins, 1990; Brusco, 1990; Castells and Hall, 1994; Porter, 1990; Storper, 1991; Cooke et al., 1997; Scott and Storper, 2007). While theoretical frameworks focusing on regional innovation differ in terminology and concentration, all continue to recognize the region-specific roles of: (1) regional factors, including culture and access to physical and human resources; (2) regional institutions, including firms, government and financial institutions; and (3) the increased interaction among actors and subsequent learning benefits derived from close physical proximity. Where concentrations of interrelated and interdependent producers operate in a localized area:

> good work is rightly appreciated, inventions and improvements in machinery, in processes and the general organization of the businesses have their merits promptly discussed; if one person starts a new idea, it is taken up by others and combined with suggestions of their own; and thus it becomes the source of further new ideas. (Marshall, 1898)

Because interactive learning requires that actors share at least a base level of competence, the innovational capacity of regions with this competence is much greater (Andersson and Karlsson, 2004). Saxenian (1990) highlights the role of competitive cooperation in Silicon Valley, and suggests that certain regional cultures can be beneficial to innovation. Other local factors, including the local availability of human capital, are extremely important for innovative capacity. The knowledge base and competence possessed by innovative regions serve as an incentive that attracts innovative and experimentation-oriented players like firms, research laboratories and business parks. Often this draw is a local phenomenon, as opposed to a national one. Successful innovative regions often act as fertile ground for spin-off enterprises from local firms. Regional government can foster innovation by creating incentives for firm location and cooperation, or it can stifle innovation by imposing cumbersome red tape. Regional financial institutions, including especially the availability of venture capital, are vital to innovation at the regional level. Learning and innovation generally benefit strongly from the relative physical proximity of actors in a network and the subsequent ability for tacit knowledge transfer (Amin and Wilkinson, 1999). Physical proximity is not a necessary or sufficient condition in itself for innovation however: it merely facilitates innovation in an RIS (Malecki and Oinas, 1999).

Following the evolutionary economic perspective, the proper functioning of these cohesive elements of an RIS can potentially also serve to reduce innovation and even stifle economic growth. When an RIS relies too heavily on inward sources of knowledge generation and transfer, it can become trapped in innovational 'lock-in' (Boschma, 2005). An overly inward orientation reduces access to outside sources of information and reduces the potential for overall knowledge diversity. Extra-local connections allow actors to: 'stay in tune with what happens in the market, what happens among other producers, customers, scientists, regulators, support agencies, and other sources of technological knowledge' (Oinas and Malecki, 2002). Successful RISs maintain at least some connections to distant regions.

The International Innovation System

Traditional notions of the innovation system have generally focused on socio-political boundaries to define their scale, and tend to ignore the international dimension of innovation systems. The inadequacy of these fixed approaches is evident in today's complex global economy: innovation today is not only a local or national process. The innovation system approach therefore has needed to recognize a new 'international innovation system' (IIS). The functioning of the IIS also includes many nuances inexplicable by any other system. While scholars have advocated various theoretical models to understanding the IIS, common themes have emerged (for example Oinas and Malecki, 2002; Coe et al., 2009). Multigovernmental organizations and other international regulatory bodies can generate incentives or reduce burdens on trade and FDI, but can also create stiffer global competition for domestic producers. For example, the World Trade Organization (WTO)'s Trade-Related Intellectual Property Rights (TRIPS) agreement, regulating the way that products are patented in its member countries, has profoundly influenced the nature of innovation in the pharmaceutical industry (Barton, 2004). Individual entrepreneurs can also alter flows of innovation on the international stage. Multinational firms, unbounded by any other spatial innovation system, are responsible for directing the flow of not only goods, but also innovation, across the globe.

INNOVATION SYSTEMS IN EMERGING ECONOMIES

While it was the more advanced Western economies that implemented the first conscious national policies designed to enhance their innovation systems, emerging economies today increasingly rely on this strategy for national economic development. But the prospects for innovation-led development are not the same for these 'latecomers': new barriers to entry impose on them significant burdens even while some unique opportunities help to reduce these burdens.

Many emerging economies have a difficult time 'jump-starting' successful innovation systems. They tend to be plagued by weak domestic knowledge bases, and lack the institutional, legal and educational infrastructure required to overcome this burden. Industrial innovation in developing countries tends to be less about formal, scientific research and development (R&D) than in developed countries (Arocena and Sutz, 2005). Economic structures in developing countries may exhibit a high degree of heterogeneity, with a low initial complexity and degree of vertical integration. Strong guards for a market-based economy in these countries are often lacking (Intarakumnerd et al., 2002). Furthermore, limited and volatile financial markets, especially in venture capital, constrain the capital inflows that innovation requires (Ernst, 2002). Furthermore, while government in much of the developed world is relatively streamlined, public institutions in the developing world are often characterized by complicated, overlapping systems of governance and decision-making, typically showing preference for government ownership as against benefiting from private entrepreneurship, especially risk-taking ability. In many developing countries, state-run firms are often the largest, but the least innovative (Dutz, 2007). These initial disadvantages mean that developing countries tend to be the most dependent on foreign sources of knowledge (Ernst, 2002). Recent empirical evidence suggests that economic growth is strongly correlated with national management of the NIS, openness of the economy and the political system and the overall quality of governance (Fagerberg and Srholec, 2008).

To make matters worse, developed countries themselves often impose their own burdens on developing well-functioning innovation systems. Large multinational corporations (MNCs), usually from developed countries, already dominate the marketplace for many technologies. They are more likely to guard their intellectual property closely than in previous decades, but are more likely to demand unimpeded access to the domestic markets of others (Nelson, 2004). New international laws and regulations mean that they are better able to guard their intellectual property yet have access to formerly protected markets.

While daunting to overcome, these disadvantages are offset by general latecomer advantages (Wong, 1999). Lower resource costs, especially in labor inputs, can give producers in the developing world an advantage over their foreign counterparts and can lead to increased magnetism for FDI. The pace of catch-up for firms in developing countries can also be greater; as technologies or methods employed by firms in existing countries become obsolete (for example, post-Fordist paradigm shift), they can be either adopted at a lesser cost or leapfrogged altogether. For growing firms in developing countries, firm information is more easily gatherable on their larger competition. Stiff competition from these larger firms in the international marketplace forces developing-country firms to innovate constantly. Furthermore, developing governments are often more willing to step in to protect domestic 'infant industries', or to provide other incentives to upgrade.

In today's economy, knowledge flows have become increasingly international in nature as institutional and cultural boundaries that serve to bound these flows have eroded. For developing countries, this means that greater opportunities exist to extract and build upon this knowledge. Previously huge R&D expenses of innovative firms are now being curtailed by moving product, service or process development to firms in offshore destinations, especially in developing countries. This facilitates technology transfer. Surpluses of skilled, educated labor combined with stronger enforcement of intellectual property rights give these locations in particular an added advantage for the MNC. Increasingly too, decreases in costs of information technology combined with this surplus have enabled researchers to communicate with others in the developed world to share information and level the innovative playing-field (Castellacci, 2006).

INDIA'S INNOVATION SYSTEMS

As an emerging economy, India has overcome many of the 'latecomer' obstacles to successful innovation-led development. Policies implemented at every level of government have been successful in harnessing positive innovation systems at the national, regional and international levels. While India has emerged as a regional leader in some areas, it remains burdened by latecomer disadvantages in others.

The following analysis comes with a caveat. Any attempt to summarize fully the evolution of India's innovation systems, even through the past few decades, would be woefully incomplete. The Indian economy is complex. Pro-development governments have instituted wide-ranging policies covering countless topics. India's regions are as diverse as they are nuanced. The scope of India's international linkages is likewise staggering. The analysis that follows is meant to be illustrative, not inclusive.

NIS Development

India's recent economic-led development began with comprehensive governmental reforms designed to strip away the latecomer disadvantages of a burdensome bureaucracy, weak human capital base and 'ock-in' of its old innovation systems. The rigid and protectionist mindset of the Indian government began to witness a profound change during the late 1980s as the country sought to keep up with the rapidly liberalizing pace of globalization. The previous protectionist attitude left the country standing on the sidelines of the booming global semiconductor business. Accordingly, the government began to rethink its position, and turned to taking calculated efforts to develop an expertise in the growing software business (Parthasarathy, 2007). The year 1991 marked the beginning of substantial economic reforms in India. Since then, successive governments have implemented strong measures to continue to liberalize the business environment and boost industrial growth led especially by innovation-oriented sectors like information technology (IT) and biotechnology (Kumar, 2001).

This movement to capture technological momentum changed India's economic trajectory in the 1990s as the IT sector moved the economy to a new level (Dossani, 2008; Sengupta, 2005). Over this decade, there was a massive change in state and bureaucratic mindset. New policies successfully aimed at growth in the financial, manufacturing and services sectors (Dossani, 2008). Economic reforms initiated in the 1990s changed industrial licensing and replaced unfavorable import regulations on most goods (Sengupta, 2005), reducing friction in the business environment. Excessive government control was replaced by a more accommodative policy framework and a more comprehensive information disclosure policy creating a more competitive and growth-oriented market stance (Dossani, 2008). The Computer Policy of 1984 and the Computer Software Export, Development and Training Policy of December 1986 were important initiatives in this reformation as they lowered import duties of software and prioritized software exports. These policies restricted the government's role to providing promotional and infrastructural backing in the sector.

India was also able to advantage its national innovation system by significantly raising its human capital base during the period. India's education system created a vast pool of engineers and skilled labor educated in English, a language which facilitated communication with foreign businesses and was a boon for India's outsourcing success. In addition, the experience that the IT professionals had gained from working on software platforms since the 1970s added to this skill advantage. As a result, India was even able to begin to support its own software projects initiated by its own professionals in the 1980s and 1990s (Parthasarathy, 2007). India has in general, however, a stronger base in supplying inputs as against outputs of technical and scientific knowledge, which is evident from its smaller contribution publications vis-à-vis researchers engaged in mainstream R&D (Wessner and Shivakumar, 2007).

Government action also attempted to overcome the latecomer disadvantage posed by dominant and restrictive multinationals. In 1974, the Indian government passed the Foreign Exchange Regulation Act (FERA), which meant that established MNC subsidiaries were forced to reduce their share of ownership to 40 percent by public sale of stock or else leave the country entirely. This policy proved critical to the future of India's domestic software industry and capacity for innovation. When the giant IBM decided to leave India, approximately 1200 former employees of the company began their own software businesses to continue to provide services for IBM's former (largely Western) customers, and these new companies found a new competitive environment which was no longer dominated by IBM (Khanna and Palepu, 2005).

Similarly, long-standing government protection of India's pharmaceutical industry allowed it to develop an initial domestic innovative capacity. India's success in the pharmaceutical and, more recently, biopharmaceutical fields is exceptional because these industries are characterized by huge barriers to entry for latecomer emerging economies. Firms are greatly dependant either directly or indirectly on the state for soft infrastructure, human resources and, more importantly, much of the basic research they use in developing their products (Bagchi-Sen et al., 2004). In India, the biotechnology and drugs and pharmaceuticals sectors are the most investment-intensive industries (Arora, 2005). These requirements generally pose significant barriers for developing countries, which generally lack these resources, but wish to stimulate innovation-led development in this sector.

During the 1960s, a network of state-owned enterprises was set up by the Indian government. These companies were highly vertically integrated, and helped to promote a domestic supplier network in the country (Reddy, 2007). National research institutes were established and tertiary education in the field was promoted to provide R&D and to build up the human resource base needed for the success of the industry. Funding of these institutions was consistent even through periods of turmoil, and can be attributed to the 'nationalist' mentality of medicinal self-sufficiency (Mytelka, 2006). Price controls on drugs were established by 1970, and most of the remaining MNCs still operating in the Indian pharmaceutical market exited or cut back their operations (Ramani and Venkataramani, 2001). The Patent Act of 1972 disallowed any patent on drugs, allowing only very restrictive process patents. This caused another exodus of TNCs from the Indian market, but helped promote the development of the indigenous Indian market, since Indian firms were now able to produce drugs that had been patented abroad (Reddy, 2007). Drugs – no matter how newly developed – quickly became cheaper generics for the domestic market and for export to other developing countries. Indian firms were able to reverse-engineer MNC products, which allowed knowledge transfer from West to East. Despite the price controls and generally low price margins, a huge number of Indian firms began to spring up. Unable to keep up with the low prices and fragmented market, the state-owned enterprises eventually went private. By 1995, Indian-owned firms held 38 of the top 50 drug-producing spots in India, and only three MNCs made it to the top ten (Ramani and Venkataramani, 2001).

While the Indian government encouraged domestic innovation in its software and pharmaceutical companies by restricting MNCs, it recognized the value of MNC presence in many other fields. Over the years more than 300 multinationals have set base in the India market in the form of setting up subsidiaries, collaborations with local firms, or setting up their own research and technical centers. This in turn has led to a healthy competition in sectors where India had domain specialty. Increased demand for better-quality goods in the international markets, a territory where MNCs usually tend to specialize, meant that the presence of these MNCs on Indian soil posed further challenges to domestic firms. This pressure saw domestic firms beginning to expand their exports to new territories, while simultaneously upgrading their standards to keep pace with those of the MNCs.

RIS Development

The development of RISs was also a key factor in to overcoming India's latecomer disadvantages. Success in these regions fostered interfirm connections between start-ups, spin-offs and MNCs which entered the arena because of distinct regional advantages and continue to provide extra-region linkages essential for preventing lock-in. By 1990, the Indian central and regional governments began setting up national Software Technology Parks (STPs) which served as export-centered zones that enabled firms to conglomerate and move into offshore activities (Parthasarathy, 2007). The idea of special economic zones that provide fiscal incentives has eventually also expanded to include biotechnology parks (Wessner and Shivakumar, 2007). In India, cluster development was widely witnessed in the cities of Bangalore, Chennai and Hyderabad in Southern India, Pune in Western India and Gurgaon in Northern India. Several transnational corporations (TNCs) established their initial development facilities in these cities (Patibandla and Petersen, 2002).

But the establishment of clusters in these areas had a secondary beneficial economic impact. By providing a large proximate network of economic agents and institutions, these cities acted as fertile ground for spin-off enterprises originating in the clusters (Dossani, 2008). Accordingly, these zones provided several benefits of cluster development which led to rapid mushrooming of factories and development centers which all had the same infrastructure, technology and processes as those at the customer's base. This process proved especially beneficial to areas such as Bangalore which were abundant in skilled labor and communication facilities (Parthasarathy, 2007).

A growing regional innovation system in Bangalore has been an exemplar of an upward move in the global value chain through the development of these clusters. Bangalore as a case has shown how a region with no background in IT, and in the absence of localized demand from users, can develop its innovative capacity from scratch. Since the software industry is relatively skill-intensive, those regions in India with a relatively abundant pool of labor with English-speaking and technical skills enjoyed a 'regional advantage' over those which did not possess such a labor pool early in India's innovation-led development. Therefore, other states such as Maharashtra in Western India; and Karnataka, Andhra Pradesh and Tamil Nadu in Southern India; which had expended greater resources early on in technical IT knowledge, dominated the software industry locations before Bangalore (D'Costa, 2003). However, years of government favoritism in locating public research institutes and several large state-run enterprises in the area created a large surplus of skilled labor in the area (Heitzman, 1999). This excess capacity not only generated an incentive for outside producers to begin to operate businesses there, but also created incentives for underemployed yet highly skilled employees to start up their own businesses (Van Dijk, 2003). Afterwards, a mix of high-quality educational institutions and the presence of multinationals with strong local linkages contributed to building competencies in indigenous firms, thereby creating a base for the emergence of a regional innovation system in Bangalore.

The Bangalore cluster has attracted most of the initial big international IT companies, like Texas Instruments, Hewlett-Packard, Oracle, Motorola and Cisco. The large technical-education industry focusing on health and engineering vocations enabled Bangalore to win out early over relatively more expensive locations such as Mumbai, which originally started as a hub of IT through the location of Tata Consultancy Services. Bangalore thus became the natural locus of this industry and the profits of IT firms began to soar as they shifted work to the IT-driven city. Bangalore became a preferred destination where the development of infrastructure under the Software Technology Park and the private IT Park helped in the agglomeration of the industry in and around the city (Patibandla and Petersen, 2002). Although Bangalore boasts the presence of a large number of TNCs, a majority of IT firms are small-scale manufacturing enterprises. One of the key factors contributing to the growth trajectory of this city has been in the form of huge software exports to global markets, primarily to the US.

Over the years, multinationals began to recognize the advantage of entering the Indian market outside of Bangalore as well, by setting up innovation centers through their subsidiaries, or acquiring firms with innovative vision, or simply by outsourcing research to Indian laboratories. Many of these Western companies started realizing the relatively higher potential that emerging countries such as India pose in terms of revenue growth. Recent estimates show that among all the MNCs entering India, about 70 percent of total investment originates from the US, followed by France, Germany, the United Kingdom, Canada, Japan, Denmark and others (Bagla and Atul, 2009). Among all the other clusters in India, cities such as Bangalore, New Delhi and Mumbai have been at the forefront to attract these set-ups. The sectors where the investment flow has primarily taken place have been IT, R&D software, biotechnology, engineering and chemical components (Bagla and Atul, 2009).

IIS Development

India's large number of qualified professionals and scientists has also allowed the country to reap the benefits of innovation stemming from the international innovation system. Successfully harnessing parts of the IIS has allowed India to reduce its latecomer disadvantages, and is important for future development. For example, Saxenian et al.'s (2002) follow-up of a 1994 study of Silicon Valley's RIS examines the important role that Western firms and native Indian entrepreneurs have played in promoting knowledge transfer and the development of India's software industry. Saxenian's (1999) study demonstrated that many Indian high-tech software entrepreneurs, usually having been educated and employed in the US market, returned to India and set up TNC subsidiaries to supply Western companies with software and other high-tech services. These Indian entrepreneurs served as a cultural bridge between East and West, and were uniquely positioned to navigate the bureaucracy, and linguistic and logistical barriers, that Western firms faced in doing business with the Indian market.

Intergovernmental partnerships have also strengthened India's prospects for future innovation. A 2006 trip to India by then President Bush prompted a communiqué announcing plans for strategic cooperation in innovation between the two countries. Following this communiqué, various agreements have been signed by the two countries, establishing organizations to promote knowledge transfer and cooperation between scientists in the public and private sectors in the two countries. These agreements include: the US–India Defense Relationship, establishing a procurement and production group; the US–India Bi-National Science and Technology Endowment, creating a fund to sponsor joint research projects for industrial potential; the US–India Knowledge Initiative on Agriculture, aimed at raising agricultural productivity in India; and the Agreement on Civil Nuclear Energy Cooperation, aimed at working together to create more environmentally friendly energy technologies; as well as various other agreements with a similar aim. What is different about this series of agreements, and the strategic partnership in general, is that it is not an assistance package, but rather a genuine opportunity for both countries to learn from one another and attempt to integrate their innovation systems (Wessner and Shivakumar, 2007). The strategic alliance has also delivered benefits more directly to the private sector, with increased protection for intellectual property rights in India, and the promotion of collaborative opportunities for businesses on both sides.

SHORTCOMINGS AND POLICY IMPLICATIONS

India has greatly strengthened its capacity for innovation at the national, regional and international levels, but some latecomer disadvantages persist. New firm and government strategies have evolved to deal with these disadvantages, but their relative success is, for now, unclear.

First, India's protection of its software and pharmaceutical industries has been a mixed blessing. While India's software industry has enjoyed great success, it evolved largely to meet the demands of foreign markets. For many years, Indian firms were stuck in the provision of low-end software services, and their profitability by exploiting the wage gap between East and West has left them little incentive to invest in R&D themselves (Saxenian, 1999). Some firms have been able to push beyond mere programming and into the fields of providing quality assurance and project scheduling for more advanced customers like retailers and banks, but domestic demand for these kinds of services is still low (Parthasarathy and Aoyama, 2006).

But concerns about this dependency are weakening. New evidence indicates that the industry is moving into the provision of R&D services involving the sale of intellectual property (IP) blocks, usually including a design for an embedded system, in exchange for payment and a royalty per volume sold (Parthasarathy and Aoyama, 2006). More highly skilled, US-educated Indian entrepreneurs are communicating their desire to return to work in India by setting up their own firms (Saxenian, 1999). Local networks of producers are forming without the presence of TNCs. Indian firms are increasingly turning to obtaining patents in the United States, and a new era of stricter enforcement of intellectual property rights in India has helped to build up the 'soft infrastructure' required for greater endogenous innovation (Parthasarathy and Aoyama, 2006).

India's compliance with the WTO's TRIPS agreement effectively ended the specific patent advantage of Indian firms in generics production for overseas markets in 2005. But this intensified global competition has pushed both Indian firms and government to help the industry upgrade. While generics still account for the bulk of domestic production, levels of R&D are on the rise, and firms are seeking new linkages with other sectors (Mytelka, 2006). Pharmaceutical firms are seeking linkages with MNCs and smaller Indian biotechnology firms to produce biopharmaceuticals. As of 2003–04, the biopharmaceuticals industry accounted for about 76 percent of all biotechnology business in India, and the country in 2010 ranks among the top 12 countries globally in its number of biotechnology firms (Arora, 2005; Chaturvedi, 2005; Bagchi-Sen and Lawton Smith, 2008). Changes in national labor laws, tax breaks, and new research parks and institutes have aimed specifically at growing the biotechnology industry (Mytelka, 2006; Bagchi-Sen and Lawton Smith, 2008).

While India has implemented many RISs, not all have succeeded, and innovation in many areas that have succeeded has not translated into economic development for the country as a whole. While Delhi's automobile cluster is a leading producer, for example, it is still highly dependent on knowledge inputs from the region's sole, large MNC (Okada and Siddharthan, 2007). Many of India's regions are still plagued by a lack of venture capital, a critical component for innovation (Dossani, 2008). Furthermore, India remains an example of uneven development. Over 30 percent of the rural population still remains below India's poverty line, while in cities it is 24.7 percent (World Bank, 2010). The top tenth of the population earns over 31 percent of the country's income, while the lowest tenth makes only 3.6 percent (World Bank, 2010).

Because innovation necessarily requires the interaction of agents with their historically molded, internationally sensitive, chance-specific environments, many necessary criteria for a successful innovation system lie outside the control of policy-makers. By critically examining the case of an emerging India, however, they can identify those criteria that they can manipulate, compare their circumstances, and identify likely outcomes to changes in those criteria.

Furthermore, certain trends of exogenous factors seem likely to prevail in the coming decade. It is likely that 'latecomer' emerging economies today will face even greater burdens. International and regional laws and regulations favoring established, often Western, businesses seem likely to continue despite the roadblock at Doha. With the increasing importance and value of intellectual property in the modern economy, multinationals are increasingly skeptical of transferring sensitive technology, and governments are being pressured to adopt tighter controls. These trends indicate that developing countries today are faced with even more formidable barriers to operating successful innovation systems. It seems likely that the days of India's process patents for pharmaceuticals or ownership regulations for software industries are over. While large economies like China may still be able to extract knowledge or ownership concessions from MNCs, smaller economies may have to rely increasingly on FDI for knowledge transfer. Developing countries will also need to work on a way to expand the innovation-led economic benefits of regional concentrations to promote even development. But new advances in information and communication technology will probably allow for an increased reliance on the international innovation system for inputs. Emerging economies may want to invest resources into fostering this kind of international interaction between distant agents. While India serves as only one example of the challenges and opportunities waiting for today's emerging economies, its experience provides at least some foundations for those undertaking the next step.

REFERENCES

Amin, Ash and Kevin Robins (1990), 'The re-emergence of regional economies? The mythical geography of flexible accumulation', *Environment and Planning: Society and Space*, **8** (1), 7–34.

Amin, Ash and Frank Wilkinson (1999), 'Learning, proximity and industrial performance: an introduction', *Cambridge Journal of Economics*, **23**, 121–5.

Andersson, Martin and Charlie Karlsson (2004), 'Regional innovation systems in small and medium-sized regions: a critical review and assessment', in B. Johansson, C. Karlsson and R. Stough (eds), *Emerging Digital Economy: Entrepreneurship Clusters and Policy*, Berlin: Springer, pp. 19–37.

Archibugi, D. and J. Michie (1997), 'Technological globalization or national systems of innovation?', *Futures*, **29** (2), 121–37.

Arocena, Rodrigo and Judith Sutz (2005), 'Innovation systems and developing countries', Danish Research Unit for Industrial Dynamics (DRUID), Working Paper No 02-05, http://www3.druid.dk/wp/20020005.pdf.

Arora, Parveen (2005), 'Healthcare biotechnology firms in India: evolution, structure and growth', *Current Science*, **89** (3), 458–64.

Bagchi-Sen, Sharmistha and Helen Lawton Smith (2008), 'Science, institutions, and markets: developments in the Indian biotechnology sector', *Regional Studies*, **42** (7), 961–75.

Bagchi-Sen, Sharmistha, Helen Lawton Smith and Linda Hall (2004), 'The US biotechnology industry: industry dynamics and policy', *Government and Policy*, **22** (2), 199–216.

Bagla, G. and Atul Goel (2009), 'Innovation from India: the next big wave', *BusinessWeek*, February.

Barton, John H. (2004), 'TRIPS and the global pharmaceutical market', *Health Affairs*, **23** (3), 146–54.

Boschma, Ron (2005), 'Proximity and innovation: a critical assessment', *Regional Studies*, **39** (1), 61–74.

Brusco, Sebastiano (1990), 'The idea of the industrial district: its genesis', in F. Pyke, G. Becattini and W. Sengenberger (eds), *Industrial Districts and Inter-firm Co-operation in Italy*, Geneva: International Institute for Labor Studies, pp. 10–19.

Carlsson, B. and R. Stankiewicz (1991), 'On the nature, function and composition of technological systems', *Journal of Evolutionary Economics*, **1** (2), 93–118.

Castellacci, Fulvio (2006), 'Innovation, diffusion and catching up in the fifth long wave', *Futures*, **38** (7), 841–61.

Castells, Manuel and Peter Hall (1994), *Technopoles of the World: The Making of the Twenty-first-century Industrial Complexes*, London: Routledge.

Chaturvedi, Sachin (2005), 'Dynamics of biotechnology research and industry in India: statistics, perspectives and key policy issues', OECD Science, Technology and Industry Working Papers, Cedex: OECD Publications.

Coe, David, Elhanan Helpman and Alexander Hoffmaister (2009), 'International R&D spillovers and institutions', *European Economic Review*, **53** (7), 723–41.

Cooke, Philip, Mikel Gomez Uranga and Goio Etxebarria (1997), 'Regional innovation systems: institutional and organizational dimensions', *Research Policy*, **26**, 475–91.

D'Costa, Anthony P. (2003), 'Uneven and combined development: understanding India's software exports', *World Development*, **31** (1), 211–26.

Dosi, G., C. Freeman, R. Nelson, G. Silverman and L. Soete (eds) (1988), *Technical Change and Economic Theory*, London: Pinter.

Dossani, Rafiq (2008), *India Arriving*, New York: AMACOM.

Dutz, M. (2007), *Unleashing India's Potential: toward Sustainable and Inclusive Growth*, Washington, DC: World Bank/International Bank for Reconstruction and Development.

Edquist, Charles (1997), 'Systems of innovation approaches – their emergence and characteristics', in Charles Edquist (ed.), *Systems of Innovation: Technologies, Institutions and Organizations*, London: Pinter, pp. 1–35.

Ernst, Dieter (2002), 'Global production networks and the changing geography of innovation systems: implications for developing countries', *Economics of Innovation and New Technology*, **11** (6), 497–523.

Etzkowitz, Henry and Loet Leydesdorff (1997), *Universities and the Global Knowledge Economy*, London: Pinter.

Fagerberg, Jan and Martin Srholec (2008), 'National innovation systems, capabilities, and economic development', *Research Policy*, **37** (9), 1417–35.

Fischer, Manfred M. (2002), 'A systemic approach to innovation', in Gunduz Atalik and Manfred Fisher (ed.), *Regional Development Reconsidered*, New York: Springer, pp. 15–31.

Freeman, C. (1982), *The Economics of Industrial Innovation*, London: Pinter Publishers.
Freeman, Christopher (1987), *Technology Policy and Economic Performance: Lessons from Japan*, London: Pinter.
Heitzman, James (1999), 'Corporate planning and strategy in the science city: Bangalore as "Silicon Valley"', *Economic and Political Weekly*, **34** (5), 2–11.
Intarakumnerd, Patarapong, Pun-arj Chairatana and Tipawon Tangchitipiboon (2002), 'National innovation systems in less successful developing countries: the case of Thailand', *Research Policy*, **31** (8), 1445–57.
Khanna, Tarun and Krishna Palepu (2005), 'The evolution of concentrated ownership in India: broad patterns and a history of the Indian software industry', in Randall Morck (ed.), *A History of Corporate Governance around the World: Family Business Groups to Professional Managers*, Chicago, IL: University of Chicago Press, pp. 283–324.
Kumar, Nagesh (2001), 'Indian software industry development: international and national perspective', *Economic and Political Weekly*, **36** (45), 4278–90.
Lundvall, Bengt-Åke (1992), *National Systems of Innovation: Towards a Theory of Innovation and Interactive Learning*, London: Pinter.
Lundvall, Bengt-Åke and Bjorn Johnson (1994), 'The learning economy', *Journal of Industry Studies*, **1** (2), 23–42.
Malecki, Edward and Paivi Oinas (1999), *Making Connections: Technological Learning and Regional Economic Change*, Aldershot: Ashgate.
Marshall, Alfred (1898), *The Principles of Economics*, London: Macmillan.
Mytelka, Lynn (2006), 'Pathways and policies to (bio) pharmaceutical innovation systems in developing countries', *Industry and Innovation*, **14** (4), 415–35.
Nelson, Richard (2004), 'The challenge of building an effective innovation system for catch-up', *Oxford Development Studies*, **32** (3), 365–74.
Nelson, Richard R. and Nathan Rosenberg (1993), 'Technical innovation and national systems', in Richard Nelson (ed.), *National Innovation Systems: A Comparative Analysis*, Oxford: University Press, pp. 3–28.
Oinas, Paivi and Edward Malecki (2002), 'The evolution of technologies in time and space: from national and regional to spatial innovation systems', *International Regional Science Review*, **25**, 102–31.
Okada, Aya and N.S. Siddharthan (2007), 'Industrial clusters in India: evidence from automobile clusters in Chennai and the National Capital Region', Chiba, Japan: Institute of Developing Economies.
Papaioannou, Theo, David Wield and Joanna Chataway (2009), 'Knowledge ecologies and ecosystems? An empirically grounded reflection on recent developments in innovation systems theory', *Environment and Planning: Government and Policy*, **27** (2), 319–39.
Parthasarathy, Balaji (2007), 'Contrasting regimes of regional development: the telecommunications equipment industry and computer software industry in India', in Allen Scott and Gioacchino Garofoli (eds), *Development on the Ground: Clusters, Networks and Regions in Emerging Economies*, London: Routledge, pp. 189–222.
Parthasarathy, Balaji and Yuko Aoyama (2006), 'From software services to R&D services: local entrepreneurship in the software industry in Bangalore, India', *Environment and Planning*, **38** (1), 1269–85.
Patibandla, Murali and Bent Petersen (2002), 'Role of transnational corporations in the evolution of a high-tech industry: the case of India's software industry', *World Development*, **30** (9), 1561–77.
Porter, Michael (1990), *The Competitive Advantage of Nations*, New York: Free Press.
Ramani, Shyama and M.S. Venkataramani (2001), 'Rising to the technological challenge: possibilities for integration of biotechnology in the Indian pharmaceutical industry', *International Journal of Biotechnology*, **3** (1), 95–115.
Reddy, Prasada (2007), 'Global biomedical industry and the emerging innovation system of India: implications for Sweden', Center for Business and Policy Studies, Oslo: University of Oslo Press.
Saxenian, Annalee (1990), 'Regional networks and the resurgence of Silicon Valley', *California Management Review*, **33** (1), 89–112.
Saxenian, AnnaLee (1999), *Silicon Valley's New Immigrant Entrepreneurs*, San Francisco, CA: Public Policy Institute of California.
Saxenian, AnnaLee, Yasuyuki Motoyama and Xiaohong Quan (2002), *Local and Global Networks of Immigrant Professionals in Silicon Valley*, San Francisco, CA: Public Policy Institute of California.
Scott, Allen and Michael Storper (2007), 'Regions, globalization, development', *Regional Studies*, **41** (1), 191–205.
Sengupta, Jati (2005), *India's Economic Growth: A Strategy for the New Economy*, New York: Palgrave Macmillan.
Storper, Michael (1991), *Industrialization, Economic Development, and the Regional Question in the Third World*, London: Pion.
Van Dijk, Meine Pieter (2003), 'Government policies with respect to an information technology cluster in Bangalore, India', *European Journal of Development Research*, **15** (2), 89–104.

Wessner, Charles and Sujai Shivakumar (2007), *India's Changing Innovation System: Achievements, Challenges, and Opportunities for Cooperation*, National Research Council Committee on Comparative Innovation Policy, Washington, DC: National Research Council.

Wong, Poh-Kam (1999), 'National innovation systems for rapid technological catch-up: an analytical framework and a comparative analysis of Korea, Taiwan and Singapore', Industrial Dynamics and Innovation Policy, DRUID Summer Conference on National Innovation Systems.

World Bank (2010), 'Data: India', http://data.worldbank.org/country/india (accessed 23 May 2010).

32 Green innovation
Philip Cooke

INTRODUCTION

In this chapter an attempt is made to present the main theoretical perspectives concerning ecological thinking about economic geography, and innovation related to it. This involves identifying, first, work that considers policy inputs and outputs favouring 'green' interests as if these formed a 'regime' of power and influence over city government decisions. It elaborates an earlier and critical view of urban governance which saw city decision-makers captured by powerful economic interests and accordingly producing outcomes that favoured economic 'booster' ideology. As reinterpreted through 'ecological modernization' perspectives that see benign influences being brought to bear by such 'green' political influence, this approach is really of only limited value to an understanding of most green innovation. However, it can be utilized to highlight forces at play in cities, more than regions, that display coherent and effective policies to seek reductions in the greenhouse gases (GHGs) that are widely understood to be major contributors to climate change. Thus the cities of Copenhagen, Denmark, Vancouver, Canada and Austin, Texas are known for their portfolios of green policies ranging from using local, organic food networks to supply municipal canteens, schools and healthcare facilities to green building codes and renewable energy consumption.

That cities mainly influence the urban practices of their citizenry by constraining consumption norms is well understood and a feature of their make-up, which historically has not emphasized production of innovation to the same extent. In the second perspective to be discussed in the chapter, this is less the case. 'Co-evolutionary transitions' thinking is a macro-approach that is concerned with society and economy-wide changes in the consciousness of citizens to change their production and consumption patterns to minimize and ultimately stop the use of GHG-inducing practices in general. This means, unless satisfactory cleansing techniques are made widely available, no more burning of fossil fuels such as coal, oil and gas. Renewable energy is the favoured mode of fuel use, meaning biomass, biogas, wind, water, solar, geothermal and tidal or wave power energy in the main. This is clearly a difficult and wide-ranging aspiration to implement, but in some countries, like Germany, the Netherlands, Denmark and Sweden, significant steps have been made in production and consumption to produce innovative ways to do this. Moreover, green production involves improving waste recycling, modes of transportation, construction and infrastructure systems, and food production as well as energy production and use. In co-evolutionary transitions thinking this involves the emergence of niches of innovations that find a market. In time these coalesce and become more important or hegemonic than the old forms of production and consumption, forming a new 'green regime'. Eventually this spreads globally, to usher in a transition to a new landscape overall and worldwide.

Some problems with this view are explored in the chapter. One of these is its general lack of a spatial perspective. This, it is argued, can be improved upon by recognition of the crucial importance to innovation of innovative regions (and cities) that bring influence to bear on wider consumption and production systems. In the empirical part of the chapter illustration of the emergence of innovative regional niches is provided and the outlines of a 'transition region' are presented. The chapter thus observes some utility in both perspectives discussed, but finds the second more appropriate to an innovation and growth agenda. However, overcoming its theoretical weaknesses is shown to be reliant on its enrichment by a spatial, specifically regional innovation systems viewpoint upon co-evolutionary transition to a green future.

THEORETICAL PERSPECTIVES

Fundamentally, there is a strictly limited literature on economic geography or regional innovation from a green perspective (Bridge, 2007). However, three subfields that engage with sustainability issues tangential to green innovation exist. Two of these begin from a clearly aspatial embarkation point, while the other takes its position from an urban viewpoint. As noted in this chapter's introduction, the three approaches involve, respectively, urban regime theory, ecological modernization theory and a co-evolutionary socio-technical transition framework. Because economic geographers attempt a synthesis between the first two, I shall here discuss them as two perspectives: the 'urban ecological modernization regime' and the 'co-evolutionary transitions' approach.

The former is a complex and ultimately contradictory synthesis of regulationist school[1] political economy. It has an established application in the urban geography literature, originally influenced by neo-elitist urban governance research, which takes the form of urban regime theory (for example Broomhill, 2001). The second is initially a more self-contained perspective, although inspired by evolutionary social theorizing to which its adherents give the designation 'system innovation'. The tradition is therefore related to but distinct from neo-Schumpeterian innovation systems thinking (see Chapters 7, 18 and 30 in this *Handbook*). System innovation concerns co-evolution of social, political, economic and scientific systems on a grand and lengthy scale, while innovation systems are more narrowly focused (Edquist, 1997). They highlight national (NIS) or technological (TIS) modes of transforming laboratory knowledge into commercial product, process or organizational novelty in use on the market. While the former claims (Geels, 2006) to be compatible with NIS and TIS perspectives, this is not entirely accepted by critics such as Hekkert et al. (2007) and Hillman et al. (2008), who take a more embedded NIS and TIS innovation systems approach in their research.

Urban Regime and Ecological Modernization Theory

As the study of urban politics evolved towards a popular focus upon urban governance in the 1990s (Stoker, 1999) it engaged with older regime theory, particularly urban regime theory (Stone, 1989, 1993; Stoker and Mossberger, 1994). A research group addressing UK urban sustainability governance deploys regulationist class analysis and urban regime theory (Gibbs et al., 2002; While et al., 2004). They conclude that a presumed contradiction between a pro-growth and a pro-green urban governance agenda may be illusory. Their focus is on the implications of environmental challenges for the composition and strategies of urban regimes. Their position and findings are as follows. Arguing against a fundamentalist perspective that saw economic globalization facing urban governance with mounting pressure on protected open space, regulatory dumping, increased levels of consumption, negative environmental externalities, and increased material flows into and through the built environment, often at the expense of poorer residents and communities, they have sought to uncover evidence that environmentalism is not simply a matter of the demands placed on local state regulation by national government, business or pressures from upper and middle-class residents.

'Ecological modernization' is a by now rather dated perspective, well critiqued by Desfor and Keil (2007). A key proponent of the conjoining of economic geography and ecological modernization is Gibbs (2006). His admirable starting point is to assist economic geography to be more 'real-world' problem-focused and policy-relevant. He holds that: 'ecological modernization, at least in its stronger formulations, can offer a substantive political challenge to neoliberal ideologies' (Gibbs, 2006, 195). The relevant stiffening is applied by reference to Gibbs's group's adherence to regulation theory, as noted above. At the heart of ecological modernization is the notion of a technological fix to the effects of pollution upon society (Mol, 1999). Hayter and Le Heron (2002) even saw the prospects of this leading to a 'green technological paradigm'. But we now know that such optimism and belief in benign productive forces is misplaced, and stronger regulation of polluters is a necessity. The focus of this attitude spread from polluting industry to the producers of 'toxic' financial investments by the 2007–09 'credit crunch'.

The present ecological crisis requires that the hydrocarbon paradigm or regime, that has underpinned industrial capitalism from the outset, itself needs transcending in a transition to a post-hydrocarbon landscape (see below; Kemp, 2002; Smith et al., 2005). Accordingly, the ecological modernization perspective tends nowadays to be critiqued for its 'reformism', failure to step outside the dominant Western, neoliberal consumptionist paradigm, and essential philosophy of 'cleaning up after capitalism' as a means to approaching broad sustainability goals (Desfor and Keil, 2007). Because 'regulationism' as described is not reformist, while ecological modernization is, it is not easy to see how they can work as complementary frameworks, and indeed most new spatial thinking about transition towards a green future now goes further than either. Thus many of the empirical findings of this work are interesting, but have relatively little theoretical purchase on an urban regime approach, largely because the use of the regulationist regime metaphor still overnarrows the research perspective to a classic and irremediable social conflict causality (While et al., 2004).

Nevertheless sensitivity to city and county governance is an advance contributed by the urban regime approach, comparing favourably to the overtly aspatial ecological modernization model and the co-evolutionary transitions approach to be discussed. It will be argued that the latter lacks any serious governance analysis, with no municipal, regional, national, federal or, as appropriate, supranational perspective in its theory of change. It is demonstrated below that the most recent green innovation and green governance approaches, especially when combined, offer superior insight into how transitions occur. Rather, 'markets' are, rather uncritically, expected to bring forth green technologies through 'strategic niche management', presumably by firms in the main. Just as the ecological modernization model betrayed a rather touching optimism about that, the transitions approach offers little in the way of a clear guide, except an undefined process of experimentation as to how that happens.

Nevertheless a redeeming feature of the co-evolutionary transitions model is that it is demonstrably evolutionary and, more than that, arguably compatible with a systems of innovation approach which, as noted, it transcends by reaching beyond 'technological paradigms'. Hence, preferable for this review is an approach in which, for example, innovative clean technology interests or social movements or networks including those of a countercultural nature may be observed to have impacted upon, for example, raising green consciousness such as green politics, 'green growth', organic farming and catering, green urbanism, climate change and/or peak oil analysis (Wolch, 2007; Guthman, 2004; Manning, 2004; Kunstler, 2005; Strahan, 2007; Kahn, 2007). This is because such a perspective moves beyond sustainable development and ecological modernization perspectives. It prioritizes anthropogenic climate change through atmospheric emissions and post-fossil fuels issues in the context of the global need to mitigate emissions through transition to a post-hydrocarbon economy and society. This improves upon a structural weakness of the more traditional sustainability discourse, where it is possible to construct an argument for sustainable utilization of, for example, hydrocarbons so that they are available for future generations to use, whereas this is not possible from a climate change perspective. This is clearly because the exploitation of hydrocarbons is seen as the cause of the potential destruction of the Earth's atmosphere. This chimes with the predominance of a theoretical and practical climate change discourse, increasingly animating social scientific and political interests, while encompassing many sustainable development concerns.

Co-evolutionary Transition Theory

This moves us forward by injecting rigour into the manner in which 'development' has to be reinvented (for example eventual removal of greenhouse gas emissions from production and consumption; see Tukker et al., 2008). As noted, much of the newer social scientific discourse on environmental issues is governed by a climate change perspective, and one that moreover questions the adequacy of long-term technological change concepts and analytical instruments as never before (see Geels, 2004, 2006; Smith, 2006). At issue here is the question of which social scientific theoretical perspective is best at capturing the long-term implications of a global response to climate change. Smith and Geels, as well as Tukker and colleagues (see also Weber and Hemmelskamp, 2005) hint at the need for a broader conception of the implications of policy intended to mitigate increases in global warming. That is, an established discourse of technological regimes (Dosi, 1982; Freeman and Perez, 1988) that explains economic change in terms of disequilibria forced by the evolving replacement of one technological regime by another, in a Schumpeterian (1975) process of 'creative destruction', seems to work well in relation to 'long waves' of development (Manning, 2004). However, this literature has not received the level of scrutiny and critique seen in the international relations regime perspective. One clear cavil would be that all Schumpeterian regimes depended upon hydrocarbon energy. Stabilization and subsequent reduction of hydrocarbon emissions requires innovative, clean technologies.

The co-evolutionary perspective presented below tentatively tackles the meta-system implications of policies to reduce utilization of hydrocarbons. This introduces novelty in the selected field of governance of climate change issues by associating them with the co-evolutionary idea of 'strategic niche management'. It presents a dynamic multilevel perspective on system innovation; here 'system' involving the co-evolution of social, economic, political, scientific and technological subsystems beyond that of the specific technological regime (Smith et al., 2005). As noted earlier, the co-evolutionary transition model envisages market niches of green innovations emerging – but has no spatial consciousness of how or where this might happen. If these innovations find sustainable markets they may eventually form a green regime of influence and political power in, for example, widespread adoption of renewable energy norms. Finally, in perhaps a generation a new green landscape may have emerged through the co-evolution of society, economy, politics and the science and technology that deliver green innovation (Rip and Kemp, 1998).

My focus on the niche level is also because this is where innovations, which may influence regimes and ultimately co-evolutionary socio-technical landscapes, begin. However, and from a critical perspective, the niche approach focuses only on how innovations are adopted in markets, a process involving uncertainty, experimentation, market probing and learning. It pays little or no attention to governance, as we have seen (Voss et al., 2006). In the proposed research, known cases of, for example, food and energy-related climate change strategies are included to explain how niche innovation is mediated by governance, including local, entailing early uptake in some settings. Thereafter, the chapter research is interested in the extent to which bottom-up and top-down processes influence the possible emergence of regional or national technological regimes. Hence the novelty in this research is that it proposes to investigate the roles of governance (government plus non-governmental organizations – NGOs) and markets (enterprises and technological innovation) as drivers of 'strategic niche management' whereas, as Voss et al. (2006) noted, hitherto these have been disconnected conceptually and empirically. Clearly, apart from the absence of a governance or security dimension, problems with this leading approach to understanding transition are its conceptual thinness, linear logic, equilibrium-mindedness and lack of spatiality. A fuller, interactive, partial or non-equilibrium transition governance model will be sought.

This perspective currently has no economic geography, evolutionary or otherwise, and cannot move forward satisfactorily until it does. Accordingly, it has no concept of 'innovation system' or 'system of innovation' as an inherently asymmetric process of regional economic development. This is far more than reading off the environmental implications of economic geography as Bridge (2007) notes. The co-evolutionary transition authors do not begin to recognize why certain concatenations of institutional, entrepreneurial and innovative interactions occur where they do and for what reasons.

But first, the notion of 'environment' must be narrowed down to the perspective denoted in the discussion so far. This does not propose to offer an overview of the spectrum of environmental interests and objects that constitute geography; rather, it is interested in the ways in which consciousness and action, whether in relation to consumption of innovation meant to mitigate hydrocarbon emissions or the production of innovation, has a distinct economic geography and from the innovation perspective a pioneering practice in some regions and an absence of recognition of its importance in others. More will be said about this in the empirical subsections that follow. But for now, the three following concepts may be previewed.

The first is path-dependence, one of evolutionary economic geography's master concepts and one in which conceptual progress has been made by economic geographers seeking to escape the 'endogeneity problem'[2] inherent in the earlier innovation economics literature (Martin and Sunley, 2006). For many decades regional economic theory and policy coincided, as resource-based or resource-exploiting regional economies evolved with relatively narrow regional specializations. Whether in the nineteenth-century industrial basins such as Germany's Ruhrgebiet, Britain's North-East England, central Scotland or South Wales, Spain's Basque Country, or Pennsylvania in the US, or the industrial districts for textiles, ceramics and footwear that Marshall (1918) and later Becattini (1978) wrote about in laissez-faire Britain or, later, contemporary Italy, it was seen as benign that the market produced relatively narrow regional industrial specialization. To counter that, when competitiveness defects brought industrial decline, an opposite discourse of regional economic development through industry diversification into often unrelated new sectors took over. Nowadays, a new discourse of regional evolution through the exploitation of 'related variety' has been emphasized, and where observed, found to be associated with reasonable regional economic success (Boschma and Wenting, 2007; Klepper, 2002; Cantwell and Iammarino, 2003; Buenstorf and Klepper, 2005).

Finally, consistent with the other key concepts is proximity, which has greater reach than simply its geographical dimension, which can involve cognitive and relational dimensions as shown in Carrincazeaux and Coris's Chapter 20 in this *Handbook* (see also Boschma, 2005), and which facilitates rapid knowledge transfer through lateral absorptive capacity among entrepreneurs and managers in related industries, assisted by knowledge spillover external economies of scope where cognitive dissonance among subsectoral actors is relatively low. In these respects I envisage the rise of regional economic 'platforms' of related industry activity, which is particularly clearly exemplified in the observed cases of green innovation. 'Green innovation' is defined as: 'diverse new and commercial products, technologies and processes which, through improvements in the clean energy supply chain from energy source through to point of consumption and recycling, result in reduction in greenhouse gases' (Cooke, 2008). In what follows, I first report some hopefully interesting and somewhat curious facts that arise when the 'tipping point' of awareness or consciousness reaches the 'green turn'.

EMERGENCE OF GREEN REGIONAL NICHES

The idea of a regional niche as a basis for mobilizing regional evolution connects directly to the related-variety argument of the previous section. Recall that of the two perspectives discussed the co-evolutionary transitions proved stronger but with problems caused by its lack of a regional innovation systems perspective. Thus how does niche experimentation occur? The two examples provided below give a more 'entrepreneurial' regional innovation system (ERIS) and a more 'institutional' (IRIS) explanation (on RISs, see Chapter 33 by Tödtling and Trippl in this volume). In Cooke et al. (2007) these were shown to be complementary to different business and institutional systems or 'varieties of capitalism'. The Californian ERIS exemplar is characteristic of 'liberal market' economies while the Danish IRIS illustration is more typical of 'coordinated market' economies where the state is a more prominent actor. In line with the thesis concerning related variety, both are cases where industry is neither overdiversified nor overspecialized, giving opportunities for revealed relatedness in new combinations of innovation at interfaces between industries. Path-dependence is important to the ways that new 'branching' from previous regional capabilities occurs.

Finally, proximity is of importance for at least three reasons: first, the accomplished regional economy works with agility and flexibility to meet increasingly user-driven demand. Second, that means user and producer interaction in proximity is territorially advantageous. Hence, third, where such conditions are met, a 'transition region' is more likely. This suggests that innovation studies in the past may have been overly 'productivist'. That is, during the years of excess, firms competed on the basis of disruptive innovation (Christensen, 1997). Following the credit crunch and widespread condemnation of the excess it bred in financial and technological innovativeness, the green turn signifies a new privileging of listening to consumer demand for more usable, less over-engineered, more sustainable goods and services.

Green Visions

John Doerr is America's leading venture capitalist. He is head of Silicon Valley's top investor, Kleiner, Perkins, Caufield & Byers. In a lecture to a Californian 'green technology' forum, TED.com, in 2007 he reported how at supper one evening his 15-year-old daughter berated him and the rest of the venture capital (VC) industry for their contribution to the destruction of the planet – and, by the way, what was he going to do to put things right?

This seems, judging from the lecture, downloadable at TED.com, to have caused Doerr to experience the kind of epiphany more normally associated with religious conversion. He immediately starts networking among his community of high-tech investors and entrepreneurs. He gets some of the smartest brains he knows to lobby the California legislature on tougher emissions controls. He takes his network to Brazil to see its successful bioethanol industry. He even goes to Wal-Mart, arch-discounter of consumption goods, to observe the implementation of its new green strategy. He discovers how petrol can be made from algae, subsequently leading the charge, in harness with Al Gore's green investment fund, Generation Investment Management, to back numerous such Californian biofuel start-ups. Yet as each scene of this narrative closes, he assesses the likely outcome of all these niche activities, declaring, 'I don't believe it's going to be enough' – to save the planet, that is. Eventually, he breaks down on-screen at the thought that he has been complicit in irretrievably poisoning the Earth's atmosphere, leaving the prospect of his daughter's generation having to survive in a world that only has that one source of oxygen.

I have shown this performance to numerous audiences, including hard-bitten environmentalists, and the consensus is that, 'he may be a venture capitalist, but he's a hell of a good actor'. To which I now respond to the effect that whether he is acting, having spotted a great market opportunity, or genuine in investing in a new 'green moral economy', does it really matter? Doerr has visibly changed his practice and evidently interacted with many of his peer-group, including persuasive Al Gore, to do the same, as Box 32.1 shows.

What is theoretically interesting and important about the data in Box 32.1 is as

BOX 32.1 MOVES BY CALIFORNIA ICT ENTREPRENEURS INTO CLEAN TECHNOLOGIES, 2008

- Shai Agassi (SAP), Founder, CEO Project Better Place, Palo Alto, SV.
- Vinod Khosla, Founder, Khosla Ventures.
- Bob Metcalfe, Partner, Polaris Venture Partners, CEO GreenFuel (Cambridge, MA).
- John Doerr, Partner, KPCB.
- Sunil Paul, Seed investor, early stage cleantech, Nanosolar, Oorja.
- Elon Musk, Chairman, Tesla, Chairman, CEO SolarCity.
- Steve Jurvetson, Partner, Draper Fisher Jurvetson.
- Bill Gross, Founder, Idealab.
- Ray Lane, Partner, KPCB.
- Steve Westly, Founder, The Westly Group.
- Dan Whaley, Founder, CEO Climos.
- David Cope, CEO of PurFresh.

- Al Gore, Founder, Generation Investment, Partner KPCB.
- Martin Eberhard, Founder, former CEO Tesla.
- Martin Roscheisen, Founder, CEO Nanosolar.
- Martin Tobias, Former CEO Imperium Renewables.
- Manny Hernandez, CFO SunPower.
- Jonathan Gay, CEO of GreenBox.
- Jeff Skoll, Founder, Skoll Foundation, investor in Tesla, Nanosolar.
- Mitch Mandich, CEO Range Fuels.
- Bill Joy, Partner, KPCB.
- Larry Gross, CEO of Edeniq.
- Bruce Sohn, President, First Solar.
- David Kaplan, Founder, V2Green.
- Raj Aturu, Partner, Draper Fisher, Jurvetson.

Source: earth2tech.

follows. First, clean technologies of the kind these investors and entrepreneurs are keen to become involved in are convergent. Convergence here means that innovations in numerous apparently not too closely related industries may open pathways to entrepreneurship in industries displaying what we may call 'revealed related variety'. Second, this relatedness works because of two important, subsidiary concepts: absorptive capacity and knowledge spillovers. In regional economic development terms, absorptive capacity is lateral, whereas in industrial economics it is vertical. Lateral absorptive capacity means that entrepreneurs in adjoining and/or revealed relatedness industries can understand each other's business models and focus, and apply tacit knowledge or even routines from the one business type or model to their own. In this way innovations might cross-fertilize and migrate from one industry to a related or revealed related one. The means by which such cross-fertilizations occur rely upon knowledge spillovers – external economies that spill over accidentally from firms located in geographical proximity that have the absorptive capacity to translate such tacit knowledge into explicit, codified, usable and repeatable knowledge in a new business context.

From Clusters to a Green Regional Innovation System

In the more institutional (IRIS) but still user-driven green economy, subsidies are increasingly to be found being made to consumption rather than only to production. Probably the most celebrated case of the success of consumer subsidy as a successful policy regime is to be found in the history of Denmark's world-leading wind turbine industry. From the beginning in the early 1970s, government subsidies were made available not to the producers but to the users of first-generation wind turbines. This sustained the industry, initially based largely upon domestic demand, and enabled the north and mid-Jutland-based cluster to outcompete its main rivals in California. The user subsidy stimulated experimentation, knowledge spillovers and niche market evolution in regionally path-dependent trajectories in both Jutland and California. But Ronald Reagan jettisoned his predecessor Governor Brown's subsidies, while in Denmark they continued until a right-wing coalition entered government in 2000. By which time the Danish design had branched considerably from its roots in agricultural and marine engineering, where the plough and the ship's propeller were the inspiration. Meanwhile the Californian design atrophied around its inspiration – propeller-driven aircraft. Already something of an anachronism, the two-blade, pointed upwind turbine design proved inferior to the three-blade, point-it-downwind Danish solution, and for once Californian ingenuity was defeated. Vestas, Denmark's national champion, has 40 per cent of the world wind turbine market and has been joined in its Aarhus–Aalborg cluster by the likes of Germany's Siemens, acquiring the other main Danish companies, Suzlon from India and Gamesa from Spain. Including home market production of turbines in Germany and Spain, these European producers, along with Denmark, have 70 per cent of world turbine production capacity with employment of 133 000 and global demand far from saturated.

To continue with the small, moderately peripheral country of Jutland a little longer, it is instructive to find that interspersed within the wind turbine cluster is another with a comparable 1970s alternative energy technology genealogy. This is its solar thermal cluster, consisting of some 20 firms of varying sizes and types, ranging from manufacturers of solar-powered water pumps for use in developing countries, to consultants designing massive solar power stations, and those that simply supply heating systems for communities, factories, offices and individual homes. One of these is EnergiPlan, whose founder Per Alex was one of a number interviewed by this author about the green energy 'platform' in North Jutland. EnergiPlan designed one of the first local solar power stations at Skorping, near Aalborg, for a communal housing scheme of some 30 houses. It is a simple mirror-collectors, pipes and covered swimming pool arrangement that supplies communal free heat and power for nine months of the year. Thereafter the commune, which operates communal dining and laundry facilities, resorts to the local biomass district heating station in the village, which commune members can access at a discount. Per Alex described how in 30 years these combinations of distinctive alternative energy technologies have helped evolve one of the first green regional innovation systems in the world.

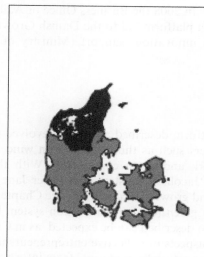

- 'Innovative Region: Flexible District Heating' Platform
- Biogas, Biomass, Solar Thermal, Wind – 'plug-ins'
- 'Social Network' >100 'system' and 'solution' firms
- Aalborg U, Municipalities, DTI, VåkstForum Fund (40 mn DK bid).
- 'Aggregators' or 'system integrators' include:
- Arcon Solar (Velux VHK), Xergi, Logstor (Pipework), Baracon (Biogas), Grundfos
- Humvel, NIRAS, EnergiPlan (consultants)

Source: Centre for Advanced Studies.

Figure 32.1   North Jutland's green regional innovation system

The demanding customers that moved most from niche to a regional transition regime for district heating in Denmark were the municipalities, most of whom run local energy supply companies which some 60 per cent of Denmark's citizens rely upon. Hence, a space for a collective 'urban regime' perspective opens up here too. Municipalities seek a balanced supply and order customized mixes of biomass, biogas, wind, solar and marine energy depending on location and the type of solution required. Enormous export markets for district heating have opened up in mature and emerging markets faced with climate change and peak oil constraints. Within north Jutland is a community of some 100–150 specialist renewable energy firms, many of which are innovative. Per Alex cited the case of Logstor, a District Heating company in north Jutland that had innovated a pre-insulated dual pipe system that minimized heat loss by fitting the cold water input pipe inside the hot water pipe. Together, the district heating firms, municipalities, university laboratories and technology transfer agencies created an association entitled Innovative Region: Flexible District Heating, with characteristics described in Figure 32.1.

This echoes the 2007 regionalization of Denmark's administration into five, one of which is North Jutland. It warrants the designation of transition regional innovation system because it consists of a commercialization subsystem and a knowledge-generation subsystem. The former consists of networks of firms in supply chains focused around the district heating engineering platform while belonging to distinctive renewable energy business segments. These are, nevertheless, capable of being system-integrated by lead aggregator firms such as solar thermal specialist Arcon, biogas contractor Xergi, green engineering firm Grundfos or consultants NIRAS into consortia for plant assembly. Supporting this subsystem is a knowledge and enterprise support subsystem consisting of public laboratories, regional development agencies, municipalities and technical agencies such as the Danish Technological Institute. In 2008 the Business Office of Aalborg had taken responsibility for leading a €5 million platform bid to the Danish Growth Fund, Väkstfonden, for 'user-driven design and innovation' support (Ministry of Foreign Affairs of Denmark, 2008).

CONCLUSIONS

It should be recalled that the regional platform described above has evolved from the earlier development of a number of clusters such as those focused on wind turbines, solar thermal and photovoltaics, pipework and green engineering. With the cross-fertilization of innovative ideas that such 'Jacobian' clusters offer (after Jane Jacobs's stress on variety in economic innovation and growth; Jacobs, 1969; see Chapters 11, 13, 14 and 26 in this *Handbook*), the rise of a green regional innovation system based on the convergent and related-variety platform described can be expected, as in California. Both California and Jutland have strong aspects of collective entrepreneurship, in the form of the venture capital and entrepreneur networks 'mutating' from information and communication technology (ICT) to 'greentech' in the former, while in the latter there is a greater emphasis on communal associativeness among firms and support organizations with a pronounced degree of informal investment by successful entrepreneurs in interesting start-up businesses.

This conclusion was reached by means of, first, a theoretical analysis of research agendas that focused upon ways in which significant change of broad societal perspectives towards more sustainable less ecologically damaging general production and consumption might be effected. One was a micro-perspective set at city government level; the other was a macro-perspective set at global level. Clearly neither was wholly satisfactory and both cried out for a 'missing middle' to be found. This was done by virtue of underlining the importance to system innovation of an innovation systems approach, notably the regional innovation systems method. This assisted understanding of how, through strong regional user–producer interaction, a 'transition region' acting as a possible 'lighthouse' to other regions might effect the move from niche experimentation towards a new green regime to ultimate overall landscape prioritization of post-hydrocarbon production and consumption by succeeding generations. Key to this were subconcepts from evolutionary economic geography about ways path-dependence, related variety and proximity can assist agile and flexible regional innovation, in this case regarding transition to the green social, political and economic landscape that many global citizens currently desire.

NOTES

1. Regulation theory analyses capitalist economic development in terms of a relationship between two key subsystems. The first is the regime of (capital) accumulation, and the second is the mode of (capitalist) regulation. It is also a theory of transition, albeit Marxist in inspiration, which was utilized particularly penetratively in analysing the 1980s transition in the predominant way of organizing factory production. This had been based on Fordist mass production means, involving repetitive work and a strict division of labour producing standardized goods for mass consumption markets under a Keynesian welfare state

mode of state regulation. A transition period denoted neo-Fordism with intense automation was a prelude to post-Fordism, which was a transition to a more flexibly specialized, even customized mode of production, with outsourcing to supply chains under a neoliberal or so-called 'Schumpeterian workfare state' mode of regulation (Lipietz, 1987; Halliday, 1990; Cooke, 1990; Amin, 1994; Jessop, 1995; Peck, 2000).

2. This occurs when the data (for example location of research and development) being used to show some geographical effect (for example differential economic growth) are distorted by these activities being concentrated in regions that display the effect already. Further, it may be that the presumed relationship is the converse of what is being presumed. Such 'chicken and egg' issues in spatial analysis are especially prone to 'endogeneity problems'.

REFERENCES

Amin, A. (ed.) (1994), *Post-Fordism: A Reader*, Oxford: Blackwell.

Becattini, G. (1978), 'The development of light industry in Tuscany', *Economic Notes*, **18**, 2–3.

Boschma, R. (2005), 'Proximity and innovation: a critical assessment', *Regional Studies*, **39**, 61–74.

Boschma, R. and R. Wenting (2007), 'The spatial evolution of the British automobile industry: does location matter?', *Industrial and Corporate Change*, **16**, 213–38.

Bridge, G. (2007), 'Environmental economic geography: a sympathetic critique', *Geoforum*, **39**, 76–81.

Broomhill, R. (2001), 'Neoliberal globalism and the local state: a regulation approach', *Journal of Australian Political Economy*, **48**, 115–40.

Buenstorf, G. and S. Klepper (2005), 'Heritage and agglomeration: the Akron Tyre cluster revisited', Papers on Economics and Evolution 2005-08, Jena: Max Planck Institute of Economics.

Cantwell, J. and S. Iammarino (2003), *Multinational Corporations and European Regional Systems of Innovation*, London: Routledge.

Christensen, C. (1997), *The Innovator's Dilemma*, Boston, MA: Harvard Business School Press.

Cooke, P. (1990), *Back to the Future: Modernity, Postmodernity and Locality*, London: Unwin Hyman.

Cooke, P. (2008), 'Cleantech and an analysis of the platform nature of life sciences: further reflections upon platform policies', *European Planning Studies*, **16** (3), 1–19.

Cooke, P., C. de Laurentis, F. Tödtling and M. Trippl (2007), *Regional Knowledge Economies*, Cheltenham, UK and Northampton, MA, USA: Edward Elgar.

Desfor, G. and R. Keil (2007), *Nature and the City*, Tucson, AZ: University of Arizona Press.

Dosi, G. (1982), 'Technological paradigms and technological trajectories: a suggested interpretation of the determinants and directions of technical change', *Research Policy*, **11**, 147–62.

Edquist, C. (ed.) (1997), *Systems of Innovation*, London: Frances Pinter.

Freeman, C. and C. Perez (1988), 'Structural crisis of adjustment, business cycles and investment behaviour', in G. Dosi, C. Freeman, R. Nelson and L. Soete (eds), *Technical Change and Economic Theory*, London, Pinter, pp. 38–66.

Geels, F. (2004), 'From sectoral systems of innovation to socio-technical systems: insights about dynamics and change from sociology and institutional theory', *Research Policy*, **33**, 897–920.

Geels, F. (2006), 'Co-evolutionary and multi-level dynamics in transitions: the transformation of aviation systems and the shift from propeller to turbojet (1930–1970)', *Technovation*, **26**, 999–1016.

Gibbs, D. (2006), 'Prospects for an environmental economic geography: linking ecological modernization and regulationist approaches', *Economic Geography*, **82**, 193–215.

Gibbs, D., A. Jonas and A. While (2002), 'Changing governance structures and the environment: economy–environment relations at the local and regional scales', *Journal of Environmental Policy and Planning*, **4**, 123–39.

Guthman, J. (2004) *Agrarian Dreams: The Paradox of Organic Farming in California*, Berkeley, CA: University of California Press.

Halliday, F. (1990), *From Kabul to Managua: Soviet–American Relations in the 1980s*, London, Pantheon.

Hayter, R. and R. Le Heron (2002), 'Industrialization, techno-economic paradigms and the environment', in R. Hayter and R. Le Heron (eds), *Knowledge, Industry and Environment: Institutions and Innovation in Territorial Perspective*, Aldershot: Ashgate, pp. 11–30.

Hekkert, M., R. Suurs, S. Negro, S. Kuhlmann and R. Smits (2007), 'Functions of innovation systems: a new approach for analysing technological change', *Technological Forecasting and Social Change*, **74**, 413–32.

Hillman, K., R. Suurs, M. Hekkert and B. Sandén (2008), 'Cumulative causation in biofuels development: a critical comparison of the Netherlands and Sweden', *Technology Analysis and Strategic Management*, **20**, 593–612.

Jacobs, J. (1969), *The Economy of Cities*, New York: Vintage.

Jessop, B. (1995), 'The regulation approach, governance and post-Fordism: alternative perspectives on economic and political change?', *Economy and Society*, **24**, 307–33.

Kahn, M. (2007), *Green Cities: Urban Growth and the Environment*, Washington, DC: Brookings Institution.

Kemp, R. (2002), 'Environmental protection through technological regime shifts', in A. Jamison and H. Rohracher (eds), *Technology Studies and Sustainable Development*, Munich: Profil Verlag, pp. 95–126.

Klepper, S. (2002), 'The capabilities of new firms and the evolution of the US automobile industry', *Industrial and Corporate Change*, **11**, 645–66.

Kunstler, J. (2005), *The Long Emergency: Surviving the Converging Catastrophes of the Twenty-First Century*, New York: Grove Press.

Lipietz, A. (1987), *Mirages and Miracles*, London: Verso.

Manning, R. (2004), *Against the Grain: How Agriculture Hijacked Civilization*, New York: North Point Press.

Marshall, A. (1918), *Industry and Trade*, London: Macmillan.

Martin, R. and P. Sunley (2006), 'Path dependence and regional economic evolution', *Journal of Economic Geography*, **6**, 395–437.

Ministry of Foreign Affairs of Denmark (2008), *Invest in Denmark*, Copenhagen: Government of Denmark.

Mol, A. (1999), 'Ecological modernization and the ecological transition of Europe: between national variations and common denominators', *Journal of Environmental Policy and Planning*, **1**, 167–81.

Peck, J. (2000), 'Doing regulation', in G. Clark, M. Feldman and M. Gertler (eds), *The Oxford Handbook of Economic Geography*, Oxford: Oxford University Press, pp. 61–80.

Rip, A. and R. Kemp (1998), 'Technological change', in S. Rayner and E. Malone (eds), *Human Choice and Climate Change*, Columbus: Battelle Press, pp. 327–99.

Schumpeter, J. (1975), *Capitalism, Socialism and Democracy*, New York: Harper.

Smith, A. (2006), 'Green niches in sustainable development: the case of organic food in the United Kingdom', *Environment and Planning C: Government and Policy*, **24**, 439–58.

Smith, A., A. Stirling and F. Berkhout (2005), 'The governance of sustainable socio-technical transitions', *Research Policy*, **34**, 1491–1510.

Stoker, G. (ed.) (1999), *The New Management of British Local Governance*, London: Macmillan.

Stoker G. and K. Mossberger (1994), 'Urban regime theory in comparative perspective', *Environment and Planning C: Government and Policy*, **12**, 195–212.

Stone, C. (1989), *Regime Politics: Governing Atlanta*, Lawrence, KS: University Press of Kansas.

Stone, C. (1993), 'Urban regimes and the capacity to govern: a political economy approach', *Journal of Urban Affairs*, **15**, 1–28.

Strahan, D. (2007), *The Last Oil Shock*, London: John Murray.

Tukker, A., M. Charter, C. Vezzoli, E. Sto and M. Munch Andersen (2008), *System Innovation for Sustainability*, Cheltenham, UK and Northampton, MA, USA: Edward Elgar.

Voss, J., D. Bauknecht and R. Kemp (eds) (2006), *Reflexive Governance for Sustainable Development*, Cheltenham, UK and Northampton, MA, USA: Edward Elgar.

Weber, M. and J. Hemmelskamp (eds) (2005), *Towards Environmental Innovation Systems*, Berlin: Springer.

While, A., A. Jonas and J. Gibbs (2004), 'The environment and the entrepreneurial city: searching for the urban "sustainability fix" in Manchester and Leeds', *International Journal of Urban and Regional Research*, **28**, 549–69.

Wolch, J. (2007), 'Green urban worlds', *Annals of the Association of American Geographers*, **97**, 373–84.

PART VI

REGIONAL INNOVATION
SYSTEM INSTITUTIONS

PART VI

REGIONAL INNOVATION
SYSTEM INSTITUTIONS

Introduction

Dafna Schwartz and Franz Tödtling

REGIONAL INNOVATION SYSTEMS ISSUES

Part VI explores the drivers of regional innovation systems and begins in Chapter 33 with Franz Tödtling and Michaela Trippl's review of the evolution and application of the concept. It draws attention to the firms, clusters, knowledge organizations and institutions of a region, as well as to the innovation interdependencies within the region and beyond. The last point is important because misinformed critique of the concept is often constrained to the 'bucket theory' of the region. But social systems are always open and this bucket lets water out and light in through its 'structural holes'. As noted in the Introduction (Chapter 1) to this *Handbook*, some inspiration for the framework came from the emergence of an interactive user–producer theory of innovation that replaced the linear model mentioned by the authors. It will be interesting to observe future adaptations to this in light of the observations there about new 'neolinear' approaches such as demand-, user- and design-driven innovation (see also Chapter 43 of this *Handbook* on these). Efforts to recognize important institutional aspects, notably 'conventions' in the earliest formulation of the regional innovation system model, will clearly be affected by such reconsiderations. This may help moderate an imputed 'fuzziness' the authors report as a critique of their treatment, perhaps not surprising in light of Sunley's (Chapter 25, this *Handbook*) recognition of the difficulty in researching them and Storper's comparison of them with astronomical 'dark matter'. This is a real future challenge for innovation research in general and regional innovation systems research particularly, not least because its methodology (comparative primary research rather than modelling secondary data sets) lends itself to exploring 'convention mutation' and 'convention displacement' as discussed in Schwartz and Cooke's 'Introduction' to Part V of this Handbook, 'Regional worlds of innovation', as cultures collide in globalizing regional innovation systems.

Apart from soft-institutional 'conventions' issues, more attention has been devoted to the regional innovation system perspective by authors seeking to elaborate harder institutional constraints. For example the authors note Asheim and Gertler's focus on knowledge dynamics and the different systemic implications if the cognitive field is 'symbolic' knowledge (creative industries) compared to 'synthetic' knowledge (engineering). Another is the authors' own differentiation of the institutional attenuation of regional innovation capabilities along a spectrum from 'fragmented' (for example Vienna's, like London's, and conceivably other metropolitan innovation deficits) to 'locked-in' (old industry regions) to 'thin' (peripheral regions) as a cause of regional innovation and broader economic underperformance. These flesh out the body of knowledge and understanding of regional evolution in ways that proliferate but do not yet reintegrate regional path trajectories or identify path-interdependence or holistic regional evolution as called for by Martin (Chapter 15 in this *Handbook*). One further elaboration proposed by the authors is to draw on a 'worlds of regional innovation' perspective after Storper, as evaluated by Sunley (Chapter 25, this *Handbook*) to specify contrasts in regional knowledge acquisition styles ranging from static, traded to dynamic, untraded, the former capturing arm's-length exchange transactions while the latter includes 'social networking' capital (as profiled by Rosenfeld, Chapter 21 in this *Handbook*). Hypothetically, the full range of these is found in accomplished regional innovation systems. What has then to be teased out is in what order for which knowledge 'convention' sets ('symbolic' compared to 'synthetic') and with what degree of 'relatedness' and even path-interdependence, so that the whole regional trajectory can be specified and, in comparative perspective, typologized. This is an exciting future research agenda for regional innovation systems analysis. Correspondingly, what other profiles, including governance as well as market failures, typify underinnovating, underperforming regions; and can learning, networking and relatedness conventions be enhanced by judicious policy intervention? Cross-border innovation systems are also inadequately studied by regional innovation systems analysts as yet. Accordingly, researching another soft institutional dimension like 'convention proximity' in relation to the 'convention mutation' and 'convention displacement' imperatives noted above, would markedly enrich understanding of key practices in regional innovation systems.

A further issue deemed worthy of more focused attention is that of regional innovation intermediaries in the changing policy arena of regional innovation systems. The novel research issues already raised point to the following evolving priorities: divergent innovation styles; distinctive innovation knowledge bases; changing and interacting convention structures; knowledge relatedness, transversality and path-interdependence; and knowledge and innovation internationalization. Each of these represents a sign that the complexity of contemporary regional innovation is best moderated by expert support in policy formation by catalytic intermediation and, to some degree, regional innovation orchestration (Chapters 23 and 42 in this *Handbook*).

Claire Nauwelaers's Chapter 34 in this *Handbook* raises a further series of important observations and issues. The first of these is the fashionable concern for policy optimization and the culling of programmes and intermediaries that have blossomed during the increasingly residual era of supply-side economics. So, increasingly, innovation agencies are faced, in a new era of budgetary restraint, with an urgent need to optimize a system that has in most cases grown somewhat anarchically and without strategic governance. However, given the priority listing above, it is clear that these roles, many of them involving cognitive switching, policy mixing and hybrid technical and policy skills, are unlikely to be well performed by functionaries inhabiting policy silos. Nauwelaers lists many traditional 'government failures' towards regional innovation: innovation infrastructure failures (including science and technology infrastructure); transition failures at firm level, for example difficulties in adapting to changing competitive environments; lock-in failures at system level, typical of old industrialized regions; institutional failures (covering supporting institutions, regulations, culture, habits, and so on); and pervasive 'learning and capability failures' (import, processing and renewal of policy knowledge; see Chapter 40 by Simmie on 'Learning regions' in this *Handbook*). All such blockages call for infusions of 'policy fluidity' to facilitate flows of knowledge and related resources to regional innovators.

Various real-time challenges are presented in Nauwelaers's Chapter 34, illustrating innovation system challenges and the roles of intermediaries in mitigating them. Among the biggest of these are cognitive and interfacing problems for actors and agents faced with high uncertainty and low versatility, as also described with solvents identified in Chapters 41 and 42 of this *Handbook*.

ENTREPRENEURSHIP AND VENTURE CAPITAL

For transition planning involving new departures for firms and regional trajectories, Schumpeter I entrepreneurship and its associated risk capital investors are key change agents and mechanisms. As much organizational change management literature stresses, nothing less than a Giddensian 'structuration' process is implied by the onset and imperatives of regional innovation paradigm and regime change. Accordingly, mechanisms for facilitating this by intermediaries and policy managers must be thoroughly understood and tested. These can include the deployment of such 'soft innovation' instruments as 'living laboratories', 'dramaturgy' and 'white spaces' identification (as discussed in Chapter 42 of this *Handbook*), some of which are routinely practised in corporate 'change management' workshops. These too are arenas in which research opportunities are ripe for observation of 'convention adjustment' to attune regions, intermediaries and firms to becoming more innovative. However, the raw material on which such institutional therapy must work has to be considered first.

Niels Bosma and colleagues Veronique Schutjens and Erik Stam perform an analysis of regional entrepreneurship in relation to regional innovation and growth in Chapter 35 of this *Handbook*. First, like innovativeness, entrepreneurship is unevenly spread across regions. But do they coincide? Giddensian thinking is again to the fore in consideration of this, as a focus on entrepreneurship means a focus on structure and agency: it is about individuals who identify, evaluate and exploit entrepreneurial opportunities within certain structures, while at the same time influencing these structures. These have spatial aspects highly familiar to students of regional innovation: localization and urbanization (dis)economies, region-specific institutions, the organization of industries in regions, and the regional availability of production factors. The fact that, nowadays, a large part of innovative change is brought about by new firms suggests regional entrepreneurship and innovation do coincide geographically proximately. Innovative firms circumvent lock-ins, at the same time incentivizing incumbents by their relative competitiveness. Accordingly, this competition has a positive effect, directly and indirectly, through (Schumpeterian) imitation, on regional productivity levels.

Nevertheless, the fact that imitators vastly outweigh innovators means the Schumpeterian distinction retains its evolutionary force and that the former is more important in, for example, agglomeration and probably cluster emergence around a few innovators. Geographical proximity is extremely important for regional entrepreneurship, almost a given. Entrepreneurs value proximity to family and friends not only for the help that those connections might offer to their ventures, but also for emotional reasons. Moreover entrepreneurs are often 'organizational products', that is, they spin-off a firm from their previous employer. Furthermore clusters are shown to be good incubators for entrepreneurship, keeping in mind that a major share of that is imitative not innovative, for example footwear. Accordingly, intermediaries are frequently entrepreneurs, or at least entrepreneurial because they practice rent-seeking competition. Equally, entrepreneurs are occasionally innovators but more commonly imitators and as such they intermediate innovation and wider, possibly global, markets.

A comparable judgement can be made for venture capitalists although their intermediary role in regional innovation is clearer. Venture capital (VC) is composed of different types of risk capital: VC funds, corporate venture companies, business angels and other private equity entities. Jesper Lindgaard Christensen's Chapter 36 in this *Handbook*, develops this theme of their importance, uneven spatial concentration and variety of profiles in his analysis of their position in the 'order' of intermediation they perform.

There are basically two convention sets here. First, they supply risk capital that facilitates entrepreneurship; second, they supply management capabilities, experience and networking which the entrepreneur or the innovator is likely to lack. Some experts consider the latter to be more important than the former function. These functions absolutely advantage metropolitan regions where venture capital habitually settles, even though metropolitan innovation is lower than ex-urban. The convention is that they usually like to locate no more than a one-hour drive from their investment, meaning that they can serve satellite clusters as well as the metropolitan ones. This might be termed the 'convention radius' of risk capital proximity, a powerful local force in the determination and reproduction of innovation-based regional inequality. Geographically asymmetric information about good prospects means venture capitalists and business angels rely on personal and professional relationships, which in turn are most often localized in close proximity to their offices. They may also specialize sectorally for example biotechnology funds. Regional innovation in non-metropolitan regions has had to evolve distinctive conventions, notably 'informal investors' *inter alia*, that is, successful regional entrepreneurs supportive of local entrepreneurship, even some business angels, but more commonly public or public–private, including specific-purpose (for example films, intellectual property rights – IPR), regional venture capital funds. Since the venture capital industry is dynamic, it is constantly evolving innovative mechanisms to exploit market opportunities.

ACADEMIC ENTREPRENEURSHIP AND INCUBATION

In the conventional order of regional innovation, notably of new technology business firms, entrepreneurs may be born in universities through a process whereby a laboratory discovery is seen to have commercial potential and its founder is advised or even trained to become an academic entrepreneur. It is not unusual for such an entrepreneur to seek accommodation in an incubator where, if in the US he or she is expected to have three assets to gain entry: a piece of intellectual property; a business plan; and seed investment of some $1 million. In Europe, the academic entrepreneur frequently must be stress-tested, possibly more than once in a screening stage that, if successful, may lead to a selection stage for which the survivor(s) may be rewarded with an incubator space and a grant to write a business plan. Surprisingly, it is sometimes wondered why academic entrepreneurship is weaker in Europe than in the US.

As is shown in Chapter 38, exceptions to the European norm such as Israel and, to a limited extent, the UK are closer to the US progenitor. But one European country that fits neither convention is Sweden, where as Magnus Kloftsen and Staffan Öberg show in Chapter 37, a highly systematic innovation chain produces regionally well-spread academic entrepreneurship and incubation based on enhancing human capital, then rewarding successful academic entrepreneurs by allowing them to retain full IPR on their innovation plus access to varieties of risk capital. Entrepreneur coaching and mentoring are crucial to this process.

Finally, the intermediating stage between academic entrepreneurship and market is occupied by incubation as discussed by Daniel Shefer and Amnon Frenkel in Chapter 38. They first discuss the role of the international technological incubators programme's visions and actions, which are: fostering entrepreneurship and innovation by channelling public and private risk funding from seed to venture capital to projects; business and marketing consultation; and provision of low-cost rent and infrastructure. Incubators number 3000 worldwide, of which nearly a third are in the US, housing some 20 000 firms. Technological incubators are also found in such emerging markets as China, Turkey, Brazil and South Korea. In Israel 26 are in operation of which 23 are techno-logical; some 200 firm 'projects' employing 2000 at a cost of $285 million were housed in Israeli incubators by 2003. The public programme was deemed successful enough that incubators could be privatized.

However, Shefer and Frenkel's evaluation showed that private incubators concentrate in innovative regions and sectors, while public incubators are more regionally sensitive and varied in the kinds of business they house. The convention set and indeed convention radius of a typical private incubator is wholly different from that of a public one. The former have a largely economic, business or administrative orientation with most origi-nating in industry and easily able to attract venture capital. Promoters of the latter have higher education levels and previous careers in academia or research institutes, but they are weaker in business and administrative skills. University incubators seek to combine both attributes but they incur higher than average budgetary deficits. Nevertheless, in Israel, the incubator programme (alongside the initially public venture capital pro-gramme) has been credited with shifting the country's path-dependence (measured by gross domestic product and exports) from an agricultural to a high-technology trajectory in less than 20 years.

Part VI brings together stimulating new regional innovation systems and policy thinking, especially, first, concerning diverse kinds and emphases for research on the issue of 'soft institutions' (for example conventions). These were opened up by Sunley's lead in Chapter 25 of Part V of this *Handbook*, followed in places throughout that part and highlighted in Tödtling and Trippl's Chapter 33 of Part VI and Nauwelaers's and Bosma et al.'s below. Among categories of regional innovation convention identified in these numerous chapters are the following: 'convention mutation', 'convention displace-ment', 'convention proximity' and 'convention radius' marking proximity constraints for special innovation services (for example academic entrepreneurship, venture capital, private incubation, patent citation). Regarding policy implications of the foregoing, key ideas with regard to policy intermediation include cognitive switching, policy mixing and hybrid technical and policy mix skills, all required as supply-side support shifts to demand-side catalysis involving regional change management, living laboratories and promotion of relatedness and transversality.

Universities remain important mechanisms because their convention sets are not (yet) narrowly profit-motivated, unlike venture capital and private incubation that clearly are. 'Ordering' such potentially related path-interdependences in regional analysis and policy promises an exciting future for researchers, intermediaries and practitioners alike, embracing key issues in regional innovation, productivity and growth analysis.

33 Regional innovation systems
Franz Tödtling and Michaela Trippl

INTRODUCTION

There is widespread agreement in the academic literature that knowledge, learning and innovation are key factors for the competitiveness of firms and the development of regional and national economies. Until the 1990s the linear model of innovation was dominant both in science and policy circles, emphasizing public and private research and development (R&D), often located in large agglomerations, leading to new products and processes and subsequent technology diffusion to peripheral regions and lower levels of the city hierarchy (see Chapter 5 by Tichy in this *Handbook*). The regional innovation system (RIS) approach (Cooke et al., 2000, 2004) has provided an alternative view of the innovation process and related policies. It draws attention to the firms, clusters, knowledge organizations and institutions of a region, as well as to the innovation interdependencies within the region and beyond. The RIS concept builds on the interactive innovation model (Kline and Rosenberg, 1986), as well as on other schools of interactive innovation such as the milieu concept (Camagni, 1991) and the studies on knowledge interdependencies in high-tech regions (Saxenian, 1994; Keeble and Wilkinson, 2000).

The RIS concept relies on the broader systems of innovation approach (see Edquist, 2005) which conceptualizes innovation as an evolutionary, non-linear and interactive process. Intensive communication and collaboration between different actors is said to be required, both among companies as well as between firms and other organizations such as universities, innovation centres, educational institutions, financing institutions, standard-setting bodies, industry associations and government agencies. Inspired by the institutionalist school of thought, the role of both 'hard' and formal institutions (that is, laws and regulations) and 'soft' institutions (practices, norms and routines) shaping the behaviour of actors and the interaction between them is stressed (see for example Edquist and Johnson, 1997). It has been argued in this context that the institutionalist emphasis has contributed to a certain 'fuzziness' of the concept (Doloreux and Parto, 2005).

Initially, the concept of innovation system was applied to the national level (Lundvall, 1992; Nelson, 1993). The national innovation system (NIS) literature revealed huge differences between countries in such attributes as economic structure, R&D base, institutional set-up and innovation performance. In the 1990s also other specifications of innovation systems emerged: Carlsson and colleagues analysed 'technological systems', arguing that systemic interrelationships are unique to technology fields (Carlsson and Jacobsson, 1997; Carlsson and Stankiewicz, 1991). Other authors emphasize the importance of a sectoral approach and examine how groups of firms develop and manufacture products of a specific sector and how they generate and utilize the technologies of that sector (Breschi and Malerba, 1997; Malerba, 2002).

More recently a growing interest in regional innovation systems has emerged (Cooke, 1992; Autio, 1998; Cooke et al., 2000, 2004; Doloreux, 2002; Asheim and Gertler, 2005;

Sternberg, 2007). Whilst not denying that national (as well as international), technological and sectoral factors are essential, it is argued convincingly that the regional dimension is of key importance. Several reasons support this view. First, regions differ with respect to their industrial specialization pattern and their innovation performance (Howells, 1999; Paci and Usai, 2000). Second, it was shown that knowledge spillovers, which play a key role in the innovation process, are often spatially bounded (Anselin et al., 1997; Audretsch and Feldman, 1996; Bottazzi and Peri, 2003). Third, the ongoing importance of tacit knowledge (Polanyi, 1966) for successful innovation has to be mentioned (Gertler, 2003; Howells, 2002). It is now well understood that its exchange requires intensive, trust-based personal contacts facilitated by geographical proximity (Morgan, 2004; Storper, 1997). Finally, policy competences and institutions are partly bound to subnational territories (Cooke et al., 2000).

THE CONCEPT OF REGIONAL INNOVATION SYSTEMS

A schematic illustration of the structuring of RISs (see Figure 33.1) is provided in Tödtling and Trippl (2005). A regional innovation system is made up by two subsystems

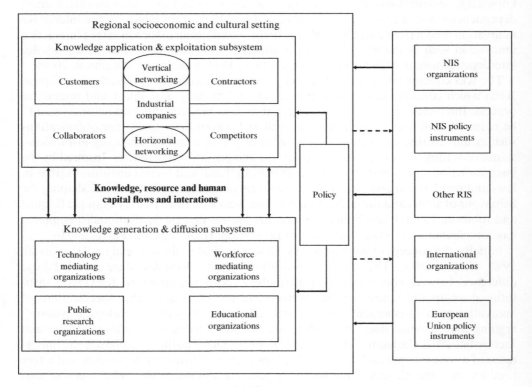

Source: Tödtling and Trippl (2005), based on Autio (1998).

Figure 33.1   Main structure of regional innovation systems (RISs)

embedded in a common regional socio-economic and cultural setting (Autio, 1998). The knowledge application and exploitation subsystem comprises the companies, their clients, suppliers and competitors as well as their cooperation partners (that is, the clusters) of the region. Ideally, these firms are linked by horizontal and vertical networking. The knowledge generation and diffusion subsystem as the second main building block of a regional innovation system consists of various organizations that are engaged in the production and diffusion of knowledge and skills. Key elements include public research institutions, technology mediating organizations (technology licensing offices, innovation centres, and so on), as well as educational institutions (universities, polytechnics, vocational training institutions, and so on) and workforce mediating organizations. Then, policy actors at the regional level can play a powerful role in shaping innovation processes, provided that there is sufficient regional autonomy (legal competencies and financial resources) to design and implement innovation policies (Cooke et al., 2000). In the ideal case, there are intensive interactive relationships within and between these subsystems facilitating a continuous flow or exchange of knowledge, resources and human capital. But, as will be pointed out further below, there are also several types of RIS problems and failures such as deficits with respect to organizations and institutions and a lack of relations within and between the subsystems.

Regional innovation systems are far from being self-sustaining entities. They usually have diverse links to national and international actors and innovation systems. We may distinguish between two important dimensions in this context. First, with respect to the innovation networks of firms, there is a widespread consensus nowadays that local connections do not suffice to sustain innovativeness (see the next section). In the context of intensifying international competition and accelerating technological change, extraregional contacts which complement local ones are of key importance (Bunnel and Coe, 2001; Oinas and Malecki, 2002). Second, in terms of public intervention it becomes apparent that regional, national and European policy actors and organizations can shape the development and dynamics of regional innovation systems (multilevel governance). This issue is further elaborated in the section on 'RISs and the role of the state'.

There exist meanwhile a number of studies on the nature, governance and performance of RISs pointing out that they are a quite heterogeneous phenomenon. Based on the literature we can distinguish between different dimensions and types of RISs:

- An interesting typology of RISs is proposed by Cooke (2004) who distinguishes these systems according to their capacity to develop dynamic high-technology sectors. He differentiates between institutional regional innovation systems (IRISs) and entrepreneurial regional innovation systems (ERISs). Whilst an IRIS is well suited to promote the development of more traditional sectors, high-technology industries such as information and communication technology (ICT) or biotechnology best flourish in ERISs. In sharp contrast to IRISs, which rely more on state and institutional support, the dynamism of ERISs is based on local venture capital, entrepreneurship, scientific excellence, market demand and incubators which support intense processes of knowledge exploitation.
- Regarding the governance dimension, Cooke (1998) classifies RISs into 'grassroots' (for example Tuscany, Catalonia), 'networked' (Baden-Württemberg, Tampere) and '*dirigiste*' (Slovenia, Singapore) types. He argues that key actors,

institutions of coordination and policy processes differ strongly between these types of RISs.

● Asheim and Gertler (2005) as well as Cooke et al. (2007) differentiate RISs according to their dominant industries and knowledge base. Distinguishing between 'analytical' (for example biotech), 'synthetic' (for example engineering) and 'symbolic' (for example cultural industries) knowledge bases and RISs, they argue that knowledge sources and interdependencies as well as policy needs differ quite markedly between these types of RIS.

● Tödtling and Trippl (2005) in a more policy-oriented paper deal with RIS problems and barriers and distinguish between 'fragmented' (metropolitan), 'locked in' (old industrial regions), and 'thin' (peripheral) types of RIS. It is argued that policies have to be addressed to these specific problems and cannot be applied in a 'one size fits all' manner.

REGIONAL INNOVATION SYSTEMS AND THE NATURE AND GEOGRAPHY OF KNOWLEDGE FLOWS

As shown in the last section, localized flows of know-how, skills and expertise are of crucial importance for the innovation capacity and competitive strength of clusters and RISs, giving rise to systemic innovation activities. Although local knowledge linkages should be regarded as key ingredients of highly innovative regions, we should bear in mind that interactions with international knowledge providers also play a central role (Amin and Cohendet, 2004; Maskell et al., 2006). They enable firms to get access to expertise which is not available within the limited context of the region. More specifically, it is the interplay between local and global knowledge flows that is vital during the innovation process.

Bathelt et al. (2004) propose the concept of 'local buzz and global pipelines' to highlight that innovation in clusters and RISs rests on both linkages at the local level and knowledge interactions with distant sources and partners: 'Local buzz refers to a thick web of information, knowledge and inspiration which circulate between the actors of a cluster. This buzz consists of specific information flows, knowledge transfer and continuous updates as well as opportunities for learning in organized and spontaneous meetings' (Bathelt, 2008, 86; see also Bathelt et al., 2004; Storper and Venables, 2004). To participate in and to benefit from buzz does not require specific investments. Firms in clusters and RISs are surrounded by a densely knit web of gossip, opinions and interpretations and therefore do not need to actively search their environment for information and knowledge (Grabher, 2002). Whilst buzz seems to be mainly about an often unintended knowledge transfer that is not related to conscious activities of cluster actors (or what below will be referred to as 'knowledge spillovers' or 'externalities'), knowledge flows through pipelines are far from automatic and participation is not free (Bathelt et al., 2004). Global pipelines are viewed as deliberately established connections to distant knowledge sources, providing access to different knowledge pools, new technologies and markets (Bathelt et al., 2004; Bathelt, 2008).

The 'buzz and pipelines' concept has enhanced our understanding of the interrelatedness of local and global knowledge linkages which underpin innovation in clusters

Table 33.1　*Types of linkages to external knowledge sources and partners*

	Static (knowledge transfer)	Dynamic (collective learning)
Formal / traded relation	Market relations ● contract research ● consulting ● licences ● buying of intermediate goods	Formal networks ● R&D cooperations ● shared use of R&D facilities
Informal / untraded relation	Spillovers ● mobility of specialists ● monitoring of competitors ● participation in fairs, conferences ● reading of scientific literature, patent specifications	Informal networks ● informal contacts ● social events ● Internet chatrooms ● virtual knowledge communities

and RISs. However, precisely which local and extralocal links involve this is not very clear (see also Asheim et al., 2007a; Wickham and Vecchi, 2008). More specifically, the channels or mechanisms by which cluster actors get access to knowledge at different spatial scales as well as their relative importance remain somewhat obscure. Recently, attempts have been made to go beyond the 'buzz and pipelines' model by proposing a differentiated typology of knowledge interactions (Table 33.1) that rests on two dimensions (Tödtling et al., 2006). The first dimension draws a distinction between traded and untraded interdependencies in the innovation process (Storper, 1997). Traded and formal relations involve monetary or other forms of compensation for particular knowledge flows, whereas in non-traded and informal relations there is no specific immediate compensation. The second dimension distinguishes between static and dynamic aspects of knowledge exchange (Capello, 1999). Static knowledge exchange refers to the transfer of 'ready' pieces of information or knowledge from one actor to the other. Dynamic knowledge exchange, in contrast, characterizes a situation, where there is interactive and collective learning among actors through, for example, cooperation or other joint activities (Camagni, 1991; Lundvall, 1992). In this case the collective stock of knowledge is increased through the interaction. Based on these two analytical distinctions we can identify four types of knowledge links: market relations, formal networks, spillovers and informal networks (see also Chapter 12 by Giuliani in this *Handbook*). Table 33.1 shows important examples for these different types of knowledge interactions.

Empirical evidence has shown that firms, particularly in knowledge-based industries, use a broad variety of these relationships (market links, spillovers, formal and informal networks) to get access to codified and tacit knowledge from specific sources (Tödtling et al., 2006; Cooke et al., 2007). It has also been shown that innovation interactions between knowledge generation and exploitation actors take place at regional, national and international levels. The sources, the kind of knowledge exchanged and the relationships differ between these levels, however. At the regional and national levels universities, research organizations and service firms are often typical knowledge sources, and there seems to be a higher share of tacit knowledge exchanged through informal relationships and spillovers. At the international level, in comparison, there is more exchange of codified knowledge along the value chain, with competitors and research organizations. Formal relations (market links, formal networks) are more important there. Regional, national and international innovation systems, thus, are strongly interconnected and play a complementary role in the development of knowledge-based sectors.

REGIONAL INNOVATION SYSTEMS AND THE ROLE OF THE STATE

Policy agents constitute an important element of RISs (see Figure 33.1). In this section we will take a closer look at the role of the state, dealing particularly with the rationale of innovation policy actions and the relevance of multilevel and multi-actor governance. How can policy interventions in RISs be justified? For a long time, the classical concept of 'market failure' has dominated the innovation policy debate, that is, underinvestment in R&D due to the existence of uncertainties, externalities and knowledge spillovers has been regarded as a key rationale for public intervention. However, from the perspective of the systems of innovation approach there is a need to go beyond the market failure approach to account also for systemic failures which can block the functioning of a regional innovation system and hamper flows of knowledge and technology (Edquist, 2002; Lundvall and Borrás, 1999, 2005). We can distinguish between different types of RIS failures (see also Tödtling and Trippl, 2005).

RIS failures may have their origin in an underdeveloped or inappropriate organizational and institutional set-up. This means that key elements of a regional innovation system are weak or even missing, leading to a curtailing of the innovation capacity of the region. Such problems include limited innovation capabilities of firms; a lack of organizations in the fields of research, education and technology transfer; as well as weakly developed or non-existent clusters. Innovation deficiencies of regions may also be caused, however, by an overspecialization in traditional industries and outdated technologies. Innovation problems in this case may result from a too strong orientation of existing knowledge organizations and schools towards outdated economic and technological structures.

Furthermore, inappropriate or missing interactions between the different actors and organizations of a regional innovation system may constitute major deficiencies. We may distinguish between two types of problem in this context. On the one hand, there may be a lack of communication and cooperation between RIS actors leading to an insufficient flow of knowledge and technology. On the other hand, too strong ties between innovation relevant organizations can lead to serious lock-in effects, undermining the innovation capabilities of regional economies. These two types of network problem can make their appearance both within the two RIS subsystems as well as between them. Finally, as we have stressed above, international connections are crucial for sustaining a region's innovativeness. If external links are poorly developed, the region suffers from a limited access to international pools of resources and knowledge. In sum, the considerations pointed out provide a sound basis to justify policy intervention in RISs and they offer implications for the scope, objectives and methods of innovation policy.

What becomes immediately clear from this discussion is that the role of the state is not confined to funding basic research but also includes support for the formation of local and non-local networks, and the establishment of new or expanded organizations such as universities, technology transfer offices, science and technology parks, and so on. The precise mix of policy instruments depends on the respective RIS and its particular deficiencies. There is no 'one size fits all' innovation policy approach applicable in every region. Instead there is a need for a 'tailor-made' innovation policy approach addressing the specific challenges, problems and opportunities found in the considered region.

This claim is in line with the recent scholarly discussion about the superiority of a platform approach to regional innovation policy (Asheim et al., 2007a; Cooke et al., 2007; Cooke, 2008) which is strongly inspired by new research on the importance of related variety as a key driver of regional growth (see, for instance, Frenken et al., 2007). It takes the specific competences and assets of regions as the starting point when diversifying the region's economic base, by promoting new fields of application that could lead to the emergence of new industries and growth paths. The distinction between related variety versus unrelated variety or related diversification and unrelated diversification (Frenken et al., 2007; and see Boschma and Frenken's Chapter 14 in this *Handbook*) is essential.

Arguably, although unrelated diversification (that is, the rise of a new industry which is not related to those already existing in an area) might have the advantage in protecting the region better against asymmetric shocks in demand, related diversification may be even more beneficial, because in this case the broadening of the economic base builds on competences present in an area, allowing for complementarities to existing industries and knowledge bases. Such an approach is helpful to escape from both overspecialization and overdiversification. To promote knowledge links between related industries to foster knowledge spillovers, to foster spin-offs or labour mobility from one sector to a related one, to promote knowledge links to international sources to get access to complementary expertise, and so on, could be regarded as key policy instruments in this respect (Asheim et al., 2007b).

The development and dynamics of RISs are influenced by a multilevel governance system formed by policy-makers at the regional, national and supranational (for example European) level. Looking at the distribution of concrete competencies between these levels, scholars have identified considerable differences within Europe (with varying degrees of political autonomy regarding formal competences and financial resources for regions) (see Cooke et al., 2000). Nevertheless, a pattern can be found indicating a complex division of labour (Cooke et al., 2000). At the regional level we can often identify competencies for the lower and medium levels of education, incubation and innovation centres, transfer agencies and, more recently, cluster policies. At the national level in many cases we find competencies for universities, specialized research organizations, and funding for R&D and innovation. At the European level there are the structural funds, the former Regional Innovation Strategies/Regional Innovation and Technology Transfer Strategies (RIS/RITTS) programmes, and the framework programmes for R&D and technological development.

The development of RISs does not only benefit from an effective vertical coordination and collaboration between regional, national and European policy hierarchies; modern forms of multi-actor governance (or, as 'associational forms of governance' as Cooke and Morgan, 1998 call it) are also regarded to be central, reflecting a rethinking of the mode of policy intervention and the role of policy actors. Interactive modes of state intervention and associational forms of governance are seen as being superior to traditional top-down policy strategies (Nauwelaers and Wintjes, 2003). Policy formulation and implementation, then, is the result of intensive communication, close interaction and consensus building between all regional stakeholders in policy networks. Policy-makers are just one actor amongst others in these networks. Consequently, the key role governments play in encouraging learning and innovation shifts from direct intervention towards stimulation, intermediation, brokering, promoting regional dialogue and building up social capital (Nauwelaers and Morgan, 1999; see also Nauwelaers's Chapter 34 in this *Handbook*).

RECENT DEVELOPMENTS AND CHALLENGES

Although a lot of research on RISs has been undertaken, there are still some issues unresolved. One of the key future topics for further research concerns various dimensions of the internationalization of RISs. Whilst there is a large body of literature on international R&D activities of firms, only a few studies have dealt with the internationalization of innovation at the system level so far (Carlsson, 2006). This issue also includes the emergence of regional innovation systems in cross-border areas (Trippl, 2010), that is, in spaces that consist of neighbour territories which belong to different nation-states. Due to regionalization tendencies in many parts of the world, the political and economic transformation of Central and Eastern Europe and the enlargement of the European Union, cross-border regions have grown in importance in recent years. Prominent examples are, amongst others, the Öresund region located at the intersection of Denmark and southern Sweden (Maskell and Törnqvist, 1999) the first Euregion (Aachen, Liege, Limburg) and the US–Mexican border region (Scott, 1999).

Their rise in significance challenges the predominant focus of the RIS concept on regions situated within a single national context. As cross-border areas stretch over one or even several national boundaries, the emergence and dynamic evolution of RISs in these regional settings often hinges on overcoming specific barriers. Recent work on 'institutional proximity' (Gertler, 2003; Boschma, 2005) is helpful to understand properly one of the core problems in this context. This literature departs from a broadly defined concept of institution that covers not only formal institutions (laws, rules, regulations, and so on) but also informal ones (such as cultural norms, habits, values, routines, and so on; see Chapters 19 by James and 25 by Sunley in this *Handbook*), and claims that a common institutional set-up shared between innovation partners (that is, institutional proximity) provides favourable conditions for knowledge interactions and positively affects innovation.

Many cross-border areas, however, are characterized by institutional distance, as a common language, a culture of shared trust, shared beliefs and values, and a common law system are often missing. Several empirical studies dealing with the nature of sociocultural impediments and their impact on transboundary relationships underline our arguments, highlighting the relevance of institutional proximity as a missing ingredient in many cross-border RISs. Van Houtum (1998), for example, identified mental distance (defined as the perception of differences between a foreign country and the home country with respect to business formalities and conventions and the perception of the consequences of these differences) as a key factor for explaining the frequency and number of cross-border economic relations. Krätke (1999) found that amongst other factors, communication barriers, fears of competition and a low-trust environment are main obstacles to interaction in the German–Polish cross-border area; and Koschatzky (2000) provides evidence showing that cultural and institutional barriers are crucial for explaining the low level of innovation links between the contiguous regions of Baden (Germany) and Alsace (France).

CONCLUSIONS

Innovation is nowadays considered as a highly interactive and systemic process. Besides sectoral innovation systems (SISs) and national innovation systems (NISs) regional innovation systems (RISs) are said to constitute a relevant setting for innovation activities and the innovation performance of firms. This is due to the fact that some key innovation factors are localized and to some extent immobile (knowledge organizations, formal and informal institutional settings, tacit knowledge, and so on), and that innovation usually requires the combination of both codified and tacit knowledge.

RISs are made up of various subsystems and elements such as knowledge-generating organizations, educational institutions and technology transfer agencies, as well as knowledge-applying organizations, that is, the firms, industries and clusters of a region. The quality of a regional innovation system depends on both the density and the capability of those organizations and on the interaction among them.

Depending on the institutional setting, leading actors and kind of governance, we can observe different types of RIS. They can be:

- entrepreneurially or institutionally driven;
- of bottom-up or top-down governance;
- based on different kinds of knowledge base (analytical, synthetic, symbolic); and
- situated in institutionally 'rich', in old industrial or in peripheral regions.

The quality and performance of RISs depends to a high degree on the knowledge interactions within and beyond the region. This refers to well-developed links, of both a traded (formal) and an untraded (informal) nature, between the subsystems of knowledge generation and application, that is, between the knowledge organizations and the firms. Often we observe a huge divide between these two subsystems. Furthermore, a large number of empirical studies show that RISs are highly open systems and that knowledge links often need to take place at an international or global level. Obviously, local and international knowledge interactions are complementing each other since highly specialized knowledge is frequently available only from international partners.

Policy actors at various levels (local, regional, national, and supranational such as the European Union) are integral elements of RISs. We observe increasingly a system of multilevel governance. Policies seem to work better when there is a bottom-up involvement of actors, and when policies are to some extent demand-oriented, that is, addressed to the problems and needs of regional companies and people. There can be different kinds of failures and problems, such as: missing or inadequate knowledge organizations;

weak industries or clusters; inappropriate or lacking institutions; and network problems such as fragmentation, lock-in, lack of global connections, and so on. The latter aspect seems to be increasingly relevant, since RISs are not autonomous or self-sufficient units but are inserted in multilevel systems (regional, national, supranational) as well as in wider neighbourhoods and cross-border systems. Although empirical evidence demonstrates that many barriers for such cross-border links exist (for example cultural and institutional barriers) they seem to become more and more important in integrating macro-regions such as Europe, North America and Asia, as the examples of the Öresund region, the area of Basel or of Baden and Alsace for Europe show.

REFERENCES

Amin, A. and P. Cohendet (2004), *Architectures of Knowledge: Firms, Capabilities and Communities*, Oxford: Oxford University Press.
Anselin, L., A. Varga and Z. Acs (1997), 'Local geographic spillovers between university research and high technology innovations', *Journal of Urban Economics*, **42**, 422–48.
Asheim, B., R. Boschma and C. Cooke (2007b), 'Constructing regional advantage: platform policies based on related variety and differentiated knowledge bases', Papers in Evolutionary Economic Geography No. 07.09, Utrecht University.
Asheim, B., L. Coenen and J. Vang (2007a), 'Face-to-face, buzz, and knowledge bases: sociospatial implications for learning, innovation, and innovation policy', *Environment and Planning C: Government and Policy*, **25**, 655–70.
Asheim, B. and M. Gertler (2005), 'The geography of innovation', in J. Fagerberg, D. Mowery and R. Nelson (eds), *The Oxford Handbook of Innovation*, Oxford: Oxford University Press, pp. 291–317.
Audretsch, D. and M. Feldman (1996), 'Innovative clusters and the industry life cycle', *Review of Industrial Organisation*, **11**, 253–73.
Autio, E. (1998), 'Evaluation of RTD in regional systems of innovation', *European Planning Studies*, **6**, 131–40.
Bathelt, H. (2008), 'Knowledge-based clusters: regional multiplier models and the role of "buzz" and "pipelines"' in C. Karlsson (ed.), *Handbook of Research on Cluster Theory*, Cheltenham, UK and Northampton, MA, USA: Edward Elgar, pp. 78–92.
Bathelt, H., A. Malmberg and P. Maskell (2004), 'Clusters and knowledge: local buzz, global pipelines and the process of knowledge creation', *Progress in Human Geography*, **28**, 31–56.
Boschma, R. (2005), 'Proximity and innovation: a critical assessment', *Regional Studies*, **39**, 61–74.
Bottazi, L. and G. Peri (2003), 'Innovation and spillovers in regions: evidence from European patent data', *European Economic Review*, **47**, 687–710.
Breschi, S. and F. Malerba (1997), 'Sectoral innovation systems, technological regimes, Schumpeterian dynamics and spatial boundaries', in C. Edquist (eds), *Systems of Innovation*, London: Pinter, pp. 130–56.
Bunnel, T. and N. Coe (2001), 'Spaces and scales of innovation', *Progress in Human Geography*, **25**, 569–89.
Camagni, R. (1991), 'Local "milieu", uncertainty and innovation networks: towards a new dynamic theory of economic space', in R. Camagni (ed.), *Innovation Networks*, London: Belhaven Press, pp. 121–44.
Capello, R. (1999), 'SME clustering and factor productivity: a milieu production function model', *European Planning Studies*, **7**, 719–35.
Carlsson, B. (2006), 'Internationalization of innovation systems: a survey of the literature', *Research Policy*, **35**, 56–67.
Carlsson, B. and S. Jacobsson (1997), 'Diversity creation and technological systems: a technology policy perspective', in C. Edquist (ed.), *Systems of Innovation*, London: Pinter, pp. 266–94.
Carlsson, B. and R. Stankiewicz (1991), 'On the nature, function and composition of technological systems', *Journal of Evolutionary Economics*, **1**, 93–118.
Cooke, P. (1992), 'Regional innovation systems: competitive regulation in the new Europe', *Geoforum*, **23**, 365–82.
Cooke, P. (1998), 'Introduction: origins of the concept', in H.-J. Braczyk, P. Cooke and M. Heidenreich (eds), *Regional Innovation Systems*, London: UCL Press, pp. 2–25.
Cooke, P. (2004), 'Integrating global knowledge flows for generative growth in Scotland: life science as a knowledge economy exemplar', in J. Potter (ed.), *Inward Investment, Entrepreneurship and Knowledge Flows in Scotland – International Comparisons*, Paris: OECD, pp. 73–96.

Cooke, P. (2008), 'Regional innovation systems: origin of the species', *International Journal of Technological Learning, Innovation and Development*, **1** (3), 393–409.

Cooke, P., P. Boekholt and F. Tödtling (2000), *The Governance of Innovation in Europe*, London: Pinter.

Cooke, P., M. Heidenreich and H.J. Braczyk (eds) (2004), *Regional Innovation Systems*, 2nd edn, London, UK and New York, USA: Routledge.

Cooke, P., C. De Laurentis, F. Tödtling and M. Trippl (2007), *Regional Knowledge Economies*, Cheltenham, UK and Northampton, MA, USA: Edward Elgar.

Cooke, P. and K. Morgan (1998), *The Associational Economy: Firms, Regions, and Innovation*, New York: Oxford University Press.

Doloreux, D. (2002), 'What we should know about regional systems of innovation', *Technology in Society*, **24**, 243–63.

Doloreux, D. and S. Parto (2005), 'Regional innovation systems: current discourse and unresolved isses', *Technology in Society*, **27**, 133–53.

Edquist, C. (2002), 'Innovation policy: a systemic approach', in D. Archibugi and B.-Å. Lundvall (eds), *The Globalizing Learning Economy*, Oxford: Oxford University Press, pp. 219–38.

Edquist, C. (2005), 'Systems of innovation: perspectives and challenges', in J. Fagerberg, D. Mowery and R. Nelson (eds), *The Oxford Handbook of Innovation*, Oxford: Oxford University Press, pp. 181–208.

Edquist, C. and B. Johnson (1997), 'Institutions and organizations in systems of innovation', in C. Edquist (ed.), *Systems of Innovation*, London: Pinter, pp. 41–63.

Frenken, K., F. van Oort and T. Verburg (2007), 'Related variety, unrelated variety and regional economic growth', *Regional Studies*, **41**, 685–97.

Gertler, M. (2003), 'Tacit knowledge and the economic geography of context, or the undefinable tacitness of being (there)', *Journal of Economic Geography*, **3**, 75–99.

Grabher, G. (2002), 'Cool projects, boring institutions: temporary collaboration in social context', *Regional Studies*, **36**, 205–14.

Howells, J. (1999), 'Regional systems of innovation?', in D. Archibugi, J. Howells and J. Michie (eds), *Innovation Policy in a Global Economy*, Cambridge: Cambridge University Press, pp. 67–93.

Howells, J. (2002), 'Tacit knowledge, innovation and economic geography', *Urban Studies*, **39**, 871–84.

Keeble, D. and F. Wilkinson (eds) (2000), *High-Technology Clusters, Networking and Collective Learning in Europe*, Aldershot: Ashgate.

Kline, S.J. and N. Rosenberg (1986), 'An overview of innovation', in R. Landau and N. Rosenberg (eds), *The Positive Sum Strategy*, Washington DC: National Academy Press, pp. 275–305.

Koschatzky, K. (2000), 'A river is a river: cross-border networking between Baden and Alsace', *European Planning Studies*, **8**, 429–49.

Krätke, S. (1999), 'Regional integration or fragmentation? The German–Polish border region in a new Europe', *Regional Studies*, **33**, 631–41.

Lundvall, B.-Å. (ed.) (1992), *National Systems of Innovation: Towards a Theory of Innovation and Interactive Learning*, London: Pinter.

Lundvall, B.-Å. and S. Borrás (1999), 'The globalising learning economy: implications for innovation policy', Luxembourg: Office for Official Publications of the European Communities.

Lundvall, B.-Å. and S. Borrás (2005), 'Science, technology and innovation policy', in J. Fagerberg, D. Mowery and R. Nelson (eds), *The Oxford Handbook of Innovation*, Oxford: Oxford University Press, pp. 599–631.

Malerba, F. (2002), 'Sectoral systems of innovation and production', *Research Policy*, **31**, 247–64.

Maskell, P., H. Bathelt and A. Malmberg (2006), 'Building global knowledge pipelines: the role of temporary clusters', *European Planning Studies*, **14**, 997–1013.

Maskell, P. and G. Törnqvist (1999), *Building a Cross-Border Learning Region*, Copenhagen: Copenhagen Business School Press.

Morgan, K. (2004), 'The exaggerated death of geography: learning, proximity and territorial innovation systems', *Journal of Economic Geography*, **4**, 3–21.

Nauwelaers, C. and K. Morgan (1999), 'The new wave of innovation-oriented regional policies: retrospect and prospects', in K. Morgan and C. Nauwelaers (eds), *Regional Innovation Strategies: The Challenge for Less-Favoured Regions*, London: Stationery Office and Regional Studies Association, pp. 224–38.

Nauwelaers, C. and R. Wintjes (2003), 'Towards a new paradigma for innovation policy?', in B. Asheim, A. Isaksen, C. Nauwelaers and F. Tödtling (eds), *Regional Innovation Policy for Small-Medium Enterprises*, Cheltenham, UK and Northampton, MA, USA: Edward Elgar, pp. 193–220.

Nelson, R. (ed.) (1993), *National Innovation Systems: A Comparative Analysis*, Oxford: Oxford University Press.

Oinas, P. and E. Malecki (2002), 'The evolution of technologies in time and space: from national and regional to spatial innovation systems', *International Regional Science Review*, **25**, 102–31.

Paci, R. and S. Usai (2000), 'Technological enclaves and industrial districts: an analysis of the regional distribution of innovative activity in Europe', *Regional Studies*, **34**, 97–114.

Polanyi, M. (1966), *The Tacit Dimension*, London: Routledge.

Saxenian, A. (1994), *Regional Advantage: Culture and Competition in Silicon Valley and Route 128*, Cambridge, MA: Harvard University Press.

Scott, J. (1999), 'European and North American contexts for cross-border regionalism', *Regional Studies*, 33, 605–17.

Sternberg, R. (2007), 'Entrepreneurship, proximity and regional innovation systems', *Tijdschrift voor Economische en Sociale Geografie*, 98, 652–66.

Storper, M. (1997), *The Regional World*, New York: Guilford Press.

Storper, M. and A. Venables (2004), 'Buzz: face-to-face contact and the urban economy', *Journal of Economic Geography*, 4, 351–70.

Tödtling, F., P. Lehner and M. Trippl (2006), 'Innovation in knowledge intensive industries: the nature and geography of knowledge links', *European Planning Studies*, 14, 1035–58.

Tödtling, F. and M. Trippl (2005), 'One size fits all? Towards a differentiated regional innovation policy approach', *Research Policy*, 34, 1203–19.

Trippl, M. (2010), 'Developing cross-border regional innovation systems: key factors and challenges', *Tijdschrift voor economische en sociale geografie*, 101, 150–60.

Van Houtum, H. (1998), *The Development of Cross-Border Economic Relations*, Tilburg: Center for Economic Research.

Wickham, J. and A. Vecchi (2008), 'Local firms and global reach: business air travel and the Irish software cluster', *European Planning Studies*, 16, 693–710.

34 Intermediaries in regional innovation systems: role and challenges for policy
Claire Nauwelaers

INTRODUCTION

Even before the advent of the 2008 economic crisis, which highlighted the value of real assets based on economic activity, innovation has been continuously rising higher on policy agendas. Being innovative is nowadays clearly acknowledged as a necessity for companies and territories alike, not as a luxury. The slogan 'innovate or die' has found its way into policy circles and, in the period 1990–2010, innovation has been established as a new and legitimate policy domain. That trend is present at all levels of governance; the regional level has certainly not escaped this wave, as many contributions in this *Handbook* witness.

The history of innovation policies in European regions, although still young, already involves a large number of experiences, and new initiatives continue to accumulate on top of traditional ones, to form a rich body of evolving policy practices. Amongst these practices, the establishment of so-called innovation intermediaries is particularly popular at the regional level.

This rather fuzzy concept of regional innovation intermediaries covers in reality a wide diversity of specific organizations, established or supported by regional authorities, with the purpose to care for companies' needs for innovation. After a period characterized by an attitude of 'letting a thousand of flowers blossom', public authorities are faced today with an urgent need to optimize a system that has in most cases grown in a somewhat anarchic way, lacking strategic governance. In many regions, both individual and collective effectiveness of the set of regional intermediaries is being called into question. This creates a need for a better understanding of the role of these intermediaries, and of new tools for policy action in this respect.

This chapter aims at elucidating the role of intermediaries in a regional innovation system, and discusses the policy implications for regional authorities. It starts with a conceptual discussion, in order to confront the concept of innovation intermediaries with what we know about innovation and innovation systems. From this, requirements are derived for regional innovation policies in general, and for regional innovation intermediaries in particular. Then, I depict the current situation within European regions, providing an overview of the diversity of organizations involved, and of the range of questions raised around them. I illustrate the debate with an example of a region having established innovation intermediaries, and comment on its recent strategy to improve their effectiveness. The last section concludes with policy options for regional authorities contemplating the option of setting up intermediaries, or faced with the necessity to reform an existing set of intermediaries.

A CONCEPTUAL BACKGROUND FOR THE ROLE OF REGIONAL INNOVATION INTERMEDIARIES AND ITS POLICY IMPLICATIONS

Before discussing the subject of regional innovation intermediaries per se, it is necessary to define a conceptual framework under which to understand the functions of these bodies. This framework provides a reference for the role, mission, mode of operation, activities and expected impacts of regional innovation intermediaries. The proposed generic framework under which to discuss regional innovation intermediaries is that of the regional innovation system, within an evolutionary perspective. The concept is presented at length in other chapters of this *Handbook* (for example, Chapters 33 and 39) and it is thus not necessary to cover this here. However, it is useful to pinpoint in a nutshell the key elements which are particularly relevant to keep in mind for the following discussion on intermediaries.

The innovation system approach pictures innovation as a complex and uncertain process, has enterprise dynamics at its core, places a premium on interactions and learning between actors, and emphasizes the importance of institutions, formal and informal, for the generation, diffusion and use of knowledge. It incorporates the idea that firms do not innovate in isolation, but rather through interactions with other firms, with users and with their environment. Such a view differs substantially from the traditional linear view of innovation, seen as the final stage of a process starting with research and ending with commercial exploitation of research results. In the systemic view, the free and efficient flow of human, financial, technical and knowledge resources is a core determinant of innovation success. And innovation is essentially the result of market opportunities rather than a by-product of technical change. Within this enlarged view on innovation, non-technological and service innovations acquire a status as growth-enhancing strategies, along with the more acclaimed forms of technology-driven product and process innovations. Easy access for firms to new technology developments is only one element of the innovation puzzle: the capacity of people and organizations to use, transform, adapt and create value from technology gets a central role in innovation (systems) performance. User-driven innovation is also receiving more and more attention, especially in sectors strongly influenced by information technology (IT) developments. Furthermore, innovation is a dynamic process, and accumulation of resources, capabilities and learning over time plays an important role in today's innovation trajectories.

Innovativeness is thus determined both by factors which are internal to the firms and by 'systemic' factors, influencing the overall effectiveness of the innovation environment. Within firms, tacit knowledge and skills, learning-by-doing processes and networking capabilities are as important as access to codified information for innovation performance. This places a heavy accent on the differences between firms, and on the role of internal firm dynamics, on innovation management practices and the quality of human resources and skills. Proximity is a favourable factor to access and capitalize on the tacit dimension of knowledge. Outside firms, the broader economic, institutional, regulatory, cultural and social context has a deep influence on firm's attitudes and strategies towards innovation; the quality of social capital in a territory is a factor difficult to measure, but nevertheless crucial for firms' innovative capacity and performance. The idea of an innovation 'ecosystem' is gaining pace; this is a system in which all components are present in a balanced way and develop positive interactions, and in which firms in particular are engaged in networks of cooperators and competitors oriented towards innovation.

The above view means that innovation takes multiple forms, and can thrive in all sectors, from the traditional to the high-tech ones, and in industry as well as in services. The Pavitt taxonomy has been widely used to characterize the diversity of innovation patterns, even within a single industry. This taxonomy distinguishes between the following categories of firms (Pavitt, 1984):

- Science-based firms: mostly large firms, innovating in regular connection with the science base (universities, research centres) and owning their internal research and development (R&D) laboratories, often engaged in patenting. These firms are responsible for more than their share of radical product innovation.
- Scale-intensive firms: large firms for which innovation comes mainly from interactions with customers, and relying on tacit knowledge much more than codified knowledge such as patents or publications.
- Supplier-dominated firms: smaller firms, with few internal R&D capacities, involved in process innovations more frequently than in product innovations, and in imitation strategies rather than genuine innovation. For these firms, technical centres are preferred partners as sources of information for innovation.
- Specialized suppliers: small or medium-sized firms, connected with the science base but for which the innovation sources are mostly the customers, which combine internal and external sources of R&D.

Many different and more elaborated typologies have been proposed since this seminal contribution – notably to incorporate a new category of small, science-based spin-offs – and cannot be described here. The important point is that an adequate policy portfolio to be adopted for fostering innovation would be very different according to the types of firms addressed by the policy. In particular, the role of R&D performers and technology providers will only be prominent for science-based firms, and to a lesser extent, for supplier-dominated and specialized supplier firms. In addition, diversity in innovation 'ecosystems' and in informal institutions also explains why similar policies work differently in different contexts.

Within this framework, what is the role of public intervention in innovation at the regional level?[1] The objective of policy intervention moves from addressing a less than optimal allocation of resources, towards ensuring the overall coherence and balance of the innovation system and improving its evolution capacity. Systemic failure, or system dysfunctions, arguments are used in addition to classical market failure arguments to justify public action in innovation. This opens up possibilities for a broader range of intervention areas than the traditional interventions to fund public research (R&D subsidies, tax incentives and the various channels for funding public research organizations). However, the concept of systemic failures is less robust than that of market failures. Two approaches towards systemic failures are presented below as a reference for regional innovation policies.

Smith distinguishes between four types of system failures (Smith, 2000): (1) infrastructural provision failures, including science and technology (S&T) infrastructure: this links up to the traditional role of governments, filling gaps in public-goods provision;

(2) transition failures at firm level: this refers to the difficulties faced by firms to adapt to changing competitive environments; (3) lock-in failures at system level: this failure is typical in old industrialized regions, which face the need to restructure their productive fabric towards new activities, requiring new skills, networks, institutions and assets, representing an important move from existing specializations; and (4) institutional failures (covering formal and informal institutions): this type of failure incorporates a broad set of inadequacies in supporting institutions, regulations, culture, habits, and so on. The idea of 'learning and capability failures' could be added to this list, in line with the above arguments of the importance of learning for innovation.

Hekkert et al. (2007) provide a typology of seven functions to be delivered by an innovation system, which can be taken as an agenda for policies intending to address system failures:

- entrepreneurial activities, encompassing both new entrants and diversification strategies from incumbents;
- knowledge development, including R&D activities, 'learning-by-searching' and 'learning-by-doing' practices;
- knowledge diffusion through networks, aiming at fostering 'learning-by-interacting' and 'learning-by-using' in the case of user–producer networks;
- guidance of the search, which refers to the process of definition of priorities amongst the variety of available technological options;
- market formation, an important function when new technologies are developed, as these create a need for transition to new regimes and new usages;
- resources mobilization, mainly the provision of finance and human resources as necessary inputs in the innovation process;
- creation of legitimacy and counteracting resistance to change, which refer to the existence of interest groups advocating new technological paths.

When a regional system presents bottlenecks or malfunctions in one or several of those functions, and there is no response from private actors, the public actor is entitled to develop strategies and instruments to address them. The seven functions open new avenues for policy intervention such as support to entrepreneurship with the help of soft mechanisms (advice, networking, and so on), targeted policies focusing on specific technology areas or industrial domains, following a variety of selection processes (clusters, competitiveness poles, and so on), or helping to overcome various kinds of 'distances' among firms and organizations (institutional, cognitive, geographical; see Boschma 2005; also Boschma and Frenken, Chapter 14 in this *Handbook*) through intermediaries.

As developed amply elsewhere in this *Handbook*, the rationale for policies to act at the regional level concerns the exploitation of the advantages of proximity to exchange and foster tacit knowledge: geographic proximity favours collaboration and cooperation, and interactive learning. Those innovation processes which are based on learning-by-doing, or learning-by-interacting, those which rely on interactions with users, and those which capitalize on local specificities, will be facilitated by geographical (and cultural) proximity. Hence the role of territory-based innovation policies is to capitalize on this potential. But these new regional advantages need to be 'constructed', based on the identification, exploitation and reinforcement of existing strengths (Asheim et al., 2007; also Chapter 23 in this *Handbook*).

There are pitfalls, too, to be avoided when adopting a regional approach to innovation promotion: the main danger lies in the development of an autarkic framework for innovation policy and the incapacity to support future-oriented development paths due to lock-in problems. This danger is present when the 'lock-in' systemic failure is at play. Innovation today flourishes when companies and other organizations are open to the world and able to access and use resources from within but also from outside their immediate environment. Too much inbreeding, lack of openness to outside sources of knowledge and ideas, difficulties in escaping the inertia of existing specializations and power balances, might be further compounded by 'parochial' approches to innovation policy. Local and regional, as well as non-regional, knowledge flows and learning interactions should be combined in order to avoid the lock-in syndrome. The 'weaknesses of strong ties' (Granovetter, 1985) should be kept in mind in regional innovation policy deployment. Adopting an open perspective for regional innovation policy also demands vertical coordination between the various levels of policy intervention.

The above discussion on the variety of innovation forms underscores the necessity for policy-makers, when designing their regional innovation policies, to build up a detailed understanding of innovation resources, strategies and problems for the different categories of firms present in a regional innovation system, and of the overall functioning of the regional innovation 'ecosystem'. Because of the diversity in regional innovation systems, there is no one-size-fits-all policy that can be applied to any region (Tödtling and Trippl, 2005; also Chapter 33, this *Handbook*); rather, policies need to be adjusted to the composition of the industrial fabric, innovation culture and prevailing political system. The profile and strength of regional innovation policies is also determined by the degree of autonomy held by regional authorities, and shaped by national policies applied in the region.

Designing and implementing innovation policies at the regional level requires adequate strategic intelligence on the system features and on the effectiveness of the policy system. System analysis, benchmarking, evaluation, foresights, strategic learning platforms, and so on form part of the infrastructure needed for designing and running tailor-made systemic policies. In particular, the question of policy evaluation acquires an important role in this framework. Policy evaluation is essentially an effort to measure additionality of public action, that is, what difference that action makes with respect to a situation where no intervention takes place. While traditional evaluations measure input additionality (new R&D investments, for example) and output additionality (new research results, patents, publications, for example), in the new framework, behavioural additionality (in terms of new innovation culture, new collaboration patterns, change in companies' organization towards innovation, for example) comes under focus with more acute intensity in reference to the policy goals as elaborated above. Also, evaluations need to pay more attention to effectiveness than to efficiency, if the goal is to improve strategic learning for policy-makers and implementing agencies.

Table 34.1 summarizes the contrasted features of innovation within a traditional linear framework versus a systemic-evolutionary one, and applies these features to regional innovation intermediaries, discussing a variety of points such as their role, targets, types of instruments used, area of action, and the kind of strategic intelligence mechanisms needed to manage (networks of) intermediaries.

Looking at regional innovation intermediaries from the angle of an innovation

Table 34.1   *Rationale and features of regional innovation intermediaries within the old linear and new systemic innovation paradigm*

Issue for intermediaries	Old paradigm	New paradigm
Policy rationale		
Role of intermediary	Technology broker	Facilitator, node in the system, change agent
Rationale for intervention	Market failures	Systems failures, learning and capability failures, transition failures
Focus of innovation support		
Innovation definition as a basis for intervention	Innovation as exploitation of technological opportunities Technology-driven process and product innovations	Wider concept of innovation, market opportunities as key driving force Organizational and service innovations
Firms as targets of intermediaries	Access to science and technology resources	Firms' absorptive capacities Learning capability People, talent, competence, creativity
System targets of intermediaries	Industry–science relationships	Enhancing social capital, facilitating all linkages and flows in the system, addressing lock-ins
Learning channels for innovation	Research providers, industry–science relationships	Firm-to-firm interactions, firms networks, users, public–private partnerships Importance of innovation environment
Territorial concept		
Territory definition, area of action	Administrative boundaries; Local networks view	Functional definition; cross-border regions A node in global networks
Constructing regional advantages		
Specialization of intermediaries system	Specialization in existing activity areas	Frontrunner in future-oriented activities; based on identification and reinforcement of strengths in the system
Sector focus	Primacy to high-tech industry and high-tech activities	All sectors including services
Policy mixes		
Configuration of instruments	Activities and instruments defined for intermediaries taken in isolation	Portfolio of interacting and coordinated instruments ('policy mix')

Table 34.1   (continued)

Issue for intermediaries	Old paradigm	New paradigm
Policy coordination		
Organization of intervention	Fragmented intervention landscape – disconnected intermediaries	Policy coordination – horizontal (types of activities) and vertical (multilevel): intermediaries 'system'
Strategic intelligence		
Goal definition of intermediary system	Based on existing structures' activities Static	Problem-oriented Based on innovation system needs and features Agile
Evidence base for mission and activity definition	Heuristic methods to inform policy on firms innovative practice	Robust evidence base on innovation in various types of firms
Accountancy and control mechanisms	Administrative and financial	Strategic, performance-oriented, additionality a strategic issue
Evaluation focus	Single-intermediary focus	System focus: intermediary network
Evaluation questions	Input and output additionality Efficiency Evaluation as control mechanism	Behavioural additionality and learning capacity Effectiveness Evaluation as learning device

Source: Adapted from OECD (2009).

system implies important changes in orientation compared to the traditional linear approach. The points listed in Box 34.1 define a strategic agenda for regional innovation intermediaries.

Adopting such an agenda has important implications with respect to the management of such intermediaries by regional authorities. First, tools and instruments used by intermediaries need to be adapted to the type of firms targeted and innovation system specificities; differentiated targets should be set by intermediaries, by types of instruments and by target groups. Second, because there is no standardized model for intermediaries, the policy should be supported by strong monitoring, analysis and evaluation activities. Third, a large range and combination of skills and competencies needs to be secured within intermediaries to accomplish their mission. This combination of skills and activities can be achieved either by specialized bodies acting in coordination, to avoid fragmentation of support, or by internalization of diversified competencies within larger bodies or agencies. Whatever the form adopted, it is crucial to implement balanced and effective mixes of instruments, so that intermediaries form an efficient system.

The most difficult challenge for regional innovation intermediaries is perhaps not only to act as reactive innovation support, responding to identified innovation needs and

---

BOX 34.1   STRATEGIC AGENDA FOR REGIONAL INNOVATION INTERMEDIARIES

- Intermediaries have a broad mission to help ensure fluidity in the innovation system, rather than a narrow one defined as brokers between 'science' and 'industry'.
- They provide support for accessing and using all innovation factors and not only access to technology.
- They capitalize on proximity to carry out their mission, but also play an important role in opening actors across the system to opportunities and resources outside of the system.
- The quality of human resources and learning capability in the system is an important target for intermediaries.
- Firm-to-firm and user–producer interactions are recognized as privileged channels for innovation promotion, and intermediaries' activities are defined with this in mind.
- Besides the direct provision or the support for access to specific resources, they also address the change process, both at firm and at system level; they do respond to immediate needs but also act as change facilitators.

---

barriers, but also to be proactive in identifying latent needs and contributing to promote new innovative trajectories, fostering changes in the system.

REGIONAL INNOVATION INTERMEDIARIES AT WORK IN EUROPE

Establishing regional innovation intermediaries is in practice a main entry point for regional authorities involved in innovation policies in Europe. This generic label covers in reality a large variety of bodies, which share the following minimum common characteristics: they aim to support innovation in regional small and medium-sized enterprises (SMEs) (even if this is not necessarily their unique goal); their mission is defined on a territorial basis (corresponding in most cases to an administrative division of a country, which we refer to as 'region'); and they benefit from public support for at least part of their activity.

The main reasons for this focus of regional policy on innovation intermediaries are twofold. First, regional authorities hold competencies in territory-based economic development, and their level of intervention is better suited to deal with SMEs than with large firms: they have developed a natural focus on innovation promotion targeting SMEs, based on the exploitation of advantages of proximity. The justification for these interventions is linked to economic development purposes, in line with the definition of regional powers. Second, most regional authorities hold limited budgetary resources to intervene in the innovation domain; establishing costly resource centres is thus in practice out of reach for most of them, even with co-funding from other levels of government. Creating intermediary institutions with the aim to facilitate access to resource centres established by these other authorities (with other goals in mind than regional innovation promotion), is for them one affordable way to develop a support infrastructure for regional SMEs.

In European regions, in line with the rise in interest towards innovation as a new policy domain, one can witness a proliferation of innovation intermediaries, funded (at least partially) by regional and local authorities. This includes a wide diversity of organizations such as technology transfer centres, university liaison offices, business advisory bodies, technology or science parks, territorial agencies involved in innovation promotion and, more recently, networks or cluster management organizations.

The examination of real practice with respect to these intermediaries reveals that there is no commonly agreed definition of what kind of organizations fall within the concept of regional innovation intermediary. In some cases, the concept is quite restricted, for example to organizations with a technology transfer mission. In other cases, it encompasses a wide range of bodies with broader business support missions, and notably cluster-type organizations. The concept of 'intermediation' itself can take two meanings: either that of a 'window' from one organization, which provides access to resources from one parent organization only (such as a university liaison office); or that of a broker, which guides the recipient not only to in-house resources (if any) but also across the wider web of resources within the region or beyond.

A typical situation in European regions is that of a proliferation of organizations, whose individual missions are defined according to diverse rationales: subterritorial development, valorization of resources from a single research organization, technology diffusion, innovation coach, sector-specific innovation promotion, and so on. As a result, most regions are faced with the existence of a set of organizations established over time on their territory, providing a host of services on an individual basis, but often lacking clarity with respect to their individual missions and targets, and in most cases with only a very limited view on the overall coherence of the system, not to mention its effectiveness.

In this context, a number of exercises have been launched across European regions (notably under the European Regional Innovation and Technology Transfer Strategies – RITTS and Regional Innovation Strategies – RIS programmes), in order to improve the situation with respect to three core questions: (1) a mapping question: what are the boundaries and components of the regional intermediaries system (or network), and who does what? (2) a relevance question: how far do these intermediaries, and their system, respond to innovation needs; are there unmet needs or redundancies? and (3) a system efficiency question: how efficient is the set of intermediaries in reaching its overall goal (and the various subgoals)?

In the following pages, I briefly report on one such exercise: a system analysis in the Belgian region of Wallonia. This example is illustrative of a number of problems and challenges at stake with regional innovation intermediaries.

The Case of Regional Innovation Intermediaries in Wallonia

At the request of the regional government, an external evaluation of the intermediary system in Wallonia was conducted in 2004–05. The starting point of the endeavour was the concern that many intermediaries had been established over time in the region, were being funded under different mechanisms and for a large variety of missions, but that an overall view of the intermediaries landscape and activities was missing, as well as a judgement on their collective efficiency. A sizeable public budget was devoted to these intermediaries but the regional authority was lacking a view on the results of its action. The establishment of a list of all intermediaries at work in the region, along with a first sketch of their missions, proved to be a demanding exercise. The study adopted a systemic approach to assess, for the first time, the intermediary system as a whole, relating its activities to the needs of local companies. It aimed at analysing the relations between the supply of services and client firms, and assessed the extent to which the system was suited to firms' needs. Hence, the study covered the three above-mentioned core questions (mapping, relevance and efficiency).

The study consisted of different phases during which the following tasks were carried out. First, the needs of companies in terms of support services and their utilization of the intermediary system were analysed thanks to a survey of 300 companies based in the region. In parallel, a map of intermediaries was established, identifying their respective functions and the interactions between them. This was done thanks to in-depth interviews realized with 25 intermediary structures and a questionnaire sent to 50 of them. Then, the matching between the needs of enterprises and the supply of services was analysed on the basis of the two previous tasks. A final phase was dedicated to benchmark the Walloon experience with other relevant examples in Europe, focusing on a number of weaker points identified through the analysis.

The different phases of the study were conducted in close interaction with a steering group established to discuss and validate the results obtained. The steering group comprised the main stakeholders in the field of intermediation and regional innovation policy. This element proved to be essential in the subsequent integration of the findings of the evaluation into further policy choices.

The study delivered a number of findings, which caused a marked change in perspective in regional innovation policy thinking. Briefly stated, the findings of the evaluation pointed towards the need for a shift from a linear conception towards a systemic approach to innovation (from 'old' to 'new' paradigm, as expressed in Table 34.1).

The results of the evaluation included the following main points. First, the original notion of 'science and technology' intermediaries was rapidly extended on the basis of the SMEs' enquiries results: it appeared that their needs went far beyond access to scientific and technology resources, to encompass a larger set of innovation ingredients. Hence the conclusion pointed towards a role for intermediaries which goes beyond establishing relations between supply and demand of S&T services. The possibility to enlarge the offer of services also to cover needs in terms of non-technological, organizational and 'gradual' innovation (marketing, human resources management, finance) was evidenced, based on the firms' feedback. Second, the analysis highlighted that the region hosted different categories of enterprises, ranging from the less innovation-aware to the most technologically sophisticated, which require different types of interventions and have different expectations (as depicted in the pyramid in Figure 34.1). The analysis of effective targets groups reached by the set of intermediaries revealed that a main challenge of the Walloon intermediary system is to reach companies which are distant from the innovation process and help them reveal their latent demand in terms of innovation support services (category C). The system was in effect overserving the needs of the most

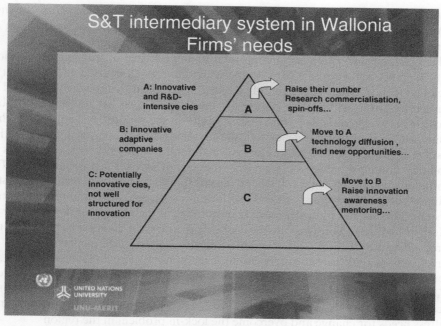

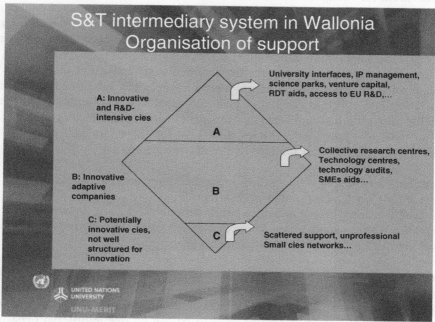

Source: UNU-MERIT.

Figure 34.1 Wallonia innovation system and strategy

advanced and technology-oriented companies (category A), and underserving the (more latent) needs of the companies which were involved in other types of innovation, and showing other types of support needs than access to technology.

A third challenge of this system concerned its high degree of fragmentation and its lack of coherence and visibility. Most of the structures are self-centred and there is a low degree of cooperation between them. Most of the intermediaries are inward-oriented and deliver services from within their parent organization. This is not so much a problem for those firms which are able to find their way within the support system, but for them, accessing resources directly is a possibility, thus diminishing the need for intermediary bodies. On the other hand, for those firms which are less aware of their own needs and possibilities, finding their way between the providers of services acting in isolation from each other is a cumbersome task. In short, intermediaries do not form a coherent system, exploiting synergies, avoiding gaps and overlaps, because there was no central piloting of the system. This caused a low degree of transparency of the system for its users.

A fourth challenge consisted in the lack of openness of intermediaries to outside resources: because of their inward-orientation, not only do intermediaries rarely seek resources outside their parent organization or the immediate regional environment, but they even more rarely investigate resources and partners outside of the regional borders. The fact that public funding of regional origin placed a premium on regional targets further compounded this lack of external openness. This creates a serious shortcoming to address needs for change and overcome the lock-in problem in the region.

A fifth result concerned the very role of this intermediary system and of public intervention for SMEs' innovation: the feedback of users (SMEs) pointed towards a limited role of the intermediary system as a whole, for innovation promotion. Private providers actually played a much more important role for providing the necessary resources, and interactions with firms appeared as the main stimulus for innovation. This fact, which is well known from innovation enquiries across Europe, was validated in this specific region. This is an important element to take into account when deciding about public funding for intermediaries, and when developing networks of intermediaries.

On the basis of these results, future directions for the intermediary system were explored. Four scenarios were retained by the steering group:

- establish a bundle of 'value-added' specialized innovation networks;
- establish a single generic entry point structure;
- establish a single specialized entry points structure;
- create a Walloon innovation intermediaries network, oriented towards technological innovation.

It has to be noted that integrating the technological and the non-technological intermediaries into a single network or structure could not be placed upfront amongst the policy options, mainly because of a fragmented governance structure, whereby a technology-oriented network would be have to be run by one ministerial department while the business-oriented network would belong to another department. The identified relevance of an integrated network or agency, offering both technological and non-technological services, was thus not immediately translated as a policy option because of institutional barriers, and inertia in the policy system.

The steering group chose the option which it considered most appropriate in the Walloon context, namely the fourth option, the creation of a Walloon network for technological innovation. This was implemented thanks to the following steps: establishment of a cental coordinating unit; joint work to define detailed missions and target groups of each network participant; setting up of a monitoring and assessment system; and implementation of performance-based funding arrangements. Despite the above-mentioned institutional barriers, over time, some providers of non-technological support such as training, or managerial advice, were integrated into the network. However, the various cluster and competitiveness poles initiatives are not considered as part of the intermediary system, while they have a clear potential to foster innovation-through-interactions. Hence, the concept of intermediaries in Wallonia is progressively moving, even if incompletely, from one of 'matching demand and supply of science and technology' towards a broader notion of innovation support, also involving managerial, human resources, financial, and so on. support. The objective of the network evolves from a linear task of 'pushing' science and technology from the public sector to companies, towards the circulation and co-generation of new knowledge by private and public organizations acting in synergy.

CONCLUSIONS AND POLICY CHALLENGES

Moving from an old towards a new paradigm of innovation has a lot of implications for regional innovation policies in general, and for the specific option of establishing regional innovation intermediaries, in particular. A new agenda for these policies has been presented in this chapter. The chapter has then briefly discussed, and illustrated through an example, the shape taken by these policies in European regions, and pinpointed the challenges they face. To sum up in this concluding section, I identify four major flaws in innovation policies as they are currently deployed in European regions, which place them at odds with the challenges to run a policy on regional innovation intermediaries.

First, and contrasting with the phenomenon of increased globalization of innovation processes, of value chains and of markets, regional innovation policies do generally exhibit an autarkic vision of innovation, confined to the regional boundaries. Policy instruments deployed at this level, and in particular (networks of) innovation intermediaries, often reveal a lack of attention to knowledge links between domestic and foreign firms, to the disintegration and integration of multinational corporations' (MNCs) and SMEs' productive activities over global value chains. They address regional firms on the basis of a location criterion and as single entities. European regions use, as a widespread type of intervention, the establishment and fine-tuning of innovation intermediary networks. As we have seen, these can take various forms, and usually consist of a set of organizations funded by the national, regional and sometimes local authorities, as well as complementary European Union (EU) funding (through the Structural Funds), which are active in the region. Approaches followed in this area suffer from a 'supply matching demand' syndrome: that is, regional intermediaries established in one region are seen as serving the needs of companies (mostly SMEs) established in that region, while there is no *a priori* reason to restrict the area of action of companies and support structures to regional boundaries.

Second, addressing the 'knowledge diffusion' function of a regional innovation system, regional authorities have endorsed various cluster, pole and 'local agglomeration' models to establish policies inspired by systemic thinking. Cluster-type organizations are playing an increasing role in innovation intermediaries systems, even if they are not necessarily recognized as such. The main goal of these instruments is to establish new linkages between various actors which together contribute to innovation processes. This generally encompasses various types of companies, of knowledge providers, training organizations, and intermediaries such as science parks and so on. A first difficulty appears with some of these policies when they are constrained by regional administrative borders, which is the case in particular for a number of cluster policies (see the previous argument). Regional support for innovative networks within regional boundaries may in certain cases still be relevant to increase local research and innovation dynamics; but especially regarding the exploitation of innovations, the bounded rationality of regional actors should be extended to international markets and (re)sources.

Another problem with clusters and network policies relates to the very goal of these strategies: when they are justified by arguments of static efficiency only (critical masses, access to a larger pool of resources, and so on), they may fail to address the entrepreneurial function of the system and the creation of new activities and new markets, that is, to act as change agents in the system. Hence it is critical that such policies are justified, designed and maintained on the basis of dynamic arguments: their potential to generate change, open new windows of opportunities and foster regional attractiveness. Static arguments for cluster policies and for intermediary systems can lead to dangerous strategies in the present context, as they might foster lock-in into dead-end activities, thus failing to act on these systemic failures.

Third, there is still a difficulty to implement a truly systemic approach in innovation policy-making. Technology-led development models persist, with notably a consequent neglect of creativity potential and organizational innovation as important dimensions of the innovation phenomenon. Regional innovation intermediaries (systems) still bear the mark of the earlier linear view on innovation, which is relevant for only a limited part of their target groups. Firm-to-firm interactions are not necessarily recognized as a priviledged channel for innovation. Combining technological and non-technological support is a difficulty, notably because of the rigidity in policy implementation agencies.

A fourth and final flaw relates to the governance of regional innovation policies. Analyses of current policy practices throughout European regions show that there is path-dependency and inertia in policy systems, which prevent swift adaptation to changes and to new challenges. This is caused by a significant amount of policy lock-in, combined with risk-adverse behaviour of regional innovation policy-makers. Regional policy-makers in Europe often manage policy portfolios, the balance of which is essentially determined by the weight of instruments which have been successful in the past. A first problem with this lies in the way in which success of a policy instrument is determined: often absorption of funds is taken as a measure of success. This is clearly insufficient to assess whether the range of instruments available contribute to policy objectives or not. A second problem is that while the composition of a policy portfolio is the product of an accumulation of instruments over time, each of them addressing a particular actor or objective, the interaction between policy instruments and the final combined effect of these instruments on the system as a whole are not taken into account.

That problem is particularly visible in the specific case examined in this chapter, that of regional innovation intermediaries, which are the product of a rather long history.

To sum up, contemporary regional innovation policies in Europe, despite the existence of a growing number of strategic exercises towards more efficient policy-making,[2] still suffer from autarkic approaches, difficulty in fostering changes in the system (as opposed to maintaining an existing system), a lack of systemic approach and deficiencies in strategic management. Those flaws are clearly visible when implementing regional innovation intermediary policies, a core type of intervention for regions in the innovation domain.

NOTES

1. See, notably, Borras and Lundvall (2004), Nauwelaers and Wintjes (2003, 2008).
2. Cf. EU-initiated RITTS and RIS exercises, and a large number of specific interregional projects focused on policy learning.

REFERENCES

Asheim, B., L. Coenen, J. Moodysson and J. Vang (2007), 'Constructing knowledge-based regional advantage: implications for regional innovation policy', *International Journal of Entrepreneurship and Innovation Management*, **7** (2–5), 140–55.

Borras, S. and B.-Å. Lundvall (2004), 'Science, technology and innovation policy', in J. Fagerberg, D. Mowery and R. Nelson (eds), *The Oxford Handbook of Innovation*, Oxford: Oxford University Press, pp. 19–34.

Boschma, R.A. (2005), 'Proximity and innovation: a critical assessment', *Regional Studies*, **39** (1), 61–74.

Granovetter, M. (1985), 'Economic action and social structure: the problem of embeddedness', *American Journal of Sociology*, **91** (November), 481–510.

Hekkert, M.P., R.A. Suurs, S.O. Negro, S. Kuhlmann and R.E. Smits (2007), 'Functions of innovation systems: a new approach for analysing technological change', *Technological Forecasting and Social Change*, **74** (4), 413–32.

Nauwelaers, C. and R. Wintjes (2003), 'Towards a new paradigm for innovation policies?', in B. Asheim, A. Isaksen, C. Nauwelaers and F. Tödtling (eds), *Regional Innovation Policy for Small–Medium Enterprises*, Cheltenham, UK and Northampton, MA, USA: Edward Elgar, pp. 120–32.

Nauwelaers, C. and R. Wintjes (eds) (2008), *Innovation Policy in Europe*, Cheltenham, UK and Northampton, MA, USA: Edward Elgar.

OECD (2009), *Governance of Regional Innovation Policy: Variety, Role and Impact of Regional Agencies Addressing Innovation (RAIs)*, forthcoming, Paris: OECD.

Pavitt, K. (1984), 'Sectoral patterns of technical change: towards a taxonomy and a theory', *Research Policy*, **13**, 343–73.

Smith, K. (2000), 'Economic infrastructures and innovation systems', in C. Edquist (ed.), *Systems of Innovation: Technologies, Institutions and Organisations*, London: Cassel.

Tödtling, F. and M. Trippl (2005), 'One size fits all? Towards a differentiated regional innovation policy approach', *Research Policy*, **34** (8), 1203–19.

35 Regional entrepreneurship
Niels Bosma, Veronique Schutjens and Erik Stam

INTRODUCTION

Many studies have shown that the occurrences of new entrepreneurial activities are une-venly spread across regions (Reynolds et al., 1994; Stam, 2005; Bosma et al., 2009). Such regional heterogeneity in entrepreneurship exerts a direct effect on regional economic development. But there are also indirect effects at play within the nexus of geography, entrepreneurship and growth: regional circumstances affect not only the intensity of new entrepreneurial activities but also the extent to which entrepreneurship interacts and interplays with regional innovation – towards regional economic growth. Understanding the mechanisms that cause regional heterogeneity in new entrepreneurial activities is thus of crucial importance for making the link with innovation and regional growth.

In this chapter we provide an overview of empirical studies on the geography of entre-preneurship, or in other words, the geographies of distinct types of new entrepreneur-ship. A focus on entrepreneurship means a focus on structure and agency; it is about individuals who identify, evaluate and exploit entrepreneurial opportunities within certain structures, while at the same time influencing these structures. These structures have spatial aspects, which are reflected in, for example, localization and urbanization (dis)economies, region-specific institutions, the organization of industries in regions, and the regional availability of production factors.

While we emphasize conditions of regional variations in distinct types of entrepre-neurship, we start this chapter by briefly assessing, from a geographical perspective, the alleged consequences of entrepreneurship in terms of economic growth. We then proceed by discussing the main conditions underlying regional differences in entrepreneurial activity.

LINKING ENTREPRENEURSHIP TO INNOVATION AND ECONOMIC GROWTH

Entrepreneurship affects economic growth via a number of mechanisms: variety, compe-tition and imitation (Wennekers and Thurik, 1999). These mechanisms entail a direct and an indirect component, as increasing firm entry also affects the economic performance and behaviour of rival incumbent firms.

Economic growth implies change and adaptation, and much of this adaptation takes place through the formation of firms that are, at least initially, small. New firms are useful devices for innovation, because they can be established at a small, experimental scale at relatively low cost, and their efforts can be intensively focused on a single innovation. The experimental and innovative aspect of new firms is reflected in the facts that they usually start small, their number is large, and as with other kinds of experimentation, most of them fail. High rates of firm entry and exit can even be regarded as a necessary price to pay in order to allow 'exploration' of new technological and market possibilities: failures at the micro level may be consistent with social benefit at the aggregate level (see March, 1991; Saxenian, 1994; Dosi and Lovallo, 1998). In short, although a large part of economic change is fuelled by the expansion and conversion of old firms, innovative change is to a large degree brought about by new firms (see Rosenberg and Birdzell, 1986). That small firms have played a large part in economic growth is not accidental; it can be explained, at least in part, by their smaller agency costs, in addition to their special suitability to the experimental stage of innovation. New firms often provide the seedbed for the emergence of new industries. A high level of new variety is needed to produce a few very successful new innovative industry leaders, like Microsoft, Google and Facebook. According to Pasinetti (1993), an economy that does not increase the variety of industries over time will suffer from structural unemployment, and will ultimately stagnate. In this view, the development of new industries in an economy is required to absorb labour that has become redundant in pre-existing industries. This labour has become redundant due to a combination of productivity increases and demand saturation in pre-existing industries, characterizing the product life-cycle dynamics in each sector.

Through a process of competition, firms with new products make firms with old products redundant; firms with more efficient modes of production push less-efficient producers out of the market. By introducing new products and methods of production and distribution, new firms directly enhance economic growth. In addition they play an important indirect role in triggering old firms to improve or restructure their activities (with liquidation as the sanction). This (potential) entry of firms acts as a disciplinary device for existing firms. New innovative firms circumvent bureaucratic rigidity and supply older firms with an incentive – self-preservation – for taking internal measures to avoid the habits and practices that eventually lead to rigidity. This competition has a positive effect on regional productivity levels (Bosma et al., 2011a).

Imitation entails the diffusion of existing products and practices to new contexts. The contexts may be explicitly geographic, such as introducing existing products in a different country or region. New contexts may also include a different consumer audience. For example an existing product, thus far only consumed by a small group of trend-watchers, may be disposed to a wider audience for a lower price. However, new producers entering the market by imitating successful innovations challenge the monopolistic position of the innovator and decrease the 'first-mover advantages'. This limits the innovator's rewards, which may even discourage innovative behaviour. It should be noted that for innovation to fuel economic growth, dissemination of innovative products and processes and their adoption by imitators is crucial (Baumol, 2004).

As for many people entrepreneurship is a risky business in a dangerous environment, imitative entrepreneurs outnumber innovative ones by far. This means that for empirically assessing the economic impact of entrepreneurship on any spatial level, this variation in entrepreneurship types should be taken into account. The great majority of the set of empirical studies that linked entrepreneurship to growth did not make distinctions between different types of entrepreneurship, or even broadened the definition to include all business owners. Now that data on entrepreneurship has become increasingly available, more sophisticated analyses are emerging showing that the degree of the impact of entrepreneurship on economic growth depends on: (1) the types of entrepreneurship considered (Wong et al., 2005; Bosma, 2011; Koellinger and Thurik, 2009); and (2) the regional context (see for example Bosma et al., 2011a; Fritsch and Schroeter, 2011). With this in mind, we now turn towards a taxonomy of the regional conditions of entrepreneurship.

REGIONAL CONDITIONS OF ENTREPRENEURSHIP

Entrepreneurship is the result of the interaction between individual actors and the surrounding environment. Still, the step to start a firm intrinsically involves an individual decision. Therefore, regional variations in entrepreneurship can be the result of two groups of factors: compositional factors, reflecting a regional over- or underrepresentation of 'entrepreneurial' population groups; and contextual factors, mainly place-specific characteristics influencing the individual entrepreneurial decisions.

Compositional Factors: An Uneven Spatial Distribution of (Potential) Entrepreneurs

We can start the explanation of regional differences in entrepreneurship by looking at the availability of (potential) entrepreneurs in particular places. Conceptually, the entrepreneurial process involves opportunity identification and exploitation (Shane and Venkataraman, 2000). Some people are more perceptive with regard to either or both elements, for instance because they possess more general or specific human capital than others. Bosma et al. (2009) show that personal characteristics such as age, education level and household income strongly contribute to the explanation of the odds of becoming an entrepreneur. Relatively high urban entrepreneurship rates can therefore be an effect of population composition, as urbanized areas are often concentrations of educated individuals with business experience in their early and middle adult years, and in that way they are a source of entrepreneurs (Glaeser, 2007). But the regional composition of corresponding population characteristics is only part of the reason why regional start-up rates vary. The other part is related to the strong inclination for entrepreneurs to locate their business in their home region. For nascent entrepreneurs the focal choice is what kind of firm to start, given their location, not so much choosing a location for a given firm (Stam, 2005). The fraction of entrepreneurs working in the region where they were born is significantly higher than the corresponding fraction for dependent workers (Michelacci and Silva, 2007). A study of Portuguese manufacturing firms found that entrepreneurs were willing to accept labour costs three times higher than in alternative locations to locate the new business in their current region (Figueiredo et al., 2002). The tendency to stay put, especially among (new) entrepreneurs, establishes the strong relation between regional population composition and regional entrepreneurship rates.

There are good reasons for the locational inertia of entrepreneurs, that all relate to the fact that the process of starting a new firm is eminently social. In other words, entrepreneurs are hardly lone individuals who rely primarily on their individually extraordinary efforts and talents to overcome the difficulties inherent to the formation of a new firm. They need other people. A first reason is the possibility to use their existing (local) network to seek partners, employees, suppliers, customers, advisors and investors (Zander, 2004; Michelacci and Silva, 2007). This decreases search costs, but it also permits them to build upon credibility and trust developed in past relationships. As the social ties of the potential entrepreneurs are likely to be localized, this induces entrepreneurs to start their firm in close proximity to their homes and to their current or former employers (Cooper and Folta, 2000; Sorenson, 2005; Stam, 2005; Parwada, 2008; see also Boschma and Frenken, Chapter 14 of this *Handbook*). The behavioural matrix of Pred (1967) is relevant here, as locational inertia can also be explained by imperfect information about alternative locations and/or limited cognitive abilities to process all information available (cf. Simon, 1957 on bounded rationality).

A second reason is of a more normative nature, as some personal relationships involve more than rational instrumental motivations, and continuing these relationships might only be possible when the entrepreneur stays within the region. Dahl and Sorenson (2009) conclude, in their empirical study of Danish entrepreneurs, that entrepreneurs appear to value proximity to family and friends not for the help that those connections might offer to their ventures, but for emotional reasons.

A third reason for locating the new firm in the home region is that entrepreneurs can start on a part-time basis (often being home-based) and delay full-time commitment until the venture seems sufficiently promising (on part-time entry as a real option strategy, see Wennberg et al., 2010). Also, locating the new firm close to home enables a spouse to keep his or her job so that income continues to flow to the family; other aspects of a founder's life can remain the same (Hanson, 2003), and the full energies of the entrepreneur can then be devoted to start-up.

Contextual Factors Influencing the Individual Entrepreneurial Decision

A broad range of relevant contextual factors explaining entrepreneurship can be identified. These factors outside the individual entrepreneur emerge from distinct perspectives, such as the nature and number of organizations in a region, the regional culture, the regional labour market structure or the employment opportunities in a region. Thus, while acknowledging that the key elements for entrepreneurship are the resources, abilities and preferences of individuals, the categorization below concerns the contextual factors. We consider the types of environment in which some individuals are more likely to start a firm than in another environment.

Entrepreneurship as a social (family) phenomenon

The positive effect of self-employed parents on the decision of their offspring to become self-employed has been confirmed in empirical research in many periods and in many places. This effect might be driven by four distinct mechanisms: a human capital effect (children learning entrepreneurial skills); a social capital effect (parents providing knowledge and other resources for their children's business); a cognitive role model effect (the entrepreneurial option is more obvious for children of self-employed parents); and a business inheritance effect (children inheriting their parent's business) (see Aldrich and Kim, 2007). This makes intergenerational transmission of self-employment an important explanation for spatial differences in self-employment (Vaillant and Lafuente, 2007), because of the locational inertia of most individuals' housing careers.

Entrepreneurship as an organizational product

Although some individuals become successful entrepreneurs without related prior experience, they are the exception rather than the rule. Entrepreneurs are often organizational products, that is, they spin-off a firm from their previous employer (Audia and Rider, 2005; Klepper, 2001). Many entrepreneurs are characterized by 'sectoral inertia': that is, they start their firm in an industry with which they are already familiar (Johnson and Cathcart, 1979; Storey, 1982; Lloyd and Mason, 1984; Vivarelli, 1991). Far from being an open choice, entrepreneurial action is relatively constrained: instead of looking around to seek the most profitable opportunity, the potential entrepreneur concentrates his or her attention on a familiar sector (Vivarelli, 1991). A person working in an industry is more likely to identify a market gap than a person without any industry experience (O'Farrell and Crouchley, 1984), irrespective of the degree of industry competition and growth prospects (Storey, 1982).

This prior experience (Shane, 2000), and personal networks, are likely to be acquired during the entrepreneur's career in existing organizations (Agarwal et al., 2004; Gompers et al., 2005; Klepper, 2001). This explains why the nature and number of organizations in a region are important determinants of entrepreneurship in a region. There is now convincing empirical evidence that spin-offs inherit knowledge from their parents that shapes their nature at birth and even their survival chances (Klepper, 2001, 2002, 2007; Klepper and Simons, 2000; Klepper and Sleeper, 2005; Buenstorf and Klepper, 2004; see also Helfat and Lieberman, 2002; Agarwal et al., 2004; Dahl et al., 2003; Buenstorf and Fornahl, 2009).

Empirical research has shown that regions dominated by small and/or young firms have relatively high new firm formation rates (Johnson and Cathcart, 1979; Reynolds et al., 1994; Mason, 1991; Audretsch and Fritsch, 1994; Mueller, 2006), and that people who work for small and young firms are more likely to become entrepreneurs (Sorenson, 2005). This stylized fact may be caused by several mechanisms: experiential learning, vicarious learning, self-selection of risk-prone workers, competition, and entry barriers. The latter two mechanisms will be discussed in the next section on the nature and localization of industries. In this subsection we will discuss experiential learning as well as vicarious learning (peer effects). The greater the proportion of an industry's labour force with direct experience of working in smaller firms, the more widespread the propensity for self-employment and hence the greater the propensity to start a new firm. Industries dominated by large plants would be expected to perform poorly as incubators of new business founders (Gudgin, 1978, 211–12; Johnson and Cathcart, 1979). In particular, young organizations that were once venture capital-backed, that focused on one segment, and whose growth has slowed, have high 'entrepreneurial spawning' levels (Gompers et al., 2005). Next to direct, experiential learning (learning how to set up and grow a business) peer effects are also important here. A study by Nanda and Sørenson (2010) showed that an individual is more likely to become an entrepreneur if his or her co-workers have been entrepreneurs before. They argue that peers matter in two ways for entrepreneurship: by structuring co-workers' access to information and resources that help identify entrepreneurial opportunities; and by influencing co-workers' perceptions about entrepreneurship as a career choice. The self-selection effect refers to individuals with particular risk preferences being more likely to choose to work for small firms and to engage in entrepreneurship at different stages of their lives (Parker, 2009).

Nature and localization of industries

Regional variations in new firm formation rates can be explained by differences in the regional composition of industries[1] and by differences in one particular industry in specific regions. The industry structure of a region affects the overall new firm formation rates in a region, as industries differ in their degree of contestability (entry barriers; Baumol et al., 1982) and the extent to which entrepreneurial opportunities emerge (for example many in business services and few in mining). Sometimes both the industry structure and the regional context are favourable for new firm formation in a particular region; this can for example be found in the South East of the UK, which has both a favourable industry mix (especially construction, services, and finance and related sectors) and favourable local conditions. In contrast, regions like Northern Ireland, Scotland and Wales suffer from a combination of both an unfavourable industry mix and unfavourable local conditions for new firm formation. Often the industry mix component dominates the local conditions component in statistical analyses of determinants of regional firm formation rates (Fotopoulos and Spence, 2001).

Several mechanisms related to the industry structure can be at work in a region, that produce something that academics and policy-makers like to call a cluster (Martin and Sunley, 2001). Two important concepts connected to clusters are localization economies and related variety. The first concept has a long history in the academic literature (Marshall, 1890; Hoover, 1948; Chinitz, 1961; Malmberg and Maskell, 2002), while the second has only recently been recognized in evolutionary economics (Frenken et al., 2007) and organizational ecology (Audia et al., 2006).

Localization economies involves agglomeration economies resulting from the concentration of the same or similar activities; for example benefits resulting from the local access to a specialized work force or the specialized reputation of a locality. Related variety emphasizes the positive effects (on entrepreneurship, innovation) of the co-presence of different but related industries or organizational populations. Regions that have a concentration of organizations of a certain kind (in a specific industry) tend to generate a relatively large number of new organizations of that same kind. This pattern has been shown for industries in general, and for specific industries like footwear (Sorenson and Audia, 2000), accounting (Cattani et al., 2004), biotechnology (Stuart and Sorenson, 2003), computer workstations (Sorenson, 2005), motorcycles (Wezel, 2005).

There are several reasons why industrial clusters foster entrepreneurship (Audia and Rider, 2005; Rocha, 2004). Clusters provide established relationships and better information about opportunities. They open up niches of specialization due to the low degree of vertical integration. Clusters foster a competitive climate and strong rivalry among firms that impose pressure to innovate due to the presence of close competitors. They provide role models with the presence of other firms that have made it (see Fornahl, 2003; Vaillant and Lafuente, 2007; Bosma et al., 2011b), and a cultural environment where establishing one's own business is normal and failure is not a social stigma. Clusters provide access to physical, financial and commercial infrastructure, easing the spin-offs of new companies from existing ones. Potential entrants will know how the local industry functions while having the technical skills to operate in it.

Industry localization may have negative effects on new firm formation: increased concentration and vertical integration raise entry barriers (Beesley and Hamilton, 1994). A shift in the direction of the effect of localization on new firm formation might be explained by the life-cycle stage of the industry: in the early stages geographical concentration has positive effects (or is even driven by new firm formation; see Feldman and Francis, 2003; Feldman et al., 2005), while in late stages (stagnant or even declining markets, and increased relevance of scale economies) the negative effects dominate. Spatial concentrations of activities in mature industries might still have high new firm formation rates, but high levels of competition lower the performance of these entrants (Sorenson and Audia, 2000). This means that there is still industry localization, but there are no localization economies any more.

Urbanization
Urban areas have important advantages for entrepreneurship (Reynolds et al., 1994; Wagner and Sternberg, 2004; Acs et al., 2003). Urban density leads to thick product, labour and real estate markets, and provides many opportunities for human interaction. The classical 'incubation hypothesis' in urban economics states that persons aspiring to go into production on a small scale have found themselves less obviously barred by a high cost structure at the centre of the urban area than at the periphery (Hoover and Vernon, 1959, 47; Chinitz, 1961; Dumais et al., 1997). In addition, cities provide contexts in which serendipitous meetings are more likely to occur than in less densely populated areas (Jacobs, 1969); these serendipitous meetings increase the likelihood of new opportunities and collaborations that might trigger the emergence of a new firm. Urban density also improves the likelihood of getting into contact with more skilled individuals in the same or related knowledge domains; learning from these more skilled peers stimulates human capital accumulation in urban environments (Glaeser, 2000) and might lead to the creation and recognition of better-quality entrepreneurial opportunities. The risks attached to starting a business are also relatively low in urban areas due to the abundant employment opportunities, which function as an occupational buffer for the entrepreneur when the firm fails. Urban areas also have important advantages for the demand for entrepreneurship (especially in retailing), as they contain demand for a rich variety of services and consumer goods (cf. Glaeser, 2007). Urbanization positively affects diversification of consumer demand. This latter phenomenon is central in flexible specialization theory (Piore and Sabel, 1984), which explains such trends in terms of the break-up of the mass market for standardized goods and services and the consequent emergence of a variety of smaller niche markets capable of exploitation by new or small businesses. This diversification is, next to urbanization, also directly driven by growth in overall demand.

Regional culture
Culture is important in the explanation of spatial variation in entrepreneurship via its effect on the attitude and values that people acquire. Social psychologists have claimed that an individual's attitudes and traits are not inherited but are developed in interaction with the social environment. Perceptions about the desirability of becoming an entrepreneur are formed and revised, given the set of information available to each person (Lafuente and Salas, 1989; Saxenian, 1990). Culture is a property of groups, and it seems that especially national (Uhlaner and Thurik, 2007), and to a lesser degree regional cultures (Davidsson and Wiklund, 1997) have significant effects on new firm formation. These cultures can change over time, but they tend to be very persistent (Beugelsdijk, 2007).

The existence of a number of entrepreneurs in a region also legitimizes the activities of nascent entrepreneurs. Differences in culture in that way affect the level to which people aspire and think about becoming an entrepreneur, which is an important phase in the process of starting a firm. One example of this is the fear of failure that might deter people from starting a new firm (Arenius and Minniti, 2005; Vaillant and Lafuente, 2007). Cognitive theories have proposed that individuals acquire information and skills by observation of (entrepreneurial) activities by others, which might trigger and enable their choice for an entrepreneurial career (Forbes, 1999; Zander, 2004).[2]

Regional knowledge production

Universities, research centres and other knowledge-intensive organizations produce new scientific and technological knowledge, which is an important source of entrepreneurial opportunities, especially in high-tech industries (Audretsch et al., 2006). Often these organizations are not fully able to recognize and appropriate the ensuing opportunities to commercialize that knowledge. Knowledge workers in these organizations respond to opportunities generated by new knowledge with starting a new firm, and in this way appropriate the expected value of their endowment of knowledge (Acs et al., 2003; Audretsch et al., 2006; Zucker et al., 1998; Feldman, 2001).[3] Geographic proximity to these sources of new knowledge is an asset, if not a prerequisite, to entrepreneurial firms in accessing and absorbing spillovers from universities and research centres (Audretsch et al., 2006). The most relevant spatial scale where these spillovers take place is not clear, as these knowledge spillovers are said to extend up to approximately 10 km (6 miles) (Baldwin et al., 2008), 50 miles (Anselin et al., 1997), 75 miles (Varga, 1998), 145 miles (Woodward et al., 2006) or even 300 km (185 miles) from their source of origin (Bottazzi and Peri, 2003). The temporal scale on which these processes take place might also range from a few months to several decades: major breakthrough inventions like the discovery of the DNA were followed by substantial entrepreneurial activity only decades later (and often in other places than the context of invention: Cambridge, UK in this instance). The creation of embodied knowledge is another example of a mechanism (through education and learning-by-doing) that generally takes multiple years and may sort out effects in multiple locations.

Regional access to financial capital

Liquidity constraints are an important factor preventing entrepreneurs from realizing their business opportunities (Holtz-Eakin et al., 1994). This is especially relevant for large new firms that require relatively large-scale investments for their initial activities. Small-scale firms can often be financed with bank loans or the support of the entrepreneur's family and friends. The entrepreneur's own home is shown to be the single most important source of collateral for bank loans. Indirectly, fluctuations in the local housing market could thus affect the availability of financial capital for new firms. New firms that require large-scale investments are more likely to enter the venture capital market. Providers of venture capital provide not only financial capital, but also knowledge of developing a business (in a particular industry). The uneven regional distribution of venture capital, means that in regions far away from the centres of venture capital, entrepreneurs might be discouraged from start capital-intensive firms. The assumption is that spatial proximity may be necessary for the formation of a venture capital relationship and that it makes monitoring of investments easier. Face-to-face contacts between the entrepreneur and the venture capital provider are necessary to identify the value of the new business and the involvement in business affairs by the venture capital provider. These contacts are hard to initiate and sustain over a large distance (Mason and Harrison, 2002; Stuart and Sorenson, 2003). Recent evidence shows that most of these contacts cannot easily be maintained over a longer distance via telecommunication; this can be used as a complement to face-to-face contacts, not as a substitute (Fritsch and Schilder, 2008).

CONCLUSION: REGIONAL ENTREPRENEURSHIP AND INNOVATION

In this chapter we have discussed the mechanisms through which entrepreneurship leads to economic growth, namely competition and selection, and variety and imitation. Next, we have provided a review of the factors explaining regional variations in entrepreneurship. These factors can be divided into compositional factors and contextual factors. Entrepreneurship concerns the interaction of particular individuals with their environment. Certain personal characteristics are connected to entrepreneurial behaviour, which means that the characteristics of the regional population, that is, the composition of a region, is an important factor in explaining regional variations in entrepreneurship. The entrepreneurial behaviour of individuals is also conditioned by their environment, ranging from their family context, to their organizational context, localization and urbanization (dis)economies, the cultural context, and access to knowledge and capital.

Regional compositional and contextual factors have a different impact on imitative entrepreneurship than on innovative entrepreneurship. Based on a large-scale study on adults in European regions, Bosma et al. (2009) show that young people, highly educated people and people with high incomes are more prone than others to have innovative ambitions in starting a firm. At the regional level, this means that an over-representation of these population groups may increase innovative entrepreneurship rates, which might eventually trigger regional economic growth in later stages. When all individual characteristics are taken into account, it seems that imitative entrepreneurship is more sensitive to regional conditions (like entrepreneurial culture and labour market conditions) than innovative entrepreneurship. The decision to start a firm is an individual one; but the ambition regarding innovation is an even more personal decision, involving courage, vision and particular personality characteristics, and being less sensitive to regional conditions than imitative entrepreneurship (Bosma et al., 2009).

NOTES

1. The regional composition of industries in itself might be thought of as a composition rather than a context effect. In line with this, Glaeser (2007) found that industry mix and demographic composition – age (older) and education (skilled) – are the most important determinants of the heterogeneity in self-employment rates across space.
2. See also the subsections above on 'Entrepreneurship as a social (family) phenomenon' and 'Entrepreneurship as an organizational product'.
3. A strong science base is not a sufficient condition for an entrepreneurial region to occur. There are multiple

regions where a strong scientific base has failed to spawn entrepreneurship – for example Ithaca (Cornell) and New Haven (Yale) – due to a lack of regional knowledge transfer.

REFERENCES

Acs, Z.J., D.B. Audretsch, P. Braunerhjelm and B. Carlsson (2003), *The Missing Link: The Knowledge Filter and Endogenous Growth*, Stockholm: Center for Business and Policy Studies.

Agarwal, R., R. Echambadi, A.M. Franco and M.B. Sarkar (2004), 'Knowledge transfer through inheritance: spin-out generation, development and survival, *Academy of Management Journal*, **47** (4), 501–22.

Aldrich, H. and P. Kim (2007), 'Small worlds, infinite possibilities? How social networks affect entrepreneurial team formation and search', *Strategic Entrepreneurship Journal*, **1**, 147–65.

Anselin, L., A. Varga and Z.J. Acs (1997), 'Local geographic spillovers between university research and high technology innovations', *Journal of Urban Economics*, **42** (3), 422–48.

Arenius, P. and M. Minniti (2005), 'Perceptual variables and nascent entrepreneurship', *Small Business Economics*, **24**, 233–47.

Audia, P. and C. Rider (2005), 'Entrepreneurs as organisation products revisited,' in J.R. Baum, M. Frese and R. Baron (eds), *The Psychology of Entrepreneurship*. Hillsdale, NJ: Lawrence Erlbaum Associates, pp. 259–76.

Audia P.G., O. Sorenson and J. Hage (2006), 'Tradeoffs in the organization of production: multiunit firms, geographic dispersion, and organizational learning', *Advances in Strategic Management*, **18**, 75–105.

Audretsch, D.B. and M. Fritsch (1994), 'On the measurement of entry rates', *Empirica*, **21**, 105–13.

Audretsch, D.B., M.C. Keilbach and E.E. Lehmann (2006), *Entrepreneurship and Economic Growth*, Oxford: Oxford University Press.

Baldwin, J.R., D. Beckstead, W.M. Brown and D.L. Rigby (2008), 'Agglomeration and the geography of localization economies in Canada', *Regional Studies*, **42** (1), 117–32.

Baumol, W.J. (2004), 'Four sources of innovation and stimulation of growth in the Dutch economy', *De Economist*, **152** (3), 321–51.

Baumol, W.J., J.C. Panzar and R.D. Willig (1982), *Contestable Markets and the Theory of Industry Structure*, San Diego, CA: Harcourt Brace Jovanovich.

Beesley, M.E. and T.T. Hamilton (1994), 'Entry propensity, the supply of entrants and the spatial distribution of business units', *Regional Studies*, **28** (3), 233–9.

Beugelsdijk, S. (2007), 'Entrepreneurial culture, regional innovativeness and economic growth', *Journal of Evolutionary Economics*, **17** (2), 187–210.

Bosma, N.S. (2011), 'Entrepreneurship, urbanization economies and productivity of European regions', in M.F. Fritsch (ed.), *Handbook of Research on Entrepreneurship and Regional Development*, Cheltenham, UK and Northampton, MA, USA: Edward Elgar, forthcoming.

Bosma, N.S., V.A.J.M. Schutjens and E. Stam (2009), 'Entrepreneurship in European regions: implications for public policy', in J. Leitao and R. Baptista (eds), *Public Policies for Fostering Entrepreneurship*, New York: Springer, pp. 129–46.

Bosma, N., E. Stam and V.A.J.M. Schutjens (2011a), 'Creative destruction and regional productivity growth: evidence from the Dutch manufacturing and services industries', *Small Business Economics*, **36** (4), 401–18.

Bosma, N.S., S.J.A. Hessels, V.A.J.M. Schutjens, C.M. Van Praag and T. Verheul (2011b), 'Entrepreneurship and role models', *Journal of Economic Psychology*, forthcoming.

Bottazzi, L. and G. Peri (2003), 'Innovation and spillovers in regions: evidence from European patent data', *European Economic Review*, **47**, 687–710.

Buenstorf, G. and D. Fornahl (2009), 'B2C-bubble to cluster: the dot-com boom, spin-off entrepreneurship, and regional agglomeration', *Journal of Evolutionary Economics*, **19** (3), 349–78.

Buenstorf, G., and S. Klepper (2004), 'The origin and location of entrants in the evolution of the US tire industry', Papers on Economic and Evolution 2004-07, Max Planck Institute of Economics, Evolutionary Economics Group.

Cattani, K.D., W.G. Gilland, and J.M. Swaminathan (2004), 'Coordinating traditional and Internet supply chains', in D. Simchi-Levi, S.D. Wu and Z.-J. Shen (eds), *Handbook of Quantitative Supply Chain Analysis: Modeling in the E-Business Era*, Boston, MA: Kluwer, pp. 643–77.

Chinitz, B. (1961), 'Contrasts in agglomeration: New York and Pittsburgh', *American Economic Review*, **51**, 279–89.

Cooper, A. and T. Folta (2000), 'Entrepreneurship and high-technology clusters', in D. Sexton and H. Landstroem (eds), *Handbook of Entrepreneurship*, Oxford: Blackwell Publishers, pp. 348–67.

Dahl, M.C., C.Ø.R. Pedersen and B. Dalum (2003), 'Entry by spinoff in a high-tech cluster', Druid Working Paper No. 03-11.

Dahl, S. and O. Sorenson (2009), 'The embedded entrepreneur', *European Management Review*, **6**, 172–81.

Davidsson, P. and J. Wiklund (1997), 'Values, beliefs and regional variations in new firm formation rates', *Journal of Economic Psychology*, **18**, 179–99.

Dosi, G. and D. Lovallo (1998), 'Rational entrepreneurs or optimistic martyrs? Some considerations on technological regimes, corporate entries, and the evolutionary role of decision biases', in R. Garud, P. Nayyar and Z. Shapiro (eds), *Foresights and Oversights in Technological Change*, Cambridge: Cambridge University Press, pp. 41–68.

Dumais, G., G. Ellison and E.L. Glaeser (1997), 'Geographic concentration as a dynamic process', NBER Working Paper 6270, Cambridge, MA: *National Bureau of Economic Research*.

Feldman, M.P. (2001), 'The entrepreneurial event revisited: an examination of new firm formation in the regional context', *Industrial and Corporate Change*, **10**, 861–91.

Feldman, M.P and J.L. Francis (2003), 'Fortune favours the prepared region: the case of entrepreneurship and the Capitol Region biotechnology cluster', *European Planning Studies*, **11** (7), 765–88.

Feldman, M.P., J. Francis and J. Bercovitz (2005), 'Creating a cluster while building a firm: entrepreneurs and the formation of industrial clusters', *Regional Studies*, **39**, 129–41.

Figueiredo, O., P. Guimaraes and D. Woodward (2002), 'Home–field advantage: location decisions of Portuguese entrepreneurs', *Journal of Urban Economics*, **52**, 341–61.

Forbes, D.P. (1999), 'Cognitive approaches to new venture creation', *International Journal of Management Reviews*, **1** (4), 415–39.

Fornahl, D. (2003), 'Entrepreneurial activities in a regional context', in D. Fornahl and T. Brenner (eds), *Cooperation, Networks and Institutions in Regional Innovation Systems*, Cheltenham, UK and Northampton, MA, USA: Edward Elgar, pp. 38–57.

Fotopoulos, G. and N. Spence (2001), 'Spatial variations in net entry rates of establishments in Greek manufacturing industries: an application of the shift-share ANOVA model', *Environment and Planning*, **31** (11), 1731–55.

Frenken, K., F.G. van Oort and T. Verburg (2007), 'Related variety, unrelated variety and regional economic growth', *Regional Studies*, **41**, 685–97.

Fritsch, M. and D. Schilder (2008), 'Does venture capital investment really require spatial proximity? An empirical investigation', *Environment and Planning A*, **40** (9), 2114–31.

Fritsch, M. and A. Schroeter (2011), 'Why does the effect of new business formation differ across regions?', *Small Business Economics*, **36** (4), 383–400.

Glaeser, E. (2000), 'The new economics of urban and regional growth', in G.L. Clark, M.P. Feldman and M. Gertler (eds), *The Oxford Handbook of Economic Geography*, New York: Oxford University Press, pp. 83–98.

Glaeser, E. (2007), 'Entrepreneurship and the city', NBER Working Paper 13551.

Gompers, P., J. Lerner and D. Scharfstein (2005), 'Entrepreneurial spawning: public corporations and the formation of new ventures, 1986–1999', *Journal of Finance*, **60**, 577–614.

Gudgin, Graham (1978), *Industrial Location Processes and Regional Employment Growth*, Farnborough, UK: Saxon House.

Hanson, S. (2003), 'Geography, gender, and the workaday world', Hettner Lectures number 6, Stuttgart: Franz Steiner.

Helfat, C.E., and M.B. Lieberman (2002), 'The birth of capabilities: market entry and the importance of prehistory', *Industrial and Corporate Change*, **11** (4), 725–60.

Holtz-Eakin, Douglas, David Joulfaian and Harvey S. Rosen (1994), 'Sticking it out: entrepreneurial survival and liquidity constraints', *Journal of Political Economy*, **102** (1), 53–75.

Hoover, E.M. (1948), *The Location of Economic Activity*, New York: McGraw-Hill.

Hoover, E.M. and R. Vernon (1959), *Anatomy of a Metropolis*, Cambridge, MA.: Harvard University Press.

Jacobs, J. (1969), *The Economy of Cities*, New York: Vintage Books.

Johnson, P.S. and D.G. Cathcart (1979), 'New manufacturing firms and regional development: some evidence from the Northern Region', *Regional Studies*, **13**, 269–80.

Klepper, S. (2001), 'Employee startups in high-tech industries', *Industrial and Corporate Change*, **10** (3), 639–74.

Klepper, S. (2002), 'Agglomeration through spinoffs: how Detroit became the capital of the US automobile industry', paper presented at the 9th Congress of International Joseph A. Schumpeter Society, Gainesville, FL.

Klepper, S. (2007), 'Disagreements, spinoffs, and the evolution of Detroit as the capital of the US automobile industry', *Management Science*, **53**, 616–31.

Klepper, S. and K. Simons (2000), 'The making of an oligopoly: firm survival and technological change in the evolution of the US tire industry', *Journal of Political Economy*, **108** (4), 728–60.

Klepper, S. and S. Sleeper (2005), 'Entry by spinoffs', *Management Science*, **51** (8), 1291–1306.

Koellinger, P. and A. Thurik (2009), 'Entrepreneurship and the business cycle', Tinbergen Institute Discussion Paper No. TI 09-032/3.

Lafuente, A. and V. Salas (1989), 'Types of entrepreneurs and firms: the case of new Spanish firms', *Strategic Management Journal*, **10** (1), 17–30.

Lloyd, P. and C. Mason (1984), 'Spatial variations in new firm formation in the UK: comparative evidence from Merseyside Greater Manchester and South Hampshire', *Regional Studies Association*, **18** (3), 207–20.

Malmberg, A. and P. Maskell (2002), 'The elusive concept of localization economies: towards a knowledge-based theory of spatial clustering', *Environment and Planning A*, **34**, 429–49.

March, J.G. (1991), 'Exploration and exploitation in organizational learning', *Organization Science*, **2** (1), 71–87.

Marshall, A. (1890), *Principles of Economics*, London: Macmillan.

Martin, R.L. and P.J. Sunley (2001), 'Rethinking the "economic" in economic geography: broadening our vision or losing our focus', *Antipode*, **33**, 148–161.

Mason, C. (1991), 'Spatial variations in enterprise: the geography of new firm formation', in R. Burrows (ed.), *Deciphering the Enterprise Culture: Entrepreneurship, Petty Capitalism and the Restructuring of Britain*, London: Routledge.

Mason, C. and R. Harrison (2002), 'Barriers to investment in the informal venture capital sector', *Entrepreneurship and Regional Development*, **14** (3), 271–87.

Michelacci, C. and O. Silva (2007) 'Why so many local entrepreneurs?', *Review of Economics and Statistics*, **89** (4), 615–33.

Mueller, P. (2006), 'Exploring the knowledge filter: how entrepreneurship and university–industry relations drive economic growth', *Research Policy*, **35** (10), 1499–1508.

Nanda, R. and J.B. Sørenson (2010), 'Workplace peers and entrepreneurship', *Management Science*, **56** (7), 1116–26.

O'Farrell, P. and R. Crouchley (1984), 'An industrial and spatial analysis of new firm formation in Ireland', *Regional Studies*, **18** (3), 221–36.

Parker, S. (2009), 'Why do small firms produce the entrepreneurs?', *Journal of Socio-Economics*, **38** (3), 484–94.

Parwada, Jerry T. (2008), 'The genesis of home bias? The location and portfolio choices of investment company start-ups', *Journal of Financial and Quantitative Analysis*, **43**, 245–66.

Pasinetti, L.L. (1993), *Structural Economic Dynamics: A Theory of the Economic Consequences of Human Learning*, Cambridge: Cambridge University Press.

Piore, M.J. and C.F. Sabel (1984), *The Second Industrial Divide: Possibilities for Prosperity*, New York: Basic Books.

Pred, A. (1967), *Behaviour and Location: Foundations for a Geographic and Dynamic Location Theory, Part I*, Lund: Gleerup.

Reynolds, P.D., D.J. Storey and P. Westhead, P. (1994), 'Cross-national comparisons of the variation in new firm formation rates', *Regional Studies*, **28** (4), 443–56.

Rocha, H.O. (2004), 'Entrepreneurship and development: the role of clusters. A literature review', *Small Business Economics*, **23**: 363–400.

Rosenberg, N. and L. Birdzell (1986), *How the West Grew Rich: The Economic Transformation of the Industrial World*, New York: Basic Books.

Saxenian, A. (1990), 'The origins and dynamics of production networks in Silicon Valley', Institute of Urban and Regional Development, UCA Berkeley, Working Paper 516.

Saxenian, A. (1994), *Regional Advantage: Culture and Competition in Silicon Valley and Route 128*, Cambridge, MA: Harvard University Press.

Shane, S.A. (2000), 'Prior knowledge and the discovery of entrepreneurial opportunities', *Organization Science*, **11** (4), 448–72.

Shane, S. and S. Venkataraman (2000), 'The promise of entrepreneurship as a field of research', *Academy of Management Review*, **25**, 217–26.

Simon, H.A. (1957), *Models of Man: Social and Rational*, New York: John Wiley & Sons.

Sorenson, O. (2005), 'Social networks and the persistence of regional innovation systems: evidence from the computer workstation industry', in S. Breschi and F. Malerba (eds), *Clusters, Networks, and Innovation*, Oxford: Oxford University Press, pp. 297–318.

Sorenson O., and P.G. Audia (2000), 'The social structure of entrepreneurial activity: geographic concentration of footwear production in the United States, 1940–1989', *American Journal of Sociology*, **106**, 424–62.

Stam, E. (2005), 'The geography of gazelles in the Netherlands', *Journal for Economic and Social Geography*, **96** (1), 121–7.

Storey, D.J. (1982), *Entrepreneurship and The New Firm*, London: Croom Helm.

Stuart, T. and O. Sorenson (2003), 'The geography of opportunity: spatial heterogeneity in founding rates and the performance of biotechnology firms', *Research Policy*, **32**, 229–53.

Uhlaner, L. and R. Thurik (2007), 'Postmaterialism influencing total entrepreneurial activity across nations', *Journal of Evolutionary Economics*, **17** (2), 161–85.

Vaillant, Y. and E. Lafuente (2007), 'Do different institutional frameworks condition the influence of local fear of failure and entrepreneurial examples over entrepreneurial activity?' *Entrepreneurship and Regional Development*, **19**, 313–37.

Varga, A. (1998), *University Research and Regional Innovation: A Spatial Econometric Analysis of Academic Technology Transfers*, Boston, MA: Kluwer Academic Publishers.

Vivarelli, M. (1991), 'The birth of new enterprises', *Small Business Economics*, **3**, 215–23.

Wagner, J. and R. Sternberg (2004), 'Start-up activities, individual characteristics, and the regional milieu: lessons for entrepreneurship support policies from German micro data', *Annals of Regional Science*, **38** (2), 219–40.

Wennberg, K., J. Wiklund, D.R. DeTienne and M. Cardon (2010), 'Human capital predictors of entrepreneurs' exit paths', *Journal of Business Venturing*, **25** (4), 361–75.

Wennekers, A.R.M. and A.R. Thurik (1999), 'Linking entrepreneurship and economic growth', *Small Business Economics*, **13**, 27–55.

Wezel, F.C. (2005), 'Location-dependence and industry evolution: founding rates in the United Kingdom motorcycle industry, 1895–1993', *Organization Studies*, **26** (5), 729–54.

Wong, P., Y. Ho and E. Autio (2005), 'Entrepreneurship, innovation and economic growth: evidence from GEM data', *Small Business Economics*, **24** (3), 335–50.

Woodward, D., O. Figueiredo and P. Guimarães (2006), 'Beyond the Silicon Valley: university R&D and high-technology location', *Journal of Urban Economics*, **60,** 15–32.

Zander, I. (2004), 'The microfoundations of cluster stickiness: walking in the shoes of the entrepreneur', *Journal of International Management*, **10**, 51–75.

Zucker, L., M. Darby and M. Brewer (1998), 'Intellectual human capital and the birth of US biotechnology enterprises', *American Economic Review*, **88** (1) 290–306.

36 Venture capital in regional innovation and growth

Jesper Lindgaard Christensen

INTRODUCTION

The history of thinking about financing of innovation and growth is often associated with the writings of Joseph Schumpeter. In order for the entrepreneur to carry out entrepreneurial activities, a capitalist is necessary to bear the risk through financing development, according to Schumpeter. As explained by Andersen (Chapter 2) in this *Handbook*, Schumpeter was also interested in regional aspects of economic evolution, although this was not at the centre of all his writings. Since then, however, the interest in geographical aspects of financing regional innovation and growth has been extremely sparse. It was not until the 1980s that spatial aspects of finance in general, and venture capital in particular, gained interest from researchers. Contributions to increase our understanding of the geography of venture capital from this decade were still few (including Wetzel, 1981, 1983, 1986; Florida and Kenney, 1988a, 1988b; Mason, 1987; Martin, 1989; Thompson, 1989). Economic geography has generally not been very concerned with financial constraints (Pollard, 2003) although there has lately been some interest in what may be denoted the geography of money (Martin, 1999; Mason and Harrison, 2002a; Zook, 2002). This research has primarily focused upon institutional venture capital, while other aspects of the geography of money have focused upon issues such as global financial centres (Agnes, 2000).

Within the new economic geography of money it has been shown that the supply of financial capital is spatially heavily skewed, with a relatively large share being invested in metropolitan areas (Martin et al., 2002; Mason and Harrison, 2002a). Some of this research has investigated how this may reinforce an uneven redistribution of capital between regions. For example, Martin and Minns (1995) find that the UK pension system is heavily concentrated in the South East regions of UK, not only in terms of the location of the pension funds which administer the pension pools, but also in terms of the firms and organizations that receive capital for investments. The implication of this according to Martin and Minns is that this process undermines the wealth of regions, and that financial power and administration of funds should be decentralized to the regions in order to retain a greater proportion of the money in the region where the money originated. Similarly, Mason (2007) argues that venture capital has been shown to spur innovation and growth, therefore an inadequate regional supply of venture capital contributes to uneven regional development. Generally, much of the literature shows that financial capital from geographically dispersed savings is not reallocated proportionally back to the regions from where it came.

Likewise, the literature on venture capital and geography has primarily focused on the distribution of the investments and the possible mismatch between the location of the

495

venture capital firms and demand. It has been discussed whether venture capital investments tend to transform savings that are widely dispersed throughout the economy into
investments mainly in metropolitan areas, where venture capital firms tend to cluster
(Murray, 1998; Mason and Harrison, 1998, 2002a).

In light of this possible source of uneven regional development, a wide array of policy
measures has been installed to level inequitable effects of this process. It has been one of
the top priorities of national, regional and European Union (EU) policies to ease firms'
access to capital, especially venture capital, and policy-makers have introduced several
measures to stimulate the development of venture capital markets (OECD, 1996). Based
on the belief that such policies spur economic growth and innovation, many regions
have claimed that access to capital is an important part of the innovation system (Cooke,
2001) and have therefore focused policies to ensure an adequate supply of risk capital.
Due to the uneven distribution of investments and investment funds, less favoured
regions have argued for regionally embedded funds to compensate for the tendency
of financial institutions to locate in metropolitan areas. The financial crisis has further
accentuated this policy debate.

Focusing upon venture, capital, this chapter discusses a number of core issues in
geographical aspects of financing investments. It is first explained why geography is
important to venture capital investments. The skewed distribution is briefly mentioned
above, and this will be elaborated in the third section. Much of the literature does not differentiate between different types of venture capital. However, as explained below in the
fourth section, there are different geographies for business angels, institutional venture
capital and private equity. Likewise, it may be argued that there are different geographies
of public and private venture capital investments and investments of different size. The
chapter also deals with how geography matters in different phases of the venture capital
cycle. The possible geographical specialization of venture capital firms is dealt with next.
Whether the above-mentioned policy initiatives are rational is also briefly discussed in
the final section.

WHY GEOGRAPHY MATTERS TO VENTURE CAPITAL INVESTMENTS

Generally, barriers to financing new ventures can be ascribed to a lack of information,
trust and competencies of the various parties involved. Venture capital is particularly
characterized by illiquid equity investments involving high degrees of information asymmetries. Financing new, risky ventures requires relatively careful selection and intense
monitoring, which in the literature has been espoused as one explanation why venture
capital firms exist. Their specialized ability to screen potential deals and to cope with
asymmetric information means that venture capital firms can invest in firms with a high-
risk, high-return profile, where returns are highly uncertain (Amit et al., 1998). Thus, the
combination of superior *ex ante* screening capabilities and *ex post* value-adding services
enables venture capital firms to perform better than other financial intermediaries in the
high-risk segment of corporate investments.

Looking more closely into the venture capital investment process, it is clear that much
of the knowledge in venture capital investments is tacit. Whereas codified information

can be transferred across distances, the often tacit knowledge related to, for example, an assessment of the trustworthiness of management may require face-to-face contact, which is facilitated by geographical proximity. Hence, geographical proximity may be important for financing such firms. Therefore, such tacit knowledge may be said to be spatially grounded (Gertler et al., 2000; Zook, 2002, 2004) because transaction costs are higher if the financier is not close to the firm. Furthermore, it may be argued that such transaction costs are higher in small firm investments. Such firms often lack managerial skills and organizational capabilities, which may render more needs for guidance.

Spatial proximity may be important in several of the phases of the venture capital investment process because of easier monitoring and learning about regionally specificities. Prior to investing, the informants of the financial institutions are often spatially bounded. Thus, Sorenson and Stuart (2001) contend that information on the potential of new, high-growth investment opportunities is not publicly available and is spatially limited. In the absence of this information, financial institutions such as venture capital firms and business angels rely on personal and professional relationships, which in turn are most often localized in close proximity to their offices (Powell et al., 2002; Florida and Kenney, 1988a; Zook, 2004). Once investment decisions have been made, ease of monitoring and involvement due to spatial proximity to the business invested in (due to more frequent face-to-face contact) means that information flows are quantitatively improved, as well as the transfer of tacit knowledge and trust-building among the parties. Investee firms as well as financial institutions operate in and rely upon networks that are spatially grounded. Spatial proximity may be important because the networks among venture capital firms themselves are also important sources of information, and this type of information is not publicly available (Shane and Cable, 2002). It may contribute to further spatial clustering if the venture capital firms themselves co-locate.

The fact that a substantial part of venture capital investments take place cross-border may at first glance be a counter-argument against the importance of geography to venture capital investments. However, most international venture capital investments are done in syndication with a local partner that acts as the lead investor. The widespread use of syndicated investments often transcends geographical distance, thus expanding the geographical radius of the venture capital activity (Sorenson and Stuart, 2001; Florida and Kenney, 1988a). Mäkelä and Maula (2008) show that these co-investments are facilitated by the local investor's contacts and specific knowledge as well as the performance of management responsibilities that are more easily done in close proximity to the portfolio firms. The argument that long-distance investors rely upon syndication with local investors to undertake value-added activities such as evaluation, monitoring and support for strategy and management purposes may be applied to regional investments within a country, rather than solely to cross-border investments.

A GEOGRAPHICALLY SKEWED DISTRIBUTION OF VENTURE CAPITAL

According to the majority of writers within the stream of literature denoted the 'geography of money', the supply of financial capital is spatially heavily skewed, with a relatively large share being managed and invested in metropolitan areas (Martin, 1999; Martin et al., 2002, 2003; Mason and Harrison, 2002a; Powell et al., 2002; Zook, 2002). This issue has been prominent specifically within venture capital research (Mason, 2007). The uneven geographical distribution of venture capital is found in most countries, with respect to the location of both the venture capital firms and the actual investments (Martin et al., 2003). In the US it is said to be concentrated in California, especially Silicon Valley, and Boston along Route 128. California accounts for a third or more of the total sum of venture capital in the US (Powell et al., 2002; Zook, 2002; Mason, 2007). Although, to a varying degree, such concentration is found in virtually all countries, Mason and Harrison (2002a) show that venture capital investments in the UK remains highly concentrated in the London and South East regions. While Scotland, Wales and the northern UK regions recently have attracted more than their expected share of the number of venture capital investments, these investments are relatively small and are primarily driven by public funds. The bulk of the money still goes into the South East where the majority of private funds operate (Mason and Pierrakis, 2009; Jones-Evans and Thompson, 2009).

One obvious explanation why investments tend to be spatially uneven is that the investment opportunities and business activities are also unevenly distributed. Different regions can have different levels of entrepreneurship, technological development, clusters, and so on (Florida and Kenney, 1998c), and both firms and intermediaries can also differ in their awareness of sources of capital from region to region (Mason and Harrison, 1998; Mason, 2007). While venture capital firms may have a preference for investing in firms near their own location, there is often a demand-induced pattern as venture capital firms concentrate their investments where economic activity is high (Stuart and Sorenson, 2003). Additionally one should expect urban areas to attract a disproportionate share of investments because these areas often host a number of institutions that may assist investment decisions and post-investment monitoring and nursing of the portfolio firms. This includes technology experts, various business services, head hunters, access to qualified staff and, not least, access to syndicate partners.

In sum, the literature has established that financial capital tends to be spatially concentrated around large metropolitan areas and in relatively prosperous regions of a country. This results in a reduction of agency costs and informational asymmetries; hence investments tend to be spatially restricted.

DIFFERENT VENTURE CAPITAL, DIFFERENT GEOGRAPHIES

Much of the literature on the geography of venture capital has treated geographical aspects such distance and proximity in rather simplistic terms. As a result, there has also been a lack of a more nuanced examination of how geography is related to different types of venture capital. Even if the literature on this is sparse, it indicates that there are quite different geographies of investments by and location of business angels (informal venture capital), institutional venture capital and private equity (Mason, 2007). Even within these three categories it may be argued that geography plays different roles. For example, publicly sponsored venture capital funds may be more willing to invest in peripheral regions (Mason and Pierrakis, 2009), partly due to the fact that some of these funds have dual objectives including both profit motives and socio-economic objectives such as stimulating even regional development. Likewise, we may see different distributions of venture capital depending on whether it is measured by the number of investments or the amount of capital supplied. In the former case we may see a more even distribution than in the latter case, as investments in peripheral areas are often smaller on average (Mason and Pierrakis, 2009; Jones-Evans and Thompson, 2009).

With respect to business angels, the general perception is that these are particularly local investments compared to other types of venture capital investments. Numerous surveys in different countries have looked into the investment preferences of angels. They generally find that a large proportion of angels prefer to invest close to their home or office.[1] A 50 mile distance or an hour's travel time is often mentioned in the surveys; however, the various studies find that a number of angels are willing to look into investment opportunities further away.

Mason (2007) reviews a number of surveys and finds that between one in ten and one-third of angel investments were more than 100 miles away, and in many cases even more than 300 miles away. The explanation why some angels do invest further away probably relates to both the specificities of such long-distance investments and the angels themselves. The former has to do with the industry specialization and distribution as well as the local size of the market for these investments. In 'thin' markets it may be necessary for narrowly specialized venture capital funds to look further away in geographical terms to find investment opportunities. The latter may be related to the reputation of the business angel and their strategy, ability and willingness to provide hands-on value-added activities. For example, proximity between the firm and the business angel might be expected to be negatively related to the degree of involvement.[2] The arguments may be applied to institutional venture capital as well, although the difference in the degree to which these arguments hold is up for debate. Thus, Avdeichikova and Landström (2005) also find that business angel investments are concentrated in metropolitan areas, but not as much as institutional venture capital investments.

Accordingly, venture capital firms generally tend to have a preference for being more involved in local firms (Lerner, 1995; Powell et al., 2002). Similarly, several studies find that funds focused upon the early-stage investments are more inclined to invest in local firms (Gupta and Sapienza, 1992; Mason and Harrison, 2000). De Clercq et al. (2001) find that, over time, venture capital firms in Finland in 1994–97 persistently diversify their investments geographically. According to the authors, one possible explanation is that when faced with constraints on opportunities for industry-specific investments, venture capital firms look for opportunities further away. Moreover, over time, venture capital firms can develop the ability to deal with local entrepreneurs and they may believe that these experiences are replicable in other geographical contexts. Powell et al. (2002) and Sorenson and Stuart (2001) support this, and find that as venture capital firms grow older, they are more inclined to invest in more distant firms. In addition, in a small market, investees know most venture capital firms. This may both increase firms' knowledge of the venture capital firm as a potential investor and elicit more invitations from other investors to participate in syndicated investments. A further possible explanation relates to the maturing of the market, which means increased specialization and abilities of investors to transcend geographical distances.

The institutional venture capital firms are concentrated in metropolitan areas in terms of their investments but also, and even more, in terms of the location of their head offices. There are several explanations for this. Many venture capital firms historically spun out of other types of financial institutions such as pension funds and banks, which in turn often have their corporate headquarters in the financial centres. Another explanation has to do with the ability to access auxiliary services to undertake the support of portfolio firms, including business services as well as technical support and advice. There is also the fact that venture capital firms have better access to highly qualified staff by locating in metropolitan areas. An important value-added activity of venture capital is to act as links to other, complementary financing sources, and being close to where such financing sources are located alleviates transaction costs associated with accessing these and potential syndication partners. There is debate about whether venture capital proceeds or follows high-tech clusters. Is the presence of venture capital the driver of industrial evolution, or does it locate according to where industrial evolution has generated investment opportunities? Zook (2005) finds that in the Internet industry entrepreneurs were willing to move to Silicon Valley to approach venture capitalists. However, a number of venture capital firms have located in Silicon Valley because of expected better deal flow. Although both forces thus may be in play, the latter mechanism seems to be the primary one (Feldman et al., 2005; Mason and Harrison, 2002b; Mason, 2007). As high-tech clusters tend to be concentrated in or near urban centres where universities are typically located, this in turn implies that venture capital firms will also be attracted to these areas (Powell et al., 2002).

Investors focusing upon the later stage, such as private equity and buy-out funds, likewise show different geographies than business angels and institutional venture capital (Mason and Harrison, 2002a), due to their different focus on types of investments in terms of stage, size of investment and the particular type of assets involved (Cumming and Johan, 2006). The type of investment often includes a complementary long-term debt component. Still, even these types of investments have been shown to be concentrated in the same Canadian provinces as the investing private equity fund, again, primarily due to agency costs involved in investing across provinces (ibid.).

GEOGRAPHICAL SPECIALIZATION OF VENTURE CAPITAL INVESTMENTS

In a much-cited paper, Gupta and Sapienza (1992) reported their study on venture capital firms' preferences regarding industry diversity and geographical scope, and claimed that there has been little interest in the specialization of venture capital firms. Venture capital firms may specialize in a number of dimensions and for different reasons. Khanin (2009) lists 15 determinants of venture capital strategies, one of them being the geographic focus, as elaborated below.

The degree of specialization of venture capital firms is closely linked to the building up of competencies. The ability to assess investment proposals and to monitor and assist management requires the build-up of skills which may be enhanced by specializing in particular segments of the market (Christensen, 2007). Industry specialization may generate competencies related to the technical features of the products and market, while geographical specialization will generate other types of competencies such as access to local networks and the ability to interpret information from the local business environment.

To a large extent the specialization choice is one of venture capital firm strategy

(Khanin, 2009). It is possible for the venture capital firm simultaneously to build up competencies in, for example, geographically diverse investments and different stages of investment. However, the investments involved in building up such competencies are substantial and should be balanced against the risk reduction achieved through diversifying into several segments. While there is likely to be a reduction in initial costs when diversifying into another area of investment, many costs cannot be eliminated, and some of these costs are not only fixed but continuous costs. This may explain why larger venture capital firms may have a more diversified profile than smaller funds, as they may benefit from scale effects in the diversification process. It may also explain why cross-border venture capital investments are primarily made through syndication with local venture capital funds, rather than directly, as costs associated with access to local information, the building up of networks, local market knowledge, and so on may not match the benefits derived from such diversification if the costs are covered by one venture capital firm alone.

One of the main problems with focusing venture capital funds in specific regions is that it involves a balance between the size of the region and the critical mass of investment opportunities needed to diversify risk. It is likely that there is a minimum efficient scale of venture capital fund investment (and there are indications that this has increased over time in recent years) which is difficult to meet for small, regionally specialized funds (Murray, 1998). This has been an issue in policy discussions about the rationale for public-funded regional funds, to which we now turn.

POLICIES TOWARDS REGIONAL VENTURE CAPITAL

The uneven distribution of venture capital financial resources laid out in earlier in this chapter means that firms in peripheral areas can be said to be disadvantaged (Murray, 1998; OECD, 1996; Mason, 2007). On the other hand, the above-mentioned demand characteristics of a region may explain parts of this phenomenon, and the ability of financial institutions to communicate and make transactions across distances may alleviate the problems. It is also debatable what are the implications of an uneven distribution of both the supply and demand for capital, and of the advantages of geographical proximity to capital sources. It is not clear if financial capital should be more concentrated around innovative clusters to gain from agglomeration effects, or if financial capital should be more regionally dispersed to stimulate regional growth of industries (Martin et al., 2002). Moreover, public funds tend to be undercapitalized and therefore may not function effectively (Mason and Pierrakis, 2009; Murray, 1998).

In addition to stimulating the supply side of the venture capital market, governments increasingly recognize that the demand side also needs to be stimulated. This includes raising awareness among small and medium-sized enterprises (SMEs) about appropriate sources of finance. Such awareness-raising is generally most efficient at the regional level. The amplitude of business cycles and the peripheral character of a region may be reduced by the active participation of regional government bodies supporting the financing of new opportunities. However, this is only likely to be successful if the required competencies exist in the market. Solely increasing the supply of venture capital may generate a return at some point in time, but it is rarely a successful strategy. The competence-building process through specialization is a long-term process which requires patience on behalf of regional government. Competencies in venture capital are not easily acquired as they rest on build-up of experience and potentially hiring experienced venture capital managers from outside, something not easily done in an expanding market with a limited number of skilled venture capital managers. Therefore, the expansion of competencies in the venture capital market has a certain inertia. Thus, according to Doran and Bannock (2000), experience from the US suggests that, for a sustainable venture capital industry to be built, publicly sponsored venture capital programmes may have to operate with a 25-year planning horizon.

There has been a debate on the design of government initiatives to stimulate regional venture capital, specifically whether they are targeting the right financing gap (Harding, 2000), and whether regional funds established are generally too small (Murray, 1998). There has even been concern as to whether it is at all possible to address regional equity gaps using general policy instruments, since the size and character of the equity gap may vary not only between regions and industries, but also over time, as underlined by the effects of the financial crisis.

The chapters in this volume have demonstrated the variety of regions even within seemingly homogeneous countries, and the present chapter has demonstrated that a nuanced view of the role of venture capital in regional innovation and growth is necessary.

NOTES

1. Wetzel (1981) and Mason (2007) show that there is often a difference between the preferences and the actual investments. In practice, the location of actual investments are closer in Euclidian distances than what is indicated by preferences.
2. See Harrison et al. (2010) for an empirical test of a range of hypotheses regarding long-distance investments by business angels in the UK. The hypotheses relate to both deal-specific characteristics and investor-specific characteristics.

REFERENCES

Agnes, P. (2000), 'The "end of geography" in financial services? Local embeddedness and territorialization in the interest rate swaps industry', *Economic Geography*, 76 (4), 347–66.

Amit, R., J. Brander and C. Zott (1998), 'Why do venture capital firms exist? Theory and Canadian evidence', *Journal of Business Venturing*, 13, 441–66.

Avdeitchikova, S. and H. Landström (2005), 'Informal venture capital: scope and geographical distribution in Sweden', Working paper presented at Babson Kauffman Entrepreneurship Conference, Babson College.

Christensen, J.L. (2007), 'The development of regional specialization of venture capital', *European Planning Studies*, 15 (6), 817–34.

Cooke, P. (2001), 'Regional innovation systems, clusters and the knowledge economy', *Industrial and Corporate Change*, 10 (4), 945–74.

Cumming, D. and S.A. Johan (2006), 'Provincial preferences in private equity', *Financial Markets Portfolio Management*, 20, 369–98.

de Clercq, D., P.K. Goulet, M. Kumpulainen and M. Mäkelä (2001), 'Portfolio investment strategies in the Finnish venture capital industry: a longitudinal study', *Venture Capital*, 3 (1), 41–62.

Doran, A. and G. Bannock (2000), 'Public sponsored regional venture capital: what can the UK learn from the US experience?', *Venture Capital*, 2 (4), 255–85.

Feldman, M.P., J. Francis and J. Bercovitz (2005), 'Creating a cluster while building a firm: entrepreneurs and the formation of innovative clusters', *Regional Studies*, 39, 129–42.

Florida, R.L. and M. Kenney (1988a), 'Venture capital, high technology and regional development', *Regional Studies*, **22**, 33–48.

Florida, R.L. and M. Kenney (1988b), 'Venture capital and high technology entrepreneurship', *Journal of Business Venturing*, **3** (4), 301–19.

Florida, R. and M. Kenney (1988c), 'Venture capital-financed innovation and technological change in the US', *Research Policy*, **17** (3), 117–37.

Gertler, M.S., D.A. Wolfe and D. Garkut (2000), 'No place like home: the embeddedness of innovation in a regional economy', *Review of International Political Economy*, **7** (4), 688–714.

Gupta, A.K. and H.J. Sapienza (1992), 'Determinants of venture capital firms', preferences regarding the industry diversity and geographic scope of their investments', *Journal of Business Venturing*, **7**, 347–62.

Harding, R. (2000), 'Venture capital and regional development: towards a venture capital system', *Venture Capital: An International Journal of Entrepreneurial Finance*, **2** (4), 287–311.

Harrison, R., C. Mason and P. Robson (2010), 'Determinants of long-distance investing by business angels in the UK', *Entrepreneurship and Regional Development*, **22** (2), 113–37.

Jones-Evans, D. and P. Thompson (2009), 'The spatial dispersion of informal investment at a regional level: evidence from the UK', *European Planning Studies*, **17** (5), 659–75.

Khanin, D. (2009), 'Strategy-shaping factors in the venture capitalist industry', *Small Business Institute National Proceedings*, **33** (1), 221–37.

Lerner, J. (1995), 'Venture capitalists and the oversight of private firms', *Journal of Finance*, **50**, 301–18.

Mäkelä, M.M. and M.V.J. Maula (2008), 'Attracting cross-border venture capital: the role of a local investor', *Entrepreneurship and Regional Development*, **20** (May), 237–57.

Martin, R. (1989), 'The growth and geographical anatomy of venture capital in the United Kingdom', *Regional Studies*, **23**, 389–403.

Martin, R. (1999), 'The new economic geography of money', in R. Martin (ed.), *Money and the Space Economy*, New York: Wiley, pp. 3–27.

Martin, R., C. Berudt, B. Klagge, P. Sunley and S. Herten (2003), 'Regional venture capital policy UK and Germany compared', Anglo-German Foundation for the Study of Industrial Society.

Martin, R. and R. Minns (1995), 'Undermining the financial basis of regions: the spatial structure and implications of the UK pension fund system', *Regional Studies*, **29** (2), 125–44.

Martin, R., P. Sunley and D. Turner (2002), 'Taking risks in regions: the geographical anatomy of Europe's emergent venture capital market', *Journal of Economic Geography*, **2**, 121–50.

Mason, C.M. (1987), 'Venture capital in the United Kingdom: a geographical perspective', *National Westminster Bank Quarterly Review*, May, 47–59.

Mason, C.M. (2007), 'The geography of venture capital investments', in H. Landström (ed.), *Handbook of Venture Capital Research*, Cheltenham, UK and Northampton, MA, USA: Edward Elgar, pp. 31–40.

Mason, C.M. and R. Harrison (1998), 'Financing entrepreneurship: venture capital and regional development', in R. Martin (ed.), *Money and the Space Economy*, New York: Wiley, pp. 157–83.

Mason, C.M. and R.T. Harrison (2000), 'The size of the informal venture capital market in the United Kingdom', *Small Business Economics*, **15**, 137–48.

Mason, C.M. and R. Harrison (2002a), 'The geography of venture capital investments in the UK', *Transactions of the Institute of British Geographers*, **27**, 427–51.

Mason, C.M. and R.T. Harrison (2002b), 'Is it worth it? The rates of return from informal venture capital investments', *Journal of Business Venturing*, **17**, 211–36.

Mason, C.M. and Y. Pierrakis (2009), 'Venture capital, the regions and public policy: the UK since the post-2000 technology crash', paper for ISBE conference, Liverpool, 3–6 November.

Murray, G.C. (1998), 'A policy response to regional disparities in the supply of risk capital to new technology-based firms in the European Union: the European Seed Capital Fund Scheme', *Regional Studies*, **32** (5), 405–19.

OECD (1996), 'Venture capital and innovation', Working Paper IV, no. 98, Paris.

Pollard, J.S. (2003), 'Small firms finance and economic geography', *Journal of Economic Geography*, **3**, 429–52.

Powell, W.W., K.W. Koput, J.I. Bowie and L. Smith-Doerr (2002), 'The spatial clustering of science and capital: accounting for biotech firm–venture capital relationships', *Regional Studies*, **36** (3), 291–305.

Shane, S. and D. Cable (2002), 'Network ties, reputation, and the financing of new ventures', *Management Science*, **48** (3), 364–81.

Sorenson, O. and T.E. Stuart (2001), 'Syndication networks and the spatial distribution of venture capital investments', *American Journal of Sociology*, **106** (6), 1546–88.

Stuart, T. and O. Sorenson (2003), 'The geography of opportunity: spatial heterogeneity in founding rates and the performance of biotechnology firms', *Research Policy*, **32**, 229–53.

Thompson, C. (1989), 'The geography of venture capital', *Progress in Human Geography*, **13**, 62–98.

Wetzel, W.E. (1981), 'Informal risk capital in New England', in K.H. Vesper (ed.), *Frontiers of Entrepreneurship Research*, Wellesley, MA: Babson College, pp. 217–45.

Wetzel, W.E. (1983), 'Angels and informal risk capital', *Sloan Management Review*, **24**, 23–34.
Wetzel, W.E. (1986), 'Informal risk capital: knowns and unknowns', in D.L. Sexton and R.W. Smilor (eds), *The Art and Science of Entrepreneurship*, Cambridge, MA: Ballinger, pp. 85–108.
Zook, M.A. (2002), 'Grounded capital: venture financing and the geography of the Internet industry, 1994–2000', *Journal of Economic Geography*, **2**, 151–77.
Zook, M.A. (2004), 'The knowledge brokers: venture capitalists, tacit knowledge and regional development', *International Journal of Urban and Regional Research*, **28** (3), 621–41.
Zook, M.A. (2005), *The Geography of the Internet Industry*, Oxford: Blackwell Publishing.

37 Regional entrepreneurship development: promoting spin-offs through coaching and mentoring*
Magnus Klofsten and Staffan Öberg

PROMOTING ENTREPRENEURSHIP FOR REGIONAL DEVELOPMENT

A common objective of economic development efforts everywhere in the world is the creation of an 'entrepreneurial region'. Such a region has the capability to move across technological paradigms and periodically renew itself through new technologies and businesses generated from its economical base (Etzkowitz and Klofsten, 2005). Good examples include the Öresund region (Sweden–Denmark), which has a high concentration of biomedical research and an emerging biomedical industry. The 'Twin Cities of Sweden', Linköping and Norrköping, have over the past 25 years succeeded in bringing new ideas emanating from research and other knowledge-intensive activities into new businesses in terms of independent firms, licensing agreements and internal ventures both in the private as well as in the public sector. Most recognized is the high amount of spin-off firms from Linköping University, which have been a strong foundation for the growth and development of the Mjärdevi and Norrköping science parks.

There is, from both a scientific and a practical point of view, an emerging interest in investigating the necessary conditions for creating new businesses. Perhaps one of the most important factors is the presence of an entrepreneurial university that both advances emerging areas of knowledge and puts this knowledge to use in developing the local region (Clark, 1998; Cooke, 2002). Therefore, has academic entrepreneurship been of high focus in spin-off creation both from the research (Lindholm, 1994; Feldman and Klofsten, 2000; Rickne, 2000) as well as from the practitioner viewpoint? Furthermore, to what extent has it resulted in the creation of various training programmes and incubators (Aaboen et al., 2008; Bergek and Norman, 2008)? A good practical example of the positive regional development effects of promoting entrepreneurship is the Entrepreneurship and New Business Development Programme (hereafter called the ENP) which is highlighted in this chapter. To understand the underlying structures and processes of entrepreneurial regional developments, this chapter addresses the use of academic entrepreneurship training, where coaching and mentoring are key tools to improve the quality and economic value of new spin-off firms.

ENTREPRENEURSHIP TRAINING AND THE USE OF COACHING AND MENTORING

Entrepreneurship is today seen as a highly relevant skill to be provided through lifelong learning. Fostering an entrepreneurial mindset as well as providing training and educational activities – starting from basic education – will greatly contribute to economic growth and regional development. Initiatives focusing on promoting entrepreneurship in the European countries have grown extensively over the decade to 2010 (Benneworth, 2007; Kirwan et al., 2008). We have also witnessed a widening of the entrepreneurship concept, focusing not just on encouraging new start-ups but also on other businesslike situations, that is, in the academic system and public sector.

Promoting entrepreneurship could be done in many different ways, but the literature shows that the following issues seem to be important in most entrepreneurship support situations (Klofsten, 2008):

- inspiring entrepreneurial behaviour and promoting positive attitudes towards change;
- providing skills and tools germane to business development;
- developing skills to handle ecological relationships with customers, financiers and other stakeholders.

A crucial content in the entrepreneurship training process is the use of coaching and mentoring (Sullivan, 2000; Regis et al., 2007). Whether we call it coaching or mentoring, the fact is that many young entrepreneurs in all type of work environments are looking to improve their skills, both personally and professionally. Choosing to work with a skilled coach or mentor can help the individuals to achieve their goals and increase their effectiveness in relation to the particular job or task they are occupied with (Evered and Selman, 1989).

The areas of coaching and mentoring have over the years been well covered in numerous articles and books with a wide range of aims and scope, for example:

- Coaching and mentoring for employee development (Minter and Thomas, 2000).
- The teacher as coach (Fiet, 2001).
- Coaching executives (Olivero et al., 1997).
- Organizational mentoring (Murray and Owen, 1991).
- Mentoring for network development (Higgins and Kram, 2001).
- Learning and mentoring (Sullivan, 2000).
- Web-based mentoring for women (Packard, 2003).

What emerges when comparing them is that both functions involve pairing a junior individual (inexperienced entrepreneur) with a more senior one outside the direct chain of command. In a study by Murray and Owen (1991), coaching is addressed as the core of the mentoring process, whereas Regis et al. (2007) see coaching as a process where the mentor contributes to increase the specific knowledge and the 'protégé's comprehension about navigating in the corporative world' (p. 8). There is however a tendency to use them interchangeably, with a high degree of overlapping (Coenders, 2001).

AIM AND SCOPE

The aim of this chapter is through a longitudinal qualitative analysis to discuss two major concepts in entrepreneurship training, namely coaching and mentoring. We are particular interested in differences, similarities and how they are interrelated. We believe there is strong theoretical and practical value in studying the coaching and mentoring processes in entrepreneurship training to understand better the underlying factors for regional development. The theoretical rationale is that there are relatively few longitudinal studies of coaching and mentoring processes in general, and those focusing on entrepreneurship training in particular. As addressed above, numerous books and papers have been written about coaching and mentoring, but most of what has been published emanates from consulting and tends to be quite anecdotic and practical. Furthermore, there seems to be a lack of consensus of what the differences (or similarities) between those functions are, or how they might be interrelated.

From the practical point of view both coaching and mentoring are strong tools, which enable inexperienced entrepreneurs, in a personal way with a more experienced colleague, to address various thoughts, opportunities, ideas and business-related issues. More systematic qualitative research in this field will help us to understand better what is going on in the coaching and mentorship process (that is, relationships, matching competences, time and resources issues), which hopefully will give us possibilities to raise relevant research questions and develop practical tools to improve those processes.

METHOD AND DATA

The data analysed below come from the ENP, for training individuals to start new technology-based or knowledge-intensive businesses. A majority of those firms are spin-off companies from an academic environment. The model was developed at the Centre for Innovation and Entrepreneurship (CIE) at Linköping University, with the help of a network of local enterprises. This programme has now spread to many districts of Sweden and, in recent years, has also been internationalized. Since the beginning of 1994, 55 programmes have been carried out, which have resulted in more than 500 new businesses as well as a dozen or more new business areas within established organizations. Today, these firms and organizations employ over 2000 people. The ENP has been analysed and data have been published in various papers (that is, Klofsten, 2000; Klofsten et al., 2010).

Both coaching and mentoring have been crucial to support the young entrepreneurs, and both functions are used as parallel and complementary activities in the ENP. The major goal of the activities has been to support the entrepreneurs in developing their first businesses plan and is a test plan on a more general level where various business issues could be addressed. The ENP is structured and has a content that will support and develop the entrepreneur, the idea (technology) and the environment (company) in parallel.

When choosing participants for the programme, two factors have been particularly been focused on. The first is that the participant can devote time to the training programme and that they possess the necessary drive and spirit to be an entrepreneur.

Secondly, the entrepreneur has to have an initial venture idea, which is going to be the base for the first business plan. As will be shown later, both these factors will strongly affect the work by the coach and mentor in their interaction with the young entrepreneur.

In this study we have access to data from 36 programmes of the total of 55 mentioned above. These 36 entrepreneurship programmes cover 450 coaching and mentoring cases at the seven Swedish universities. When collecting data the following main sources have been used:

- 360 written evaluations of participants' judgement of the training programme, where the coaching and mentoring could be commented up on;
- documentation from meetings in 520 coached projects;
- 60 personal interviews with participants;
- 40 personal interviews with mentors;
- other documents from the programmes, that is, protocol for choosing the award winner for the best idea, and best business plans.

In analysing coaching and mentoring we have used a checklist to gather information, including the following 21 items listed in four categories linked to: (1) structural issues (mission, form and task); (2) process issues (connection to programme content, meeting environment, problem-solving, assessing the opportunity or idea, operative role, confidentiality and networking); (3) relationships (extent, meeting, initiative, homework, documentation and follow-up); and (4) character of the coach and mentor (background and experience, engagement, integrity, social competence and role/ethics).

ANALYSIS AND DISCUSSION

As shown in Table 37.1, there are both similarities and differences between coaching and mentoring. When it comes to the structural issues it could be said that both the coach and mentor are there to guide and support the entrepreneur, often from a situation where the individual is stuck and cannot see the way to commercialize their idea. The entrepreneur will confirm that someone else believes in the idea. Both roles aim to support the entrepreneur in creating a business-oriented platform for long-term survival and growth where fragments are put together.

There are however structural differences when comparing coaching and mentoring. The coach is working much closer to the programme management of the training programme and is monitored to a higher degree by this function than the mentor. A coach has also the responsibility of assuring that the participants put the theory learnt at the different workshops into practice. The coach will also check that the young entrepreneur uses the mentor and stays focused. A coach employs process thinking, and is at the same time keen on what is going on in the entrepreneur's mind. The mentor is given more freedom to act and transfer personal experiences and advice based on similar business situations.

There are several process-oriented issues to take into consideration. When a coach or a mentor gets involved in an entrepreneurship training programme it is clearly stated that they are not allowed during the programme to be engaged financially in the businesses

Table 37.1   Similarities and differences between coaching and mentoring

Item	Coaching	Mentoring
Structural issues		
Mission	Make the idea more concrete and understandable – develop a first version of a business plan	Improve the quality of the first business plan – create a foundation for doing profitable business
Form	Process orientation	Situation orientation
Task	Develop a structure and a platform through guidance	Transfer personal experiences of doing business and solve specific problems
Process issues		
Connection to programme content	Strong connection	Weak connection
Meeting environment	Neutral	Neutral
Problem solving	Guidance	Suggest
Assessing the opportunity or idea	No role	No role
Operative role	No	No
Confidentiality	Orally agreed	Orally agreed
Networking	Door opener	Door opener (more active)
Relationships		
Extent	Scheduled meetings	Non-scheduled meetings
Meeting	Individually	Individually or in groups
Initiative	Schedule based	Demand driven
Home work	Yes – a natural part of the process	No demand – not a natural part of the process
Documentation	Yes – a natural part of the process	No demand – not a natural part of the process
Follow-up	Yes – a natural part of the process	No demand – not a natural part of the process
Character of the coach and mentor		
Background and experience	Generalist	Often a specialist with a background in a particular industry
Engagement	High	High
Integrity	High	High
Social competence	High and credible	High and credible
Role (ethics)	Neutral and independent	Neutral and independent

they are supporting. The consequence is that neither of them can have an operative role in the entrepreneur's business, and the balance between being involved, but not too involved, is hard to manage. When training the entrepreneurs it is of great importance that the entrepreneur is in the driver's seat, not the coach or mentor. This rule creates a neutral arena of positive learning, which facilitates openness, and avoidance of particular financial interest. Both the coach and, especially, the mentor are expected, through their relationships with the business world, to support the individual with contacts and to open doors, giving access to resources the young entrepreneur does not have. Neither the coach or the mentor should assess the opportunity or idea – their task is to support what the entrepreneur has in hand. It is up to the entrepreneur to decide whether to take the idea further, or to close down the project.

The process that the coach is acting from and the work task given to the participants are strongly connected to the content of the entrepreneurship training programme (workshops and other educational activities). The coach provides guidance, whereas the mentor suggests experienced-based solutions. A mentor also has the mandate to process questions not directly connected to the programme content. When meeting a coach or a mentor the young entrepreneur has the opportunity to discuss various questions, to help realize personal goals. It is not uncommon that the discussion is about issues not directly related to the business, and some of them could deal with very sensitive and personal matters such as family issues or personal relationships.

There are several differences between coaching and mentoring in the relationships with the individual. The coach takes the initiative to meet the individual, and at the start of a programme a schedule is handed out. In this particular case there are three meetings during the half-year programme. Each meeting takes about 1–1.5 hours and there might also be sporadic mail or telephone contact between the meetings. To get the most out of the meetings it is important that the participant has done their homework, and that the coach documents and follows up the continuous development and progress of the entrepreneur. The coach will support the programme leader with status reports based on the documentation from the coach meetings. A participant is expected to take initiate meetings with the mentor at least three times during the training programme. Sometimes the mentoring meetings are organized in smaller groups of participants, mainly for efficiency reasons – good mentors are busy people. To limit the mentor's administrative work, homework between meetings, documentation and a follow-up procedure is not demanded.

When recruiting coaches and mentors it is crucial to get people who show engagement, integrity and have high social competence. The meeting between the participant and a coach or mentor might be the only moment where the young entrepreneur meets a person in a business situation who does not have a personal interest in the project, and in a totally neutral arena. This can lead to the entrepreneur opening up in a way that they normally would not. A coach should preferably be a generalist with a business-minded approach. The mentor should be a generalist with a background in a particular industry, and have the ability to work in depth with the entrepreneur's business issues. The mentor's experience of industry complements the process skills of the coach.

CONCLUSIONS AND IMPLICATIONS

This chapter focuses on two important concepts in entrepreneurship training, namely coaching and mentoring. Particular interest has been paid to differences and similarities between them, and how they are interrelated. As a basis for the analysis we have dealt with various structural, process and relationship issues, and issues dealing with the personal character of the coach and mentor. We have shown that there are differences as well as similarities connected to all four of these functions. The following major conclusions can be drawn from the chapter:

First, there are structural differences between a coach and mentor and they are related to mission, form and task. There are notable process differences due to their connection to programme content and problem-solving. The relationship with a coach is to a larger extent schedule-based, and meeting the mentor is demand-driven. Coaching is based on generalist competence whereas mentoring comes from a specialist. Since the coach has a number of tasks, in relation to the entrepreneur and to the programme management, his work is similar to that of a project manager, but without involving decision-making, only guidance.

Second, similarities are in process items such as the opportunity or idea assessment, meeting environment, operative role and confidentiality. The extent of the relationship is basically the same and there are similarities when it comes to personal engagement, integrity, social competence and credibility.

The authors are convinced that the coach and the mentor have different roles for supporting the young individual to be a better entrepreneur. Coaching and mentoring are two parallel activities, which complement each other. Another angle on this subject is whether differences exist between the sexes in coaching and mentoring entrepreneurs. There is an ongoing debate in Sweden about why women start so few firms, and why few firms started by females expand. Perhaps coaching and mentoring processes could be developed and become important tools to support the female entrepreneur better.

A crucial factor in all coaching and mentoring processes is to respect the individual drive and engagement of the entrepreneurs. The more active the entrepreneur is in relation to the project, the more easy and efficient the coaching and mentoring will be. Experiences from the entrepreneurship training programmes show that active participation by the entrepreneur makes the work between the coach and mentor more synchronized. The successes of the coach and the mentor are highly dependent on the relationships they create with entrepreneur.

So what implications do our conclusions have for entrepreneurship and regional development? One major implication is to secure the supply of skilled and experienced coaches and mentors – they are crucial players when training new spin-off firms. One way of getting access to those groups is to create networks of successful experienced entrepreneurs who are prepared to share their experiences. A good example of such a network is the Management Leader Group connected to the ENP. To increase their interest in participating, they are offered competence development activities through regular seminars.

Other implications are connected to the coaching and mentoring processes per se. The form of the process is independent of the backgrounds of the entrepreneurs which means that coaching and mentoring are delivered in the same form to all type of individuals. This way of looking at coaching and mentoring as general processes goes against the traditional way of thinking to some extent. In that way, different types of entrepreneurs are offered tailor-made activities dependent on their background, university spin-offs, corporate spin-offs, academic status and sex.

Finally, we are convinced that coaching and mentoring are such critical resources for the development of new firms that they should automatically be treated as part of a regional development strategy. There is, from both a scientific and a practical point of view, emerging interest in investigating the necessary conditions for creating new businesses, and the renewal capabilities of a supporting infrastructure on a regional basis. Perhaps one of the most important factors is the presence of an entrepreneurial university that both advances emerging areas of knowledge and puts this knowledge to use in developing the local region (Clark, 1998). As shown in this study, the university has been the driver to develop the ENP, including the coaching and mentoring functions. The emergence of university–industry–government interactions – sometimes described as the 'Triple Helix' – can also be identified as a key factor in entrepreneurial regional development (Etzkowitz, 2005). Beyond the research capacity in emerging and interdisciplinary fields with potential for the development and realization of new ideas is the capability to effectively utilize these knowledge resources of experiences entrepreneurs who can act as good examples in coaching and mentoring of inexperienced entrepreneurs.

NOTE

*   This chapter is a revised version of the paper 'Coaching versus mentoring: are there any differences?', presented at the 16th Annual High Technology Small Firms Conference at the University of Twente, Enschede, The Netherlands, 22–23 May 2008, which will be published in the forthcoming conference proceedings.

REFERENCES

Aaboen, L., P. Lindelof and H. Lofsten (2008), 'Incubator performance: an efficiency frontier analysis', *International Journal of Business Innovation and Research*, **2** (4), 354–80.
Benneworth, P. (2007), 'Seven samurai opening up the ivory tower? The construction of Newcastle as an entrepreneurial university', *European Planning Studies*, **15** (4), 487–99.
Bergek, A. and C. Norman (2008), 'Incubator best practices: a framework', *Technovation*, **28**, 20–28.
Clark, B. (1998), *Creating Entrepreneurial Universities: Organizational Pathways of Transformation*, New York: Pergamon.
Coenders, M.J.J. (2001), 'Coaching by colleagues: a scalable HRD tool for the adhocracy', in J. Streumer (ed.), *Perspectives on Learning at the Workplace: Theoretical Positions, Organisational Factors, Learning Processes and Effects, Proceedings Second Conference HRD Research and Practice across Europe*, 26–27 January, UFHRD, Euresform, AHRD, Enschede: University of Twente, pp. 231–6.
Cooke, P. (2002), 'Regional innovation systems: general findings and some new eveidence from biotechnology clusters', *Journal of Technology Transfer*, **27**, 133–45.
Etzkowitz, H. (2005), *Triple Helix*, Stockholm: SNS Press.
Etzkowitz, H. and M. Klofsten (2005), 'The innovative region: toward a theory of knowledge-based regional development', *R&D Management*, **35** (3), 243–55.
Evered, E.D. and J.C. Selman (1989), 'Coaching and the art of management', *Organizational Dynamics*, **18** (2), 16–32.
Feldman, J.M. and M. Klofsten (2000), 'Medium sized firms and the limits to growth: a case study in the evolution of a spin-off firm', *European Planning Studies*, **8** (5), 631–50.
Fiet, J.O. (2001), 'The pedagogical side of entrepreneurship theory', *Journal of Business Venturing*, **16** (2), 101–17.
Higgins, M.C. and K.E. Kram (2001), 'Re-conceptualizing mentoring at work: a developmental network perspective', *Academy of Management Review*, **26** (2), 264–88.
Kirwan, P.M., P. van der Sijde and M. Klofsten (2008), 'Supporting high-tech companies: using the business platform as a practical instrument', *International Journal of Innovation and Regional Development*, **1** (1), 48–65.
Klofsten, M. (2000), 'Training entrepreneurship at universities: a Swedish case', *Journal of European Industrial Training*, **24** (6), 337–44.
Klofsten, M. (2008), 'Supporting academic enterprise: a case study of an entrepreneurship programme',

in A. Groen, R.P. Oakey, P. van der Sijde and G. Cook (eds), *New Technology-Based Firms at the New Millennium*, vol. 6, Oxford: Elsevier Science, pp. 55–67.

Klofsten, M., P. Heydebreck and D. Jones-Evans (2010), 'Transferring good practices beyond organisational borders: lessons from transferring an entrepreneurship programme', *Regional Studies*, **44** (6), 791–9.

Lindholm, Å. (1994), 'The economics of technology-related ownership changes: a study of innovativeness and growth through acquisitions and spin-offs', PhD dissertation, Chalmers University of Technology, Gothenburg.

Minter, R.L. and E.G. Thomas (2000), 'Employee development through coaching, mentoring and counselling: a multidimensional approach', *Review of Business*, **21** (1), 43–57.

Murray, M. and M.A. Owen (1991), *Beyond the Myths and Magic of Mentoring*, San Francisco, CA: Jossey-Bass.

Olivero, G., K.D. Bane and R.E. Kopelman (1997), 'Executive coaching as a transfer of training tool: effects on productivity in a public agency', *Public Personnel Management*, **26** (4), 461–9.

Packard, B.L. (2003), 'Web-based mentoring: challenging traditional models to increase women's access', *Mentoring and Tutoring*, **11** (January), 1–30.

Regis, H.P., J.A. Falk and S.M.R.C. Dias (2007), 'Mentoring entrepreneurial networks: mapping conceptions of participants in technological-based business incubators in Brazil', *Journal of Business Venturing*, **13** (7), 275–94.

Rickne, A. (2000), 'New technology-based firms and industrial dynamics: evidence from the technological systems biomaterials in Sweden, Ohio and Massachusetts', PhD dissertation, Chalmers University of Technology, Gothenburg.

Sullivan, R. (2000), 'Entrepreneurial learning and mentoring', *International Journal of Entrepreneurial Behaviour and Research*, **6** (3), 1355–2554.

38 Regional innovation and incubation: the technological incubators programme for entrepreneurship and innovation
Daniel Shefer and Amnon Frenkel

INTRODUCTION

The development of high-tech industry and the rate of innovation adoption have often been linked to rapid economic growth. Although a general framework for technological entrepreneurship as a means of economic growth was advanced by Schumpeter back in the 1930s (Schumpeter, 1934), it was only in the 1980s that interest was renewed in this area. The rationale for public support of high-tech industry is based on two assumptions. First, that high-tech industry is a desirable activity for the economy of any country in that it gives a high added value, has many positive externalities that influence other branches of the economy, and is strongly export-oriented (particularly important to small economies). The second assumption describes the different market failures associated with high-tech industry, such as the difficulty or inability of enforcing intellectual property rights and, therefore, reap the benefits from the new discoveries; and the need for a critical mass of knowledge and funds in specific areas.

Particular attention has been given to new technology-based firms in recent decades (Cooke and Morgan, 1998; Moore and Garnsey, 1993). In an evolutionary perspective, small new firms provide the pool from which the big industries of the future will emerge. They have proved to be much more flexible and adaptable to new technologies than big firms, thereby helping innovation to reach the market faster (Garnsey et al., 1994).

The spatial distribution of high-tech industry has been the focus of many studies. Agglomeration of industries, such as found in Silicon Valley, California (Saxenian, 1983) or in Cambridge, England (Segal Quince, 1985; Casper and Karamanos, 2003; Cooke, 2003), appears to be the most common distribution pattern (Audretsch, 1998; Audretsch and Feldman, 1996), although some studies report a dispersal trend (Keeble, 1994). Among the factors associated with the location of high-tech establishments, most common are the need for highly skilled manpower, the availability of venture capital, and proximity to a university or a research institution.

In spite of its tendency to agglomerate, high-tech industries are also very attractive as a means of local economic development for a number of reasons (Shefer and Frenkel, 1998; Shefer and Bar-El, 1993; Cooke and Morgan, 1998; Malecki, 1991). One major advantage lies in the fact that high-tech industries generally cause much less pollution than traditional industries, especially as sensitivity to environmental impact grows and monetary sanctions against polluting industries become more popular almost everywhere. Furthermore, high-tech industries are only minimally affected by transportation costs since the price–weight ratio of products is relatively high, implying that, at least in this respect, peripheral regions are still suitable for the location of such industries.

Finally, there are positive effects that hold at a national level, such as high 'added value', and positive externalities that hold at the regional and local levels, as well.

A variety of programmes have been proposed in different countries and regions to provide incentives to attract new high-tech firms. These can be divided roughly into four categories, each focusing on a different aspect of new-firm formation: fiscal programmes, direct financing programmes, consulting programmes and infrastructure-oriented programmes.

The technological incubators programme is a complementary programme that overlaps all four categories and provides several services that differ based on the definition and sponsor of the incubator. These services include the funnelling of public and private venture capital to projects, business and marketing consultation, and the provision of low-cost rent and infrastructure. At a national level, the technological incubators programme may be seen as filtering and developing valuable, original ideas and for providing seed-capital. At a local level, the incubator may be viewed as a means of local economic development since it can induce the creation and development of new firms in a specific location.

It is important to point out that the technological incubators programme is an economic development programme that aims at fostering both entrepreneurship and innovation from the very beginning of a project's inception. The programme can help create a healthy entrepreneurial culture by empowering initiators and encouraging them to develop their own firms. The incubator located in a remote region is able to supply a number of functions that are seldom found in peripheral areas, including venture capital, business and legal consulting and the filtering of valuable ideas. Nevertheless it cannot help in increasing the supply of skilled labour.

This chapter presents an overview of the technological incubators programme, which is designed to promote entrepreneurship and innovation. We present the technological incubator as a viable programme in a period of rapid technological progress and high-tech development. We draw heavily on the remarkable Israeli Public Technological Incubator Program that in 2010, after almost two decades of operation, can be labelled as a success story. First, we describe the way the technological incubators operate and function. Next, the Israeli Technological Incubator Program is presented, and we discuss the ongoing process of privatization of the technological incubators. The university-based technological incubator is presented, and the specialized biotechnology incubator is discussed, emphasizing the unique features of biotechnology networking and its industrial cluster. We end the chapter with a few concluding remarks concerning the technological incubators programme as a vehicle that helps to promote entrepreneurship, innovation, and local and regional economic development.

THE TECHNOLOGICAL INCUBATORS IDEA: AN OVERVIEW

The idea of the technological incubators programme emanated from the desire to encourage and support budding new start-ups in their critical years before reaching maturity. The incubator increases the chances of survival of small firms graduating from the incubator by supplying them with such basic services as assistance and consultation in varying areas, thereby helping to accelerate their rate of survival and growth

(Sherrod, 1999). Enterprises that began their life in an incubator have been found to have a higher rate of success than those that did not. This is due to an increase in the number of employees and a reduction of labour and operational costs, as well as an increase in gross sales, net profits, net value and overall benefit to the entrepreneurs (Mian, 1996). Cutbill (2000) reported that start-up firms that began their life in a supported milieu (for example in a technological incubator) had an 87 per cent chance of success, in contrast to an 80 per cent failure rate among start-ups that chose not to be in such a supportive milieu in their first five years of operation. Research in the UK found that managers of firms within incubators or firms that had graduated from incubators strongly believed that this attachment had been important to the development of their business (Hannon and Chaplin, 2003).

Technological and business incubators are a worldwide phenomenon. In the US the number of incubators exceeds 800 and more than 20 000 companies that have graduated from them are still in operation (Applegate, 2000). Structural changes and globalization smoothed the ground for the establishment of technological and business incubators in Europe in the early 1980s, in particular in Britain, France, Germany and Italy (Bird, 1989). The objectives of these incubators vary from place to place. In Spain and Belgium, the first incubators were established in order to attract branches of international companies; in Germany, to promote the creation of new jobs and to encourage potential entrepreneurships. In France, the first incubator was erected in proximity to a university in order to transfer technology from academia to industry and to commercialize university research outputs. In Italy, the incubator is considered a regional economic development tool; and in Britain it is a tool for the creation of new jobs (OECD, 1997).

Technological incubators also exist in the Far East. In Japan, for example, they operate within innovation centres and science parks (Kawashima and Stöhr, 1988). They were established for the first time in 1989 as part of research centres that were meant to serve primarily as incubators for small and medium-sized high-tech firms (Kawashima and Stöhr, 1988). By 1994 there were 45 technological incubators in operation. The incubators in Japan, in contrast to those in the US and Europe, do not limit the time that projects are allowed to operate in the incubator. Japanese incubators act more like a real-estate business, renting areas and supplying technical and administrative services. Their main weakness is the absence of access to sources of funding, including venture capital (VC) funds, and the lack of their connection to business and financial firms (OECD, 1997).

Technological incubators are not limited only to the industrialized world; they can now be found in such countries as China, Turkey, Brazil, South Korea and Indonesia, where the economy has been undergoing structural changes. Among the developing countries, the largest technological incubators programme exists in China, encompassing 85 incubators and more than 2000 projects. Thanks to generous and intensive government support, the programme has proved successful and contributes to the development of the country's economy (OECD, 1997).

It is estimated that there are today some 3000 incubators spread all around the world, more than half of them established during the 1990s (Reynolds, 2000). Most of the incubators are affiliated with and activated by such public or private bodies as government agencies, universities, research centres and large technological firms (Culp, 1990). The growing number of technological incubators internationally points to the importance ascribed by governments to the development of business as a basis for the creation of economic activities, and as a tool for promoting entrepreneurship and innovation, and creating new jobs.

The principal objective of the technological incubators programme, as a development initiative 'from below', is to foster entrepreneurial activities and innovation from the very inception of a project (Peter et al., 2004). On the one hand, the programme can help to create a healthy entrepreneurial culture by empowering local people and encouraging them to develop their own firms locally. On the other hand, it works very slowly: at least 10–15 years are needed in order to assess the actual impact of the programme on employment and economic development.

THE ISRAELI PUBLIC TECHNOLOGICAL INCUBATOR PROGRAM

In the early 1990s, Israeli high-tech industry blossomed in an unprecedented manner. The electronics industry, which accounts for most of the high-tech sector, increased its sales from $2 billion in 1986 to $13.1 billion in 2003 (www.iael.org.il). Formal Israeli venture capital funds, internal and external, almost non-existent until 1990, totalled some $4.2 billion in 2000 (Avnimelech and Teubal, 2004; Avnimelech et al., 2007). The exceptional growth of Israeli high-tech firms in the civilian sector began in 1986 with the closure of the 'Lavi' project (the Israeli-designed fighter airplane), which caused several thousand engineers to leave the military industry for the civil sector and, often, to become technological entrepreneurs. The boom was bolstered by the massive immigration from the former Soviet Union in the early 1990s.

Start-ups have played a crucial role in Israel's high-tech growth. According to the Office of the Chief Scientist (OCS), which operates Israel's public sector research and development (R&D) incentives programmes), Israel produces the second-highest absolute number of technological start-up companies per year in the world after the US (OCS, 2007). Although start-up capital is usually provided by venture capital funds, seed capital is often supplied by the technological incubators.

The Israeli Public Technological Incubator Program was initiated by the OCS in Israel's Ministry of Industry and Trade in the wake of the large influx of immigrants from the former USSR, many of whom were scientists and engineers. Between 1990 and 1993, 28 incubators were established throughout the country; in 2010 26 incubators were in operation (more than half in peripheral areas, with the rest in or near metropolitan areas). Of these, 23 were technological incubators; one was dedicated to biotechnology and two to technology-based industries. The OCS grants are for a two-year term, amounting to between $350 000 to $600 000. For biotech projects it may be up to $1.8 million for three years. The level of the grant (or a soft loan) is up to 85 per cent of the approved budget of the project (80 per cent for biotechnology projects) (OCS, 2007). The additional 15 per cent, 'complementary financing', is to be supplied by the entrepreneur or by strategic partnerships (for example VC) in exchange for equity in the project. Each incubator is a not-for-profit entity, usually sponsored by a university, a municipality or a large firm. There is no sector limitation, and any one incubator can support between eight and 12 projects. The principal criteria for project selection are that it is product-oriented, primarily export-oriented, based on R&D and feasible with the available resources.

From a small annual budget of $2 million at the beginning in 1991, the Israeli Public Technological Incubator Program increased its annual budget to $32 million in 2002. As of 2003, total government grants to the programme amounted to $285 million (see www.incubators.org.il). At the end of 2003, more than 200 projects were in operation in incubators, which employed more than 2000 workers. One-third of the initiatives were based on ideas brought by new immigrants, all of whom had an academic education (most with a Master's or PhD degree).

Shefer and Frenkel (2003) evaluated the Israeli Public Technological Incubator Program ten years after its establishment. They found that, in general, the programme had fulfilled its promise: 86.4 per cent of the projects in 1999–2001 graduated from the programme, and 78 per cent of these were able to secure financial support after graduation, which is regarded as an indication of success. In this context, the incubators located in the periphery presented lower rates of success, compared with those in the central regions of Israel.

Ten years after the establishment of the Israeli Public Technological Incubator Program, it was discovered that incubators are capable of enlarging their budget from non-governmental sources – mostly in the form of royalties, sale of shares and dividends, and strategic partnerships. These new sources of funding suggest that the vast government support needed at the initial stage can gradually be reduced over time, once outside private funding sources are developed and attained. Once again, technological incubators located in peripheral regions require more public support, and for a longer period of time, than do those located in the central regions of the country (Shefer and Frenkel, 2003).

The Israeli Public Technological Incubator Program is regarded as a success story and a model to be imitated worldwide. Many visitors come to Israel to study the programme in order to implement it abroad. Since 1995, a joint project has existed between the Israeli programme administration and Sweden, in order to establish a similar programme there. Shefer and Frenkel's (2003) study of the Israeli programme was part of a large, European Union (EU)-sponsored research project to develop a methodology for creating seed and start-up capital for high-tech firms. The project follows the Israeli success story of the technological incubators programme and tests its applicability to EU countries, Italy in particular.

In most developed countries the capital market operates in a competitive environment, based on supply and demand. A market failure, though, interferes with the capital market. The government is then forced to regulate the market and to devise policies that will direct investment to worthwhile initiatives. The VC market is a central financial resource in the new global economy in general, and for high-tech industry in particular. Access to VC sources has a critical effect on promoting innovation initiatives, the establishment of new technological firms, and economic growth as a whole. Public intervention in the VC market is acceptable in many countries. Most of the time, it is only a partial intervention, focusing especially on regions where the VC market has not yet developed (Ber, 2002). In the US and UK, for example, the VC industry tends to concentrate in the large business centres. In order to bring about a geographically balanced distribution of capital, governments intervene by adopting different strategies, such as tax remission, government guarantees, and even support of private VC funds (Doran and Bannock, 2000; Hood, 2000).

This kind of government intervention started in 1991 with the Government Insurance Company, Inbal, which provided VC funds that were traded on the stock market, with a

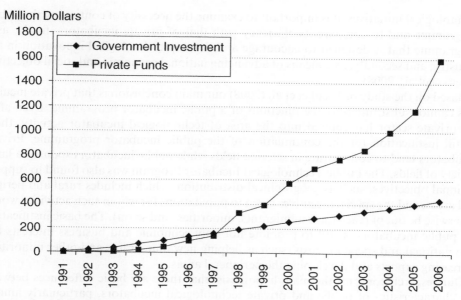

Million Dollars

Source: Ministry of Industry, Trade and Labor, Office of the Chief Scientist.

Figure 38.1   Government investment vs private investment in Israeli incubators' projects 1991–2006

70 per cent guarantee. The government VC program Yozma, based on a $100 million fund, began operating in 1992. The basic idea was to promote, through government support and the involvement of foreign financial and investment institutions, the establishment of Israeli VC funds that invested in young Israeli high-tech start-ups. In 1997, the government sold Yozma to the private sector, indicating the end of government intervention in the VC market. During its period of operation, Yozma led to the establishment of ten VC private funds, which raised $2.7 billion up to the end of 2002, thereby triggering Israel's VC market (Avnimelech and Teubal, 2004). The total investment of VC funds in Israel from 1998 to 2002 amounted to $8.1 billion. The peak came in 2000, before the high-tech market collapsed, when 62 companies operated 100 VC funds with a total capital of $5 billion, estimated to be 3 per cent of gross domestic product (GDP) (by comparison, VC funds' share of US GDP is estimated at only 0.7 per cent (Ber, 2002). This government intervention model in a situation of market failure, which ended when the market started to supply needs efficiently, calls for an examination of the Public Technological Incubator Program and a comparison with privately run programmes (Figure 38.1).

PRIVATIZING THE TECHNOLOGICAL INCUBATORS

Private technological incubators began operating in Israel in 2000 as a result of the readily available private VC to sectors that traditionally had been funded solely by the public sector. With Israel's private sector assuming a central role in financing technological initiatives, it is important to examine the necessity of continuing the public programme and to compare its efficiency with that of private incubators: firstly, as a programme that is designed to encourage and develop technological innovation in the industry; and secondly, as a means of advancing national economic and social objectives (Frenkel et al., 2008).

Based on the study of Frenkel et al. (2008) our main conclusion is that private incubators cannot substitute fully the functions of a public incubator programme. Even after the private sector has entered into the area of technological incubator activity, there is still justification for the continuation of the public incubator programme. Private incubators tend to concentrate in selected fields while public incubators sponsor a large variety of fields. The Public Technological Incubator Program was also found to support national objectives, such as geographical distribution, which includes rural and peripheral areas, and the special incentives given to populations for whom such activities would otherwise be out of reach (new immigrants, minorities, and so on). The basic justification for public incubators is still to promote not only economic and business interests but also national and social interests, such as helping new immigrants and other minorities, increasing exports and developing the peripheral areas.

Our research confirms the main hypothesis, that there are basic differences between the characteristics of public and private technological incubators, particularly among their initiators. Initiators of private incubators are characterized by an economic, business and administrative orientation; most of them come from industry, thus requiring less support in these areas. On the other hand, initiators of public incubators are characterized by a higher level of education; most come from academia or research institutes, and lack business and administrative skills. However, great unanimity was found among project initiators from both private and public incubators with respect to factors contributing to the success of projects.

Private incubators are not able to replace their public counterparts. Firstly, the number of projects within the private incubators is smaller by far than in the public incubators. Secondly, although the technological incubator (in both types) by definition serves as a helping framework for the initiator, particularly in order to mobilize capital resources, initiators in private biotechnology incubators must finance their initial development stages before being admitted into the incubator. Thirdly, private biotechnology incubators also depend on government support. Fourthly, it is still not clear whether private incubators are a phenomenon that will survive in the long term.

Our study results indicate the role played by VC funds and private investment companies that invest in technological incubator projects. VC funds tend to invest more in projects within private incubators than in the public incubators. However, they are only of secondary importance compared to the role of the OCS in public incubators and to the owner or sponsor in private incubators. Therefore, these sources serve as complementary rather than substitutive sources of funding for projects.

Unlike the private sector, the public sector is a source of stability and can be a reliable anchor for long-term planning. A good example of such a situation can be found in the worldwide crisis that has plagued high-tech industry continuously since 2000. The crisis has pushed the whole Israel economy into an unstable, precarious situation, and some markets have ceased to function independently. In order to fill the vacuum, government intervention was needed at different levels. Moreover, as a result of the ongoing recession, there has been a sharp decrease in private investment. The consequent need for government intervention created a new demand and justification for the existence of the Public Technological Incubator Program.

UNIVERSITY-BASED TECHNOLOGICAL INCUBATORS

University-based technological incubators are initiatives that facilitate knowledge flows from the university to the incubator's firms. They provide a mechanism for technology transfer, promote the concept of growth through innovation and the application of technology, support local economic development strategies for small business development, and encourage growth from within local economies (Mian, 1996). It is not surprising therefore that universities and other research organizations are major developers of technology incubator programmes (Phillips, 2002).

Past evidence indicates that technology incubators associated with universities typically focus on commercializing university discoveries while also providing local economic development benefits (Rothaermel and Thursby, 2005). Other reasons for the increase of technology incubators as an approach to economic development may be due in part to a larger number of technology-based start-up companies, and the desire of state and local governments to encourage technology-based businesses in their respective regions. In general, technology incubators used as an economic development approach appear to have emerged from two influences: (1) an increasing interest in fostering indigenous business development, particularly small business entrepreneurship, as an economic development strategy (Shefer and Bar-El, 1993); and (2) the desire to lure high-technology business development (Malecki, 1991).

Incubators associated with universities typically offer access to advanced technology laboratories, equipment, and other research and technical resources such as faculty, staff, students and libraries. Many of the first incubators in the United States were sponsored by universities. The advantages of being near a university campus include access to library facilities, access to student labour, a creative environment and exposure to state-of-the-art technical equipment (laboratories) and expertise (Rothaermel and Thursby, 2005). Companies within university-based incubators were perceived to benefit from these advantages. Moreover, in recent years the networked incubator has emerged as an effective mechanism that fosters partnerships between high-technology-based firms (spin-out HTBFs) and other external parties such as government support agencies and founders, thus facilitating technology transfer from universities to the market (McAdam and McAdam, 2006). In their study on of the operation of entrepreneurial networking within 12 entrepreneurial firms in the US based in a university science park incubator, and with related stakeholders in the Republic of Ireland, McAdam and McAdam (2006) found that the incubator environment enhances the development of social networks that support new entrepreneurs during the vital, initial stages of a firm's formation. These networks play a key role in facilitating the design and implementation of a firm's growth strategies within the university science park incubator.

University-based incubators originating in the USA have spread to Latin America, Europe, Asia, Australia and Africa (Rice and Matthews, 1995). Incubation in these various parts of the world has developed according to distinctive trajectories; there has been a focus on reverse engineering and adapting to imported technology in Eastern Europe, spin-offs from faculty research in the USA, and an emphasis on student-organized firms in Sweden (Etzkowitz, 2002). Etzkowitz argued that incubation is part of the bi-evolution of the university, an expansion of mission and focus. It exemplifies the growth of academic objectives to incorporate a 'third mission' of economic and social development. It also involves a shift in focus, from individuals to organizations, in the teaching function of the university. Academic incubation is increasingly part of a broader complex of university–industry relations including technology transfer licensing and liaison offices. These various programmes are currently being reorganized into a common administrative authority, on the one hand, and decentralized into individual academic units, on the other.

Through analysis of data collected in the 1992 National Business Incubation Association survey, Phillips (2002) found that university-based technology incubators had higher rates of employment and revenues among tenant companies, as well as a larger number of patent applications per tenant firm. However, costs appeared higher for university-based technology incubators, and the average operating deficit was higher for these incubators than for other incubators.

SPECIALIZED TECHNOLOGICAL INCUBATORS: THE BIOTECHNOLOGY INCUBATORS

A specialized technological incubator is classified as such when all the projects within the incubator belong to one field of activity. In a recent study in Israel it was found that all the private incubators were specialized: half of them specialized in biotechnology, and half in software (Frenkel et al., 2008). Only one public incubator, Bioline, was found to be specialized exclusively in biomedicine. Bioline is a consortium comprising Teva Pharmaceuticals, Giza Venture Capital and Hadasit – a subsidiary of Haddassah Medical Organization, which is affiliated to the Hebrew University in Jerusalem. Bioline Incubator was established in January 2005 in response to a call from the OCS Israeli Minister of Trade and Labor to erect two specialized biotechnology public incubators. Bioline was the sole bidder in that tender.

Biotechnology firms require certain types of networks for their success (Kaufmann and Schwartz, 2009). At the early stage of development these firms are highly dependent on regional networks closely linked to academic and/or research institute (Kaufmann et al., 2003; Niosi and Bas, 2001; Monitor, Inc., 2001). Over time, the level of networking expands to cater to more complex business and technological needs; it shifts from the local or regional level of networking to national and international networking, collaborations and corporations (Lemarié et al., 2001; Cooke et al., 2006). The unique characteristics of biotech firms stress the importance of networking – a major portion of these firms emerge from academic or research institutes and this tie is therefore paramount for them. Most of the biotech entrepreneurs come directly from these entities and they like to continue their affiliations or contacts with their former places of work. Nevertheless their business experience is meagre and they are in desperate need of external business assistance. The biotechnology industry in Israel concentrated around three leading universities and research institutes: the Weizmann Institute in Rehovot, the Hebrew

University in Jerusalem and Tel-Aviv University. A close association was found between the specialty of the academic institute in biotechnology related fields and the number of the biotechnology firms located in the region (Kaufmann et al., 2003).

In order to carry advanced research stages, including clinical trials, the biotech firms often require well-equipped research facilities (laboratories) and strong financial backing. Furthermore, because of the lengthy development process (often ten years and more) solid strategic partners are required well in advance in order to assure smooth progress, eventually leading to the development of a new approved (Food and Drug Administration –FDA) marketable product.

CONCLUDING REMARKS

In the past few decades, the high-tech industries have undergone tremendous expansion worldwide, stimulating a new wave of industrial growth. Innovations and knowledge spillovers (externalities), particularly in the high-technology industries, were found to be very important for regional development and growth. Regions with a high level of innovation have become a destination for highly skilled labour and an impetus for improved educational infrastructure. Policy-makers often view high-technology industries as a crucial component of regional economic growth and, increasingly, as an important part of regional export base. Consequently, to attract high-technology industries to outlying regions is now in vogue.

The technological incubators programme is an economic development programme that aims at fostering both entrepreneurships and innovations from the very beginning of a project's inception. The programme can help to create a healthy entrepreneurial culture by empowering initiators and encouraging them to develop their own firms. The incubator located in a remote region is able to supply a number of functions that are seldom found in peripheral areas, including venture capital, business and legal consulting, and the filtering of valuable ideas. Nevertheless it cannot help in increasing the supply of skilled labour. The technological incubators programme is a worldwide phenomenon that can now be found in countries around the globe. Nevertheless there are different types and kinds of incubators.

In the early 1990s, the Israeli high-tech industry blossomed in an unprecedented manner. The electronics industry, which accounts for most of the high-tech sector, was leading the pack. Start-ups have played a crucial role in Israel's high-tech growth. The Israeli Public Technological Incubator Program was initiated by the OCS in the wake of the large influx of immigrants from the former USSR, many of whom were scientists and engineers. Between 1990 and 1993, 28 incubators were established throughout the country; in 2010 26 incubators were operating throughout the country.

Based upon our studies and the studies of many other scholars around the globe there is no doubt that the technological incubator programmes serves as an important tool in the economic development arsenal. The programme fulfils several important objectives: it promotes entrepreneurship and innovations, it helps create start-ups that are crucial for high-tech industry, provides seed money and helps to explore external funding through strategic partnerships. The programme helps new immigrants and other minority populations, and can help promote the growth of outlying areas.

REFERENCES

Applegate, J. (2000), 'Founder of incubator goes from rock stars to start ups', *Los Angeles Business Journal*, http://www.findarticles.com.

Avnimelech, G., D. Schwartz and R. Bar-El (2007), 'Entrepreneurial high-tech cluster development: Israel's experience with venture capital and technological incubators', *European Planning Studies*, 15 (9) 1181–98.

Avnimelech, G. and M. Teubal (2004), 'Venture capital start-up co-evolution and the emergence and development of Israel's new high tech cluster', *Economics of Innovation and New Technology*, 13 (1), 33–60.

Audretsch, D. (1998), 'Agglomeration and the location of innovative activity', *Oxford Review of Economic Policy*, 14, 18–29.

Audretsch, D. and M.P. Feldman (1996), 'R&D spillovers and the geography of innovation and production', *American Economic Review*, 86, 630–40.

Ber, H. (2002), 'Is venture capital special? Empirical evidence from a government initiated venture capital market', Working Paper, Bank of Israel, Jerusalem.

Bird, B.J. (1989), *Entrepreneurial Behavior*, New York: Scott Foresman & Company.

Casper, S. and A. Karamanos (2003), 'Commercializing science in Europe: the Cambridge biotechnology cluster', *European Planning Studies*, 11 (7), 805–22.

Cooke, P. (2003), 'Editorial: the evolution of biotechnology in three continents: Schumpeterian or Penrosian?', *European Planning Studies*, 11 (7), 757–63.

Cooke, P., D. Kaufmann, C. Levin and R. Wilson (2006), 'The biosciences knowledge value chain and comparative incubation models', *Journal of Technology Transfer*, 31, 115–29.

Cooke, P. and K.K. Morgan (1998), *The Associational Economy: Firms, Regions and Innovation*, Oxford: Oxford University Press.

Culp, R.P. (1990), 'Guidelines for incubator development', *Economic Development Review*, 8 (4), 19–23.

Cutbill, D. (2000), 'Incubators: the blueprint for new economy companies', *Los Angeles Business Journal*, http://www.findarticles.com.

Doran, A. and G. Bannock (2000), 'Publicly sponsored regional venture capital: what can the UK experience?', *Venture Capital: An International Journal of Entrepreneurial Finance*, 2 (4), 255–85.

Etzkowitz, H. (2002), 'Incubation of incubators: innovation as a Triple Helix of university–industry–government networks', *Science and Public Policy*, 29 (2), 115–28.

Frenkel, A., D. Shefer and M. Miller (2008), 'Public versus private technological incubators programmes: privatizing the technological incubators in Israel', *European Planning Studies*, 16 (2), 189–210.

Garnsey, E., S.C. Galloway and S.H. Mathiesen (1994), 'Flexibility and specialization in question: birth, growth and death rates of Cambridge new technology-based firms from 1988–92', *Entrepreneurship and Regional Development*, 6, 81–107.

Hannon, P.D. and P. Chaplin (2003), 'Are incubators good for business? Understanding incubation practice – the challenges for policy', *Environment and Planning C:Government and Policy*, 21 (6), 861–81.

Hood, A. (2000), 'Public venture capital and economic development: the Scottish experience', *Venture Capital: An International Journal of Entrepreneurial Finance*, 2 (4), 313–41.

Jim, Telesis and S. Tilles (1987), *Export-Led Growth Strategy for Israel*, Jerusalem: Jerusalem Institute of Management.

Kaufmann, D. and D. Schwartz (2009), 'Networking strategies of young biotechnology firms in Israel', *Annals of Regional Science*, 43 (3), 599–613.

Kaufmann, D., D. Schwartz, A. Frenkel and D. Shefer (2003), 'The role of location and regional networks for biotechnology firms in Israel', *European Planning Studies*, 11 (7), 823–40.

Kawashima, T. and W. Stöhr (1988), 'Decentralized technology policy: the case of Japan', *Environment and Planning C: Government and Policy*, 6 (4), 427–39.

Keeble, D. (1994), 'Regional influences and policy in new technology-based firm creation and growth', in R. Oakey (ed.), *New Technology-Based Firms in the 1990s*, London: Routledge, pp. 204–18.

Lemarié, S., V. Mangematin and A. Torre (2001), 'Is the creation and development of biotech SMEs localised? Conclusions drawn from the French case', *Small Business Economics*, 17, 61–76.

Malecki, E.J. (1991), *Technology and Economic Development*, New York: John Wiley.

McAdam, M. and R. McAdam (2006), 'The networked incubator: the role and operation of entrepreneurial networking with the University Science Park Incubator (USI)', *International Journal of Entrepreneurship and Innovation*, 7 (2) 87–97.

Mian, S.A. (1996), 'Assessing value-added contributions of university technology business incubators to tenant firms', *Research Policy*, 25 (3), 325–35.

Monitor, Inc. (2001), 'Israeli Biotechnology Strategy Project, realizing our potential', Final Report, the Chief Scientist.

Moore, I. and E.W. Garnsey (1993), 'Funding for innovation in small firms: the role of government', *Research Policy*, **22**, 507–19.

Niosi, J. and T. Bas (2001), 'The competencies of regions: Canada's clusters in biotechnology', *Small Business Economics*, **17**, 31–42.

OECD (1997), 'Technology incubators: nurturing small firms', http://www.oecd.org/pdf/M000014000/M00014673.pdf, Paris.

Office of the Chief Scientist (OCS) (2007), *The Israeli Economy at a Glance*, Jerusalem: OCS.

Peter, L., M. Rice and M. Sundararajan (2004), 'The role of incubators in the entrepreneurial process', *Journal of Technology Transfer*, **29**, 83–91.

Phillips, R.G. (2002), 'Technology business incubators: how effective as technology transfer mechanisms?', *Technology in Society*, **24**, 299–316.

Reynolds, K. (2000), 'Poplar incubators help hatch fledgling firms', *Los Angeles Business Journal*, http://www.findarticles.com.

Rice, M. and J. Matthews (1995), 'Growing new ventures, creating new jobs: principles and practices of Successful Business Incubation', Kauffman Center for Entrepreneurial Leadership, Kansas City.

Rothaermel, F.T. and M.T. Thursby (2005), 'University–incubator firm knowledge flows: assessing their impact on incubator firm performance', *Research Policy*, **34**, 305–20.

Saxenian, A. (1983), 'The genesis of the Silicon Valley', *Built Environment*, **9** (1), 7–17.

Schumpeter, J. (1934), *The Theory of Economic Development*, New York: Oxford University Press.

Segal Quince (1985), *The Cambridge Phenomenon*, Cambridge: Thetford Press.

Shefer, D. and E.L. Bar-El (1993), 'High-technology industries as a vehicle for growth in Israel's peripheral regions', *Environment and Planning C: Government and Policy*, **11**, 245–61.

Shefer, D. and A. Frenkel (1998), 'Local milieu and innovations: some empirical results', *Annals of Regional Science*, **32**, 185–200.

Shefer, D. and A. Frenkel (2003), 'An evaluation of the Israeli Public Technological Incubator Program and its projects – final report', S. Neaman Institute for Advanced Studies in Science and Technology, Technion-IIT, Haifa, Israel.

Sherrod, L. (1999), 'Incubating your business', *Essence*, http://www.findarticles.com.

PART VII

REGIONAL INNOVATION POLICY

Introduction

Philip Cooke and Ron Boschma

REGIONAL GOVERNANCE AND LEARNING

Part VII, the final Part of the *Handbook of Regional Innovation and Growth*, focuses on regional innovation policy. To a limited extent some such implications arose in Part VI on regional innovation institutions, especially intermediaries (Tödtling and Trippl's Chapter 33 and Nauwelaers's Chapter 34 in respect of 'relatedness' and 'conventions' that are marked features of the new regional innovation challenge). These pose interesting tasks for modes of governance of regional innovation and demands for new kinds of learning, both more proactive than the 'institutional borrowing' that characterized the supply-side era when markets became perceived as the solutions to developmental dilemmas. Main results of this in many countries have involved social polarization, financial market collapse, continued regional deindustrialization, if not industrial 'desertification', with only regional public sector employment excess to mitigate the resulting imbalances. Faced with the budgetary reckoning of this neoliberal experiment, regional governance, where it exists or survives, must perforce itself become innovative. Coordinated market economies have recognized this for some time, as exemplars from the chapters that follow make clear. The task is harder in liberal market economies, where injunctions that state intervention was the problem rather than the solution penetrated most deeply into the governance fabric.

Martin Heidenreich and Knut Koschatzky's Chapter 39 reviews the literature on regional governance of innovation, pointing to some fallacies and open questions about the manner of its conception and execution. Both authors inhabit Germany's coordinated market regime and are accordingly comfortable with federal norms that devolve some innovation and other knowledge responsibilities (for example universities) to the meso-level. They identify key efficiencies from knowledge recombination coordinated in regional institutions from the outset, primarily lower transaction costs, learning advantages from spatial proximity, and direct provision of 'collective competition goods'. 'Governance' moves beyond a region's 'soft institutions' such as conventions by addressing its 'harder' government plus civic or associational rules and regulations. These can involve the nature of financial support for innovation (this can range from grants to loans); university coordination (for example regional mergers or centres of excellence); sectoral, cluster or platform stimulus (see Harmaakorpi et al.'s Chapter 41); training and skills formation; foreign direct investment; and regional promotion abroad, a non-trivial package of innovation instruments.

REGIONAL GOVERNANCE AND POLICY LEARNING

Building social capital is a target of regional governance and variety in the interactions between these exerts a strong influence on the distinctiveness of regional governance idiosyncracies, which extend to regional innovation system configurations. Although for complex systems to function effectively there must be considerable system articulation, especially those involving multilevel regional–national–supranational strata, Heidenreich and Koschatzky refer to studies that see considerable friction among such levels. This is caused by networks negotiating and bargaining according to distinctively layered democratic politics. Thus, although not hierarchically organized in a top-down manner, the supranational can withhold resources from the national or regional levels if proposals to access policy funds infringe the 'rules of the game' being targeted. Occasionally a region can reject national policy inclination, clarify that it has reserved powers, or move ahead with its own projects where the state has abdicated a national strategic responsibility or allowed it to fall into disarray, conceivably for ideological reasons. 'Real service' provision to small and medium-sized enterprises (SMEs) by Italian regional administrations was a case of the last-named, which was subsequently forced into privatization by a hostile right-wing national government. The authors refer to Sabel's 'regional experimentalism' as characterizing aspects of such friction resolution. In general, friction of the kind noted is a minority pastime.

Regional agglomeration and associated regional advantage arising from spatially proximate innovation, productivity and growth also partly explain the success of ideas and practices promoting regional innovation governance. So, argue Heidenreich and Koschatzky, does recognition by evolutionary social scientists and practitioners (for whom neoclassical theorems can seem other-worldly) of the difficult-to-measure value of social networking and 'untraded interdependencies', Storper's regional 'dark matter' measurable only by its gravitational influence. Enough is understood of these at least to see their effects in rapid regional mobilization that can swiftly translate identity into action, showing a region has 'got its act together'. Is this an immutable regional comparative advantage for some or can it be 'learned' for wider regional practice? The generic design for this is portrayed in Heidenreich and Koschatzky's conclusion as dilemmas surrounding regional economic structure, regional networks, regional institutions and regional policies. The 'big shift' for new regional innovation policy is to attend to the content and multidimensional interrelationships of the second and third of these, rather than mapping the first onto the fourth, and vice versa. Regional intelligence and policy learning suggest that a more proactive catalytic or orchestrating role is required of regional innovation governance in future.

One perspective that promised this is 'the learning region', a concept anatomized by James Simmie in Chapter 40 of this *Handbook*. Somewhat disappointingly, the promise of this notion has not materialized, partly because as Simmie shows it got bifurcated into a normative idea resting on the injunction that learning was a desirable end for regions to aspire to, on the one hand, and more empirically that it was an action line in regional innovation strategy, on the other. Accordingly, it has never developed analytically even though as foregoing chapters make clear there is a clearly perceived need for 'regional policy learning' to tackle issues such as: 'cognitive switching' by entrepreneurs and policy functionaries; 'convention analysis' of regional production culture; policy mixing to stimulate 'path creation'; and the hybrid skills to facilitate relatedness and transversality (see Chapter 42 by Philip Cooke in this *Handbook*). In its origins, in the work of Richard Florida in 1995, 'learning region' is a response to the rise of the knowledge economy, as is even more the case in a rapid follow-up article by Björn Asheim which grounds the notion in Lundvall and Johnson's advocacy of building a 'learning economy' to face the exigencies of the same phenomenon. Michael Storper did not write about 'learning regions' as such, but devoted research time to comparing 'technological learning' in clusters with different convention sets or modes of untraded interdependence, which were probably the most fruitful theory and practice lines to follow. Finally, probably the most-cited variant of the 'learning region' idea was Kevin Morgan's paper of 1997. Here, Simmie shows the key to regional regeneration and improved social welfare lay in strengthening a region's social capital and institutional capacity to support learning.

Critique of the concept has ranged from ascribing it the status of 'fuzzy', an 'impressionistic neologism', 'unlikely', 'over-localized', and challenged by 'learning asymmetries'. This is reminiscent of the many critiques aimed at the cognate concept of 'organizational learning' in firms. Here problems concerning how to sample, from where or whom to learn, whether what might be learned was applicable, and indeed whether it was yesterday's knowledge, meaning the learner would be engaged in a permanent failure to 'catch up', were all raised. This all seems rather unfair to what – if the concept had been better specified, perhaps in terms of learning the region's paradigm and regime uniqueness and how it might be 'nudged' towards path-interdependence – we now see to be a fundamental cognitive need in accomplishing regional innovation and growth. This seems to be the thinking in recent attempts to revisit the concept by Rutten and Boekma who are cited in Simmie'schapter . However, the kind of conceptual and policy instruments needed to achieve such endogenous regional change are nowhere specified.

REGIONAL PLATFORMS, METHODS AND NEW INNOVATION POLICIES

This task is undertaken by Vesa Harmaakorpi, Tomi Tura and Helinä Melkas in Chapter 41 of this *Handbook* with their 'platform' concept of regional innovation and renewal. The roots of this model are found in recognition of basic Schumpeterian insights into the nature of innovation as a product of cross-fertilization of knowledge and ideas. This is something which the cluster idea, as the apotheosis of proximate specialization, obscured for academics and policy-makers alike for two decades or more. Accordingly, there has been a lack of policy measures to foster practice-based, networked innovation processes that combine diverse knowledge bases. It could be added that until recently, and in the process of being articulated into a synthesis in this *Handbook*, there has been relatively little intellectual leadership of an alternative perspective either. One reason for this is that although the Lundvall line that policy learning is for policy-makers not academics seems a little harsh, it is difficult to think out and design policy in the 'ivory tower', an otherwise excellent location for reflection and critique. Harmaakorpi and associates have the privilege of occupying both 'worlds': academia and innovation policy-making simultaneously. This enabled them to conduct 'regional experiments' à la Charles Sabel. One criticism they have of the 'proximity' perspective is that it fails to explain how learning from knowledge spillovers actually happens, and that this may be negative. They find the distance implied in the notion of diversity more appealing because it avoids negatives like involuntary spillovers, opportunism and lock-in. Accordingly their aim is to create an efficient balance between the contradictory purposes of enhancing proximity and distance. The cluster model is seen to be suboptimal in this respect and accordingly inferior to a platform model of regional innovation policy.

The 'platform' model of regional innovation policy displays the following key characteristics: its network morphology is one based on loose-coupling of weak ties engaging with 'structural holes', that is, areas where network interactions may produce innovations if the holes can be filled with innovation discourse, action and content; social capital is thus of the institutional 'bridging' kind; knowledge production is transversal; knowledge conversion is by means of cross-fertilization; regional absorptive capacity is future-oriented; experience-based learning is favoured over science-based learning; external economies are those of 'urbanization' rather than 'localization' in kind; and innovation systems are regional and national. On this basis structured experiences of challenges and change of conventions, competences and capabilities are induced by articulation of discourses among firms and stakeholders combining related knowledge from inside and beyond the region. The aim of this is to create a regional platform based on relatedness and supported by platform policies that optimize it.

Facilitation of the required articulation of discourses that may valorize or change conventions, and build up firm and intermediary competences and capabilities, is by instigating a structure of learning institutions and processes in the region. The key spatial process aims here are: to clarify the nature and forms of regional related variety; to facilitate the recombination of knowledge; to identify the 'structural holes' or 'white spaces' where innovation opportunity may lie; and to evolve regional platforms that combine knowledge, clusters and sectors for purposes of innovation. Complementing these in a new regional innovation systems perspective are four policy concepts. First, 'enlightenment' may be diffused through the deployment of dramaturgy, literally acting out scripts of representative 'convention sets' under challenge. Second, having a mode of 'orchestrating' dramaturgy and other learning facilities, such as 'ideas incubators', 'living laboratories' and 'improvization sessions'. Orchestration here implies promotion of such assets and conducting their articulation into a coherent narrative. Third, achieving 'transversality', or the cross-pollination of intercluster or sector-cluster innovation potentials within and beyond the region; and finally, evolving methodologies, such as technology or creativity matrices to concretize commercializable innovation actions and outcomes.

The exemplar of this is engineering-rich Bavaria but it is also practised in the design-driven innovation context of Lombardy with its creative and innovative design-intensive domestic furnishing, lighting and kitchenware clusters, as described (after Verganti) by Philip Cooke and Arne Eriksson (Chapter 43 of this *Handbook*). Here, the innovation paradigm is changed relatively frequently and radically in the 'episodic' sense by articulation of discourse that changes conventions by changing the meanings prioritized in the prevailing socio-cultural regime. This demands inputs from inside and well beyond the region, as well as inside and well beyond the specific cluster. It requires strong articulation of regional firms and stakeholder institutions and it is orchestrated in ways that 'propose' innovations to markets. It can thus be vulnerable to overestimation of the market appeal of new lines but such 'practical reasoning' is also built into the articulation of discourse process.

Accordingly, a new paradigm for regional innovation and growth has been evolved in ways that meet the criticisms of the weaknesses and lacunae of inherited models, rooted as these initially were in manufacturing supply chain thinking of the 1990s. This is by no means the only way forward but it resonates completely with the main threads of the discourse from its Schumpeterian origins to the modern day. As Arnoud Lagendijk shows in the final chapter of this *Handbook*, Chapter 44, the new agenda for regional innovation policy is different from the old. As others have noted, endogenous innovation policy with the regional agency in a more catalytic role is now expected to replace the backstop functions it had in responding to market failures and welfare enhancement imperatives in the neoliberal, supply-side era. This is conceived as the appropriate posture in the context of a global knowledge economy regime assailed by seemingly intractable crises of economy and ecology.

The region where innovation platform methodology was pioneered was a declining economy within Finland; the region where pulp and paper relatedness evolved into cross-media clustering is a relatively poor, peripheral region in Sweden; London and other metropoles may not be as innovative as presumed because they bask in conventions of entitlement, expectation and privilege. Accordingly, the 'innovation paradox' reported by Lagendijk as least absorptive capacity in regions needing most innovation is clearly somewhat shaky and in need of measured reflection. He also draws attention to 'smart specialization' as an appropriate response, building on regions' own paradigm and regime assets rather than aping those of inappropriate exemplars. With this we would agree, except that we would elaborate the concept to 'smart diversification' in light of the relatedness, path-interdependence, conventions and transversality imperatives central to the concerns of this *Handbook* and to evolutionary economic geography more generally.

39 Regional innovation governance
Martin Heidenreich and Knut Koschatzky

Economic regions can be an efficient way of organizing distributed innovation processes which require the development, accumulation and recombination of heterogeneous knowledge under conditions of economic, technical and scientific uncertainties. These advantages have been explained by transaction cost savings; by the private or public provision of products, services and qualifications that fit the specific needs of the regional companies; by the opportunity to establish and stabilize interaction-based trust relationships; or by learning advantages, because spatial proximity is supposed to facilitate the exchange of implicit, experience-based, uncodified knowledge and the recombination of previous knowledge (Scott, 1998; Cooke, 2002a). Regional institutions play a crucial role for these advantages, because they may contribute to the provision of 'local collective competition goods' (for example qualified employees, research and development services, technology transfer, reliable legal or technological norms, information on new markets and technologies, consultancy and other 'real services'; see Le Galès and Voelzkow, 2001). Regional governance structures, composed of: 'a control and regulatory structure that brings governmental and societal actors together, has both formal and informal levels, and is characterised by hierarchical, competitive, and cooperative inter-actor relations' (Benz, 2001), are therefore crucial for the innovative capabilities of a region.

In the following, we will discuss first this concept of regional (innovation) governance, then the role of regional governance structures in different theoretical approaches, and finally the link between regional policy, regional learning and regional governance structures.

THE CONCEPT OF REGIONAL INNOVATION GOVERNANCE AND ITS IMPLICATIONS

Governance

The theoretical discussion on regional innovation systems (RISs) is closely connected to the term 'governance' (Cooke, 2002a; Cooke et al., 2004). From an economic perspective, governance is defined as the existence of rules and the way they are enforced in economic transactions. The starting point of the new institutional economics, which was firmly established in the scientific debate by Oliver Williamson's contribution *Markets and Hierarchies* in 1975, is the assumption that bounded rationality and behavioural uncertainty are the most significant barriers and limitations for human decision-making behaviour. 'Bounded rationality' and 'genuine uncertainty' prevent the perfect coordination of complete contracts to reduce uncertainty (Williamson, 1985, 46). Uncertainty arises in part through opportunistic behaviour ('moral hazard') by actors, that is, by pursuit of self-interest with guile or through artificially caused information asymmetries to gain advantage (Williamson, 1985, 47–8). Depending on the expected opportunistic behaviour, different protective arrangements are required, for example contracts or laws, and rights emerging therefrom (for example property rights), which must be protected (North, 1990, 3–4). The state is interpreted thereby as a powerful organization which sets up rules and standards, as well as institutions, and is not dependent on consensus in this endeavour.

From a political science viewpoint, governance refers to the analysis of the balance of power in relationships and thus to collective action in different fields of activity (Fürst, 2001, 371). According to a definition of governance given by the Commission on Global Governance (1995, 4), it is:

> the sum of the many ways individuals and institutions, public and private, manage their common affairs. It is a continuing process through which conflicting or diverse interests may be accommodated and cooperative action may be taken. It includes formal institutions and regimes empowered to enforce compliance, as well as informal arrangements that people and institutions either have agreed to or perceive to be in their interest.

Mayntz (1993, 11) defines governance as the social coordination of collective action by systems of norms and order. Collective action thus plays an important role in governance.

Due to the significance of collective action in political coordination, close ties exist between governance and the concept of social capital (Rosenfeld's Chapter 21 in this *Handbook*). Social capital is formed by characteristics of civic social organization such as trust, norms and networks, which can improve societal efficiency and make coordinated action possible (Putnam et al., 1993; Putnam, 1995). Social capital facilitates the cooperation of societal actors in order to reach common goals. Due to its meaningful role for social, economic and technological development, the accumulation of social capital is a target of public governance (Aldridge et al., 2002, 51). Governments as the most important organizations for public coordination are, like other organizations and their members, part of a social system and thus dependent on the social capital of the social system.

Regional Governance

Regional governance is aimed at complex and intermediary regulatory structures in regions (Benz and Fürst, 2003, 12) and can be understood as complementary to state, private sector or communal regulation (Fürst, 2004). It starts with the typical structural characteristics of the regions, consisting of market, hierarchy and associations and in particular the interdependency of these structures (Fürst, 2001, 374). Voelzkow et al. (2007) propose a more fine-grained typology of governance modes: the state and companies (as two forms of hierarchical coordination), markets, associations, communities and networks, which shape policies in such different fields as corporate governance, finance, vocational training, research and development (R&D), and industrial relations. These governance structures are the basis of institutional learning processes because they regulate the interaction between people, private and public associations and companies: 'By reducing uncertainty and, thus, the amount of information needed for individual and collective action, institutions are fundamental building blocks in all societies' (Johnson, 1992, 26).

Resulting from the regional contexts of these structural characteristics, specific regional governing styles emerge, so that regional governance: '[is] not a standardisable form of self-government, but each region . . . [develops] its own idiosyncratic form' (Fürst, 2004, 375). Thus the political regulatory competences of regions are unequal and, due to the connection to the inherent regional structures, also path-dependent. Accordingly, different regions distinguish themselves by region-specific governance structures, each of which grew out of the respective economic, political and social environment and in the course of the region's specific history.

Focusing on regional autonomy and competences, Wiehler and Stumm (1995, 244–245) differentiate the following regional governance types in Europe:

- regions with wide-ranging powers (for example German *Länder*);
- regions with advanced powers (for example Spanish autonomous communities);
- regions with limited powers (for example Dutch provinces); and
- regions without power (for example Portuguese planning regions).

The heuristic concept of regional innovation systems (Iammarino, 2005) provides a suitable basis to analyse the contextual structures of regional governance. Cooke (2004) in particular has proposed a complex typology of more or less centralized governance forms of enterprise innovation support (see also Asheim and Gertler, 2005 for the related distinction of territorially embedded, regionally networked and regionalized national innovation systems).

First, grassroots systems:

> In terms of technology transfer action the *initiation* process in this modality is locally organised, at town or district level. *Funding* will be diffuse in origin, comprising a mix of local banking, local government, possibly local Chamber of Commerce capital, grants and loans. The *research* competence is likely to be highly applied or near-market. The level of technical *specialisation* will be low and generic problem-solving is more likely than significant, finely-honed, technological expertise. Finally the degree of supra-local *co-ordination* will be low because of the localised nature of the initiation. (Cooke, 2004, 11)

Examples of this type can be found in the central Italian regions with industrial districts or in states with film, design, biotechnology and information technology (IT) clusters, for example in Southern California.

Second, network systems:

> *Initiation* of technology transfer action in a network modality is multi-level . . . *funding* is more likely to be guided by agreement amongst banks, government agencies and firms. The *research* competence in a networked innovation architecture is likely to be mixed, with both pure and applied, 'blue-skies' and near-market activities geared to the needs of large and small firms. System *co-ordination* is likely to be high because of the large number of stakeholders and the presence of associations, fora, industry clubs and the like. *Specialisation* within such a system is likely to be flexible. (Cooke, 2004, 12)

Examples of this type are the regional innovation systems in Baden-Württemberg, North-Rhine Westphalia and the regions of Denmark.

Third, dirigiste systems:

Technology transfer activities in a *dirigiste* innovation model are animated mainly from outside and above the region itself. *Initiation* of actions is typically a product of central government policies. *Funding* is largely centrally determined although the agencies in question may have decentralised locations in the regions. The kind of *research* conducted in *dirigiste* systems is often rather basic or fundamental and it may be expected to relate to the needs of larger, possibly state-owned, firms in or beyond the region in question. The level of *co-ordination* in such a RIS is very high, at least potentially, since it is state-run, and the level of *specialisation* is also likely to be high. (Cooke, 2004, 13)

French regions, but also Singapore and Slovenia, are examples of this type.

An important topic in the debate on regional governance structures is the interaction of different regulatory levels, because regional development processes are also shaped by national and sometimes also local and supranational political actions and institutions. Therefore, 'multi-level governance relationships' play an important role. Cooke et al., 2000, 96) stresses:

> [the] complementarity of regional, national and EU networks and support structures . . . The services of universities, technology transfer and training are often easiest to access at the level of the region. The national level often has most of the relevant funds for innovation support, also specialized research organizations and training institutions are there. The EU level might focus on generic research activities.

Such a multilevel governance system creates the preconditions for regional openness, the penetrating into supraregional, national and supranational policy levels and the integration of regional innovation systems in globally operating technological and enterprise systems (see Cooke, 2002b, 136–7). Such a view of the interaction of different governance levels is called into question by Voelzkow et al. (2007), who demonstrate the frictions especially between the regional governance structures – which often focus on specific sectors and technologies – and the national level.

In a democratic system, policy-making does not take place in the form of top-down decision-making, but is a result of networking and bargaining between different societal actors, interest coalitions and systems, that is, in 'multi-actor innovation policy arenas' (Kuhlmann, 2001, 961). Usually, there is no dominant player, but the policy arena is composed of a variety of political, corporate, social and scientific bodies. Since the beginning of the 1990s, regional governments have become an additional and important actor in this policy arena. According to Cooke (2003, 414), this move towards regional innovation 'brought a stronger emphasis from the sub-national, mainly regional level of intervention as animator of a public–private process of interactive and mainly incremental learning-based innovation'. In regions, not only multiactor arenas exist, but they are also an object of multilevel governance structures. Due to the complexity of intervening factors at the regional level (besides the upper hierarchical policy levels, corporate and technology regimes for instance play an important role):

> necessary adaptation and integration processes of the innovation systems can obviously not be carried out completely and exclusively by the original innovation actors in industry and science on their own . . . [but] . . . state-based mediating and regulatory capacities of political systems will remain indispensable. (Kuhlmann, 2001, 966)

Regional Innovation Governance

In view of the move towards regional innovation, new disruptive technologies opened a 'window of opportunity' for the self-contained configuration of the regional science and innovation system (Charles et al., 2004), for the creation of interfaces with national policies and for a stronger participation in measures formerly mainly oriented towards the national level. In this political context, those regions which are the object of national and European policy support are privileged. In the framework of the general policy that aims at concentrating on excellence within the European Research Area (European Commission, 2001) regional equality is of no concern (Héraud, 2003). On the other hand, for many regions the fight for public funds becomes harder: strongly relying on knowledge resources for economic and social development, they enter a new form of global competition with similar regions. In this respect, the formulation and implementation of new policy concepts and the use of strategic intelligence are necessary for creating a supportive environment which attracts innovative companies – and human capital for research and development as well (Fürst, 2001). Depending on the economic situation of a region and its degree of exploitation of regional innovation potential, either more catalytic (that is, support of network formation) or more interventionalist (that is, direct intervention and governance) policy approaches are appropriate (Enright, 2003). In a catalytic approach, the role of a (regional) government should be confined to the setting of a favourable legal and institutional environment, and should stimulate but not govern processes. According to Charles et al. (2004, 13), three key roles are attributed to regional governments:

- setting regional priorities for research on the basis of small units of excellence not necessarily recognized at the national scale;
- negotiating with central actors to shape central policies for the benefits of their regions;
- building linkages from all elements of the regional science system into innovation, commercialization and technology transfer.

Cooke et al. (2000, 104) distinguish between knowledge application and exploitation subsystems on the one hand (for example horizontal and vertical network linkages between firms) and knowledge generation and diffusion subsystems (universities, research institutes, technology transfer agencies, and regional and local innovation support agencies) on the other hand (see Figure 39.1). On the basis of 11 regional case studies, the authors distinguish regions with high, medium and low infrastructural and policy organizational capacities for developing regional innovation potential, with Baden-Württemberg, Styria, Wales and the Basque Country on the higher, and Centro (Portugal), Féjer (Hungary) and Lower Silesia on the lower side of the spectrum.

With reference to the ability for regional governance, social capital plays a crucial role, when the learning capabilities and absorptive capacities of regional policy and promotional organizations and the openness for collective action are sufficiently developed (Koschatzky, 2001, 334; Marin and Mayntz, 1991, 18). Therefore, economic governance aims at the strengthening of networks of association, the encouragement of voice and negotiation, the mobilization of a plurality of autonomous organizations and context-sensitive, local, procedural rationalities of behaviour (Amin, 1999, 368).

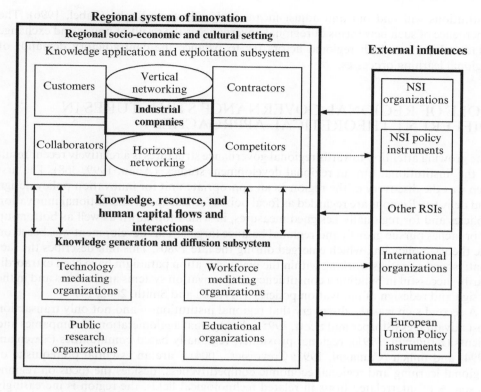

Figure 39.1   Regional knowledge generation, diffusion and exploitation

Such a procedural approach has been described as 'regional experimentalism' (Sabel, 1996; Heidenreich, 2005; see also Chapter 1, 'Introduction', in this *Handbook*)). Its basic assumption is that the renewal of an economic region requires a simultaneous reinvention of organizational and regional capabilities. Complementary to the restructuring of regional firms, the region, its boundaries, its identities, its governance structures, its 'collective competition goods' and its political and associational actors have to be 're-invented' in order to face the uncertainties of international competition on costs and innovation. A classical role of regional institutions was the public provision of collective competition goods or 'real services' for smaller firms that could not afford their own departments (for marketing, quality assurance, consulting and so on). This however requires that the regional associations know what type of public goods are required. Given the openness of networked processes of regional cooperation – which have been described as 'pragmatic collaboration' (Helper et al., 2000, 445) – this assumption is highly unrealistic. Sabel (2004, 86) therefore observes the emergence of a new, processural type of regional governance, whereby 'learning' regional institutions which create the conditions for a creative interpretation of new situations and opportunities become crucial for the support of innovative networks of enterprises: 'experimentalist institutions will find out and adjust means and ends accordingly' (Sabel, 1996). The emergence of such new forms of regional governance is the result of power and exchange relationships, in which regional actors try to balance the contradictory demands of regional learning processes.

ROLE OF REGIONAL GOVERNANCE STRUCTURES IN DIFFERENT THEORETICAL APPROACHES

The growing attention towards regional governance structures is a relatively recent result of the 'institutional turn in regional development studies' (Amin, 1999, 368). The first step was the discovery of the region as an appropriate unit for innovation policy design and delivery. Regions are regarded as focal points for European and national innovation policies and for regionally designed measures, in which top-down as well as bottom-up approaches pursue growth and regional balance targets. This development was based on the theory–policy link which emerged during the late 1980s. This link describes the fact that: 'social scientists working within the new innovation paradigm have been extraordinarily successful in building a constituency for innovation systems approaches and in the design and redesign of innovation policies' (Mytelka and Smith, 2002, 1477).

A second step was the discovery that regional institutions – and not only transaction cost advantages (Storper and Scott, 1995), the regional agglomeration of companies and clients (Krugman, 1991), regional proximity, regionally based communities (Saxenian, 1994) and milieu (Camagni, 1991; Crevoisier, 2004) – are an essential prerequisite of regional learning and regional economic competitiveness. Besides the focus on regions as spaces of interrelated firms in related technological fields, the region is increasingly analysed also as a space for subnational institutions and governance structures.

In earlier studies, the advantages of regional proximity were analysed, on the one hand, as a result of transaction cost advantages (see von Thünen, 1966 [1826]; Christaller, 1933) or the availability of natural resources (coal, ore, wood, sun, fertile land; Vatne's Chapter 4 in this *Handbook*). Krugman (1991), as one of the protagonists of the 'new economic geography' (see Koschatzky, 2001), explains the emergence and consolidation of regional agglomerations by the reduction of procurement and distribution costs, that is, by the cost advantages of territorially concentrated forward and backward linkages. These advantages are also crucial for the Californian school of regional studies (see Storper and Scott, 1995). On the other hand, other regional advantages are the possibility to exploit the experience, knowledge and skills of proximate companies and institutions. These learning and network effects have often been analysed as the quasi-natural result of proximity (see, for example, Marshall, 1982 [1890], 225, taking the example of the textile industry in Lancashire: 'The mysteries of the trade become no mystery, but are as it were in the air'). Porter (1998) systematizes this intuition by explaining the competitive advantages of regionally concentrated clusters by four factors: the proximity to competitors; challenging clients; efficient regional suppliers and service providers; and the availability of a qualified workforce. In this perspective, regional advantages are not only the result of transaction cost savings, but also the result of mutual learning facilitated by geographic, social and institutional proximity: 'knowledge creation is supported by the institutional embodiment of tacit knowledge' (Maskell and Malmberg, 1999, 167).

In the 1980s, the seminal study of Piore and Sabel (1984) drew attention to the institutional bases of regional learning and innovation. They describe regional institutions as the essential basis for cooperation between competing companies. Besides the disproved prediction of the 'end of mass production', the concept of flexible specialization focuses the attention to industrial districts and postulates a revival of regionally embedded forms of production. They describe industrial districts as a promising, innovative type of a spatially distributed division of labour, which are characterized by: (1) the production of highly specialized products for diversified markets (economies of scope); (2) the use of flexible technologies; and (3) regional institutions, which balance cooperation and competition between companies, thus stimulating them to continuous innovation. Examples of such institutions are trade unions, guilds and purchasing cooperatives, marketing cooperatives, vocational schools, regional business associations and regional savings banks (Zeitlin, 2008).

While Piore and Sabel (1984) still conceptualized regional governance structures mainly as stable communities, and underlined the importance of personal, direct, trust-based interactions, Storper (1997) proposed a less 'personalized' concept of regional governance. He analyses regional economic relations as conversation and coordination and points to the crucial role of 'untraded interdependencies', that is, non-market relations, conventions, informal rules and habits that coordinate an economy faced with uncertainty. He designates regions as 'worlds of production'. The basis of regional identities, relations and networks are 'conventions', that is: 'taken-for-granted mutually coherent expectations, routines, and practices, which are sometimes manifested as formal institutions and rules, but often not' (Storper, 1997, 38). These conventions can be understood as regional institutional orders or governance structures, which shape the 'action capacities' of economic agents and the economic identities of territories and regions.

In comparison with the 'relational perspective', and similar to (but largely independently of) the concept of national innovation systems (Edquist, 2005), the concept of regional innovation systems (RISs) (Cooke et al., 2004) emphasizes more strongly the role of formal regional institutions; an RIS: 'consists of interacting knowledge generation and exploitation sub-systems linked to global, national and other regional systems for commercialising new knowledge' (Cooke, 2004, 3). Similarly to the distinction between knowledge exploitation and knowledge diffusion subsystems, Asheim and Isaksen (2002, 83) characterize their version of innovation systems firstly by:

> firms in the main industrial cluster in a region including their support industries. Secondly, an institutional infrastructure must be present, i.e., research and higher education institutes, technology transfer agencies, vocational training organisations, business associations, finance institutions etc., which hold important competence to support regional innovation.

The first part of this definition may be too restrictive, because an RIS is not necessarily characterized by a dominant industrial cluster. An RIS may contain many clusters or no clusters at all. The second part of this definition stresses the fact that regional innovation systems are not only integrated through production and value chains (for example by supplier and buyer networks), but also by institutions and regional cultures. The potential strengths of these systems consist in the capability to provide collective resources which stimulate and stabilize communication and cooperation between regional companies, schools, universities, technology transfer, research and development facilities, and political and administrative actors, which may contribute to organizational, technical and social innovations.

Thus the crucial 'output' of regional governance structures is the provision of regional collective goods – for example the access to specialized technological knowledge, information about new markets, the vocational training of qualified and motivated manpower adapted to the needs of regional industry; but also the stabilization of regional networks and patterns of cooperation: 'Provision of such goods must be ensured by social or political arrangements, that is by forms of local governance' (Le Galès and Voelzkow, 2001, 1). In general, these collective goods cannot be provided only by regional firms. Especially in countries with stronger regional governments and decentralized political competences (for example in Spain, Germany or Italy), the provision of these regional collective competition goods and thus regional innovativeness is facilitated by political institutions (Crouch et al., 2001, 2004).

In conclusion, at least five different foundations for regional economic advantage have been discussed in regional studies: regionally available (natural) resources; transaction cost savings; specialization advantages in regional clusters; learning and innovation advantages due to geographical, social and institutional proximity; and last but not least, institutionally stabilized regional orders. The last two advantages can be interpreted as outcomes of regional governance structures. This implies also that regional governance structures are not the only source of regional advantage. While the relational perspective focuses on untraded interdependencies between reflexive actors and thus the crucial role of networks, regional identity, reputation and trust, the RIS approach stresses the complementarity between interorganizational networks and (mostly formal) institutions. Le Galès and Voelzkow (2001) show that the crucial function of these institutions is the provision of local collective competition goods.

CHALLENGES FOR REGIONAL INNOVATION GOVERNANCE

Regional innovation governance has to take the peculiarities of innovation activities into account, namely uncertainty, complexity and interactivity (Dosi, 1988). Compared to other forms of regional governance, innovation governance faces the dilemma that it should govern a phenomenon which is highly uncertain, unpredictable, complex and of systemic nature. On the one hand, regional actors and governance structures have to open up to new demands, challenges and technologies; on the other hand, the relative closure of regions is a precondition for regionally concentrated social and industrial networks and the incremental accumulation of competences.

This dilemma is translated in four different dilemmas of regional innovation systems (Heidenreich, 2004). First, businesses must assert themselves under increasingly globalized competition. Paradoxically, this is accompanied by the increasing importance of local, experience-based, context-bound knowledge. Second, innovative firms are dependent on distributed knowledge of innovation networks, that is, on trust-based patterns of cooperation between firms, schools, research institutes, political authorities and users, as these networks facilitate the recombination of technical knowledge and the embeddedness of new technologies. However, these networks may also be the source of lock-in effects (Grabher, 1993). Third, strong linkages between scientific, economic, political, technical and cultural actors may facilitate mutual learning processes between regional actors. These regional networks, however, may also hamper radical scientific, economic or technical innovations. Fourth, regional competitiveness is based on the accumulation and path-dependent development of competences. This, however, may also impede new technological trajectories. These four dilemmas shape the regional economic structure (between regionalization and globalization), regional networks (between fragility, regional learning and lock-in-effects), regional development and technology transfer institutions (between learning and inertia), and regional policies, which are characterized by the tension between the preservation of previous strengths and the development of new technological and economic opportunities.

The fourth dilemma is a crucial challenge for the design of regional policies and governance structures. On the one hand, regions are successful in a short-term perspective if the innovation-supporting institutional infrastructure (education and research, bank systems, technology transfer, industrial policy) is adjusted to the dominant industrial specialization. In this way, regional governance structures can contribute to the preservation and incremental development of accumulated industrial experiences and competences. Cluster policies, for example, may stimulate and stabilize 'networks of production of strongly interdependent firms (including specialised suppliers), knowledge producing agents (universities, research institutes, engineering companies), bridging institutions (brokers, consultants), and customers linked to each other in a value-adding production chain' (Boekholt and Thuriaux, 1999, 381). This, however, may impede the exploitation of new technological and market opportunities. While the existing technological and organizational patterns of specialization must be supported by regional institutions, new technological fields can only be reached if the region and its firms and institutions open up to new perspectives, cooperation partners and technologies. This, however, requires a diversification of regional competences beyond the established networks and technological trajectories.

This tension between new technological and market opportunities and the lock-in effects of regional networks, institutions and patterns of specialization confronts regional policies with considerable uncertainties, which can no longer be dealt with by top-down decisions. Innovation policy as one of the most important forms of innovation governance requires learning experiences, social capital and strategic intelligence in policy-making. Strategic intelligence is: 'a set of – often distributed – sources of information and explorative as well as analytical (theoretical, heuristic, methodological) tools employed to produce useful insight in [sic] the actual or potential costs and effects of public or private policy and management' (Kuhlmann, 2002, 17). According to Nauwelaers (2000; and see her Chapter 34 in this *Handbook*), 'policy learning' can be understood as: 'the capacity of policy-makers to grasp the trajectories taken by firms in their knowledge governance modes . . . and the capacity to respond to such changes by developing flexible policy approaches in instruments'. It appears necessary to combine regional intelligence (that is, the ability to understand the socio-economic context and enterprises' needs); with policy learning, that is, the possibility to permit and support further developments in political goals and instruments (see also Simmie's 'Learning regions' Chapter 40 in this *Handbook*). These 'political opportunity structures' (Fürst, 2001, 375) represent a seedbed for regional governance, especially when an implicit demand for regional policy steering already exists, due to special problem situations and challenges.

Policy design and implementation thus involves the participation of a broad spectrum of actors. It also requires new forms of coordination like networks or clusters (Porter, 1998; Martin and Sunley, 2003). The diversity of economic and social actors in a system is seen as being important to its long-term survival and growth. Indeed, it could be argued that many disadvantaged regions are lacking a diverse set of actors which hinders their growth and development. Little attention has been paid so far to the understanding of the diversity of economic and social actors relevant to innovation within an innovation system. Very little is known about how to characterize the relevant key actors, in terms of their interests, motivations, functions and connectivity within systems. A higher diversity will also provide a more diverse set of functions in terms of innovation activities. For example, research on intermediaries points to a wide variety of new functions and frameworks provided by these actors (Howells, 2006). The diversity of actors involved adds further complexity to decision-making processes. From a policy perspective, questions emerge on how to integrate these actors in the policy arena and how to align and reach consensus across different (even conflicting) interests and objectives. The participation of a variety of new actors in social spaces of science and technology policy-making, for example in the form of regional foresight, has also become an important issue (Renn and Thomas, 2002; Koschatzky, 2005). The field is thus dynamic and displays an evolving research agenda.

REFERENCES

Aldridge, S., D. Halpern and S. Fitzpatrick (2002), 'Social capital: a discussion paper', London: Performance and Innovation Unit, Cabinet Office.
Amin, Ash (1999), 'An institutional perspective on regional economic development', *International Journal of Urban and Regional Research*, **23**, 365–78.
Asheim, B. and M.S. Gertler (2005), 'The geography of innovation: regional innovation systems' in J. Fagerberg, D.C. Mowery and R.R. Nelson (eds), *The Oxford Handbook of Innovation*, Oxford: Oxford University Press, pp. 291–317.
Asheim, B.T. and A. Isaksen (2002), 'Regional innovation systems: the integration of local "sticky" and global "ubiquitous" knowledge', *Journal of Technology Transfer*, **27**, 77–86.
Benz, A. (2001), 'From associations of local governments to "regional governance" in urban regions', *German Journal of Urban Studies*, **40** (2), 139–54.
Benz, A. and D. Fürst (2003), 'Region – "Regional Governance" – Regionalentwicklung', in B. Adamaschek and M. Pröhl (eds), *Regionen erfolgreich steuern. Regional Governance – von der kommunalen zur regionalen Strategie*, Gütersloh: Bertelsmann, pp. 11–66.
Boekholt, P. and B. Thuriaux (1999), 'Public policies to facilitate clusters: background, rationale and policy practices in international perspective' in OECD (ed.), *Boosting Innovation: The Cluster Approach*, Paris: OECD, pp. 381–412.
Camagni, R. (ed.) (1991), *Innovation Networks: Spatial Perspectives*, London: Belhaven.
Charles, D., B. Perry and P. Benneworth (eds) (2004), *Towards a Multi-Level Science Policy: Regional Science Policy in a European Context*, Seaford: Regional Studies Association.
Christaller, W. (1933), *Die zentralen Orte in Süddeutschland*, Jena: A. Fischer.
Commission on Global Governance (1995), *Our Global Neighborhood: The Report of the Commission on Global Governance*, Oxford: Oxford University Press.
Cooke, P. (2002a), *Knowledge Economies: Clusters, Learning and Cooperative Advantage*, London: Routledge.
Cooke, P. (2002b), 'Regional innovation systems: general findings and some new evidence from biotechnology clusters', *Journal of Technology Transfer*, **27**, 133–45.
Cooke, P. (2003), Economic globalisation and its future challenges for regional development', *International Journal of Technology Management*, **26**, 401–20.
Cooke, P. (2004), 'Introduction: regional innovation systems. An evolutionary approach', in P. Cooke, M. Heidenreich and H.-J. Braczyk (eds), *Regional Innovation Systems*, 2nd edn, London, UK and New York, USA: Routledge, pp. 1–18.

Cooke, P., P. Boekholt and F. Tödtling (2000), *The Governance of Innovation in Europe*. London, UK and New York, USA: Pinter.

Cooke, P., M. Heidenreich and H.-J. Braczyk (eds) (2004), *Regional Innovation Systems*, 2nd edn, London: Routledge.

Crevoisier, O. (2004), 'The innovative milieus approach: toward a territorialized understanding of the economy?', *Economic Geography*, **80**, 367–79.

Crouch, C., P. Le Galès, C. Trigilia and H. Voelzkow (2001), *Local Production Systems in Europe: Rise or Demise?*, Oxford: Oxford University Press.

Crouch, C., C. Trigilia, H. Voelzkow and P. Le Galès (2004), *Changing Governance of Local Economies: Responses of European Local Production Systems*, New York: Oxford University Press.

Dosi, G. (1988), 'The nature of the innovative process', in G. Dosi, C. Freeman, R. Nelson, G. Silverberg and L. Soete (eds), *Technical Change and Economic Theory*, London, UK and New York, USA: Pinter, pp. 221–38.

Edquist, C. (2005), 'Systems of innovation: perspectives and challenges', in J. Fagerberg, D.C. Mowery and R.R. Nelson (eds), *The Oxford Handbook of Innovation*, Oxford: Oxford University Press, pp. 181–208.

Enright, M. (2003), 'Regional clusters: what we know and what we should know', in J. Bröcker, D. Dohse and R. Soltwedel (eds), *Innovation Clusters and Interregional Competition*, Berlin: Springer, pp. 99–129.

European Commission (2001), *The Regional Dimension of the European Research Area*, Brussels: European Commission (COM(2001)549 final).

Fürst, D. (2001), 'Regional governance – ein neues Paradigma der Regionalwissenschaften?', *Raumforschung und Raumordnung*, **59**, 370–80.

Fürst, D. (2004), 'Regional governance', in A. Benz (ed.), *Governance Regieren in komplexen Regelsystemen. Eine Einführung*, Wiesbaden: Verlag für Sozialwissenschaften, pp. 45–64.

Grabher, G. (1993), 'The weakness of strong ties: the lock-in of regional development in the Ruhr area' in G. Grabher (ed.), *The Embedded Firm*, London: Routledge, pp. 255–77.

Heidenreich M. (2004), 'The dilemmas of regional innovation systems', in P. Cooke, M. Heidenreich and H.-J. Braczyk (eds), *Regional Innovation Systems: The Role of Governance in a Globalized World*. 2nd edn, London, UK and New York, USA: Routledge, pp. 363–89.

Heidenreich, M. (2005), 'The renewal of regional capabilities: experimental regionalism in Germany', *Research Policy*, **34**, 739–57.

Helper, S., J.P. MacDuffie and C.F. Sabel (2000), 'Pragmatic collaborations: advancing knowledge while controlling opportunism', *Industrial and Corporate Change*, **9** (3), 443–83.

Héraud, J.-A. (2003), 'Regional innovation systems and European research policy: convergence or misunderstanding?', *European Planning Studies*, **11**, 44–56.

Howells, J. (2006), 'Intermediation and the role of intermediaries in innovation', *Research Policy*, **35**, 715–28.

Iammarino, S. (2005), 'An evolutionary integrated view of regional systems of innovation: concepts, measures and historical perspectives', *European Planning Studies*, **13**, 497–519.

Johnson, B. (1992), 'Institutional learning', in B.-Å. Lundvall (ed.), *National Systems of Innovation*, London: Pinter, pp. 23–44.

Koschatzky, K. (2001), *Räumliche Aspekte im Innovationsprozess. Ein Beitrag zur neuen Wirtschaftsgeographie aus Sicht der regionalen Innovationsforschung*, Münster: Lit Verlag.

Koschatzky, K. (2005), 'Foresight as a governance concept at the interface between global challenges and regional innovation potentials', *European Planning Studies*, **13**, 619–39.

Krugman, P. (1991), *Geography and Trade*, Cambridge, MA: MIT Press.

Kuhlmann, S. (2001), 'Future governance of innovation policy in Europe – three scenarios', *Research Policy*, **30**, 953–76.

Kuhlmann, S. (2002), *Governance and Intelligence in Research and Innovation Systems*. Utrecht: Universiteit Utrecht.

Le Galès, P. and H. Voelzkow (2001), 'Introduction: the governance of local economies', in C. Crouch, P. Le Galès, C. Trigilia and H. Voelzkow (eds), *Local Production Systems in Europe: Rise or Demise?* Oxford: Oxford University Press, pp. 1–24.

Marin, B. and R. Mayntz (eds) (1991), *Policy Networks: Empirical Evidence and Theoretical Considerations*, Frankfurt/Main, Germany and Boulder, CO, USA: Campus.

Marshall, A. (1982), *Principles of Economics*, 9th edn, London: Macmillan (1st edn 1890).

Martin, R. and P. Sunley (2003), 'Deconstructing clusters: chaotic concept or policy panacea?', *Journal of Economic Geography*, **3**, 5–35.

Maskell, P. and A. Malmberg (1999), 'Localised learning and industrial competitiveness', *Cambridge Journal of Economics*, **23**, 167–85.

Mayntz, R. (1993), 'Governing failures and the problems of governability: some comments on a theoretical paradigm', in J. Kooiman (ed.), *Modern Governance*, London: Sage, pp. 9–20.

Mytelka, L.K. and K. Smith (2002), 'Policy learning and innovation theory: an interactive and co-evolving process', *Research Policy* **31**, 1467–79.

Nauwelaers, C. (2000), 'Policy learning for innovation in European regions', paper presented at the RESTPOR conference, 5–7 September, Kashikojima.

North, D.C. (1990), *Institutions, Institutional Change and Economic Performance*, Cambridge: Cambridge University Press.

Piore, M.J. and C.F. Sabel (1984), *The Second Industrial Divide. Possibilities for Prosperity*, New York: Basic.

Porter, M.E. (1998), 'Clusters and the new economics of competition', *Harvard Business Review*, November/December, 77–90.

Putnam, R.D. (1995), 'Tuning in, tuning out: the strange disappearance of social capital America', *Political Science and Politics*, **28**, 664–83.

Putnam, R.D., R. Leonardi and R.Y. Nanetti (1993), *Making Democracy Work: Civic Traditions in Modern Italy*, Princeton, NJ: Princeton University Press.

Renn, O. and M. Thomas (2002), 'The potential of regional foresight', Final Report of the STRATA-ETN Expert Group, Luxembourg: European Communities.

Sabel, C.F. (1996), 'Experimental regionalism and the dilemmas of regional economic policy', paper presented to the conference on Socio-Economic Systems, Institute of Fiscal and Monetary Policy, Tokyo, Japan; www2.law.columbia.edu/sabel/papers/ExpReg.html: (accessed 17 January 2009).

Sabel, C.F. (2004), 'Pragmatic collaboration in practice', *Industry and Innovation*, **11** (1–2): 81–7.

Saxenian, A. (1994), *Regional Advantage*, Cambridge, MA, USA and London, UK: Harvard University Press.

Scott, A.J. (1998), *Regions and the World Economy: The Coming Shape of Global Production, Competition, and Political Order*, Oxford: Oxford University Press.

Storper, M. (1997), *The Regional World: Territorial Development in a Global Economy*, New York, USA and London, UK: Guilford Press.

Storper, M. and A.J. Scott (1995), 'The wealth of regions: market forces and policy imperatives in local and global context', *Futures*, **27** (5), 505–26.

Voelzkow, H., S. Elbing and M. Schröder (2007), *Jenseits nationaler Produktionsmodelle? Die Governance regionaler Wirtschaftscluster*, Marburg: Metropolis.

Von Thünen, J.H. (1966), *Der isolierte Staat in Beziehung auf Landwirtschaft und Nationalökonomie*, Stuttgart: G. Fischer (first edition 1826).

Wiehler, F. and T. Stumm (1995), 'The powers of regional and local authorities and their role in the European Union', *European Planning Studies*, **3**, 227–50.

Williamson, O. (1975), *Markets and Hierarchies*, New York: Free Press.

Williamson, O.E. (1985), *The Economic Institutions of Capitalism: Firms, Markets, Relational Contracting*, New York: Free Press/Macmillan.

Zeitlin, J. (2008), 'The rediscovery of industrial districts: a disciplinary paradox', in G. Jones and J. Zeitlin (eds), *The Oxford Handbook of Business History*, Oxford: Oxford University Press, pp. 219–41.

40 Learning regions
James Simmie

INTRODUCTION

'Learning regions' are one of a family of concepts known as territorial innovation models (TIMs) that evolved from the late 1970s onwards. They were inspired by a growing debate about why localities still mattered in the context of the rapid internationalization of the global economy from around the 1960s. This was combined with a concern with shifts in standardized mass production manufacturing from what were seen as high-labour-cost areas in the First World to low cost areas in newly industrializing countries (NICs). In this context it was argued that the international competitiveness of local and regional economies in the First World increasingly rested on their relative abilities to adopt flexible, networked, knowledge-based and innovative production systems.

Varying combinations of these characteristics were developed to explain either the continued competitive success of particular regions mostly in the US or Europe, or what policies were needed to insure the survival or renewal of less-favoured regions (LFRs). These included 'new industrial districts' in Italy (Bagnasco, 1977; Becattini, 1981), 'innovative milieux' in France (Aydalot, 1986), 'new industrial spaces' in the US (Storper and Scott, 1988), 'spatial clusters of innovation' (Porter, 1996) and 'regional innovation systems' in Europe (Braczyk et al., 1998).

These theoretical developments were driven by three main debates. The first was the argument that the fusion of information and communications technologies was lessening the significance of geography, as information could be passed instantaneously from one part of the world to another as could many of the weightless products of the knowledge economy such as financial services. This was to be summed up later as 'the death of distance' (Cairncross, 1997). All the TIMs argued that the opposite was in fact the case. They showed that the knowledge economy was much more concentrated and successful in some regions rather than others. They sought explanations for the continued significance of regions in the light of this finding.

A second debate was taking place within economic geography. Here the conventional wisdom was that economic activities located in particular places in order to minimize the costs of their transactions. Again, some of the TIMs took issue with this view, arguing that in knowledge-based economies, important interactions took place that were not based on markets and payments. They stressed the significance of networks in facilitating learning and the exchange of knowledge. These were shown to differ in different localities and also to be 'embedded' in or tied to those places. As a result one local economy could have a comparative advantage over another because of its conventions, culture and social institutions, and not simply its geographical position in the web of traded transactions.

These two debates led to an academic definition of the learning region. This is that: 'In a learning region, regional actors engage in collaboration and coordination for mutual benefit, resulting in a process of regional learning. Regional characteristics affect the degree to which the process of regional learning leads to regional renewal' (Rutten and Boekema, 2007a, 136). Here the focus is on the processes of learning in a region.

A third debate surrounded the disappointing results achieved after decades of regional policy in the UK and Europe designed to close the economic gaps between rich and poor regions. There was evidence to suggest that if anything these gaps were 'diverging' rather than 'converging'. New policies were clearly required. These sought to address the issue of how to accelerate the generation of knowledge and innovation in LFRs. It was argued in this context that what they needed was a set of institutions that could galvanize local learning, knowledge and innovation.

Starting from this policy perspective, a second definition of the learning region has emerged. This is that:

> A learning region can be defined as a regional innovation strategy in which a broad set of innovation-related actors (politicians, policy makers, chambers of commerce, trade unions, higher education institutes, public research establishments and companies) are strongly but flexibly connected with each other and who stick to a certain set of 'policy principles'. (Hassink, 2001; quoting OECD, 2001, 24)

Here the focus is on regional innovation strategies.

The schizophrenic definition of what is meant by a learning region has limited both its development as an analytical tool and its ability to differentiate itself in both theoretical and policy terms from other TIMs. This has led to some confusion over its objects of study on the one hand, and its distinction from, for example, regional innovation system policies on the other. Some of these confusions arise from the different agendas of the founding fathers of the concept.

In this chapter, I shall examine the ideas of the founding fathers of the learning region concept. This will be followed by a brief look at what some of the main critics have to say about the concept. A further section will look at a contemporary view of what learning regions are and what they should do. Finally I shall draw together some general conclusions.

THE FOUNDING FATHERS OF THE LEARNING REGION CONCEPT

The founding fathers of the learning region as a distinctive TIM in its own right were Storper (1993), Florida (1995), Asheim (1996) and Morgan (1997). In the US, Richard Florida is generally credited with coining the term 'learning region'. He was concerned to explain the implications for systems of production of the transition of the capitalist economy, from one based on land, labour and capital to one based primarily on knowledge. He argued that in these new circumstances networks would be the dominant organizational mode of production.

He argued that on the one hand the world economy would see the rise of global networks of companies, but that on the other hand, these companies would be dependent on their home regions because they would be the locations of concentrations of key knowledge assets. These home regions would provide the underlying environment and infrastructure facilitating the essential transfers of knowledge, the generation of ideas and learning. As a result, learning in networks is dependent on the characteristics or infrastructure particularly of the global companies' home regions.

Infrastructure may differ from one region to another. It follows from this that one of the reasons why some regions do better than others in the world economy is because of differences in the performance and functioning of their learning and knowledge infra-structures. These cannot be transferred to other regions and so are 'embedded' in their particular localities. As such, they are subject to the cultural and institutional norms and practices of those places.

Despite coining the term 'learning region', Florida was not primarily interested in geographic regions per se. Instead his focus was primarily on the organizational arrange-ments of transnational companies (TNCs) in a knowledge-based economy. Here he was concerned with their global rather than local networks. The main role of key regions in this argument was as the home base of the headquarters and research and development (R&D) functions of TNCs. As such, they formed nodes in a global system of production.

Also in the US, Michael Storper (1993) was concerned to explain the new forms of production organization emerging with the growth of the knowledge-based economy. He was influenced by the work of Piore and Sabel (1984) in their book *The Second Industrial Divide*. In it, they argued that large conglomerates were beginning to break themselves up, or to 'deverticalize', into smaller units. The relationships between these smaller units and between small companies in general were then managed as networks.

Initially Storper (1993) sought to distinguish the characteristics of new networked forms of industrial organization from the traditional transaction cost logic used in eco-nomic geography. His argument was that, given the importance of knowledge in the new economy, learning is key and qualitatively different requirement from simple market transactions. The essential difference is that knowledge creation or learning is essentially a social rather than a market process. It involves, among other things, the development and exchange of tacit and underdeveloped knowledge for which there are no existing markets. Instead networks are the means by which such learning takes place.

Storper (1993) based his arguments on a series of empirical case studies. These were conducted: in north-east central Italy, focusing on design-intensive or craft-based indus-tries, producing mostly fashion goods such as clothing, leather, fabrics, furniture and personal accessories; in Paris on fashion clothing and the Ile-de-France high-technology aerospace, electronics and nuclear reactors; and in Californian high-technology districts concentrating on electronics and aerospace. He found that within these industrial sectors in these particular places technological learning could be seen as a social process heavily influenced by the conventions, culture and informal institutions of the local networks that they were a part of. In this context learning took place on the basis of 'untraded interdependencies'. These pertained to specific networks and places and so distinguished the mode of learning between one network in one locality, and another. Storper (1993) described these differences in different places as 'separate worlds of production'.

It should be borne in mind, however, that Storper's (1993) case studies were conducted in three different countries. As a result the cultural and conventional differences between the learning production networks that he identified owed as much to national as to local differences. Furthermore, the technological districts in his study had all followed different pathways of development to arrive at similar results in terms of networked forms of production. For these reasons it has proved difficult to identify learning regions empirically and subject them to comparative empirical analysis.

Like Florida (1995), Storper (1993) was primarily interested in firms and industries rather than regions as a whole. His case studies were conducted on industrial sectors in particular places rather than on those places themselves. In contrast Asheim (1996), working in Norway, started from the question of why another form of locality-based TIM, namely industrial districts, were not necessarily also good at technological learning. He went on to focus on the nature of successful learning in particular places.

Like both Florida (1995) and Storper (1993), he argued that in a knowledge-based economy networks are the key organizational form facilitating technological learning. In addition, agglomeration provides advantages with regard both to the formation of local networks and consequential learning. Like Storper (1993), Asheim (1996) argued that learning is a social and interactive activity and therefore can only be understood in its institutional and cultural context. He also argued in favour of quasi-integrated regional networks as the best organizational context for interactive learning. Like Storper (1993) he believed that the way in which such networks were organized was based on informal conventions and local cultural norms.

In addition to these informal arrangements, Asheim (1996) also argued that learning regions required a formal institutional set-up. This included a region's innovation policy and support organizations. These formal institutions for learning and innovation were what, for Asheim (1996), distinguished a learning region from an industrial district. As a result of the addition of formal institutions a learning region, in Asheim's (1996) view, could function as a regional innovation system. For him in a learning region geographically concentrated learning networks, territorially embedded conventions, regional innovation policy and support organizations work together as part of a coherent system.

These arguments, however, far from distinguishing learning regions from industrial districts, created further confusion between these and regional innovation systems. The introduction of a requirement for formal institutions to stimulate learning made the Asheim (1996) view much more akin to the concept of a regional innovation system than a learning region. This more policy-oriented approach to learning regions was developed in Wales by Morgan (1997).

In Wales, one of the UK's LFRs, Morgan (1997) confronted the UK and European failure to close the gap between rich and poor regions on the basis of traditional regional economic policy. His main purpose was to link the concepts of the interactive model of innovation and the networked or associational economy, to define a new way to tackle the problems confronting LFRs like Wales. Morgan (1997) linked innovation to economic development and regarded it as an instrument to further social welfare. This gave the learning region a policy agenda in addition to its theoretical one. Following evolutionary economic theory, he argued that innovation was an interactive process influenced by a variety of institutions and conventions. In a given region these constituted its 'social capital' (Putnam, 1993; Rosenfeld, Chapter 21, this *Handbook*). Social capital is a feature of social organization and includes networks, norms, trust and the conventions that facilitate informal coordination and cooperation for mutual benefit.

Morgan (1997) made social capital pertaining to regions a key factor in explaining the difference between successful regions and LFRs. It followed from this argument that the key to regional regeneration and improved social welfare lay in strengthening a region's social capital and institutional capacity to support learning.

Unlike the previous founding fathers, one of Morgan's (1997) main objects of study was the region. The two reasons for this were, first, that physical proximity facilitates the development of trust and person-embodied knowledge; and second, that social capital can best be developed within a region because it requires regular interactions to build and maintain trust.

Although Morgan (1997) does focus on the geographic region as the locus for building the social capital that facilitates learning, his interests overlap those of other TIMs such as regional innovation systems. Thus the founding fathers of the both the theoretical and the policy-oriented versions of the learning region do not provide a definition of the concept or its objects of study that clearly distinguishes it from other TIMs. This definitial imprecision has led some critics to argue that the concept of the learning region is so 'fuzzy' that it amounts to little more than vague and impressionistic neologism (Martin, 2001; Simmie, 1997).

CRITICS OF THE LEARNING REGION

Critics of the learning region concept include Hudson (1999), Simmie (1999, 2003), Hassink (2001) and Cooke (2005). Hudson (1999) argues that the social and structural constraints imposed by the capitalist system of production set the limits of what is possible in such a system. One feature of this system is spatially uneven economic development. This is partly based on carefully guarded economically valuable tacit knowledge. Hudson (1999) sees the development and use of new knowledge in a capitalist system as a zero-sum game in which one firm or locality's gain is another's loss. He argues that the prospect of generating convergence between different regions on the basis of a policy focus on learning is unlikely to succeed in the face of the forces driving uneven economic development.

Hassink (2001) argues that the concept of the learning region suffers from definitional fuzziness, its normative character, the fact that it overlaps with other TIM concepts, and its uncertain position between national innovation systems and global production networks.

Simmie (1999) found in a study of innovative firms in the South East of England that they learned as much from national and international networks as they did from their local regional networks. He went on to argue (Simmie, 2003) that, far from regions relying mainly on the transfer of knowledge and learning within locally confined networks, the more innovative among them formed nodes in global systems of learning, knowledge generation and innovation. In this respect what distinguished successful regions from LFRs was often not only the social capital embodied in their local networks, but also the level and quality of their international linkages as well.

Cooke (2005) argues that the learning region is unlikely to last as a policy framework because of asymmetries rather than equality in local collaborations using different forms of economically valuable knowledge. He distinguishes between symbolic, synthetic and abstract forms of knowledge and argues that these are unequally distributed between actual and potential users in localities. This militates against the sharing of such knowledge in collaborative networks.

CONTEMPORARY VIEWS OF THE LEARNING REGION

In response to some of these criticisms, Rutten and Boekema (2007b) refined the learning region concept. They argued that: 'The learning region is a concept of endogenous regional development; i.e. it puts the spotlight on processes within regions (. . . learning and networking) and on how regional context factors affect these processes' (Rutten and Boekema, 2007b, 139). For them, a truly learning region is characterized by two key phenomena. These are, first, that mutually beneficial collaboration and coordination between regional actors must function as a coherent system; and second, that the resulting regional renewal must lead to changes for the 'better' in the regional context.

The conceptualization of the region does not necessarily correspond to administrative or geographical boundaries. Local networks define the boundaries of the system. This represents a functional definition of the region which could stretch to encompass the whole of Silicon Valley, or be as small as the haute couture district of Paris.

For Rutten and Boekema (2007b) the purpose of the learning region is to promote regional development by enabling regional companies to introduce product and process innovations. They focus on the regional context of this activity. For them this is composed of three main factors. These are spatial proximity, regional interfirm networks and the institutional set-up of a region. With respect to spatial proximity they argue that traditional agglomeration advantages provide economies of scale with respect to labour markets and transactions. Regional interfirm networks are the key instruments through which regional learning is achieved. The characteristics of these networks are critical to the success of regional learning. Finally, the formal institutional set-up of a region is regarded as the most visible element of the regional context affecting learning. Rutten and Boekema also follow Morgan (1997) in arguing that local animators are important in stimulating local learning.

Rutten and Boekema (2007b) also follow Morgan (1997) in arguing that social capital is an important variable in the conceptualization of the learning region. For them this refers to the regional institutional capacity, the local networking capability and locally embedded conventions. These kinds of social capital affect both the processes of regional learning and the regional context.

DISCUSSION AND CONCLUSIONS

Starting around the late 1970s, inspired by theoretical debates both among heterodox evolutionary economists and among some orthodox economists, and by the lack of success of traditional regional economic policy to close the gap between rich and poor regions, there was a growing interest in the possibilities for endogenous regional economic growth. In Europe, Aydalot and the GREMI laid the foundations for a regional endogenous development approach in their work on innovative milieux. Learning processes in such milieux were seen as becoming increasingly based on endogenous factors. From an orthodox economic theory perspective Barro and Sala-i-Martin (1992) developed a regional version of an endogenous growth model. In both cases the potential contributions of localities to their own economic development was asserted against control and policy prescriptions devised by the national state.

These debates and policy problems inspired common threads in both the conceptual and policy-based definitions of learning regions. These were the significance attached to the interactive model of innovation combined with the importance of local networks and institutions (social capital). But while there is some consistency in the understanding and use of the interactive model of innovation, there is a dual use of the concept of institutions. At an intangible and informal level they are defined as: 'common habits, routines, established practices, rules or laws that regulate the relations and interactions between individuals and groups' (Edquist and Johnson, 1997). In this conception they are said to promote, in a particular locality, sets of shared values, meanings, understandings and tacit knowledge that are historically unique to that place and also facilitate the further development of the types of knowledge found there. Geographic proximity is said to facilitate such local forms of learning and to distinguish them from those of other places.

Institutions are also equated, at a more tangible and formal level, with organizations and structures. In this case they are defined as firms, universities, technical institutes, trade associations, chambers of commerce and professional associations (Morgan, 1997). These are regarded as the structural assets that produce and reproduce the informal institutions peculiar to a given locality. It should be borne in mind, however, that many places will have an array of most of these types of institution. So it is not so much the list of formal organizations that makes the key difference between different regions, but the nature of the informal shared values, meanings, understandings and tacit knowledge that they generate over time that influences their distinctive capacities for learning and innovation.

Storper (1993) recognized the paradox that although, in his case studies, local conventions were important in determining the nature and quality of successful local learning, they had all arrived at this point by significantly different pathways of development. The concepts of path-dependence and lock-in drawn from evolutionary economics have been invoked to understand these long-term development pathways. They stress the importance of the historical pathways taken to arrive at a current set of circumstances. They also show that there is no necessary reason why such developments should lead to learning success. Interactive learning that used to be a distinctive strength of a particular regional economy can also turn into a weakness. The examples of industrial decline in the Ruhr Area (Grabher, 1993), and the Swiss mechanical watch industry (Maillat, 1996), have led to the general conclusion that in a 'learning' region policy-makers should learn from errors made in the past and in so doing avoid path-dependent development.

Nevertheless, learning in a particular region depends to a large extent on what is already known in that region. This is closely related to the historical production structure of the economy. Knowledge is accumulated over time through the production experiences of this structure. Once this structure goes into decline, especially if it is dominated by a single industry, it is quite possible for politicians and policy-makers in the public sector to recognize the problem but not to be in a position to do much about it. Breaking out of conventions that lead to less successful forms of learning is no easy task.

Although continual reference is made to the region as a unit of analysis by the advocates of the learning region concept, they seldom mean geographically or administratively defined regions. In his case studies Storper (1993), for example, analyses mainly industrial sectors concentrated in particular districts of large urban agglomerations. Morgan (1997) discusses regions in terms of the 'nexus of processes'. If the region is defined in terms of the functional extent of particular local networks, then there is a danger of ending up with the circular argument that local learning networks are the key to learning within the geographical extent of local learning networks.

Within the family of TIMs the learning region concept in both its theoretical and policy-based forms has drawn attention to the need to learn, generate new knowledge and innovate in modern spatial economies. It has broken with traditional neoclassical economics and economic geography in arguing that learning is essentially a social and cultural phenomenon rather than one that is based on market transactions. It has also drawn attention to the fact that there are significant differences in the conventions and informal institutions that determine the ways in which collaborative learning takes place in different companies, industrial sectors and places. The combination of these differences is a key driver of the economic success or failure of different places.

REFERENCES

Asheim, B. (1996), 'Industrial districts as "learning regions": a condition for prosperity', *European Planning Studies*, **4** (4), 379–400.

Aydalot, P. (1986), *Milieux Innovateurs en Europe*, Paris: GREMI.

Bagnasco, A. (1977), *Tre Italia: La Problematica Territoriale Dello Sviluppo Economico Italiano*, Bolognia: Il Mulino.

Barro, R.J. and X. Sala-i-Martin (1992), 'Public finance in models of economic growth', *Review of Economic Studies*, **59** (4), 645–61.

Becattini, G. (1981), 'Le district industriel: milieu creative', *Espaces et Societies*, **66–67**, 147–64.

Braczyk, H.-C., P. Cooke and M. Heidenreich (eds) (1998), *Regional Systems of Innovation*, London: UCL Press.

Cairncross, F. (1997), *The Death of Distance*, Cambridge, MA: Harvard Business School Press.

Cooke, P. (2005), 'Learning regions: a critique', paper presented at the 4th European Meeting on Applied Evolutionary Economics, Utrecht, 19–21 May.

Edquist, C. and B. Johnson (1997), 'Institutions and organizations in systems of innovation', in C. Edquist (ed.), *System of Innovation: Technologies, Institutions and Organizations*, London, UK and Washington, DC, USA: Pinter, pp. 41–63.

Florida, R. (1995), 'Toward the learning region', *Futures*, **27** (5), 527–36.

Grabher, G. (1993), 'The weakness of strong ties: the lock-in of regional development in the Ruhr area', in G. Grabher (ed.), *The Embedded Firm: on the Socioeconomics of Industrial Networks*, London: Routledge, pp. 1–31.

Hassink, R. (2001), 'The learning region: a fuzzy concept or a sound theoretical basis for modern regional innovation policies?', *Zeitschrift fur Wirtschaftsgeographie*, **45** (3–4), 219–30.

Hudson, R. (1999), 'The learning economy, the learning firm and the learning region: a sympathetic critique of the limits to learning', *European Urban and Regional Studies*, **6**, 59–72.

Maillat, D. (1996), 'From the industrial district to the innovative milieu: contribution to an analysis of territorialised productive organisations', IRER Working Paper No. 9606b, Neufchâtel, Université de Neufchâtel.

Martin, R. (2001), 'Geography and public policy: the case of the missing agenda', *Progress in Human Geography*, **25** (2), 189–210.

Morgan, K. (1997), 'The learning region: institutions, innovation and regional renewal', *Regional Studies*, **31**, 491–503.

OECD (2001), *Cities and Regions in the New Learning Economy*, Paris: OECD.

Piore, M.J. and C.F. Sabel (1984), *The Second Industrial Divide: Possibilities for Prosperity*, New York: Basic Books.

Porter, M. (1996), 'Competitive advantage, agglomeration economies and regional policy', *International Regional Science Review*, **19**, 85–94.

Putnam, R.D. (1993), 'The prosperous community: social capital and public life', *American Prospect*, **13**, 35–42.

Rutten, R. and F. Boekema (2007a), *The Learning Region: Foundations, State of the Art, Future*, Cheltenham, UK and Northampton, MA, USA: Edward Elgar.

Rutten, R. and F. Boekema (2007b), 'The learning region: a conceptual anatomy', in R. Rutten and F. Boekema (eds), *The Learning Region: Foundations, State of the Art, Future*, Cheltenham, UK and Northampton, MA, USA: Edward Elgar, pp. 127–42.

Simmie, J.M. (ed.) (1997), *Innovation, Networks and Learning Regions?* London: Jessica Kingsley.

Simmie, J.M. (1999), 'Innovation projects and local production networks: a case study of Hertfordshire', *European Planning Studies*, **7** (4), 445–62.

Simmie, J.M. (2003), 'Innovation and urban regions as national and international nodes for the transfer and sharing of knowledge', *Regional Studies*, **37** (6–7), 607–20.

Storper, M. (1993), 'Regional "worlds" of production: learning and innovation in the technological districts of France, Italy, and the USA', *Regional Studies*, **27** (5), 433–55.

Storper, M. and A.J. Scott (1988), 'The geographical foundations and social regulation of flexible production complexes', in J. Wolch and M. Dear (eds), *The Power of Geography*, London: Allen & Unwin.

41 Regional innovation platforms
Vesa Harmaakorpi, Tomi Tura and Helinä Melkas

INTRODUCTION

Mainstream economic development policy in Europe has relied on a cluster approach and on the power of knowledge and research as the sources of innovation. Innovation policy has been to a great extent equivalent to science and technology policy. Cluster policies have aimed at building competitive advantage with strong regional and national clusters based on the logic of proximity and agglomerations. Recent discussions have, however, emphasized other forms of economic order and origins of innovation.

Innovation increasingly appears to follow the logic of cross-fertilization and use of distance rather than proximity as a fuel in innovation processes. In this context, cluster policy seems to have its weaknesses. Regions that have enough related variety in their economic structure appear to be successful in building constructed competitive advantage (Boschma, 2005a). This leads to the need to focus the analysis on platforms rather than clusters.

According to innovation surveys, only 4 per cent of innovations are based on scientific sources (CIS, 2004). The logic of practice-based innovation differs crucially from the logic of science-based innovation. A practical context and interaction between the two subsystems of an innovation system – acquisition and assimilation of knowledge; and transformation and exploitation of knowledge – seem to offer a lot of unused potential for innovation (Autio, 1998; Zahra and George, 2002). This potential remains largely untouched due to lack of policy measures to foster practice-based, networked innovation processes that combine diverse knowledge bases (Harmaakorpi and Melkas, 2005).

The objective of this chapter is to set the basis for and outline the concept of regional innovation platforms as an alternative to clusters. First, we look into the interplay between the concepts of proximity and distance in practice-based innovation and the two forms of regional innovation: the cluster model and the regional innovation platform model. After comparing those, we move on to discussing a practical case of building regional innovation platforms with the help of the Regional Development Platform Method in the Lahti region in Finland. The chapter displays the state of the art in the field of regional innovation platforms by pondering upon this issue both conceptually and empirically.

PROXIMITY AND DISTANCE: CHALLENGING OR SUPPORTING REGIONAL INNOVATION?

Since the 1990s, there has been increasing interest in the notion of proximity in the context of economic development in general – and innovation in particular. As such, the notion of proximity is a sort of 'umbrella' concept (Boschma, 2005a) consisting of different dimensions. The general idea behind this umbrella is that proximity, in whatever form, somehow reduces the uncertainty of economic activity, contributes to solving the problem of coordination between different actors, and facilitates interactive learning and innovation (Boschma, 2005b, 62; and see Boschma and Frenken's Chapter 14 in this *Handbook*).

When analysing the logic and dynamics of innovation, at least four functions of proximity have been identified. First, being close to each other helps companies to develop an efficient division of labour and coordinate their actions, facilitating the development of a core of specialized suppliers and partners. Second, there are externalities of proximity available to all within a region. In particular, these externalities are related to the localized human resources (workforce) and know-how (Feldman, 1994; Torre and Gilly, 2000, 172). Third, there is evidence that when companies of the same industry are located close to each other, it forces them to innovate by creating an environment where companies compete, in a positive sense, with each other (see, for example, Porter, 1990). Fourth, and perhaps most importantly, proximity is relevant for the appearance of knowledge spillovers and learning processes between the actors (Audretsch and Feldman, 2003; Malmberg and Maskell, 2002).

It is not clear, however, what the role of physical proximity is in contrast to the other forms of proximity in innovation activities. In his discussion on the relevance of proximity for learning, Boschma (2005b) argued that geographical proximity per se is neither a necessary nor a sufficient condition for learning. Moreover, as Audretsch and Feldman (2003, 13) argued in the context of knowledge spillovers, empirical evidence on the correlation between physical proximity and learning gives us no understanding about the ways in which knowledge spillovers really occur between the relevant actors. The relevance of physical closeness lies in two effects: it enables cost-efficient and relatively easy transactions between the actors (traded interdependencies; Storper, 1997), and it contributes to the other forms of proximity by strengthening the chance to rely on the local, relatively common culture and strong personal ties (untraded interdependencies).

From the point of view of innovation, proximity in its different forms has contradictory effects. There are the apparent positive effects of proximity, but on the other hand it has been persuasively argued that there is a phenomenon of 'having too much proximity', that is, a negative side of proximity. These negative effects relate to different forms of lock-in, involuntary spillovers, a certain lack of flexibility and a possibility of opportunism (see, for example, Boschma, 2005b; Tura and Harmaakorpi, 2005, 1120; Adler and Kwon, 2000, 106–7).

The possibility of negative effects of proximity suggests that there are equally important conditions of innovation connected to the idea of physical, cognitive or functional distance or diversity between actors. Such models of innovation emphasize the generation and maintenance of social, cultural and cognitive diversity as basic functions of innovation policy. Boschma (2005b) identified two basic features of distance that are relevant for innovation processes: (1) by enhancing physical, cognitive, social and structural openness, distance enables new ideas and information to be triggered and thus fosters renewal of the regional knowledge base; and (2) distance enables the implementation of new ideas by the formation of an efficient combination of control and flexibility.

When discussing the roles of proximity and distance in innovation policy, we thus face a critical dilemma: on the one hand, there is a need for mechanisms for enhancing physical, social and cognitive proximity between the relevant actors of innovation processes. This is the basic idea behind most of the modern innovation policies and, for example, behind the different models of technology centres and science parks. On the other hand, innovation policy has to include mechanisms for enhancing social and cognitive diversity, openness of innovation networks and the ability of an innovation 'network' to connect itself to the wider national and global knowledge base – that is, mechanisms for ensuring sufficient distance between the actors.

This perspective is not unfamiliar to innovation policy-makers, but it has not attracted the attention of its opposite. In particular, when focusing on the practical models and methods of innovation policy, this imbalance is striking. The main intention of innovation policy models appears to be the generation of different forms of closeness. However, if the above argument is accepted, the central challenge is not to maximize proximity, but to create an efficient balance between the contradictory purposes of enhancing proximity and distance. This balance is, in fact, at the core of the idea of regional innovation platforms.

Several efforts have been made to identify and analyse the different dimensions of proximity and distance (for example, Rallet and Torre, 1999; Torre and Gilly, 2000). In this chapter, we draw from the analysis of Boschma (2005b) but describe the relevant dimensions somewhat differently. First, the geographical dimension refers to pure physical proximity or distance between actors. As we argued, it does not in itself contribute positively or negatively to innovation but it may, for instance, facilitate social proximity. Second, the cognitive dimension refers to closeness or differences in ways of thinking and knowledge bases. Cognitively close actors are able to assume a certain common knowledge base that does not have to be defined or negotiated. On the other hand, cognitive distance enables the adaptation of new information and the questioning of existing cognitive assumptions. Third, the communicative dimension refers to closeness or differences in concepts and professional languages. For instance, when making a new idea understandable, communicatively distant concepts from other fields or sciences may be utilized.

Fourth, an additional dimension of distance and proximity refers to organizational arrangements to coordinate transactions and enable exchange of information within and between organizations. The importance of organizational proximity lies in the need for efficient organization of utilization of knowledge and other resources owned by a variety of actors. On the other hand, an organization should have both strong and weak links (see the next section) in its network. Differences in expertise in different industries or clusters refer to the fifth, functional dimension of distance. On the other hand, functionally close actors act in areas of expertise that are close to each other – for example, in the same industry. It is useful to obtain novel information and experiences also from outside of one's own field of operations. In such cases, the information often needs to be adapted to the field of operations in question.

Cultural distance refers to differences in (organizational) cultures, values and so on. Cultural proximity thus deals with closeness of cultural habits and values – 'rules of the game'. The challenge of cultural distance is to get people working in different organizational cultures to collaborate. Finally, there is a social dimension of distance and proximity, referring to intensity of trust-based social relations, such as friendship or kinship. The notion of social proximity comes close to the concept of social capital and is also

Table 41.1 Dimensions of proximity and distance in innovation networks

Distance	Source	Innovation potential
1. Geographic	Physical proximity/ distance between actors.	Does not automatically lead to innovations but may, for instance, facilitate social proximity.
2. Cognitive	Closeness/ differences in ways of thinking and knowledge bases.	Cognitive closeness helps to assume a certain common knowledge base. Cognitive distance enables adaptation of new information.
3. Communicative	Closeness/ differences in concepts and professional languages.	When making a new idea understandable, concepts from other fields or sciences may be utilized.
4. Organizational	Arrangements to coordinate transactions and enable exchange of information within and between organizations.	Contributes to efficient organization of utilization of knowledge and other resources. An organization should have both strong and weak links in its network.
5. Functional	Differences or closeness in expertise in different industries/clusters.	Functional distance brings novel information from outside of one's own field of operations. Information often needs to be adapted.
6. Cultural	Differences or closeness of cultural habits and values; 'rules of the game'.	The challenge is to get people working in different organizational cultures to collaborate.
7. Social	Intensity of trust-based social relations, such as friendship or kinship.	Innovation requires interaction among different kind of actors. Trust helps in creation of radical ideas.

closely connected to trust. In innovation processes, when bringing together socially distant actors, the question of trust creation is central for the success of these processes.

The seven central dimensions of distance and proximity, as well as their relevance to innovation, are summarized in Table 41.1.

THE INTERPLAY BETWEEN PROXIMITY AND DISTANCE IN PRACTICE-BASED INNOVATION

Achieving innovations was earlier seen mostly as a linear process leading from scientific work to practical innovative applications. Nowadays, innovation is often considered to be a result of cooperation in normal social and economic activities (Kline and Rosenberg, 1986; Lundvall, 1988). Innovation processes are created by many triggers and take place in multi-actor innovation networks. These processes occurring within a practical context are here called 'practice-based innovation processes'. We define them as innovation processes triggered by problem-setting in a practical context and conducted in non-linear processes utilizing scientific and practical knowledge production and creation in cross-disciplinary innovation networks. In such processes there is a strong need to combine knowledge interests from theory and practice, as well as knowledge from different disciplines. A new kind of characterization of expertise is also needed. Experts in innovation processes cannot just 'pour knowledge' into innovating partners and then disappear; they must be interactive partners in collective learning processes that lead to successful innovations (Harmaakorpi and Mutanen, 2008).

Before moving on to discuss two models of regional innovation, we briefly summarize important discussions and theoretical frameworks that are relevant for innovation policies focusing on the above-mentioned basic dilemma of creating an efficient balance between the purposes of enhancing proximity and distance. These frameworks are summarized in Table 41.2 and focus on:

- strong links, weak links and structural holes;
- social capital;
- knowledge production, creation and conversion;
- absorptive capacity;
- STI and DUI modes of innovation;
- agglomeration economies;
- innovation systems.

The interplay between proximity and distance is a very challenging task to manage with regard to supporting practice-based innovation. Practice-based innovation is often hybrid by nature, and its effectiveness may only become visible after quite some time has passed. Therefore, methods and approaches to managing the interplay between proximity and distance successfully require considerable attention also in research. As shown by Table 41.2, there are many levels and details to be taken into account. By means of building regional innovation platforms, this challenging task may be aided in practice.

TOWARDS REGIONAL INNOVATION PLATFORMS

Two Models of Regional Innovation

The relation between proximity and distance has been an important question in many of the current discussions on innovation and regional innovation systems, as shown by Table 41.2. This question is far from being purely theoretical. The practical innovation policy is, from the point of view of individual regions, very much about attracting different actors to locate close to each other, organizing the forms of closeness efficiently and effectively, and helping the actors to take advantage of the others close to them. Thus, the problem of efficient and effective forms of proximity is at the core of regional innovation policies.

It may be assumed that different regional innovation policies react to the dilemma of the balance between proximity and distance in different ways. In order to identify the practical effects of the dilemma we identify two ways to solve it – two basic models of regional innovation policy. This distinction is not aimed at being a comprehensive analysis of different policies, nor is it intended to be 'the' correct way to analyse innovation policy models. Rather, the distinction between these two policy models illustrates two

Table 41.2   Proximity and distance in innovation according to certain theories and frameworks

Theory/ framework	Description	Innovation considerations	Theorists include, for instance
Network morphology	Innovation environment consists of network morphology of strong ties and weak ties in social networks. Structural holes are found between the dense network structures.	More novel information flows through weak ties (including the element of distance) than through strong ties. However, a regional innovation system in which strong ties are lacking could be incapable of utilizing the potential of structural holes.	Granovetter (1973, 2005) Burt (1992, 2004)
Social capital	Social capital (SC) refers to features of social organization that facilitate coordinated actions. Bridging SC creates bonds across diverse horizontal groups, whereas bonding SC connects members of homogeneous groups.	It is essential both to build an atmosphere of trust and proximity (bonding social capital) in an innovation network, and to keep the network open and diverse (bridging social capital) to allow the necessary diverse flows of information to take place.	Coleman (1988) Putnam (1995) Tura and Harmaakorpi (2005)
Two modes of knowledge production	Traditional knowledge production based on single disciplines (mode 1) is homogeneous and primarily cognitive knowledge generation. Mode 2 knowledge production takes place in broader, heterogeneous and interdisciplinary socio-economic contexts within an applied setting.	Mode 1 knowledge production sets the basis for scientific innovations in science-push innovation processes characterized by cognitive proximity. Mode 2 knowledge production is important in practice-based middle-ground innovations that often take place in networked nonlinear innovation processes.	Gibbons et al. (1994) Howells (2000)
Knowledge creation and conversion	Knowledge is not always a product-like outcome of an active, specified activity; there are also other ways to create knowledge. Knowledge creation and conversion processes and different types of knowledge need to be taken into account in regional innovation systems.	Regional innovativeness may be increased by supporting knowledge creation and conversion processes by means of, for instance, creativity tools based on the interplay of proximity and distance.	Howells (2002) Harmaakorpi and Melkas (2005)
Absorptive capacity	Absorptive capacity is an organization's ability to value, assimilate and apply new knowledge. Potential absorptive capacity is important in acquiring and assimilating external knowledge; realized absorptive capacity in transformation and exploitation of the knowledge that has been gathered.	Potential absorptive capacity is crucial when a company tries to secure the richness of information flows in order to create middle-ground innovations. Without realized absorptive capacity it is impossible to operationalize the new knowledge into innovations.	Cohen and Levinthal (1990) Zahra and George (2002)

561

Table 41.2 (continued)

Theory/ framework	Description	Innovation considerations	Theorists include, for instance
STI and DUI modes of innovation	The STI (science, technology, innovation) mode of innovation is based on the production and use of codified scientific and technical knowledge. The DUI (doing, using, interacting) mode is based on an experience-based mode of learning.	The STI mode refers to the way firms use and develop the body of science-like understanding and explicit knowledge in their innovation activities. The DUI mode refers to know-how and 'know who' that are tacit and often highly localized. It can be intentionally fostered by building structures and relationships that enhance and utilize learning by doing, using and interacting.	Berg Jensen et al. (2007)
Location and urbanization economies	Location economies assess agglomeration as a process external to the company but internal to the industry; urbanization economies as a process external to the industry and internal to the region.	Location economies rely strongly on physical, cognitive, functional, cultural and social proximity. Urbanization economies are based on physical and functional proximity, but also benefit from cognitive, cultural and social distance that are important for middle-ground innovations.	Marshall (1916) Christaller (1933) Lösch (1954) Chinitz (1961)
Innovation systems	An innovation system is a system of private and public companies, universities, and public agencies, characterized by embeddedness, and regular and strong internal interaction promoting the innovativeness of the entire system.	A sectoral innovation system, based on a specific knowledge base, technologies, inputs and demand, includes a relatively high amount of cognitive and organizational proximity, whereas regional and national innovation systems are prone to possess social and cultural proximity and – especially regional innovation systems – functional proximity.	Freeman (1987) Lundvall (1992) Cooke et al. (1997) Malerba (2002)

different approaches to the current concrete challenge of the balance between proximity and distance.

The discussion above underlines the relevance of diverse forms of proximity. This is also a starting point of many modern innovation policies. Glaeser et al. (1992), for instance, suggested that knowledge spills over locally only within a certain industry or other definite, functionally close set of businesses. This view that combines geographical and functional proximity is an important theoretical basis for the model of innovation policy commonly known as the 'cluster model of regional innovation policy'.

The basic idea of the cluster model is that businesses closer to one another have advantages unavailable to businesses farther away. Clusters are traditionally defined as a mode of organization of productive systems, characterized by a geographical concentration of economic actors and other organizations, specialized in a common field of activities, developing interrelations of a market and non-market nature, and contributing to the innovativeness and competitiveness of their members and the territory. Porter (1990) emphasized the importance of place from the perspective of a company – how a company's location affects its strategy and performance. Firms are real competitors in the world economy, but their success is strongly related to features of their home base.

In line with Porter's work, clusters have become the hegemonic way of outlining regional innovation policy. Cluster policy may help in clarifying economic strengths and challenges of a region. The strength of cluster policy lies in the way in which that kind of a policy takes into account efficient knowledge spillovers, learning and innovation activities between functionally close actors. Cluster policy may also enable and foster accumulation of other forms of proximity and their combinations.

The cluster model has however been challenged by, for instance, Boschma (2005a). Critical studies have shown that agglomerations in sharp regional clusters do not increase regional competitiveness. Neither can competitiveness be promoted effectively by decentralizing scarce development resources in very many different industries without cooperation between these industries. Instead, regions that allow different industries to grow and focus on synergies between those industries seem to succeed better. The concept of 'related variety' developed by Boschma, and its exploitation as a driver of innovative capability, seem to create a new direction for innovation policy – leading us to the second model of modern regional innovation policy: the framework of regional development platforms or regional innovation platforms (Harmaakorpi, 2006; Cooke, 2006, 2007; Lazzeretti et al., 2010). The concepts of innovation platform and development platform have the same meaning in this chapter.

The dynamic of regional development or innovation platforms lies in the logic of urbanization economies that emphasizes the power of related variety. It has its intellectual roots in the frameworks of regional innovation systems and evolutionary economics. The concept of regional development platform is strongly bound to the institutional (formal and informal) set-up of a region and may thus be a useful tool in exploring existing business potentials in manifold regional resource configurations. While the concept of regional innovation platform is related to the concept of clusters, it has several features in its basic logic that differ from the cluster policy.

There are three defining features of the concept of regional innovation platform. First, it aims to solve the dilemma of proximity and distance in a particular way, illustrated by the concept of 'related variety'. Cooke (2007) underlined the promotion of related variety in local economic activities as a necessary step to build up competitive advantage within a regional innovation system. Related variety implies existence of cognitive relationships among different industries. The main advantage of 'related industries' is higher capacity to absorb innovations from neighbouring sectors through cross-fertilization.

Second, regional innovation platforms are based on identification of the existing regional resource basis rather than on identification of existing clusters. The practical organization of a regional innovation system based on platforms may thus be radically different from the cluster-based organization. Regional development platforms often emerge from very unorthodox combinations that exploit regional related variety. Third, regional development platforms are fundamentally future-oriented. The platforms are formed on the basis of identified future societal, technological and business trajectories. The competitive advantage of platforms is thus based on their capability to identify future business potential and combine different resource bases.

According to these features, regional innovation or development platforms may be defined as regional resource configurations based on past development trajectories, but presenting future potential to produce competitive advantage existing in the defined resource configurations. The central power of development platforms may be found in exploiting distance as innovation potential, but synergy in the platforms is emphasized in terms of related variety (cf. Harmaakorpi, 2004, 2006).

Possible competitive advantage is based on the dynamic capabilities of actors working for a platform. The actors of a regional innovation platform are firms, technology centres, expertise centres, research centres, educational organizations and so on, contributing to the defined development platform. A regional development platform must be separately defined each time. A development platform is often based on an industry, area of expertise or future megatrend, or a combination of those. A development platform is connected to past trajectories, but the concept describes the future potential of the platform. Technological development may create totally new platforms. However, they are usually based on accumulated work done within existing platforms. Identification of new innovation platforms requires a special regional dynamic capability – visionary capability – as well as continuous resource-based futures research (Harmaakorpi and Uotila, 2006; Uotila et al., 2007).

In Table 41.3, the regional cluster model and regional innovation platforms are assessed with the help of the framework of Table 41.2.

Building Regional Innovation Platforms: The Regional Development Platform Method (RDPM) in Lahti Region, Finland

Thinking related to regional innovation platforms is quite young. It has been implemented as a tool for identifying and outlining constructed competitiveness in the Lahti region in Finland during the decade to 2010, when the Regional Development Platform Method was developed in the region to support competitiveness policy (Harmaakorpi, 2006). The RDPM was presented as an institutional and social innovation, and a tool for regional innovation policy (Harmaakorpi, 2006). The tool is based on the resource-based view of regional development, but it has been planned to make regions sensitive to adapting to changes in the techno-economic paradigm. Another central basis for the

Table 41.3 The cluster model versus the regional innovation platform model

Theory/ Framework	The Cluster Model – Agglomeration	The Regional Innovation Platform Model – Related variety
Network morphology	The cluster model promotes, in particular, strong ties of a regional innovation system. The ties are strengthened by organizing activities inside the cluster and trying to form a joint vision for the cluster.	The 'fuel' of regional innovation platforms consists of weak ties of regional networks (especially interregionally). Structural holes are actively utilized.
Social capital	The cluster model emphasizes aspects of bonding social capital by, for example, promoting a common vision for a cluster.	The objective of the regional innovation platform model is to bridge different groups regionally and interregionally.
Two modes of knowledge production	The cluster model tends more likely to foster Mode 1 knowledge production since the companies and university members in cluster meetings are from the same branch.	Mode 2 knowledge production in practical contexts is the main business of the regional innovation platform model. The innovation potential is explored among different fields of knowledge.
Knowledge creation and conversion	The cluster model tends to foster knowledge being produced as product-like outcomes of active, clearly specified activities. Information and explicit knowledge are more likely to be produced than contextualized, tacit knowledge.	Cognitive relationships among different industries and cross-fertilization enable effective information sharing and contextualization between individuals. More radical changes in the knowledge-base of an individual or a group may take place.
Absorptive capacity	The cluster model is adequate in increasing realized absorptive capacity in regional innovation networks due to promotion of bonding social capital.	The regional innovation platform model attempts to increase potential absorptive capacity particularly by new methods of futures research and foresight. Particular attention is paid to assimilating foresight information and converting it into future-oriented innovation knowledge.
STI and DUI modes of innovation	The cluster model promotes, in particular, the STI (science, technology, innovation) mode that is based on the production and use of codified scientific and technical knowledge.	The DUI (doing, using, interacting) mode is intentionally fostered by building structures and relationships that enhance and utilize experience-based mode of learning.

Table 41.3 (continued)

Theory/ Framework	The Cluster Model – Agglomeration	The Regional Innovation Platform Model – Related variety
Location and urbanization economies	The cluster model takes advantage mainly of location economies that combine companies in the same industry.	The regional innovation platform model takes advantage of urbanization economies by spillover processes among industries inside of a region.
Innovation systems	The cluster model primarily enhances the sectoral knowledge base. It also binds regional clusters into international sectoral innovation systems.	The regional innovation platform model is based on the theories of regional and national innovation systems.

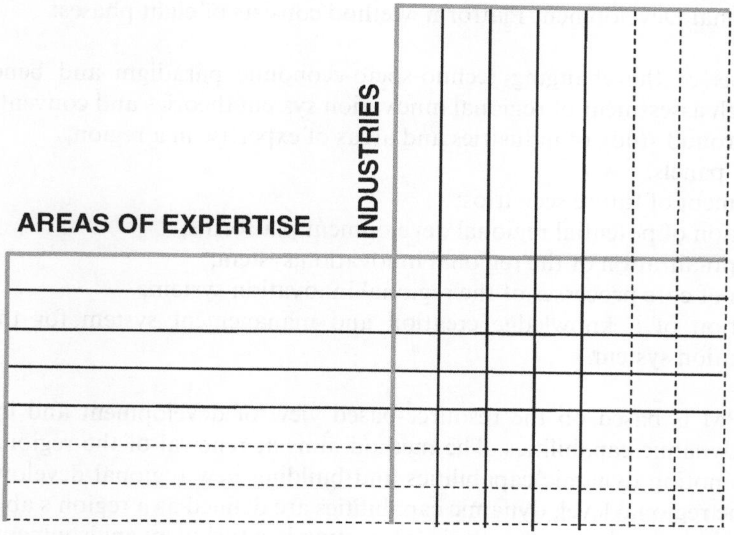

Source: Harmaakorpi (2006).

Figure 41.1 *The principle of combining industries and areas of expertise in the Regional Development Platform Method*

tool is recognition of networked regional development environment. Particular attention is paid to an interactive manner of designing and running the regional innovation system. All the phases of the method are planned so that they can be conducted in networked interaction, where participation is possible for various people and organizations – without forgetting the importance of leadership roles in the process.

The RDPM helps to look for regional business potential upon which it is possible to build future competitive advantage of a region. The dominating idea in developing the RDPM was the importance of individual regional development paths in designing development strategies. The strategies should be based on a thorough assessment of regional resources, capabilities and competencies as well as future possibilities leading to business potential that can give regional competitive advantage (Teece et al., 1997; Scott, 2000; Pekkarinen and Harmaakorpi, 2006). An essential part of the method is core process thinking that was designed to form innovation networks aiming at exploiting business potential existing in the regional development platforms. Moreover, the RDPM may be seen as a network leadership tool that helps regional actors to interact during a development process and to promote social capital and dynamic capabilities in the region.

In Figure 41.1, the principle of industries and areas of expertise forming resource configurations in the RDPM is presented. Areas of expertise are formed by skills, capabilities and competencies that are considered to be important regardless of industry. Industries are marked in the columns, and the areas of expertise chosen for each individual study are marked in the rows. The RDPM aims to define business potential that can give regional competitive advantage based on the industries, areas of expertise and, especially, on their combinations.

The Regional Development Platform Method consists of eight phases:

- analysis of the changing techno-socio-economic paradigm and benchmarking through assessment of regional innovation system theories and conventions;
- background study of industries and areas of expertise in a region;
- expert panels;
- assessment of future scenarios;
- definition of potential regional development platforms;
- conceptualization of the regional innovation system;
- search of core processes of the regional innovation system;
- definition of a knowledge creation and management system for the regional innovation system.

The RDPM is based on the resource-based view of development and includes the concept of dynamic capabilities. The method aims at renewal of the regional resource base by promoting dynamic capabilities and building new regional development platforms. At the regional level, dynamic capabilities are defined as a region's ability to generate competitive development paths in interaction in a turbulent environment. Dynamic capabilities aim to reform regional resource configurations based on the history of the region in question and opportunities emerging from the techno-socio-economic development. Five dynamic capabilities are considered to be essential in a networked regional innovation environment: (1) innovative capability; (2) learning capability; (3) networking capability; (4) leadership capability; and (5) visionary capability (see Figure 41.2).

The regional development platform thinking in the Lahti region is nowadays intertwined with network-facilitating innovation policy (Harmaakorpi and Tura, 2008). It has gained interest also elsewhere in Europe, and Cooke (2006), for instance, has outlined development platforms for Scania, Sweden and Hedmark, Norway. In addition, the RDPM has been implemented as a tool for regional innovation policy in South Africa and Tasmania.

Figure 41.3 illustrates a practical application of the RDPM, the age business core process in the Lahti region. Areas of expertise, industries and relevant regional actors have been identified to form a whole to respond effectively to the megatrend of ageing of population. The main areas of expertise in the region concerning ageing are design and well-being. The central industrial sectors, again, are plastics, construction, furniture and metal industry. The age business core process is based on those areas of expertise and sectors. Relevant regional actors that contribute to and benefit from the core process aiming at successful responses to ageing are companies in the industrial sectors in question, innovation intermediaries, educational institutions, and expertise and development centres. The 'owner' of the core process also needs to be identified; in the case of the age business process it has been the Regional Development Centre Programme. All these elements form an important regional development platform as well as a network. Figure 41.3 provides an example; industries or actors, for instance, may change over time, but identification and design of a core process are useful for innovation policy.

It seems that development platform-related thinking has good opportunities to become an efficient tool for competitiveness policy. Its central challenge lies in moving further away from scientific debate to become a practical tool for developing innovation

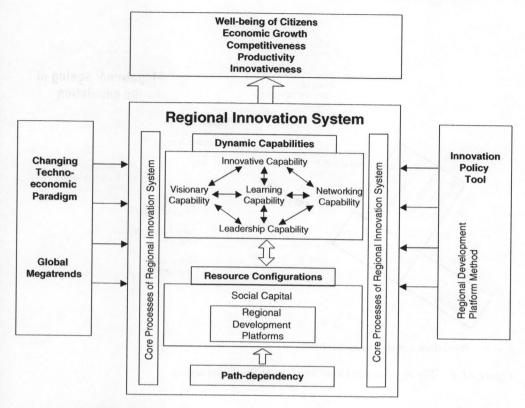

Source: Harmaakorpi (2004, 2006).

Figure 41.2   A systemic framework for development of a regional innovation system

platforms and mechanisms to utilize and benefit from related variety. Crucial questions to answer in this process are the following: How do these platforms develop? Which actors play key roles in these processes? What is the role of the public sector in the development of platforms? Which interventions are needed to create development platforms? When an increasing number of well-justified answers are given to these questions, implementation of regional constructed competitiveness policy may gain entirely new, different forms along with development platform thinking.

CONCLUSIONS

Clusters have been the central framework of regional development in the 1990s and the beginning of the twenty-first century. The cluster theory has indeed been quite useful, but it has recently been challenged strongly by the novel emphasis on the role of innovations, the increasing complexity of innovation processes, and the change in the sources of competitiveness. The theories of innovation systems appear to provide a new

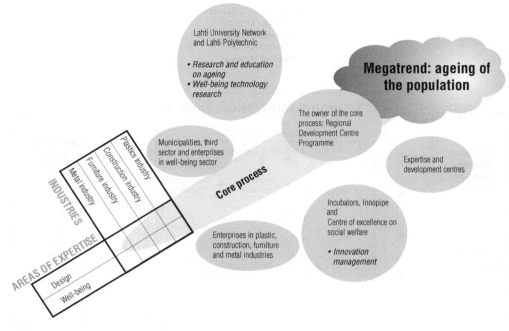

Source: Pekkarinen and Harmaakorpi (2006).

Figure 41.3   The age business core process in the Lahti region

kind of viewpoint into developing competitiveness, but they also require a new kind of framework for assessing structures of regional competitiveness.

In this chapter, we presented the innovation platform thinking as a feasible framework for developing the regional economic future. It is related to the cluster model, but it takes into account the significance of the element of distance – which is central particularly in innovation activities – as part of development efforts. The regions that manage to create a limited amount of innovation platforms based on related variety appear to succeed best in the competition between regions. These regions are able to utilize in a synergic manner the innovation potential lying in between and at the interfaces of the platforms. Policies to promote competitiveness should thus allow diversity and divergence in order to enhance innovativeness, but manage to link diversity into a force that promotes growth. Diversity at all levels – from, for instance, individual innovation tools, to diverse types of knowledge, to organizations, industries and sectors – is important in this regard.

REFERENCES

Adler, P. and S.-W. Kwon (2000), 'Social capital: the good, the bad and the ugly', in E.L. Lesser (ed.), *Knowledge and Social Capital Foundations and Applications*, Boston, MA: Butterworth-Heinemann, pp. 89–115.
Audretsch, D.B. and M.P. Feldman (2003), 'Knowledge spillovers and the geography of innovation', in J.V.

Henderson and J. Thisse (eds), *Handbook of Urban and Regional Economics*, Vol. 4, Amsterdam: North-Holland, pp. 2713–39.

Autio, E. (1998), 'Evaluation of RTD in regional systems of innovation', *European Planning Studies*, **6** (2), 131–40.

Berg Jensen, M., B. Johnson, E. Lorenz and B.-Å. Lundvall (2007), 'Forms of knowledge and modes of innovation', *Research Policy*, **36**, 680–93.

Boschma, R. (2005a), 'Role of proximity in interaction and performance: conceptual and empirical challenges', *Regional Studies*, **39** (1), 41–5.

Boschma, R. (2005b), 'Proximity and innovation: a critical assessment', *Regional Studies*, **39** (1), 61–74.

Burt, R.S. (1992), *Structural Holes: The Social Structure of Competition*, Boston, MA: Harvard University Press.

Burt, R.S. (2004), 'Structural holes and good ideas', *American Journal of Sociology*, **110** (2), 349–99.

Chinitz, B. (1961), 'Contrasts in agglomeration: New York and Pittsburgh', *American Economic Review*, **51**, 279–89.

Christaller, W. (1933), *Die Zentralen Orte in Suddeutschland*, Jena, Germany: Gustav Fischer Verlag.

CIS (2004), 'Innovation Europe – results for the third Community Innovation Survey for the EU, Norway and Iceland', Luxembourg.

Cohen, W. and L. Levinthal (1990), 'Absorptive capacity: a new perspective on learning and innovation', *Administrative Science Quarterly*, **35**, 128–52.

Coleman, J. (1988), 'Social capital in the creation of human capital', *American Journal of Sociology*, **94**, Issue Supplement: Organizations and Institutions: Sociological and Economic Approaches to the Analysis of Social Structure, 95–120.

Cooke, P. (2006), 'Global bioregional networks: a new economic geography of bioscientific knowledge', *European Planning Studies*, **14**, 1265–85.

Cooke, P. (2007), 'To construct regional advantage from innovation systems first build policy platforms', *European Planning Studies*, **15**, 124–46.

Cooke, P., M. Uranga and G. Etxebarria (1997), 'Regional innovation systems: institutional and organisational dimensions', *Research Policy*, **26**, 475–91.

Feldman, M.P. (1994), *The Geography of Innovation*, Boston, MA: Kluwer.

Freeman, C. (1987), *Technology and Economic Performance: Lessons from Japan*, London: Pinter Publishers.

Gibbons, M., C. Limoges, H. Nowotny, S. Schwarzman, P. Scott and M. Trow (1994), *The New Production of Knowledge*, London: Sage.

Glaeser, E., H. Kallal, J. Scheinkman and A. Shleifer (1992), 'Growth of cities', *Journal of Political Economy*, **100**, 1126–52.

Granovetter, M. (1973), 'The strength of weak ties', *American Journal of Sociology*, **78**, 1360–80.

Granovetter, M. (2005), 'The impact of social structure on economic outcomes', *Journal of Economic Perspectives*, **19** (1), 33–50.

Harmaakorpi, V. (2004), 'Building a competitive regional innovation environment – the regional development platform method as a tool for innovation policy', Doctoral dissertation, Espoo: Helsinki University of Technology.

Harmaakorpi, V. (2006), 'The regional development platform method as a tool for regional innovation policy', *European Planning Studies*, **14** (8), 1085–184.

Harmaakorpi, V. and H. Melkas (2005), 'Knowledge management in regional innovation networks: the case of Lahti, Finland', *European Planning Studies*, **13** (5), 641–59.

Harmaakorpi, V. and A. Mutanen (2008), 'Knowledge production in networked practice-based innovation processes: interrogative model as a methodological approach', *Interdisciplinary Journal of Information, Knowledge, and Management*, **3**, 87–101.

Harmaakorpi, V. and T. Tura (2008), 'Verkostoja palveleva innovaatiopolitiikka', in V. Harmaakorpi and H. Melkas (eds), *Innovaatiopolitiikkaa järjestelmien välimaastossa*, Acta series no. 200, Helsinki: Suomen Kuntaliitto & Lappeenrannan teknillinen yliopisto (in Finnish), pp. 149–58.

Harmaakorpi, V. and T. Uotila (2006), 'Building regional visionary capability: futures research in resource based regional development', *Technological Forecasting and Social Change*, **73**, 778–92.

Howells, J. (2000), 'Knowledge, innovation and location', in J.R. Bryson, P.W. Daniels, N. Henry and J. Pollard (eds), *Knowledge, Space, Economy*, London, UK and New York, USA: Routledge, pp. 50–62.

Howells, J. (2002), 'Tacit knowledge, innovation and economic geography', *Urban Studies*, **39**, 871–84.

Kline, S. and N. Rosenberg (1986), 'An overview on innovation', in R. Landau and N. Rosenberg (eds), *The Positive Sum Strategy*, Washington, DC: National Academy Press, pp. 275–305.

Lazzeretti, L., F. Capone and T. Cinti (2010), 'The regional development platform and "related variety": some evidence from art and food in Tuscany', *European Planning Studies*, **18** (1), 27–45.

Lundvall, B.-Å. (1988), 'Innovation as an interactive process: from user-producer interaction to the national system of innovation', in G. Dosi, G. Freeman, R. Nelson, G. Silverberg and L. Soete (eds), *Technical Change and Economic Theory*, London, UK and New York, USA: Pinter, pp. 349–69.

Lundvall, B.-Å. (ed.) (1992), *National Systems of Innovation: Towards a Theory of Innovation and Interactive Learning*, London: Pinter Publishers.

Lösch, A. (1954), *The Economics of Location*, New Haven, CT: Yale University Press.

Malerba, F. (2002), 'Sectoral systems of innovation and production', *Research Policy*, **31**, 247–64.

Malmberg, A. and P. Maskell (2002), 'The elusive concept of localization economies: towards a knowledge-based theory of spatial clustering', *Environment and Planning A*, **34**, 429–49.

Marshall, A. (1916), *The Principles of Economics*, London: Macmillan.

Pekkarinen, S. and V. Harmaakorpi (2006), 'Building regional innovation networks: definition of age business core process in a regional innovation system', *Regional Studies*, **40** (4), 1–13.

Porter, M.E. (1990), 'Cluster and the new economics of competition', *Harvard Business Review*, November–December, 77–90.

Putnam, R.D. (1995), 'Bowling alone: America's declining social capital', *Journal of Democracy*, **6** (1), 65–78.

Rallet, A. and A. Torre (1999), 'Is geographical proximity necessary in the innovation networks in the era of the global economy?', *GeoJournal*, **49**, 373–80.

Scott, A.J. (2000), *Regions and World Economy: The Coming Shape of Global Production, Competition and Political Order*, New York: Oxford University Press.

Storper, M. (1997), *The Regional World: Territorial Development in a Global Economy*, New York: Guilford Press.

Teece, D.J., G. Pisano and A. Shuen (1997), 'Dynamic capabilities and strategic management', *Strategic Management Journal*, **18** (7), 509–33.

Torre, A. and J.P. Gilly (2000), 'On the analytical dimension of proximity dynamics', *Regional Studies*, **34**, 169–80.

Tura, T. and V. Harmaakorpi (2005), 'Social capital in building regional innovative capability', *Regional Studies*, **39** (8), 1111–25.

Uotila, T., V. Harmaakorpi and H. Melkas (2007), 'A method for assessing absorptive capacity of a regional innovation system', *Fennia*, **184** (1), 49–58.

Zahra, A.Z. and G. George (2002), 'Absorptive capacity: a review, reconceptualization, and extension', *Academy of Management Review*, **27** (2), 185–203.

42 Regional innovation policy and dramaturgy
Philip Cooke

INTRODUCTION

Very few regional innovation agencies have either informal or informal methodologies aimed at getting innovators to cross-pollinate their specific knowledge (for those that do, see Chapter 23 on transversality in this *Handbook*). There are very few Venn diagrams showing overlapping intercluster horizontal knowledge dynamics. But there are some that practice such transversality and a few others that understand it and aspire to evolve appropriate methods to take advantage of cross-sectoral knowledge dynamics and open up the 'white spaces' as they are sometimes referred to, or what Burt (1992) refers to as 'structural holes', where innovation opportunities are at their most tempting and potentially abundant. This fits well with Schumpeter's (1975) concept of innovation as recombinations of knowledge. In Andersen's Chapter 2 in this *Handbook* on Schumpeter's regional innovation theory, it is made clear that Schumpeter radically separated the role of innovator and entrepreneur. The innovator recombines knowledge from ideas and knowledge that already exist, while the entrepreneur separately undertakes the innovation, deploying commercial skills.

Under the circumstances to be described, the regional innovation agency takes on more of an 'innovator' role and even edges into a more entrepreneurial role, especially where fees are charged for innovation services. Accordingly, catalytic innovation, which is what this model implies on the part of the innovation agency, is far more than mere 'support' or such equivalent supply-side roles as to promote, encourage, assist or partner firms in their quest for innovation. Supply-side economics was the neoliberal mantra, adopted by regional, national, multilateral and supranational agencies everywhere in the form of 'spatial specialization' policies like clusters and clustering. Now, demand-driven innovation is back to pick up the pieces left by the failures of supply-side neoliberalism. Anne Golden has articulated the innovation policy dilemma as follows: 'Should reliance be placed on urban specialisation – as Harvard professor Michael Porter claims? . . . Or should we trust in diversity – as the late urban expert Jane Jacobs believed?' (Golden, 2009). This chapter looks beyond Porter towards concepts inspired by Jacobs, notably diversity as a wellspring of innovation and growth, as represented in the evolutionary economic geography of 'related variety' (Jacobs, 1969; Frenken et al., 2007).

The chapter is constructed as follows. It begins in the next section with a theoretical overview of some of the key spatial process concepts associated with transversality. However, this is done contextually, with an emphasis on the discourse of communicative competence and moderation of cognitive dissonance. Hence there is an outline of the concept of 'related variety' which underpins the whole analysis (for full treatment see Boschma and Frenken's Chapter 14 in this *Handbook*). In the spatial process subsystem to be articulated below, it is thus intimately connected to Schumpeterian 'recombination' sought by identification of 'structural holes' (Burt, 1992) or 'white spaces' to create innovation platforms. In the second half of the chapter attention is drawn more to policy concepts and practical instruments such as transversality itself, 'orchestration' (Wallin, 2006), matrix methodologies and dramaturgy. The last is particularly innovative and some effort is made to elicit key elements in which creativity of this kind is deployed in the orchestration of regional innovation. This is displayed diagrammatically in Figure 42.4 below. Representative models are briefly discussed and reasons for this 'cultural turn' in practice adduced. Amongst the principal contributory elements, it will be argued are: the rise of creative industries as progenitors of services innovation; the need for innovation 'orchestrators' to move beyond mere advertising into the 'experience economy'; and the cognitive assets of dramaturgy in translational knowledge activities. The chapter ends with concluding remarks.

A CONCEPTUAL FRAMEWORK FOR ADVANCED REGIONAL INNOVATION POLICY PRACTICE

This chapter is interested in the framing process, whereby predominant ideas pervade consciousness in only partially recognized ways. This is comparable to the way that language users adopt new words that fit a broader narrative or discourse of power, status or influence (Davenport and Leitch, 2009). Although a seminal text introducing the discourse may not exist, or may be unread even if it does, a practitioner may absorb such discourse in many ways and utilize it for good or ill. Practitioners are avid networkers, for whom language is the key medium of exchange; they attend workshops, seminars, conferences and exhibitions, and consult websites. They reflect, communicate and interact on what they have heard or seen, and decide which discourse makes most practical sense, or answers difficult professional questions; discourse is, accordingly, viral. It is possible that this has occurred in relation to the core evolutionary economic geography concept of 'related variety', given the fact that advanced practitioners of regional innovation policy are behaving as though they had read, for example, Frenken et al. (2007).

Spatial Process Concepts

Related variety
The articulation of discourse process described earlier is rather poorly understood or analysed in innovation studies. By analysing some of the methods developed by advanced innovation policy orchestrators, we may get a clearer understanding of the problem of translation. This means translation of tacit into codified knowledge, interdisciplinary dialoguing, and mechanisms that make clients value the authenticity of their mind-opening experience to the extent that they transform discourse into action. Below are summarized five key points that may assist understanding of the policy power of a new, value-adding innovation concept. The basic idea of related variety is that economic development is caused by interactions between elements in regional economies displaying relatedness in technology or industry. This has a number of implications. First, applying the notion of related variety has led to new insights in the externalities literature. Empirical studies tend to show that it is not so much regional specialization or regional diversification regarding externalities that induces knowledge spillovers and enhances

regional growth, but a regional economy that encompasses related activities in terms of competences (that is, regions well endowed with related variety). Second, it has provided additional insights to the question of whether or not extraregional linkages matter for regional growth. Adopting a relatedness framework, empirical studies on trade patterns tend to show that it is not inflows of knowledge per se that matter for regional growth, but inflows of knowledge that are related (not similar) to the existing knowledge base of regions. Related flows concern new knowledge that can be understood and exploited and, thus, be transformed in regional growth.

Third, relatedness is now also investigated in network analysis because tracing movements of knowledgeable persons can reveal relatedness in action. For instance, studies show that collaborative research projects tend to create more new knowledge when they consist of agents that bring in complementary competences (Wenting, 2008). Fourth, the notion of relatedness refreshes recognition of the importance to regional growth of labour mobility. This too is often regarded as one of the key mechanisms through which knowledge diffuses. Recent studies show that neither inflows nor outflows of labour are properly assessed if how these knowledge flows match the already existing knowledge base of firms and regions is not also considered. Fifth, relatedness may also show its relevance through entrepreneurship dynamics of the kind indicated by Schumpeter (1975). Experienced entrepreneurs (those that have acquired knowledge in related industries), as opposed to spin-off companies, may play a crucial role in the regional diversification process. More generally speaking, longitudinal studies show that long-term development of regions depends on their ability to diversify into new sectors while building on their current knowledge base (Harmaakorpi, 2009).

However, at least two problems exist methodologically in the application of related variety to economic processes. What might be called simple related variety may predict regional innovation potential by *ex ante* analysis of regional industrial composition. Hence similar industries, like varieties of engineering, may reveal actual evidence of high innovation, and high spin-off and labour mobility factors assisting it. For example, a UK study shows engineering to be the most innovative industry category, ahead of highly innovative categories like other manufacturing, creative industries; and knowledge-intensive business services (KIBS; Chapain et al., 2010). But there is a strong element of unpredictability regarding innovative crossovers between unrelated industries. This is extremely hard, to the point of impossibility, to predict and may only be observable *ex post* as something akin to 'revealed related variety'. Equally so, the issue of related variety outside the region or even country probably also only allows for *ex post* understanding. In these respects, fascinating as it is to see advanced innovation emerging from cooperations between, for example, otherwise unrelated agricultural and automotive research, as occurs regarding biofuels, the practical implications of this for regional policy are unclear – but may become less so as the chapter proceeds.

Recombination

The second key spatial process concept concerns 'recombinant methods' of innovation, as proposed by Schumpeter. How does this occur? Veblen (1898) held the view that the ultimate source of innovation lay in dissatisfaction with the status quo on the part of the innovator. This is highly likely to be user-driven in the sense that the innovator themselves may experience the initial dissatisfaction, or may learn of the dissatisfaction of a third party such as a doctor with respect to a drug's efficacy, or that of a quite widespread segment of the community, for example concerning pollution or environmental degradation. Dissatisfaction reveals prospects of a 'lead market' that can be exploited entrepreneurially if the innovator comes up with a workable improvement.

In the history of innovation, numerous world-class novelties arose unexpectedly when a different innovation target was being aimed at. The Post-it note is the classic 'useful innovation' of this kind. As a 'repositionable' or 'releasable adhesive' it began as a solution in search of a problem. Initially conceived of as a better kind of bookmark, consumer demand after a marketing trial showed that its real value lay as a visual reminder listing device. In Cooke and Morgan (1998) the example is given of Borg Warner the US steering gear firm needing to cut cost by stamping rather than milling components, which led it to innovate an advanced stamping machine that created more demand than the product it made. Prosthetic joints became more efficient when discoveries made in aerospace ceramics were applied to inadequate pre-existing solutions. Very many other innovations are explicable in terms of these crossover effects in contexts of dissatisfaction with existing combinations of knowledge. Proximity to the initial user may be advantageous but many such crossovers occur at trade exhibitions (Maskell et al., 2006).

Structural holes or white spaces

This brings us to the third of our spatial process concepts, the identification of 'white spaces' or 'structural holes' where innovation opportunities and potential are argued to lie, according to this approach (Burt, 1992). Burt contrasts two types of interaction that may create the social capital underpinning innovation opportunities. The first is that it occurs among strongly interconnected network members, a contrast made earlier by Granovetter (1973) with his notion of strong network ties, which may in practice turn out to be too inward-looking and specialized to avoid 'lock-in'. The weight of past relations and interactions among actors and institutions under a strong ties regime can be innovation-inhibiting. The second possibility is that social capital for innovation may be better served where the network has actors who can broker interconnections between disconnected interests. This is cognate to the 'weak ties' argument advanced in Granovetter (1973) where 'lock-in' is avoided because the burden of obligations, favour exchanges and traditionally strong and regular social capital interactions is missing. This leaves greater scope for new interactions that might be desirable for innovation to ensue. This is consistent with the innovation mechanism embodied in the concept of 'recombinant methods' discussed above.

Two interesting and important theoretical insights are then discussed in Burt (1992). First he demonstrates the widely assumed prevalence of sociological and social psychological research insights that intragroup knowledge circulation predominates over intergroup knowledge circulation. This is shown for work groups, divisions of firms and, indeed, whole industries where no actor is simultaneously aware of innovation opportunities resting with other actor networks. However, while agreeing that 'silos' are inefficient, whether in business divisions or in industrial clusters, not least for the time they waste in diffusing knowledge, Burt (1992) recognizes that knowledge eventually reaches everyone of consequence to it. The second important observation is that while it may seem that innovation-inhibiting tight networks need to be replaced in their entirety by innovation-promoting looser networks with good internetwork antennae, both have a

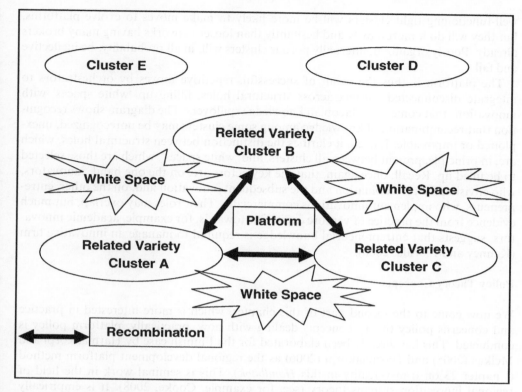

Figure 42.1   Regional intercluster innovation platform model

key role to play. But how are structural holes identified from tight networks? Burt (2000) draws a distinction between structural holes outside the network and those inside it. The latter exert a negative effect on the network's ability to reach consensus. It is also empirically frequently the case that some hierarchy prevails, as well as good internal network communication and cohesion. These constraints allow the tight network to reach conclusions about the need to seek innovation elsewhere than inside the network or specialization setting. Hence strong cluster organizations are valuable but limited in their horizons, while looser ones tend on all criteria analysed in Burt (2000) to be superior.

Platforms

This leads to the final process concept, edging towards a practice concept, which is the notion of 'platform' (discussed in more depth in Chapter 23 on transversality in this *Handbook*. This is represented in spatial process terms by Figure 42.1. I have mapped a set of four conceptual relations that connect 'relatedness' as a condition of industry coexistence that is potentially value-adding for innovation strategy, to 'recombination' as the means by which innovation results in the commercialization of new knowledge. Recombination involves crossing 'structural holes' among networks and filling 'white spaces' between clusters. If the network or cluster itself is internally well integrated and led, this enhances efficiencies, leading to recognition of the need for network brokership. Hence well-functioning tight clusters will be more likely to make moves to evolve platforms, but they will do it more slowly and hesitantly than looser networks having many brokers already. Poorly organized, internally porous clusters will, in all probability, be ineffective and fail.

The platform is thus the result of successful, repetitive moves by orchestrators to integrate disconnected clusters across structural holes, filling up 'white spaces' with innovations that come from Jacobian knowledge spillovers. The diagram shows recognition that recombination of knowledge among some clusters may be unrecognized, unexploited or impossible. Indeed, it clarifies the distinction between structural holes, which are, in principle, present between all clusters, and 'white spaces', which are those selected to be filled up. Recall, once again, that the key actors are, on the one hand, innovators, who envision the recombination and the subsequent innovation and, on the other, entrepreneurs, who implement innovations commercially. Their roles may overlap, but much evidence from the practice of venture capitalists towards, for example, academic innovators, suggests that entrepreneurial knowledge is required to manage an innovative firm (Kenney and Florida, 2000).

Policy Theory Concepts

We now come to the second part of this chapter, which is more interested in practice and concerns policy theory concepts dealing with how, practically, platform policy is conducted. This has already been elaborated for the Finnish case by Harmaakorpi and Melkas (2005) and Harmaakorpi (2006) as the regional development platform method (Chapter 23 on transversality in this *Handbook*). This is seminal work in the field of regional innovation systems theory (see, for example, Cooke, 2008). It is empirically based in a study of regional resilience in the Finnish furniture industry region of Lahti (on resilience, see Bristow, 2010; Simmie and Martin, 2010). However, this is not the only type of regional innovation context; indeed platform policy in support of exploiting white spaces has been more evident in relatively prosperous European regions, although it is also practised in some peripheral regions. Hence, there is a need for a conceptualization of this practice approach as it is deployed in different regional settings. Nevertheless, returning to the Finnish original, heralding a Mark 3 regional innovation system approach that moves beyond mainly 'institutional' (Mark 1) or mainly 'entrepreneurial' (Mark 2) models (see Cooke, 2004) here we see the early processes and institutions of dramaturgy appearing in regional innovation policy practice.

Dramaturgy

Dramaturgy is a branch of the theatrical arts which involves bringing productions to life on the stage. The role of a dramaturg in a production can be quite varied, depending on their training 'school' and the philosophy of the theatre the dramaturg is working for. Different national theatre traditions also have differing beliefs on the role of dramaturgy in theatre production. In Harmaakorpi's exposition of the 'toolkit' utilized in recombination stimulation in Lahti (Figure 42.2), among numerous innovations involving more than one 'living laboratory', is Innolink. This is part of the organizational process to integrate regional platform policy approaches among technological and other experts, value networks and client firms.

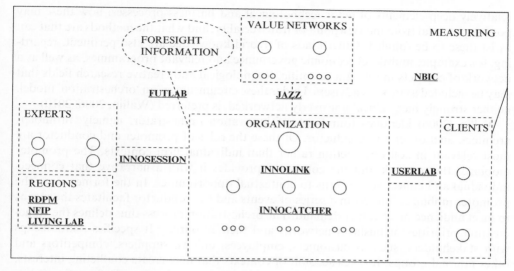

Source: Harmaakorpi (2009).

Figure 42.2 *The Lahti regional innovation system platform policy toolkit*

One means of identifying possible future developmental trajectories and giving them regional relevance is the use of creative methods. One of the most interesting and successful of these has been the use of theatrical drama to connect ideas to a systematic analysis of knowledge, resources and the potentialities and possible pitfalls of cooperation. Scripts are written by professional dramatists in the form of short sketches articulating mentalities, blockages, barriers and change requirements in contexts where the drama involves simulations of real-world experiences of firms and institutions confronting the need for innovation. The short dramas or sketches are then acted out to an audience of potential users of the ideas and solutions presented. The cognitive plateau achieved collectively by users then feeds into the succeeding phases of the innovation process, such as 'Jazz', where improvization on any emergent opportunity themes is encouraged, Innocatcher, where potentially creative notions and concepts are articulated, captured and integrated, and Userlab, a 'living lab' where testing and trialling of ideas occurs and process outcomes are simulated. Living labs are used elsewhere in Nordic regional innovation settings, notably Värmland region in Sweden, as test-beds, demonstration centres or what might be termed 'rehearsals for reality' in relation to innovation.

Orchestration

For such an innovation policy process to be enacted requires organization and management. This is for three reasons: first, the users of innovation involved in the quest for innovation may be diverse in sectoral terms, although they probably consist of sectoral sub-blocks rather than having wholly individualized capabilities. Second, the central task of dramaturgy is to open up the prospects for cross-pollination of knowledge and capabilities in as harmonious a manner as possible. Finally, there is a need for the special skills, sometimes called 'hybrid' skills, of an animator or facilitator who is cognizant of relatively deep elements of actor technological and business processes, how these may possess potential from the viewpoint of transversality, and what the methods are that can assist these to be fulfilled. Other kinds of hybrid knowledge are also pertinent, regarding, for example, multilevel economic governance and relevant programmes, as well as a network of contacts in relevant scientific, technological and creative research fields that may be included as process advisers. Under these circumstances an 'orchestration' model, neither strongly hierarchical nor overly networked, is preferred (Wallin, 2006, 2010).

Wallin (2006) identifies four kinds of innovation orchestrator, namely: promoter, architect, auctioneer and conductor. Of these the roles of promoter and conductor are most relevant in collective action rather than individual firm contexts. The promoter mobilizes the network and the conductor provides it with a narrative that connects individual and collective concerns to contextual opportunities. In the former sense the promoter mobilizes interest in a series of events and the conductor facilitates the means to meet audience or customer demand. The orchestration process thus defines the value-creation priorities of business networks and their resources. It specifies relationships with stakeholders, such as customers, employees, unions, suppliers, competitors and other internal groups. It takes account of contexts that may create conflicting interests, or impose risks to firm networks. It seeks to identify innovative means of creating value. The orchestration process model is itself subject to continual review as a response to actual and possible changes in perceived business conditions. In regional innovation policy settings, the ideal promoter and conductor of proceedings is the specialist innovation agency, whose interest may still be in profitability for itself but only in relation to selling its specific skills rather than competing with its business customers. Such an agency may house the infrastructural knowledge discussed above to assist promotion and the transversality knowledge to stimulate innovation. As will be shown in the empirical part of the chapter, orchestration can also usefully be assisted by narrative, if not dramaturgy, in both its promotion and conducting roles.

Transversality

In discussing the conducting aspect of orchestration policy, transversality has been mentioned more than once (also see Chapter 23 on transversality in this *Handbook*). It is vital to see it in relation to the evolutionary economic geography insight regarding the extra value that accrues to urban or regional economies displaying related variety (Frenken et al., 2007; Boschma and Frenken, 2003). However, two important things were noted in the subsection discussing the concept. The first is that the mere existence of related variety does not automatically mean that it will be exploited. Market failure may prevail due to asymmetric information, resulting in knowledge spillovers and mutual absorptive capacity being underused for well-known reasons of satisficing, first articulated by Simon (1957). Firms may not have the resources, time or priority to look outwards at narrow transversality as much as they ideally should. Here, as in other situations, market failures warrant third-party interventions that, in this instance for a fee, bring opportunities for potential innovation gains to their attention. Second, it was noted that transversality in the broader sense can also be a source of useful interactions among firms leading to innovation. Where such search and selection behaviour is prioritized by the firm in one cluster or sector seeking to fill a 'white space' by connecting to firms in wholly other clusters or sectors, they may be successful, even within their region. However, achieving 'revealed

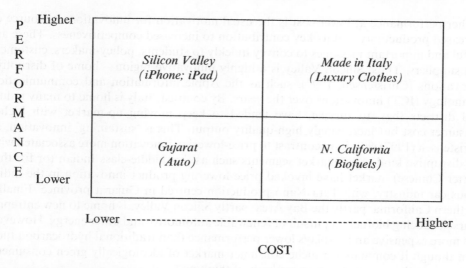

P **E** **R** **F** **O** **R** **M** **A** **N** **C** **E**	Higher *Silicon Valley* *(iPhone; iPad)* *Gujarat* *(Auto)* Lower	*Made in Italy* *(Luxury Clothes)* *N. California* *(Biofuels)*

Lower -- Higher

COST

Figure 42.3   Regional innovation quadrants

related variety' in this way is even more demanding, so for the innovation agency here is where 'story-telling' skills may be utilized to the utmost to create a 'red thread' of narrative that might appeal to the broadest possible innovation-seeking audience.

As noted earlier, this is when the regional innovation agency takes on a catalytic role in the innovation process. The interaction of the key concepts of relatedness, recombination, structural holes and white spaces, platforms, dramaturgy, orchestration and transversality endow the third-party brokerage capability with a special resonance compared to the past. Earlier models of regional innovation have focused on supply-side measures like attracting foreign investment, designing science parks and incubators, or building clusters as main means of promoting regional innovation. Now innovation is moving towards demand-side drivers, with a focus on lead markets, public procurement and consumer preference for ethical production and consumption. Helping to identify revealed related variety opportunities to meet demand-driven innovation is the key new challenge faced by regional innovation policy and its practitioners.

Matrix methods
One of the simplest yet most effective instruments for facilitating transversality and its associated innovation opportunities is 'the matrix' (see Eriksson et al., 2010). This is an elaboration of the technique of the 2 x 2 quadrant or double-entry tabulation that social scientists and management theorist find useful as heuristic devices in both teaching and research. Where concepts interact, illumination, clarification or even innovation may be achieved, as shown in Figure 42.3. The interest in this illustrative quadrant is that it shows innovation is found in many and diverse locations, at different positions in global markets, and with different drivers in terms of relations between cost and performance.

One of the generic findings from empirical studies of innovation is that much of it is driven by the twin contradictory forces of cost reduction and quality improvement.

Higher performance at lower cost is the usual motivation for innovation, its source of increased productivity and its key contribution to increased competitiveness. These are useful and important messages to convey quickly to students, policy-makers, customers and suppliers. Thus, Silicon Valley is a highly innovative region – home of disruptive innovations (Christensen, 1997), such as the Apple information and communication technology (ICT) innovations over the years. By contrast, Italy is home to many industrial districts that, to survive, have tended to keep moving up-market with higher consumer cost but increasingly high-quality output. This is 'sustaining' innovation, as Christensen (1997) calls it, in contrast to price-lowering innovation more associated with the disruptive kind. New market segments such as the middle-class Indian (or for that matter Chinese) market have invoked price-lowering product innovation in the indigenous car industry, with Tata Nano production centred in Gujarat province. Finally, northern California, partly the Bay Area, partly Silicon Valley, is home to new entrepreneurs producing biofuels in pursuit of renewable automotive and other energy. However, it is more expensive and displays lower performance than traditional hydrocarbon fuels even though it commands a niche consumer market of ideologically green consumers. Thus we see the power of matrix methods of thinking.

However, the use to which matrix thinking has been put in innovation practice is thus far twofold. First, some regional innovation practitioners have compared their industry mix along the y axis with their toolbox of innovation support instruments along the x axis and categorized cases accordingly. Thus, for example, firms in one sector might tend to be supported by access to technical university laboratories, while firms in another might be recipients of clustering policy, as appropriate. An alternative matrix approach has been to adopt a policy perspective, for example 'sustainable development', and to identify industries appropriate to different aspects of that perspective. Thus green construction might be included on the production side, organic food on the consumption side and green logistics at the intersection of the two. Finally, regional industries have been compared with technologies known to be utilized by one industry or cluster but not by others. Innovation policy here is to have innovations developed in one industry demonstrated to other industries through workshops, exhibitions and conferences. The key aim is innovation transfer. The orchestrating agency then brokers conversations, dialogues and meetings among interested potential innovation adapters and adopters, and assists as needed with extra expertise, for example from university or private laboratory research establishments. In each of these applications, a narrative is evolved, whether from a sustainable development viewpoint or a healthier living perspective that endows the promotion and conducting of the innovation process an attractive storyline 'hook'.

This exposition facilitates representation of these process interactions by means of a conceptual framework, generalizing the concepts and practices described into a frame of reference for academics and policy-makers alike to test out in other contexts to determine the extent to which dramaturgy plays any role in evolving regional innovation policy formulation processes. In Figure 42.4 a relatively straightforward attempt is made to illustrate connectivity among groups of concepts and practices using a regional innovation systems framework. This shows the full working of the model between the process subsystem in the upper level and the policy and practice subsystem at the lower level. Two-way interactions occur between and within the subsystems. This model achieves three important things of relevance to modern regional innovation policy. First, it shows

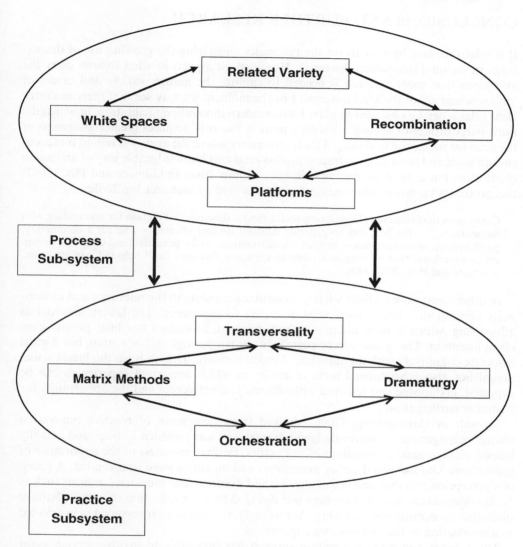

Figure 42.4   Transversality: key process and practice conceptual framework

a high degree of overlap between spatial processes of both related variety and revealed related variety and policy mechanisms to further exploit these for regional innovation purposes. Second, it recognizes in its incorporation of dramaturgy in the policy toolbox, that regional innovation policy-makers should raise their game in terms of popular appeal to economic actors and utilization of dramaturgy in the economic actor–policy-maker interface. Finally, it demonstrates the new demand-side role of the regional innovation policy system as a catalyst and orchestrator of regional innovation opportunity, rather than a mere provider of supply-side support as has been the case for most of the neoliberal era since about 1980.

CONCLUSIONS AND FURTHER RESEARCH

It is relatively easy by now to see the rationales underlying the growing use of dramaturgy in regional innovation discourse. However, all aspects of what follows carry the injunction that more research is needed to capture the nature, variety and extent of 'policy rehearsal' of the kind outlined. For the moment we may see that there are three clear roles it can be observed to play. First, modern innovation facilitation, in which the third-party broker or agency takes on a more active role, requires greater awareness of the need for successful branding. This is imperative where the agency is reliant on fees to sustain itself and must demonstrate a professional and knowledgeable way of attracting client attention against competing calls on customer time. In Gilmore and Pine (2007) this process is known as 'placemaking', a term coined by architect Jon Jerde:

> Companies that embrace placemaking understand a fundamental dictum for contending with authenticity . . . the best way to generate demand for any offering – whether a commodity, good, service, other experience, or even transformation – is for potential (and current) customers to experience that offering in a place so engaging that they can't help but pay attention. (Gilmore and Pine, 2007, 149)

In other words, clients filter what to prioritize according to the relevance and authenticity of what they have experienced or expect to experience. The fakery involved in advertising, which is both ubiquitous and oversold, nowadays has little purchase on client attention. The 'place' can be permanent or temporary, real or virtual, but it must associate cognitively with an authentic, lived experience. Drama is, in the literal sense, unreal but also a heightened form of reality in which important experiences can be captured, juxtaposed and resolved with efficiency, effectiveness and the opportunity for customer participation.

Second, as Harmaakorpi (2006) showed from experience of reactive innovation change management, scenario-designed dramaturgy was intended to help, and actually helped, change basic assumptions of key actors, raising awareness of the importance of institutions. Old industrial policy mentalities and measures were transcended. A previous perception was that absence of clusters and dynamic lead industries or firms such as Nokia doomed the region. This view was changed by the application of policy platform discourse concerning transversality. Accordingly, the power of transversal networks led to a revaluation of the region's own capabilities.

Third, more and more innovation support has inevitably to involve service-sector innovation since service employment and businesses are the majority in virtually all economies. Such businesses are themselves either creators or users of dramaturgy in their core business models. Accordingly they are acutely aware of the authenticity and creativity dimensions of the innovation services they may be purchasing. This means the innovation agency having a portfolio of experience-oriented services on offer in the form of a permanent demonstration space or specific types of innovation service availability. It also means having access to appropriate enterprise and innovation support personnel who understand and utilize dramaturgy where appropriate and together make the agency's premises a site to be trusted to provide value-adding innovation and creativity-optimizing opportunities.

Finally, it is worth noting that, although there are relatively few regional innovation agencies engaging with these new orchestration, recombination and 'white spaces' quests to enhance regional innovation potential, a few others that are beginning to work in this way deserve mention. Thus Skåne is a second Swedish example that pioneered the 'white spaces' concept and has established a 'sounding board' model of deliberation among regional innovation stakeholders concerning identification of likely candidate white spaces. This is echoed in the ways its 'Moving Media' cluster has shown strong transversality among new media like computer games, the film industry and film-based tourism. Moreover, policy has been devoted from both national economic development and innovation promotion agencies to enhance creative and innovative infrastructures in relation to the film, TV and video drama industry evolving in the region. As was shown also in the Chapter 23 on transversality (this *Handbook*) a further example is the French region of Midi-Pyrénées where transversality has been adopted as its new regional innovation system approach. The process by which transversality was arrived at as a policy development exercise was orchestrated by the regional governance system. The processes are open-ended, but a platform of transversality among agrofood, healthcare biotechnology and aerospace exists in which transversality is to be imagined and implemented by firms selected as high-potential innovators, many acting as supply-chain hubs or *'firmes pivots'*. This strategy aims to secure regional prosperity by enhancing platforms for innovation and their transversality.

REFERENCES

Boschma, R. and K. Frenken (2003), 'Evolutionary economics and industry location', *International Review of Regional Research*, **23**, 183–94.

Bristow, G. (2010), 'Resilient regions: re-"place" ing regional competitiveness', *Cambridge Journal of Regions, Economy and Society*, **3**, 153–67.

Burt, R. (1992), *Structural Holes: The Social Structure of Competition*, Cambridge, MA: Harvard University Press.

Burt, R. (2000), 'The network structure of social capital', in I. Sutton and R. Staw (eds), *Research in Organizational Behaviour*, Greenwich, CT: JAI Press, pp. 345–431.

Chapain, C., P. Cooke, L. De Propris, S. MacNeill and J. Mateos-Garcia (2010), *Creative Clusters and Innovation: Putting Creativity on the Map*, London: NESTA.

Christensen, C. (1997), *The Innovator's Dilemma*, Boston, MA: Harvard Business School Press.

Cooke, P. (2004), 'Introduction: regional innovation systems – an evolutionary approach', in P. Cooke, M. Heidenreich and H. Braczyk (eds), *Regional Innovation Systems*, London: Routledge, pp. 1–18.

Cooke, P. (2008), 'Regional innovation systems: origin of the species', *International Journal of Technological Learning, Innovation and Development*, **1**, 393–409.

Cooke, P. and K. Morgan (1998), *The Associational Economy*, Oxford: Oxford University Press.

Davenport, S. and S. Leitch (2009), 'Creating space for the successor: the discourse strategies of pro- and anti-GM factions regarding the future of agriculture in New Zealand', *European Planning Studies*, **17**, 943–62.

Eriksson, A., V. Allee, P. Cooke, V. Harmaakorpi, M. Sotarauta and J. Wallin (eds) (2010), *The Matrix: Post Cluster Innovation Policy*, Stockholm: VINNOVA.

Frenken, K., F. van Oort and T. Verburg (2007), 'Related variety, unrelated variety and regional economic growth', *Regional Studies*, **41**, 685–97.

Gilmore, J. and J. Pine (2007), *Authenticity*, Boston, MA: Harvard Business School Press.

Golden, A. (2009), 'Foreword', in D. Wolfe (ed.), *21st Century Cities in Canada: The Geography of Innovation*, Canada, Conference Board, pp. 1–8.

Granovetter, M. (1973), 'The strength of weak ties', *American Journal of Sociology*, **78**, 1360–80.

Harmaakorpi, V. (2006), 'Regional development platform method as a tool for regional innovation policy', *European Planning Studies*, **14**, 1093–1112.

Harmaakorpi, V. (2009), 'Platforms to develop regional capabilities', presentation to Vinnova Policy Review workshop, 24 February.

Harmaakorpi, V. and H. Melkas (2005), 'Knowledge management in regional innovation networks: the case of Laths', *European Planning Studies*, **15**, 641–60.

Jacobs, J. (1969), *The Economy of Cities*, New York: Vintage.

Kenney, M. and R. Florida (2000), 'Venture capital in Silicon Valley: fuelling new firm formation', in M. Kenney (ed.), *Understanding Silicon Valley: Anatomy of an Entrepreneurial Region*, Stanford, CA: Stanford University Press, pp. 98–123.

Maskell, P., H. Bathelt and A. Malmberg (2006), 'Building global knowledge pipelines: the role of temporary clusters', *European Planning Studies*, **14**, 997–1013.

Schumpeter, J. (1975), *Capitalism, Socialism and Democracy*, New York: Harper.

Simmie, J. and R. Martin (2010), 'The economic resilience of regions: towards an evolutionary approach', *Cambridge Journal of Regions, Economy and Society*, **3**, 27–43.

Simon, H. (1957), *Models of Man: Social and Rational*, London: Wiley.

Veblen, T. (1898), 'Why is economics not an evolutionary science?', *Quarterly Journal of Economics*, **12**, 373–97.

Wallin, J. (2006), *Business Orchestration*, London: Wiley.

Wallin, J. (2010), 'Business orchestration for regional competitiveness', in A. Eriksson V. Allee, P. Cooke, V. Harmaakorpi, M. Soratauta and J. Wallin (eds), *The Matrix: Post-cluster Innovation Policy*, Stockholm: Vinnova, pp. 46–53.

Wenting, R. (2008), *The Evolution of a Creative Industry: the Industrial Dynamics of Fashion Design*, Utrecht: University of Utrecht Press.

43 Design-driven regional innovation
Philip Cooke and Arne Eriksson

INTRODUCTION

It is commonplace in innovation studies to reference the shift in the predominant approach to innovation practice and theory from a traditional linear to a more recent interactive model. The critique of the linear model probably began with Kline and Rosenberg (1986) although it was clear that their 'cascade' model of supply chain interactions only captured an aspect of the non-linear nature of innovation at that time. It was Lundvall (1988, 1992) who examined the importance of user–producer innovation interactions more generally, and set the scene for a new, more sociologically nuanced approach centred on the concept of interactive learning, and finally (Lundvall and Johnson, 1994) the learning economy. The last broad concept recognized that one of the reasons why the linear model of innovation was withering on the vine was because of a transition then beginning in economic affairs more widely. This was the onset of what they called 'knowledge society' in which firm and individual competence at learning would determine the competitive advantage of nations. The need to revitalize learning in the economy was much influenced by the global rise of information and communication technologies (ICTs) and later the Internet in economic, social and political life. Accordingly, much retooling of worker skills was implied, academics having been among the first to have to do this as many were intensive users of computer power, e-mail and digital media more generally.

However, the 'interactive' perception of innovation (also highlighted by Nelson, 1993 and Edquist, 1997), which yielded a massive amount of research and associated discovery in the decades that followed, has received challenges from three quarters, 20 years on. From a critical perspective, these could be termed 'neolinear' innovation models because they privilege unidirectional causality, somewhat against the relational social interactions shown to characterize user–producer innovation relations. The latter posited a new role for the innovation user against the old unidirectional 'technology push' view of innovation, where it emanated from the research and development (R&D) laboratories of great corporations, through their engineering departments where basic research became applications research and prototyping, to the sales and marketing department whose job it was to identify markets for the innovation in question. The product life cycle captured the logistic curve of this process (Chapter 5 by Tichy in this *Handbook*). In transitional theoretical terms, 'technology push' and 'market pull' retained importance in the work of Dosi (1982), who argued that the former is associated with radical innovation, while the latter is associated with incremental innovation. We shall see how this distinction is used creatively in the newer of the three perspectives to be discussed, namely design-driven innovation (DDI; Verganti, 2009). Dosi's important contextual idea of the sociocultural regime (technological regime) which is ushered in by radical innovation, or alternatively embeds incremental innovation, also receives refreshment in DDI. In what follows, the next section contrasts demand-driven and user-driven innovation, while the succeeding section presents and explores design-driven innovation models. All three have been applied, either conceptually or practically, to issues of regional innovation strategy.

DEMAND-DRIVEN AND USER-DRIVEN INNOVATION

In its earlier forms the idea of demand-driven innovation was indistinguishable from user (or customer) driven innovation. Recognizing the critique of the linear innovation model, Jovanovic and Rob (1985) also noted that there was a spatial dimension to it whereby firms get information about their products from customers who would like to see future improvements, and firms market innovations accordingly. However, since then, influenced by the rise and demise of neoliberal 'supply-side' policy thinking, a change in the meaning of 'demand-driven innovation' has occurred, which also separates it from user-driven innovation (Aschhoff and Sofka, 2009). Recall (see Chapter 42 on dramaturgy in this *Handbook*) that the neoliberal experiment began almost from its first days in the Reagan–Thatcher era with policies to remove state regulation from regional development. Accordingly, enterprise zones in the US and UK represented the suspension of planning rules in the belief that such areas would stimulate entrepreneurship. Entrepreneur-led Training and Enterprise Councils (TECs) were formed in the UK, modelled on the US Private Industry Councils (PICs). Moreover, there was a big push to change the sociocultural regime by creating an 'enterprise culture' in society (shareholding; housing owner-occupation) and economy (entrepreneurship; tax-free zones). In both countries, deregulation led to deindustrialization and the tertiarization and specialization of economies in financial services and retailing associated with a growing social polarization. This extreme market vulnerability and its sociocultural regime of recklessness, greed and excess were the proximate cause of the financial catastrophe of 2007–09, the subsequent nationalization of many banks, and the demise of supply-side economics.

Once the state reasserted itself against such depredations, discourse turned to new roles for state agencies in rebalancing economic structures away from knowledge-intensive services (KIBS; see Chapter 28 on services innovation in this *Handbook*) like investment banking and towards, for example, 'green manufacturing' (see 'Green innovation', Chapter 32 in this *Handbook*). However to usher in such regime change or 'co-evolutionary transition' requires concerted demand-driven innovation stimulated by state regulation, identification of 'lead markets' like renewable energy, clean technologies and waste recycling that only the state, including its regional and local variants, can protect through 'strategic niche management' and 'infant industry' protection (Geels, 2004, 2006). Other lead markets are healthcare and education, for both of which there is burgeoning demand for what is fundamentally public provision. So stimulating innovation through mobilizing efficiencies in meeting such vast public demand has become a large part of what is conventionally understood as demand-driven innovation (Edler and Georghiou, 2009). However, this is an enormous challenge because innovation is not necessarily cheap in the short or even medium term, despite Christensen's (1997) injunctions to the contrary. In pharmaceuticals, which is a direct supplier industry to public healthcare, new drugs can easily cost 500 per cent more than the ones they replace.

The whole life-cycle analysis of a completely new drug suggests it costs $1 billion to get it from laboratory bench to the ultimate patient (Goozner, 2004). Similarly, inducing demand for electric cars is challenging and replete with market failure. Successful demand-driven innovation is clearly in its infancy and poses the greatest challenge to twenty-first century innovation policy.

Moreover, demand-driven innovation policies must promote both technological and sociocultural change, something that states have had limited experience in doing (Breznitz et al., 2009). Accordingly, demand-driven innovation can involve nearly the entirety of public sector powers to accelerate knowledge production and resulting innovations through public demand, including private demand to achieve it (Klinger, 2005).

This is nowadays contrasted with the neighbouring concept of customer- or user-driven innovation (CDI or UDI). It is a more limited concept, close to that adumbrated by Jovanovic and Rob (1985). Central to this kind of innovation is the notion of the role of the intermediate (for example in a supply chain) or final customer in a store. How this occurs is a matter of great concern and careful study by marketing research and consumer studies experts. In Chapter 23 on transversality in this *Handbook* it can be seen how, regionally, a whole panoply of interface organizations has been put in place to, for example, trial concepts in a consumer testbed laboratory, track customer eye movements when confronted with a variety of branding designs, and have university research conducted on consumer behaviour, response and preference, all under one roof.

User-driven innovation is accordingly more structured than demand-driven innovation because it is in the interests of producers to understand better the ways in which customers or users interact with innovation. In Verganti's (2009) critique of user-driven innovation he draws attention to four aspects that he later differentiates from design-driven innovation norms. These are: its research methodologies; its structured and embedding innovation markets; its incremental nature; and the absence of sociocultural regime change in association with user-driven innovation. In turn, the typical observational methodologies of customer- or user-driven demands are surveys, interviews, simulation and a variety of other market research techniques that he calls 'applied ethnography'. He sees the kind of markets such innovation finds comfort in to be highly structured, non-turbulent and moderately predictable for strategy, like those assumed in Porter (1998). Innovation in these circumstances is always incremental, building on refinements of already marketed products and services. By definition such innovation does not unsettle the calm waters of the status quo, even if the focus of discussion is a relatively narrow submarket for consumer goods rather than the whole mental landscape of humans raised in the hydrocarbons era. Nevertheless, it is important to stress that most innovation is indeed incremental, and that incremental innovation is the type that regional innovation policy is more able to animate. From a transversality viewpoint, regions will have few industries among which to stimulate innovative cross-fertilizations, and few resources to facilitate exploration of 'structural holes' outside the 'white spaces' that may be tractable innovation candidates. International programmes supporting multinational corporations will have more 'technology push' capability than the 'market pull' of incremental innovation.

DESIGN-DRIVEN INNOVATION

In recent years, a number of writers have begun rejecting a good deal of the conventional wisdom about user–producer innovation interaction, with its connotations of Nordic consensus and inclusivity, as well as the North American tradition of seeing innovation as firms meeting what market researchers, armed with clipboards and interview schedules, say the customer wants. Particularly, it rejects the inversion of the linear model whereby users lead producers in innovation matters (for example in somewhat limited products like snowboards or mountain bikes, associated with the likes of Von Hippel, 2005). Writers such as Boisot (2006) and Martin (2009) have expressed strong interest in the discipline of design as a means to understanding the nature of innovation. Martin (2009) rests the weight of his case on 'design thinking', which he defines as a counterpoint to the two dominant modes of thinking evolved in academe and used beyond. The two dominant forms of logic are deductive and inductive reasoning. These allow determination of the truth or falsehood of truth-statement claims. Deductive logic is rooted in empirical generalization and reasons from the general to the specific. Contrariwise, inductive logic argues from the specific to the general.

Aligning himself with American pragmatist philosophy, Martin asserts that how one declares a statement true or false is less important than how we know and understand. This involves evolving interaction with and practical experience of a context or environment. This 'experiential' turn was addressed in Chapter 42 on dramaturgy in this *Handbook*, whereby authenticity and experience that convinces are revalued upwards in the determination of what is important and worthy of prioritization by users and producers of innovation; 'seeing is believing', as it might be summarized. Pragmatists were interested in the origins of new ideas, seeing them as neither deductively nor inductively originated. Rather, new ideas came from logical leaps of the mind in a form of reasoning named 'abductive', which involves elements of critique and speculation rather than strictly declarative reasoning. Martin suggests that designers inhabit this world. They do this because they seek new or unexpected observations, critique conventional wisdom and make inferences about different sociocultural regimes.

Some abductive thinkers fail to heed the requirement that the design must be matched to what is technologically feasible, launching products that do not yet have supporting technology. Consider the software designers who inferred from the growth of the Internet that consumers would want to do all their shopping online, from pet supplies to toys to groceries. Online security and back-end infrastructure had not yet caught up to their ideas, dooming them to failure. For this approach to work, the 'creatives' in a business setting need to be constrained by the innovation norm that the new knowledge must be commercializable. Within that frame, it may be disruptive, at least to relatively settled markets, or even radical if it is also regime-changing. This, in simple terms, is Martin's (2009) take on 'design thinking'.

Verganti (2009) is interesting to the project of this *Handbook* for two reasons. First, he actively seeks to relate design thinking to innovation standbys like 'technological paradigms and regimes' through his use of 'sociocultural regimes', seeing in the process a conjunction of design and innovation discourses. Second, he has utilized his research and reflection to design a regional innovation strategy for Lombardy in Italy. He says that 'design-driven innovation' aims radically to change the emotional and symbolic content of products, that is, their meanings and languages, through a deep understanding of broader changes in society, culture and technology. Unlike Martin (2009), therefore, Verganti sees design not as a process of individual abduction but as a collective process, involving knowing what knowledgeable others think about society as well as being creative regarding series rather than one-off innovations. Accordingly, a manufacturer's ability to understand, anticipate and influence the emergence of new product meanings is built by engaging external interpreters (designers, firms in other industries, suppliers, schools, artists, the media and so on) who share the same problem: to understand the evolution of new socio-cultural models, and propose new visions and meanings. In this way, management of the innovation process regarding sociocultural meaning mirrors that in technological innovation. They are thus, collectively, capable of learning from each other's key processes in, on the one hand, design-driven innovation in meanings and, on the other, technological innovation.

Verganti contrasts DDI with UDI as follows: user-driven design implies that product development should start from a deep analysis of user needs. Such analysts observe customers as they use existing products and track their behaviour in consumption processes (for example the Packaging Media Lab in Chapter 23 on transversality, this *Handbook*). However, firms that Verganti (2009) takes as exemplars of DDI including Lombardy domestic goods and appliances firms such as Alessi, Artemide and Kartell (also non-Italian design-intensive firms such as Apple and B&O) practise 'design-driven innovation'. These propose innovations that radically redefine what a product means to the consumer. An example is the Alessi kitchenware product line which was transformed from simple tools to 'transition objects' that embodied transgressive forms thought likely to appeal to child-like affections dormant in adults. The innovation model of a firm such as this means that it pushes DDI onto the market, so there is little overlap with CDI (Shane and Ulrich, 2004). The discourse is one of making proposals to the potential consumer or user of the innovation. This is not 'technology push' but 'design push', and conceivably 'regime push'.

Consider the following: in the early years of the present millennium, Italian fashion designers quickly developed a 'script' that questioned the trajectory of men's business fashion. This had been locked into a quality model of consumption involving high-priced designer suits in dark colours, similarly expensive shirts, silk ties and lasted shoes. It was the apotheosis of an Anglo-American men's office wear taken to its utilitarian extreme in the conservative suiting typically worn by 'IBM man'. As postmodernism displaced foundationally modernist conceptions everywhere, the sociocultural regime for officewear also became transgressed. This involved a number of distinctive elements being pulled together. First, the T-shirt had been appropriated in the 1950s, initially through the US film industry's iconography, and then by the orders for such sportswear placed with industrial district producers (Cooke and Morgan, 1998). Later, Milan-based casualwear firm Diesel subverted the smart-casual denim market by deliberately ripping and painting such products (Cooke and Piccaluga, 2006) with great market effect, and emulated by other producers. Finally, the imagery of besuited New York female office-workers walking to work in Nikes then changing into heels in the office triggered off the subversive notion that traditional footwear could be designed like modern sports footwear. Tod's and others even produced luxury variants on this theme. Thus, armed with T-shirt, Diesels and designer trainers, the new Italian executive dress-wear code was

Table 43.1   Lombardy design cluster: leading firms' financial performance

	Ten-Year Growth, 1994–2003 (%)	Revenue (2003, US$)
Alessi (Home Furnishings)	81	US$104 mn
Artemide (Lighting)	59	US$110 mn
B&B Italia (Furniture)	54	US$165 mn
Cassina (Furniture)	117	US$163 mn
Flos (Lighting)	106	US$75 mn
Kartell (Furniture)	211	US$70 mn

Source: Verganti (2006).

born. So how is this researched industrially and academically? In Cooke and Schwartz (2007) we showed Italian design consultants making excursions to teenage nightclubs in Rome to make notes on street fashion and relay this to suppliers of the youth fashion retailer Miss Sixty. Verganti (2009) proposes for both customer and retailer a DDI research meta-model in which DDI is a result of a networked research process where knowledge of languages and meanings is shared among firms and external interpreters. It is 'meta' because bridging meaning innovation and technological innovation.

Design is defined as dealing with the meanings people give to products and the messages and product languages that can be devised to convey meaning (Krippendorf, 1989) – 'de-sign', 'signing it', and giving it 'sign-ificance': 'design is making sense of things'. It also has a semantic, stylistic, symbolic, iconic representation in design languages. Thus innovation of meanings is incremental if framed within existing aesthetic norms. It can be radical with significant reinterpretation of meanings. DDI tends to be radical within, for instance, the fashion or domestic-ware market niches, but nevertheless hugely revenue-earning. Verganti (2006) gives performance indicators of the key design cluster firms focused upon in the Lombardy Innovation Strategy, as shown in Table 43.1. Radical innovations in meaning are not immediate and imply profound changes in sociocultural regimes (Geels, 2004). DDI is reconstructionist or social constructivist not fitting a given structured market (Porter, 1998) – it involves a dialogue with, and modification of, the market.

Accordingly, breakthrough changes in Italian design explore new routes, satisfy latent needs and aspirations, move the frontiers of design languages, set new standards of interpretation and eventually strengthen the brand value. As already noted, DDIs make proposals, they do not study markets or answer user needs. This is cognate with Dosi (1982) on the relationship between technological innovations and technological paradigms or sociocultural regimes. The clear implication of this work is that radical technological innovations are mainly technology push; incremental ones remain within existing technological paradigms and are largely market pull. Knowledge of the subtle and unexpressed dynamics of sociocultural models is tacit not codified. Nor, as with UDI is it to be found in sociological scenarios that normally extrapolate current phenomena. DDI assumes a modification of the scenario. Moreover, and importantly, knowledge is distributed among users, firms, designers, products, media, cultural centres, schools and artists (network of actors), which creates a continuous design discourse on sociocultural regime change and its implications for consumption. Interpreters are extremely important to these capabilities and training and maintaining them is key to any future DDI regional innovation strategy. Key issues are: how to find and use them; which ones are important as gatekeepers; which are key as brokers; and which are expert at moving across industries, different sociocultural worlds, through acculturation with other countries, including being from other regions or countries.

THE LOMBARDY DDI INNOVATION STRATEGY

Although it is widely believed that Lombardy is a unique region with a high social consciousness and valuation of design, and a globally excellent design expertise among its firms, entrepreneurs and employees, Verganti (2006) suggests that the capabilities the region displays are also to be found elsewhere. Moreover, in a telling case study of New York's Finger Lakes region he provides an instructive analysis of how that subregion has the asset specificity to be a platform of transversally interacting clusters, but for socio-anthropological reasons, it is not. In respect of design cluster regions he lists Helsinki, Finland; London, UK; Stockholm, Sweden; Copenhagen, Denmark; Catalonia, Spain and Rhône-Alpes, France. In the case of Helsinki, it has numerous small design studios, several designers' associations, research centres focused on design, a design museum and the Aalto Design University. Aalto University was established on 1 January 2010, when the Helsinki University of Technology, Helsinki University of Economics and the University of Art and Design Helsinki were merged. Aalto University aims to create a new science and arts community by bringing together three existing universities of technology, economics and art. The combination of three universities is thought to open up new possibilities for strong transversality in education and research. The new university's goal is to be one of the leading institutions in the world in terms of research and education in its own distinctive disciplines. These elements are key to a regional DDI strategy, echoing Foray's (2009) idea of 'smart specialization' (see also Francis and Bessant, 2005).

Verganti (2005, 2006) displays a lengthy period of involvement as a consultant to IReR, the regional development agency of Lombardy. His work began with advice on the region's scientific and technological infrastructure needs but later moved into Lombardy's chief value-adding design clusters. It is shown that Lombardy is a key centre of furniture manufacturing, that the region possesses about 25 per cent of all Italian furniture companies and that Italy is Europe's largest furniture exporter, with 45 per cent of its output exported. Regional furniture growth rates exceeded both the Italian and European Union levels from 1994 to 2003. In the design cluster study reported in Verganti (2006), focused on the lighting, kitchen furnishing, furniture and kitchenware clusters, the reported views of 26 international design experts were that Lombardy's schools, studios, manufacturers and research centres were little better than in other design clusters. However, the region was distinctive for the number and strength of links between diverse actors in the regional innovation system. This well-known feature of Italian industrial districts (see Chapters 10, 8, 13 and 12 by Breschi, Capello, De Propris and Crevoisier, and Giuliani, respectively, in this *Handbook*) seems, if anything, to be more pronounced in these transverse industries than elsewhere. The skills interface of entrepreneurs and their territorial identities are also quite mixed. Thus the founders of

Alessi and Cassina are lawyers; that of Artemide is an aerospace engineer; others are from such disciplinary backgrounds as economics. Leading designers include Israeli Ron Arad, American Michael Graves, Philippe Starck from France, Richard Sapper (German) and Ettore Sottsass (Austrian). Accordingly, combinative rather than primarily cumulative knowledge is the source-code for the Lombardy design platform. Verganti (2006) is strongly convinced that cross-pollination from outside the country and profession in which DDI operates is crucial, and cites UK designer Jonathan Ive, designer of the iMac and most subsequent Apple innovations, as a case in point. He previously designed bathrooms.

For another take on the key ingredients of a successful design-based innovation platform upstate New York is taken as a model of a region that fails to exploit its design-intensive regional innovation assets. Its main city, Rochester, was home to Xerox and the Gannett media firm. Bausch & Lomb, a leading lens maker, is present, as is Eastman Kodak. Corning fibreglass is nearby, alongside numerous specialist optical networks companies. The state of New York established the Center for Electronic Imaging Systems as a collaboration between Xerox, Kodak and Rochester University's optical engineering school. Rochester Institute of Technology is a leading print media college, while Alfred University excels in ceramics and glass sculpture. Eastman House is a pre-eminent museum of photography. However, despite these institutional riches, there is little interaction among the regional assets; 'cross-town rivalries' predominate over creative collaboration, even among artists and designers, let alone manufacturers. Large firms like Corning scarcely interact with specialist glass acquisitions like Steuben and if the former changes specifications there is outcry. Accordingly, with almost zero social networking going on among the potential digital optical platform, it is not surprising that the subregion displays low job growth and that the data show that the majority of new residents in the region are prisoners.

CONCLUSIONS

What do we learn from this account of the emergence of three apparently new perspectives on regional innovation that seem to question the insights of the interactive learning innovation model developed in the late 1980s and 1990s? The first and most striking thing is that possibly the most sophisticated, the design-driven innovation model, is thoroughly saturated with innovation interactions of a kind without which there would likely be no innovation in domestic wares in Lombardy. That this is as unthinkable for Lombardy as its opposite for optronics in New York is believable, tells us an enormous amount about the nature of regional culture (James's Chapter 19 and Lazzeretti's Chapter 26 in this *Handbook*) or regional sociocultural production regimes, as it does about industry culture. For there is an insightful article by Orsenigo (2001) about the failure of Lombardy's biotechnology cluster for precisely the reasons the New York State optronics cluster failed: namely, low networking and poor institutional interfacing capability. Associative practices clearly do not always cross industries even in otherwise highly associative regional cultures. Industrial mix, in other words related variety, seems to be the missing ingredient in these narratives of weak and strong business ecosystems.

Of the two other types of neolinear innovation models under inspection, the one we called demand-driven innovation seemed much more challenging than mere user-driven innovation, even if the latter can really convincingly be said to exist. The huge task of turning whole societies away from their life-long love affair with hydrocarbons, and the management of a process of substituting renewable energy, clean technology and high-grade waste recycling in its place, is a daunting challenge indeed. That it is intimately bound up with processes of regional innovation is discussed elsewhere in this book (see Chapter 32 on green innovation). There is a lengthy research agenda into the successes and failures of some regions and municipalities to support and promote green consumption and production regimes. Why some succeed and others fail needs meticulous unravelling. Preliminary research suggests once more regional sociocultural regimes may have some part in explaining this. Older industrial regions tend to score low on both sustainability and creativity criteria, which in a burgeoning knowledge economy gives serious cause for reflection.

REFERENCES

Aschoff, B. and W. Sofka (2009), 'Innovation on demand – can public procurement drive market success of innovations?', *Research Policy*, **38**, 1235–47.

Boisot, M. (2006), 'Organizational versus market knowledge: from concrete embodiment to abstract representation', *Journal of Bioeconomics*, **8**, 219–51.

Breznitz, D., M. Ketokivi and P. Rouvinen (2009), 'Demand- and user-driven innovation', in Ministry of Education (ed.), *Evaluation of the Finnish National Innovation System – Full Report*, Helsinki: Helsinki University Press, pp. 71–102.

Christensen, C. (1997), *The Innovator's Dilemma*, Boston, MA: Harvard Business School Press.

Cooke, P. and K. Morgan (1998), *The Associational Economy*, Oxford: Oxford University Press.

Cooke, P. and A. Piccaluga (eds) (2006), *Regional Development in the Knowledge Economy*, London: Routledge.

Cooke, P. and D. Schwartz (eds) (2007), *Creative Regions*, London: Routledge.

Dosi, G. (1982), 'Technological paradigms and technological trajectories: a suggested interpretation of the determinants and directions of technical change', *Research Policy*, **11**, 147–62.

Edler, J. and L. Georghiou (2009), 'Public procurement and innovation: resurrecting the demand side', *Research Policy*, **36**, 949–63.

Edquist, C. (ed.) (1997), *Systems of Innovation*, London: Pinter.

Foray, D. (2009), 'Understanding "smart specialization"', The Questions of R&D Specialization: Perspectives and Policy Implications, IPTS Report, EC-Seville.

Francis, D. and J. Bessant (2005), 'Targeting innovation and implications for capability development', *Technovation*, **25**, 171–83.

Geels, F. (2004), 'From sectoral systems of innovation to socio-technical systems: insights about dynamics and change from sociology and institutional theory', *Research Policy*, **33**, 897–920.

Geels, F. (2006), 'Co-evolutionary and multi-level dynamics in transitions: the transformation of aviation systems and the shift from propeller to turbojet (1930–1970)', *Technovation*, **26**, 999–1016.

Goozner, M. (2004), *The $800 Million Pill*, Berkeley, CA: University of California Press.

Jovanovic, B. and R. Rob (1985), 'Demand driven innovation and spatial competition over time', Economic Research Reports, Starr Centre for Applied Economic Research, New York University.

Kline, S. and N. Rosenberg (1986), 'An overview of innovation', in R. Landau and N. Rosenberg (eds), *The Positive-sum Strategy*, Washington, DC: National Academy Press, pp. 275–305.

Klinger, D. (2005), 'Demand-driven innovation diffusion', *Comparative Technology Transfer and Society*, **3**, 6–9.

Krippendorf, K. (1989), 'On the essential contexts of artifacts or on the proposition that "design is making sense (of things)"', *Design Issues*, **5**, 9–39.

Lundvall, B. (1988), 'Innovation as an interactive process', in G. Dosi, C. Freeman, R. Nelson, G. Silverman and L. Soete (eds), *Technical Change and Economic Theory*, London: Pinter, pp. 330–48.

Lundvall, B. (ed.) (1992), *National Systems of Innovation,* London: Pinter.

Lundvall, B. and B. Johnson (1994), 'The learning economy', *Journal of Industry Studies*, **1**, 23–42.

Martin, R. (2009), *Design for Business*, Boston, MA: Harvard: Business Press.

Nelson, R. (ed.) (1993), *National Innovation Systems*, Oxford: Oxford University Press.
Orsenigo, L. (2001), 'The (failed) development of a biotechnology cluster: the case of Lombardy', *Small Business Economics*, **17**, 77–92.
Porter, M. (1998), *On Competition*, Boston, MA: Harvard Business School Press.
Shane, S. and K. Ulrich (2004), 'Technological innovation, product development and entrepreneurship in management science', *Management Science*, **50**, 133–44.
Verganti, R. (2005), 'Regional action in research, innovation and technology transfer', Rapporto IReR, Milan: IReR.
Verganti, R. (2006), 'Innovating through design', *Harvard Business Review*, December, Reprint R0612G, 1–9.
Verganti, R. (2009), *Design Driven Innovation*, Boston, MA: Harvard Business School Press.
Von Hippel, E. (2005), *Democratizing Innovation*, Cambridge, MA: MIT Press.

44 Regional innovation policy between theory and practice
Arnoud Lagendijk

INTRODUCTION

Over the three decades to 2010, regional innovation policies have gained a prominent position in the wider field of economic support. This applies in particular to the European Union (EU), where much of the structural support is channelled through the regional development funding, of which a growing part is aimed at innovation support (Bachtler et al., 2007). Regional initiatives have also been tied more closely to the EU's innovation and competitiveness policies (Soete, 2009). In other parts of the world, regional innovation has been used as an inspiring concept notably for substantial regional clustering and knowledge transfer initiatives (Blien and Maier, 2008). This chapter will first provide a historical overview of policy development, with emphasis on the European case, followed by a more in-depth discussion of the theoretical and policy rationales behind the policy. The latter will also serve to highlight some dilemmas and issues surrounding regional innovation policy, which will be discussed in the final section.

REGIONAL INNOVATION POLICY: FROM LOCAL EXPERIMENTS TO A MULTILEVEL FRAMEWORK

The concept of regional innovation policy dates back to the 1960s and 1970s, when the first attempts were made to apply national innovation policy practices to the regional level. The concept can be traced back to initial attempts in France to boost the technological potential of regional growth poles (Cooke, 1985). Consequently, the concept has made inroads through its adoption and diffusion by the European Community (Molle, 1983). After providing some key definitions, this section will provide a historical sketch of this process.

In general terms, regional innovation policy stands for those policy initiatives and practices aiming at improving the capacities of firms within particular region(s) to develop new products and processes, to enter new markets and to adopt new business practices, by the successful application of knowledge. In simple terms, the label 'regional' can either refer to particular regions that set out to develop a 'bespoke' policy to boost their own economy, or to the way a national policy or research framework is geared towards a subnational division, such as the EU 'NUTS 2' level. In terms of policy-making, the first case corresponds to a 'bottom-up', and the second case to a 'top-down' approach to regional innovation policy (Howells, 2005).

The way innovation yields something 'new' can take two basic forms. It can mean products or practices either new to the world or new to the region. The first form is most manifest in nascent, high-tech (sub)sectors and knowledge-intensive services. It is often associated with a more linear, and technologically oriented view of innovation. Scientifically produced knowledge ('invention') is valorized and turned into commercial outputs ('innovation'). The second form, innovation as new to the region, refers to the process in which 'local' firms absorb new knowledge and practices from elsewhere, to tailor their products and services better to a wider market area, and to increase productivity. Such a broader, more entrepreneurial definition of innovation tends towards a system perspective, emphasizing the importance of mutual interaction between firms, research and business support organizations, market agents, consultancies, banks, local authorities and so on.

In the 1970s and 1980s, the regional innovation challenge was primarily associated with the first form, with an emphasis on developing and valorizing new technologies. In response to deteriorating economic circumstances, regions were urged to move their industrial basis towards nascent, high-tech sectors, such as microelectronics and chemistry, or to the high-technology segments of traditional industries. Moreover, these ambitions were aligned with the contemporaneous orientation of regional policy towards the locational strategies of large, multiplant business and state-funded organizations. Confiding in the 'engine' function of subsidiaries of multiplant enterprises and state-funded organizations such as research institutions, policy measures targeted the research intensity of these establishments and their embedding in the regional 'growth pole'. This aim was pursued primarily in two ways, namely through making regional innovation policy more innovation-oriented, and through the regionalization of national research policies. The latter ranged from taking regional spatial effects of national decisions on the allocation of research funding into account, to a more thorough spatial decentralization of research policy and support for regional research and development (R&D).

From the 1980s onwards, inspiration was found in upcoming literature on the innovative capacities of locally clustered small and medium-sized entreprises (SMEs) (Nauwelaers and Wintjes, 2002; Ewers and Wettmann, 1980), triggering a shift to a more system-oriented approach to innovation. A focus on the role of SMEs instead of that of large enterprises and state activities also met the upcoming anti-interventionist and pro-market stance prevalent in national and international economic policies. While the support for basic invention and technological innovation was relegated to research policy, (regional) innovation policy turned to knowledge accessibility and absorption, and the embedding of SMEs in regional innovation networks and systems.

Alongside the shift in the policy object from the locational practice of large organizations to the clustering and embedding practices of SMEs, a shift took place in the nature of policy intervention. What prompted this shift was the growing realization that because of regional specificities and complexities, blanket solutions would not work, and that innovation policies need to be designed and shaped at the regional level itself. In Cooke's (1985, 259) words: 'There has to be a regional-level policy development with national government playing coordinative and supportive roles'. Initially, the regional level was associated primarily with implementation, that is, the fine-tuning and adaptation of national R&D policies and instruments. In other words, the policy focus expanded from the level of policy instruments, targeting technology development and absorption, to the level of policy formulation, with emphasis on more decentralized forms of innovation and economic development policy (Ewers and Wettmann, 1980). In addition, the focus on technological innovation was complemented with an interest in management practices, the provision of joint services and sector studies (Bachtler et al., 2003; Molle, 1983).

For the European Commission, the shifts in orientation from large to small organizations and from policy implementation to formulation meant that regional innovation policy held particular appeal, for a variety of reasons. Most importantly, to complement and justify its market integration ambition, the Commission sought to develop policies targeting spatial and social disparities. In these so-called 'cohesion' policies, regional policy has taken a prominent position. While largely oriented towards classical redistributive, infrastructure-oriented investment approaches, the European Commission developed a keen interest in promoting new approaches to regional innovation, notably those targeting local capacities to participate in Europe's Common Market. Alongside a growing interest in innovation in general, this promotion can be attributed to three factors. First, the new innovation approaches, with their emphasis on improving the conditions for SME development, met the Commission's interest in developing supply-side measures that are market-conforming that is, that do not benefit single firms. Second, the Commission was also keen to support strategic capacity-building at the regional level through developing, testing and exchanging policy practices geared to the brokering and facilitation of intelligence (including foresight and benchmarking exercises), monitoring, communication and evaluation. Third, regional innovation provided a highly appropriate platform to experiment with policies that, besides cohesion, would target another major ambition of the EU, namely competitiveness. The key challenge thus became to develop a kind of regional innovation policy that would both enable lagging regions to catch up and contribute to the Union's innovation capacities as a whole.

In response to these ambitions, the Commission developed a joint programme of regional and industrial policy-making based on the Community's Innovation Programme and Article 10 of the European Regional Development Fund. In 1993, a double initiative was launched entailing:

- Regional Technology Plans (RTPs), followed by Regional Innovation Strategies (RISs), destined for less-favoured regions – European Regional Development Fund (ERDF)-assisted NUTS-2 areas ('cohesion regions'); and
- Regional Innovation and Technology Transfer Strategies (RITTS), open to all (kinds of) regions, with explicit focus on innovation support structures ('competitiveness regions').

Enabled by a relatively small amount of seed money (around € 0.5 million, with 50 per cent European support), these initiatives were set up to experiment with the governance and substance of regional innovation practices. So key aspects of the programme were learning and dissemination. This was facilitated, in particular, by a variety of platforms and networks such as the Innovating Regions in Europe (IRE) network and its Mutual Learning Platform (IRE, 2006). IRE has played a major role in fine-tuning, advocating and diffusing the EU 'RIS methodology', as a holistic, system-based approach to regional development, amongst participating but also many other (including non-EU) regions (see EC, 1994).

The EU's Lisbon Strategy (2000) gave a further impetus to infuse the Union's policies with an emphasis on innovation. This led to three major trends of policy integration. First, innovation features more in cohesion policies, manifested for instance by a general ambition to raise the innovation content from about 6 per cent to 20 (European Communities, 2006), and by an innovation-oriented track in the Community Programmes such as Interreg (European Commission, 2009). Second, links between industrial and regional policy have been strengthened through the elaboration of 'place-based' cluster approaches (Barca, 2009). Third, there is a strong interest in connecting research policy, including the development European Research Area, to 'place-based' innovation approaches (Soete, 2009). To facilitate this, the EU research framework programmes have been oriented towards business participation, while research themes have become more focused on the Union's competitiveness agenda. The EU has thus been working towards a stronger alignment of regional policy, industrial policy and research policy, in which the focus on competitiveness and cohesion should lead to a 'balanced development' of Europe's regional space (Tewdwr-Jones and Morais Mourato, 2005).

In the following years, however, the adoption of 'place-based' solutions was curbed by the eastward expansion of the EU. The expansion produced the 'statistical effect' that whole blocks of countries, rather than of regions, became primarily eligible for regional assistance. Moreover, in most accession countries regional governance structures were generally absent or lacking. Combined with an increased emphasis in policy-making on efficiency, management and accountability, this prompted the EU to implement more centralized (national) structures to administer regional aid. At the same time, certain old member states, notably the UK and the Netherlands, lobbied for a renationalization of regional innovation policy, which could then become better aligned with national policy initiatives. An example is the Dutch spatial innovation policy focusing on 'Knowledge Peaks', although this is partly rooted in the Dutch experiences with the Regional Innovation Strategies – Regional Innovation and Technology Transfer Strategies (RIS–RITTS) programme (Minez, 2004).

The conditions for EU regional innovation policy thus changed significantly (Bachtler et al., 2003; Bachtler et al., 2007). After 2000 the RIS programme was centred on the accession countries, promoting learning between regions from 'old' to 'new' member states. A final round of RIS was launched in 2005, and the IRE network was closed in 2008. The experimental and learning approach was embedded within the new programme of DG-Regio 'Regions for Economic Change' (RfEC) geared to testing and exchanging 'best practices' within and between regions and cities (building on Interreg and Urbact financing) (EC, 2006). By sharing excellence, RfEC seeks to contribute to cohesion and convergence between regions, as well as to overall competitiveness, in line with the RIS–RITTS programme. The network activities have been further elaborated in the context of the PRO INNO innovation policy initiative of DG Enterprise and Industry. What these developments demonstrate, overall, is a movement of regional innovation policy from a hotchpotch of local projects to an embedding of initiatives in a broader multilevel and multisector governance context.

The remainder of this chapter will discuss this shift, particularly its conceptual roots, in more detail. The next section will explain the conceptual framework for this debate, drawing in the notions of meta-rationales, theoretical rationales and policy rationales.

THE RATIONALES OF REGIONAL INNOVATION POLICY

Rationales underpinning policy development come in different shapes and guises (Laranja et al., 2008). In a broad sense, policy is informed by 'meta-rationales', that is, basic ideas about the role of the state and its scope and capacities for policy action (PRO INNO, 2009).

Concerning meta-rationales, economic policies are dominated by the (neo)liberal idea that intervention is only warranted in two cases, namely: (1) when markets or networks do not function properly; or (2) when welfare distribution is found wanting. Both conditions apply to knowledge production and use (PRO INNO, 2009). While considered increasingly vital for economic development and wealth creation, knowledge production and use are prone to a variety of market and network 'failures', justifying concerted state actions in the form of science, technology and innovation policies. Yet, mainstream, neoliberal thinking also prescribes that these policies should help businesses to (co-) produce and absorb knowledge, without providing undue advantages to single firms. Place-based policies avoid such unfair treatment, since they support disadvantaged areas through activities focusing on brokering, facilitation and policy learning, benefiting whole groups (clusters) of firms. Moreover, this ambition accords with the second justification for policy interventions, namely the objective of reducing spatial inequality. For 'pro-market' institutions such as the EU, World Bank or the Organization for Economic Co-operation and Development (OECD), the neoliberal approach has held much appeal in their search for 'balanced' competitiveness and cohesion policies.

Beyond general meta-rationales, policies are informed by 'policy rationales', which in turn build on 'derived theoretical rationales' (Laranja et al., 2008). Policy rationales consist of cogent and endurable ideas on how to pursue particular goals, in terms of organization, processes and instruments. In the case of regional innovation policy, much significance is attached to (public–private) collaboration, network-building, foresight, and clustering, amongst others. These notions draw on simplified accounts of academic abstractions, on 'theoretical' rationales, that highlight and conceptualize, in particular, the role of knowledge, proximity, spatial embeddedness, institutions, absorptive capacities and social capital. While generalization is inevitable for ideas to perform in a policy setting, they may tend to what Richardson (2006) calls 'thin simplifications' of complex realities. The remainder of the chapter will provide an overview of how theoretical and policy rationales have been articulated, selected, linked and used, and what kind of tensions and dilemmas this has generated.

THEORETICAL RATIONALE: ENDOGENOUS GROWTH

From a scientific angle, innovation policies are based on an evolutionary, Schumpeterian outlook on economic development, which sees the disrupting effects of technological change as more important than the equilibrium tendencies of 'market forces'. Echoing these ideas, a prevailing 'derived theoretical rationale' that has emerged from the 1980s onwards is the perspective of endogenous growth (Ács, 2000; Howells, 2005). The crux of this perspective is threefold:

1. The production of technology should be seen as part of (not external to) economic development; in other words, knowledge production does not just 'happen' but can be aimed at as part of private and social agendas of economic growth.
2. Economic growth is induced by increasing returns to knowledge and technology: the more they are used, the more benefits accrue.
3. State intervention can serve to boost the production of knowledge and technology, because of the problem of market failure noted before: private actors refrain from investing in and trading new knowledge because they are insufficiently able to recoup their costs, resulting in a loss of social value.

Rather than tending to equilibrium, economies follow particular trajectories (Storper, 1997). Once a particular direction is taken, increasing returns and accompanying policy measures will result in a self-reinforcing process of specialization and concentration. This involves the development of particular technologies and associated economic activities, embedded in specific national and local settings. An important role is played by Marshallian advantages such as the pooling of labour and knowledge spillover. While this may bring important economic benefits for a considerable time, it may also result in a negative form of lock-in. Because of the role played by time and place, it is very difficult and costly to change track even when a particular set of technologies and specializations starts to lose their economic significance (Boschma and Lambooy, 2002). As a result, economic disparities can persist for a long time, between nations as well as between regions. As argued before, besides the market failure argument, this unequal distribution of welfare provides another justification for state intervention through place-based innovation policy.

In addition to the dominant role of technology, evolutionary perspectives draw the attention to the particular role of institutions. 'Institutions' refers to the organizational make-up of an economy as well as the rules and conventions that guide action and interaction, in a formal and informal sense. They are important in non-trivial ways for at least four reasons:

- Knowledge is produced and valorized through a particular configuration of firms, the state and other organizations, notably education and research organizations, trade associations and financial organizations.
- The interactions within this configuration are guided by a much broader arrangement than market transaction, comprising collaborative planning, networking and contracting.
- The interactions also depend on what is called 'soft infrastructure' (MacLeod 1999, IRE 2008), which includes attitudes towards risk-taking, collaboration and exchange of information; this in turn, has a strong impact on the nature and extent of knowledge spillover occurring in a particular territory.
- Institutional development is highly time- and place-specific in two ways: institutions bear the marks of the time and place they evolve in, while they, in turn, have an impact on the historical development of particular places. The implication is that innovation policies should be tailored to local conditions and challenges (Fritsch and Stephan, 2005).

POLICY RATIONALES: RIS, DISTRICTS, CLUSTERING

The 'endogenous growth' perspective, elaborated along spatial-evolutionary and spatial-institutional lines, presents the prime intellectual foundation for policy thinking on regional innovation. This has broadly resulted in three closely related policy rationales.

First, a merger between the 'system' perspective on innovation and the emphasis on place-based institutional (inter)action has resulted in the notion of 'regional innovation systems' (RISs). The latter can be characterized as: 'a set of interacting private and public interests, formal institutions, and other organizations that function according to organizational and institutional arrangements and relationships conducive to the generation, use, and dissemination of knowledge' (Doloreux and Parto, 2005, 134–5). Policy initiatives have thus sought to nurture links and arrangements amongst the 'users' (firms) and 'producers' (universities and other research organizations) of knowledge, notably in the form of collaborative projects, as well as links between business, the research community and state support more generally. In particular, those regions aiming at a stronger interaction between the local higher education sector and business community have taken such initiatives.

Second, the emphasis on place-based knowledge development and pooling of labour has inspired initiatives specifically dedicated to raising the innovation capabilities of SMEs. Such a 'district' (or 'Marshallian') approach generally aims at improving the absorptive capacity of SMEs (the propensity and ability to acquire and use state-of-the-art knowledge), and at nurturing a process of collective learning, whilst often targeting particular sectors. Whereas RIS approaches focus on particular knowledge-intensive firms and organizations, here a wider regional segment is aimed for, with the aspiration to increase the performance of local SMEs more broadly. More attention is paid to cognitive aspects of innovation, and to how these can be affected by a region's 'soft infrastructure' (Loasby, 1998; Boschma, 2005). Such a policy is often adopted in regions with an over-representation of poorly performing and weakly connected SMEs.

Adopting more an evolutionary line of thinking, the third perspective focuses on structural change. How can regions, through developing new innovative capabilities and the reallocation of resources, provoke a shift in their economic specialization more towards growth sectors? This perspective takes on board key insights and methods from cluster approaches, such as cluster mapping, sectoral strategies focusing on networking and innovation, and institutional capacity-building aiming at reorienting a region's economic infrastructure (education, research, business support) towards a modified sectoral (or 'cluster' profile) (see CLOE, 2007). This approach appeals, in particular, to regions suffering from industrial decline or other structural problems.

The way in which such rationales are employed and combined illustrates the extent to which underlying theoretical accounts are simplified and instrumentalized. In general, policy rationales tend to favour simple means–ends logics in which the build-up of a regional collective order (system, district or institutional capacity) is believed to boost a region's innovative capacity. What is often ignored, at the level of the region, is the way such orders depend on a range of social, cultural and political factors that take a long time to change (Uyarra 2007). Moreover, what is problematic at the (inter)national level is the way that endogenous growth thinking is tweaked towards the ambition of cohesion. While the theoretical work on endogenous growth approaches depict a world of disequilibrium, lock-in and polarization, in policy thinking each place is considered to have sufficient 'opportunities' for fostering innovation and, through that, economic wealth. One only needs to articulate and meet these opportunities, by nurturing and using the appropriate forms of 'intelligence', collaboration and strategic action. In effect, this celebration of 'ubiquitous' opportunities presents one of the key vulnerabilities of the policy approach, an issue discussed in more detail below.

A FOCUSING CONCEPT: THE KNOWLEDGE ECONOMY

A discourse straddling the academic and policy debates on regional innovation is that on the 'knowledge economy'. This concept has played an important role in giving knowledge a particular strategic meaning. Echoing core ideas from endogenous growth theory, one key insight underpinning the 'knowledge economy' is that wealth creation is based less on the build-up and efficient deployment of scarce resources (industrial and human capital), but more on the valorization of new knowledge. Thus adopting an absolute rather than a relative approach to competitiveness, this has translated into policy rationales for regional innovation policy advocating the creation of knowledge-based distinctiveness and the prevention of critical knowledge to competitors. Under the label of achieving regional 'excellence', it has also boosted the build-up of strategic intelligence (foresight, benchmarking) and the exchange of 'good' or 'best' practices for regional knowledge creation and valorization (IRE, 2006; EC, 2008).

It should be noted, however, that theoretical views on how to foster regional development in the 'knowledge-based economy' are mixed. The significance of 'distinctiveness' is supported by theoretical work that sees the erosion of knowledge assets through their tendency to become 'ubiquitous' as a threat (Maskell 1999). The danger of leakage is disputed, however, by accounts that argue that codified, easily transmittable knowledge only plays a partial role in sustaining competitive advantage. And where it does, it is often well secured by (inter)state regulation of (intellectual) protection rights. More specifically, competitive advantage is dependent on how a heterogeneous set of different kinds of codified and tacit knowledge is developed, deployed and combined – and it is the capacity of governing this process that is crucial to economic success (Barney and Hesterly, 1999). Economic success, as a result, is very difficult to emulate even when some core information 'leaks out'. What is more, the emphasis on the role of knowledge combination explains why regions can actually prosper by innovating on the basis of absorbing knowledge new to the region, rather than creating and using knowledge new to the world. In such a case, it is the skilful combination of knowledge, rather than its distinctive nature, that underpins competitive advantage.

Moving from theory to policy practice, more ambiguities arise. The basic policy rationale reads that regions should share and absorb an ubiquitous policy knowledge basis to foster unique (economic) knowledge sustaining their competitive advantage (Reid, 2008). In other words, knowledge new to the region should nurture knowledge new to the world. Admittedly, policy-makers and analysts have been at pains to argue that there is no magic bullet, that each guideline or script needs to be locally adapted, implemented and monitored, and that the key to success is learning not copying (IRE, 2008; 2006). One consequence of this insight is that the focus has moved away from success stories to learning from both success and failure (Reid, 2008). Yet pregnant questions remain. If achieving success in the knowledge economy is so challenging, to what extent can the circulation of 'best practices' really make a difference? To what extent can 'best practices' serve locally tailored, 'bespoke' policy approaches (see Howells, 2005; Tödlting and Trippl, 2005)? Taking a more strategic stance, if regional agents discover that a certain practice proves to be effective, would they then not be tempted to protect and valorise this form of knowledge (see IRE, 2008)? In other words, how is a boundary to be drawn between 'ubiquitous' public knowledge, which regions are expected to share amicably and improve jointly, and competitive knowledge, that regions should keep to themselves?

Finally, there is a geographical conundrum. It is a well-known fact that peripheral regions generally possess less capacities to absorb knowledge, even when this is publicly available. What is more, peripheral regions seem to lack the resources to make adequate plans for, and provide the matching of, European funding for regional innovation support. Oughton et al. (2002, p. 98) label this the 'innovation paradox': 'The regional innovation paradox refers to the apparent contradiction between the comparatively greater need to spend on innovation in lagging regions and their relatively lower capacity to absorb public funds earmarked for the promotion of innovation and to invest in innovation related activities, compared to more advanced regions'. Peripheral regions often lack the institutional capacity, internal funding and opportunities to respond adequately to the policy options intended to serve them. And even when capacities suffice, the range of opportunities conceived by regions appears rather limited. Across the world, regions tend to chase the same dreams of becoming the next hotspot in biotech, information and communication technology (ICT), business services, and so on, through hosting world-class research hubs, science parks, clusters of excellence, and so on.

ADDRESSING THE INNOVATION PARADOX THROUGH 'SMART SPECIALIZATION' AND 'MULTILEVEL GOVERNANCE'

Current debates indicate at least two ways out of these dilemmas. The first one starts with a search for a more realistic approach to 'opportunities'. Accepting that only a limited number of regions can be at the frontier of research and innovation, most regions need to find alternative routes to position themselves in the knowledge economy. Following an evolutionary approach, Foray (2006) and Soete (2009) make a case for 'smart specialization'. Rather than just targeting similar sectors or technology segments, regions should explore how promising technologies can be applied in certain domains where there is scope for enduring market potential. This means, to start with, that a distinction should be made between 'leading' regions that primarily engage in the valorization of new, frontier technology, and 'follower' regions that search for specific combinations and applications meeting market opportunities. Such a differentiation, moreover, should by accompanied by an 'unbounded view' of the regional economy, paying due attention to the critical role played by external economic and research linkages, and the position of regions in 'global' value chains.

Such a 'relational' view ties in with the second possible response to the innovation paradox, namely a change in spatial governance structures (Kuhlmann, 2001). Within the context of the EU, a discussion is going on as to what extent one should move from a division of responsibilities between spatial levels (as implied by the EU principle of subsidiarity) to a division and alignment of tasks (Soete, 2009). The latter entails a vertical model of coordination and collaboration, resulting from a process of mutual recognition and blending of strengths and opportunities at different levels rather than one resulting from a strict principle of political and administrative separation. In such a view, a regional innovation policy forms an integral part of a multilevel governance approach to innovation. Instead of seeing regions as a kind of generic laboratories producing 'best practices' for the community at large, regional innovation initiatives should become strategically tied to specific (combinatory) research and innovation networks and programmes at (inter)national levels. The consequence is that smart specialization in research networks and value chains should be accompanied by smart specialization in governance. Instead of focusing on 'best practices', policy should focus on an assessment of missing strategic connections and other development constraints (Soete, 2009).

Moving again from such theoretical insights to policy practice and rationales, a multilevel approach to innovation based on 'smart specialization' poses a major challenge. Guided by neoliberal meta-rationales, European policies have become more and more dominated by top-down goal-setting, managerial and financial control, and evaluation, with project tendering as the main vehicle for engaging with bottom-up initiatives. This is consistent with the neoliberal preference for limited state intervention, competition-based forms of governance, financial accountability and performance assessment. This is also consistent with the notion that the state should refrain from 'picking winners', something which should be left to the 'market' (or what is close to the market). Multilevel governance, in contrast, requires more long-term vision and strategy-making at a central level of policy-making, and thus calls for a move towards a more programmatic, and longer-term policy style. Moreover, rather than being imposed solely in a top-down way, such a strategy should be articulated and attuned with visionary as well as practical developments 'on the ground' (Howells, 2005). This takes us to the final challenge: the move from a selective 'knowledge economy' to an inclusive 'knowledge society'.

OUTLOOK: REGIONAL INNOVATION POLICY IN THE KNOWLEDGE SOCIETY

The knowledge economy offers unprecedented scope for economic development across the globe. Yet, its geography features spikes and networks, rather than diffusion and distribution. Knowledge is produced in, and flows through, core agglomerations and their connecting spaces, rather than trickling down from central to peripheral areas. Against this background, regional innovation policies serve a double purpose. They intend to support and draw lessons from knowledge 'spikes' as well as to reduce spatial inequalities in capacities to produce and use knowledge. So far, these initiatives have only met limited success. One of the key problems, as mentioned above, has been the incapacity of regions most in need to partake fully in the project carousel through which state organizations seek to address spatial inequality: the innovation paradox. Not unexpectedly, in Europe the evidence on the spatial distribution of knowledge production points out a certain degree of convergence across Europe, but also at persistent gaps (De Bruijn, 2009; Howells, 2005; Mulas-Granados and Sanz, 2008). Overall, while cohesion policies in general have served to disperse infrastructure and wealth, innovative capacities continue to be concentrated in core urban agglomerations.

This chapter has reviewed various responses to these challenges. A promising route is suggested by the ideas of 'smart specialization' and policy integration along both horizontal lines (between regional, industrial and research policies), and vertical lines (multilevel governance). To put it in more fashionable terms, one could interpret this as an attempt to counter the selective forces of the 'knowledge economy' through the inclusive and empowering ambitions of the 'knowledge society' (Felt and Wynne, 2007; Svanfeldt, 2009). Raising the governance capacities needed to develop and exchange policy expertise, and setting this process in a democratic setting with strong civic and business commitment, may better serve to tackle the conundrum of 'balanced development' and the 'innovation paradox' by fostering place-based innovation.

REFERENCES

Ács, Z.J. (2000), 'Endogenous technical change, entrepreneurship and regional growth', in M.M. Fischer and J. Fröhlich (eds.), *Knowledge, Complexity and Innovation Systems*, Berlin: Springer-Verlag, pp. 228–47.

Bachtler, J., F. Wishlade and C. Méndez (2007), 'New budget, new regulations, new strategies: the 2006 reform of EU Cohesion Policy', Glasgow: European Policies Research Centre, University of Strathclyde.

Bachtler, J., F. Wishlade and D. Yuill (2003), '*Regional policies after 2006: complementarity or conflict?*', Glasgow: European Policies Research Centre, University of Strathclyde.

Barca, F. (2009), 'An agenda for a reformed cohesion policy. A place-based approach to meeting European Union challenges and expectations. Independent Report prepared at the request of Danuta Hübner, Commissioner for Regional Policy', Brussels: Commission of the European Communities.

Barney, J.B. and W. Hesterly (1999), 'Organizational economics: understanding the relationship between organizations and economic analysis', in S. Clegg and C. Hardy (eds), *Studying Organization: Theory and Method*, London: Sage Publications, pp. 111–48.

Blien, U. and G. Maier (eds) (2008), *The Economics of Regional Clusters: Networks, Technology and Policy*, Cheltenham, UK and Northampton, MA, USA: Edward Elgar.

Boschma, R.A. (2005), 'Proximity and innovation: a critical assessment', *Regional Studies*, 39, 61–74.

Boschma, R.A. and J.G. Lambooy (2002), 'Knowledge, market structure, and economic coordination: dynamics of industrial districts', *Growth and Change*, 33, 291–311.

CLOE (2007), *Cluster Management Guide: Guidelines for the Development and Management of Cluster Initiatives*, Karlsruhe: Clusters Linked Over Europe.

Cooke, P. (1985), 'Regional innovation policy: problems and strategies in Britain and France', *Environment and Planning C – Government and Policy*, 3, 253–67.

De Bruijn, P.J.M. (2009), 'The spatial industrial organization of innovation', Nijmegen, Radboud University: Department of Human Geography.

Doloreux, D. and S. Parto (2005), 'Regional innovation systems: current discourse and unresolved issues', *Technology in Society*, 27, 133–53.

European Commission (EC) (1994), *Regional Technology Plan Guide Book*, Brussels: European Commission, DG XVI / DG XIII.

European Commission (EC) (2006), 'Communication from the Commission. Regions for economic change', Brussels: Commission of the European Communities, Directorate-General for Regional Policy.

European Commission (EC) (2008), 'Good practice in the field of regional policy and obstacles to the use of the Structural Funds', Brussels, Commission of the European Communities. Directorate-General for Regional Policy, Policy Department Structural and Cohesion Policies.

European Commission (EC) (2009), *Interreg IVC. Interregional Cooperation Projects*, Brussels: European Commission, European Regional Development Fund.

European Communities (2006), *Creating an Innovative Europe. Report of the Independent Expert Group on R&D and Innovation appointed following the Hampton Court Summit and chaired by Mr. Esko Aho*, Luxembourg: Office for Official Publications of the European Communities.

Ewers, H.J. and R.W. Wettmann (1980), 'Innovation-oriented regional policy', *Regional Studies*, **14**, 161–79.
Felt, U. and B. Wynne (2007), 'Taking European knowledge society seriously', Brussels: European Commission, DG Research.
Foray, D. (2006), 'Globalization of R&D: linking better the European economy to "foreign" sources of knowledge and making EU a more attractive place for R&D investment', Brussels: European Commission.
Fritsch, M. and A. Stephan (2005), 'Regionalization of innovation policy – introduction to the special issue', *Research Policy*, **34**, 1123–7.
Howells, J. (2005), 'Innovation and regional economic development: a matter of perspective?', *Research Policy*, **34**, 1220–34.
IRE (2006), 'Mutual learning platform. Synthesis report', Luxembourg: Innovating Regions in Europe.
IRE (2008), 'The IRE Network: Inspiring Innovation Innovating Regions in Europe (IRE)', Luxembourg: Innovating Regions in Europe.
Kuhlmann, S. (2001), 'Future governance of innovation policy in Europe – three scenarios', *Research Policy*, **30**, 953–76.
Laranja, M., E. Uyarra and K. Flanagan (2008), 'Policies for science, technology and innovation: translating rationales into regional policies in a multi-level setting', *Research Policy*, **37**, 823–35.
Loasby, B.J. (1998), 'Industrial districts as knowledge communities', in M. Bellet and C. L'Harmet (eds), *Industry, Space and Competition: The Contribution of the Economists of the Past*, Cheltenham, UK and Lyme, NH, USA: Edward Elgar, pp. 70–85.
MacLeod, G. (1999), 'Reflections on the New Regionalism in economic development', Durham: Dept. of Geography, University of Durham.
Maskell, P. (1999), 'Globalisation and industrial competitiveness: the process and consequences of ubiquitification', in E.J. Malecki and P. Oinas (eds), *Making Connections: Technological Learning and Regional Economic Change*, Aldershot: Ashgate, pp. 35–60.
Minez (2004), *Pieken in de Delta*, Den Haag: Department of Economic Affairs.
Molle, W.T.M. (1983), 'Technological change and regional development in Europe', *Papers of the Regional Science Association*, **52**, 23–38.
Mulas-Granados, C. and I. Sanz (2008), 'The dispersion of technology and income in Europe: evolution and mutual relationship across regions', *Research Policy*, **37**, 836–48.
Nauwelaers, C. and R. Wintjes (2002), 'Innovating SMEs and regions: the need for policy intelligence and interactive policies', *Technology Analysis and Strategic Management*, **14**, 201–15.
Oughton, C., M. Landabaso and K. Morgan (2002), 'The regional innovation paradox: innovation policy and industrial policy', *Journal of Technology Transfer*, **27**, 97–110.
PRO INNO (2009), *Annual Report 2008–2009. Working towards more Effective Innovation Support in Europe*, Brussels: Commission of the European Communities, European Regional Development Fund.
Reid, A. (2008), 'Analysing ERDF co-financed innovative projects. Final report prepared in the framework of the European Commission study on the ERDF co-financed innovative projects and comparative analyses', Brussels: Technopolis Group.
Richardson, T. (2006), 'The thin simplifications of European space: dangerous calculations?', *Comparative European Politics*, **4**, 203–17.
Soete, L. (2009), 'The role of community research policy in the knowledge-based economy. Expert Group Report', Brussels: European Commission, Directorate-General for Research.
Storper, M. (1997), *The Regional World*, New York: Guildford Press.
Svanfeldt, C. (2009), 'From research to regional policy – using regional foresight to reconcile seemingly opposing European perspectives', Brussels: Commission of the European Communities. Directorate-General for Regional Policy.
Tewdwr-Jones, M. and J. Morais Mourato (2005), 'Territorial cohesion, economic growth and the desire for European "balanced competitiveness"', *Town Planning Review*, **76**, 69–80.
Tödlting, F. and M. Trippl (2005), 'One size fits all? Towards a differentiated regional innovation policy approach', *Research Policy*, **34**, 1203–19.
Uyarra, E. (2007), 'Key dilemmas of regional innovation policies', *Innovation-the European Journal of Social Science Research*, **20**, 243–61.

Index

absorptive capacity 183, 211–19
academic entrepreneurship and incubation
452–4
Academic Ranking of World Universities 319,
324
adaptability of firms 185, 240–41, 243, 250,
257, 373
Africa 521, 568
agglomeration 31
disequilibrium theory and 61–3
economic activity spatially unevenly
distributed 54
emphasis on localized knowledge spillovers
65
general equilibrium theory and 59–61
information-rich contact and 122
innovative outgrowth 29
internationalization and 30–31
location theory and 56–8
scale economies and 55–6
agglomeration economies, linkages across
regions neglected 143, 148
agglomeration externalities, stem from
specialization 144, 151
Airbus aeroplanes, servicing and 382–3
alliance formation, twofold motives 223
alternative model of economic development 65
Amazon.com 369
American competitiveness in international
trade 68, 381
anchoring 105–6, 167, 170–76, 184, 267, 322
anti-nuclear energy discourse 11
Apple 30, 410, 582, 591, 594
Asia 8, 94, 323, 409, 521
asymmetric knowledge capabilities 50
ATMs (automatic teller machines) 366
Austin, Texas (green policies) 434
Australia 287, 521
Austria 161, 312, 355, 538
autopoiesis or self-organization 19
average wage, measure of productivity 127

behavioural economics, non-rational
behaviour and 345
Belgium 321, 516
'best practices' 370, 600, 605–6
biotechnology 4, 6, 7, 106, 137–8, 148, 171, 385
clusters 294, 296, 307, 317, 320–34

firms 333, 385–9, 396, 411–12, 457
medical 412
black box 135, 140, 141, 230
Boston 161, 317, 322, 385, 385–7, 386–7, 395,
412
Boston's Route 128 248–50, 259, 315, 318, 498
bounded rationality, uncertainty and 534
Brazil 243, 408, 416, 440, 453, 516
broadband access, less populated places 286
budget airlines, service industry innovation
and 381
'building boom' 378
business angels, investment capital 499, 502
business-cycle conference, Schumpeter (1949)
32–3

California 250, 283, 286, 549
Californian school 159, 248, 250
Cambridge 20, 319, 375, 386–7, 412, 415
biotech industry 170, 257, 324, 386, 481, 514
research 318–19, 321–2
Canada 412, 428, 434
capabilities accumulation, identification of
commonalities 146
capitalism
emergence and evolution of 8
evolutionary development under 55
fuelled by innovation 3
regional varieties 183
waveform evolution of 12
capitalist system, new knowledge a zero-sum
game 551
Cardiff University, Networks of Innovators 2
catastrophic agglomeration, overconcentrated
spatial results 5
Cayman Islands 373
CBS Labour Force Survey employment data
125
Center for Information Technology Research
in the Interest of Society (CITRIS) 375
centrality of learning, knowledge frontier
moving rapidly 446
Centre for Innovation and Entrepreneurship
(CIE) 507
Centres of Excellence 395
Chilean wine cluster 229
China 30, 91, 258, 320, 407, 410, 453
FDI 412, 414–15

science parks 323
technological incubators 516
climate change crisis 304
'Cluster Chairs', to promote regional
    innovation transversality 311
cluster concept 246, 306
cluster development, policy planning at
    'governance' level 51
cluster literature, role in bridging capabilities
    149
cluster model, versus regional innovation
    platform model 565–6
cluster policies 175, 289
cluster renewal, regional regime governance
    and 267
cluster theory, challenged by role of
    innovations 569
cluster-management team 20
clusters 293–4, 298–9, 300
co-evolutionary transition, envisages market
    niches 438
co-invention networks, role of 138–9
coaching and mentoring 506–11
coal mining regions, acid test in 16
Cobb–Douglas production function 132–3
cognitive approach 107–8, 111–13, 115–16
collective learning process 4, 46, 49, 108, 114,
    224, 318
combinations of knowledge, innovation
    platforms 51
communication cost, scale and 122
communication techniques 285–6
comparative advantage 13, 29, 224, 240–41
comparative statics, Schumpeter's
    evolutionary version 35
comparing different networks 161
competence theories, link with comparative
    advantage 240
competition 10, 33, 35–6, 38–9, 48–9, 59–60,
    241, 452
'Competitive Capitalism', 'Trustified
    Capitalism' 40
competitiveness 109, 185, 234, 238
computerization, 'epochal' innovation 14, 17
computers 44, 249, 283, 296, 360, 381, 487
concept of regional innovation governance
    534–40
conceptual framework for advanced regional
    innovation policy practice 574
  conclusions and further research 584–5
  dramaturgy 578–9
  matrix methods 581–3
  orchestration 579–80
  platforms 577–8
  policy theory concepts 578

recombination 575–6
related variety 574–5
structural holes or white spaces 576–7
transversality 580–81
constructing regional advantage (CRA) 309
constructive advantage, impact of open
    innovation strategies on regional growth
    397
contemporary globalization, innovation
    challenges and 81–3, 87
'convention proximity', 'convention radius'
    453
conventions, definitions 339–40, 344
conventions and relations, interchangeable
    343–4
Cornwall, automotive engineering 182
counterfeit brands and misleading advertising
    83
creative capacity of culture (CCC) 350
'creative destruction' 15, 32, 303, 437
'creative disruption', agglomeration housing
    innovations 104
creative industries 384
creative industry innovation rates 385
creativity, thrives with face-to-face interaction
    290
Cuba, bioscience cluster 248, 258
cultural approaches, relations between
    cognition and behaviour 346
'cultural economy' 247
cultural influences on firms' learning and
    innovative behaviours 254–6
cultural milieu, exist in regions with innovation
    253
'cultural turn' 247
cultural–economic relationships, demystifying
    253, 259
culture 168, 255, 350–52, 354, 359
Culture and Regional Embeddedness (CURE)
    19
cumulative mutation/adaptation 206
'customized innovation' 367
cyclical replacement/regeneration 206

Danish Technological Institute 444
'death of distance' 285
Delft 317
Delhi 412, 428, 430
demand-driven innovation 10, 68, 588–9
dematuring IDs 86
'democratization', personal computers 17
Denmark 11, 80, 193, 339, 403, 428, 462, 505,
    536, 593
  Copenhagen and 434
  wind turbines industry 17, 310, 442, 444

deregulation, deindustrialization and 588
design, definition 13–14
'design paradigm', speeds up application of
what began life 19
design-driven innovation 8–9, 13, 30, 286, 449,
587–8, 590–91, 594
design-related activities (KIBS), service
industries and 335
developing countries, could be innovative 258
different venture capital, different geographies
498–500
digitization, credit cards and 28
diminishing returns from partnerships 310
direct-foreign-investment activities, so-called
product cycle 69
dirigiste systems of governance 536–7
disadvantaged regions, lack diverse set of
actors 544
discontinuous adjustment 84, 88
disruptive innovation, sustaining innovation
and 13
disruptive technologies, 'window of
opportunity' 538
distance, two basic features of 557
distance decay factor 71
diversity 104, 106, 143
division of labour 32, 54, 56, 58, 222–3, 246,
541
dominant design 69, 72, 75
domination thesis, key sectors of '*industrie
motrice*' 61
dominant firm, keeps temporary monopoly
profit 62
dramaturgy 583–4, 590
Dublin, gendered work–life conflict in 257–8,
410
Dutch government, service innovation 367,
375
Dutch State Mining (DSM), diversification 16
dynamic competitiveness of a region, depends
on adaptability 241
dynamic force of innovations, Schumpeterian
understanding 61
dynamic forces, economies arrived through 54
dynamic knowledge exchange 459
dynamics of proximity in spatial innovation
272–7

'ease of learning' 212
East Germany, 'regional experimentalism' 19
Eastern Europe 8, 91, 218
economic activities, effect of proximity and
human contacts 63
economic context of (2007–09) 309–10
economic crisis, connected to globalization 304

economic geographers, need to know
conventions and knowledge 347
economic geography, future of 32
economic growth 61, 64, 107, 482
economic revolution, irreversibility of 28
economic and spatial planning 15
economy of cities, Jane Jacobs's work 50,
143–4, 147, 151
electrification epoch, R&D labs and 18
embedded clusters, competitiveness of firms
and competitive advantages 54
embeddedness 172, 174, 227, 251
emerging economies, innovative systems in 423
employees, most change jobs within same
economic area 191
employment dynamics, caused by
technological change 145
enabling and enhancing open innovation 397
'end of mass production' 541
endogenous growth 60, 104, 144, 601–3
energy crisis 304
ENP 505, 507, 511–12
entrepreneur
active intermediary 15
in driver's seat not the coach or mentor 509
entrepreneurial regional innovation systems
(ERISs) 323, 457
entrepreneurs 484–6
entrepreneurship
conduit of knowledge spillover 226
geography of 482
interaction of individuals with environment
490
key transfer mechanism 192
leads to economic growth 490
peers matter in two ways for 486
promoting done in different ways 506
risky business in dangerous environment 483
tolerance of failure necessary for 315
what it depends on 484
why clusters foster 487
Entrepreneurship and New Business
Development Programme, *see* ENP
entrepreneurship and venture capital 451–2
entropic uniformity, milieu death and 114
'environment' 438
episodic radical innovations 14, 182–3
epochal passages of incremental innovation
13, 183
equilibrium, based on the railroad 37
EU 8, 69, 150, 211, 230, 290
academic commission 303
Community Survey 380, 384
Lisbon Strategy (2000), major trends 600
policies to ease firms' access to capital 496

EU-25 proximity for 228
Europe 150, 158
    decentralization (1980–2010) 50
    distance knowledge can travel 228, 230
    Eureka and development R&D 284
    four major flaws deployed in regions 479–81
    governance types in 536
    incubators and 452, 516, 521
    islands of innovation 318
    low profile for venture capital 320
    nanotechnology 317
    policies to build cooperation and trust 282
    regional policy 548
    Silicon Valley reactions in 322
    universities and open innovation and
        collaboration with industry and 393
European Commission, three factors for
        innovation 599
Euroregion 462
evolutionary economic geography 6, 120, 181,
        194, 439
examples of service innovation 367–8
    contract R&D services 371–2
    financial innovation 372
    logistic innovation 370
    retail innovation 368–9
    tourism innovation 370–71
    user-led innovation 369–70
experiential learning 486
'exploitation subsystem', denotes variety 19
export flows 94
externalities in Perroux's mind, dynamic force
        62

failure, fear of might deter new firm set-up 489
failures at micro-level, social benefit at
        aggregate level 483
FDI 82, 94–6
    automotive industry and 409
    China and 337, 430
    conducted by multinational corporations
        (MNCs), 406
    inward and outward 149
    magnetism of 424
    policies and direct sponsorship 421
    regions that have attracted 412
fifth Kondratieff wave 366
filtering down 73–4
financial capital, supply spatially skewed 495
financial crisis 304
Finland 17, 188
    developmental policy trajectories in 304–5
    innovative platform methodology 533
    region of Lahti 308–9, 564–9, 568–9, 570,
        578–9

Turku and 321
    venture capital 499
firm-level studies 214–16
'first-mover' advantage 295
first-movers, clusters and 316
'flagship catalysts' 171
'flexible specialization' 30
foreign direct investment, *see* FDI
foreign partners 83, 88
fossil fuels paradigm, renewable fuels
        paradigm and 1
framework, geared to EU 'NUTS 2' level 597
France 2, 16–17, 321–2, 516, 537, 597
    IDs 80
    Sophia-Antipolis 161
free-riders 223, 387
French research group (GREMI) 2, 157
French School of Proximity 269, 271–2, 277
function-based approach 109, 115

game theory and spatial competition, Harold
        Hotelling and 60
gatekeepers 284
    role in absorptive capacity 215, 218
general equilibrium modelling, evolutionary
        dynamics of Marshall's externalities and
        60
geographical proximity
    advantage to service platforms 387–8
    coordination through proximity 271–2
    ease of communication and 68
    'external economies' of industrial clustering
        58
    favours collaboration and cooperation and
        470
    important for regional entrepreneurship
        451
    innovation and 48, 269
    interinstitutional fit 29
    local forms of learning and 553
    matters for innovation 269–71
    matters in mediating knowledge spillovers
        139
    may be determinate of M&As 191
    moulded by relational proximity 265
    productivity gain and 4
    regional services innovation variations 382
    tacitness gives *raison d'étre* 185
    three key advantages for service industries
        388
geographical scale, weakness in understanding
        by Porter 305
geographical and socio-cultural proximity
        31
geographical space, major function of 145–6

geography
  matters in labor markets 288
  mediating knowledge flows 138
geography of innovation 132
German–Polish cross-border area, obstacles
    to 463
Germany 2, 8, 16, 193–4, 304, 321, 369
  Baden-Württemberg 144, 150, 457, 536,
    538
  Bavaria 382, 532
  Bayern Innovativ (BI) 312
  Canada and 256
  coordinated market regime 529
  Liepzig's media cluster 199
  Munich high-tech region 322
  national innovation during Industrial
    Revolution 420
  Ruhr Area industrial decline 553
  technological incubators 516
Giddensian thinking 451
Glass–Steagal Act, repealed by Clinton 9
globalization 30–31, 48, 78
  anchoring and 173
  can produce new geographic space 97
  challenges and opportunities 175
  competition from newly industrialized
    countries 270
  economic crisis and 304
  forces networks to look for international
    strategies 225
  ineluctable process 234–5
  neo-Marshallian industrial districts and
    106
  service innovation and 373–4
  urbanized vision of world 351
  venture capitalism initiatives and 91
good specialization, machine specialization 86
governance, definitions 535–6
governance of regional innovation, mix of
    public and private organizations 49
government policies, market failures and 51
Greater London metropolitan region 124
'green innovation' 205, 338, 439
'green' products and services 383
green regional niches 439–40
  from clusters to green regional innovation
    system 442–4
  green visions 440–42
greenhouse gases (GHGs) 434
GREMI (French research group) 2, 157, 270,
    552
  'innovative milieu' 251
Grenoble 317, 321–2
growing clusters, firms benefit from
    information 296

growth
  land rent theory of 29
  regional 74
  regional innovation and 103
  social process 3
growth 'pole' concept, focus on technological
    change 62

'hard' agglomeration economies, 'traded'
    material linkages 246
'hard' economic institutions, patterns of
    economic growth 247
Harvard Multinational Enterprise Project
    1965, FDI and 68
heterogeneity
  leads to 'creative abrasion' 224
  shown 91
'high cultural' hubs, culturally distinctive 335
high-income regions, produce 'new' products
    continuously 70
high-skilled labour, effects of 130
high-tech industries, cause less pollution than
    traditional 514
higher-skilled workers, lower costs and higher
    returns from migration 124
history of concept of absorptive capacity 211
  in development literature 212
  extensions to the concept 213–14
  as firm-level concept 212–13
'how radical is radical?' 11, 182
HP and chipset designer Weitek, partnership
    between 392
human capital 119
  decisions 122
  effect 125
  endogenous source of economic growth
    123
  'flow through' role of university system 124
  lagged effect of education 127
  mobility is international 124
  regional knowledge base and 129
human capital variable, often operationalized
    215
Human Genome project 387
hydrocarbons
  challenge of turning to clean technology 595
  price rises in 304

IBM and Siemens, service activities 364, 367,
    369
ICT 5, 96, 148, 170, 225, 272, 276, 311, 444,
    587
Illinois Central Railroad 34–5
IM and MID models 168–9
imperfect competition, 'dynamic effect' 61

'increasing returns', path-dependent positive 'lock-in' 29
increasing returns to scale, Marshall's focus on 61
'incubation hypothesis', urban economies and 488
India 91, 258, 320, 393, 413, 419, 425–30
    Bangalore, international IT companies 428
    Bollywood 354
    brain drain with Silicon valley 337
    car industry 583
    education in English 425, 427
    Foreign Exchange Regulation Act (FERA) 426
    'latecomer' obstacles 424, 426
    regions lack venture capital 430
    semiconductor and software business 425
India's innovation systems 424–5
    IIS development 428–9
    NIS development 425–7
    RIS development 427–8
industrial agglomerations, three overlapping critiques 249
industrial districts
    egalitarian societies 295
    strength tied to exchange of information 283
industrial districts (IDs) 78–9, 87
    firms in have two distinct typologies 94–5
    internationalization of 92
    lack of social and business consensus 87
    modern and distance-learning processes 91
    organizational form 90
industrial revolution, spatial concentration of economic activities 54
industrialized countries, polarization 110
industry-focused evolution from path-dependence 16
Information Age, universities and academic entrepreneurship 18
information and communication technology, *see* ICT
Innovating Regions in Europe (IRE) network 599
innovation
    across 15 nations 46–7
    definitions 17, 531
    'democratization' of 13
    depends on growth 3–4
    engine of economic growth 155
    geographic proximity and 284
    grounded in intergenerational transfers of know-how 252
    inclusiveness spurs 290
    interactive learning and 46
    land use and transport interconnections 1

locational advantages in 394
    measured by patents and competitive exports 318
    neo-Schumpeterian perspective 184
    new firms as useful devices for 482
    nothing automatic about 38
    Schumpeterian definition 148, 573
    specialist professionals to manage 14
    two forms to yield something new 597–8
    where demand for new products highest 70
innovation governance, requires learning experience 543
innovation and growth 145
innovation system
    relationships among components 45
    seven functions 470
innovation systems: concept and scales 419–20
    international innovation system 423
    national innovation system 420–21
    regional innovation system 421–3
innovation and technical progress, complex set of structures 43
innovative activity, returns on concentration of 110, 116
innovative capacities, do not operate in isolation 51
innovative 'ecosystem', gaining pace 468–9
innovative governance, four different dilemmas of RIS 542–3
'Innovative Materials', vehicle and new materials manufacturers 312–13
innovative milieu, definition of 252
innovative milieux (IMs), 'sets of localised players' 168
innovative networks: new approaches 160–62
innovative networks 160
    focus on regional networks 155, 162
'innovative paradox', place-based innovation and 607
innovative processes
    many triggers 559
    systemic nature of 109
    uncertainty and 114
innovator, monopoly and scale economies, demand increases 68
inside technology clusters 316–17
    advantages of urban areas 317–19
    dispersion of R&D: centres of excellence 320–21
    importance of venture capital 319–20
    universities: key institutions of technology clusters 319
institutional proximity 462
institutional regional innovation systems (IRIS) 457

institutional thickness
  four elements of 252
  three overlapping frameworks 252–3
'institutional turn in regional development
    studies' 540
institutional venture capital firms,
    metropolitan areas 499
insurance services, innovation services and 381
intellectual capital reports, complement
    financial reporting 29
intellectual property 371–2
intellectual property (IP) blocks 429
intellectual property rights 452
  capabilities idea and 146
interactive learning 2, 29, 46, 90, 106–7, 143,
    147–8, 187, 323, 394, 394–5, 587
interconnectedness of firms, increases over
    time 194
internal scale economies, diminishing marginal
    cost of production 58
internalization and recontextualization 184
International Association of Science Parks
    (IASP) 322–3
International Computers Limited (ICL) 364
international innovation system (IIS) 423
internationalization, models of 94
international venture capital investments, done
    in syndication 497
Internet and email 225
Internet, the 368–70
  software designers and 590
interregional growth rates, more sensitive than
    international 238
intra-industry spillovers 144–5
inward-looking RIS, negative lock-in
    situations 301
Ireland 171, 408–11, 414, 416, 487, 521
Iron and Steel Trades Confederation in
    Teesside 256
irreversibility, emerges from given situation 37
irreversibility, externalities and institutional
    fit 28–9
'isodapanes', Weber and 57
Israel 124–5, 320, 385, 413–15, 452–3, 517–20,
    522
  biotechnology and software incubators
    522–3
  capital–labour ratios 125–7
  high-tech mini-clusters 268
  incubators 452–3, 519
  Model 1 and homogenous specification 128
  Model 2 human capital allowed to vary by
    region 129
  Model 3 the most heterogeneous form of
    estimation 129

observations on six regions for 12 time
    periods 127–8
  private technological incubators 519–20
  spatial panel data 125
  venture capital 320, 518, 520
Israeli Public Technological Incubator
    Program 517–18, 523
Italy 188
  23 districts analysed 92–4, 97
  ceramic tile industry 305
  CERVED archive and IDs 92, 97
  economies of scale in large corporations 2
  Emilia-Romagna and Tuscany 2
  empirical case studies 549
  fashion designers 591
  governance types 536
  IDs 78, 80, 82, 85, 90–91, 95, 298, 322, 342
    internationalization of 95
  industrial districts 200, 293
  Lombardy 9, 532, 590–94
  Lux Ottica 92, 94, 95
  Milan and personal relationships for design
    286
  north-east and central 247
  northern and industry 282, 289
  Piedmont 150
  Prato Chinese district 306, 313, 337
  'real service' to SMEs 530
  study of industrial districts 158, 536
  technological incubators 516
  'Tuscan', 'Emilian' and 'Marche' models 267

Jacobian tradition, knowledge transfer and
    119
'Jacobs externalities' 58–9, 104, 181, 187–8,
    190, 373
Japan 74, 80, 217, 276, 409, 413, 428
  Flamenco 359
  ICT 410
  lean production 383
  point-of-sale (POS) system 368–9
  technological incubators 516
JTH experiment, modified, citations of patents
    of mobile inventors 138
JTH results 136–7
Jutland 11, 338, 444
  energy 442–3
  forestry 183
  wind turbines 17, 442

k-innovations 40–41
'Keep It Simple Stupid' (KISS principle) 41
knowledge
  bedrock of innovation 125
  public nature of 224

source of regional economic development
    and growth 222
'sticky' properties 122
transferred by individuals 136–7
knowledge capabilities, residing in networks
    and open innovation 396
knowledge circulation, complementary to that
    across regions 148
knowledge diffusion processes 110
knowledge economy 169
    competitive advantage of nations 270
    demise of Fordist model 160
    economic development across the globe
        606–7
    regional development mixed 604
    weightless products of 547
'knowledge entrepreneurs', dealing in
    intellectual property 416
knowledge externalities, source of regional
    productivity gains 129
knowledge filter theory 110
knowledge flow, decreases with social distance
    among inventors 138
knowledge flows
    agglomeration externalities literature and
        189
    characterized as spillovers 132
    global map of 174
    increasingly international 424
    not only spatial but socially bounded 140
    reason they are spatially bounded 136
knowledge generation innovation 120
knowledge labour, major outflows and inflows
    30
knowledge links, four types 459
knowledge sharing, dilemmas of 223
knowledge spillovers 50, 103–4, 122, 182
    agglomeration of economic activity and 63
    difficult to trace 129
    geographically localized 187
    localization of 137–8
    mechanisms of 227–8
knowledge transfer, challenge to investigate
    key mechanisms 195
knowledge-based 'gatekeeper' firms,
    knowledge filters empirically through
    184
knowledge-based innovation
    territorially embedded process 226
    three theoretical approaches 226–7
knowledge-intensive business services (KIBS)
    335, 366, 384–6, 390, 588
    importance of geographical proximity
        388
Korea 321

labour market 'churning' mechanism 124
labour mobility 119, 124, 193
Lancashire, textile industry 540
Latin America 521
lead firms, role to 'pollinate' the local context
    175
lead markets, healthcare and education 588
leadership, problem of overpersonalized 20–21
'lean production' 7, 15, 337, 383
learning
    concept, institutional aspect 49
    from both success and failure 605
    in a milieu 113–14
    outcome of social capital 290
learning by doing 5, 28, 121, 183, 346, 470, 489
'learning by interacting' 183, 470
'learning', 'creative' or 'innovative' region 121
learning regions 530–31
    concept of endogenous regional
        development 552
    contemporary views of 552
    definitions 548
    discussion and conclusions 552–4
    founding fathers 548–51
    TIMs 547
Lehman Bros 20
Leontief paradox 68
less-favoured region (LFR) 547, 550–51
lifelong learning 111
Limburg, coal mining region prospers 16
Linwood and Bathgate, path-dependence and
    183
Liverpool–Manchester railroad 37
'living laboratory' 309, 532, 579
local amenities, to encourage socialization and
    networking 290
local milieu 113
local *recentrage* of social organization 80
localization economies, agglomeration
    economies 487
localization externalities, scale economies and
    246
localized knowledge spillovers (LKS) 270–71
locally based determinants of
    entrepreneurship, neo-Schumpeterian
    accounts 251
location and 'anchoring' of lead firm,
    beneficial 173
location process, nature of tacit knowledge 270
location theory 55–6
locational evolution 27–8
'lock-in' 79, 104, 106, 201, 471, 576
'lock-out' of firms, not investing in absorptive
    capacity 184
London 144, 336, 385–6

long-wave-inducing innovation 13
low-wage destinations, production shifted to 68
lower communication costs 54
Lower Silesia 538

machine-tool industry, mobility of mature industries 72
macroeconomics growth literature (1960s) 212
'Made in Italy' districts 96
mail-coach firms 35–6
Management Leader Group, connected to ENP 511
manufacturing *filières* 81, 87
MAR 104–6
Mark I model, model of economic evolution 38, 40–41
Mark II model, innovative oligopolistic competition 38–40
'market failure', innovation debate and 460
'market processes', not suitable for sociological study 156
market relationships, networks and 159
'Marshallian industrial district' (MID) 78–80, 83–6, 87, 90, 168
Marshall's triad of external economies of industrial localization 247
mass immigration, may not have adverse effect on manufacturing 124
Massachusetts
    decline of computer business 283
    services innovation 386
Massachusetts Biotechnology Council 20
Massachusetts Institute of Technology (MIT) and Stanford 315–16, 387
matrix thinking, use twofold 582–3
mature clusters, three characteristics 297–8
'mature' IDs 78–83, 86
mature Western IDs 91
measurement of knowledge flows 136
    evidence from surveys 139
    markets for technologies 137
    mobility of skilled workers 136–7
    social networks 137–9
    use of patent citations 136
mergers and acquisitions (M&As), technologically related knowledge bases 190–91
Metropolis 1985 study 7, 67–9, 72
metropolitan areas, large have more inventors than smaller 139
metropolitan statistical areas (MSA), new products at level of 134
micro-nationals 416
microelectronics, Sematech and research 284

Middle West, railroadization 34
migration, human capital investment decision 123
milieu, 'cognitive engine' 113
milieu innovateur theory (1980s) 113–14
mobility 173, 175–6
Model 'T' Ford 37
'mooring', to access embedded knowledge 172
multilevel governance, long-term vision and strategy-making 606
multilevel governance systems, important role 537
multinational corporations (MNCs) 428
    dominate marketplace for technologies 424
    more 'technical push' than 'market pull' 589
multinational enterprises (MNEs)
    generators of new knowledge 151
    geographical reach by overseas subsidiaries 69
    'internal' actors 149
    new sources of cheap labour, capital and land 81
    purchasing R&D 371–2
    spur diversification of regional knowledge base 150
multinationals
    concentrate FDI on sectors with low R&D 73–4
    shift manufacture of products 69

nanotechnology, cutting-edge research and 317, 411
national competitiveness, move from obscurity to meaninglessness 235
national innovation system (NIS)
    difference between countries 455
    framework for science and technology 315
national innovation systems (NISs) 420, 463
national systems of production, national institutions and 45
national-specific factors, role in shaping technological change 420
neo-mercantile image of international trade, zero-sum game 235–6
neo-Schumpeterian, concerns about innovation and policy 182–3
neo-Schumpeterian perspective, commercialization of new knowledge 44
neoclassic theory, labour migration and rate of economic growth 123
neoclassical approach, innovation as an exogenous variable 43
neoclassical modelling, agglomeration and 61
neoliberal epoch 9, 588

'neolinear' innovation models 8–10, 19, 587, 594–5
Netherlands 16, 188, 400–403, 412–13, 434, 600
network, reciprocal linkages and 49
network evolution over time, analysing 161
network paradigm, corporate and spatial dimensions of 48
network position, firms' characteristics and 161
network systems of governance 536
networked regional innovation environment, five dynamic capabilities 568
networks
  advantages in innovation processes 156, 161
  benefits associated with 223
  different forms and structures 231
  dynamic systems 231
  forms of learning in 228
  four dimensions 105
  knowledge diffusion and 193
  knowledge-intensive exchange 227
  proximate relations between economic actors 222
  proximity and 225
  spatially grounded 48
  stronger strategic behaviour of firms within 224
networks of innovation 155–6
  degree of formalization 156–7
  geographic scope 157–8
  method or approach to analysis 157
  types of actors 157
'Neutron Jack' Welch (CEO General Electric) 19–20
'new', restricted sense of 72–3
new cluster theory, 'old' agglomeration theory and 63–4
new economic geography (NEG) 5, 60–61, 119–20, 265, 269
new equilibrium, mix of railroad and horses 35
new era of capitalist economic development (1970s) 246
new firms, entrepreneur with pre-entry background in industry 190
new forms of FDI in the knowledge economy 412–13
  entrepreneurship by R&D FDI centres 414–15
  financial FDI 413–14
  micro-multinational firms 415–16
new growth theory (NGT) 6, 103, 119–20
'new industrial districts' 246
new industries, ICT and biotechnologies 170

new industry, anchoring, transforming mobile into immobile factors 172
new knowledge 63
new labour-saving devices 68
new Marshallian districts, learning systems 97
'New Men' 38
new millennium, culture as strategic resource 350
new path creation, path-dependent process 204
new principle, invention of is rare event 72
new products, enhancements of existing products 72–3
new regional development paths 203–4
'new regionalism' literature 227
new technology-based firms (NTBFs) 315, 319–20
'new trade theory' 60
New York
  competitiveness, difficulties of explaining 67
  failure of optronics cluster 594
newly developing countries, unspecialized IDs 95
newly industrialized countries, developed countries and 270
newly industrializing countries (NICs) 547
NIRAS consultants 443
non-governmental organizations (NGOs) 438
Nordic countries 8, 183, 296, 304, 570, 590
  'green innovation' 17
North America, industrial districts 158
North Carolina, Research Triangle Park 315, 319
North Jutland 183, 443
North-Rhine Westphalia 536
Northern Ireland 487
Norway 299, 568
  locally based TIM 550

OCS 517, 520, 523
OECD 218
OECD–EU policy model, high-income agglomerations and 72–3, 75
Office of the Chief Scientist, *see* OCS
Ohio greenhouse cluster 229
'old institutionalism' 251
old Marshallian model 90
open innovation
  corporate outsourcing 336
  importance of global competitiveness of RIS 395
  relatively new model 403
opportunistic behaviour, isolation and punishment for 115–16, 534

orchestration 583
  awareness that process may affect innovation
    environment 412
  model subject to continual review 580
  regional innovation 450
  role of 21, 30
organizational learning 228–9
organizational proximity 274
Oslo, lock-in favouring traditional oil-rigs 267,
  299
outsourcing 14, 313, 395
  cars 74
  decentralized production 7–8
  industrial R&D 365
  international, strategy of diffusion 96
  specific tasks and 75
Oxford's Motorsport Valley 248, 253–4, 318,
  321, 385

'The Packaging Arena' (TPA) 311
paradigm, denotes 'dominance' 19
'paradigm shifting' 7, 10–11
partial equilibrium model, Weberian model
  57–8
Patent Act (1972) 426
patent citations 136
patent data 161
  innovation and 133, 270
patenting activities 109
patents, only small proportion are
  commercialized 285
path-dependence
  across different industries, need not be
    isomorphism 200–201
  arising in economic history 181
  depth, memory in regional development
    process 202
  'foundational concept' 198
  identification of policy action 207
  strength of historical causality 201
  two main types 205
path-interdependence or holistic regional
  evolution 449
paths to cultural enhancement 352
  cross-fertilization 355–6
  cultural enhancement of economy 354
  economic enhancement of culture
    352–3
  economic renewal 355
  serendipity 256, 356
  urban renewal 354–5
pecuniary externalities 59, 61–2, 103, 106,
  135–6, 168
performance of sampled district firms (2000–
  2002) 93

peripheral regions, less capacity to absorb
  knowledge 605
pharmaceuticals, direct supplier industry of
  public healthcare 588–9
place-based policies, support disadvantaged
  areas 601
'platform' concept, regional innovation and
  renewal 531
platform model, regional intercluster 577
'platform' model of regional innovation,
  characteristics of 532
'pole' concept, transformed from French to
  English connotation 63
poles of growth ('*pôles de croissance*'),
  economic growth 61
policy-driven ties, networks and 159–60
Portland's high-tech industries, Intel and Tek
  Tronix 171
Portugal 2, 80
positive externalities 54
post-Fordist economy 167, 246, 253, 259, 424
Post-it note, classic 'useful innovation' 576
post-Schumpeterian researchers 32
private incubators, differ from public ones 453
PRO INNO innovation policy initiative 600
process innovation, involves labour-shedding
  4–5
Proctor & Gamble 395
product cycle
  two Vernons 69
  what is left of Vernon's regional version 71
    filtering down 73–4
    new products and importance of
      dominant design 72–3
    where does innovation occur? 71–2
product innovation, creates employment 4
'product life cycle' 30
product or process innovation of firms (2004–
  06) 384
product-cycle hypothesis 67, 75
  Vernon and 68
product-cycle literature, demand elements in
  70
production
  concentrated in industrial districts 2
  reagglomeration of 246
productivity gains, knowledge and commercial
  exploitation 4
productivity growth, between US and EU 5
proximities and internal–external interactions
  277
proximities to proximities 277
proximity
  deals with coordination 276
  diverse forms 563

important to user-driven innovation and
     creativity 286
key concept 439
reduces uncertainty in innovative activity
     123
'umbrella' concept, four functions 556–7
proximity approach, isolates two key
     dimensions of complexity of knowledge
     base 271
proximity and distance
   dimensions of 558–9
   theories and frameworks 560–62
proximity and innovation, relationship
     between 265
Proximity School 265
public sector support, cluster associations and
     289
'punctuated equilibrium' 205–6
'punctuated evolution', 'creative destruction'
     and 15
pure and pecuniary externalities, distinction
     between 135

'quality of place' 393
questions and open debates
   articulating approaches, articulating levels
     278
   determination of knowledge 278
   local and the global 277
   negative effects of proximity 277–8
   proximity and internal/external interactions
     277
   proximity to proximities 277
QWERTY keyboard 12–13, 16, 201

R&D 7, 17, 50, 62, 96, 104, 109, 110, 112,
     114–15
   -based clusters 294–5
   development 335
   fine-tuning of national 598
   functions of TNCs 549
   geography proximity and 265
   government centres 124
   hypothesis 218
   incubator projects and 126
   industrial relations and 535
   institutes 293
   intensity 133, 135, 225
   international 462
   investment in 212–13, 216
   laboratories 587
   locations of new sites 320
   low activity in Oslo firms 299
   networks 395
   organizations 211

pecuniary 266
   private 134, 140, 217, 226
   role in building absorptive capacity 214–15
   services 429
   of spillovers 132
   teams 229
   technological clusters and 316
   university spending 135, 296
   US consortia 284
radical innovation 10, 11–14, 146
'railroadization' 28, 33–4, 36, 40
RDPM 564, 567
   eight phases 568
'real services' 539
recent developments and challenges 462–3
recent path-dependence, form of historicity
     202
'recombinant methods' of innovation, spatial
     process concept 575
recombination, crossing 'structural holes' and
     filling 'white spaces' 577
'Red Flag Act' 12
'regime-push' 14
regional, focus of 49
regional absorptive capacity 149
regional advantage, regional competitiveness
     and open innovation 392
   competitive advantage 393–4
   interregional 393
   intraregional 392–3
regional anchors 167, 170–71
regional capabilities, regards knowledge
     complementarities 147
regional cluster of flamenco 357, 360
regional clusters
   decline of and concept of negative lock-in
     298
   networks and 157
regional comparative advantage 172
regional competitive advantage
   clustering externalities and 239
   theory of heavily criticized 237
regional competitiveness
   determined by productivity 236, 239
   no clear definition 235
regional conditions of entrepreneurship 484
   compositional factors 484–5
   contextual factors influencing individual
     entrepreneurial decision 485
   entrepreneurship as organized product 486
   entrepreneurship as social (family)
     phenomenon 485
   nature and localization of industries 487–8
   regional access to financial capital 489–90
   regional culture 488–9

regional knowledge production 489
urbanization 488
regional cultural economy, learning,
    innovation and development 248
regional culture, ethereal and eternal 253
'regional culture of production', dimension of
    comparative advantage 185
regional culture structures, innovative activity
    in some regions 253
regional development, stickiness of innovation
    285
regional development agency (RDA), catalyst
    for innovation 312–13
Regional Development Centre Programme 568
regional development platform method 305–7
    constructing regional advantage 309
    regional development methodology 307–8
    regional development platform
        implementation 308–9
    regional development theory 307
regional dynamic comparative advantage
    241–2
regional economies
    competition and 235
    subject to structural change 189
    'unbounded view' 605
regional governance
    policy learning and 529–31
    variability in powers of 18–19
regional governance structures, 'output'
    regional collective goods 542
regional governments, three key roles 538
regional growth 74
    how open innovation can be identified 391–2
regional industrial agglomerations, threefold
    argument 248–9
regional industrial systems, gendering of
    innovation and learning 257
regional inequalities 121
regional initiatives, tied to EU's innovation
    and competitive policy 597
regional innovation
    role of social capital 266
    Schumpeterian origins 27
    taught in universities 1
regional innovation governance, challenges for
    542–4
regional innovation intermediaries
    role of 467–8
    table 471–3
regional innovation intermediaries at work in
    Europe 474–5
    case of regional innovation intermediaries in
        Wallonia 475–9
regional innovation platform model 556

regional innovation quadrants 581
Regional Innovation Strategies/Regional
    Innovation and Technology Transfer
    Strategies, *see* RIS/RITTS
regional innovation system, *see* RIS
Regional Innovation and Technology Transfer
    Strategies (RIS-RITTS) programme 600
regional innovation theory
    Marshallian and neo-Marshallian
        perspectives 30
    and tailored empirical research 18
regional innovations systems issues 449–51
regional knowledge
    anchoring capacities 174
    contrasts in 450
    generation 538–9
    spillovers and 123
regional literature, filtering-down process 70
regional 'lock-in' 308
regional networks
    not self-contained and self-sufficient entities
        230–31
    transregional flows of knowledge 230
regional open innovation, can be double-edged
    sword 402
regional path-dependence, 'depth' is of
    importance 207
regional path-dependence concept 199–200
regional policy and incentives 407–8
'regional regime', variety, cluster evolution
    and 267
regional science, regional innovation systems
    and 2
regional services innovation 380
regional socio-technical paradigm changes 16
regional specialization, regional anchor and
    171
regional systems of innovation, *see* RSIs
regional variations in new firm formation,
    differences in regional industries 487, 490
regional variety, different forms of 147
regional venture capital, policies towards
    501–2
regional worlds of innovation 336
regional worlds of production 341–5
regionally specific cultures, importance of 247
'Regions for Economic Change' (RfEC) 600
regions of high-related variety, 'biotech
    clusters' 387
related diversification, regional level 191
related variety
    allows higher absorptive capacity of regions
        300
    driver of innovative capability 563
    implications of 574–5, 583

spatial externalities literature 188
treated as static and given 189
two things of importance to 303
relatedness, knowledge spillovers and 187
'relative absorptive capacity' 213–14
relocation, globalization challenges 82
Renfrewshire and East Lothian (Scotland),
late path-dependence 182–3
revolutionary innovations, implemented in
new agglomerations 71
Ricardian comparative advantage, incomplete
explanation for competitiveness 238
RIS 169, 455, 541
consists of institutional infrastructure 64
differs from NIS 421–2
failures 460
governance and business structure 50
must be innovation-prone 315
narrow and broad definition 296–7
relevance of regional networks of firms 49
roots in innovation system approach 217
systematic framework for development of
569
two subsystems 293–4
types 463
risk capital proximity, 'convention radius' 452
risk-finance, dried up 310
RISS and nature and geography of knowledge
flows 458–60
role of the state 460–62
rivalry and competitive advantage, Porter and
306–7
'Romer externalities' of urbanization 181–2,
187
rotating leadership 20
Royal Bank of Scotland 20
RSIs 149–50
rules and conventions, important for four
reasons 602

S&T intermediary system in Wallonia 476–7
Salt Lake City 248
Mormon ethics and 254
San Diego and Boston, local universities
anchoring players 170–71, 319
scale economies 54
externalities and 58–9
Marshall and 55–6
Schumpeterian disequilibrium and
evolutionary perspectives 29, 451
science and technology (S&T) policy 51
science-based methodology, competence centre
and 230
science-intensive innovation activities 4
Scotland 416, 487, 498

sectoral and functional approach 107–8
sectoral innovation systems (SISs) 463
sectoral system of innovation, definition 48
securitization, first collateralized mortgage
bond (CMB) 9
self-employed parents, positive effect on
offspring 485
semiconductor patents 136, 319
service industries, innovation in 335–6
service industry innovation, quite extensive
389
service innovation 363
expanding notion of innovation 366–7
R&D and service innovation 365–6
reverse product life-cycle theory 366
what is service innovation? 364–5
what is service? 363–4
service innovation and regions 372–4
services geographical proximity, enhances
knowledge spillovers 386
services innovation, regional dimension 384,
386
services and manufacturing, borderline can be
fragile 383
Services, Science, Management and
Engineering (SSME) 375
services-oriented architecture (SOA) 367
Silicon Valley 4, 11, 18, 161, 182, 190, 199
active networking and 318
agglomeration of industries 514
biotechnology and 395
evolved through ICT 317
high-tech clusters 159
immigrants and open boundaries 393
innovative region 582
interpersonal world 342
learning region 552
new Argonauts 258
open information flow and learning 392–3
R&D 321
regional development 248–50
research university and 296
satellite status 385
services innovation 386
social capital and 287
successful growth of 253, 315
venture capital 320, 324, 498, 500
Silicon Valleys of dissimilar types 54
Silicon Valley's exceptionalism 185–6
Silicon Valleys and Research Triangles 129–30
'simultaneous engineering', matrix
management 8
Singapore 537
Slovenia 537
small and medium-sized enterprises, *see* SMEs

smart specialization 605–7
SMEs 2, 7, 30, 71, 78, 81–3, 85, 289, 474
  Chinese in Italy 337
  clustering and embedding practices of 598
  collocation and 226
  FDI and 407
  quality products and 295
  venture capital and 501
SNA, economic geographers and 162
social capital
  can reduce transaction costs 297
  embedded in memberships not community
    or region 289
  impact on learning and innovation 282
  limitations and cost of 288
  measurement of 266
  must encompass global pipelines and local
    buzz 291
  outcome is innovation 284
  racial inequality and? 288
  societal actors and 535
  stimulates cooperation 266–7
social capitalism, less-favoured and less-
  populated regions 290
'social filters' 227
social network analysis (SNA) 157, 162
social ties, networks and 159
socio-cultural 'innovative milieu', 'nexus of
  untraded interdependencies' 252–3
soft-institutional 'conventions' issues 449, 453
Software as a Service (SaaS), 'virtual
  businesses' and 415
Software Technology Parks (STPs), India 427
solar energy, now uses thin-film polymers but
  also silicon 310
Sophia-Antipolis 161
South East of England 150
South Korea 258, 516
Southeast Asia, consumer electronics and 74
Southern California 536
space, source of knowledge creation 113
Spain 2, 80, 188
  Andalusian culture 334–5, 350, 357–60, 371
  economia de la fiestas 357, 360
  Feria de Abril 357–8
  Museo del Baile Flamenco (Museum of
    Flamenco) 358–9
  Semana Santa festivities 358
  technological incubators 516
  Zara 368
spatial clustering, understanding goes back to
  Marshall 64
spatial clustering of persons, advantages of 56
spatial externalities, labelled localized
  economies 187

spatial proximity, venture capital and 489
spatial spillovers, Marshallian externalities and
  122
spatially bounded knowledge 228
specialization, versus diversification 143
specialization and diversification, dynamics of
  growth and agglomeration 181
specialization and diversity, cumulative path
  150
specialization of venture capital firms, building
  up competencies and 500–501
specialized knowledge, European and Japanese
  firms 71
specialized labour markets, localized 56
Standard Industrial Classification (SIC) 188
standardization phase, 'less developed
  countries' start production 69
star scientist, external knowledge from 137,
  228
static knowledge exchange 459
Stockholm, ICT cluster 318–19
'strategic niche management' 10–11
structural approach 107, 110–11, 115
'structural holes' or 'white spaces' 573
structural unemployment, if no increase in
  variety of industries 483
subprime mortgage demand, Florida and
  California 9
sustainability, regions seek 10
Sweden 2, 17, 188, 191–2
  IDs 80
  incubation and 453
  knowledge-intensive industries 505
  Packaging Arena laboratories 311, 383
  Skäne and 'white spaces' concept 585
  study of different sectors of 47
  Värmland in 183, 311, 579
Switzerland 2, 106, 175, 251, 395, 553
system failures, four types 469–70
systems of innovation approach, nature of
  systemic interactions 43–4
systems of innovation perspective 45
  national systems of innovation 45–7
  regional systems of innovation 48–51
  sectoral and technological systems of
    innovation 47–8

tacit knowledge 121, 172
Taiwan 258, 320–21, 393, 412
  Hsinchu Science-based Industrial Park
    (HSIP) 323
'tangible' and 'intangible' resources, culture
  and 35
Tasmania 568
tautological reasoning 111

'technical push' and 'market pull' 587
technological change
    cumulative and irreversible character 44–5
    foreign firm and 171
    formal economic modelling 63
technological change and economic growth,
        neo-Schumpeterian approach 65
technological complexity, renewal frequency of
        knowledge base 271–2
technological development, cyclical process
        205
technological externalities 59, 63
technological filières 108–9
technological incubators idea 515–17
technological innovations (2000–2003) 94–5
technological paradigm shifts 16, 169
technological relatedness, might be relevant
        189
technological specialization 55
technological systems, focus of 47–8
technologies
    common structure 44
    transferred to subsidiaries are about ten
        years old 71
technology, key elements of knowledge, skills
        and artefacts 44
technology clusters
    complex 324
    immature stages of 'cluster life cycle' 268
    tied to early stages of industry life cycle 315
    'well-functioning' RISs 316
technology spillovers 145
technopoles, 'cathedrals in the desert' 171
technopolis, 20 to 30 years to develop 324
territorial innovations models, *see* TIMs
theoretical perspectives 435
    co-evolutionary transition theory 437–9
    urban regime and ecological modernization
        theory 435–7
theory of land rent 54
'Third Italy' 2, 30, 79, 266–7, 295, 297
TIMs 547–8, 550, 551, 554
towards regional innovation platforms 560–69
    Regional Development Platform method in
        Lahti Region Finland 564–9
    two models of regional innovation 560–64
Trade Related Intellectual Property Rights
        (TRIPS) 423, 429
translocal specific public goods 86–7
transmission of ideas, interfirm mobility of
        workers 283
transnational companies (TNCs) 549
transnational corporations (TNCs) 427, 429
transversality 106, 182–3, 309–10
    'joined-up governance' 268

quest for found new literature on 'policy
        mix' 310
    role of RDAs 313
    source of useful interaction among firms 580
    spatial process concepts and 573, 583
    variety of types 310–13
transversality and platforms, two elements of
        regional innovation thinking 303–4
'Triple Helix' 396, 411–12, 421, 512
Turkey 188, 453, 516
tweeting, important complement but does not
        replace talking 291
Twente 317

UK 188
    automobile sector 199
    clean energy clusters 204
    light industry in old industrial regions 16
    media companies in East and West Sussex
        286
    Merseyside Rainhill Trials 383
    National Endowment for Science,
        Technology and the Arts (NESTA)
        384
    regional policy 389, 548
    spillovers and 218
    technological incubators 516
    technology transfer a third stream for
        universities 321
    Training and Enterprise Councils (TECs)
        588
    West Midlands automotive industry 8, 183
    West Midlands and North West 150
uncodified knowledge, imitation and reverse
        engineering 109
United Nations 191, 360, 406
universities
    anchor tenant 170
    entrepreneurial opportunities 110, 489
    important mechanisms, convention sets not
        profit-motivated 453–4
    three functions of 319
universities and venture capital, role of 316
University of Birmingham, Services and
        Enterprise Research Unit 375
University of California
    semiconductors and computer science 296
    SSME program 375
university laboratories, localized knowledge
        spillovers 133
university research, 50 miles from MSA 134
US 68–9, 94, 321
    automobile industry 199
    banks buy more computers than European
        381

basic spatial unit of analysis 133–4
'bioscience megacenters' 317, 415
Capitol biotechnology cluster in Maryland 295
clean energy clusters 204
clusters of innovation in five metropolitan areas 284
distance knowledge can travel 228, 230
foreign investment mainly from 408–9
high-tech locations 186
Private Industry Councils (PICs) 588
Stanford Industrial Park 322
Technological incubators 452, 453, 516, 531–2
Troubled Relief Programme (TARP) 20
US–India Bi-National Science and Technology Endowment 429
US–India Defense Relationship 429
user needs, marketing manager and 8

user producer innovation 14–15
user-driven innovation 10, 589

venture capital, geographically skewed 320, 452, 495, 497–8
venture capital market, certain inertia 502

Wal-Mart, 'every-day-low-price' (EDLP) 368, 373, 440
Wales 384, 408–9, 439, 487, 498, 538, 550
Wallonia, regional intermediaries in 475–9
waste recycling 434, 588, 595
waveform economic evolution 28, 33
'white spaces' or 'structure holes' 576
'work–life balance' (WLB) arrangements 257–8
workshop systems, Industrial Age 18, 28, 79
World Trade Organization (WTO) 423, 429
worlds of production 334, 339, 340, 347–8

Printed and bound by CPI Group (UK) Ltd, Croydon, CR0 4YY

16/04/2025

14658387-0003